Nineteenth-Century Literature Criticism

Guide to Gale Literary Criticism Series

When you need to review criticism of literary works, these are the Gale series to use:

If the author's death date is: **You should turn to:**

After Dec. 31, 1959
(or author is still living)

CONTEMPORARY LITERARY CRITICISM

for example: Jorge Luis Borges, Anthony Burgess,
William Faulkner, Mary Gordon,
Ernest Hemingway, Iris Murdoch

1900 through 1959

TWENTIETH-CENTURY LITERARY CRITICISM

for example: Willa Cather, F. Scott Fitzgerald,
Henry James, Mark Twain, Virginia Woolf

1800 through 1899

NINETEENTH-CENTURY LITERATURE CRITICISM

for example: Fedor Dostoevski, Nathaniel Hawthorne,
George Sand, William Wordsworth

1400 through 1799

LITERATURE CRITICISM FROM 1400 TO 1800 (excluding Shakespeare)

for example: Anne Bradstreet, Daniel Defoe,
Alexander Pope, François Rabelais,
Jonathan Swift, Phillis Wheatley

SHAKESPEAREAN CRITICISM

Shakespeare's plays and poetry

Antiquity through 1399

CLASSICAL AND MEDIEVAL LITERATURE CRITICISM

for example: Dante, Homer, Plato, Sophocles, Vergil,
the Beowulf Poet

Gale also publishes related criticism series:

CHILDREN'S LITERATURE REVIEW

This series covers authors of all eras who have written for
the preschool through high school audience.

SHORT STORY CRITICISM

This series covers the major short fiction writers of all nationalities
and periods of literary history.

ISSN 0732-1864

Volume 27

Nineteenth-Century Literature Criticism

*Excerpts from Criticism of the
Works of Novelists, Poets, Playwrights,
Short Story Writers, Philosophers, and Other
Creative Writers Who Died between 1800
and 1899, from the First Published Critical
Appraisals to Current Evaluations*

Janet Mullane
Laurie Sherman

Editors

Marie Lazzari
Thomas Ligotti
Joann Prosyniuk

Associate Editors

Gale Research Inc. · *DETROIT* · *NEW YORK* · *LONDON*
Toll-free Telephone Number: 1-800-347-GALE

Contents

Preface

Since its inception in 1981, *Nineteenth-Century Literature Criticism* has been a valuable resource for students and librarians seeking critical commentary on writers of this transitional period in world history. Designated an "Outstanding Reference Source" by the American Library Association with the publication of its first volume, *NCLC* has since been purchased by over 6,000 school, public, and university libraries. With this edition, volume 27, the series has covered more than 300 authors representing 22 nationalities and over 15,000 titles. No other reference source has surveyed the critical reaction to nineteenth-century authors and literature as thoroughly as *NCLC*.

Scope of the Series

NCLC is designed to serve as an introduction for students and advanced readers to the authors of the nineteenth century, and to the most significant interpretations of these authors' works. The great poets, novelists, short story writers, dramatists, and philosophers of this period are frequently studied in high school and college literature courses. By organizing and reprinting the enormous amount of commentary written on these authors, *NCLC* helps students develop valuable insight into literary history, promotes a better understanding of the texts, and sparks ideas for papers and assignments. Each entry in *NCLC* presents a comprehensive survey of an author's career or an individual work of literature and provides the user with a multiplicity of interpretations and assessments. Such variety allows students to pursue their own interests; furthermore, it fosters an awareness that literature is dynamic and responsive to many different opinions.

NCLC continues the survey of criticism of world literature begun by Gale's *Contemporary Literary Criticism (CLC)* and *Twentieth-Century Literary Criticism (TCLC)*, both of which excerpt and reprint commentary on authors of the twentieth century. For additional information about *TCLC*, *CLC*, and Gale's other criticism series, users should consult the Guide to Gale Literary Criticism Series preceding the title page in this volume.

Coverage

Each volume of *NCLC* is carefully compiled to present:

- criticism of authors who represent a variety of genres and nationalities

- both major and lesser-known writers of the period (such as non-Western authors increasingly read by today's students)

- 8 - 12 authors per volume

- individual entries that survey the critical response to each author's works, including early criticism to reflect initial reactions, later criticism to represent any rise or decline in the author's reputation, and current retrospective analyses. The length of each author entry also indicates an author's importance, reflecting the amount of critical attention he or she has received from critics writing in English, and from foreign criticism in translation.

An author may appear more than once in the series because of the great quantity of critical material available or because of a resurgence of criticism generated by such events as an author's centennial or anniversary celebration, the republication or posthumous publication of an author's works, or the publication of a new translation. Usually, one or more author entries in each volume of *NCLC* are devoted to individual works or groups of works by major authors who have appeared previously in the series. Only those works that have been the subjects of extensive criticism and are widely studied in literature courses are selected for this in-depth treatment.

Organization of the Book

An author entry consists of the following elements: author heading, biographical and critical introduction, principal works, excerpts of criticism (each preceded by explanatory notes and followed by a bibliographic citation), and a bibliography of further reading.

- The **author heading** consists of the name under which the author most commonly wrote, followed by birth and death dates. When the name under which an author published is a pseudonym or a variation of his or her full name, the complete real name is given in parentheses on the first line of the biographical and critical introduction. Also located at the beginning of the introduction are any name variations under which an author wrote, including transliterated forms for authors whose languages use nonroman alphabets.

- A **portrait** of the author is included when available. Many entries also feature illustrations of materials pertinent to an author's career, including manuscript pages, letters, book illustrations, and representations of important people, places, and events in an author's life.

- The **biographical and critical introduction** contains background information that introduces the reader to an author and to the critical debate surrounding his or her work. When applicable, biographical and critical introductions are followed by references to additional entries on the author in other literary reference series published by Gale, including *Short Story Criticism, Dictionary of Literary Biography, Children's Literature Review,* and *Something about the Author.*

- The list of **principal works** is chronological by date of first book publication and identifies the genre of each work. In those instances where the first publication was in a language other than English, the title and date of the first English-language edition are given in brackets. Unless otherwise indicated, dramas are dated by the first performance, rather than first publication.

- **Criticism** is arranged chronologically in each author entry to provide a useful perspective on changes in critical evaluation over the years. All titles by the author featured in the critical entry are printed in boldface type to enable the user to ascertain without difficulty the works being discussed. Also for purposes of easier identification, the critic's name and the publication date of the essay are given at the beginning of each piece of criticism. Anonymous criticism is preceded by the title of the journal in which it appeared. Publication information (such as publisher names and book prices) and parenthetical numerical references (such as footnotes or page and line references to specific editions of works) have been deleted at the editors' discretion to provide smoother reading of the text.

- Critical excerpts are prefaced by **annotations** providing the reader with information about both the critic and the criticism that follows. Included are the critic's reputation, individual approach to literary criticism, and particular expertise in an author's works. Also noted are the relative importance of a work of criticism, the scope of the excerpt, and the growth of critical controversy or changes in critical trends regarding an author. In some cases, these notes include cross-references to excerpts by critics who discuss each other's commentary.

- A complete **bibliographic citation** designed to facilitate the location of the original essay or book follows each piece of criticism.

- An annotated bibliography of **further reading** appearing at the end of each author entry lists additional secondary sources on the author. In some cases it includes essays for which the editors could not obtain reprint rights.

Cumulative Indexes

Each volume of *NCLC* includes a cumulative index listing all the authors who have appeared in *Contemporary Literary Criticism, Twentieth-Century Literary Criticism, Nineteenth-Century Literature Criticism, Literature Criticism from 1400 to 1800, Classical and Medieval Literature Criticism,* and *Short Story Criticism,* along with cross-references to the Gale series *Children's Literature Review, Authors in the News, Contemporary Authors, Contemporary Authors Autobiography Series, Dictionary of Literary Biography, Concise Dictionary of American Literary Biography, Something about the Author, Something about the Author Autobiography Series,* and *Yesterday's Authors of Books for Children.* Useful for locating an author within the various series, this index is particularly valuable for those authors who are identified with a certain period but who, because of their death dates, are placed in another, or for those authors whose careers span two periods. For example, Fyodor Dostoevsky is found in *NCLC,* yet Leo Tolstoy, another major nineteenth-century Russian novelist, is found in *TCLC* because he died after 1899.

Each new volume in Gale's Literary Criticism Series includes a cumulative topic index, which lists all literary topics treated in *NCLC, TCLC, LC 1400-1800,* and the *CLC Yearbook.* In addition, each volume of *NCLC* contains a cumulative nationality index in which authors' names are arranged alphabetically under their respective nationalities.

Title Index

Each volume of *NCLC* also includes an index listing the titles of all literary works discussed in that volume. Foreign language titles that have been translated are followed by the titles of the translations—for example, *Notre-Dame de Paris (The Hunchback of Notre-Dame).* Page numbers following these translated titles refer to all pages on which any form of the title, either foreign-language or translated, appears. Titles of novels, dramas, nonfiction books, and poetry, short story, or essay collections are printed in italics, while all individual poems, short stories, and essays are printed in roman type within quotation marks. The first volume of *NCLC* published each year contains a cumulative index to all titles discussed in the series since its inception. The cumulative index last appeared in *NCLC* in volume 25.

A Note to the Reader

When writing papers, students who quote directly from any volume in Gale's Literary Criticism Series may use the following general forms to footnote reprinted criticism. The first example pertains to material drawn from periodicals, the second to material reprinted from books.

[1]T. S. Eliot, "John Donne," *The Nation and the Athenaeum,* 33 (9 June 1923), 321-32; excerpted and reprinted in *Literature Criticism from 1400 to 1800,* Vol. 10, ed. James E. Person, Jr. (Detroit: Gale Research, 1989), pp. 28-9.

[1]Clara G. Stillman, *Samuel Butler: A Mid-Victorian Modern* (Viking Press, 1932); excerpted and reprinted in *Twentieth-Century Literary Criticism,* Vol. 33, ed. Paula Kepos (Detroit: Gale Research, 1989), pp. 43-5.

Suggestions Are Welcome

In response to suggestions, several features have been added to *NCLC* since the series began, including annotations to excerpted criticism, an index listing authors in all Gale literary criticism series, entries devoted to a single work by a major author, more extensive illustrations, and an index to titles.

Readers who wish to suggest authors to appear in future volumes, or who have other comments regarding the series, are cordially invited to write the editors or call our toll-free number: 1-800-347-GALE.

Authors to Be Featured in Forthcoming Volumes

Matthew Arnold (English poet and critic)—The author of such major poems as "The Scholar Gypsy" and "Dover Beach," Arnold was also one of the most influential thinkers of the Victorian era. His writings on culture, religion, and literature have been particularly esteemed. This entry will include essays written for the 1988 centenary of Arnold's death.

Charles Baudelaire (French poet)—Baudelaire is considered one of the greatest poets in world literature. His influential collection *Les fleurs du mal* (*The Flowers of Evil*), which has earned him recognition as the first modern poet, candidly reflects his obsession with moral, physical, and psychological corruption.

Charles Darwin (English naturalist and scientific writer)—While not the originator of the theory of evolution, Darwin gave it extensive support in his *On the Origin of Species by Natural Selection.* In addition to the disturbing effect this work had on religious convictions and institutions, something which Darwin did not intend, it also inspired an optimistic belief in the historical progress and improvement of human life.

Toru Dutt (Indian poet and translator)—Dutt was one of India's first prominent women writers. She is best known for her English translations of French poetry and her original English poems adapted from Hindu epics.

William Hazlitt (English critic and essayist)—Hazlitt was one of the most important and influential commentators during the Romantic age in England. In his literary criticism and miscellaneous prose he combined discerning judgment with strongly stated personal opinion, producing essays noted for their discursive style, evocative descriptions, and urbane wit.

Felicia Hemans (English poet)—Hemans was one of the most popular poets of the early nineteenth century. Focusing on religious, patriotic, and domestic subjects, her verse was memorized and declaimed by several generations of English and American school children.

Francis Jeffrey (Scottish journalist, critic, and essayist)—An influential literary critic, Jeffrey was also a founder and editor (1803-1829) of the prestigious Edinburgh Review. A liberal Whig, Jeffrey often allowed his political beliefs to color his critical opinions, and his commentary is judged the most characteristic example of "impressionistic" critical thought during the first half of the nineteenth century. Today, he is best remembered for his brutal attacks on the early Romantic poets, exemplified by the first sentence of a review of William Wordsworth's *Excursion:* "This will never do."

Charles-Marie-René Leconte de Lisle (French poet)—Leconte de Lisle was the leader of the Parnassians, a school of French poets that rejected the tenets of Romanticism in favor of emotional restraint, clarity of expression, and attention to artistic form. Inspired by the civilizations of ancient Greece, Scandinavia, and India, as well as by his love of nature, Leconte de Lisle's poetry has been described as impassive and pessimistic yet sensitive and acutely attuned to beauty.

Herman Melville (American novelist, novella and short story writer, and poet)—A major figure in American literature, Melville is recognized for his exploration of complex metaphysical and moral themes in his novels and short fiction. *NCLC* will devote an entry to his novella *Billy Budd,* a symbolic inquiry into the nature of good and evil, innocence and guilt.

John Henry Newman (English theologian and writer)—An influential theologian, Newman was a key figure in the Oxford movement, whose adherents advocated the independence of the Church of England from the state and sought to establish a doctrinal basis for Anglicanism in the Church's evolution from Catholicism. Newman's subsequent conversion to Roman Catholicism inspired his best-known work, *Apologia pro vita sua,* an eloquent spiritual autobiography tracing the development of his beliefs.

Alfred Tennyson (English poet and dramatist)—Often regarded as the poet whose work is most representative of the tastes and values of the Victorian era, Tennyson remains one of the most popular authors in the history of literature. The prosodic skills demonstrated in such memorable poems as "The Charge of the Light Brigade" and *In Memoriam* have especially contributed to his high standing among critics and readers.

Acknowledgments

The editors wish to thank the copyright holders of the excerpted criticism included in this volume, the permissions managers of many book and magazine publishing companies for assisting us in securing reprint rights, and Anthony Bogucki for assistance with copyright research. We are also grateful to the staffs of the Detroit Public Library, the Library of Congress, the University of Detroit Library, Wayne State University Purdy/Kresge Library Complex, and University of Michigan Libraries for making their resources available to us. Following is a list of the copyright holders who have granted us permission to reprint material in this volume of *NCLC*. Every effort has been made to trace copyright, but if omissions have been made, please let us know.

COPYRIGHTED EXCERPTS IN *NCLC*, VOLUME 27, WERE REPRINTED FROM THE FOLLOWING PERIODICALS:

American Anthropologist, v. 64, October, 1962 for a review of "The Lost Eden" by Charles Kaut. Copyright 1962 the author. Reprinted by permission of the author.—*American Literature,* v. XLVIII, May, 1976. Copyright © 1976 Duke University Press, Durham, NC. Reprinted with permission of the publisher.—*Eire-Ireland,* v. X, Winter, 1975 for " 'Dark Rosaleen' as Image of Ireland" by Diane E. Bessai; v. XI, 1976 for " 'In Wreathed Swell': James Clarence Mangan, Translator from the Irish" by Robert Welch. Copyright © 1975, 1976 Irish American Cultural Institute, 2115 Summit Avenue, No. 5026, St. Paul, MN 55105. Both reprinted by permission of the publisher and the respective authors.—*Germano-Slavica,* n. 6, Fall, 1975. Reprinted by permission of the publisher.—*Neuphilologische Mitteilungen: Bulletin de la Société Neophilologique* v. LXXVIII, 1977. © Modern Language Society, Helsinki, 1977. Reprinted by permission of the publisher.—*Russian Literature* v. XIV, November 15, 1983 for "A Lesson for Novelists; or, The Dramatic Structure of 'Eugene Onegin' " by Roberta Clipper Sethi. © 1983, Elsevier Science Publishers B.V. (North-Holland). All rights reserved. Reprinted by permission of the publisher and the author.—*The South Atlantic Quarterly,* v. 43, January, 1944. Copyright 1944, renewed 1971 by Duke University Press, Durham, NC. Reprinted by permission of the publisher.—*Studies in American Fiction,* v. 7, Autumn, 1979. Copyright © 1979 Northeastern University. Reprinted by permission of the publisher.—*Studies in English Literature, 1500-1900,* v. VI, Autumn, 1966 for "Arthur Hugh Clough: The Modern Mind" by Frederick Bowers. © 1966 by William Marsh Rice University. Reprinted by permission of the publisher and the author.—*Victorian Poetry,* v. 16, Spring-Summer, 1978; v. 20, Spring, 1982. Both reprinted by permission of the publisher.

COPYRIGHTED EXCERPTS IN *NCLC*, VOLUME 27, WERE REPRINTED FROM THE FOLLOWING BOOKS:

Arcilla, Jose S., S.J. From "Once More the 'Noli'—with Understanding," in *Understanding the "Noli": Its Historical Context and Literary Influences.* Edited by Jose S. Arcilla, S.J. Phoenix Press, Inc., 1988. Copyright 1988 by Phoenex Publishing House, Inc., and Ateneo de Manila University. All rights reserved. Reprinted by permission of the publisher and the author.—Barker, Stephen F. From "The Style of Kant's Critique of Reason," in *The Philosopher as Writer: The Eighteenth Century.* Edited by Robert Ginsberg. Susquehanna University Press, 1987. © 1987 by Associated University Presses, Inc. Reprinted by permission of the publisher.—Beck, Lewis White. From an introduction to *Critique of Practical Reason and Other Writings in Moral Philosophy.* By Immanuel Kant, edited and translated by Lewis White Beck. The University of Chicago Press, 1949. Copyright 1949 by The University of Chicago. Renewed 1976 by Lewis W. Beck. All rights reserved. Reprinted by permission of the author.—Beck, Lewis White. From an introduction to *Perpetual Peace.* By Immanuel Kant, edited by Lewis White Beck. Liberal Arts Press, 1957. Copyright © 1957 The Bobs-Merrill Company. Renewed copyright © 1985 by Lewis White Beck. All rights reserved. Reprinted with permission of Macmillan Publishing Company.—Beck, Lewis White. From "What Have We Learned from Kant?" in *Self and Nature in Kant's Philosophy.* Edited by Allen W. Wood. Cornell University Press, 1984. Copyright © 1984 by Cornell University Press. All rights reserved. Used by permission of the publisher, Cornell University Press.—Belinsky, V. G. From and extract translated by M. A. Nicholson in *Fenimore Cooper: The Critical Heritage.* Edited by George Dekker and John P. McWilliams. Routledge & Kegan Paul, 1973. Reprinted by permission of the publisher.—Bergmann, Frank. From *Upstate Literature: Essays in Memory of Thomas F. O'Donnell.* Edited by Frank Bergmann. Syracuse University Press, 1985. Copyright © 1985 Syracuse University Press. All rights reserved. Reprinted by permission of the publisher.—Biswas, Robindra Kumar. From *Arthur Hugh Clough: Towards a Reconsideration.* Oxford at the Clarendon Press, 1972. © Oxford University Press, 1972. Reprinted by permission of Oxford University Press.—Brown, Ford K. From *Fathers of the Victorians: The Age of Wilberforce.* Cambridge at the University Press, 1961. Reprinted with the permission of Cambridge University Press.—Cassirer, Ernst. From *Kant's Life and Thought.* Translated by James Haden. Yale University Press, 1981. Copyright © 1981 by Yale University. All rights reserved. Reprinted by permission of the publisher.—Clayton, J. Douglas. From *Ice and Flame: Alexsandr Pushkin's "Eugene Onegin".* University of Toronto Press, 1985. © University of Toronto Press 1985. Reprinted by permission of the

Marie Bashkirtseff

1859?-1884

(Born Maria Konstantinovna Bashkirtseva) Russian diarist and artist.

Variously described by critics as a "freak of nature," an "egomaniac," and a "true genius," Bashkirtseff gained widespread recognition in the late nineteenth and early twentieth centuries for her psychological self-portrait, *Le journal de Marie Bashkirtseff* (*The Journal of Marie Bashkirtseff*). The *Journal,* spanning Bashkirtseff's young adult life, is a precocious and forthright account of the aspirations and self-doubts of an adolescent struggling to find an identity. Scholars note that Bashkirtseff is unique among nineteenth-century women diarists in her candor, self-consciousness, and brazen egotism; as Rozsika Parker and Griselda Pollock remarked, "Never before had a woman so urgently proclaimed her ambition to excel, her hunger for public fame. Never before had a woman so coolly analysed her emotions." Written in French and published posthumously according to Bashkirtseff's wishes, the *Journal* caused a sensation when it appeared in 1887 and within two years was a best-seller in Europe and America. The public was intrigued by Bashkirtseff's extravagant life-style, frank self-revelation, and tragic struggle with tuberculosis. Despite questions concerning the veracity of the work (the original manuscript differs greatly from the highly edited published version), Bashkirtseff is recognized today as an important figure in the history of nineteenth-century autobiographical writing.

Bashkirtseff was born in Gavronzi in the Ukraine. Her parents, Constantine Bashkirtseff and Marie Babanine, despite claims in the *Journal* that they were descended from a long line of Russian nobility, came from families of wealthy, but untitled, landowners. After two years of marriage, Bashkirtseff's mother left her husband and moved with her two children back to the Babanine estate. In 1870, Bashkirtseff, her mother and brother, a wealthy aunt, and a cousin, left Russia to travel in Europe. Their two-year tour included stays in Vienna, Baden-Baden, Geneva, and Nice, where the family took up permanent residence and where, in 1873, Bashkirtseff began writing her journal. Throughout her travels, Bashkirtseff had been educated by various governesses. Her instruction was intensive; she learned to speak Italian, English, and French and could read Horace, Plato, Dante, and Shakespeare in their original languages. In 1876 the family spent the summer in Rome, which proved to be an important period in Bashkirtseff's life. Inspired by the city's architecture and history, she wrote in her journal, "The beauties and the ruins of Rome are going to my head . . . I wish to be a Caesar, Augustus, Marcus Aurelius, Nero, Caracalla, the Devil, the Pope." Indeed, evidence of Bashkirtseff's desire for fame is present throughout her journal. At another time she wrote: "To marry and have children! Any washerwoman can do that . . . What do I want? Oh, you know well enough. I want glory." A developing love for art coupled with her overwhelming ambition to become famous prompted Bashkirtseff's decision to study painting. In 1877, the family moved to Paris so that Bashkirtseff could enroll at the esteemed Atelier Julian. The discovery in 1880 that she was

dying from tuberculosis further fueled her desire to achieve renown as an artist. Despite a symptomatic loss of hearing and instructions from her doctor to reduce her activities, Bashkirtseff increased her hours at the studio. In the end, she achieved moderate recognition for her work. Between 1881 and 1884, several of her paintings were displayed at the highly prestigious Paris Salon. Her most famous painting, a depiction of Paris street urchins entitled "The Meeting," received much critical praise and is now in the collection at the Louvre.

In 1884, Bashkirtseff engaged in a series of brief correspondences with several prominent French writers, including Alexander Dumas (fils) and Guy de Maupassant, in an attempt, many critics believe, to ingratiate herself with the authors and possibly procure an editor for her journal, which she planned to have published. However, Dumas promptly broke off the correspondence, declaring that too much novel reading had "turned her head." Her communication with Maupassant was equally futile. Bashkirtseff was disappointed with the "bourgeois" quality of his letters—Maupassant seemed more interested in her physical appearance than in her autobiography—and abruptly ended the correspondence. During the final years of her life Bashkirtseff did, however, establish a close friendship with the prominent painter Jules Bastien-

1

Lepage, who was also suffering from a fatal illness. Greatly influenced by his painting, Bashkirtseff adopted his realistic style in much of her own work. Many biographers indicate that Bastien-Lepage was the only true love of Bashkirtseff's life, the one person who could have helped her to overcome her preoccupation with herself and her disillusioned view of men. After several earlier liaisons and numerous marriage proposals Bashkirtseff had written: "I shall not love, for candidly, in my inmost heart, I am convinced of the villainy of men. Not only that, I do not find anyone worthy of my love, either morally or physically." Other scholars believe that, after Bashkirtseff's death, her mother embellished the account of her friendship with Bastien-Lepage in an attempt to make her daughter appear to have had a closer relationship with the respected artist than was the case. Nevertheless, Bastien-Lepage's name dominates the last pages of the journal. The concluding words of the work describe the extreme difficulties the artist overcame in order to visit Bashkirtseff's bedside. She died eleven days after this final entry.

Before Bashkirtseff died, she outlined detailed instructions for an extravagant funeral and burial, including a plan for the construction of a chapel in her honor where every year on the anniversary of her death she requested that "beautiful and sad music be sung there by great artists." Bashkirtseff also gave specific orders for her journal to be published posthumously. Five months before her death she wrote a preface to the diary in which she declared, "If this book be not the *exact,* the *absolute,* the *strict* truth, it has no right to exist." Ironically, in the process of condensing the voluminous journal into two publishable volumes, Bashkirtseff's mother made several major alterations to the text. One of the most serious discrepancies between the original and the edited text concerns Bashkirtseff's age. Throughout the edited journal, dates were changed to make Bashkirtseff appear younger than she actually was. Critics cite several probable reasons for this falsification, including Madame Bashkirtseff's desire to present her daughter as a child prodigy (she even corrected grammar to make the entries sound less juvenile) and her wish to heighten the pathos of Bashkirtseff's early death. There were other more subtle changes made to the original manuscript: all references to a scandalous law suit involving Bashkirtseff's aunt were carefully deleted, the drunken behavior of an uncle was downplayed, and many of Bashkirtseff's cruel and derogatory remarks about her family were softened. Those who have studied the original manuscript, which was finally made available to the public in 1936, feel that, in general, Bashkirtseff's mother presented her daughter in a much more favorable light than she deserved.

William Gladstone's laudatory 1889 review of the *Journal,* in which he praised Bashkirtseff's candor and intelligence, is said to have sparked the work's widespread popularity in England and America. The publication of Bashkirtseff's letters two years later further fueled interest in the diary. Critical reaction to Bashkirtseff's *Journal* has been varied. Some late nineteenth- and early twentieth-century reviewers presented Bashkirtseff as a romantic heroine, contributing to a highly sentimentalized view of the author and her work. Many praised her descriptive powers, commenting that, had she focused her creative energies on fiction, she might have become a celebrated author and in this way satisfied her desire for fame. Other critics, however, found little merit in Bashkirtseff's diary, regarding it as nothing more than the egotistical and foolish whimperings of a spoiled teenager. Critical interest in the *Journal* decreased in the middle of the

twentieth century, and although the original manuscript has been available for over fifty years, no comprehensive study of it has yet been published in English. However, modern critics agree that, despite the numerous alterations made to the original text, the edited journal has considerable merit of its own. Bashkirtseff's strong-willed demeanor, her straightforward manner of expressing her feelings, and her audacious self-promotion were extremely uncharacteristic for women of her era and the *Journal* continues to be regarded as one of the few truly uninhibited accounts of a woman's intellectual and emotional self to emerge from the period. A recent reprint of the 1890 English translation has received moderate interest from feminists, who have praised Bashkirtseff for her bold ambition and unwillingness to conform to the social pressures of her day, which typically required women to dedicate their lives to marriage and children. Because of her candid self-analysis and the fascination surrounding her unusual life and tragic death, Bashkirtseff is today considered one of the most intriguing diarists of the nineteenth century.

PRINCIPAL WORKS

Le journal de Marie Bashkirtseff (journal) 1887
    [*The Journal of Marie Bashkirtseff,* 1890]
Lettres de Marie Bashkirtseff (letters) 1891
    [*Letters of Marie Bashkirtseff,* 1891]
Nouveau journal inédit, accompagné de la correspondance inédite avec Guy de Maupassant (journal and letters) 1901
    [*The Further Memoirs of Marie Bashkirtseff, Together with a Correspondence between Marie Bashkirtseff and Guy de Maupassant,* 1901]

MARIE BASHKIRTSEFF (essay date 1884)

[*In the following preface to her* Journal, *written five months before her death, Bashkirtseff describes her upbringing and characterizes the work as a "document of human nature."*]

Why tell lies and play a part? Yes, it is clear that I have the wish, if not the hope, of remaining on this earth by whatever means in my power. If I do not die young, I hope to survive as a great artist; but if I do, I will have my *Journal* published, which cannot fail to be interesting. But as I talk of publicity, this idea of being read has perhaps spoilt, nay, destroyed, the sole merit of such a book? Well, no! To begin with, I wrote for a long time without a thought of being read, and in the next place it is precisely because I hope to be read that I am absolutely sincere. If this book be not the *exact,* the *absolute,* the *strict* truth, it has no right to exist. I not only say all the time what I think, but I never contemplated hiding for an instant what might make me appear ridiculous, or prove to my disadvantage; for the rest I think myself too admirable for censure. Rest assured, therefore, kind reader, that I reveal myself completely, entirely. I, personally, may, perhaps, possess but a feeble interest for *you;* but do not think that it is I: think, here is a human being who tells you all its impressions from childhood. It cannot help being interesting as a document of human nature. Ask M. Zola, even M. de Goncourt, or Maupassant. My diary begins at twelve years of age, and begins to have some meaning from the age of fifteen or sixteen. Therefore a hiatus remains to be filled up, and I will write a kind of preface which will enable the reader to follow this human and literary document.

There—suppose me famous. We begin:—

I was born on the 11th November, 1860. It is fearful even to have to write it; but at any rate, it comforts me to remember that when you read this I shall no longer be of any age.

My father was the son of General Paul Grégorievitch Bashkirtseff, who belonged to the gentry, and was a brave, obstinate, hard, and even cruel, man. My grandfather was raised to the rank of general after the Crimean war, I believe. He married a young girl, the adopted daughter of a great nobleman; she died at the age of eight-and-twenty, leaving five children—my father and four sisters.

My mother got married at one-and-twenty, having previously refused many excellent offers. Mamma's maiden name was Babanine, and by her we belong to the old provincial nobility; her father always made a boast of his Tartar origin, which dated from the first invasion—*Baba Nina* are Tartar words—but for my part, I laugh at it. . . . Grandpapa was the contemporary of Lermontoff, Poushkine, &c. He had been a Byronian, a poet, soldier, scholar; he had been to the Caucasus. Very early in life he married a Miss Julia Cornélius, a very gentle and pretty girl of fifteen. They had nine children, if you please, no more!

After two years of marriage mamma returned to her parents with two children. I was always with my grandmother, who idolised me. Aunt followed her example when my mother did not take her with her; she was younger than mamma, but not pretty, and sacrificed herself and was sacrificed for everybody.

In the month of May, 1870, we started on our travels. My mother's cherished dream was at last carried out. We spent a month in Vienna, enchanted by its novelties, its fine shops, and theatres. We reached Baden-Baden in June, at the height of the season, astir with Paris and all its luxury. Our party consisted of grandpapa, mamma, Aunt Romanoff, my first cousin Dina, Paul, and myself. We were also accompanied by Lucien Walitzky, our angelic and incomparable doctor. He was a Pole, but without exaggerated patriotism, with the kindest heart, the most caressing manners, and given to caricaturing. He was doctor of the district at Achtirka; had studied at the University with my mother's brother; and always made one of the family. When we left Russia we wanted a physician for grandpapa, and carried off Walitzky. At Baden-Baden I began to get an insight into the fashionable world, and was tortured by vanity. . . .

But I have not said enough of Russia, nor myself, which most concerns us. According to the practice of our gentry I had two governesses, one Russian and the other French, The Russian lady, whom I well remember, was a Madame Melnikoff, a woman of the world, well educated, and romantic, who, being separated from her husband, had elected to turn teacher after the perusal of numerous novels. She became the friend of the family, and was treated like one of us. Every man paid court to her, and she ran away one fine morning after I know not what romantic episode. We are very romantic in Russia. She might easily have said goodbye, and left in the usual way; but the *Slav* character inoculated with French civilisation and romantic literature is a curious product. This governess, acting up to her part of unhappy wife, naturally

adored the little girl entrusted to her care; and I, already entering into the spirit of the thing, returned her adoration. Indeed, the whole family affected to think that her disappearance must make me ill; everybody looked at me pityingly that day, and I believe that my grandmother had some special soup prepared for me which is usually given to invalids. I felt myself growing quite pale before such a show of sympathy. I was, in truth, rather frail, delicate, and not pretty—a fact which did not prevent everybody from considering me as a being inevitably destined by fate to become one day everything that is beautiful, brilliant, and magnificent. My mother went to a Jewish fortune-teller.

"You have two children," said he; "the son will be like the rest of the world, but your daughter will be a star." . . . .

One evening at the theatre a gentleman said to me, laughing:—

"Show me your hands, young lady. . . . Oh! To judge from her gloves there's no doubt she'll be a terrible flirt."

It made me quite proud. Since I can remember, since the age of three (I had a wet-nurse till I was three-and-a-half), I had aspired to future greatness. All my dolls were kings and queens; and my thoughts, and all that was talked of in our family, seemed continually to have some reference to the triumphs which must inevitably come to me.

At five I dressed myself in my mother's laces, with flowers in my hair, in order to dance in the drawing-room. I was the famous ballet-dancer Pepita, and all the family came and looked at me. Paul was hardly noticed, and Dina bore me no grudge, though the daughter of the favourite George. One story more. When Dina was born, grandmamma, without so much as saying by your leave, took her from her mother, and kept her ever afterwards. This happened before my birth.

Mme. Melnikoff was succeeded by Mlle. Sophie Dolgikoff, a young lady of sixteen. Holy Russia! After her came another French lady, Mme. Brenne, with pale blue eyes and hair dressed in the style of the Restoration—a sad creature with her fifty years and her consumptive habit. I liked her very much. She taught me drawing, and I drew a little church in outline with her. In fact, I sketched a great deal; while the old ones played at cards I sat by and drew on the card-table.

Mme. Brenne died in 1868 in the Crimea. The little Russian governess, treated like one of us, was on the eve of getting married to a young man whom the doctor had introduced, and who was known as having been jilted repeatedly. On this occasion everything seemed to go on swimmingly, when, on going into Mlle. Sophie's room one evening, I found her dissolved in tears with her nose buried in the cushions.

"Everyone's come," I cried. "What on earth's the matter?"

At last, after copious tears and sobs, the poor child confessed that she never could—no, never! . . . and fresh tears.

"But why?"

"Because, because I can't get used to his face."

The young man heard all this from the drawing-room. An hour afterwards he packed his trunk, weeping bitterly, and departed. It was the seventeenth time he had been jilted. How well I remember the girl's words—"I can't get used to his face!" It came from the bottom of her heart, and I understood perfectly what a horrible thing it would be to marry a man whose face one couldn't get used to.

All this carries us back to Baden-Baden in 1870. War having been declared, we hurried off to Geneva; I, full of discontent and determined to have my turn. Every day, before going to bed, I added the following words in a low voice to my prayer:

"Grant, O Lord, that I may never have the small-pox, that I may be pretty, and have a fine voice; that I may be happy in my married life, and that mamma may live long!"

In Geneva we stayed at the Crown Hotel, near the Lake. I had a drawing-master, who brought me sketches to copy— little châlets whose windows were drawn like trunks of trees, not a bit like the real windows of real châlets. So I would have none of them, not seeing how a window could look thus. Whereupon the good old man bade me simply copy the view from my window. Just then we left the Crown Hotel and went to board with a family from whose house one had a view of Mont Blanc. So I scrupulously copied what I saw of Geneva and the lake, and the thing stopped there, I can't remember why. In Baden we had had time to have our portraits taken after some photographs, and they appeared ugly to me by dint of being smooth and prettified. . . .

When I am dead people will read my life, which to me seems very remarkable. Were it not so it would be the climax of misery. But I hate prefaces and editors' notes, and have missed reading many excellent books on this account. That's why I've wished to write my own preface. It could have been dispensed with had the whole diary been published; but I think it best to begin with my thirteenth year, the preceding part being too long. The reader, however, will find sufficient data to go upon in the course of this narrative, for I frequently make references to the past, now for one reason, now for another. Suppose I were to die now quite suddenly, seized by some illness; perhaps I should not know of my danger; they would conceal it from me; and, after my death my drawers would be ransacked, and my family would discover my *Journal,* and, having read, would destroy it. Soon afterwards nothing would remain of me—nothing . . . . nothing . . . . nothing! . . . It is this which has always terrified me. To live, to have so much ambition, to suffer, weep, struggle—and then oblivion! . . . . oblivion . . . . as if I had never been. Should I not live long enough to become famous, this *Journal* will be of interest to naturalists; for the life of a woman must always be curious, told thus day by day, without any attempt at posing; as if no one in the world would ever read it, yet written with the intention of being read; for I feel quite sure the reader will find me sympathetic. . . . And I tell all, yes, all. . . . Else what were the use of it? In fact, it will be sufficiently apparent that I tell everything. . . . (pp. xxxv-xl)

> Marie Bashkirtseff, in a preface to her The Journal of Marie Bashkirtseff, Vol. I, *translated by Mathilde Blind, Cassell & Company, Limited, 1890, pp. xxxv-xl.*

W. E. GLADSTONE (essay date 1889)

[*Gladstone was a distinguished nineteenth-century statesman and literary commentator. Four times prime minister of Britain, he was largely responsible for the rise of the late-Victorian Liberal party. His diverse intellectual interests are illustrated in the numerous essays and pamphlets written throughout his prolific career. In the following review of the* Journal, *he calls Bashkirtseff a "true genius" and describes her thoughts on, among other subjects, fame, art, love, and religion.*]

However tightly we may draw the definition of 'noticeable books,' any book must be noticeable which opens a new chapter in the experiences of human nature, or which adds a page to a chapter already opened. Such a condition is at once satisfied by the *Journal de Marie Bashkirtseff.* It may even be pronounced a book without a parallel. It is, however, one hardly possible to represent in brief, for there is nothing contained in any one part of it that is not contradicted by another. But the authoress says of it, with the *naïveté* which never abandons her, in the short preface, dated only five months before her death, 'C'est très intéressant comme document humain' [see essay dated 1884].

A reader has, indeed, to approach it under circumstances of very considerable disadvantage. It has to be judged, like the poems of Homer, from internal evidence. We are not told who has given it to the press; and, like the human infant, it comes into the world utterly unclothed. Editorial labour has in this case been confined to an obituary notice at the close, and to the composition of a title-page, neither of which would fill two lines. A panegyrical poem by Theuriet is prefixed to the *Journal,* and there is a photograph which exhibits a strong countenance precociously developed, and shows how, at the age of twelve, the owner of it worshipped her own hands for their beauty. In the *Journal,* personal references are scanty and curtailed, and important facts, such as domestic relations, are left in seemingly purposed obscurity; upon neither the one nor the other of them is there a glimmer of elucidation. Fortunately, there is to be found in the *Woman's World* of June and August 1888 a vivid and striking paper, signed 'Mathilde Blind,' which furnishes much needful information for such as may desire to obtain it.

This is not a book which will reward the seeker of mere pleasure. It does not possess the interest attaching to such a character as the Italians call *avvenente,* or winning. Wonder it will stir, but not confidence; admiration, but not quite a loving admiration. Mlle. Bashkirtseff attracts and repels alternately, and perhaps repels as much as she attracts. It is only when, at the age of not yet twenty-four full years, death cuts the thread of her intense and overwrought existence, that as the pall is cast over her the reader becomes absorbed in deep sympathy, while he contemplates the mournful arrest of such diversified and powerful faculties, the extinction of such a fresh and brilliant light. But when the tale is surveyed as a whole, even its tragic interest subsides in comparison with its commanding singularity as a psychological study. She tells us in the preface, which was really a postscript, it had been her intention all along unrelentingly to strip her very self before the world by recording *tout, tout, tout.* She exhibits to us an imposing tapestry in reverse. Possessed of a phenomenal personality, and spurred by an audacious sincerity, she sounds incessantly her own inner depths, and brings to the surface what she finds at the bottom, which is mapped out in hills and valleys like the bed of ocean. Oftentimes she stops in a sentence, but commonly, as it appears, because even her great command of language refuses to answer fully to the force and vehemence of her thought. It is not a picture of herself which she has given, so much as a demonstration in anatomy. The lines of this deep-cut image are wrought out in so sustained a fashion, by an unremitting exercise of force, that they run over its entire surface. The scope and temper of her composition are everywhere discerned, and though the pages are a thousand, and present scores of apparent contradictions, almost every page is a moral epitome of the book. The word 'psychology' is too cold and technical to indicate the workings of this abnormally uplifted and yet profoundly harrowed soul. They really supply an object-lesson in human nature, and tell us things new and strange about its widest and wildest contrasts.

Her exterior history may be briefly sketched. She is a Russian, and she is intensely Russian, for whatever she is she is intensely. Her life is passed almost wholly out of her country, at first from the circumstances of her family, and afterwards also for health. The chief shares of it fall to Nice, which opens out her sense of the glories of nature, and to Paris, where she undergoes the discipline and practises the worship of art. Even from the time when the *Journal* begins with her teens, her life is a perpetual strain: not an effort only, but an effort of abnormal violence. The dance, at five years old, as the ideal of movement; then the song as the sovereign implement of sound; and lastly the painter's and the sculptor's art as the representation, nay within limits the production, of life; each of these in turn cast over her its powerful spell. At the same time her mind wrought continuously in every other direction, inwards and outwards, social, acquisitive, reflective. With all this she joins a steady pursuit of her prescribed purpose of self-record, and the *Journal,* if it stood alone, would be no mean monument of labour for so short a life. It is no wonder that with such action, and such friction, 'the sword was consumed before the sheath.' At Nice, when still only fourteen years old, she had a sort of pain in the right lung, where two years later a doctor at some German watering-place pronounced that there was mischief. She weeps at nineteen over the departure of her voice, which she had at one time thought would make her mistress of the world, which is attested by others than herself. She more than suspects the mortal disease, and desires only that it may make short work of her. Before this time she slowly began to be sensible of an almost habitual though far from total deafness, which it seems occasionally accompanies the pulmonary complaint. And she frets far more under this inconvenience than at her mortal malady, evidently because the one interfered with the activity of social communion, while she daringly defied and suppressed the monitions of the other. She begins the systematic pursuit of art in the *atelier* at sixteen. In September 1884, when twenty-three, she is still at work. On October 9 she complains that she is too weak, though, as she thinks, her lungs are no worse. On the 20th the *Journal* drops into silence, and on the 31st she dies.

And so we bid adieu to one of those abnormal beings who in this or that country seem to be born into the world once or twice in a generation, oftener perhaps women than men, and who commonly succumb to the strain of life long before the natural term. They may seem to warn us common mortals to beware how we handle them roughly or lightly, because they are above and beyond us: our arms do not encompass them. And yet as they are meant for this among other purposes, to give us lessons, and as we cannot learn without trying to understand, something like judgments must perforce be passed upon them, with whatever deference and reserve. And indeed there is one remark, obvious enough to make, which seems to cover the whole case of this extraordinary person. She was a true genius, though some of her judgments in letters and in art seem to be eccentric. But while her powers in every direction unfolded themselves with superlative and precocious ra-

pidity, the great quality which we call character was of slow and immature growth; and girls of twelve or less than twelve abound everywhere around us who are riper in this capital respect than was Marie Bashkirtseff when she died. To do her justice, she saw the anomalies of her own composition: and she cries, looking upwards:—

> Pourquoi dans ton ouvre céleste,
> Tant d'éléments si peu d'accord?

As she had earlier said (in 1879): 'Je ne peux pas vivre: je ne suis pas crée régulièrement: j'ai un tas de choses de trop, puis un tas qui manquent, et un caractère qui ne peut pas durer.'

Whether she had actual beauty may be questioned. She herself frequently debates it, and commonly, not uniformly, decides in the affirmative. She certainly had energy, fascination, and command. Womanish she was in many of woman's weaknesses; and she did not possess the finer graces which we signify by the epithet feminine. Of this she was sufficiently conscious. 'Oh si j'étais seulement un homme!' But death would be better still. More roundly she declares, 'Je n'ai de la femme que l'enveloppe.' Her emotions were portentous in strength and activity: her affections but moderately strong. On the death of the family physician, whom she loved, she asks, 'Was it the first time I ever shed tears but from self-love or anger?' Her family were her slaves; but, they being wholly beneath and behind her, she was not in sympathy with them; and even with the invalid grandfather she carried on habitually the war of words. She has not been brutal with him, she has only treated him as an equal. Her greatest defect seems to have been her want of the sentiment of reverence. Her endowments were splendid and universal. As a child she is the wonder of the dance; and she dances only to be seen. Her voice is reported by others as well as by herself to have been magnificent. She acquired languages with such facility that she seems to pass through no stage of difficulty or stumbling. She is surprised at finding herself speak Italian so well. The ancient tongues are learned, apparently without a teacher; and she reads her Homer seriously, for no modern composition, sensational or other, impresses her like the catastrophe of Troy. Her passion for reading was insatiable, her power of work immense. All subjects were food for her: for politics she could lose her sleep. After the development which she undergoes when about sixteen, the *Journal* everywhere bears testimony to her powers alike of observation and reflection.

Art was her master-passion: and she clung to it, and bent the course of her life to it, with a desperate fidelity to the very end. She had a true conception of her work, as that which attains by striving after the unattainable. 'Il ne faut jamais être content de soi.' At the outset she astonished her teachers, who even questioned her as to the authenticity of her works, since they could not conceive a novice to be capable of such performances. Yet here, as in the case of all other accomplishments which could be made subjects of observation, she loved them with an ulterior motive. All these things were conceived of in a manner peculiar to herself. She sought in them excellence indeed, and sought it intensely, but excellence for the sake of renown, and not renown simply to be enjoyed at some uncertain date, but renown made palpable and brought home in celebrity, in homage visible and sensible, in the glances of the crowd there and then: she sought, with an incessant hunger,

> Digito monstrari, et dicier Hæc est.

She dealt in the market of fame, but dealt only for cash.

And so not unnaturally there were peculiarities and perhaps inconsistencies in her ideal. She has intense unquestioning admiration for Watteau and for Greuze, but she criticises and renounces Raphael, though she adores his country. Her enthusiasm for progress in art was unbounded: but her object was reality, not beauty. Of her ultra-realism as an artist there is a small but significant indication in one of the two works by her which are preserved in the Luxembourg. A group of *gamins* are in confabulation together, near a building, on the blank wall of which has been scratched the figure of a gallows. Presumably this seemed to her the fittest subject for an urchin's initial effort. If there was an idea which lay at the root of all her aspirations, that idea was power. This intense realism penetrated also into her literary tastes, and may probably explain her pronounced and violent admiration for Zola, although she appears to have known some of the most exceptional works of this author, who pushes realism into sheer brutality. With this passion for art only her love of visible worship could maintain at least a qualified rivalry. An evening at the theatre has been an evening lost, though she laughed incessantly, for she has neither studied, nor been seen. And again, at a great party, 'I did not produce all the effect I intended.'

Love, as might be expected, flits across the scene in its various forms. At the outset, in a childish and transient but passionate affection; sometimes as coquetry; sometimes, as in the case of Bastien Le Page, the painter and like herself a realist, a form of admiration which looks as if it might almost be love. When, however, there is an idea of marriage, her view suddenly becomes matter of fact, or even mercantile. She would like to be an ambassadress. On the whole, wedlock would have been a troublesome incident, and she holds it at arm's-length.

Where the sources of susceptibility were so redundant, it could not but be that religion should attract a share of the emotions. And so it was; in the earlier periods more, however, than in the latest. As late as in 1878, when her sad fate is apparently in her view, she says, in all earnestness, 'que la volonté de Dieu soit faite;' and, when about to enter upon the course of study in the *atelier,* she makes a solemn dedication of herself and her work to 'the Father, and the Son, and the Holy Ghost.'

The idea of the Deity after this seems to have deteriorated, learn 'what is that good, and acceptable, and perfect will of God,' and to find in that search the regulative principle of character, and the secret of peace. She is apt to treat the Almighty as she treated her grandfather, *en égal.* It was to be a relation of *do ut des;* or perhaps of *da ut dem.* If things are not disposed as she wishes, she threatens as a penalty that she will have done with believing. Sometimes *Dieu est méchant.* And 'jusqu'à présent je me suis toujours adressée à Dieu, mais comme il ne m'entend pas du tout, je n'y crois . . . presque plus.' But she then adds her sense of the absolute necessity of belief in God, unless for the very fortunate, as the sole stay of the human spirit, and adds, with her proper and portentous *naïveté,* 'Cela n'engage à rien.' Everywhere, however, in this book, and especially here, we must bear in mind that the **Journal** is a work of self-accusation as much as of self-worship, and that she clothes in words, which are of course vivid words, what passes through the minds of others but lies there only in embryo and unformed suggestion.

Among the lessons which a perusal of this record must bring home is a feeling of thankfulness that we have not been con-

stituted the judges of one another. Judgment indeed there must be, for without it we cannot learn; but it should always be conditioned, tentative, provisional, and never authoritative, never final. To be understood, the history here detailed leads us up to the words of Tennyson:—

> There's somewhat in this world amiss
> Shall be unriddled by and by.

Marie Bashkirtseff reminds me powerfully of the ruins of Selinunti, which are unlike any other ruins I ever saw. The temple is so shattered that it may be said to be reduced to a mass of single stones: but every stone by itself is majestic. Here were great powers, amassed in an abundance like that of the materials for the rearing of Solomon's temple. They have been lost in a double disappointment—for there is surely a disappointment apart from the too early death. It is not a case for elaborate laments.

> Let not high verse, mourning the memory
> Of that which is no more, or painting's woe,
> Or sculpture, speak in feeble imagery
> Their own cold powers.

The lesson is one to learn in silence, and the book one to close with a sorrowful but reverent sympathy for one who, in the striking language of M. Theuriet, was 'faite pour beaucoup souffrir, et pour beaucoup faire souffrir.' (pp. 602-07)

W. E. Gladstone, "'Journal de Marie Bashkirtseff','" in The Nineteenth Century, *Vol. XXVI, No. 152, October, 1889, pp. 602-07.*

ANATOLE FRANCE   (essay date 1889-92)

[*France was a French novelist and critic of the late nineteenth and early twentieth centuries. According to literary historians, France's best work is characterized by clarity, control, perceptive judgment, and tolerance. In the following essay, he sympathetically reviews Bashkirtseff's* Journal, *calling her a "troubled soul" and a "poor child whose misfortune it was to have had no childhood." This essay originally appeared in French in the four-volume collection* La vie littéraire, *published between 1889 and 1892.*]

Marie Bashkirtseff, whose journal has just been published, died at the age of twenty-four, on October 31st, 1884, leaving several canvases and some pastels which show a sincere feeling for nature and an ardent love of art. Granddaughter of General Paul Gregorievitch Bashkirtseff, one of the defenders of Sebastopol, she used to boast of having, through her mother, old Tartar blood in her veins. She had a fair complexion, magnificent red hair, prominent cheekbones, a short nose, a piercing look, and infantile lips. She was small and perfectly formed—a reason, doubtless, why she loved to look at statues. At Rome, when she was sixteen years old, she used to pass long hours before the marbles of the Capitoline Museum. We need not wonder, either, that at the same time she was also delighted with a riding-habit "in black cloth, made in one piece, by Laferrière . . . a dress in the Princess style, fitting closely everywhere."

Her hands, though slender and very white, were not of a perfect shape, but a painter has said that there was a beauty in the way in which she rested them on anything. Marie Bashkirtseff worshipped them. She knew that she was pretty, yet she seldom describes herself in her private diary. I have noted only, under the date of July 17th, 1874, this portrait, very prettily arranged: "My hair, knotted in Psyche fashion, is redder than ever. With a thin woollen dress of a particular shade of white, graceful and becoming, and a fichu of lace around my neck, I have the appearance of one of those portraits of the first Empire. To complete the picture, I ought to be under a tree, and holding a book in my hand." And she adds that she loves solitude in front of a mirror.

She was vainer of her voice than of her beauty. That voice was of a compass of three octaves, all but two notes. One of Marie Bashkirtseff's first dreams was to become a great singer.

She wished to show herself in her journal such as she was, with her faults and her merits, her continual restlessness, and her perpetual contradictions. M. Edmond de Goncourt, at the time he was writing the story of Chérie, used to ask young girls and women for confidences and confessions. Marie Bashkirtseff has given hers. She has, if we are to believe her, told us everything; but she was not of a disposition to address herself to a single confessor, however distinguished he might be. Her vanity could only be satisfied with a public confession, and it is before the world that she has opened her soul.

Who would not take pity and compassion on this poor child, whose misfortune it was to have had no childhood? That, doubtless, was nobody's fault, but Marie Bashkirtseff was never like those whom the God to whom she prayed every day designated as alone worthy of entering into the Kingdom of Heaven. She never knew the ineffable sweetness of being small and humble. At fifteen years of age, she had wings, but not the remembrance of the nest. Naïve gladness and simplicity she never possessed.

The first confidences that she makes us are those of a little love affair which she had at Rome during the Carnival, and which had no other result than a kiss on the eyelids. The young girl showed in it a considerable amount of coquetry and skill.

"You do not love me," sighed, one day, the young nephew of a Cardinal whom she allowed to be her patient admirer, "Alas! you do not love me."

"No."

"I must not hope?"

"Good Heavens! Yes! hope always. Hope is in the nature of man; but as for me, I will not give you any."

The priest's nephew displayed marked inclination, but Marie Bashkirtseff did not allow herself to be caught by it. "I should be at the pinnacle of joy if I believed him," she says, "but I doubt, in spite of his genuine, courteous, and even naïve manner. *That is what comes of being vulgar oneself.*"

And she adds:

"Besides, it is the better way."

She had not the least desire to marry poor Pietro.

"If I were his wife," she thought, "the riches, the villas, the museums of the Ruspoli, of the Dorias, of the Torlonias, of the Borghese, of the Chiaras, would crush me. I am ambitious and vain above everything. And to say that he loves such a creature simply because he does not know her! If he knew her, this creature . . . Ah! pshaw! he would love her all the same."

To show herself, to be in evidence, to shine, that is her perpetual dream. Pride devours her. She repeats incessantly: "If I

were a queen!" She exclaims as she walks in Rome: "I want to be Cæsar, Augustus, Marcus Aurelius, Nero, Caracalla, the Devil, the Pope!" She finds beauty only in the princes, in the Duke of H—, in the Grand Duke Wladimir, in Don Carlos. The rest are not worth a look.

The most incoherent ideas mingle together in her head. It is a strange chaos. She is very pious; she prays to God morning and evening. She asks from Him a duke for a husband, a beautiful voice, and her mother's recovery. She exclaims, like Shakespeare's Claudius: "There is nothing more awful than not to be able to pray." She has a special devotion to the Blessed Virgin; she practises the orthodox religion, and she reads the future in a broken mirror, in which she sees a multitude of little figures, the floor of a church in black and white marble, and perhaps a shroud. She consults Alexis the diviner, who in his trance sees Cardinal Antonelli; she has her fortune told for a louis by Mother Jacob. She has every superstition. She is persuaded that Pope Pius IX. has the evil eye. She fears a misfortune because she has seen the new moon with her left eye. Her ideas change every moment. At Naples she suddenly asks herself what sort of thing an immortal soul can be since it must retire before an indigestion caused by eating lobster. She does not see how a stomach-ache can put the celestial Psyche to flight, and she concludes that there is no soul, that it is "a pure invention." Some days later she puts a rosary round her neck, in order to look like Beatrix, she says, and also because "God in His simple grandeur does not suffice. We must have images to look at and crosses to kiss." She is coquettish, she is scatter-brained, but her linnet's head is furnished like that of an old librarian. At seventeen years of age, Marie Bashkirtseff has read Aristotle, Plato, Dante, and Shakespeare. Amédée Thierry's stories of Roman history captivate her. She recalls with pleasure "an interesting work on Confucius." She knows Horace, Tibullus, and the maxims of Publius Syrus by heart. She feels Homer's poetry deeply. "Nobody, it seems to me," she says, "can escape this adoration for the ancients. . . . No modern drama, no romance, no sensational comedy of Dumas or of George Sand, has left in me as clear a remembrance and as profound and natural an impression as the description of the taking of Troy. I seem to have been present at those horrors, to have heard the cries, seen the fire, been with Priam's family, with those wretches who hid themselves behind the altars of their gods, where the sinister blaze of the fire which was devouring their town was going to search them out and betray them . . . and who can escape a shudder whilst reading of the apparition of the phantom of Creusa?" Her mind is a storehouse into which she thrusts pellmell Madame de Staël's *Corinne*, the "Homme-Femme" of M. Alexandre Dumas fils, "Orlando Furioso," the novels of M. Zola, and those of George Sand. She travels incessantly, going from Nice to Rome, from Rome to Paris, from Paris to St. Petersburg, to Vienna, and to Berlin. Continually wandering, she is continually bored. Her life seems bitter and empty to her. "In this world," she says, "everything that is not sad is stupid, and everything that is not stupid is sad." She is without anything, because she wishes to have everything. She is in frightful distress, she utters cries of anguish, and yet she loves life. "I find it good," she says; "would one believe it? I find everything good and agreeable, even tears, even pain. I love to weep, I love to be in despair. I love to be grieved and sad . . . and I love life in spite of everything. I want to live. It would be cruel to make me die when I am so easy to please." At certain hours she has an obscure and terrible consciousness of the evil that broods over her. From the spring of 1876 onwards she feels herself stricken. "Just now," she wrote, under the date of June 3rd, "as I went out of my dressing-room I was superstitiously frightened. I saw beside me a woman dressed in a long white robe, a light in her hand, with her head a little bent, and plaintive-looking like those phantoms of the German legends. Reassure yourself, it was only I myself reflected in a mirror. Oh! I am afraid that a physical evil may proceed from all these moral tortures."

In 1877 a single passion took possession of this troubled soul. Marie Bashkirtseff devoted herself entirely to painting. At last she collected the scattered treasures of her intellect. All her dreams of fame melted into a single one, and henceforth she lived only to become a great artist. She studied with ardour in Julien's Academy, and she soon became one of its best pupils. It was, if I dare say so, one of those sudden conversions of which the lives of the saints offer so many examples, and which reveal a sincere, unrestrained, unstable nature. Henceforth princes were nothing to her. She became a Republican, a Socialist, and even a bit of a revolutionary. She put on no more of Laferrière's riding-habits, and gaily wore the black smock-frock of the woman-artist. She discovered the beauty of those who are wretched. She was a new creature. At the end of six months she was, along with Mademoiselle Breslau, at the head of the class. She has drawn a portrait of her rival which is certainly not a flattering one; "Breslau is thin, outlandish, wasted, although with an interesting head, no charm, like a boy, and—all alone!" She flatters herself that if she had Mademoiselle Breslau's talent, she would make use of it in a more feminine fashion. She would then be unique in Paris. In the meantime she works furiously. It is on January 21st, 1882, that for the first time she sees Bastien Lepage, whose painting she admired and imitated. "He is quite small," she says, "quite fair, wears his hair in the Breton style, has a turned-up nose, and the beard of a young man." He was already smitten with the disease of which he was soon to die. She herself felt that it had overtaken her. For two years she had been a prey to a racking cough. She grew thin. She became deaf. This infirmity drove her to despair. "Why," said she, "why does God make us suffer? If it is He who created the world, why has He created evil, suffering, wickedness? . . . I shall never get better. . . . There will be a veil between me and the rest of the world. The wind in the branches, the murmur of water, the rain dropping on the window-panes, words pronounced in a low voice, I shall hear nothing of all that!" Soon she learns that she is in consumption, and that her right lung is attacked. She exclaims: "Let me have ten years more, and fame and love during those ten years! and I shall die content at thirty. If there were any one with whom to come to terms I would make it a bargain—to die at thirty, after having known what it is to live." The consumption follows its fatal course. Marie Bashkirtseff writes on August 29th, 1883: "I cough all the time in spite of the heat, and this afternoon, during the model's rest, as I was half asleep on the divan, I *saw* myself stretched out, and a great taper lighted by my side. . . . "

"To die? I am very frightened of it."

Now that life is escaping her, she loves it to distraction. Arts, music, painting, books, society, dresses, luxury, noise, quiet, laughter, sadness, melancholy, love, cold, sunshine, all the seasons, the calm plains of Russia, and the mountains of Naples, the snow, the rain, the spring and its intoxications, the tranquil days of summer and its beautiful starlit nights, she adores, she admires them all! And she must die. "To die, it

is a word that one says, and that one writes easily, but to think, *to believe* that one is going to die soon? Do I believe it? No, but I *fear* it."

And some days later, brushing aside those illusions that plant themselves so obstinately at the bedside of consumptives, she sees death distinctly:

"Here is then the end of all our troubles! So many aspirations, so many desires, so many projects, so many . . . to die at twenty-four on the threshold of everything."

While she was dying, Bastien Lepage, also dying, had himself carried to her almost every day. The journal stops at Monday, October 20th. Even on that day, Bastien Lepage had come, supported by his brother, to the bedside of the dying woman. Marie Bashkirtseff expired eleven days afterwards, "on a foggy day," says M. André Theuriet, "like that which she had painted in one of her last pictures, 'L'Allée.'"

It is always a touching spectacle, when nature shows us Love and Death, the one beside the other, in a terrible epitome. But there is in Marie Bashkirtseff's all too short life something bitter, something which contracts the heart. We think as we read her ***Journal*** that she must have died still unsatisfied, and that her shade yet wanders somewhere, laden with heavy desires.

As I reflect on the agitations of that troubled spirit, and follow the course of that life, uprooted and flung to all the winds of Europe, I murmur with the fervour of a prayer this verse of Sainte-Beuve:

> To be born to live and to die in the same house!

(pp. 146-54)

Anatole France, "Marie Bashkirtseff," in his On Life & Letters, *translated by A. W. Evans, 1911. Reprint by Dodd, Mead and Company, 1924, pp. 146-54.*

MATHILDE BLIND (essay date 1890)

[*In the following excerpt from an introduction to her English translation of the* Journal, *Blind discusses Bashkirtseff's multi-faceted personality, which made her "a born critic of life."*]

An autobiography such as this ***Journal of Marie Bashkirtseff***—a book in the nude, breathing and palpitating with life so to say—has never, to my knowledge, been given to the world. In some sense, therefore, its publication may be looked upon as a literary event. To read it is an education in psychology. For in this startling record a human being has chosen to lay before us "the very pulse of the machine," to show us the momentary feelings and impulses, the uninvited back-stair thoughts passing like a breath across our consciousness, which we ignore for the most part when presenting our mental harvest to the public. Is it well, is it ill done to make the world our father confessor, to take it into our most intimate and secret confidence? Difficult to say, but in any case it is supremely interesting. For it is like possessing one of the much envied fairy gifts which enabled one to see through stone walls and to hear the thoughts as they passed through a man's head. We may like this book or not; we may find the personality revealed in it adorable or repellent; but no one can deny that it is a genuine addition to our knowledge of human nature. "In any case," as its young author says, with striking penetration, "it is at least interesting as a human document" [see essay dated 1884], and more particularly so as a document about feminine nature, of which as yet we know so little. Indeed, most of our knowledge comes to us second-hand, through the medium of men with their cut-and-dried theories as to what women are or ought to be.

Now here is a girl, the story of whose life as told by herself may be called the drama of a woman's soul; at odds with destiny, as such a soul must needs be, when endowed with great powers and possibilities, under the present social conditions; where the wish to live, of letting whatever energies you possess have their full play in action, is continually thwarted by the impediments and restrictions of sex. A girl with the ambition of a Cæsar—as she herself says—smouldering under her crop of red golden hair, has a hard time of it though her head repose on down pillows edged with the costliest of laces; such a girl may well be fretted into a fever by the loving care of her affectionate aunts and uncles, and grandparents, &c. &c. Did we but know it the same revolts, the same struggles, the same helpless rage, have gone on in many another woman's life for want of scope for her latent powers and faculties.

But Marie Bashkirtseff is too complex and versatile a nature to be taken in illustration of any particular theory; she is made up of heterogeneous elements, and her mutability of mood is a constant surprise to the reader. She never wholly yields herself up to any fixed rule of conduct, or even passion, being swayed this way or that by the intense impressionability of her nature. She herself recognises this anomaly in the remark: "My life can't endure; I have a deal too much of

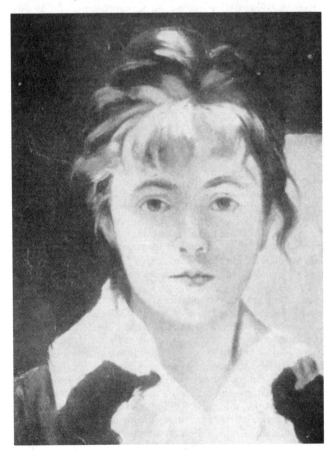

Self-portrait of Bashkirtseff.

some things and a deal too little of others, and a character not made to last." The very intensity of her desire to seize life at all points seems to defeat itself, and she cannot help stealing side glances at ambition during the most romantic *tête-à-tête* with a lover, or of being tortured by visions of unsatisfied love when art should have engrossed all her faculties. For she wants everything at once—whatever success Fortune has to offer its favourites, the glamour of youth and beauty, rank and wealth with their glittering gifts, the artist's fame, the power of a queen of society—all, all, or nothingness! She hardly realised in her passionate self-absorption and egotism how much she asked, or what a niggard Fate is to the claims of individual man. I was strangely reminded of her on my return from Paris last autumn, where I had been to see her pictures and the house with its splendid studio where the last years of Marie Bashkirtseff's life were spent. Near me, on the Calais boat, sat a beautiful little French boy between three and four years old, staring intently at the sea below. Suddenly he looked round and asked, as if the thought had just struck him, "Is this the sea, Mamma?" On her replying in the affirmative, he said in the most matter-of-fact tone, "Mamma, I want to drink up the whole sea."

"Maman, je voudrais boire toute la mer," said this delicate, golden-haired mite of a boy, his earnest eyes fixed on the welter of waters just lit for a moment with the stormy crimson of a sudden sunset. This wish—childish but not unnatural where the limits of personality are unrealised—seemed like an echo, the mocking echo of Marie Bashkirtseff's life.

Did not she too want to drink up the whole sea, the whole of life, embracing the entire circle of sensations, but finding only a few poor pitiful spoonfuls doled out to her instead, dash herself to pieces, in her ineffectual rage at the obstacles she encountered. How well she knew herself is shown by her saying, "If I could keep a little quieter I might live another twenty years." But she was too intensely modern for repose. Born in an age of railways and electric telegraphs, she wanted to live by steam. Terribly moving, when we remember the sequel, is that bitter cry of hers, the very burden of her *Journal:* "Oh, to think that we live but once and that life is so short! When I think of it I am quite beside myself, and my brain reels with despair." . . .

"We live but once, and my time is being wasted in the most unworthy fashion. These days which are passing are passing never to return."

"We live but once! And must life, so short already, be shortened still further; must it be spoilt—nay, stolen—yes, stolen by infamous circumstances?"

This violent temperament, full of stress and tumult, may be partly due to the opposing tendencies of heredity and actual circumstances. For Marie Bashkirtseff, although in a measure the product of modern French life, and moulded by cosmopolitan influences, is nevertheless intensely Russian. Her personality is a singular mixture of untutored instincts joined to an ultra-modern subtlety of brain and nerves. She has the wild Cossack blood in her veins, but on her back the last fashionable novelty by Worth. Her religion offers the same curious compound of primitive idolatry and philosophical reasoning. Not only is she apt, as Mr. Gladstone so happily expresses it [see review dated 1889], "to treat the Almighty as she treated her grandfather, *en égal,*" the nature of her prayers is essentially similar to a savage's worship of his idol—inclined to be extremely devout if his requests are granted; but likely to turn restive and make away with his fetish if the latter remains deaf to him. And the singularity is that while she is acting her religious part with immense fervour, devoutly saying her prayers as she kneels on the floor, she doesn't believe in God at all. Indeed, she acutely dissects the nature of religious beliefs, while continuing in her half-belief; for, as she says in her naïve cynicism, *"cela n'engage à rien."* Yet she was full of profound intuitions—unexpected flashes of insight that opened out perspectives into the infinite mysteries of spiritual experience. She startles the reader every now and then in the very midst of her wounded vanities and lamentations over her wasted life of sixteen summers by assuring him that she is not to be taken quite seriously, that, after all, it is not so very sad, and that the sadness itself and the sighs, the tears and the wringing of hands, are part of the play at which the other Ego—the over-soul as Emerson would say—is all the time present as at a spectacle. This unknown factor of human consciousness, aloof and indifferent to misery and pain—nay, even enjoying misery and pain—is often referred to by the youthful writer, showing that Marie was above all a born critic of life—love and sorrow, passion and pain serving but as the raw material for the development of thought and analysis. In this respect her *Journal* is a far more complete expression of her individuality than her pictures are. And it is possible that the novel—the most modern of all forms of art—might have afforded the fullest scope for the development of her genius. For the novel, treated with the conscientious precision of scientific analysis, is the distinctive feature of Russian literature. But the question is whether she was not too much taken up with herself to enter into other lives with the sympathetic insight required for the delineation of human character. Be that as it may, she has produced a book of more absorbing interest than any novel can ever be—a book with all the attraction of romance, and yet a mirror reflecting life in its passage from day to day. Indeed, the unique interest of this *Journal* arises from the fact that the writer, in the very ardour of the moment, finds relief in recording her impressions; and while in the act of experiencing a variety of sensations, she is yet able to treat herself, and others in contact with herself, as objects of dispassionate observation, to be used with minute fidelity in the representation of human existence. (pp. vii-xi)

Could Marie Bashkirtseff have known what a sensation she has produced since her untimely end, even her thirst for renown might have been appeased. Could she have known that her chief picture was bought by the State within a year of her death, and now hangs in the Luxembourg along with the masterpieces of modern French art; could she have known that her *Journal* is an enthusiasm to the few, a curiosity to the many, and is taking rank among the autobiographies the world will not willingly let die; could she have known of the essay which the spell of her personality has drawn from the grand old humanitarian leader of England—could she have known all this, it might have compensated her for much in her life, and would have spared her that haunting dread of perishing with nothing to show that she had been—*"rien, rien, rien!"* (p. xxxiv)

> *Mathilde Blind, in an introduction to* The Journal of Marie Bashkirtseff, Vol. I, *translated by Mathilde Blind, Cassell & Company, Limited, 1890, pp. vii-xxxiv.*

WILLIAM STEAD   (essay date 1890)

[*In the following excerpt from a review of the* Journal, *Stead declares the work "interesting and instructive beyond most other books of our time," but criticizes Bashkirtseff for her "unwomanly" self-centeredness and lack of patriotic feeling for her native Russia.*]

In this *Journal* you see a good deal of the wilful Marie, more perhaps than many of us have been permitted to see of most women, even in our own families; more, indeed, than most women see even of themselves, but we do not see the whole woman, nor do we ever feel that even in her case, there is an exception to the rule laid down by the sombre author of "Night Thoughts":—

> God spares all beings, save Himself, the sight.
> That hideous sight, a naked human heart.

The human creature has far too much eye for effect ever to reveal itself quite naturally. The Journal—the private secret journal—which so many of us have kept, was well-named long ago by John Forster the "Devil's Vanity Trap." We write for ourselves alone, we say, and even as we write that pious lie, we see the eye of the critic glancing over our shoulder, and despite all our efforts we assume a pose. Marie Bashkirtseff, no doubt, tries resolutely to photograph her varying phases of emotion from day to day, but there is an element of theatricality about it also. Even in her undress she poses and folds about her with artist's instinct whatever scrap of a garment she retains—even if it be only a dressing gown—with a constant eye to effect. And, above all, she never really leaves go of her dressing-gown; hence an element of unreality about the *Journal* which, nevertheless, with all its drawbacks, is interesting and instructive beyond most other books of our time. Here, at least, a young and gifted girl does at least try to set down night by night how she felt, what she thought, and what things she longed for; and how few there are of human kind of all those who have ever undertaken the task have written as well as she or written so sadly. Women, like men, for the most part, are happily too busy to find time to turn the microscope upon their vitals and to spend hours, like a Hindoo fakir, absorbed in self-contemplation. Those who have time for the task have, as a rule, little or nothing to tell us. The moanings of a do-nothing lady of wealth would bore us exceedingly, nor would her journal—the mere eructation of mental flatulence—be of interest to a living soul. But poor Marie was in herself supremely interesting. To begin with, she was a woman, a young woman, and a young Russian woman. In Slavonic countries woman, who elsewhere is the inferior or the equal of man, is his superior. The brain of the Slav woman weighs more than that of the man, and she excels him in most of the human qualities. Two Russian types of womanhood, portrayed by great artists, have impressed themselves indelibly upon the imagination of the Western world. One is the Lisa of Turgenieff, the other the Anna Karenina of Tolstoi. Side by side with these heroines, whose exquisite femininity makes us revolt passionately against the tragic pathos of their doom, we have the dark and sombre but heroic gallery of female Nihilists—who have taught Europe more than it cares to acknowledge of the terrible grandeur of self-immolation—the brilliant and energetic Princess Lieven, and here in this journal a Russian girl of artistic genius and copious articulation, who pours out in the ear of the world the confidences, the self-reproaches, the self-appreciation, which most people blush even to mutter in the solitude of their own room. But what a charm there is about them all, speaking as they do of marvellous youth and inexhaustible vitality. Marie Bashkirtseff's *Journal* carries us back into the heart of Russia, with the exuberance of its spring-like beauty, the fierce heat of its noonday when the young green leaves seem to faint and wither in the sun rays, and the indescribable charm of the gloaming when the voices of the peasant girls singing in chorus on their way to the well swing in the air like the low-toned music of the Russian bells. She is a true child of her country—Russian crossed with a Tartar strain, with nerves all tremulous as aspen leaves, but capable of sudden tension as if steel. Like the Steppe, which loses itself in a dim horizon where earth and sky mingle, and are lost, there is ever a mystical background encompassing her life, in the midst of which are signs and portents and superstitions not unworthy the moujiks who tilled her father's land. Fierce, too, and passionate, as a child, there is in her life something not unlike the short brilliant summer of Muscovy. You go to sleep in the train amidst snow and frost and a desolate forest, in which the perennial green of the fir alone breaks the black expanse of leafless boughs. You wake next morning in the midst of the luxuriant spring verdure of an English May. The birds are singing in midheaven, the frogs are chanting in the marsh, the delicate green leaves of the silvery birch are shining in the sunlight. Everywhere there is light and gladness, the warmth and the glow of light. For a time it lasts, and then almost with equal suddenness the icy grasp of winter freezes the land into the silence and darkness of death. The birds sing no more, the waters are shrouded deep with ice, the very animals hybernate, and all Russia is one wintry grave. Marie Bashkirtseff's life was just like that—the sudden burst into consciousness, the brief hot day, and then the long cold nights.

Marie Bashkirtseff has been compared to Rousseau. But she is no "self-torturing sophist." She is Russian—Russian in her infantile directness and energy of nature, who chronicles as she goes instead of philosophising after the event. But even more than this, she is a woman. A Rousseau in petticoats, a Rousseau from whom the dominating element of Jean Jacques seems to have been eliminated, has little left of Rousseau, except intense self-consciousness, supreme egotism, and a certain relief in wailing in the market-place. Far more than a Rousseau, Marie Bashkirtseff is the preacher in Ecclesiastes. Vanity of vanity all is vanities, written at large in every page of this "human document." Youth she had, and beauty, wealth and boundless ambition—a career that offered endless vistas of success; fame, love, all that she most longed for, she tasted, and then saw it dashed from her lips. Seldom has there been a more pathetic record of disappointments since the days of the Preacher who, having looked on all the works that his hands had wrought, and saw the labour that he had laboured to do, and behold! all was vanity and vexation of spirit, and there was no profit under the sun. (pp. 539-40)

Marie Bashkirtseff, although a genius, is as wayward, as fitful, as passionate, as imperious, as vain, and, withal, as indifferent as any coquette of any age. "It is only the envelope of me that is feminine, deucedly feminine," she says, and the envelope does not go deep down. Of the distinctively womanly there is in her but little trace. She was Russian with a trace of Tartar blood; her temper was uncontrollable. On one occasion, her nerves getting the better of her, she flung a clock into the sea as a relief to her overstrung feelings; on another she tore up her gloves. But of genuine passion, of overpowering affection, she may have been capable, but she died before it blossomed in her, and she seems to have been equally devoid

of tenderness even to those who spent their lives for her. She was a spoiled child, tyrannically selfish, and therefore the very antithesis of the true woman.

It is curious to see how eager she is to have her lovers tell her how they love her, to describe when the malady began, and so forth—as a spectator curious and interested, but without sympathy or corresponding sentiment. Yet she can write:—

> Ah! how sweet it is to be loved! There is nothing in the world so sweet . . .
>
> I wished to know how he came to love me, and since when. It seems that he loved me from the first.

Yet she never loved him back, although, as she notes, "his fire warms my heart." She coolly tells one adorer who had just assured her that he loved her as no one else did, and that he was devoted to her body and soul, "I generally inspire feelings of that kind." The impassivity of soul, the absence of all response beyond the vulgar love of triumph, that is not even saddened by the ravages which it inflicts—these do not charm us with Marie Bashkirtseff. They were probably due to immaturity. Her intellect developed in advance of her heart. If she had lived but ten more years all this unripeness of heart might have disappeared. In this she was true to nature. A woman who has not learnt to feel is apt to be as cruel and ruthless in her way as a schoolboy is in his. But so far from regarding her as a full and perfect woman revealed all undraped before the astonished eyes of mankind, she is hardly to be regarded as a woman at all in the full sense of the word. There was in her an intense fever of life, but it did not flow in the normal channels. She was artist, musician, wit, philosopher, student, anything you like but a natural woman with a heart to love, and a soul to find its supreme satisfaction in sacrifice for lover or for child. In her the natural yields to the artificial. She is self-conscious to an absurd extent, and her egotism is sublime. On one occasion she is overwhelmed by a consciousness of her own beauty that for twenty minutes she gazed enraptured on her own charms, and chronicles the fact in her diary. "I compare myself," she says on another occasion, "with all the statues I see." She is always comparing herself with everyone, always thinking of herself, her thoughts always eternally revolving round her own personality. Poor Marie—it seems hard to say such things of one so young, so gifted, and so charming—but we tremble at the thought of the deluge of egotistic sentimentalities with which the success of her journal will flood the world if every ambitious school-girl is taught to regard Marie Bashkirtseff as a type and example of the supremely interesting woman. Not the less do we regret the spread of the conviction in the minds of men that these women folk in the secret heart are always dreaming and longing and gushing *à la* Bashkirtseff.

There is nothing to prove that she ever felt the inspiration and the glow of that passion which lifts the humblest of her sisters into an ideal world. Men were always falling in love with her. She tried sometimes to make believe that she was in love with them, but it was always a failure. As she neared the end of her life, she felt this, but could not act on the feeling.

> I consider I am very foolish for not being seriously preoccupied with the only thing worth troubling about—the only thing which gives all sorts of happiness which obliterates all sufferings—love, of course, love. Love performs the miracle of the mingling of souls. It's an illusion. No matter! That

which you believe exists for you. I tell you so. Love makes the world appear as it ought to be.

But of love Marie Bashkirtseff was utterly destitute until the very last, when she, herself dying, began to feel love for one already half-dead. Even in the one great-love scene in the journal, in which she met at midnight on the bottom of the stairs in her Roman palace one of the most dissolute of the young Roman nobles, and spent two hours with him in the darkness alone, listening to his protestations of affection, there is no thrill, there is no touch of real feeling. She was very clever, no doubt, very fascinating, but woman she was not. In all the journal there is no truer word than this entry:—

> If I dish you up moving phrases, don't let yourself be caught by them. Of the two selves who are trying to live, one says to the other, But in heaven's name, have a veneration of some kind. And the other one who attempts to feel something is always dominated by the first. The *Moi Spectateur* which continues observing and absorbing the seconds, and will it always be so? And love?
>
> Well, to tell you the truth, it seems impossible when you see human nature through the microscope. The others are very happy, they only see what is necessary. Would you like to know? Well, then, I am neither painter, sculptor, nor musician; neither woman, nor daughter, nor friend. Everything reduces itself with me into subjects of observation, reflection, and analysis. A look, a face, a sound, a joy, a sorrow are immediately weighed, examined, verified, classified, noted down. And when I have said or written it I am satisfied.

That assuredly is not typical woman.

If Marie Bashkirtseff is thus lacking in the supreme quality of her sex, she is equally lacking in the supreme quality of a Russian. She is a poor patriot, although, of course, she does feel towards Russia a certain admiration and even affection. She speaks of her Russian heart leaping for joy when the *Revue des Deux Mondes* devotes an article to "my great and admirable native land." But Russia—beautiful, great, and sublime though she regarded it—bored her extremely, and the exclamation that she worked in Paris for the glory of her country was a poor excuse. I admit that had she been other than Russian, her modicum of patriotic feeling would have sufficed; but with Russians patriotism holds a far higher place among the elemental virtues than in the West, and Marie Bashkirtseff was a poor patriot for a Russian. She was, it must be remembered, brought up abroad. But her journal during the war of 1876-8 shows how little she was in sympathy with the overpowering emotion which throbbed in the heart of all good Russians. She arrived at St. Petersburg when the sensation produced by the heroic death of young Kireeff, Madame Novikoff's brother, in the Servian war, was thrilling the nation's heart. She notes the widespread feeling, but it leaves her unmoved. At Moscow, a fervid appeal on behalf of the Servians rouses her to ask indignantly why the Tzar does not declare war, but beyond this there is hardly a trace in her voluminous journal of any interest in the great world-drama which has unfolded itself before her eyes in Eastern Europe. The singing at the station when the volunteers depart for Servia thrills her, but the fate of the brave fellows is never alluded to. The declaration of war, for which she had longed, passed without comment. Only once during that terrible year when the Russians were slaughtered in hecatombs before Plevna, and Shipka was being held by the skin of their teeth,

does her journal show any trace of patriotic emotion. She remains silent a whole night in order to secure the despatch of reinforcements to her veterans of Shipka, and she records with gratification that the reinforcements arrived. She says an immense number of prayers, but she says nothing of the other incidents of the war. Even the conclusion of peace within sight of Constantinople is to her less than the death of a pet dog or the shape of an ill-fitting dress. No one, but for a couple of entries for 1877 to 1878, would ever imagine that the voluminous writer belonged to a nation, which was in the throes of its destiny. She never names Skobeleff or Gourko, and as for the Berlin Congress and the treaty which ended the war, Marie Bashkirtseff does not so much as allude to them. Even from the mere point view of one who hunted insatiably after sensations, this indifference to the fate of her country is somewhat disappointing, especially when the young lady was so susceptible as to weep for thirty-six hours over the death of the Prince Imperial.

But a truce to fault-finding and criticising this fair and fascinating girl, who, although deficient in the two master passions of a Russian woman, nevertheless possessed so much charm both of body and of mind. There is nothing more interesting in the journal than the entries in which this frank, unsophisticated child-woman puts down with characteristic bluntness her ideas about God. Some people say that she did not believe in God. No doubt, at times, from her as well as all others, He seemed to have hidden His face, to have been evaporated out of existence by philosophical speculations, or to be disproved by the logic of facts. But at bottom there was always the child-like faith or passionate yearning for God, a real live God, a father to one who never knew what it was to have a father's care, a confidante, a friend who never failed. Merely to string together the entries in the journal on this subject suffices to show how child-like was her faith, how simple and natural the outpouring of her soul to the Infinite, how sad and cold she found the world when faith in God went out, and left her alone in the dim and dreary gloom of approaching death. (pp. 544-46)

Marie Bashkirtseff complained once that her parents had not systematically educated her. She might with much more reason have complained that they had over-trained her, overstrained her, or taught her the ordinary lessons of unselfishness and self-control, which are essential to the making of a tolerable human character. Marie Bashkirtseff might have been a splendid woman if she had ever been broken in. Her magnificent will would then have been an instrument by which she might have attained almost any height in the artistic profession. But, untrained as she was, or rather trained as she was to be self-indulgent, vain, selfish, not even her indomitable devotion to a study for which but little original aptitude could do more than bring her to the threshold of success. The *Journal* is the tragedy of a spoiled life, and Marie Bashkirtseff deserved a better fate. There is pathos enough no doubt in the gradual deprivation, first of her hearing, and then of her young, impulsive life, but there is more pathos in the evidence with which every page abounds of the life poisoned at its source by vanity, egotism, and absolute indifference to the welfare of others. Except to her dogs, there is no trace in these pages of a considerate act. Mother and aunt slaved for her, she queened it over them like an empress, and showed herself absolutely indifferent to their happiness. Her envy and hatred of her rivals was only too much in keeping with the rest of her character. Had she been but a little more careful to avoid giving others pain she might have been living now. It is sad to think that an early death should have carried her off before the spoiled child had time to mend her spoiled life. (p. 549)

William Stead, " 'The Journal of Marie Bashkirtseff': The Story of a Girl's Life," in The Review of Reviews, *Vol. 1, No. 6, June, 1890, pp. 539-49.*

LIONEL JOHNSON (essay date 1891)

[*An English poet and critic, Johnson is considered one of the most important figures associated with the Decadent and Aesthetic movements of the 1890s. Like many of his contemporaries, he lived an eccentric life and died young, producing a small but distinguished body of works that reflects his deep interest in medieval literature and thought and demonstrates two major influences: Walter Pater's aestheticism and the poetry of the Celtic Revival. In the following essay he insists that Bashkirtseff's journal and letters have been overrated, denouncing them as the foolish outpourings of a silly, vulgar, and conceited girl. Johnson's remarks first appeared in the* Anti-Jacobin *on 10 October 1891.*]

Had the diaries and letters of Mdlle. Bashkirtseff been the work of another woman, she would have criticised them something in this manner:—"I have read the celebrated diary, the wonderful letters. Oh, the happy woman! To long, long, long for things all her life, and to die of consumption! the beautiful death! at twenty-three! That is my idea of success in this terrible world. To long passionately for fame, adoration, triumph; and to die before she found out that there is nothing, nothing, nothing, in all the world! I am mad with jealousy. Oh, my God! help me, Thou! That is quite a simple prayer. They have not sent home my white dress, and tonight the Prince will think me hideous: he, with his drooping moustache and pale brow! Oh! the poor girl that I am. And she, the other, had so much! And Aunt Mary has actually forgotten to have the dogs washed."

The journal and the letters of Mdlle. Bashkirtseff have won the admiration of this singular age by utterances precisely in that tone and style. So frank, so fearless, so human, so true: veritable records of a mind touched by all our modern influences: those wonderful influences which no one will be good enough to explain, which every one "in the movement" is only too anxious to experience. After reading these volumes, the poor disbeliever in the movement is left with a sense of profound disgust. Silly petulance, ill-bred ostentation, unfathomable conceit, offensive vulgarity, and no trace of affection or of thought: these are the gifts and qualities which we are called upon to study and to admire. Fine phrases are invented for it: the revelation of a soul, the true history of a modern mind, the exhibition in all their crudity of passions and desires, hopes and despairs, which modesty or shame is accustomed to conceal. Few persons have gone to the extreme of asking us to admire Mdlle. Bashkirtseff: she was vain, foolish, and so forth: but then she did not mind saying so! And the spectacle of a young Russian lady suffering the *maladie de siècle,* and boldly exposing its symptoms to the world, is a spectacle that appeals to our sympathies or excites our curiosity. So say the wise teachers of our time. But apart from the sorry taste evinced in admiration of these writings, we can but wonder at the surprise and excitement felt over them. For the explanation of their character is perfectly simple, and nothing new. Every man, by the natural constitution of his mind, thinks about his thoughts, and not only is conscious of his emotions, but has a further consciousness of that consciousness. Take a man at his devotions, a man of real and simple religious nature: he performs them with perfect sincerity, but he is also conscious of his devotional emotion, as though he were a dispassionate critic outside himself. Look at a beautiful scene or work of art: you genuinely admire and enjoy, but you also reflect upon your admiration and enjoyment. And the process may be indefinitely prolonged. A man who is perpetually analysing his motives, thinking of his thoughts, examining his emotions, runs a fair chance of becoming imbecile: but the process is none the less a natural one. Some years ago a Catholic priest wrote an account of his novitiate in a religious order. At the ceremony of profession it was customary for the prior to crown the professed with white flowers. The writer says: "Even at that solemn moment the ludicrous could not be entirely banished, and the thought of my bald head and grizzled tonsure called up irresistibly thoughts of Greek philosophers at a symposium, and inspired me with a frantic desire to conclude the ceremony." That is innocent enough, but to encourage this natural tendency of reflection till it becomes a very torment of perpetual self-consciousness, is sure to end in an unnatural state of mind. Mdlle. Bashkirtseff, being by nature quick and keen of mind, became, in sober truth, a monomaniac, unable to think of anything but herself. In her art, her dress, her acquaintance, her every thought and feeling, she was consumed with a passion for analysing her motives and emotions, for appearing effective, for creating a situation. So that in her journal and letters there is not one single line of simple, unsophisticated writing. Yet we are told of her spontaneous, genuine, frank confessions: of her yearning for a great life, for fame, for manifold experience. Hers is only a case of childish precocity, bad training, and consequent craziness.

She visits Père Didon, the great Dominican. "One would like to see him with a moustache. One can see plainly that he is fully aware of his popularity, that he is accustomed to adoration; that he is sincerely delighted with the sensation he creates everywhere!" So *naïve!* and so penetrating! She goes to confession: and because it was "singular" she records its details in her diary with a positive relish. She writes to her mother: "I am going to tell you about my childish doings. This morning I went for a walk and entered a Catholic church. I availed myself of the absolute solitude of the place to go up into the pulpit, to go into the choir, to go on the altar" (surely a mistranslation here), "and to read the prayers placed on the tablet of the altar: I did all this by way of prayer, for I have a multitude of projects in which I need the assistance of Heaven. But the thought that I have read a Mass transports me! Only think, I rang the bell as the priests do during Mass!" (They do not: but no matter.) "At all events my intentions were not bad."

So much for Mdlle. Bashkirtseff's religion, which does not seem to have been one of her more cherished emotions. It is in her letters to her relatives, mother, grandfather, brother, that the perfection of her trivial selfishness appears. She informs a friend that "Mamma was very good to-day. In the end I really believe I shall grow fond of her." She leaves her mother to go to Paris, against her mother's wish. "I am a naughty girl; I left my mother, saying I was delighted to depart with my uncle. That made her feel unhappy, and people do not know how much I love her, and they judge me by appearances. Oh! according to appearances I am not very affectionate." That is very true: her affections never display themselves in deeds. She leaves her grandfather without taking any notice of him, and explains that she did it in her hurry to get away. She worries her aunt with perpetual clamour for money, and with perpetual commissions about her dresses and her dogs. To her father: "You have always been prejudiced against me, although I have never done anything to justify such a feeling on your part. I have never lost the love and esteem for you, however, which every well-born girl owes to her father." To her brother she sends an elaborate description of her dress: "A gown of a clinging and elastic material that modestly revealed the outline of my figure": "you should be proud, my dear boy, to have a sister like me." But the most unpleasant things in the book are her accounts of men and of her interest in them. She is enchanted with the coarse admiration of strangers who stare at her in the theatre, or follow her in the streets. She describes them with the vulgar silliness of a romantic shop-girl. One of them "is dark, has very fine eyes, a slight drooping moustache, a velvety skin, such as I do not think I have ever before seen in a man; a handsome mouth, a regular nose, neither round nor pointed, nor aquiline nor classic—a nose of which, too, the skin is delicate, a thing which is exceedingly rare," etc. Then there are her letters to distinguished writers unknown to her, more foolish and impertinent than one could have thought possible. Of *Faust* she writes that "the subject is disgusting. I do not say immoral, hideous: I say *disgusting.*" And that is what we say of her letters. They disgust us, because they are so hopelessly foolish and so unspeakably undignified: so full of petulant vanity and of pretentious affectation. Arnold said of a certain letter by Keats, that "it is the sort of love-letter of a surgeon's apprentice which one might hear read out in a breach of promise case, or in the Divorce Court." These letters are the letters of an hysterical lady's-maid in point of manner, of an undisciplined female novelist in point of matter. To paraphrase Arnold, "they have in their relaxed self-abandonment something underbred and ignoble, as of a girl ill brought up, without the training which teaches us that we must put some constraint upon our feelings and upon the expression of them." And Mdlle. Bashkirtseff was very badly brought up: that is obvious. It would have been a saving discipline for her to have known the severity of wise parents, or even of cruel: she might have learned endurance, if not reverence.

To those who affect an admiration of her character let us suggest the question: What would life become were most women like Mdlle. Bashkirtseff? Could any man wish to have a wife, a daughter, a sister, like her? Is it for her qualities that any man honours and loves his mother? Philistine questions, but worth asking. And if the answer must be No, how are we to justify this fervent interest in a diseased and silly soul?

Such souls are merely miserable, pitiable: not admirable nor estimable. It is in vain for them, as Massillon has it, *"se consoler d'une passion par une autre passion nouvelle; d'une perte par un nouvel attachement; d'une disgrace par de nouvelles espérances; l'amertume les suit partout; ils changent de situation mais ils ne changent pas de supplice."* Some lovers of extravagance and of perversion may enjoy these dismal pages, with all their outcries and affectations: to those who love the natural beauty of the natural mind, and to those who know the strength and sternness of a real sorrow, these pages must seem false and wretched, and the liking for them a melancholy sign of disordered times. (pp. 245-50)

Lionel Johnson, "Marie Bashkirtseff," in his Post Liminium: Essays and Critical Papers, *edited by Thomas Whittemore, Elkin Mathews, 1911, pp. 245-50.*

BOJIDAR KARAGEORGEVITCH   (essay date 1903)

[*Karageorgevitch was a Russian nobleman and longtime friend of the Bashkirtseff family. In the following essay, he discusses the alterations made to the original manuscript of the* Journal *and the resulting misconceptions surrounding Bashkirtseff's life.*]

"What is the use of lying and posing? To begin with, I wrote for a long time without ever thinking that I should be read by others, and now it is just because I do hope to be read that I am absolutely truthful. If this book were not the *exact, absolute and faithful truth,* there would be no reason for its existence."

Marie Bashkirtseff thus opens the preface of her *Diary* [see essay dated 1884]. It seems to me that my poor, charming friend did not need this preamble. When there is anything that deviates from the strict truth in a memoir it becomes a romance, the title of the book thus becomes inaccurate and makes it lose much of its value.

I had already read Marie Bashkirtseff's *Diary* when the first two volumes of it appeared in print, but during that first perusal of it, I was still too full of emotion, of sorrow, to be able to criticise the book and grasp the wrong impression it gave of its author. She seemed to live again in certain details, certain scenes in which in nearly every case the actors and the setting were familiar to me, but I could not judge of the *tout ensemble* of the book, and of the effect that such a work would produce on the indifferent reader. In spite of this, it seemed to me that I did not find in the book the Marie I had known—the best and most intelligent of women, the rare soul to whose advice I owe nearly all the good fortune I have had in my life.

A third volume of Marie Bashkirtseff's *Memoirs* appeared recently. I then reread the three volumes, and was disagreeably surprised to discover several mis-statements that had escaped me at the first reading, and which, I am sure, were quite unintentional on the part of the authoress.

In 1879 Marie owned to her *Diary* that she was nineteen, and spoke of the marriage of her brother Paul, who had then attained his majority. Now, though it is not mentioned in any part of the *Diary* as now published, yet it is a fact that Marie was older than her brother Paul. Again, in the book Marie is present at the Michael Angelo centenary fêtes at Florence, and the date is given as the 14th September, 1874. Unfortunately for the book, I will not say for Marie, these fêtes were celebrated in 1875. People do not think of all these things in arranging.

After this incontrovertible instance, it seems difficult to credit the dates of the book. We are astonished at the precocity, the maturity, the depth of soul with which Marie wrote at the age of twelve. Her reflections on the Duke of Hamilton, reflections of a little girl of twelve, if we are to trust the veracity of the book, provoked the admiration of Lombroso and other specialists. Doctors have gone into this "case" from the beginning, they have put down this unheard-of precocity to atavism, have discovered a humpbacked aunt, consumptive tendencies, extraordinary circumstances of birth, etc., etc. All this has increased the sale of the book and has interested the reader, whilst the real truth, which is better proved by the trickery of the book than even by the publication of Marie's birth certificate, is that Marie at the moment of her fancy for the Duke of Hamilton was sixteen or seventeen years of age, and that the "freak" who has puzzled all the mind specialists was simply an ordinary young girl waiting for the Prince Charming whom all girls expect at that age.

In the light of the *real, plain, unvarnished* truth, Marie is no longer a "freak," a phenomenon; she leaves Barnum's show for the ranks of ordinary people, and if she loses something in novelty I am quite sure that she gains greatly in interest. Again in the book certain things are made to stand out, the smallest occurrences in the St. Julian Studio are repeated and enlarged indefinitely, whilst in reality, after the first six months of studio life, Marie grew weary of this tittle-tattle, and did not even repeat it to those who, like myself, were her daily confidants.

On the other hand, other pages of the *Diary* are entirely omitted, or very nearly so. Marie was one of the first apostles of feminism. She aided in the publication of the *Citoyenne,* a feminist paper which preceded the *Fronde,* and which has since disappeared, and for which she wrote the art criticism for a year or two. For awhile she was devoted, body and soul, to feminism. She used to be present at the meetings in the Petrelle Hall, and scolded me as if I were the lowest of creatures, because my interest in these questions was not sufficiently lively, and because on one occasion I pushed my indifference so far as to tell her that I had been present at a meeting to which she had sent me, and at which I had not appeared, while I related to her what I had read of the proceedings in the *Citoyenne.* "You are a wretch," she said, "you have no right to refuse to be interested in a question which is going to change the face of the earth, etc., etc." It is true that her interest in feminism was but a fire of straw, but, nevertheless, it was real, and in Marie's "soul-journey," to borrow the delightful expression of one of the most justly celebrated of her biographers, this phase of her life was worthy to be recorded otherwise than by the simple mention of two visits that Marie paid to Hubertine Auclert, whose portrait she wished to paint.

In 1882 Marie spent two months at the Villa Misé Brun, near Nice. She led there a life of strenuous work, hardly ever going into Nice, and receiving no visits. A great peace descended upon her rather anxious nature. The memory of those two months passed near her is infinitely precious and dear to me. Monsieur and Madame Bashkirtseff, Madame Romanoff, and Paul and his wife, who were all there with us, went in every day to Monte Carlo by the midday train, and did not return till Marie, Dina and myself had been long in bed. Marie painted all day; then, after a little walk in the twilight, she would shut herself up in her room, where she wrote until dinner time. At table she used to announce to Dina and myself that she had just written pages, compared to which the writings of all the so-called æsthetics, philosophers, and other literary men were nothing but nonsense. After dinner we would draw, and Marie never retired to rest without writing a few more pages of her *Diary.* Not a word concerning this visit has been judged worthy of publication, and I am sorry for it, as it is the only time in her life when Marie, whose personality was so wonderfully interesting and original, could be her real self, freed from the pettiness and the exactions of worldly society, whose meannesses constantly irritated her. But at Misé Brun we were alone, we did not enter a single drawing-room at Nice; there was at this period no famous name to mention in the *Diary,* and these pages thus appeared uninteresting to those who were concerned in the publication

of it. They have simply extracted an attack on Breslau inspired in several pages by Albert Wolff's praise of her.

I know that it must have been a difficult task to condense into two volumes the memoirs of Marie Bashkirtseff which, printed *in extenso,* would have filled ten or twelve volumes at least. I except from blame M. Andre Theuriet, who edited the *Diary,* and this all the more freely as I know that he never met Marie, nor saw the real manuscript of her *Diary,* but only a copy which had been edited before he received it. I grant that the question of the moment was to make the book interesting. Marie was quite unknown at the moment of her death, and the mention of celebrated persons in her memoirs would naturally greatly augment the interest of her *Diary* and increase its sale. Marie, however, in herself, was interesting enough, and real enough; she was much more interesting than can be imagined by those who credit the absurd stories of her precocity which, instead of representing her as the good, amiable and clever girl she really was, make her out to be a "case" or an insupportable and neurotic *arriviste.*

Maurice Donnay, in *L'Autre Danger,* wishing to describe an insupportable young snob, speaks of her as "of the Marie Bashkirtseff order." Maurice Donnay never knew Marie Bashkirtseff personally, and only judges her from what he has read about her. Alphonse Daudet, in an interview with the *Figaro,* speaking of Madame Weiss, a Russian who murdered her husband in Algeria, says: "She reminds one of Marie Bashkirtseff. Heaven preserve our families from Franco-Russian unions." Poor Marie! How abominably false is this statement concerning an exquisite being such as you were.

This is all that she has gained by her pretended precocity, the irritating repetition of the Julian meetings, and the Breslau success. And what proves more clearly than anything that M. Theuriet was not to blame for the mis-statements in the first two volumes, the third volume, published without his supervision, is full of the same errors. These errors are to be found not only in the text, but also in the illustrations.

Under the title "Marie Bashkirtseff's Studio," we are shown a little house in the Rue Hégésippe Moreau, where Marie never was, and which was taken by Madame Bashkirtseff ten years after the death of her daughter, in order to place there some of Marie's pictures. There are many beautiful photographs of Marie's studio taken at the Rue Ampère the day after her death. Why were these not published?

There appeared some years ago in *Black and White* an interesting article which has never been contradicted. This article proved that there is an error of four years in the dates of Marie's *Diary.* But it came too late. The legend still prevails of the sentimental freak only twelve years of age, yet noting down her impressions with the ripe judgment of a grown woman. Marie's admirers have been even more cruel to her than Daudet and Donnay; and the mis-statements of the book have given rise to others. Legend has seized hold of Marie Bashkirtseff and daily defaces more and more her real character. Among these traditions the most firmly established is that of Marie Bashkirtseff's love for Bastien-Lepage.

For years, whenever M. Theuriet has mentioned Bastien-Lepage in his articles, he has always spoken of Marie Bashkirtseff in connection with the great painter, who was his intimate friend, and in return, whenever he has written on the subject of Marie Bashkirtseff, he has mentioned Bastien-Lepage. In Marie's *Diary everything* she says concerning Bastien-Lepage has been printed. During the last two years of her life his name recurs on nearly every page; whilst the names of people whom Marie had been in the habit of seeing for years, such as A. de M., for instance, who proposed to her, not once, but three times, are not even mentioned. I know that Marie could not but be charmed with the great painter who united in his personality such a delightful being as Jules Bastien-Lepage. Eager as she always was for artistic society, she used to speak with enthusiasm of the man and his works; but it is going rather too far to deduce from this fact that their names should always be coupled together. The visit of Jules Bastien-Lepage to Marie only a few days before the young girl's death is also a dramatic incident well calculated to make an impression on the romantic reader, but even legend could hardly gather from it that there had ever been a love affair between the two, or that Marie, whose ideas of honour were of the strictest, was ever anything more than the painter's sincere admirer. Taking everything together—visits, meetings in the Bois de Boulogne or at the Salon—Marie and Bastien-Lepage saw each other a dozen times at the most; and I am not alone in asserting this. My statement is confirmed by the brother of the great painter, who was with him constantly at the time of his acquaintanceship with Marie. Another clear proof that Marie did not see much of Bastien-Lepage is the way in which she speaks of his mother, who, like his brother, was constantly with her son at the time he met Marie. All of us who were in the habit of visiting the Bastien-Lepage household, fell under the spell of her whom we used to call "the little mother," an exquisite creature, at the same time so good, so gentle, and so intelligent. Well, Marie, speaking of her in her *Diary,* says, "She is a woman of sixty who looks as if she were forty-five or fifty. Her hair is of a pretty, fair colour, with hardly any white in it, and she has a kindly smile. In fact, she is a very sympathetic woman whose whole bearing is well in keeping with her black and white dress. She does very beautiful embroidery, for which she designs her own patterns."

"The little mother" might have created this superficial impression on a stranger, but it is absurd to think that Marie would not have amended this description if she had seen this unique woman but three times. Besides, in the third volume, Marie owns in the last days of her *Diary* that she hardly knew Bastien-Lepage at all. But the legend has rolled on, biographers have found copy in it, and the intimacy, nay, more—the love affair of Marie and Bastien-Lepage have become notorious and incontestable facts.

At the time of the Exhibition of Children's Portraits at the Grafton Gallery in London one of my friends showed me a water-colour by Bastien-Lepage, representing a little girl of eight or ten years of age keeping a cow in a meadow. "It is a portrait of Marie Bashkirtseff, by Bastien-Lepage," said my friend, a well-known English novel-writer of the new school. I thought he was joking, and began to laugh. But my friend repeated his assertion in a serious tone.

"But look! The water-colour is dated 1880, and Marie owns to being twenty, in her *Diary,* at that period. I know the model—she is a girl called Chandeau de Damvillers, who was ten years old in 1880. Besides, Bastien-Lepage had given up painting when he met Marie."

"That is true?" answered my friend; "but I assure you that Bastien-Lepage painted a beautiful portrait of Marie Bashkirtseff. Every one knows that he did."

Maurice Barrès, a great writer and one of the most clear-headed thinkers of our time, once rented the apartment where Jules Bastien-Lepage died. That was twelve years ago. Naturally, he was haunted by the memory of the great painter of Lorraine, and this led him to occupy himself with Marie Bashkirtseff. The eminent writer set to work and put together a biography of Marie Bashkirtseff. I quote M. Barrès's words:—

> There are certain spots, famous in the history of human feeling, that carry our souls beyond their own feelings and give us a presentiment of the troubles that will agitate them one day. Such a spot is the terrace at Elsinore where the obscure Hamlet mourned over the death of his father.
>
> They are the psychological spots that act as powerfully upon the imagination as hot springs upon certain physical temperaments; and Catholic pilgrimages of a similar nature show in a marvellous degree that this kind of intellectual exaltation contains all the conditions necessary for elevating curiosity and respect into real passions. But each generation chooses its own particular places of devotion, and it is by these preferences that the variations of feeling are revealed. Who among the younger of our new men would be moved at the sight of the house in the Avenue d'Aylau which witnessed the close of so splendid a life? The older men, such as M. Catulle Mendès, or M. Camille Pelletan, must pity us for our coldness; and in spite of all their sympathetic comprehension, they would suspect us of bad faith if I added that, though we are indifferent to the last dwelling-place of Victor Hugo, a certain little house in the Monceau quarter has power to move us. Marie Bashkirtseff lived for some years and finally died at 61, Rue de Prony. She was well calculated to arouse the interest of this group of liberal minds whose tone, irritating and yet attractive, has interested critics for some years past.
>
> I approached the house by the short road that the young girl herself traversed so many times, when she visited Bastien-Lepage, dying in that house in the Rue Le Gendre, in which, by a touching accident, I have succeeded the good painter, whom she loved as a brother. The disconsolate mother of the girl whose memory we are recalling told me that when Bastien-Lepage learned the fatal news he hid his tears in the pillows among which he was still to wait three months for death. Marie Bashkirtseff was struck down by one of those miasms that float about Paris. I saw volumes of Kant and Fichte lying on her desk opened at passionate pages which death prevented her perusing.

M. Maurice Barrès starts on this pilgrimage in a little book entitled *Trois Stations de Psychotherapie,* and describes Marie Bashkirtseff, whom he had known, whose personality he had grasped and sounded in the visit he paid the little house where she lived and died, where ten years after her death he found lying open the Kant and Fichte upon which the girl nourished herself. M. Barrès constitutes himself the biographer of Marie, talks of her in numerous articles that have appeared in the *Figaro* and elsewhere, and draws her portrait *ne varietur,* because he has often passed along a road that Marie had to traverse to reach the house of Bastien-Lepage.

Marie Bashkirtseff never lived in the Rue de Prony; she died at 30, Rue Ampère, and all the details that interested M. Barrès so deeply, the books open on the desk, are due to the chances of unpacking. M. Barrès does not tell us who showed him the house into which he cannot have entered haphazard, nor does he tell us who pointed him out the desk upon which the open books were lying.

M. Maurice Barrès, after having devoted a number of articles to the subject of Marie Bashkirtseff, learned one day that he had been taken in, that there was more artificiality than reality in the cult that was paid to Marie in the little hotel in the Rue de Prony, and after having offered too much incense before the young girl, he threw her aside in an article in the *Figaro,* which Marie certainly did not deserve. Following his example, others, romantically interested in Marie, on learning that certain things they had repeated about her were false, slandered her in their turn, and those who hold her memory dear have each time felt an unpleasant shock. Is Marie to blame for what has happened? Certainly not; we can only feel sorry that the truth she loved so much should have been so minimised in the parts of the **Diary** that have been published, and that her charming figure should not have been presented to us in its true colours. (pp. 647-53)

Bojidar Karageorgevitch, "Legend and Marie Bash-kirtseff," in The Fortnightly Review, Vol. LXXIV, No. CCCCXLII, October 1, 1903, pp. 647-53.

AUGUSTINE BIRRELL (essay date 1904)

[*Birrell was an English statesman and essayist. Although his political career was always his primary interest, he earned a reputation for reflective humor, insightful observation, and judicious pronouncement in such collections of miscellaneous essays and literary criticism as* Obiter Dicta *(1884) and* Et Cetera *(1930) and in his critical biographies of Charlotte Brontë, William Hazlitt, and Andrew Marvell. Birrell's writing style—scholarly, personal, and socially conscious—led to the coinage of the verb "to birrell," defined as: "to comment on life in a combination of irony and kindly mordancy, with apparent irrelevance, but with actual point." In the following excerpt from an essay that first appeared in 1904, Birrell discusses Bashkirtseff's extreme egotism.*]

Miss [Mathilde] Blind is, no doubt, correct in her assertion that, as a painter, Mlle. Bashkirtseff's strong point was expression. Certainly, she had a great gift that way with her pen. Amidst a mass of greedy utterances, esurient longings, commonplace ejaculations, and unlovely revelations, passages occur in this journal which bid us hold. For all her boastings, her sincerity is not always obvious, but it speaks plainly through each one of the following words:

What is there in us, that, in spite of plausible arguments—in spite of the consciousness that all leads to *nothing*—we should still grumble? I know that, like everyone else, I am going on towards death and nothingness. I weigh the circumstances of life, and, whatever they may be, they appear to me miserably vain, and, for all that, I cannot resign myself. Then, it must be a force; it must be a *something*—not merely "a passage," a certain period of time, which matters little whether it is spent in a palace or in a cellar; there is, then, something stronger, truer, than our foolish phrases about it all. It is life, in short; not merely a passage—an unprofitable misery—but life, all that we hold most dear, all that we call ours, in short.

People say it is nothing, because we do not possess eternity. Ah! the fools. Life is ourselves, it is ours, it is all that we possess; how, then, is it possible to

say that it is *nothing?* If this is *nothing,* show me *something.*

To deride life is indeed foolish. Prosperous people are apt to do so, whether their prosperity be of this world or anticipated in the next. The rich man bids the poor man lead an abstemious life in his youth, and scorn delights, in order that he may have the wherewithal to spend a dull old age; but the poor man replies: "Your arrangements have left me nothing but my youth. I will enjoy that, and *you* shall support me in a dull old age."

To deride life, I repeat, is foolish; but to pity yourself for having to die is to carry egotism rather too far. This is what Mlle. Bashkirtseff does.

I am touched myself when I think of my end. No, it seems impossible! Nice, fifteen years, the three Graces, Rome, the follies of Naples, painting, ambition, unheard-of hopes—to end in a coffin, without having had anything, not even love.

Impossible, indeed! There is not much use for that word in the human comedy.

Never, surely, before was there a lady so penetrated with her own personality as the writer of these journals. Her arms and legs, hips and shoulders, hopes and fears, pictures and future glory, are all alike scanned, admired, stroked, and pondered over. She reduces everything to one vast common denominator—herself. She gives two francs to a starving family.

It was a sight to see the joy, the surprise of these

Bashkirtseff at the age of twenty.

poor creatures. I hid myself behind the trees. Heaven has never treated me so well; heaven has never had any of these beneficent fancies.

Heaven had, at all events, never heard the like of this before. Here is a human creature brought up in what is called the lap of luxury, wearing purple and fine linen, and fur cloaks worth 2000 francs, eating and drinking to repletion, and indulging herself in every fancy; she divides a handful of coppers amongst five starving persons, and then retires behind a tree, and calls God to witness that no such kindness had ever been extended to her.

When Mlle. Elsnitz, her long-suffering companion—"young, only nineteen, unfortunate, in a strange house without a friend"—at last, after suffering many things, leaves the service, it is recorded:

> I could not speak for fear of crying, and I affected a careless look, but I hope she may have seen.

Seen what? Why, that the carelessness was unreal. A quite sufficient reparation for months of insolence, in the opinion of Miss Marie.

It is said that Mlle. Bashkirtseff had a great faculty of enjoyment. If so, except in the case of books, she hardly makes it felt. Reading she evidently intensely enjoyed; but, though there is a good deal of rapture about Nature in her journals, it is of an uneasy character.

> The silence that is in the starry sky,
> The sleep that is amongst the lonely hills,

do not pass into the souls of those whose ambition it is to be greeted with loud cheers by the whole wide world.

Whoever is deeply interested in himself always invents a God whom he can apostrophise on suitable occasions. The existence of this deity feeds his creator's vanity. When the world turns a deaf ear to his broken cries he besieges heaven. The Almighty, so he flatters himself, cannot escape him. When there is no one else to have recourse to, when all other means fail, there still remains—God. When your father, and your mother, and your aunt, and your companion, and your maid, are all wearied to death by your exhaustless vanity, you have still another string to your bow. Sometimes, indeed, the strings may get entangled.

> Just now, I spoke harshly to my aunt, but I could not help it. She came in just when I was weeping with my hands over my face, and was summoning God to attend to me a little.

A book like this makes one wonder what power, human or divine, can exorcise such a demon of vanity as that which possessed the soul of this most unhappy girl. Carlyle strove with great energy in *Sartor Resartus* to compose a spell which should cleave this devil in three. For a time it worked well and did some mischief, but now the magician's wand seems broken. Religion, indeed, can still show her conquests, and, when we are considering a question like this, seems a fresher thing than it does when we are reading *Lux Mundi*.

"Do you want," wrote General Gordon in his journal, "to be loved, respected, and trusted? Then ignore the likes and dislikes of man in regard to your actions; leave their love for God's, taking Him only. You will find that as you do so men will like you; they may despise some things in you, but they will lean on you, and trust you, and He will give you the spirit

of comforting them. But try to please men and ignore God, and you will fail miserably and get nothing but disappointment."

All those who have not yet read these journals, and prefer doing so in English, should get Miss Blind's volumes. There they will find this "human document" [see preface by Bashkirtseff dated 1884] most vigorously translated into their native tongue. It, perhaps, sounds better in French.

One remembers George Eliot's tale of the lady who tried to repeat in English the pathetic story of a French mendicant— "J'ai vu le sang de mon père"—but failed to excite sympathy, owing to the hopeless realism of Saxon speech. But though better in French, the journal is interesting in English. Whether, like the dreadful Dean, you regard man as an odious race of vermin, or agree with an erecter spirit that he is a being of infinite capacity, you will find food for your philosophy, and texts for your sermons in the ***Journal of Marie Bashkirtseff.*** (pp. 264-68)

> *Augustine Birrell, "Marie Bashkirtseff," in his* The Collected Essays & Addresses of the Rt. Hon. Augustine Birrell: 1880-1920, Vol. 2, *J. M. Dent & Sons Ltd., 1922, pp. 262-68.*

MARY L. BREAKELL (essay date 1907)

[*Breakell was one of Bashkirtseff's fellow art students at the Atelier Julian. Noting that the confusion surrounding the accuracy of the* Journal *does not diminish Bashkirtseff's unusual insight, Breakell reflects on her intellectual and emotional qualities, comparing her abilities as an artist and a writer and discussing her consuming interests.*]

It is twenty years since Marie Bashkirtseff played her short part on the world's stage and passed from the scene, and now may we gauge her truly in the balance of her surroundings?

In those intervening years half the world of art and a great portion of the world of letters have heard of, if they have not read, her journal, and been moved by the story of the sad undercurrents in her young, brilliant life. The veracity of the dates of the journal have been questioned more than once. Yet, after all, to the public, the interest of the *Diary* does not depend on the age of the diarist. It does not lose in interest even if the young girl be three or four years older than we all supposed her to be when she 'fell in love with the Duke of Hamilton,' even though her history may become less piquant to the few, who, like Lombroso, have scientifically considered the poor child as a 'freak of nature.' Her falling in love at twelve years of age does not seem half so extraordinary as some of her deep reflections on things in general uttered at sixteen. The flashes of true insight she reveals in profound observations on men and things might be the expression of a high order of mind and intellect at any age over, not under, twenty-five, so that the wonder is not in the questionable three or four years of difference, but in the thoughts at all, considering she died not at twenty-three, but at the still early age of twenty-eight at the oldest.

But unique as the journal is to those who accept it, on trust as being what Marie seems to have intended it to be, a faithful 'human document,' apart from its psychological interest to students of human nature, it will hold an abiding and universal fascination for all young art-students so long as the passionate dream of the art-life holds men and women in thrall. And there are few dreams so deep, so absorbing, as that young dream of art, none founded more on the imaginings of others in books and stories, and exaggerated lives of the great painters, which depict chiefly the sun-gilded edges on the waves of life, slurring its dark under-flood. Romance hangs in thick folds round the painter's art, often beneath them there is but a skeleton of poverty and want, or a beautiful embalmment of a life's wasted energies such as that of Marie Bashkirtseff as revealed in her *Diary,* a warning figure of death swathed in the semblance of life, a sacrifice of false ambitions. For Marie Bashkirtseff's reputation has been mistaken for the fulfilment of her own ambitions. She stands on a pedestal in the eyes of aspiring students as one of Art's great geniuses. Yet, if Marie were truly an artist, it was not as a painter, and looking beneath the semblance, rather than as a genius in any art, does not Time point to her as an historic human object-lesson?

Marie has been too much regarded as a curiosity, an amusement to the world at large. The meaning of such lives as hers lies deeper. Time and Death do not strike the strings of life at random. There is, there was a *motif*—we can feel it as we look at her, in focus now with her surroundings, now that that space of twenty years lies between us and her.

Was it for nothing but the amusement of our idle moments that, out of so many millions of women's lives, her life is singled out in the interest of its brilliant setting of beauty, wealth, and position haloed by romance? Was it but to satisfy a morbid curiosity and her own intense egoism that this most self-conscious child was impelled or inspired to write a journal from her early years, and that the fate that wills such things should permit her fame to be so widely circulated?

Of the keeping of this journal she writes in an entry, dated the year before she died: 'It is a necessity without motive, like the necessity of breathing.'

What was the meaning, then, of Marie's life? From the standpoint of use, in the economy of Providence, is she to be regarded as a positive force, or, indeed, as a negative warning?

Marie was not an artist—that is, a true artist; she herself has said it more than once. It would seem that the constant and not unconscious purpose, the thread upon which her days were strung, was the *Diary*—this book of which she says, 'It is a woman with all her thoughts, her illusions, hopes, weaknesses; her charms, sorrows, and delights. I am not yet a complete woman, but I shall be one. You will be able to trace my life from the cradle to the grave.' Of this *Diary,* we are told, 'it might have filled five or six volumes, not merely one.' What, then, has been left out of it?

Would she have appeared in truer colour had its pages not been deleted?

Will it be possible, when all the actors in the drama of her life are dead, for the world at large to read an edition containing the whole as she left it? Should we, indeed, then judge her differently?

In reading the journal as it is published, the foremost impression one receives is that this young Russian had a wonderfully magnetic power of attraction for both sexes of those she came in contact with. The next, that her intellect in its strength and mathematical grasp was of a masculine order. It would seem that she wrote absolute truth when she jotted down in its pages that there was nothing of the woman about her but the 'envelope.' Veritably it would seem that the *woman* was all on the surface, for in face, form, and contour she was the most intensely womanly creature; her influence with men of the most feminine nature. Her influence over women must have been through the masculine intellect.

She wrote once in playful mood that she had two hearts—really she had none. She had the mastery, method, powers of comparison, the grasp of a man's mind combined with the intuition of the woman's, but lacking the heart of either. And the secret of her fascination and influence over both sexes probably lay in this lack of heart of either.

For in thus lacking heart she could coldly analyse and calculate to a nicety the effect of a word, a look, on a lover of the opposite sex, or a friend of her own, to lead him or her on; or to repel. She wrote and spoke much of love in the abstract, continually dissecting what she thought was love in herself for others or other's love for herself; and certainly she could write beautifully of the passion, though she was incapable of feeling it. One might have thought that her intellectual qualities of mind and her pose as a blue-stocking on all subjects would have repelled ordinary men. But these qualities were counterbalanced by that intensely feminine exterior which disguised her masculine understanding, and her complete, cold-blooded, masculine mastery of feminine wiles. I believe no man could have withstood her charm had she so willed (nor woman either).

To a man there seemed so much to be gained in loving her; but as what should have been her heart was in reality only a great capacity or reservoir for absorbing—with no outlet— love was never returned. It remained in the reservoir which merely reflected one image more deeply, more clearly; *not his,* but that of her own charming self.

Like a child she skirmished on the brink of passion, fancying herself in love, but never falling in. And then came the time when, as she exclaimed in the retrospect of her journal of 1875 to 1877:

> I complain in them of I know not what, spending my strength in fury and despair, in trying to find *what to do*. Go to Italy, Paris, get married, paint? What was to be done? I wanted to be everywhere at once. What vigour there was in it all! As a man I should have conquered Europe. . . . There are moments when we naïvely fancy ourselves capable of anything. It is a fire that consumes you, and death is at the end inevitable.

Then a momentous visit to Paris, the metropolis of art, and she indeed comes on 'L'Etoile' of the crossways, and with a visionary Arc de Triomphe at the end of all of them. She has to make her decision; there are innumerable roads branching out in every direction; there are many signposts before her— hands pointing. Which shall she follow? Writ large, there is the way of matrimony, of which she notes in scorn:

'To marry and have children? Any washerwoman could do that.'

Pleasure? No; that alone will not satisfy her. Philanthropy? Religion? She but scans the latter through the distorted mirror of superstition. Politics draw her greatly, and she writes of them:

> I must not go often to the Chamber of Deputies, it might draw me away from the studio; you get interested and you go on and on; every day is a fresh page of the same book. I could become so passion-

ately interested in politics that I should lie awake; but my politics are there at the Rue Vivienne.

(Paris, 1877)

For she has stepped into the charmed circle of Art, the very starland of forgetfulness and ignorance of all the great issues of life. Thence onwards to the end she is fired with enthusiasm for Art as a means to gain the glory that she covets. And yet even in the midst of the fever of Art-life she writes as though in spite of her absorbing studies she is aware of the futility of it all:

> 1878. September 13.—I am not in my right place in the world. I waste, in idle talk, energy enough for the making of a man. . . . I am nothing, and the capabilities which might have developed into real qualities are nearly always wasted or misapplied.

And she within the same year writes, for with her choice of Art her death-knell was sounded:

> I am desperately sad! Oh, terrible, despairing, horrible, and frightful word! To die! My God, to die! To die, without leaving anything behind me! To die like a dog, just as a hundred thousand women have died, whose names are barely inscribed on their tombstones.

> Fool, fool that I am not to see what God wills. God wills that I should renounce everything and give myself up entirely to Art. In five years I shall still be quite young—perhaps beautiful; but if I should become only an artistic mediocrity, as so many are!

Thence onward she wore her life to a thread in a feverish, unworthy desire to emulate, to outstrip others. There was something intensely small and childish in this envy and despair at any success of her rivals—rivals who, having none of her prestige and advantages of family and fortune, still eclipsed her.

> Breslau's picture [she writes after the Varnishing Day at the Salon] is quite skied, and the effect is quite deplorable. I was so disquieted at the success which she appeared certain to obtain that it is a great consolation.

> I won't conceal it. . . . God was very good to me in not suffering me to be killed outright by Breslau; at all events, to-day I do not know how to express myself so as to avoid the appearance of mean sentiments.

Then, later, in 1882:

> To be celebrated and to be loved, as Balzac says, that is happiness. . . . Breslau is lean, crooked, and worn-out; she has an interesting head, but no charms; she is masculine and solitary! She will never be anything of a woman unless she has genius; but if I had her talent I should be like no one else in Paris. . . . That must come.

'I am smarting. Wolff [the art critic] dedicates ten lines of extreme flattery to Mademoiselle Breslau.' Of this she writes three days later: 'The blow was so severe that I have spent the last three days in real misery.'

Probably this childish envy on the part of one who could make such sage observations on life as those recorded in the journal may be partly explained by the fact that Marie, entirely educated at home, was for the first time, in this *atelier* life, brought into actual and imminent competition with others.

An only daughter, made much of by her family from childhood, who idolised her as a prodigy of genius, she could not suffer anyone to be preferred above herself. In working against her fellow-students she worked against time also, for she knew her years were numbered. She had worn her frail life to a thread in this feverish haste after fame; and ultimately she snapped it in her reckless disregard of all ordinary precautions of health, in her passionate pursuit of *la gloire*. And the pity of it—that Marie, though she might be a painter, was not an artist in the true sense of painting! She was an artist of a sort by nature, as most observant children are in common with savages. Both make their earliest efforts in the graphic art as distinct from literature.

But, reversing the order, she was a literary artist first from her babyhood, a philosopher, a thinker. She was also a voracious reader and must have had an extraordinary memory. She had a capacity for seeing the obvious essentials of any undertaking, and so things came easy to her. In consequence, apart from any special gift, she could achieve a high plane of accomplishment in most things; and so, for instance, in painting, her merely technical attainment was far above the average of the ordinary professional in that art.

She says herself: 'I am not an artist. I have drawn without any difficulty, just as I do everything.'

But she could see with the artist's eye if she could not feel with the artist's heart, and in her written words she could bring a scene before you in all the brilliancy of nature. Her vivacious account of her first visit to Russia, as from the woman's standpoint, is a valuable addition to other descriptive literature on the subject of her native country by the great Russian novelists. Her description of the crumbling beauties of Old Spain and the picturesque incidents of her travel, as an artist, through that sunny land of deep contrasts in character and colouring, makes us wish we could have more of Marie in such unintrospective moods. In a few trenchant words she brings the whole arena of the bullfight and its horrors before us. Her pen, like a Spanish dart pointed in blood, imparts the strange and terrible fascination the sport has for those who frequent such scenes. 'Oh,' she concludes, 'it makes your flesh creep and your head feel ironbound; it's a school for assassins.'

Her description of the death chamber and the funeral of Gambetta is a fine literary picture, if you will. In that she seized, besides spectacular appearance, the high-wrought spirit of the Paris of the moment. There she was at her best. Her grasp of the character of the man is a noble tribute to the dead statesman. There is more original genius in such a piece of writing than in her much-talked-of picture, 'Le Meeting,' in the Luxembourg—a mere gallery transcript of the surface of things, seen through the eyes and put down on canvas, in the borrowed manner of another, even though that other might be a Bastien-Lepage.

Marie, indeed, was a writer first, a painter last; the reputation she gained as a painter was but antecedent to that she should have attained had she lived to lead the literary life, and fired by the inspiration of her native country, become, perhaps, Russia's great woman-novelist. And so to have had it in her power to help some tremulous, flickering movement of thought which might only be coaxed and guided into action by the breath and hand of a woman. Had she not taken up painting, probably, despite her consumptive tendencies, she would have been living now, possibly, a life of usefulness, not rejoicing in the failure of others, not competing with those poorer than herself, but helping them over the rough places on the road of life.

For she had her nobler moments in which faint glimmerings of true aspiration after better things seemed possible. She had generous impulses sometimes, not for the sole sake of righteousness, be it said, but generally with an eye to the main chance in Heaven. When a picture is hung in the Salon she writes: 'A week ago I gave a thousand francs to the poor. . . . Heaven is rewarding me for my money.'

Truly, she was a curious mixture of the sage and the savage, of intellect and superstition. She reviled her God when things went ill with her; she tried to bribe Him. She thanked Him, as we have seen, for the misfortunes of her rivals. But she was no hypocrite. Her one great virtue was honesty; an honesty that frankly owned its faults, because being Marie Bashkirtseff she had a right to them.

And, lacking heart, she was chaste because she had no impulse to be otherwise. There is no need to say of her 'She loved much, therefore to her much shall be forgiven'; and on the score of loving 'not wisely, but too well' she cannot be reproached. She had the virtue of her greatest fault—lack of heart and sympathy.

In summing up the characteristics of this extraordinary girl one may say that among them were all the qualities that go to the making of the successful man or woman (of genius or not of genius) including intense egoism. She had a determined will and a mathematical mind, and, of a surety, to an artist such a mind and will mean a sure hand. She had also a remarkable memory, some sensibility and æsthetic taste, and an entire lack of sympathy for others—excepting as to their attitude of mind towards herself. Moreover, in order to succeed her strong will needed not the spur of poverty, and she was born in the environment and conditions (though she girded at them) that conduce to make the worldly success, in any line, of a person with much less force of will and intellect than hers.

Some of less force of character and as little real sympathy for the life of the true artist would find such luxuries, social surroundings of life, and pleasure, as hers, absorb their interest and energies, but this young Russian, typical of the primitive race of the Steppes, savagely self-conscious of high mental powers and faculties in their dawn, needed a wider outlet. She needed a world to conquer. Her relatives and friends had made themselves her abject slaves and adorers; and, in the social circles she moved in, even at the early age of sixteen, her wit, charm, and riches made her queen. Matrimony offered little attraction to her, partly because she could have married at any moment. In Paris she came in contact with the sphere of Art, which in its profession offered more difficulties and obstruction and opposition to her *as a woman* than some other professions, and for that very reason it attracted her. Young (only twenty-one) and beautiful, if charm be counted as beauty, full of life, in all the fire and energy of unbroken human will, she determined, though a woman, to conquer that Kingdom of Art which showed itself so incredulous of a woman's gifts and powers. But cold Death, indomitable, despite the radiant girl's young life, interposed his barrier—a wall which would not fall at her behest, though blasted by youth, with fire of beauty, gold, and genius. And Death prevailed. . . . Surely life may well end when the purpose for which its torch was lighted is ignored and unfulfilled. If we

are so self-willed, self-centred, as to disregard the signposts of the better ways, writ large by Providence on the road of life, is it not probable that we may become mere stumbling-blocks to others, and that the same Providence in the interests of those other wayfarers may remove us from their path? Marie, as she had mapped out her path, would have become a stumbling-block to others; for the success she might have gained as a woman-artist, however merited, would almost universally have been attributed by those captiously critical of woman's capabilities as due to her social advantages of wealth and position, added to beauty and extreme sexual attraction. For, indeed, that same indomitable Death is almost the only power of this world that we can be quite sure will withstand all these. The cause of woman would in no way be advanced by the social success in art of such an one.

Had Marie Bashkirtseff, with all her powers and the opportunities life gave her, but had the heart to see beyond her own reflection, a heart to see and feel for others, and the courage to brave the conventions of the social world she moved in—for she was a coward—had she had the heart to take up life's thread in a stronger part, for her (as a Russian) than that of Art, she might have been living now, a great social force for good. She had the brain and the hand, and these alone can do something clever, but only 'head, hand, and heart' together can do the truly great things of life.

It may be asked, 'What other paths lay open at the cross-roads when this young gifted Russian chose her way?'

Was there not a hand that pointed eastwards towards the distant Steppes? And that watchword 'Patriotism,' at the same time, was it not ringing in her ears?

Did Russia and the needs of its people, *her* people, emerging out of open serfdom into the sinister new forms of indirect slavery of a wider civilisation, mean nothing to her—and she one of Russia's most gifted daughters? She is condemned by her own pen, for in 1884 she writes in her ***Diary:***

> And you, wretch! You live in France, you prefer being a foreigner to remaining at home! Since you love your beautiful, great, sublime Russia, go thither and work for her. . . . But if it were not for my painting I would go. . . . My work absorbs all my faculties, and the rest is merely an interval, an amusement.

She was dreaming, like so many, on high enchanted ground, and she did not heed though she heard the cries of those beneath her—of those who helped by their toil to make the golden setting that she gleamed in at Nice, Paris, and Rome. She had in reality no sympathy with her struggling fellow country people groaning under the burdens of life. If she regarded them other than as necessary adjuncts to the comfort and prosperity of herself and her kind, it was merely in a pictorial light, as incidental to the landscape, that she so regarded them. Yet she was not ignorant of the state of things in Russia; for in an earlier letter (June 1880), dated from an estate of her father's in that country, she writes to M. Julian after describing her father's *fête* and the feast to the peasantry:

> They made me take off my hat and veil to get a better look at me, and after they had looked at me it was my turn to be cheered and carried in triumph. I was obliged to embrace a number of them. . . . Then when all the crowd had drunk and danced, they spoke of donations of lands, but someone let them see plainly that it was of no use, and that

ended this episode. They distribute among these good people, it appears, so-styled ukases of the Emperor, compelling the land-owners to give them dozens of things. A price has also been set on the heads of the nobles—fifty roubles a head. Do you not fancy you see mine already at the end of a pike? In short, if you recall the history of your *ancien régime* you will understand how things are here, and the resemblance between the two periods is striking—from the frightful condition of the people to the stupid blindness of the nobles. The French peasant sacking the château, saying that it grieves him to the heart to do so but that the King commands it, is the brother of the Russian who pretends to have received orders to massacre the Jews.

This excerpt from her letters shows that she was a cold, clear, observant spectator of exterior life. Even if she gave alms it was with no real charity or sympathy for the recipient, but because her religion enjoined it as a duty, or out of curiosity or display. This curious aloofness is illustrated by an incident she records in the *Diary,* of her gift of two francs to a family of tramps, father, mother, and children, who in wretched plight, half-clothed, half-starved, wandering homeless, came into view in the landscape she was sketching. Having given the coin, she hid behind a tree to watch, unseen herself, the extreme delight of these poor people at the unexpected gift.

'Heaven has never treated me so well! Heaven has never had any of these beneficent fancies!' she adds in recording the incident.

Then besides Patriotism and Philanthropy there was another movement in her day, which, as touching her own sex, we might suppose would have offered great attraction to a woman of Marie's strong views. But her lack of sympathy with her kind made her interest in the *Feminist* movement again merely cold and curious. It appears from the *Diary* that she held the votaries of Feminism up to scorn. Yet she could understand, as a woman, some of the difficulties in Art with which woman had to contend—that is, she understood with the limited vision of a *rich* woman, poor in practical experience of the poor one, who knows too well the narrow, pinching ways of poverty, and as a woman she wrote with some appreciation of their difficulties in another letter to M. Julian. But she cared nothing for *woman* in the abstract. Her sympathy with woman's cause was merely sympathy for the sex of Marie Bashkirtseff. Else would she have shown such lamentable and small jealousy at the small successes of other girls? If death had spared her it is more than probable that she would never have really conquered the innermost kingdom of Art, for lacking heart she lacked poetry and humour and all the fine shades and tones between. She would always have met more than her match in these. Still, though she cannot fairly occupy a niche in the temple of fame as a great artist, she will keep it in our memory as a wonderful child, a girl Narcissus, who, born with great gifts and capabilities, yet lacking heart and blinded by unwise training, found naught in life to love, or live for, but her own reflection.

Yet we may well ask again, in the light of recent Russian events, from the point of Patriotism would she not have appeared differently had her journal not been deleted? Has the day come when those responsible may do her justice, in giving more of that journal to the world? (pp. 116-25)

Mary L. Breakell, "Marie Bashkirtseff: The Reminiscence of a Fellow-Student," in The Nineteenth Century and After, *Vol. XIX, No. 365, July, 1907, pp. 110-25.*

BERNARD SHAW   (essay date 1913)

[*Shaw is generally considered the greatest and best-known dramatist to write in the English language since William Shakespeare. He is closely identified with the intellectual revival of the British theater, and in his dramatic theory he advocated eliminating romantic conventions in favor of a theater of ideas grounded in realism. During the late nineteenth century, Shaw was a prominent literary, art, music, and drama critic, and his reviews were known for their biting wit and brilliance. In the following excerpt, Shaw challenges William Stead's contention that Bashkirtseff was "unwomanly" (see excerpt dated 1890) and praises her for breaking through the double standard that implies only men should be self-motivated. Shaw's comments are drawn from a revised version of an essay that originally appeared in 1891.*]

In 1890 the literary sensation of the day was the **Diary of Marie Bashkirtseff.** An outline of it, with a running commentary, was given in *The Review of Reviews* by the editor, the late William Stead, who, having gained an immense following by a public service in rendering which he had to simulate a felony and suffer imprisonment for it in order to prove that it was possible, was engaged in a campaign with the object of establishing the ideal of sexual "purity" as a condition of public life. He had certain Ibsenist qualities: faith in himself, wilfulness, conscientious unscrupulousness, and could always make himself heard. Prominent among his ideas was an ideal of womanliness. In support of that ideal he would, like all idealists, make and believe any statement, however obviously and grotesquely unreal. When he found Marie Bashkirtseff's account of herself utterly incompatible with the picture of a woman's mind presented to him by his ideal, he was confronted with the dilemma that either Marie was not a woman or else his ideal was false to nature. He actually accepted the former alternative. "Of the distinctively womanly," he says, "there is in her but little trace. She was the very antithesis of a true woman." William's next difficulty was, that self-control, being a leading quality in his ideal, could not have been possessed by Marie: otherwise she would have been more like his ideal. Nevertheless he had to record that she, without any compulsion from circumstances, made herself a highly skilled artist by working ten hours a day for six years. Let anyone who thinks that this is no evidence of self-control just try it for six months. William's verdict nevertheless was "No self-control." However, his fundamental quarrel with Marie came out in the following lines. "Marie," he said, "was artist, musician, wit, philosopher, student, anything you like but a natural woman with a heart to love, and a soul to find its supreme satisfaction in sacrifice for lover or for child." Now of all the idealist abominations that make society pestiferous, I doubt if there be any so mean as that of forcing self-sacrifice on a woman under pretence that she likes it; and, if she ventures to contradict the pretence, declaring her no true woman. In India they carried this piece of idealism to the length of declaring that a wife could not bear to survive her husband, but would be prompted by her own faithful, loving, beautiful nature to offer up her life on the pyre which consumed his dead body. The astonishing thing is that women, sooner than be branded as unsexed wretches, allowed themselves to be stupefied with drink, and in that unwomanly condition burnt alive. British Philistinism put down widow idealizing with the strong hand; and suttee is abolished in India. The English form of it still flourishes; and Stead, the rescuer of the children, was one of its high priests. Imagine his feelings on coming across this entry in a woman's diary: "I love myself." Or this, "I swear solemnly—by the Gospels, by the passion of Christ, by MYSELF—that in four years I will be famous." The young woman was positively proposing to exercise for her own sake all the powers that were given to her, in Stead's opinion, solely that she might sacrifice them for her lover or child! No wonder he was driven to exclaim again, "She was very clever, no doubt; but woman she was not."

Now observe this notable result. Marie Bashkirtseff, instead of being a less agreeable person than the ordinary female conformer to the ideal of womanliness, was most conspicuously the reverse. Stead himself wrote as one infatuated with her mere diary, and pleased himself by representing her as a person who fascinated everybody, and was a source of delight to all about her by the mere exhilaration and hope-giving atmosphere of her wilfulness. The truth is, that in real life a self-sacrificing woman, or, as Stead would have put it, a womanly woman, is not only taken advantage of, but disliked as well for her pains. No man pretends that his soul finds its supreme satisfaction in self-sacrifice: such an affectation would stamp him as coward and weakling: the manly man is he who takes the Bashkirtseff view of himself. (pp. 566-68)

*Bernard Shaw, " 'The Quintessence of Ibsenism',"
in his* Selected Prose, *edited by Diarmuid Russell,
Dodd, Mead & Company, 1952, pp. 534-694.*

E. LEIGH MUDGE (essay date 1921)

[*In the following essay, Mudge discusses the importance of the* Journal *as a representative account of adolescent development.*]

Marie Bashkirtseff has been called by Maurice Barrès "Our Lady Never Satisfied." A divine discontent is characteristic of the genius and also of the adolescent; and this young artist was both. In her journal we have a remarkable record of self-confessions, beginning at the age of twelve, at the very outset of the adolescent period, and continuing until a few days before her death at twenty-three, when adolescence is gradually merging into adulthood. To say that Marie Bashkirtseff was precociously mature need not be interpreted to mean that she had no youth. Her life was *all* youth, crowded with experiences, endowed with unusual intellectual power, force of will and potency of feeling, but youthful through and through. Some have said that she did not develop and mature; that the artist of twenty-three is the same erratic and temperamental child as the schoolgirl of twelve. This is surely a misconception. She matured as an adolescent matures. She did not live to attain adulthood; perhaps had she lived she would have preserved the youth-spirit through other years; but there was a many-sided development that made her the promising young artist she was toward the end of her short life.

Many who read the journal of Marie Bashkirtseff will consider it the record of a morbid and abnormal mind. Unusual it certainly was,—the mind of a genius, a highly temperamental young woman,—but may not its abnormality consist in its being so clearly revealed to the world? Other girls have similar emotions and ambitions and ideas, but they have repressed them conventionally and grown away from them into the saner development of middle age. Doubtless the characteristics of adolescence are exaggerated in the young artist,

as in any other unusually vivid and vigorous personality. It is this exaggeration of adolescent traits that makes her journal of high value to students of psychology. Just as any human tendency may be more clearly examined in its most highly developed form, so the feelings which are usually hidden in the reticent adolescent heart may be clearly seen in the open magnification of this unusual personality.

Marie Bashkirtseff is, like all young people, distinctly and often painfully self-conscious. She seems to be constantly thinking of herself, her abilities, her personal appearance, her feelings. She is childishly pleased, even within the last fortnight of her life, with her clothes and her face. In the earlier years of the journal she frequently makes such confessions as, "I love to be alone before a looking glass." "My photographs are never like me." "I compare myself with all the statues I see." In her twentieth year she made the following entry:

> Since yesterday my complexion has been wonderfully fresh and clear and beautiful, and my eyes brilliant and animated. Even the contour of my face is more delicate and more perfect than before. Only it is a pity that this is at a time when there is no one to see me. It is a silly thing to say, but I remained standing for half-an-hour before the glass for the pleasure of looking at myself; it is a long time since this has happened.

Many an adolescent girl fancies herself a genius. Marie knew herself a genius and devoted herself zealously to doing the things for which she felt the ability. "I long to go into society," she writes. "I long to shine. I long for high rank, for riches, pictures, palaces, jewels. I long to be the center of a brilliant circle." "I desire glory." "I am resolved on being famous whether it be as an artist or in any other way." "I long to see everything, to know everything, to learn everything."

A tumult of varying emotions is expressed throughout the journal, doubtless a very original and individual torrent, but perhaps not altogether unlike the experience of other girls in this introspective age. Mlle. Bashkirtseff is continually examining herself, often in a curiously objective and disinterested manner.

> The woman who writes these words and the woman she is writing about are two different persons. What do all these sufferings matter to *me?* I write them down; I analyze them; I transcribe my daily life but to *me*, to *me myself*, all that is completely indifferent. It is my pride, my self-love, my interests, my complexion, my eyes that suffer, that weep, that rejoice; but *I*, I take part in it all only to observe, to narrate, to write about and reason coldly concerning all these trifles, like Gulliver among the Lilliputians.

At other times, she writes: "I like to sob and despair, to indulge myself in sadness. It is a form of diversion." "However much I may cry and fall into a rage, I am always conscious of what I do." "I suffer genuinely, but something deep within me remains calm and observant. I watch myself and am interested. I never entirely forget." This apparent paradox of actual emotion under one's own dramatic scrutiny is typical of adolescence, and so is the ability to hide one's feelings under a mask, as when Marie says: "it is my nature to laugh; it is sometimes altogether independent of the humor I am in."

Her first love affairs are typical of early adolescence. She falls in love with an English duke whom she has never met, and believes herself heartbroken when she hears of his marriage, while she is yet in her thirteenth year. Later she fascinates an Italian youth and so far yields to his love-making as to give him a single kiss, for which she long continues to reproach herself. It is only near the end of life that a normal love experience begins to emerge, and even this she does not seem to recognize for what it is, although she reminds herself of a possible danger to her self-ambitious principles.

> I am vexed to think I should have let my thoughts dwell upon him personally—he is not sufficiently great for that. He is not a demi-god in art, like Wagner, and it is only in such a case that it would be admissible to entertain a profound admiration for him.

Indeed she gives her growing interest in Bastien-Lepage, whose life ended within a few weeks of her own, a mystical interpretation as well as the more obvious interest in a fellow-craftsman. She describes the mystery in the eyes of his Jeanne d'Arc, and says of the painter that he has looked into the eyes of the Maid.

Many typical adolescent traits were magnified in this remarkable girl. She was ambitious, self-assertive, high-spirited, finicky in tastes, often restless and irritable, intellectually critical and still highly suggestible. She justly felt, as most young people do, that her friends did not understand her. Indeed she does not understand herself. She has the typical dream life and vivid imagination of adolescence, together with unusual power to make her dreams concrete and clear both to herself and to others. She manifests the curiously mature attitude which is often seen in young people. Even at the age of twelve, she makes such sage remarks as: "The expectation of an unpleasantness is more terrible than the thing itself." "I have a horror of trivial, every day annoyances, so I let them pass with a smile." "Work is the cure of everything. How can the hand be busy and the mind idle?" "True wisdom can be learned only from personal experience."

What have been termed "contradictory characters" are characteristic of all vigorous personalities, and especially of those who may be called geniuses, and also appear normally in adolescence. In many respects the nature of Marie Bashkirtseff was of this paradoxical sort. She is deeply religious and also highly superstitious, and still she is cynical, skeptical, and intellectualistic. Her mother's veneration of images is foolishness to her, but a broken mirror is an omen of misfortune, and a strong current of mysticism runs through her entire life. Early in her fourteenth year she already considers herself quite *blasé* and is developing the attitude of introspection and dramatic objectiveness already mentioned. "I compare myself to a piece of water that is frozen in its depths, and has motion only on the surface, for nothing amuses or interests me in my DEPTHS." But within a few days she is in raptures over the recovery of her voice, which is at this time her artistic hope. "I receive it with tears in my eyes, and I thank God for it on my knees. I said nothing, but I was cruelly grieved. I did not dare to speak of it. I prayed to God, and He has heard me!"

Moods of gaiety and hopefulness are closely followed by periods of melancholy and despair. To be sure, the progress of disease may account for some degree of this in her later years, but she has the true adolescent shifting of moods. At fifteen she utters this melancholy wail, which seems almost too self-conscious to be convincing:

> Just now I fell on my knees, sobbing, and praying

to God with outstretched arms, and eyes fixed straight before me, just as if He were there in my room. It appears that God does not hear me. Yet I cry to Him loudly enough.

> Shall I ever find a dog on the streets, famished, and beaten by boys; a horse that drags behind him from morning till night a load beyond his strength; a miller's ass, a church mouse, a professor of mathematics without pupils, an unfrocked priest, a—poor devil of any kind sufficiently crushed, sufficiently miserable, sufficiently sorrowful, sufficiently humiliated, sufficiently depressed, to be compared to me? The most dreadful thing with me is that humiliations, when they are past, do not glide from my heart, but leave their hideous traces.

A few days later she is saying: "I don't know what to do with myself for joy."

Many times, in the frankness of her journal, Mlle. Bashkirtseff commends herself, her appearance, her ability, her motives, her character. In spirit as well as in attitude she is a coquette. She is no shrinking wall-flower. She has endless confidence in herself. But this trait also has its foil, and again and again she is as self-condemnatory as the ascetic saints. At one time she writes of a voice that often whispers to her that she will achieve success: "I believe this voice. It has never yet deceived me, and it has too often predicted misfortune for it to speak falsely this time." Yet in a few days she says: "My projects, my hopes, my little vanities are fallen to pieces. I have deceived myself in everything." She is both a coquette and severely moral, and she continues for a long time her self-castigation for the kiss given her ardent Italian lover. Her frequent fits of melancholy, and sometimes of violent passion at her failures and misfortunes, are doubtless exaggerated by ill health, but still they are typically adolescent phenomena, and so are the wistful ambitions, the impulsively extravagant emotions, the shifting likes and dislikes, and the passionate idealism which are revealed throughout her journal.

Marie Bashkirtseff did not live long enough to attain the full fruitage of her artistic ambitions. She accomplished some work that was worthy; perhaps, had she lived, she might have produced something really great. But her greatest service to the world is not as a painter. In her journal she has rendered a distinguished service not only to our knowledge of an artistic temperament but to our knowledge of the spirit of youth. In giving the world her faithful transcription of her intimate life experiences, she has painted a masterpiece. What the world lost by her early death we do not know, but by leaving this remarkable record she has attained a worthy place in the world's memory. Marie Bashkirtseff is eternally young. (pp. 78-82)

> *E. Leigh Mudge, "An Adolescent Genius," in* The Pedagogical Seminary, *Vol. XXVIII, No. 1, March, 1921, pp. 78-82.*

ERNEST DIMNET (essay date 1925)

> [*In the following essay, Dimnet claims that the intrigue surrounding Bashkirtseff's* Journal, *as well as her public image as a "princess with artistic tastes," is a result of the highly selective editing of her original manuscripts, which has left readers with a distorted impression of her personality.*]

Marie Bashkirtseff died, at the age of twenty-four, in 1884. By 1890 the publication of her *Diary* and its multitudinous translations had made her famous all over the world. There was about her much the same halo which gave unexpected duration to the aristocratic but effaced heroes of *Le Récit d'une Sœur.* People did not realize how much of an artist there was in the Russian girl; they would see in her, above all, a princess with artistic tastes and the something sovereign which the possession of rank, combined with talent and wealth, confers upon a few privileged beings. When Barrès showed her to us, in one of his daring fore-shortenings, as Our Lady of the Sleeping Car, he was merely summing up a universal impression of social prestige of a rare quality.

Yet, there were, at the time, rumours tending to counteract this simplified and banal notion. People who had known the girl intimately said that had her *Diary* been less carefully edited by Theuriet—an admirer and a poet—a much more interesting, if a less refined, figure would have appeared. They hinted that violence would seem a much more appropriate description of her nature than charm.

To-day the publication of a completely uncensored volume of the *Diary* by a well-known Nice journalist, M. Pierre Borel, enables us to judge for ourselves, but once more there are problems still unsolved. M. Borel is as reticent an editor as Theuriet, whose sole preface to the original two volumes was a poem. Why should M. Borel begin his *in extenso* publication with the year 1877 when we know that the girl began to keep her *Diary* at the age of thirteen, in 1873? Why do some passages—among others an unexpected interview of Marie with King Vittorio Emmanuele, on an hotel staircase—which appear in Theuriet's selection vanish from the so-called complete text? Honest curiosity having induced the present writer to ask M. Borel for an explanation, a courteous but unsatisfactory answer came to the effect that the MS. used for the preparation of the volume was a copy made by Marie Bashkirtseff's mother. Here again a problem arises: why does this copy begin in 1877, and how trustworthy a copyist was Madame Bashkirtseff?

However, M. Borel has the right to boast that we now know enough about Marie's life to realize that the impression rashly gathered thirty years ago by insufficiently informed people was wide of the mark. There is a good deal of the Oriental semi-barbarian in the girl who shows herself—resolutely and, in one way, heroically shows herself—in a diary she wanted to be placed before the public. But there is more that savours of immature and not always sweet seventeen. Marie Bashkirtseff loved writing and wrote everything. Like the Surréalistes of to-day she often pours out her ideas without caring to sift them in advance, and goes on writing till she hits on something that pleases her (the bits which also pleased Theuriet). She writes in full of long and trivial conversations—once or twice squabbles—she has had with nobodies. Her social life is apparently all-absorbing, but so is the literary life she enters upon the moment her other occupation releases her. Her sincerity is absolute: no rouge is put on, no feminine secrecy is ever suspected. Marie Bashkirtseff uses the frankest, not infrequently the most abusive language.

This first volume is full of people, society people. She cares for nobody else and admits she is a snob. She is shocked to find in some novel a princess who is in love with a painter. She delights in enumerations of Italian titles (most of the four months covered by the volume are spent at Naples and Florence) which make some pages look like a dance card. No poetry dares peep in. Eugénie de Guérin is a thousand miles off. No landscapes, no night pieces, nothing that is usually associated with a girl's diary. Religion appears a little at Easter, Russian superstitions at every corner, and queer little prayers sometimes come out when a suppressed yawn might as well, but no interior life of the kind to which diaries have accustomed us. Marie loves towns, palaces, ballrooms and international trains, nothing else. We see her practise her piano or her singing, and she alludes to painting, but not a line has been quoted, or could be quoted, showing real appreciation of literature or art. A ravenous appetite for men and women, especially men of course, seems to kill all other tastes.

Quite a hundred pages are devoted to an affair with a Florentine nobleman of French descent, Count de Larderel, now certainly deceased. He is twenty-three, has a mistress and a child, and enjoys the worst reputation, even that of not fighting duels, which, however, he improves in course of time by getting rather badly wounded. This hero fascinates her. As no reticence is ever used we see Marie doing very unprincely things, like peeping in at the gentleman's keyhole and pumping his valet. She is everlastingly trying to see him, and as she is at the time, and tells us she is, the handsomest and most fascinating woman in Naples, she succeeds pretty easily. All this is told in the tone of a hardened society woman of forty or rather reminds us of the days when girls came out at twelve and married at thirteen, but strangely enough all the liberties taken are taken in writing. Larderel never can boast of the least advantage, and has pretty promptly to propose for marriage, adding that he hopes Marie will mother his little girl. The *dénouement* is an extraordinary anti-climax. Marie has no wish to mother anybody. She is only a girl of seventeen who plays at being in love without knowing love any better than the year before (see Theuriet) when she was playing the same game with the "dog son of a priest," Cardinal Antonelli's nephew. We have been, as Larderel has been, deluded by a flirt.

What should the conclusion be? That honest Theuriet not only did Marie Bashkirtseff a wonderful service by so bravely editing her notebooks, but actually created the notoriety which makes us to-day read every line of this trivial narrative. Without him Marie Bashkirtseff would have remained a seductive but queer vision in the minds of two score of people. (pp. 89-90)

Ernest Dimnet, "The Real Marie Bashkirtseff," in The Saturday Review, *London, Vol. 140, No. 3639, July 25, 1925, pp. 89-90.*

EDWARD WAGENKNECHT   (essay date 1944)

[*Wagenknecht is an American literary historian, novelist, anthologist, and biographer. His best-known works are* Cavalcade of the English Novel *and* Cavalcade of the American Novel, *literary histories of the development of the novel in England and America. In the following excerpt, he reflects upon Bashkirtseff's writings, focusing on her reputation as an egomaniac, her talent as an artist, her views on love and religion, and her intense energy for life.*]

No woman in history ever waged more relentlessly than [Marie Bashkirtseff] what Professor Wilbur C. Abbott once very happily described . . . as the conflict with oblivion. This is a type of mind less common among women than among men: it is the temper to which we owe the great conquerors, the great explores, the great pioneers. Cunningly, craftily, she set her woman's wit to work to conquer death, to hoodwink oblivion. "Of what use were pretense or affectation? Yes, it is evident that I have the desire, if not the hope, of living upon this earth by any means in my power. If I do not die young I hope to live as a great artist; but if I die young, I intend to have my journal; which cannot fail to be interesting, published" [see essay dated 1884].

And because death had marked her for his own, she loved life. "I should like to be Caesar, Augustus, Marcus Aurelius, Nero, Caracalla, Satan, the Pope! I should like to be all these—and I am nothing!" So to a Napoleonic passion for eminence, she adds a Byronic hunger for breadth and depth of experience, a passionate longing to know, to feel, all that can be felt and known in human experience, yet at the same time she holds herself to a passionate purity, an undeviating, heroic rectitude. A girl Byron without sin! A Napoleonic egomaniac who never harmed a living thing!

Egomaniac is not too strong a word, and since it is along this line that Marie is generally attacked it may be well to have her egoism before us at the outset. She frankly and innocently admires everything about herself, and she expresses her admiration with a childish naïveté that is at once dismaying and disarming. "There is nothing more beautiful in the world than my body and . . . it is a true sin, an infamy, not to have myself sculptured or painted." She has herself photographed at any rate, photographed in every conceivable attitude. But better than any picture was her mirror, and she could spend hours before it, gazing enraptured upon herself. Quite as much as her beauty she admires her character—"the truest, the most admirable, the most just, the greatest, and the most loyal creature in the world"—"this wonderful and unique *me,* who fills me with delight, and whom, like Narcissus, I adore!"

To be sure, many think such things without saying them, and Marie has resolved to write "everything, everything, everything." The plain truth is that there are no limits to her egoism, yet there are times when she achieves an almost complete objectivity. "As a subject of interest for you, *I* may appear to you of little consequence; but forget that it is *I;* think simply that a fellow-being is recounting to you her impressions from her infancy."

The value of Marie's journal is often impeached on the score of her incessant affectations. She pretends to be telling the truth about herself, urge her critics, but she does not actually tell it, for she is always posing. What these persons overlook is that it was natural for her to pose, as natural as it was to breathe. She is not insincere because she poses; she would be insincere if she did not pose! In other words, we are dealing with one of those unusual persons to whom only artificialities are thoroughly natural.

Such a personality must inevitably repel many readers, yet those who love Marie Bashkirtseff—and she is far from being unlovable—are likely to feel even her egoism as part of her charm. It is only as she compares herself with others that she is satisfied; when she measures herself against her own ideal, she is nothing. (pp. 63-5)

It is interesting to study her egoism as it affected her relations with others. Her thought of humanity in general is, on the whole, one of wise kindliness. She takes the broad view, admires generosity and unselfishness, and she is utterly revolted by gossip and intrigue and will have no part in them. In a day of rampant nationalism she disdains patriotism altogether. With money she is extravagantly generous. That there was nothing mean in her egoism we see clearly in the light of her extravagant tendency towards hero-worship. Even when her keen mind told her that the object of her adoration was a futility, her imagination would set to work to rebuild a secret shrine for her devotions.

In the family circle she was something of a tyrant. She could rebuke her good-for-nothing father like an archduchess on the rare occasions when he condescended to grace the family circle with his presence, but everything she told him was true, and she seems on the whole to have thought of him a good deal more kindly than he deserved. Her mother and her aunt petted and spoiled her shamefully; from babyhood she was consistently the object of enough unintelligent and undiscriminating adulation to have ruined a saint.

As for others outside the family circle, it may be, as those who knew her in life are always inclined to insist, that her *Journal* does not quite do her justice. One of her fellow-students, Miss Mary L. Breakell, testifies [in the essay "Marie Bashkirtseff: The Reminiscence of a Fellow-Student" (see excerpt dated 1907)]: "In spite of the discomforts she caused us, I think we all loved Marie Bashkirtseff, as one loves a charming, wilful child. Indeed, the Marie I knew was a much more charming person than the writer of the *Diary,* though that writer was herself." Miss M. H. Dixon adds, more warmly [see Further Reading], "I have seen her aiding the least promising newcomer in the *atelier* Julian, giving her time, when she had already begun to guess that her working days were numbered." Still more cogent are the words of Prince Bojidar Karageorgevitch [see essay dated 1903], who knew her so much better than either of the women: "I did not find in the book the Marie I had known—the best and most intelligent of women, the rare soul to whose advice I owe nearly all the good fortune I have had in my life."

What Marie Bashkirtseff would have achieved as a painter if she had had a longer time to work, it is of course impossible to say definitely. The work that she did is certainly immensely creditable when one considers the circumstances under which it was produced, yet I incline to doubt any genuine vocation for painting on her part. She deceived herself and she sometimes deceives us along this line because what she had was a genuine aesthetic sensitiveness and aptitude generally. She played four instruments; she is said to have been an excellent interpreter of Chopin. Her critical judgments in art, too, are always interesting; making due allowance for her bent towards naturalism, one might speak of them as often penetrating, even when they were not wholly just. Strangely enough, her aestheticism fails her when she approaches poetry, which seems to have meant nothing to her whatever.

Yet Marie never thinks of art as the chaste mistress to which the artist must concentrate his all. It is a tool, a vehicle for her own ambitions, a cunning device to be used as a means of bringing her fame. And she seems almost indifferent in her choice of the particular form of art that shall achieve this end. As a child she dreamed of being a famous dancer; later she thought of herself as a great singer, with side glances, from time to time, at the possibility of winning social success through a brilliant marriage. When her voice failed her, she turned to painting instead, and—impatient at fame's tarrying—she was already, before the end, on the verge of transferring her interests to sculpture.

Whatever she essayed she worked at as faithfully as artist has ever worked, but she was not working for art, she was working for Marie Bashkirtseff. As time went on and her illness

The interior of Bashkirtseff's tomb in Paris.

increased, she became increasingly impatient in her race against time, and it would be very unfair to take all her despairing self-depreciations at their face-value. "I shall never paint, I have never been able to paint a picture well." "If I wish to become an artist, it is for the same reason that malcontents become republicans."

No, what she had was not real creative power, it was the passion for self-expression. It is no accident that she lives in the world's imagination through the direct impression of herself that she achieved in her *Journal* while her paintings are neglected. "I feel unable to write tonight, and something compels me to write. So long as I leave something unsaid, something torments me." Even in the early days, she is inclined to view the world in terms of "copy." "And when I have spoken or written, I am satisfied." Towards the end, she feels the itch for writing taking possession of her more and more.

Not all Marie's writing was done in her *Journal.* There is the correspondence she conducted, generally under an assumed name, with the most famous writers of the day. Most interesting is the famous interchange with Maupassant, in which this amazing girl and her manifold enthusiasms so mystified and bewildered the blasé, extracautious man of the world. She wrote too to Zola, to Dumas, *fils,* to Sully-Prudhomme. In a sense her correspondence is intimate, revealing. She is as

frank in her letters as she is in her *Journal.* But only rarely is there any genuine *interchange* of thought and feeling: she is almost exclusively preoccupied with her own concerns. These were her innocent liaisons with famous men, or as she puts it in Maupassant's case: "I woke up one beautiful morning with the desire of getting the pretty things I know how to say appreciated by a connoisseur. I searched and chose him."

I have already glanced at Marie Bashkirtseff's feeling that she was running a race with time. It was indicative of her nature that this girl, so madly aflame with life and the love of it, should have lived her whole life under the shadow of the fear of death. Premonitions always haunted her. As early as 1878, long before she knew the nature of the disease that finally killed her, she wrote, "It would be absurd; and yet I think I am going to die. It is impossible that I should live long. I am not constituted like other people; I have a great deal too much of some things in my nature, a great deal too little of others, and a character not made to last."

She was right; in spite of all her endowments the end was inevitable, as in such cases it always is. She foreordained to destruction in a far deeper sense than ever souls were foreordained to damnation under the old Calvinistic theology.

The fashionable society in which she lived was the kind of society least adapted to the needs of such a being as she was. Moving as she did through one Continental hotel after another, she early acquired a cosmopolitanism which contributed importantly to the maturity of her mind, but she acquired at the same time a hectic instability which made her problem of adjustment far more difficult than it need otherwise have been. Not that Marie was ever essentially a worldly person. She lived in the realm of her own imagination, and for all her precocious maturity, the appeal she makes is often that of the helpless child. Nevertheless, the mad whirl placed an unnecessary strain upon a physique far too delicate to withstand it, and the whole existence offered stimuli to self-conscious pride, to artificiality of thought and feeling, to morbid introspectiveness, which she, of all the women of her time, did not need, and which she was least able to resist. "Mme. Gavini came again today to tell mamma that I am wearing myself out; that is true, but it is not with painting; to avoid wearing myself out it would be only necessary to go to bed every night at ten or eleven o'clock, while, as it is, I stay up till one, and waken in the morning at seven." But escape from it alone she could not, and the people around her had no real grasp of her problem. Her inbred shortcomings made her susceptible, her environment reinforced her shortcomings; thus she traveled around a vicious circle.

When we turn to the higher problems of the spirit, she seems no more enviably placed. Take, first, love. If you are to judge by the *Journal* alone, you will feel that nobody was ever preoccupied with it more. She seeks out the love passages in her favorite novels and reads them again and again. She dreams herself to sleep every night with dreams of love. Yet she can, when she chooses, be quite cynical about marriage. She dreams of an alliance that shall raise her to a high, to a dominating position. "That is why I wish to go into the world—to find a rich husband and to free myself for studying, to frequent learned men, writers, and artists."

But she would never really have married for that reason, nor, indeed, I think, for any other. The procession of her fancies trails its way through her *Journal,* but one cannot seriously think of her as married to any one of them. Sometimes, as in the case of the Duke of Hamilton, for whom she conceived a schoolgirl affection when she was twelve, she was content to worship from afar, without ever attempting to establish a contact. Sometimes, as with Lardarel and Antonelli, she enjoyed the thrill of conquest. And sometimes, as with the Bonapartist journalist, Paul de Cassagnac, she worked herself up into a dreadful state, principally, one suspects, because the man was utterly indifferent to her.

Marie felt herself very badly used in the Antonelli matter, for Pietro's uncle, a cardinal, opposed the affair, principally because Marie was not a Roman Catholic but a member of the Greek Orthodox church. But it was her pride that was hurt, not her heart, and she was clear-sighted enough when, five years later, she wrote in the margin of her *Journal:* "I never loved him; all this was but the effect of an excited imagination in search of romance."

The inspiration came always from within, never from without. Lardarel was an utterly disreputable man-about-town, with a bad history, a vulgar mistress, and an illegitimate child, and Marie finally came to her senses about him when he insisted that if they were to marry, she would be obliged to look after the child! It is amusing to note the mixture of jealousy, indignation, and shocked virginal modesty in her response to this suggestion: "The left-over of a courtesan, of a dancer!!! and he regrets her still." After he had gone out of her life, she named her mandolin case "the sarcophagus of Alexandre."

Paul de Cassagnac hurt her far more deeply than Lardarel, but even here I think the real trouble is the humiliating reflection that she is not wanted. When her dog disappears in the midst of her agony, she finds herself more concerned over the animal than she is over love. "I write that I love, I act as if I loved, I say that I love to a confidante, and I do not believe it myself."

No, she is not a lover. She is too busy, for one thing, too tremendously occupied with that conflict with oblivion, while the natural tendency of the lover is to forget everything there is in the world except love, to forget the world and let the world forget him. "My future glory prevents me from thinking about him seriously; it seems to reproach me for the thoughts I devote to him."

Moreover, Marie was, if I may so express it, temperamentally a virgin, or, as we sometimes say, she was born an "old maid." The physical side of love made absolutely no appeal to her. "I have not been in the world and I know nothing, I say it without irony." What did appeal to her was the dream side; she toys with the idea of conquest; but she has no intention whatever of giving up her lovely body to any man. Her friends told her that she could never have a confidante because she had none of the guilty secrets that other girls love to share, and they were right. She did not hold men to a particularly rigid standard: she even finds Casanova-like proclivities rather fascinating in a Cassagnac, but such things were simply not to be thought of in connection with herself. Nor did she feel—as so many felt in her time—that marriage makes everything right. Once one of her friends got into trouble. For heaven's sake, urges Marie, hold your head high. "He doesn't love you enough to marry you and if you dare to love him knowing that, it is no longer love, it is bestiality." Even her brother's marriage, quite respectable according to conventional standards, had something about it that shocked her. It was not on a sufficiently idealistic level to suit her austere tastes: there was no delicacy, no morality, no modesty in it.

Once she allowed a man to kiss her. As soon as the spell of the kiss wears off, a cold chill passes over her, and for months afterwards she hates herself, tortures herself with the accusation that she has been false to her ideals. "God! how could I have kissed him on the face? . . . Mad, execrable creature! Ah, this is what makes me weep and tremble with rage!" She exaggerates of course; she always exaggerates; but fundamentally she is sincere. And when a comparative stranger gallantly kisses her hand, she is disgusted to find that the action gives her pleasure. "I thank God that I am a good girl and not in love with anybody. If I were I should probably kill myself with rage."

Yet even without this passionate puritanism, marriage must have been very difficult for her, for in love as in all else she was the thoroughgoing idealist. She lives in the ivory tower, and marriages, while they may be made in heaven or in hell, must be lived in this world. Marie Bashkirtseff believed, perhaps rightly, that no man could possibly be worthy of her, and her ideal was impossibly high. "It would be necessary that not a word, not a look, of his should be at variance with the idea I have formed of him. Not that I demand in him an impossible perfection, or that he should be a being superior to humanity; but I require that his caprices should be interesting caprices that would not lower him in my eyes; that he should be in conformity with my ideal—not the hackneyed ideal of an impossible demigod, but that everything of him should please me, and I should not unexpectedly discover in him some stupid, dull, weak, foolish, mean, false, or mercenary trait; one such blemish, only, no matter how small it might be, would be sufficient to ruin him in my eyes."

I have not, of course, forgotten Bastien-Lapage. As an artist Marie worshiped him, he influenced her profoundly, and during her last days they grew very close together. Bastien-Lepage fought a losing fight with cancer that ran parallel to her own struggle with tuberculosis, and he outlived her by little more than a month. As long as Marie was able to go out, she was taken to call on him, and the *Journal* reaches heights of almost unbearable pathos in its account of how the man and the girl—both young, highly gifted, with everything to live for—lay helpless, day after day, watching each other die. Yet to ferret out a romance between Bastien-Lepage and Marie Bashkirtseff is to betray a sex-obsessed imagination. There was a world of sympathy and understanding, and that is all.

Where love fails, religion often succeeds. "Where there is nothing, there is God." But Marie is even more uncertain about faith than she is about love. Sometimes she accepts all—the obscurantism of the Greek church, plus a world of superstitious belief and practice that belongs to no church. Sometimes she plays with the idea of faith-healing, dreams of making a pilgrimage. And at all times she turns God into an ally of her own petty irritations. "Who knows what God reserves for us? He will be punished perhaps in his old age for having been so insulting to me."

That she was desperately in need of God, she never, never forgot, and sometimes—especially in the early days—she achieves a genuine utterance of faith. "I am under the protection of God, I am almost sure of it, I have prayed to him so much about it." Yet even here we have the rather vulgar idea that religion consists primarily in getting things through supernatural agency, and as time went on with Marie Bashkirtseff, and it became increasingly clear that she was not going to get the things she wanted most of all, as moreover she read nihilistic or naturalistic books, frankly skeptical of the existence of God altogether, it was inevitable that her belief, never firmly founded, should waver.

There are times when she tries to discriminate between the essential and the inessential in religion. "I believe in God, our Savior, the Virgin, and I honor some of the saints, not all, for there are some that are manufactured like plum cakes." She speculates on the influence upon Jesus of "his humanity, his environment, and his country." She differentiates between the God of the Bible and the God of modern thought. Once she asks a smart young man if he believes in God. He replies, "I believe only what I understand." And Marie comments, "Oh, the stupid beast! All the boys that are beginning to grow a moustache think like that."

But more poignant than any of the problems of intelligent speculation, there was suffering and frustration, and here is the rock on which at last she foundered. Not that she ever definitely abandoned her faith. Rather, she wavers incessantly, at one moment throwing herself upon God with fierce reproaches and fiercer petitions, at the next turning against Him altogether as the author of all her miseries. Sometimes

the fires of faith will burn brightly, as in a noble passage on immortality inspired by the death of Gambetta: "There must be something beyond the grave; this transitory existence cannot be all; it does not satisfy either our reason or our aspirations; there must be something beyond; if there were not, this life would have no meaning, and God would be an absurdity." But in another mood she can write: "He [God] takes cognizance of nothing. Besides, it is very evident that God is not what we imagine him to be. God is, perhaps, nature; and all the events of life are directed by chance, which sometimes brings about those strange coincidences and events that make us believe there is a Providence. As to our prayers to God, our communion with Him, our faith in Him, I have learned to my cost that there is nothing in them."

But even in her bitterest moods she manifests a fundamentally religious nature. When she gives up the hope of God's help, she even derives a grim pleasure from the thought that God has made her a special object of vengeance. Quite clearly she perceived a truth which just now "all the sad young men" of the present day are just beginning to realize, that "Without God there can be neither poetry, nor affection, nor genius, nor love, nor ambition." And even when she thought her faith was gone, she continued to pray, as mankind has always prayed, because she could not live without prayer: "Though there be no God to hear my evening prayer, yet I pray to him every night in despite of my reason." But all this is to speculate on what might have been. Her world being what it was, Marie Bashkirtseff's religion was, in the last analysis, not a source of comfort to her but an added stimulus to struggle, all the more harrowing because she took it seriously, and none the less severe because it was often naïve and a little crude.

Yet it was not the failure of love that killed Marie Bashkirtseff, nor the failure of God, nor was she killed by tuberculosis. She died of sensation, of the tremendous intensity of the life that she led. Had she been willing to live as other people live, had she learned how to take reasonable precautions, her life might have been prolonged indefinitely. Her whole life was an orgy of sensibility: she received, she transmitted stimuli with destructive rapidity and intensity. "I am an exaggerated person; it is like a piano a half-tone higher, it is exact, but it is exaggerated." She tells us that she has pictured to herself "every human feeling, every earthly pleasure," and there is no doubt that the statement is essentially true. "I believe the candle is cut in four," she says, "and burns at every end."

Sometimes this intensity took the form of a feverish joy in life, and then she was comparatively safe, though even here the tendency was toward destructive intemperance: "I fancy that there is no one who take so intense a delight in all things as I do—art, music, painting, books, society, dress, luxury, gayety, solitude; tears and laughter, sadness and rejoicing; love, cold, heat; the solemn plains of Russia and the mountains that surround Naples; the snows of winter, the rains of autumn, spring with its intoxicating joys, the calm days and glorious starlit nights of summer—I love them and delight in them all." Sometimes there is a touch of barbarism in her intensity, as in her rather horrible account of the bullfight in Spain. And sometimes she performed curious feats of inversion. She had the hypochondriac's delight in illness, and she had a wonderful time being thoroughly miserable. In 1880, when the presence of tuberculosis was first discovered, she was rather pleased at the prospect of enjoying a new sensation: she is, she finds, still at an age when one can discover a thrill even in dying. This was the period when she deliberately neglected her health, flew into wild rages on the slightest provocation, insanely exposed herself for a whim, refused to use poultices because they might spoil the color of her skin. Indeed, at this time Marie Bashkirtseff was much more concerned about the deafness that accompanied her tuberculosis than she was about the tuberculosis itself. Tuberculosis was rather romantic, but deafness struck her as stupid, humiliating; to be obliged to confess that she could not hear wounded her vanity; she could see nothing interesting in that! Afterwards she changed her mind about all this, but afterwards it was too late.

This mad hunger for life, this ardent desire for experience and yet more experience, this flaming energy burning itself out through its own intensity—it is in these things that the real tragedy of Marie Bashkirtseff lies. "I came home at half-past six so exhausted with fatigue that the sensation was delicious. Perhaps you may not believe it, but for me every overpowering sensation, even the sensation of pain, is a joy. I remember once when I hurt my finger, some years ago, that for half an hour the pain was so acute that I took pleasure in it." This was her "tragic flaw," not sin nor transgression, but simply her too great eagerness to accept the gift of being. "Here it is at last, then, the end of all my miseries! So many aspirations, so many hopes, so many plans—to die at twenty-four, on the threshold of everything." (pp. 65-74)

Edward Wagenknecht, "Marie Bashkirtseff in Retrospect," in The South Atlantic Quarterly, *Vol. 43, No. 1, January, 1944, pp. 63-75.*

ROZSIKA PARKER AND GRISELDA POLLOCK (essay date 1985)

[*In the following excerpt from their introduction to a 1985 reprint of the* Journal, *Parker and Pollock emphasize the feminist qualities of Bashkirtseff's work, examining her refusal to conform to sexual stereotypes and the ways in which contemporary response to the diary reflects the "sexual divisions" of nineteenth-century society.*]

The *Journal* of a Russian woman, painter, sculptor, musician who died very young in 1884 took the world by storm when it was first published in France in 1887 and in England in 1890. It caused a sensation in Europe and even more so in America, and all reviewers confirm the fame it brought to its author: "It is this *Journal* with which the world is now ringing, and which it is hardly too much to say is likely to carry the fame of Marie Bashkirtseff over the face of the civilised globe" [see entry by Marion Hepworth Dixon in Further Reading].

Never before had a woman so urgently proclaimed her ambition to excel, her hunger for public fame. Never before had a woman so coolly analysed her emotions and questioned woman's guiding purpose—love. Never before had a woman so openly revolted against all that woman was meant to be— where she should have been self-sacrificing, she was egotistical; where she should have longed for home and hearth, she desired knowledge and education; where she should have patiently waited for marriage, she equivocated about that option: where she should have been content to live as some man's wife, she longed to be famous for herself. All this makes it understandable why *The Journal of Marie Bashkirtseff* caused a sensation and why women have continued to read the *Journal* as a cult text throughout the twentieth

century though never without equivocation. There had been young ladies' journals, true enough, but what the *Journal* gave was more than anyone at that date permitted themselves to expect from a young lady. Yet women readers like Marion Dixon welcomed the *Journal* precisely because it transgressed its genre. In it, she wrote, we find "a woman self-revealed, a woman who almost for the first time in history has had the courage to present us with a real woman, as distinguished from the sham women of books".

The *Journal* broke the mould and depending on its readers' gender and ideology, shocked, horrified, fascinated or thrilled them.

The heart of the *Journal* and of its public notoriety is the matter of sexual difference. It is first and foremost the representation of a woman's life, or, put in another way which transcends a purely biographical interpretation, the representation of the life women were offered at that date and in that social milieu. The *Journal* is a protest against that life and its central figure, the lady. The rebellion which generated the text undermines the ideologies of femininity which strive to secure their propositions about the nature, calling and feelings of women as natural and therefore unquestionable. The resistance in these pages against the conventions which ruled women's sexuality and denied women, especially those young and unmarried, social mobility and freedom exposes the social regulation of women as a disciplinary system based on almost constant surveillance. Thus, although the diary form suggests an intimate world of private reveries and personal confessions, at all points the text is shaped by the pressure of the outside, the constraints of the social. The diary therefore comes into existence as an imaginary realm of freedom for its author, a freedom experienced in the writing of that which is always in excess of the permitted and possible world, a writing which invents a sympathetic listener in its readers, and makes a demand for total acceptance—an uncomfortable position. So that in reading the *Journal* the reader is asked to be other than the "social others" through whose exclusion, surveillance or disapprobation the author suffers an acute sense of being split, fragmented and invalidated.

The *Journal* offers the reader, therefore, a position against the grain of the conventional notions of women. But this is not because the *Journal* is a highly formulated feminist critique of femininity. It is rather a living of femininity within the specific structures of a provincial Russian emigré nobility living in France without full acceptance into respectable French society and yet, by virtue of wealth and social habits, cut off from any other social world. It is in addition a writing across femininity, which is exposed as a series of often contradictory positions. The stereotype of femininity ideologically proposed is an illusion of coherence and consistency— woman's nature spontaneously lived. The *Journal,* conceived not in meditated opposition, but out of a struggle to live that myth, simultaneously exposes femininity both as imposed from outside, a regulation of women's lives and as internalised, coterminous with a body and a self. The author of the *Journal* negotiates this by multiple splittings. For instance, one of the most quoted passages states:

I have nothing of the woman about me but the envelope and that envelope is diabolically feminine. As for the rest it is quite another matter. It is not I who say this, since it seems to be that all women are like myself.

Under the dominant regime of sexual difference, a different

and better condition can only be imagined in terms of being a man, and frequently the writer cries out, "If only I were a man." Man is the agent of freedom in matters sexual, intellectual, and social. Woman is, as it were, a confining envelope within which a potential human person is housed but that "personness" is permitted only to men. Another kind of split is identified in this passage:

> Indeed the woman who is writing and her whom I describe, are really two persons. What are all her troubles to me? I tabulate, analyse, and copy the daily life of my person; but to *me myself,* all that is very indifferent. It is my pride, my self love, my interests, my envelope, my eyes, which suffer, weep or rejoice; but *I myself,* am there only to watch, to write, to relate and to reason calmly about these great miseries, just as Gulliver must have looked at the Lilliputians.

This statement underwrites the very modern notions of representation to which the text is available. That is to say the *Journal* is about a woman, a narrative of a life, but the writing itself produces another subject and sets the surveyor and analyst into a fractured relation to her whose life is told. This itself should prevent us from slipping into the illusion of searching the *Journal* for the real and true Marie Bashkirtseff screened behind the text. There have been many authors who have used the Journal as a resource precisely for this kind of biographical reconstruction and their products appear inevitably as a kind of fiction. There is no originating personality revealed in an unmediated fashion by the *Journal.*

All such diaries are a form of literature conforming to a set of codes and conventions. The mode of writing is shaped within an imaginary bond of a confessing subject and confessor/reader which in this particular *Journal* comes remarkably close to the kind of modern forms of confessions which Foucault has characterised in the analytical relationships of psychoanalysis.

But the author is also commentator, the *Journal* the locus of acts of critical reflection, a means to gain a perspective on the contradictions whose effect she was. Herein lies the "political" activity of the *Journal* in whose writing an Other is imagined and addressed with and through whom knowledge can be derived. This process importantly echoes the manner of feminist analyses where the telling of lived experience is transformed into political understanding by placing those experiences in a larger context of women's lives.

In our culture we privilege the notion of the unified subject, we imagine the individual as a coherent and conscious self who is the origin and cause of both actions and such things as art or literature. Psychoanalysis has proposed a radically different view of human subjectivity, arguing that the human subject is split between conscious and unconscious. The subject is fragmented and therefore written texts or artifacts are not the expression of a unified self but moments in the *process* which is the human subject. *The Journal of Marie Bashkirtseff* is, as a text, uneven and often incoherent. This is a product of the author's struggle as a subject, which was shaped by the historical forces which determined what it was to be a feminine subject at that date. Modern feminist historians have identified the division between the public and the private in the nineteenth century as a major social split which produced the particular form of bourgeois femininity and its oppressive features. *The Journal of Marie Bashkirtseff* dramatises what it meant to live that split which was experienced

in one way as a prohibition on women's free access to the public sphere of work and knowledge:

> What I long for is the freedom of going about alone, of coming and going, of sitting in the seats of the Tuileries, and especially in the Luxembourg, of stopping and looking at the artistic shops, of entering churches and museums, of walking about the old streets at night: that's what I long for; and that's the freedom without which one cannot become a real artist. Do you imagine that I get much good from what I see, chaperoned as I am, and when, in order to go to the Louvre, I must wait for my carriage, my lady companion and family?

The mediating point between the public and the private is the family. At its most immediate, the writing of the *Journal* was an escape from that family, the cutting out of a space apart, through which to construct an identity separate from them. Yet there was no escape—except the ones endlessly debated in the *Journal*—marriage or fame. Only the latter could ensure freedom for marriage entailed another kind of servitude, however much it could be dreamed of in the ideal of mutual respect from a great and brilliant man. Ironically it was through the family that the *Journal* came to be published to secure for its author the renown that would have made her free of both the social marginality she suffered and the isolation within her family.

It was the family, however, which imposed upon the *Journal* its published form. Selecting from the eighty-four exercise books of handwritten manuscripts, a particular figure of Marie Bashkirtseff was incised by omission, alteration and suppression. This "Marie" was in many ways a figure restructured to confirm all that against which the diary's subject struggled in the writings. This is the claim of the most recent study of *The Journal of Marie Bashkirtseff* by Colette Cosnier.

Cosnier records her emotions of shock, stupor and anger as she leafed through the original manuscript in the Bibliothèque Nationale in Paris and discovered that the date of birth and age of Marie Bashkirtseff had been falsified, by two years throughout, her expressions—such as studio slang censored, whole passages suppressed for indecency and her violently critical attitude to women's conditions softened so that her feminism is all but erased. Cosnier argues that a legendary Marie Bashkirtseff has been built up, initially produced by the expurgated text and enlarged by unscrupulous writers in the 1920s, who freely used the materials which became available after the death of Madame Bashkirtseff in 1920 to fashion an image of an angelically pure, divinely gifted and fascinating but enigmatic woman. Cosnier quotes large sections of hitherto unpublished *Journal* to reveal an affectionate, creative and sexual woman. Cosnier considers her a woman born a hundred years too soon. Prisoner of her own times, she becomes for Cosnier a woman for ours.

Every reading of the *Journal* has been partial and overdetermined by the competences and interests of the readers. Cosnier gives us a feminist Marie Bashkirtseff, which is a valuable corrective to the excesses of the edited *Journal* 's fashion-conscious egotist. It will be important for any one reading the *Journal* now to be aware of Cosnier's material. It does not invalidate the *Journal* as it is currently published, for its very form is itself a historical evidence of the struggle over femininity of which the name Marie Bashkirtseff has become a symbol both for her detractors and supporters. It is moreover only a further aspect of both the inevitable incoherence of the *Journal* and the marking of history—via the family—across its pages. Cosnier's text thickens the thin lines of discourse in the *Journal* at precisely those points where it falters for reasons that are not the writer's.

Marie Bashkirtseff's date of birth is usually given as 11 November 1860. During her life her father revealed to her that she had in fact been born on 28 November 1858, only seven months after her parents' marriage. This fact had been concealed by suggesting that she had been premature (which was not the case), and by dating her birth from January 1859. It was then altered to November 1860. To maintain the fiction, all ages given in the *Journal* were doctored with the effect that instead of being thirteen at the age of her infatuation for the Duke of Hamilton she was closer to fifteen and her desire to marry the fellow was not the childish fantasy whose piquancy troubled the readers. She died at the age of twenty-six, an age when she recognised she could no longer be considered tragically young.

The second major area of revision of the published *Journal* is the excision of almost all references to the exact composition of the household in which Marie Bashkirtseff was brought up. There is no reference in the published text to the depraved, drunken Uncle Georges, the father of cousin Dina, a public scandal, frequently in prison or coming up before the magistrates and police. His antics were a major cause of the social ostracism which the Bashkirtseff family suffered in both Nice and Paris where they were not accepted by polite society, the passport to which was ensured by being received by the Russian ambassador. This never happened because of the scandals of Uncle Georges as well as the pall which hung over the family because of the strange affair of the marriage of Aunt Sophie to the rich man, Romanoff who, having wanted to marry Marie's mother, had been duped into wedding Sophie. After a year of marriage he died in mysterious circumstances and a case was brought against the Babanines (Marie's mother's family) by the disinherited Romanoff heirs who spread unpleasant rumours about the connivings of the Babanine brothers. Also cleaned out of the *Journal* are references to Madame Bashkirtseff's own somewhat dubious friendships and flirtations, and her moral irresponsibilities towards her daughter. Cosnier prints a letter written—in uncharacteristic fury it must be admitted—to her mother on 10 February 1881:

> Being the voluntary or involuntary cause of all my troubles because it is your fault if I have passed and do now pass my youth locked up without seeing any one except the Mouzays or the aged Gavinis or other people of this sort, thus being the cause of my moral death, you should at least try not to inflict on me the nuisance of my physical death. . . . Before the pretext for dramas was Georges, at present it is me. Instead of talking to me about your love for me, remember that you have morally assassinated me, you and your Georges. . . . But because I am not dying from illness, I would find it very different when I shall have definitely lost hope of escaping from the atrocious and abominable life which you have made for me.

Cosnier draws attention to the references to sexuality which must have figured for the author as one of the *Journal*'s claims for shocking honesty. Marie Bashkirtseff not only writes of the sexual excitements she experiences in physical contact with the young men she was involved with (and there are many more than the expurgated diary allows) but she is frank about the way in which the double standard forces women to imagine themselves in love when all they are experiencing is desire. Of Antonelli, the man she was courted by during her stay in Rome in 1876, the entry for 10 March 1876 reads: "I cannot say that I love him but I can certainly say that I desire him. . . . It is in the arms of Pietro that I would like to be . . . eyes closed, I achieve such an illusion that I almost believe myself there and then and then . . . I am furious." The freedom to enjoy sexual relations without the implications of love or marriage (or babies) was a repeated theme of Marie Bashkirtseff's *Journal.* Men enjoyed this liberty and she envied it.

Many of her thoughts about the relative position of men and women have been abbreviated or altered, though it remained a constant issue which informed her feminism. The published *Journal* allows us a glimpse of a visit paid by Marie Bashkirtseff to the apartment of Hubertine Auclerc, organiser of the militant suffrage movement, Le Droit des Femmes (founded 1876), in December 1880. Edited out are her repeated visits to the meetings of this group which she joined and her financial investment in the socialist and feminist journal *La Citoyenne* in which, under the name of Pauline Orell, she published several salon reviews and an incisive article on the restrictions placed on women artists on 20 February 1881. These revelations indicate that Marie Bashkirtseff was a much more ardent and conscious feminist than the *Journal* allows.

While the published journal provides insights into the constraints within which a woman of Marie Bashkirtseff's marginal social position lived, these very pressures and conventions become all the more vivid once the fact of her revolt is restored by the publication of these unknown passages. Her feelings of being sexually aroused makes the outrage at women's lack of freedom more concrete, her resistance to marriage becomes more explicable and less the folly of a contrary young woman, her hunger for a career emerges as a means to escape the inadequacy of the familial environment and the limitations placed upon an unmarried woman in a dubious social position. It is important to read the *Journal* in the light of the omissions and these restrictions of our understanding provided by Cosnier's research.

But there is a match between what has been taken out and what Cosnier's rereading restores. Across this seam can be discerned the figure of woman as she has ideologically changed between the late nineteenth-century feminist campaigning against bourgeois norms of femininity and the late twentieth-century women's movement. Sexuality is privileged in modern feminism as a symbolic expression of women's claim for autonomy, self-expression and self-knowledge. For Marie Bashkirtseff sexual licence was entwined with other more vital forms of liberty, the freedom to learn and to be assessed in terms of being someone and not something, to escape the bartering of women in marriage.

Most reviewers of the 1890s read the *Journal* within the prevailing ideological systems and struggled to find ways to accommodate Marie Bashkirtseff within them. There is, however, an interesting contrast between the reading of the *Journal* by men and by women.

The French edition of the *Journal* was reviewed for *The Nineteenth Century* by the eminent English statesman William Ewart Gladstone in 1889 [see essay above]. "Mlle Bashkirtseff attracts and repels alternately, and perhaps repels as much as she attracts." Yet Gladstone claimed the book as one without parallel, written by a true genius because "when the tale is viewed as a whole, even its tragic interest subsides in comparison with its commanding singularity as a psychological study." There were two ways to respond, one through the stereotype of the tragic life of an exceptional woman, the other through a scientific interest in the human condition. Marie Bashkirtseff, however, was fascinating but dangerous because of her excess, waanting to be more than a woman. There is, however, comfort for Gladstone in the fact that it is tuberculosis—a disease almost mythically identified with women's physical inferiority in the nineteenth century—and not social conventions which confounded her desire to be more than she should. Gladstone also names the book a psychological study but the images employed to expand this notion reveal a more cutting edge. "It is not a picture of herself which she has given so much as a demonstration in anatomy. The lines of this deep-cut image are wrought out in so sustained a fashion, by an unremitting exercise of forces, that they run over the entire surface." The text is thus transformed into a body, a woman's body, a body cut and pared, left exposed, through death to an objectifying observer. It is clear that despite the appeal in the *Journal* for a sympathetic reader, Gladstone cannot identify with Marie Bashkirtseff and draws back into a medical distance. Yet, "Psychology sounds too cold and technical for the workings of this uplifted and yet profoundly harrowed soul". Once again etherealised as Woman, as soul, Marie Bashkirtseff is returned to a place of ideological safety for Gladstone who concludes by projecting a destructive wish. He compares the *Journal* with the ruins at Selinunti, a Greek temple which has suffered total destruction and is reduced to a mass of single broken stones.

The testimony of women who had known Marie Bashkirtseff as a fellow art student at the Académie Julian does not provide us with a corrective or truer picture of the artist or author, but reminds us of an important aspect of the *Journal*'s popularity in the later nineteenth century, the meanings of the *Journal* offered to readers who were women. Both Marion Dixon and Mary Breakell wrote "reminiscences" based on the claim to personal acquaintance with the *Journal*'s writer, but both in different ways express a disappointment in the published book. "The woman was so much more human than the portrait," was Marion Dixon's comment. "With a fine scorn in real life, for bourgeois pretensions and middle class prejudices, she could be kind and helpful, almost tender with the ignorant and ill advised. I have seen her aiding the least promising new-comer in the *atelier* Julian . . ." Mary Breakell insisted [in the essay "Marie Bashkirtseff: The Reminiscence of a Fellow-Student" (see excerpt dated 1907.)]: "The Marie I knew was a much more charming person than the writer of the *Diary* although the writer was herself." The Marie Bashkirtseff these women knew was the one who escaped the family and its dubious social milieu to the sustaining air of a studio of serious artists. Their testimony is further evidence of the splitting Marie Bashkirtseff experienced when she joined a community of women at work. In that environment of different social and professional relationships another place in the continuum of subjectivity was possible. The authors all attest to their own and others' suspicions about the integrity of the published journal (and its dates), lamenting an unspecifiable lack in the edited volume compared with what they remembered. But what is also noticeable in the reviews by women writers is the acceptance of the imperfect

heroine, the indulgence in the inconsistencies and contradictions, a pardon for extreme self love and egotism. Helen Zimmern's article is typical [see Further Reading].

> No one can lay down without emotion the pages of this diary, in which a human soul has voluntarily laid its very inmost fibres here before us. She was not a faultless heroine, far from it, but we love her none the less for that. The more, perhaps, because it approaches her to our common humanity. And think of her what we will, we cannot refuse her the tribute that she was a valiant soul, who acted up to the motto she herself had chosen. *"Jusqu'au bout"*.

It is interesting to find a reflection of the *Journal* in another young woman's diary, Julie Manet, daughter of the Impressionist painter. Berthe Morisot read the *Journal* in 1897 and was interested in the life of this intelligent and open-minded young woman. Julie Manet wrote that she found Marie Bashkirtseff a curious and not a disagreeable character as she had been led to expect, not so full of pride as she had been told. Julie Manet wrote in a sympathetic manner about Marie Bashkirtseff's struggle to be someone.

> I remember Mother and Father read the *Journal* at Mézy, they talked a lot about it and had numerous discussions. Papa, far from finding like Monsieur Degas that she was a woman who should be publically whipped, admired her, while Mother said to him, "I can just see you with such a woman, you would find her insupportable." She [Berthe Morisot] would have found Marie Bashkirtseff extraordinary . . . but I think one must not judge her on what she said, in fact she did not have such excessive admiration for herself.
>
> In opposition to the generality of books (according to what is said) this one must be better understood by a young girl who can enter into the spirit of the girl who recounts her life and thoughts and compares them with her own.

These few examples from the numerous published responses to the *Journal* underline the sexual divisions of later nineteenth-century society of which the *Journal* was so telling a product. (pp. vii-xvii)

> *Rozsika Parker and Griselda Pollock, in an introduction to* The Journal of Marie Bashkirtseff, *translated by Mathilde Blind, Virago Press Limited, 1985, pp. vii-xxx.*

JANE MARCUS (essay date 1988)

[*In the following excerpt, Marcus discusses various aspects of the* Journal, *including the relationship between Bashkirtseff and her reader, her reputation as an artist, and the misconceptions surrounding her life due to the editing of her diary.*]

The relationship between reader and writer established immediately by Marie Bashkirtseff is intense and demanding. She is the victim and we are her saviors. By reading her we make her live and fulfill her desires, and in a curious way we are asked to be her sexual partners. She has never been loved, she cries, and one rushes to assure her that she is loved. Here Woolf's claim that as readers we like to see ourselves romantically as deliverers is powerfully evoked, and all chivalrous readers—most male, but, I suspect, some female—are inspired by this text to see themselves charging to her rescue on white horses:

This poor journal, the confidant of all my strivings toward the light, all these outbursts, which would be regarded as the outbursts of imprisoned genius if my aspirations were to be finally crowned by success, but which will be regarded as the vain ravings of a commonplace creature if I am destined to languish forever in obscurity. To marry and have children? Any washerwoman can do that. What then do I desire? Ah, you know well what I desire—I desire fame. It is not this journal that will give it to me, however. This journal will be published only after my death for I show myself too *nakedly* in it to wish it to be read during my lifetime.

Bashkirtseff knows very well that she consciously creates herself in the diary:

> I must repeat to myself again that no advice in the world—nothing but *personal experience*—could ever have kept me from doing anything I wished to do. That is because the woman who writes these words and the woman she is writing about are two different persons. What do all these sufferings matter to *me?* I write them down; I analyze them; I transcribe my daily life, but to *me*, to *me myself*, all that is completely indifferent. It is my pride, my self-love, my interests, my complexion, my eyes, that suffer, that weep, that rejoice; but *I*, I take part in it all only to observe, to narrate, to write about and reason coldly concerning all these trifles, like Gulliver among the Lilliputians.

Bashkirtseff demands pity: "Can you not fancy you already see me feeble, emaciated, pale, dying, dead? It is not atrocious that this should be so? But, dying young, I shall at least inspire everyone with pity. I am myself touched with compassion when I think of my fate." At the time these words were written, Bashkirtseff was suffering from tuberculosis and was growing deaf; she had already lost her voice and given up her ambition to sing in favor of painting. Bashkirtseff's translator says she has "all the cynicism of a Machiavelli and the naiveté of an ardent and enthusiastic girl." Despite winning a medal at the Salon, Marie's fame as a painter quickly receded as the fame of Impressionists increased. "The Meeting," a large realistic painting of Paris street urchins, was found abandoned in the attic of the Newberry Library in Chicago in 1973. When I ask feminist art historians why Bashkirtseff is not included in their books, they cite the vanity of the diary as a reason. In a preface written in 1884 (see essay above), just before her death, Bashkirtseff asserts the power of her diary as "a human document" that would interest Zola, Goncourt, or Maupassant. The expressive realism or naturalism of her writing is as much of the period as her paintings and those of her beloved Bastien-Lepage—now thoroughly overshadowed by Impressionism. Marie herself looks down on the "childishness" of Manet and all those who paint "pretty subjects," and yet the diary bursts with details of her concern over her appearance: dresses, hats, flowers, decorations for her room, even the white leather cases for the very diary in which she writes. She jumps from philosophizing to boasting that she owns seven hundred books. In the preface she worries that publishing the diary might destroy its value and proclaims her *sincerity*:

> If this book is not the *exact*, the *absolute*, the *strict* truth, it has no *raison d'être*. Not only do I always write what I think, but I have not even dreamed, for a single instant, of disguising anything that was to my disadvantage, or that might make me appear ridiculous. Besides, I think myself too admirable

for censure. You may be very certain, then, charitable readers, that I exhibited myself in the pages *just as I am.*

She grudgingly reveals her birth date (11 November 1860): "Only to write it down is frightful. But then I console myself by thinking that I shall be no age at all when you read this journal." She prepares the journal for publication, fearing that her family might destroy it on her death:

> and soon nothing would be left of me—nothing—nothing—nothing! This is the thought that has always terrified me. To live, to have so much ambition, to suffer, to weep, to struggle, and in the end to be forgotten;—as if I had never existed. . . . The record of a woman's life, written down day by day, without any attempt at concealment, as if no one in the world were ever to read it, yet with the purpose of being read, is always interesting. I am certain that I shall be found sympathetic, and I write down everything, everything, everything.

At age sixteen (although the dates may have been changed later to make her appear younger than she was), Bashkirtseff wrote:

> What ever I may become in the future, I bequeath my journal to the world. I offer you here what no one has ever yet seen. All the memoirs, the journals, the letters, which are given to the public are only inventions glossed over, and intended to deceive the world; I have neither any political action to gloss over, nor any unworthy action to conceal. No one troubles himself whether I am in love or not, whether I laugh.

Bashkirtseff's journal enjoyed several years of fame and then it—and she—disappeared from history. But in 1911 it was still popular enough to inspire an anonymous parody: *Super Soul: The Memoirs of Marie Mushenough.* Bashkirtseff's myth was taken up by Maurice Barrès as "the representation of the eternal force which calls forth heroes in each generation" and by "Our Lady Who is Never Satisfied," a right-wing idealization of certain forms of womanhood that also used the figure of Joan of Arc, who was not canonized until the 1920s. It is unfortunate that we do not have a reliable text of the diary as Bashkirtseff wrote it. According to her friend Bojidar Karageorgevitch [see essay dated 1903], the enormous manuscript was cut by her mother and by Theuriet, a friend of Bastien-Lepage who wished to stress Marie's relationship with the painter. Karageorgevitch deplores the changing of the dates to make her appear as "a sentimental freak only twelve years of age" and complains that "legend has seized hold of Marie Bashkirtseff and daily defaces more and more her real character." The omissions in the diary are also important:

> Marie was one of the first apostles of feminism. She aided in the publication of the *Citoyenne*, a feminist newspaper which preceded the *Fronde* . . . for which she wrote art criticism. . . . For a while she was devoted, body and soul, to feminism. She used to be present at the meetings in the Petrelle Hall, and scolded me as if I were the lowest of creatures, because my interest in these questions was not sufficiently lively. . . . "You are a wretch," she said, "you have no right to refuse to be interested in a question which is going to change the face of the earth."

Despite these problems with the text, Bashkirtseff's journal remains the great lyric outpouring of the striving woman artist. (pp. 134-37)

> *Jane Marcus, "Invincible Mediocrity: The Private Selves of Public Women," in* The Private Self: Theory and Practice of Women's Autobiographical Writings, *edited by Shari Benstock, The University of North Carolina Press, 1988, pp. 114-46.*

FURTHER READING

Blind, Mathilde. "A Study of Marie Bashkirtseff." In *Jules Bastien-Lepage and His Art, etc.,* by André Theuriet and others, pp. 149-90. London: T. Fisher Unwin, 1892.

A study of Bashkirtseff's life, focusing on her reputation as an artist. The essay includes a complete listing of her paintings.

Cahuet, Albéric. *Moussia: The Life and Death of Marie Bashkirtseff.* New York: Macaulay Co., 1929, 300 p.

The first full-length biography, based on information from the edited manuscript of Bashkirtseff's *Journal.* Cahuet's work originally appeared in French in 1926.

Cronin, Vincent. "Marie Bashkirtseff." In his *Four Women in Pursuit of an Ideal,* pp. 215-74. London: Collins, 1965.

Examines Bashkirtseff as a "self-conscious" Romantic, noting that the publication of her journal fulfilled her claim: "I am my own heroine."

Dixon, Marion Hepworth. "Marie Bashkirtseff: A Personal Reminiscence." *The Fortnightly Review* n.s. XLVII, No. CCLXXVIII (1 February 1890): 276-82.

A sentimental assessment of Bashkirtseff's talents by one of her fellow art students.

Gribble, Francis. "Marie Bashkirtseff." *The English Review* XLII (June 1926): 800-07.

Discusses Bashkirtseff's attitude toward love, recounting several of her amorous relationships.

Moore, Doris Langley. *Marie and the Duke of H.: The Daydream Love Affair of Marie Bashkirtseff.* Philadelphia: J. B. Lippincott Co., 1966, 304 p.

Analyzes the first year of Bashkirtseff's *Journal,* particularly her account of her infatuation with the Twelfth Duke of Hamilton. This is the first study in English based on the original manuscript.

Moorman, Lewis J. "Marie Bashkirtseff." In his *Tuberculosis and Genius,* pp. 59-99. Chicago: University of Chicago Press, 1940.

Discusses the effect of tuberculosis on Bashkirtseff's life and writings.

Zimmern, Helen. "Marie Bashkirtseff: A Human Document." *Blackwood's Edinburgh Magazine* CXLVI, No. DCCCLXXXVII (September 1889): 300-20.

A biographical sketch describing Bashkirtseff's love affair with Pietro Antonelli and reunion with her father in Russia.

Arthur Hugh Clough

1819-1861

English poet and essayist.

Formerly regarded as an author whose works were of value only to the extent that they reflected the ideological crises and conflicts of English society in the nineteenth century, Clough is today esteemed as a highly accomplished poet of the Victorian period. While he has been praised as a lyric poet, it is primarily in his skills as a satirist that critics now find his strength. In such works as *The Bothie of Tober-na-Vuolich: A Long-Vacation Pastoral, Amours de Voyage,* and *Dipsychus,* Clough displays the candor and irony with which he questioned the beliefs and conventions of his time concerning such subjects as religion, love, and marriage.

The son of a cotton merchant, Clough was born in Liverpool. He began his formal education in 1828, studying for a year at a preparatory school in Chester before attending Rugby, where he earned several academic honors, distinguished himself as an athlete, and from 1835 to 1837 edited the *Rugby Magazine.* He also contributed several of his earliest writings to the magazine, and his first published work, *The Close of the Eighteenth Century: A Prize Poem,* appeared in 1835. The following year, Clough was awarded a scholarship to study classics at Balliol College, Oxford, which he entered in 1837. He graduated with a bachelor's degree in 1841 but failed to obtain a Balliol Fellowship necessary to begin further studies. Clough regained his postion at Oxford the next year, winning a fellowship to Oriel College. At Oriel, Clough found that his personal ideals were in conflict with the college's requirement that all students subscribe to the Thirty-Nine Articles of the Anglican Church before taking degrees. While Clough remained a lifelong Christian, biographers point out that he did not passively accept the precepts of established institutions and believed that individuals should actively formulate and continually reassess their own convictions. With some reservation, he signed the Articles in 1843 to receive his M.A.; however, his principles forced him to withdraw from the college in 1848, a year before he would have had to resubscribe in order to obtain his doctorate.

Soon after leaving Oxford, Clough published his first significant poem, *The Bothie of Toper-na-Fuosich* (later renamed *The Bothie of Tober-na-Vuolich,* after he discovered that the original title was a bawdy Gaelic toast). Whereas *The Bothie* was highly praised by both English and American critics, his second volume, *Ambarvalia,* a collection of the poems Clough and his friend Thomas Burbidge had written in college, was not well received when it was published in 1849. Shortly afterward, Clough was appointed principal of a student hall at the University of London. In 1851, Clough resigned from the university and the following year he left for the United States at the invitation of Ralph Waldo Emerson, whom he had met while Emerson was on a lecture tour of England. Clough remained in the United States until 1854, when he returned to England and took a position as an examiner in the London Education Office. In 1860, he became ill and traveled to the Continent, where he hoped to regain his health. He died in Italy in 1861.

While Clough experimented in his poetry with different styles, meters, and techniques, most of his poems were either lyrical or satiric. As a lyric poet, Clough portrayed subjects with seriousness and attention to formal beauty. Two of his best known poems, "Say Not the Struggle Naught Availeth" and "Qua Cursem Ventus," are in this manner. The former, which was inspired by Clough's witnessing the fall of Giuseppe Mazzini's Roman Republic in 1849, marks with sadness the failure of ideals, while "Qua Cursem Ventus" laments the dissolution of a friendship over conflicting beliefs. Although Clough's lyricism has long been praised by critics, his ability as a satirist is more highly esteemed today. With satire sometimes bluntly incisive and at other times humorously ironic, Clough attacked many of the ills he saw afflicting Victorian society, among them religious hypocrisy, materialism, and extremes of both skepticism and religious orthodoxy. Clough's satirical works include such poems as "The Latest Decalogue," "In the Great Metropolis," and "Epi-Straussium," as well as his longer and, according to critics, more significant poems, *The Bothie, Amours de Voyage,* and *Dipsychus.*

Of Clough's long poems, *The Bothie* was the most popular with Victorian critics. A pastoral love story written in hexameters, this poem has been praised for its vivid characterization, compelling narrative, and skillful use of a meter uncommon in English verse. The poem concerns a Scottish student who marries a girl below his social class. In this marriage critics have found a reconciliation between the bookish ideals of young intellectuals, who are often presented ironically, and the natural values of the Scottish peasants. In the later *Amours de Voyage*, Clough showed the emptiness of idealism if not practically applied. Set in Rome during the revolution of 1848-49, the poem focuses on Claude, an equivocating intellectual whose continual self-analysis and skepticism prevent him from any action, particularly from asking his lover to marry him; by the time he decides to propose, she has already left him. One of Clough's most complex poems, *Amours de Voyage* is written as a series of letters between several characters. Using this structure, Clough achieved what critics consider a brilliant effect of symbolically relating the Italians' valiant efforts to protect their crumbling republic to Claude's attempts to overcome his uncertainties about love, marriage, politics, and art. While the satire of Claude's personal and ideological equivocations in this poem is somewhat subdued by a frequently sympathetic treatment of his emotional and intellectual problems, that in *Dipsychus* is relentless. This poem is structured as a debate between the excessively moral title character and the cynical "Spirit," who tries to tempt Dipsychus into accepting socially expedient attitudes towards sex, religion, and money by making him see the impracticality of scruples in what the Spirit depicts as a corrupt society. Generally interpreted as a reconciliation of the inner conflict of the individual whose conscience inhibits participation in a society that he or she perceives as immoral, *Dipsychus* concludes with the protagonist becoming a stronger person by affirming, in opposition to the Spirit, the positive qualities of humanity, qualities from which he was once blinded by the inflexibility of his moral code.

Clough's place in English literary history is a matter of critical dispute. The talents for storytelling and characterization displayed in *The Bothie* and *Amours de Voyage* have led some commentators to argue that Clough made a greater contribution to English fiction than to poetry, while others contend that such an interpretation ignores the complex poetic effects he achieved in these poems. Still others assert that his unconventional candor and his use of experimental techniques and meters link him more closely with the modernist poets of the twentieth century than with his contemporaries; however, many regard his moral commitment, style, techniques, and subjects as quintessentially Victorian. Although these critical conflicts remain unresolved, Clough and his writings continue to be studied with respect and enjoyment. In the words of Isobel Armstrong, "Clough's work is still important and relevant. He was one of the first poets to write about the intellectual; the searching, buoyant sanity he brought to problems still familiar will always be refreshing."

(See also *Dictionary of Literary Biography,* Vol. 32.)

PRINCIPAL WORKS

The Close of the Eighteenth Century: A Prize Poem (poetry) 1835

A Consideration of Objections against the Retrenchment Association at Oxford during the Irish Famine in 1847 (essay) 1847

The Bothie of Toper-na-Fuosich: A Long-Vacation Pastoral

(poetry) 1848; also published in revised form as *The Bothie of Tober-na-Vuolich* in *Poems,* 1862

Ambarvalia [with Thomas Burbidge] (poetry) 1849

*Amours de Voyage (poetry) 1858; published in the periodical *Atlantic Monthly*

Mari Magno; or, Tales on Board (unfinished poetry) 1862; published in *Poems*

Poems (poetry) 1862

†Dipsychus (unfinished verse dialogue) 1865; published in *Letters and Remains*

Letters and Remains (poetry, verse dialogue, essays, lectures, and letters) 1865

‡Adam and Eve (verse drama) 1869; published in *The Poems and Prose Remains of Arthur Hugh Clough*

§The Poems and Prose Remains of Arthur Hugh Clough with a Selection from His Letters and a Memoir. 2 vols. (poetry, verse drama, verse dialogue, essays, lectures, and letters) 1869

The Poems of Arthur Hugh Clough (poetry) 1951; revised edition, 1974

The Correspondence of Arthur Hugh Clough. 2 vols. (letters) 1957

Selected Prose Works of Arthur Hugh Clough (essays and lectures) 1964

Selected Poems (poetry) 1987

---

*This work was written in 1849.

†Clough began writing *Dipsychus* in 1850.

‡Critics speculate that Clough began writing this work in 1845.

§The memoir is by Clough's wife, Blanche Smith Clough.

CHARLES KINGSLEY (essay date 1849)

[*An English clergyman and novelist, Kingsley was the recognized leader of the Christian Socialism movement in the first half of the nineteenth century. His so-called brand of "muscular Christianity"—a term he himself deplored—urged a renunciation of the Calvinistic doctrine of rewards and punishments and instead advocated the development of a religious organization that stressed the positive qualities in God and humanity and strove to improve the social, moral, and spiritual condition of all people. Kingsley's work had a marked influence on his age, particularly his novels* Alton Locke *(1850) and* Yeast *(1850), and his criticism of other writers was often determined by the same moral and social standards he applied successfully in these two works. Here, Kingsley lauds* The Bothie of Toper-na-Fuosich *for Clough's fitting treatment of a novel and deserving subject.*]

'And when I tell ye I saw a glazier,' writes Thomas Hood's Irish footman from Mont Blanc, 'ye'll be thinking I mane a fine boy walking about wid putty and glass at his back, and ye'll be mightily mistaken; that's just what a glazier isn't like at all. And so I've described it to yees.'

Even so say we of Mr. Clough's **Bothie.** When our readers hear of an Oxford poem, written, too, by a college fellow and tutor, they will naturally expect, as usual, some pale and sickly bantling of the *Lyra Apostolica* school; all Mr. Keble's defects caricatured, without any of his excellences—another deluge of milk-and-water from that perennial fount of bad verses, which, if quantity would but make up for quality, would be by this time world-famous,—and that is just what *The Bothie* is not like, 'at all at all.'

Mr. Clough's poetic *début* would have been certainly an easier one had he followed in the track of the reigning Oxford school. The only conditions of initiation into that guild have been lately, that a man should be a thorough bigot; that his conceptions should be sufficiently confused, and his style likewise; and, above all, that he should be melancholy. Werterism, now expelled from all other grades of society, has taken refuge, alas! in the institution which ought to be leading the age, not dragged grumbling in its rear; and thus has arisen a second and, we hope, last 'Poetry of despair,'—on strictly Church principles. To extract tears from sunshine; to bear the wailings of remorse in the song of a skylark; and prove the eternal perdition of Dissenters from the down on a dandelion—is, with these gentlemen, to see into the deepest spiritual symbolism of nature. But the thing is past a jest.

As for style, the prevailing problem with the Oxford poets has seemed to be, how best to hide the farthing rushlight of bigotry under the bushel of mystification; how an author, having no definite meaning, or, if he have one, being frightened at it, may so jumble his words as to mean nothing, or anything except what is cheerful, or manly, or expressive of real faith that God has anything to do with the world, or, indeed, has had since Astræa and the Stuarts vanished together in 1688.

Now, as we said before, the best possible way of describing Mr. Clough's poem, is to say, that all this is just what it is *not*.

But this negative method of description, *per modum tollendi,* as the schoolmen would have said, though pleasantly compendious for the reader, is hardly fair on the critic, to whom it gives no chance of displaying his æsthetic acumen at the author's expense: we shall, therefore, proceed to say something about what the *Bothie* is.

The poem sets forth, in playful earnestness, how a party from Oxford, with their tutor, went to read in the Highlands for the long vacation; how 'they bathed, read, and roamed, all in the joy of their life and glory of shooting-jackets;' and how, there and then, 'the eager, impetuous Hewson,' poet and ultra-ultra-Radical, realised his theories of the nothingness of rank, and the dignity of dirty work, by flirting with Highland lassies—casting himself, in a sudden revulsion of feeling, at the delicate feet of 'Lady Maria'—and finally falling in love with 'Elspie Mackaye.' The incidents and arguments which flow out of Hewson's strange sayings and doings, together with his most deep and truly poetical 'love-story,' make up the staple of the poem.

And here we must notice, first of all, the author's vivid and versatile faculty for drawing individual character. Adam, the tutor; Hobbes, 'contemplative, corpulent, witty;' Lindsay, clever, brilliant, do-nothing; even the characters of whom little but the names appear—Arthur, Hope, and Airlie, Sir Hector, the old chieftain, David Mackaye, the old army farrier, are each and every one of them living, individual persons— you could swear to them if you met them in the street. Hewson the Poet is more a type of a class than an individual—so far right. But the women are as vividly sketched as the men. 'Katie,' the open-hearted child of nature, who thinks no shame to commence a fresh innocent flirtation with every fresh acquaintance, and, like a butterfly,

. . . . Takes pleasure in all, as in beautiful weather,

Sorry to lose it, but just as we would be to lose fine weather.
And she is strong to return to herself, and to feel undeserted,
For she always keeps burning a cheerful fire inside her,—

might pass for a type of the Celtic girl, such as you will meet with in every village in Wales and Ireland, as well as the Highlands. And as a contrast, Elspie Mackaye, really a noble ideal of the true Scotchwoman, with all her rich Norse character, her wild Dantesque imagination, her shrewd, 'canny' insight, her deep and strong affections, yet all crushed into order by that calm self-restraint which indicates, not coldness, but intense and victorious energy—we must say, that we know no recent fiction of a female character so genial, so original, and yet so natural. (pp. 103-04)

Mr. Clough has all the advantage of a novel subject, and one, too, which abounds in fantastic scenery and combinations, as it were, ready-made to his hands. On such ground he need only be truthful to be interesting. The strange jumble of society which the Highlands would present in the summer to such a party—marquises and gillies, shooters and tourists— the luxuries and fopperies of modern London amid the wildest scenery and a primitive people—Aristotle over Scotch whisky—embroidered satin waistcoats dancing with barelegged hizzies—Chartist poets pledging kilted clansmen— Mr. Clough was quite right in determining to treat so odd a subject in a correspondingly odd manner. Such a Cockneysavage Walpurgis-dance does exist. It may be seen, we are informed, every summer in the ancient haunts of Rob Roy and 'the Children of the Mist.' It is a 'great fact of the age;' and in our judgment, a very significant, and not unpleasing one, and, because it exists, Mr. Clough was quite right in telling us all about it; and quite right, also, in telling his story in his own way, and in no one else's. What possible model could he have followed? An Oxford colony in Cockneyised Highlands! Conceive writing a pastoral thereon, after the manner of Theocritus, or Bion, or Virgil, or anybody else! Would Catullus's *Atys* have done? or Apuleius? or Aristophanes with modifications? . . .

All which classic models considered, we confess our opinion that Mr. Clough could not have well embodied his conceptions in a form more thoroughly natural to them. He found the sublime and the ridiculous hand-in-hand, as they usually are, not only in Cockneyised Highlands, but every where else, we suspect, on this earth; and, like greater men than himself, he has not been ashamed to draw them in the same picture. He has dared to set down honestly just what he saw, never caring whether it happens to be the fashion just now to talk of such things, or to skip them, and then fancy they don't exist: and he has been rewarded. There runs all through the poem a general honesty, a reverence for facts and nature—a belief, that if things are here, they are here by God's will or the devil's, to be faced manfully, and not to be blinked cowardly; in short, a true faith in God—which makes Mr. Clough's poem, light as may seem the subject and the style, and coming just now, as it does, from noble old Oxford, anything but unimportant, because they indicate a more genial and manly, and therefore a more poetic and more godly spirit, than any verses which have come out of Oxford for a long time past.

How shamefully we have wandered! and we had just conceived the most gracefully turned period, now, alas! resolved into its mother element, to set forth how the *bizarrerie* of the subject was so charmingly expressed in the *bizarrerie* of the style; how a playful, mock-heroic key gave scope for all sorts of variations into the bucolic, sentimental, broad-farce, pathetic, Hebrew-prophetic, what not. Seriously, it is most refreshing, in turning over page after page at random, to tumble, in these mannerist days, on such a variety as this. (p. 105)

O si sic omnia!—the worshippers of *Hermann and Dorothea,* and pure classic form, will cry; and not without a show of reason, for indeed Mr. Clough has fully justified the warning which is given to readers in his introductory note, to 'expect every kind of irregularity in these modern hexameters;' 'spondaic lines,' he says, 'are almost the rule;' and, as we humbly think, a very good rule. But a large proportion of his hexameters are, to use the very mildest word, abnormal. The scandalised scansionist stumbles on occasional trochees in every foot in a verse, to stop at last, horror of horrors! at a line which will not scan at all,—forward, backward, or sideways. We will not quote an instance, we will spare the nerves of classical readers: their existence we must mention, if only to fulfill the reviewers' eleventh commandment—'Thou shalt find every possible fault with thy neighbour, and more too;' and to prove, as bound, our own æsthetic talents. How shocking, if readers should suspect from a critic's silence that he did not know a mistake when he saw it!

Mr. Clough may demand, not beg, pardon for these slips, sown rarely, as they are, up and down among some of the most perfect hexameters, in our humble opinion, which we have yet seen in the English language. When the author has given himself fair play, he has shewn a complete mastery over the metre, and a faculty as yet, we fancy, all but unique, not of Græcising or Germanising his English, as most hexameter-writers have to do, but of Anglicising the metre, of harmonising not English to it, but it to English. For instance, in almost the first lines that come to hand . . . :

> But, O Muse, that encompassest earth like the ambient
>   ether,
> Swifter than steamer, or railway, or magical missive electric,
> Belting, like Ariel, the sphere with the star-like trail of thy
>   travel,
> Thou, with thy Poet, to mortals mere post-office second-
>   hand knowledge
> Leaving, wilt seek in the moorland of Rannoch the wandering hero.

Yet, after all, we do not think that Mr. Clough has been quite fair to himself in this respect. A high artistic finish is important for more reasons than for the mere pleasure which it gives to readers. There is something sacramental in perfect metre and rhythm. They are outward and visible signs (most seriously we speak as we say it) of an inward and spiritual grace, namely, of the self-possessed and victorious temper of one who has so far subdued nature as to be able to hear that universal sphere-music of hers, speaking of which, Mr. Carlyle says somewhere, 'that all deepest thoughts instinctively vent themselves in song.' And an author is, therefore, unfair to himself, who leaves any lines which may give a perverse and evil-speaking generation a handle for imputing to him, not want of skill, which in this case they cannot, but confusion of thought or haste of execution.

Thus much in our reviewer's right of taking our betters to task; to all which, if Mr. Clough should answer, that he does not care; that he left the said lines as a testimony that an author has a right to say his own say in his own way; that metre

was made for thoughts, not thoughts for metre; that he has as much right to put in spondees where he likes, as Aristophanes had; that trochees fit a great deal better into English hexameters than anapæsts ever did into Greek iambics; that his verses are not properly hexameters at all, but a fire-new discovery of his own genius, to be christened henceforth, *Bothiaics*; that as somebody, some time or other, must have invented each new metre, he has as good a right as his neighbours to make one, provided his manufacture be worthy; if he shall gently protest against the popular belief that the devil is, and has been, the only inventor since the beginning (when every thing made itself); if he shall denounce once for all the pedantry of metre-mongers, and call them in grimmest earnest Scribes and Pharisees, letting the spirit of verse starve while they haggle for the letter; if he shall assert boldly his belief that old Homer wrote by ear, and not by *Gradus,* and cared no more for 'longs and shorts' than Shakspeare and Burns did; and that, while Hermann was wasting his wits over his great unreadable *De Metris,* the ghost of Aristophanes stood behind his chair watching the bewildered German's *Bacchics* and *Brachycatalectics,* and *Graidiocolosyrtics,* too, with thumb on nose, and grindings of Elysian coffee-mills;—to all this we can only answer,—that we most thoroughly agree with him.

The author entitles his poem, *A Pastoral*; a classic title, from which we expect a classic poem, and, as we think, have one, in the spirit rather than in the letter. He has wisely tried to write, not as old Greeks wrote, but as they would have written now in his place; and there is a truly Greek, and, what is better, a truly English tone, all through the poem; a healthy, simple admiration of what is simple and beautiful wherever he finds it. He rejoices, like Homer or Theocritus himself, in eatings and drinkings, in sunshine, in bathing and dancing, in kissings and innocent flirtations, and in a good racy joke, too, now and then,—some of which last, as we hear, have roused much pious horror at Oxford, a place where prudery is tolerably rampant, as it generally is wherever a good many young men get together. It is remarkable, by the bye, and we have verified it, too, in the matter of this very poem, how the first person to discover any supposed impropriety in a book is sure to be an unmarried man, and the very last a married woman; whether from the superior pure-mindedness of the former class, the public may judge. It is a pity that men will not remember that the vulture's powers of scent, which could wind a dead sparrow among all the rose gardens of Damascus, are not indicative of cleanliness in that most useful bird. Would that they bore in mind the too-often-forgotten dictum of Dean Swift, who had had experience enough, certainly, in that time, 'that the nicest man has the nastiest thoughts,' and, moreover, that *Honi soit qui mal y pense* is the motto not only of English chivalry, but, we had almost said, of Protestantism itself; and that those who wish just now to be true Englishmen, would do well to abide by it.

But to return. The poem evinces also a truly Greek spirit in its sense of the dignity of the every-day relations, and the humblest employments of life, a truth which is cleverly separated from the absurdities which are often jumbled with it, by occasional sly caricatures of the school which consecrates potato-forks and wash-tubs, and which, in its disgust of the evils of luxury, conceives itself bound to fall in love with the merely accidental vulgarities of poverty. The question of what is, or is not, truly dignified, runs through the whole poem, and helps to raise it gradually above mere Greek animalism into the region of the Christian nineteenth century, into disquisitions on rank and marriage, man and Providence, often of great vigour, depth, and pathos. The author indulges, too, in those frequent repetitions of the same line, or part of a line, which are so common in the Greek poets, both epic and pastoral; and, we think, with a very pleasing effect. These repetitions act like the burden of a song, or the recurrence of the original air in music, after wandering variations. They make one feel, as in the old Greek poets, that the author is in earnest, and enjoys his conception, and likes to take it up, and look at it, and play with it again and again, lingering over it almost reverently, as if conscious that there was something more in it than he could bring out in words—an Infinite hidden under the most trivial Finite, which must be felt for again and again ere it reveal itself. (pp. 106-08)

The exclusively Oxonian allusions and phrases may be objected to, and certainly a glossary of a dozen words or so would have been a convenient appendage. But we think the author perfectly right in having introduced his Oxford slang. The thing existed—it was an integral part of his subject. Oxford men have peculiar phrases, peculiar modes of life and thought—he had no right to omit them. For ourselves, we cannot sympathise in the modern cosmopolitan spirit, which cries down all local customs, phrases, and costume; and wants to substitute a dead level uniformity for that true unity which is only to be found in variety; which prefers, as Archdeacon Hare well instances, the dead blank regularity of a modern street, to the rich and harmonious variety of a pile of old Gothic buildings; which would civilise Highlanders by making them abjure kilts and take to paletots, and is merciless to all peculiarities—except its own.

We recommend this whole story, as a fair and characteristic specimen of Oxford life, to those whose whole notions of the universities are drawn from the shallow Cockney cavillers of the day. We are no more contented than they are with the present state of the Universities. No more, for that matter, are the rising generation of the University men themselves, both masters and bachelors; they are as clamorous for reform as the mob can be, with, as we think, rather better notions of what reform ought to be. But though Oxford is not our Alma Mater, we must in her defense assert, once and for all, that the young men there, and in Cambridge, too, taken *en masse,* will be found far superior in intellect, earnestness, and morality,—not to mention that most noble and necessary part of manhood, much sneered at in these Cockney days, physical *pluck,*—to any other class of young men in England. Compare them with the army, with the navy, the medical students. Compare them with the general run of shopkeepers' sons in town or country; compare them with the rising generation of young men in London, with their prurience, their effeminacy, their quill-driving commercialism, joining (we speak from experience) too often the *morale* of an old rake with the *physique* of a puling girl. Again we may recommend our readers to look at this picture of what an Oxford tutor, and an Oxford reading party, in most cases, are. And even if it should prove a little too favourably drawn to hold good in every case, it may serve as a fair set-off against the exaggerations on the opposite side of the question. (p. 109)

'But what, after all, is the purpose of Mr. Clough's poem?'

This, at least, is its purpose,—'*To make people do their duty in that state of life to which God has called them.*' Whether the author attaches exactly the same meaning to those words as his readers do remains to be proved. Further, we shall say

nothing, for the author has said nothing; and he, doubtless, knows a great deal better than we what effect he intends, and we have no wish, or right either, to interfere with him. He seems to think, as indeed we do, that it is far better to give facts and opinions on different sides, and let the reader draw his own conclusion from them, than to tack a written moral to the last page of his poem, as you sew a direction-card on a little boy's back when you send him off to school. Let the reader try to crack the nut himself; and not, as is usual in these lazy days, expect reviewers to do it for him. It will be wholesome exercise; and we will warrant the kernel worth the trouble. (p. 110)

> *Charles Kingsley, in an originally unsigned review of "The Bothie of Toper-na-Fuosich," in* Fraser's Magazine for Town & Country, *Vol. XXXIX, No. CCXXIX, January, 1849, pp. 103-10.*

RALPH WALDO EMERSON (letter date 1849)

[*Emerson was one of the most influential figures of the nineteenth century. An American essayist and poet, he founded the Transcendental movement and shaped a distinctly American philosophy that embraces optimism, individuality, and mysticism. His philosophy stresses the presence of ongoing creation and revelation by a god apparent in everything and everyone, as well as the essential unity of all thoughts, persons, and things in the divine whole. Emerson and Clough began corresponding in November 1847 while Emerson was on a lecture tour in England, commencing a friendship that lasted throughout Clough's life. In the following letter to Clough, Emerson extols* The Bothie of Toper-na-Fuosich *as a "noble" work and also transcribes favorable comments on the poem by fellow American poet Henry Wadsworth Longfellow. For further commentary by Emerson, see letter dated 1858.*]

My dear Clough,

I cannot tell you how great a joy to me is your poem [*The Bothie of Toper-na-Fuosich*]. It came to me on the very day when a frightful calamity had come into the house of a dear friend here, whom I was on the way to visit,—and I had that night a strange balance to adjust, of grief & joy. For this poem is a high gift from angels that are very rare in our mortal state. It delights & surprises me from beginning to end. I can hardly forgive you for keeping your secret from me so well. I knew you was good & wise, stout of heart & truly kind, learned in Greek, & of excellent sense,—but how could I know or guess that you had all this wealth of expression, this wealth of imagery, this joyful heart of youth, this temperate continuity, that belongs only to high masters. It is a noble poem. Tennyson must look to his laurels. It makes me & all of us richer, and I am recalling every passage of speech & action of my staid & reticent friend, to find the hints & parallels of what I read. I have no time now to write at all, much less to tell you what I think. But I sent the poem to many friends, each for one night, & have the best report from all. Three of them have ordered copies immediately, & you shall have a sale here quickly. Longfellow I sent it to, & he writes moderately enough, yet I will transcribe his note, as Longfellow is prized on your side the water. "Altogether fascinating, & in part very admirable is the poem of Mr Clough. Tom Appleton read it aloud to us the other evening, the audience consisting of my wife; my brother, an engineer; Lowell, the poet; a German friend, a man of letters, well versed in our vernacular; & myself. All were much delighted with the genial wit, the truth to nature, & the extreme beauty of various passages

& figures; all agreed that it was a poem of a very high order of merit; no one criticised.—In the morning, I found Appleton reading it again to himself; in the afternoon, my wife doing the same thing, &c"—then he praises "the fine delineation of the passion of love," & congratulates himself on the hexameters, &c &c

Well, Carlyle has written me, & never mentioned this. I looked into your journals, & find no notice yet. It is named somewhere, but they have not found out that they have got a new book! Well, keep your secret if you can, & as long as you can. Alas for you! Your silent days, I believe, are now nearly ended. Thanks & joy & love to you!

R. W. EMERSON.

Ralph Waldo Emerson, in a letter to Arthur Hugh Clough on January 16, 1849, in Emerson-Clough Letters, *edited by Howard F. Lowry and Ralph Leslie Rusk, 1934. Reprint by Archon Books, 1968.*

MATTHEW ARNOLD (essay date 1849)

[*Arnold is considered one of the most influential authors of the later Victorian period in England. While he is well known today as a poet, in his own time he asserted his greatest influence through his prose writings. Arnold's forceful literary criticism, which is based on his humanistic belief in the value of balance and clarity in literature, significantly shaped modern poetic theory. Although Arnold and Clough were classmates at Oxford and friends throughout their lives, their views on poetry often clashed. Many critics believe that their arguments, some of which are still preserved in letters, poems, and reviews, helped Arnold to formulate his theories. The following excerpt represents one facet of this debate. Arnold, reviewing Clough's poems in Ambarvalia, strongly censures his friend on moral and aesthetic grounds for the poetic display of what Arnold calls "morbid self-consciousness." Arnold's remarks first appeared on 28 March 1849 in the* Guardian. *For further commentary by Arnold, see poem dated 1866.*]

Mr. Clough is already known to our Oxford readers as the author of a **Long Vacation Pastoral,** not very intelligible, and hardly to be recommended, beyond the walls of the University. His present work [**Ambarvalia**], if less witty and amusing, is far more powerful, even in its fragmentary nature, more profound, more interesting, more rich in 'the thoughts that shake mankind'. Scintillations, as the abrupt little pieces are, they shed a light around, deep and wide, on human nature. Rarely relieved as the book is, by the boldly yet finely traced characters that stand out in such roundness from the **Pastoral,** yet is their loss atoned for by glimpses into those mysterious cells of the heart, which, as they lie deepest, so are most common to mankind at large. Mr. Clough must be content with 'fit audience, though few'. Those readers who are fond of 'poetry made easy',—who like the even tenor of superficial faultiness, the tinsel of glittering diction, and a 'false gallop' of thought—such we warn not to run the risk of bewilderment and a headache over these pages. Besides, the book is even more tantalising than it need be—there are very few headings to enable one to stand at the writer's view-point, and thence gaze around with him; no obvious arrangement, if any; not even marked pauses to prevent the shock of plunging from a Polkish love song into a metaphysical reverie (sometimes both are combined into one piece) with the versatility of a barrel-organ; and, at times, an hieroglyphical abruptness of expression which better suits the *déshabille* of an author's note-book than his appearance in public.

The first poem ['**The Questioning Spirit**'] is a good specimen of the whole. There is in it a silvery melody, very dependent on due emphasis, and hence linked closely to the sense, as in old English poets, and a plaintive sweetness, both worthy of Tennyson. It well represents, too, the tone of anxious heart-felt inquiry after truth which pervades the book, soothed, however, and calmed here, as in other places, by allusions to the only remedy, fulfilment of immediate duties. . . . (pp. 79-80)

Perhaps it might be objected that the question—What duty is? is left untouched in this poem; but Poetry is not bound to teach explicitly: she neither can nor ought to do more than point the way. Other passages, however, in his poems, must, we fear, make us add that the complaint from which Mr. Clough is thus sheltered as a poet, might be made with but too much truth against him as a thinker.

In almost every line of the poems there is great power and promise. A finished work they are not, as a whole, nor yet singly. They are the wild sad outpourings of an Aeolian harp, or the broken murmurings of a brook over rough places. Metaphors are said to be the test of a true poet. Here is one, beautiful and original:—

Ah love, high love, she said and sighed,
She said, the poet's love;
A star upon a turbid tide,
Reflected from above;
A marvel here, a glory there;
But clouds will intervene,
And garish earthly noon outglare
The purity serene.

(p. 80)

'**When Israel came out of Egypt**', is one of the least incomplete and grandest things in the book; but its apparent moral, that scepticism is the road to faith, is rather a strange one, and, though true in a certain sense, dangerous and unreasonable at a time, when, among persons likely to be readers, there is more liability to morbid restlessness than to apathetic quietism. Also, it is a slight inaccuracy, but one bearing on the subject, and so very tempting, to call Aaron the brother-*priest* at the time of the golden calf. The '**Silver Wedding**' sadly wants explanation, without which its drift is hard to understand. Many are not acquainted with the custom of styling the twenty-fifth anniversary of the wedding-day, the silver, and its venerable successor in the fiftieth year, the golden wedding. But the poem is one of the most beautiful in the volume, and we heartily wish we had room to quote it. (pp. 80-1)

Mr. Clough's style is very racy. He uses single words with peculiar aptness, and this, if done by impulse, is a sure mark of the true poet. And yet the words do not glare with a too prominent consciousness, like those in Coleridge's prose, nor give the idea of petty precision. Altogether the author seems to have a vigorous grasp on the English language, wielding it, with the boldness and ease of a master-hand, to great and little things; and skilfully enriching it now and then with adventitious idioms, terse and new. In a word, the style, although slip-shod here and there, is well suited for the utterance of free original thoughts.

But, with all these merits, there are grave liabilities to censure, aesthetical and moral. Doubt, it may be urged, is not a Poet's mood. At all events, states of minds and feelings, however interesting, want to be associated with outward realities, or rather to be expressed in and by them. In this Mr.

Clough falls very far short of the author of *Locksley Hall.* It is true that all real poetry must emanate from the heart; but also it must fasten its tendrils on the outer world; its business is to wed the material of the one to the living spirit of the other. Lastly, he is guilty often of too didactic an exposé of abstract truth—e.g. in the recipe for love, as it might be called:—

> Let Reason first her office ply;
> Esteem and Admiration high, &c. &c. . . .

There is a want of substance, shape, and colour, for the imagination to feed upon.

Morally, the charge is similar, but, of course, more serious. The danger of autobiographical revelations is notorious, especially for minds of a certain constitution. We have no right to attach, definitely, autobiographical character to these poems—for certain positions of mind may be transient, though genuine while they last—however strong the appearance of it which they wear. In that light they would be as sacred from criticism as a published work can be. We are speaking of likely effects from reading them. The disgust at shams—the weariness of unmeaning conventionalities—the ardent longing for truth, and sense of duty—generous sympathy with fellow workers in the great cause of truth, whose conscience forces them to a different path from the writer's own—the noble elevation of sentiment over the Fetish worship of money or pleasure into a contemplation of the awful meaning of life—all this is truly grand and good. But through the book there runs a morbid self-consciousness, a critical and sensitive distrust of self, which are the very opposite of action, and direct hindrance to it:—

> Unless above himself he can
> Erect himself, how mean a thing is man!

Always to be mapping out the foundations on too vast a scale, and with an eye too curious and fastidious, is not the way to rear a goodly superstructure. Nor is it for human intellect to set about analysing and proving the ultimate principles—facts they are, and nothing more or less—of the reason or emotions. Weariness and vexation can only ensue. Nor is it for man to reject this or that system because it is not faultless. Better for us, perhaps, that we must put up with imperfection. In this world we must work: if we wait for symmetrical theories, whose beauty is marred by no troublesome incongruities, there is danger of evaporating in sentimentality, or stagnating in indifference:—

> The fruit of dreary hoping,
> Is waking blank despair.

The poems bear far more decided traces of thinking, than of reading—a fault, if any, on the right side. But is not this, insufficiently qualified by the other, apt to destroy the balance of the mind? Above all, of course, we who are firmly convinced that what we see so often alluded to, by thinkers of that class to which Mr. Clough belongs, as *mere* forms—worthy of the greatest hatred if they were so—are in reality the channels of important verities, in some instances effete in appearance from neglect or misuse, must be excused if we warn our readers against the bad philosophy which now-a-days ministers with so much subtilty and success to intellectual pride. Moreover, it may be asked, whether it be not merely a more subtle and elevated form of selfishness, that amiable and genial weakness which lays bare to the inspection of others the melancholy workings of its own breast—troubles not

peculiar to the complainer—as if leaning helpless on their support and sympathy? Then, too, the excess of self-distrust is almost equally a want of faith with excess of self-confidence. That self-distrust alone has humility for its parent, which leans, for the support it cannot find in itself, upon something external, worthy of being the prop of the human soul. If it be said, that it is possible for men, without any fault of their own, never to have met with this 'something external', we answer, that indeed it is so, but it is equally possible, and far more usual, for men to reject the true prop, having constituted themselves the judges of its unworthiness. Great, indeed, is the sympathy due both to the voluntary and the involuntary wanderer: but the latter only has any excuse—the sufferings of the latter alone can be contemplated without danger by others. *Qui laborat, orat,* is a beautiful thought concerning one who has never been taught to pray, a pernicious falsehood about one who has rejected the practice. With such a one it will soon be *Qui non orat, nec laborat!* We are not, in these remarks, treating these poems so much as autobiographical revelations, as thoughts thrown before the minds of many readers not unlikely, from the fashion that now prevails among men of intellect and cultivation—especially those who have come under the influence of a popular writer lately deceased, as remarkable for self-reliance as for moral honesty and straightforwardness—to awaken echoes that may, in some cases, deepen into the knell of faith and religion. Byronian mawkishness is no longer in vogue: the fresh upright morality of the teaching of which we speak would dissipate in a moment such unhealthy exhalations. A mixture of misanthropy and debauchery is no longer the obvious way to be thought interesting: nor, when sensuality links itself with opposition to religion instead of hatred of mankind, is it much more popular. The vice now is to fancy oneself 'one of no common intellect, no common feelings,' and to reject, because men of less fine natures have abused them, the means of happiness with which Nature and Providence have furnished the humble as well as the intellectual of mankind. We are very far from hinting that this is applicable to the causes which have produced the painfully real traces of morbid struggling before us: but considering the probable effect upon some of the readers of these poems,—given to the world, we venture to say, without the slightest thought of influencing any one either way,—and remembering also the number of minds that are hampered by too much self-consciousness from fresh impulsive action, we cannot doubt that their indiscriminate circulation will do far more harm than good. (pp. 81-3)

> *Matthew Arnold, in an excerpt from* Clough: The Critical Heritage, *edited by Michael Thorpe, Routledge & Kegan Paul, 1972, pp. 78-84.*

J. C. SHAIRP   (letter date 1849)

[*An English educator and minor poet, Shairp attended Balliol College, Oxford, with Clough. The following excerpt is from the first of four letters exchanged between Shairp and Clough in November 1849 about* Amours de Voyage, *the completed manuscript of which Clough had sent Shairp the previous October. Excerpts of the three other letters immediately follow.*]

My dear Clough

The latter half [of *Les Amours*] as being more downright pleases me more than the former. But taken as a whole—bating some few pages—it does not give me much pleasure.

The state of soul of which it is a projection I do not like. It strikes me as the most Werterish (not that I ever read Werter) of all you have yet done. There is no hope, nor strength, nor belief in these;—everything crumbles to dust beneath a ceaseless self-introspection and criticism which is throughout the one only inspiration. The gaiety of manner where no gaiety is, becomes flippancy. In the **Bothie,** though I was not its warmest admirer, there was strength and something positive in the men's characters and the Highland Hills—but here this fresh element is wanting and blasé disgust at men and things rampant. The **Ambarvalia,** if Werterish, was honest serious Werterism—but this is Beppoish or Don Juanish (if I remember them right). The Hexameters still do not go down with me. They give me a sense of Travestie—which is their place I think. The snatches of longs and shorts are very nice, but they would not do to be more than snatches. One page or two of the Hexameters rise into music—that 'Falling Falling still to the ancient Lyrical cadence' and that about the statues on Monte Cavallo. But I need not go on to enumerate minor things which I liked. No, I would cast it behind me and the spirit from which it emanates and to higher, more healthful, hopeful things purely aspire. I won't flatter; but you were not made, my dear Clough, to make sport before The Philistines in this way, but for something else.

Write to me soon—else I shall think you are offended at my abusiveness.

[P.S.] Why this superabundance of oaths and other sweary words? They weaken the lines, are in bad taste and not good for yourself, if I may say so. On the whole I regard **Les Amours** as your nature ridding itself of long-gathered bile. Once cleared off I hope you have done with bile. Don't publish it—or if it must be published—not in a book—but in some periodical. For if you live, you will leave this mood of mind behind I hope, and then books which are its echo might be a clog about your neck. (p. 275)

Post. No. 2. You see I have caught infection from Mary Trevellyan's P.S.S. [Trevellyan is a character in **Les Amours.**] Should it strike you that my estimation of the amours comes from my 'rosewaterish sentimental' nature—that though I may go that way nature has not meant you nor do you intend to go that but another road—should this occur to you, I may add that I doubt much whether **Les Amours** will arride the public as much as either of your two former works.

It is hard to speak out and yet to seem friendly, but forgive any seeming bluntness or hardness of speech. (p. 276)

> *J. C. Shairp, in a letter to Arthur Hugh Clough in November, 1849, in* The Correspondence of Arthur Hugh Clough, Vol. I, *edited by Frederick L. Mulhauser, Oxford at the Clarendon Press, 1957, pp. 275-76.*

ARTHUR HUGH CLOUGH   (letter date 1849)

My dear Shairp

Good Heaven! don't be afraid.—You are a very gentle beast and of a good conscience and roar me like any sucking dove—Parturiunt montes—You are not half trenchant enough. You don't at all sting, I assure you. Yet your criticism is not exactly what I wanted. What I want assurance of is in the way of execution rather than conception. If I were only half as sure of the bearableness of the former as I am of

the propriety of the latter, I would publish at once. Gott und Teufel, my friend, you don't suppose all that comes from myself!—I assure you it is extremely *not* so.

You're a funny creature, my dear old fellow—If one don't sing you a ballant or read you a philosophic sermonette, if one don't talk about the gowans or faith—you're not pleased. However I believe that the execution of this is so poor that it makes the conception a fair subject of disgust—Farewell—and . . . and believe that if there is one thing I really like it is *dis*praise. (p. 276)

> *Arthur Hugh Clough, in a letter to J. C. Shairp in November, 1849, in* The Correspondence of Arthur Hugh Clough, Vol. I, *edited by Frederick L. Mulhauser, Oxford at the Clarendon Press, 1957, p. 276.*

J. C. SHAIRP   (letter date 1849)

My dear Clough

Your friend Goëthe says in Eckerman—'Yes—Such things one has to suffer from friends—How few men are capable of understanding the proper law of a production! Instead of taking its ground, and seeing what it should be, they praise or blame according as it harmonizes with their own condition.' I confess I have always done so and pace Goëthe intend to continue to do so. That is if I do not like the 'law of any production' I cannot like the carrying out of that law, however faithfully this may [be] done. Making reserve of some passages which I should willingly preserve, I do not like the conception. There is nothing hearty and heart-whole in it—no strength except in its raillery at all men and things and in its keen, ceaseless self-introspection. I do not like the point of view nor atmosphere from which it looks out on the world. It does not seem true or at least very partially so: and certainly is not refreshing. Every feeling of love for M. Treveyllian [*sic*] as it rises is cut to shreds by this; if carried out it would cut the whole world up into shreds and oneself to the bargain. I *can* like other things besides a Ballad and a Sermonette but one has supped one's fill of negations and now would prefer a draught of something stronger.

As to the execution I am not a good judge because the Hexameter does not take me, but has always a feeling of parody. But even for Hexameters many of them are slovenly. Not that I dislike your roughness, but then it should be more rock-like ruggedness not so slip slop—not so many Well's and other monysyllables [*sic*], and not so many *oaths* above all.

The execution too is wanting in dramatic power, scenes, and scenery. The analysis *is too absorbing.* You see I am getting rather truculent, but you say you like dispraise. (pp. 276-77)

> *J. C. Shairp, in a letter to Arthur Hugh Clough in November, 1849, in* The Correspondence of Arthur Hugh Clough, Vol. I, *edited by Frederick L. Mulhauser, Oxford at the Clarendon Press, 1957, pp. 276-77.*

ARTHUR HUGH CLOUGH   (letter date 1849)

My dear Shairp

You cannot possibly be too severe and truculent about the execution—and I agree quite as to the correctness (which is the only question) of what you say.—Except that I am not sure that Scenes and Scenery, after which you always go awhoring, would exactly improve the matter.

But do you not, in the conception, find any final Strength of Mind in the unfortunate fool of a hero? I have no intention whatever of sticking up for him, but certainly I didn't mean him to go off into mere prostration and defeat. Does the last part seem utterly sceptical to your sweet faithful soul?—

Goodbye—Your censure of the conception almost provoked me into publishing—because it showed how washy the world is in its confidences. There is a Roland for your Oliver,—my boy.—

But I probably shan't publish for fear of a row with my Sadducees. (pp. 277-78)

> *Arthur Hugh Clough, in a letter to J. C. Shairp in November, 1849, in* The Correspondence of Arthur Hugh Clough, Vol. I, *edited by Frederick L. Mulhauser, Oxford at the Clarendon Press, 1957, pp. 277-78.*

RALPH WALDO EMERSON (letter date 1858)

[*In the following excerpt from a letter to Clough, Emerson expresses profound disappointment with the ending of his friend's* Amours de Voyage. *For further commentary by Emerson, see letter dated 1849.*]

I cannot forgive you for the baulking end or no end of the **Amours de Voyage.** I esteemed the *Atlantic Monthly* worth the founding, when I heard that you would write. I read the first *livraison* of your poem with joy, & said, Behold that is what cannot be written here. Tis the sincerity of British culture. Here is a man tremulous all over with sensibility, and he holds a fine pen that delicately finds the right word,—gift that brings with it all other gifts. We watched from month to month our beloved star. The hexameters frightened some citizens. But all the good readers I know gave this poem every advantage over all the rest. And when we began to build securely on the triumph of our poet over all gainsayers, suddenly his wing flags, or his whim appears, & he plunges to a conclusion, like the ending of the Chancery suit in *Bleak House,* or like the denouement of Tennyson's *Princess.* How can you waste such power on a broken dream? Why lead us up the tower to tumble us down? There is a statute of Parnassus, that the author shall keep faith with the reader; but you choose to trifle with him. It is true a few persons compassionately tell me, that the piece is all right, and that they like this veracity of much preparation to no result. But I hold tis bad enough in life, & inadmissible in poetry. And I think you owe us a retribution of music, & to a musical argument. As I wish now to give due emphasis to my objection, I shall say nothing of all the merits that shine in the poem.

> *Ralph Waldo Emerson, in a letter to Arthur Hugh Clough on May 17, 1858, in* Emerson-Clough Letters, *edited by Howard F. Lowry and Ralph Leslie Rusk, 1934. Reprint by Archon Books, 1968.*

GEORGE HENRY LEWES (essay date 1862)

[*A versatile and prolific Victorian man of letters, Lewes wrote philosophical works, scientific studies, dramatic and literary criticism, plays, and novels, and served as editor on two prominent nineteenth-century periodicals, the* Leader *and the* Fortnightly Review, *both of which he also helped to establish. Critics often cite Lewes's influence on the novelist George Eliot, to whom he was companion and mentor, as his principal contribution to English letters, but they also credit him with critical acumen in his literary commentary, most notably in his dramatic criticism. Here, Lewes maintains that Clough's renown as a poet reflects his friends' respect for him as a person more than the intrinsic worth of his poetry.*]

Certain books have an indirect interest, personal or historical, which renders them more attractive than many that are intrinsically better. The **Poems of Arthur Clough,** for example, claim but a very modest place as poems, but they are attractive as the writings of a man of sweet, sincere, sensitive nature, and of high culture. A poet he was not; neither by the grace of God, nor by the acquired cunning of ambitious culture, could he become a singer; and it is mere rhetorical evasion in his friendly biographer, to say that "Clough *lived* his poem instead of writing it" [see Palgrave entry in Further Reading]. Yet the feeling which prompted this evasion suggests the source of interest we feel in this volume; it is the intense conviction, produced in friends, of some supreme excellence which Clough *might* have achieved, *ought* to have achieved, but somehow *did* not. In a word, he was one of the prospectuses which never become works: one of that class whose unwritten poems, undemonstrated discoveries, or untested powers, are confidently announced as certain to carry everything before them, when they appear. Only they never do appear. Sometimes attempts are made; they fail, and the failure is "explained," the attempts being repudiated as any real indication of the man's genuine powers. "Under happier circumstances," we are assured . . . as if the very seal and sign of genius were not precisely the regal superiority to circumstances, making them aids and ministers to success, instead of becoming their captive and slave! (p. 398)

[In] spite of biographers, the world will persist in awarding superiority to the men who achieve success. Had Arthur Clough never written a line, we could have better understood the expectations of his friends. But he has written enough to furnish a tolerably decisive estimate of his quality. As a man, he was doubtless loveable and loved; as a writer, he can claim but a very modest place. He was thoughtful and cultivated, and all thoughtful, cultivated minds will recognize this in his poems. They will also recognize a sincere and sensitive nature, shrinking from the rough and ready acquiescences of conventional beliefs, and withdrawing from the conflicts of life, conscious of being unfitted for them. But as to poetry, there is little or none. The nearest approach to poetry is perhaps in the following:—

"Qua Cursum Ventus."

As ships becalmed at eve, that lay,
With canvas drooping, side by side,
Two towers of sail at dawn of day
Are scarce long leagues apart descried;

When fell the night, up sprung the breeze,
And all the darkling hours they plied,
Nor dreamt but each the self-same seas
By each was cleaving, side by side:

E'en so—but why the tale reveal
Of those whom, year by year unchanged,
Brief absence joined anew, to feel
Astounded, soul from soul estranged?

At dead of night their sails were filled,
And onward each, rejoicing, steered—
Ah, neither blame, for neither willed
Or wist what first with dawn appeared!

To veer, how vain! On, onward strain,
Brave barks! In light, in darkness, too,
Through winds and tides one compass guides—
To that, and your own selves, be true.

But oh, blithe breeze! and oh, great seas,
Though ne'er, that earliest parting past,
On your wide plain they join again,
Together lead them home at last.

One port, methought, alike they sought,
One purpose hold where'er they fare—
Oh, bounding breeze! oh, rushing seas!
At last, at last, unite them there!

We shall have misled the reader if he have understood us to say that this volume is only interesting as an example of the actual work achieved by a man who greatly impressed his friends. It is interesting, though less so, for its own sake. The verses are not good, but they are far from commonplace. They express real thoughts and real feelings, and in the **Bo-thie of Tober na Vuolich** there is considerable promise; for, in spite of its being exclusively a bit of Oxford-student life, in spite of its intentional imitations of Homer and Goethe, and its classical allusions, there is enough humour and fancy, and enough originality, to make it popular in a wider circle, and suggest that the writer, in ripening years, might have produced a remarkable work in prose. His later writings, however, are inferior to it. (pp. 399-400)

> *George Henry Lewes, in an originally unsigned essay titled "Our Survey of Literature, Science, and Art," in* The Cornhill Magazine, *Vol. VI, No. 33, September, 1862, pp. 398-400.*

WALTER BAGEHOT (essay date 1862)

[*Bagehot is regarded as one of the most versatile and influential authors of mid-Victorian England. In addition to literary criticism, he wrote several pioneering studies of politics, sociology, and economics. As editor of the London* Economist, *he was instrumental in shaping the financial policy of his generation. Despite their diverse subject matter, Bagehot's works are unified by his emphasis on factual information and his interest in the minds and personalities of literary figures, politicians, and economists. In the following excerpt, Bagehot reviews the 1862 edition of Clough's* Poems. *While valuing Clough's works for reflecting the intellectual character of his age, Bagehot believes they will only appeal to a limited few: "the solitary, the meditative, and the calm."*]

No one can be more rigid than we are in our rules as to the publication of remains and memoirs. It is very natural that the friends of a cultivated man who seemed about to do something, but who died before he did it, should desire to publish to the world the grounds of their faith, and the little symptoms of his immature excellence. But though they act very naturally, they act very unwisely. In the present state of the world there are too many half-excellent people: there is a superfluity of persons who have all the knowledge, all the culture, all the requisite taste,—all the tools, in short, of achievement, but who are deficient in the latent impulse and secret vigour which alone can turn such instruments to account. They have all the outward and visible signs of future success; they want the invisible spirit, which can only be demonstrated by trial and victory. Nothing, therefore, is more tedious

or more worthless than the posthumous delineation of the possible successes of one who did not succeed. (p. 310)

If we did not believe that Mr. Clough's poems, or at least several of them, had real merit, not as promissory germs, but as completed performances, it would not seem to us to be within our province to notice them. Nor if Mr. Clough were now living among us, would he wish us to do so. The marked peculiarity, and, so to say, the *flavour* of his mind, was a sort of truthful scepticism, which made him anxious never to overstate his own assurance of anything; disinclined him to overrate the doings of his friends; and absolutely compelled him to underrate his own past writings, as well as his capability for future literary success. He could not have borne to have his poems reviewed with "nice remarks" and sentimental epithets of insincere praise. He was equal to his precept [expressed in **Dipsychus**]:

> Where are the great, whom thou wouldst wish to praise
>   thee?
> Where are the pure, whom thou wouldst choose to love
>   thee?
> Where are the brave, to stand supreme above thee,
> Whose high commands would cheer, whose chiding raise
>   thee?
> Seek, seeker, in thyself; submit to find
> In the stones bread, and life in the blank mind.

To offer petty praise and posthumous compliments to a stoic of this temper is like buying sugar-plums for St. Simon Stylites. We venture to write an article on Mr. Clough, because we believe that his poems depict an intellect in a state which is always natural "to such a being as man in such a world as the present," which is peculiarly natural to us just now; and because we believe that many of these poems are very remarkable for true vigour and artistic excellence, although they certainly have several defects and shortcomings, which would have been lessened, if not removed, if their author had lived longer and had written more.

In a certain sense there are two great opinions about every thing. There are so about the universe itself. The world as we know it is this. There is a vast, visible, indisputable sphere, of which we never lose the consciousness, of which no one seriously denies the existence, about the most important part of which most people agree tolerably and fairly. On the other hand, there is the invisible world, about which men are not agreed at all, which all but the faintest minority admit to exist somehow and somewhere, but as to the nature or locality of which there is no efficient popular demonstration; there is no such compulsory argument as will *force* the unwilling conviction of any one disposed to denial. As our minds rise, as our knowledge enlarges, as our wisdom grows, as our instincts deepen, our conviction of this invisible world is daily strengthened, and our estimate of its nature is continually improved. But—and this is the most striking peculiarity of the whole subject—the more we improve, the higher we raise, the nobler we conceive the unseen world which is in us and about us, in which we live and move, the more unlike that world becomes to the world which we *do* see. (pp. 310-11)

There are plenty of minds like that of Voltaire, who have simply no sense or perception of the invisible world whatever, who have no ear for religion, who are in the technical sense unconverted, whom no conceivable process could convert without altering what to bystanders and ordinary observers is their identity. They are, as a rule, acute, sensible, discerning, and humane; but the first observation which the most ordinary person would make as to them is, that they are "limit-ed;" they understand palpable existence; they elaborate it, and beautify and improve it; but an admiring bystander who can do none of these things, who can beautify nothing, who, if he tried, would only make what is ugly uglier, is conscious of a latent superiority which he can hardly help connecting with his apparent inferiority. We cannot write Voltaire's sentences; we cannot make things as clear as he made them; but we do not much care for our deficiency. Perhaps we think "things ought not to be so plain as all that." There is a hidden, secret, unknown side to this universe, which these picturesque painters of the visible, these many-handed manipulators of the palpable, are not aware of, which would spoil their dexterity if it were displayed to them. Sleep-walkers can tread safely on the very edge of any precipice; but those who see, cannot. On the other hand, there are those whose minds have not only been converted, but in some sense *inverted*. They are so occupied with the invisible world as to be absorbed in it entirely; they have no true conception of that which stands plainly before them; they never look coolly at it, and are cross with those who do; they are wrapt up in their own faith as to an unseen existence; they rush upon mankind with, "Ah, there it is! there it is!—don't you see it?" and so incur the ridicule of an age.

The best of us try to avoid both fates. We strive, more or less, to "make the best of both worlds." We know that the invisible world cannot be duly discerned, or perfectly appreciated. We know that we see as in a glass darkly; but still we look on the glass. We frame to ourselves some image which we know to be incomplete, which probably is in part untrue, which we try to improve day by day, of which we do not deny the defects,—but which nevertheless is our "all;" which we hope, when the accounts are taken, may be found not utterly *unlike* the unknown reality. This is, as it seems, the best religion for finite beings, living, if we may say so, on the very edge of two dissimilar worlds, on the very line on which the infinite, unfathomable sea surges up, and just where the queer little bay of this world ends. We count the pebbles on the shore, and image to ourselves as best we may the secrets of the great deep.

There are, however, some minds (and of these Mr. Clough's was one) which will not accept what appears to be an intellectual destiny. They struggle against the limitations of mortality, and will not condescend to use the natural and needful aids of human thought. They will not *make their image*. They struggle after an "actual abstract." They feel, and they rightly feel, that every image, every translation, every mode of conception by which the human mind tries to place before itself the Divine mind, is imperfect, halting, changing. They feel, from their own experience, that there is no one such mode of representation which will suit their own minds at all times, and they smile with bitterness at the notion that they could contrive an image which will suit all other minds. They could not become fanatics or missionaries, or even common preachers, without forfeiting their natural dignity, and foregoing their very essence. To cry in the streets, to uplift their voice in Israel, to be "pained with hot thoughts," to be "preachers of a dream," would reverse their whole cast of mind. It would metamorphose them into something which omits every striking trait for which they were remarked, and which contains every trait for which they were not remarked. On the other hand, it would be quite as opposite to their whole nature to become followers of Voltaire. No one knows more certainly and feels more surely that there is an invisible world, than

those very persons who decline to make an image or representation of it, who shrink with a nervous horror from every such attempt when it is made by any others. All this inevitably leads to what common practical people term a "curious" sort of mind. You do not know how to describe these "universal negatives," as they seem to be. They will not fall into place in the ordinary intellectual world any how. If you offer them any known religion, they "won't have that;" if you offer them no religion, they will not have that either; if you ask them to accept a new and as yet unrecognised religion, they altogether refuse to do so. They seem not only to believe in an "unknown God," but in a God whom no man can ever know. Mr. Clough has expressed, in a sort of lyric, what may be called their essential religion:

> O Thou whose image in the shrine
> Of human spirits dwells divine!
> Which from that precinct once conveyed,
> To be to outer day displayed,
> Doth vanish, part, and leave behind
> Mere blank and void of empty mind,
> Which wilful fancy seeks in vain
> With casual shapes to fill again!
>
> O Thou, that in our bosom's shrine
> Dost dwell, unknown because divine!
> I thought to speak, I thought to say,
> "The light is here," "behold the way,"
> "The voice was thus" and "thus the word,"
> And "thus I saw," and "that I heard,"—
> But from the lips that half essayed
> The imperfect utterance fell unmade.
>
> O Thou, in that mysterious shrine
> Enthroned, as I must say, divine!
> I will not frame one thought of what
> Thou mayest either be or not.
> I will not prate of "thus" and "so,"
> And be profane with "yes" and "no,"
> Enough that in our soul and heart
> Thou, whatsoe'er Thou mayest be, art.
>
> [from **"A hymn, yet not a hymn"**]

It was exceedingly natural that Mr. Clough should incline to some such creed as this, with his character and in his circumstances. He had by nature, probably, an exceedingly real mind, in the good sense of that expression and the bad sense. The actual visible world as it was, and he saw it, exercised over him a compulsory influence. The hills among which he had wandered, the cities he had visited, the friends whom he knew,—these were his world. Many minds of the poetic sort easily melt down these palpable facts into some impalpable either of their own. To such a mind as Shelley's the "solid earth" is an immaterial fact; it is not even a cumbersome difficulty—it is a preposterous imposture. Whatever may exist, all that *clay* does not exist; it would be too absurd to think so. Common persons can make nothing of this dreaminess; and Mr. Clough, though superficial observers set him down as a dreamer, could not make much either. To him, as to the mass of men, the vulgar outward world was a primitive fact. "Taxes *is* true," as the miser said. Reconcile what you have to say with green peas, for green peas are certain; such was Mr. Clough's idea. He could not dissolve the world into credible ideas and then believe those ideas, as many poets have done. He could not catch up a creed, as ordinary men do. He had a *straining*, inquisitive, critical mind; he scrutinised every idea before he took it in; he did not allow the moral forces of life to act as they should; he was not content to gain a belief "by going on living." He said [in **Amours de Voyage**],

Action will furnish belief; but will that belief be the true
     one?
This is the point, you know.

He felt the coarse facts of the plain world so thoroughly, that
he could not readily take in any thing which did not seem in
accordance with them and like them. And what common idea
of the invisible world seems in the least in accordance with
them or like them?

A journal-writer, in [**Amours de Voyage**], has expressed this:

   Comfort has come to me here in the dreary streets of the
        city,
   Comfort—how do you think?—with a barrel-organ to
        bring it.
   Moping along the streets, and cursing my day as I wan-
        dered,
   All of a sudden my ear met the sound of an English psalm-
        tune.
   Comfort me it did, till indeed I was very near crying.
   Ah, there is some great truth, partial very likely, but need-
        ful,
   Lodged, I am strangely sure, in the tones of the English
        psalm-tune:
   Comfort it was at least; and I must take without question
   Comfort, however it come, in the dreary streets of the city.

   What with trusting myself, and seeking support from
        within me,
   Almost I could believe I had gained a religious assurance,
   Formed in my own poor soul a great moral basis to rest
        on.
   Ah, but indeed I see, I feel it factitious entirely;
   I refuse, reject, and put it utterly from me;
   I will look straight out, see things, not try to evade them;
   Fact shall be fact for me, and the Truth the Truth as ever,
   Flexible, changeable, vague, and multiform, and doubt-
        ful.—
   Off, and depart to the void, thou subtle, fanatical tempter!

Mr. Clough's fate in life had been such as to exaggerate this
naturally peculiar temper. He was a pupil of Arnold's; one
of his best, most susceptible, and favourite pupils. Some years
since there was much doubt and interest as to the effect of Arnold's teaching. His sudden death, so to say, cut his life in the
middle, and opened a tempting discussion as to the effect of
his teaching when those taught by him should have become
men and not boys. The interest which his own character then
awakened, and must always awaken, stimulated the discussion, and there was much doubt about it. But now we need
doubt no longer. The Rugby "men" are *real* men, and the
world can pronounce its judgment. Perhaps that part of the
world which cares for such things has pronounced it. Dr. Arnold was almost indisputably an admirable master for a common English boy,—the small, apple-eating animal whom we
know. He worked, he pounded, if the phrase may be used,
into the boy a belief, or at any rate a floating, confused conception, that there are great subjects, that there are strange
problems, that knowledge has an indefinite value, that life is
a serious and solemn thing. The influence of Arnold's teaching upon the majority of his pupils was probably very vague,
but very good. To impress on the ordinary Englishman a general notion of the importance of what is intellectual and the
reality of what is supernatural, is the greatest benefit which
can be conferred upon him. The common English mind is too
coarse, sluggish, and worldly to take such lessons too much
to heart. It is improved by them in many ways, and is not
harmed by them at all. But there are a few minds which are
very likely to think too much of such things. A susceptible,

serious, intellectual boy may be injured by the incessant in-
culcation of the awfulness of life and the magnitude of great
problems. It is not desirable to take this world too much *au
sérieux*; most persons will not; and the one in a thousand who
will, should not. Mr. Clough was one of those who will. He
was one of Arnold's favourite pupils, because he gave heed
so much to Arnold's teaching; and exactly because he gave
heed to it was it bad for him. He required quite another sort
of teaching: to be told to take things easily; not to try to be
wise overmuch; to be "something beside critical;" to go on
living quietly and obviously, and see what truth would come
to him. Mr. Clough had to his latest years what may be noticed in others of Arnold's disciples,—a fatigued way of looking at great subjects. It seemed as if he had been put into them
before his time, had seen through them, heard all which could
be said about them, had been bored by them, and had come
to want something else.

A still worse consequence was, that the faith, the doctrinal
teaching which Arnold impressed on the youths about him
was one personal to Arnold himself, which arose out of the
peculiarities of his own character, which can only be explained by them. As soon as an inquisitive mind was thrown
into a new intellectual atmosphere, and was obliged to na-
turalise itself in it, to consider the creed it had learned with
reference to the facts which it encountered and met, much of
that creed must fade away. There were inevitable difficulties
in it, which only the personal peculiarities of Arnold prevented his perceiving, and which every one else must soon perceive. The new intellectual atmosphere into which Mr.
Clough was thrown was peculiarly likely to have this disenchanting effect. It was the Oxford of Father Newman; an Oxford utterly different from Oxford as it is, or from the same
place as it had been twenty years before. A complete estimate
of that remarkable thinker cannot be given here; it would be
no easy task even now, many years after his influence has declined, nor is it necessary for the present purpose. Two points
are quite certain of Father Newman, and they are the only
two which are at present material. He was undeniably a consummate master of the difficulties in the creeds of other men.
With a profoundly religious organisation which was hard to
satisfy, with an imagination which could not help setting before itself simply and exactly what different creeds would
come to and mean in life, with an analysing and most subtle
intellect which was sure to detect the weak point in an argument if a weak point there was, with a manner at once grave
and fascinating,—he was a nearly perfect religious disputant,
whatever may be his deficiencies as a religious teacher. The
most accomplished theologian of another faith would have
looked anxiously to the joints of his harness before entering
the lists with an adversary so prompt and keen. To suppose
that a youth fresh from Arnold's teaching, with a hasty faith
in a scheme of thought radically inconsistent, should be able
to endure such an encounter was absurd. Arnold flattered
himself that he was a principal opponent of Mr. Newman; but
he was rather a principal fellow-labourer. There was but one
quality in a common English boy which would have enabled
him to resist such a reasoner as Mr. Newman. We have a
heavy apathy on exciting topics, which enables us to leave dilemmas unsolved, to forget difficulties, to go about our pleasure or our business, and to leave the reasoner to pursue his
logic: "any how he is very *long*"—*that* we comprehend. But
it was exactly this happy apathy, this commonplace indifference, that Arnold prided himself on removing. He objected
most strenuously to Mr. Newman's creed, but he prepared
most anxiously the very soil in which that creed was sure to

grow. A multitude of such minds as Mr. Clough's, from being Arnoldites, became Newmanites. A second quality in Mr. Newman is at least equally clear. He was much better skilled in finding out the difficulties of other men's creeds than in discovering and stating a distinct basis for his own. In most of his characteristic works he does not even attempt it. His argument is essentially an argument *ad hominem*; an argument addressed to the present creed of the person with whom he is reasoning. He says: "Give up what you hold already, or accept what I now say; for that which you already hold involves it." Even in books where he is especially called on to deal with matters of first principle, the result is unsatisfactory. We have heard it said that he has in later life accounted for the argumentative vehemence of his book *against* the Church of Rome by saying: "I did it as a duty; I *put* myself into a state of mind to write that book." And this is just the impression which his arguments give. His elementary principles seem *made,* not born. Very likely he would admit the fact, and yet defend his practice. He would say: "Such a being as man is, in such a world as this is, *must* do so; he must make a venture for his religion; he may see a greater probability that the doctrine of the Church is true than that it is false; he may see before he believes in her that she has greater evidence than any other creed; but he must do the rest for himself. *By means of his will* he must put himself into a new state of mind; he must cast in his lot with the Church here and hereafter; *then* his belief will gradually strengthen; he will in time become sure of what she says." He undoubtedly, in the time of his power persuaded many young men to try some such process as this. The weaker, the more credulous, and the more fervent, were able to persevere; those who had not distinct perceptions of real truth, who were dreamy and fanciful by nature, persevered without difficulty. But Mr. Clough could not do so; he felt it was "something factitious." He began to speak of the "ruinous force of the will," and "our terrible notions of duty." He ceased to be a Newmanite.

Thus Mr. Clough's career and life were exactly those most likely to develop and foster a morbid peculiarity of his intellect. He had, as we have explained, by nature an unusual difficulty in forming a creed as to the unseen world; he could not get the visible world out of his head; his strong grasp of plain facts and obvious matters was a difficulty to him. Too easily one great teacher inculcated a remarkable creed; then another great teacher took it away; then this second teacher made him believe for a time some of his own artificial faith; then it would not do. He fell back on that vague, impalpable, unembodied religion which we have attempted to describe.

He has himself given in [*Amours de Voyage*] . . . a very remarkable description of this curious state of mind. He has prefixed to it the characteristic motto, *"Il doutait de tout, même de l'amour."* It is the delineation of a certain love-passage in the life of a hesitating young gentleman [Mr. Claude], who was in Rome at the time of the revolution of 1848; who could not make up his mind about the revolution, who could not make up his mind whether he liked Rome, who could not make up his mind whether he liked the young lady, who let her go away without him, who went in pursuit of her, and could not make out which way to look for her, who, in fine, has some sort of religion, but cannot himself tell what it is. The poem was not published in the author's lifetime, and there are some lines which we are persuaded he would have further polished, and some parts which he would have improved, if he had seen them in print. It is written in conversational hexameters, in a tone of semi-satire and half-belief. (pp. 312-19)

The plot of the poem is very simple, and certainly is not very exciting. The moving force, as in most novels of verse or prose, is the love of the hero for the heroine; but this love assuredly is not of a very impetuous and overpowering character. The interest of this story is precisely that it is not overpowering. The over-intellectual hero, over-anxious to be composed, will not submit himself to his love; over-fearful of what is voluntary and factitious, he will not make an effort and cast in his lot with it. He states his view of the subject better than we can state it:

I am in love, meantime, you think; no doubt you would think so.
I am in love, you say, with those letters, of course, you would say so.
I am in love, you declare. I think not so; yet I grant you
It is a pleasure indeed to converse with this girl. Oh, rare gift,
Rare felicity, this! she can talk in a rational way, can
Speak upon subjects that really are matters of mind and of thinking,
Yet in perfection retain her simplicity; never, one moment,
Never, however you urge it, however you tempt her, consents to
Step from ideas and fancies and loving sensations to those vain
Conscious understandings that vex the minds of mankind.
No, though she talk, it is music; her fingers desert not the keys; 'tis
Song, though you hear in the song the articulate vocables sounded,
Syllabled singly and sweetly the words of melodious meaning.
I am in love, you say; I do not think so, exactly.
There are two different kinds, I believe, of human attraction:
One which simply disturbs, unsettles, and makes you uneasy,
And another that poises, retains, and fixes and holds you.
I have no doubt, for myself, in giving my voice for the latter.
I do not wish to be moved, but growing where I was growing,
There more truly to grow, to live where as yet I had languished.
I do not like being moved: for the will is excited; and action
Is a most dangerous thing; I tremble for something factitious,
Some malpractice of heart and illegitimate process;
We are so prone to these things, with our terrible notions of duty.
Ah, let me look, let me watch, let me wait, unhurried, unprompted!
Bid me not venture on aught that could alter or end what is present!
Say not, Time flies, and Occasion, that never returns, is departing!
Drive me not out, ye ill angels with fiery swords, from my Eden,
Waiting, and watching, and looking! Let love be its own inspiration!
Shall not a voice, if a voice there must be, from the airs that environ,
Yea, from the conscious heavens, without our knowledge or effort,
Break into audible words? And love be its own inspiration?

(pp. 319-20)

The same defect which prevented Mr. Claude from obtaining his bride will prevent this poem from obtaining universal popularity. The public like stories which come to something; Mr. Arnold teaches that a great poem must be founded on a great action, and this one is founded on a long inaction. But Art has many mansions. Many poets, whose cast of thought unfits them for very diffused popularity, have yet a concentrated popularity which suits them, and which lasts. Henry Taylor has wisely said "that a poet does not deserve the name who would not rather be read a thousand times by one man, than a single time by a thousand." . . .

Little deep poetry is very popular, and *no* severe art. Such poetry as Mr. Clough's, especially, can never be so; its subjects would forbid it, even if its treatment were perfect: but it may have a better fate; it may have a tenacious hold on the solitary, the meditative, and the calm. It is this which Mr. Clough would have wished; he did not desire to be liked by "inferior people"—at least he would have much distrusted any poem of his own which they did like.

The artistic skill of these poems, especially of [*Amours de Voyage*] . . . , and of a long-vacation pastoral published in the Highlands [*The Bothie of Tober-na-Vuolich*], is often excellent, and occasionally fails when you least expect it. There was an odd peculiarity in Mr. Clough's mind; you never could tell whether it was that he would not show himself to the best advantage, or whether he *could* not; it is certain that he very often did not, whether in life or in books. His intellect moved with a great difficulty, and it had a larger inertia than any other which we have ever known. Probably there was an awkwardness born with him, and his shyness and pride prevented him from curing that awkwardness as most men would have done. He felt he might fail, and he knew that he hated to fail. He neglected, therefore, many of the thousand petty trials which fashion and form the accomplished man of the world. Accordingly, when at last he wanted to do something, or was obliged to attempt something, he had occasionally a singular difficulty. He could not get his matter out of him.

In poetry he had a further difficulty, arising from perhaps an over-cultivated taste. He was so good a disciple of Wordsworth, he hated so thoroughly the common sing-song metres of Moore and Byron, that he was apt to try to write what will seem to many persons to have scarcely a metre at all. It is quite true that the metre of intellectual poetry should not be so pretty as that of songs, or so plain and impressive as that of vigorous passion. The rhythm should pervade it and animate it, but should not protrude itself upon the surface, or intrude itself upon the attention. It should be a latent charm, though a real one. Yet though this doctrine is true, it is nevertheless a dangerous doctrine. Most writers need the strict fetters of familiar metre; as soon as they are emancipated from this, they fancy that *any* words of theirs are metrical. If a man will read any expressive and favourite words of his own often enough, he will come to believe that they are rhythmical; probably they have a rhythm as he reads them; but no notation of pauses and accents could tell the reader how to read them in that manner; and when read in any other mode they may be prose itself. Some of Mr. Clough's early poems . . . are perhaps examples of more or less of this natural self-delusion. Their writer could read them as verse, but that was scarcely his business; and the common reader fails.

Of one metre, however, the hexameter, we believe the most accomplished judges, and also common readers, agree that

Mr. Clough possessed a very peculiar mastery. Perhaps he first showed in English its *flexibility*. Whether any consummate poem of great length and sustained dignity can be written in this metre, and in our language, we do not know. Until a great poet has written his poem, there are commonly no lack of plausible arguments that seem to prove he cannot write it; but Mr. Clough has certainly shown that in the hands of a skilful and animated artist it is capable of adapting itself to varied descriptions of life and manners, to noble sentiments, and to changing thoughts. It is perhaps the most flexible of English metres. Better than any others it changes from grave to gay without desecrating what should be solemn, or disenchanting that which should be graceful. And Mr. Clough was the first to prove this, by writing a noble poem, in which it was done.

In one principal respect Mr. Clough's two poems in hexameters, and especially the Roman one, from which we made so many extracts, are very excellent. Somehow or other he makes you understand what the people of whom he is writing precisely were. You may object to the means, but you cannot deny the result. By fate he was thrown into a vortex of theological and metaphysical speculation, but his genius was better suited to be the spectator of a more active and moving scene. The play of mind upon mind; the contrasted view which contrasted minds take of great subjects; the odd irony of life which so often thrusts into conspicuous places exactly what no one would expect to find in those places,—these were his subjects. Under happy circumstances he might have produced on such themes something which the mass of readers would have greatly liked; as it is, he has produced a little which meditative readers will much value, and which they will long remember.

Of Mr. Clough's character it would be out of place to say any thing, except in so far as it elucidates his poems. The sort of conversation for which he was most remarkable rises again in the ***Amours de Voyage***, and gives them to those who knew him in life a very peculiar charm. It would not be exact to call its best lines a pleasant cynicism; for cynicism has a bad name, and the ill-nature and other offensive qualities which have given it that name were utterly out of Mr. Clough's way. Though without much fame, he had no envy. But he had a strong realism. He saw what it is considered cynical to see—the absurdities of many persons, the pomposities of many creeds, the splendid zeal with which missionaries rush on to teach what they do not know, the wonderful earnestness with which most incomplete solutions of the universe are thrust upon us as complete and satisfying. "*Le fond de la Providence,*" says the French novelist, "*c'est l'ironie.*" Mr. Clough would not have said that; but he knew what it meant, and what was the portion of truth contained in it. Undeniably this *is* an *odd* world, whether it should have been so or no; and all our speculations upon it should begin with some admission of its strangeness and singularity. The habit of dwelling on such thoughts as these will not of itself make a man happy, and may make unhappy one who is inclined to be so. Mr. Clough in his time felt more than most men the weight of the unintelligible world; but such thoughts make an instructive man. Several survivors may think they owe much to Mr. Clough's quiet question, "Ah, then you think—?" Many pretending creeds, and many wonderful demonstrations, passed away before that calm inquiry. He had a habit of putting your own doctrine concisely before you, so that you might see what it came to, and that you did not like it. Even now that he is gone, some may feel the recollection of his society a check on unreal theories and half-mastered thoughts. (pp. 323-26)

Walter Bagehot, in an originally unsigned essay titled "Mr. Clough's Poems," in The National Review, *London, Vol. XV, No. XXX, October, 1862, pp. 310-26.*

MATTHEW ARNOLD   (poem date 1866)

[*The following is Arnold's "Thyrsis," a poem written in 1866 in memory of his friend Clough and the years they shared at Oxford. Considered one of Arnold's best poems, "Thyrsis" has been blamed by critics for perpetuating the image of Clough as an irresolute person who retreated from life. For further commentary by Arnold, see excerpt dated 1849.*]

How changed is here each spot man makes or fills!
In the two Hinkseys nothing keeps the same;
The village street its haunted mansion lacks,
And from the sign is gone Sibylla's name,
And from the roofs the twisted chimney stacks—
Are ye too changed, ye hills?
See, 'tis no foot of unfamiliar men
Tonight from Oxford up your pathway strays!
Here came I often, often, in old days—
Thyrsis and I; we still had Thyrsis then.

Runs it not here, the track by Childsworth Farm,
Past the high wood, to where the elm tree crowns
The hill behind whose ridge the sunset flames?
The signal-elm, that looks on Ilsley Downs,
The Vale, the three lone weirs, the youthful Thames?—
This winter eve is warm,
Humid the air! leafless, yet soft as spring,
The tender purple spray on copse and briers!
And that sweet city with her dreaming spires,
She needs not June for beauty's heightening,

Lovely all times she lies, lovely tonight!—
Only, methinks, some loss of habit's power
Befalls me wandering through this upland dim.
Once passed I blindfold here, at any hour;
Now seldom come I, since I came with him.
That single elm tree bright
Against the west—I miss it! is it gone?
We prized it dearly; while it stood, we said,
Our friend, the Gypsy Scholar, was not dead;
While the tree lived, he in these fields lived on.

Too rare, too rare, grow now my visits here,
But once I knew each field, each flower, each stick;
And with the countryfolk acquaintance made
By barn in threshing time, by new-built rick.
Here, too, our shepherd pipes we first assayed.
Ah me! this many a year
My pipe is lost, my shepherd's holiday!
Needs must I lose them, needs with heavy heart
Into the world and wave of men depart;
But Thyrsis of his own will went away.

It irked him to be here, he could not rest.
He loved each simple joy the country yields,
He loved his mates; but yet he could not keep,
For that a shadow loured on the fields,
Here with the shepherds and the silly sheep.
Some life of men unblest
He knew, which made him droop, and filled his head.

He went; his piping took a troubled sound
Of storms that rage outside our happy ground;
He could not wait their passing, he is dead.

So, some tempestuous morn in early June,
When the year's primal burst of bloom is o'er,
Before the roses and the longest day—
When garden walks and all the grassy floor
With blossoms red and white of fallen May
And chestnut flowers are strewn—
So have I heard the cuckoo's parting cry,
From the wet field, through the vexed garden trees,
Come with the volleying rain and tossing breeze:
The bloom is gone, and with the bloom go I!

Too quick despairer, wherefore wilt thou go?
Soon will the high Midsummer pomps come on,
Soon will the musk carnations break and swell,
Soon shall we have gold-dusted snapdragon,
Sweet-william with his homely cottage smell,
And stocks in fragrant blow;
Roses that down the alleys shine afar,
And open, jasmine-muffled lattices,
And groups under the dreaming garden trees,
And the full moon, and the white evening star.

He hearkens not! light comer, he is flown!
What matters it? next year he will return,
And we shall have him in the sweet spring days,
With whitening hedges, and uncrumpling fern,
And bluebells trembling by the forest ways,
And scent of hay new-mown.
But Thyrsis never more we swains shall see;
See him come back, and cut a smoother reed,
And blow a strain the world at last shall heed—
For Time, not Corydon, hath conquered thee!

Alack, for Corydon no rival now!—
But when Sicilian shepherds lost a mate,
Some good survivor with his flute would go,
Piping a ditty sad for Bion's fate;
And cross the unpermitted ferry's flow,
And relax Pluto's brow,
And make leap up with joy the beauteous head
Of Proserpine, among whose crownéd hair
Are flowers first opened on Sicilian air,
And flute his friend, like Orpheus, from the dead.

O easy access to the hearer's grace
When Dorian shepherds sang to Proserpine!
For she herself had trod Sicilian fields,
She knew the Dorian water's gush divine,
She knew each lily white which Enna yields,
Each rose with blushing face;
She loved the Dorian pipe, the Dorian strain.
But ah, of our poor Thames she never heard!
Her foot the Cummer cowslips never stirred;
And we should tease her with our plaint in vain!

Well! wind-dispersed and vain the words will be,
Yet, Thyrsis, let me give my grief its hour
In the old haunt, and find our tree-topped hill!
Who, if not I, for questing here hath power?
I know the wood which hides the daffodil,
I know the Fyfield tree,
I know what white, what purple fritillaries
The grassy harvest of the river fields,
Above by Ensham, down by Sandford, yields,
And what sedged brooks are Thames's tributaries;

I know these slopes; who knows them if not I?—
But many a dingle on the loved hillside,
With thorns once studded, old, white-blossomed trees,
Where thick the cowslips grew, and far descried
High towered the spikes of purple orchises,
Hath since our day put by
The coronals of that forgotten time;
Down each green bank hath gone the plowboy's team,
And only in the hidden brookside gleam
Primroses, orphans of the flowery prime.

Where is the girl, who by the boatman's door,
Above the locks, above the boating throng,
Unmoored our skiff when through the Wytham flats,
Red loosestrife and blond meadowsweet among
And darting swallows and light water-gnats,
We tracked the shy Thames shore?
Where are the mowers, who, as the tiny swell
Of our boat passing heaved the river grass,
Stood with suspended scythe to see us pass?—
They all are gone, and thou art gone as well!

Yes, thou art gone! and round me too the night
In ever-nearing circle weaves her shade.
I see her veil draw soft across the day,
I feel her slowly chilling breath invade
The cheek grown thin, the brown hair sprent with gray;
I feel her finger light
Laid pausefully upon life's headlong train;
The foot less prompt to meet the morning dew,
The heart less bounding at emotion new,
And hope, once crushed, less quick to spring again.

And long the way appears, which seemed so short
To the less practiced eye of sanguine youth;
And high the mountaintops, in cloudy air,
The mountaintops where is the throne of Truth,
Tops in life's morning sun so bright and bare!
Unbreachable the fort
Of the long-battered world uplifts its wall;
And strange and vain the earthly turmoil grows,
And near and real the charm of thy repose,
And night as welcome as a friend would fall.

But hush! the upland hath a sudden loss
Of quiet!—Look, adown the dusk hillside,
A troop of Oxford hunters going home,
As in old days, jovial and talking, ride!
From hunting with the Berkshire hounds they come.
Quick! let me fly, and cross
Into yon farther field!—'Tis done; and see,
Backed by the sunset, which doth glorify
The orange and pale violet evening sky,
Bare on its lonely ridge, the Tree! the Tree!

I take the omen! Eve lets down her veil,
The white fog creeps from bush to bush about,
The west unflushes, the high stars grow bright,
And in the scattered farms the lights come out.
I cannot reach the signal-tree tonight,
Yet, happy omen, hail!
Hear it from thy broad lucent Arno vale
(For there thine earth-forgetting eyelids keep
The morningless and unawakening sleep
Under the flowery oleanders pale),

Hear it, O Thyrsis, still our tree is there!—
Ah, vain! These English fields, this upland dim,
These brambles pale with mist engarlanded,
That lone, sky-pointing tree, are not for him;
To a boon southern country he is fled,
And now in happier air,
Wandering with the great Mother's train divine
(And purer or more subtle soul than thee,
I trow, the mighty Mother doth not see)
Within a folding of the Apennine,

Thou hearest the immortal chants of old!—
Putting his sickle to the perilous grain
In the hot cornfield of the Phrygian king,
For thee the Lityerses song again
Young Daphnis with his silver voice doth sing;
Sings his Sicilian fold,
His sheep, his hapless love, his blinded eyes—
And how a call celestial round him rang,
And heavenward from the fountain brink he sprang,
And all the marvel of the golden skies.

There thou art gone, and me thou leavest here
Sole in these fields! yet will I not despair.
Despair I will not, while I yet descry
'Neath the mild canopy of English air
That lonely tree against the western sky.
Still, still these slopes, 'tis clear,
Our Gypsy Scholar haunts, outliving thee!
Fields where soft sheep from cages pull the hay,
Woods with anemones in flower till May,
Know him a wanderer still; then why not me?

A fugitive and gracious light he seeks,
Shy to illumine; and I seek it too.
This does not come with houses or with gold,
With place, with honor, and a flattering crew;
'Tis not in the world's market bought and sold—
But the smooth-slipping weeks
Drop by, and leave its seeker still untired;
Out of the heed of mortals he is gone,
He wends unfollowed, he must house alone;
Yet on he fares, by his own heart inspired.

Thou too, O Thyrsis, on like quest wast bound;
Thou wanderedst with me for a little hour!
Men gave thee nothing; but this happy quest,
If men esteemed thee feeble, gave thee power,
If men procured thee trouble, gave thee rest.
And this rude Cumner ground,
Its fir-topped Hurst, its farms, its quiet fields,
Here cam'st thou in thy jocund youthful time,
Here was thine height of strength, thy golden prime!
And still the haunt beloved a virtue yields.

What though the music of thy rustic flute
Kept not for long its happy, country tone;
Lost it too soon, and learnt a stormy note
Of men contention-tossed, of men who groan,
Which tasked thy pipe too sore, and tired thy throat—
It failed, and thou wast mute!
Yet hadst thou alway visions of our light,
And long with men of care thou couldst not stay,
And soon thy foot resumed its wandering way,
Left human haunt, and on alone till night.

Too rare, too rare, grow now my visits here!
'Mid city noise, not, as with thee of yore,

Thyrsis! in reach of sheep-bells is my home.
—Then through the great town's harsh, heart-wearying roar,
Let in thy voice a whisper often come,
To chase fatigue and fear:
Why faintest thou? I wandered till I died.
Roam on! The light we sought is shining still.
Dost thou ask proof? Our tree yet crowns the hill,
Our Scholar travels yet the loved hillside.

(pp. 1361-67)

Matthew Arnold, "Thyrsis," in The Norton Anthol-
ogy of English Literature, Vol. 2, *edited by M. H.*
Abrams and others, third edition, W. W. Norton &
Company, Inc., 1974, pp. 1361-67.

WILLIAM ALLINGHAM   (essay date 1866)

[*A minor nineteenth-century Irish poet, dramatist, and essay-*
ist, Allingham is best known for his lengthy narrative poem
Laurence Bloomfield in Ireland, *which movingly portrays the*
plight of the Irish peasant class under the domination of En-
glish absentee landlords. An acquaintance of Clough, Al-
lingham here describes some of the general characteristics of
his verse and personality.]

The name of Arthur Hugh Clough is held in regard by many
readers of books in England and America, and in affection by
his personal friends. He was an Englishman of our own day
with its novelties and problems, intellectual, cultivated, thoroughly honest and singleminded, and possessing moreover a
marked degree of originality, which after all is the truly interesting thing. Originality or 'genius,' that which is born with
a man, and peculiarly distinguishes him from all others, is
what we seek in every one; this *is* the man.

Clough's mind, naturally of a grave reflective turn, was occupied in early life with the studies of a public school and college career, and a good deal at the same time with moral and
theological questions; English ecclesiasticism had a large
share in his training; later, he took interest in politics, though
not in parties; the picturesque in nature attracted him much,
and he delighted in rambles afoot; first and last he had a constant literary impulse, which expressed itself mainly in poetic
forms, in part perhaps because his habitually reserved mind
had thus the advantage of a thicker veil when venturing into
public view. Reserved and reticent, cautious almost to a fault
in forming opinions, everything Clough said, did, and wrote
was genuine—was from himself, and imbued with his truthful, generous, and manly nature. (p. 525)

Clough's poems . . . consist of two long poems in hexameters—the *Bothie,* and *Amours de Voyage;* a set of five stories
in rhyme grouped under the general title of *Mari Magno;* and
some threescore minor effusions. Of all the larger compositions, and several of the smaller, the main subject matter is
the same, namely, Love, as seen from one point of view,
though with various circumstances, by an educated young
Englishman of the present day,—neither 'platonic' love by
any means, nor on the other hand sensual or lawless, but love
as a desire and search for what is truest and best in matrimonial union. This love, as our poet represents it, this hoping
and longing for hymeneal happiness, is self-questioning, self-
tormenting, fearing shams, fearing self-deception, fearing to
lose what is solid through over-refinement, a substance for a
shadow; fearing still more to sell its birthright for a mess of
pottage. The hero of the *Bothie,* an Oxford man, yet a radical,
is troubled chiefly, both in his general views, and particularly

in his character of aspirant to matrimony, by his thoughts as
to the condition, duties, and mutual relations of the upper
and the lower classes.

The *Amours de Voyage* (first published in America) was all
but unknown in England during the author's lifetime, and is
still much less widely known than the *Bothie.* This poem (to
which one of the mottoes is 'Il doutait de tout, même de
l'amour.' *French Novel,*) recounts the slight adventures of one
Claude, a young Englishman of our time, one of the—

Feeble and restless youths born to inglorious days.

Sick of London, he makes a tour to Italy and Switzerland. He
is disappointed or dissatisfied, or at best unsatisfied, with almost everything and every one he sees,—not ignobly, but
with the discontent of a subtle, inquiring, and aspiring soul,
which is least of all contented with *itself.* At Rome he meets
three Miss Trevellyns, and likes them, especially Mary, not
forgetting, however, to remind himself—

Well, I know there are thousands as pretty and hundreds
    as pleasant,
Girls by the dozen as good, and girls in abundance with
    polish
Higher and manners more perfect than Susan or Mary
    Trevellyn.
Well, I know, after all, it is merely juxtaposition,—
Juxtaposition, in short; and what is juxtaposition?

Claude's attitude throughout is that of a questioner. He is,
perhaps, the best type yet given us in literature of the scepticism of modern England. He is highminded, pure, benevolent, intellectual; but he questions of religion, of morals, of
love, of men and women, of history and art, and above all of
himself. He is not an ingenious quibbler, he has no touch of
affectation; to question and doubt, to consider and reconsider, is as natural to him as thinking or breathing. . . . As
Georgiana Trevellyn remarks, 'he really is too shilly-shally.'
Does he care very much for Mary Trevellyn? Does she care
very much for him? He cannot decide, and in his indecision
allows her and her party to travel northwards without him.
Then he pursues, but, by a series of misadventures, fails to
find them, and gives up the pursuit, saying by and by—

After all, do I know that I really cared so about her?
Do whatever I will, I cannot call up her image;

. . . . .

After all, perhaps there was something factitious about it;
I have had pain, it is true: I have wept, and so have the
    actors.

Meanwhile Mary Trevellyn, who has been anxiously looking
for Claude, submits on her part, 'although in a different manner,' to the closing of their acquaintance. In a letter of
Clough's of June 1858, he says:

I have had, mirabile dictu, a letter from Emerson,
who reprimanded me strongly for the termination
of the *Amours de Voyage* [see excerpt dated 1858],
in which he may be right, and I may be wrong; and
all my defence can only be, that I always meant it
to be so, and begun it with the full intention of its
ending so; but very likely I was wrong all the same.

Love, and Self-questioning, singly or in combination, form
the staple of the minor poems, whereof the following may be
named as very characteristic:—**'Duty,' 'When panting sighs**
the bosom fill,' 'O tell me, friends,' 'The questioning Spirit,'

'**O thou whose image.**' Several short pieces printed in the [1862 *Poems*] reappear embodied in the long composition, which remains a fragment, given in the volume of *Letters and Remains* and entitled *Dipsychus,* that is, the two-souled or two-minded, a man who cannot come to an agreement with himself, 'This way and that dividing the swift mind.' Some of the pieces in question assume a different meaning as part of the long composition. . . . There is a kind of bitter humour, a sarcastic philosophy, of which we find traces in Clough's other poems, appearing in larger measure in this *Dipsychus,* as in the lines ' "There is no God" the wicked saith;' or 'How pleasant it is to have money,' &c.; or these:—

> This world is very odd we see,
> We do not comprehend it;
> But in one fact we all agree,
> God won't, and we can't mend it.
>
> Being common sense, it can't be sin,
> To take it as I find it;
> The pleasure to take pleasure in;
> The pain, try not to mind it.

On one side of his mind, at least, Clough had a good deal of sympathy with the way of looking at life which we find in such poets as Horace, Goethe, Byron, Béranger.

Dipsychus is tormented by 'twisted thinkings,' he fears action, and also fears lest he may drone and dream away his life:

> Is it a law for me
> That opportunity shall breed distrust,
> Not passing till that pass?

The Spirit taunts him:

> Heartily you will not take to anything;
> Whatever happen, don't I see you still,
> Living no life at all? . . . .
>   Will you go on thus
> Until death end you? if indeed it does.
> For what it does, none knows. Yet as for you,
> You'll hardly have the courage to die outright;
> You'll somehow halve ev'n it. Methinks I see you,
> Through everlasting limbos of void time,
> Twirling and twiddling ineffectively,
> And indeterminately swaying for ever.

Clough's last work comprises five love-stories under the general title of *Mari Magno, or Tales on Board,* being supposed to be told by certain passengers in a steamer during the voyage from England to Boston U.S. They are all very modern and matter-of-fact both in style and substance, and include many characteristic and interesting remarks on life.

Clough's poetry is in every part full of matter and meaning; of mere beauty and melody for their own sakes there is but little. Picturesque he often is, but (to compare one art with another) it is in the style of Clarkson Stanfield, never in that of Turner or of David Cox. He was comparatively inattentive to the subtle effects of language and metre, caring much for conveying his thought strongly and clearly, and but little for giving delight by the way. Indeed, he generally felt metre as a hindrance, and was very impatient of the bonds of rhyme. Yet, in writing in verse, he doubtless felt also that he had more scope for originality: there was less risk of seeming odd in manner, or of 'committing himself' in matter. This criticism, however, is partly opinion, partly surmise; the main fact is that he *has* expressed himself effectively, has spoken to the world out of the thought and experience of a man, and a 'man of genius,' *unus e multis,* a true word which remains.

Dr. Thomas Arnold, Clough's schoolmaster at Rugby.

From the higher mind of cultivated, all-questioning, but still conservative England, in this our puzzled generation, we do not know of any utterance in literature so characteristic as the poems of Arthur Hugh Clough, 'sometime fellow of Oriel College, Oxford.' Freely he thinks and speaks; yet always as an Englishman. His sympathies are general, but his tastes and standards are still national. (pp. 532-35)

> *William Allingham, "Arthur Hugh Clough, 1819-1861," in* Fraser's Magazine for Town & Country, *Vol. LXXIV, No. CCCCXLII, October, 1866, pp. 525-35.*

HENRY SIDGWICK   (essay date 1869)

[*A prominent ethical philosopher in the Victorian era, Sidgwick also wrote on politics, economics, and literature. In the following excerpt, Sidgwick discusses the three dominant moods Clough expressed in his poetry: "religious skepticism," "ethical skepticism," and "amatory skepticism."*]

[Clough] was a philosophic poet; a being about whose nature and *raison d'être* the critical world is not thoroughly agreed. Philosophic poetry is often treated as if it was versified philosophy, as if its primary function was to "convey ideas," the only question being whether these should be conveyed with or without metre. Proceeding on this assumption, an influential sect maintains that there ought to be no philosophic poetry at all; that the "ideas" it "conveys" had much better seek the channel of prose. To us it seems that what poetry has to communicate is not ideas but moods and feelings; and that if a feeling reaches sufficient intensity, whatever be its specific quality, it is adapted for a poetical form, though highly intellectual moods are harder to mould to the conditions of metrical expression than others. The question is often raised, especially at the present day, when our leading poets are philo-sophic, whether such and such a poem—say Browning's "Christmas Eve," or parts of *In Memoriam*—would not have been better in prose. And the question is often a fair one for discussion, but a wrong criterion is used for determining it. If such a poem is really unpoetical, it is not because it con-tains too much thought, but too little feeling to steep and pen-etrate the thought. Tried by this test, a good deal of Brow-ning's thought-laden verse, and some of Tennyson's, will ap-pear not truly poetical; the feeling is not adequate. Although Clough sometimes fails in this way, it may generally be said that with him the greater the contention of thought, the more intense is the feeling transfused through it. He becomes unpo-etical chiefly when he becomes less eagerly intellectual, when he lapses for a moment into mild optimism, or any form of languid contentment; or when like Wordsworth he caresses a rather too trivial mood; very rarely when the depths of his mind are stirred. He is, then, pre-eminently a philosophic poet, communicator of moods that depend on profound and complex trains of reflection, abstract and highly refined spec-ulations, subtle intellectual perceptions, and that cannot be felt unless these are properly apprehended. He is to a great extent a poet for thinkers; but he moves them not as a thinker, but as a poet.

We do not mean to say that Clough was not a thinker; but the term is somewhat indefinite, and in one sense he was not. His mind brooded over a few great questions, and was rather finely receptive than eagerly discursive; he did not enjoy the mere exercise of thought for its own sake. . . . But though he was too much of a poet to care greatly for the mere exer-cise of the cognitive faculties, though no one could less have adopted the "philosopher's paradox" of Lessing, we may still Call him philosophic from his passionate devotion not to Search after Truth, but to Truth itself, absolute, exact truth. He was philosophic in his horror of illusions and deceptions of all kinds; in his perpetual watchfulness against prejudices and prepossessions; against the Idols, as Bacon calls them, of the Cave and the Theatre, as well as of the Tribe and the Mar-ket-place. He was made for a free-thinker rather than a scien-tific inquirer. His skill lay in balancing assertions, comparing points of view, sifting gold from dross in the intellectual prod-ucts presented to him, rejecting the rhetorical, defining the vague, paring away the exaggerative, reducing theory and ar-gument to their simplest form, their "lowest terms." "Lumen Siccum," as he calls it in one of his poems, is the object of his painful search, his eager hope, his anxious loyalty.

The intellectual function, then, which Clough naturally as-sumed was scepticism of the Socratic sort, scepticism occu-pied about problems on which grave practical issues depend-ed. The fundamental assumptions involved in men's habitual lines of endeavour, which determined their ends and guided the formation of their rules, he was continually endeavouring to clear from error, and fix upon a sound basis. He would not accept either false solutions or no solutions, nor, unless very reluctantly, provisional solutions. At the same time, he saw just as clearly as other men that the continued contemplation of insoluble problems is not merely unpractical, but anti-practical; and that a healthy and natural instinct forces most men, after a few years of feverish youthful agitation, resolute-ly to turn away from it. But with this instinct Clough's fine passion for absolute truth conflicted; if he saw two sides of a question, he must keep seeking a point of view from which they might be harmonized. In one of the most impressive of

the poems classed in this edition as "Songs of Absence," he describes his disposition

To finger idly some old Gordian knot,
Unskilled to loosen and too weak to cleave;

but the reluctance to cleave knots, in the speculative sphere, does not proceed from weakness.

It is this supreme loyalty to reason, combining and conflict-ing with the most comprehensive and profound sympathy with other elements of human nature, that constitutes the pe-culiar charm of Clough's scepticism, and its peculiar adapta-tion to poetical expression. Towards the beliefs to which other men were led by their desires, he was as strongly, or more strongly, impelled than others; the assertions in which they formulated their hopes he would gladly have made with the same cheerful dogmatism. His yearning for the ideal he never tried to quench or satisfy with aught but its proper sat-isfaction; but meanwhile the claims of the real, to be accepted as real, are paramount. He clings to the "beauty of his dreams;" but—two and two make four. It is the painfulness, and yet inevitableness of this conflict, the childlike simplicity and submissiveness with which he yields himself up to it; the patient tenacity with which he refuses to quiet his hold of any of the conflicting elements; the consistency with which it is carried into every department of life; the strange mixture of sympathy and want of sympathy with his fellow-creatures that necessarily accompanies it, that makes the moods which he has expressed in verse so rare, complex, subtle, and in-tense.

We may classify these moods . . . into first, those of religious scepticism, where the philosophic impulse is in conflict with the mystical; secondly, those of ethical scepticism, where it contends with habitual active principles; thirdly, those where it is perplexed with the most clamorous and absorbing of human enthusiasms, the passion which forms the peculiar topic of poetry. It is this latter division that at once completes the consistency of Clough's scepticism, and forms its most novel, original, and least understood application. As he him-self says, not only "saint and sage," but also "poet's dreams,"

Divide the light in coloured streams;

the votary of truth must seek "lumen siccum."

The personal history of Clough's religious scepticism has rather to be guessed than known from the records of his life that life before us. . . . At Rugby he seems to have yielded himself entirely to the influence of Arnold, and to have em-braced with zealous docility the view of life which that re-markable man impressed so strongly, for good or for evil, on his more susceptible pupils. But though somewhat over-solemn and prematurely earnest, like many Rugby boys of the time, he was saved from priggishness by his perfect sim-plicity. At Balliol he shows nothing of the impulsiveness, ve-hemence, and restlessness, the spirit of dispute and revolt, which are supposed to precede and introduce deliberate infi-delity. Thrown upon Oxford at the time when the "New-manitish phantasm," as he calls it, was startling and exciting Young England, he writes of the movement to his friends with a mild and sober eclecticism—a tranquil *juste-milieu* temper which would become a dean. He is candidly obser-vant, gives measured admiration for good points, notes ex-travagances, suggests the proper antidotes, seems disposed, on the whole, to keep out of the atmosphere of controversy and devote himself to his studies. Nothing could give smoother promise of untroubled orthodoxy. It is true that he speaks of being "exhausted by the vortex of philosophism;" and he must have been much more powerfully influenced by Newmanism than these letters indicate. He said afterwards, that for two years of this time he had been "like a straw drawn up the vortex of a chimney." His mind seems habitually to have been swayed by large, slow, deep sea currents, the surface remaining placid, even tame; such a steady hidden movement it seems to have been that floated him away from his old moorings of belief. Gradually or suddenly the theologico-juridical, ecclesiastico-mystical dialectics that went on around him became shadowy and unreal; all his religious needs, hopes, aspirations remaining the same, a new view of the universe, with slowly accumulating force, impressed itself irresistibly on his mind, with which not only the intellectual beliefs entwined with these needs and aspirations seemed incompatible, but even these latter fundamentally incongruous. And thus began a conflict between old and new that was to last his life, the various moods of which the series of his religious poems, solemn, passionate, and ironical, accurately expresses.

Perhaps the first characteristic that we notice in these is their rare reality and spontaneity. We feel that they are uttered, just as they appear, from an inner necessity; there was no choice to say them or not to say them. With some poets religious unbelief or doubt seems an abiding attitude of intellect, but only occasionally to engross the heart; their utterances have the gusty force of transitory passion, not the vitality of permanent feeling. But with Clough it is different: the whole man is in the poems, they spring from the very core of his being. The levity of some of them is as touching as the solemnity of others; it is a surface-mood, showing explored depths beneath it, in which an unrestful spirit finds momentary relief. Another characteristic is, that over the saddest cries of regret and struggles of checked aspiration is spread a certain tranquillity—not of hope, still less of despair, but a tranquillity that has something Aristotelian in it, the tranquillity of intellectual contemplation. (pp. 366-70)

The known order of the world, even without the certainty of a personal God, source or correlate of that order, afforded somewhat of philosophic satisfaction, however little it could content the yearnings of his soul. It was a sort of *terra firma,* on which he could set his feet, while his eyes gazed with patient scrutiny into the unanswering void. Further, we remark in these moods their balanced, complex character; there is either a solemn reconciliation of conflicting impulses, or a subtle and shifting suggestion of different points of view. . . .
[An example of the former, **"Qui laborat, orat,"**] is one of Clough's most perfect productions; there is a deep pathos in the restrained passion of worship, and the clear-cut exactness of phrase, as it belongs to the very essence of the sentiment, enhances the dignity of the style. Somewhat similar in feeling, but more passionate and less harmonious, is the following fragment [**"Hidden Love"**]:—

> O let me love my love unto myself alone,
> And know my knowledge to the world unknown:
> No witness to the vision call,
> Beholding, unbeheld of all;
> And worship Thee, with Thee withdrawn apart,
> Whoe'er, whate'er Thou art,
> Within the closest veil of mine own inmost heart.
>
> . . . . .
>
> Better it were, thou sayest, to consent:
> Feast while we may, and live ere life be spent;

> Close up clear eyes, and call the unstable sure,
> The unlovely lovely, and the filthy pure;
> In self-belyings, self-deceivings roll,
> And lose in Action, Passion, Talk, the soul.
>
> Nay, better far to mark off so much air,
> And call it Heaven: place bliss and glory there;
> Fix perfect homes in the unsubstantial sky,
> And say, what is not will be by-and-bye.

Sometimes the intellectual, or as we have called it, philosophical element, shows itself in a violence of sincerity that seems reckless, but is rather, to use a German word, rücksichtslos; it disregards other considerations, not from blind impulse but deep conviction. The tone of the poem is then that of one walking firmly over red-hot ploughshares, and attests at once the passion and the painfulness of looking facts in the face. In the fine poem called **"Easter Day"** (where a full sense of the fascination of the Christian story and the belief in immortality depending on it, and of the immensity of its loss to mankind, conflicts with scientific loyalty to the modern explanation of it), the intensity of the blended feeling fuses a prosaic material into poetry very remarkably. (pp. 371-72)

The complex and balanced state of Clough's moods shows itself in an irony unlike the irony of any other writer; it is so subtle, frequently fading to a mere shade, and so all-pervading. In the midst of apparently most earnest expression of any view, it surprises us with a suggestion of the impossibility that that view should be adequate; sometimes it shifts from one side of a question to the other, so that it is impossible to tell either from direct expression or ironical suggestion what the writer's decision on the whole is. . . . The truth is, that though Clough from time to time attempts to reconcile and settle, his deepest conviction is that all settlement is premature. We meet continually phrases like the

> Believe it not, yet leave it not,
> And wait it out, O man,

of one of his earlier poems. To use a favourite image of his, the universe, by our present arithmetic, comes to much less than we had fondly imagined. Our arithmetic is sound, and must be trusted; in fact, it is the only arithmetic we have got. Still the disappointing nature of the result (and let us never pretend to ourselves that it is not disappointing) may be taken as some evidence of its incompleteness.

This irony assumes a peculiar tone when it is directed to vulgar, shallow, unworthy states of mind. It is not that Clough passionately repudiates these, and takes up a censorial position outside and over against them; these, too, are facts, common and important facts of humanity; *humani nihil*—not even Philistinism—*a se alienum putat.* His contempt for them is deep, but not bitter; indeed, so far from bitter that a dull pious ear may misperceive in it an unpleasing levity. His mode of treating them is to present them in extreme and bald simplicity, so that the mind recoils from them. A penetrating observer describes something like this as a part of Clough's conversational manner. "He had a way," says Mr. Bagehot, "of presenting your own view to you, so that you saw what it came to, and that you did not like it" [see excerpt dated 1862]. A good instance of this occurs in an unfinished poem, called the **"Shadow".** . . . We quote the greater part of it, as it also exemplifies Clough's powerful, though sparingly exercised, imagination; which here, from the combination of sublimity and quaintness, reminds one of Richter, only that we have antique severity instead of romantic profuseness:—

> I dreamed a dream: I dreamt that I espied,
> Upon a stone that was not rolled aside,
> A Shadow sit upon a grave—a Shade,
> As thin, as unsubstantial, as of old
> Came, the Greek poet told,
> To lick the life-blood in the trench Ulysses made—
> As pale, as thin, and said:
> "I am the Resurrection of the Dead.
> The night is past, the morning is at hand,
> And I must in my proper semblance stand,
> Appear brief space and vanish,—listen, this is true,
> I am that Jesus whom they slew."
>
> And shadows dim, I dreamed, the dead apostles came,
> And bent their heads for sorrow and for shame—
> Sorrow for their great loss, and shame
> For what they did in that vain name.
>
> And in long ranges far behind there seemed
> Pale vapoury angel forms; or was it cloud? that kept
> Strange watch; the women also stood beside and wept.
> And Peter spoke the word:
> "O my own Lord,
> What is it we must do?
> Is it then all untrue?
> Did we not see, and hear, and handle Thee,
> Yea, for whole hours
> Upon the Mount in Galilee,
> On the lake shore, and here at Bethany,
> When Thou ascended to Thy God and ours?"
> And paler still became the distant cloud,
> And at the word the women wept aloud.
>
> And the Shade answered, "What ye say I know not;
> But it is true
> I am that Jesus whom they slew,
> Whom ye have preached, but in what way I know not."
>
>   . . . . .
>
> And the great World, it chanced, came by that way,
> And stopped, and looked, and spoke to the police,
> And said the thing, for order's sake and peace,
> Most certainly must be suppressed, the nuisance cease.
> His wife and daughter must have where to pray,
> And whom to pray to, at the least one day
> In seven, and something sensible to say.
>
> Whether the fact so many years ago
> Had, or not, happened, how was he to know?
> Yet he had always heard that it was so.
> As for himself, perhaps it was all one;
> And yet he found it not unpleasant, too,
> On Sunday morning in the roomy pew,
> To see the thing with such decorum done.
> As for himself, perhaps it was all one;
> Yet on one's death-bed all men always said
> It was a comfortable thing to think upon
> The atonement and the resurrection of the dead.
> So the great World as having said his say,
> Unto his country-house pursued his way.
> And on the grave the Shadow sat all day.

The effect of the latter part is like that of stripping an uncomely body, familiar to us as respectably draped and costumed, and showing it without disguise or ornament. That "the world" has never seen himself in this nakedness we feel: but we also feel that here is the world which we know. The two lines before the three last show the felicitous audacity with which Clough sometimes manages metre: nothing could

more sharply give the shallowness of the mood in contrast with the solemnity of the subject than the careless glibness of the lines

> It was a comfortable thing to think upon
> The atonement and the resurrection of the dead.

The longest of the religious poems is an unfinished one called the *Mystery of the Fall.* The fundamental idea seems to be this. The legend of the Fall represents a permanent and universal element of human feeling, the religious conviction of sin, but only one element: the beliefs corresponding to it, even if intuitive consciousness is relied upon as their evidence, are not affirmed by the sum total of valid consciousness—taking "Sunday and work-days" together. Not only do our practical necessities and active impulses require and generate other conceptions of the universe which seem incompatible with the religious, but the latter is unsatisfying in itself: the notions of perfect creation, lapse, wrath, propitiation, though they correspond to a part of our religious experience, yet do not content our religious feeling as an adequate account of the relation of God to man. This Clough has tried to express, keeping the framework of the old legend, in dialogues between Adam, Eve, Cain, and Abel after expulsion from the garden. The transitions and blendings of the different moods are given with a close and subtle fidelity to psychological truth: and this putting of new wine into old bottles is perhaps justified by the prominence in human history of the Hebrew legend. There is no reason why Adam and his family should not be permanent machinery for serious fable, as Jove and his subordinates are for burlesque. Still the incongruity between the modern moods (and especially the perfect self-consciousness accompanying them) and the antique personages and incidents is here too whimsical: and, for poetry, the thought is too predominant, and the feeling not sufficiently intense; to some parts of the subject, as the murder of Abel, Clough's imagination is inadequate: and on the whole the result is interesting rather than successful, and we doubt whether the poem could ever have been completed so as to satisfy the author's severe self-criticism.

We take a very different view of the other unfinished long poem, *Dipsychus.* If it had received the author's final touches, a few trivialities and whimsicalities would no doubt have been pruned away: but we doubt whether the whole could have been much improved. It has certain grave defects which seem to us irremovable, and we should rank it as a work of art below either of his hexameter poems. There is not sufficient movement or evolution in it; the feeling is too purely egoistic to keep up our sympathies so long; and it is not sufficiently framed. The Venetian scenes in which the dialogue goes on, though appropriate to some of the moods, have no particular connexion with the most important: whereas in *Amours de voyage,* and still more in the *Bothie,* the harmonizing of external and internal presentments is admirably managed. At the same time the composition is one of great interest. The stress of feeling is so sustained, the changes and fluctuations of mood are given with such perfect propriety, the thought and expression are so bold and novel yet free from paradox, so subtle without a particle of mere ingenuity. The blank verse too in parts, though only in parts, seems to have been carefully studied, and, though a little too suggestive of Elizabethan models, to attain a really high pitch of excellence. Perhaps no other poem of Clough's has so decidedly this one 'note' of genius, that its utterances are at once individual and universal, revealing the author to the reader, and at the same time the reader to himself. (pp. 372-76)

We turn now to what we may call the amatory scepticism. This is a more proper subject of poetry, as thought here is in no danger of being too predominant over feeling; at the same time it is more novel and original, as on no subject do poets in general less allow thought to interfere with feeling. Poets, in fact, are the recognised preachers of the divinity, eternity, omnipotence of Love. It is true that with some of them fits of despair alternate with enthusiasm, and they proclaim that Love is an empty dream: but the notion of scrutinizing the enthusiasm sympathetically, yet scientifically, and estimating the precise value of its claims and assertions, probably never entered into any poetic soul before Clough. (p. 377)

The fascination of the ideal was as strong for him as for other poets, but not stronger than the necessity of making it real. Hence in that period of youthful forecast and partial experience of passion, in which the finest love-fancies of most poets are woven, he perpetually feels the need of combining clear vision with exaltation. He keeps questioning Love as to what it really is, whence it comes, whither it goes: he demands a transcendental evaluation of it.

> Whence are ye, vague desires?
> Whence are ye?
>
> From seats of bliss above,
> Where angels sing of love,
> From subtle airs around,
> Or from the vulgar ground;
> Whence are ye, vague desires?
> Whence are ye?

"Is love spiritual or earthly?" is the passionate perplexity that tinges many of his songs. Or if this pearl of great price is to be found on earth, how shall we know it from its counterfeits, by what criterion discern the impulses that lead us to the true and the false? In one of the finer passages of the **Mari Magno** tales, this longing for direction is uttered.

> Beside the wishing gate which so they name,
> 'Mid northern hills to me this fancy came,
> A wish I formed, my wish I thus expressed:
> *Would I could wish my wishes all to rest,*
> *And know to wish the wish that were the best!*
> Oh for some winnowing wind, to the empty air
> This chaff of easy sympathies to bear
> Far off, and leave me of myself aware!
> While thus this over-health deludes me still,
> So willing that I know not what I will;
> Oh for some friend or more than friend austere
> To make me know myself and make me fear!
> Oh for some touch, too noble to be kind,
> To awake to life the mind within the mind.

But if love be after all only "a wondrous animal delight" in which nature's periodic blossoming culminates, the philosophic spirit, however deep its yearning, cannot submit to it, but has to contemplate it from the outside with tender and curious sympathy. This mood tinged with playfulness inspired the charming song in which he describes how he

> Watched in pleasant Kensington
> A 'prentice and a maid.
> That Sunday morning's April glow,
> How should it not impart
> A stir about the veins that flow
> To feed the youthful heart?

The rapture of this sympathetic contemplation is expressed in *Amours de Voyage.*

> All as I go on my way, I behold them consorting and coupling;
> Faithful it seems and fond: very fond, very possibly faithful,
> All as I go on my way with a love and contentment unmingled.
> Life is beautiful, Eustace, and could we eliminate wholly
> This vile hungering impulse, this demon within us of craving,
> Life were beatitude, living a perfect divine satisfaction.

This leads us to the deepest issue of all—a thoroughly Platonic problem. Be this love as noble as it may, is its exaltation compatible with clear vision? Does not this individualized enthusiasm of necessity draw away from the centrality of view and feeling after which the philosophic spirit aspires? Is it not unworthy of us, for any pleasure's sake, to be tricked by its magic and take its coloured light for white?

But we are tired of reducing to prose the various phases of this subtle blending and conflict of enthusiasms. As expressed by Clough they have the perfect vitality and reality of all his moods. None of these perplexities are arbitrarily sought; the questions raised must each have been raised and decided by many human beings since self-consciousness began. If no poet has uttered them before, it is because in most men the state of mind in which they were felt is incompatible with the flow of feeling that poetry requires. Clough's nature was, perhaps, deficient in passion, but it had a superabundant tenderness and susceptibility to personal influence, which made him retain the full feeling of personal relations while giving free scope to his sceptical intellect.

In one of the two long hexameter poems published in his lifetime, *Amours de Voyage,* Clough has given a dramatic embodiment to the motives that we have been analysing. The poem is skilfully composed. Thoroughly apprehending the aversion which practical humanity feels for these perplexities, he somewhat exaggerates the egotism of the hero of the piece to whom he attributes them, handles him with much irony throughout, and inflicts a severe but appropriate Nemesis at the close. The caricature in "Claude" is so marked that we are not surprised that Clough, the least egoistical of men, was indignant when a friend appeared to take the poem as an account of the author's own experiences. "I assure you," he writes, "that it is extremely not so" [see first letter by Clough dated 1849]. Still this attitude of the author could not reconcile the public to a hero who (as the motto has it) *doutait de tout, même de l'amour.* That the poem never attained the success of the **Bothie** we are not surprised. It has not the unique presentations of external nature which give such a charm to the earlier poem: it wants also the buoyant and vivacious humour which is so exuberant in the **Bothie,** and of which the fountain in Clough's latter years seems almost to have dried up. But it shows greater skill in blending and harmonizing different threads of a narrative, and a subtler management of the evolution of moods; it has deeper psychological interest, and in its best passages a rarer, more original imagination. The **Amour** is very closely interwoven with the incidents of the French siege of Rome (of which, by the way, Clough's letters give us interesting details) so that the two series of events together elicit a complete and consistent self revelation of the hero. The amative dubitations turn principally on two points—the immense issues that depend on amative selection compared with the arbitrary casual manner in which circumstances determine it, and the imperious claim of passion for a concentration of interest which to the innermost, most self-conscious, self is profoundly impossible. These play into one another in the following very characteristic passage.

> Juxtaposition, in fine; and what is juxtaposition?
> Look you, we travel along in the railway carriage or steamer,
> And, *pour passer le temps,* till the tedious journey be ended,
> Lay aside paper or book, to talk with the girl that is next one;
> And, *pour passer le temps,* with the terminus all but in prospect,
> Talk of eternal ties and marriages made in heaven.
> Ah, did we really accept with a perfect heart the illusion!
> Ah, did we really believe that the Present indeed is the Only!
> Or through all transmutation, all shock and convulsion of passion,
> Feel we could carry undimmed, unextinguished, the light of our knowledge!
>
> . . . . .
>
> But for the steady fore-sense of a freer and larger existence,
> Think you that man could consent to be circumscribed here into action?
> *But for assurance within of a limitless ocean divine, o'er*
> *Whose great tranquil depths unconscious the wind-tost surface*
> *Breaks into ripples of trouble that come and change and endure not,—*
> But that in this, of a truth, we have our being, and know it,
> Think you we men could submit to live and move as we do here?
> Ah, but the women—God bless them! they don't think at all about it.
> Yet we must eat and drink as you say. And as limited beings
> Scarcely can hope to attain upon earth to an actual abstract,
> Leaving to God contemplation, to His hands knowledge confiding,
> Sure that in us if it perish, in Him it abideth and dies not,
> Let us in His sight accomplish our petty particular doings,—
> Yes, and contented sit down to the victual that He has provided.

The three lines that we have italicized seem to us almost perfect specimens of the English Hexameter, showing the extreme flexibility which the metre has in Clough's hands, and his only, and none of the over-accentuation which neither he nor any one else can generally avoid. Very opposite opinions have been delivered as to the merits of this hexameter. Some most appreciative readers of the poems declare that they read them continually under protest; that no interest in the subject and no habit can make the metre tolerable. Mr. Arnold, however, on this subject an especially Rhadamanthine critic [see Further Reading], considers the success of Clough's experiment to be so decided as to form an important contribution to the question (which has occupied a most disproportionate amount of human intellect in our time), How Homer is to be translated? We do not take either view. We think Clough's metre, as he uses it, felicitous; but we do not think that this proves anything as to the appropriateness of the hexameter for translating Homer, or for any other application of 'the grand style.' Clough has not *naturalized* the metre. He has

given it ease, but not simplicity; he has not tried to give it simplicity, and therefore he has succeeded with it. All English hexameters written quite *au sérieux* seem to us to fail; the line ought to be unconscious of being a hexameter, and yet never is. But Clough's line is, and is meant to be, conscious of being a hexameter: it is always suggestive of and allusive to the ancient serious hexameters, with a faint but a deliberate air of burlesque, a wink implying that the bard is singing academically to an academical audience, and catering for their artificial tastes in versification. This academic flavour suits each poem in a different way. It harmonizes with the Oxonian studies of the *Bothie,* and here, indeed, the faint burlesque inseparable from the metre becomes from time to time distinct mock-heroic. In *Amours de Voyage,* it suits the over-culture, artificial refinement of the hero's mind: he is, we may say, in his abnormal difficulties of action and emotion, a scholastic or academic personage. In short the metre seems to belong to a style full of characteristic selfconscious humour such as Clough has sustained through each of the poems; and we cannot analyse its effect separately. Clough we know thought differently; but we are forced to regard this as one instance out of many where a poet takes a wrong view of his own work. His experiment of translating Homer into similar hexameters is nearly as much a failure as Mr. Arnold's, or any other; and his still bolder experiment of writing hexameters by quantity and not accent results, in spite of the singular care and even power with which it is executed, in a mere monstrosity.

We consider then that it was a happy instinct that led him to the metre of the *Bothie.* In more ordinary metres he often shows a want of mastery over the technicalities of verse-writing. He has no fertility of rhymes, he is monotonous, he does not avoid sing-song, he wearies us with excessive, almost puerile, iterations and antitheses. It is very remarkable, therefore, how in this new metre, self-chosen, he rises to the occasion, how inventive he is of varied movements, felicitous phrases, and pleasant artifices of language, how emphatically yet easily the sound is adapted to the sense, in a way which no metre but blank verse in the hands of a master could rival. Another evidence of the peculiar fitness of this instrument for his thought is the amount that he can pack without effort into his lines; as e.g. in the following description of one of the members of the Oxford reading party—

> Author forgotten and silent of currentest phrase and fancy,
> Mute and exuberant by turns, a fountain at intervals playing,
> Mute and abstracted, or strong and abundant as rain in the tropics;
> Studious, careless of dress, inobservant, by smooth persuasions
> Lately decoyed into kilt through example of Hope and the Piper,
> Hope an Antinous man, Hyperion of calves the Piper.

It is hard to imagine so much said so shortly in any other style.

The flexibility of the metre aids in bringing out another great excellence of these poems; the ease and completeness with which character is exhibited. There is not one of the personages of the *Bothie,* or even of *Amours de Voyage,* where the sketching is much slighter, whose individuality is not as thoroughly impressed upon us as if they had been delineated in a three-volume novel by Mr. Trollope. We are made to understand by most happily selected touches, and delicately illustrative phrases, not only what they are in themselves, but precisely how they affect one another. It becomes as impossible for us to attribute a remembered remark to the wrong person as it would be in a play of Shakespeare. To say that Clough's dramatic faculty was strong might convey a wrong impression, as we imagine that he was quite devoid of the power of representing a scene of vivid action; but the power of forming distinct conceptions of character, and expressing them with the few touches that poetry allows, is one of the gifts for displaying which we may regret that he had not ampler scope.

The descriptions of natural scenery in the *Bothie* form probably the best-known and most popular part of Clough's poetry. In this, as in some of his most important poetical characteristics, he may be called, in spite of great differences, a true disciple of Wordsworth. His admiration for the latter appears to have been always strongly marked; and one of the more interesting of the prose remains now published is ["**Lecture on the Poetry of Wordsworth**"], perhaps somewhat meagre, but showing profound appreciation, together with the critical propriety and exactness of statement characteristic of Clough. His simplicity, sincerity, gravity, are all Wordsworthian; but especially his attitude towards nature. Through a manner of description quite different we trace the rapt receptive mood, the unaffected self-abandonment, the anxious fidelity of reproduction, which Wordsworth has taught to many disciples, but to no other poet so fully. (pp. 378-83)

There is a peculiar combination of simplicity and subtlety in [Clough's] best things, the simplicity being as it were the final result and outcome of the subtlety, so that the presence of the latter is felt and not distinctly recognised, which we find in no other poet except Goethe. It is this combination that fits him for his peculiar function of rendering conscious the feelings that pass half unconsciously through ordinary minds, without seriously modifying them. There is a pretty instance of this in an idyllic song which we will quote. Most of the song is rather commonplace; a peasant girl driving she-goats homeward thinks alternately of the scene, and of her absent lover. Suddenly we are surprised with this very Cloughian sentiment.

> Or may it be that I shall find my mate,
> And he returning see himself too late?
> *For work we must, and what we see, we see,*
> *And God he knows, and what must be, must be,*
> When sweethearts wander far away from me.

The excellence of the lines that we have italicized we should describe paradoxically by saying that their naïveté is at once perfect and, as naïveté, impossible. (p. 384)

[If] Clough has many of Wordsworth's excellences, he certainly has his full share of the cognate defects. It is natural, perhaps, to the man who values the individuality of his thought and feeling so much as to spend great care on its expression, to want the power of discriminating between those parts of it that are, and those which are not worth expressing. Certainly Clough has not, any more than his master, the selective faculty that leads to the sustained elevation and distinction which we expect from a great poet, and which the adoption of a simple manner renders peculiarly indispensable. Commonplace thought and feeling in strikingly simple language does not make, perhaps, more really worthless poetry than commonplace thought and feeling in ornate language; but its worthlessness is more patent. There is this one advantage, that the critic is not forced to dwell upon it: no one's taste is perverted, except perhaps in the first charm of the poet's novelty. No one now pretends to admire the dulness

and twaddle in Wordsworth; and in Clough even more than in Wordsworth the expression rises and falls with the matter: the dullest and most trivial things are the worst put. We will only say that the genius of twaddle, which often hovers near his muse, makes its presence especially felt in his last poems, the *Mari Magno* tales. These must, of course, be judged as unfinished productions; but no retouching could have enabled them to rank very high as poetry. They are easy, pleasant, even edifying reading, and they essentially want effectiveness. They are written in obvious emulation of Crabbe; and in a natural and faithful homeliness of style, which occasionally becomes a transparent medium for a most impressive tenderness, they certainly rival Crabbe; but their general level is much lower. The charm of Crabbe, when he is not tender, lies in the combination of unobtrusive dignity, and a certain rustic raciness and pregnancy, with a fair share of the artificial point and wit that properly belong to the Popian measure. Clough has nothing of this; and though in the best passages his characteristic fineness of apprehension makes amends, on the dead levels of narration the style is much inferior to Crabbe's: its blankness is glaring. In the first tale especially the genius of twaddle reigns supreme; it reminds us of—we will not say the worst, for it has no bad taste, but—the second-rate portions of Coventry Patmore.

The inferiority of these poems is due, as we before hinted, to a deeper cause than a temporary defect of vigour or a mistaken experiment of style. It is evident that we have here Clough without his peculiar inspiration—his talent, we may say, but not his genius. As an artist he is noteworthy—his production has many high qualities, viewed as technically as possible; it is not, however, as a mere artist, but as an utterer of peculiar yet representative moods, that he has the power to excite our deepest interest. But these moods are the moods, in the main, of youth; and when Clough, after a period of more than usually prolonged adolescence, finally adopted the adult attitude towards life, they ceased to dominate his habitual thought and feeling. Not that any abrupt change shows itself in him. There were two tempers singularly entwined in him throughout: his letters for the most part present a striking contrast to the contemporary poems. In the latter we find chiefly absorbing effort after an ideally clear vision, a perfect solution of problems: in the former mild practical wisdom, serene submission to the imperfections of life, cheerful acquiescence in "the best under the circumstances." And this quieter tone naturally grew upon him. Not that he could ever separate speculation from practice, or in either sphere settle down into smooth commonplace: but he grew tired of turning over the web of commonplace notions and rules, and showing their seamy side: he set himself rather to solve and settle instead of raising and exposing difficulties. At the same time the sincerity which had led him to emphasize his passionate perplexities, still kept him from exaggerating his triumph over them: he attains no fervour of confident hope, nor expansion of complacent optimism: he walks in the twilight, having adapted his eyes to it somewhat, but he does not mistake it for dawn. Whether in such twilight he would ever have seemed to see with sufficient clearness to impel him to utter his vision to the world, is doubtful: at any rate the utterance would, we imagine, have taken a prosaic and not a poetical form. He was looking at life steadily till he could see it whole: aspiring, as he says in an early poem,

> To bring some worthy thing
> For waiting souls to see.

But the very loftiness of this aspiration, and the severity with which he would have judged his own claims to be a teacher, incline us to think that he would never have uttered the final outcome of his life's thought. What he wished to do for the world no one has yet done: we have scarcely reason to believe that he could have done it: and he would have been content to do nothing less. (pp. 384-86)

Henry Sidgwick, in an originally unsigned review of "The Poems and Prose Remains of Arthur Hugh Clough," in The Westminster Review, n.s. *Vol. XXXVI, No. II, October 1, 1869, pp. 363-87.*

RICHARD HOLT HUTTON   (essay date 1877)

[*Hutton was an influential mid-Victorian man of letters who wrote primarily on theological questions and literary subjects. In the following excerpt, he describes the general characteristics of Clough's thought and poetry, comparing his works to those of Johann Wolfgang von Goethe, William Wordsworth, and Geoffrey Chaucer. Hutton's remarks were first published in 1877.*]

[*The Poems and Prose Remains of Arthur Hugh Clough, with a selection from His Letters, and a Memoir* contains] as adequate a picture of the singular but large, simple, and tender nature of the Oxford poet as is attainable, and it is one which no one can study without much profit, and perhaps also some loss; without feeling the high exaltation of true poetry and the keen pleasure caused by the subtlety of true scholarship, at every turn; nor also without feeling now and again those "blank misgivings of a creature moving about in worlds not realised," which are scattered so liberally among these buoyant ardours, disappointed longings, and moods of speculative suspense, and which characterise these singular letters of reticent tenderness and rough self-satire.

Every one who knew Clough even slightly, received the strongest impression of the unusual breadth and massiveness of his mind. Singularly simple and genial, he was unfortunately cast upon a self-questioning age, which led him to worry himself with constantly testing the veracity of his own emotions. He has delineated in four lines the impression which his habitual reluctance to converse on the deeper themes of life made upon those of his friends who were attracted by his frank simplicity. In one of his shorter poems he writes—

> I said my heart is all too soft;
> He who would climb and soar aloft
> Must needs keep ever at his side
> The tonic of a wholesome pride.

This expresses the man in a very remarkable manner. He had a kind of proud simplicity about him, singularly attractive, and often singularly disappointing to those who longed to know him well. He had a fear, which many would think morbid, of leaning much on the approbation of the world; and there is one characteristic passage in his poems, in which he intimates that men who lean on the good opinion of others might even be benefited by a *crime* which would rob them of that evil stimulant:—

> Why so is good no longer good, but crime
> Our truest best advantage; since it lifts us
> Out of the stifling gas of men's opinion
> Into the vital atmosphere of Truth,
> Where He again is visible, though in anger.

So eager was his craving for reality and perfect sincerity, so morbid his dislike even for the unreal conventional forms of life, that a mind quite unique in simplicity and truthfulness represents itself in his poems as

> Seeking in vain, in all my store,
> One feeling based on truth.

Indeed, he wanted to reach some guarantee for simplicity deeper than simplicity itself. I remember his principal criticism on America, after returning from his residence in Massachusetts, was that the New Englanders were much simpler than the English, and that this was the great charm of New England society. His own habits were of the same kind,— sometimes almost austere in their simplicity. Luxury he disliked, and at times his friends thought him even ascetic.

This almost morbid craving for a firm base on the absolute realities of life was very wearying to a mind so self-conscious as Clough's, and tended to paralyse the expression of a certainly great genius. As a rule, his lyrical poems fall short of complete success in delineating the mood which they are really meant to delineate, owing to this chronic state of introspective criticism on himself in which he is apt to write, and which, characteristic as it is, necessarily diminishes the linearity and directness of the feeling expressed, refracting it, as it were, through media of very variable density. As he himself,—no doubt in this stanza delineating himself,—says of one of his heroes in **"The Clergyman's First Tale":**—

> With all his eager motions still there went
> A self-correcting and ascetic bent,
> That from the obvious good still led astray,
> And set him travelling on the longest way.

And in the same poem there are descriptive touches which very skillfully portray the nature of those dispersive influences, as I may call them, in his character, which, while they may injure his lyrical, add a great wealth of criticism to his speculative and disquisitional poems:—

> Beside the wishing-gate, which so they name
> 'Mid Northern hills, to me this fancy came;
> A wish I formed, my wish I thus expressed:
> *"Would I could wish my wishes all to rest,*
> *And know to wish the wish that were the best!*
> Oh, for some winnowing wind to th' empty air
> This chaff of easy sympathies to bear
> Far off, and leave me of myself aware!"

That is clearly self-portraiture, and it describes an element in Clough's nature which, no doubt, contributed greatly to diminish the number of his few but exquisite lyrical poems, and sometimes to confine even those to the delineation of feelings of a certain vagueness of drift. Yet there was, besides this most subtle and almost over-perfect intellectual culture in Clough, much of a boyish, half-formed nature in him, even to the last; and this, when fully roused, contributed a great deal of the animation, and, when least roused, contributed not a little of the embarrassed, shy, half-articulate tone to some of the most critical passages of his finest poems. He describes this side of boyish feeling admirably in one of his *In Mari Magno* tales:—

> How ill our boyhood understands
> Incipient manhood's strong demands!
> Boys have such trouble of their own
> As none, they fancy, e'er have known,
> Such as to speak of, or to tell
> They hold were unendurable:

Religious, social, of all kinds,
That tear and agitate their minds.
A thousand thoughts within me stirred
Of which I could not speak a word;
Strange efforts after something new
Which I was wretched not to do;
Passions, ambitions, lay and lurked,
Wants, counter-wants, obscurely worked
Without their names, and unexplained.

And even in his latest and most finished poems you see the traces of this half-developed element of Clough's massive and rich but to some extent inert imagination; and you see, too, how powerfully it operated to discontent him with his own productions, to make him underrate vastly their real worth. Rapidly as his genius ripened at an age when, with most men, the first flush of it would have passed over, there was something of conscious inertia, not unlike immaturity, in it to the last, which gives a tone of proud hesitation, a slowness of hand, to the literary style of his finest poems. He calls himself, in [*The Bothie of Tober-na-Vuolich: A Long Vacation Pastoral*], "the grave man, nicknamed Adam," and there is really something of the flavour of primeval earth, of its unready vigour and crude laboriousness, about his literary nature. Even when he succeeds best, the reader seems to see him "wipe his honourable brows bedewed with toil." And yet he is impatient with himself for not succeeding better, and despises his own work.

The *Long Vacation Pastoral* belongs to a class of poems that is scarcely naturalised in England—the class of which Goethe's *Hermann and Dorothea* is, perhaps, the most perfect specimen, though in vigour and breadth of imagination, Clough's pastoral is certainly superior. Goethe's influence over the school of poetry of which Matthew Arnold and Clough have been the most considerable English disciples, is very powerfully marked. There is the same longing after the old Homeric simplicity,—less successful perhaps in a cultivated Englishman than in the more childlike German,—the same love of homely naturalness of manner, of the wholesome flavour of earth, an even deeper desire to tame or exercise all romance that is alien to common sense, and the same intellectual disposition to give common sense the casting vote, wherever there seems to be a conflict between it and the thirst of their own natures for something deeper. Moreover, in Clough's poem there is the same underlying theme which haunted Goethe so constantly,—the wish to analyse the true secret of womanly fascination; and, finally, the keynote of the answer given in the *Long Vacation Pastoral* is also the keynote of the *Hermann and Dorothea*, that the highest charms of women consist in a certain union between homely usefulness and classical beauty, in the graceful cutting of bread-and-butter, like Werther's "Charlotte," or graceful "potato-uprooting," like Philip's heroine in Clough's *Pastoral*. As one of his "reading" party expresses it—

All cathedrals are Christian, all Christians are cathedrals:
Such is the Catholic doctrine; 'tis ours with a slight variation.
Every woman is or ought to be a cathedral,
Built on the ancient plan—a cathedral pure and perfect,
Built by that only law, that Use be suggester of Beauty;
Nothing concealed that is done, but all things done to
adornment;
Meanest utilities seized as occasions to grace and embellish.

But if the school of art and the predominant thought which marks Goethe's *Hermann and Dorothea* and Clough's poem

are the same,—if they both alike seek and find their ideal of women in "the freshness of the early world," in some well-born or well-taught maiden,

Milking the kine in the field; like Rachel watering cattle,
Rachel, when at the well the predestined beheld and kissed
her;
Or with pail upon head, like Dora beloved of Alexis,
Comely, with well-poised pail over neck arching soft to
the shoulders,
Comely in gracefullest act, one arm uplifted to stay it,
Home from the river or pump moving stately and calm to
the laundry;

—yet all the imaginative form and framework of Clough's poem are entirely his own,—entirely original, and marked strongly with the stamp of its Oxford origin.

The almost Homeric vigour with which all the characteristics of the reading party are dashed off, the genial humour with which their personal peculiarities are coloured-in, the buoyant life of the discussions which arise among them, the strength with which the Highland scenery is conceived and rendered in a few brilliant touches, the tenderness and simplicity with which now and then the deeper pathos of life is allowed to be seen in glimpses through the intellectual play of the poem, are all Clough's own. He is far more terse, far less prolix, than the great German poet in his style of painting homely nature. There is none of that relaxed fibre which makes scoffers say that Goethe is a little spooney on his Charlotte's bread-and-butter, and his Dorothea's proficiency as a waggoner. Clough's poem is masculine throughout, though the sentiment is, perhaps, not entirely healthy, and the humour certainly is of a kind of which Goethe had little trace. (pp. 286-92)

I have said that, in [Clough's] dread of the romantic school, and his longing for that antique type of nobility in which the simpler and more homely tasks are associated with classical grace and dignity, he had borrowed much from Goethe. But his mind had been also deeply influenced by the very different poetry of Wordsworth in its strong love for a frugal, hardy, and simple industry as the highest school of human character. And perhaps, too, in spite of his steady preference of Aristotle to Plato, of common sense to what he thought idealism, of what is common to what is high, the deep and sometimes transcendental musing of Wordsworth's meditative mind had a charm for him of which he was almost ashamed. At all events, there is a gleam of transcendental depth and subtlety here and again in this poem, shyly—almost apologetically—put forth, and scarcely put forth but to be withdrawn. The lines in which Elspie confesses her love for Philip, the radiant poet, are couched in a very different key from that of Goethe's naturalistic school,—a different, and I think a higher, key:—

And she was silent some time, and blushed all over, and
answered
Quietly, after her fashion, still knitting, "Maybe I think
of it,
Though I don't know that I did"; and she paused again.
"But it may be;
Yes, I don't know, Mr. Philip, but only it feels to me
strangely
Like to the high new bridge they used to build at, below
there,
Over the burn and glen on the road. You won't under-
stand me.

But I keep saying in my mind—this long time, slowly with
    trouble,
I have been building myself up, up, and toilfully raising,
Just like as if the bridge were to do it itself without ma-
    sons,
Painfully getting myself upraised one stone on another,
All one side, I mean; and now I see on the other
Just such another fabric uprising, better and stronger,
Close to me, coming to join me. And then I sometimes
    fancy,—
Sometimes I find myself dreaming at night about arches
    and bridges,—
Sometimes I dream of a great invisible hand coming down
    and
Dropping the great key-stone in the middle; there in my
    dreaming
There I felt the great key-stone coming in, and through it
Feel the other part,—all the other stones of the archway,
Joined into mine, with a strange happy sense of complete-
    ness. But, dear me,
This is confusion and nonsense. I mix all the things I can
    think of,
And you won't understand, Mr. Philip."

This is a definite addition to the great doctrine of the poem,
that women, like flowers, must be "rooted in earth" to be either beautiful or useful—a definite addition and a noble addition. Here we have something of Wordsworth's conception
of the poet:—

> The outward shows of sky and earth,
> Of hill and valley, he has viewed,
> And impulses of deeper birth
> Have come to him in solitude.

There are "impulses of deeper birth" struggling with the naturalism of Clough's chosen school of thought. Still, the great
sea, and the wide omnipresent sunlight, are his favourite symbols of what is divine,—what is broad, bright, and simple,
rather than what is lofty, mysterious, and dim.

Clough always seems to have needed external stimulus, something of excitement in the atmosphere, for his best poetic success. Thus, the siege of Rome during his residence there in
1849 was the stimulus which gave rise to his very original and
striking poem, *Amours de Voyage,*—a poem brimful of the
breath of his Oxford culture, of Cardinal Newman's metaphysics, of classical tradition, of the political enthusiasm of
the time, and of his own large, speculative humour, subtle
hesitancy of brain, and rich pictorial sense. Yet so ill-satisfied
was he with this striking poem, that he kept it nine years in
MS., and published it apologetically at last only in an American magazine, the *Atlantic Monthly.* He himself says that
what he doubted about in it was not its truth of conception,
but its vigour and execution [see letters by Clough dated
1849]. Yet no execution could have been more perfect of the
picture—a picture of inchoacy, I admit—which he intended
to draw. Mr. Emerson has in some cases shown himself a fine
critic; but he never made a more egregious blunder than when
he found fault with Clough for not making this poem end
more satisfactorily [see letter dated 1858]. The whole meaning and drift of it would have been spoiled if it had so ended.
His idea was to draw a mind so reluctant to enter on action,
shrinking so morbidly from the effects of the "ruinous force
of the will," that even when most desirous of action it would
find a hundred trivial intellectual excuses for shrinking back
in spite of that desire. His own explanation of the poem is
contained in the final verse:—

> So go forth to the world, to the good report and the evil!
> Go, little book! thy tale, is it not evil and good?

> Go, and if strangers revile, pass quietly by without answer.
> Go, and if curious friends ask of thy rearing and age,
> Say, "I am flitting about many years from brain unto brain
>   of
> Feeble and restless youths born to inglorious days:
> But," so finish the word, "I was writ in a Roman chamber,
> When from Janiculan heights thundered the cannon of
>   France."

And it is this brain of what the author chooses to call "feeble
and restless youths born to inglorious days" that the poem
is meant to delineate throughout,—its speculative discontent,
its passion for the abstract, its dread of being committed to
a course, its none the less eager craving for action and for the
life that can only be reached through action, its driftings and
reactions;—and all this is artistically contrasted with the
great Roman stage on which so many great dramas had been
enacted in years gone by, and whereon one great revolutionary drama was going forward at that very moment. To my
mind, the poem would lose half its character and meaning if
the hero's incipiency of passion had been developed into anything but incipiency, if it had not faded away, just as it is represented as doing, with the first difficulties, into a restless but
still half-relieved passiveness. The irony of the poem, with its
background of Mazzinian and Garibaldian achievement,
would have been utterly spoiled by any other conclusion.
How perfect a picture of the paralysis caused by too subtly
speculative a nature is there in such lines as these, for example, in which the hero declares his intention to abide by the
indications of the first adverse throw of fortune:—

> Great is Fate, and is best. I believe in Providence partly.
> What is ordained is right, and all that happens is ordered.
> *Ah, no, that isn't it! But yet I retain my conclusion.*
> I will go where I am led, and will not dictate to the
>   chances.

Amours de Voyage would indeed have been spoiled, if it had
ended "prettily," like any other novel.

The oftener I return to Clough's unfinished but striking
poems, the more I am struck by something in their fresh natural handling, and a certain lustre of sunlight on their surface, which suggests to me a modern and intellectualised
Chaucer; and I think the same homely breadth and simplicity
were strongly marked in his countenance. Of course, the
whole essence of such genius is changed by the intellectual
conditions of Clough's age, and the still higher intellectual
conditions of his personal career. But the characteristic is
only the more strongly marked for such striking and fundamental variations; and had he lived to fill more completely
with his individual genius, and to complete the beautiful fragments of tales which are entitled *In Mari Magno,* every one
would have noticed not merely an external resemblance in
structure and scheme, but a very close analogy in genius between the *Canterbury Tales* by the father of English poetry,
and the series by this later representative of our academic
school. His Chaucer-like love of the natural simplicities of life
was probably Clough's strongest creative impulse; his mode
of describing is in the same style of bold, direct, affectionate
feeling for the earth and the true children of the earth; and
the homely though polished pathos of his stories have again
and again filled me with like haunting associations, even
when the analogy was so much disguised by the different intellectual accent of our time that its secret was not easy to
catch. . . .

Look, again, at Clough's feeling for women's beauty; the mingled breadth and tenderness of his drawing, his keen sense of the healthy simplicity of true womanliness, his constant preference for the true woman rather than the true lady, his evident bias for that which has its root in the homely earth, though it attains a beauty which earth alone could never give; it is Chaucer become conscious of the difference between his own inner mind and the taste of our modern intellectual day. Chaucer describes his ideas of feminine loveliness in the person of Blanche, wife of John of Gaunt, thus:—

> I sawgh hir daunce so comeley,
> Carole and synge so swetely,
> Laughe and pleye so womanly,
> And loke so debonairly;
> So goodely speke, and so friendly;
> That, certes, I trow that evermore
> Nas [was not] seyne so blysful a tresore.
> For every heer on hir hede,
> Sothe to seyne, hyt nas not rede,
> Ne nouther yelowe, ne browne, hyt nas,
> Me thought most lyke golde hyt was.
> And whiche eyen [eyes] my lady hadde!
> Debonaire, goode, glade, and sadde [grave],
> Symple, of goode mochel, nought to wide.
> Therto hir looke was not asyde,
> Ne overtwert, but besette to wele,
> It drew and took everydele,
> Alle that on hir gonne beholde.

And now let me take an extract from one of Clough's tales to compare with this picture of Chaucer's:—

> A highland inn amongst the western hills.
> A single parlour, single bed, that fills
> With fisher or with tourist as may be;
> A waiting maid as fair as you can see,
> With hazel eyes and frequent blushing face,
> And ample brow, and with a rustic grace
> In all her easy ample motions seen,
> Large of her age, which haply is nineteen;
> Christian her name, in full a pleasant name,
> Christian and Christie scarcely seem the same.
> A college fellow who has sent away
> The pupils he has taught for many a day,
> And comes for fishing and for solitude,
> Perhaps a little pensive in his mood,
> An aspiration and a thought have failed,
> Where he had hoped, another has prevailed,
> But to the joys of hill and stream alive,
> And in his boyhood yet at twenty-five.
>
> A merry dance that made young people meet,
> And set them moving both with hands and feet:
> A dance in which he danced and nearer knew
> The soft brown eyes, and found them tender too.
> A dance that lit in two young hearts the fire,
> The low soft flame of loving sweet desire,
> And made him feel that he could feel again;
> The preface this what follows to explain.

Of course the parallel must not be pushed too far, for even Chaucer, if possessed of all the new culture, and striving to harmonise it with his large, simple, healthy, human tastes, would become quite a new man. And no doubt Clough's poetry is in nature and essence intellectual. Still there is no poet of our generation whose intellectuality gives less of the effect of a thinning and refining away of life to a shadow, than Clough.

Such subtlety as there is in Clough is of a broad, sweeping, comprehensive kind; not the fine instinct with which Tenny-

son, for instance, follows out one by one a hundred shadowy paths of imaginative reasoning, but the wide subtlety which hovers hither and thither over one or two of the greater chasms that separate thought from action. The ground quakes under Clough's feet at points where generally it would be supposed firm; and where ordinary men's imaginative doubts begin, his scarcely reach. The effect on his poetry is to exercise his imagination in depicting not so much universal feelings as the craving of the cultivated mind for *permission* to surrender itself to them. In some of his most characteristic verses he asks:—

> What we, when face to face we see
> The Father of our souls, shall be,
> John tells us, does not yet appear;
> Ah! did he tell what we are here!
>
> A mind for thoughts to pass into,
> A heart for loves to travel through,
> Five senses to detect things near,
> Is this the whole that we are here?
>
> Rules baffle instincts—instincts rules,
> Wise men are bad—and good are fools;
> Facts evil—wishes vain appear,
> We cannot go, why are we here?
>
> O may we for assurance' sake,
> Some arbitrary judgment take,
> And wilfully pronounce it clear
> For this or that 'tis we are here?
>
> Or is it right, and will it do,
> To pace the sad confusion through,
> And say: "It doth not yet appear,
> What we shall be, what we are here"?
>
> Ah! yet when all is thought and said,
> The heart still overrules the head;
> Still what we hope we must believe,
> And what is given us, receive;
>
> Must still believe; for still we hope
> That in a world of larger scope,
> What here is faithfully begun
> Will be completed, not undone.
>
> My child, we still must think, when we
> That ampler life together see,
> Some true result will yet appear
> Of what we are, together, here.

This [poem, **"Through a Glass Darkly"**], like almost all Clough's poems of this class, presents the effect of a homely, simple, human beauty, half undermined by fundamental doubts,—doubts suggested, indeed, only to be partially abandoned, but also to be partially maintained, as a preservative against the blind eager confidence of presumptuous faith. The massive and genial sympathy which Clough feels with the universal instincts of human nature, alike religious and social, is the first marked feature that strikes us in all his poems: then the sifting process begins of tracing them to their roots, showing how much wider is the trust placed in them in the practical conduct of modern life, than it is possible to justify intellectually; and then when he has pared these instincts down to their minimum of meaning, and we have been shown how impossible our whole life would be if they were given no greater validity than that, they are permitted, though with hesitation and a doubtful or rather hypothetical confidence, to take back something of their natural authority, now that it is fairly shown to be liable to all kinds of presumptuous error.

No doubt, this sort of large, half-genial suspense of judgment, that looks upon natural instincts with a sort of loving doubt, and yields with cautious hand a carefully stinted authority to human yearnings in order not wholly to lose a share in the moving forces of life, is not likely to be widely popular. With Clough this suspense of human judgment was unfortunately not supplemented by any confident belief in a divine answer to those vague yearnings, and consequently his tone is almost always at once sweet and sad. It is saturated with the deep but musical melancholy of such thoughts as the following, whose pathos shows how much more profoundly and deeply Clough thirsted for truth than many of even the most confident of those of us who believe that there is a living water at which to slake our thirst:—

> To spend uncounted years of pain,
> Again, again, and yet again,
> In working out in heart and brain
> The problem of our being here;
> To gather facts from far and near,
> Upon the mind to hold them clear,
> And, knowing more may yet appear,
> Unto one's latest breath to fear
> The premature result to draw—
> Is this the object, end, and law,
> And purpose of our being here?

Yet even in poetry of this kind, which abounds in [*Poems and Prose Remains*], there is something of the same large hesitating melancholy that we should expect, if once a mind of homely Chaucer-like wisdom fell under a cloud of modern doubt. Instead of applying itself, like the ordinary scepticism, to particular riddles, it would touch the whole substance of life, not unkindly, with Clough's questioning finger; treat the fundamental instincts which guide us into our human relations with the same half-confidence; try to separate, even in dealing with "love," the real affinity of nature from the "juxtaposition" of habit, and show the problem to be indeterminate with the same quaint humour. And in things divine it would state the problem as fairly, and substitute a sigh of pathetic hope for the solution, with the same sad fidelity. It may be something of a fancy, but it is at all events a fancy that touches the border of truth, if I recognise even in the type of Clough's genial scepticism something not entirely unlike the scepticism which might pervade the mind of a Chaucer, watching, with the old homely shrewdness as well as the rich modern culture, the swaying tides of our theological debate, and clinging too closely itself to the human forms of beauty and goodness, to come with any clear personal conviction out of the strife.

However, Clough's great literary powers never manifested themselves even to his most intimate friends by any outward sign at all commensurate with the profound belief they had in his genius. But if his powers did not, there was much in his character that did produce its full effect upon all who knew him. He steadily refrained from looking, even in time of severe trial, to his own interest, when what seemed to him higher interests were at issue. He never flinched from the worldly loss which his deepest convictions brought on him. Even when clouds were thick over his own head, and the ground beneath his feet seemed crumbling away, he could still bear witness to an eternal light behind the cloud, and tell others that there is solid ground to be reached in the end by the feet of all who will wait to be strong:—

> Say not, the struggle nought availeth,
> The labour and the wounds are vain,
> The enemy faints not, nor faileth,
> And as things have been, they remain.
>
> If hopes were dupes, fears may be liars,
> It may be, in yon smoke concealed
> Your comrades chased e'en now the fliers,
> And, but for you, possess the field.
>
> For while the tired waves, vainly breaking,
> Seem here no painful inch to gain,
> Far back, through creeks and inlets making,
> Comes silent, flooding in, the main.
>
> And not by eastern windows only,
> When daylight comes, comes in the light:
> In front the sun climbs slow—how slowly!
> But westward, look, the land is bright.

I do not think that any competent judge who really studies Clough's *Remains* will doubt for a moment that he was one of the most original men of our age, and perhaps its most intellectual and buoyant, though very far, of course, from its richest or most musical and exquisite, poet. There is a very peculiar and unique attraction about what I may call the physical and almost animal buoyancy of these subtly intellectual rhythms and verses, when once the mass of the poet's mind—by no means easy to get into motion—is fairly under weigh. Matthew Arnold and Clough both represent the stream of the modern Oxford intellectual tradition in their poems, but how different is their genius. With all his intellectual precision, there is something of the boyishness, of the simplicity, of the vascular Saxon breadth of Chaucer's poetry in Clough; while Mr. Arnold's poetical ancestor is certainly no earlier than Wordsworth. There are both flesh and spirit, as well as emotion and speculation, in Clough; while, in Mr. Arnold, soul and sentiment guide the emotion and the speculation. There is tenderness in both; but Clough's is the tenderness of earthly sympathy, and Mr. Arnold's the lyrical cry of Virgilian compassion. Both fill half their poems with the most subtle intellectual meditations; but Clough leaves the problems he touches, all but where they were, not half settled, reproaching himself for mooning over them so long; while Mr. Arnold finds some sort of a delicate solution, or no-solution, for all of them, and sorts them with the finest nicety. Finally, when they both reach their highest poetical point, Mr. Arnold is found painting lucidly in a region of pure and exquisite sentiment, Clough singing a sort of pæan of buoyant and exultant strength:—

> But, O, blithe breeze, and O, great seas,
> Though ne'er, that earliest parting past,
> On your wide plain they join again,
> Together lead them home at last!
> One port, methought, alike they sought,
> One purpose hold where'er they fare.
> O, bounding breeze, O, rushing seas,
> At last, at last, unite them there!

(pp. 294-309)

Richard Holt Hutton, "Arthur Hugh Clough," in his Literary Essays, *third edition, Macmillan and Co., Limited, 1888, pp. 286-309.*

JOHN MACKINNON ROBERTSON   (essay date 1887)

[*Robertson contends that, despite their poetic form,* The Bothie of Tober-na-Vuolich *and* Amours de Voyage *bear a strong re-*

lation to English fiction and had a significant impact on its development. In an unexcerpted portion of his essay, Robertson examines the history of English fiction until the time Clough wrote his poems. Robertson's comments first appeared in 1887.]

To some readers of the various appreciative criticisms which have been passed upon Arthur Hugh Clough, it must have seemed odd that the friendly writers should have so little to say of the poet's measure of success in a pursuit which bulked largely in his artistic work—the writing, in the verse form, of what is none the less analytic fiction. Setting aside the ***Mari Magno: or, Tales on Board,*** which are also character studies, about half his verse is made up simply of ***The Bothie of Tober-na-Vuolich*** and ***Amours de Voyage;*** and to the critic of fiction the latter production cannot well fail to be at least interesting, while the former is known to have interested a good many readers who would not profess to be specially critical. So silent, however, has criticism been on the subject, that there is probably an air of extravagance about an attempt to show that Clough was a great and original artist in fiction. (p. 301)

If . . . British fiction in 1848-9 was on the whole . . . imperfectly intellectual, so much the more would be the merit of any man who at one stride attained the higher level; and this achievement it is that I venture to claim for Clough, in respect of these two works of his which are in form hexameter poems, but are in essence works of narrative, analytical, psychological fiction. Little read as they still are in proportion to their merits, I will rather assume them to be known to my readers than recapitulate their contents, as the mere telling of their simple stories would reveal nothing of their charm and power, which can only be gathered from a deliberate perusal. What really needs to be pressed is the relation that such works bear to the contemporary novel, and the faculty for fiction to which they testify. In the criticism of Clough's own generation one finds indeed some tribute to the power of the character-sketching in both the ***Bothie*** and the ***Amours;*** but—and this is the special point—no clear perception that just this merit, in the circumstances, took the two works out of the list of poetic successes and placed them high among the fictional, where alone could any analogous art be found, and where, further, it would be hard to find anything equally subtle in the same line. Doubtless it was the simple fact of Clough's having written in hexameters that stood mainly in the way of the proper classification; and it will be necessary to consider what that fact substantially amounts to.

What seems to me to have been done by those who say that Clough proved we could have good English poetry in hexameters is: having found that a work in hexameters may be entirely successful in its art, to assume that it is therefore first-rate hexameter verse. Now, the literary question raised by Clough's hexameters is rather too complex to be so simply disposed of. It includes, to begin with, the old question as to what the technical "values" of poetry really are; and on this there is need to guard against obscuring the issue by discussing the kind of impression we get from those classic poets to whom the hexameter was native. Asking rather what are the constituent elements of our own best poetry, we find that they may be resolved into effects of cadence, consonance, and concentrated and charming verbal expression; that without these the verse form has no value, whatever be its metre; and that no metrical form, as such, gives the least permanent security for their presence. It almost follows from this that true poetic values, unalloyed by effects which are not such as to justify the verse form, can only be had from short poems—that all

lengthy works in verse inevitably involve much inferior performance, and that such works must rely for their acceptance on the reader's pleasure in the successful passages inducing him to tolerate the others. For a variety of reasons, I believe that Clough quite felt all this, at least in his younger days; and I accordingly do not believe that in writing the ***Bothie*** and the ***Amours*** he was aiming at strictly poetical effects at all. . . . On the face of the matter, very much of the ***Bothie*** and of the ***Amours*** is humorous; in fact, humour, buoyant in the first and sombre and subtle in the second, pervades the whole conception of the two works; which is as much as to say that they are not to be classed as poetry proper, if indeed they are to be called poetry at all. I am, however, sufficiently conscious of the psychological difficulties of the problem to prefer waiving the last challenge, and simply to say that where verse is humorous its effects, granting them to have certain analogies with those strictly poetic, certain properties which clearly belong to the verse form, are nevertheless of a distinctly different order from those others. This may seem at bottom a truism, but on the acceptance of it there depends such a point of practice as the deciding not to give the same name to horse and ass because both are cattle for riding. Humorous verse has undoubtedly this quality in common with beautiful verse, that when it is quite successful we return to it on the sheer strength of the fascination of the words, in their kind; and such charm over us is assuredly a special credential of the finest verse. It is the words, and the order of the words, that make the poetry; not the ideas as it might be paraphrased in any prose form, however accurately. But since the "rhythmical creation of beauty," to use Poe's phrase, has thus so inexpressibly different an effect from that of the rhythmical creation of amusement, an effect so much more different from the latter than from that of fairly elevated prose, one hardly cares to give the name of poetry to both. I would finally say, then, that Clough wrote in hexameters because there was a certain artistic effect he was able to get from hexameters, which served his purpose, but which he never regarded as the same in kind with that which he aimed at in his finer rhymed poetry. And this particular artistic effect, accruing to the hexameter as he handled it, was not, as I take it, a strictly metrical or cadencial effect at all, but one of delicately humorous parody—so delicate that while the humour was often effusive it could be refined away at need till it put no check on a perfectly serious intonation and purpose. Clough, in short, wrote in hexameters not because he thought that special metre, *quâ* metre, tractable to serious verse, but because the hexameter was the metre of Homer and Virgil to begin with, and thus afforded endless opportunities for jests of style that would appeal to academic readers; and because further there was no blank measure in which pungency and piquancy could be better maintained at less cost of enforced dignity. He had thus the two resources of parody of classic manner and parody of rhythm in general; a combination, I suppose, the more difficult to analyse and describe truly because it is so unique. (pp. 306-10)

Why did Clough write in verse at all if his purpose was to any extent serious fiction? I would say, on that, that he happened at a particular period to be steeped in Greek verse, and at the same time overflowing with "criticism of life" as he saw it around him; and that he found in these works of his the fittest expression possible for him at the moment. It so happened that he could write elastically and spontaneously at the given time in the given manner; the manner being in itself a stimulus peculiarly fit in his case. He seems never to have written prose with any such facility as is shown in the ***Bothie,*** which would appear to have taken only somewhere about a month in the writing: his prose essays are mostly laboured and ineffectual; heavily packed with culled passages of Latin verse; never seeming to kindle all along the line, or to be written because of a clear sense of something to say. They never write themselves: they are composed; and smack of Carlyle and I know not how many other intellectual fashions of his young days. But in the *Bothie* we seem to have the exuberance of a holiday-making undergraduate with the keen judgments, the wide observation, and the musings, of the ripening man. Hence, an artistic success without parallel in its kind. There is, I venture to say, no piece of fiction in the language, within similar compass, which can compare with this for quantity and quality, in its combination of truth, force, and variety of character-drawing, truth of environment, depth of suggestion, and range of association and sympathy. No English writer has yet appeared who has shown the skill to pack such a picture and commentary as that of the opening banquet-scene into anything like the same space of prose. Told in prose at the same length, indeed, the multifold description and episode would have an air of crowding, of willed terseness, such as we have in Flaubert's *Salammbô;* whereas the verse, with all its load of significance, seems positively to loiter by the way, in the mock-Homeric and Miltonic iterations of epithets and dallyings with phrases and descriptions. It seems to be written for the sheer humour of the thing; and yet Thackeray could not have better have turned the humour to the account of the portraiture. Admiring notice has been taken by Mr. W. M. Rossetti [see Further Reading] of one line which conveys a whole story:

> Pipers five or six, among them *the young one, the*
> *drunkard.* . . .

The tutor, "the grave man, nicknamed Adam," so admirably exhibited by a series of incidental, effortless dramatic touches as the story goes on, is already permanently outlined by that phrase and the lines on his dress; the "shrewd ever-ciphering factor" is as it were henceforth identifiable; the whole cast of character of each of the students seems to be known definitely once for all; even the *attaché* and the Guardsman are individualised by an imperceptible touch; the Marquis of Ayr gesticulates before us; and Sir Hector, in particular, is at once photographed and permanently revealed by a few lines of burlesque comment and the incomparable report of his toast-speech on *The Strangers,* the entire creation being accomplished in a sort of unconscious addendum to the scholar's smiling apostrophe:

> Bid me not, grammar-defying, repeat from grammar-
> defiers
> Long constructions strange and plusquam-Thucydidean.

—the last epithet a paragraph in itself. There lacks nothing to indicate the entire Highland environment; and with the all-round allusion there is thrown in one entirely sufficient vignette of the student's living-place and bathing-place:

> Where over a ledge of granite
> Into a granite basin the amber torrent descended,
> Only a step from the cottage, the road and the larches be-
> tween them.

So matchlessly vivid is it all that one could almost swear it a faithful transcript from actual fact; but the chances are that the total opening section, like the piece as a whole, is an artistic combination of various recollections and various fancies. In the first edition the "pastoral" is thus dedicated: "My

long-vacation pupils will I hope allow me to inscribe this trifle to them, and will not, I trust, be displeased if in a fiction, purely fiction, they are here and there reminded of times we enjoyed together." It could be wished that some of these pupils had put on record, for the enlightenment of future critics, some note as to the element of traceable fact in the artistic whole.

The easily evolving story of the *Bothie* is so steadily pregnant from first to last that to touch on all its good points would be to make a commentary much longer than the book; and it must suffice me here to touch on one or two points only before turning to the *Amours de Voyage.* One is, the success with which Clough has given us, in Hewson, a type of hot-headed young enthusiast, in such a way as to secure abundant sympathy and full understanding, without for a moment turning him into a hero and challenging our homage. Where before had anything of the kind been done? I cannot recall a youthful Radical in English fiction who is not either intellectually magnified, or handled with a hostile animus, or thrust down our throats. In Clough there is no such malpractice: the lad is treated with absolute insight and absolute kindliness, yet without a shade of flattery, and becomes for us, enthusiast as he is, as absolutely real as Sir Hector, or as any observed personage in any novel; and how much fictional skill went to doing this can only be indicated by suggesting a comparison of Hewson with any other imagined young democrat the reader can think of, Felix Holt included. Another noteworthy feature is the presentment of the girl Elspie Mackaye, a study which may be suspected of idealism, but which is yet wonderfully true, as those who have known the Highlands at all widely or intimately can testify. Elspie is perhaps specifically the Highland girl of a fine type as one sees her in vacation-time; but, granting that, she is charmingly well drawn; and the proportion of idealisation is, it may be said without hesitation, much below that infused in Dorothea Brooke or Maggie Tulliver, not to speak of Myra and Romola. It may be doubted, indeed, if she is not to the full as true as Ethel Newcome. Now, this again constitutes a great success, when it is considered how lightly, how dramatically, Clough has laid his touches on. Girls of the people we have had in abundance in more recent fiction; but one so estimable and yet so little idealised, or one drawn with such strong simplicity, it will not be easy to call to mind; and I can think of nothing so good of earlier date.

A power to paint women of another type might very safely have been inferred from the sketch of Elspie in the *Bothie;* but the *Amours de Voyage* furnishes the decisive proof. Having the encouragement of the judgment of most of his readers to consider the *Bothie* a success, Clough made his next attempt at fiction an essay in hexameters likewise; this time, however, so obviously disclaiming a poetic purpose, by throwing his story into the form of letters, that the fact of its not having been generally dealt with as a novel is a little surprising. The power of the character studies in the *Amours,* as in the *Bothie,* has not been overlooked; but what has been awanting is the distinct recognition that in both works the versifier has surpassed the existing prose fiction on its own ground. For the whole work of these Italian letters is no less fine, if less brilliant in form, than that of the earlier composition; the quieter tone being in fact the outcome of the greater subtlety of the study. What he attempted in this case was a study of the mind of a cultured and original Englishman in Rome, as acted upon on the one hand by the historic associations of the city and the contemporary problems connected with that history, and on the other by his intercourse with the inevitable person of the other sex, with whom he gradually falls in love, though the affair, so far as the story goes, comes to nothing. Told in its scanty detail, the narrative is about as slight as a fiction could well be; but it is just the investing of such a plot with permanent interest that makes the work the masterpiece it is. As in the earlier piece, the workmanship is perfect nearly all round. There is no inadequacy. The commentary on Rome and its history; the sketch of the acquaintances whose appearance on the scene begins the story; the man's self-criticism and self-satire; the woman's reticent self-revelation; the prattle of the sister; the interludes on the Roman political situation; the chimes of half-elevated song that seem to lend themselves subtly to the note of passion, at first obscure, afterwards swelling to something of a lyric strain, only to die away finally in the minor—it is all masterly, as perfect as it is original. We shall not see just such another performance. Hexameter stories in imitation of Clough would be by many degrees more unsatisfactory than imitations of Whitman, for the simple reason that his work is so infinitely more difficult to equal; but it seems to me to-day, looking first at Clough's work and then at the developments fiction has taken and is taking in Russia, France, and America, that here in England this merely privately famous man of the schools had curiously anticipated later tendencies and achievements by a whole generation. All that is most characteristic of the best new work—the graded half-tints, the simple drawing, the avoidance of glare and melodrama, the search for the essential interest of the normal—all of it belongs to these experiments in hexameters. There has been no equally good portraiture of feminine character *in minimis* and in whole before or since. But, what is more, Clough had really philosophised his fiction in a style quite beyond the faculty of all but one or two of the moderns; contriving to make an intellectual man both ideally impressive and artistically true; a rare feat in the novel, where the anatomy of the higher grades of mind has hitherto been attempted with so little real success. The forceful simplicity of the unpretentious drawing of Claude can be best appreciated when contrasted with the labour bestowed on Daniel Deronda—and the result. Clough's work has the masculine weight and precision that in Turguénief make a short story live in the reader's mind like a great experience. Much tolerable workmanship will be forgotten before this.

There is, indeed, an air of paradox in saying that one of the ablest performances in modern fiction, which at its best is above all things naturalistic, is one cast in the artificial form of letters in verse; and certainly the phenomenon is fitted to make us very careful how we theorise about right and wrong in art forms. Say what we will about hexameters, it is clear that these verse-novels of Clough's are "idealised" work as beside prose realism: so far as treatment goes, the method is obviously not that of naturalist fiction. In fact, Clough is at times not careful to preserve verisimilitude even within his artistic limits; as when he makes one of Mary Trevellyn's letters to Miss Roper begin thus:

> You are at Lucca baths, you tell me, to stay for the summer;
> Florence was quite too hot; you can't move further at present.
> Will you not come, do you think, before the summer is over?

Since the letter could obviously have been made to read in a less impossible manner and yet convey all the facts required,

the workmanship here must be pronounced faulty. But, making allowance for such faults of detail, which belong to inexperience in an uncommon method, what could be more essentially naturalistic than the whole presentment of the women's cast of mind and way of taking things? It is singular how perfectly the contents of actual letters are suggested in Clough's hexameters; so scrupulously sunk to the strictly prosaic level, wherever necessary, as to stop just short of the flavour of burlesque. Lines which in themselves are absolutely *banal*, conveying epistolary phrases also *banal* in themselves, yet curiously retain just the needful artistic value for the suggestion of a girl's femininely veiled emotions and hopes and fears; the commonplace letter becomes alive for us by its burden of narrative implication, very much as it would in a novel as realistic as sifted prose could make it. Indeed we may search a hundred prose novels in vain for such delicate fidelity of suggestion. The touches in the portrait are as refined as any of Mr. Henry James; and yet how much more real is the lady than some of that artist's presentments!

But no less essentially true, on the other hand, does the painting remain when it rises above the commonplace into sheer poetry, as in these fine lines in which Claude comments on the failure of the Italian rising:

> Whither depart the souls of the brave that die in the battle,
> Die in the lost, lost fight, for the cause that perishes with them?
> Are they upborne from the field on the slumberous pinions of angels
> Unto a far-off home, where the weary rest from their labour,
> And the deep wounds are healed, and the bitter and burning moisture
> Wiped from the generous eyes? or do they linger unhappy,
> Pining, and haunting the grave of their bygone hope and endeavour?

If there were any danger of this apostrophe lessening our sense of the reality of the sceptical, critical young Englishman, unrestfully musing at Rome, it would be sufficiently averted by the unflinching fall of key and pitch that follows:

> All declamation, alas! though I talk, I care not for home nor
> Italy; feebly and faintly, and but with the lips can lament the
> Wreck of the Lombard youth, and the victory of the oppressor.
> Whither depart the brave?—God knows; I certainly do not.

The snatch of poetry, equally with the half-real half-affected cynicism, and with the general mordant criticism on Rome and humanity and its ways, is part of the presentation of the young man's mind; a true product of the century in its restless analysis of its instincts. Nothing in the story is more dramatically convincing than the hero's passage from the analytical mood to that of charmed surrender to the feminine attraction he had just been analysing. Half-way, we have this:—

> Allah is great, no doubt, and Juxtaposition his prophet.
> Ah, but the women, alas! they don't look at it in that way.
> Juxtaposition is great;—but, my friend, I fear me, the maiden
> Hardly would thank or acknowledge the lover that sought to obtain her,
> Not as the thing he would wish, but the thing he must even put up with . . . .
> Ah, ye feminine souls, so loving, and so exacting,

Since we cannot escape, must we even submit to deceive
    you?
Since, so cruel is truth, sincerity shocks and revolts you,
Will you have us your slaves to lie to you, flatter and—
    leave you?

The girl indeed did not "look at it that way;" the one sex
being as faithfully reproduced as the other. Her first judgment is perfectly "observed":

I do not like him much, though I do not dislike being with
    him.
He is what people call, I suppose, a superior man, and
Certainly seems so to me; but I think he is terribly selfish.

Later we learn from the silly sister that

Mary allows she was wrong about Mr. Claude *being self-
    ish;*
He was *most* useful and kind on the terrible thirtieth of
    April.

And in a postscript:

Mary has seen thus far.—I am really so angry, Louisa—
Quite out of patience, my dearest! What can the man be
    intending?
I am quite tired; and Mary, who might bring him to in a
    moment,
Lets him go on as he likes, and neither will help nor dis-
    miss him.

He indeed did not make rapid progress, for before the doctrine of Juxtaposition we had this:

I am in love, you declare. I think not so; yet I grant you
It is a pleasure indeed to converse with this girl. Oh, rare
    gift,
Rare felicity, this! she can talk in a rational way, can
Speak upon subjects that really are matters of mind and
    of thinking
Yet in perfection retain her simplicity . . . .
No, though she talk, it is music; her fingers desert not the
    keys; 'tis
Song, though you hear in the song the articulate vocables
    sounded,
Syllabled singly and sweetly the words of melodious
    meaning.
I am in love, you say; I do not think so, exactly.

And still the woman is woman, as in this postscript to a letter
of the silly sister:

. . . . All I can say for myself is, alas! that he rather repels
    me.
There! I think him agreeable, but also a little repulsive.
So be content, dear Louisa; for one satisfactory marriage
Surely will do in one year for the family you would estab-
    lish;
Neither Susan nor I shall afford you the joy of a second.

To which the silly sister adds a post-postscript:

Mr. Claude, you must know, is behaving a little bit better;
He and Papa are great friends; but he really is too *shilly-
    shally,*
So unlike George! Yet I hope that the matter is going on
    fairly.
I shall, however, get George, before he goes, to say some-
    thing.
Dearest Louise, how delightful to bring young people to-
    gether!

And yet again the girl, after a "let us say nothing further

about it" as to a deviation of Mr. Claude from the agreed-on
travelling plan of the party, half opens her heart thus:

Yes, my dear Miss Roper, I certainly called him repulsive;
So I think him, but cannot be sure I have used the expres-
    sion
Quite as your pupil should; yet he does most truly repel
    me.
Was it to you I made use of the word? or who was it told
    you?
Yes, repulsive; observe, it is but when he talks of ideas
That he is quite unaffected, and free, and expansive, and
    easy;
I could pronounce him simply a cold intellectual being.—
When does he make advances?—He thinks that women
    should woo him;
Yet, if a girl should do so, would be but alarmed and dis-
    gusted.
She that should love him must look for small love in re-
    turn; like the ivy,
On the stone wall, must expect but a rigid and niggard
    support, and
E'en to get that must go searching all round with her hum-
    ble embraces.

And he too had his reasons:

Is it my fault, as it is my misfortune, my ways are not her
    ways?
It is my fault that my habits and ways are dissimilar whol-
    ly?
'Tis not her fault; 'tis her nature, her virtue, to misappre-
    hend them;
'Tis not her fault; 'tis her beautiful nature not ever to know
    me.
Hopeless it seems—yet I cannot, though hopeless, deter-
    mine to leave it:
She goes—therefore I go; she moves—I move, not to lose
    her.

And then comes the swerving aside, the result of the silly sister's George having said

Something to Mr. Claude about what they call his atten-
    tions;

and Mary's postscripts multiply, and Miss Roper explains,
and Mr. Claude eagerly decides to follow and propose; and
the travellers journey at cross purposes and never meet; and
the foiled lover, half content to accept the decision of Fate,
decides to winter in Egypt, while the now heart-sore Mary
returns with her party to England. There is something peculiarly modern in this ending that is no ending; something indefinitely in advance, technically speaking, of the symmetrical *denoûments* of previous fiction; something artistically in
advance of much good fiction of our own time. Alike artistically and philosophically the whole is closed by one of the
half-lyric strains which begin and end the cantos:

So go forth to the world, to the good report and the evil!
Go little book! thy tale, is it not evil and good?
Go, and if strangers revile, pass quietly by without answer.
Go, and if curious friends ask of thy rearing and age,
Say "I am flitting about many years from brain unto brain
    of
Feeble and restless youths born to inglorious days:
But," so finish the word, "I was writ in a Roman chamber,
When from Janiculan heights thundered the cannon of
    France."

The end is thus fittingly on the plane of idealist art; and yet
who will say that the whole has not been as rigorously true

a presentment of the literal life as the most determined naturalist could achieve? It is English naturalism, certainly: Clough, whose "name is handed down in William Arnold's *Rules of Football* as the best goal-keeper on record," was substantially English in his tastes. But all the same he had here succeeded in putting into an unlikely enough and ostensibly idealist art-form a piece of character fiction more essentially naturalistic than anything produced anywhere up to his time; nay, more deeply so than anything done in the forty years since, for he had contrived to handle a man's philosophy and a woman's emotions in a love-story with equal ease and verisimilitude, and to give his tale in hexameters a philosophic ripeness without a tinge of pedantry. The critical lesson is the old one that there are no rules for geniuses; that, as it has been put afresh by a gifted though faulty fictionist of our own day, Mr. Moore, "art is eternal; that it is only the artist that changes; and that the two great divisions—the only possible divisions—are, those who have talent, and those who have no talent."

For most men verisimilitude in fiction and drama will be best attainable by the most strictly natural media; but Shakspere, again, could put more reality into blank verse dialogue than the Nashes and Lylys could put into prose; and there is no calculating the capacity of an original faculty to innovate in method, or to lead captive the captivity of form. And I do not scruple to risk derision by thus mentioning Clough in the same breath with Shakspere, being satisfied that he had some measure of Shakspere's endowment; though the scanty recognition of it among his countrymen promises small acceptance for such a view.

It may well be that it is the smallness of Clough's product that has hindered the recognition of his real greatness; mere volume counting for so much in the impression made on the world even by fine work; and it may be too that his comparative failure in serious poetry has affected the general attitude toward his whole remains. I say comparative failure; for his poetry well-nigh makes up by its deep intellectual interest for its lack of the true poetic charm. *Dipsychus* and the rest of it is indeed better worth reading than a good deal of verse of much wider vogue. It has not, however, truly caught either the trained or the untrained ear; and this, with the habit of treating his hexameters as being equally with the rest essays in the poetic art, goes far to account for the limited character of his reputation. Then his *Mari Magno: or, Tales on Board* must have helped to subdue the critical tone in his regard, for here, there can be no doubt, the artistic failure is as complete as the earlier success. To account for it, we must fall back on the accounts we have of Clough's mental constitution—the slowness of his mind to set to work at all times, and the conditions of his health in his later years. He had written his good things under the two strong impulses of physical vigour and Italian travel; and in the absence of similarly happy conditions he produced nothing more that could be ranked beside them. In the *Mari Magno* we have an all too decisive test of the fitness of rhymed verse as a vehicle for narrative that aims at being serious without being archaic; and a proof of Clough's wisdom in choosing the hexameter even where his purpose was not tinged with humour. In that, the freedom of the medium allowed him to be serious and impressive when he wanted; in the rhymed pentameter, applied to fictional purpose, verisimilitude was far harder to reach; and even the simple seriousness that was all he now had in his mind is continually turned to absurdity by the pitfalls of the rhyme. When a man gravely writes in the couplet measure of "A

beauteous woman at the table d'hôte;" and tells how, on board ship, he

> amid a dream
> Of England, knew the letting-off of steam—

artistic charm is over and done with. The couplet, like the hexameter, might have been used humorously; but for a sober, matter-of-fact tale, as Crabbe had sufficiently shown, it is the fatallest of all metrical conveyances.

And yet in these hopeless verses are contained two tales which, in their structure and detail, still betray the mind of a born fictionist; a mind which sees characters instantaneously as organic wholes, and has no more difficulty in presenting them with all their specific differences than a good portraitist has in giving the lines of different faces. We are told that Clough had a wonderful eye for scenery, remembering the hang and lie of roads and hills, streams and valleys, in a fashion that surprised his friends. He had just such a faculty for discriminating character. The slightly-sketched tale-tellers in the *Mari Magno* are like drawings by Keene; and through the racking couplets the people of the stories, especially of the second, keep their form and colour with the same steadiness that is seen in the hexameter novels. The old curious felicity of indicating a character by a few touches is not gone; and the reader, when he can forget the versification, seems to have gained some new knowledge of life from the few pages he has turned over. The people are "observed:" we feel that we have been reading transcripts from actual private histories. . . . Why, with this genius for a great art, Clough did so little in it, and never seemed even to realise clearly where his genius lay—this is a question the answering of which raises divers points as to his total idiosyncrasy, his training, and his intellectual environment.

Something has to be allowed for a constitutional lack of productive energy, otherwise definable as intellectual fastidiousness, the physical side of which is perhaps to be looked for by the clue of the paralysis which finally struck him down after a fever. Of his character as seen in childhood his sister testifies: "One trait I distinctly remember, that he would always do things from his own choice, and not merely copy what others were doing." And again: "Arthur even then was too fastidious to take off his shoes and stockings and paddle about as we did." [see Blanche Smith Clough entry in Further Reading]. The child was father to the man. Nor was native fastidiousness the only force at work. In his prime he gives, in a letter to a friend, this account of his hard schooling:

> I may, perhaps, be idle now; but when I was a boy, between fourteen and twenty-two throughout, I may say, you don't know how much regular drudgery I went through. Holidays after holidays, when I was as school, after a week or so of recreation, which very rarely came in an enjoyable form to me, the whole remaining five or six weeks I used to give to regular work at fixed hours. That wasn't so very easy for a schoolboy spending holidays, not at home, but with uncles, aunts, and cousins. All this and whatever work, less rigorous though pretty regular, that has followed since during the last ten years has been, so far as external results go, perhaps a mere blank and waste; nothing very tangible has come of it; but still it is some justification to me for being less strict with myself now. Certainly, as a boy, I had less of boyish enjoyment of any kind whatever, either at home or at school, than nine-tenths of boys, at any rate of boys who go to school,

Inside a schoolroom at Rugby.

college, and the like; certainly, even as a man I think I have earned myself some title to live for some little interval, I do not say in enjoyment, but without immediate devotion to particular objects, on matters as it were of business.

And to that picture of destructive education he adds another touch in the **"Passage on Oxford Studies"** extracted in the *Prose Remains,* describing the sickness of heart that overtook him on going to the university, at the prospect of endless classics: "An infinite lassitude and impatience, which I saw reflected in the faces of others, quickly began to infect me." Such a youthful experience must have told on the adult man, laming the springs of creative energy and dispiriting the abnormal genius. But it is with a sense of fresh exasperation that one thinks of such a faculty being further weakened for practical performance by the effeminate ecclesiastical atmosphere of the Oxford of the Newman epoch, when currents of febrile mysticism and timorous scepticism drew young men this way and that; not one in a hundred of those affected being able to attain a stable and virile philosophy. Clough himself said afterwards that for two years he had been "like a straw drawn up the draught of a chimney" by the Newman movement; and it would not be going too far to say that if he were not one of those "wrecks" declared by Mr. Gladstone to have been "strewn on every shore" by the academic tempest in question, he was at least left less seaworthy for life. It has become a little difficult to think either of the mystics or of the half-hearted sceptics as men of high intellectual power: it seems a trifle strange in these days that one such as Clough, having once realised the force of the rational criticism of the popular creed, should be unable to robustly readjust his life to the sane theory of things. But so it was. The character-student suffered as much from the disintegration of his inher-

ited faith as did any hectic disciple of them all; and when he found he could be neither Catholic nor Protestant he seemed to lapse into a sense of intellectual homelessness. The English universities, in which the nation's best educational endowments are turned mainly to the account of training men to preach to the illiterate or the unquestioning the religious system of the Dark Ages, seem to unfit men systematically for any independent appraisement or application of their natural powers. (pp. 312-28)

The relevant facts for us here are that Clough, missing what seemed his natural career as a priest, had yet been so permeated by the ecclesiastical and university view of human activity as to be in a measure unfitted to apply his powers in any other way. He could not settle down peacefully in intercourse with men who had definitively turned their backs on an impossible faith: there is evidence that he found such men uncongenial in their decided rationalism, as they doubtless found him in his melancholy retrospectiveness. One feels that just twenty years earlier the same Clough could have quietly found his way into the clerical grooves, like many another man of potential genius, leaving no literary legacy of any importance to his countrymen, and living to face alike Strauss and Newman with the sheathing prejudices of profession and habit. In fine, we may say that he stood in religion and philosophy as he did in his fiction—between two widely-different generations; sundered from the past, but slow to begin to face the future. But whereas his religion had been a profound prepossession, the removal of which taxed his whole moral nature and left him lamed with the struggle, his spontaneous and hardly purposive excursion into the field of intellectual art yielded a remarkable result, suggestive no less of the manifold intellectual forces that lie cramped or latent around us, than of the power of certain institutions and conventions to keep them down.

It is not fitting, however, that the last word on such a personality as Clough's should be a suggestion of frustration. Frustration, after all, is a matter of comparison, and whatever impression he may make on later readers, he was to his own generation, which in that way could best judge him, an impressive and not a weak figure. Let us remember him by the words of one whose name will live with his longer than these comments [see first entry by Mathew Arnold in Further Reading]:

> I mention him because, in so eminent a degree, he possessed these two invaluable qualities—a true sense for his object of study, and a single-hearted care for it. He had both, but he had the second even more eminently than the first. He greatly developed the first through means of the second. In the study of art, poetry, or philosophy, he had the most undivided and disinterested love for his object in itself, the greatest aversion to mixing up with it anything accidental or personal. His interest was in literature itself; and it was this which gave so rare a stamp to his character, which kept him so free from all taint of littleness. In the saturnalia of ignoble personal passions, of which the struggle for literary success, in old and crowded communities, offers so sad a spectacle, he never mingled. He had not yet traduced his friends, nor flattered his enemies, nor disparaged what he admired, nor praised what he despised. Those who knew him well had the conviction that, even with time, those literary arts would never be his. His poem [*The Bothie*] . . . has some admirable Homeric qualities—out-of-door freshness, life, naturalness, buoyant rapidity. . . . But that in him of which I think oftenest, is the Homeric simplicity of his literary life.

Homeric simplicity is perhaps not the description which would suggest itself to most men; but whatever words can serve the literary memory of the author of *The Bothie of Tober-na-Vuolich* and *Amours de Voyage* will be ungrudgingly allowed by those who can appreciate the singular independence of his work. (pp. 329-30)

> *John Mackinnon Robertson, "Clough," in his* New Essays Towards a Critical Method, *John Lane, The Bodley Head, 1897, pp. 301-30.*

STOPFORD A. BROOKE (essay date 1908)

[*Brooke was an Anglo-Irish clergyman, poet, critic, and educator whose* Primer of English Literature *(1876) was popular with generations of students. In the following excerpt, he discusses the poetry and thought of Clough, whom he believes "has been too much neglected" but whom he does not consider a major poet.*]

Of all the poets who played on England as on a harp, Clough was one of the most personal. He was even more personal than Arnold, who could detach himself at times from himself. But Clough was never self-detached in his poetry, even when he tried to be so. He contemplated his soul and its sensitive and bewildered workings incessantly, and saw in them the image of that which was going on in the soul of the younger men in England. Sometimes he is intensely part of the spiritual strife he is conscious of, because he is so conscious of it in himself; sometimes he watches it from without, as a press correspondent might the battle he describes; sometimes, in the course of a single poem, he flits from the inside to the outside position, or from the outside to the inside; but always it is the greater image of his own soul that he watches in the struggle of the whole; always he is intimately close to the trouble or calm, the wondering or the anchoring of the eager, restless, searching, drifting being within, whom he did not wish to be himself. No one is more intimate, more close, more true to this inward life. It is this which makes him so interesting and so much a favourite with those who like him. They see a man in much the same condition as they are, or have been, themselves; they feel that he has been quite true to himself in it, and has done his very best to tell the truth—and to read true things said truly is always a keen, if sometimes a sorrowful pleasure. Moreover, no obscurity, no vagueness, troubles the reader. We are conscious that he has striven with all his might to render the matter in question into the most lucid form he can; and few have put remote and involved matters of the soul into such simple words as Clough.

Again, we see, through all the confused trouble he describes, and in spite of all the wavering and uncertainty, that he has one clear aim—that of getting out of the storm, if possible, into some bright light and quiet air. He does not like the confusion and the questioning, and the trouble, but desires to be quit of them, if this can be done truthfully. He will not shut his eyes to any difficulty, nor retire to his tent while the battle is going on, nor pretend there is no confusion, for the sake of light and sweetness. Truth to himself first—then he will be fit to see the Truth itself, if it be possible. But it is his aim, his hope, his impassioned desire, even in despair, to see it at last. That Truth *is*, he believes; and he sets himself to work his way to it through the tangled forest of life.

> It fortifies my soul to know
> That, though I perish, Truth is so:
> That, howsoe'er I stray and range,
> Whate'er I do, Thou dost not change.
> I steadier step when I recall
> That, if I slip, Thou dost not fall.

To a certain degree then, he was above scepticism. He did not think it a fine condition; the last thing he imagined was that there was any reason for being proud of it; nevertheless he would not move one inch out of it till his reason and conscience together told him he might leave this or that question behind. The only thing he knew was that there was a clear solution to be found somewhere, sometime, in the Truth itself. Even the star of that knowledge was sometimes overwhelmed in clouds. He kept his head and heart however; he was finally master in his soul. He moved amid the disorganised army of his thoughts and emotions, like a great captain who sees and knows the troubled state of his army, and the desperate and broken ground over which it has to advance; who visits every regiment and knows the wants of each; who has entered every tent, who is aware of the fears, doubts, failures, and despairs of every man—but who is determined to lead the army on, because he knows that, far away, there is a safe and quiet resting-place—soft grass and clear streams within a fortified defence—where he can camp them at last, order them, and restore their spirit. Sometimes he is all but hopeless; whence he has brought the armies of his soul he cannot tell; whither they are going he cannot tell; all is doubt and trouble; but again, there are hours of rest when the place whither he is going and its far off light are clear; at times he feels a proud joy in the fighting forwards; at times nothing lives but exhaustion, yet he never thinks of surrender. Here is a poem which puts this life of his into clear, gentle, but impassioned form:

> Where lies the land to which the ship would go?
> Far, far ahead, is all her seamen know.
> And where the land she travels from? Away,
> Far, far behind, is all that they can say.
>
> On sunny noons upon the deck's smooth face,
> Linked arm in arm, how pleasant here to pace;
> Or, o'er the stern reclining, watch below
> The foaming wake far widening as we go.
>
> On stormy nights when wild north-westers rave,
> How proud a thing to fight with wind and wave!
> The dripping sailor on the reeling mast
> Exults to bear, and scorns to wish it past.
>
> Where lies the land to which the ship would go?
> Far, far ahead, is all her seamen know.
> And where the land she travels from? Away,
> Far, far behind, is all that they can say.

Whence and whither our ship came, and goes, and the ship of all humanity, we cannot know, though we may hope to know. We live by faith, not knowledge. Sometimes the battle is illuminated and rejoiced by sudden outflamings of faith; again it is darkened by absolute despair. Faith in God rushes up one day through the crust of doubt and drowns every sceptical thought; the next day, there is no God. Christ is not risen; the day after He is risen. There is no rest, no clear heaven, no knowledge of whence and whither—nothing but tossing to and fro. Even when he falls back on duty, a voice in his heart tells him it is not enough. He must find the unknown Perfect his soul desires.

At last, he is enraged with his condition. Life is slipping away in overthinking, in this way and that dividing the swift mind. The soul, while he is young, is growing old in a diseased confusion. Is this life, he asks, this the end of our stay on earth?

"Perchè Pensa? Pensando S'Invecchia"

> To spend uncounted years of pain,
> Again, again and yet again,
> In working out in heart and brain
> The problem of our being here;
> To gather facts from far and near,
> Upon the mind to hold them clear,
> And, knowing more may yet appear;
> Unto one's latest breath to fear
> The premature result to draw—
> Is this the object, end, and law,
> And purpose of our being here?

There are those who are not troubled by any such questions, simple folk who believe and have peace, and Clough praises their life and thinks them true and happy; at moments he can feel with them, but not for long. There are others who find peace and power to live and work by giving up all questions of this kind as hampering life and useless for good. But Clough was not of that temper, and could not enter its regions. He did his duty, but a tender intensity of passion urged him beyond it to find the rest in perfection. He was the image and the expression of thousands who lived in that disturbed time, when criticism and science set the battle in array against the old theology. It is the image and the expression, even now, after the battle has raged for sixty years, of the condition of a number of persons who are impassioned to find a truth by which they can live, who desire to believe but are unable, who are equally unable to find peace in unbelief. Thus moving, like a Hamlet, through the strifes of theology and religion, he resembles Hamlet in another way. When the Prince is suddenly flung into the storm of action, he takes momentarily a fierce part in it, and enjoys it, till overthinking again seizes on him. Clough repeats this in his life, and his poetry is touched with it.

These are the causes of the pleasure with which we read Clough's earlier poetry—its clear image of a certain type of men and women in a spiritually troubled time, its close contact with and intimate expression of the constantly debating soul, its truthfulness, its sanity amid scepticism, its statement of all sides of the matter in hand, its personal humanity, and its sympathy with man, its self-mastery and its clear aim. There is also plenty of good matter of thought and of emotion worthily controlled—great things in poetry, provided they are expressed poetically. But the poetry itself is not of a high quality; its level is only a third of the way towards greatness; it is imaginative, but the imagination in it never soars and never is on fire, never at a white heat; on the contrary, its play is gentle, soft, touched, like an autumn evening when summer has just died, with tender, clear, brooding light. The greater number of these poems are such as a man who lived in a constant atmosphere of trouble and battle might write, when, wearied with the strife, he enjoyed an hour of forgetful rest after trouble, and of sheathing of the sword after battle; and I do not know of any other poet of whom this may be said so truly. In that he is alone—that is the distinction of these early poems. And this clear, soft, brooding note is just as clearly struck in the poems which have nothing to do with the trouble of the soul, but with matter of the affections. I quote this little idyll: how grave it is, and tender; what an evening light rests upon it; not the light of Italy, but of the northern sky among the mountains. What self-control breathes in it; what a quiet heart, quiet, not by the absence of passion, but by self-restraint, and by that on which Clough so often dwelt and which subdued his poetry so often—by the sense of the inevitable, of a fate which, hemming us in on every side, imposes on us its will, and ignores our struggle and our pain:

"Ite Domum Saturæ, Venit Hesperus"

> The skies have sunk, and tied the upper snow,
> (Home, Rose, and home, Provence and La Palie.)
> The rainy clouds are filing fast below,
> And wet will be the path, and wet shall we.
> Home, Rose, and home, Provence and La Palie.
>
> Ah dear, and where is he, a year agone,
> Who stepped beside and cheered us on and on?
> My sweetheart wanders far away from me,
> In foreign land or on a foreign sea.
> Home, Rose, and home, Provence and La Palie.
>
> The lightning zigzags shoot across the sky,
> (Home, Rose, and home, Provence and La Palie.)
> And through the vale the rains go sweeping by;
> Ah me, and when in shelter shall we be?
> Home, Rose, and home, Provence and La Palie.
>
> Cold, dreary cold, the stormy winds feel they
> O'er foreign lands and foreign seas that stray.
> (Home, Rose, and home, Provence and La Palie.)
> And doth he e'er, I wonder, bring to mind
> The pleasant huts and herds he left behind?
> And doth he sometimes in his slumbering see
> The feeding kine, and doth he think of me,
> My sweetheart wandering whereso'er it be?
> Home, Rose, and home, Provence and La Palie.

The thunder bellows far from snow to snow,
(Home, Rose, and home, Provence and La Palie.)
And loud and louder roars the flood below.
Heigh-ho! but soon in shelter shall we be:
Home, Rose, and home, Provence and La Palie.

Or shall he find before his term be sped,
Some comelier maid that he shall wish to wed?
(Home, Rose, and home, Provence and La Palie.)
For weary is work, and weary day by day
To have your comfort miles on miles away.
Home, Rose, and home, Provence and La Palie.

Or may it be that I shall find my mate,
And he returning see himself too late?
For work we must, and what we see, we see,
And God he knows, and what must be, must be,
When sweethearts wander far away from me.
Home, Rose, and home, Provence and La Palie.

The sky behind is brightening up anew,
(Home, Rose, and home, Provence and La Palie.)
The rain is ending, and our journey too;
Heigh-ho! aha! for here at home are we:—
In Rose, and in Provence, and La Palie.

There may be, he thinks, inevitable partings, however true men and women be to one another. Life moves us to an end of which we know nothing, which we cannot master.

This is a favourite motive of his, as indeed it was of Matthew Arnold. They must have discussed it a hundred times at Oxford. We may exercise our will on circumstance, but it is of no avail. We try, and try again and yet again, but a little thing, of which we take no note, turns us from the goal. At last we grow wearied of being baffled, and give up the thing we desired; and then, in the hour when we have released ourselves from pursuing, we wonder, as we look back, whether we really cared for the thing we pursued, or whether the person we pursued cared for us. A series of slight pressures of circumstance on a dreamy and sensitive soul drifts the will away from its desired goal, and each of the drifts is accepted. Clough must have felt that this was the position of a part of his soul, perhaps with regard to matters of thought, certainly so far as the affections were concerned; or, if that is assuming too much, he must at least have sympathised keenly with this position in others. At any rate, he knew all about it. It is a frequent motive in his poems, and one whole poem, the **Amours de Voyage,** is a careful study of this matter of the heart. Clough seems to take a personal delight in the slow, subtle, close drawing, week by week, of the wavering, wandering, changeful drifting of the heart of the hero in love, into pursuit, and out of love—never one moment's resolution, never an hour of grip on circumstance, never one bold effort to clench the throat of Fate. Many are involved in similar circumstances, and have a similar temper; and the result in the poem is the exact result of a soul in that condition. And it seemed, I suppose, to Clough that it would be well to paint their condition, to show its folly, its evil, and its end. "Go, little book," he says—

Go, and if curious friends ask of thy rearing and age,
Say, "I am flitting about many years from brain unto brain
of
Feeble and restless youths born to inglorious days."

Of course, we need not believe in the inevitableness of the position, nor indeed did Clough finally. When he recorded it, he recorded what he had felt and known in himself, but he had passed out of it. Only, what he had then attained—for

I think he speaks of himself—"that happiness was to be found in knowledge, that faith passed, and love passed, but that knowledge abided"—was not, it seems, a much better position. Knowledge, to be sure, is a good thing, but it is a foundation for life which is always shifting. Its abiding is only for a short time, and its professors have to relay their foundations. And in the moral realm, in the conduct of life, to say nothing of the spiritual realm, knowledge, or what passes for knowledge, is frightfully insecure, and is attended with one fatal comrade, with pride in itself.

This is always true: "Knowledge puffeth up, but Love edifieth"; and if I may judge from the bulk of his poetry, Clough came to that at last. As to this insistence on fate, on the inevitable in circumstance, it is not an image of true life. Man is not master of the whole of fate, for he is not able to see all, but a great deal of what he thinks inevitable is in his hands. If he cannot climb over obstacles, he can get round them; that is, if he have courage, and chose to exercise his will, to be what he was made to be—a cause in the universe. Fate, as they call it, seems herself to remove the obstruction, if we take her gaily and boldly. If we march up to the barrier, we find it to be mere cloud through which we go easily to the other side. It is always wise to disbelieve in obstacles.

If the gentleman in the **Amours de Voyage,** when he found that he had just missed his love at Florence, had not waited to analyse his feelings, and then arrived too late at the next town where she had been, and then paused to analyse again his sensations, and then was the victim of a misdirected letter, and then gave up his pursuit; had he knit his heart into any resolution, instead of saying "Whither am I borne," he would easily have found the girl, and found his happiness. Fate? nine-tenths of fate are in our own hands, but we let the other tenth master us, and then fate fills the nine-tenths which was in our power with her own sombre self. This is our punishment, and we deserve it.

Well, it is a good thing to have the whole matter laid before us with such remarkable closeness and veracity as Clough has done in this poem. Its hero is a characteristic type: cultivated, retiring, disliking society. He has been thrown in the past, like Clough, into a world of jarring strife and noise, of mental and spiritual disturbance. Sensitive, refined till he thrills at a touch, angry with the circumstances of life which call him to act—when action, which forces him into contact with vulgar reality out of philosophic dreams, is as repugnant to him as it was to Hamlet "a cursed spite" of fate—he welcomes any change, any chance, which takes him out of the world of strife and effort. This also was the case with Clough himself, from whom the hero of the poem is partly drawn.

He was wearied with the strife within; he sought the world without; he welcomed the chance of employment elsewhere. He left Oxford, and afterwards went to America. There he gathered pupils around him at Cambridge, and wrote for the reviews. The things he wrote were not of any high quality; they have not even subtlety; they have no distinction. Uncontent still, he came back to England, his friends having found him a place in the Education Office. And then, his career being decided for him, and his drifting boat anchored by another hand than his own, he settled down to the prim ways, and regular work, and consistent routine of a government office, with its pleasant holidays. And then, too, he married, and loved his wife, his children, and his home; and gathered love around him, and found that love *did* abide and edify. His humour was set free from sorrow. The questions which had so deeply perplexed him were still subjects of careful thought, but they tormented him no more. He passed, we are told, "from the speculative to the constructive phase of thought," and would have, had he lived, expressed his matured conceptions of life in a more substantial way. He was happy and useful. He was always oppressed with the "sadness of the world, and the great difficulties of modern social life," but he turned his mind steadily, in this atmosphere of love and happiness, and with the deep experience they gave him, to help towards this solution. I wish he had had time to record in poetry his conclusions, but office work is a great disintegrator of poetic creation, and very little was done, and that not good as poetry, before the blind Fury came with the abhorred shears, and slit the thin-spun life.

He was only forty-three years old. The tales published under the title of **Mari magno** were written during the last holidays of his life, while he searched for health, and the last of them when he was dying. They are for the most part concerned with the question of marriage: its true end, its trials, fitness for it, and other matters. They have their own interest, but their main interest, like that of all the poems, is Clough's revelation of his character. He was, with that sensitive nature of his, a reserved man; but when he wrote poetry, the unconscious disclosure of his soul—the piece of human nature he knew best, and in which he was most interested—was so fine and accurate and all the more attractive because it was done unawares—that it fascinates even those readers who do not think highly of the poetry.

There is, however, another element in it which has its own fascination. This is the ceaseless change of mood within one atmosphere, like the ceaseless change of cloud scenery in a day of the same kind of weather from morning to evening. We never can tell what is coming in a poem, what the next verse will bring out, what new turn will be given to the main matter. Moreover, from day to day his mood varied. He might be sarcastic on Monday, depressed on Tuesday, gently humorous with life on Wednesday, despairing on Thursday, joyous with hope and strong in fortitude on Friday, idyllic on Saturday, sceptical on Sunday morning, religious on Sunday evening, and subtle, delicate, and tender every day. This has its own attraction for certain people, and those who like him, like him dearly.

Then, he had an excellent, light-flitting, kindly humour. Sometimes it was broad enough, as in that poem in [**Dipsychus**] about money, written in Venice, in the character of a vulgar rich man. . . . Sometimes his humour touches lightly and softly the comfortable, thoughtless life. . . . (pp. 30-44)

The **Bothie** also is full of quaint, observant humour. All the Oxford elements of his day are there; liked, even loved, but held up to gentle, subtle ridicule, delicately touched, but touched home. Oxford's young enthusiasm is pictured in the pupils, its quiet temper in the tutor, its dress, its ways of talk, the beginning of its æstheticism, its hereditary self-satisfaction, its variety of youthful intellect, its high sense of honour and morality, its manliness, its noisy athleticism, its sense that Oxford is, on the whole, though a doubt may now and then intrude, the mother, and the father, too, of the intellectual universe; and its reading parties, with a tutor, the incubator of statesmen, poets, philosophers, radical emigrants, and conservative squires, all fitted to replenish the earth and subdue it, to counsel and lead the world. (p. 45)

There is a true love of nature, especially of Highland scenery,

in the poem. Clough loved the mountains. Wales and the Highlands were dear to him. He wandered alone, meditating, among the glens; it was his great pleasure to have his contemplation broken by nature's sudden shocks of mild surprise, and to weave what he saw into what he thought. His friend, Frank Palgrave, who wrote a gentle, distinguished memoir of him, said that his mind was "haunted like a passion" by the loveliness of poetry and scenery; that by his "acceptance in the natural landscape, he had inherited a double portion of the spirit of Wordsworth. He loved nature, not only for its earthly sake, but for the divine and the eternal interfused with it" [see Further Reading]. This seems too strongly said, but it is the judgment of a friend. Clough may have loved nature as much as Wordsworth, but he had not Wordsworth's power of expressing his love. His descriptions are ill-composed; the spiritual passion he felt slightly appears in them. In the **Bothie,** the halting metre mangles the description; indeed, here, as in the whole of his poetry, the execution lags behind the conception. Art had not thrown her mantle over this man; the language does not enhance or uplift the thought; it rather depresses and lowers it; and, though we always understand him, which is a blessed gift to us, considering what we suffer from others, we wish that the clearness of the poem had been accompanied by a finer composition and workmanship. Palgrave even goes so far as to say that "one feels a doubt whether in verse he chose the right vehicle, the truly natural mode of utterance." If that means that Clough would have perhaps done better to write in prose, I am sure, though it sounds bold to say so, that the critic is wrong. I have been surprised by the inferiority of Clough's prose to his poetry. His prose does not rise beyond the level of the ordinary review; his soul is not living in it. On the contrary, in his poetry, though it does not want art, and does not seek for it, there is a spirit always moving—a delicate, fantastic, changing spirit; a humanity, with a touch here of Ariel, and there of Puck; a subtle sound and breathing such as one hears in lonely woods and knows not whence it came, and a melody of verse which his friend Matthew Arnold never arrived at; and these qualities prove, as I think, that prose was not the true vehicle of his thought, and that poetry was. I cannot conceive that even the mocking arguments of the Fiend in **Dipsychus** would be half as well expressed in prose. There is a short prose dialogue at the end of that poem. To read it and compare it with the poetry is proof enough of this. As to the impassioned utterances of the soul in **Dipsychus** struggling to hold its immortal birthright against the tempter who cries: "Claim the world; it is at your feet,"—some passages of which are quite remarkable in spiritual, I do not mean religious, poetry—they would be impossible in prose. Prose could not reach their feeling, nor the delicate interlacing of their thinking. It is in describing the half-tones of the spirit's life as well as of the life of the heart, in touching with the delicate finger the dim, delicate regrets and hopes and fears which flit before us like moths in twilight, in following with soft and subtle tread the fine spun threads of a web of thought, in recording the to and fro questions and answers of our twofold self within, and passing from one to another, each different as light and darkness—with distinctive power and pleasure in the play—it is in these remote, unsailed-on seas of feeling and contemplation that Clough's best work is done, and very few have done the same kind of work so well. The best of this kind is written in the region of the spirit, but he loved also to write of remote and unvisited regions of the affections, where Destiny, as it were, played her part in bringing together, and in parting, lovers and friends; and the pathetic quiet, the still submission to the parting, and the silent, sorrowful hope that Destiny may again unite those she has divided, are as simply told as they are tenderly felt. . . . I may have quoted more of this poetry than is in proportion in a short essay, but I feel that Clough has been too much neglected; and the reading of the whole of this intimate history of a soul, struggling to light in a time of great spiritual trouble, is likely to be of use to many who, in our changed circumstances, are going through a similar kind of trouble, and for similar reasons, which Clough went through.

The trouble did not last all his life. He attained a harbour of peace when he took life by the right handles. The inward storm retreated over the mountains, and at eventide there was a clear quiet. Had he lived, he might have made music for us out of the peace as soft and clear as his earlier music was sad and harsh, and yet, in the harshness, tender. When he was less within his own soul—that ill-fortuned dwelling for us—and moved in and out among men, his hopes for man, his faith in God, his love of natural humanity, revived, and with them came restoration of the calm he had lost. Even in 1849, about the year he left Oxford, where self-contemplation has her natural seat for those who care for it, he had begun to look beyond his inner soul to humanity, and to think that if he did not get on, others might; if truth did not dawn on him, it might have risen on others; that in the world there might be fighters who had won the field, though he had been put to flight; that his strife might have unconsciously helped them to their victory; that the struggle, though so dark and despairing, was not without its good;—and he used concerning this more hopeful thought a noble image in the poem I now quote ["**Say Not, the Struggle Nought Availeth**"]. What the image suggested became true as the years of the century went on. It is even truer now. We have a closer, more faithful grasp on truth than Clough could have; we have a diviner and a clearer hope. And what the last verse says was realised also, one is glad to think, in his own life.

Say not, the struggle nought availeth,
The labour and the wounds are vain,
The enemy faints not, nor faileth,
And as things have been they remain.

If hopes were dupes, fears may be liars;
It may be, in you smoke concealed,
Your comrades chase e'en now the fliers,
And, but for you, possess the field.

For while the tired waves, vainly breaking,
Seem here no painful inch to gain,
Far back, through creeks and inlets making,
Comes silent, flooding in, the main.

And not by eastern windows only,
When daylight comes, comes in the light;
In front, the sun climbs slow, how slowly,
But westward, look, the land is bright.

These happier, more hopeful words belong to 1849. He died in 1861. A kinder, gentler, more delicate soul has rarely lived among us. The Tennyson children used to call him the Angel-child. His fantastical spirit, his finer thought which would have liked to have danced on life's common way, the Ariel in him, would seem to have fitted him for fairyland, were it not that the sore trouble of the world, and the mystery of God's way with it, were, in that tempest-tossed time, too much for him. He was forced to enter the battle with eyes which saw too many things at the same time. The confusion might have overwhelmed him, but the other side of his nature came to his help. His light-heartedness, it is true, departed,

save at happy intervals, but he never allowed its absence to injure his association with his friends. And then, to meet his distress, he had great allies within—profound love of and belief in truthfulness, no self-deceit ever touched his soul; a set and honest manliness, a rooted scorn of the temptations and the base things of the world; a great love of freedom and a deep sympathy with men who strove for it; a soul which honoured the ideals and the vital causes of humanity; a love of natural life and a longing to see the divine in it; a fresh delight in the sweetness and beauty of earth and sky and sea; and a humility which touched with its grace all whom he met. His sarcasm, which grew out of the bitterness of his struggle, out of his silent, passionate, tormented inner life, bit only on himself, and spared the world; and when it fell on the world's follies, it was so mixed with happy humour that it half-healed the wound it gave. He had his martyrdom, but he was martyred for us, and the blood of these martyrs is the seed of that invisible Church which rises yearly, beyond all our creeds and scepticisms, into fuller weight and power.

His literary position is rather a solitary one. He has no parents and no children. I seem, however, to trace in some of his religious poems the poetic influence of Keble. What is plain is: that he stands between the absence of art in poetry which marked men like Bailey and Alexander Smith—in their long, uncomposed, intemperate, and self-conscious poems—and a man like Matthew Arnold, who made a study of his art, who was excessively conscious of being an artist, who worked out a theory of his art on the bed of which, like Procrustes, he strained out or shortened his poems; who rarely, therefore, was spontaneous; who questioned his emotion till it grew cold instead of yielding to the angels of impulse whose wings brushed his shoulder, and whose celestial colours glimmered before his eyes. (pp. 46-54)

Clough wrote side by side with Arnold, but was not influenced by Arnold's demand for artistic excellence. He wrote what came to him with all the carelessness, but without the natural genius of Walter Scott. He did not obey, though he knew, what noble art demanded. Yet, he reached a certain place among the poets. And he owed this, I think, to the steady, informing, temperance-insisting culture of a great university. He was a scholar and had studied and loved the Greek and Roman models of what high poetry is. He might— since he had no poetic genius, only a gentle and charming talent—have been enslaved by a scientific art, a slavery from which genius saves a man, and have become one of the literary prigs of poetry who prate of art but cannot practise it; who gain the whole world of a clique's applause and lose their soul as poets. He was saved from this by the strength of the passion with which he wrote, by his truthfulness which did not condescend to modify his work and by his love of clearness. But though he had this one artistic merit of clearness, he was, unlike a true artist, indifferent to beauty, to excellence, to delicate choice and arrangement of words and music. He spent no trouble on his work. His poetry, therefore, with all its personal charm, remains in the porch, not in the temple of the Muses. (pp. 54-5)

Stopford A. Brooke, "Arthur Hugh Clough," in his
Four Victorian Poets: A Study of Clough, Arnold,
Rossetti, Morris, *1908. Reprint by Russell & Russell, 1964, pp. 30-55.*

EDMUND GOSSE (essay date 1921)

[*Gosse's importance as a critic is due primarily to his introduction of Henrik Ibsen's "new drama" to English audiences. He was among the chief English translators and critics of Scandinavian literature and was decorated by the Norwegian, Swedish, and Danish governments for his efforts. Among his other works are studies of John Donne, Thomas Gray, Sir Thomas Browne, and important early articles on French authors of the late nineteenth century. Although Gosse's works are varied and voluminous, he was largely a popularizer, with the consequence that his commentary lacks depth and is not considered in the first rank of modern critical thought. However, his broad interests and knowledge of foreign literatures lend his works much more than a documentary value. In the following excerpt, Gosse offers a harshly negative view of Clough as a poet and as a person.*]

The life of literature is so wide and the interests of a particular generation are often so narrow, that it is salutary every now and then to take a dose of verse or prose which has entirely ceased to be popular. It was popular once, and among persons, we are apt to forget, quite as enthusiastic and as intelligent as we are ourselves. In this spirit, as one who takes from the hand of Mr. J. I. Osborne [Clough's biographer (see Further Reading)] a glass of sarsaparilla, I hasten to sip a critical blood-purifier which I certainly should not apply to for idle pleasure, since it is difficult to think of a single imaginative writer of the Victorian Age more widely remote from us to-day than Arthur Hugh Clough. He has been dead nearly sixty years, and the circle of his personal friends, who adored and admired him, has ceased to exist. We habitually think of the writers among whom he lived without remembering him, and Lord Morley is said to have refused to allow a volume on him to be added to the "English Men of Letters" series on the ground that Clough was not a Man of Letters. Mr. Osborne has composed his monograph in the form of an "English Man of Letters" volume, perhaps in order to supplement this void. He has done his work exceedingly well, not without some irony at the expense of his subject, since it is undeniable that a protracted study of Clough is apt to be fatiguing.

Clough was a contemporary of Ruskin, Froude, Charles Kingsley, and George Eliot, and he had certain characteristics in common with those persons. But there was one great distinction between them and him; while each of them in his or her way got a tremendous return for their energy, Clough got hardly anything out of life at all. His friends, who watched him with growing dismay, were confident at first, and then, alas! less confident, that he would ultimately do something really illustrious, but he did not. . . . Clough began with the highest hopes, the purest aspirations; nothing was too lofty for his spiritual ambition. But it all petered out, and, after the slight achievements which we know, we find him correcting the exercises of the infant Tennysons and tieing up parcels for Florence Nightingale, and then quietly passing out of the world.

The only years in his life when he was really successful were those which he spent at Rugby, flushed and exhilarated by the magnetism of the magnificent Dr. Arnold. Mr. Osborne gives a study of Clough's enthusiasm as the typical prize schoolboy. He was a leader, a prophet, an immensely influential moral teacher at Rugby, which is a paradox, because Clough in later life never led anybody anywhere. Mr. Osborne notes this strange fact, but offers no explanation. Is it not probable that the strenuousness of Dr. Arnold blew through his docile pupil as through a flute, and that in

Clough's "sermons and admonitions," and in all the extraordinary zeal with which he proselytised at Rugby, he was really more passive than active?

At all events, when he went to Oxford, where he stayed for ten years, as there was no one to lead him, he entirely ceased to be a leader. It has been alleged that he took part in the Tractarian Movement, but, as Mr. Osborne shows, he sat completely aloof from it in his garret at Balliol, subduing the flesh by ascetic practices which had no ecclesiastical meaning, plunging into the frozen Cherwell, sitting through the winter without a fire, and eating coarse and scanty food. Why did he do this? Not as Newman or Keble might have done it, because the extremity of spiritual ecstasy burned up all bodily desires, but "with an eye to self-discipline." "A mental struggle was going on in him all his life," and he regarded it "as a guarantee of the rightness of a course of conduct that it should lead away from, rather than toward, the attainment of any concrete good." So he wrestled with himself under the cold roof, singing "O let me love my love unto myself alone," until large bunches of his brown hair came out. He was gentle and inoffensive; he was pious and irritatingly meek; and he sat counting the pulse of his own conscience until he heard no other sound.

Then he burst away from Oxford, and rushed off to Chelsea to sit at the feet of Carlyle, who welcomed so susceptible a victim, and dropped the vitriol of Teufelsdröckh on Clough's quivering spirit.

In later years Clough was accustomed to say that Carlyle "took him into the wilderness and left him there." In that solitude the conscience of Clough ate him out like a white ant; it completely hollowed him, so that if any one leaned against him for spiritual support, Clough sank in dust under the pressure. He suffered from a horrible recurring fear that perhaps "there is no God." This takes its best, perhaps its only tolerable form, in the well-known song in *Dipsychus,* and in the "Christ is not risen" ode ["**Easter-Day: Naples, 1849**"]. By 1848 he had grown exhausted with this particular torment, and took up the Revolution, but when Matthew Arnold suggested to him that "the millennium is not coming this bout," he went to Rome to see for himself. He then wrote to F. T. Palgrave "Farewell, politics, utterly! What can I do?" One of his old friends said of Clough that his mind was "habitually swayed by large, slow, deep-sea currents." This was meant as praise, but it suggests the image of a derelict schooner.

Obviously no lasting memory of this amiable and unselfish man could be based on his opinions or his actions. Yet, nearly sixty years after his death, he is still remembered, and in no danger of being forgotten. He is remembered by his poems, which, although they are amateurish in form and dry in texture, have an element of faint perennial interest. It is a valuable critical exercise to try to discover in what this permanent interest consists, since Clough's verse is almost the negation of poetry, and in particular is devoid of all the qualities which are admired at the present moment. Nevertheless, it has that power of arresting and diverting attention which is given only to living literature. When the body of his verse has been winnowed, not much remains, but there is a handful of golden grains, and they are pure wheat. He wrote short lyrics, some of which appeared in the slender *Ambarvalia* of 1849, and were continued till the end of his life; and he composed those long poems in which the journals of his holidays were roughly versified.

Of these *The Bothie of Tober-na-Vuolich* was the most important. . . . *The Bothie,* a record in hexameters of the vacation of an Oxford reading party in the Western Highlands, is Clough's most solid claim to immortality. It is very crude and dull in some parts, but in others it has not merely a startling vividness and picturesqueness, but it is sensuous and almost passionate to a surprising degree. His other works were mainly posthumous; he wrote a sort of novel called *Amours de Voyage,* which also is in hexameters, and he left unfinished *Mari Magno,* a series of tales in verse, supposed to occupy the leisure of a Transatlantic voyage. In 1861 Clough read *Mari Magno* to Tennyson, and "cried like a child over it." We are not told whether Tennyson wept.

Among the lyrics which Clough produced up to the age of thirty, we find but few which have stood the test of time. These are characteristic of three principal moods: **"Qua cursum ventus"** is an ethical or gnomic piece of reflection, very gracefully turned; **"Lo, here is God, and there is God"** is an ironic disquisition of the kind that Clough delighted in, but written with quite unusual sprightliness; and the fragment beginning "Farewell, my Highland lassie," which I conjecture to have been cast aside when he determined to write *The Bothie* in hexameters, has a picturesque warmth hardly to be found elsewhere. Here then, perhaps, is Clough at his very best:—

> I fall to sleep with dreams of life in some black bothie spent,
> Coarse poortith's ware thou changing there to gold of pure content,
> With barefoot lads and lassies round, and thee the cheery wife,
> In the braes of old Lochaber a laborious homely life;
> But I wake—to leave thee, smiling, with the kiss upon the brow,
> And the peaceful benediction of—ο θεοσ μετὰ σου!

Later—as I suppose, for dates are lacking—he wrote **"The Hidden Love"** and that truly admirable hymn, almost Clough's only faultless piece, **"Say not the struggle nought availeth."** These and some pages of *The Bothie* preserve the memory of their author, and promise to continue unassailable. They have far greater value for us than such purely intellectual verses as **"Qui laborat, orat,"** which Mr. Osborne is inclined to over-estimate.

It used to be customary to speak of Clough as a disciple of Wordsworth, and recent critics have seemed ready to take the same view. It is obvious that Clough, as a schoolboy, imitated the simpler numbers of *Lyrical Ballads,* but in his mature work I agree with Mr. Osborne in finding not a trace of Wordsworth's attitude to Nature or of the majesty of Milton's vision. On the other hand, I think no one has observed the strange and direct influence which Longfellow exercised over Clough's form, although the accent of the latter is more thoughtful and more completely swayed by the desire for veracity than that of the once-popular American. But almost everything in *Ambarvalia* seems to start from Longfellow's *Voices of the Night* (1839). It was immediately after reading *Evangeline* that Clough abandoned his effort to write his Scotch "pastoral" in rhyme, and adopted hexameters, while it is recorded that he received *The Courtship of Miles Standish* just before he began *Amours de Voyage.* We are almost driven to suppose, when once we have observed these coincidences, that there was something sympathetic to Clough in the New England atmosphere, and particularly in the elegance of Longfellow. Clough, proceeding from Oxford and

London, welcomed in Emerson such an impression of "perfect intellectual culture" as he thought he had not found elsewhere. Though Clough was a product of the finest English humanism and the bosom friend of Matthew Arnold, he developed a much closer fellowship with Lowell and Whittier than with Browning and Rossetti.

Mr. Osborne has approached his difficult task with candour and taste, and has not allowed himself to be unduly trammelled by the Middle Victorian tradition. He finds it more difficult to know what to make of the elegy in which Matthew Arnold flung a garment of purple and gold round the shoulders of his deceased friend. Yet if we read "Thyrsis" carefully [see poem dated 1866], and do not allow the sumptuous beauty of the scene and the ornament to divert our attention from what is directly said about the subject, we may see that Arnold, in spite of his lifelong affection for Clough, was well aware what a negation his intellectual and imaginative experience really was. Clough

> Learn'd a stormy note
> Of men contention-tost, of men who groan,
> Which task'd his pipe too soon, and tired his throat—
> It fail'd, and he was mute!

But we turn from this clairvoyance, and from Clough's harsh numbers, to the Dorian pipe and the Cumnor cowslips, to the resuscitated Lityerses-song in the Phrygian cornfield, and poor Thyrsis fades away into an echo. "Man gave thee nothing!" (pp. 129-35)

> *Edmund Gosse, "Clough," in his* Books on the Table, *Charles Scribner's Sons, 1921, pp. 127-35.*

F. L. LUCAS (essay date 1930)

[*A twentieth-century English man of letters, Lucas is best remembered as a literary critic, a scholar and translator of classical Greek literature, and the editor of Jacobean dramatist John Webster's works. Lucas's poetic ideal stressed, according to John Sparrow, "the proper appreciation of the relation between form and matter, feeling and its artistic expression, which inspired alike the poetry and the criticism of the Greeks." Noted for what another critic termed the "eighteenth-century" qualities of "bluff common sense and man-of-the-world manners" in his criticism, Lucas was antagonistic to modernist trends in poetry and criticism. In the following excerpt, Lucas regards Clough as an amateur poet who "took life too seriously, and art not seriously enough."*]

[Clough] had, one may say, two ruling passions—one, for going his own way and thinking his own thoughts; the other, for going, and for thinking, straight. The moral conscientiousness of the model pupil of Arnold is of no great interest: young prigs, never rare, were particularly plentiful then. But the intense intellectual conscientiousness into which it grew is a far rarer quality: it remains one of the central things in the worth of Clough's poetry and in the unhappiness of his life.

It was, indeed, this unresting critical honesty of mind that rescued him from the effects of a system of education about which he later retained no illusions. Seventy years before Mr Strachey [see Further Reading], whom some have thought so unfair, Arnold's own pupil criticized no less incisively, through the mouth of the Uncle in *Dipsychus,* Arnold's treatment of schoolboys as miserable little sinners with souls to be saved: "They're all so pious . . . they seem to me a sort of hobbadi-hoy cherub, too big to be innocent, and too simple for anything else. They're full of the notion of the world being so wicked, and of their taking a higher line as they call it. I only fear they'll never take any line at all. . . . Why didn't he flog them and hold his tongue? Flog them he did, but why preach?" From this Rugbeian elephantiasis of the conscience Clough recovered; but he seems himself to have doubted whether he recovered completely. One cannot be too careful about teasing fiction into autobiography; but the hero of **Dipsychus** is certainly in part a self-portrait:

> He was a sort of moral prig, I've heard,
> Till he was twenty-five: and even then
> He never entered into life as most men.
> That is the reason why he fails so soon.

Similarly, in **Mari Magno:**

> He now, o'ertasked at school, a serious boy,
> A sort of after-boyhood to enjoy
> Appeared. . . .
> With all his eager notions still there went
> A self-correcting and ascetic bent,
> That from the obvious good still led astray,
> And set him travelling on the longest way.

Whatever this may be as poetry, as psychology it rings true enough. How much of Clough's final character came to him from birth, how much from Rugby, only a modern biographer would be rash enough to estimate. Certainly Clough believed in an inherited lack of vitality. "Take care", he writes to his brother, "you never say 'It's too much trouble'—'I can't be bothered', which are tolerably old favourites of yours, and, indeed, of all who have any Perfect blood in them." (Perfect was his mother's maiden name.) The peculiar misfortune was that one by nature so scrupulous and doubtful should have been thrown by destiny first into the most overscrupulous of schools, and then into a society hag-ridden by religious doubt. This child of Diffidence was bred up by Too-good, then sent to live in Doubting Castle. Poor relations of Hamlet are tediously numerous; but Clough was no ignoble member of that family. He too lacked, not will, but eyelids—the power to stop looking and shut his eyes and leap. And he too found his malady completed by his own awareness of it, by the self-knowledge that he was born

> To finger idly some old Gordian knot,
> Unskilled to sunder and too weak to cleave.

Sceptics should take care to inherit a sanguine temperament. Clough lacked the wise frivolity of Lucian or Montaigne or Voltaire—"I do not greatly think about Montaigne". Nature had denied to that earnest soul the animal spirits that enable happier men to be as foolish as a foolish world requires. In the words of "Thyrsis" [see poem by Matthew Arnold dated 1866]:

> Some life of men unblest
> He knew, which made him droop and filled his head.
> He went: his piping took a troubled sound
> Of storms that rage outside our happy ground;
> He could not wait their passing, he is dead.

It was not only religious uncertainty that tormented him. Even in love, where few men find any difficulty in being foolish enough, his intellectual conscience pursues him with doubts whether his passion is not (characteristic word) "factitious". The real Clough did in the end get happily married (how much by his own doing we cannot know); but the hero of **Amours de Voyage,** one of his many self-portraits, ends more deeply lost than ever in the doubt that stands inscribed

on its title-page—"Il doutait de tout, même de l'amour". The "factitious" pursues him as the Furies Orestes. Love, to meet his demands, has to be far too true ever to run smooth:

> I tremble for something factitious,
> Some malpractice of heart, some illegitimate process.
> We are so prone to these things with our terrible notions
>   of duty.

He certainly feels something: but what is it?

> Well, I know after all it is only juxtaposition.
> Juxtaposition in short: and what is juxtaposition?

What, indeed? He might have found an answer in a poetess he knew, the first of poetesses, in that quivering poem which begins:

> God is not more blessèd than is the lover
> Sitting, looking into thy face before him.

But it would have been no use. The unhappy ending of **Amours de Voyage** is a foregone conclusion:

> After all perhaps there was something factitious about it;
> I have had pain, it is true: I have wept, and so have the
>   actors.

As with love, so with politics. Clough is that "Republican Friend" to whom Arnold addressed his sonnets of 1848. But in the republican Rome of 1849 Clough was not one of the heroic geese who might perhaps save the Capitol. He sympathized; he understood; indeed, he understood far too well.

> Victory! Victory! Victory!—Ah, but it is, believe me,
> Easier, easier far, to intone the chant of the martyr
> Than to indite any paean of any victory. Death may
> Sometimes be nobler; but life, at the best, will appear an
>   illusion. . . .
> The smoke of the sacrifice rises to heaven
> Of a sweet savour, no doubt, to Somebody, but on the
>   altar,
> Lo, there is nothing remaining but ashes and dirt and ill
>   odour.

Some of us may, perhaps, find that odour not unfamiliar, remembering 1919: and, seeing Mussolini stand where stood Mazzini, may wonder if Clough was, after all, so wrong as our fathers must have thought. (pp. 60-5)

"He that looks too long into the abyss", said Nietzsche, "in the end the abyss shall look into him." But that, through life, was the one thing Clough never hesitated to do, long and steadily, come what might. Honesty, coupled with a sense of humour which first appears in his mature writing, like a sun first seen at noon on a grey day, is what ennobled the vision of life which he expressed so often in verse and sometimes in poetry. Like Samuel Butler, he too pursued "the understanding that surpasses any peace"; like Bishop Butler, he also passionately felt—"Things are what they are and the consequences of them will be what they will be; why then should we wish to be deceived?" In his own homely phrase:

> But play no tricks upon thy soul, O man,
> Let fact be fact, and life the thing it can.

Or again, in one of his finer flashes:

> It fortifies my soul to know
> That, though I perish, truth is so.

Or yet once more, in a typical letter: "I think I must have been getting into a little mysticism lately. It won't do: twice two are four, all the world over, and there's no harm in its being so; 'tisn't the devil's doing that it is; *il faut s'y soumettre,* and all right". No wonder he loved the eighteenth century and thought it a good training for a poet to copy out some Goldsmith every day; no wonder pupils of his remembered how at some wild opinion in their essays he would only say in his quiet searching way: "Ah then, you think so?"

The result of too much good sense is disillusion: the sugar for disillusion is irony. It is a bitter sweetening; but it serves. Eighteenth-century France can illustrate that. And Clough, though he could never be epicureanly gay, developed a pleasantly ironic humour; genial in the *Bothie,* more flippantly bitter in *Amours de Voyage,* bitterer still in *Dipsychus,* but most pointed of all perhaps in **"The Latest Decalogue,"** with that admirable climax of sneering feminine rhymes:

> Thou shalt not covet: but tradition
> Approves all forms of competition.

But Clough can never play Mephistopheles for long; there is too much of the tenderer Margaret in him, too much of that wistfulness which finds its utterance in the three poems of his that all the world still knows—**"Peschiera," "Qua Cursum Ventus,"** and **"Say not the struggle naught availeth."**

It is, then, as a human document rather than as literature that much of Clough's work can be enjoyed to-day—as the utterance of a mind preserved from softness by its wit, from ineffectiveness by its courage and good sense. Technically, Clough's verse can at times be atrocious—

> Had miscellaneous experience had
> Of human acts, good half, and half of bad.

But he is sometimes lovely, seldom dull, never false. Thus *The Bothie of Tober-na-Vuolich,* if read, as it should be read, for nothing more serious than amusement, has a way of startling one every now and then with glimpses of sudden beauty, or with sudden depths—

> Perfect as picture, as vision entrancing that comes to the
>   sightless
> Through the great granite jambs, the stream, the glen, and
>   the mountain.

The next instant, like his mountain-stream, his hurrying hexameters will tumble laughing down bathos after bathos; until they foam out again into some momentary loveliness, or run more deeply and slowly through a stretch of quiet reflection. For even here in the wilderness, though less harshly, echo the cryings of Carlyle and the questionings of 1848: even here is debated that eternal problem of the price of civilization in terms of human misery. (pp. 65-8)

Clough put a good deal into this poem; for, indeed, it contained a good deal of himself. He had taken a reading-party to Glen Urquhart the year before; several of the characters are portraits. . . . But I suppose *The Bothie* finds few readers to-day: and *Amours de Voyage* even fewer, though it seems to me better still. The idea of a novel in hexameter letters hardly stirs the blood; yet I feel Clough's hexameters to be the only successful specimens of their kind in English. For English hexameters cannot be taken seriously. That is exactly why they suit so well the half-mocking tone of these two poems; and just because their tone is so largely burlesque, when it does at moments become serious, the contrast is strong enough to make us for a moment take them seriously too. This contrast runs all through the action of *Amours de*

Voyage—the abortive, very English love affair of this "too quick despairer", seen against the background of the vain heroism of the brief Roman Republic. It is a slight, amusingly told story, made to serve as a thread for Clough's reflections on life, which form the real heart of the poem up to its stoical conclusion:

> Shall we come out of it all, some day, as one does from a
>   tunnel?
> Will it be all at once, without our doing or asking,
> We shall behold clear day, the trees and meadows about
>   us,
> And the faces of friends, and the eyes we loved looking at
>   us?
> Who knows? Who can say? It will not do to suppose
>   it. . . .
> Not as the Scripture says, is, I think, the fact. Ere our
>   death-day,
> Faith, I think, does pass, and Love, but Knowledge abideth,
> Let us seek Knowledge;—the rest may come and go as it
>   happens,
> Knowledge is hard to seek, and harder yet to adhere to.
> Knowledge is painful often; and yet when we know we are
>   happy.
> Seek it, and leave mere Faith and Love to come with the
>   chances.
> As for Hope—to-morrow I hope to be starting for Naples.

So too, under the Roman Empire, Virgil's scholiast likewise concluded, "All things grow a weariness, except to understand"—"omnia lassant praeter intellegere": so too, under the Third Republic, Proust likewise turned away from the world—to understand. Is it really the wisest course? That is another question. But I have an affection for *Amours de Voyage.* It is not the sort of work to appeal to either the popinjays or the pedants in modern criticism. It is too human. So much the better. One may like a poet to wear other than daisy-chains, even though at times he clanks and stumbles in them. Pure Beauty left too long alone is always liable to be found fondling hairy ears, in a union of null perfection and perfect nullity.

The two other long poems published after Clough's death are both unfinished and both inferior. *Dipsychus,* "the Doubled-souled", an adaptation of the idea of *Faust,* with a characteristic twist leaves it in doubt whether its Mephistopheles is really a devil, or simply the Spirit of Good Sense. But though there are moments when here too Clough's irony rings home, as in the passage where Mephistopheles insists that the hero shall take holy orders, the poem as a whole goes too much in dressing-gown and slippers. Similarly, *Mari Magno,* with its remote mixture of Chaucer and Crabbe, is to-day but a barren ocean to plough: yet there remain fine things, now widely forgotten, in the shorter poems—among them that fragment **"The Shadow",** whose opening dignity Clough never equalled again:

> I dreamed a dream: I dreamt that I espied,
> Upon a stone that was not rolled aside,
> A Shadow sit upon a grave—a Shade
> As thin, as unsubstantial, as of old
> Came, the Greek poet told,
> To lick the life-blood in the trench Ulysses made—

Then once more the serious features relax into the old ironic smile, the agonized flippancy of Hamlet; for the shade of the risen Jesus cannot explain Himself; the priests alone show no tremor of doubt in themselves or of belief in Him—

As for the Shade, who trusted such narration?
Except, of course, in ancient revelation.

To-day, as we look back, Clough seems the poet of a promise unfulfilled—of a promise cut short, not like that of Keats by death, but by lack of vitality. His later work steadily weakens; and there is little reason to suppose that longer life would have meant for him longer memory. At times he seems made to fit his friend's phrase of Shelley—"an ineffectual angel"—and yet Clough was of sturdier stuff than that implies. His was less the faint heart that wins no fair lady, than the eternal doubt which lady was indeed fair. It was no mere "angel" that impressed the critical Matthew Arnold with the sense that there had never been "purer or more subtle soul", and left his mark even on the rough granite of Carlyle's mind. For us he remains the impersonation of an age when religious doubt was not, as now, a rare and mild greensickness, but a crippling, even a fatal malady. We are not cleverer; we are harder, disillusioned, indifferent. The age of crusades is over: few lament it. But a crusade was what Clough longed for:

> We ask action
> And dream of arms and conflict; and string up
> All self-devotion's muscles; and are set
> To fold up papers.

The Crimean War came: but it set Clough to string up, not "self-devotion's muscles", but (as Mr Strachey's readers will remember) the brown-paper parcels of Miss Florence Nightingale. Perhaps the truth is that he took life too seriously, and art not seriously enough. The air of the amateur clings about him: he could not, like happier artists, forget the whole round globe in carving some cherry-stone. He seems at times a half-hewn Matthew Arnold, left lying in the quarry. He *is* Hamlet, Hamlet with a touch of Polonius—not Shakespeare. His sadness grows monotonous. "Laugh, my young friends", says Nietzsche again, "if you are at all determined to remain pessimists."

Laughter indeed is easy for the insensitive, the world provides no lack of subjects.

> But men at whiles are sober
> And think by fits and starts;
> And, when they think, they fasten
> Their hands upon their hearts.

(pp. 69-74)

F. L. Lucas, "Clough," in his Eight Victorian Poets, *Cambridge at the University Press, 1930, pp. 55-74.*

FRANCIS W. PALMER (essay date 1943)

[*Challenging the popular critical conception of Clough as a person whose overwhelming indecisiveness led to personal and social failure, Palmer argues instead that Clough developed and maintained positive moral convictions and political ideals that are expressed in his poetry and prose writings.*]

Like his friend Matthew Arnold, Arthur Hugh Clough came to the belief that morality constitutes the most essential part of religion. His review of Francis Newman's *The Soul* contains these instructive lines: "Your religious experience will *not* have been idle if you come forth with but the one conviction that *the Kingdom of God is without us,* and, in one sense, does come of observation." A growing conviction that this is true accounts for the positive ground which underlies the apparent skepticism of much of his verse. To the unresolved doubt of an early poem like **"The Questioning Spirit"** suc-

ceeds the calm assurance that permeates the **Mari Magno.** Nor is that certitude absent from any of the longer poems, though its presence in them has not always been recognized. Even in an historical estimate of Clough as an exponent of doubt, however, it ought to be recognized that Clough rightly belongs among the friends and aiders of those who would live in the spirit.

Disproportionate emphasis generally has been laid on Clough's skeptical habits of mind. During the decade after his death, in the excitement that followed publication of Darwin's theory of natural selection, everyone was ranged without qualification in the ranks of Faith or the ranks of Doubt. Classification of Clough in the second category, though it denotes at best a half-truth, hardened into tradition. Critics who subscribe to this theory read in Clough the story of failure, and speculate, as J. I. Osborne does, on why he failed [see Further Reading]. The causes, Osborne decides, consist in a "disposition to sit forever on large problems he could not solve" and a fatal physical limitation of not being strung finely enough for genuine poetic enthusiasm and great creative effort. Evidently Osborne assumes that Clough had exhausted his poetic output at the age of forty-two. A similar assumption underlies a recent study by Townsend Scudder, published under the caption "Incredible Recoil" [see Further Reading]. Comparing Claude, hero of the **Amours de Voyage,** with the life-loving, buoyant-spirited Philip of the **Bothie,** he sees this newer Clough as "the indecisive, questioning nonparticipant, the victim of an extraordinary recoil, who stood irresolute between offered actions, and then passed, defeated, through the portals of his own dissolution." Whether these conclusions are just depends largely on the validity of assuming that Clough had "beat his music out" and of further taking for granted, as Scudder does, that Clough's heroes are photographic portrayals of himself. I do not mean to urge, what would at most be idle conjecture, that had he been spared to the longevity of a Tennyson he might have become a poet of first magnitude. Against the contrary assumption, however, I think it only right to adduce some facts that go far to invalidate it. It should not be forgotten that in his last illness Clough was engaged in writing the tales of **Mari Magno,** a series of poems which show an increasing mastery of his medium, a deepening poetic insight, and a ripening attitude toward life. Nor do his resignation from Oxford, his marriage and happy family life, or his self-sacrifice in aiding Florence Nightingale during the Crimean War, very effectively bear out the charge of irresolution. In some recent criticism, it is therefore encouraging to see a departure from the traditional view with a shift of emphasis to Clough's narrative power and his subtle analysis of social problems and questions of love and marriage [see Garrod entry in Further Reading].

We shall undoubtedly be nearer the truth if we weigh Clough's poems by Arnold's definition of poetry as a criticism of life. Without denying that Clough put much of himself into his verse, we may yet perceive in **Dipsychus** and the **Amours** amusing dissections of the mind, profound analyses of what elsewhere he himself calls an "over-educated weakness of purpose in Western Europe," arising from a "disposition to press too far the finer and subtler intellectual and moral susceptibilities." These companion studies of introspection, wherein "thought wheels round on thought," comprise in their distinctive way tracts for the time. Their vacillating heroes, beset by

> some craven scruple
> Of thinking too precisely on the event,

share the enervating weakness of the time that holds its victim in the "easy chair of Use and Wont." What was needed, and needed imperatively in time of change, was rather resolution and action. But Clough, although he does not bring his characters to a solution of all their problems, does not leave them in hopeless stalemate. The rebellious attitude with which Dipsychus yields to the spirit of circumstance forecasts action and change rather than repose. The outcome of the *Amours,* however unusual in fiction, is equally positive in temper. The situation of the hesitant lover Claude, who cannot assure himself that he loves the girl of the story until she passes out of his life, and who then pines for what is not, parallels in general outline of plot the tale of young Werther. With it, this tale shares the theme of romantic yearning for an inaccessible love. In Goethe's story, Werther finds his desire thwarted by the marriage of his loved one to another; whereas in Clough's poem mere geographical separation permanently divides the two lovers. It is characteristic that Clough rejects as factitious the supreme discontent of Goethe's lover, whose logical and actual end was suicide. Claude, after probing his own soul and admitting to himself his cowardliness toward life, achieves something like victory. Would not a true coward have manufactured excuses to himself instead of facing self-criticism? He emerges little scarred and much stronger for his experience, concluding that

> Knowledge is painful often, and yet when we know we are happy.

It hardly seems credible that the poet was less honest with himself than was the hero he created.

Clough's answer to criticism that the ending of the *Amours* was weak, is to be found, I think, in the **"Lawyer's First Tale"** of the *Mari Magno.* If none but himself, not even Emerson, could perceive any strength in Claude, he was not one, surely, to defend his work. But in the later poem he returns to the same theme, treating it objectively and omitting the introspectiveness of Claude. It is another tale of love that came to naught, as childhood acquaintances very frequently do. It came to naught for the rarer reason that the girl, wiser than her cousin in her perception of the intellectual gulf that separated them, married another before ever the cousin summoned up resolution to declare his own devotion. When quite by accident they met in Switzerland, it was with real shock that he learned of her marriage. Nor was he, on invitation at her home later, wholly able to conceal his disappointment, which she in turn firmly but kindly rebuked, urging him to aim higher in life and to quit college and seek his success in the world. Cruel though her judgment seemed at the time,

> As she had counselled, I had done,
> And a new effort was begun.
> *Forth to the war of life I went,*
> *Courageous, and not ill content.*

In this repeated rejection of Werther's Byronic dissatisfaction, Clough reveals an imagination fundamentally healthy, morally sound. Although H. W. Garrod chides Emerson for missing the point of the *Amours,* he himself seems partly to have missed Clough's purpose in these two poems. It somewhat misleads to say that Clough "liked a hero who could not bring his resolution to the sticking-point." Clough liked a hero who had about him the stuff to repair loss or failure and to carry on. Although he was naturally of introspective turn,

criticism rather than morbidity lay behind even his most speculative verse—criticism nicely tempered by the tenderness and nobility that Palgrave tells us distinguished his character [see Further Reading].

Further hints that when death occurred Clough was still growing in stature as a poet of the moral life, may be discerned in another of the *Mari Magno* series, the clergyman's second tale. The moving human sympathy with which the man of religion delivers this story of an act of sin and the feeling of guilt and the expiation which at last restores the offender to the broken circle of love is a lively commentary on theologians who lightly use phrases like "atonement by a crucified Saviour." It incorporates the poet's belief that life is constant struggle against the forces, oftenest in insidious guise, which assail it and threaten man's happiness:

> Something there is, we know not what, in man,
> With all established happiness at strife,
> And bent on revolution in his life.

But the struggle is not unavailing. Defeat in this perpetual battle of the human to achieve its highest capabilities is never final. The route to strength and victory leads the Edward of the tale an "unblest wanderer" through the thoroughfares of London that are to him "the flaming streets of hell." Work and separation from family for the space of a year constitute the severe penance by which he satisfies the voice of conscience, which Clough equates with God's justice. It may be said, of course, that Clough's puritanism, as his moral earnestness has loosely been called, is narrowly Victorian. May it not also be said that either present-day or Victorian world, if it "lightly treat such slips," comes short of the highest range of experience?

Nor was Clough's concern with problems of right and wrong limited to *personal* problems, as distinct from what may be termed *social* morality. The same disinclination to range himself under a party banner, the unshrinking honesty and realism, and the incisive grasp of fundamentals that characterize his religious and moral ideas mark also his social and political attitudes.

The closest approach to a party designation for Clough would be, I fancy, to adopt another phrase of Arnold's and label him a *Liberal of the Future* [from the essay "The Future of Liberalism"], though the phrase is merely suggestive, not definitive. Two principles underlay his generally fugitive statements that bear on matters of politics or society. He evinces an earnest sympathy with victims of oppression or poverty and, conversely, a desire for the triumph of genuine liberty. In an increasingly industrial order of civilization, he could not help seeing that economic insecurity was steadily growing and that human rights were more and more being infringed upon. Nor did statesmanship have any adequate solution to the seeming dilemma. Whatever their theoretical distinctions, in actual practice both Liberals and Conservatives were driven by interests not essentially different. Nineteenth-century reform is in the main a story of conservatism acquiescing in half-hearted changes to forestall revolution. In the words of Dr. Arnold, most were "reforms not upon principle, but upon clamour." The policies of both parties were opportunist, intent on preserving anciently held or newly won privileges. Clough speaks of them as "aristocratic parties," kept in a state of separation chiefly by personal differences. He seems to have sympathized more with the aims of Bright and the Radical party, considering them sincerer exponents of liberalism, than with either "the party of Yorke or the party of Pratt."

If the spreading movement for democracy exalted the individual, inherent tendencies of the economic system in which industrialism operated made for new forms of oppression and depreciated human worth. It needed no Engels or Marx to see that actuality tended by "iron laws" in a direction opposite to the democratic ideal. The aim of democracy to extend the benefits of social coöperation to all, instead of a fraction, became remote of fulfillment as capital correspondingly centralized and labor came more and more to depend on the mercies of the market.

So far as the hopes of democracy seemed rational, Clough shared them. His sympathies went wherever he saw the oppressed struggling to freedom.

> There are two kindreds upon earth, I know—
> The oppressors and the oppressed. But as for me,
> If I must choose to inflict wrong, or accept,
> May my last end, and life too, be with these.

Dipsychus' statement, together with his compassion for the "slaving brother" who propels the gondola while he takes his idle pleasure, rings with conviction. How strongly Clough felt where justice was at issue emerges at many points in his work. That he made the hero of the *Bothie* a Chartist supplies a notable instance. Philip's disquisitions on the dignity of labor, on equality, on rich and poor, and the evils of factitious rank, if they do not merit the stigma of "communistic," do at all events indicate that the sympathy of the poet with the ill-starred efforts of the Chartists was real.

Some of Clough's finest poetry came out of the inspiration of the continental revolutions. Emerson spoke of the *Amours* as "the sincerity of British culture," a poem written by "a man tremulous all over with sensibility . . . a fine pen that delicately finds the right word" [see letter dated 1858]. But more than literary interests took Clough to Paris in 1848 and to Rome in 1849 to witness the struggles with his own eyes. His letters home betray his hopes that a more equitable arrangement might ensue than hitherto had obtained. They bear out the lines of the *Amours* in which Claude speculates on the issues of war:

> Should I incarnadine ever this inky pacifical finger,
> Sooner far should it be for this vapour of Italy's freedom,
> Sooner far by the side of the d—d and dirty plebeians.

His reporting of events to his friends back in England shows an incisive grasp of realities. Historians agree with his diagnosis that the Parisian uprising was a middle-class movement. "This present assembly," he writes, "is extremely shopkeperish and merchantish in its feelings, and won't set to work at the organization of labour at all: but will prefer going to war to keep the people amused, rather than open any disagreeable social questions." Few will presume to question that his insight into the real cause of war was sound. With Old Testament fervor he expresses his disappointment at the turn taken by the revolution:

> Ichabod, Ichabod, the glory is departed! Liberty—
> Equality and Fraternity, driven back by shopkeeping bayonets, hides her red cap in dingiest St. Antoine. Well-to-do-ism shakes her Egyptian scourge to the tune of "Ye are idle, ye are idle: the tale of bricks will be doubled; and Moses and Aaron of Socialism can at the best only pray for plagues; which

will come, paving stones for vivats, and emeutes in all their quarters.

In May he predicted "another emeute" within three months, and his gloomiest presentiments were borne out during the "June days," when stern measures closed both the National Workshops and the Socialist headquarters. Clough discounted most of the tales of cruelty that circulated abroad, and was disposed to think of the revolt "in the same light as a great battle, with, on the whole, *less* horror, and certainly more meaning, than most great battles that one reads of."

During the summer of the following year, the gallant stand of the tiny Roman republic against the superior power of France called forth his admiration ("unto this has come our grand Liberty-Equality-and-Fraternity Revolution!"). He approved of Mazzini, and in general of the cause he was promoting—the deliverance of Italy from disunion and foreign domination by welding the whole peninsula in one republic. Clough agreed that the papacy—organ of oppression in the Roman states—stood as the main obstacle to realization of this aim. He apparently regarded the division of church lands among the peasants as a wholesome measure. Later, in 1859, he expressed not only his continuing sympathies with Garibaldi but his devout hope "that, with French influence predominating in Italy, the Pope will go to the dogs, with all his canaille accompanying." Clough has been arraigned as a mere spectator of stirring events—curious, but unconcerned as to the outcome. That he preferred to wage the conflict on an other than physical plane, however, argues simply that he thought the pen of more lasting efficiency than paving stones or swords.

Nothing of the fanatic, though, marked Clough's hopes of social betterment. As he expected less immediate advantage from any single attempt than Wordsworth and the Lake poets had of the Revolution of '89, so he experienced no great recoil at a comparative failure. Not at a single bound did he expect to attain "the good time." There is, he deemed [in his essay **"Recent Social Theories"**], no "royal road to human happiness" unmarked by continuing effort and struggle. Once achieved, Democracy must perennially seek out its wisest leadership. "The millennium, as Matt says, won't come this bout," he wrote from Liverpool in 1849, recalling his experiences of the previous year as he signed himself Citizen Clough. He felt that this knowledge, however, need not deter men from striving.

On the other hand, it does denote the necessity for defining justice according to the conditions which it presupposes and under which it has to exist. He recognized that force has its proper place in an organized community. Both for attaining justice and for developing the noblest traits of character, "coercion met by a mixture of resistance and submission" is requisite. He reminds enthusiasts that liberty is never absolute, but conditioned. More or less of liberty, is the real question. Since good is that which appeals to the highest self, liberty consists not merely in "doing as I please," which is the popular conception, but in acting according to an ideal of service. Such an ideal must guide a really successful revolt. Experience abundantly teaches that one tyranny may fall only to give way to another not less onerous, perhaps, for being different.

Clough's idea of the functional nature of property grows from this conception of liberty. His brave pamphlet on the Irish famine [*A Consideration of Objections against the Retrench-*

ment Association], denouncing the "sublime indifference" of the propertied classes to want and starvation, has wider application than the occasion which called it forth. We need not misrepresent Clough's intention if for the starving Irish we substitute ill-paid Lancashire operatives or undernourished and overworked mill children of Birmingham. Ownership of property, he insisted, entails commensurate responsibilities. It is at most a loan from the Giver of all things, "saddled with indefinite rent-charges, reservations, and reversional interests"; the needy have a lien which must be recognized. The earth, our ultimate wealth and subsistence, "hath he given to the children of men." One right—not to own property, but to work and receive the just wages of work—contravenes all others. Although Clough appeals to the conscience of the wealthy, the consequences to "sublime indifference" are not hard to draw. "Some one, I fear, might be found to look up your title-deeds, and to quote inconvenient Scriptures."

The ills which fell upon industrial workers, to be sure, sprang from a cause different from that of the Irish famine. The gradual but inevitable process by which labor was frequently reduced to conditions of slavery came about as a result of the competitive market. Though Englishmen in the main still clung to the doctrine of *laissez faire,* Clough condemned it in pointed satire. He thus parodies the Tenth Commandment in the concluding lines of his **"Latest Decalogue":**

> Thou shalt not covet, but tradition
> Approves all forms of competition.

It would be difficult to find anywhere else so concise and effective a statement of the basic hypocrisy of modern life. At one time Clough avowed his intent to become the "Apostle of anti-laissez-faire." That he gave up the ambition, we may perhaps regret; why he did so, we can merely guess.

That government must become increasingly instrumental in maintaining and promoting the general welfare, a deduction implicit in his rejection of *laissez faire,* may be fairly inferred also from Clough's remarks on education. He favored the extension of the secular system as rapidly as practical considerations would allow, although he did not think that the cause could prevail for the country in general on account of popular apathy in educational matters. But he believed that a start could be made in municipalities. He was convinced, moreover, that exclusion of secular schools from receiving government subsidies should cease. It was his opinion, based on unhappy experience, that propagation of knowledge ought to be freed of religious controls. He confided to Emerson his feeling that "all education is in England, and I think in America, so mixed up with religious matters, that it is a great difficulty."

Today it is no easy matter to realize, amid opportunities for universal secular education, that so recently as the 1850's the very idea was being debated in Victorian circles. The ease with which Clough's opinions might be dismissed as commonplace must not blind us to the fact that frequently they were radical in his own time. This ease owes itself, paradoxically, to the fact that time has borne out the soundness of Clough's instincts.

The chief bar to a true understanding of Clough appears to be merely that we lack from him a body of criticism such as Arnold left. Yet I think it would not be impossible to reconstruct Arnold's principles on the basis of an amount of evidence equal to that which Clough has left us. It takes patience, care, and sympathy; but this is the business of criticism. Granted this effort, Clough will be seen to have held positive moral convictions and positive social attitudes and

Oriel College, Oxford, which Clough attended from 1842 to 1848.

to have given them expression in his work as in his own life. (pp. 58-68)

Francis W. Palmer, "Was Clough a Failure?" in Philological Quarterly, Vol. XXII, No. 1, January, 1943, pp. 58-68.

MARTHA HALE SHACKFORD   (essay date 1946)

[*Shackford considers* Dipsychus *as a work of social criticism attacking the spiritual complacency and materialistic values that Clough perceived in English society during the time of the Oxford Movement.*]

Essentially a man of his epoch yet deeply critical of it, Clough must be studied in relation to the Victorian Age, which was dominated by a rapidly growing industrialism and a more or less autocratic science. Men were absorbed in problems relating to mechanical matters and physical laws; railways, steamboats, telegraph lines, mills, and merchandise seemed nearer and more real than questions of faith and truth. To be sure there were great reforms in this period; slavery in the colonies was abolished, the corn laws were repealed, factory acts were passed, the Catholics emancipated, and steady slow progress in civic betterment was made. But, as regards the average man, life was so full of material things that he had scant time for things spiritual. . . . Clough had none of this tendency to shirk the moral issue, he had none of the superstitious reverence for virtue by mechanics not by choice. And the very source of Clough's power as a poet lies in his eternal protest against spiritual smugness and mere compliance.

The general reader knows Clough as the author of several short poems which voice the spiritual unrest and aspiration of his days, but his position as a poet is not as firmly established as is that of his friend Matthew Arnold whose poems have deservedly won a wider audience. Various stumbling blocks do stand in the way of enjoyment of Clough's works. His poems are too centered in intellectual question, too abstract as compared with the imaginative "lucidity" and lyrical poignancy of "The Forsaken Merman," "Dover Beach," and "The Youth of Nature" which show Arnold's poetic birthright. Moreover, Clough has been called the poet of hopeless doubt, provoking pessimism and despair. Clough did doubt; he sought rational proof to support faith, he wore himself out in debate, but his actual belief is shown, inequivocally, in the short poem best known of all his work:

"With Whom is no Variableness, neither Shadow of Turning"

It fortifies my soul to know
That, though I perish, Truth is so:
That, howso'er I stray and range,
Whate'er I do, Thou dost not change.
I steadier step when I recall
That, if I slip, Thou dost not fall.

(pp. 47-8)

Another reason for difficulty in enjoying his poetry is the fact that he was perhaps the most pleasantly ironical poet of the whole nineteenth century. The literal-minded reader is baffled by a style which is subtle, based upon the desire to ridicule false, meretricious ideas by gravely seeming to champion these ideas. In **"The Latest Decalogue"** he lashes iniquity with a potent vigor, but he does it indirectly, professing to accept standards which we know are abhorrent to him. Yet who can fail to understand his meaning in

Honour thy parents; that is, all
From whom advancement may befall;
Thou shalt not kill; but need'st not strive
Officiously to keep alive.

Still another deterrent to reading Clough's poems with pleasure is his frequent use of a semi-mystical tone and mood in which he expresses his deep awareness of the individual's constant struggle to renounce the dear and pleasant familiar things of life in favor of invisible spiritual verities. Perhaps his most characteristic poem is the short lyric of five stanzas, on the Beautiful, beginning.

I have seen higher, holier things than these,
And therefore must to these refuse my heart,
Yet am I panting for a little ease;
I'll take and so depart.
Ah, hold! the heart is prone to fall away
Her high and cherished visions to forget,
And if thou takest, how wilt then repay
So vast, so dread a debt?

Before discussion **Dipsychus** which is thoroughly representative of all these aspects of his work, it is well to take a glance at . . . how the Oxford Movement of the eighteen forties affected him, for surely **Dipsychus** is related to that would-be renaissance in religion. . . . (pp. 48-9)

As a tutor and a Fellow, at Oriel, he came very closely into the atmosphere of Tractarianism, for Newman, whom he called "the Arch-Oxford-Tractator," was then at the height of his influence and power. Oxford reverberated to the footsteps of pilgrims toward an intensified religious life, based on a return to the ardor and the authority of the Early Church. Clough was quick to respond to the genuine appeals of this renovated purpose but he did not share all the aspirations of these men. The Tractarian Movement swept on its way carrying Newman into the Roman Catholic Church, in 1845,—the logical result of the ideas he had expressed in Tract Ninety. Of Newman's strong influence on both Arnold and Clough there is no doubt, though the admiration they felt was for Newman's great intellectual gifts rather than for his arguments on particular points of doctrine. (pp. 49-50)

[Clough] was disturbed, as early as 1843, about the precise meaning of the thirty-nine Articles of the Church which every Oxford student was then required to subscribe to, and which he did sign before taking his Master's degree. The questions in his mind were more insistent however; he admitted to friends that he was not satisfied with what seemed to him a merely passive acceptance of doctrine. Clough, already interested in "Germanized" scholarship, was impressed by the new ideas brought back from Germany by Jowett, tutor at Balliol since 1842, from visits there in 1845 and 1846. His conception of religion was already shaping towards that of "the Board Church," the title he inaugurated as defining a communion which permitted liberty of conscience based on vigilance of spirit. More and more he grew distrustful of dogmatic formulas. Being heir to Plato and Kant, as well as to the French Revolution he was an individualist in religion, feeling the necessity of a personal awareness of God, without any interfering ritual or creed. The poem beginning, "O Thou whose image," shows his mystical approach to the Divine:

O Thou, in that mysterious shrine
Enthroned, as I must say, divine!
I will not frame one thought of what
Thou mayest either be or not.
I will not prate of "thus" and "so,"

And be profane with "yes" and "no,"
Enough that in our soul and heart
Thou, whatso'er Thou mays't be, art.

In *Notes on the Religious Tradition,* a late prose work, Clough pleaded for tolerance and understanding, believing that he was not justified "in neglecting those pulsations of spiritual instinct which come to me from association at one time with Unitarians, at another with Calvinists, or again with Episcopalians and Roman Catholics." Not only as regards religious questions did he plead for breadth; he wrote to a friend (June 19, 1850), "It continues to strike me how ignorant you and I, and other young men of our set are . . . Enter the arena of your brethren, and go not to your grave without knowing what common merchants and solicitors, much more sailors and coalheavers are acquainted with. Ignorance is a poor kind of innocence. . . . When you get to the end of this life, you won't find another ready-made, in which you can do without effort what you were meant to do with effort here."

In the spring of 1848, at the height of his usefulness, he resigned his tutorship, and in October, his fellowship, because he felt that he could not honestly subscribe to these Articles of faith. The scrupulousness of his action is the more remarkable because he did not deny any of the Articles, he merely found it impossible to affirm them as positively as he thought an honest thinker should. Without making a show, or seeming to demand sympathy, he quietly renounced the intellectual and social life of Oxford, and departed to seek some other post. Perhaps his action helped toward the abolition, later, of the required signing of the Articles.

Such quiet heroism is seldom applauded; Clough was regarded not as a hero but as a problem. To-day we see more clearly how nobly he acted in refusing to be a hypocrite in order to make sure of benefits while he was conscious of uneasy doubts and incomplete loyalty. His renunciation involved the loss of almost all the associations and the friendships he valued. Detaching himself from the place that he loved he became the resident of a world crude, hard, difficult to a man of fine sensibility and a lover of old-established customs and traditions. The Oxford world represented fullness and depth of life. The stateliness of the old gray buildings, the quiet beauty of green "quad," and of gently flowing river, the sound of mellow chimes coming across the soft air, the almost visible and audible tradition of the place had appealed to him with keenest power. To go away, to feel that loneliness and longing, embittered always by a sense of estrangement due to misunderstanding on the part of his friends tested the very fiber of his spiritual life. Most of all he missed the zest and stimulus of his friendships there, the interchange of ideas, the pursuit of knowledge, the daily contact with men of like tastes and energies. To give up these was essential tragedy. (pp. 50-1)

It was during a visit to Venice in 1850 that Clough began *Dipsychus,* never completed, but a fragment of very great interest because it so suggestively pictures the Victorian conflict between comfort and the higher life. The poet presents, in a series of loosely woven scenes, the idealism and the spiritual irresolution of a typical young intellectual who, visiting Venice and delighting in the shimmering beauty of the city, fascinated by the gay irresponsible life is continually debating with himself as to whether the appeal of ease is the appeal of materialism or of good, honest common sense. The *dramatis personae,* Dipsychus and the Spirit, are merely the two sides of the "double-souled" young man. There is little action, only such as is needed to view the city. The more aspiring mood of the thinker is satirized by the Spirit of *laissez-faire* in the world of moral duty, until at the end of Part one, Dipsychus surrenders to the Mephisto within himself, and complies with worldly-wiseness. Part two is very Faustian, and has lost the zest of literary manner which characterizes the first Part. It cannot be claimed that *Dipsychus* is a great poem, it is only an experiment, yet singularly alive and important as diverging from the Oxford Movement.

The scene opens in the Piazza of St. Mark's where Dipsychus is pondering over the problem of the Resurrection, but interrupted by the Spirit who calls his attention to the picturesque sights and sounds near, so much more significant than empty musings about religion. So the semi-drama continues in and around Venice. There are charming pictures of the city in a vivid word or two which suggest the unique beauty of "this eldest child of Liberty" so beloved by Byron, Goethe, Shelley, Browning, and other poets. The hero wanders from scene to scene, now in the Public Gardens, now in the Academy of Art, in a gondola, whose motion is praised in an onomatopoetic lyric, now at the fashionable bathing beach, *The Lido,* now within St. Mark's church. Without seeking for effects, Clough gives pictures of the dim color, the marble, the palaces and churches, mellowed and harmonized by Adriatic tides, and conjures up in alluring variety the gaiety of the people whose talk and laughter mingle with the murmur of the water.

But always there is in the mind of Dipsychus an undercurrent of speculative thought, he is asking questions such as these: Is there evidence to prove the authenticity of the *Bible?* And if the *Bible* is true, is its teaching sufficient for the needs of the yearning human soul? Does philosophy, being more distinctly based on reason, prove a substitute for religion? Are Berkeley and Kant right: is sensuous experience only an illusion? Is thought the only reality? If philosophers prove too abstract, are poets and artists better guides to living? And, in the last analysis, are we so ringed around by necessity that we have no choice at all? Does the iron law of life compel us to conform? Or, divinest of dreams, has the individual perfect liberty, the power and the right to live his own life in the sanctity of spirit gained from communion between the Creator and the single soul? Clough's religious individualism finds expression in a stanza which reveals his essential longing for complete freedom in this mystical approach of mortal to divine:

O let me love my love unto myself alone,
And know my knowledge to the world unknown;
No witness to the vision call,
Beholding, unbeheld of all;
And worship thee, with thee withdrawn, apart,
Whoe'er, whate'er thou art,
Within the closest veil of mine own inmost heart.

One of his basic problems is whether the individual ever is at one with himself, free from cross currents of impulse or judgment which seem to defeat his centrality of being. Even if for a time, a man possesses this assured consciousness of a single harmonious identity does that consciousness continue? Is man's life anything more than a series of experiences, spasmodic, transitory, fugitive? Granting that the self is a centralized, self directing unit, there is another question,—what is the self's presumptive place in the unity of all life? Who can prove that this *is* a world of unity and purpose?

> . . . one would drudge
> And do one's petty part, and be content
>   . . . solaced still
> By thinking of the leagued fraternity,
> And of co-operation, and of the effect
> Of the great engine. If indeed it work,
> And is not a mere treadmill! Which it may be.
> Who can confirm it is not?

And what shall Dipsychus do,—the educated, scrupulous, philosophising youth, who seeks the *summum pulchrum* both in idea and in conduct? Can one make the perfect choice, achieve the absolutely right and suitable action? For the old familiar friends, after all, *are* eternally true,—faith, hope, love lead us on to duty, positive, courageous, constructive action. By every implication Clough asserted his belief in a sort of Pragmatism, not utilitarian but symbolic:

> Yet if we must live, as would seem,
> These peremptory heats to claim,
> Ah, not for profit, not for fame,
> And not for pleasure's giddy dream,
> And not for piping empty reeds,
> And not for colouring idle dust;
> If live we positively must.
> God's name be blest for noble deeds.

As a Critique of Pure Worldliness *Dipsychus* is most successful; as a work of art it fails. Readers justly complain that it is too casual, too disconcerting, a medley of blank verse and of various stanzas; that it moves not logically but chronologically. All this is true. From the literary point of view it is as a satire that *Dipsychus* is most interesting, and it should be judged as a satire on character. Many people make the mistake of censuring it because it has not the dramatic intensity of *Hamlet* or *Le Misanthrope* or because it does not lead inexorably onward as does Swift's *Argument Against Abolishing Christianity,* or because it has not the sustained tone of such satire as Dryden's terrible *Mac Flecknoe* with its rapier thrust,

> Trust nature, do not labour to be dull.

Clough, it seems, is closest in method and in purpose to Byron. Of course the difference between Byron, as a man and Clough needs no discussion; it is the moral fastidiousness and uncompromising idealism of Clough which makes him so memorable a person. But Clough enjoyed Byron's satires, especially the best of *Don Juan,* was impressed by his attack on Cant and Hypocrisy, and [was] delighted, in an almost undergraduate fashion, by Byron's tricks, his jaunty, adroit manipulation of puns, antitheses, double, triple, broken, and forced rimes, his insolent wit, and ironic anti-climax:

> But *"carpe diem"*, Juan, *"carpe, carpe!"*
> To-morrow sees another race as gay
> And transient, and devour'd by the same harpy.
> "Life's a poor player,"—then "play out the play,
> Ye villains!" and above all keep a sharp eye
> Much less on what you do than what you say:
> Be hypocritical, be cautious, be
> Not what you *seem,* but always what you *see.*

The doubts and restless cogitations of Dipsychus are expressed in the bland words of the worldy *Spirit,* whose somewhat undergraduate facetiousness and love of *reductio ad absurdum* give amusing contrast with the moral problems of Dipsychus. The comments vary from boyish pleasantry to more mature criticism. "Perfectibility" is glanced at by the wistful Dipsychus,

> Life it is beautiful truly, my brothers, I grant it you duly,
> But for perfection attaining is one method only, abstaining.

The Spirit, however, is the satirist, usually. Victorian conventionality he laughed at:

>   one perfect prayer
> For savoir-vivre and savoir-faire.

He gives mock advice to those who prefer sentiment to performance:

> Be large of aspiration, pure in hope,
> Sweet in fond longings, but in all things vague.

which reminds us of Blake's *Jerusalem,* though Clough did not read that:

> He that would do good to another must do it in Minute
>   Particulars.
> General Good is the plea of the scoundrel, hypocrite, and
>   flatterer.

There is playful jesting at Oxford's faith in athletics as the cure-all:

> But you, with this one bathe, no doubt,
> Have solved all questions out and out.

Men's futile and cowardly evasions of direct action are noted:

>   Yet as for you,
> You'll hardly have the courage to die outright;
> You'll somehow halve even it.

There seems a gradual increase in the cynicism of the Spirit, he grows more persuasive, and here Clough shows considerable dramatic power, especially in the pseudo-choruses with the refrain, "Submit, submit." These are so consummately ironical that they delude many readers into the belief that Clough approves of compliance, whereas, in truth, he was almost savagely contemptuous of the man who yields placidly to custom and comfort.

>   Submit, submit!
> 'Tis common sense, and human wit
> Can claim no higher name than it.
> Submit, submit!
> Devotion, and ideas, and love.
> And beauty claim their place above;
> But saint and sage and poet's dreams
> Divide the light in coloured streams,
> Which this alone gives all combined,
> The *siccum lumen* of the mind
>
> Called common sense: and no high wit
> Gives better counsel than does it.
> Submit, submit!

These stanzas sum up the materialistic philosophy of the tempting Spirit who seeks to beguile the scholar. If they are interpreted in the sense opposite to what they say, we see that in this bitter ironic way Clough is protesting at easy compliance with mere worldly common-sense. What he said, by implication, is "Rebel, aspire, follow ideals, and avoid the cheap compromise dictated by the power of this world? Beauty, truth, love, holiness, wisdom, imagination, art are eternal and desirable." The "dry light" of true wisdom, in the Heracleitean sense, is that nearest the fire, for "fire is at the top of the upward way."

In *Dipsychus* we see Clough's withering scorn for futile eva-

sions and cowardice in meeting life. The placid citizen who
goes out each morning, thinking:

> Men's business-wits, the only sane things,
> These and compliance are the main things,

will learn from Clough that there are "higher, holier things
than these." This poet believed in the individual's duty, in the
individual's obligation to take a vigorous part in the larger
life. His collected poems bear witness, on almost every page,
to the faith that

> Life loves no lookers-on at his great game.

He believed that man must progress, not by shambling along
following the conventions of the day, but by judicial fearless
scrutiny of these conventions, followed by individual action
and aspiration toward the *summum pulchrum*. But, although
the individual has his moral obligations, it is not for his own
salvation he must seek:

> Our gaieties, our luxuries,
> Our pleasures and our glee,
> Mere insolence and wantonness,
> Alas! they feel to me.
>
> How shall I laugh and sing and dance?
> My very heart recoils,
> While here to give my mirth a chance
> A hungry brother toils.
>
> The joy that does not spring from joy
> Which I in others see,
> How can I venture to employ,
> Or find it joy for me?

                                              (pp. 52-5)

*Martha Hale Shackford, "Clough's 'Dipsychus'," in
her* Studies of Certain Nineteenth Century Poets,
The Suburban Press, 1946, pp. 47-55.

DORIS N. DALGLISH (essay date 1952)

[*Dalglish analyzes Clough's shorter poems, concentrating her
discussion on the poet's religious beliefs.*]

If Clough's fragments entitled **The Mystery of the Fall** were
to be anonymously re-published or produced on the stage
today, the critics might make some strange guesses as to the
date of this apparently modern piece of drama. An 'early Victorian' Biblical play sounds strange enough, but the opening
of the **Mystery** does not date at all:

> *Adam.* Since that last evening we have fallen indeed!
> Yes, we have fallen, my Eve! O yes!—
> One, two, and three, and four;—the Appetite,
> The Enjoyment, the aftervoid, the thinking of it—
> Specially the latter two, most specially the last.
> There, in synopsis, see, you have it all:
> Come, let us go and work!
>   Is it not enough?
> What, is there three, four, five?

Adam's remark that "a first baby is a strange surprise' is in
the same tone, but Clough made no other attempts at this colloquialism. The slow evolving of consciousness and conscience in both Adam and Eve, their naive ponderings on the
Fall, and the strife of Cain and Abel, and the consequent ar-
guings round the problem of atonement, are presented in a
stark, tentative blank verse:

> If it be so, why are we here?—the world,
> Why is it as I find it? The dull stone
> Cast from my hand, why comes it not again?
> The broken flow'ret, why does it not live?
> If it be so,
> Why are we here, and why is Abel dead?
> Shall this be true
> Of stocks and stones and mere inanimate clay,
> And not in some sort also hold for us?

The fragments are unique among Clough's work and offer yet
another proof of the versatility of his talent. He wrote other
poems based on Old Testament history, short narratives, but
they are not remarkable. It is more interesting to examine the
work inspired by that frenzied disbelief in miracles which
raged among thoughtful Englishmen in the eighteen-fifties
much as psychoanalysis raged in the nineteen-twenties:

> As of old from Sinai's top
> God said that God is One,
> By Science strict so speaks He now
> To tell us, there is None!
> Earth goes by chemic forces; Heaven's
> A Mécanique Celeste!
> And heart and mind of humankind
> A watch-work as the rest!

Science was not the enemy whom Clough had particularly to
face, but the lines serve to show how far he was from accepting materialism with any but a satiric welcome. His religious
poems illuminate those years, so troubled for English religion, during which he knew Oxford and felt 'like a bit of
paper blown up the chimney by a draught', while W. G.
Ward did his best to prove to his pupil what lovely logical fun
the Catholic Church must be. After Clough was dead, Ward
repented of having forced the subtle problems of his own soul
upon the younger man. 'There goes Ward,' men had said in
Oxford, 'mystifying poor Clough, and persuading him that
he must either believe *nothing* or accept the whole of Church
doctrine.' One cannot imagine that Clough was temperamentally fond of ecclesiastical history. Such attraction as Tractarian views held for him was probably born of instinct and emotion. To Clough the psychological soundness of the system
advocated by Ward would be perfectly acceptable. His nature
was attuned to that generous wholeness of existence which
sheer individualism misses and for which the humanist constructs an impressive, and in some ways more comfortable,
substitute which no one finds it possible to enjoy. (pp. 38-9)

Clough's ardent and gifted nature came under the opposing
influences of contemporary religious thought, and his reactions are evident in his poetry. Take the lines which begin,

> Across the sea, along the shore,
> In numbers more and ever more,
> From lonely hut and busy town,
> The valley through, the mountain down,
> What was it ye went out to see,
> Ye silly folk of Galilee?
> The reed that in the wind doth shake?
> The weed that washes in the lake?
> The reeds that waver, the weeds that float?—
> A young man preaching in a boat.

Nothing could express better the Liberal and Christocentric
religion of Dr. Arnold which had been an inspiration to
Clough's boyhood.

The incomplete poem, **'The Shadow,'** and the significant
poem, **'Easter Day,'** both deal with the negations of the Gos-

pel which became current with the appearance, in 1835, of Strauss's life of Jesus. The shadow who says, 'I am that Jesus whom they slew', sits upon the grave:

> The subtle Jesuit cardinal shook his head,
> And mildly looked and said,
> It mattered not a jot
> Whether the thing, indeed, were so or not;
> Religion must be kept up, and the Church preserved
> And for the people this best served, . . .
>
> And English canons heard,
> And quietly demurred.
> Religion rests on evidence, of course,
> And on inquiry we must put no force.
> Difficulties still, upon whatever ground,
> Are likely, almost certain, to be found.
> The Theist scheme, the Pantheist, one and all,
>
> Must with, or e'en before, the Christian fall.
> And till the thing were plainer to our eyes,
> To disturb faith was surely most unwise.
> As for the Shade, who trusted such narration?
> Except, of course, in ancient revelation.
>
> And dignitaries of the Church came by.
> It had been worth to some of them, they said,
> Some hundred thousand pounds a year a head.
> If it fetched so much in the market, truly,
> 'Twas not a thing to be given up unduly.

The first part of **'Easter Day'** consists of a long emphatic denial of the Resurrection, expressed in some of the most passionate, fluent, flexible verse Clough ever wrote. Christian argument in poetry is something which passed in the seventeenth century from the common stream of English poetry. Christopher Smart and Cowper and the Wesleys had no desire to argue. Penitence and praise and adoration were their incentives. The poems which Newman wrote on his Mediterranean voyage were autobiographical when they did not recall the early Christian associations of the scene. Keble was avowedly a denominational poet. Until Clough wrote, in the middle of the century, no poet had, for over a hundred and fifty years, seen the relations of Christian dogma and contemporary thought as the centre of imaginative discussion. Browning's *Christmas Eve and Easter Day* is magnificent, but it is not theology; it is a rich piece of humanistic drama, and if Browning were alive now, he would, no doubt, lavish his energy on any powerful 'ideology' with the same enthusiasm. *Christmas Eve and Easter Day* anticipated those people whose unregulated zeal for a God of nothing but social love has helped to fling theology into the arms of Karl Barth. But Clough was neither a sectarian nor an advertisement writer. He wrote **'Easter Day'** in that spirit of 'trying to go into and at the bottom of an object' which, Arnold warned him, was fatal to the sensuousness of poetry. He knew that no man can ever escape from the shaping and moulding to which the creeds which he accepts or disowns subject the raw materials of his manhood. He possessed that good characteristic, the capacity for admiration. It had been aroused by Dr. Arnold's sincere Liberalism, but the 'young man preaching in a boat' Christianity could never have satisfied him. A mind as original and creative as Clough's knows that it dare not accept that moving figure of the historic Jesus merely as the figure of 'a young man preaching in a boat', dare not accept it at all unless it safeguard the miracle by institutional religion. And then he had had to admire the dialectics of Ward as they scintillated round the Catholic ideal. Clough himself was able to understand the resources of the Faith:

> O happy they whose hearts receive
> The implanted word with faith; believe
> Because their fathers did before,
> Because they learnt, and ask no more.
> High triumphs of convictions wrought,
> And won by individual thought;
> The joy, delusive oft, but keen,
> Of having with our own eyes seen,
> What if they have not felt nor known
> An amplitude instead they own,
> By no self-binding ordinance prest
> To toil in labour they detest:
> By no deceiving reasoning tied
> Or this or that way to decide.
>
> O happy they! above their head
> The glory of the unseen is spread;
> Their happy heart is free to range
> Thro' largest tracts of pleasant change;
> Their intellects encradled lie
> In boundless possibility.
> For impulses of varying kinds
> The Ancient Home a lodging finds:
> Each appetite our nature breeds,
> It meets with viands for its needs.

It is difficult to understand how any critic who has read **'Easter Day'** can continue to label Clough as the typical Victorian sceptic. The vehemence with which he paints the universal effects that follow from a denial of the Resurrection is the vehemence springing from abhorrence of a world unprotected by that holy fact. The varied and, for him, intricate rhetoric of the changing metrical form must spring from this suppressed passion:

> Eat, drink, and die, for we are souls bereaved:
> Of all the creatures under heaven's wide cope
> We are most hopeless, who had once most hope,
> And most beliefless, that had most believed.
> Ashes to ashes, dust to dust;
> As of the unjust, also of the just—
> Yea, of that Just One too!
> It is the one sad Gospel that is true—
> Christ is not risen!
>
> Ye men of Galilee!
> Why stand ye looking up to heaven, where Him ye ne'er
>   may see,
> Neither ascending hence, nor returning hither again?
> Ye ignorant and idle fishermen!
> Hence to your huts, and boats, and inland native shore,
> And catch not men, but fish;
> Whate'er things ye might wish,
> Him neither here nor there ye e'er shall meet with more.
> Ye poor deluded youths, go home,
> Mend the old nets ye left to roam,
> Tie the split oar, patch the torn sail:
> It was indeed an "idle tale"—
> He was not risen!

The conclusion seems almost weak after that outpouring of despair:

> Whate'er befell,
> Earth is not hell;
> Now, too, as when it first began,
> Life is yet life, and man is man.
> For all that breathe beneath the heaven's high cope,
> Joy with grief mixes, with despondence hope.
> Hope conquers cowardice, joy grief:
> Or at least, faith unbelief.
> Though dead, not dead;
> Not gone, though fled;

Not lost, though vanished.
In the great gospel and true creed,
He is yet risen indeed;
Christ is yet risen.

That faith 'at least' conquers unbelief seems a timorous answer to the sustained hypothesis of frustration which makes up the first part of the poem. The necessary corollaries to this bare statement have to be looked for in Clough's more personal and intimate poems; in such verses as this:

O Thou, in that mysterious shrine
Enthroned, as I must say, divine!
I will not frame one thought of what
Thou mayest either be or not.
I will not prate of "thus" and "so",
And be profane with "yes" and "no",
Enough that in our soul and heart
Thou, whatsoe'er Thou may'st be, art.

'Qui Laborat, Orat' is a poem which almost too carefully avoids suggesting Christianity. Yet it is not merely, as might appear on a first reading, a theistic version of Wordsworth's *'Ode to Duty.'* It is written by a man who worships.

O only Source of all our light and life,
Whom as our truth, our strength, we see and feel,
But whom the hours of mortal moral strife
Alone aright reveal!

Mine inmost soul, before Thee inly brought,
Thy presence owns ineffable, divine;
Chastised each rebel self-encentred thought,
My will adoreth Thine.

. . . . .

Nor times shall lack, when while the work it plies,
Unsummoned powers the blinding film shall part,
And scarce by happy tears made dim, the eyes
In recognition start.

At one point, it is true, Clough comes near the characteristic fastidiousness of Liberal thought.

It dare not dare the dread communion hold
In ways unworthy Thee,

does somehow remind one of Stopford Brooke's description of Arnold as making it his aim 'to clear away from religion those forms of it which violated intellectual and moral truth, and to establish what was eternal in it, beyond controversy, and fitted for God to be'. But Clough's mind was far too healthy to demand a model universe and grace which should be unfailingly comprehensible to mortals. And his nature was too rich to be truly satisfied with his own Stoical understatement:

It fortifies my soul to know
That, though I perish, Truth is so.

'My will adoreth Thine' was his native idiom.

It is not easy to define from his poems Clough's exact attitude towards the new critical and historical treatment of Christianity. It is improbable that a complete sceptic—Clough as the literary text-books see him—would have entitled a poem **'Epi-Strauss-Ium'** and exclaimed in it:

Matthew and Mark and Luke and holy John
Evanished all and gone . . .
Lost, is it, lost, to be recovered never?
However,

The place of worship the meantime with light
Is, if less truly, more sincerely bright,
And in blue skies the Orb is manifest to sight.

In one of his letters he wrote, 'I do not see that it is a great and noble thing, a very needful or very worthy service, to go about proclaiming that Mark is inconsistent with Luke, that the first Gospel is not really Matthew's.' But his sensitive conscience corroborated what his critical powers and sense of history would anyway have told him—that one Strauss does not make a new heaven and a new earth:

"Old things need not be therefore true",
O brother men, nor yet the new;
Ah! still awhile the old thought retain,
And yet consider it again!

The souls of now two thousand years
Have laid up here their toils and fears,
And all the earnings of their pain,—
Ah, yet consider it again!

We! what do we see? each a space
Of some few yards before his face;
Does that the whole wide plan explain?
Ah, yet consider it again!

One feels that it would have taken more than one work of destructive criticism to make Clough sit down limply and exclaim,

While we believed, on earth he went
And open stood his grave . . .
Now he is dead. Far hence he lies
In the lorn Syrian town.

If it is true that you cannot have an infidel astronomer, it is equally true that you cannot have an infidel satirist. It would take more than a Strauss to defeat a Clough and condemn him to languish in humanism. If he appeared to his contemporaries to be undecided, hesitating and even slack, it certainly was not from excess of indifference and scepticism. His fine faculties must have come very near exhaustion after passing from one deep whirlpool of religious emotion to another. Both the Liberalism of Dr. Arnold and the Tractarianism of Oxford had insisted upon introspection:

God's most deep decree
Bitter would have me taste: my taste was me.

But there was a world of difference between the two forms of introspection: the difference between examining oneself to see whether one is improving and examining oneself to ensure that one does not grow worse, is greater than it appears. After all, Dr. Arnold, 'waking up each morning', as has been said, 'with the conviction that everything was an open question', is one of the leaders of that procession whose participants today cherish optimistic little books on the psychology of religion. To pass from his influence to that of W. G. Ward must have been no inconsiderable shock.

We need to remind ourselves frequently that Clough was only forty-two at the time of his death. He had had a deep experience of that 'mortal moral strife' in which, more clearly than in any less exacting atmosphere, he declared, man is conscious of the divinity by which he lives. But Clough was neither old nor exhausted. He was approaching the crucial years of life when he died. The varying atmospheres of religious enthusiasm and prejudice in which he had spent so many years might well have drained from his spirit belief and energy, admiration and love, leaving him at the mercy of seven spirits of crankiness or indifference. Cranks, however, did not arise until later in the century, when humanitarianism and other reforms were more intensively developed, and indifference could never, even in his most depressed moments, have found a home in Clough's heart.

Any careful study of Clough leaves one marvelling at the indifference and neglect which have allowed him to be deposed to the rank of an earnest poet of meagre output, who moralized in a gentlemanly way because Dr. Arnold had been his headmaster. Inevitably one is left not only marvelling but exposed to a peculiarly strong temptation to belittle Tennyson. To find fault with him for not being Clough is even less sensible than to join in the wholesale depreciation of him which was evident in the nineteen-twenties, for those who depreciated had at least some right on their side. Nevertheless, it is exasperating to see so much rough-hewn excellence, even loveliness, lying unread while (apart from *In Memoriam* which, along with certain lyrics, will never abide our question) the pale or hectic dreams of Tennyson, all elongated and involved like the Nouveau Art of a later day, remain unquestioned.

Consider, for example, that plain and simple poem which Clough puts into the mouth of a French girl, one of Millet's peasants as it might be, who is driving her cows home.

> For work we must, and what we see, we see,
> And God He knows, and what must be, must be;
> When sweethearts wander far away from me,
> Home, Rose, and home, Provence and La Palie.
>
> The sky behind is brightening up anew
> (Home, Rose, and home, Provence and La Palie),
> The rain is ending, and our journey too:
> Heigho! aha! for here at home are we:—
> In, Rose, and in, Provence and La Palie.

We have proof in **Mari Magno** that Clough had observed very closely not only peasant girls but everybody whom he had met while making the commonplace Continental tours of the educated man of his time. Tennyson, on the other hand (it was not his fault), seems to have gained nothing from such travel but the purely subjective sensations of each moment. It would probably have been very good for him had he travelled much more widely and actually seen India and Mexico, instead of having to satisfy his imagination with tropical dreams of scarlet flowers and purple sunsets.

That Clough should trouble to write a poem of 46 lines, giving his idea of what might be passing through the peasant girl's mind, is another proof of what has to be rather regrettably called the progress of poetry as social history. It is a very significant change. Wordsworth was much more familiar with peasants than was Clough, but he saw them so exclusively as symbolic figures and as adjuncts to his own soliloquies that the poet probably did not know as much about them as the Oxford don knew. When Wordsworth wrote about them, he took personality away from them. Either they illustrated, as did the French girl with her knitting and her 'hunger-bitten heifer', what man had made of man, or they unconsciously helped the poet who chanced to meet them to understand how much hidden virtue there still was in man. But that their emotions could have any aesthetic value apart from his own appreciation of them would have been to Wordsworth a subversive idea. Clough's poem is not very ambitious—we have only to consider what Browning would have made of Ermyntrude, or whatever he would have named the heroine—but, like Rossetti's *Jenny,* it clearly marks a phase

of evolution in nineteenth-century poetry. More than fifty years were to pass before young Charles Sorley, filled with hero-worship of Masefield, exclaimed that it was 'the most awfully sad thing in history' that poetry had become a kind of upper-class preserve. When Clough wrote of peasants, Scottish or French, he too was in revolt against static conceptions of human worth. He was reverting to that earlier ideal of the importance of the individual which the spacious freedom of Protestantism had helped to destroy. For him the girl driving Provence and La Palie had in herself meaning and dignity, and in composing verses which she might have recited he acted in the spirit of the medieval poet who had never heard of 'Humanity' rather than in that of 'Humanity's' modern devotees. Here is another proof that to view Clough as the complete sceptic is entirely to misread his writings. That unconscious and unselfconscious admission of some other person's right to think and feel, an independent and solitary right, argues a humility which the sceptic is not, indeed, debarred from feeling, but which in the moment of its birth uproots his scepticism. In a poet the result is a willingness to enter into the communal, brotherly, scarcely differentiated experience of the race and to use without mediation or embellishment as much as the soul can there accept.

A more familiar poem which reveals the same depth of feeling is **'Qua Cursum Ventus.'** The revelation is one of more intimate and really passionate feeling, and it is hardly clear on a first reading. Indeed with much of Clough's poetry a second or a third reading is necessary before one can dig through the sheer solidity of thought and discover the spring of imagination. He demands concentrated reading, for he usually lacks surface attraction.

We do not know for certain what friend Clough had in mind when he wrote this poem of separation which suggests nothing so much as Wordsworth's 'There is a change and I am poor'. Was he Arnold? Was he W. G. Ward? At any rate Clough endured a wound which cut to the very heart; and Victorian friendships could suffer pangs which our age of compromise and indifference too rarely encounters. A companionship, one of those companionships round which the life that Oxford knows sheds its distinctive light, had to undergo human cleavage and Clough had to write,

> To veer, how vain! On, onward strain,
> Brave barks! In light, in darkness too,
> Through winds and tides one compass guides—
> To that, and your own selves, be true.
>
> But O blithe breeze! and O great seas,
> Though ne'er, that earliest parting past,
> On your wide plain they join again,
> Together lead them home at last.
>
> One port, methought, alike they sought,
> One purpose hold where'er they fare,—
> O bounding breeze, O rushing seas!
> At last, at last, unite them there!

The first part of the poem is calm and matter of fact, but at this point emotion will have its say and even dictates the additional emphasis of the internal rhymes. One can forgive the slight extra jingle of 'where'er they fare', because the general level of Clough's expression of courage and hope and wistful longing for happiness past as well as unrealized is so high. And because there is no 'period' feeling anywhere in the poem, one cries out yet again with wonder and sorrow that a man could have written like this nearly a hundred years ago and been so deplorably neglected.

The fact that the poems written at the end of Clough's short life possess so much of the spirit of English satiric narrative indicates that he knew no prolonged exile from the realistic universe of faith with its more honest laughter and its nobler pain. In short, he never essentially departed from the position in which one attacks, instead of constructing, a world which is not in fact either brave or new.

At other times a more embittered realism provoked him, and he burst out into satiric verse which must have been inspired by dislike of the wealthy parvenu and the inevitable creation, in an industrial society, of a new middle class as yet lacking in tradition. The dislike is one which he shared with Tennyson. Every couplet of **'The Latest Decalogue,'** from

> Thou shalt have one God only; who
> Would be at the expense of two?

onwards, condemns a spirit of competition and profit-making. A new and powerful element was present in English society, dominant over what Clough had called, in the *Bothie*

> the whole great and wicked artificial civilized fabric—
> All its unfinished houses, lots for sale, and railway outworks.

We should not forget that his early years had been spent in America, where the various potentialities, both good and evil, of a younger and more democratic constitution must have been symbolized, for the mind of a child, in persons and objects outwardly unimpressive. He could speak as the satirist of society, and he could also speak as the satirist of human nature. Rebellion burns furiously in that impetuous poem, **'Duty.'**

> Duty—that's to say, complying
> With whate'er's expected here;
> On your unknown cousin's dying,
> Straight be ready with the tear;
>
> . . . . .
>
> Duty—'tis to take on trust
> What things are good, and right, and just;
> And whether indeed they be or be not,
> Try not, test not, feel not, see not:
> 'Tis walk and dance, sit down and rise
> By leading, opening ne'er your eyes;
> Stunt sturdy limbs that Nature gave,
> And be drawn in a Bath chair along to the grave.

His prejudice against rank individualism elevated to a social principle was as strong as Arnold's, but he was lacking in the didactic impulse which produced *Culture and Anarchy*. Clough's mind did not, we feel, move easily among those irrational political circumstances and exasperating social accidents which caused his friend to suffer. He was not compelled to encounter middle-class Nonconformity in his professional life, as was Arnold. Nevertheless, even if the two men had changed places, it is doubtful whether we should have found Clough using such phrases as 'the hideous and grotesque illusions of middle-class Protestantism'. For all its truth, *Culture and Anarchy* makes rather painful reading. One sympathizes and one wishes that Arnold's protests had been able to check the equally 'hideous and grotesque' illusions of the academic Liberals which were to develop so disastrously, both outside and in the Church, in years to come. At the same time, one

is conscious of his unpreparedness and of the inadequacy of the weapons which he brought with him. Much of his habit of repetition may have been due to his own consciousness of resources which might have been more solid. It needs something far stronger and more primitively simple than culture to withstand the anarchy of Liberalism. However, 'not deep the poet sees but wide'—one sort of poet. There was abundance of thought in the England which Arnold knew, but the story of both history and aesthetics has since been enriched by research and theory of which he did not know. At a time when criticism and counter-criticism of one another's poems were exchanged between the two friends, Arnold complained that Clough was not *natural* and had a trying habit of *solving* the universe. (The italics are Arnold's.) Clough retorted that Arnold was 'confined within the dismal circle of his Hindoo-Greek philosophy', and blamed him for turning and twisting his eyes 'in the hope of seeing things as Homer, Sophocles, Virgil, or Milton saw them'. In these words he asserted his own independent nature and his own preference for what was deep, although not necessarily in opposition to what was wide. Even if he might have chosen to oppose to Liberalism the forces which Arnold opposed, one may doubt whether it would have entered his head to give them the titles of Hebraism and Hellenism. Names did not mean much to Clough, for he had not the temperament which makes phrases. He would have gone back, as usual, to first principles and to that simple human sympathy which illuminated his narrative poems. (pp. 40-52)

> *Doris N. Dalglish, "Arthur Hugh Clough: The Shorter Poems," in* Essays in Criticism, *Vol. II, No. 1, January, 1952, pp. 38-53.*

WALTER E. HOUGHTON (essay date 1963)

[*Analyzing* The Bothie of Tober-na-Vuolich, *Houghton argues that the poem continues to appeal to modern audiences because of its masterful synthesis of story and ideas, the breadth of its portrayal of young adulthood, and its sheer ability to delight.*]

When Clough published **The Bothie of Tober-na-Vuolich** in November 1848, his friends were astonished, partly because they expected a defense of his resignation (whether a theological pamphlet or an **Adam and Eve**), but mainly, I think, because they could not identify the author with the work. The prize pupil of Dr. Arnold had written a poem that was called "indecent and profane, immoral and Communistic." The reticent man who had been struggling with religious doubts and composing intellectual lyrics for **Ambarvalia** had produced a comedy of Oxford undergraduates. Emerson's reaction was hardly unique [see letter dated 1849]:

> It delights and surprises me from beginning to end.
> I can hardly forgive you for keeping your secret
> from me so well. . . . I am recalling every passage
> of speech and action of my staid and reticent friend,
> to find the hints and parallels of what I read.

The hints and parallels were there, of course, even if not generally known. After the intellectualism of Oxford and the long indecision ("Shall I resign?" involving "What shall I do?" involving "Who am I?") and after the confession of faith he had made in **Adam and Eve,** Clough could now respond unequivocally to the objective tendencies of his nature, and release the buoyant, even boyish, spirits so long suppressed. Furthermore, waiting to be turned from theory to realization, there lay in his mind the idea of a large modern poem capturing the spirit of the age, wrestling with its problems, reflecting its complex experience, and speaking its idiom. (pp. 92-3)

The Bothie is no longer modern. It has lost the contemporary appeal of its realism and its radical ideas—radical in the 1840s—on social equality, the duty of work, and the role of woman, whether peasant or fine lady. (Chartism, Christian Socialism, and Tennyson's *Princess,* published in the previous year, are in the immediate background.) No one today will find the hexameters a point of angry attack or eloquent defense. And though there are signs of its revival, the narrative poem is not in vogue. What keeps *The Bothie* fresh and alive is its masterly fusion of plot, character, setting, and ideas; its suggestion, because of the range of feeling and variety of tone, of a broad picture of life, at any rate youthful life; and most of all, its sheer charm, or whatever it is that makes it one of the most delightful poems in English literature.

In itself the action is handled with quiet suspense and forward thrust. Clough never forgets he is telling a story, at least not until Canto IX when the story is over. The characterization, though not so subtle as it is in *Amours de Voyage,* is remarkably deft, hitting off temperament, speech, and dress with graphic economy, and sharpening the sketch of individuals by the clash or comparison of personalities: Hewson vs. Lindsay, Hewson and Adam, Lindsay and Arthur, Kitty vs. Elspie. Moreover, the reading party as a whole is vividly created. Though the subject has often been attempted, undergraduates have perhaps never been caught with better success—swimming, reading, dancing, and endlessly talking (about politics and women and love and philosophies of life), arguing, debating, telling stories, in the latest slang and the typical wit (a mixture of sexual jokes and academic puns)—the whole shot through with a spirit of gaiety and friendship that is suddenly touched, here and there, by a note of irritation or dislike.

Philip Hewson, the hero, is a Chartist with social ideals of equality and the duty of work, but he has the "eager, impetuous" temperament of the reformer, which can sometimes make him "wild and flighty." This blending of wisdom with exaggeration is nicely recorded in his fiery speech of Canto II. For after satirizing the artificialities of courtship ("evening parties, shooting with bows . . . turning the leaves on the dreary piano, offering unneeded arms") and pleading for women to be helpmates instead of dolls, he rushes on to demand that ladies abandon ballroom, carriage, and satins for "washing, cooking, and scouring, or . . . uprooting potatoes," and dress in "plain linsey-woolsey"; for what is useful, he claims, is graceful, and "labour alone, can add to the beauty of women." But Philip's ideas are not just those of a Chartist with what the Piper calls his "confounded *égalité.*" They are also those of a young man whose experience counts as heavily as his thinking. "One day," he says, when I was

> strolling, ungainly in hobbadiboyhood,
> Chanced it my eye fell aside on a capless, bonnetless maiden,
> Bending with three-pronged fork in a garden uprooting potatoes.
> Was it the air? who can say? or herself, or the charm of the labour?
> But a new thing was in me; and longing delicious possessed me,
> Longing to take her and lift her, and put her away from her slaving.
> Was it embracing or aiding was most in my mind? hard question!

> But a new thing was in me; I, too, was a youth among maidens:
> Was it the air? who can say? but in part 'twas the charm of the labour.
>
> (II, 42-50)

Hewson's theories are beautifully connected with his passions, and both are interwoven in his prediction of what household work and homespun clothes can accomplish:

> So, feel women, not dolls; so feel the sap of existence
> Circulate up through their roots from the far-away centre of all things,
> Circulate up from the depths to the bud on the twig that is topmost!
> Yes, we should see them delighted, delighted ourselves in the seeing,
> Bending with blue cotton gown skirted-up over striped linsey-woolsey,
> Milking the kine in the field, like Rachel, watering cattle,
> Rachel, when at the well the predestined beheld and kissed her,
> Or, with pail upon head, like Dora beloved of Alexis,
> Comely, with well-poised pail over neck arching soft to the shoulders,
> Comely in gracefullest act, one arm uplifted to stay it,
> Home from the river or pump moving stately and calm to the laundry.
>
> (II, 92-102)

The beauty of labor is wonderfully fused with the beauty of feminine posture.

After an outburst of Lindsay's, and Hobbes' amusing description of Hewson as "a Pugin of women" (having the same scorn of the purely ornamental and the same belief in the union of "use and grace"), Adam the tutor, who sees the truth in Philip's view, disliking luxurious living himself and believing on moral grounds in the duty of work, also sees its excesses, which he calls "distortions." One should seek only the good, he says, and not the attractive, and since inequality is a fact of creation, one should remain in his station. To which Hewson replies, acidly:

> Alas! the noted phrase of the prayer-book,
> *Doing our duty in that state of life to which God has called us,*
> Seems to me always to mean, when the little rich boys say it,
> Standing in velvet frock by mama's brocaded flounces,
> Eying her gold-fastened book and the watch and chain at her bosom,
> Seems to me always to mean, Eat, drink, and never mind others.
>
> (II, 202-07)

The education of Philip Hewson that follows through the next cantos is the education of both the young radical and the young man, for doctrine and experience continue to interact in a living character. In Canto III the incipient affair with Katie, the farmer's daughter at Rannoch, is the meeting point of advanced theory and masculine susceptibility:

> But tell me, said Hobbes, interposing,
> Did you not say she was seen every day . . . washing, cooking, scouring?
> How could he help but love her? nor lacked there perhaps the attraction
> That, in a blue cotton print tucked up over striped linsey-woolsey,
> Barefoot, barelegged, he beheld her, with arms bare up to the elbows,

Bending with fork in her hand in a garden uprooting potatoes?

(III, 228-34)

The following Canto is not entirely successful. In Philip's
moral struggle to resist temptation, the admonitory vision of
the ruined girl turned prostitute is a Victorian convention
now outmoded. Adam's lecture on the weakness of women
and the difference between gaining wisdom by intuition and
by experience—though entirely in character—seems too
long, or it seems too much like a lecture from Clough. But
Adam seizes effectively on the opportunity to drive home his
earlier advice ("seek only the good," and seek it "in your station"); and the saving glance of Elspie, with its elaborate
meaning (lines 135-44), is a skilful projection of Philip's conscience. What is more, his passionate longing to return to
Katie has the specificity of mixed emotions and oblique sexuality:

Spirits escaped from the body can enter and be with the
living;
Entering unseen, and retiring unquestioned, they bring,—
do they feel too?—
Joy, pure joy, as they mingle and mix inner essence with
essence;
Would I were dead, I keep saying, that so I could go and
uphold her!

. . . . .

Is it impossible, say you, these passionate, fervent impul-
sions,
These projections of spirit to spirit, these inward em-
braces,
Should in strange ways, in her dreams, should visit her,
strengthen her, shield her?
Is it possible, rather, that these great floods of feeling
Setting-in daily from me towards her should, impotent
wholly,
Bring neither sound nor motion to that sweet shore they
heave to?
Efflux here, and there no stir nor pulse of influx!
Would I were dead, I keep saying, that so I could go and
uphold her!

(IV, 40-43, 48-55)

Thus, if Philip chooses the good in Canto IV, he is far from
ignoring the attractive; indeed, he is the more exposed, after
this frustration, to the attraction of someone of his own class.
Furthermore, to the extent that his radical ideas are exaggerated, they are the more easily abandoned under contrary
pressure. It is only momentarily, therefore (but long enough
for the impact to arrest attention), that we are surprised by
the rightabout-face in Canto V. Philip is still dancing but
"dancing in Balloch . . . in the castle with Lady Maria."
And being Philip, he proceeds at once to erect a new theory—
or is it a rationalization? Because his distaste of idle luxury
and his sympathy for the poor are entirely genuine, he reveals
his skepticism in the very act of profession:

What of the poor and the weary? their labour and pain is
needed.
Perish the poor and the weary! what can they better than
perish,
Perish in labour for her, who is worth the destruction of
empires?

. . . . .

Dig in thy deep dark prison, O miner! and finding be
thankful;

Though unpolished by thee, unto thee unseen in perfection,
While thou art eating black bread in the poisonous air of
thy cavern,
Far away glitters the gem on the peerless neck of a Princess,
Dig, and starve, and be thankful.

(V, 51-53, 64-68)

The extravagant phrasing betrays an act of the will! Indeed,
that is all but implied by the opening line: "Often I find myself saying, and know not myself as I say it." His praise of
Lady Maria has the same ambiguity:

Suffer that service be done you, permit of the page and the
valet,
Vex not your souls with annoyance of charity schools or
of districts,
Cast not to swine of the sty the pearls that should gleam
in your foreheads.
Live, be lovely, forget them, be beautiful even to proud-
ness,
Even for their poor sakes whose happiness is to behold
you;
Live, be uncaring, be joyous, be sumptuous; only be lovely.

(V, 72-77)

That could hardly be spoken straight by Philip Hewson the
Chartist unless he were madly in love. Otherwise it would be
half ironic. The opening line gives the answer: "Often I find
myself saying, in irony is it, or earnest?" But under the circumstances, it *is* half earnest too, and he gives the last command a qualification that makes it his own:

Live, be uncaring, be joyous, be sumptuous; only be lovely,—
Sumptuous not for display, and joyous, not for enjoyment;
Not for enjoyment truly; for Beauty and God's great
glory!

(V, 77-79)

In similar fashion the next paragraph, in which he comes
round to Adam's philosophy and wonders if God has not,
after all, disposed his works "in a wonderful order" and made
"man, as the beasts, to live the one on the other," begins with
the warning: "It seems inspiration—of Good or of Evil!"
Plainly, a new Katie with more character will have no trouble
displacing Lady Maria, especially in a man and a thinker
who, in both roles, is "the eager, impetuous Philip."

Clough drew his hero with a sure hand, but he was anxious
about his heroine and the speech of the lovers, never an easy
thing for a young writer to handle, and here complicated by
distinctions of class. His success in this area is now difficult
to judge, because literary fashions and actual mores, too, can
change so much that what is natural for one generation may
seem stilted to another. Allowance must be made for some
Victorian sentimentality: Philip's tears are especially trying.
Elspie must be read within the context of Romantic primitiv-
ism and the need of the Victorian intellectual to find in
woman an incarnation of the simplicity and force of elemental nature. After describing a city at dawn as "resumed to Primal Nature and Beauty," Philip adds, "Such—in me, and to
me, and on me the love of Elspie!" That explains her commanding presence in Cantos VII-VIII and her complete domination of her social and intellectual superior, not noted for
his timidity or shyness. But her speech is, and was, a problem.
Many will agree with Froude that she has "too great command of language and metaphor, and that very few women
and no young girls ever did talk in finished simile, however

clever they were." One might answer that not many Roman soldiers talked of Antony and Cleopatra in the brilliant metaphors of Enobarbus. If the artist may not put the right words into mouths that otherwise would be dumb or fumbling, a good deal of literature must be devalued. But "right" must mean not only expressive but also in keeping, that is, blended into the texture. In this story, Elspie's speech, side by side with the other voices, had to be realistic. It could show great command of language and metaphor, but the particular idiom had to be one which, like Enobarbus's, we could imagine her using. No one was ever as witty as Millamant, but her wit becomes her so well we suspend our disbelief; whereas Elspie's elaborate similes, thrown off in conversation, seem incongruous and, therefore, unbelievable. Only their form, however, not their content, is out of keeping. As she considers her possible union with Philip, Elspie thinks of the new bridge over the burn:

> I have been building myself, up, up, and toilfully raising,
> Just like as if the bridge were to do it itself without masons,
> Painfully getting myself upraised one stone on another,
> All one side I mean; and now I see on the other
> Just such another fabric uprising, better and stronger,
> Close to me, coming to join me: and then I sometimes fancy,—
> Sometimes I find myself dreaming at nights about arches and bridges,—
> Sometimes I dream of a great invisible hand coming down, and
> Dropping the great key-stone in the middle: there in my dreaming,
> There I feel the great key-stone coming in, and through it
> Feel the other part—all the other stones of the archway,
> Joined into mine with a strange happy sense of completeness.
>
> (VII, 61-72)

The phrasing of the final lines makes it plain that the keystone is a phallic image, and the dream is "Freudian." The next day she explores the relationship with Philip in another simile equally revealing:

> You are too strong, you see, Mr. Philip! just like the sea there,
> Which *will* come, through the straits and all between the mountains,
> Forcing its great strong tide into every nook and inlet,
> Getting far in, up the quiet stream of sweet inland water,
> Sucking it up, and stopping it, turning it, driving it backward,
> Quite preventing its own quiet running: and then, soon after,
> Back it goes off, leaving weeds on the shore, and wrack and uncleanness:
> And the poor burn in the glen tries again its peaceful running,
> But it is brackish and tainted, and all its banks in disorder.
> That was what I dreamt all last night. I was the burnie,
> Trying to get along through the tyrannous brine, and could not;
> I was confined and squeezed in the coils of the great salt tide, that
> Would mix-in itself with me, and change me.
>
> (VII, 120-32)

And then she concludes,

> And I struggled, and screamed, I believe, in my dream. It was dreadful.

You are too strong, Mr. Philip! I am . . .

. . . . .

quite afraid and unwilling.

(VII, 133-34, 136)

This is clearly a sexual nightmare in which the manifest content is so thin it could only pass unanalyzed in a modest and "pure minded" young woman living in 1848. By an extraordinary piece of daring, Clough has put the most suggestive language into the mouth of a person who could not possibly be suggestive, and by so doing has not only underlined her simplicity but revealed the unconscious mode in which sexual fears find verbal expression.

But when Philip meekly promises to depart tomorrow, Elspie at once forgets her dread, and boldly taking his hand kisses the cold fingers. This reversal of feeling is brilliantly expressed in the same imagery, with the masculine tide now ebbing and the feminine burn rushing after it:

> That great power withdrawn, receding here and passive,
> Felt she in myriad springs, her sources, far in the mountains,
> Stirring, collecting, rising, upheaving, forth-outflowing,
> Taking and joining, right welcome, that delicate rill in the valley,
> Filling it, making it strong, and still descending, seeking,
>
> . . . . .
>
> With a delicious forefeeling, the great still sea before it.
>
> (VII, 157-161, 163)

In Canto VIII, however, a new revulsion comes over "the spirit of Elspie" as she feels a new terror, that of "deserting her station." The ensuing argument, recalling an earlier pattern of ideas, stresses equality, now of husband and wife (contra Tennyson's *Princess*), and the democratic distaste for "the old solemn gentility stageplay." Elspie refuses to become a "lady" waited upon by footmen, not because she cannot fill the role, but because she wants to abide by her training and continue to work; to which Philip answers, "God forbid you should ever be aught but yourself."

It is characteristic of Clough's success in blending character and theme that Canto IX opens, a few lines later, with Philip erecting this remark into an abstract principle and connecting it with his equalitarian theory of labor. Regardless of class or of sex, let each of us "do the thing we are meant for": Lady Marias *perhaps* to be lovely and idle; other women (again, contra Tennyson) to have careers in teaching and nursing. And true to his temperament, Philip pushes his latest idea to extremes:

> If you were meant to plough, Lord Marquis, out with you, and do it;
> If you were meant to be idle, O beggar, behold, I will feed you.
> If you were born for a groom, and you seem, by your dress, to believe so,
> Do it like a man, Sir George, for pay, in a livery stable;
>
> . . . . .
>
> Hast thou for cooking a turn, little Lady Clarissa? in with them,
> In with your fingers! their beauty it spoils, but your own it enhances;
> For it is beautiful only to do the thing we are meant for.
>
> (IX, 18-21, 37-39)

This is too much for Adam the grave man with his caution and his common sense. He reiterates the social theory he had expounded in Canto II:

> When the armies are set in array, and the battle beginning,
> Is it well that the soldier whose post is far to the leftward
> Say, I will go to the right, it is there I shall do best service?
> There is a great Field-Marshal, my friend, who arrays our battalions;
> Let us to Providence trust, and abide and work in our stations.
>
> (IX, 41-45)

Philip's retort to that, with its sharp question pointed at the weak sides of conservatism, renews the earlier debate. How, he asks, can we distinguish between the circumstance we should take arms against and the circumstance we should accept as an act of Providence? Specifically, in the Victorian battle of ideas, which Arnold, too, was picturing at the same time in the same imagery,

> What are we to resist, and what are we to be friends with?
> If there is battle, 'tis battle by night: I stand in the darkness,
> Here in the mêlée of men, Ionian and Dorian on both sides,
> Signal and password known; which is friend and which is foeman?
> Is it a friend? I doubt, though he speaks with the voice of a brother.
>
> (IX, 50-54)

Indeed, the situation is even worse.

> O that the armies indeed were arrayed! O joy of the onset!
> Sound, thou Trumpet of God, come forth, Great Cause, to array us,
> King and leader appear, thy soldiers sorrowing seek thee.
>
> . . . . .
>
> Neither battle I see, nor arraying, nor King in Israel,
> Only infinite jumble and mess and dislocation,
> Backed by a solemn appeal, 'For God's sake do not stir, there!'
>
> (IX, 59-61, 63-65)

But Philip is no longer the Philip of Canto II. He is able now, now that he has looked with pleasure into the castle at Balloch, to accept a philosophy of order—at any rate in theory. In the middle of this radical passage he says:

> Still you are right, I suppose; you always are, and will be;
> Though I mistrust the Field-Marshal, I bow to the duty of order.
>
> (IX, 55-56)

But the phrasing is dubious, and his concluding words seem to reiterate his own position:

> Yet you are right, I suppose; if you don't attack my conclusion,
> Let us get on as we can, and do the thing we are fit for;
> Every one for himself, and the common success for us all, and
> Thankful, if not for our own, why then for the triumph of others,
> Get along, each as we can, and do the thing we are meant for.
> That isn't likely to be by sitting still, eating and drinking.
>
> (IX, 66-71)

The last line reveals a continuing distaste for aristocratic life; and in the next letter his "soul of souls" is filled with "the old

democratic fervour" for an equalitarian society where no one should sit still and everyone should work—preferably, he seems to feel, with his hands. Certainly, he himself, after taking a first class degree at Oxford, married a farmer's daughter and in New Zealand "hewed, and dug; subdued the earth and his spirit." Still, he was not insincere in telling Adam he supposed he was right. He thought he was—the Oxonian in him thought he was—and yet he lived by another creed, being committed deeply to the anti-aristocratic radicalism of the 1840s.

A modern poem that would capture the spirit of the age had to aim at a synthesis of elements hitherto kept apart for reasons of simplicity or decorum. It had to have range of experience and diversity of tone, and perhaps a mixture of genres. For the age had not only felt the romantic delight in plenitude, it was itself, as Clough noticed, crowded with "new books and new events." The self-consciousness that accompanied the decay of established ideas and turned the individual back upon himself had opened up new areas of feeling and observation. Life was more complex, and one was more aware of the complexity. Less than a year before *The Bothie* was written, Arnold was saying to Clough that had Shakespeare and Milton been writing now, they would have had "the multitude of new thoughts and feelings to deal with a modern has"; while Clough himself a little later was telling Allingham that one should write not "short things" but narrative poems because "a large experience . . . is necessary to attract the modern world to poetry. Shakespeare and Milton should meet together as Rousseau and Voltaire have in Goethe and in Beranger."

Compared with "The Rape of the Lock" or "Michael" or

Clough's friend, American poet Ralph Waldo Emerson.

Marmion, Clough's **Bothie** has far greater breadth: gentlemen and peasants at work and play, the beauties of autumn scenery, the sentiment and the passion of love, a large pattern of social and political ideas, and a mass of literary allusion and learned puns. What gives this range of material a special quality was noticed by Kingsley in his perceptive review. Calling attention to "the strange jumble" of "marquises and gillies, shooters and tourists—the luxuries and fopperies of modern London amid the wildest scenery and a primitive people—Aristotle over Scotch whiskey—embroidered satin waistcoats dancing with bare-legged hizzies—Chartist poets pledging kilted clansmen," he praised Clough for picturing "the sublime and the ridiculous hand-in-hand, as they usually are," and daring "to set down honestly just what he saw" [see excerpt dated 1849].

In what may be called tone or mood, there is a similar range with similar incongruities. The modern poetry of Goethe had blended "Earnestness and Sport," and the modern poems of Byron had been "droll or pathetic, descriptive or sentimental, tender or satirical, as the humour strikes me,"—all qualities of Clough's temperament that had already been expressed separately. The tradition of the "new poem" united them. Also, as Kingsley observed, the "playful, mock-heroic key gave scope for all sorts of variations into the bucolic, sentimental, broad-farce, pathetic, Hebrew-prophetic, what not."

For that scope the hexameters were particularly useful. More than one critic has praised their effective expression of both the familiar realities of daily life or political discussion, and at the same time subjects like autumn landscape and the sentiment of love that require "poetical grace and ideal elevation." . . . One might argue that blank verse would have been as malleable; but the endless objections to Clough's hexameters because they are not proper hexameters, that is, classical hexameters (as Clough, of course, was well aware), seem silly. The ancient metric is no longer in our ears, and in any event we are prepared to judge the form of a poem, however irregular, by its effectiveness. As Kingsley put it, if Clough has not written hexameters, he *has* written "*Bothiaics,*" and very good ones too. (pp. 99-114)

The meter was primarily an imitation of Homer, but if we try to classify **The Bothie,** we think not only of the epic—and of Dryden and Pope in their mock-heroic vein—but also of Wordsworth and Tennyson. For the poem is a mixed genre: it is a modern idyll written in the epic manner, partly "straight," partly comic. Its muse was not Calliope nor the Thalia of pastoral poetry. She was, as she should have been, a hybrid. "Muse of the Epos and Idyll," Clough calls her, "Muse of great Epos, and Idyll the playful and tender."

The repeated epithets and the elaborate similes, along with the hexameters, are the obvious Homeric elements. But more important are the two things that for Arnold made **The Bothie** more like the *Iliad* than any other English poem: "the rapidity of its movement, and the plainness and directness of its style." As a result, it "produces a sense in the reader which Homer's composition also produces . . . the sense of having, within short limits of time, a large portion of human life presented to him, instead of a small portion" [see *On Translating Homer* in Further Reading]. In this respect, the form supports the range of material and variety of tone in giving the impression of breadth.

Though the term idyll still meant a country story, usually about love, in a setting of field and stream, it had come to mean something more realistic than the classical work of Theocritus or Virgil. . . . [But] the idyll continued to be bathed in something of an ideal light, never quite seen on land or sea—or Scotch Highland.

Both criteria are suggested, respectively, by the title (a bothie is a farmer's hut or cottage) and the subtitle, *A Long-Vacation Pastoral.* Interpenetrating the realism is a fine strain of Arcadian unreality. The character of Elspie, the somewhat "dreamy" ending in which the Oxford gentleman marries the peasant girl and lives happily ever after—in faraway places—and even the wit and gaiety of the reading party are not to be scrutinized too closely by "fact and common sense." Nor should they be. "To glorify the life he yet faithfully represents" is a legitimate purpose for a poet, and entirely true to our imaginative experience. And it was also true to Clough's experience at the time. He was writing from Liverpool in the autumn of 1848, the first autumn in twenty years that he had not been at school or university. He was on vacation, no doubt of it, and enjoying at long last "a sort of afterboyhood." In this mood, Oxford undergraduates and Highland lassies could not be treated with the severity of Crabbe.

This delicate heightening of reality is part of the charm of the poem. Because the sense of actual life is so firmly created, the touch of idealism is made to seem real, and this is far more winning than outright fantasy. Then there is the portrayal of youth, which can be enormously attractive if it is free from sentimentality. Newman described the age in a famous sermon:

> How beautiful is the human heart, when it puts forth its first leaves, and opens and rejoices in its spring-tide. Fair as may be the bodily form, fairer far, in its green foliage and bright blossoms, is natural virtue. . . . Generosity and lightness of heart and amiableness, the confiding spirit, the gentle temper, the elastic cheerfulness, the open hand, the pure affection, the noble aspiration, the heroic resolve, the romantic pursuit, the love in which self has no part,—are not these beautiful?

Much of that spirit is found in **The Bothie,** but not all of it. For there the temper of the young is a little less ardent, a little more earthy. And it has a further quality overlooked by Newman, a quality which runs through the whole poem and is, I think, its most charming feature: a wonderful freshness and vivacity. Clough spoke of the Oxonians reading, talking, roaming, "All in the joy of their life, and glory of shooting-jackets"; or, more compactly, of "the joy of eventful living." The description of swimming in the mountain pool catches this quality in symbolic action. When exploring the upper reaches of a stream, the Reading Party had seen

> on a sudden before them
> Slabs of rock, and a tiny beach, and perfection of water,
> Picture-like beauty, seclusion sublime, and the goddess of bathing.
> There they bathed, of course, and Arthur, the Glory of headers,
> Leapt from the ledges with Hope, he twenty feet, he thirty;
> There, overbold, great Hobbes from a ten-foot height descended,
> Prone, as a quadruped, prone with hands and feet protending;
> There in the sparkling champagne, ecstatic, they shrieked and shouted.
>
> (III, 55-62)

Champagne indeed! The same kind of joyful energy pervades

their conversation; and Hobbes is equally bold and amusing, though far more skilful, as he descends on Philip with the witty analogy between his theory of women and Pugin's theory of Gothic.

These various qualities are brought together in a letter written to Clough by Garth Wilkinson: "Full to brimming, as it is, of youthhood and external nature, I yet feel that my greatest gratitude to it arises from the manner in which it takes one's tenderest experiences back into their native air. . . . It is 'long vacation' all over, alike for soul and sense." That comes as close as one could expect to defining the complex charm of *The Bothie of Tober-na-Vuolich.* (pp. 115-18)

> Walter E. Houghton, in his The Poetry of Clough: An Essay in Revaluation, *Yale University Press, 1963, 236 p.*

FREDERICK BOWERS   (essay date 1966)

[*In the following excerpt, Bowers highlights the modern qualities of Clough's poetry, suggesting that his contemporaries may have perceived him as a "failure" because they misunderstood his unconventional verse.*]

In her book *Arthur Hugh Clough—The Uncommitted Mind* Katharine Chorley sets out to solve the "problem of Clough"—the question raised by Clough's having failed to "make his mark in the world of affairs . . . in the world of letters" after a brilliant career at Rugby School and a competent one at Oxford [see Further Reading]. As many critics before her, Lady Chorley goes to his life for the answer to this "problem": "this brings us . . . to the enigma of his personality. His poetry cannot be fully understood until the solution of this enigma has been found." Having examined the various pressures on Clough's life, his early separation from his parents, of Dr. Arnold's over-development of Clough's sensitive conscience, of the proselytising of Wilfred Ward, Lady Chorley concludes that Clough had a strong unconscious desire to return to the safety of the womb and that his indecisiveness came from the exaggerated *anima* of his personality formed by his isolated, over-disciplined childhood and adolescence.

This may all be correct but it adds to the already large biographical study of Clough's poetry. Clough's life, it is true, presents an interesting case in many ways: he came into contact with many of the important Victorian movements; he reflects the Victorian intellectual aesthete's growing distaste for contemporary materialism and prejudice; in his letters and poetry he is ready made for psychoanalysis and neat classification in both Freudian and Jungian terms. But it is his poetry that is important, and this positive aspect of Clough is worthy of far more attention than it has received. Instead of joining the band of Clough sympathisers whose work seems to betray a maternal protectiveness and pity for the sensitive youth, the critic would do well to leave biography on one side and look at what the poet left as his permanent contribution to literature.

The "problem" in any case is as much one of his friends and reviewers as it is of Clough himself. For excellent documentation of this hostile criticism of Clough's work one can do no better than consult the work of Walter E. Houghton, who rightly singles out Arnold's "Thyrsis" [see poem dated 1866] as the major and seminal denigration. Arnold's criticism is historically and biographically interesting coming as it does from one who was closest to Clough personally, who had a unique interest in excusing Clough's education under Dr. Arnold from being considered a cause of Clough's "failure," and who was a rival poet. Behind Arnold's criticism (in his letters to Clough and in "Thyrsis") there is the energy of personal grudge. The tone of his letters is schoolmasterish and pedantic, as if he wished to continue his father's headmasterly control of Clough beyond his schooldays. He is particularly resentful of Clough's individuality, and on occasion descends to barely controlled envy: "hearing Sellar and the rest of that clique who know neither life nor themselves rave about your poem [*The Bothie of Tober-na-Vuolich*] gave me a strong almost bitter feeling with respect to them, the age, the poem, even you." (pp. 709-10)

Arnold's poetic notions were clearly revealed by Leavis thirty years ago: as a writer "who regarded himself as a critic of the ideas about poetry in his day" and who discounted "wit, play of intellect, stress of cerebral muscle" he does not surprise us in his antipathy to Clough's individual vision and realism. Clough's reaction to "this strange disease of modern life" is not to escape from it by indulging in daydreams but to meet and recognize it for what it is. He emerges a more mature . . . man and poet than do most of his contemporary writers. He is more sensitive to his age than either Arnold or Tennyson, and his reaction to it makes him return poetically to the more technically perfect and emotionally restrained verse of Homer, Chaucer, and the English Augustans—a divergence from contemporary taste which found Clough few friends among his reviewers.

There is to our ears a distinctly modern ring to much of Clough's poetry; passages of *Amours de Voyage* anticipate the style and tone of Eliot and Pound:

> I do not like being moved; for the will is excited and action
> Is a most dangerous thing; I tremble for something facitious,
> Some malpractice of the heart and illegitimate process;
> We are so prone to these things with our terrible notions of duty.
>> (*Amours de Voyage,* 1862)

> What you call the normal
> Is merely the unreal and the unimportant.
> I was like that in a way, so long as I could think
> Even of my own life as an isolated ruin,
> A casual bit of waste in an orderly universe.
>> (*Family Reunion,* 1939)

The didactic, measured stress-beat in these passages (the six-beat of Clough's hexameters and the four-beat of Eliot's verse) is set against a deliberately chosen tone of speech. The combination of a precise orderly verse and the unpoetic tone of speech is the characteristic voice of the best modern poetry. In Clough, the conversational tendency lends itself to that different, hesitant, and qualified tone that seems to be peculiarly twentieth century:

> There have been times, not many, but enough
> To quiet all repinings of the heart;
> There have been times, in which my tranquil soul
> No longer nebulous, sparse, errant, seemed
> Upon its axis, solidly to move
> Centred and fast.
>> (*Dipsychus,* c. 1850)

> So I have seen a man killed! An experience that, among others!
> Yes, I suppose I have; although I can hardly be certain,

And in a court of justice could never declare I had seen
  it.
But a man was killed, I am told, in a place where I saw
Something; a man was killed and I saw something.
                                    (*Amours de Voyage*, 1862)

This tone has much in common with that of puzzlement and self-questioning in

And indeed there will be a time
To wonder, "Do I dare?" and "Do I dare?"
Time to turn back and descend the stair,
With a bald spot in the middle of my hair—
(They will say: "How his hair is growing thin!")
                                    (*Prufrock*, 1917)

                                    (pp. 710-12)

The dispassionate, serious-flippant, "throw-away" tone of Pound's

Unaffected by the 'march of events',
He passed from men's memory in *l'an trentiesme
De son eage;* the case presents
No adjunct to the Muses 'diadem.'

is heard in Clough's "However, one can live in Rome as also in London. / Rome is better than London, because it is other than London," and "Am I prepared to lay down my life for the British female? / Really, who knows?" (*Amours de Voyage*) Other less striking parallels may be seen between Clough's characteristic tone of qualified, intelligent diffidence (and its technical expression in the long line) and much of the poetry of Auden. Particularly in the sinewy prosaic language and syntax set over a firm controlling accentual structure are the two poets similar, producing a resemblance in the detached tone—fastidious in Clough, clinical in Auden. Clough's wit has obvious parallels with that seen in some of MacNeice's work; both poets use doggerel and audacious rime for satiric effect and there is, moreover, a similar use of colloquialism and prosaic tone.

When the *Guardian* reviewed Clough's *Ambarvalia* [see excerpt by Arnold dated 1849] the reviewer was worried by the diffidence and doubt of the poet: "Doubt, it may be urged, is not a Poet's mood." In his longer poems this doubt becomes a tired scepticism which contributes to a tone which is found later in the detachment of *Hugh Selwyn Mauberley* and much of Eliot's poetry. There is a superciliousness and fastidiousness about Clough's work which reflect a violent break with the enthusiastic and confident emotionalism of his contemporaries' poetry. One is particularly struck by his distaste for the flaccid sentimentality of his time; *Dipsychus* ridicules the religiosity, respectability, prudery, and Gothic vagueness of his century; Claude in *Amours de Voyage* socially rejects the material grossness of the mercantile class, at the same time deprecating its taste for rubbish which Rome supplies in plenty. Claude is a forerunner of Mauberley: "Rome disappoints me much; I hardly as yet understand, but *Rubbishy* seems the word that most exactly would suit it." He is out of touch with his time just as Mauberley is:

The "age demanded" chiefly a mould in plaster,
Made with no loss of time,
A prose kinema, not, not assuredly, alabaster
Or the "sculpture" of rhyme.

Indeed, in Clough's **"Letters of Parepidemus II"** Pound's deprecation of the "classics in paraphrase" is exactly anticipated by Clough's criticism of bits "of rhythmical prose,"

"lengthy straggling, irregular slips of *prose mesurée*" which characterized contemporary translation. Both Pound and Clough feel superior to their age—one as a youth "born to inglorious days," the other as a cultural (and actual) exile, punished for "non-esteem of self-styled 'his betters'."—and to the "accelerated grimaces" and "gewgaws" which formed the standards of their time's taste. Clough's "Anglo-savage" is Pound's "half-savage."

Claude's contempt for the bourgeoisie strikes a modern note:

Middle class people these, bankers very likely, not wholly
Pure of the taint of the shop: will at table d'hôte and restaurant
Have their shilling's worth, their penny's pennyworth
  even.

Claude cannot help wincing at Mary Trevellyan's "mercantile accent" as she discusses the Romantic poets; both the manner and the matter depress him. One feels that Eliot's image in *The Waste Land* would have been congenial to him: "One of the low on whom assurance sits / As a silk hat on a Bradford millionaire." As Pound and Eliot, Clough is depressed by the coarsening of sensibility to which he finds the Anglo-savages prone; in **"Letters of Parepidemus II"** he writes: "And the whole Anglo-Saxon world of the future will, it is greatly to be feared, go forth on its way, clearing forests, building clippers, weaving calicoes and annexing Mexicos, accomplishing its natural manifest destiny, and subsiding into its primitive aboriginal form."

But it is not only in attitude and consequent poetic tone that Clough's work anticipates the best of twentieth century poetry; his poetry is a return to the intelligence of the line of wit which runs on to Eliot. This is not to say that in Clough we have a poet who has Hopkins's quality of metaphysicality where the "intellect is at the tip of the senses." Clough is not a sensuous writer, but his poetry does evince a return to that poetry of intellect which in his own time hardly passed for poetry at all; he leaves the heart-crying school of verse for something more seventeenth century, Augustan, and deflating: "To move on angel's feet were sweet; / But who would therefore scorn his feet?" (*Dipsychus*). The antithetic and epigrammatic nature of much of his work is accompanied by an intellectual rejection of uncritical sentiment: "Sweet it may be and decorous, perhaps, for the country to die; but / On the whole we conclude the Romans won't do it, and I shan't."

Technically, he reflects the intellect rather than the heart in his interest in, and perfectionist approach to, prosody. In the "Letter to Parepidemus" already quoted, he discusses the nature of classical prosody, noting that in Latin the quantitative system of the verse deliberately violates the stress of spoken language; it is at the strain between verse accent and colloquial stress that Clough aims in his first long poem in hexameters, *The Bothie of Tober-na-Vuolich:* the verse is not smooth—as for instance is the saccharine *Evangeline* of Longfellow—but is remarkably vital, achieving a feeling of spontaneity that hides precise attention to the verse; the *Amours de Voyage* has smoother hexameters to reflect a different tone, but smoothness never becomes monotony. Clough's hexameter system is accentual, using six stressed syllables and an indeterminate number of intervening unstressed syllables; it anticipates in many ways the stress regularity of much modern verse, and in a similar way it has stretched across its regularity a colloquial, sometimes racy, language. Beneath the conversational tone lies a verse sophisticated and precise.

In imagery too there are hints of a twentieth century mind. His use of it is sparing, as the main burden of meaning is carried by a hard, muscular syntax which recalls (Sonnet VI particularly so) the logical complexity of seventeenth-century verse. When he does present an image, however, it is the unpoetic, contemporary illustration of modern verse; machinery, railways, coitus, and urban degradation supply his images and reflect his reaction against poetic decorum and contemporary prudery alike. He is sometimes bawdy and rough in his language, which must have dearly offended the heart criers. He uses all materials for his poetry and his language is modern in its eclecticism, showing as it does, sources technical, scientific, philosophical and even mathematical:

> Or let me see a mighty Work, a Volume,
> The Complemental of the inferior Kant,
> The Critic of Pure Practic, based upon
> The antinomies of the Moral Sense; for look you
> We cannot act without assuming x,
> And at the same time y, its contradictory.

His language deliberately avoids cosiness and can achieve a directness rare in nineteenth-century verse:

> Even as now
> An o'er grown Baby, sucking at the dugs
> Of Instinct, dry long since.

In **Dipsychus** the Spirit ridicules the poet's use of the word "moiety" as too poetic; frequently he mocks pomposity where it creeps into the verse.

Even in a minor detail Clough anticipates a technique of Pound and Eliot; he frequently uses quotations, foreign and Shakespearean, for the purposes of deflatary contrast: "There is a tide, at least, in the *love* affairs of mortals . . ." or to present tradition's view, as when the Spirit sings "It was a lover and his lass" to ridicule Dipsychus's modesty.

If it is not certain that Clough's poetry had any direct influence on twentieth century poets, it is at least clear that it anticipated the tone, technique, and attitude of later poets, and that this perspicience made Clough something of an enigma to his contemporaries. In so many ways he did not belong to his age; his poetry shows and appeals to an intelligence which his age preferred to use on other things. Under such circumstances, Leavis tells us, "poetry will cease to matter much" to the age. To Clough as to Hopkins poetry did matter; it was not a graceful accompaniment to other, more practical, pursuits. It may not be entirely true, therefore, to cite Hopkins as the originator of "the only influential poetry of the Victorian age," and, although one would not wish to suggest that Clough was the only poet of his age really in step with poetic tradition, one cannot refrain from remarking that his "problems" were as much those of a good poet's being misunderstood by an age of coarse sensibility as those which most of Clough's chroniclers seem to believe. (pp. 712-16)

> Frederick Bowers, "Arthur Hugh Clough: The Modern Mind," in Studies in English Literature, 1500-1900, Vol. VI, No. 4, Autumn, 1966, pp. 709-16.

MICHAEL TIMKO (essay date 1966)

[*Timko asserts that Clough's significance for modern readers derives from his philosophy of "passive naturalism," his insistence on truth and realism over artificiality and his belief that mankind is endowed with "native goodness." Culling a poetic theory from Clough's various prose writings, Timko further argues that Clough believed the purpose of all poetry should be essentially moral.*]

As both man and artist Clough has not fared well at the hands of critics; indeed, over the years the myth of the Clough "failure" has been preserved until now the question is no longer whether Clough failed, but why he did. Some critics have seen him as a frustrated Carlylean, others as a frustrated satirist, others as a frustrated believer. His latest biographer [see Chorley entry in Further Reading], accepting the myth, finds still another reason for his failure: Clough always had the desire to return to the womb! Even those who have tried to "rescue" Clough have succeeded in preserving the tradition, for they have been so intent on "defending" him, on making him all things to all people so that he can be acceptable, that they have managed to convey the impression that there must after all be some solid basis for the myth. J. M. Robertson, for instance, insisted that Clough's poetry be read as fiction, that Clough be regarded as novelist rather than poet [see excerpt dated 1887]. The latest study, Walter Houghton's *The Poetry of Clough* [see excerpt dated 1963], keeps the focus on the poetry, but in the attempt to make Clough "contemporary" it emphasizes the "modern" techniques at the expense of the moral aesthetic that is the basis for Clough's poetry, its *raison d'être*. It is as fruitless to talk of Clough's poetry from the standpoint of technique only as it is to dismiss it as fiction or to see it as the final product of a Jungian sublimation. (pp. 3-4)

In order to understand Clough fully, we must know the quality of his thought and character. First, Clough was a Victorian, living in a period which made certain assumptions about life and art. To say this is not to say that Clough was in complete agreement with these ideas and assumptions; but the fact remains that he was influenced by and did agree with many of them, particularly so in his poetic theory and practice. Second, Clough was an artist, and to deny him this, as some have done, is to do him an injustice. He worked at his writing; he knew exactly what he was trying to do and revised and rewrote to achieve the effects that he wanted. He was also familiar with literary theory and criticism. His poetry, criticism, and writings demonstrate that he should not be dismissed as a "rough versifier" who was more interested in getting down his thoughts than in putting them down in the best possible way. Third, it is important to recognize that in his poetic theory and practice Clough was more a Victorian than a modern, and no amount of analysis will make him a "modern." It is true that his satiric poetry reveals some "modern" tendencies, but, on the whole, Clough was committed to a poetic theory that was not too far removed from most of the accepted conventions of his day, particularly in his view of the poet and in his insistence that the poetry be "moral." Clough was not a "radical" in his poetic theory and practice.

Finally, and it is in this area that one could make a claim for "radicalism" (in the sense that he was fighting the accepted beliefs of the time), Clough had ideas, and very positive ones, on the major concerns of his age, ideas that form the foundation for much of his satiric poetry and many of his actions during his lifetime. Living in an age when conformity, custom, and convention seemed to play a dominant part in man's life, Clough insisted on the importance of "the natural" over the artificial, on the real over the false. It is true, of course, that other Victorian writers were doing this, but what distinguishes Clough most clearly from his contemporaries is the basis of his thought, his "positive naturalism." What makes him significant in our day, and also marks his unique contribution to his own, is his "acceptance of the human fact as we know it now." (pp. 6-8)

"It is the virtue of man to know and love the ideal. / It is the wisdom of man to accept and love the real," Clough once wrote, and it is this love and acceptance that make his writing seem so fresh and vital today. In an age of "compromise" Clough refused to advocate easy solutions or timid compromises. In this respect, certainly, he is a realist whose positive qualities have not yet been fully recognized. Dissatisfied with life about him, as were most of his contemporaries, Clough, unlike some others, still retained his "innocence" and a firm belief in the "native goodness" of human nature and the dignity of the human spirit.

It is at this point that misunderstandings of Clough's thought and art often arise. His acceptance of human nature, his refusal to deal in absolutes, to condemn on rigid moral and ethical grounds, are taken to be signs of weakness or lack of conviction. This has often led to misinterpretations of his poems, particularly **"It fortifies my soul to know," "Epi-Strauss-ium,"** the two parts of the **"Easter Day"** poem, and *Dipsychus,* the "submission" of whose hero has consistently been misjudged. Clough's refusal to be arbitrary also has been seen as a sign of a total objectivity, an indication of his willingness only to point out difficulties rather than to suggest positive solutions as well. Again, although Clough was able to see both (or all) sides of a question, he was writing with a firm moral commitment, not with the intent merely to display verbal wit or poetic pyrotechnics. At the core of his life and work are a resiliency and toughness and an integrity found in few others writing during his own time.

Certainly it would have been easier to allow himself to be seduced by alien visions or by such high-sounding words as "custom," "authority," or "tradition." It would have been much simpler to resort to "base mechanical adroitness." However, Clough recognized and tried to demonstrate in his writing that man also had within him this "interfering, enslaving, o'ermastering demon of craving," as well as nobility, honor, and the capacity for love and endurance. It is precisely this recognition that makes the term "positive naturalism" so fitting; for, in addition to his insistence on man's need to pursue the "truth" and his belief in the "essence" of Christianity, Clough was also a "naturalist" who refused to deny the validity of man's emotions and desires, "natural" as well as ideal. He was also positive in this naturalism with his insistence that these emotions and desires, when given full recognition and not suppressed, could lead to a fuller and more satisfying life here on earth. It is because of this view that he insists that we stop dreaming of what might be and work with what we have. Man's salvation depends not on illusion, but on reality, not on creating new heavens for himself, but on making the best of this world. The quality that makes Clough a significant Victorian is his clear recognition of the paradoxical, yet ultimately admirable, nature of man. (pp. 8-10)

To Clough, man, as a human, necessarily has to suffer, but he also has to grow. "Earthy as well as godlike," he is bound to develop until his native goodness asserts itself and he learns to live as befits him. Clough was keenly aware of that "irreducible part of each of us." In his *Mystery of the Fall,* an artistic failure but a valuable poem for providing insight

into his thought, Clough has Adam try to describe this very idea:

>   yet still
> I, or a something that is I indeed,
> A living, central, and more inmost I
> Within the scales of mere exterior me's,
> I—seem eternal, O thou God, as Thou;

And Clough's "metaphor that is symbolic of the inalienable part of every man" is one that indicates clearly his optimistic attitude towards human nature, for his imagery concerning man is usually that of growing, natural objects, such as seeds, trees, and flowers. Adam tells Eve:

> That which we were, we could no more remain
> Than in the moist provocative vernal mould
> A seed its suckers close, and rest a seed.
> We were to grow.

In this characteristic image Clough indicates both his realistic appraisal of the world, with its "vernal provocativeness," and his optimistic faith in man's eventual development and full maturity as a human being. And his concern is always with man in this world, the here and now; the focus is always on "the contradictions, paradoxes and dangers of living the moral life," and the intention is "the better understanding of the inextricable tangle of good and evil and of how perilous moral action can be." (pp. 10-11)

His positive naturalism is nowhere more apparent than in the responses he makes to the problems of his age, particularly those brought on by the changes taking place in the social, political, economic, and religious spheres. Change has been cited as the dominant characteristic of the Victorian period; and it is Clough's ability to retain his realistic view of human nature in the face of this change and to assert consistently and positively his principles that characterizes his work and makes his contribution to Victorian literature so significant. Sensitive, sympathetic, perceptive, at times brilliantly witty, at others bitterly ironic, Clough was able to see through the thick smoke that covered the battleground of Victorian controversy and to distinguish the real—i.e., the true. The consistent theme of his work is his condemnation of the false, the artificial, the insincere, and his praise for the real, the natural, the good.

This approach is pervasive in all of his writing. In the political sphere, both domestic and international, he refused to be trapped into accepting either of the attractive extremes of complete freedom or authoritarianism; he was, instead, a "liberal of the future" [see excerpt by Francis W. Palmer dated 1943], concerned not with systems or parties but with the individual's relationship to others and with the development of the human spirit. Avoiding jingoism or paternalism, Clough insisted that a government was to be judged only on the basis of its granting "genuine liberty" to its people. Hence his condemnation of both parties in England, each of which seemed to be interested only in furthering its own fortunes; his support of the Italians against the Austrians; and his disgust with Napoleon III, who seemed to him the symbol of tyranny and oppression. His statements on social and economic questions were predicated on the same principles that inspired his political ideas: a sincere sympathy for those suffering from oppression and a genuine desire to serve and help them. Disturbed by the pernicious philosophy underlying laissez-faire, the thought of placing relationships of individuals on a cash-nexus basis only, Clough insisted on the need for new definitions of liberty. Basing his solutions on the essential dignity of the human spirit, Clough refused to view men as "hands" or "machines" or "servants"; from the vantage point of his humane realism, he insisted that men combine for higher objects than the mere "culinary" one of securing equal apportionments of meat and drink. Service, not liberty, equality, or fraternity, was the watchword.

Clough's avoidance of unreasonable dogmatism and irrational emotion, his insistence on knowledge and reasonableness are seen to best advantage in his comments on religion, perhaps the area that caused the most violent reactions in the Victorian period. It is also in this area that Clough's distinction between natural and artificial is most evident. For Clough, the great gap between religion and life was the heart of the matter. Religious experiences of all types seemed to prove that religion was sadly impracticable in daily life, and the problem became one of the necessary adjustment (not compromise) between the two. In his attempts to show the results of religious hypocrisy that enabled people to place great emphasis on outward forms and customs and make no attempt to come to a genuine understanding of the true meaning and spirit behind them, Clough consistently stressed the necessity to make religion not a theological creed, but a way of life. Basic to this point of view was, again, his recognition that man did not need to look for new virtues, but needed to order and distribute his native goodness in this world. One of the statements that Clough has the hero of the poem *Dipsychus* make is especially significant in the context of his own belief: "It seems His newer will / We should not think of Him at all, but trudge it, / And of the world He has assigned us make / What best we can." To Clough this was more than just a poetic utterance; it summed up his religious position. (pp. 13-15)

If the problem with Clough's religious and social thought has been one of learning to understand exactly what he meant rather than taking for granted that since he was not an orthodox believer he was therefore a skeptic and a failure, the problem with his art is one of learning to take him at his word rather than believing what critics, and sometimes sympathetic ones, have insisted that he meant to say or do. He has to be rescued from those who are so eager to have his poetry read and appreciated that they make him either into their own image or into some image that they feel is more appealing to the modern reader. (p. 93)

For Clough, as for many of his contemporaries, poetry was basically the disclosure of a man's character, the reflection of his nature, the verbal expression of his innermost being. In his lecture ["**The Development of English Literature**"] he states that the works of Shakespeare and Milton reflect their characters. Shakespeare wrote the plays that he did because he was characteristically of a "balanced speculative" nature. Milton, on the other hand, wrote the poetry that he did because he was "strongly, deliberately, seriously, irreversibly committed; walking as in sight of God, as in the profound almost rigid conviction, that this one, and no other of all those many paths is or can be, for the just and upright spirit possible—self-predestined as it were, . . . to a single moral and religious aim."

But Clough's concept of the nature of poetry is complicated by the moral and ethical basis of his poetic theory. The end of poetry for Clough is primarily moral; therefore, since poetry is the reflection of a man's essential nature, the value of the poetry becomes dependent on the character of the poet,

and it becomes necessary to examine the poet's "character and his view of life" to see if he has sincerely and accurately expressed this character and this view in his poetry. If the poet is of a virtuous nature, the more accurately he is able to reflect this "virtue" in his poetry, the better his poetry will be. This belief is behind Clough's implication [in his "**Lecture on Wordsworth**"] that Wordsworth is a great poet because he "succeeded beyond the other poets of the time . . . in making his verse permanently true to his genius and his moral frame."

It is important, however, to see that Clough's concept of the moral or virtuous man is not simply the view of an outwardly pious or religious individual; it is much closer to Carlyle's view of the "moral" individual, the man virtuously related to the universe: "To know a thing," Carlyle wrote in *Heroes and Hero-Worship*, "what we can call knowing, a man must first love the thing, sympathize with it; that is, be *virtuously* related to it. If he have not the justice to put down his own selfishness at every turn, . . . how shall he know?" Clough echoes Carlyle's words as, after condemning Byron's "hot career of wilfulness" and Scott's "easy existence," he praises Wordsworth's "dignified, elevated, serious, significant, and truly human . . . homely and frugal life in the cottage at Grasmere." The emphasis remains here, as elsewhere, on the acceptance of and sympathy for the "truly human" rather than the pretentiously artificial.

Clough's view of the poet and the nature of poetry is most clearly brought out in his lecture on the poetry of Wordsworth, for it is principally because of this approach that he prefers Wordsworth to almost any other poet. Clough inquires into "the worth of that genius and moral frame[,] the amount of the real significance of his character and view of life," and he finds that while Byron exhibits an "ebullient overflowing life, refusing all existing restrictions," and while Scott exhibits a "free vigorous animal nature ready to accept whatever things Earth has to offer," Wordsworth's preeminence consists in having "attained a law," and in exercising "a lordship by right divine over passions and desires." The similarity of this statement to Carlyle's admiration for the man who has the justice to "put down his own selfishness at every turn" is obvious.

His admiration for the character of Wordsworth becomes transferred to the poetry of Wordsworth. Wordsworth is a greater artist than either Byron or Scott precisely because his poetry more perfectly expresses his essentially moral nature. "His poems," writes Clough, "do more perfectly and exquisitely and unintermittedly express his real meaning and significance and character than do the poems of either Scott or Byron." Contrasting Wordsworth with the two "lesser" writers, Clough cites what for him is indisputable proof of Wordsworth's superiority. Wordsworth did not "sweep" or "carry" away with him the "exulting hearts of youth," as did Byron; he did not "win the eager and attentive ear of high and low, at home and abroad in the entertainment of immortal Waverley novels"; but he did "lay slowly the ponderous foundations of pillars to sustain man's moral fabric"; he did "fix a centre around which the chaotic elements of human impulse and desire might take solid form and move in their ordered ellipses"; he did "originate a spiritual stability." And all this, to Clough, was "greater than sweeping over glad blue waters or inditing immortal novels."

The belief that the poet must be "moral" and that poetry is the reflection of his virtuous nature directly affects Clough's thinking on the two closely related questions of subject matter and function. Clough felt that poetry should deal with what he called the "obvious facts of human nature"; that is, with subjects that have some significance to all men, rather than with pastoral scenes or with stories from the classical past that might be of some interest to only a select few. Alexander Smith is praised for writing about and using images from the present, while Arnold and even Wordsworth are condemned for making too much of classical myths and of nature. "Is it not . . . an easy matter," asks Clough [in his **"Recent English Poetry"**], "to sit under a green tree by a purling brook, and indite pleasing stanzas on the beauties of Nature and fresh air?" Or, he asks, is it "so very great an exploit to wander out into the pleasant fields of Greek or Latin mythology, and reproduce, with more or less of modern adaptation,—'the shadows / Faded and pale, yet immortal, of Faunus, the Nymphs, and the Graces?' " Should not poetry, he says, to gain the ear of the multitudes, to shake the hearts of men, "deal more than at present it usually does, with general wants, ordinary feelings, the obvious rather than the rare facts of human nature?" Smith's *A Life-Drama* has the advantage of not being "mere pastoral sweet piping from the country," and the images of the poem are praised because they are drawn from "the busy seats of industry" and are "lifelike, immediate and firsthand." And Arnold's *Tristram and Iseult* is better than his *Empedocles on Etna* because Clough prefers the "human passions and sorrows of the Knight and the Queen" to the "high, and . . . pseudo-Greek inflation of the philosopher musing above the crater, and the boy Callicles, singing myths upon the mountains." Both Arnold and Wordsworth, according to Clough, are inclined to put too much stress on nature. In the former he notes a disposition to "assign too high a place to what is called Nature"; the latter, instead of using the phenomena of external nature as analogies of what is truly great—human nature—is guilty of regarding these phenomena as being the truly great, all important, and pre-eminently wonderful things of the universe. "The Poet of Nature he may perhaps be," concludes Clough [in his **Lecture on Wordsworth**], somewhat sharply, "but this sort of writing does justice to the proper worth [and] dignity neither of Man *nor* Nature."

To Clough the greatness of poetry lies in its application to life. Specifically, poetry has two principal aims. First, it should teach the significance of and give some purpose to our own petty lives and works. Second, it should indicate to us our relationship to the "purer existence." Could not poetry, he asks:

> attempt to convert into beauty and thankfulness, or at least into some form and shape, some feeling, at any rate, of content—the actual, palpable things with which our every-day life is concerned; introduce into business and weary task-work a character and a soul of purpose and reality; intimate to us relations which, in our unchosen, peremptorily-appointed posts, in our grievously narrow and limited spheres of action, we still, in and through all, retain to some central, celestial fact? Could it not console us with a sense of significance, if not of dignity, in that often dirty, or at least dingy, work which it is the lot of so many of us to have to do, and which some one or other, after all, must do? Might it not divinely condescend to all infirmities; . . . exclude nothing, least of all guilt and distress . . . ; not content itself merely with talking of what may be better elsewhere, but seek also to deal with what *is* here? . . . Cannot the Divine

> Song in some way indicate to us our unity, . . . with those happier things; inform us, and prove to us, that though we are what we are, we may yet, in some way, even in our abasement, even by and through our daily work, be related to the purer existence.

Although poetry must have a "message," Clough does not use the word in its modern pejorative sense to indicate a poet's preaching to his readers or giving his readers some facile solution to a pressing immediate problem. The message of the poem is that which gives the reader some new or added insight into his life in general, or into one vital aspect of his life, such as love, death, or friendship. It interprets the significance of all that we do or part of what we do here on earth; it is that which consoles us by showing us how, in our limited and narrow spheres, we still "retain to some central and celestial fact." By defining them in universal terms, the message gives new meaning to those actions, those movements, those ideas that we, in our limited worlds, see only as particulars. Poetry, for Clough, is a criticism of life.

If the poet has the moral responsibility of criticizing life, he must be able to fact facts, and the poetry that he writes must be neither remote nor sentimental. The love of truth, as has been seen, was the cornerstone of his entire outlook on life itself, as well as of his criticism. The crucial place it holds in his poetic theory is indicated by his remarks on the age of Dryden and the poetry of Wordsworth. He praises the spirit of Dryden's era as one which had an "austere love of truth," a "righteous abhorrence of illusion," a "rigorous uncompromising rejection of the vague, . . . the merely probable," and a "sternconscientious determination . . . to admit, if things are bad, that they are so." "Such a spirit," he concludes [in **"The Development of English Literature"**], "claims more than our attention,—claims our reverence." The veneration for truth also enabled Clough to see, in spite of his great admiration for Wordsworth, that the poet was guilty of both sentimentality and a certain seclusion from the actual world. "Retiring early from all conflict and even contact with the busy world, he shut himself out from the elements which it was his business to encounter and to master. This gives to his writings . . . a certain appearance of sterility and unreality." Clough also deplores Wordsworth's "mawkish sentimentality." . . . These faults in Wordsworth's poetry detract from its essential function, the moral one. "People in busy streets," comments Clough [in **Lecture on Wordsworth**], "are inclined I fear to contemn the wild precepts of the rural moralist."

Clough's remarks on the nature, function, and subject matter of poetry and on the character of the poet must, of course, be understood in the light of his thought, for they lose their special meaning when taken from the context his idealism and positive naturalism. His admiration of Wordsworth's "moral" character and poetry and his lack of praise for Byron reflect the great value he placed on the belief in God, the essentials of Christianity, and the native goodness of man; Wordsworth's poetry was able to "sustain man's moral fabric" and to "originate a spiritual stability." But his condemnation of Wordsworth for assigning too high a place to nature and of Scott for his "free animal nature" and his commendation of Alexander Smith and of Dryden and his age for being closer to life and truth, for rejecting the vague and illusory, illustrate his realistic determination to see things as they are, including the realization that man has some devil as well as deity in him. Clough's wish, of course, as we have already seen, was for man to accept things as they really are rather than avoid coming to grips with the world by resorting to conventional behavior, to "mawkish sentimentality," or to animal actions. He valued the "real" or the "natural" over the artificial or "unnatural"; and he was especially aware of the need to keep these separate. While his opposing the artificial with the natural is logical enough, too often his opposing the natural with the "unnatural" has not been understood. Clough shows in his lyrics and satires, especially in *Dipsychus,* that the natural, when it takes extreme forms, is as enervating and debilitating as the artificial. This view is the basis for his rejection of Byron and Scott and his praise of Wordsworth for exercising a "lordship by right divine over passions and desires." *Moral* or *virtuous* must be seen, then, as synonyms for natural, with the understanding that natural implies a balance of the idealistic and realistic, of the head and heart; it is, in short, a positive "naturalism."

The moral basis of his theory led Clough to assign a prominent role to style, a role as prominent, for instance, as that which Matthew Arnold gave; for the style, according to Clough, contributed to the moral effect of the poem. Like Arnold, Clough had a twofold theory of style. On the one hand, he regards style as the expression or the reflection of the character of the poet; accordingly, he admires Wordsworth, for example, because his poems "more perfectly and exquisitely and unintermittedly express his real meaning and significance and character than do the poems of either Scott or Byron." On the other hand, he regards style as the form itself, that which he calls [in **"Lecture on Wordsworth"**] "that permanent beauty of expression[,] that harmony between thought and word, which is the condition of 'immortal verse' "; and it is under this aspect that he discusses the importance of the unity of the poem and the proper place of diction and imagery.

His attitude towards the style as the reflection of the poet's character is convincingly shown by his rejection of poets who are content to imitate rather than labor to develop their own distinctive stylistic note, one which would reflect their essential natures. In his review of Arnold and Smith [in **"Recent English Poetry"**], he objects to their imitativeness; Smith is too much a disciple of Keats, but there is hope that he is young enough to free himself from his present manner, "which does not seem his simple and natural own." Arnold, too, has failed to develop a style which reflects his particular character; he needs to stop "turning and twisting his eyes, in the hope of seeing things as Homer, Sophocles, Virgil, or Milton saw them"; he needs, instead, to look at things, accept them, and depict them as he sees them. Only in this way will he attain that style uniquely suited to him.

Clough's thoughts on the other aspect of style—the form that the poet gives to his material—are very similar to those of Arnold; both are in complete agreement regarding imagery, diction, and the essential unity of a poem. For both, style in this sense—the permanent beauty of expression, that harmony between thought and word, which is the condition of immortal verse—means not "mere accessories," not "the unneeded but pleasing ornament," but rather the "clearness of arrangement, rigor of development" of the poem [as he wrote in **"Lecture on Wordsworth"**]. The content of the poem being the most important element, the form (style) must not detract in any way from the message. The sum of the individual parts of a poem must not be greater than the sum of the whole: the

diction and imagery must not call attention to themselves, but only contribute to the total impression of the piece.

Clough at all times insists on the importance of not distracting the reader from the central theme. In the course of his review of the poems of Smith he subjects the poet to severe criticism for his excessive fondness for figurative language. By telling his similes and metaphors out as a clerk might sovereigns at the Bank of England, Smith is incessantly calling off "the attention, which the reader desires to devote to the pursuit of the main drift of what calls itself a single poem, *simplex et unum*." In addition, he is so intent on imitating the "exuberant expressions" of the Elizabethans and Keats that he falls at times into the error of using what Clough labels "vicious expressions." After quoting a passage from Smith's *Life-Drama,* he comments: "Our author will not keep his eye steady upon the thing before him; he goes off, and distracts us, and breaks the impression he had begun to succeed in giving, by bidding us look now at something else"; and he concludes with the wish that Smith would learn to use "simpler epithets" and "plainer language."

Clough's advice to Smith to acquaint himself with and use models other than the Elizabethans and Keats is his solution to what he thought the most pressing critical problem of his time: the lack of unity in the works of the poets. Finding that Keats, Shelley, and Coleridge, "with their extravagant love for Elizabethan phraseology," have led to this "mischief," to excessive imagery and extravagant diction, Clough, concentrating on plainer language, pointed to the late seventeenth and the eighteenth centuries for guidance. In his lecture [**"Dryden and His Times"**] he remarks that in Dryden's time people found themselves reading words "easy at once and graceful; fluent yet dignified; familiar, yet full of harmony" and that this state of affairs was due mainly to Dryden himself who "organized the dissolving and separating elements of our tongue into a new and living instrument, perfectly adapted to the requirements . . . of the age." He concludes with the lamentation: "Have we any one who speaks for our day as justly and appropriately as Dryden did for his? Have we anything that will stand wear and tear as well and be as bright and unobsolete in a hundred and fifty years, as Alexander's feast is today?" He repeats this plea for greater simplicity in his review of Smith and Arnold. After commenting on Smith's diction, he deplores the poet's apparent lack of familiarity with an important period of English language and literature, the period between Milton and Burns. "To write out, as a mere daily task, passages, for example, of Goldsmith," Clough advises [in **"Recent English Poetry"**], "would do a verse-composer of the nineteenth century as much good, we believe, as the study of Beaumont and Fletcher."

In the light of these ideas, it would seem at first sight that the lyric rather than satire would be the genre in which Clough the poet would most successfully carry out the ideas of Clough the critic. [The critic adds in a footnote: In addition to the three long poems, the *Bothie, Amours,* and *Dipsychus,* I include in the satiric canon (as distinguished from the lyric) the following "shorter" poems: **"Look you, my simple friend, 'tis one of those," "To the Great Metropolis," "It is true, ye gods, who treat us," "Duty—that's to say complying," "I give thee joy! O worthy word!" "The Latest Decalogue," "O land of Empire, art and love!" "Sa Majesté très Chrétienne," "I dreamed a dream," "In the Great Metropolis,"** and **"O qui me."** . . .] Certainly, for instance, the subject matter and the purpose of the lyrics reflect his critical ideas. The poet,

Clough states, should deal with meaningful subjects, vital in their appeal and timeless in their interest, and this is what Clough the lyricist does, treating most often man's relationship to nature, to country, to fellow human beings, and to truth or God. And the end for which they are written is to provide a criticism of life, to show that man is capable of living a meaningful life. In matters of style, too, Clough the poet follows the dictates of the critic, employing the more traditional forms, striving for simple diction, and being very sparing in the use of imagery. Following the recommendations of the critic, the lyric poet demonstrates the strong influence that the period between Milton and Burns had on him. There is some influence by later poets, particularly Wordsworth and Tennyson, but, on the whole, Clough's lyrics reflect the critic's praise of neo-classical writing, particularly the qualities of lucidity, plainness, and moral concern.

But save for some notable exceptions, Clough the lyricist failed to achieve the goal of Clough the critic. It remained for Clough the satirist to do this, and the reasons for his success in this genre lie ultimately in the poet's own intellectual and moral attitudes. While both genres rest on his belief that poetry should be primarily moralistic, the satires more clearly reflect this belief and thus more effectively demonstrate Clough's great concern with the individual's role in the world and his failure to measure up to an ideal that may be expressed by the term "organic" or "natural" as opposed to the "mechanic" or "unnatural." The satires concern themselves much more specifically than do the lyrics with the "general wants, ordinary feelings, the obvious rather than the rare facts of human nature"; they concern themselves more with the here and now. They are in fact Clough's attempts to "fix a centre around which the chaotic elements of human impulse and desire might take solid form and move in their ordered ellipses." Also, the satires, unlike most of the lyrics, contain that harmony of thought and word which Clough found so essential to poetry. Reflecting the more vigorous aspects of the neo-classical tradition rather than the plainness and simplicity found in the lyrics, the satiric poems are written in that style which reveals the moral aesthetic so central to his prosodic theory. With its irony, indirection, and ambiguity, Clough's satire became for him the most direct and effective way of expressing his deep concern over man's plight. In his satiric poems, thought and art became one. (pp. 94-110)

> *Michael Timko, in his* Innocent Victorian: The Satiric Poetry of Arthur Hugh Clough, *Ohio University Press, 1966, 198 p.*

WENDELL V. HARRIS   (essay date 1970)

[*In the following excerpt, Harris analyzes Clough's poems in* Ambarvalia, *discerning in them early patterns of the intellectual struggle that characterizes Clough's later poetry.*]

As the product of his years of self-questioning at Oxford, Clough's contributions to [*Ambarvalia*], all probably in their final state before the writing of the *Bothie,* reveal many issues in the conflict which had come to a temporary resolution at the time of his resignation from Oxford. Though not a defense of his resignation or a manifesto, the poems reveal the precise nature of the radical uncertainties with which Clough was struggling and the entire conscientiousness with which he attempted to face every question; thus, in a sense, they provide that explanation which his friends had expected of the

Bothie. The reaction of most of his friends does not, however, indicate that they were able either to enter sympathetically into Clough's perplexities or to see for what purpose he was using his poetry. (p. 52)

The title of the volume is taken from the ancient Roman festival at which animals were sacrificed to insure the fertility of the fields. The reasons behind the choice of the title must remain conjectural; it has little apparent relevance to the poems included by either Clough or Burbidge. To those familiar with Clough's life and poetry, however, the title can perhaps be recognized as having a certain significance beyond whatever Clough intended; his portion of the volume, for the most part, represents the sacrifice of an enormous amount of painful energy in the attempt to propitiate the spirit, or demon, of absolute intellectual honesty which Clough so honored.

The opening poem of the volume, for which Clough later suggested the title **"The Questioning Spirit,"** introduces in its first stanza an emblem of Clough's intellectual life:

> The human spirits saw I on a day,
> Sitting and looking each a different way;
> And hardly tasking, subtly questioning,
> Another spirit went around the ring
> To each and each: and as he ceased his say,
> Each after each, I heard them singly sing,
> Some querulously high, some softly, sadly low,
> We know not,—what avails to know?
> We know not, wherefore need we know?
> This answer gave they still unto his suing,
> We know not, let us do as we are doing.

That each man indeed pursues his own goals while unwilling to entertain and unable to answer fundamental questions of what or how or why, represents the human condition as many besides Clough have seen it. But this vision, from which many another thinker has pushed forward to found a system satisfactory at least to himself in giving the answers to how or why, Clough found enormous difficulty in transcending. This particular poem comes to a resolution in approval for the seventh spirit's devotion to a duty the larger meaning of which he cannot know. It is, however, just here that Clough in other poems confesses himself balked: how can one know what is duty when one is in "true ignorance" of all else? Furthermore, the questioning spirit itself, clearly intended in this poem to present the doing of one's duty as the best guide amid human ignorance, is later seen ambivalently; perhaps that spirit tempts to destruction.

Clough's contributions to **Ambarvalia** answer variously the problems raised by such questioning. Some, like the **"Commemorative Sonnets," "Alcaics"** and **"When soft September,"** seem practice exercises; but most strike one not so much as either carefully finished esthetic objects or powerfully stated formulations of the poet's beliefs as so many instances of the trying-out of ideas in poetic form. The inconsistency of the lines of argument in these poems demonstrates the seriousness and the difficulty of the problems raised. This use of poetry as a medium for the expression of problems makes Clough a philosophic poet in an almost unique sense.

In one of his undergraduate essays [**"The Moral Effect of Works of Satire"**] Clough distinguished satire from "genuine Poetry," describing the latter as "careless of the present" and as "impatient in its love for the end of the anxieties and struggles of the pursuit." Clough's own employment of poetry as a means of speculation is, like satire, too concerned with present problems, with discords and struggles, to achieve the finished surface and integrated view one associates with "genuine Poetry" or, that is, poetry which takes beauty as its object.

The attempts which have been made to argue that Clough either was, or should have been, primarily a satirist, are to some extent based on a partial recognition of this point. Finding considerable portions of his work satirical, certain critics have tended to explain as in some way satiric the other portions which obviously do not aim at poetic beauty; they fail to recognize that what Clough aimed at in these poems was neither the lyric nor the satiric. This is not to say that Clough was not at times very witty and at other moments quite the opposite of prudish in his irony. A collection of all those passages excised, as the phrase is, "pro pudore," either by the poet himself or his wife in her capacity as editor, would prove a valuable corrective to the usual view of Clough as a prime representative of inhibited Victorianism.

The human problems considered in *Ambarvalia* are of the broadest import. There is, first, a whole array of attitudes toward the vexed question of duty. The well-known **"Qui Laborat, Orat,"** argues that life properly lived and work properly done are in themselves a perpetual prayer; God is known aright in "the hours of mortal moral strife" and not presumably by abstract meditation. Work is thus prayer, worship, and the means of achieving "The beatific supersensual sight."

Thomas Arnold has referred the genesis of this poem to an evening's discussion of the dangers of vocal prayers, but it almost surely owes as much to Carlyle as to that conversation. "Admirable was that of the old Monks, *'Laborare est Orare,'* work is worship," is the burden of Chapter XII of *Past and Present.* But we know from other poems of *Ambarvalia* that the Carlylean faith is not sufficient for Clough; in the background lies the question: "what *is* the work which is worthy?"

The pitfalls of blindly following what seems to be duty are presented in a pair of poems. That which begins **"Thought may well be ever ranging"** warns of the danger of mistaking duty for love—

> Men and maidens, see you mind it;
> Show of love, where'er you find it,
> Look if duty lurk behind it!
> Duty-fancies, urging on
> Whither love had never gone!

The poem beginning **"Duty—that's to say complying"** looks forward to *Dipsychus* in its irony and prosody. Duty, it argues, can be simply compliance with social norms, or worse, the excuse for sacrificing "all that's truest, noblest, best" in a refusal to follow the soul in its questing and guessing. The fear of acquiescing in a partial truth, of compromising, and of accepting duties readymade appears also in **"Come back again my olden heart"** which prefers a courageous refusal to make questionable affirmations to the attitude which proudly wills to "climb and soar aloft" above doubts and fears.

One begins to see running through all these poems two patterns of thought which go far to explain what is too easily interpreted as mere indecisiveness and fruitless questioning. The first is a fear of making irrevocable decisions—not only decisions which might lead to practical tragedies, as in the possibility of confusing love and duty, but also decisions which might begin to corrupt the freedom and purity of the mind. "Skepticism is the chastity of the mind" says Santayana, and Clough seems to have been one who would take this statement in an almost literal sense. Premature decisions and

unconscious compromises are dangerous not only because they preclude other possible views and beliefs, but because, in a sense which can be expressed only metaphorically, they clutter, sully, and finally destroy the temple of the mind in which Clough hopes some day a revelation will occur. This attitude is discoverable in a letter dating from 1836, when Clough was in the fifth form at Rugby, in which he speaks of feeling "triumphant" in knowing that his heart "was sanctified for a temple of God's spirit." However unnaturally pious the sentiment may seem in a boy of seventeen, such phrases in Clough's letters were not merely conventional pieties but represented the basis of his later attitude toward the world.

The poetic cry **"Come back again, my olden heart!"** questions whether the "heavenly light" which reveals "the truly right" can still be expected to reveal itself once he has dismissed the doubting heart which kept the world and compromise at bay. But, if the mind preserves itself uncluttered and inviolate, then—and this is a position to which Clough tenaciously holds at this time—the light, the revelation, and the vision will appear. Viewed in this way, **"Qui Laborat, Orat"** expresses the hope that some form of direct knowledge of God will be granted to one who expresses his devotion through work, and thus avoids speculation about or egoistic claims on the deity.

The clearest statement of this view is perhaps in the brief poem beginning **"Away, haunt not thou me."** Vain philosophy, which offers only "to perplex the head, / and leave the spirit dead," is contrasted with the Wisdom and Power "welling, bubbling forth, unseen, incessantly." The last four lines are probably more often quoted than fully understood within the context of Clough's thought:

> Why labour at the dull mechanic oar,
> When the fresh breeze is blowing,
> And the strong current flowing,
> Right onward to the Eternal Shore?

The poem dismisses mechanic philosophy to wait on direct inspiration and revelation—but, despite the cheering tone, the bulk of Clough's treatments assume that the wait may be a long and dreary one. For all his evocation of "secret treasure-depths below, / Fed by the skiey shower, / And clouds that sink and rest on hill-tops high," he cannot share the faiths held by the Romantic poets who might well have written those lines.

Clough was a great admirer of Wordsworth, not only in his Rugby days but at Oxford. . . . But for this very reason, nothing shows the doubting temper of Clough's mind better than comparison with the younger Wordsworth. For the Romantic poet, the glimpses of Eternity were to be encountered on all sides, in the meanest flower that blows as well as in the sublimity of the Alps. But, for Clough, the times when "Unsummoned powers the blinding film shall part, / And scarce by happy tears made dim, the eyes / in recognition start" are extremely rare, and more anticipated than experienced. Clough seems to have had an ironic sense of this difference, for when he most closely and intentionally echoes Wordsworth, the echo becomes mocking:

> Here am I yet, another twelvemonth spent,
> One-third departed of the mortal span,
> Carrying on the child into the man,
> Nothing into reality
>
> . . . . .

So was it from the first, so is it yet;
Yes, the first kiss that by these lips was set
On any human lips, methinks was sin—

The child may well be father of the man, but this thought is hardly comforting to one unable to look back upon a childhood trailing any discernible clouds of glory. Indeed, the poem from which the above lines are taken is one of a series bearing the title **"Blank Misgivings of a Creature moving about in Worlds not realized"**—a phrase taken from Wordsworth's "Ode: Intimations of Immortality," where it is charged with much more hopeful connotations than it conveys standing alone as Clough's title. Similarly, the last section of **"When panting sighs the bosom fill,"** which contains such Wordsworthian lines as "A glory on the vision lay;/A light of more than mortal day / About it played, upon it rested," is introduced by a mockingly phrased answer to the question of whether it is true love that is felt: "I cannot say— the things are good: / Bread is it, if not angel's food; / But Love? Alas! I cannot say; . . ." And indeed whether a glory lay on the vision or not, Clough is unsure whether its source is not "Fancy's brook, or [sexual] Passion's river."

Despite his admiration, the mature Clough was not prepared to admit that Wordsworth's affirmations were based on entirely solid ground; and his criticism in his [**"Lecture on Wordsworth"**] reflects his own fears of premature decision: "There may be moreover a further fault in Wordsworth's high morality . . . which I shall characterize by the name of false or arbitrary Positiveness. There is such a thing in Morals as in all Science, as drawing your conclusion before you have properly got your premises. It is desirable to attain a fixed point: but it is essential that the fixed point be [the] right one."

Thus doubting the power of philosophical reason, unsure of how to validate what seem the claims of duty, and trusting that skepticism is not only a purer but a more likely prelude to the great revelation he desires than any affirmation, Clough clings to his doubts, using poetry as a means of exploring possible positions without committing himself to them: "Why should I say I see the things I see not, / Why be and be not? / Show love for that I love not, and fear for what I fear not?" In the poem of which these lines are the opening, Clough again states the danger of going along with the values and beliefs of those all around him. One may choose to "keep amid the throng. / And turn as they shall turn, and bound as they are bounding," but "Alas! Alas! alas! and what if all along / The music is not sounding?" The poem then contrasts the loud but wholly illusory music with the soft inner melody which sounds only fitfully.

Finally, in one of the most impressive of the poems of **Ambarvalia, "When Israel Came Out of Egypt,"** Clough uses a striking figure to carry the same burden: like those Israelites who would not wait for Moses' return, but created the Golden Calf to worship, Man in his rash impatience rushes to worship the first convenient deity rather than await the truth:

The clouded hill attend thou still,
And him that went within.
He yet shall bring some worthy thing
For waiting souls to see:
Some sacred word that he hath heard
Their light and life shall be;
Some lofty part, than which the heart
Adopt no nobler can,
Thou shalt receive, thou shalt believe,
And thou shalt do, O Man!

In her "Memoir," Mrs. Clough says that "his scepticism was of no mere negative quality—not a mere rejection of tradition and denial of authority, but was the expression of a pure reverence for the inner light of the spirit, and of entire submission to its guidance" [see Further Reading]. This praise is not merely that of an admiring wife; it is an accurate summation of his position as developed in the early poems. Nevertheless, what Mrs. Clough does not mention is how long and weary was the watch for the inner light to shine brightly enough for Clough to make out the road he was to travel.

Clough's questioning in **Ambarvalia** extends not only to the nature of duty and religious truth, but also to that of true love. Clough searches for the signs, the certifying marks, as it were, of the essence of love. As in his questioning of how to recognize duty or distinguish the true attributes of the deity, it is essentially an epistemological question Clough raises. His need is not to know what the essence of love is; that would be finally as presumptuous as to ask the essence of God. What he wishes rather is a way of distinguishing the effect produced by an ideal and essential love from that produced by sheer sexual drive or romantic fancy. Perhaps to the modern temper Clough may seem to have made a radical mistake in assuming that there is indeed an isolable something which is love, but one must remember that he is speaking directly out of the Christian Platonic tradition which assumes that there exists a love ordained by God to purify man, to set his feet on the steps which lead to the vision in which the good, the true, and the beautiful blend into one.

Clough's idealism about love is seen in **"With graceful seat and skilful hand," "The Silver Wedding,"** and to some extent in **"God be with You!"** . . . The first two especially express the ennobling and purifying powers of love and marriage. But against these more or less occasional pieces must be set three more searching poems. **"Ah what is love, our love, she said,"** questions whether all human love and the poet's expression of idyllic love are not indeed illusions. **"When panting sighs"** and **"Natura Naturans"** give form to the doubts thus expressed, pursuing analysis in strange ways which must have caused readers of the time to murmur "'Twere to consider too curiously, to consider so." The former poem asks whether what seems the delicious thrill of love is a prelude to the love of which the angels sing, or merely the "same song" the beasts know, modified only in that the "soul and spirit add / To pleasures, even base and bad, / A zest the soulless never had"—a speculation which sounds curiously like an anticipation of the ironic *fin de siècle* discussion Richard Le Gallienne later gave of decadence as adding the joys of corrupting the soul to those of corrupting the body. The idealism with which Clough invests love causes him to be wary and suspicious. The question which **"When panting sighs"** poses is simply whether the particular complex of emotions there described measures up to the vision of ideal love. Reason is called in to speak to the question, but how can reason distinguish the "halo of the soul" from the: "Phosphoric exhalation bred / Of vapour, steaming from the bed / Of Fancy's brook or Passion's river"?

One must always bear in mind that Clough was using poetry as a means of clarifying to himself questions, problems, and possible answers; otherwise, the multitude of viewpoints suggested in the poems of *Ambarvalia* appears chaotic. In the midst of the many poems which try to separate the ideal from the impure and earthy, one of Clough's most lyrical and intensely vivid poems, **"Natura Naturans,"** denies the premise of a radical difference between the ideal and the mundane, asserting that human love between the sexes is indeed part of a universal sexual force. The poem is startling coming from Clough's pen, for it identifies the passing pleasures of a young man and woman sitting beside each other "in casual second class" with the force operative in "Hymen's shrine" and with "The Power which e'en in stones and earths / By blind election felt, in forms / Organic breeds to myriad births." The sensations of sexual attraction are described as the flowering within each of the full force of nature:

> Flashed flickering forth fantastic flies,
> Big bees their burly bodies swung,
> Rooks roused with civic din the elms,
> And lark its wild reveillez rung;
> In Libyan dell the light gazelle;
> The leopard lithe in Indian glade,
> And dolphin, brightening tropic seas,
> In us were living, leapt and played:

Before its close, the poem has doubly accounted for the whole phenomenon: first, in terms of a guarded evolutionary theory; second, in terms of a somewhat heretical account of the "primal prime embrace" in the garden of Eden.

Of course not all the poems of *Ambarvalia* take philosophical or theological problems as their center. Such a poem as **"On Latmos,"** . . . for instance, is a conventional handling of the Endymion-Selene legend; but, while not a poem of which Clough had any reason to be ashamed, it, like most of his writing which does not bear directly on an intellectual problem, is slacker in both thought and technique than that which derives its interest from a tension between points of view. One of Clough's biographers, Lady Chorley, had indeed pronounced that " 'On Latmos' can surely be read only as a personal love poem," referring to it again as "that mysterious poem whose source and object elude conjecture" [see Further Reading]. As has been seen, there is some evidence for thinking that Clough may have experienced a love affair around 1846-47, but whether or no **"On Latmos"** was inspired by it, the poem does not, when considered by itself, convey a sense of personal passion. The same is true of **"God be with you"** for which the claim of a personal emotional inspiration seems even stronger. These and the few other poems in the volume which do not deal directly with intellectual conflict tend to stand out by contrast with the majority not because they express strong personal sentiments but because they seem pale and conventional.

Unlike Tennyson, Clough was unequal to or uninterested in taking a scene or an old legend as the subject of a poem and creating an esthetically beautiful object from it—"The Kraken," "Mariana," and "Tithonus" were outside his poetic range. Indeed, though he somewhat ambiguously vindicated the reality of poetic imagination in **"Is it true, ye gods?"** in another poem, **"A golden key on the tongue,"** Clough expresses his reservations about devoting one's life to poetry. If a sense of happiness and human kindliness comes amid our "cheerless wanderings," it is not, he says, to be wasted on "the trifler, Poesy":

> Heaven grant the manlier heart, that timely, ere
> Youth fly, with life's real tempest would be coping,
> The fruit of dreamy hoping
> Is, waking, blank despair.

The sense of the seriousness of life which here causes him to wonder if life is not of too great import to devote much of it

to poetry underlies Clough's impatience with all that is superficial, illusory, and less than of sterling goodness and truth. The same impulse leads him in **"Look you, my simple friend"** to find the evil and the crime that lead men to recognize God through his anger to be preferable to devoting one's life to the exercise of mere wit and cleverness.

Thus, lying beneath the variously inconsistent themes of the poems of *Ambarvalia,* we find Clough's dedication to the serious duties of life, to the necessity of waiting for insight and revelation, and to the refusal to accept any emotional or intellectual coin without subjecting it to a rigorous, if finally inconclusive, examination. But with man's duties not yet fully identified, the infallible signs of emotional and intellectual truth not yet discovered, and the revelation not yet come, it is hardly surprising that Clough gave the title **"Blank Misgivings of a Creature moving about in Worlds not realized"** to the sequence of ten poems which sum up the anxieties felt during the ten years at Oxford. . . . The note which runs through the whole group is repentance, but it is a repentance that does not quite ring true because the poems are far too abstract, too speculative, to suggest that any real sin is being reflected upon:

> So in they came,
> A noisy band of revellers,—vain hopes,
> Wild fancies, fitful joys; and there they sit
> In my heart's holy place, and through the night
> Carouse. . . .

Such lines sound as false as similar ones of Oscar Wilde, but for a rather different reason: one doubts Wilde's repentance, but one doubts Clough's sins. But the tone of Clough's anxious questioning comes through convincingly enough. Through many of these poems also runs the metaphor of debt, expressing the fear that to enjoy life before finding and entering upon one's duties is to incur an enormous debt, as well as to lose the hoped-for higher insights. The tenth poem of the group, beginning "I have seen higher holier things than these, / And therefore must to these refuse my heart" comes only to an uneasy resolution when it affirms "Do thou, as best thou mayst, thy duty do: / Amid the things allowed thee live and love" with the promise that the Summum Pulchrum will yet be seen. The answer seems as provisional as the others that Clough has essayed in *Ambarvalia.*

Read as completely serious statements, many of the lines in these ten poems exaggerate the desperation of Clough's mood; actually their seriousness is leavened with irony. The Wordsworthian echoes are at least partially lighthearted, and the source of the title suggests that Clough was perhaps attempting to follow Wordsworth in constructing a poem that, like the "Ode," would work through a series of doubts and questionings to a limited affirmation. (pp. 52-63)

The reviews of *Ambarvalia,* though not entirely damning, were almost unanimous in finding Clough's poems too obscure and too fragmentary. The expectations of the reviewers were, of course, that a poem should be a finished artifact, polished in expression, rounded in form, lucid in content, and unambiguous in point of view. We recognize today that the surface of a good poem may very well at first appear disorganized; and we can also see, looking back, that a good many Victorian poems were less unambiguous than they were thought to be. Modern readers have, moreover, been led by the whole trend of twentieth-century poetry to feel that a little obscurity is no bad thing in a poem. For these reasons, we may very well feel that Clough was simply ahead of his critics' appreciation. However, the reviewers were not speaking simply for the peculiar critical standards of their time; instead, they were championing one perennial kind of poetry over another: that which creates beauty, not that which simply attempts to express with absolute fidelity an individual response to life. It is the second goal we must value if we are to appreciate Clough, and it is only honest to admit that Clough rarely produces the first type, and almost never that highest kind of poetry which combines both.

It was perhaps his devotion to an absolute, almost philosophic, accuracy of phrasing that prevented Clough from often forging the memorable lines and phrases one recalls from other poets' works. The quotation of brief passages from Clough generally suggests a degree of prosaicness not felt when the poems from which they are taken are read complete—the delights of his poetry come not from his abilities as a phrase maker, but from his ability to convey with integrity the breadth and depth of the questions on which his intellect has been brought to bear.

At the time he was writing his poems, Clough himself was probably too much preoccupied with the process of objectifying his intellectual conflicts in poetry to worry about the world's evaluation of it; and at the time of the publication of *Ambarvalia* he was too relieved at having conclusively made his decision to leave Oxford to care much about the reviewers. The response of the world, or even of his friends, to his poetry presumably troubled him much less than his sense of loneliness in having travelled so considerable a distance from the convictions of his friends. **"Sic Itur"** and **"Qua Cursum Ventus"**—the latter one of his best-known poems (it probably records the termination of close friendship with W. G. Ward)—testify to his sense of sadness at the parting of intellectual ways and to his faith that men honestly pursuing truth may have to pursue different paths ("To veer, how vain! On, onward strain"). But the very honesty and integrity which compel them to differ may well see them through to the same goal:

> One port, methought, alike they sought,
> One purpose hold where'er they fare,—
> O bounding breeze, O rushing seas!
> At last, at last, unite them there!

(pp. 64-5)

Wendell V. Harris, in his Arthur Hugh Clough, *Twayne Publishers, Inc., 1970, 175 p.*

ROBINDRA KUMAR BISWAS (essay date 1972)

[*In this excerpt from his critical biography of Clough, Biswas discusses* Amours de Voyage, *demonstrating how the relationship between the elegiac passages and those in hexameter add to the complexity, depth, and significance of the poem.*]

Amours de Voyage is concerned with the search for meaning. Its aims are twofold: first, to create the figure of Claude as a particular, historically rooted instance of the hypersensitive intelligence, quick to see through conventional values and detect the throttling simplifications on which they rest; second, to observe him in the act of criticism and analysis, also attempting to convert perception into meaning and re-establish a syntax of experience—to recognize 'this' and 'that' and put the two together. The modified dramatic form of the poem is exactly fitted to these aims. Claude writes nearly all the letters. Those written by the Trevellyn girls provide only an oc-

casional change of perspective—a necessary one, since both Georgina's fussy, utterly mindless conventionality, and Mary's subdued suggestions of a more enduring substantiality and worth, help to locate Claude. The drama, after all, is wholly his, the only real dialogue is 'of the mind with itself'. And yet the drama is not exactly the drama of interior monologue: Claude is defined by the personal letter, that oblique and yet most self-conscious of verbal forms. His existence is inseparable from his capacity for considered verbalization, his capacity to find the exactly answering, discriminating phrase. He is at once the text and the gloss: he is the creature, not of spontaneous utterance, but of the deliberate, inevitable, afterthought. The letter form, approaching the intimacy and directness of private self-revelation, can place us sufficiently close to the cutting-edge of Claude's consciousness to involve us in the involutions, the hesitations, the revisions, and the circuits, of his responses:

> Yet it is pleasant, I own it, to be in their company; pleasant,
> Whatever else it may be, to abide in the feminine presence.
> Pleasant, but wrong, will you say? But this happy, serene coexistence
> Is to some poor soft souls, I fear, a necessity simple,
> Meat and drink and life, and music, filling with sweetness,
> Thrilling with melody sweet, with harmonies strange overwhelming,
> All the long-silent strings of an awkward, meaningless fabric.
> Yet as for that, I could live, I believe, with children; to have those
> Pure and delicate forms encompassing, moving about you,
> This were enough, I could think; and truly with glad resignation
> Could from the dream of romance, from the fever of flushed adolescence,
> Look to escape and subside into peaceful avuncular functions.

(I. ix. 168-79.)

Intimidated by the directness of the first statement, the mind burrows hastily into qualification—'pleasant, whatever else it may be'—and into the safe, comfortably abstract, and unlocalized 'feminine presence'. Issuing forth once more to grapple with felt experience, the statement strengthens from 'meat and drink' to 'life', from the minimum of the necessary to the plenitude of the essential, and from mere 'coexistence' to the 'overwhelming' reciprocity of musical harmony. Once again the affirmation has been pushed too far, and the mind, withdrawing to the refuge of the safely asexual, adds a new motive to the general fear of illusion ('the dream of romance') in Claude's uneasiness about his association with Mary Trevellyn. In this letter Claude enforces an inward view; he can equally impose a distance, and, by holding himself far enough, elicit and record an almost wholly critical response to his own idling mind, moving aimlessly back and forth along itself, outrageously, comically, resolute only in its refusal to engage with experience, trapped in and isolated by its awareness of miscellaneousness and indeterminacy.

> So we stand in the sun, but afraid of a probable shower;
> So we stand and stare, and see, to the left of St. Peter's,
> Smoke, from the cannon, white,—but that is at intervals only,—
> Black, from a burning house, we suppose, by the Cavalleggieri;
> And we believe we discern some lines of men descending
> Down through the vineyard-slopes, and catch a bayonet gleaming.

Every ten minutes, however,—in this there is no miscon-
ception,—
Comes a great white puff from behind Michael Angelo's
dome, and
After a space the report of a real big gun,—not the
Frenchman's?—
That must be doing some work. And so we watch and con-
jecture.

Shortly, an Englishman comes, who says he has been to
St. Peter's,
Seen the Piazza and troops, but that is all he can tell us;
So we watch and sit, and, indeed, it begins to be tire-
some.—
All this smoke is outside; when it has come to the inside,
It will be time, perhaps, to descend and retreat to our
houses.

(II. v. 117-31.)

Moving between two such contrary potentialities the form
becomes a subtly controlling and directing instrument.

All this, however, is only on the outskirts of the poem's existence. The centre is the poetry itself and in this the Roman
background is inseparably involved. At an obvious level the
heroic defence of the Mazzinian Republic provides an ironic
commentary on Claude's fastidious hesitancy, but the setting
penetrates much further into the poem's life and creates
much more profoundly significant ironic patterns. For underlying this undetermined Rome of present political violence,
there is another Rome felt as an organic presence—Rome as
the Eternal City, the seat of civilization, the embodiment of
achievement and culture, where the tides of history have been
stilled into the poised and mythic tranquillity of art. The evidences of this Rome are everywhere and they bring memories
of wholeness and of meaningful continuities which mock the
perspiring, inchoate, distracted, and dislocated present. Once
he has shed his initial languidly clever superiority, Claude responds positively to the community of meanings and values
which this Rome represents; only, he is a fragment in a fragmented world and history separates him from that
community. . . . The poetry which re-creates Claude's often
ludicrous, often tragic attempt to achieve meaning displays
a precise awareness of the crisis in culture that gives to his
attempt a relevance extending beyond the purely personal.
(pp. 310-12)

Unwittingly Shairp laid his finger on something basic in the
poetic structure and method of ***Amours de Voyage*** when he
excepted from his general condemnation the 'snatches of
longs and shorts' and the 'page or two' of the hexameters
which 'rise into music' [see first letter by Shairp dated 1849].
For two distinct kinds of poetry are immediately discernible
in the poem, and the active, complexly ironic relationship between them is centrally important in creating the sensitive
and mobile wakefulness which distinguishes the work as a
whole. The elegiacs that frame each canto have a consistent
and clearly recognizable poetic life, which consciously recalls
the ideal past and is permeated by it.

Is it illusion? or does there a spirit from perfecter ages,
Here, even yet, amid loss, change, and corruption abide?
Does there a spirit we know not, though seek, though we
find, comprehend not,
Here to entice and confuse, tempt and evade us, abide?
Lives in the exquisite grace of the column disjointed and
single,
Haunts the rude masses of brick garlanded gayly with
vine,

Clough about the time he left Oxford and moved to London.

E'en in the turret fantastic surviving that springs from the
ruin,
E'en in the people itself? is it illusion or not?

(II. 1-8.)

Saturated in the Rome of Antiquity and controlled by its
presence, this self-possessed voice, which gives to that Rome
its high imaginative valency, translates Claude's hesitant,
self-conscious wanderings and perplexed conflicts into an
ironically distanced, recognizably 'poetic' experience.

Yet to the wondrous St. Peter's, and yet to the solemn Ro-
tonda,
Mingling with heroes and gods, yet to the Vatican walls,
Yet may we go, and recline, while a whole mighty world
seems above us
Gathered and fixed to all time into one roofing supreme;
Yet may we, thinking on these things, exclude what is
meaner around us;
Yet, at the worst of the worst, books and a chamber re-
main;
Yet may we think, and forget, and possess our souls in re-
sistance.—
Ah, but away from the stir, shouting, and gossip of war,
Where, upon Appenine slope, with the chestnut the oak-
trees immingle,
Where amid odorous copse bridle-paths wander and wind,
Where under mulberry-branches the diligent rivulet spar-
kles,
Or amid cotton and maize peasants their water-works ply,
Where, over fig-tree and orange in tier upon tier still re-
peated,
Garden on garden upreared, balconies step to the sky,—
Ah, that I were, far away from the crowd and the streets
of the city,
Under the vine-trellis laid, O my beloved, with thee!

(III. 1-16.)

Clearly the ironic traffic runs both ways. If these gracefully finished, traditionally accomplished elegiacs mock at the sprawling libertinage of the hexameters, the exceptional openness of the hexameters, their receptiveness to process, exposes, in turn, the illusory and unreal quality of this kind of loveliness. The two kinds of poetry, in fact, organize two radically different modes of experience. Their confrontation dramatizes the crisis in meaning.

Yet, opposed as these two kinds of poetry are, they are not discontinuous. The hexameters and the elegiacs are linked by a common pattern of imagery which, in drawing them together, only emphasizes the absolute difference between them. The language of the hexameters seems to reach out to that of the elegiacs and to the kind of rest which that language organizes; the attempt, ironically, proves its own impossibility. Two main classes of image predominate in *Amours de Voyage,* and their centrality in a poem concerned so fundamentally with the search for meaning and integrity and with the discrimination of historical continuity will be immediately apparent. To describe them in their most general and inclusive aspect, these are the continually recurring images of solidness and fixity and of fluidity and movement. Most frequently they appear as images of land and water, but they appear in many other forms as well—as images of voyaging and travel, of arrival and departure, the flow of a crowd, the fixity of a relationship, the flow of emotions: the list can be expanded quite easily. In themselves the images are important, of course, but even more important is the difference in their treatment and function in the two kinds of poetry, and the emotional significance with which they are invested.

In the elegiacs these leading images are absorbed into serenely balanced, ideally harmonious landscapes from which they derive an unobtrusive stability and completeness of meaning:

> Therefore farewell, ye hills, and ye, ye envineyarded ruins!
> Therefore farewell, ye walls, palaces, pillars, and domes!
> Therefore farewell, far seen, ye peaks of the mythic Albano,
> Seen from Montorio's height, Tibur and Aesula's hills!
> Ah, could we once, ere we go, could we stand, while, to ocean descending,
> Sinks o'er the yellow dark plain slowly the yellow broad sun,
> Stand, from the forest emerging at sunset, at once in the champaign,
> Open, but studded with trees, chestnuts umbrageous and old,
> E'en in those fair open fields that incurve to thy beautiful hollow,
> Nemi, imbedded in wood, Nemi, inurned in the hill!
>   (III. 293-302.)
> There is a city, upbuilt on the quays of the turbulent Arno,
> Under Fiesole's heights,—thither are we to return?
> There is a city that fringes the curve of the inflowing waters,
> Under the perilous hill fringes the beautiful bay,—
> Parthenope do they call thee?—the Siren, Neapolis, seated
> Under Vesevus's hill,—are we receding to thee?
>   (V. 1-6.)

Exempt from the press and complexity of particulars, this poetry of evocation accumulates its pictures into a perfect poise and simplicity of meaning—sea balances land, mountain plain, nature civilization, movement stillness. The harmony of the landscape is the outward and visible sign of an inner grace of uncomplexity—love is sure here and totally convinced, travel is purposeful, even loss has meaning.

In the elegiacs the poetic significance of these images of solidness and fluidity is stabilized by their poetic context. Significantly, it is primarily when Claude responds most simply and unreservedly to the spell of Roman antiquity that the hexameters approach most nearly the poetic quality of the elegiacs, and, in doing so, sustain a similar kind of equilibrium in these images.

> Ye, too, marvellous Twain, that erect on the Monte Cavallo
> Stand by your rearing steeds in the grace of your motionless movement,
> Stand with your upstretched arms and tranquil regardant faces,
> Stand as instinct with life in the might of immutable manhood,—
> O ye mighty and strange, ye ancient divine ones of Hellas,
> Are ye Christian too? . . .
>
> And ye, silent, supreme in serene and victorious marble,
> Ye that encircle the walls of the stately Vatican chambers,
> Juno and Ceres, Minerva, Apollo, the Muses and Bacchus,
> Ye unto whom far and near come posting the Christian pilgrims,
> Ye that are ranged in the halls of the mystic Christian Pontiff,
> Are ye also baptized? are ye of the kingdom of Heaven?
>   (I.x. 186-91; 194-9.) . . .

Normally this kind of stability is as foreign to the hexameters as is the lucid, contemplating, Horatian voice, for the characteristic idiom of the hexameters and the mode of being out of which that idiom emerges provide no such continuously supporting and equilibrating context. Claude can no more find absolute rest in the 'positive, calm, Stoic-Epicurean acceptance' (I. iv. 76) of Classical and Renaissance humanism than he can free himself completely from the stark, neurotic dualisms of Protestantism,

> With its humiliations and exaltations combining,
> Exaltations sublime, and yet diviner abasements,
> Aspirations from something most shameful here upon earth and
> In our poor selves to something most perfect above in the heavens,—
>   (I. iv. 66-9.)

or exorcize himself of the anguishing injunction, 'Except ye be converted, and become as little children, ye shall not enter into the kingdom of heaven': his desire for the safe, sinless, and asexual company of children (I. ix. 175-80) acquires wicked ironic point from being interposed between his rejection of 'the Martyrs, and Saints, and Confessors, and Virgins, and children' in favour of the 'mightier forms of an older, austerer worship' (I. viii. 159-60), on the one side, and, on the other, his apostrophe to the 'immutable manhood' of the Horse Tamers on the Monte Cavallo.

Normally the implications and the emotional equivalents of the leading images of fixity and fluidity are in a constant state of transformation in the hexameters. Images of fixity are used, for instance, to represent the strangling effect of civilization on the natural life (I. ii), the tyranny of regimented devotion (I. v), the closed, limpet-like life of selfish withdrawal (II. ii), the safe familiarity of the present and the near at hand (II. iv), the rest and steadiness of achieved human relationship (II. xi), the serene contemplation of the spectator withdrawn from any relationship (II. xii), an escape from the flux of living (III. vii), a hard and naked rock to which to cling amid loss and change (V. v). Images of fluidity can represent the wandering, chaotic seas of theological controversy, historically disastrous because their invasion denies and perverts pure growth (I. v), the transformation of a peaceful crowd into a violent mob (II. ix), the life of primitive organisms in the Aqueous Ages of the world (II. ii), the limitless ocean of possibility when one is freed from the circumscription of action (III. vi), the ebb and flow of love's fortunes (IV. iii). This crudely descriptive and merely illustrative list is useful only quantitatively in indicating something of the range and pervasiveness of these sliding significances. Only the poetry itself gives us the experience of these transformations in meaning:

> But I am in for it now,—*laissez faire,* of a truth, *laissez aller.*
> Yes, I am going,—I feel it, I feel and cannot recall it,—
> Fusing with this thing and that, entering into all sorts of relations,
> Tying I know not what ties, which, whatever they are, I know one thing,
> Will, and must, woe is me, be one day painfully broken,—
> Broken with painful remorses, with shrinkings of soul, and relentings,
> Foolish delays, more foolish evasions, most foolish renewals.
> But I have made the step, have quitted the ship of Ulysses;
> Quitted the sea and the shore, passed into the magical island;
> Yet on my lips is the *moly,* medicinal, offered of Hermes.
> I have come into the precinct, the labyrinth closes around me,
> Path into path rounding slyly; I pace slowly on, and the fancy,
> Struggling awhile to sustain the long sequences, weary, bewildered,
> Fain must collapse in despair; I yield, I am lost, and know nothing;
> Yet in my bosom unbroken remaineth the clue; I shall use it.
> Lo, with the rope on my loins I descend through the fissure; I sink, yet
> Inly secure in the strength of invisible arms up above me;
> Still, wheresoever I swing, wherever to shore, or to shelf, or
> Floor of cavern untrodden, shell-sprinkled, enchanting, I know I
> Yet shall one time feel the strong cord tighten about me,—
> Feel it, relentless, upbear me from spots I would rest in; and though the
> Rope sway wildly, I faint, crags wound me, from crag unto crag re-
> Bounding, or, wide in the void, I die ten deaths, ere the end I
> Yet shall plant firm foot on the broad lofty spaces I quit, shall
> Feel underneath me again the great massy strengths of abstraction,
> Look yet abroad from the height o'er the sea whose salt wave I have tasted.
>
> (I. xii. 227-52.)

The rate and density of change are dizzying; the images of fixity and movement, of solidity and fluidity, draw together, interpenetrate, fall apart, change emotional colour and even actual reference. This oscillating, helplessly open poetry places us at the vertiginous centre of consciousness, where meaning is in constant process, solidifying, dissolving, reforming into new shapes, and where large significances have to be painfully extracted from an unremitting flux.

This tension and ambiguity in meaning is achieved through—

and regulated by—Clough's deceptively casual hexameters. Spilling more frequently into enjambement and running to longer verse-paragraphs, infinitely more subtle in movement than the hexameters of ***The Bothie,*** these long, untwisting lines achieve a remarkable range and flexibility of expressiveness and a delicate command over pause and cadence. Without the least strain they can rise to a quiet understated lyricism, drop to the informal rhythms of natural colloquial speech, or record deftly the empty talkativeness of Georgina Trevellyn's letters. What distinguishes them most clearly, however, is their brilliant syntactical strategy. . . .

> So, I have seen a man killed! An experience that, among others!
> Yes, I suppose I have; although I can hardly be certain,
> And in a court of justice could never declare I had seen it.
> But a man was killed, I am told, in a place where I saw Something; a man was killed, I am told, and I saw something
>
> (II. vii. 164-8.)
> Great is Fate, and is best. I believe in Providence partly.
> What is ordained is right, and all that happens is ordered.
> Ah, no, that isn't it. But yet I retain my conclusion.
>
> (V. viii. 176-8.)

The punctuation is not heavily grammatical. It reproduces, rather, the rhythmic patterns of reflective speech, and the loosely strung phrases reach out to one another through these light pauses, each phrase picking up the meaning at the point at which it has been deposited by the preceding one and pushing it—comically in the first example, pathetically in the second—one unexpected stage further. The curiously open syntax, delicately following every curve and nuance of response, gently—and ironically—disconnects 'this' from 'that' and disperses statement into nonstatement. In this deftly controlled, fastidiously self-inspective poetry of afterthought even the single line can become the subtle record of ambivalence:

> I am in love, you say: I do not think so, exactly.
>
> (II. x. 265.)

This sensitive syntactical fidelity to the tentative and the provisional in human response not only enables the hexameters to hold meanings and rhetorics in suspense and observe their incipience and dissolution, but gives to Claude's recognitions, when he does arrive at them, a movingly precise, exact, veracity:

> She goes,—therefore I go; she moves,—I move, not to lose her.
>
> (II. xiii. 291.)

It is this rhetorically validated veracity, this minimal utterance, which ensures that Claude emerges from the poem as something more than a mere fool or an absolute failure. The story of his love ends 'in smoke' and he loses Mary Trevellyn. Unable to relate himself to himself or, through decision, to the world which surrounds him, he submits to the rule of necessity;

> Ah, the key of our life, that passes all wards, opens all locks,
> Is not *I will,* but *I must.* I must,—I must,—and I do it.
>
> (V. viii. 154-5.)

Mainly because of his interminable speculativeness, his incessant 'fiddle-faddling' (IV. iii. 38), partly because he is genuinely, as Clough called him, an *'unfortunate* fool' and the victim of circumstances, two lives lose an opportunity for what might have been mutual enrichment. But something valuable is not merely rescued but born out of loss and futility and misunderstanding and personal failure, something deeper, less spectatorial than his once threatened allegiance to the life of the intellect, and quite distinct from his 'wilful unmeaning acceptance' (V. v. 65) of necessity. We see it forming in the fifth letter of the last Canto, when, reduced to an almost complete degradation by his recognition of loss and failure, Claude yet refuses the strangely moving consolation offered by a homely symbol of all that is simple and familiar, conventional and reassuring—a barrel-organ grinding out an English psalm-tune.

> What with trusting myself and seeking support from within me,
> Almost I could believe I had gained a religious assurance,
> Found in my own poor soul a great moral basis to rest on.
> Ah, but indeed I see, I feel it factitious entirely;
> I refuse, reject, and put it utterly from me;
> I will look straight out, see things, not try to evade them;
> Fact shall be fact for me, and the Truth the Truth as ever,
> Flexible, changeable, vague, and multiform, and doubtful.—
> Off, and depart to the void, thou subtle, fanatical tempter!
>   (V. v. 95-103.)

The toughened movement of the verse, the purposive, abrupt, accumulating syntax, enacts the strengthening resolve in the face of realized inadequacy. In despair of meaning, yet refusing to be overwhelmed by his desire for meaning, Claude is, like his hexameters, shortening his syntactic reach. The process is completed when he comes to rest in his final crippled but splendid affirmation:

> Not as the Scripture says, is, I think, the fact. Ere our death-day,
> Faith, I think, does pass, and Love; but Knowledge abideth.
> Let us seek Knowledge;—the rest may come and go as it happens.
> Knowledge is hard to seek, and harder yet to adhere to.
> Knowledge is painful often; and yet when we know, we are happy.
> Seek it, and leave mere Faith and Love to come with the chances.
> As for Hope,—to-morrow I hope to be starting for Naples.
>   (V. x. 197-203.)

Claude has come to terms with syntax: he has begun to acquire 'the temper or disposition of mind which can look at a *gap* or chasm without shuddering'. The hexameters no longer reach out to one another in search of meaning.

> As for Hope,—to-morrow I hope to be starting for Naples.

In the wintry finality of that utterance **Amours de Voyage** faces unflinchingly the human consequences of Claude's bleak commitment. The poem ends with the French guns of the closing epilogue and their comment on the individual failure which yet seems so akin to victory.

The superbly original artistry of these hexameters, restlessly alive with implication beneath their off-hand surface, is, of course, the most immediately striking single achievement of **Amours de Voyage**. . . . It seriously diminishes both the hexameters themselves and the poem as a whole, however, if we lose sight of the larger artistic strategy which contains this new and exciting poetic voice. For by playing off what we might call the poetry of the background against that of the

foreground Clough establishes an intricate structure of ironic and poetic relationships which creates the whole point of the hexameters, and establishes the validity of the artistic revolt they represent. It is only when we put this local idiom back into its validating framework that we can begin to take the measure of Clough's achievement, of the depth and complexity of the poem and its scrutiny of contemporary history and contemporary values. (pp. 313-21)

Robindra Kumar Biswas, in his Arthur Hugh Clough: Towards a Reconsideration, *Oxford at the Clarendon Press, 1972, 489 p.*

PATRICK GREIG SCOTT   (essay date 1978)

[*Scott disputes claims that Clough's verse is modern, arguing that his sensibilities and the portrayal of such subjects as religion and sexuality in his poetry were conventionally Victorian.*]

The poetry of Clough, and the critical response to it over the past thirty or so years, present a particularly interesting instance against which to test present-day understandings of Victorianism. After years of being treated simply as an exemplum of the mid-Victorian religious dilemma, Clough has been accorded striking revaluation by more recent critics, who almost unanimously applaud him for his "modernity." However, the last thirty years have also seen, for Clough as for other Victorian writers, an enormous increase in the sheer quantity of scholarly study; the amount of information available to the Clough critic—biographical, textual, bibliographical, and contextual—greatly complicates, if we use it, the reading responses which we can make and thus deepens, for the specialist if not for the average student, our understanding of Clough's relation to his time, the true quality of his Victorianism. There is a near-schizophrenia between the critical and historical interpretations of Clough's poetry, and he thus becomes a compelling instance of that general problem in modern discussion of the great Victorians which Michael Timko has recently brought out into the open: while our knowledge about the Victorians has grown quantitatively, our critical interpretation of their literature still largely draws on ideas of literary excellence and even of literary intention which are romantic or modernist in origin rather than specifically Victorian. (p. 32)

It seems time . . . to explore the possibility that the "modernist" label itself may have outlived its revaluative and pedagogic usefulness, and may now actually be distorting our response to some crucial areas of Clough's work. One such area is his treatment of sexuality, for it has become a commonplace that Clough, at least in the drafting of his poems if not in the early published versions, was one of the frankest of Victorian poets. Frederick Bowers, for instance, in his essay "Arthur Hugh Clough: The Modern Mind," refers to Clough's ridicule of "prudery," his "reaction against . . . contemporary prudery," his "bawdy and rough" language, and the fact that his poetry is "sometimes racy" [see excerpt dated 1966]. Such a response rests essentially on a few speeches from the early scenes of **Dipsychus,** which seem to take one away from family proprieties into the world of the other Victorians:

> one can pick up in one's walking
> In the Strand Street in London town
> Something quite nice for half a crown.
> But—in the dark what comes amiss?
> Except bad breath and syphilis.

It is worth noting, however, that in these scenes Clough is deliberately contrasting the smoking-room coarseness of the Spirit with the disturbed high-mindedness of Dipsychus himself, and that the Spirit, who is morally "in the dark," and equates sexual fulfillment with prostitution, is as much the object of Clough's satire as is Dipsychus. Elsewhere in Clough's work, the treatment of sexuality is rather different, not so much direct as poetic and idealized. In "Natura naturans," for instance, he presents the growing sexual awareness of two young Victorians in a second-class railway carriage through a sustained description of the developmental force of nature:

> In me and her—sensation strange!
> The lily grew to pendent head,
> To vernal airs and mossy bank
> Its sheeny primrose spangles spread,
> In roof o'er roof of shade sun-proof
> Did cedar strong itself outclimb,
> And altitude of aloe proud
> Aspire in floreal crown sublime;
>
> . . . . .
>
> Yea, close comprest in human breast,
> What moss, and tree, and livelier thing,
> What Earth, Sun, Star of force possest,
> Lay budding, burgeoning forth for Spring.

From such images, Clough directs the reader, not to the sexual knowingness of the Strand or the Haymarket, but to the innocence of "sinless" Eden, and the "primal prime embrace." In the use of natural imagery, in the adoption of the language of the Song of Solomon (cedars, aloes), and above all in its evocation of the role of the subconscious in human sexuality, Clough's picture here seems closer to Tennyson's in the garden in *Maud,* than to T. S. Eliot's in the typist's bed-sittingroom in *The Waste Land.* Clough's integration of sexual awareness into some of his poetry was not, in fact, a lonely gesture of anti-Victorianism, but, as Robindra Biswas argues [in *Arthur Hugh Clough: Towards a Reconsideration* (see excerpt dated 1972 for an extract from this work)], was part of a fairly widespread attempt by the poets of the eighteen-forties and fifties to create a moral idealization of sexual energy. At one level, the "message" of Clough's *Bothie* is just such an attempt to transcend the undergraduates' socially bound views of sexuality, and to express the true "sexual glory," but it is reticence, and a veiled or symbolic presentation of sexuality, which are more characteristic of Clough's work than bawdy or "frankness." In *The Bothie,* for instance, the treatment of Elspie's growing love for Philip Hewson is presented entirely through extended passages of imagery, of the burnie's current, and of bridge-building, and even though the reader can hardly escape the sexual nature of their attraction, its presentation is implicit rather than explicit.

The modernist claim that Clough's best poetry is his most explicit has had some effect on the way even textual scholars approach his poems, since it has long been recognized that neither Clough himself, nor his rather proper wife and literary executor Blanche, put into print the less decorous of his manuscripts. Richard M. Gollin has argued that the pressures of Victorian sexual morality operated to produce a damaging censorship. Professor Gollin writes:

> The manuscripts, and even the texts published in Clough's life-time, often reflect two distinct stages of writing. In the first stage, Clough wrote his poem as it required itself to be written, a poem reflecting the thoughts and feelings he had at the time; in the second, Clough wrote and revised to make the poem respectably presentable to the Victorian tastes and judgments he increasingly accepted after his marriage.

In fact, Clough tended to draw back from explicitly sexual references long before he had even met his future wife. As early as 1844, Clough consciously revised one of his "erotico-philosophical" poems away from the erotic and towards the philosophical; the veiled language of "Natura naturans" dates from 1847; and in *The Bothie,* where Clough had originally included among the utilitarian tests of human beauty a line, "So but the bed be well-made, who made it is worthy to fill it," he deleted the reference from his first rough manuscript before making his fair copy for the printer. Other such instances could be cited from later poems such as *Amours de Voyage,* but the pattern seems to go much more deeply into Clough's mode or writing, and to start much earlier, than the "censorship" argument implies. Even in the notorious case of *Dipsychus,* where Clough at one point considered discarding from Scene III the whole of the discussion of prostitutes on which the movement of the poem depends, the bawdiest lines come from sections which were never integrated into any coherently arranged text of the poem, and their abandonment, like Clough's eventual abandonment of the work as a whole, may have been because of the intractable aesthetic problems they presented, rather than merely from prudishness. In the "second revision" of the poem, Clough had been creating increased space and sympathy for Dipsychus at the expense of the worldly Spirit, and the Spirit's bawdy interjections were especially subject to cutting as they had tilted the balance of sympathy against Dipsychus. The curious result of the modernist urge to deVictorianize Clough, and to include more bawdiness from the early drafts, is to put pressure on the textual scholar to incorporate material from different revision stages into his text: the new Oxford edition prints a hybrid text of *Dipsychus* for the early scenes, presenting the editor's own conflation of Clough's unfinished "third revision" and the longer "second revision" to forestall criticism that he had been timid in 1951 about printing Clough's references to the prostitutes. The result is that there is duplication of lines between scenes drawn from different manuscripts, and a text has again been produced which Clough himself never envisaged. A modern, consciously "uncensored," Clough edition, which drew from unfinished and fragmentary early drafts, would result in an even more unsatisfactory text than the posthumous censorship occasionally imposed by Mrs. Clough.

A second area in which the "modernist" label has led to a distortion of Clough's achievement is that of religious poetry. Mrs. Clough and the circle of Clough's admirers who reviewed her posthumous editions had maintained, for the most part, that, though Clough resigned his Oxford fellowship in 1848 in an Emersonian protest against religious restrictions, and though he wrote occasional poems expressing skepticism about traditional religious attitudes, he retained a positive religious belief throughout his life. Rather defensively, Mrs. Clough stressed in her memoir her disappointment that Clough had not lived longer, to express these "mature convictions in works of a more positive and substantial kind." By and large, modern scholarly study has vindicated Mrs. Clough's general position: though Clough was consistently critical of historical claims for the scriptural records, and skeptical of subjective assertions about particular religious experiences, he held with equal strength that it is "impossible for any Man, to live, act, and reflect without feeling the significance and depth of the moral and religious teaching which passes amongst us by the name of Christianity." Clough's attitude was, from early in the eighteen-forties, like that of his protagonist Claude:

> No, I am not, you may trust me, in any true sense a Sceptic,
>
> . . . . .
>
> I am, believe me, at bottom nor sceptic nor unbeliever,
> Misbeliever perhaps, as I go the wrong way about it;
> So it would seem; yet rather account me an over-believer.

Clough is perhaps more searching in his exposure of the self-deceptions possible in religious experience, but at root his religious belief stayed very close to that of such contemporaries as Tennyson, predicated on "the existence of some sort of absolute spiritual reality that is more than a mere projection of [man's] feelings."

Yet even though scholars may now recognize the continuing idealism of Clough's beliefs, and have disregarded the Stracheyan stereotype of Clough as ineffectual doubter [see Strachey entry in Further Reading], the critical implications of such recognition are seldom followed out. Most twentieth-century critics have emphasized the skepticism in his poetical treatment of religion to the neglect of other qualities. Every Victorian anthology includes Clough's satire on Victorian complacency, **"The Latest Decalogue,"** and every reader remembers the scorn of the Spirit in *Dipsychus* for the insincerity of Victorian belief:

> "There is no God, or if there is,"
> The tradesman thinks, "'twere funny
> If he should take it ill in me
> To make a little money."
>
> "Whether there be," the rich man says,
> "It matters very little,
> For I and mine, thank somebody,
> Are not in want of victual."

What is often forgotten is that the sociological reductionism here implied is put into the Spirit's mouth, and is therefore itself to be suspect, and that the ironic tone of the verse changes as Clough turns to less grudging believers. The border between irony and idyll is narrow when Clough writes of "country folks who live beneath / The shadow of the steeple" and of "Youths green and happy in first love" in the sixth and seventh stanzas of the song; and the jaunty rhythm of the opening stanzas seems also to become slower and more wistful:

> And almost every one when age,
> Disease, or sorrows strike him,
> Inclines to think there is a God,
> Or something very like Him.

If such a tension of attitudes can happen even when Clough is avowedly giving an ironic treatment to Victorian religion, we must recognize that most of Clough's religious poetry is engaged and serious, with the will to believe predominating over the skeptical, ironic unbelief which has attracted critical attention. Any reader of Clough needs to be aware not only of the quantity but also of the strength of passages such as this one, from the *Ambarvalia* volume:

> One Power too is it, who doth give
> The food without us, and within

The strength that makes it nutritive:
He bids the dry bones rise and live,
And, e'en in hearts depraved to sin,
Some sudden, gracious influence
May give the long-lost good again,
And wake within the dormant sense
And love of good.

Now a similar case to that sketched here about Clough's poetic treatment of sexuality and of religion could also be made about other areas in which his attitudes were alleged to be modern. His treatment of the Victorian city, for example, is not only controlled and satiric (as in the two **"Great Metropolis"** poems, or the song **"As I sat at the cafe"**), but can also express, without apparent irony, a conventionally Victorian and emotional horror at the moral side-effects of urbanization (especially in *Mari Magno*), and rise to a highly poetic idealization of the organic society he glimpsed beyond the surface dislocation of urban development (in the concluding section of *The Bothie*). The essential argument should, however, already be clear, that the "modernist" label encourages an over-selective approach to Clough's poetry, and obscures the emotionality and the ultimately unironic idealism which suffuse his work.

There are implications in this case for the reading of Clough's longer poems. In *The Bothie,* for instance, the satire on the undergraduate reading party in the opening books has attracted much more favorable comment than the more idyllic later books, where Philip's quest for the Good Time Coming begins to have fulfillment in his marriage to Elspie, and where the famous mock-Homeric style gives way to an almost Tennyson-like Virgilian pastoral; we can only make sense of the poem if we recognize the authenticity both of Philip's personal development and of the stylistic development, as man and style together move from *dégagé* to *engagé*. Likewise, in *Amours de Voyage,* Claude's alienated monologues, those in which his self-irony is destroying the hope of certainty or action, have attracted all the praise, to the virtual disregard both of the consistently affirmative elegiacs which begin and end each canto, and of the sheer lyricism (about liberty, the Alban hills, and Mary herself) which sustains Claude in the face of practical frustration. In many of the epistemological debates of Clough's poetry, the reality as well as the elusiveness of idealistic belief or intuitive knowledge is represented by his very poeticness, which serves as a stylistic counter-argument to irony and doubt. The ultimate failure of a poem like *Dipsychus* stems from the fact, not that the irony was too daringly unprintable, but that, because Dipsychus himself was divided and uncertain, the poetic counter-argument in his speeches was not strong enough to make the reader believe in any genuine alternative to the Spirit's worldly, amoral skepticism.

The whole strategy of Clough's poetry is to exploit the tension between the ironies of the fragmented phenomenal world and the integrative possibilities, uncertain though they may be, of that intuitive vision which could only be presented through the resources of traditional, often lyric, poeticism. A typical Clough poem will often start by breaking up some traditional poetic form (for instance, the sonnet), replacing it with a poetry of fragmentation; it will, however, almost invariably then turn back to a renewal of lyric meter for a concluding expression of the will to believe. A good example is the sequence **"Blank Misgivings,"** but many, both of the longer and shorter poems, exhibit this pattern. As Clough writes in the middle of **Amours de Voyage,** he might say farewell in the middle of a poem to "the mythic Albano" or poetic traditionalism, yet he departed "but to behold [it] again" before his conclusion. Such a strategy lies, of course, behind much of Tennyson's work: both *In Memoriam* and *Maud* exploit a similar tension between the fragmentation of experience and the integrative possibilities of belief. Clough's distinctiveness lies, I think, not in any rejection of Victorian idealism, but in the thoroughness with which his poetry makes us experience the sheer difficulty, the healing power, and the overwhelming significance of the Victorian quest for transcendent meaning.

Of course, it could be claimed that to emphasize the Victorianism of Clough is to ignore a qualitative distinction, thought to be obvious to all discerning critics, between his disengaged, drily ironic poetry and the dully traditionalist rhetoric of his liberal belief—rhetoric in which he is, inevitably, nearer to the language of his lesser as well as his greater contemporaries. There are two arguments against this. First, readings which take account of Clough's Victorianism seem to be more inclusive and to explain more about individual poems than those which rest on a modern response to a few selected images or lines. Secondly, the "modernist" presupposition has, to a large extent, prevented critics from examining Clough's non-ironic passages with the same scrupulous care that has led to such a striking revaluation of, say, Tennyson's poeticism in recent years: we may not yet know the variety of strength in Clough's poetry, because our very expectations about Clough's modernity may prevent our responding adequately to the lyrical or the abstract within his work. Clough was, I think, a striking and innovative and essentially serious poet, but his was a modernity of the mid-nineteenth not of the twentieth century. Even as a slogan for the classroom, the "modernist" label on Clough's poetry has come to obscure far more about his achievement than it usefully highlights, and a more integrated understanding of his poetry will best be reached by frank recognition of his Victorianism. (pp. 36-42)

> *Patrick Greig Scott, "The Victorianism of Clough,"* in Victorian Poetry, *Vol. 16, Nos. 1 & 2, Spring-Summer, 1978, pp. 32-42.*

JEFFREY M. JESKE (essay date 1982)

[*In the following essay, Jeske reassesses* Mari Magno, *considering it the most mature expression of Clough's inner conflict between idealism and naturalism.*]

Continuing controversy attends the **Mari Magno,** Arthur Clough's last long poem, composed, but not completed, during the six months before his death. Two main issues have traditionally divided readers. Regarding the purpose of the group of marriage-related stories, some suggest that Clough was attempting incisive social commentary. Others, confronting the "intellectual suicide" represented by Clough's marriage to Blanche Smith, argue that the collection contains only pleasant little tales treated within a cozily conventional framework of Victorian moral attitudes: hence Henry Sidgwick's characterization of the poem as "the genius of twaddle" [see excerpt dated 1869]. A second concern involves the rank of the **Mari Magno** in Clough's canon. Juxtaposing the work with the **Bothie, Amours,** and **Dipsychus,** readers such as H. W. Garrod argue that, if completed, the **Mari Magno** would have been Clough's masterpiece [see Further Read-

ing]. A more frequent assessment, however, is that in substituting simple objectivity and homey didacticism for the more subjective focus of the earlier works, the **Mari Magno** is the most dated and least successful of Clough's longer poems—that the truly creative poetic period ended when Clough completed **Dipsychus.** Recent critical silence suggests acceptance of the proposition that the **Mari Magno,** given its conventional moralizing and apparent inferiority to the earlier work, deserves little attention. This essay will demonstrate, however, that because it contains perhaps the maturest and most subjective presentation of the conflict between idealism and "positive naturalism," the poem requires reappraisal.

The key to Clough's accomplishment lies in his adaptation of a Chaucerian framework. Notwithstanding the well-documented influence of Crabbe and Patmore on the style and content of the **Mari Magno,** it is Clough's choice and, more importantly, his modification of Chaucer which result in an unique form of narrative tension, one enabling Clough to deal in a new way with a conflict familiar not only to his earlier works, but to the *Canterbury Tales* as well. Chaucer, of course, uses a panorama of characters having widely different attitudes toward reality to show the fundamental conflict of the late fourteenth century, a period when the dominance of Christian Platonism was challenged by a form of "this-worldliness" championed by the rising bourgeois classes, who were oriented to the immediacy of the material world. Thus the Knight's Tale is followed by the Miller's Tale, idealism by naturalism; the tales, reflecting the assumptions of their tellers, clash, as do the characters themselves in the links between tales.

Clough achieves a related effect, juxtaposing the same philosophical positions in a hierarchy of characters: as in the earlier long poems, the essential theme of the **Mari Magno** involves the discord between two sets of values, the one Platonic, requiring detachment in a search for transcendent order, the other Aristotelian, requiring participation and posing a this-worldly rather than otherworldly ethic. For Clough, however, the problem is individual rather than societal; there is, then, a major difference in the hierarchic structure. Because he is illustrating *inner* conflict, Clough does not base tension primarily in the external juxtaposition of characters—hence the weak links among them. Instead, conflict inheres in the relationship *between teller and his tale.* The stories embody philosophical values which are the opposite of those the respective narrators profess. Clough employs form to create a surface which indeed suggests the "absence of tension" and "balanced and reposeful mental state" critics have traditionally found in the poem. But the surface belies the intense divisions in his characters' psychology, the presentation of which is remarkably modern.

Clough's gallery contains only five storytellers: the lawyer, clergyman, American, ship's mate, and narrator. Nevertheless, the small size of this "mixed multitude" sufficiently defines the central philosophical conflict, with each member representing a position in the Platonic / Aristotelian spectrum. Their plan is for each to tell two tales. In fact, the lawyer and clergyman tell two, and the other three characters one apiece. But although the plan is in apparent disarray, Clough's arrangement of the tales is not. The seven tales form two triads, separated by the central **"My Tale."** The two groups proceed in opposite order. The first tale of the first triad is told by the lawyer, the most Platonic of the group. Balancing him on the other end of the philosophical spectrum—and triad—is the American, advertised as having "racy tales of Yankee-land"—i.e., a teller of naturalistic tales. Separating these two is the English clergyman, "in black and white," who "miscellaneous large experience had / Of human acts, good, half and half, and bad." The second triad begins with the ship's mate, a surrogate for the American. A second tale by the clergyman follows, and finally, the lawyer's second. In philosophical terms, there is a movement throughout the triads beginning with the ostensibly Platonic lawyer, through an apparent representative of synthesis, to an Aristotelian; then, in the second triad, a return through these two latter positions to the Platonist.

The tales themselves can also be arranged in a philosophical hierarchy. But this hierarchy is in an inverse relationship to the one already established. That is, the lawyer, portrayed as the most dedicated to Platonic idealism, tells a realistic tale redolent with Aristotelian values and world view. And on the other hand, the storytellers most nominally Aristotelian—the American and the mate—tell tales whose high level of abstraction and sparse detail argue a Platonic interpretation of reality. Only the clergyman's tales accurately reflect their teller, and here, verisimilitude is rooted in the same Platonic/Aristotelian conflict. Given the outright juxtaposition of philosophical tendencies, one recalls *Dipsychus,* but in the *Mari Magno,* the dramatic situation is more subjective, with conventional tales freighting repressed desires. [The critic adds in a footnote: In *Dipsychus,* the tension is represented in the dialogue between Dipsychus and the Spirit, the latter linked in the Epilogue with "subjective imagination."] And here, Clough does not resolve the conflict of the two eternally warring tendencies. His form holds them in balance. If one looks to the organizational pattern, the circular movement and teller/tale conflict prevent absolute judgment. If one examines the central **"My Tale,"** one encounters enigma. Beneath the unfinished domestic tales of the *Mari Magno* Clough plots for the last time the irreconcilable philosophical coordinates of his art's core.

The lawyer is a fitting emblem of the abstract idealism often characterized as Clough's bête noire. His commitment to absolutes presupposes a Platonic interpretation of reality. He is an embodiment of standards, "always there to guide" and, appropriately, is the narrator's "guardian friend." The role is, of course, questionable; there is something insidious in this man's commitment, a product of highmindedness and detachment akin to those of Dipsychus, who dies a "lawyer acute." Despite being to "gentlest thoughts" inclined, "To the severe [he] had disciplined his mind" (ll. 58-59). Because of this seeming violation of nature, he is wracked by the same tension plaguing Dipsychus and Claude, here expressed in psychosomatic symptoms: "he suffered from some pain / Of mind, that on the body worked again" (ll. 71-72). Despite his rising success, the lawyer, at thirty-three, is ripe for crucifixion, for "The world with him her lesson failed to teach / To take things easily and let them go" (ll. 75-76).

Were the *Mari Magno* superficial in conception, the stuff of the lawyer's tales would be consistent with his professed values; as the man "forced you to your best" in company, the stories, position papers in a friendly shipboard debate concerning the nature of marriage, would didactically espouse Platonic idealism. But both tales indict the abstractedness which the lawyer himself represents. The protagonists of both, college students, fail to materialize desired love relationships, presented as positive goods, because of over-

intellectuality. The first tale quickly introduces the fundamental opposition between transcendent and naturalistic values. The protagonist, a student whose anonymity symbolizes his loss of identity in books, finds a truly Edenic situation in a visit to his third cousins at a vicarage which, adjacent to a luxuriant garden, teems with life. The vicar himself, "every inch a man," is virtually planted in the earth, as are his "blooming" daughters, who surround him "As vines around an ancient stem" (III. 17).

The protagonist falls in love with Emily, who epitomizes connectedness and manifests a wisdom derived not from books, but from experience. She is a "queen" moving serenely "Amid the living, heaving throng . . . divining by a glance, / And reading every countenance" (II. 75ff.). Brimming with potentiality, invested with a "scarce-exerted power," Emily, with her life values, is clearly superior to the student. Ruefully, he observes that

> For all I read and thought I knew,
> She simply looked me through and through.
> Where had she been, and what had done,
> I asked, such victory to have won?
> She had not studied, had not read,
> Seemed to have little in her head,
> Yet of herself the right and true,
> As of her own experience, knew.
>
> (II. 42-49)

Despite recognizing Emily's superiority, however, the protagonist will not compromise, as the lawyer probably would not, and thus repeats Claude's refusal in the *Amours* to "enfasten the roots of my floating existence / In the rich earth." Instead, the protagonist rigidly adheres to his own abstract ideas. During his annual visits he becomes introspective, taking greater pleasure in gazing into a lake than upon any female face; or he acts the intellectual prig, talking in superior tone "of much I thought I knew" while lacking "any teaching of the heart" (III. 27, 35). Occasionally, he shows signs of relenting, but always too late, as when pleasant memories of a preceding evening's dance finally spur an impulse to participate—"when the opportunity was past." Finally, he makes himself positively unwelcome, by exercising "The busy argufying brain / Of the prize schoolboy" (III. 37-38).

Two years later, post-degree travel brings the protagonist to Switzerland, and here occurs the final indictment of the abstractedness which the lawyer-narrator represents. While staying in the mountains, meditating upon a lake and fleeing into the woods whenever the tourist-laden steamer arrives, the protagonist unexpectedly encounters Emily. Revealing the depths of his feeling, he addresses her, "Emilia, whom I love," only to be interrupted by her introduction of her husband. Checked, he announces a plan to stay at the university. Emily forcefully demurs. College is only "play," she insists, where "Fellows grow indolent, and then / They may not do as other men" (V. 25-26). To counteract this sterility, Emily admonishes him to leave school and his detachment, to marry. She insists that her instinctive wisdom, approved throughout the tale, is correct here:

> [I] . . . certainly am slow.
> And yet some things I seem to know;
> I know it will be just a crime
> If you should waste your powers and time.
>
> (V. 54ff.)

She urges him to *do,* to participate in life. His commitment to the "argufying brain," the lawyer's chief tool, stirs Emily's declaration, "You're twenty-three, I'm twenty-five, / And I am so much more alive" (V. 70-71). They part. But Emily's advice becomes "cogent on [his] will." Retrospectively, he observes that "As she had counselled, I had done, / And a new effort was begun" (V. 109-110). The tale finished, the lawyer apologizes for having opened a "youthful, ancient, sentimental vein," and applies to the clergyman, who "knows for what we live," for "correction." Obviously, he has committed a gaffe, telling a tale which indicts his conscious motivations.

The lawyer's second story, "A tale of human suffering and tears," has much in common with the first. The protagonist is another college student whose over-commitment to mind prevents a love relationship. Again, a surrogate lawyer fails at life by refusing to exchange Platonic idealism for a healthier Aristotelian participation, and again looks silly juxtaposed with a superior female. The heroine of the tale, Christian, resembles Emily. A combination of Chaucer's Constance and Griselda, being made to suffer yet enduring all, Christian is unschooled, yet naturally wise; Philip finds her "so charming in the ore." Fecund, bearing seven children by the conclusion of the story, she exerts a magnetic power over Philip, who discovers her in a search for solitude in the Highland hills.

Philip destroys the relationship, however. His meddling brain appears in "experiments" designed to take "The measure of her intellect," leading to denigrating comparisons of her actual person with his idealized image of it. Sure of her when together, he is crippled by reasonings when apart, and these become determinative. Hesitant to declare openly his desire to marry, Philip returns temporarily to the university to perform his bursar's office. There, he learns that Christian's aunt intends taking her to Australia. Instead of returning to Glasgow immediately, he sends a note whose message, "In no case . . . let Christian go" (l. 235), is belied by the ten pounds accompanying it. When he does return she is gone, and, reminiscent of Claude, he curses his guilty tardiness, acknowledging that "He should have owned her when he left her first" (l. 256). Despite a personal search in Australia, he does not see her again until years later, when, as in the first tale, he finds her lost to him—married to another man and a mother. He himself has married, for the "right" reasons, a wealthy noblewoman. But the marriage is barren. Only the discovery of the son Christian had borne him en route to Australia, a child who is the product of a fleeting act of participation, modifies his grief.

Before the end of the story, the clergyman interrupts, declaring it to be "mere pain," and ruefully asserts that "if the women don't sustain / The moral standard, all we do is vain" (ll. 243-244). And, upon continuing, the lawyer himself suggests a moral interpretation of the story, based upon the illicit sexuality between Philip and Christian; he proposes, for example, that because of "lawless loving," Christian "did not dare to think how dear she was" (l. 254), and hence went to Australia. Even a perfunctory reading reveals, however, that little in the tale supports such an interpretation—which, of course, is the interpretation we should expect the always-didactic lawyer consciously to stress. The protagonist's choice is not between conventional morality and immorality. Rather, it is between the barren intellectual life the lawyer himself has chosen and a life of actualizing those emotions and qualities which the story demonstrates to be most salutary: Christian's unselfishness, for example. Philip can either remain aloof, or "find his joy in children and in wife" (l. 197);

the tragedy of the tale lies in his choosing, as the lawyer would likely have advised, the first avenue. The tale amply displays the mistake of that decision. Christian's long letter at the end of the story, one of Clough's most poignant passages, is a paean to the opportunities blighted by Philip, who now finds limited joy in the fact that through the child "Father and Mother are as one."

The lawyer's tales are balanced in the two triads by the tales of the American and the mate, respectively, both of which, highly moral in tone, reveal the philosophical assumptions one would expect of the lawyer but not of these narrators. Once again there is direct opposition between teller and tale. The American, for example, appears to be analogous to the Wife of Bath or the tellers of Chaucer's fabliaux. Returning to New England, he is "unspoilt" by either Europe or his own accomplishments in letters; the **Mari Magno** narrator alludes to stories suggestive of Boccaccio, stories of rustics and clergy which the narrator himself cannot tell. In fact, it is the American who proposes the story rounds: apparently he has become bored with the intellectualized discourse of the others. Thus, if the lawyer nominally represents Platonic idealism, the American seems Aristotelian, given his New World preferences for ideas imbedded in matter and for the multiplicity of creation rather than the supposed unity transcending it.

And yet the American's tale is the shortest of all, its 35 lines scarcely complementing the 740 of the lawyer's first tale. The content is similarly surprising. There is a superficial resemblance to Chaucer's Reeve's tale, with a girl mistakenly entering the bed of a stranger. But she hurriedly leaves upon discovering her error and, soon thereafter, marries the virtuous bed-partner when he returns a watch she had abandoned in her flight. Hardly one of the "racy tales of Yankeeland" we had been led to expect, the story is actually a moral exemplum, a demonstration of a strictly Platonic concept of Providence:

> Love begins not when lovers meet and kiss,
> They were intended for each other's bliss
> When souls began: what do we know of this?
> Something there is, to which a statesman grave
> Vague title of *Superior Order* gave:
> Something subsists behind each petty deed,
> Each casual-seeming chance, which is indeed
> The fact from whence our showy facts proceed.
>
> (ll. 48-55)

In fact, the tale is the most abstract in the group, its view of Providence linking the American with the lawyer-like Claude, the "cold intellectual being" who declares that "What is ordained is right, and all that happens is ordered."

The same inversion of form and content occurs in the second triad, where the 73-line mate's story, with its theme of rigidly controlled providence, is juxtaposed with the 511-line lawyer's second tale, surprisingly a hymn to opportunities missed through the misuse of the protagonist's free will. The mate is undescribed, but his profession suggests the naturalistic, Aristotelian mode; nevertheless, like the American, he presents an epigrammatic, highly moral tale, whose scarcity of concrete detail belies a hearty love for the natural realm. In the story a servant girl, en route to her French home, misses a monthly steamer and faces possible mischief in a bad town. Happily, though, a kindly sea captain interposes himself and offers to marry her, saving her reputation and demonstrating the active intervention of Providence. Once again, we have a tale one would expect the lawyer to tell but which actually occurs at the other pole of the triad.

The character who seems to blend the two philosophical extremes is the clergyman, whose central tales balance each triad, as shown in their median size (282 and 261 lines). He himself is described, in the prologue, as dual. Though he looks the dignitary, he is a virile figure—"Manly his voice and manly . . . his air" (l. 41)—and the narrator points out that he "Had not known / The things pertaining to his cloth alone" (ll. 42-43). Given the clergyman's rank in the hierarchy of characters, his tales should mesh abstraction and concreteness, and they do. Both tales offer a Platonically inclined protagonist who, in the conflict between idealism and life, finally makes decisions validating the principle of connectedness represented by marriage. The first tale begins, for example, much like the lawyer's first, with a "serious boy" having a familiar frailty: "a touch / Of something introspective overmuch" (ll. 39-40).

His spontaneity braked by a "self-correcting bent," Edmund cannot fully assent to and materialize his feelings for Emma, who has appealed to his "soft eye" and stirred his blood. He flees the "obvious good," fearing that his love is "not a joy where soul and soul unite" but a "wondrous animal delight" (ll. 115-116); he will not commit himself to a bliss that does not transcend the spring songs and blossoms which are its natural analogues. He seeks some superadded spiritual component in order for love to be "all in all." Responding with instinctive wisdom, Emma, much like Emily in the lawyer's first tale, dismisses the protagonist's confused intellectualizing, and in particular his false idealization of her, demanding that he seek her as she is if at all. It is not her arguments that conciliate, however, nor his perceiving the "weight of intellect" in her brow when the two meet after five years. Rather, "Morn's early odorous breath perchance in sooth, / Awoke the old natural feeling of their youth" (ll. 259-260). Years of wandering have weakened Edmund's resistance to natural feeling, and to the "mystic virtue" which had underlain their original meetings. After a few "sweet" weeks, they marry, and Edmund ostensibly relaxes into life, validating the proposition of the story that a love, in expressing Aristotelian connectedness, can indeed satisfy other than merely the "nought else seeking soul."

To the end of this very satisfactory tale, however, the clergyman tacks an absurd bit of instruction, repeating it three times for emphasis: "love is fellow-service, I believe." Essentially, he re-roots love in abstraction, and hence instead of fully synthesizing idealism and natural life, he preserves the source of conflict. The same tension recurs in his second tale, which begins with an already-existing happy marriage, and analyzes its near destruction through the application of abstract principles. Here, the husband, Edward, is seduced while convalescing at a health resort and condemns himself to a life of ascetic atonement, repudiating his wife and children. The clergyman highly approves this course of action; noting that there are others who "lightly treat / Such slips," he observes, "God be thanked, this was not one of those" (l. 160).

As a result of his self-inflicted penance, Edward, living in a garret and working in his old office, though now the "worst companion in the place," becomes "So cold a husband, cold a father," that only news of his daughter's serious illness sparks a reunion. Despite the clergyman's endorsement of his protagonist's behavior, the wife's lengthy speech on the occasion of Edward's homecoming provides a damning commentary on her husband's moral otherworldliness. Another example of an Aristotelian heroine, Jane demonstrates that he has left his family defenseless through his "unnatural plan," that his daughter probably caught her fever through want of him, and most importantly, that in neglecting his duty, "both to God and man," he is guilty of the sin often imputed to Platonic idealists, overweening pride: "after all, you know we are but dust, / What are we, in ourselves that we should trust?" (ll. 313-314). In this tale, as in the clergyman's first, the actual content contradicts its teller's interpretation and a tension emerges reflecting the same philosophical dualism dividing the other tellers (the lawyer inconsistently condemns Edward's behavior, while the American is supportive).

Mediating the symmetrical order of the triads, the narrator's central **"My Tale"** is critically important. Certainly, if there is a definitive statement on marriage, or a resolution of the philosophical dualism of the other stories, it should be here. And yet actually there is no tale at all, at least nothing resembling the others. Instead Clough presents, in seemingly disorganized fashion, juxtapositions which reinforce the conflict governing the whole *Mari Magno.* The narrator begins, as the subtitle of the tale indicates, with a "Modern Pilgrimage," describing a trip he had made in the Auvergne, in a group bearing a striking correspondence to Chaucer's band of pilgrims, complete with priest, soldier, and conductor. Unlike the shipbound passengers whose pilgrimage provides the macrocosmic structure of the *Mari Magno,* these overland travelers do not tell an organized round of tales, but they do interact in a much more Chaucerian fashion: the brief treatment focuses on a contrast of the "demure" priest with the "lusty" *conducteur.* The first relates a short "Miracle of the Virgin," in which a sick little girl is saved by prayer. Noting that love, here depicted as essentially transcendent, is the interceding Virgin's attribute, the priest demonstrates a Platonic conclusion, that we are surrounded by a "superior power." In response, the conductor does not tell a tale, but instead sings a song posing a different interpretation of love, as "gay amours." The conductor bids these goodbye because of his advancing age, and now jocularly pledges to "do my very utmost to be wise" (l. 152); obviously, though, abstract wisdom is but a second choice. His preferred mode of living is Aristotelian, fecund, non-intellective. Neither he nor the priest has the ascendancy.

The narrator's companions interrupt him—as well we might—seeking a story more appropriate to the them: "In Hamlet give us Hamlet, if you please" (l. 208). In particular, the American encourages him to tell a story about a peasant beauty he once met, and the lawyer actually begins recounting the story, which he has already heard, hoping that his young friend will continue it. But the narrator refuses to tell that story, again depriving us of a touchstone with which to evaluate the others. Instead he offers some Pyrenaean verses, which contain not a narrative but an impressionistic vision. Briefly, he describes a girl leading a donkey on a country road. She is beautiful, colorfully dressed, and frequently turns to show him her face. But then he notices a priest following, reading a book: the narrator cautions him to keep reading, lest he be beguiled by the girl. Then he notices, "succeeding in a row," a "motley train [of] Musicians," who stop to ask directions to Spain. As he converses with them, however, he observes that his "dearer friends," the dark-eyed maiden and her beast, are gone. The narrator bids them adieu, and ends his vision.

Here at the core of Clough's creative effort, in sight of "Green pastoral heights that once in lava flowed, / Of primal fire the product and abode" (II. 11-12), we encounter a paradigmatic riddle. Challenged to approach more closely his thematic meaning, the narrator has generated a vision evoking the essence of mutable life: "More evanescent than the snow / The pictures come, are seen, and go" (ll. 242-243). In the procession we find the basic foci of Clough's life and art. First there is the rustic girl, met repeatedly, representing the allure of natural life, of active participation in the multiplicity which an Aristotelian outlook defines as good. Behind her follows the priest, attentive not to the girl or the surroundings but to the abstract realm his book suggests; he is yet capable of being beguiled, like the host of Clough idealists who are compromised or "corrupted" when they take notice of natural beauty. Finally there are the musicians, representing Art, who, while offering a mode of communication with the world, distract the narrator. As a result, instead of establishing wished-for rapport with the girl, he loses her and must sublimate his desires in song.

The invocation of Art here, in conjunction with the organizational structure of the entire work, seems to suggest a preference for the Platonic, otherworldly attitude toward experience which Chaucer likewise exemplifies. Chaucer begins the *Canterbury Tales* with the chivalric Knight's Tale, ends with the pious Parson's Tale, and postscripts the entire collection with an apology for his "translacions and enditynges of worldly vanitees, the which I revoke," claiming that "Al that is writen is writen for oure doctrine." Although the sincerity of this "retraccioun" is questionable, it has been well-argued that despite Chaucer's love for the "great middle" of the *Tales,* his dominant concerns were the spiritual quest, salvation, and the final rejection of the physical world. Clough also begins and ends with tales told by a Platonic character. But a conflict exists within the lawyer which complicates our assessment of what he truly stands for. Neither the lawyer nor the others exhibit any solidity, any unambiguous position with respect to the central philosophical conflict of the work. In this last work, Clough hardly gives grounds for the conclusion that marriage and stability had subdued his spirit, turning him away from the inner life and the exploration of his earlier works. As has been said of *Dipsychus,* the **Mari Magno** is "in the fullest sense investigative." [*Arthur Hugh Clough—Towards a Reconsideration* by Robindra Kumar Biswas. For an extract from this work, see excerpt dated 1972.] Like the lyrics, the **Mari Magno** details the universality of the inner conflicts of human beings, cast here and in the other long poems as the conflict between idealism and naturalism. But unlike the other works, the **Mari Magno** offers not even partial resolution. Clough's final and most subjective statement of the problem occupying his entire creative life presents an unbearable, because unsolvable, tension. Perhaps this is why, when shortly before death he read the work to Tennyson, Clough wept like a child over it. (pp. 21-32)

Jeffrey M. Jeske, "Clough's 'Mari Magno'; A Reassessment," in Victorian Poetry, *Vol. 20, No. 1, Spring, 1982, pp. 21-32.*

FURTHER READING

Armstrong, Isobel. *Arthur Hugh Clough.* Bibliographical Series of Supplements to *British Book News* on Writers and Their Work, edited by Bonamy Dobrée, no. 148. London: Longmans, Green, and Co., 1962, 48 p.
    Pamphlet providing a general introduction to the study of Clough.

Arnold, Matthew. *On Translating Homer.* London: Smith, Elder, and Co., 1896, 178 p.
    Includes both *On Translating Homer* (1862) and *On Translating Homer: Last Words* (1862), essays that include discussion of Clough's use of hexameter.

————. *The Letters of Matthew Arnold to Arthur Hugh Clough.* Edited by Howard Foster Lowry. London: Oxford University Press, 1932, 192 p.
    Arnold's letters to Clough, useful for Arnold's views on Clough's poetry and insight into their relationship. Lowry's introduction is also a valued contribution to Clough and Arnold studies.

Arnold, Thomas. "Arthur Hugh Clough: A Sketch." *Nineteenth Century* XLIII, No. CCLI (January 1898): 105-16.
    Reminiscences by Clough's friend and Matthew Arnold's brother.

Beatty, J. M., Jr. "Arthur Hugh Clough As Revealed in His Prose." *The South Atlantic Quarterly* XXV, No. 2 (April 1926): 168-80.
    Concludes from a reading of Clough's prose that, although he held liberal beliefs, "tradition and reason" prevented him from acting on them.

Bowers, Frederick. "Arthur Hugh Clough: Recent Revaluations." *The Humanities Association Bulletin* XVI, No. 2 (Fall 1965): 17-26.
    Examines Clough's critical reputation.

Chew, Shirley. Introduction to *Selected Poems,* by Arthur Hugh Clough, edited by Shirley Chew, pp. 9-35. Manchester: Fyfield Books, 1987.
    Discusses Clough's personality, opinions, and poetry.

Chorley, Katharine. *Arthur Hugh Clough, the Uncommitted Mind: A Study of His Life and Poetry.* Oxford: Clarendon Press, 1962, 372 p.
    A psychobiographical exploration of Clough as a failure, both as a poet and as a person.

Clough, Blanche Smith. "Memoir of Arthur Hugh Clough." In *The Poems and Prose Remains of Arthur Hugh Clough,* Vol. I, by Arthur Hugh Clough, edited by Blanche Smith Clough, pp. 1-54. London: Macmillan and Co., 1869.
    Biographical account by Clough's wife.

Cockshut, A. O. J. "Clough: The Real Doubter." In his *The Unbelievers: English Agnostic Thought, 1840-1890,* pp. 31-43. London: Collins, 1964.
    Maintains that Clough "never developed any coherent attitude to religion, to marriage, to work, or to life itself."

Dean, Paul, and Moore, Jacqueline. " 'To Own the Positive and Present': Clough's Historical Dilemma." *The Durham University Journal* LXXVI, No. 1 (December 1983): 59-62.
    Extends and modifies an earlier discussion by Dean and Jacqueline Johnson (see entry below) to include commentary on *Amours de Voyage* and *Dipsychus.*

Delaura, David J. "Arnold, Clough, Dr. Arnold, and 'Thyrsis'." *Victorian Poetry* VII, No. 3 (Autumn 1969): 191-202.
    Suggests that a reading of Clough's *Letters and Remains* in December 1865 while in the midst of writing "Thyrsis" (see poem dated 1866) prompted Arnold to soften the poem's satire of Clough in the concluding stanzas.

Enright, D. J. *"A Kidnapped Child of Heaven": The Poetry of Arthur Hugh Clough.* Nottingham Byron Lecture. Nottingham: University of Nottingham, 1972, 23 p.

General appreciation of Clough's verse.

Fairchild, Hoxie Neale. "Clough." In his *Religious Trends in English Poetry.* Vol. IV: *1830-1880, Christianity and Romanticism in the Victorian Era,* pp. 505-27. New York: Columbia University Press, 1962.

Examines Clough's spiritual questioning.

Garrod, H. W. "Clough." In his *Poetry and the Criticism of Life: The Charles Eliot Norton Lectures for 1929-1930,* pp. 109-27. Cambridge: Harvard University Press, 1931.

Cursory discussion of Clough's work praising his gifts for story-telling and satire but condemning his religious poetry.

Gollin, Richard M. "The 1951 Edition of Clough's *Poems:* A Critical Reexamination." *Modern Philology* LX, No. 2 (November 1962): 120-27.

Questions the completeness and reliability of the 1951 edition of Clough's poems.

———; Houghton, Walter E.; and Timko, Michael. *Arthur Hugh Clough, A Descriptive Catalogue: Poetry, Prose, Biography, and Criticism.* New York: New York Public Library, 1967, 117 p.

Extensive bibliography of primary and secondary sources.

Goode, John. "*Amours de Voyage:* The Aqueous Poem." In *The Major Victorian Poets: Reconsiderations,* edited by Isobel Armstrong, pp. 275-97. Lincoln: University of Nebraska Press, 1969.

Contends that *Amours de Voyage* should not be regarded as a minor classic but rather as a "major masterpiece."

Greenberger, Evelyn Barish. *Arthur Hugh Clough: The Growth of a Poet's Mind.* Cambridge: Harvard University Press, 1970, 270 p.

Focuses on Clough's prose to trace the development of his thought. Greenberger appends several previously unpublished poems and a list of Clough's undergraduate essays with dates and comments by his professors.

Hardy, Barbara. "Clough's Self-consciousness." In *The Major Victorian Poets: Reconsiderations,* edited by Isobel Armstrong, pp. 253-74. Lincoln: University of Nebraska Press, 1969.

Examines how Clough's personal dilemmas and intellectual detachment are expressed in his poems.

Hewlett, Maurice. "Teufelsdröckh in Hexameters." *Nineteenth Century and After* XCI, No. DXXXIX (January 1922): 68-75.

Responds to Edmund Gosse's attack on Clough (see excerpt dated 1921), defending *The Bothie of Tober-na-Vuolich* and discussing the influence of Thomas Carlyle's philosophy on Clough.

Hudson, William Henry. "Arthur Hugh Clough." In his *Studies in Interpretation: Keats, Clough, Matthew Arnold,* pp. 75-149. 1896. Reprint. Folcroft, Pa.: Folcroft Press, 1969.

Culls Clough's philosophy of life from his writings.

Johnson, Jacqueline, and Dean, Paul. " 'Paradise Come Back': Clough in Search of Eden." *Durham University Journal* LXIX, No. 2 (June 1977): 249-53.

Discusses Clough's "repeated use of the Eden-myth and the related story of Jacob, Rachel and Leah, as mediators for his statements about the human condition," focusing on *Adam and Eve* and *The Bothie of Tober-na-Vuolich.* This work is a companion piece to the study cited above by Dean and Moore.

Johnson, Robert. "Modern Mr. Clough." *The Arnoldian* 13, No. 1 (Winter 1985/86): 1-9.

Argues that in *Dipsychus* Clough anticipates modern writers by asserting that "human endeavor necessarily must be rooted in the physical world and not in the shadowy realm of ideals."

Johnson, W. Stacy. "Parallel Imagery in Arnold and Clough." *English Studies* XXXVII (February 1956): 1-11.

Explores the repeated images of seas, ships, and rivers in Arnold's and Clough's poetry.

Locke, James R. "Clough's *Amours de Voyage:* A Possible Source for 'The Love Song of J. Alfred Prufrock.'" *Western Humanities Review* XXIX, No. 1 (Winter 1975): 55-66.

Presents textual evidence to show that T. S. Eliot was influenced by Clough's poem.

MacCarthy, Desmond. "Clough." In his *Portraits,* pp. 63-7. New York: Oxford University Press, 1954.

Attempts to correct the misconception that Clough was a weak-willed, irresolute doubter, particularly countering Lytton Strachey's negative assessment of the poet (cited below).

Machann, Clinton. " 'The Centre Is No Centre': Astronomical Imagery in Clough's Prose." *The Arnoldian* 12, No. 1 (Fall 1984): 22-31.

Purports that "Clough's use of astronomical imagery and the epistemological assumptions associated with it helps the reader, not to re-evaluate what has been called his unique position among Victorian agnostics, but to better understand the underpinnings of that position."

McGhee, Richard D. " ' "Blank Misgivings" ': Arthur Hugh Clough's Search for Poetic Form." *Victorian Poetry* VII, No. 2 (Summer 1969): 105-15.

Argues that Clough's " 'Blank Misgivings' " reflects how the poet reconciled the conflict between his Wordsworthian aesthetic principle of spontaneity with his concern for classical poetic form.

McGrail, John P. "Three Image Motifs in Arthur Hugh Clough's *The Bothie of Tober-na-Vuolich.*" *Victorian Poetry* 13, No. 1 (Spring 1975): 75-8.

Discusses the function that the image motifs of water, trees, and a keystone perform in *The Bothie.*

Micklus, Robert. "A Voyage of Juxtapositions: The Dynamic World of *Amours de Voyage.*" *Victorian Poetry* 18, No. 4 (Winter 1980): 407-14.

Explores how "juxtaposition," here defined as "a dynamic vision of life . . . of contrasting opposites in continual flux," is important to the meaning, imagery, theme, structure, and characterization of the poem.

Miyoshi, Masao. "Clough's Poems of Self-Irony." *Studies in English Literature, 1500-1900* V, No. 4 (Autumn 1965): 691-704.

Shows that Clough often portrayed his intellectual and spiritual dilemmas in his poetry with playful irony.

Osborne, James Insley. *Arthur Hugh Clough.* Boston: Houghton Mifflin Co., 1920, 195 p.

Study of Clough's life and works. Osborne accepts the interpretation of Clough as a person whose self-questioning led to artistic and personal failure.

Palgrave, F. T. "Memoir." In *Poems,* by Arthur Hugh Clough, pp. v-xxiv. Cambridge, England: Macmillan and Co., 1862.

Sensitive biographical account by a friend of Clough that has been blamed for initiating the trend in Clough criticism of esteeming his life above his writings.

Rossetti, William Michael. Review of *The Bothie of Toper-na-Fuosich: A Long Vacation Pastoral. The Germ,* No. 1 (January 1850): 34-46.

Laudatory contemporary review of *The Bothie,* concluding with a few favorable comments on *Ambarvalia.*

Ryals, Clyde de L. "An Interpretation of Clough's *Dipsychus.*" *Victorian Poetry* 1 (November 1963): 182-88.

Regards *Dipsychus* as a humorous satire "on the author himself, on the anguish which he suffered during the process of growing up, and on Romantic metaphysics.''

Scudder, Townsend. "Incredible Recoil." In his *The Lonely Wayfaring Man: Emerson and Some Englishmen,* pp. 154-67. London: Oxford University Press, 1936.

Delves into the relationship between Ralph Waldo Emerson and Clough, providing insights into Emerson's views on his friend's poetry.

Sharp, Amy. "Arthur Hugh Clough and Matthew Arnold." In her *Victorian Poets,* pp. 121-56. 1891. Reprint. Port Washington, N.Y.: Kennikat Press, 1970.

Discusses the life and works of these two poets.

Strachey, Lytton. "Florence Nightingale" and "Dr. Arnold." In his *Eminent Victorians,* pp. 133-204, 205-42. 1918. Reprint. Garden City, N.Y.: Garden City Publishing Co., n.d.

Contains only brief, disparaging mention of Clough in relation to Nightingale and Dr. Arnold, but Strachey's commentary has inspired much critical controversy.

Symonds, John Addington. "Arthur Hugh Clough." *Fortnightly Review* n.s. IV, No. XXIV (1 December 1868): 589-617.

Insightful examination of Clough's thought and poetry.

Thorpe, Michael, ed. *Clough: The Critical Heritage.* The Critical Heritage Series, edited by B. C. Southam. London: Routledge and Kegan Paul, 1972, 411 p.

Excerpts from early reviews, letters, and essays about Clough from 1847 to 1920.

Timko, Michael. "Arthur Hugh Clough: Palpable Things and Celestial Fact." In *The Victorian Experience: The Poets,* edited by Richard A. Levine, pp. 47-66. Athens: Ohio University Press, 1982.

Attempts to account for the large amount of critical attention that has been devoted to Clough by analyzing Clough's views on the purpose of poetry and showing how he applied them in *Amours de Voyage.*

Trilling, Lionel. *Matthew Arnold.* New York: Columbia University Press, 1949, pp. 19ff.

Critical biography of Arnold that provides insights into his relationship with Clough.

Waddington, Samuel. *Arthur Hugh Clough: A Monograph.* London: George Bell and Sons, 1883, 333 p.

The first book-length biography of Clough. Waddington based most of this work on and quotes extensively from letters, reviews, and notices by people acquainted with the poet.

Weinstock, Donald J. " 'Say Not We Are on a Darkling Plain': Clough's Rejoinder to 'Dover Beach'." *Victorian Poetry* 19, No. 1 (Spring 1981): 73-80.

Contends that "Say Not the Struggle Naught Availeth" was written in direct response to Arnold's "Dover Beach."

Williams, David. *Too Quick Despairer: A Life of Arthur Hugh Clough.* London: Rupert Hart-Davis, 1969, 166 p.

Biographical study arguing that Clough had purposefulness, strength of mind, and integrity and that the "outward appearance of a sickly self-questioner being pushed around is deceptive."

Williams, Stanley T. "Clough's Prose." In his *Studies in Victorian Literature,* pp. 235-52. 1923. Reprint. Port Washington, N.Y.: Kennikat Press, 1967.

Traces the development of Clough's beliefs through his prose writings, arguing that they supplement the incomplete record left by his poetry.

Wolfe, Humbert. "Arthur Hugh Clough." In *The Eighteen-Sixties: Essays by Fellows of the Royal Society of Literature,* edited by John Drinkwater, pp. 20-50. Cambridge: Cambridge University Press, 1932.

Sympathetic study asserting that "in Clough a great natural satirist and story-teller was smothered not by his own doubts but by the doubts thrust upon him by his friends."

James Fenimore Cooper

1789-1851

American novelist, essayist, historian, travel writer, and satirist.

The following entry presents criticism of Cooper's Leatherstocking novels: *The Pioneers; or, The Sources of the Susquehanna: A Descriptive Tale* (1823), *The Last of the Mohicans: A Narrative of 1757* (1826), *The Prairie* (1827), *The Pathfinder; or, The Inland Sea* (1840), and *The Deerslayer; or, The First War-Path* (1841). For discussion of Cooper's complete career, including criticism of the Leatherstocking novels, see *NCLC,* Volume 1.

Cooper was one of the first American novelists to undertake the creation of a distinct national literature, appropriating his country's history as the central theme of his work. In his most enduring achievement, the five novels of the Leatherstocking series, Cooper presented a fictional rendering of United States history that has become fused with historical record as part of the national consciousness. These novels established a number of cultural archetypes, including that of the noble native American, as well as the savage and treacherous counterpart of this figure, and, in Nathaniel "Natty" Bumppo—frontiersman, hunter, tracker, and scout—created a fictional paradigm of the American character.

Cooper was born in Burlington, New Jersey, and raised in Cooperstown, an upstate New York village founded and governed by his father that served as a model for the frontier communities of Cooper's fiction. His undistinguished academic career ended with expulsion from Yale in 1805 for engaging in pranks. He subsequently served on a merchant vessel and then in the United States Navy. An inheritance from his father enabled Cooper to leave the Navy in 1811, marry, and lead a leisured existence for about a decade, during which time he fell deeply in debt. Popular legend holds that Cooper wrote his first novel, *Precaution* (1820), in response to a challenge by his wife to write a better novel than one they had been reading; biographers theorize that he hoped the venture would be financially successful. *Precaution,* modeled on the English novel of manners, was not remunerative. Cooper quickly began work on a second novel, *The Spy* (1821), featuring American characters and situations, which he hoped would prove more successful. With his third novel, *The Pioneers,* Cooper took as his model the historical romance made popular by Sir Walter Scott, telling a story of the American frontier in a form that had traditionally depended on the cultural background of European history. The uniquely American characters, settings, and themes of *The Pioneers* engaged the nation's nostalgia for an appealing and historically rich period of the recent past, and Cooper developed the frontier romance and the central character of Leatherstocking further in *The Last of the Mohicans* and *The Prairie.* There are indications that he intended to conclude the series with *The Prairie,* which depicts Leatherstocking's death and the retreat of the westward vanguard of settlers. For more than a decade thereafter, Cooper espoused republican social and political convictions in fiction and nonfiction which criticized European forms of government and condemned American reliance on foreign culture. These works were not well received: the

readers and critics who extolled Cooper as America's first historical romancer did not accept him in the role of social and political critic. Some commentators suggest that he returned to the Leatherstocking saga with *The Pathfinder* and *The Deerslayer* primarily to recoup the critical and popular regard that had attended the earlier novels in the series.

The first three Leatherstocking novels are often regarded as a trilogy in which Cooper established the conventions of the frontier romance and began codifying the American historical experience. *The Pioneers, The Last of the Mohicans,* and *The Prairie* share vividly described wilderness settings; suspenseful plots involving kidnap, pursuit, and rescue; and striking characterizations that derived from such mythical-historical accounts as John Filson's biography of Daniel Boone. The novels are linked thematically by Cooper's exploration of the moral implications of colonization, which are often exemplified in the clash between the dictates of personal freedom and the mandate of the community to impose restrictions on individual rights. Many critics concur with Edwin Fussell that "Cooper's power lay in his assurance that one direction was morally right and the other practically inevitable." The solitary Leatherstocking—who, according to historian Henry Nash Smith, was "conceived in terms of the antithesis between nature and civilization, between freedom and law, that has governed most American interpretations of the westward movement"—is the central moral referent of the series. Although his superior skills as a hunter and tracker enable settlers to follow him into the wilderness, his opposition to man-made institutions leads him into conflict with the authorities of the frontier communities. The encroachment of civilization is portrayed in an increasingly negative way throughout the first three novels of series. In *The Pioneers,* for example, Cooper described the depletion of game around frontier settlements, and in *The Prairie* he detailed the destruction left by a party of pioneers felling trees indiscriminately. At the close of *The Prairie,* the westward progression temporarily halts. The significance of this conclusion is widely debated: some critics consider it Cooper's rejection of the desirability of westward expansion, while others contend that it represents Cooper's exploitation of national nostalgia for the time when an American wilderness still existed and men like Leatherstocking were needed to push the frontier further. The final two Leatherstocking novels, *The Pathfinder* and *The Deerslayer,* offer an idealized account of early United States history, recounting details of Leatherstocking's past in heroic terms appropriate to a mythic figure. Some critics consider these last two Leatherstocking novels superior to the first three, contending that they contain Cooper's most effectively realized themes, settings, and characters.

Throughout the latter part of the nineteenth century and in the first part of the twentieth, the Leatherstocking novels were regarded primarily as adventure books. Literary historians generally acknowledged Cooper as a leading figure in the development of American literary nationalism, but considered his actual achievement of little importance. Beginning in the 1960s, however, Cooper's works have undergone a revaluation, focusing for the most part on the Leatherstocking novels. Individual studies have examined Cooper's use of historical sources; his treatment of women and native American characters; his facility with landscape description, an aspect of Cooper's literary art that is almost universally commended; and the explication of the hierarchy of class distinctions that is a salient feature of the series. Many commentators suggest that Cooper has been undervalued, contending that as America's first popularly successful man of letters, his contribution to the literary and cultural life of his country was considerable. The principal characteristics of Cooper's prototypical American hero, Leatherstocking, recur in American popular culture in the cowboy, the Wild West lawman, and the twentieth-century private investigator. Richard Slotkin summarizes this mythic figure "as a man armed and solitary, plebeian but worthy somehow of nobility, fronting a native wilderness and seeking in action his heart's desire." The Leatherstocking novels are moreover recognized as a source of the imagery that infuses popular conceptions of early United States history, and Cooper is celebrated as the author who, in the words of Howard Mumford Jones, "fixed the image of the virgin American wilderness and of the frontiersman upon the imagination of mankind."

(See also *Dictionary of Literary Biography,* Vol. 3; *Concise Dictionary of American Literary Biography 1640-1865;* and *Something about the Author,* Vol 19.)

THE PORT FOLIO   (essay date 1823)

[*In the following excerpt from a review of* The Pioneers, *the critic commends Cooper's vivid descriptions of frontier settlement life and praises the novel's characterizations.*]

[In **The Pioneers**] the scene is laid in a frontier village, inhabited by ordinary personages, who have exchanged the abodes of civilization for a sylvan life. The reader, therefore, must not expect to be astonished by a succession of prodigious adventures, or perplexing incidents and harassing entanglements. His feelings will not be excited by any romantic trials of friendship or love. These the author has avoided, although **The Spy** contains ample evidence that he possesses the power of delineating tender scenes with great pathos and effect. We think a few pages of this description would have increased his popularity: but he seems to have turned away with a sort of churlishness, not belonging to his character, from our gratification in this respect. But let us be grateful for what we have.

The work is truly, what it professes to be, "a descriptive tale;" and it is by the laws of that species of composition that its merits are to be scanned. It might, indeed, be called historical; for the historian can scarcely find a more just and vivid delineation of the first settlements of our wilderness.

The dangers, difficulties, and pinching privations, encountered and endured, by the hardy adventurers, who first broke the silence of our interminable forests, and opened a passage for the beams of the sun to the face of the earth, which they had not visited for centuries;—the strange mixture of men of all countries, characters and occupations, who found themselves, they knew not how, assembled around the same fire, and bound together by the same fortunes;—the hardihood and perseverance with which they met and tamed the rudeness of savage nature,—and the incredible progress of their victories and improvements—these are the novel themes of **The Pioneers**—and they are described in these volumes with the knowledge of a witness and the hand of a master. In Europe the scenes of this tale may be viewed as the wild creations of fancy, and the actors as the phantoms of an ingenious imagination; but the American, who has ample evidence of their truth, will recur to them with deep interest and pride, unmingled with a tinge of incredulity. We have been on the very spot, where the author has placed his village;—we have bathed in the same water where old Mohegan paddled his light canoe—we have witnessed the wilderness in flames, and contended successfully on the lake with the pride of the forest. The removal of forests of immense magnitude; the creation of flourishing towns and cultivated fields, where but a few years before those forests stood, are events now so familiar to us, that they scarcely excite surprise. But we perceive the effects without an exact knowledge of the means by which they have been produced. **The Pioneers** affords us much of this information, imparted with a fidelity and vividness that carry the reader into the midst of the scenes, and make him acquainted with every individual who is introduced. These individuals will all be found in good keeping; not deformed by caricature nor frittered away by extravagance. Each one speaks and acts with perfect fitness and congruity, and they are, as we can testify from personal observation, the very kind of persons who may be expected to be found in such situations. (pp. 230-31)

The descriptions throughout of the appearance and scenery of the country, are highly wrought and very striking. The opening scene of the work, the shooting of the buck, the sudden appearance and appropriate deportment of Leather-stocking and the young Hunter, so admirably contrived to excite and fasten curiosity—the generous intrepidity of the latter in stopping the horses on the brink of a precipice—and the subsequent ride to Templeton, are all . . . exceedingly well done, and, in most parts, highly impressive. (p. 235)

In comparison with *The Spy*, we think it will be found that *The Pioneers* is a more finished composition and of a higher order; it may not, however, be as popular, because, as we have already remarked, the subject is less captivating, and it wants the interesting plot which enriches its predecessor. (p. 248)

A review of "The Pioneers," in The Port Folio, *Vol. 15, No. 251, March, 1823, pp. 230-48.*

JOHN MILLER   (essay date 1826)

[*In the following excerpt from a review of* The Last of the Mohicans, *Miller praises Cooper's depiction of native American life and discusses the plot and characterizations of the novel, finding the characters Uncas, Chingachgook, and Bumppo (here called Hawk-eye) to be especially well presented.*]

[In *The Last of the Mohicans* Cooper has] attempted to offer a picture of Indian character and life; and we may be justified, by a personal acquaintance with the aboriginal tribes of the North-American wilderness which falls to the lot of few Europeans, in pronouncing with confidence that it is a representation of admirable fidelity. That the author has availed himself of the narrative of John Hunter and of the notices of the missionary Heckewelder, is extremely probable; but we are convinced that the tale could never have been written, with the peculiar graphic truth which marks every page of his delineations of Indian manners, unless he had himself mingled with the red children of his country's forests. Elaborate relations of their general usages, and even imitations of their nervous and figurative language, might be copied from books: but here we have a thousand little peculiarities of habit, gesture, tone, and attitude, thrown as it were incidentally and unconsciously into the narrative, but which could not possibly have been noted except by familiar and watchful observance from the life. We are particular in remarking the easy and perpetual recurrence of these little characteristic touches, because they serve to determine the pretensions of the work to the highest praise which can be bestowed upon it. They certify that it is all that it claims to be,—an authentic exhibition of the wildest and most fearfully romantic state of society, which the world has ever known.

The structure of the tale itself is sufficiently simple, but the narrative is frequently worked up to an intensity of horror and an agony of suspense which are really much more than interesting: the anxiety of the reader becomes engrossed, and his imagination excited, in many of the situations of the story, to a degree which is absolutely painful. Indeed it is a positive fault in the romance that the personages, for whom our sympathies are keenly awakened, encounter one unrelieved and perpetual crisis of terrific danger through three whole volumes of adventure. They are never for an instant secured from the appalling contingencies of a conflict with the Indian. Throughout the entire tale, the lair and ambush are around them and the war-whoop in their ears: the death-shot from the unerring rifle is the least of their dangers; and the tomahawk, the scalping knife, and the demoniac refinements of savage torture, appear as their hourly and impending lot. The first volume is filled with the thrilling details of an encounter with the Indians, which should seem to terminate, after a quick succession of imminent perils and as many sudden escapes, in the temporary safety of the rescued victims. These adventures are conceived with vivid invention, and the circumstances are told with amazing animation and force of description. Through this first volume we are led by the author in breathless rapid interest: our attention is never off the stretch; and yet we seek no relief, until we have seen the objects of our sympathy beyond their first series of dangers. But then it is that we encounter the prominent defect of the work. The second volume resembles the first, and the third is a repetition of the second. Without respite, without variety of interest, and almost without any change of scene, machinery, or action, we are led in an uniformity of horror through two volumes more of Indian ambushes, pursuits, battles, massacres, and scalpings. (pp. 123-24)

[The characters of Chingachgook, Uncas, and the white hunter] prove conspicuous actors . . . and are, beyond all comparison, the most remarkable and best drawn characters in the book. One of them, the white hunter, who is introduced to us only by his *noms de guerre* of Hawk-eye and La Longue Carabine, is a specimen (of the better sort, indeed,) of a class of men still to be found in the American forests. His qualities are adroitly elicited by a hundred little characteristic niceties of opinion and action, which, though perhaps they might not be quite understood by our home-bred readers, are all struck off from the original with most admirable tact. In the strange mixture of the habits of civilised and Indian life, the corresponding confusion of moral opinions and principles, an enthusiastic respect for the finer qualities of the red people, coupled always with the superior pride of pure European blood, and the perpetual boast of being 'a man without a cross;' in all these points, he who is familiar with the population of the American forests will at once recognise Hawk-eye for the true exemplar of a whole class. He is the genuine representative of the white hunter, who has naturalised himself among the red people, preserving some of the lingering traits and humaner features of civilised man, but acquiring the stern insensibility to danger and suffering, the patient endurance of privation, the suppleness and activity of limb, and even in part the wonderful sagacity of the senses, by which the native warrior supports and guards his life, and tracks out his path in the darkness, and solitude, and bewildering mazes of his gigantic forests.

The two Indian companions of Hawk-eye are father and son, 'the Last of the Mohicans,' a once celebrated tribe of the Delaware nations. Mr. Cooper will not be accused, by those at least who know any thing of the Indian character, of having, with any undue and foolish partiality for the virtues of savage life, depicted it too favourably for truth. But as in Magua he has displayed all the worst and most revolting features of the Indian mind, so may his portraits of the two Mohicans, Chingachgook and Uncas, be received as accurately representing in their persons all that is dignified and estimable,—and the amount of this is far from small,—in the simple children of the lake and forest. (p. 126)

John Miller, in an originally unsigned review of "The Last of the Mohicans," in The Monthly Review, *London, Vol. II, No. VII, June, 1826, pp. 122-31.*

C. S. SEALSFIELD (essay date 1831)

[*"Charles Sealsfield" was the pseudonym of Moravian monk Karl Postl, who traveled extensively in the United States in the early nineteenth century and published two books of essays about his travels. In the following excerpt, he comments on* The Pioneers *and* The Prairie *and summarizes the defects and strengths of Cooper's fiction.*]

[*The Pioneers* is] to our taste one of the most pleasing of all the productions of our author. The subjects undertaken to be described in this work are evidently such as he had been familiar with in that period of life when the deepest impressions are received; and he has delineated them with a truth and nature seldom surpassed. The sketches of rural scenery, rural manners, and rural sports, the changes of our seasons, and every object and incident characteristic of our early settlements, are, for the most part, admirable. There is also a rich variety in this work. Natty Bumppo is an original, "not to be found in any of the books," and, with one exception, a faultless original—he talks too much and too long. The story is, however, marvellously lame; and the hero, as well as the heroine, somewhat uninteresting. There is a childish mystery in the conduct of this tale, of which the author seems to be enamoured, since he has incorporated others, if possible, still more flimsy, into his subsequent productions. Take it, however, all in all, we think it a charming performance, in spite of numerous blemishes, which would have been fatal to its reputation, had they not been redeemed by equal beauties.

The Prairie has the same faults in full, and the same beauties in a lesser degree. It is evidently written to follow up the success of *The Pioneers;* a dangerous experiment, since an author seldom if ever succeeds a second time in introducing a favourite character. The cream is generally skimmed the first time, and either the scum or sediment is served up at the second table. Our old acquaintance, Natty Bumppo, verifies this observation. He appears again in *The Prairie,* but with increased garrulity, and becomes heavy and tedious by repetition. Of this the writer seems to have been aware, for he kills him by a natural death at the conclusion of the story, apparently apprehensive that he might be tempted to murder him by inches in a future work. One of the faults of our author in fact, is a habit of copying himself, of giving his readers a second edition of the same characters. (p. 252)

In the power of delaying a catastrophe, which seems every moment inevitable, and lengthening a tale that appears obstinately determined to come to an end, he is also peculiarly distinguished. He travels with a drag-chain to his wheel; and contrives by the most studious, provoking delays, to excite a fidgety impatience to get on, which doubtless many readers mistake for an intense interest in the story. Like travellers on a deep and miry road, we are half mad to arrive at the end, not so much on account of any anticipated pleasure, as from the intolerable fatigue of the journey.

The main causes of the slow progress of the narrative, and the paucity of incidents in the story, are a love of talking, and a habit of unfeeling minuteness in his descriptions, that, if not soon corrected, will undermine and eventually destroy his popularity. Natty Bumppo, who is represented as enamoured of solitude, is incessantly making long speeches; his Indians talk like members of congress, or city aldermen at a meeting of the common council; men, women, and children, black, white, and copper-coloured, all talk, while the story either makes *lee-way,* as we sailors say, or stands stock still. This is perpetually occurring at moments when the crisis of the narration demands that it should proceed rapidly, without looking either to the right or to the left. . . .

The talent of our author for description is superior to his talent for conversation. What he has seen he describes with great truth; we almost feel inclined to say, with too much truth. Monsieur Voltaire observes, with strict justice, that "the secret of being dull, is to say all that can be said on a subject." To our taste there is too much of excessive minuteness, too much of enumeration, of uninteresting and insignificant particulars in almost all his descriptions of land, water, ships, men, women, dress, &c.; in short, of every material object. He seems to dwell on every thing that comes in his way, after the manner of people who talk for hours upon one single topic, however uninteresting, simply because they don't know what to talk about next. . . .

Our author certainly can write English, though his style wants simplicity as well as brevity. There is a mannerism about it which savours of affectation, and produces stiffness. He seldom goes directly towards his object, but *purrs* round, and round, and round, seemingly afraid he will catch it, and peradventure burn his fingers. He approaches it in circles, and is a long time getting to the centre. It is not that he stops to indulge his feelings, exercise his imagination, or give a momentary sport to his humour and vivacity. These are delightful interruptions of a story; they embellish its incidents; and we hold a man cheap who does not sometimes exhibit them in his writings. But the delays here alluded to are not of this sort; they are the embarrassments of long dialogues and minute descriptions, given in a style redundant with words, neither happily disposed nor very expressive. . . .

With the same frankness with which we have pointed out the faults of this writer, and with far more pleasure to ourselves, we will now proceed to state where, in our opinion, his chief strength lies. No one that we are acquainted with, has described the peculiar features of American character and scenery, so far as he has gone, with more truth and exactness. Within certain limits he is a man of keen discrimination, of sagacious observation. Setting aside the fault of excessive minuteness and eternal repetition, his descriptions are admirable. Deficient as he is in the conception and conduct of a story, he excels in particular scenes, where he concentrates his recollections and experience upon one single object, and one single moment. (p. 253)

In thus pointing out what we conceive to be the faults of our author, we have been influenced principally by a hope that he will condescend to mend them, as well he can, we do not doubt. He owes it to his country, of whose literary reputation abroad and at home he is one of the pillars, to do all in his power to maintain his station, and even to rise still higher. If he only give himself time, and take ordinary pains, we have no doubt but he will be able, being an excellent navigator, to *steer* clear of those really exemplary blemishes, which have made it sometimes a matter of wonder to us, that he has escaped condign punishment in the courts of criticism. The talent of describing professional scenes is certainly a very desirable one; but, though a powerful ingredient in the composition of a tale of fiction, something more than this is required to constitute a claim to stand almost at the head of the writers of his country, and close by one of the most successful authors the world ever saw—we mean Sir Walter Scott. To constitute a great writer in the walks of fiction, he must unite, with the knack of describing what he has seen, the power to invent; the faculty of judgment to arrange; and the combination of all the constituents of a consummate intellect, in bringing about, by striking and natural means, a striking yet natural catastrophe. Hitherto we think our author has been much overrated. It remains to be seen whether, by any future efforts, he will be able to make good a lasting title to the elevated rank which has been conferred upon him. (p. 254)

C. S. Sealsfield, in an originally unsigned essay titled "The Works of the Author of 'The Spy'," in New York Mirror, *February 12, 1831, pp. 252-54.*

NEW YORK MIRROR   (essay date 1841)

[*In the following review, the critic praises Cooper's achievement in completing the Leatherstocking saga with* The Deerslayer, *which is held to contain none of the flaws of the earlier Leatherstocking novels.*]

Mr. Cooper is an exception to the general rule, that an author's last works are generally inferiour to his first. [**The Deerslayer**] is certainly the best which has issued from his pen in many years. There is so much real merit in Mr. Cooper that it gives us great pleasure to praise him whenever he puts it in our power to do so, which, we regret to say, has not always been the case. He is the most original thinker of any of our American novelists; the manliest, most vigourous and independent spirit of them all, unrivalled in descriptive powers, and unapproached in the heartiness of his patriotic feelings. If, with all these eminent qualities, he has defects and weaknesses, which, with the tenacity of his character, he too pertinaciously adheres to, it is matter of regret, and for no worse feeling. In the present work, we are happy to say, none of those peculiarities are to be met with which some critics, and ourselves among the number, have found so offensive. Its principal personage, as the public are already aware, is our old friend Leatherstocking, who is drawn in the vigour of early manhood, thus completing the history of his life and death. Mr. Cooper could not have chosen a more popular hero, and he has felt that no apology was necessary for bringing so general a favourite on the stage again, though for the fifth time. The scene is laid on the borders of that beautiful lake near which the author himself resides. His descriptions of that fine sheet of water and the hills that encircle it are in his best style, that is, remarkably clear and minute, and exquisitely true to nature. We can almost fancy ourselves looking down on the unruffled surface of Otsego, and feel the night-breeze rising, damp and heavy with the odours of the forest. Mr. Cooper cannot delineate fashionable life, nor catch the tone of modern society, but here he has attempted nothing of the kind; "his foot is on his native heath," and he seems to breathe the freer for it; at least his style is certainly more easy and flowing than it was wont to be. The sketches of Indian character strike us as peculiarly masterly, and the surprises, scuffles, "skrimmages," and other incidents of border warfare, are of course capital. If there is any fault in the book, and one at least a reviewer must find, or the public will deem him unfit for his task, it is in the love of Judith for the Deerslayer, and the apparent coldness with which he repulses it. It seems too bad that so brilliant a beauty, with so many generous impulses and good qualities too to enhance her outward advantages, should throw herself at the head of a rough hunter only to be rejected; and, moreover, the Deerslayer, trained in Indian habits of observation, could hardly have remained so long ignorant of what was going on in his pretty neighbour's heart as to render so many pages of broad hints and circumlocutions necessary on her part. But, on the whole, the author is perhaps right, for a wife like Judith would have been a sad incumbrance to Natty; and, besides, her unhappy fate is such as the warmest feelings, when uncontrolled by principle, are too apt to lead to. Indeed, throughout the work there is more knowledge of human nature and more successful delineation of character than Mr. Cooper has generally had credit for. There is little of that heavy dialogue which encumbers most of his former works, and indeed every where we see signs of a better taste and kindlier feeling. We are glad to be able to say thus much of one whom we have always delighted to honour; who, whatever may be his errours of judgment, has shown a genuine American feeling which is unfortunately too seldom met with in American writers. Let him go on and write a few more such works as **The Deerslayer,** illustrating American history, scenery and manners, and identifying himself with his subject, and he cannot fail to reach a higher reputation than he has yet enjoyed. His own country will, of course, be the last to appreciate him, but, after his renown has been endorsed by England, France and Germany, it will begin to pass current here; and, it being proved already that he is a man of genius, it will go near to be thought so shortly.

A review of "The Deerslayer," in New York Mirror, *September 11, 1841 p. 295.*

V. G. BELINSKY   (essay date 1841)

[*Belinsky was the first and most influential of the Russian Civic Critics, a group of nineteenth-century cultural commentators who demanded that works of literature also advance progressive philosophical, social, and political ideals. In the following excerpt from a review of* The Pathfinder *first published in 1841, he commends Cooper's creative power in presenting uniquely American landscapes and themes. The extended analysis of the novel that Belinsky projected never appeared.*]

Since he did not begin writing novels until after Walter Scott, Cooper is regarded as Scott's imitator, or even as an outstanding novelist, albeit after Scott. But this is a gross error, the opinion of the masses, who draw their conclusions not from the heart of the matter itself, but from external circumstances; that is to say, not from *how* this or that novelist writes, but from *when* he started writing, how his novels are selling, who praises them or who inveighs against them. Cooper is not in the least inferior to Scott. Yielding to him in abundance and complexity of content, and in vividness of colour, he excels him in that intensity of feeling which powerfully grips the soul of the reader before he is aware of it. Cooper surpasses Scott in creating vast, majestic edifices seemingly out of nothing, amazing us with the apparent simplicity of materials and poverty of resources from which he creates something great and boundless. (p. 191)

Cooper's genius derives much of its originality from the fact that he is a citizen of a young state, which sprang up in a young land, quite unlike our own old world. Consequently Cooper's works bear a certain special stamp: one thinks of them and is at once transported to the virgin forests of America, to her boundless prairies, covered with grass taller than a man—prairies across which roam herds of buffalo, where the red-skinned children of the Great Spirit hide, locked in relentless conflict one with another, and with the conquering palefaces. . . . (p. 192)

Many figures have been created by the brush of the great Cooper, and limned with considerable originality and interest: the mere mention of John Paul, the Red Rover and Harvey Birch is sufficient for one to lose himself in contemplation of the infinite . . . But not a single figure of all the multitude of his marvellous creations moves the reader to such wonder and sympathy as does the colossal image of that man—so great in his natural simplicity—whom Cooper has made the hero of four of his novels: *The Last of the Mohicans, The Pathfinder, The Pioneers* and *The Prairie.* Even his creator is so taken with, so captivated by the wonderful image which has sprung from his fantasy, and loves so ardently this finest creature of his genius that, after presenting him in three novels as a character indispensable to the continuity of the action, Cooper conceived the idea of a new novel with him as hero. And from all this there emerged a wonderful tetralogy, a vast and splendid poem in four parts. Cooper spent a long time preparing himself for this novel, as for a mighty exploit; many years elapsed from the first gleam of an idea up to the moment of actually writing *The Pathfinder*—so deeply aware was Cooper of the importance of the work he had conceived. Consequently, of all famous novels one can scarcely point to a single one which is distinguished by so profound an idea, so daring a conception, such richness of life and such nature genius! Many scenes from *The Pathfinder* would enhance the beauty of any of Shakespeare's dramas. It is based on the idea of one of the greatest and most enigmatic acts of the human spirit: the act of *self-abnegation,* and in this respect the novel represents the *apotheosis of self-abnegation.* But enough of this. *The Pathfinder* is the kind of work about which one should either say everything, or say nothing at all. We look forward, in the near future, to discussing *The Pathfinder* in a separate essay. Nor, indeed, shall our words lack a subject: life and its undiscovered mysteries, which the novel invests with poetic form, will provide us with the finest of themes, and the epigraph to the novel: 'Here the heart may give a useful lesson to the head, and Learning wiser grow without his books,' will set the tone for our essay. (pp. 192-93)

> *V. G. Belinsky, in an extract translated by M. A. Nicholson from* Fenimore Cooper: The Critical Heritage, *edited by George Dekker and John P. Mc-Williams, Routledge & Kegan Paul, 1973, pp. 191-93.*

G. S. HILLIARD (essay date 1862)

[*In the following excerpt from an overview of Cooper's novels, Hilliard notes some salient aspects of Cooper's fiction, drawing examples from the Leatherstocking tales.*]

No one of our great writers is more thoroughly American than Cooper; no one has caught and reproduced more broadly and accurately the spirit of our institutions, the character of our people, and even the aspects of Nature in this our Western world. He was a patriot to the very core of his heart; he loved his country with a fervid, but not an undiscerning love: it was an intelligent, vigilant, discriminating affection that bound his heart to his native land; and thus, while no man defended his country more vigorously when it was in the right, no one reproved its faults more courageously, or gave warning and advice more unreservedly, where he felt that they were needed.

This may be one reason why Cooper has more admirers, or at least fewer disparagers, abroad than at home. On the Continent of Europe his novels are everywhere read, with an eager, unquestioning delight. His popularity is at least equal

to that of Scott; and we think a considerable amount of testimony could be collected to prove that it is even greater. But the fact we have above stated is not the only explanation of this. He was the first writer who made foreign nations acquainted with the characters and incidents of American frontier and woodland life; and his delineations of Indian manners and traits were greatly superior in freshness and power, if not in truth, to any which had preceded them. His novels opened a new and unwrought vein of interest, and were a revelation of humanity under aspects and influences hitherto unobserved by the ripe civilization of Europe. The taste which had become cloyed with endless imitations of the feudal and mediæval pictures of Scott turned with fresh delight to such original figures—so full of sylvan power and wildwood grace—as Natty Bumppo and Uncas. European readers, too, received these sketches with an unqualified, because an ignorant admiration. We, who had better knowledge, were more critical, and could see that the drawing was sometimes faulty, and the colors more brilliant than those of life. (p. 52)

In constructive skill Cooper's rank is not high; for all his novels are more or less open to the criticism that too frequent use is made in them of events very unlikely to have happened. He leads his characters into such formidable perils that the chances are a million to one against their being rescued. Such a run is made upon our credulity that the fund is soon exhausted, and the bank stops payment.

For illustration of the above strictures we will refer to a single novel, *The Last of the Mohicans,* which everybody will admit to be one of the most interesting of his works,—full of rapid movement, brilliant descriptions, hair-breadth escapes, thrilling adventures,—which young persons probably read with more rapt attention than any other of his narratives. In the opening chapter we find at Fort Edward, on the head-waters of the Hudson, the two daughters of Colonel Munro, the commander of Fort William Henry, on the shores of Lake George; though why they were at the former post, under the protection of a stranger, and not with their father, does not appear. Information is brought of the approach of Montcalm, with a hostile army of Indians and Frenchmen, from the North; and the young ladies are straightway hurried off to the more advanced, and consequently more dangerous post, when prudence and affection would have dictated just the opposite course. Nor is this all. General Webb, the commander of Fort Edward, at the urgent request of Colonel Munro, sends him a reinforcement of fifteen hundred men, who march off through the woods, by the military road, with drums beating and colors flying; and yet, strange to say, the young ladies do not accompany the troops, but set off, on the very same day, by a by-path, attended by no other escort than Major Heyward, and guided by an Indian whose fidelity is supposed to be assured by his having been flogged for drunkenness by the orders of Colonel Munro. The reason assigned for conduct so absurd that in real life it would have gone far to prove the parties having a hand in it not to be possessed of that sound and disposing mind and memory which the law requires as a condition precedent to making a will is, that hostile Indians, in search of chance scalps, would be hovering about the column of troops, and so leave the by-path unmolested. But the servants of the party follow the route of the column: a measure, we are told, dictated by the sagacity of the Indian guide, in order to diminish the marks of their trail, if, haply, the Canadian savages should be prowling about so far in advance of their army! Certainly, all the sagacity of the fort would seem to have been concentrated in the person of the Indian. How much of this improbability might have been avoided, if the action had been reversed, and the young ladies, in view of the gathering cloud of war, had been sent from the more exposed and less strongly guarded point of Fort William Henry to the safe fortress of Fort Edward! Then the smallness of the escort and the risks of the journey would have been explained and excused by the necessity of the case; and the subsequent events of the novel might have been easily accommodated to the change we have indicated. (pp. 56-7)

In the delineation of character, Cooper may claim great, but not unqualified praise. This is a vague statement; and to draw a sharper line of discrimination, we should say that he is generally successful—sometimes admirably so—in drawing personages in whom strong primitive traits have not been effaced by the attritions of artificial life, and generally unsuccessful when he deals with those in whom the original characteristics are less marked, or who have been smoothed by education and polished by society. It is but putting this criticism in another form to say that his best characters are persons of humble social position. He wields his brush with a vigorous hand, but the brush itself has not a fine point. Of all the children of his brain, Natty Bumppo is the most universal favorite,— and herein the popular judgment is assuredly right. He is an original conception,—and not more happily conceived than skilfully executed. It was a hazardous undertaking to present the character backwards, and let us see the closing scenes of his life first,—like a Hebrew Bible, of which the beginning is at the end; but the author's genius has triumphed over the perils of the task, and given us a delineation as consistent and symmetrical as it is striking and vigorous. Ignorant of books, simple, and credulous, guileless himself, and suspecting no evil in others, with moderate intellectual powers, he commands our admiration and respect by his courage, his love of Nature, his skill in woodland lore, his unerring moral sense, his strong affections, and the veins of poetry that run through his rugged nature like seams of gold in quartz. (pp. 57-8)

Cooper, as we need hardly say, has drawn copiously upon Indian life and character for the materials of his novels; and among foreign nations much of his reputation is due to this fact. Civilized men and women always take pleasure in reading about the manners and habits of savage life; and those in whom the shows of things are submitted to the desires of the mind delight to invest them with those ideal qualities which they do not find, or think they do not, in the artificial society around them. Cooper had enjoyed no peculiar opportunities of studying by personal observation the characteristics of the Indian race, but he had undoubtedly read everything he could get hold of in illustration of the subject. No one can question the vividness and animation of his sketches, or their brilliant tone of color. He paints with a pencil dipped in the glow of our sunset skies and the crimson of our autumn maples. Whenever he brings Indians upon the stage, we may be sure that scenes of thrilling interest are before us: that rifles are to crack, tomahawks to gleam, and arrows to dart like sunbeams through the air; that a net of peril is to be drawn around his hero or heroine, from the meshes of which he or she is to be extricated by some unexpected combination of fortunate circumstances. We expect a succession of startling incidents, and a rapid course of narrative without pauses or languid intervals. We do not object to his idealizing his Indians: this is the privilege of the novelist, time out of mind. He may make them swift of foot, graceful in movement, and give them a form like the Apollo's; he may put as much expression as he pleases into their black eyes; he may tessellate their

speech as freely as he will with poetical and figurative expressions, drawn from the aspects of the external world: for all this there is authority, and chapter and verse may be cited in support of it. But we have a right to ask that he shall not transcend the bounds of reason and possibility, and represent his red men as moved by motives and guided by sentiments which are wholly inconsistent with the inexorable facts of the case. We confess to being a little more than skeptical as to the Indian of poetry and romance: like the German's camel, he is evolved from the depth of the writer's own consciousness. The poet takes the most delicate sentiments and the finest emotions of civilization and cultivation, and grafts them upon the best qualities of savage life; which is as if a painter should represent an oak-tree bearing roses. The life of the North-American Indian, like that of all men who stand upon the base-line of civilization, is a constant struggle, and often a losing struggle, for mere subsistence. The sting of animal wants is his chief motive of action, and the full gratification of animal wants his highest ideal of happiness. The "noble savage," as sketched by poets, weary of the hollowness, the insincerity, and the meanness of artificial life, is really a very ignoble creature, when seen in the "open daylight" of truth. He is selfish, sensual, cruel, indolent, and impassive. The highest graces of character, the sweetest emotions, the finest sensibilities,—which make up the novelist's stock in trade,— are not and cannot be the growth of a so-called state of Nature, which is an essentially unnatural state. We no more believe that Logan ever made the speech reported by Jefferson, in so many words, than we believe that Chatham ever made the speech in reply to Walpole which begins with, "The atrocious crime of being a young man"; though we have no doubt that the reporters in both cases had something fine and good to start from. We accept with acquiescence, nay, with admiration, such characters as Magua, Chingachgook, Susquesus, Tamenund, and Canonchet; but when we come to Uncas, in *The Last of the Mohicans,* we pause and shake our heads with incredulous doubt. That a young Indian chief should fall in love with a handsome quadroon like Cora Munro—for she was neither more nor less than that—is natural enough; but that he should manifest his passion with such delicacy and refinement is impossible. We include under one and the same name all the affinities and attractions of sex, but the appetite of the savage differs from the love of the educated and civilized man as much as charcoal differs from the diamond. The sentiment of love, as distinguished from the passion, is one of the last and best results of Christianity and civilization: in no one thing does savage life differ from civilized more than in the relations between man and woman, and in the affections that unite them. Uncas is a graceful and beautiful image; but he is no Indian. (pp. 60-1)

Cooper would have been a better writer, if he had had more of the quality of humor, and a keener sense of the ridiculous; for these would have saved him from his too frequent practice of introducing both into his narrative and his conversations, but more often into the latter, scraps of commonplace morality, and bits of sentiment so long worn as to have lost all their gloss. In general, his genius does not appear to advantage in dialogue. His characters have not always a due regard to the brevity of human life. They make long speeches, preach dull sermons, and ventilate very self-evident propositions with great solemnity of utterance. Their discourse wants not only compression, but seasoning. They are sometimes made to talk in such a way that the force of caricature can hardly go farther. For instance, in *The Pioneers,* Judge Temple, coming into a room in his house, and seeing a fire of maple-logs, exclaims to Richard Jones, his kinsman and factotum,—"How often have I forbidden the use of the sugar-maple in my dwelling! The sight of that sap, as it *exudes* with the heat, is painful to me, Richard." And in another place, he is made to say to his daughter,—"Remember the heats of July, my daughter; nor venture farther than thou canst *retrace before the meridian.*" We may be sure that no man of woman born, in finding fault about the burning of maple-logs, ever talked of the sap's "exuding"; or, when giving a daughter a caution against walking too far, ever translated getting home before noon into "retracing before the meridian." (p. 64)

Every author in the department of imaginative literature, whether of prose or verse, puts more or less of his personal traits of mind and character into his writings. This is very true of Cooper; and much of the worth and popularity of his novels is to be ascribed to the unconscious expressions and revelations they give of the estimable and attractive qualities of the man. [William Cullen Bryant], in his admirably written and discriminating biographical sketch, originally pronounced as a eulogy, and now prefixed to **Precaution** . . . , relates that a distinguished man of letters, between whom and Cooper an unhappy coolness had for some time existed, after reading **The Pathfinder,** remarked,—"They may say what they will of Cooper, the man who wrote this book is not only a great man, but a good man." This is a just tribute; and the impression thus made by a single work is confirmed by all. Cooper's moral nature was thoroughly sound, and all his moral instincts were right. His writings show in how high regard he held the two great guardian virtues of courage in man and purity in woman. In all his novels we do not recall a single expression of doubtful morality. He never undertakes to enlist our sympathies on the wrong side. If his good characters are not always engaging, he never does violence to virtue by presenting attractive qualities in combination with vices which in real life harden the heart and coarsen the taste. We do not find in his pages those moral monsters in which the finest sensibilities, the richest gifts, the noblest sentiments are linked to heartless profligacy, or not less heartless misanthropy. He never palters with right; he enters into no truce with wrong; he admits of no compromise on such points. How admirable in its moral aspect is the character of Leatherstocking! he is ignorant, and of very moderate intellectual range or grasp; but what dignity, nay, even grandeur, is thrown around him from his noble moral qualities,—his undeviating rectitude, his disinterestedness, his heroism, his warm affections! No writer could have delineated such a character so well who had not an instinctive and unconscious sympathy with his intellectual offspring. (pp. 64-5)

> *G. S. Hilliard, in an originally unsigned essay titled "James Fenimore Cooper," in* The Atlantic Monthly, *Vol. IX, No. LI, January, 1862, pp. 52-68.*

T. E. KEBBEL (essay date 1899)

[*In the following excerpt, English critic Kebbel assesses some characteristics of the Leatherstocking novels.*]

The publication of illustrated editions of Cooper's Leather-Stocking Tales, simultaneously in London and New York, affords an opportunity of saying something on the merits of a writer who, as a master of healthy and manly fiction, deserves to be better remembered than he seems to be at the present day, especially as the novel of romantic adventure has, for the time at least, regained its vogue. It is at present proposed to

deal only with the five Indian tales, commonly known as the Leather-Stocking Series from the name of the wild hunter who is the hero of them all. In those, of which the scenes are placed among the lakes and forests inhabited down to the end of the last century almost exclusively by the Red Man, we have a set of original pictures with as marked an idiosyncrasy as the Highland stories of Sir Walter Scott. What Scott did in *Waverley, Rob Roy,* and *The Legend of Montrose* for a race of men scarcely known to the English public of ninety years ago, this Fenimore Cooper did for the Delawares, Mohicans, and Iroquois, of whom only very vague ideas existed on this side of the Atlantic, but who had no little in common with the Mac Ivors, the Macgregors, the Camerons, and the Children of the Mist. This is Cooper's title to fame. He saw the poetic and dramatic elements which lurked in the life of the Red Man, and only required drawing out by the hand of genius to form a valuable and unique addition to the national literature. (p. 191)

Cooper began the Leather-Stocking Series, in his thirty-third year, with the story of **The Pioneers** published in 1822. But this, although the first that was written, is the fourth in order of time if we look to the life of the hero. It finds the hunter an old man of seventy-six, if we are to trust his own account of his age given in **The Prairie,** of which the date is understood to be 1804, when he says that he is eighty-seven. From **The Pioneers,** the events of which are supposed to have occurred in 1793, our author takes a leap backwards of nearly forty years, introducing us again to his hero (then bearing the name of Hawkeye) in 1755, at the beginning of the Seven Years' War when Montcalm was in command of the French forces in Canada. This, the second tale of the series, is **The Last of the Mohicans,** and is followed by **The Pathfinder,** a story of the same war. Next comes **The Prairie,** when the author carries us forward again to the year of the hunter's death; and following this, and published in 1841, we have at last **The Deerslayer,** which takes us back again more than sixty years, when that was the title borne by the young novice who was known to be a dead shot at game, but who had not yet drawn trigger on a human enemy. **The Deerslayer** then, though the last in publication, is the first in order of events; and it is with this that we must begin if we would follow the career of Leather-Stocking from youth to manhood, and from manhood to extreme old age.

Leather-Stocking is a white man by birth and a Christian, his real name being Nathaniel, or Natty, Bumppo. Before he became a forester he had served with the English army under a Major Effingham . . . ; but, at some period prior to 1740, he had quitted the service, taken to the woods, and been adopted by the tribe of Delawares. At the opening of the story we are to suppose that he was about twenty-three, and had been leading this wild life for some four or five years. At the breaking out of the war of the Austrian Succession hostilities recommenced, if they could ever be said to have ceased, between the French and English in America, and Deerslayer, who had not yet abandoned all connection with the army, was employed by the English as a scout. The Delawares were a tribe friendly to this country, while the Mingoes, called indifferently Iroquois, Hurons, and Maquas, were in alliance with the French. Both sides alike offered rewards for the enemies' scalps; and one of Chatham's finest speeches was directed against this barbarous system, which was continued down to 1763.

At the opening of the story we find the Deerslayer on his way to meet a young Delaware chief, known as the Great Serpent, with whom he is to go upon his first war-path in the service of the English. The Serpent is the head of the ancient tribe of the Mohicans, now absorbed into the Delawares, but once powerful and renowned, and with what reverence the family were still regarded we shall see in the next act of the drama. While on the road Deerslayer falls in with a frontier man Harry March, commonly known as Hurry Harry, with whom he embarks on Lake Oswego (Glimmerglass), and is introduced to a curious character living upon the lake with his two daughters, Judith, a great beauty but one who has "tripped in her time," and Hetty, thoroughly pure and good but of slightly weak intellect. At one end of this lake is the spot where Deerslayer and the Indian are to meet. This has been chosen because the Serpent has a love-affair on hand as well, the Indian maiden, his betrothed, having been stolen by the Iroquois who are supposed to be lying in ambush not very far from the lake. . . . How Floating Tom and his family, sometimes in a fortified building raised on piles in the open lake and called the Castle, sometimes in a floating scow called the Ark, are attacked by the hostile Indians, with the varying fortunes of the struggle which went on upon the lake and in the woods till the arrival of some English soldiers; how the Serpent recovered his bride; how old Tom and his daughter Hetty met their death; the rescue of the Deerslayer at the last moment when in the hands of his enemies and about to be put to the torture, the reader will discover for himself.

Three out of the other four tales are built on much the same lines. (pp. 191-93)

Cooper troubled himself very little with the construction of his plots. It might be said indeed, with small exaggeration, that he made one do for all. His two girls captured by savages, and rescued in each case by the same hero or heroes, reappear punctually in four out of the five stories; and in the fifth, though the danger is different, the deliverance is the same. Unquestionably this is a defect, and if our interest in the story depended on the machinery, on the means, that is to say, by which the heroines are first entrapped and afterwards extricated from the toils, nobody would read any one of them a second time. But Cooper doubtless knew where his own strength lay, and confident in his powers of description may have relied on them to compensate not only for all want of variety in his situations, but for any other faults which professional critics might discover; and there are some to be mentioned presently which it would seem that he mistook for beauties. But who can think of these things when standing by the side of Deerslayer on the banks of Oswego, and contemplating the lovely scene which even the untutored hunter cannot view without emotion? Who can remember, when reading the thrilling story of the fight on the river and the siege of the block-house in *The Pathfinder,* that he has practically read it all before in *The Last of the Mohicans*? Does the fact that Judith and Hetty, Alice and Cora have undergone exactly the same sufferings and perils as the heroine of *The Prairie* lessen for one moment the interest which absorbs us in the fortunes of Inez? In what way does Hardheart at the stake differ from the Deerslayer when bound for torture? Yet we watch the fate of the Pawnee warrior with as keen an anxiety as if we saw the scene for the first time. Not only does the vivid reality with which these incidents are depicted engross our attention for the time to the exclusion of all such mental processes as comparison or discrimination, but the exquisite setting in which each is presented to us, the picturesque combination of rock, stream, and waterfall, of hills clothed with

virgin forests reaching down to the water's edge, where the oaks fling their untamed branches into the bosom of the lake, or form a natural arch across the narrow bed of the brook as it hurries down the glen, the boundless and unbroken canopy of the forest, on which the traveller looks down from some mountain-top, stretching on every side as far as the eye can reach, and hiding in its recesses the Huron or Iroquois watching like a tiger for his prey,—these wild woodland glories, with all the charm of mystery and danger superadded, effectually prevent us from wishing for one moment that anything in the picture could be different. We rather hug the monotony, than turn away from it. This constant succession of stirring incidents, one very like another, environed with scenery in which there is never any great variety, never palls upon us. They are always fresh, rekindling hope and fear and rousing the imagination to renewed activity as often as we read them.

As the descriptive powers of the Leather-Stocking Tales do so much towards redeeming the sameness of the plots, they have been taken next in order, though according to all established rules and forms of criticism the second place should have been reserved for the characters. Let us now glance at these. It will be allowed on the threshold that in stories of savage, or half savage, life we cannot expect to encounter those complex or eccentric characters which seem to be the growth of civilisation, far less those compounds of folly, vanity and meanness which it is the business of the modern novelist to reproduce. But in Leather-Stocking himself, in Ishmael of *The Prairie,* and in Judith of *The Deerslayer* Cooper shows considerable knowledge of human nature, and a skilful touch in the delineation of it. The relations between Judith Hutter, the daughter of Old Tom, and the young hunter himself at the outset of his career, are made extremely interesting; and as a study in psychology they deserve more attention than perhaps has yet been bestowed on them.

Judith is a girl of great beauty, high spirit, and no small mental powers. While living for a time near the settlements, as they were called, she had acquired manners above her station, which would all tend to increase her powers of fascination for a half savage nature. She had been seduced by an English officer at one of the forts, and though nobody knew of the fact, many suspected it. Her whole soul was in revolt against the baseness with which she had been treated, and when she first met the hunter she was in a mood to prize simple honesty and straightforwardness above all other qualities. These she found in Deerslayer, and was seriously prepared to abandon all her former social ambitions and pass her life with him in the wilderness. In a word, she fell passionately in love with him; though the rude young woodsman, dressed in skins and unable to read or write, presented as wide a contrast to the smart uniforms, gallant demeanour, and polished manners which she had met with at the garrison as could well be imagined. The gradual growth of her feelings is well described. (pp. 195-96)

Ishmael in *The Prairie,* the other character I have mentioned as displaying those lights and shades which the modern novel-reader expects to find in some at least of the personages introduced to him, is perhaps from one point of view the best drawn in the series. He is the leader of the band of emigrants with whom we find ourselves at the beginning of the story, a rough, vindictive, unscrupulous man, apparently bent only on gain. But gleams of light are occasionally thrown upon his character in the course of the story to prepare us for the better traits which show themselves at the end of it. He appears suddenly awakened to a sense of justice, owns that he was wrong in being a party to the kidnapping of Inez, dismisses all his prisoners freely, and completes his part of the sternly just man by putting to death his brother-in-law, who had been convicted of murdering one of Ishmael's sons. Altogether he is certainly an impressive character, and the skill with which his latent good qualities are gradually revealed to us through the coarser and more savage outside, which is all that we see on our first acquaintance with him, deserves high praise. Nearly as much perhaps may be said of his wife Esther, who till the last moment has appeared only as a scolding termagant. The death of their favourite son seems to have softened both, and the communing together of husband and wife over their great loss and over the necessary punishment of the assassin, the woman's brother, is full of genuine pathos, and touches a deeper key than Cooper generally strikes.

In the rest of his white characters there is little individuality, if we except the old sailor Cap in *The Pathfinder,* and he after all is only an ill-drawn copy of Commodore Trunnion. In fact, Cooper's attempts at comedy are usually failures, Dr. Elnathan Todd in *The Pioneers,* for instance, Gamut in *The Last of the Mohicans,* and the Doctor, Obed, in *The Prairie.* He is only at his best with the grave and dignified savage who, as Peacock says, "never laughs, because he has nothing to laugh at." It is only civilisation which produces the ridiculous; and his Indian Braves, though they all belong to one of two types, and there is little of what we call character to be got out of either, are nevertheless noble specimens of a very interesting people, who with all the ruthless ferocity and vindictive passions of the true savage combined certain virtues not common to all uncivilised races, and seeming as if they might have been inherited from some remote ancestry acquainted, it might be, with higher codes of morality. Chingachgook, the Great Serpent, who plays so prominent a part in the three earliest novels, Uncas, and the young Pawnee chief who comes on in *The Prairie,* represent the best side of the Indian character, while in Renard, Mahtoree, and Arrowhead we have the worst. But they are all five such embodiments of manhood as must be regarded with very deep interest, whether their skill, fortitude, and daring be combined only with that cruelty which was the Red Man's gift, or with the treachery and villainy, to which, as we are led to believe, he was not universally addicted. Certainly both in Hardheart and the Serpent Cooper has given us characters which command our sympathy and admiration, and such as, allowance being made for the traditions of savage life, may fairly be called heroic. (pp. 197-98)

Besides the want of variety in his plots, which is of course a technical fault, Cooper has two others of more practical importance. One is that he is apt to overcrowd his canvas. His tales want thinning like an overgrown plantation, that the leading incidents may stand out in bolder relief and in their true proportions. But this is nothing to the prosy moralising which he introduces in season and out of season, in the shape of conversation especially between Deerslayer and the Serpent, and various other characters, respecting what they call "white gifts" and "red gifts" and what it is lawful for the Red Man to do and not for the White. Sometimes these long palavers are introduced in the very middle of an acute crisis when the parties to it are hiding for their lives and hostile rifles or tomahawks are within a few yards of them. "Stranger, is this a time to ask conundrums," was the serious question of a wounded American soldier when he overheard a clergyman examining a fellow-sufferer as to his religious faith. This is

what one would have liked to say to Deerslayer. A little of it is all very well. It was a point with Cooper to contrast the Christian and Indian morality and to illustrate what had been done on the Indian frontier by missionary effort. But there is a time for everything; few people, and least of all savages, would discuss nice questions of casuistry while their hair was trembling on their heads. (pp. 198-99)

On reading over the Leather-Stocking Series afresh, I have sometimes been struck with the absence of all wild animal-life in the forests, especially bird-life, in which, according to Audubon and Wilson, the western woodlands were particularly rich. Hawkeye tells us, in *The Last of the Mohicans,* that "he has listened to all the sounds of the woods for thirty years as a man will listen whose life and death depend on the quickness of his ears." There is no whine of the panther, no whistle of the cat-bird with which he is not familiar. This of course was only to be expected; but Cooper was true to nature in not representing Leather-Stocking as taking that interest in zoology which belongs rather to a state of advanced civilisation. He might however, one would think, have made some use of materials which would have greatly enhanced the effect of many of his scenes. The gloomy croak of the raven, supposed by so many races of mankind to be an omen of evil, and the hideous wail of the horned owl heard in the forest solitude, must often have startled the watchers during those nights of terror so graphically described in these novels. But we see no trace in Cooper of any of those tastes or sympathies which would have led him to seek fresh elements of interest in the sources here indicated. The want of them is more apparent now than it would have been eighty years ago; but perhaps even now such accessories will be little missed by the great majority of his readers. (pp. 200-01)

> *T. E. Kebbel, "Leather-Stocking," in* Macmillan's Magazine, *Vol. LXXIX, No. 471, January, 1899, pp. 191-201.*

LOUISE POUND   (essay date 1927)

[*Pound, an American linguist and critic, cofounded the periodical* American Speech *and served as its editor from 1925-33. She edited and contributed to several other publications, and her essays on literature, linguistics, vocabulary and diction, folklore, and education were collected in* The Selected Writings of Louise Pound *in 1949. In the following excerpt, she examines the dialect used by the character of Natty Bumppo in the Leatherstocking novels.*]

The speech of James Fenimore Cooper's frontiersman, Nathaniel Bumppo, he of the sobriquets Leather-Stocking, Deerslayer, Hawkeye, Pathfinder, La Longue Carabine, is far from being the most important feature of his characterization. Yet it has no little interest for present-day students of speech, an interest that is partly historic and partly intrinsic. Leather-Stocking has taken his place among the classic characters of the world. He belongs alongside Don Quixote and Gil Blas in European literature and Robinson Crusoe and Lemuel Gulliver, Parson Adams and Dr. Primrose, Mr. Pickwick and Sir Willoughby Patterne in British literature. With Rip Van Winkle and Uncle Tom he begins the list of unforgettable characters for American literature. It is possible that future generations will place next on the roll of permanent heroes of our fiction George F. Babbitt, the realtor, who is perhaps as characteristic of our period as the frontiersman was of Cooper's. It is not unthinkable that in the twenty-first century those interested in linguistic retrospection may seek to analyse the speech of Sinclair Lewis's business man much as we examine the speech of Leather-Stocking; partly because of the historic place of the book and partly because it reflects some features of our speech selected by the writer as characteristic.

Cooper explains in the preface to the Leather-Stocking Tales, prefixed to *The Deerslayer* in 1841, that there is not perfect harmony or consistency between the tales because of their fortuitous manner of composition. In the order of their production Cooper wrote *The Pioneers* (1823), *The Last of the Mohicans* (1826), *The Prairie* (1827), *The Pathfinder* (1840), and *The Deerslayer* (1841). Thus there were nineteen years between the first volume and the last. In *The Pioneers, The Last of the Mohicans,* and *The Pathfinder,* Cooper's hero is in his prime. In *The Prairie,* the third to be written, he is an old man. In *The Deerslayer,* written last, he is in his youth. The order in which the stories belong as recounting the life of their hero is the alphabetical order, *The Deerslayer, The Last of the Mohicans, The Pathfinder, The Pioneers,* and *The Prairie.* Tennyson sought in much the same manner to bring unity to the *Idylls of the King* long after he had launched them independently. Cooper, on the whole, is as successful as Tennyson in his late attempt to achieve unity.

When Cooper brought forward his frontiersman in *The Pioneers* (1823) he told us little or nothing of his past life. We know that he was of white parentage, "a man without a cross," and was brought up among the Delaware Indians. Was he of English, Scotch, or Irish progenitors? Probably he was of English stock although we are not told this specifically. In the preface of *The Deerslayer* Cooper says of his hero: "He was removed from everyday inducements to err which abound in civilized life while he retains the best and simplest of his early impressions." Cooper is often said to have had the life of Daniel Boone partly in mind when he created his character, but his idea of the unsocial Leather-Stocking, shunning the haunts of men, displaying more zest for the companionship of savages in the woods than for civilized man, plainly emerges from the post-Rousseau dissatisfaction with civilization and sublimation of voluntary social exile which characterized European and American literature of more than a hundred years ago. Tired of hearing of nature only when refined and artificialized by man, tired of hearing of man only when tamed by society and civilization, the public transferred its interest to nature in her primitive aspects and to human beings in their most independent, solitary, and protesting attitudes. Cooper has his Bumppo wax enthusiastic over nature's wonders in the best manner of the Wordsworthian decades from which he derives. Leather-Stocking is capable of high flights of poetical eloquence when talking of nature, although before and after these passages he may speak as an illiterate. Consider the following which is surely book speech rather than that of a woodsman.

> ". . . . The seasons come and go, Judith; and if we have winter with storms and frosts, and spring, with chills and leafless trees, we have summer, with its sun and glorious skies, and fall, with its fruits, and a garment thrown over the forest that no beauty of the town could rummage out of all the shops in America."

(pp. 479-80)

There are times also when Cooper's frontiersman becomes Ossianic. This passage from *The Prairie* is almost pure Ossian transferred to the American scene.

> ". . . . It is the fate of all things to ripen, and then to decay. The tree blossoms, and bears its fruit which falls, rots, withers, and even the seed is lost! Go count the rings of the oak and of the sycamore; they lie in circles, one about the other, until the eye is blinded in striving to make out their numbers; and yet a full change of the seasons comes round while the stem is winding one of these little lines about itself, like the buffalo changing his coat, or the buck his horns; and what does it all amount to? There does the noble tree fill its place in the forest, loftier and grander and richer, and more difficult to imitate than any of your pitiful pillars, for a thousand years, until the time which the Lord hath given it is full. Then come the winds, that you cannot see, to rive its bark, and the waters from the heavens, to soften its pores; and the rot, which all can feel and none can understand, to humble its pride and bring it to the ground. From that moment its beauty begins to perish. It lies another hundred years, a moldering log, and then a mound of moss and earth; a sad effigy of a human grave."

Passages like these and illiterate speeches may come from Leather-Stocking on the same page. It was this incongruity that led Mark Twain to remark that "when a personage talks like an illustrated, gilt-edged tree-calf, hand-tooled seven-dollar Friendship's Offering in the beginning of a paragraph, he shall not talk like a negro minstrel at the end of it."

The example of Sir Walter Scott whose lower class characters use dialect as part of their "local color" was immediately behind Cooper in his handling; though the use of dialect in fiction was of course far older than Scott. Cooper is no such skilful employer of dialect as was his master. He handles it more or less amateurishly; but his results equal those of his contemporaries, and he does as well relatively with his dialect as with his book English. For poetry the florescence time of dialect writing lasted from the *Biglow Papers* through James Whitcomb Riley and Eugene Field. Toward the end of the century young poets wrote it and newspapers printed it much as, in these days, our popular writers are preoccupied with slang. But in prose the use of dialect was already established, and Cooper wrote it without introducing novelties or bringing in changed modes. He was no linguistic innovator like O. Henry or Ring W. Lardner. The illiterate speech of his lower class characters resembles that in the works of his contemporaries.

What were the stock marks of unlettered speech to the novelists and dramatists of the early nineteenth century? What devices did Cooper rely on? In these days we are accustomed to eccentric diction, in the illiterate or informal speech of our fiction, and to spellings showing word-liaison and slovenly pronunciation in general. An analysis of a present-day bestseller would reveal a liberal usage of slang expressions, the transient variations from the standard that rise in vogue, have their day, and are replaced by the new. Dialect on the other hand has permanence. Its users speak it seriously and unconsciously, not deliberately or flippantly. Cooper places dialect not slang in the mouths of his characters while our contemporary fiction writers like both. Slang has taken on more and more importance. The heroes and heroines of Cooper's period may never speak it but it is relied upon by the most patrician characters of present-day popular writers.

The volume which Cooper wrote last, *The Deerslayer,* is that in which Leather-Stocking's speech is most heavily weighted with dialect. *The Prairie* which he wrote while in Europe has least dialect. The hero's language improved with age. He speaks by far the best English of his life when he has become an octogenarian! It is to be borne in mind, however, that in *The Deerslayer,* the frontiersman has the central role. He nearly monopolizes the conversation in this book and hence Cooper gave his language greater attention. He is a minor character in *The Pioneers* and on the whole is subordinated in *The Pathfinder.* That Cooper was in Europe when he wrote *The Prairie* probably accounts for the more bookish character of his speech in this tale.

Cooper's divergences from standard English may come from first-hand memories of characters known in his childhood at Cooperstown, or from his reading. Very likely they come from an amalgam of experience and reading, with possibly a little invention here and there. Bumppo's speech is not to be looked on as specifically New York speech. Dialect of much the same type comes from the mouths of New England characters and from the pens of other authors.

An analysis of the dialect of Leather-Stocking reveals the following as its leading features.

SOUNDS

Vowels

Non-standard pronunciation plays a larger rôle in Leather-Stocking's dialect than breaches of grammar or misuses of words. The lapses from the standard are not uniform in the five books of the series but interest in pronunciation maintains a chief place in all. Especially, Bumppo's faults of speech belong in the category of archaisms. As already remarked, they are much the same faults as those in other fiction of the time, when the speech of unlettered characters is to be reflected. Many are identical with those exhibited in Lowell's *Biglow Papers.* Moreover the same faults are exhibited by other characters in the Leather-Stocking Tales themselves. Deerslayer's dialect does not differ noticeably from that of Hurry Harry in *The Deerslayer* or from that of Ishmael Bush in *The Prairie,* or from that of characters in works outside the Leather-Stocking series.

Easily the most striking and frequent variation from the standard is the substitution of *ar* for *er, ir (sarmon, vartue),* that change which began in England toward the end of the fifteenth century and was completed in the next century. In the eighteenth century, as many documents testify, the educated usually have *er* and the uneducated *ar.* In the earlier nineteenth century the usage is relied upon as an indication of dialect, the *Biglow Papers* having, for example, *narves, varsed, vartue.* Instances of this substitution from the five tales of the Leather-Stocking series are:—

Pioneers: sartin, sartain, sartainty, unsartain (but uncertain, i) l'arned, larn't, unl'arned, unl'arnt, l'arning, sarved, yarbs, sarpent, disarnable, intarpret, desarts, varmint, consarns, consarning, sarvice, parson (= person), s'arch, etarnity, 'arth.

Last of the Mohicans: sarpints, sarpents, disconsart, (disconcerts, viii, disconcerted, vi), divarsions, pervart, 'arth, prefarment, varmints, vartue, l'arn, karnel, desarts, sartain (certain viii, circumvent v).

Prairie: varmints, (vermin, xxix), l'arning unl'arns, 'arth, uns'archable, (but deserts, circumvent, circumventions, etc.).

Pathfinder: sartain, sart'in, sartainty, sartainly, unsartain, onsartainty, sarve, sarvice, sarvices, sarv-

ing, sarvent, marcy, marciless, prefar, prefars, prefarred, 'arth, consarn, consarning, consarned, convarse, l'arn, l'arns, l'arning, l'arnt, l'arned, unl'arned, expart, tarms, sarcumvent, sarcumvented, sarcumventions, sarpent, starn, infarnals, pervarted, s'arch, s'arching, narves, narvous, resarve, presarve, obsarvent, obsarved, desarves, desarved, desarving, undesarvedly, parsecuted, sarcumstances, desarts, desarted.

Deerslayer: 'arth, 'arthly, 'arnestly, 'arly, 'arliest, 'arned, 'arnest, (airnest, xiv), consarting, disconsarts, consarn, consarns, consarned, consarnin', consarning, consarting, sarving, disparsed, varsed, parceive, sarcumvention, sarcumventions, sarcumvent, sarcumvents, sarcumvented, convarse, convarsing, univarsal (universal, xv), tarminate, tarmination, sarmons, sartain, sartainly, sartainty, onsartain (unsartain, xiii) unsartainly, sarcumstance, sarcumstances, tarms, tarmed, expart, expartest, arn'nd infarnal, sarve, sarving, avart, avarse, avarsion, advarsities, larn, larned, larnt, alart, services, larnin', larning, sarviceable, detarmined, marcy, marciful, obsarvable, parceptible, desarter, desarves, desarved, desarving, intarpreted, vartue, vartues, obsarve, obsarved, parvarse, Sarpent, s'arch, prefar, parch, desarts, desarted, presarves, sartified, swarving, (eternal, xxvi, universal, xv).

Next in abundance are examples of the fluctuation between *e* and *i,* also a characteristic of uneducated speech in the later eighteenth century. Today we usually associate *i* for *e* with Irish English, but it once belonged to English speech generally. As often noted, Benjamin Franklin said *git* for *get.* The closer vowel appears most frequently in *The Deerslayer,* which was written last. In *The Prairie* it plays no rôle.

Deerslayer: fri'nd, fri'nds, fri'ndly, (friendly, xxii), fri'ndship, ind (end, xxvi), indivors, ag'in, gin'rally, gin'rous, gin'ral, gin'rals, gin'ralizing, ginerosity, inimy, inimies, inmity, ricommend (as noun, v), riptyles, indivor, endivors, endivoring, chist, rijiment, invy, diviltries (deviltries, xxx), vinerable, ripresentatyve.

Pathfinder: rijiment, ind, endivors, riptyle, inimy, squinched, diviltry, (devil, xxiv), risolute, ginerous, befri'nded, ginirals, giniral, gin'ral, gin'rally, inmity, ag'in, ag'inst.

Mohicans: ag'in,

Pioneers: gin'rous, ag'in, ind, inimy, wilcome, squinch, sintence.

(pp. 480-83)

Some individual words showing non-standard pronunciation are—

we'pons (*Mohicans,* viii), 'ither (*Pioneers.* Not a recognized pronunciation till later), ende'vored (*Pathfinder,* vii), amboosh (*Deerslayer*), f 'erceness (*Deerslayer,* xiv), and the fronted kear, kearful, kearless (*Pioneers*), skear (*Pioneers, Prairie*).

A stock mannerism in *The Deerslayer* is the use of *on-* for *un-.* Dickens and others make abundant use of this mannerism in the speech of their uneducated characters. It appears frequently in *The Pathfinder* but is not relied on in the earlier books, *The Pioneers* and *The Prairie,* and it is little used in *The Last of the Mohicans.*

Deerslayer: onequal, onjust, onfit, onsartain (but

unsartain, xxiii, unsartainty, xvii), ondergo, onjus-tifiable, onreasonable, onbecoming, onexpected, onexpectedly, onlawful, ontimely, oncommon, on-true, ondo, ongin'rous, onpossibility, onhuman, on-calculated, onthoughtful, onpleasant, onbeknown, oneasy, onless, onexpected, onaccountable, on-called for, onmeaningly, onlikely, oncomprehensi-ble, oncivilized, onequalled, onharmless (xiii), onfit, onknowingly, oncomely, onqualified, on-meaningly, onsteady, onknown, onskilful, uncom-mon and onequalled (xii). But unl'arned (xxiv), un-humanize (v).

Pathfinder: onwise, onbecoming, onreasonable, on-practysed, onsteady, onthoughtful, oncreditable, But uneasy (xix).

Mohicans: onlimited, oncommon. But unhuman act (xiv). *Pioneers,* unl'arned man, uncertain. *Prai-rie:* unl'arned hunter, uneasy, etc.

Retention of a secondary accent on the last syllable results in the preservation of length in that syllable for certain words now having a shortened vowel in the standard language. Cooper suggests this pronunciation to the eye by spelling them with a *y* which he often italicizes. He makes free use of this device in *The Pathfinder* and *The Deerslayer* but not in the three earlier books.

Pathfinder: actyve, natyve, riptyle, favoryte, prac-tysed, onpractysed.

Deerslayer: captyve, captyves, actyve, instinctyve, riptyle, riptyles, practyce, practyces, practyse (verb) natyve, captyvement, representatyve, coward-dyce.

Among vowel changes, that most commonly exhibited is *syncope.* The following are staple instances—

Deerslayer: ingen'ous, nat'ral, partic'lar, frivol'ties, cur'ous, cur'osity, exper'ence, exper'enced, inex-per'enced, ongin'rous, gin'rous, gin'ral, gin'rally, gin'ralizing, ven'son (but venison, xxv).

Pathfinder: gin'ral (giniral, viii), gin'rally, exp'erence, exper'enced, nat'ral, nat'rally, cur'osity. But particular, i, ginerous, xviii.

Pioneers: gin'rous, cur'ous, consid'ring, posteerum (i).

The words *whosoever* and *howsoever* are contracted to *whosever* and *howsever* in *The Deerslayer.* A whole syllable, consonant as well as vowel, is omit-ted in Bumppo's *gran'ther* in his speeches to Mid-dleton in *The Prairie.*

There are many instances of vowel *weakening,* especially of final syllables. Witness *Ontary, Pennsylvany, Virginny,* and *fever-an-agy* in *The Pioneers.* In *The Deerslayer* appears *valie* for value and *idee* with apocope of *-a* (idea, xiv). *The Prairie* has *thankee, harkee.* Forms like *natur', ventur', crea-tur'* (*cretur Pioneers,* i, creature also, i) *scriptur', futur', for-tun'* are common in all five tales. Weakening of a middle syl-lable appears in *repitation* (*Deerslayer*) *edicate, edication, un-edicated* (*Pathfinder*). *The Prairie* (xxii) has *education.*

Vowel *glides* appear occasionally. The forms *commerades* (*Mohicans,* xii) and *Patteroon* (patroon, patron, *Mohicans,* xiii) show glides; and glides or analogical vowels appear in *thataway,* (*Deerslayer*), *thisaway* (*Deerslayer*), *hereaway,* (*Deerslayer*) *thereaways* (*Mohicans,* vi).

Consonants

Consonant changes involve fewer words and may be reviewed more quickly than vowel changes, for Cooper's series. In-stances of added consonants are—

Prosthesis: t'other (*Pathfinder,* xxviii, *Deerslayer,* xxvi).

Epenthesis: lovyer (*Deerslayer,* ix), howsomever (*Pioneers, Prairie*), and instances of intrusive *r,* inter mates (*Pathfinder,* ii) plauserble, conterpla-tion (*Deerslayer,* xxvi), darter (*Deerslayer,* xii). Possibly the intrusive *r* of the last word is meant merely to indicate vowel quality, but compare da'hter (*Pathfinder,* xii).

Epithesis: varmint, gownd (*Deerslayer*).

Consonant *substitution* appears in a few words. *Injin* occurs regularly for Indian in *The Deerslayer* but in other books (*Pi-oneers,* xvi, etc.; *Prairie,* v, etc.), Leather-Stocking pro-nounces the word in the usual way. *The Last of the Mohicans* has *handkercher* for handkerchief. Dental *n* for back *n* (*ng*) appears in many words throughout the series.

Consonant *loss* (of *w, f, r, l, s, d*) appears in a few instances.

trainin', clearin', longin's, feelin's, comin', cun-nin'est, meetin', etc.

backard (*Deerslayer*), a'ter, a'terwards, a'ternoon (*Deerslayer*), gal (*Pathfinder, Deerslayer*), galish, soger, sogers, sogerizing (*Pathfinder,* xiii), sin' (*Pi-oneers,* etc.).

extrornary (*Pioneers,* xvi), "This is an extr'ornary garment, too; and extr'ornary things get up exta'ornary feelin's" (*Deerslayer,* xii).

GRAMMATICAL FORMS

For nouns may be noted the occurrence of many *nomina agentis* now unfamiliar. In *The Prairie* all the characters use the plural *Siouxes,* doubtless then the current plural. *Fren-chers* appears in *The Prairie* and in *The Last of the Mohi-cans, Welshers* in *The Prairie* and *Dutchers* in *The Last of the Mohicans* and *The Pioneers.* *The Pathfinder* has *ignoranters* (iii), *The Prairie* linguisters and admirators and *The Last of the Mohicans* admirators (vi), *physicianer,* and *musicianer.* Not all these forms would count as dialectal in Cooper's day. *Physicianer* is not entered in the *Oxford Dictionary,* nor *igno-ranter.* Its quotations show that *linguister* and *musicianer* had contemporary currency and that *admirator* was obsolete or rare. Of somewhat different character are *non-composser* (*Mohicans,* xxii) and a *non-plusser* (*Deerslayer,* xxv).

The plural *pair,* "three pair of moccasins" (*Mohicans,* xxl) persists in present dialect speech.

For *pronouns* the usage of *ye* for *you* and of the possessives *their'n, our'n, his'n, your'n* (present-day editors omit the apostrophe) and of *them* as a demonstrative are frequent. There is much confusion of the nominative and the accusa-tive.

ye (*Pioneers,* xxx, xli, etc. Used to a dog, *Pioneers,* xxx, *Prairie,* etc.). your'n (*Pioneers*). But yours (*Pathfinder,* xxix). our'n (*Pioneers, Pathfinder*). their'n (*Pathfinder*). his'n (*Deerslayer,* etc.).

"them troops," "them knaves the Sioux," "Among them hills," (*Prairie*), "them hills" (*Pioneers*), "them regions," "them islands," "them miscreants," "them matters," "them rapids" (***Pathfinder***), "them riptyles," "them sort of feelin's," "them echoes," "them elephants," "them clouds" (***Deerslayer***), "that there gownd" (***Deerslayer***, xii).

"they was all them Yaqua Indians," "there's them living" (***Pioneers***), "there are them in the camp" (***Mohicans***), "there's them, etc." (***Deerslayer***), "them that live in the settlements" (***Pathfinder***).

Certain dialectal prepositions and adverbs are used pretty consistently in the series. Instances are too numerous to deserve individual citation. The archaic *afore, atween, atwixt* appear often with occasional *before's* and *between's* interspersed. *Ag'in* abounds, and *a'ter* for after; *a'terwards, a'ternoon* appear in ***The Deerslayer***. Leather-Stocking uses the adverb *easierly* (***Deerslayer***, xxv) and remarks to Judith, "You're wonderful handsome," (xxiv). In ***The Pioneers*** (i) he refers to "thirty years agone," and uses "topsyturvylike." The prepositional phrase "at othersome" occurs in ***The Last of the Mohicans*** (vi) and "watch anights" in ***The Pioneers*** (i).

Wrong verbal usages are the least obsolete among the marks of dialect in Leather-Stocking's speech, especially the employment of analogical principal parts. Some of these wrong usages, notably the confusion of the preterite and the past participle, yet persist. ***The Pioneers*** and ***The Last of the Mohicans*** make much use of the archaic *'tis, 'twas, 'twouldn't.* Another archaism is *be* for *are:* "where be ye?", "you be," "we be," etc. *Used to could* occurs in ***The Pioneers*** (xli) and ***The Pathfinder*** (xxix), and *lay* for *lie* in ***The Pioneers*** (xxvi) and ***The Pathfinder*** (iv). *Ain't* appears occasionally. An interesting verb usage is exhibited in Deerslayer's "rendezvous'd an app'intment" (viii), "to rende'vous a fri'nd" (v).

> ***Pioneers:*** "you was," "times is," "I doesn't," "them that hasn't l'arning." ***Deerslayer:*** "Our ways doesn't agree," "things doesn't," "you was," "your answers doesn't," etc.

> ***Pioneers:*** druv, fou't, knowed, seed, catched, drawed, mought, teached. ***Mohicans:*** bursted, fou't, knowed, come (came). ***Pathfinder:*** knowed, know'd, druv, fi't, fou't.

VOCABULARY

A few matters of vocabulary deserve mention. A glossary of Leather-Stocking's unusual or unfamiliar words, dialect terms, archaisms, or coinages, might seem brief when set over against one from some analogous series of tales of the present-day. On the whole his vocabulary is narrow and hard-worked rather than rich and varied. In addition to the words or forms involved in preceding entries, certain others should be taken into account. A majority are adjectival.

> atomy (***Pioneers***, xiii), trampooses (***Pathfinder***, viii), ambushment (***Mohicans***, v), younker (***Mohicans***, xiii), exaltification (***Deerslayer***, xii), horrifications (***Prairie***, xxiv), "Isn't he a queerity?" (***Pathfinder***, ii).

> afeard (***Deerslayer***, ***Pathfinder***), timmersome (***Deerslayer***), untimmersome (***Pathfinder***), frighty, gaunty, twisty, wasty (***Pioneers***), oversightful (***Deerslayer***, vii), disremembering, judgmatical (***Mohicans***), (adverb judgmatically, ***Pathfinder***), adrye (***Pioneers***), skeary (***Deerslayer***), compass (***Deerslayer***), despisable (***Mohicans***), opinionated

(biassed, ***Deerslayer***), misfortinate (***Pathfinder***, i), misfortunate (***Pathfinder***, xxvii, ***Deerslayer***, xxx), gallantifying (***Deerslayer***, ii).

> captivate (capture), unteached, (***Deerslayer***), "my eyes never a-weary" (***Deerslayer***, ii), musickate (***Mohicans***), horrified (made horrible, ***Prairie***, xxiv), "to make a man solemnize" (***Pioneers***, xxvi), "has never behappened me" (***Deerslayer***, iv).

One of Leather-Stocking's most annoying and hard-worked mannerisms is his use of the exclamation *Anan* when he does not understand or prefers not to understand. This is relied on throughout the series. *Ah's me!* is another of his persistent exclamations. His *harkee* and *thankee* are used by other characters in the series and in many other works of the period. *For why?* is one of his favorite questions.

Pleonasms in the speech of Leather-Stocking are "human man" (***Mohicans***) and "new beginner" (***Prairie***). Folk-etymology curiosities are "buck-and-near" (***Deerslayer***, xxiv), "my-hog-guinea chairs" (***Mohicans***, vi), "baggonet," "baggonetmen" (***Pioneers***, xiii). A comment in the ***Deerslayer*** (xxiv) is "That's a moral impossible." "I peppered the blackguards intrinsically like," he remarks in the ***Pathfinder*** (xxvii).

When Bumppo talks to the Indians and is supposed to be speaking in the Indian tongue, there is often no dialect in his English. In ***The Prairie***, in which little dialect appears anyway, few faults of language are exhibited when he addresses the Pawnees. But there is little consistency. In the same book (*e.g.*, ***Deerslayer***), his speeches to the Indians may show dialect in one passage and literary or book English in another.

Leather-Stocking's terms of disparagement for the Indians show more variety and resourcefulness than might be expected from a speaker whose vocabulary in general is no large one. He calls them—

> varmints (***Prairie***), riptyles (***Deerslayer***, etc.), imps (***Prairie***), varlets (***Mohicans***), devils (***Prairie***), knaves (***Mohicans, Prairie***), wily sarpints, infarnals (***Pathfinder***), vagabonds (***Mohicans, Deerslayer***), disremembering hounds (***Mohicans***), blackguards (***Pathfinder***).

His terms for women are the often-cited "females," "the gentles," "the pretty ones," etc. Readers find these monotonous.

In ***The Last of the Mohicans***, hardly elsewhere, Cooper's frontiersman likes striking or poetical comparisons from nature—

> ". . . . and like a rattler that has lost his fangs," ". . . . screeching like a jay that has been winged," "like so many fettered hounds or hungry wolves," "brushing the dry leaves like a black snake," "much the same as one of you spurs a horse" ". . . . losing moments that are as precious as the heart's blood to a stricken deer."

The citations in the preceding pages show the leading characteristics of Leather-Stocking's speech, but they are not exhaustive. To make them such would protract this paper, without corresponding increase in its interest or its value.

An excursion through the Leather-Stocking Tales with special attention to the speech of the characters shows plainly that Cooper's forte was not dialogue. His characters are tiresome talkers. They never forget their hobbies and they have a stock round of mannerisms. Some writers of fiction are at their best when their dialogue is examined. Here Cooper is probably at his worst. (pp. 483-87)

Louise Pound, "The Dialect of Cooper's Leather-Stocking," in American Speech, *Vol. II, No. 12, September, 1927, pp. 479-88.*

HENRY NASH SMITH (essay date 1950)

[*Smith is an American educator and critic who has written extensively on the works of American novelists. In the following essay, he examines the conflict presented in the Leatherstocking novels between individual desire for freedom and the need of the community to impose restrictions on the behavior of its members. He also assesses the function of a character's social status in the novels.*]

Although [the American frontiersman Daniel] Boone was not exactly the prototype of Cooper's Leatherstocking, there is a haunting similarity between the two figures. Cooper based a part of chapters X and XII of *The Last of the Mohicans* on a well-known exploit of Boone in conducting the rescue of Betsey and Fanny Callaway and Jemima Boone, his daughter, from the Cherokees. Betsey Callaway, like Cora Munro in Cooper's novel, tried to aid her rescuers by breaking twigs to mark the trail, and was detected by her Indian guards. The rescue also furnished Cooper with several other details for his story.

Near the opening of *The Prairie* Cooper sets his stage by describing the migration of Americans from Ohio and Kentucky across the Mississippi immediately after the Louisiana Purchase. Although Boone actually settled in Missouri in 1799, Cooper names him among the emigrants of 1804:

> This adventurous and venerable patriarch was now seen making his last remove; placing the "endless river" between him and the multitude, his own success had drawn around him, and seeking for the renewal of enjoyments which were rendered worthless in his eyes, when trammelled by the forms of human institutions.

In a footnote added to the revised edition, Cooper elaborates this passage with the remark that Boone emigrated beyond the Mississippi "because he found a population of ten to the square mile, inconvenient." The aged Leatherstocking has likewise "been driven by the increasing and unparalleled advance of population, to seek a final refuge against society in the broad and tenantless plains of the west. . . . "

The similarities between Boone and Leatherstocking were analyzed at length by a perceptive writer in *Niles' Register* in 1825, when Leatherstocking had appeared in only one novel, *The Pioneers.* The critic points out that both these heroes love the freedom of the forest, both take a passionate delight in hunting, and both dislike the ordinary pursuits of civilized men. As testimony to the fidelity of Cooper's characterization, the writer quotes a letter from a traveler through the Pennsylvania mountains who came upon herdsmen and hunters reminiscent both of Boone and of Leatherstocking. One of their number, celebrated throughout the West as having once been a companion of Boone, had set out for Arkansas when he was almost a hundred years old, and was reported to be still alive, a solitary hunter in the forest. A nephew of the emigrant who remained in Pennsylvania, himself athletic and vigorous at the age of seventy, shared Leatherstock-

Natty Bumppo in his prime (illustration by James Daugherty for The Last of the Mohicans.

ing's love of hunting and his antipathy for "clearings" to such a marked degree that the traveler felt he must have sat as a model for Cooper. A similar point was made by the poet Albert Pike [in his *Prose Sketches and Poems, Written in the Western Country*], who after graduating from Harvard went out the Santa Fé Trail and later settled in a very primitive Arkansas. "I cannot wonder that many men have chosen to pass their life in the woods," wrote Pike in 1834, "and I see nothing overdrawn or exaggerated in the character of Hawkeye and Bushfield." He listed as the prime attractions of the lonely hunter's life its independence, its freedom from law and restraint, its lack of ceremony.

For at least one section of the reading public, then, Leatherstocking, like Boone, was a symbol of anarchic freedom, an enemy of law and order. Did this interpretation conform to Cooper's intention in drawing the character?

The original hunter of *The Pioneers* (1823) clearly expresses subversive impulses. The character was conceived in terms of the antithesis between nature and civilization, between freedom and law, that has governed most American interpretations of the westward movement. Cooper was able to speak for his people on this theme because the forces at work within him closely reproduced the patterns of thought and feeling that prevailed in the society at large. But he felt the problem more deeply than his contemporaries: he was at once more strongly devoted to the principle of social order and more vividly responsive to the ideas of nature and freedom in the

Western forest than they were. His conflict of allegiances was truly ironic, and if he had been able—as he was not—to explore to the end the contradictions in his ideas and emotions, the Leatherstocking series might have become a major work of art. Despite Cooper's failures, the character of Leatherstocking is by far the most important symbol of the national experience of adventure across the continent. The similarities that link Leatherstocking to both the actual Boone and the various Boones of popular legend are not merely fortuitous.

The Pioneers illustrates these aspects of Cooper's work with almost naïve directness. After a negligible first novel, *Precaution*, he had turned to the matter of the American Revolution in *The Spy,* which had had a sensational success. The Preface to *The Pioneers,* his next book, has a jaunty air bespeaking the apprentice novelist's growing confidence. Cooper announces that he is now writing to please himself alone. We may well believe him, for the scene is the Cooperstown of his childhood, and the character of Judge Marmaduke Temple, patron of the infant community, landed proprietor, justice of the peace, and virtual lord of the manor, has much in common with that of the novelist's father William Cooper. Not only did both William Cooper and Judge Temple buy land on the New York frontier and oversee the planting of a town on the shores of Lake Otsego; they resemble one another even in the minor detail of springing from Quaker forebears but having given up formal membership in the sect. When an author turns to autobiographical material of this sort and introduces a central character resembling his father, one does not have to be very much of a Freudian to conclude that the imagination is working on a deeper level than usual. This is certainly the case in *The Pioneers.*

Still very much an amateur in the externals of his craft, Cooper contrived for his story of Cooperstown a flimsy plot that hinges upon a childish misunderstanding about Judge Temple's administration of the property of his old friend Major Effingham, but the plot is merely a framework to hold together a narrative focussed about an entirely different problem. The emotional and literary center of the story is a conflict between Judge Temple and the old hunter Leatherstocking which symbolizes the issues raised by the advance of agricultural settlement into the wilderness. In the management of this theme Cooper is at his best. From the opening scene, when Judge Temple claims as his own a deer that Leatherstocking's young companion has shot, until the moment when the Judge sentences the old hunter to a fine and imprisonment because of his resistance to the new game laws, the narrative turns constantly about the central issue of the old forest freedom versus the new needs of a community which must establish the sovereignty of law over the individual. One aspect of the conflict is of course the question of a primitive free access to the bounty of nature—whether in the form of game or of land—versus individual appropriation and the whole notion of inviolable property rights. Not far in the background are the further issues of the rough equality of all men in a state of nature as against social stratification based on unequal distribution of property; and of formal institutional religion versus the natural, intuitive theology of Leatherstocking, who has little regard for theological niceties or the minutiæ of ritual.

The profundity of the symbol of Leatherstocking springs from the fact that Cooper displays a genuine ambivalence toward all these issues, although in every case his strongest commitment is to the forces of order. The social compact,

with all its consequences, is vividly and freshly realized, as it had to be realized with every new community planted in the wilderness. And all the aspects of authority—institutional stability, organized religion, class stratification, property—are exhibited as radiating from the symbol of the father. But if the father rules, and rules justly, it is still true that in this remembered world of his childhood Cooper figures as the son. Thus he is able to impart real energy to the statement of the case for defiance and revolt.

But we are not concerned with Cooper's personal relation to his materials so much as with his treatment of the themes arising from the advance of the agricultural frontier. The broader setting for the story is indicated in an exclamation of Elizabeth Temple: "The enterprise of Judge Temple is taming the very forests! How rapidly is civilization treading on the footsteps of nature!" When Elizabeth, with a burst of womanly sympathy for the imprisoned Leatherstocking, declares he must be innocent because of his inherent goodness, her father makes a crucial distinction: "Thou hast reason Bess, and much of it too, but thy heart lies too near thy head." The Judge himself means to pay Leatherstocking's fine, but he cannot brush aside the sentence of imprisonment which he imposed as the spokesman of necessary justice. He sends Elizabeth with a purse to visit the hunter and comfort him: ". . . say what thou wilt to the poor old man; give scope to the feelings of thy warm heart; but try to remember, Elizabeth, that the laws alone remove us from the condition of the savages; that he has been criminal, and that his judge was thy father."

Another interesting scene occurs when the sonless Judge Temple invites Oliver Effingham to enter his household as a secretary. Oliver hesitates. Richard, the Judge's pompous factotum, says in an aside to Elizabeth, "This, you see, cousin Bess, is the natural reluctance of a half-breed to leave the savage state. Their attachment to a wandering life is, I verily believe, unconquerable." The Judge remarks that the unsettled life of a hunter "is of vast disadvantage for temporal purposes, and it totally removes one from within the influences of more sacred things." But this rouses Leatherstocking, who bursts out:

> No, no, Judge . . . take him into your shanty in welcome, but tell him the raal thing. I have lived in the woods for forty long years, and have spent five years at a time without seeing the light of a clearing, bigger than a wind-row in the trees, and I should like to know where you'll find a man, in his sixty-eighth year, who can get an easier living, for all your betterments, and your deer-laws: and, as for honesty, or doing what's right between man and man, I'll not turn my back to the longest winded deacon on your patent.

This states the issue as succinctly as possible. Cooper is unable to solve it, and resorts to a compromise statement that represents exactly his unwillingness or inability to accept the full implications of the conflict he has stated. The Judge answers, "nodding good-naturedly at the hunter": "Thou art an exception, Leatherstocking; for thou hast a temperance unusual in thy class, and a hardihood exceeding thy years. But this youth is made of materials too precious to be wasted in the forest."

The Judge's reply expresses the unfailing regard for status which qualified Cooper's attitude toward the idea of nature as a norm. Leatherstocking, noble child of the forest, is nevertheless of inferior social status; whereas even in disguise, Oliver's gentle birth is palpable to the Judge's Falstaffian instinct. Leatherstocking began life as a servant of Major Effingham, and he is wholly illiterate. The fact that he speaks in dialect is a constant reminder of his lowly origin. It is true that the social status of the old hunter was not to prove significant during the long passages of adventure in *The Last of the Mohicans* and *The Prairie,* which deal with Indian warfare and the rescue of Cooper's distressed heroines from their captors. Here Leatherstocking's prowess with the rifle, his talents as a strategist, and his skill in following trails could be exploited with little regard for gradations in rank. But the problem of the hunter's status could not be permanently ignored. The response of readers to this symbol of forest freedom and virtue created a predicament for the novelist by revealing to him that his most vital character occupied a technically inferior position both in the social system and in the form of the sentimental novel as he was using it. The store of emotion associated with the vast wilderness in the minds of both Cooper and his audience was strikingly inharmonious with the literary framework he had adopted.

A more self-conscious or experimentally inclined writer might have found in this situation a challenge to devise a new form proceeding functionally from the materials. But Cooper was not the man to undertake a revolution, either in life or in literature. He chose a different course of action; he set about modifying the traditional form of the novel as far as he could without actually shattering it, and at the same time altering his materials as much as possible to make them fit.

Cooper's efforts to solve his problem can be traced in the last two novels of the Leatherstocking series, *The Pathfinder* and *The Deerslayer,* which appeared in 1840 and 1841. In *The Prairie,* published thirteen years before, he had described the death of Leatherstocking, and had at that time meant to abandon the character forever. This decision seems to have been due in part to the technical difficulty mentioned above, for in later years Cooper told his daughter he wished he had left out of *The Prairie* the genteel hero and heroine, Inez de Certavallos and Captain Middleton, retaining only those characters who properly belonged to the locale. But if the upper-class hero and heroine were to be omitted, and Leatherstocking was to be promoted to the post of official hero, how was the plot to be managed? It is at this point that Cooper's reluctance to break with the conventions of the sentimental novel becomes most glaringly apparent. A novel, according to canons which he considered binding, was a love story. The hero of the novel was the man who played the male lead in the courtship. If Leatherstocking was to be promoted to this rank, he must be made to fall in love with a heroine. In *The Pathfinder,* Cooper accordingly sets to work with great good will to exhibit Leatherstocking in love. The problem was to construct a female character, sufficiently refined and genteel to pass muster as a heroine, but sufficiently low in social status to receive the addresses of the hunter and scout without a shocking and indecent violation of the proprieties.

The object of Leatherstocking's affection, Mabel Dunham, is the daughter of a sergeant—not an officer—in the British army. When she is first introduced in the company of Cap, her seafaring uncle, who occupies "a station little, if any, above that of a common mariner," Cooper is careful to point out that Mabel is "a maiden of a class in no great degree superior to his own." She is, therefore, technically accessible to the lower-class Leatherstocking. But before she can qualify as a heroine Mabel has to be given some of the attributes of gentility. Cooper explains elaborately that upon the death of her mother Mabel had been taken in charge by the widow of a field-officer of her father's regiment. Under the care of this lady Mabel had acquired "some tastes, and many ideas, which otherwise might always have remained strangers to her." The results of this association

> were quite apparent in her attire, her language, her sentiments, and even in her feelings, though neither, perhaps, rose to the level of those which would properly characterize a lady. She had lost the coarser and less refined habits and manners of one in her original position, without having quite reached a point that disqualified her for the situation in life that the accidents of birth and fortune would probably compel her to fill.

In particular, Mabel had acquired a degree of sensibility that caused her to respond in approved fashion to the beauty of landscape—an index in Cooper almost as infallible as that of language for distinguishing the upper classes from the lower.

Ironically enough, the novelist's care in refining Mabel creates a fresh problem for him. The modifications of her character that qualify her for the role of heroine raise her somewhat above the actual range of Leatherstocking's manners and tastes. When Mabel's father proposes the marriage Leatherstocking is timid about it. He fears that a "poor ignorant woodsman" cannot hope to win the girl's affection. The sergeant compels the scout to admit that he is a man of experience in the wilderness, well able to provide for a wife; a veteran of proved courage in the wars; a loyal subject of the King. But Leatherstocking still demurs: "I'm afeard I'm too rude, and too old, and too wild like, to suit the fancy of such a young and delicate girl, as Mabel, who has been unused to our wilderness ways, and may think the settlements better suited to her gifts and inclinations." Pressed still further, Leatherstocking makes an avowal that throws a flood of light on Cooper's conception of the social relationships prevailing within his standard tableau of a captured heroine in the process of being rescued by Leatherstocking and a genteel hero:

> I have travelled with some as fair, and have guided them through the forest, and seen them in their perils and in their gladness; but they were always too much above me, to make me think of them as more than so many feeble ones I was bound to protect and defend. The case is now different. Mabel and I are so nearly alike, that I feel weighed down with a load that is hard to bear, at finding us so unlike. I do wish, serjeant, that I was ten years younger [the scout was then presumably in his early thirties], more comely to look at, and better suited to please a handsome young woman's fancy!

In short, "I am but a poor hunter, and Mabel, I see, is fit to be an officer's lady." She is indeed, as appears in the course of the story when the regimental quartermaster wants to marry her: or is she? Cooper subsequently causes this officer to prove a traitor, perhaps because of an unconscious impulse to punish him for his subversive disregard of class lines. In any event, when the actual moment of Leatherstocking's proposal arrives, Mabel's superior refinement is so unmistakable that it decides the issue. One of Cooper's very few valid comic inventions causes her, in her confusion, to use a more and more involved rhetoric that Leatherstocking cannot follow at all. He has to resort to his characteristic query, "Anan?" The match is quite unsuitable and in the end Leatherstocking has the exquisite masochistic pleasure of giving his blessing to her union with Jasper Western, the young, handsome, and worthy Great Lakes sailor.

If Leatherstocking could hardly be imagined as married, however, a feeling for symmetry would suggest that he at least might be shown as himself hopelessly beloved. This is the formula of the last novel of the series, *The Deerslayer,* which removes the obstacle of the hero's age by going back to the period of his early youth and thus represents the utmost possible development of Leatherstocking into a hero of romance. In this story he is loved by Judith Hutter, beautiful daughter of a somewhat coarse backwoodsman. But Judith's reputation is stained by past coquetries: she is obviously not an appropriate mate for the chaste Leatherstocking, and eventually is consigned to an offstage marriage with a British officer.

Despite these late experiments in depicting Leatherstocking in his youth, the persistent image of the hunter was that of his first appearance, as a man of venerable age. This trait of Leatherstocking was strengthened by whatever parallels were felt to exist between him and Daniel Boone. When John Filson's biography of Boone appeared in 1784, the Kentuckian, at fifty, already seemed a patriarchal figure, his active days of fighting in the past. The folk cult of Boone that developed after 1815 emphasized the picturesque conception of an octogenarian huntsman. Cooper himself gives testimony to the popular tendency to exaggerate Boone's age when he remarks in a note to the revised edition of *The Prairie* that the famous hunter emigrated to Missouri "in his ninety-second year." Boone was actually sixty-five when that event occurred. The many Western hunters created in the image of Leatherstocking who people Western fiction through most of the nineteenth century are characteristically of advanced age.

If Leatherstocking was, so to speak, intrinsically aged, this fact hindered his transformation into a hero of romance as seriously as did his low social status. Cooper was thus led to experiment with younger heroes who had Leatherstocking's vital relation to the forest, but were more easily converted into lovers. The character of Oliver Effingham in *The Pioneers* had early suggested the idea of a young hunter, wearing the garb and following the vocation of Leatherstocking. In *The Prairie* the impulse to double the role of the hunter in this fashion yields the character of Paul Hover, who, like Oliver, appears as an associate of Leatherstocking but is a real instead of merely a pretended child of the backwoods. Paul is a native of Kentucky and has a dialect that is the unmistakable badge of lowly status. It is true that he is merely a bee hunter rather than a hunter of deer and bear, but his sentiments concerning the rifle and his skill at marksmanship arouse Leatherstocking's enthusiastic approval. The most interesting thing about Paul is that, despite the presence in this novel of the official genteel hero and heroine, he is treated as an embryonic hero himself. He is young and handsome and virtuous, and in the end is allowed to marry Ellen Wade, who has carefully been given appearance, manners, speech, and sensibility superior to those of her crude companions—a distinct foreshadowing of Mabel Dunham's status and character in *The Pathfinder.* The Paul-Ellen love affair in *The Prairie,* in fact, seems to have furnished Cooper with the germ of his experiments in the two later novels.

Near the end of his life the novelist made a final effort to construct a story with a Western hero in *The Oak Openings* (1848). Like Paul Hover twenty years earlier, Ben Boden is a bee hunter of admirable character. In the absence of a genteel hero, however, he has to be refined somewhat beyond Paul Hover's level. This process is indicated in terms of the significant criterion of language. We are told twice in the first chapter that he used surprisingly pure English for one in his social class, and he has the further genteel trait of highly moral views concerning whiskey. Margaret Waring, the heroine, like Ellen Wade, is related to a coarse frontiersman, but is made as refined as possible within the iron limits of her status. Although *The Oak Openings* is one of Cooper's weakest novels, the fault lies in his uncontrollable tendency to preach on any current topic that happens to come into his mind. The basic conception is very promising.

The novel begins as if Cooper were determined to see what might have been made of *The Prairie* if he had carried out his project of omitting the genteel hero and heroine. If this conjecture is valid, then Ben Boden represents Cooper's ultimate achievement in trying to use a man of the wilderness as a technical hero. After the dangers of Indian warfare in early Michigan have been endured by the young lovers, the novelist feels compelled to add an epilogue that exhibits Ben Boden in his old age as a substantial farmer, a man of influence in the community, and a state senator. This career "shows the power of man when left free to make his own exertions." But if Boden's Jacksonian rise in the world gives retroactive sanction to Cooper's choice of him as a hero, it dissolves whatever imaginative connection he may have had with the mysterious and brooding wilderness.

Cooper's twenty-five years' struggle to devise a Wild Western hero capable of taking the leading role in a novel yielded the following results: (1) Since the basic image of Leatherstocking was too old for the purposes of romance, the novelist doubled the character to produce a young hunter sharing the old man's habits, tastes, skills, and, to some extent, his virtues. (2) The earliest of the young hunter companions of Leatherstocking, Oliver Effingham, could be a hero because he was revealed as a gentleman temporarily disguised as a hunter. That is, the hero retained all his genteel prerogatives by hereditary right, and at the same time claimed the imaginative values clustering about Leatherstocking by wearing a mask, a *persona* fashioned in the image of the old hunter. But this was so flagrant a begging of the question that Cooper could not be satisfied with it. He therefore undertook further development of the young hunter produced by doubling the character of Leatherstocking, and this process yielded (3) the Paul Hover-Ben Boden type of hero, a young and handsome denizen of the wilderness, following the gentler calling of a bee hunter and thus free from even the justifiable taint of bloodshed involved in Leatherstocking's vocation. This young Western hero is given a dialect less pronounced than that of Leatherstocking except in Leatherstocking's most exalted moments. His actual origin is left vague. He is not a member of the upper class, but he is nowhere specifically described as having once been a servant. Finally, the young hero has none of the theoretical hostility to civilization that is so conspicuous in Leatherstocking. These changes make it technically possible for a Wild Westerner to be a hero of romance, but they destroy the subversive overtones that had given Leatherstocking so much of his emotional depth. (pp. 59-70)

Henry Nash Smith, "Leatherstocking and the Problem of Social Order," in his Virgin Land: The

American West as Symbol and Myth, *Cambridge, Mass.: Harvard University Press, 1950, pp. 59-70.*

HOWARD MUMFORD JONES (lecture date 1955)

[*A distinguished twentieth-century American critic, Jones was awarded the Pulitzer Prize in literature for his study of the formation of American culture in* O Strange New World *(1964). He is also acclaimed for criticism in which he examines the relationship between America's literary and cultural development. In the following excerpt from a lecture delivered in Israel in 1955, he discusses Cooper's representation of the American frontier in the Leatherstocking novels.*]

[In the five Leatherstocking novels Cooper] fixed the image of the American wilderness upon the imagination of mankind. I have no sooner said this, however, than I must warn you that Cooper is much more than the author of these five novels. He published some fifty works, of which thirty-one are fiction; he is taken seriously by social historians as an interpreter of the social history of his time; and scholars are nowadays interesting themselves in his writing as first-rate material for intellectual history. Cooper's fictional technique is out-of-date, and his style falls into that awkward period between the clarity of eighteenth-century prose in America and the flexible and supple prose of the great nineteenth-century men—another reason why he is not now read as he once was read. It is not his merits or defects as a stylist that now concern us, but his interpretation of the frontier in the American sense of the term.

Of Cooper's many novels about a dozen present our theme. Of these the central group is the Leatherstocking Tales, written between 1823 and 1841. The order of their publication is not the chronological order of Leatherstocking's own life; and it is interesting to note in this connection that *The Deerslayer,* on which, so to speak, the dew of youth and innocence forever lies, was written only ten years before Cooper's death, whereas *The Pioneers,* which presents Natty Bumppo (Leatherstocking) in a rather unidealistic light, was published early. The order in which the novels should be read and the dates of their appearance are given in the following table:

(1)	*The Deerslayer*	1841
(2)	*The Last of the Mohicans*	1826
(3)	*The Pathfinder*	1840
(4)	*The Pioneers*	1823
(5)	*The Prairie*	1827

(p. 34)

[The] first fact to be noted concerning these famous novels is that they fixed the image of the virgin American wilderness and of the frontiersman upon the imagination of mankind. The frontiersman is, of course, Natty Bumppo or Leatherstocking. The image of the virgin land was equally powerful and may be illustrated from any number of passages in the novels. Here, for example, is the picture of the untouched American forest as presented in *The Last of the Mohicans:*

> The eye could range, in every direction, through the long and shadowed vista of the trees; but nowhere was any object to be seen that did not properly belong to the peaceful and slumbering scenery. Here and there a bird was heard fluttering among the branches of the beeches, and occasionally a squirrel dropped a nut, drawing the startled looks of the company, for a moment, to the place; but the instant the casual interruption ceased, the passing

air was heard murmuring above their heads, along that verdant and undulating surface of forest which spread itself unbroken, unless by stream or lake, over such a vast region of country. Across the tract of wilderness which lay between the Delawares and the village of their enemies, it seemed as if the foot of man had never trodden, so breathing and deep was the silence in which it lay.

Such was the endless American forest.

But if with Cooper we cross the Mississippi River and explore the Great Plains region which extends some four or five hundred miles from the base of the Rocky Mountains eastward, we have another image of immensity, this time from *The Prairie:*

> In the little valleys, which, in the regular formation of the land, occurred at every mile of their progress, the view was bounded on two of the sides by the gradual and low elevations which give name to the description of prairie . . . ; while on the others, the meagre prospect ran off in long, narrow, barren perspectives, but slightly relieved by a pitiful show of coarse, though somewhat luxuriant vegetation. From the summits of the swells, the eye became fatigued with the sameness and chilling dreariness of the landscape. The earth was not unlike the ocean, when its restless waters are heaving heavily, after the agitation and fury of the tempest have begun to lessen. There was the same waving and regular surface, the same absence of foreign objects, and the same boundless extent of the view. . . . Here and there a tall tree rose out of the [river] bottoms, stretching its naked branches abroad, like some solitary vessel; and, to strengthen the delusion, far in the distance appeared two or three rounded thickets, looming on the misty horizon like islands resting on the waters.

(pp. 35-6)

The Leatherstocking Tales are uneven, they are sometimes absurd, and the modern reader can only wish they were better written. Nevertheless, they are the prose epic of the American frontier. In them, if we read them in the order of Leatherstocking's biography, we can follow the receding frontier from east to west, and grow high-hearted as we look forward, melancholy as we look into the past. For in Cooper, as in most writers of frontier stories, the frontier is forever passing away—as, for instance, it is seen passing in that classic cowboy story, *The Virginian* by Owen Wister.

We make some general observations on these novels as works of art. We note, for example, that Cooper's landscape descriptions are carefully composed; and we are not surprised to learn that they are composed after the fashion of the first important school of American landscape painters, the so-called Hudson River artists, who strove on canvas for the same epic sweep, the same panoramic effect that Cooper achieves in such passages as the two I have just quoted. We note likewise that the structure of these novels is naif and that Cooper's management of the story is seldom more than an alteration of captures and escapes rising to a simple climax and resolution at the end of the book. But these captures, these thrilling escapes are problems in masculine action (except perhaps in *The Pioneers*); and though there are woman characters like Judith and Hetty (in *The Deerslayer*); though Cooper's female characters are not all tiresome examples of brainless gentility, as is sometimes alleged, this world of hunters, fighters and adventurers is, inevitably, almost overwhelmingly a world of men. Only in the case of Hester Bush, in *The Prairie,* do we have an adequate treatment of the frontier woman, and Hester is perhaps more like an avenging Old Testament heroine than she is like the actual American woman on the frontier.

Indeed, it is among his male characters that Cooper's triumphs are found. Not to dwell upon the unforgettable Leatherstocking, who is not so much a person as he is a mythological being like Uncle Tom, one can point to the equally unforgettable Ishmael Bush, husband of Hester, and to his sons; or to Hurry Harry and Tom Hutter in *The Deerslayer,* who sum up the paradox of the frontiersmen, compounded as they were of incongruous good and evil traits. Then there are the Indians. In later novels—for example, in *The Oak Openings*—Cooper took a far more disillusioned view of the red man than he took in the Leatherstocking series. His noble savage has been endlessly attacked as anthropological nonsense; and yet if Uncas is idealized, if Magua is too much an incarnation of villainy, how excellent they are as imaginative creations! To reduce them to the test and measurement of the social scientist or the historian is like taking the Jean Valjean of Victor Hugo as a case study in the French labor movement. For good or ill, certain character creations in these novels are permanent additions to the imaginary population of world literature.

One can, of course, go further in one's complaint. Not only are Cora and Uncas idealized, but the frontier is idealized also. Except in *The Pioneers* it is forever summer in these novels. The wilderness is without the terrific storms characteristic of North America, it is without mud, it is without sleet and snow and ice, just as it is without squalor, filth or depravity. Food is always plentiful and always available. No one thirsts. There is no human obscenity. The only cruelty is the clean cruelty of Indian warfare and Indian custom, which Cooper, or Leatherstocking for him, continually explains away as the product of the savage's peculiar "gifts." The frontier settlements are too clean for the realist, the sexual habits of the pioneers have, with minor exceptions, the prudishness of Victorianism, no one gets drunk, and no one is the worse for the eye-gouging, hand-to-hand conflicts among primitive-minded white men, which furnish occasion for comic sketches by the so-called humorists of the Southwestern frontier.

But we must take Cooper as we find him; and I am almost prepared to say that the dominant note of these novels is the note of melancholy at the perpetual passing of what was transient and beautiful. The frontier is presented as a kind of Eden, an earthly paradise that is forever being destroyed by the greed and malevolence of man. Again and again, as Leatherstocking moves westward before the advance of "civilization," he complains of the "wasty ways" of the settlements. Indeed, as we shall see, no small part of the dramatic conflict of *The Pioneers* arises from the tension between the careless village, destroying its own natural resources, and the farsighted plans of Judge Temple to preserve them. The judge is a premature conservationist and so, too, oddly enough, is Natty Bumppo, though the two disagree as to the nature of the conservation to be practised. But Leatherstocking's lament over the passing of the wilderness in this novel merely anticipates and does not contradict the melancholy of his old age as expressed in *The Prairie.* It is, if you will, the melancholy of all romanticism.

Recent scholarly and critical interest in Cooper has called at-

tention to certain intellectual elements in his work, which now figures importantly as material for the study of the history of ideas in American culture. Reserving *The Pioneers* for special discussion, let me turn to three important doctrines that tend to dominate the Leatherstocking tales: the theory of divine governance of the world; the theme of the ruins of empire; and the question of the moral cycle in the life of the individual.

It is said that Beethoven arrived at the knowledge of God through the love of nature, which is the school of the heart. Leatherstocking (and, oddly enough, the Indians) arrive at the same doctrine in the same way. In *The Last of the Mohicans* Leatherstocking is made to say, in reproof of David Gamut, the New Englander, who represents a false pedantry:

> Books! what have such as I, who am a warrior of the wilderness . . . to do with books? I have never read but in one, and the words that are written there are too simple and too plain to need much schooling . . . [This book] is open before your eyes . . . and he who owns it is not a niggard of its use. I have heard it said that there are men who read in books to convince themselves there is a God. . . . If any such there be, and he will follow me from sun to sun, through the windings of the forest, he shall see enough to teach him that he is a fool.

Is not this attitude towards the divine in nature reminiscent of many passages in the Book of Psalms? The influence of the Old Testament upon Cooper has never been calculated, but I suggest it is immense. The famous death-scene in *The Prairie* exhibits this same untroubled faith in the God of nature as it came from the hand of the Creator. This God it is who, amid the beauties of the sunset, calls Leatherstocking to his eternal home, the God to whom, in his last second on earth, the aged scout answers: "Here!" Immediately after this an aged Indian interprets the scene when he says:

> A valiant, a just, and a wise warrior, has gone on the path which will lead him to the blessed grounds of his people! . . . When the voice of the Wahconda [God] called him, he was ready to answer.

Here the revealing phrase is "the blessed grounds of his people." Obviously a simple appeal to the God of nature created unexpected difficulties for our novelist. Was the God of nature the God of the Indians, the God of Leatherstocking, or the God of organized Christianity in the settlements? The problem was to account for this diversity of interpretation and belief; and if it cannot be said that Cooper solved his dilemma, we must remember that he is an artist, not a metaphysician. His solution is emotional, not philosophic.

Cooper vaguely felt that Indian religion was all of a piece. All Indians, he assumed, worshipped the Great Spirit—the Wahconda of the passage just quoted. The anthropological incorrectness of this view is unimportant here; what is important is to realize that for Cooper, product of a romantic generation, primitive religion was an important generalized fact. Primitive religion, as exemplified by his Indians, has many virtues and many defects, but, at least as Cooper pictures it, Indian religion was consistent with itself. It accounted for Indian morality, Indian warfare, Indian tribal customs; and again and again we hear Leatherstocking explain (without condoning) Indian cruelty as the product of Indian religious notions. To Leatherstocking the Indian divinity was inferior to his own God, but Leatherstocking, unlike Christian missionaries, was perfectly able to tolerate, because he could understand, Indian action in the light of Indian belief.

The God of Leatherstocking was, so to speak, a somewhat more developed deity. Leatherstocking's schooling had been among the Moravians, so that the basis of his belief was a vague and diffused Christian concept, yet essentially Leatherstocking's God is the God of nature tinctured by Christianity but unconfined by Christian theology. To the extent that Leatherstocking read nature with the eyes of his schooling, God was the God of Hebraic and Christian tradition; to the extent that he read, as he says, in the book of nature, his God was a God who corresponds, in a queer way, to the Earth Spirit in *Faust*. The inherent incompatibility of these two interpretations is less important than Cooper's (and Leatherstocking's) belief that God is on the side of human dignity, that He favors individualism in the sense that to create an individual soul is to endow that soul with responsibility for conduct. For Leatherstocking the beauty of the universe (that is, of the unspoiled wilderness) was entirely consonant with this wide charity of his attitude towards Indian religion. What puzzled Leatherstocking was to discover that the white man, who ought to know better, abandoned responsibility and charity when he created the settlements from which the scout perpetually fled.

Cooper was a devout member of the Episcopal church. He did not, in his earlier novels, forget this fact—Episcopalianism is an important element in *The Pioneers,* and the satiric picture of David Gamut in *The Last of the Mohicans* is an expression of Cooper's Episcopalian distrust of New England Calvinism. And as he grew older, it seemed to him more and more important to insist upon the Trinitarian Deity of his particular faith. Only in the theological teachings of the *via media* of Anglicanism (and it should be remembered that the Oxford movement was launched in 1833, when Cooper was half-way through his creation of the Leatherstocking series) could he find a clearly defined deity and a firm control of human folly. The problem of converting the Indians and the frontiersmen to Trinitarian Christianity intervenes between the reader and the God of nature in *The Pioneers,* and becomes increasingly important in later novels—for example, in *The Oak Openings;* and in a very late novel, *The Sea Lions* (which, to be sure, has nothing to do with the American frontier) it is pushed to the verge of absurdity—the hero, originally a Unitarian, visits the Antarctic and becomes converted to a Trinitarian faith in the God of nature!

The Leatherstocking series turns not only upon a concept of deity but also upon a concept of history. We who in the Western world have been imaginatively stirred by theories of the wax and wane of cultures as set forth in the writings of Burckhardt, Spengler, and Toynbee have to remember that there is nothing specifically new in a cyclic doctrine of history. Immensely influential in the United States, where it enjoyed numerous printings in translation, Volney's famous study commonly called *The Ruins of Empire,* originally published in 1791, touched the literary imagination. Doubtless the vogue of the ruins of empire theme was increased by the cosmic drama of the French Revolution and the rise and fall of the Napoleonic empire. And of course the way for Volney had been prepared by the independent statement of the cyclical theory by such writers as Thomas Jefferson.

What is striking in connection with the frontier theme is the paradoxical application of this doctrine to the unpeopled wilderness. The human imagination was apparently unable to conceive of an empty New World. That was, so to speak, sheer waste of creative talent. If the earth was the Lord's, the fulness thereof was man's; and if the wilderness were empty, that emptiness was not aboriginal, it was merely a phase in the cycle of history. One should search the wilderness for evidence of vanished empires; and this, obediently enough, a poet like William Cullen Bryant, contemporary and friend of Cooper, set himself to do. In his youthful masterpiece, "Thanatopsis," he projects himself in imagination to the vast, unknown reaches of the Columbia River in the Pacific Northwest (he calls the river the Oregon), and yet, he says, the dead are there—that is, kings and peoples long since dissolved in dust. So in another notable poem, "The Prairies," descriptive of the Illinois country, Bryant interprets the fabulous moundbuilders, whose earthworks may be seen in Ohio and other parts of the Old Northwest, as if they were like the Aztecs or the Incas, creators of a lost and splendid empire that fell by virtue of the moral law which brings about the ruin of all states by time and folly.

Cooper adopts the same doctrine; and rather incongruously, in *The Prairie* (and the term here refers to the Great Plains), he sets the aged Leatherstocking to debating with another pedant, this time not a New England Calvinist, the theme of the ruins of empire. Dr. Obed Battius is a learned archaeologist, who tries to explain to Leatherstocking the ruins of empire idea. Leatherstocking thereupon seeks to fuse this doctrine with the doctrine of a natural God operating through the majestic processes of natural law. He tells Dr. Battius:

> Time was made by the Lord, and they were made by man. This very spot of reeds and grass, on which you now sit, may once have been the garden of some mighty king. It is the fate of all things to ripen, and then to decay. The tree blossoms, and bears its fruit, which falls, rots, withers, and even the seed is lost! Go, count the rings of the oak and of the sycamore; they lie in circles, one about another, until the eye is blinded in striving to make out their numbers, and yet a full change of the seasons comes round while the stem is winding one of those little lines about itself, like the buffalo changing his coat, or the buck his horns, and what does it all amount to? There does the noble tree fill its place in the forest, loftier, and grander, and richer, and more difficult to imitate, than any of your pitiful pillars of a thousand years, until the time which the Lord hath given it is full. . . . From that moment its beauty begins to perish. It lies another hundred years, a mouldering log, and then a mound of moss and earth; a sad effigy of a human grave. . . . As if that were not enough to convince man of his ignorance; and as though it were put there in mockery of his conceit, a pine shoots up from the roots of the oak, just as barrenness comes after fertility, or as these wastes have been spread, where a garden may have been created. Tell me not of your worlds that are old! it is blasphemous to set bounds and seasons . . . to the works of the Almighty . . .

I earlier remarked on the profound influence upon Cooper's imagination of the Old Testament. The influence of the Book of Job seems to me evident enough in a passage like this. You will note, moreover, that Leatherstocking (or Cooper) is not interested in the cyclic theory of history as a mechanical explanation of an empty wilderness, he tries to equate it with the moral law he finds in nature on the frontier. And whether or no one accepts this compound of cosmic ethics and historical explanation, no one who lives in Israel or who familiarizes himself with the exploration of the ruins of dead cities and ancient empires but must be struck by the parallel between, oddly enough, the frontier of the American wilderness, supposed by Cooper and Bryant to exemplify the ruins of empires, and the archaeology of Israel, where the ruins of empires theme is clearly and cogently exemplified.

But there is for Cooper in the frontier situation a second moral cycle: the moral cycle of the individual life. The unspoiled wilderness is innocent and lovely, and yet death lurks in this green innocence. How does it feel to kill in this new Eden? How shall man reconcile himself to the necessity of murder? The American critic, Yvor Winters, was, I think, the first to point to the importance Cooper gives this topic in *The Deerslayer* [in "Fenimore Cooper, or the Rains of Times," in his *In Defense of Reason*]; and I cannot do better than follow Mr. Winters' teaching as I try to explain the significance of this theme for an understanding of the American frontier.

Mr. Winters calls our attention to the importance of Chapter VII of *The Deerslayer.* Leatherstocking (here known as Deerslayer, since he has hitherto been only a hunter of animals, not a hunter of men) has spent the night asleep in a canoe on a tranquil lake, Glimmerglass. He wakes and starts into life another Adam, says Mr. Winters, an Adam in the midst of innocent nature. Writes Cooper:

> His rest had been deep and undisturbed: and when he awoke, it was with a clearness of intellect and a readiness of resources that were much needed. . . . The sun had not risen . . . but the vault of heaven was rich with the winning softness that 'brings and shuts the day,' while the whole air was filled with the carols of birds . . .

Deerslayer must now capture another canoe that has drifted to shore. This he attempts to do.

But an Indian now tries to kill him. Says Mr. Winters:

> The Indian in ambush fires and misses, attacks, and then, being outwitted by Deerslayer but allowed to escape, retreats to cover. Deerslayer is quickly on shore and behind a tree. Then commences the series of hesitations on the part of Deerslayer to kill this man, hesitations which arouse the wonder and then the contempt of the Indian. Deerslayer has never killed a man, yet he has embarked upon the career of a professional scout, and this Indian is his enemy. His wonder, his hesitation, the infallibility of his instincts and muscular reactions, the immense passivity of the morning wilderness, give the scene something of the tenderness and wonder of idyllic first love. But this is first death. . . . Deerslayer's consciousness of the significance of the fact which he momently withholds, and the pure spiritual isolation of the consciousness, the quiet clarity with which the whole is rendered, constitute . . . one of the most remarkable passages in . . . literature.

Deerslayer slays the Indian, decently arranges the body, gazes down upon it, and says:

> I didn't wish your life, red-skin, but you left me no choice between killing or being killed. Each party acted according to his gifts, I suppose, and blame can light on neither. . . . Well, this is my first battle with a human mortal . . . this is the beginning with the red-skins. . . . Why should I wish to

boast . . . ? It's slaying a human, although he was a savage; and how do I know he was a just Indian; and that he has not been taken away suddenly to anything but happy hunting-grounds.

Upon the untouched wilderness intrudes the perplexity of human motives, human emotions, and human imperfections, and what we have in this passage is a vague anticipation of Gide's gratuitous act with all its immense train of implications for happiness or evil. But the act is not wholly gratuitous. Death has been forced upon Leatherstocking by his choice of a human occupation—that of scouting; and though he might have anticipated the necessity of killing, he could not anticipate the necessity of killing this particular human being. In sum, the intricate question of human responsibility for a crucial act enters the wilderness. If man invades nature, by what code shall he live? Cooper refers to the problem in *The Prairie,* in the dramatic episode wherein Ishmael Bush stages his necessary, yet illegal, trial and condemnation of a murderer within his own family circle. Whether, in short, one considers the vast drama of history or the tiny circle of human life, the question of the intrusion of man into nature becomes central as the frontier is discovered, fought for, and settled.

I have remarked that *The Pioneers* stands apart from the other novels in the series, not only because it was written in 1823 and before Cooper had discovered the mythic possibilities in Leatherstocking, but also because this novel turns not upon the question of individual exploit but upon the problem of settlement. In what manner shall the wilderness be taken over? How shall the frontier area be controlled? This is, in part, the theme of the first of the stories.

The time runs from a snowy Christmas time in 1792 to a hot August of 1793. The place is Templeton in central New York, really the Cooperstown of the novelist's youth. We study the third or fourth stage of the development of the frontier—that which comes after the village as a social and economic entity has rendered obsolescent the hunter and the scout. This particular village has been created on a great landed estate; and the novel involves two principal conflicts: that between the unthinking mass of villagers and the proprietor of this estate—a conflict between populism and benevolism; and that between order, law, and propriety characteristic of settled communities, and the "natural" ethics of the wilderness as exemplified by Natty Bumppo and Indian John (the Chingachgook of *The Last of the Mohicans*). And Cooper, who is more impartial than some of his critics allow him to be, sees the claims of all four elements in the conflict. For example, the law of the wilderness cannot conquer the civil code by which social man must live; and yet, in some sense, the hunter and the Indian retain a higher ethical sanction inasmuch as they shelter young Effingham and his father, whom they wrongly believe to have been despoiled by Judge Temple.

In the language of contemporary criticism the texture of *The Pioneers* is "denser" than that of its successors; that is, the novel, upon inspection, reveals a series of layers of meaning. The plot structure, however, does not differ essentially from that in other Cooper novels. We have the same succession of rescue, escape, capture and revelation, and the motheaten device of mistaken identity serves us, as the climax and resolution appear. But *The Pioneers* is more than another adventure story. The autobiographical element is strong. Judge Temple is modeled upon Judge Cooper, the novelist's father, and the account of the relations between the village and the proprietor owes much to the actual history of Cooperstown. Moreover, the charm of the story partly lies in the nostalgia of the writer for what has vanished. Finally, more than any other of the series, *The Pioneers* is in the tradition of Smollett. Indian John and Natty Bumppo are not only far from being romanticized, there is even in them a touch of surliness such as one finds in the novels of the Scotsman. The Smollett influence is especially felt in the creation of the minor figures, who are grotesques as Commodore Trunnion is a grotesque. There are a comic Frenchman, a comic German, a comic doctor, ill-natured comic servants, and a comic "projector" or universal genius in the case of Richard Jones.

But these are aesthetic rather than philosophic considerations; and I desire, in concluding this discussion, to call your attention to the two or three leading intellectual issues of *The Pioneers.* The first may be phrased as finding the answer to the question: what is the proper political form of a frontier settlement? Cooper does not believe in pure democracy. Templeton is composed of elements from Europe, from New England (Cooper distrusted New Englanders), and from what I may call the backwash of the frontier—men who, in an earlier phase of the frontier, might be acceptable because they live under natural law, but who, not realizing that civic responsibility now enters the problem, tend to lawlessness. The talk in the tavern and around the lake during the fishing scene shows both the danger such a society holds because of the opportunity for demagoguery, and the need for wise leadership. By and large the populace is ungrateful to Judge Temple, and this notion that the people are always ungrateful is to increase in importance in other, later books by Cooper. The novelist conveys to us an acute sense of the cultural gap between the hall and the village—between, that is, the small ruling group, and the democratic many, and so dramatizes the question of leadership. Judge Temple makes his mistakes—for example, he is so poor a judge of men as to make the flighty Richard Jones a sheriff, but the novelist's sympathy is clearly with him, and not with the many-headed multitude. Cooper is here unable to solve the problem of communication between the governing group and the uncultivated majority; the novel ends in melodrama, rather than in genuine cultural reconciliation.

But the problem of the frontier settlement is not only one of political form, it is also one of economic policy. Temple—and Cooper—insist upon conserving natural resources. The villagers are gravely at fault. They waste the wild game, the birds, the fish, and the lumber. So far the drama is simple. But the group around Natty Bumppo is caught between these two forces. It is too much to expect the old hunter to acquiesce in the, to him, artificial prohibition against killing deer; yet Leatherstocking is essentially of the judge's party, though neither he nor the judge is aware of it. A naked policy of *laissez faire,* Cooper seems to say, must bring about the speedy ruin of the frontier settlement. But how impose a wise restraint upon men accustomed to follow the law of nature, not the law of the land?

This leads to the third ideational problem of the book: the moral adaptation of the new settlement. The ebullient individual must be controlled, but what forces are to control him? Obviously, law and religion; and Cooper presents and dramatizes both these elements. Thus the proprietor is *Judge* Temple; that is, his traditions are the traditions of Anglo-Saxon law. He is the embodiment of civil order—that civil order which leads to Bumppo's imprisonment. The civil order is capable of misinterpretation, since in Bumppo's view Temple is the proprietor of Templeton only by legal chicanery; but as if to vindicate the ideal nature of justice, we learn that Temple is in fact merely holding the title until the legitimate owner appears. From this point of view Natty is totally wrong.

The other guardian of moral order is the church; and here many readers of *The Pioneers* miss the central significance of Chapter xi, which describes the service in Richard Jones's rather rickety church building. The service is in form Episcopalian, and Cooper wants us to understand that this chapter is to furnish the moral base from which to measure ethical deviation and ethical norm. For this reason he gives the sermon in full. The rector's address is filled with charity for all, but it concludes with a firm insistence upon the disciplinary nature of religion and of the church. He says:

> Wise and holy men, the fathers of our religion, have expended their labors in clearing what was revealed from the obscurities of language, and the results of their experience and researches have been embodied in the form of evangelical discipline. That this discipline must be salutary, is evident from the view of the weakness of human nature. . . .

This is a far remove from Leatherstocking's scorn of bookishness, expressed in the passage from *The Last of the Mohicans* I earlier quoted. That Cooper took Trinitarian Christianity seriously is evident if one reads the novels of his later years.

The great task of the law and of the church was to hold human selfishness in check. An agrarian society was, Cooper thought, less liable to be a selfish society than is a commercial one; and what is wrong in Templeton is the entrance of the trading spirit into what might have been an agrarian utopia. To understand his thinking in this respect one can usefully refer to that strange anti-Utopia of his later years, *The Crater.* On that imaginary island a balanced agrarian economy is developed under the equivalent of a landed gentleman (like Judge Temple), but there, as in Templeton, the spirit of trade—that is, of exploitation—creeps in. What is trade? By 1847, when he published this book, Cooper was clear about the evil nature of trade, which occasions "an exaggerated estimate of self." He drops all pretense at fiction to declare in his own person:

> Trade, perhaps the most corrupt and corrupting influence of life—or, if second to anything in evil, second only to politics—is proclaimed to be the great means of humanizing, enlightening, liberalizing, and improving the human race! Now against this monstrous mistake in morals, we would fain raise our feeble voice in sober remonstrance. That the intercourse, which is a consequence of commerce, may, in certain ways, liberalize a man's views, we are willing to admit; though at the same time, we shall insist there are better modes of attaining the same ends.

In sum, for Cooper a balanced and happy national life can be developed out of frontier conditions by the rich development of an agrarian economy, but woe to the nation that sacrifices agriculture to commerce and to an exploitative and spending economy!

What Cooper does is in curious ways to illustrate by anticipation certain elements in the frontier theory of Frederick Jackson Turner. He shows in dramatic action the force of the frontier in molding a society. He is not, however, content

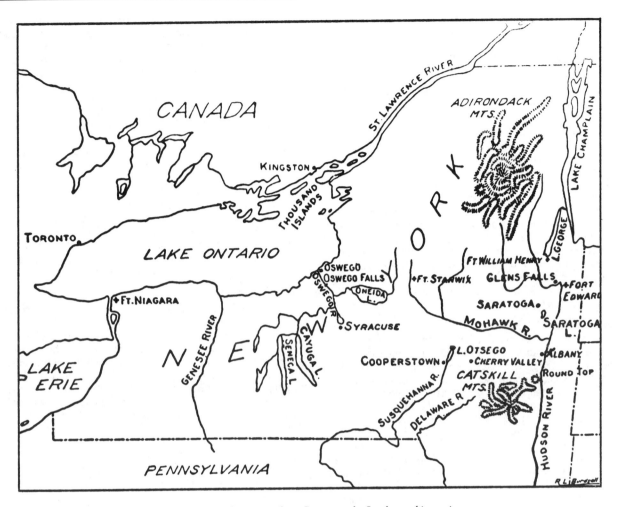

Map depicting the region where Cooper set the Leatherstocking series.

with the play of economic determinism. He believes that sagacity should direct the process of developing the frontier settlement, and for him, at least, sagacity is a direct function of certain ideal, certain non-deterministic elements. Among these are the perpetual recognition of God as the creator of nature, and the continual guidance of the new community by ancient traditions of law and of religion. (pp. 37-50)

> Howard Mumford Jones, "James Fenimore Cooper," in his The Frontier in American Fiction: Four Lectures on the Relation of Landscape to Literature, *The Magness Press, The Hebrew University, 1956, pp. 26-50.*

EDWIN FUSSELL (essay date 1965)

[*Fussell is an American educator and critic. In the following excerpt, he examines Cooper's development of an increasingly complex historical view of westward migration in the Leatherstocking novels.*]

Of the five Leatherstocking Tales, three were composed in the 1820's and two in the early 1840's. The development of the series is usually described as a movement from the realistic to the Romantic; from personal experience to myth (though the last novel reverts to the Cooperstown region of the first);

from the hard facts of old age to the pleasing possibilities of youth. Each of these descriptions is true, but it is more comprehensively true that Cooper increasingly generalized his materials, and in doing so advanced from a fairly conventional American account of the Westward Movement to a far more imaginative, complex, and critical view. The first novel opens with an optimistic account of pioneering: "The whole district is hourly exhibiting how much can be done, in even a rugged country, and with a severe climate, under the dominion of mild laws, and where every man feels a direct interest in the prosperity of a commonwealth, of which he knows himself to form a distinct and independent part. . . . Only forty years have passed since this whole territory was a wilderness." The last one ends: "We live in a world of transgressions and selfishness, and no pictures that represent us otherwise can be true; though, happily for human nature, gleamings of that pure Spirit in whose likeness man has been fashioned, are to be seen relieving its deformities, and mitigating, if not excusing, its crimes." As Leatherstocking remarks in the same book: " 'What a thing is power! . . . and what a thing it is, to have it, and not to know how to use it!' " After a trip to Michigan in 1847, Cooper moralized again in the preface to ***The Oak Openings; or, The Bee-Hunter*** (1848): "There is nothing imaginary in the fertility of the west. . . . Time may lessen that wonderful fertility, and bring the whole country more on a level; but there it now is, a glorious gift from God, which it is devoutly to be wished may be accepted with due gratitude, and with a constant recollection of His unwavering rules of right and wrong, by those who have been selected to enjoy it." Moral accountability was the gist of Cooper's letter to his countrymen.

The Pioneers; or, The Sources of the Susquehanna (1823), in which Cooper drew most heavily on memories of his Cooperstown boyhood, stands somewhat apart from the other Leatherstocking Tales. It is not an adventure story, but . . . a pastoral, closer to sketch than to romance, and more expository than narrative. Except toward the end, there is little plot, but rather a series of loosely-connected episodes illustrating the rough charms of life in a frontier community. There is little of the open violence which dominates the later Tales, but instead an almost continuous air of comedy. In *The Pioneers,* Cooper concentrates on the amity and near-amity existing among men joined in a struggle with nature. Despite their fallings out, Leatherstocking and the aristocratic Judge Temple are more often than not on the same side—especially with respect to the conservation of natural resources—and it is difficult to tell which of them is meant by the title. Very likely it refers to both.

Within the relatively simple and apparently innocuous overview of happy pioneering, Cooper is quietly subversive. At the end, the villainous scamp Hiram Doolittle pulls up stakes and departs for the farther West, presumably as one of "that band of Pioneers, who are opening the way for the march of our nation across the continent." That phrase, which magniloquently and sentimentally concludes the novel, ostensibly refers to Leatherstocking, who has been driven from his home of forty years by a civilization in which Doolittles thrive, and who has no intention whatever of opening the way for the march of any such people. Throughout *The Pioneers* the Americans are said to have "dispossessed" the Indians, and indeed the novel slyly hints that the Fall of Man and private land ownership are practically coterminous, at least in this country; if so, then further progress will entail further costs. (" 'I never know'd preaching come into a settlement, but it made game scarce, and raised the price of gunpowder.' ") (pp. 31-3)

The Pioneers is for the most part a comic story, and the comedy derives from the incompetence of its presumably civilized citizenry. In the opening scene, the Great Land Chief (Temple) "with a practised eye and steady hand, drew a trigger; but the deer dashed forward undaunted, and apparently unhurt." The deer is killed by Leatherstocking's rifle, whose owner thereupon "drew his bare hand across the bottom of his nose, and again opened his enormous mouth with a kind of inward laugh." This silent, ironic laughter is continuous throughout the Leatherstocking Tales, and signifies the hero's superiority to his betters. As it turns out, Judge Temple has accidentally shot Oliver Edwards. On the way home, Richard Jones cannot manage the horses, and the whole party must be rescued from his jaunty ineptitude by the victim of the first accident. The doctor who dresses Edwards' wound has acquired reputation (and a medical education) by repairing the wounds of woodcutters, on whom the trees they were felling have unaccountably fallen; the same doctor steals his best remedies from Indian John Mohegan, to whom he condescends. (pp. 34-5)

The farce of incompetence is counterpointed by the tragedy of misunderstanding. Some of the misunderstandings are factitious and remediable, such as the confusions about Ed-

wards' identity and Temple's probity. Through most of the novel, the Judge is viewed in a false light, enabling Cooper perpetually to insult him and then exonerate him in the end. But if Temple's rectitude is ultimately vindicated, his intelligence is not. His overestimation of the law is a serious error in philosophy, and his nearly total inability to assess the character and control the behavior of his underlings is an equally serious defect of moral prudence. Deluded by superficial notions of justice, he relentlessly pursues a course of action whose injustice is apparent to the meanest intelligence. Apparently Cooper already sensed the truth he was to articulate a decade later, upon returning to the United States from Europe: "Every hour I stay at home convinces me more and more that society has had a summerset, and that the *élite* is at the bottom!" Temple's legal proceedings against Natty Bumppo are simply one long train of judicial errors, while Natty Bumppo's indictment of the society which permits such persecution is unanswerable. At the end, with almost inconceivable stupidity, Temple benevolently orders a "pursuit" of Leatherstocking, who, knowing better, has already entered the forest.

But if Judge Temple is not the hero of the book, he is clearly at its center, as the representative American faced with the problem of Leatherstocking; it is not Leatherstocking's failure to adapt himself to American civilization that constitutes the problem, however, as it would have for a conformist like Crèvecœur, but the fact that Leatherstocking's existence prefigures the possibility of a morally higher American civilization. We are told that Marmaduke Temple's knowledge "was eminently practical, and there was no part of a *settler's* life, that he was not familiar with"; in this dimension, Temple is the William Cooper of *A Guide in the Wilderness,* but there, probably, the resemblance ends, for otherwise this fictional guide in the wilderness is hopelessly lost. He defines Leatherstocking as " 'an exception . . . for thou hast a temperance unusual in thy class,' " unwittingly describing the transcendence (of limitation or of contradiction) which is the inner principle of Cooper's hero and the real reason Judge Temple, who has no such talent for development, will never understand him. In a social situation characterized by bewildering change, Temple's steady good sense and fixed good intentions are worthless or worse. (pp. 35-6)

Leatherstocking does not dominate *The Pioneers,* as he dominates the later Tales, however fervently Cooper may subscribe to his opinions. Whereas in every subsequent Tale the other characters depend on Leatherstocking, in this one he helplessly depends on them, and especially on their intelligence, imagination, and good will, which are not invariably forthcoming. How easily he can be victimized in such a place as Templeton is suggested by the weakness of the people who victimize him. And perhaps as a result of the subsidiary role, his many incipient virtues are adulterated with faults typical of a testy, old, conservative crank; indeed, in several ways, Leatherstocking is a burlesque of Judge Temple's Federalist obsessions. Although in Elizabeth Temple's eyes, he is her knight, Sir Leatherstocking, he is by other people as maliciously slandered as the Judge; but, on the whole, he is too isolated from Templeton to affect its communal life one way or another. Like Indian John, he is a pathetic figure, first in his hut, then in his cave, and finally in his flight from the settlements, their questionable denizens, their wasty ways, and the sound of their axes and hammers. Upon Elizabeth Temple he invokes the blessing of " 'the Lord that lives in clearings as well as in the wilderness,' " a singular concession for him; and then, waving his hand, he disappears. We never see him in the settlements again.

The scene of *The Last of the Mohicans: A Narrative of 1757* (1826) is notably different from the scene of *The Pioneers.* Although "since the period of our tale, the active spirit of the country has surrounded it with a belt of rich and thriving settlements . . . none but the hunter or the savage is ever known, even now, to penetrate its rude and wild recesses." The increase in violence is also notable, for this is "emphatically, the bloody arena, in which most of the battles for the mastery of the colonies were contested"; typically, none of the various contestants was by 1826 in possession of it. Elsewhere, Cooper speaks of "romantic, though not unappalling beauties," and indeed the word for this country, the behaviors it engenders, and the novel which records them, is *implacable.* It is thus at least triply ironic that the woods into which small bands of warriors disappear—and sometimes reappear—seem "as still . . . as when they came fresh from the hands of their Almighty Creator." Of all the Leatherstocking Tales, *The Last of the Mohicans* is most unrelentingly bloody, cruel, and savage.

Superficially considered, forest violence is natural for red men but unnatural for white, as Hawkeye remarks after one of Chingachgook's more sophisticated scalpings. On this assumption, forest violence indirectly reveals the white man's inability to adapt to a realm of existence for which his virtues and experiences have all too inadequately prepared him; throughout the novel, he is portrayed as irrelevant, ineffectual, and irresponsible. Captain Duncan Heyward, the presumed conventional hero, is frequently a comic target not essentially different in function from such an obvious one as David Gamut, the Puritan singing-master. " 'Is there nothing that I can do?' demanded the anxious Heyward," ever eager to assume a heroic role for which he is not cut out. " 'You!' repeated the scout, who, with his red friends, was already advancing in the order he had prescribed; 'yes, you can keep in our rear, and be careful not to cross the trail.' " Another time, Leatherstocking is obliged to warn him: " 'If you judge of Indian cunning by the rules you find in books, or by white sagacity, they will lead you astray, if not to your death.' " Throughout *The Last of the Mohicans,* the respectable white characters commit one act of folly after another, from the consequences of which they must be rescued by Hawkeye, Chingachgook, or Uncas. (pp. 39-40)

The genuine heroes are determined both pragmatically (by competence) and ethically (by loyalty to their "gifts"). In a rare moment of insight, Heyward enunciates the official doctrine of moral judgment: " 'As bright examples of great qualities are but too uncommon among Christians, so are they singular and solitary with the Indians; though, for the honour of our common nature, neither are incapable of producing them.' " Uncas is the ultimate hero of this novel, and in nearly every respect Leatherstocking's superior. " 'I, who am a white man without a cross,' " Leatherstocking proudly declares himself, page after tedious page, with no awareness of the ironic pun he always makes on "cross," once even assuring us that his blood is not tainted " 'by the cross of a bear.' " Insofar as miscegenation is a major theme of this tragic novel, the attitudes of Colonel Munro and of his daughter Cora are controlling. Cora's all-too-white half-sister Alice is no more the heroine than Heyward is the hero, as even her language shows (" 'Father! father! . . . it is I! Alice! thy own Elsie! spare, oh! save, your daughters!' "). Cora, on the contrary,

commands a style so sharply pertinent that it survives even errors of judgment, such as her initial confidence in Magua: " 'Should we distrust the man, because his manners are not our manners, and that his skin is dark!' coldly asked Cora." She is the only person in the novel who makes the same point with sufficient force about Uncas: " 'Who, that looks at this creature of nature, remembers the shades of his skin!' " Everybody else, it seems. "A short, and apparently an embarrassed, silence succeeded this characteristic remark."

Far from attacking miscegenation, as has often been alleged, Cooper surreptitiously advocates it. On the one hand, *The Last of the Mohicans* presents for our dismayed contemplation example on example of pure and bloody savagery, red and white; on the other hand, it presents for our admiring recognition the noble Uncas nobly in love with the nobly dark Cora. (pp. 41-2)

In the course of a long harangue, Magua assures his people that God created Negroes to be slaves, and white men to be exploiters. " 'Some the Great Spirit made with skins brighter and redder than yonder sun,' continued Magua . . . 'and these did he fashion to his own mind.' " If Cooper sometimes seems nearly to espouse Magua's view, it is not only because Cooper has so thoroughly identified himself with Uncas, and with the elegiac tone promoted by Uncas' premature death, but because Cooper is bent on deriving from this tragic and elegiac action as many ominous ambiguities as he can. Uncas is often a surrogate of the author. "The Mohican chief maintained his firm and haughty attitude; and his eye, so far from deigning to meet her [an old squaw's] inquisitive look, dwelt steadily on the distance, as though it penetrated the obstacles which impeded the view, and looked deep into futurity." The ancient Tamenund is another spokesman for the novelist. Sympathetically responding to the appeal of Cora, whose mention of her own tainted blood has touched the old man's heart, Tamenund speaks out until it hurts: " 'I know that the pale-faces are a proud and hungry race. I know that they claim, not only to have the earth, but that the meanest of their colour is better than the Sachems of the red man.' " It is perhaps for this reason that the white man does *not* have the earth, as the novel so abundantly demonstrates. " 'The dogs and crows of their tribes,' continued the earnest old chieftain, without heeding the wounded spirit of his listener, whose head was nearly crushed to the earth, in shame, as he proceeded, 'would bark and caw, before they would take a woman to their wigwams, whose blood was not of the colour of snow. But let them not boast before the face of the Manitto too loud. They entered the land at the rising, and may yet go off at the setting sun!' " In the last paragraph of the book, Tamenund speaks again; the tenor of his speech is the same, the application of it even more mysteriously alarming: " 'The pale-faces are masters of the earth, and the time of the red-men has not yet come again.' " Whatever else this speech is taken to mean, it surely means Cooper's recognition that the nobility of the outraged American Indian is now passing to the major American writer, defined as major by his moral antipathy to the Westward course of American empire and by his acts of enlightened counteraggression against it. According to Leatherstocking, " 'Nothing but vast wisdom and unlimited power should dare to sweep off men in multitudes.' " *The Last of the Mohicans* shows us limited power, and almost no wisdom at all.

The various themes of the novel are joined, and more or less resolved, in the closing chapter. Peace has finally been restored to the wilderness, but Cora, Uncas, and Magua have been killed in the process. (Uncas dies "with a look of inextinguishable scorn.") Of Magua, nothing more is said; of Cora and Uncas, much. Delaware girls strew with forest flowers the corpse of "ardent, high souled, and generous Cora." At "the opposite space of the same area" sits Uncas, "as in life." Soon the Delaware maidens commence "a sort of chant in honour of the dead," in which they observe that Cora's and Uncas' deaths, so nearly coincident, "render the will of the Great Spirit too manifest to be disregarded." Then "they advised her to be attentive to the wants of her companion, and never to forget the distinction which the Manitto had so wisely established between them." The Manitto's distinction is between male and female, not between Indian and white man. "That she [Cora] was of a blood purer and richer than the rest of her nation, any eye might have seen." The Delaware girls allude but briefly to the weeping Alice. "They doubted not that she was lovely in the eyes of the young chief [Heyward], whose skin and whose sorrow seemed so like her own; but, though far from expressing such a preference, it was evident, they deemed her less excellent than the maid they mourned."

Hawkeye piously rejects the Indian view "of the future prospects of Cora and Uncas"; Colonel Munro, who has been unable to follow the exact meaning of the funeral chant, responds with greater magnanimity: " 'Say to these kind and gentle females, that a heart-broken and failing man, returns them his thanks. Tell them, that the Being we all worship, under different names, will be mindful of their charity; and that the time shall not be distant, when we may assemble around his throne, without distinction of sex, or rank, or colour!' " The dubious scout transmits the message in such a form "as he deemed most suited to the capacities of his listeners." Then, as in the beginning, "all the white men, with the exception of Hawk-eye, passed from before the eyes of the Delawares, and were soon buried in the vast forests of that region." And so, "deserted by all of his colour," Hawkeye remains, with Chingachgook, the bereaved father of the last of the Mohicans, who calls himself " 'a blazed pine, in a clearing of the pale-faces.' " But there is one final word. " 'No, no,' cried Hawk-eye . . . 'not alone. The gifts of our colours may be different, but God has so placed us as to journey in the same path. I have no kin, and I may also say, like you, no people. He was your son, and a red-skin by nature; and it may be, that your blood was nearer;—but if ever I forget the lad. . . .' " At the end of the novel, Hawkeye alienates himself from his people, transcends the limits of American civilization (as understood by Parkman and such types), and becomes the true hero of the new American civilization hopefully coming into existence through his renunciation and transcendence. The nobility of Uncas passes to him, as the nobility of Uncas' race passes to Cooper.

American civilization continued to wander Westward, and Cooper with it. Much more explicitly than any other Leatherstocking Tale, *The Prairie* (1827) is dominated by the Westward Movement. The action is latest in time—soon after the Louisiana Purchase—and therefore farthest West, in the absolute sense of the term (location). It is also farthest West, in the relative sense of the term (direction), for in no other Leatherstocking Tale is so much attention paid to emigration. As soon as the United States were in possession of Louisiana, "swarms of that restless people, which is ever found hovering on the skirts of American society, plunged into the thickets. . . . The inroad from the east was a new and sud-

den out-breaking of a people, who had endured a momentary restraint, after having been rendered, nearly, resistless by success." Following the trail of Daniel Boone and his fictional follower Leatherstocking, settlers from Ohio and Kentucky file "deeper into the land, in quest of that which might be termed, without the aid of poetry, their natural and more congenial atmosphere." It is as one particular exemplification of this general exodus that we first behold the notorious Bush family, "a band of emigrants seeking for the Eldorado of their desires." On first acquaintance, their desires seem to be almost wholly for destruction; making a camp, "they stripped a small but suitable spot of its burden of forest, as effectually, and almost as promptly, as if a whirlwind had passed along the place."

Cooper halfheartedly pays homage to the social-stages-of-history theory. "The march of civilization with us, has a strong analogy to that of all coming events, which are known 'to cast their shadows before.' The gradations of society, from that state which is called refined to that which approaches as near barbarity as connection with an intelligent people will readily allow, are to be traced from the bosom of the states, where wealth, luxury and the arts are beginning to seat themselves, to those distant, and ever-receding borders which mark the skirts, and announce the approach, of the nation, as moving mists precede the signs of day." Traveling Westward, the Bushes almost automatically descend from one social stage to the next lower: " ' 'Tis time to change our natur's,' he [Ishmael Bush] observed to the brother of his wife . . . 'and to become ruminators.' " The Indians also descend the social stages, thanks to "that engrossing people who were daily encroaching on their rights, and reducing the Red-men of the west from their state of proud independence to the condition of fugitives and wanderers." As early as 1804, Leatherstocking has reached the Pacific Ocean and recoiled, thus anticipating the achievement and return of Lewis and Clark, whose expedition is in progress simultaneously with the action of *The Prairie* and is several times alluded to.

" 'I have seen the waters of the two seas! . . . America has grown, my men, since the days of my youth, to be a country larger than I once had thought the world itself to be.' " As Leatherstocking adds, in a passage worth meditating: " 'I came west in search of quiet. It was a grievous journey that I made.' " Leatherstocking is also an avatar of the god Terminus, a deity Western orators were fond of invoking to allay the fears of the anxious. He is first seen in *The Prairie* as a man against the sky, outlined "between the heavens and the earth," with the intention and effect of blocking further American headway. He dies at a Pawnee village in a scene strongly resembling the scene of his advent, with "the light of the setting sun" falling "upon the solemn features." Unquestionably, this is his country, which perhaps partly explains Cooper's confounding prairies, plains, and Great American Desert, a concept recently bequeathed the public through erroneous reports from the Long Expedition. The mere fact of Cooper's misinformation about Western American topography is far less significant than the zeal with which he prosecutes a golden opportunity to frustrate the Great American Ego. "Nature," he is pleased to proclaim, and endlessly to reiterate, "had placed a barrier of desert to the extension of our population in the west." Obviously Cooper thought, as Leatherstocking thinks, that " 'the Lord has placed this barren belt of prairie, behind the states, to warn men to what their folly may yet bring the land!' " As Leatherstocking rhetorically inquires: " 'What will the Yankee

Choppers say, when they have cut their path from the eastern to the western waters, and find that a hand, which can lay the 'arth bare at a blow, has been here and swept the country, in very mockery of their wickedness. They will turn on their tracks like a fox that doubles, and then the rank smell of their own footsteps will show them the madness of their waste.' "

As a consequence of Cooper's idiosyncratic view of the Westward Movement, and of his identification of it with Leatherstocking as a sort of moralistic *ne plus ultra,* the West—what remains of it—becomes an idealized neutral territory or testing ground for heroes. Except for Leatherstocking, all the white characters are in the end, by Cooper's dispensation, backtrailers. Following his gift, which is small, the comic pedant Dr. Bat becomes "a *savant* in one of the maritime towns." The Bushes are also turned back, and are last seen "pursuing their course towards the settlements. As they approached the confines of society, the train was blended among a thousand others." Middleton and Inez return home (presumably Louisiana), taking with them Ellen Wade (several times called a girl of the settlements) and Paul Hover. This former borderer, bee-hunter, and game-cock of the wilderness, "is actually at this moment a member of the lower branch of the legislature of the State where he has long resided." In *The Pioneers* a wide variety of types, none of them excessively heroic, was happily engaged in taming the wilderness; *The Prairie* suggests that taming the wilderness is the prerogative of those who have tamed themselves, and that these, paradoxically, neither wish nor need to tame it. Here is an aristocracy for which practically no one will ever desire to qualify, and a vastly different world of assumptions from the property-centered *Pioneers.* From that world, Leatherstocking was exiled to the West as a nuisance; now he takes his revenge. He *is* the West, and the other Americans have not caught up with him. Most of them never will. Those who do will not like it. Cooper's Western landscape—Far Western, in 1827—is flat, treeless, semi-arid, empty, silent; more particularly, it seems to be associated with moonlight, driving clouds, birds of prey, and, in episode after episode, wind. " 'For here may natur' be seen in all its richness, trees alone excepted. Trees, which are to the 'arth, as fruits to a garden; without them nothing can be pleasant or thoroughly useful.' " The landscape of *The Prairie* is the basic metaphorical landscape of the entire series, its special starkness dependent on Cooper's studied removal from it of all signs of fruition.

For the third successive time in the Leatherstocking Tales, there is a Last Survivor, Leatherstocking himself, who dies after announcing: " 'I am without kith or kin in the wide world! . . . When I am gone, there will be an end of my race.' " (Whatever he means by race, it is neither family nor nation.) Perhaps Cooper's desire to mitigate an increasing sense of loss and loneliness explains the extraordinary number of "father images" in the novel, which derive not only from the relations of patriarchal Ishmael Bush with his many sons, but more importantly from Natty Bumppo's attempts to establish a continuous relation with humanity before he dies. He adopts the heroic young Pawnee Hard-Heart (" 'I have no son, but Hard-Heart' "), though to do so he must thwart the rival intentions of an elderly Sioux. " 'I have made him my son,' " Leatherstocking explains, " 'that he may know that one is left behind him.' " (Of course, it is Hard-Heart who is left behind.) (pp. 43-50)

Leatherstocking's death is rendered through symbolism reminiscent of the frontier tableau defining Oliver Edwards in

The Pioneers. "Middleton [officer and gentleman in the United States Army, and link with Leatherstocking's early career along the frontiers of white civilization] and Hard-Heart [inheritor of the roles of Chingachgook and Uncas] placed themselves on the opposite sides of his seat and watched with melancholy solicitude the variations of his countenance. . . . There were moments, when his attendants doubted whether he still belonged to the living. Middleton . . . fancied he could read the workings of the old man's soul in the strong lineaments of his countenance. Perhaps what the enlightened soldier took for the delusion of mistaken opinion did actually occur, for who has returned from that unknown world to explain by what forms and in what manner, he was introduced into its awful precincts!" Death is inevitably a retroactive definition, and in *The Prairie,* Cooper achieves much his best definition of Leatherstocking so far. Middleton says it: " 'Unlike most of those who live a border life, he united the better, instead of the worst qualities, of the two people.' " Here is the heart of the Leatherstocking Tales and of early American literature: the constitutive antithesis of white man and red, civilization and nature (or almost any other antithesis), is mediated and transcended by a figure—a character who is also a figure of speech—who incarnates the best of both worlds, is born of their deathlock, and is very much himself. The series of Tales is the tragic story of this man's life, death, and apparent defeat; alternatively, or simultaneously, it is the heroic story of his eventual triumph in what Romantic writers liked to call "the world of mind."

As in all the Tales after *The Pioneers,* the genteel characters are unimportant. Captain Middleton is only a *deus ex machina* and Inez ("the beau idéal of female loveliness") rather a cause of plot than a person in it. More than ever our interests are enlisted in the fate of Leatherstocking, and then in the affairs of the Bush family, whose sorry mismanagement reminds us that Cooper is again treating his civilization-nature polarities in terms of different kinds of law (prairie or Indian law vs. American law, and then both vs. divine law). Particularly in the first half of the novel, Cooper obviously finds distasteful this crude squatter and his crude family, who live closer to instinct than to reason; this is a severe limitation, as Leatherstocking is forever pointing out, though he is also forever praising instinct. Within the space of three paragraphs, Cooper defines the Bushes as "a race who lived chiefly for the indulgence of the natural wants," defends a "great principle of female nature" (maternal love) in Esther Bush, and then describes her as behaving "with that sort of acuteness which is termed instinct, in the animals a few degrees below her in the scale of intelligence." For all their dullness, the Bushes are frequently spoken of as exceptionally competent within the range of their experience. The Bush girls "promised fairly to become . . . no less distinguished than their mother for their daring, and for that singular mixture of good and evil, which, in a wider sphere of action, would probably have enabled the wife of the squatter to enrol her name among the remarkable females of her time." In many ways the Bushes resemble Leatherstocking, as in Cooper's generic description of them: "It would have been a curious investigation, for one skilled in such an inquiry, to have traced those points of difference, by which the offspring of the most western European [the American] was still to be distinguished from the descendant of the most remote Asiatic [the Indian], now that the two, in the revolutions of the world, were approximating in their habits, their residence, and not a little in their characters."

Surely it is not Cooper's final intention to belabor the brutishness of the Bushes, but rather to demonstrate how in people of almost no education, existing almost entirely outside society, there remains a fund of moral knowledge and a connatural sense of justice. Increasingly Cooper was taking his stand on the bedrock of human dignity, man as a divinely created rather than a socially conditioned being. As he did so, the values of his fiction gradually shifted from one side of the frontier to the other, from civilization to nature. The sequence in which the squatter, who knows no law but family, must assume responsibility to sentence and execute his wife's brother for the murder of his eldest son, and then finds it in his heart not only to forgive the man but through his absolution to help his wife find forgiveness—this sequence is widely held to be Cooper's finest achievement. What the action most memorably says is that the divine attributes of justice and mercy are man's attributes too, and that they are not wholly the result of civilization—which is rather the culture of them—but of nature. Perhaps the particular civilization which assisted in the formation of Ishmael Bush is less than perfect, and perhaps his feelings of claustrophobia arise from a subliminal awareness of the imperfection. He always feels himself confined, and seeks a kind of breathing space he never really understands; in this, and in much else, he is less a foil to Natty Bumppo than a variant on a lower plane.

For emphasis on the Indian, *The Prairie* is among the Leatherstocking Tales second only to *The Last of the Mohicans.* " 'The rightful owners of the country,' " as Leatherstocking regularly calls them, are Plains Indians on horseback, but as Leatherstocking also remarks (more for literary than for anthropological reasons), " 'Red-natur' is red-natur', let it show itself on a prairie, or in a forest!' " The allegory of good and evil continues unchanged by the change of tribes or location. Mahtoree (fundamentally a Mingo) stalks through the Bushes' camp "like the master of evil"; Hard-Heart is "Apollo-like." If Hard-Heart is Uncas resurrected, he is also a red Leatherstocking. " 'Look at that noble Pawnee,' " says Leatherstocking, " 'and see what a Red-skin may become, who fears the Master of Life and follows his laws.' " Red men and white are regularly seen as analogues of one another. After all, "little apology is needed for finding resemblances between men, who essentially possess the same nature, however it may be modified by circumstances." Mahtoree leans from the saddle "like some chevalier of a more civilized race," and speaks "in the haughty tones of absolute power," as if he were an American demagogue. "In a state of society, which admitted of a greater display of his energies, the Teton would in all probability have been both a conqueror and a despot." Escorting Middleton to the Pawnee village, Hard-Heart and his braves "set an example of courtesy, blended with reserve, that many a diplomatist of the most polished court might have strove in vain to imitate." Throwing himself on a horse, Hard-Heart makes a sign "with the air of a prince to his followers." Hard-Heart is richly endowed with the capacity to transcend his circumstances, and even the freethinker Mahtoree is ambiguously said to be "much in advance of his people in those acquirements which announce the dawnings of civilization."

As Hard-Heart explains, with his usual tact: "The Wahcondah sometimes veiled his countenance from a Red-man. No doubt the Great Spirit of the Pale-faces often looked darkly on his children. Such as were abandoned to the worker of evil could never be brave or virtuous, let the colour of the skin be what it might." Whether the Great Spirit of the Pale-faces

was in 1827 looking darkly or brightly on his children is a question that only the Great Spirit can answer; unquestionably, the Pale-faces were a success, and had long since learned to argue from success to desert to virtue. But an aged Indian asks Leatherstocking about the Americans: " 'Why cannot his people see every thing, since they crave all?' " And Hard-Heart tells Leatherstocking: " 'Your warriors think the Master of Life has made the whole earth white. They are mistaken. They are pale, and it is their own faces that they see.' " Only Hard-Heart and Leatherstocking transcend historical conditioning to achieve a relation based on their common humanity. (pp. 50-4)

When he returned to the Leatherstocking Tales thirteen years later, Cooper continued the development implicit in the first three with remarkably little change of direction. *The Pathfinder; or, The Inland Sea* (1840), takes place on and about Lake Ontario, "in the year 175-, or long before even speculation had brought any portion of western New-York within the bounds of civilization." The inland sea enabled Cooper to realize an old idea of writing within one set of covers his two favorite kinds of fiction. "Nature," he says, meaning also himself, "appeared to delight in producing grand effects, by setting two of her principal agents in bold relief to each other." Occasionally lake and surrounding forest fuse in a figure of speech, as when we see "an ocean of leaves," or when we are told that the *Scud* resembles "a man threading the forest alone" and that her meeting with another ship "was like that of two solitary hunters beneath the broad canopy of leaves that then covered so many millions of acres on the continent of America." Pathfinder also finds it reasonable to think that God provided " 'lakes of pure water to the west, and lakes of impure [i.e., salt] water to the east,' " for as usual the local scene is emblematic of the national predicament. "At the period of our tale, and, indeed, for half a century later, the whole of that vast region which has been called the west, or the new countries, since the war of the revolution, lay a comparatively unpeopled desert, teeming with all the living productions of nature, that properly belonged to the climate, man and the domestic animals excepted." Paradoxically, as Cooper remarks in the preface, "there are isolated spots, along the line of the great lakes, that date, as settlements, as far back as many of the older American towns, and which were the seats of a species of civilization, long before the greater portion of even the older states was rescued from the wilderness." The species of civilization to which Cooper alludes is the new American civilization emerging from the figurative frontier in the mythical West.

In *The Pathfinder,* genteel characters are on the whole conspicuous by their welcome absence. "The reader is to anticipate none of the appliances of people of condition in the description of the personal appearances of the group in question." Instead, the reader is to anticipate increased attention to Leatherstocking, the figurative frontier in person. At first sight, Mabel Dunham takes him for an Indian, and only later sees "that she was about to be addressed by one of her own colour, though his dress was so strange a mixture of the habits of the two races, that it required a near look to be certain of the fact." His face is sunburnt "bright red," we are several times told; morally, he is distinguished by "that stoicism which formed so large a part of his character, and which he had probably imbibed from long association with the Indians." Quartermaster Muir is not far wrong when he calls him " 'wild, half-savage, or of a frontier formation,' " though of course we must discover in these epithets implications other than the villainous quartermaster intends. " 'I may say,' " Pathfinder is always saying, " 'that my own feelings towards a Mingo' "—and toward everything else, he might have added—" 'are not much more than the gifts of a Delaware grafted on a Christian stock.' " (pp. 54-5)

More than in the Tales of the 1820's, Cooper is eager to define discursively the nature of the mysterious Leatherstocking, paragon of probity, stability, self-discipline, simplicity, faith, energy, courage, integrity, prudence, sincerity, truthfulness, freshness of sensibility, and, over all, of a "beautiful and un-erring sense of justice." He is America as America ought to be, and it is significant that as Cooper's sense of what America ought to be developed from the 1820's to the 1840's, he not only augmented and magnified Leatherstocking's virtues but gave them an increasingly aesthetic orientation. This development was to be completed only with *The Deerslayer* in the following year; at this penultimate stage, "the most surprising peculiarity about the man himself, was the entire indifference with which he regarded all distinctions that did not depend on personal merit." He also possesses "a natural discrimination, that appeared to set education at defiance"; that is, he constitutes a living proof that intelligence, imagination, and conscience, key to the other virtues, are rather innate than acquired. "In short, it was said of the Pathfinder . . . that he was a fair example of what a just-minded and pure man might be, while untempted by unruly or ambitious desires, and left to follow the bias of his feelings, amid the solitary grandeur and ennobling influences of a sublime nature; neither led aside by the inducements which influence all to do evil amid the incentives of civilization; nor forgetful of the Almighty Being, whose spirit pervades the wilderness as well as the towns." (Cooper was doubtless tempted to say "more than the towns.") Leatherstocking is a paradigm of the ideal democratic ethos in the Era of Good Feeling and Age of Jackson, the new man of the New World miraculously uncorrupted by (as it is ironically called) free enterprise.

Late in the novel, Pathfinder tells how he overcame three great temptations. Since the temptations are not great, and the morality used to circumvent them eccentric, the anecdote is primarily comic in effect. His real temptation is naturally Mabel Dunham, though it is not, strictly speaking, her rejection of him that, as Cooper says, "might be termed the most critical [instant] in our hero's life," but the possibility of her acceptance. This marital temptation is not at all comic, but in many ways painful, for surely being in love is the most improbable of all the improbable situations in which Leatherstocking is placed by his creator. Of course, there is no serious doubt of the outcome: Leatherstocking is a saint, with a vocation to celibacy. Throughout *The Pathfinder,* Cooper touches on Leatherstocking's limitations of personality, education, and background, which, superficially considered, might be thought to unfit him for domestic life with a beautiful young girl. He is also defined as a man preeminently susceptible to education of a more profound kind, and learn his lessons he assuredly does. Even before the final recognition scene, he has an uneasy sense that something has gone wrong with his life. To Mabel's question, " 'And our own Delaware, Pathfinder—the Big Serpent—why is he not with us, to-night?' " he replies: " 'Your question would have been more natural, had you said, why are *you* here, Pathfinder?—The Sarpent is in his place, while I am not in mine.' " Later he tells her: " 'I have indeed been on a false trail, since we met!' " Finally taking leave of Mabel and her lover Jasper Western, he says sadly: " 'I shall return to the wilderness and my Maker.' " In

this way only can he be saved, for the path into the wilderness leads to the City of God which is his ultimate destination. Jasper and Mabel settle in New York, for there are, indeed, gifts and gifts. That Leatherstocking, possessor of the highest gifts within the compass of Cooper's imagination, is also provincial, superstitious, ignorant, and verbose, signifies Cooper's recognition of the obvious truth that even the highest gifts exist in, through, and sometimes despite, particular conditions. (pp. 56-8)

The Deerslayer; or, The First War-Path (1841) is much the most Romantic of the Tales. The civilized folk who dominated *The Pioneers,* and then lingered along the margins of the next three Tales, chiefly as military personnel, are gone. Cooper had apparently come to understand that the unifying conception of the frontier metaphor, with its mediating embrace of opposites, enabled him to comprehend in a single character both the civilized and the natural virtues. As he grows ever younger, Leatherstocking assimilates the better qualities of Judge Temple's civilization (foresight, prudence, responsibility), detached from implications of social, economic, or educational class. Leatherstocking now stands for nature *and* civilization *and* their dynamic interplay, which is greater than either alone. Cooper's progress was also a roundabout reversion in time from the alleged 1794 of *The Pioneers* to the alleged 1740 of *The Deerslayer;* as he retreated from contemporary civilization, he inevitably left behind the world of upper-class America and arrived in a simpler world where he could ignore such distinctions. Even more clearly than in *The Pioneers,* Cooper now saw that the real problem was not what American civilization might do with its Leatherstockings, but what American civilization might do with its Judge Temples. Cooper's best insight was that Judge Temples were expendable.

In the fresh purity of youth, Leatherstocking is surrounded by Indians good and evil, and by white frontiersmen conspicuously less admirable than the better Indians, or even, in certain respects, than the worst Indians. The central conception of *The Deerslayer* is the Double Frontiersman, represented by the opposition between Leatherstocking on the one hand, and Floating Tom Hutter and Hurry Harry March on the other. But the distinction between them must not be interpreted as primarily a distinction between ideal and real, for in that interpretation Leatherstocking's efficacy would be lost; and as the narrative carefully demonstrates, his enactment of the borderer's role, even before his initiation into the full horrors of border life, is quite as authoritative as March's and Hutter's. The proper distinctions are both aesthetic and ethical. The low frontiersmen, foils to the greater glory of Leatherstocking, are undeveloped human beings, even though they live in a setting singularly conducive to what Cooper regards as natural human development.

This apathy is disastrous, as we learn from the very different uses to which nature is put by Leatherstocking:

> We have written much, but in vain, concerning this extraordinary being, if the reader requires now to be told, that, untutored as he was in the learning of the world, and simple as he ever showed himself to be in all matters touching the subtleties of conventional taste, he was a man of strong, native, poetical feeling. He loved the woods for their freshness, their sublime solitudes, their vastness, and the impress that they everywhere bore of the divine hand of their creator. He seldom moved through them, without pausing to dwell on some peculiar

beauty that gave him pleasure, though seldom attempting to investigate the causes; and never did a day pass without his communing in spirit, and this, too, without the aid of forms or language, with the infinite source of all he saw, felt, and beheld. Thus constituted, in a moral sense, and of a steadiness that no danger could appal, or any crisis disturb, it is not surprising that the hunter felt a pleasure at looking on the scene.

Leatherstocking is further characterized by "the freshness of his integrity, the poetry and truth of his feelings," and Chingachgook by "the poetry and truth of nature." The novel is full of natural beauties, usually called "holy," and the poetic characters' responses to them validate their credentials as true American heroes. "Most of the influence that such a scene is apt to produce on those who are properly constituted in a moral sense, was lost on Hutter and Hurry; but both the Delawares, though too much accustomed to witness the loveliness of morning-tide, to stop to analyze their feelings, were equally sensible of the beauties of the hour, though it was probably in a way unknown to themselves." As Cooper never tires of saying, "the whole was lost on the observers [Hutter and Hurry], who knew no feeling of poetry, had lost their sense of natural devotion in lives of obdurate and narrow selfishness, and had little other sympathy with nature, than that which originated with her lowest wants." *The Deerslayer* depends on the ethics of Emerson, which in turn depend on the aesthetics of Wordsworth; as in the later aesthetic ethics of Henry James, Leatherstocking is *par excellence* the man on whom nothing is lost. His superiority appears to be a matter of election, for the aesthetic response plainly presupposes ethical awareness, and vice versa.

The more the issues of the novel are seen as ethical rather than as aesthetic, the more cleanly the image of the Double Frontiersman splits into polar opposites, until finally Tom Hutter is revealed as despicably insensible to Leatherstocking's captivity and probable death, "for while he knew how material his aid might be in a defence, the difference in their views on the morality of the woods, had not left much sympathy between them." Differences in moral view have been evident throughout. Leatherstocking spends his best energies in the avoidance of even necessary bloodshed, while Hutter and Hurry devote their worst talents to the pursuit of scalps. (In Cooper's view, they are clearly worse than the misguided Bushes.) For these "men who dreaded the approaches of civilization as a curtailment of their own lawless empire," Indians are fair game, and their extermination is legally justified by the scalp bounties the colony offers. Since the crime extends into the highest places, it is both colony and frontiersmen whose approaches Leatherstocking dreads. " 'I'm glad it has no name,' " he says of the lake, " 'or, at least, no pale-face name; for their christenings always foretell waste and destruction.' " Since practically all the action of *The Deerslayer* results from Indian-hating, whether regarded as regressive barbarism or as political policy, the fitting climax of the novel is the horrific vision of Tom Hutter: "The quivering and raw flesh, the bared veins and muscles, and all the other disgusting signs of mortality, as they are revealed by tearing away the skin, showed he had been scalped, though still living." So, in a manner of speaking, has America been scalped by Cooper; with some justice, he defends this savage act of poetic justice as one of the "decrees of a retributive Providence."

Significantly, the Double Frontiersman (Indian-hater and forest-philosopher) issues from a single situation. The novel is full of realistic details drawn from border life—house-raising, strange mixtures of furniture, love of sports and outdoor activities, freedom and familiarity of manners—and these realistic details compel us to attend to the fact of man's ability to choose between alternative modes of behavior within the same set of circumstances. Like Leatherstocking, Hurry Harry is a "creature equally of civilization and barbarism," but in nearly every other respect he is Leatherstocking's antithesis. Even the "physical restlessness that kept him so constantly on the move" is rather the opposite than the same kind of restlessness inspiring Deerslayer's geographical and spiritual mobility. There is a world of meaning in Leatherstocking's remark: " 'Never talk to Hurry about these things; he's only a borderer, at the best.' " His best is not good enough, for he is all too representative of a class. " 'Take 'em as a body, Judith, 'arth don't hold a set of men more given to theirselves, and less given to God and the law.' " Hurry Harry's clothing has "the usual signs of belonging to those who passed their time between the skirts of civilized society and the boundless forests," but he has learned nothing from either, or from their admixture. He is a frontiersman only in appearance, only, as it were, sartorially. He is a costumed adolescent, and the American woods are full of him. (pp. 59-63)

In the course of his frontier novels, Cooper had all along been disengaging himself from American civilization, as understood by the world into which he was born, in order to create an American civilization worthier of the name, as he had also been disengaging the frontier metaphor from its literal origins, in order to apply it to more significantly ethical and religious situations. Now he transcends American civilization altogether. On the frontiers of Heaven, rather than on the Far Western plains where Leatherstocking dies, the Tales come to an end. Cooper had traveled a long way from Cooperstown, and clearly could go no further.

At the heart of the Leatherstocking Tales is Cooper's vision of cultural relativism and pluralism, which in turn is sustained by a basic distinction between the reign of nature and the works of man; after all, for there to be an admixture, there must first have been a distinction. Nature is anterior, more stable, and thus more directly—or at least more simply—related to God; nature is the proximate, though not the ultimate, ground of being. In that sense—as the non-ethical, or the pre-ethical—nature is in contrast with the nightmare behavior of man; and as cyclical recurrence, nature is in contrast with the linear forms of human history, whether progressive or regressive. But since all men have available to them the same immediate access to nature, and through nature mediately to God, they may if they choose move back toward their single source and reaffirm an essential brotherhood. Paradoxically, nature, in itself neither good nor bad, is also the source of a spectrum of ethical behaviors, works of man, and civilizations.

Invaluable as they are, civilizations, or cultures, separate groups of men from each other. In Leatherstocking's conversation, the antithesis between "natur' " (as given) and "gifts" (as second nature, in traditions, mores, manners, styles) is almost never-ending. " 'I am too christianized to expect any thing so fanciful as hunting and fishing after death,' " he announces in *The Deerslayer,* discriminating his faith from the faith of his Indian friends, but not on that account diminishing his sympathy with them; " 'nor do I believe there is one Manitou for the red-skin, and another for a pale-face. You find different colours on 'arth, as any one may see . . . but

only one natur'. . . . A natur' is the creatur' itself. . . .
Now, gifts come of sarcumstances.' " As he explains to Cap
in *The Pathfinder,* in a still more catholic formulation:
" 'With me, it is as oncredible for a white man not to be a
Christian, as it is for a red-skin not to believe in his happy
hunting-grounds; indeed, after allowing for difference in traditions, and in some variations about the manner in which the
spirit will be occupied after death, I hold that a good Delaware is a good Christian, though he never saw a Moravian;
and a good Christian a good Delaware, so far as natur' is consarned.' " In the light of such remarks, the Double Indian
and the Double Frontiersman split and realign themselves,
and the deplorably disastrous relations in the United States
between Indians and frontiersmen are replaced by the eternal
warfare of opposing principles.

Increasingly insisting on Leatherstocking's conscience, Cooper's argument circles back to its beginnings, where everything comes together, for the sense of right and wrong is at
once nature and the source of the highest civilization. The
doctrine of cultural relativism was obviously encouraged and
sharpened by such American conditions as life in the woods
and encounter with the Indian; it was, in fact, demanded by
them, and by the sense of human decency, the necessity for
self-respect, both for the times in which the Leatherstocking
Tales were written and for posterity. The doctrine of cultural
relativism was also an absolute religious principle, considerably antedating the birth of even the noblest concept of American civilization, and, conceivably, surviving its eventual decline or disappearance. In *The Deerslayer* we learn that it
was the Moravians who first taught our hero " 'that all are
to be judged according to their talents, or l'arning; the Indian,
like an Indian; and the white man, like a white man.' "
(Clearly, it was St. Paul who taught *them*.) As the dying Leatherstocking says to Hard-Heart: " 'There are many traditions concerning the place of Good Spirits. It is not for one
like me, old and experienced though I am, to set up my opinions against a nation's. You believe in the blessed prairies,
and I have faith in the sayings of my fathers. If both are true,
our parting will be final; but if it should prove, that the same
meaning is hid under different words, we shall yet stand together, Pawnee, before the face of your Wahcondah, who will
then be no other than my God.' "

With three of the Leatherstocking Tales behind him, Cooper
wrote, curiously, in *Notions of the Americans,* that "all the
attempts to blend history with romance in America, have
been comparatively failures, (and perhaps fortunately,) since
the subjects are too familiar to be treated with the freedom
that the imagination absolutely requires. Some of the descriptions of the progress of society on the borders, have had a
rather better success, since there is a positive, though no very
poetical, novelty in the subject." The preface he supplied for
the entire series of Leatherstocking Tales in 1850 was more
assured. "In a moral sense," he said, minimizing the tortuous
development of his insight,

> this man of the forest is purely a creation. The idea
> of delineating a character that possessed little of
> civilization but its highest principles . . . and all of
> savage life that is not incompatible with these great
> rules of conduct, is perhaps natural to the situation
> in which Natty was placed. He is too proud of his
> origin to sink into the condition of the wild Indian,
> and too much a man of the woods not to imbibe as
> much as was at all desirable, from his friends and
> companions. . . . Removed from nearly all the

temptations of civilized life, placed in the best associations of that which is deemed savage, and favorably disposed by nature to improve such advantages, it appeared to the writer that his hero was a
fit subject to represent the better qualities of both
conditions, without pushing either to extremes.

Cooper was an inventive genius, not a literary critic, and it
is useless to demand more of him than this final recognition
that Leatherstocking was purely and simply that new man,
the generic American, the metaphor of the Western frontier
fleshed out as a human being; whatever additional instruction
we wish must be sought in the Tales themselves, and then in
the literature they inspired. Cooper's achievement was perhaps limited by its being so intuitive, so much an affair of trial
and error; certainly it was limited by hasty production, by
novelistic conventions unworthy of his matter, and by a prose
style only intermittently brilliant. Still, in the center of his
rambling, disjointed narratives we can find, if we look for
them, germs of a rich development. For all his shortcomings,
Cooper's integrity and passion enabled him to nurture his
basic figure until it grew beyond him—grew, in fact, to be
nearly synonymous with early American literature. Thus he
defined the age and became (insofar as any one man can be)
the improbable founder of the national expression. The Leatherstocking Tales are not in any ordinary sense great art; but
the rest of American writing through Whitman is a series of
footnotes on them. (pp. 64-8)

> *Edwin Fussell, "The Leatherstocking Tales of
> James Fenimore Cooper," in his* Frontier: Ameri-
> can Literature and the American West, *Princeton
> University Press, 1965, pp. 27-68.*

WILLIAM H. GOETZMANN (essay date 1969)

[*Goetzmann, an American historian and critic, received the
Pulitzer Prize in history for his* Exploration and Empire: The
Explorer and the Scientist in the Winning of the West (*1967*).
*In the following excerpt, he examines Cooper's delineation of
the historical process in the Leatherstocking novels, focusing on*
The Prairie.]

The Prairie, which Cooper wrote in 1826-1827 in Paris, was
the third book in the Leatherstocking saga which chronicled
the adventures of Natty Bumppo, a forest hunter and frontiersman who resembled Daniel Boone, immortalized by
John Filson in a biography in 1784. It was apparently to be
the third and last volume of a trilogy which was artfully
structured. The first volume, entitled *The Pioneers,* Cooper
had published in 1823. It introduced Natty Bumppo as
"Deerslayer," a relatively old man who, in killing a deer on
Judge Marmaduke Temple's New York estate, violated civilized law and was punished. From the beginning, it was clear
that Natty Bumppo had a past, and a rather noble one at that,
consisting of adventures with the Indians in the forest wilderness, and going back beyond the Revolution to the French
and Indian War. Cooper thus placed his major character just
beyond the middle of life. In so doing, he began his epic clas-
sically *in medias res.* The next volume, *The Last of the Mohicans* (1826), is a flashback that pictures Natty in the prime
of life, in the midst of his glorious past. *The Prairie,* written
right on the heels of the previous book and suggesting that
Cooper was rapidly spinning out the conclusion to his woodsman's odyssey, is clearly a finale—the grand curtain scene of
Leatherstocking, now an old man well past eighty, and waiting serenely for death out in nature beyond the reaches of civ-

ilization. From a point just past the center of his hero's life, Cooper had thus flashed backward and forward. He had, through the medium of Leatherstocking, told the story of frontier America.

Critics, preoccupied with apologizing for his stilted language, have generally missed the skill and subtlety with which the trilogy was structured. Over all three books hangs a cloud of mortality, of inevitable death and change with its inescapable sadness and elegiac tone. In the first book, the deer is killed, but even worse, possessed as property under law. The trees are cut down and the forest is rapidly disappearing. Mighty Deerslayer himself is tried and convicted of the humiliating crime of poaching, and hence suffers spiritual death at the hands of Judge Temple, the agent of civilization. Leatherstocking's day, like that of the wilderness he loves so much, is clearly past. One can only leave it to the Freudian critics to decide whether Judge Temple was meant to be Cooper's own father, and if this is then a novel of emotional rebellion as well as a novel of social commentary.

The Last of the Mohicans, a story of Leatherstocking's prime years, also tells a tale of dying and thus sustains the tone, if not the theme of the first book. This time, of course, the victim is the noble Uncas, last of his tribe which had been virtually wiped out by vicious New Englanders years before. Thus we have a sequence of doom: first the Indian, then the forests, then the hunter. *The Prairie* is the last in this somber sequence. It is entirely a novel of death, but appropriately enough, death and resurrection, for it ends on that ambiguous Easter note of sadness and hope. It chronicles the death of one way of life and the birth of another which is not altogether bad.

At this point, Cooper had created a subtle structural masterpiece; then, as D. H. Lawrence so astutely but only halfway perceived, Cooper began the "sloughing of the old skin" [see *NCLC,* Vol. 1, pp. 214-16]. He went back in 1840 and 1841 and wrote two more books in the Leatherstocking series, *The Pathfinder* and *The Deerslayer,* which took Natty Bumppo back by successive stages through young manhood to youth and the beginning of his career. The spell of death was broken. In a different sense, another resurrection had occurred, and Leatherstocking once again roamed the forests and the glimmerglass lakes. These books had a place, certainly, in proportion to Natty's very long life, and they did make clear to the reader in the age of Manifest Destiny and march of empire just what the attractions of the unspoiled wilderness had been. They also recalled the pioneering exploits of an older heroic generation that had given hard birth to the country and which was in danger of being forgotten except in the formalistic orations of Daniel Webster.

There was something so basic about Cooper's five Leatherstocking tales that they received the supreme accolade. They were taken up by the generations and read as children's books for nearly a hundred years. They sustained themselves on the magic level of story and character down through all the years when Americans lost their self-consciousness in a preoccupation with work, industrial development, and the growth of great cities where the forest and the longhouse once stood. They outlasted the dime novel and hundreds of imitations which blossomed into a whole new genre called "westerns." They survive even today in the era of the cinema and the "horse opera," holding their own against the best of John Ford.

But since 1950, at least, with the work of Henry Nash Smith in *Virgin Land; The American West as Symbol and Myth* [see excerpt above], literary critics and students of culture have begun to see the larger meaning of Cooper's work. Cooper now stands forth clearly as the great novelist of changing America, and at the heart of his work stands the ambivalence and paradox that are central to the American historical experience. Cooper, along with many other Americans, could never make up his mind whether he preferred nature or civilization. Nature was God's pure handiwork. It was beauty, the vast, silent sublimity of forest and lake and prairie. It was innocent and noble and free. It was America's one great spiritual and material resource, and it set us off during a crucial period of national self-identification from the feudal, class-ridden industrial society of "civilized" Europe. On the other hand, nature was crude, lawless, the home of violence, danger, and terror. Most of all it stood in the way of progress. Over and over again in his Leatherstocking tales, Cooper posits the contrast between nature—time stood still—and progress—the relentless, and in many ways inviting, wave of the future. The problem was to tame nature and bring it under control for good without degenerating into the callous over-civilization of Europe. This was the mission of America, to create a new society, efficient and orderly and civilized, but based closely upon the beneficent laws of nature and hence free. So Cooper, like most Americans, while always aware of the nature versus progress dilemma, invariably had it both ways.

In his books he celebrated *both* nature and civilization; time *and* progress stood still. The Leatherstocking saga catches all of this so perfectly because it is a myth or story of heroic proportions that chronicles the emerging historical identity of the American people. Cooper knew, as some social scientists of the present appear to have forgotten, that individual and collective identities can only be derived from history. His great achievement was to render the historical process of change during a period of cultural genesis somehow timeless and permanent while at the same time capturing all of the ambiguities, dislocations, and anomalies of a culture in the throes of a process of acceleration more rapid than any ever seen before. It was because he was so sensitive to the historical process bound up in the frontier movement that Cooper, of course, found Dr. Edwin James's narrative of the cutting edge of civilization on the prairies so utterly fascinating.

The Prairie, as befitting the final act of a great drama, has most of Cooper's symbolic characters onstage in a vastly greater panorama than any of his other books. The tone and many of the characters in the book are reminiscent of Shakespeare's valedictory play, *The Tempest.* There is never any doubt but that this is to be the finale. The landscape, Mark Twain notwithstanding [see *NCLC,* Vol. 1, pp. 208-10], is a real landscape derived from James's careful account, but it is bizarre and skillfully managed by Cooper. It is a "bleak and solitary place" with "bruised and withered grass," offering little "that was flattering to the hopes of an ordinary settler of new lands." It was colored by the "hues and tints of autumn," suggesting age, and the great fortress rock which was to shelter the Bush family stood out upon the autumnal prairie like a tombstone.

Leatherstocking, wrinkled and old, makes his sudden appearance on the prairie silhouetted against the setting sun, an awe-inspiring nature god about to pass from the face of the earth:

> The sun had fallen below the crest of the nearest wave of the prairie, leaving the usual rich and glowing train on its track. In the center of this flood of fiery light, a human form appeared, drawn against the gilded background, as distinctly, and seemingly as palpable, as though it would come within the grasp of any extended hand. The figure was colossal, the attitude musing and melancholy, and the situation directly in the route of the travellers. But embedded, as it was, in its setting of garish light, it was impossible to distinguish its just proportions or true character.
>
> The effect of such a spectacle was instantaneous and powerful. The man in front of the emigrants came to a stand, and remained gazing at the mysterious object with a dull interest, that soon quickened into superstitious awe.

Throughout the book, this godlike quality of Leatherstocking is maintained. His wisdom, constantly thrust before the reader and the other characters in the story, is a function of his great age and long experience. His powers, now no longer physical (even his "hawkeye" has grown dim), derive from his great intuitive understanding of nature and men. But so great are these powers, especially those of intelligence and mortality, that he largely influences the actions of all the others in the story.

More important than his powers, however, are his values for they denote what he represents in Cooper's myth of America's beginnings. The twin keys to Leatherstocking's values are freedom and a reverence for nature. Having been arrested by Judge Temple for making free use of nature's bounty when he killed a deer, Natty rejects "the law of the clearings" for the most part, favoring instead the freedom of nature's laws—even as applied to the Indians who make "free" with the settlers' horses because, being natural beings, they have little feeling for or need of private property. Leatherstocking does not, however, violate nature or nature's laws, and, embodying Cooper's basic ambivalence in this matter, he does not entirely scorn civilization's laws. Speaking to Ellen Wade, he declares, "The law—tis bad to have it, but I sometimes think it is worse to be entirely without it. Age and weakness have brought me to feel such weakness at times. Yes-yes, the law is needed when such as have not the gifts of strength and wisdom are to be taken care of." Here Cooper gets at the heart of his theme, and for that matter the theme of most "westerns" down to the present day. This is the role of law and order which is synonymous with the best aspects of civilization in that it provides justice and protection for the weak against the vicious, the violent, and the rapacious—in short the spoiler who is in Cooper's terms the unnatural man. The good law is, by implication, Jeffersonian law which is in harmony with nature, indeed derives from it, but which nevertheless allows a man to be as free as possible without injury to his fellow creatures. It depends fundamentally upon tolerance and mutual respect.

These qualities are sadly lacking in Ishmael Bush who might be considered the main character in the story. Bush is a brute who has killed a man back in "civilization" in a fight over land. Gathering his numerous brood about him like some tribal leader, he has set out on his exodus across the forbidding prairie to get as far as possible beyond the restraints of law for which he has only contempt. As evidence of this, he has added kidnapping to his crimes. In partnership with his evil brother-in-law, Abiram White, he has abducted Inez de Certavallos, daughter of a decadent but rich Spanish colonial grandee. Improbable as it seems at first reading, Bush and White expect to collect a ransom for Inez out in the wilderness. On this point the reader might possibly be deceived by a geographical "eclipse" in Cooper's story, since if the emigrant band were heading across the prairie on or near the Spanish trail from Santa Fe to St. Louis, they might well have been, by Cooper's (and James's) logic, in a position to contact Spanish authorities in the matter of the ransom. Cooper simply neglected to mention the occasional Spanish outposts along the way such as those near the base of the southern Rockies, on the Red River between Oklahoma and Texas, and the trading camps along the Platte River as well as the temporary camps of the comancheros operating out of Santa Fe.

Bush's important role, however, is not that of kidnapper. He is Ishmael the outcast and outlawed wanderer. He is a kind of gypsy Caliban of brutish and powerful strength doomed to suffer in his own private dungeon of ignorance, unless he learns. We first see him crashing across the prairie in one of Cooper's best descriptive passages:

> He was a tall, sunburnt man, past the middle age, of a dull countenance and listless manner. His frame appeared loose and flexible; but it was vast, and in reality of prodigious power. It was only at moments, however, as some slight impediment imposed itself to his loitering progress, that his person, which in its ordinary gait seemed so lounging and nerveless, displayed any of those energies which lay latent in his system, like the slumbering and unwieldy, but terrible, strength of the elephant.

Resorting to then fashionable phrenological description, Cooper adds, "The inferior lineaments of his countenance were coarse, extended and vacant; while the superior, or those nobler parts which are thought to affect the intellectual being, were low, receding and mean." He dresses like a gypsy, absurdly loaded with the plunder of a hundred brushes with hated civilization: a silken sash, a silver-hafted knife, a marten's-fur cap, Mexican coins for buttons, three worthless watches slung around his neck, a rifle with a mahogany stock banded in precious metal; and he carries the prime symbol of evil—the spoiler's axe. Like Lennie in Steinbeck's *Of Mice and Men,* he is ignorant, but possessed of terrible and menacing potential for destruction which he can barely control. He stands for the great barbarian melting pot of America, unleashed, in Cooper's aristocratic view, upon the prostrate body of nature.

Cooper's story, however, is really the story of how Ishmael Bush learned to value the ways of civilization, how he redeemed himself and rose up out of his brutishness to wisdom and sanity and maturity, how out in nature he exchanged the role of Caliban for that of Prospero who in the end puts all things right. *The Prairie* is therefore very much Bush's story, though it is again a measure of Cooper's ambivalence that Bush is forced to compete throughout with Leatherstocking for the reader's attention because Cooper cannot finally make up his mind about nature versus civilization. In a sense, Bush and the bee hunter, Paul Hover, of the next generation, are to be seen as Leatherstocking's successors in a maturing America, with all the sad and sentimental connotations that that condition brings with it.

Despite twists and turns of plot, the course of Bush's education is relatively simple. One of his stalwart but stupid sons is mysteriously murdered. Bush thrashes about in a thicket of accusations and misdirected Old Testament tribal wrath. First he believes the Indians did it, then poor, good Leatherstocking. Finally, however, he learns that it was Abiram White, his own brother-in-law. Since there is no law out in the wilderness (some say, west of the Pecos) he is forced to create his own court of justice, conduct a trial, convict, condemn, and hang Abiram White. It is as a result of this experience that the tribal patriarch repents his own evil ways, learns the value of law, and civilization comes at last to the prairie. He is finally seen as the dispenser of justice, setting free Inez, giving his ward, Ellen, to Paul Hover, freeing Captain Middleton, coming to terms with the Indians, and in general making peace with civilization.

The Indians form a counter-story to that of Ishmael Bush. Both Pawnee and Sioux, though fierce, no-quarter fighters, have codes of honor and justice. This is symbolized by the dramatic passage of arms between Mahtoree and Hard-Heart on an island in the river between the two warring Indian armies that so much resembles the chivalric duel between Richard the Lion-Hearted and Saladin in Walter Scott's *The Talisman*. Cooper also goes to great lengths, some say absurd lengths, to indicate how the Indian's closeness to nature and his intuitive grasp of its ways makes him the supremely appropriate inhabitant of the great prairie no-man's land. He repeats, on several occasions in the book, Dr. James's conclusion that the Great American Desert should form a permanent and healthy barrier to American expansion. It should be left to nature's noblemen, the wild, free, yet honorable redmen with whom Leatherstocking elects to spend his declining years. But alas, the reader realizes sadly that Leatherstocking and his Indian friends are destined, like Uncas the last Mohican, to vanish before the march of empire—however good that empire may be.

The two pairs of younger characters in the book deserve further mention. Inez de Certavallos and her sleepy Spanish father represent, of course, decadent Europe and its feeble colonial culture in America. Captain Middleton, full of youthful excitement bordering on hysteria, is nonetheless a brave representative of the upper-class military aristocracy, making him a fit companion in Cooper's blue book for Inez who is of gentle birth. Ellen Wade and Paul Hover are the rising energetic middle-class generation. Little orphan Ellen is a girl scout, a combination Tess Trueheart and Doris Day, brave, bubbly-clean, and reverent who nevertheless works her "womanly wiles" on the naive bee hunter who has followed her halfway across the continent with an only vaguely defined purpose in mind. Paul Hover, of course, finds happiness. He has his Ellen in the end, he has his bee business, and best of all, he is Leatherstocking's designated successor. He receives the magic laying on of hands. On the latter point, however, Cooper somehow fails to convince. One is left to wonder if Paul Hover represents a truly apostolic successor, especially since Cooper did not continue *his* story (as a "son of Leatherstocking," so to speak) in 1840, but rather went back to the young manhood of Natty Bumppo himself. And further, in *The Pathfinder* Cooper created a similar character, still unsatisfactory as a surrogate—the young sailor, Jasper Western. The aristocratic Cooper, it seems, never could really reconcile himself emotionally to the middle class.

With most of the characters accounted for, we are left with only the ridiculous Dr. Obed Bat. The good doctor is clearly Cooper's attempt to write one of Shakespeare's "low" or comic characters into his story. Dr. Bat is a distant kin to Justice Shallow, Ancient Pistol, perhaps even in some ways to Doll Tearsheet. In his great pretension and corresponding lack of wisdom or common sense, he slightly resembles Falstaff, though Cooper's character falls far short of any such lofty literary attainment.

Yet, Dr. Bat adds an important dimension to Cooper's story that is commonly overlooked. For one thing, the impractical naturalist very probably reflects Cooper's personal reaction to Dr. James's overly scientific account of Major Long's adventure. The James narrative is studded with official and sober scientific descriptions that do not enhance the belletristic quality of the story and are real-life counterparts to Dr. Bat's penchant for Linnean nomenclature on any and every occasion. Dr. James's businesslike descriptions of bizarre, potentially colorful phenomena must be ranked with Dr. Bat's obtuseness in mistaking his own donkey (Asinus domesticus) for a buffalo (Vespertilio horribilis). Consider for instance this absurd visual image so soberly presented by Dr. James as a typical scene in the "Bad Heart" village: " 'I saw one mother,' Dr. James carefully recorded, 'apparently thirty years of age and of usual stature, suckling her infant who *stood* upon the ground. She found it necessary to stoop but little and stood observing us almost erect while the child of about two years was nursing.' " But Dr. Bat was not intended solely as a figure of humor, nor simply as a vehicle for Cooper's impatience. He also embodies Cooper's comment on science and the validity of the abstract scientific view of nature as opposed to Leatherstocking's common-sense intuitive outlook. Major Long's staff, preoccupied with measuring Pikes Peak, overlooked its grandeur. Dr. Bat errs in the same direction: " 'I made my own base, knew the length of the perpendicular by calculation, and to draw the hypotenuse had nothing to do but to work my angle,' said the busy Dr. Bat describing how he was rescued after being lost from camp. 'I supposed the guns were fired for my benefit, and changed my course for the sounds—not that I think the senses more accurate or even as accurate as a mathematical calculation, but I feared some of the children might need my services.' "

Dr. Bat sees nature only in the abstract. He is a collector out of context, a systematizer, a classifier. He does not know true nature and he is consequently a virtually helpless tenderfoot. And he does not learn. He misses life itself. In Cooper's view, he is the most ignorant of all, beyond even the redemption afforded Ishmael Bush. Clearly Cooper, the artist and romantic, detested the world of science and abstract reasoning. As early as 1827, out on the boundless prairies of Cooper's imagination, the "two cultures" stood unalterably opposed.

One could not arrive at truth through science, but one could do so in the most profound sense through history, the literary imagination, romance, and myth. Though Leatherstocking faded away into the sunset, broken twig, toothless hound, and all, Cooper could never forget him. He was too much a part of Cooper's own, and changing America's, basic experience. He lives on today, out of time, out of space, far out of the course of ordinary "realistic" experience, perhaps in the realm of what J.R.R. Tolkien called "Faërie," but in any case ever so much more historical than history itself. Whatever "literary offenses" Fenimore Cooper committed, lack of insight, broad vision, profundity, imagination, and genius were not among them. (pp. 68-77)

William H. Goetzmann, "James Fenimore Cooper: 'The Prairie'," in Landmarks of American Writing, *edited by Hennig Cohen, Basic Books, Inc., Publishers, 1969, pp. 66-78.*

JOEL PORTE (essay date 1969)

[*Porte is an American educator and critic who has written extensively on the life and works of Ralph Waldo Emerson and edited collections of Emerson criticism. In the following excerpt, he examines the role of women in the Leatherstocking novels.*]

When we think of Cooper's treatment of women in the Leatherstocking Tales, our first impulse usually is to share Mark Twain's scorn for the woodenness of Cooper's "females," or perhaps to remember James Russell Lowell's couplet: " . . . the women he draws from one model don't vary / All sappy as maples and flat as a prairie" [see *NCLC*, Vol. 1, p. 205]. Unfortunately, the verse is catchier than it is accurate, and suggests that Lowell had not read Cooper's books very attentively. Cooper offers many examples of clever, buxom, and passionate brunettes to balance his sexless and silly blonde ingénues, establishing, as Leslie Fiedler says [in *Love and Death in the American Novel*], "once and for all the pattern of female Dark and Light that is to become the standard form in which American writers project their ambivalence toward women." But Cooper achieved more, in his treatment of women, than simply to set for future American writing two invaluable archetypes. The dark and fair ladies function in the Leatherstocking Tales as an essential part of the myth of the American Adam, Natty Bumppo.

These archetypal females make their appearance in purest form in *The Last of the Mohicans,* where they are represented by Alice Munro and her half-sister Cora—the two aspects of woman. Alice, notably blonde and blue-eyed, is first seen riding through the forest, when she "artlessly suffered the morning air to blow aside the green veil" that covers her face. She is young (just adolescent enough to be believably nubile) and markedly without guile (since cunning, as we shall see, always implies sexuality), and she suffers no one but nature (*innocent* nature, symbolized by her green veil) to touch her purity. Cora, on the other hand, conceals her charms with "care" and is "rather fuller and more mature" than Alice. The fair sister is simply frightened by the evil Magua, but Cora looks at him with "pity, admiration, and horror" combined, "as her dark eye followed the easy motions of the savage. The tresses of this lady were shining and black, like the plumage of the raven. Her complexion was not brown"—she is not *literally* a squaw—"but it rather appeared charged with the color of the rich blood, that seemed ready to burst its bounds." As we should expect, she has a "dark, thoughtful eye" (she is described as "more thoughtful" than Alice) and is ripe, almost rampant, with female carnality.

Between Cora and her sister there exist officially all the requisite love and devotion, but we are made aware of a barely suppressed sense of rivalry—the yearning felt by a presumably experienced woman to return to the pristine state of the innocent virgin. (" 'That I cannot see the sunny side of the picture of life, like this artless but ardent enthusiast,' she added, laying her hand lightly, but affectionately, on the arm of her sister, 'is the penalty of experience, and, perhaps, the misfortune of my nature.' ") By clear implication a fully sexual woman, Cora harbors a not-so-secret sympathy for the darkly attractive savage—officially contradicted, of course, by her public statements of horror whenever Magua mentions marriage—

N. Orr illustration for The Pathfinder.

and it is she who is forced to bear the "fierce looks," "wavering glances," and other expressions "that no chaste female might endure" of the lustful savage. Even the reserved and noble Uncas is committed by nature to showing a preference for Cora: he treats Alice with "sufficient courtesy," but when faced with Cora, "his dark eye lingered on her rich, speaking countenance."

What Cora's countenance utters, of course—even, as Cooper would have it, in spite of her conscious intentions—is the dark secret of human sexuality. (Cora's slight admixture of Negro blood, received from a slave ancestress from whom she is "remotely" descended, surely is intended as a kind of folk-shorthand for establishing her claim, not to Negro racial identity, but to passion. However, one cannot absolve Cooper of hedging on the question of female sexuality by trying to convince us—and himself—that it is a "Negro" characteristic and thus not to be thought of in connection with the blonde Alice or any pure white woman.) It is not just the evil Indian, Magua, who is attracted to Cora, but theoretically any Indian, for sexuality in Cooper's mythic scheme of things is the "redskin" element in human nature—an element which, as we have seen, Cooper cannot help but discover in the paleface also.

The universality of this mythos reveals the narrowness of Fiedler's notion that miscegenation is the "secret theme" of *The Last of the Mohicans* and of the Leatherstocking Tales generally. Despite Cooper's obvious interest in and horror of racial mixing, the not very secret theme of *The Last of the Mohicans* seems more truly to be the Miltonic one, that sex brought and brings death into the world, with all our woe and loss of Eden. Magua/Satan (the connection is made explicitly by Cooper) brings about the destruction of Uncas/Adam and Cora/Eve, to say nothing of his turning all of Fort William Henry into a fallen world of death and desolation. The only ones really exempt from the effects of sin are Natty and Chingachgook, who have substituted ideal friendship and devotion to manly duty for the baser passions, and seal their compact of purity with almost religious zeal (a firm handshake and scalding tears) over the monitory grave of Uncas, who was noble but tainted by desire.

The archetypal blonde and brunette appear again, this time in a slightly comic form, in *The Deerslayer,* where they are incarnated in the Hutter sisters, Hetty and Judith. With a show of wit that improbably combines a conventional Elizabethan conceit and Indian insight, Chingachgook names the girls, respectively, the Drooping Lily and the Wild Rose: "Drooping" for Hetty, because she is simple-minded, a wilted version of the normally alert and strong-willed blonde heroine; and "Wild" for Judith, because with her reputation for looseness she is a kind of wood nymph, a sylvan version of the normally (but usually covertly) passionate dark lady.

Hetty, "a subdued and humble copy" of her sister, is so far removed from the notion of sex that she is scarcely described by Cooper at all, except for his saying that she is "guileless, innocent, and without distrust." Judith, however, is convincingly presented as a delicious morsel, fit "only for a man whose teeth show the full marks." She is a woman who "has had *men* among her suitors, ever since she was fifteen," and the brutally masculine Hurry Harry March waxes eloquent over her endowments: "The hussy is handsome, and she knows it. Boy, not a tree that is growing in these hills is straighter, or waves in the wind with an easier bend, nor did you ever see the doe that bounded with a more nat'ral motion." Natty's reaction to March's tempting description of Judith is defensive—"For my part, I feel more cur'osity about the feeble-witted sister than about your beauty"—and his warning to March makes an interesting suggestion about this passionate creature: "I would think no more of such a woman, but turn my mind altogether to the forest; *that* will not deceive you, being ordered and ruled by a hand that never wavers."

For Natty the fundamental choice is between women, with their blandishments, and the innocent forest. But his way of stating this truth clearly suggests that, whereas the forest is God's creation, the dark lady is not. She is the devil's child, associated, as we should expect, with cleverness and redskins. ("Judith," reveals March, "is as full of wit, and talk, and cunning, as an old Indian orator.") For as Natty insists, "the Evil Spirit delights more to dwell in an artful body, than in one that has no cunning to work upon." Here Cooper not only institutes an association of sex with the head that was to become standard in the American romance, but also combines in Natty's reaction our national ambivalence toward sexuality and what many observers consider our native anti-intellectualism.

Other important characteristics of the two women are suggested when Natty enters the Ark of the Hutter family and finds himself in the girls' bedroom. Hetty's "homely vestments" remind him of his mother (the standard connection is thus established between the fair lady and motherhood, the hearth and the heart); but on seeing Judith's fancy clothes, "he bethought himself of a sister, whose incipient and native taste for finery had exhibited itself somewhat in the manner of that of Judith." The identification between the dark lady

and the figure of the sister—to be developed in the fiction of Poe, Melville, and Faulkner as the maddeningly tantalizing and forbidden incest wish—is very faint, but it is certainly present. Cooper only tells us that "these little resemblances opened a long-hidden vein of sensations; and as he [Natty] quitted the room, it was with a saddened mien." The vein of Natty's sensations is presumably one of tenderness; but since Judith and his sister are clearly associated in Natty's mind, we are free to consider the more complex implications of the passage. Is Natty forced to recall a sister who, like Judith, was also a fallen woman? Or is he saddened by being confronted, in the opposing images of mother and sister—fair lady and dark lady—with his own complicated reactions, usually submerged, to the dual figure of woman?

What is certain, in any case, is that in rejecting Judith's marital overtures at the end of *The Deerslayer,* Natty is rejecting not only the general notion of marriage but also, and more particularly, the strong suggestion of sexuality provided by Judith's escapades at the garrison. Marriage to Judith represents the threat of mixing sex and sentiment—the threat of discovering, within oneself, a moral ambiguity. Ultimately Natty flees the moral "messiness" implied by the female character itself, and chooses to push off into the forest so that he can wrestle instead, as Lawrence says, with "the American wild, as a hermit wrestles with God and Satan," in a realm where the adversary is external and the categories of good and evil more clearly delineated [see D. H. Lawrence excerpt, *NCLC,* Vol. 1, pp 214-16].

It might seem a flat contradiction of the foregoing formulation that we find Natty Bumppo in *The Pathfinder* actually offering himself to Mabel Dunham in marriage. But a close scrutiny of the story reveals no contradiction at all; on the contrary, the essential fable of Leatherstocking and Cooper's underlying intention in his treatment of women in the series are here most clearly brought to the surface. In *The Pathfinder* the belief in the essential duality of the female nature is embodied, not in the familiar two ladies, but in the two roles between which Mabel Dunham must choose in the course of the action: either the religiously devoted daughter of her father, or the sinful (because sexual) wife of a lusty young man.

The first alternative is contained, surprisingly but with a ruthless logic, in Natty's offer of marriage to Mabel. Cooper's intention should be unmistakable—to the reader, at least. Natty and Sergeant Dunham, Mabel's father, have been "tried, sworn, and constant" friends for twenty years, beginning before Mabel was born, and the idea for the match largely originates with the father. "Although necessarily much weaned from the caresses and blandishments that had rendered his child so dear to him, during the first year or two of his widowhood, he had still a strong, but somewhat latent, love for her," and he clearly intends to gratify that love by choosing a mate for her who will really be a surrogate father. When Natty exhibits diffidence at his abilities in courtship, the Sergeant reassures him by saying, "Tut, tut, man; I foresee I must do half this courting for you!"

Mabel is not slow at realizing that marrying Natty would be like marrying her father, and she receives his proposal with manifest horror: "While I esteem, respect—nay, reverence you, almost as much as I reverence my own dear father, it is impossible that I should ever become your wife. . . . a match like that would be unwise—unnatural, perhaps." And Natty himself sees the justice of Mabel's complaint: "Yes, unnat'ral—ag'in natur'; and so I told the serjeant, but he *would* have it otherwise." Yet Mabel is almost convinced to do as her father wishes:

> Trained like a woman [as a woman should be!], to subdue her most ardent feelings, her thoughts reverted to her father, and to the blessings that awaited the child who yielded to a parent's wishes. "Father," she said quietly, almost with a holy calm—"God blesses the dutiful daughter! . . . certainly the man is not living for whom I have more respect than for Pathfinder; not even for you, dear father."

All the while that Mabel is making this speech of holy sacrifice, her face, Cooper tells us, seems "angelic," but a practiced eye "might have traced something wild and unnatural in it." And this intimate interview between father and daughter reaches its conclusion in a climax of tears: "Mabel threw herself into her father's arms—it was the first time in her life—and sobbed on his bosom like an infant. The stern old soldier's heart was melted, and the tears of the two mingled; but Serjeant Dunham soon started, as if ashamed of himself," and Mabel goes sobbing to bed.

It is difficult to know just how conscious Cooper was of this (as it now appears) unabashed toying with the notion of incest; it surely casts a strange light on his own role as the father of daughters. But the obvious intent here is quite other: like the protagonist of a Restoration tragedy, Mabel must choose between love (passion) and honor. It is as if the Serjeant and Natty were combining in an attempt to convince women to choose a life of "purity" and renunciation, rather than the expression of their physical and emotional natures. But the implications of this situation for Natty Bumppo himself are even more interesting. It is worth noting, first, that the only time in the Leatherstocking series when Natty seems in serious danger of marriage, the danger is more apparent than real. We *know* that Mabel Dunham will never marry the Pathfinder; and we have good reason to suspect that Natty knows this too and thus has offered himself, for the first and last time, *safely,* in a situation where he does not really run the risk of being accepted (the whole episode ultimately affording Natty the acceptable emotional outlet of a shameless indulgence in self-pity). Furthermore, Natty sees very clearly just what sort of marriage offer he is making. "You're more befitting to be my daughter than to be my wife," he finally admits to Mabel; and at the very moment when he asks her to choose between himself and Jasper Western, he attempts to encourage her to speak freely by saying, "I told him [the Serjeant] that I would be a father to you, as well as a husband, and it seems to me no feeling father would deny his child this small privilege. Stand up, Mabel, therefore, and speak your thoughts as freely as if I were the Serjeant himself." Standing-in for her father, he urges her to choose him as a husband!

Natty is thus manifestly offering himself only as the most parental of spouses, since Cooper is aware that any other kind of marriage would damage Natty's mythic status. "I'm sometimes afear'd," the Pathfinder says early in the book, "it isn't wholesome for one who is much occupied in a very manly calling . . . to form friendships for women,—young women in particular." If he is to remain, as Mabel originally sees him, "above, beyond, superior to all infirmity . . . a man . . . little liable to the weaknesses of nature," he must, in Cooper's words, be "untempted by unruly or ambitious desires . . . neither led aside by the inducements which influence all to do evil." Chief among these inducements, of course, is sex.

Women are a danger because, through sex appeal, they weaken the moral fibre and would make Natty give in to "evil"—would show it, in fact, to be an integral part of his nature. Desire would prove him an irretrievably fallen man. Therefore, if Natty is to marry Mabel, he can do so only as a father—a guide and protector. He must believe always in the sentimental love religion—in woman's purity, in her right to remain holy, inviolate, and unsexual. For Natty to accept Mabel otherwise would be to admit his own sexuality. Therefore, he cannot acknowledge that he has a pleasure phallus to offer a woman; Killdeer is a symbol of law, order, chastisement, and food-getting. One might say that Natty revenges himself on female sexuality by insisting on treating women unsexually. The kind of marriage he offers Mabel Dunham is a punishment for the eternal Eve in all women.

Cooper, as a matter of fact, closes *The Pathfinder* on an explicitly Miltonic note. As Mabel prepares to leave Natty and cleave unto Jasper, the young lovers look "like a pair of guilty beings":

> Jasper and Mabel sat, resembling Milton's picture of our first parents, when the consciousness of sin first laid its leaden weight on their souls. Neither spoke, neither even moved; though both at that moment fancied they could part with their new-found happiness [Eros], in order to restore their friend [Natty] to his peace of mind. Jasper was pale as death; but, in Mabel, maiden modesty [!] had caused the blood to mantle on her cheeks, until their bloom was heightened to a richness that was scarce equalled in her hours of light-hearted buoyancy and joy.

Sin and death have entered the world again, and Pathfinder/God is suffering, as is Jasper/Adam. Only Mabel/ Eve/Lilith is pleased. Or, to put it another way, Natty is the old Adam confronted with a young pair who willingly "fall" all over again, and his peace of mind is accordingly disrupted. Yet Natty's anguish is a necessary component of his character. He must be continually reminded of the nearness of danger, so that he can avoid it at all costs. He knows that sin brings death and loss of Paradise, and if he would remain worthy of the American Eden, he must be careful.

"This being," Cooper tells us, with profound insight into his own creation, "in his peculiar way, was a sort of type of what Adam might have been supposed to be before the fall, though certainly not without sin." This paradox defines Natty Bumppo, the American Adam, who combines prelapsarian virtue with postlapsarian knowledge. He is aware that he can maintain his goodness in a fallen world only by means of a strict moral code, devilish cunning, and a deadly weapon. His is a goodness that takes evil tacitly into account, a militant goodness that protects its purity by being always on guard against the enemy. He believes the civilized world to be evil and separates himself from it; he is self-righteous and wary. As Cooper explains:

> The affinities of such a character were, as a matter of course, those of like for like. His associates and intimates . . . were generally of the highest order, as to moral propensities; for he appeared to possess a species of instinctive discrimination that led him insensibly to himself, most probably, to cling closest to those whose characters would best reward his friendship

—better, to cling closest to those whose characters would

least endanger his position. Women, with their ambiguous natures, are of course the primary threat.

We are now in a position to spell out the essential fable of Natty's celebrated friendship with Chingachgook, the "Big Sarpent" (so called, as Natty never tires of explaining, after "a sartain sarpent at the creation of the 'arth that outwitted the first woman"). The American Adam knows intuitively how to avoid the error of his archetypal ancestor: he can only hope to retain possession of his American Eden if he makes a pact with the devil and they jointly exclude women from the virgin forest. "Where is the man to turn this beautiful place into . . . a garden of Eden for us?" Judith Hutter demands of her sister Hetty. The harsh answer is given throughout the Leatherstocking Tales: the American Eden (to paraphrase Melville) is a Paradise for bachelors only. (pp. 20-8)

Joel Porte, "Cooper," in his The Romance in America: Studies in Cooper, Poe, Hawthorne, Melville, and James, *Wesleyan University Press, 1969, pp. 3-52.*

MICHAEL D. BUTLER   (essay date 1976)

[*In the following essay, Butler finds that the narrative structure of* The Last of the Mohicans *echoes a pattern of historical development in the United States: the decline of the native American and European immigrant and the rise of a distinctly American type.*]

The Last of the Mohicans is commonly thought the most exciting of the Leatherstocking tales; a number of critics also consider it the least significant of them. Yvor Winters, for one, declared it "the best single plot of adventure in Cooper," but added that it "nowhere rises to a level of seriousness" [see *NCLC*, Vol. 1, pp. 220-22]. James Grossman characterized it as "pure adventure story," "deliberately superficial" and set in "an arbitrarily simplified world" where "everything happens for the sake of the excitement of the action" [see Further Reading]. Their opinions are representative; they are also perfectly understandable. Supposedly, serious historical fiction must, like the epic, deal with events of great importance to race or nation. From an American standpoint, the action in Cooper's novel instead appears almost perversely insignificant. Despite its precise subtitle—"A Narrative of 1757"—and its use of specific geographical settings, actual characters and events, in terms of historical consequence *The Last of the Mohicans* seems to float free of real place and time. Characteristic—perhaps symbolic—of all is the fall of Fort William Henry, the most significant actual event in the novel. It is a French victory in a war won by the English, a war "waged," according to Cooper, "for the possession of a country that neither was destined to retain." A like air of futility surrounds most action in Cooper's tale. Characters take what turn out to be fruitless precautions; they lay out and follow what prove to be foolish plans. They put faith in empty authorities, practice useless skills. Nearly all of them end the novel dead or isolated in the wilderness. Indeed, at first glance, the common denominator of all those situations Cooper gathered together into his book seems to be chaos. "But everything depends," as Hawkeye says, "on what scale you look at things." In *The Last of the Mohicans,* an admirably constructed adventure story tends to obscure an equally well-structured argument. As we should expect, the novel is less a narrative of particular events than the illustration of universal principles. While on one level it depicts the chaotic vio-

lence of an apparently meaningless struggle, on another it demonstrates the well-ordered process of historical change. In general, the events of *The Last of the Mohicans* embody a theory of human progress. In particular, they compress into two weeks the three most crucial developments in our nation's past: the decline of both Indian and European on the continent, and the consequent creation and rise of the American.

No matter what its ultimate order, however, *The Last of the Mohicans* is at least superficially the most violent of the Leatherstocking tales, a story filled with the pursuit, torture, and bloody—for some readers gratuitous—slaughter of defenseless men, women, children, and small animals. Quite appropriately, therefore, the novel contains a number of obvious borrowings from Gothic fiction. Terrifying, apparently unearthly, cries ring out in the night. Young virgins fleeing the threat of rape take refuge in grottoes, are imprisoned in caves. Demonic savages—their leader a corrupt aristocrat at times less Huron than Italian—skulk through the woods carrying out the sinister commands of a master intelligence. Men constantly slide in and out of disguise as they alter identities, rank, loyalties. Of greater significance—because it suggests Cooper was interested in more than merely borrowing literary conventions—the world of *The Last of the Mohicans* is, like the nightmare landscape of the Gothic, a place of broken barriers where the boundaries between rational and irrational, natural and supernatural, seem to have given way. It is a world apparently operated by chance and what might be termed "fatal inertia." Near the middle of the novel Cooper placed a scene in which Montcalm is pictured contemplating Magua and "brooding deeply on the temper" of "his ungovernable ally." "As he mused," the novel states, "he became keenly sensible of the deep responsibility they assume who disregard the means to attain their end, and of all the danger of setting in motion an engine which it exceeds human power to control." The passage is strikingly like the confession of Carwin, a ventriloquist in Charles Brockden Brown's *Wieland,* who by thoughtlessly misusing his talent begins a process which culminates in a man's murdering wife and children. Of his responsibility, Carwin says, "Surely my malignant stars had not made me the cause of her death; yet had I not rashly set in motion a machine, over whose progress I had no controul, and which experience had shewn me was infinite in power?" Supposedly those lines at least in part inspired Mary Shelley's *Frankenstein,* which, like *Wieland,* deals with the chaos man-made monsters bring to the religion, society, or science creating them. Both books also demonstrate a process in which monsters once set in motion stay in motion, uncontrolled until their course has been run. Man has the power to set his creations going, the lesson runs, but not to stop them or even alter their direction. Attempts to do either merely intensify the violence made inevitable by his original act. The process begun by the experiments of Doctor Frankenstein ends in the Arctic after the destruction of the scientist's family, his monster, and himself. At the climax of Brown's novel, Carwin's attempt to check Wieland's homicidal progress by once again throwing his voice immediately precipitates a horrific suicide.

The Last of the Mohicans is filled with analogous monsters in analogous motion. Although less violent, David Gamut is one. He is introduced as the embodiment of chaos. A "false superstructure of blended human orders . . . so profanely reared," he lacks the "proportions" of other men and is characterized by a "contrariety in his members." A similar contrariety lies in the conflict between his instincts and his education, between the beauty of his singing voice and the flat prosiness of his lyrics. Like Frankenstein's monster, Gamut is both the twisted product and the emblem of man's attempts to impose himself upon the external world. In Cooper's work, Gamut specifically reveals the inherent falsity of American Puritanism's arrogant suppressions and redefinitions of Nature. More generally, his inability to master his surroundings or himself is, in varying degrees and with varying implications, typical of all characters in the novel. On a lesser level, the artificial gait of the Narragansett walkers represents another perversion of nature—as does bringing the societally bred horses into the wild where they do not belong. That act creates a chaotic situation which neither Heyward nor Bumppo—nor Magua in his turn—can control. More tragically, Cora embodies the chaos resulting from a violation of the integrity of race. She is the consequence of slavery, of one man's imposition of his will on another, and, in Munro's mind, "a curse entailed on Scotland by her unnatural union with a foreign and trading people." The most conventionally monstrous of grotesques, however, is Montcalm's confederation of traditional Indian enemies. The French general's helplessness at its nightmarish eruption into the butchery of Fort William most graphically exemplifies the Gothic process operating in the novel. There are other and perhaps more significant engines, however. Magua is one. Not wholly Montcalm's creation, he is in one sense the culmination of an evolutionary process begun when the Dutch first used whiskey to further trade with the Indian. In another sense, he is a consequence of Munro's "imprudent severity," a fruitless attempt to alter that process. In his own turn, the Huron is both monster and helpless keeper of a monster. Like Montcalm, he attempts to direct a disordered band of savages to serve his own end—a confused mixture of lust for revenge and lust for Cora. Like Montcalm he is unable to maintain control.

The greatest monster of all, however, is the world of *The Last of the Mohicans,* a grotesque created like the rest by man's will to impose. Thrown out of balance by Dutch, French, and English attempts to impress European names, policies, ideals, traditions on American lands and peoples, it is a chaotic mixing of savage and civilized, red and white. Within its boundaries no man can be certain of anything—least of all himself. The frequently cited inadequacies of Duncan, Munro, and Montcalm underscore the impotence of the civilized. Less often noted lapses of Cooper's "warriors of the woods" emphasize their inability to cope with this hybrid world. When confronted by the unfamiliar shriek of frightened horses, for example, Bumppo is unmanned by superstition. Lost in a fog, he follows a cannon ball's furrow toward rather than away from danger. In the final chase, Uncas is likewise undone when his uncharacteristic love of Cora overcomes Indian restraint. Overanxious, he rushes ahead, slips, falls and—lying face down—is stabbed in the back.

The best expression of the chaotically gathered world and of the nature and significance of action taking place within it is Bumppo's description of Glens Falls:

> " . . . look at the perversity of the water. It falls by no rule at all; sometimes it leaps, sometimes it tumbles; there, it skips; here, it shoots; in one place 't is white as snow, and in another 't is green as grass; hereabouts it pitches into deep hollows, that rumble and quake the 'arth; and thereaway it ripples and sings like a brook, fashioning whirlpools and gulleys in the old stone, as if 't was no harder than trodden clay. The whole design of the river seems disconcerted. First it runs smoothly, as if meaning to go down the descent as things were ordered; then it angles about and faces the shores; nor are there places wanting where it looks backward, as if unwilling to leave the wilderness, to mingle with the salt! Aye, lady, the fine cobweb-looking cloth you wear at your throat is coarse, and like a fish net, to little spots I can show you, where the river fabricates all sorts of images, as if, having broke loose from order, it would try its hand at everything. And yet what does it amount to? After the water has been suffered to have its will, for a time, like a headstrong man, it is gathered together by the hand that made it, and a few rods below you may see it all, flowing on steadily towards the sea, as was foreordained from the first foundation of the 'arth!"

Significantly the perversity of the falls lies in its sublimity—in its mingling of extreme contrasts. It is therefore a natural analogue for the world of the French and Indian War. The water's conflict of sounds, colors, movements corresponds to the turmoil of race, policy, tradition within the bloody arena bordered by the headwaters of the Hudson and the holy lake. Like the falls, the war world fabricates all sorts of confused and contradictory images; both are temporary collections of disconnected and ultimately inconsequential elements. The falls is therefore to the river what the war was, in Cooper's mind, to American history. In spite of Glens' impressive grandeur or sublime terror, when compared to the predestined flow of the entire river, it stands revealed as a brief passage, a momentary departure from the greater design. It is, in other words, a chaos of the surface only.

That is true of all disorder in *The Last of the Mohicans.* The novel may be the bloodiest of the Leatherstocking tales but its violence proves insignificant when compared to its essential order. Actually, individual characters and events are the only chaotic elements in the book, and they are ultimately overwhelmed by a scene, style, and structure which embody and demonstrate the truth of universal order. Nature presents the most immediate contrast to those violent elements. The first paragraph of *The Last of the Mohicans* sets out the conflict between man's desire for battle and the country in which he must wage it.

> It was a feature peculiar to the colonial wars of North America, that the toils and dangers of the wilderness were to be encountered before the adverse hosts could meet. A wide and apparently an impervious boundary of forests severed the possessions of the hostile provinces of France and England. The hardy colonist, and the trained European who fought at his side, frequently expended months in struggling against the rapids of the streams, or in effecting the rugged passes of the mountains, in quest of an opportunity to exhibit their courage in a more martial conflict.

The ironic contrast of the passage is maintained throughout the novel. Action is frequently put into historical perspective as Cooper asserts that "what was wilderness then is wilderness still." Men and armies are "swallowed" by the woods. Violent scenes almost always give way to panoramas, word versions of Hudson River paintings and therefore in subject, composition, and technique the very embodiments of natural order.

On another level, style functions in a similar way. Characterized by an abstract vocabulary set into extended and syntactically balanced complex sentences, Cooper's manner of writing is so fundamentally decorous and rational it often seems at odds with the graphic action it describes. In most cases style deadens or de-emphasizes violent event—as in the case of the grisliest scene in the novel, the murders of mother and baby during the Fort William massacre. There the potential effect of braining the child and tomahawking the parent is wholly undercut by the alliteration, balance, and generally anti-climatic movement of the paragraph. A better example of the message Cooper's style could communicate comes at the end of Chapter 2 in this description of the unsuspecting party riding into a forest full of hostile Indians:

> A gleam of exultation shot across the darkly painted lineaments of the inhabitant of the forest, as he traced the route of his intended victims, who rode unconsciously onward; the light and graceful forms of the females waving among the trees, in the curvatures of their path, followed at each bend by the manly figure of Heyward, until, finally, the shapeless person of the singing-master was concealed behind the numberless trunks of trees, that rose, in dark lines, in the intermediate space.

Here abstract language undercuts the immediacy of the scene. Furthermore, by stressing line and shape, Cooper's writing directs attention away from the subject of the picture to its art, an ordered set of techniques and processes. It therefore emphasizes that character and event are not mirrorings of real life but elements in an arrangement governed by a definite set of artistic principles. In this case then, by its very nature Cooper's style argues the existence of laws, ideals, truths, beyond the concrete. It suggests that action is less meaningful than its context and that behind the apparent chaos of immediate scene may lie a more real order.

A similar suggestion is communicated by the structure of the novel. Although contemporary publishing practices determined in advance that *The Last of the Mohicans* would be two volumes long, Cooper seems to have made a special attempt to balance his halves. He manipulated actual chronology, for one thing, to place Fort William's fall exactly in the middle of his tale. The first volume covers the seven days before the surrender, the second the seven after. Imprisonment in a cave centers each volume. Each climaxes with a massacre: the first, the slaughter of whites at Fort William; the second, the defeat of the Hurons—a "destruction of a whole community." Even the major dissimilarities of the two halves suggest the mirrored balance of opposites. The first part is set in a world dominated by civilized consciousness. Here the identities of the whites are fixed, and Magua plays the imposter. The second is set within the red world. There Magua's identity is certain; Natty and, more particularly, Duncan slide in and out of disguise.

The cast of characters as a whole is, however, the greatest single argument for the hidden order of the novel's world. The characters are fairly evenly divided into savage and civilized, red and white, moral and immoral; each major figure has at least one counterpart or correspondent. Most obvious is the relationship of Uncas and Magua, who, bound together by love of Cora, seem mirror images of one another. Both are chiefs in search of a tribe. For good or bad, both are in some way in advance of other red men. Each is a courageous warrior and skilled orator. Each is also, in a sense, a solitary man. Magua has lost wife and children and so, like Uncas, is the last of a line. There is of course an essential difference here.

Uncas has been isolated by history; as the last of the unmixed people, he is racially superior to all other Indians. Magua has been cast out of his tribe. While Uncas stands above the Delaware, therefore, Magua—as Cooper's descriptions stress—merely sits apart from the Huron. That difference is reflected in their contrasting attitudes toward Cora. Uncas loves chastely with a "sympathy that elevated him far above the intelligence, and advanced him probably centuries before the practices of his nation." Magua acts out those practices. In his eyes, Cora finds "an expression that no chaste female might endure." It is on the fundamental level of morality, therefore, that Uncas and Magua are most clearly opposite. Pure-blooded and virtuous, the Mohican is literally the Indian race's highest point of development, a realization of all its potential for good. Magua on the other hand represents the Indian in decline, still possessing physical and intellectual skills but morally degraded by mongrel blood and whiskey.

Uncas's moral correspondent is the white, Duncan Heyward. Early in the novel, there appears a scene in which those two clasp hands. No doubt Cooper intended that the act draw attention to the many similarities between the men whose names nearly rhyme and who are also bound by love—this time of sisters. Both are young chiefs and, in their proper worlds, skilled warriors. Uncas is master of the wild; neither Hawkeye nor Chingachgook can match his talent for reading signs. In council, he is eloquent enough to sway Delaware elders; by the end of the novel he has become their youngest war chief. Duncan enters the book the youngest officer in King George's Royal Americans, and, whatever his problems in the woods, he is the master of civilization. "A gallant gentleman" of "vast riches," he has distinguished himself on conventional battlefields. Munro defers to his diplomatic skills; Montcalm finds him an equal in the art of diplomatic banter. Within their separate worlds, then, Uncas and Duncan possess equivalent skills and occupy analogous positions. More important, they are also bound by similar racial purity and moral superiority.

Standing in contrast is the less obvious but equally significant correspondence of Magua and Montcalm. As in the case of Uncas and Duncan, Cooper appears to have designed several scenes primarily to draw attention to the relationship. When Montcalm enters the novel, Duncan signals the connection as, "turning his eyes from the malign expression of Magua, [he] suffered them to rest with pleasure on the smiling and polished features, and the noble military air, of the French general." Later, in Chapter 17, Cooper brings the two villains together in another episode centered by the touching of hands and apparently serving no purpose other than to reemphasize the link between them. Like Duncan and Uncas, Montcalm and Magua are white and red versions of one another. Both are chiefs; both are courageous. Montcalm will prove his bravery, the novel tells us, on the Plains of Abraham; Magua's defiant death dominates the end of the book. Both are cunning politicians. "In a more advanced state of society," we are told, the subtle fox Magua would have been entitled "to the reputation of a skilled diplomatist." The "Jesuitical" Montcalm is "expert in those political practices which do not always respect the nicer obligations of morality, and which so generally disgraced the European diplomacy of that period." The two even share the petty deceptions of schemers; each enters the novel feigning ignorance of English. More important, both disregard means in pursuing ends. Each uses the Indian for his own purposes; each sets in motion a red engine he cannot control.

Besides maintaining a balance of red and white, savage and civilized, the correspondence of Magua and Montcalm also suggests that the Frenchman is more important to *The Last of the Mohicans* than he at first seems. The comparison emphasizes that because of greater power and possibility, Montcalm—and the Europe he represents—is a greater villain. That is supported by Bumppo's frequent assertions that the bloody arena is the Frenchman's creation. That fact, in turn, necessarily renders Magua a more complexly perceived character, and enhances Duncan Heyward's position in the book. He is, of course, Montcalm's proper counterpart or adversary. Like Uncas and Magua, Duncan and Montcalm share military and diplomatic skills. But also like Mohican and Huron, the men are in spite of many similarities fundamentally opposite, and once again the distinguishing qualities are blood and morality. Duncan is pure Anglo-Saxon; Montcalm is not. Despite some early slips, Duncan is essentially a Christian gentleman; Montcalm is "deficient in that moral courage without which no man can be truly great."

At the conclusion of the novel, Cooper predicts the future relationship of Hawkeye and Chingachgook as they clasp hands over Uncas's grave. For most of the book, however, Chingachgook is a less obvious correspondent for the scout than is David Gamut. The two white men are similarly named; both carry lower-class Christian names taken from the Old Testament. They are physically alike. Gamut may be wholly uncoordinated but he resembles Bumppo enough to pass for him in the Huron camp. Both men are likewise extremely conscious of "gifts"; each uses the word when proclaiming his being true to his talents. Although both are white, the two are—like Magua and Montcalm, Uncas and Duncan—savage and civilized versions of each other. Furthermore, both are variations of a literary type—the garrulous bore whose thought is controlled more by association than reason. Because the more conventional—galloping onto the scene one-spurred like his antecedents, the Puritan knights Hudibras and Ichabod Crane—Gamut is the more obviously comic character. But he is not the only one. The singer's introduction to the novel, a convoluted discourse on the Narragansett walking horse, Old England, and New Haven is often matched by Bumppo's windy treatises. During the final stalking of the Huron, for example, Hawkeye launches forth on the future of the horse in wilderness warfare. Heyward's reaction and the scout's sulky reply reveal Cooper's comic intentions:

> "This is a subject that might better be discussed at another time," returned Heyward; "shall we charge?"

> "I see no contradiction to the gifts of any man, in passing his breathing spells in useful reflections," the scout replied.

In another scene, Bumppo arrives at a mineral spring and, unable to find a drinking gourd, rants and raves. Once again, another character's reaction points up the intended humor of the episode:

> ". . . the vagabonds have thrown away the gourd! This is the way with benefits, when they are bestowed on such disremembering hounds! Here has the Lord laid his hand, in the midst of the howling wilderness, for their good, and raised a fountain of water from the bowels of the 'arth, that might laugh at the richest shop of apothecary's ware in all the colonies; and see! the knaves have trodden in the

clay, and deformed the cleanliness of the place, as though they were brute beasts, instead of human men."

> Uncas silently extended towards him the desired gourd, which the spleen of Hawkeye had hitherto prevented him from observing, on a branch of an elm.

As these passages emphasize, scout as well as singer is a grotesque. While Gamut is obviously too much the creature of an unnatural and irrational Puritan society, Bumppo, the novel suggests, is too much a warrior of the woods. Despite Hawkeye's constant assertions of his "crosslessness," Magua for one considers him a half-way man—"one whose skin is neither red nor pale." In addition, Bumppo evidences at least one sign of the degeneration Crèvecoeur believed an inescapable effect of frontier life. He possesses a "secret love of desperate adventure which had increased with his experience, until hazard and danger had become, in some measure, necessary to the enjoyment of his existence." Hawkeye, Cooper intimated, is a proud killer, one who boasts there is not "the space of a square mile atwixt Horican and the river that Killdeer has n't dropped a living body on, be it an enemy or be it a brute beast."

The most significant correspondence between Gamut and Bumppo is their nearly equal inability to cope with the nightmare world of *The Last of the Mohicans*. In fact, despite the scout's gibes, Gamut's humble dependence often proves a more effective guide through chaos than Hawkeye's vaunted skills. A number of episodes therefore imply that Bumppo is unwarrantedly proud of his abilities. Despite his authoritative discourse on the art of bear imitation, had he, the book states, "been aware of the low estimation in which the more skillful Uncas held his representations, he would probably have prolonged the entertainment a little in pique." More dramatically to the point are those occasions when the scout is rendered helpless by things beyond his "cunning or experience"—by the screams of the horses at Glens Falls or the fog before Fort William. Not particularly intellectual and thus incapable of innovation, Bumppo is, Cooper stressed, a limited man. Uncas more quickly understands new signs. He recognizes the characteristic mark of the Narragansett, for example, and associates it with the sisters even as Hawkeye commits himself to a false trail. Cora is more imaginative. After firing his last shot in the fight at Glens Falls, Bumppo sits down to die; the girl's plan saves him. In many ways, therefore, Bumppo is at least as big a fool as David Gamut, and so, while the correspondence of the two maintains the balance of the cast by providing savage and civilized versions of the bore, it also argues that no matter what the future awaiting him in later Leatherstocking Tales, Hawkeye is not the hero of *The Last of the Mohicans*.

In all, the balanced division of the novel's cast into white and red, savage and civilized, reflects Cooper's social ideal, the hierarchical order of the great chain of being. It also suggests the dynamic version of that chain, a rising spiral in which civilized and savage are analogous but superior and inferior rings. That is, in fact, the pattern of historical change depicted in the book as possession of America passes upward from a red to a white nation. At first glance, of course, there seems to be nothing ascending about the action of the novel. Instead of transitions, it seems to offer only dead ends. Most obviously it portrays the end of the Mohicans and portends the extinction of all red men. As Tamenund announces in the closing lines:

> "The pale-faces are masters of the earth, and the time of the red-men has not yet come again. My day has been too long. In the morning I saw the sons of Unamis happy and strong; and yet, before the night has come, have I lived to see the last warrior of the wise race of the Mohicans."

Besides mirroring Cooper's method, the ancient Delaware's compression of his life—and by extension the history of the Indian—into a single day also establishes the proper meaning of Uncas's death. As the embodiment of Indian virtues, the Mohican points up what is to be lost with the passing of his people. More accurately, because he enters the novel a miraculously preserved artifact of an evolutionary peak reached years before, Uncas reveals what has already been lost. The future of the Indian lies with the Huron whose continuing degradation predicts the fate of the race. Set in contrast to the melodious harmony of Uncas's voice and character is the chaotic squalor of the Huron village, a place planned and constructed with less care than a beaver dam. As the last of the unmixed people, Uncas represents the particular perfection attainable only in the integrated world of a tribe held together by "the claims of a common origin, a similar language, and . . . moral interest" (preface to the first edition). In contrast, the Huron—contaminated by indiscriminate mixing of blood and by contact with the whites—project the brutalization attending the violation of those natural categories.

Because both Uncas and the Huron represent different phases in the same history, that history is not tragic. The existence of the two renders the red man's decline a gradual process rather than an abrupt fall. What is more, tragedy supposedly requires choice; Cooper gave the Indian none. The Mohican's superiority depends upon the purity of his blood; because no unmixed women remain, his race can have no future. Furthermore because the red race realized its potential in Uncas and because change is the rule of Nature, the Indian's decline is both inevitable and right. "Does not," Tamenund asks, "the egg become a worm—the worm a fly, and perish?" That truth is implicit in the many conventional signs of mutability and mortality scattered throughout the novel. Dead trees, ruined forts, and grown-over mounds all preach the same general lesson. The last, however, point an even more specific moral. Because they were widely accepted as artifacts of a city-building people who had ruled America before the invasion of nomadic red men, the mounds here serve as signs of national change. Likewise when coupled with frequent references to the Oriental origin and character of the red race, they also argue that no Indian—not even Chingachook—can be considered the God-appointed eternal owner of North America. They therefore help to place the red race within the context of a cyclical history and by so doing necessarily alter the reader's attitudes toward both the disappearance of the Indian and the ensuing rise of the white American nation.

That is also true of the other cycle ended in *The Last of the Mohicans,* the European. Throughout his novel, Cooper constantly if unobtrusively reminded his reader of the continent's colonial past. *The Last of the Mohicans* contains references to the Dutch and their brief rule over New York. Montcalm embodies those North American ambitions of France that died with him on the Plains of Abraham. More interesting, Munro acts out the less dramatic decline of British power. Early in Chapter I, Cooper wrote:

> The imbecility of her military leaders abroad, and the fatal want of energy in her councils at home, had lowered the character of Great Britain from the proud elevation on which it had been placed by the talents and enterprise of her former warriors and statesmen. No longer dreaded by her enemies, her servants were fast losing the confidence of self-respect. In this mortifying abasement, the colonists, though innocent of her imbecility, and too humble to be the agents of her blunders, were but the natural participators.

> They had recently seen a chosen army from that country, which, reverencing as a mother, they had blindly believed invincible—an army led by a chief who had been selected from a crowd of trained warriors, for his rare military endowments, disgracefully routed by a handful of French and Indians, and only saved from annihilation by the coolness and spirit of a Virginian boy. . . .

The process lined out in the passage is certainly that to which Munro is subjected. Deprived of "the confidence of self-respect" by the cowardice of fellow officers, having suffered "mortifying abasement" in the dishonor of the Fort William massacre, he wanders through the second half of the book a shattered imbecile, the constant reminder of Britain's decayed power. In addition, like the Indians, the Scottish officer is from the beginning of the novel associated with the past. To Magua, he is "the old chief," "the gray-head." A warrior closer to Hawkeye or the Huron than to Duncan or Montcalm, he is an offensive fighter who distrusts defensive tactics and is like Bumppo afraid that advancing civilization means the end of "manly" battle. "If the settlements should ever spread far from the two rivers," Natty says, "both hunting and war would lose their beauty." "The beauty and manliness of warfare," says Munro, "has been much deformed, Major Heyward, by the arts of your Monsieur Vauban. Our ancestors were far above such scientific cowardice!"

In response to Munro's lament, Duncan says, "It may be very true, sir; but we are now obliged to repel art by art." Here Cooper clearly showed that the future lies with the American. Munro's "your Monsieur Vaubin" seems his recognition of the fact. In like fashion, Bumppo's prediction of the horse's future in wilderness warfare seems his. Magua's intense hatred is his; nothing else could explain his emotion. Duncan would appear to be the least of his enemies, yet, in the Delaware camp, the Huron looks around and "on Hawkeye he cast a glance of respectful enmity; on Duncan, a look of inextinguishable hatred." Clearly Cooper intended that Duncan be seen as an important "natural participator" in the historical process of the novel. Although the passage describing the decline of British power refers specifically to Washington, Duncan too is a Virginian boy. What is more, his progress is analogous to that of Washington and the American colonies during the French and Indian War. At the outset of the novel he is subordinate to Munro but as the Scot declines, Duncan rises. In so doing he transforms himself from a dependent Anglo-American to a self-reliant American. He enters the novel a rank-proud and often helpless youth; he leaves it Hawkeye's acknowledged superior, in control of himself and his situation. Duncan is the book's major argument for a theory of progressive history. Cooper's description of the elevating effect of Uncas's love for Cora suggests the existence of a natural level above the highest an Indian can attain; Duncan lives on that level. Montcalm, Magua, Uncas, Chingachgook, and Hawkeye end the novel dead, dying, or isolated in the wilderness. Only Duncan—and Alice—have futures. Beyond race the one truly significant difference between Duncan and Uncas is that between a beginning and an end. The Mohican is the last of his people; he must look to the past for his family. Duncan, an orphan, must look to the future for his. Within the compressed world of *The Last of the Mohicans,* he is, like the better known Virginian boy, the father of his nation.

In early parts of the novel, however, Duncan is more Anglo than American. Like the armies and policies of England and France, he is no more than something imposed upon the American wild. Like Montcalm, he has more style than substance. His attitudes are European; his attempt to bribe Magua with liquor particularly smacks of morally bankrupt European diplomacy. At this point, Duncan possesses only the confidence of rank, not the authority of knowledge or skill. Judging himself by his position in the British army, he introduces himself to Bumppo not by name but as the youngest major of the Royal Americans. The meaninglessness of that identity in the New York woods is underscored by the inexperienced youth's incompetence there. He is out of place; his weapons prove to be little more than ceremonial badges of rank. His light sword snaps; his pistols shoot wide. His intelligence serves him no better. Given to foppish posturing, he too often relies on false pride rather than reason to determine his conduct. Losing faith in Magua's guiding, for example, Duncan takes command and gets lost. "It was because I suspected him," runs his absurdity, "that I would follow no longer; making him, as you see, follow me."

As the novel continues, however, Duncan changes. An early sign of improvement comes at the beginning of Volume 2 when he arrives on scene, his scarlet coat traded for "vestments adapted, both in quality and color, to their present hazardous pursuit." The key word is "adapted" for as the first paragraph of the novel makes clear, *The Last of the Mohicans* is in part about learning to cope with the wilderness by "emulating the patience and self-denial of the practiced native warriors." Throughout the second volume, Duncan increasingly conforms to the requirements of necessity and, as illusions fostered by artificial rank give way to a real sense of situation and self, he uncovers some American talents. Although, for example, he early prefers short sword and pistols, the shooting match with Hawkeye reveals his competence with the American weapon, the long rifle. What is more important, too proud in the first volume, he agrees in the second to play the fool in order to free Alice from the Huron camp. There, he rescues Uncas with an unobtrusive trip. In the final battle with the Huron, he is content to lie back, "imitating the necessary caution of his companions." All represent significant concessions made to reality by a character who formerly preferred headstrong courage to reasoned cunning and who, at least partly a comic character, was the subject of passages which set him up as a boy given to grand but ill-taken gestures. In one Indian fight, for instance,

> Encouraged by this slight advantage, the impetuous young man continued his onset, and sprang upon his enemy with naked hands. A single instant was enough to assure him of the rashness of the measure, for he immediately found himself fully engaged, with all his activity and courage, in endeavoring to ward the desperate thrusts made with the knife of the Huron.

In another, when told by Bumppo to be sensible and duck:

> Heyward smiled, as he answered,—
> "It would be but an ill example for the highest in rank to dodge while the warriors were under fire!"

In *The Pioneers,* the first of the Leatherstocking Tales, Cooper defined his hero, Oliver Edwards, by means of a scene in which the disguised aristocrat stood in Templeton Hall, clad in buckskin—one hand clutching a rifle, the other fingering a piano. The point of the picture is Edwards's familiarity with both society and the wild—and his ability to slide easily from one to the other. Cooper obviously hoped that Duncan be seen to attain the same ability in *The Last of the Mohicans.* In the first volume, the young American proves his civilized superiority by taking the lead away from Munro when negotiating with Montcalm. By the beginning of the second volume, with Munro shattered, Duncan has taken charge and become "the highest in rank." Still helpless in the woods, however, he must defer to Bumppo, who orders him to "keep in our rear, and be careful not to cross the trail." At the Huron camp, Heyward asserts himself and resumes command. "Hawkeye regarded the young man a moment in speechless amazement," the novel states; "But Duncan, who, in deference to the other's skill and services, had hitherto submitted somewhat implicitly to his dictation, now assumed the superior, with a manner that was not easily resisted." Here Duncan repeats his behavior toward Magua but now instead of a fool's act, it is, the novel implies, a proper resuming of natural authority. Heyward's adventures in the Indian village further support that implication as he proves a more effective spy than Natty, who can speak neither Huron nor French. Significantly, the men's roles are reversed; Duncan is now the man between and acts as translator for the helpless Bumppo.

By retaking his rightful position, Heyward restores the social order that had disappeared in the Fort William massacre. During the episode set within the Delaware encampment, a description of the party concludes: "Hawkeye had placed himself a little in the rear, with a deference to the superior rank of his companions, that no similarity in the state of their present fortunes could induce him to forget." It was crucial to Cooper's vision of a naturally hierarchical society that Heyward end the book Bumppo's acknowledged superior. It was just as crucial to his theory of progressive history that Duncan and, by extension, the white race be accepted as naturally superior—in potential at least—to the Indian they replace. In part Duncan's ability, unshared by Bumppo or Uncas, to operate in both society and the wild argues that point. In larger part, however, Cooper pointed out the superiority of the white by emphasizing the inferiority of the red. At the top of Nature's hierarchy, as delineated in *The Last of the Mohicans,* sits the rational white man; on the bottom the "sagacious" beaver, a being whose "admirable structures" lead Duncan to conclude that "the brutes of these vast wilds were possessed of an instinct nearly commensurate with his own reason." Standing between them is the Indian, whom both Cooper and his characters often think of more as animal than man. In particular, there runs through the novel a tendency to associate him with the dog. "I will watch the bushes," says Hawkeye to Uncas, "while your father shall run with a low nose to the ground." "His head was turned aside," reads a description of Magua, "his nostrils expanded, and his ears seemed even to stand more erect than usual." Even so, the Indian is raised above the beasts by a power of concrete reasoning which makes him master of signs but not symbols. A literalist, he directs his life and culture toward immediate situations. Indians do not, according to Cooper, waste time in idle speculation. In a moment of repose, Chingachgook's face reveals "the quiet, vacant composure, which distinguishes an Indian warrior, when his faculties are not required for any of the greater purposes of his existence."

"The white man," says Heyward, "may, and does often, forget the burial-place of his fathers; he sometimes ceases to remember those he should love, and has promised to cherish; but the affection of a parent for his child is never permitted to die." The Indian will die for the graves of his fathers; the white for the life of his child. The Indian, in other words, looks to the past, the white to the future. Analogously, the white is master of future thought; that is, he speculates or reasons abstractly. Within *The Last of the Mohicans,* that trait is his curse, his salvation—and the source of his superiority. Uncas and Chingachgook, for example, consistently agree to Bumppo's plans. Cora's cool rationality saves the party at Glenn's Falls and after. In the last battle with the Huron, Duncan proves himself a tactician able to predict and prepare for the flow of battle. That ability is particularly significant, for the novel repeatedly demonstrates that the red man is, in contrast, exclusively an offensive warrior who cares nothing for trenching and fortification, the white arts of anticipatory warfare. Indian combat is immediate man-to-man struggle, the outcome of which is determined by physical strength, skill, cunning, and—as Uncas's death makes clear—chance. Perhaps the exact nature of the distinction between white and red reasoning is best shown in a scene so ludicrous Cooper must have included it to make a serious point. Natty sights down on a buck partly hidden by brush:

> "It cannot be!" said the young Indian, springing to his feet with youthful eagerness; "all but the tips of his horns are hid!"
> "He's a boy!" said the white man, shaking his head while he spoke, and addressing the father. "Does he think when a hunter sees a part of the creatur', he can't tell where the rest of him should be!"

Although knowing where "the rest of him should be" sometimes pitches the civilized man into the chaos of national aspiration and diplomatic intrigue, it also lifts him spiritually beyond the Indian. Despite Bumppo's doctrine of gifts, which seems to preach a separate but at least equal relationship between the two races, the novel makes clear that the Indian is morally inferior. Living by an Old Testament ethic, he demands an eye for an eye, or, in Magua's words, "what a Huron loves—good for good; bad for bad!" The New Testament concept of mercy is understood only by whites. They alone ask it; they alone offer it.

That distinction is tied to the last and perhaps most interesting difference between white and red in *The Last of the Mohicans*—the greater femininity of the civilized world. Within the novel, women seem to act as fundamental expression and generating force of their societies. Even in the masculine culture of the Huron, women define and drive the tribe. The most cruel, the most brutal, the most skilled at torture and abuse, they are the violent exhorters of the nation. The role of the white woman is the same but her effect different. She is the leading point of the ascending spiral. In her purity, gentility, and spirituality, she embodies the future toward which civilization in America rises. In the Huron culture, manliness is defined by the ability to kill—to hunt and make war. In Cooper's white world, it seems defined by the ability to protect "females." "It would not be the act of men," says Hawkeye at a crucial moment, "to leave such harmless things to

their fate." "The pale-faces" says Magua, "make themselves dogs to their women," and within the novel society does seem designed primarily to serve them—as all the white men in the book serve Cora and Alice. Duncan is devoted to the girls. Bumppo gives Cora an "affectionate shake of the hand," takes "open pleasure" in Alice. David Gamut follows them into captivity like a faithful dog; during the funeral scene, the novel speaks of "secret emotions" in the singer. Perhaps most telling of all, however, is the revelation made during the shooting match between Bumppo and Heyward. In an enthusiastic response to Duncan's shot, Hawkeye gives away the ultimate meaning of his life in the woods. "It may do for the Royal Americans!" he shouts, "but had my gun often turned so much from the true line, many a marten, whose skin is now in a lady's muff, would still be in the woods."

Of course it is Alice whom Bumppo serves. She is the future of America. Even if Duncan's preference were not enough, Cooper's descriptions of the two girls leave no doubt as to their proper roles. When introducing the younger sister, Cooper quite specifically associated her with nature. "The flush which still lingered above the pines in the western sky was not more bright nor delicate," the novel reads, "than the bloom on her cheek; nor was the opening day more cheering than the animated smile which she bestowed on the youth." There is nothing comparable in Cora's description—unless it be mention of her "tresses . . . shining and black, like the plumage of a raven" that associates her only with death, with the ravens that fly over corpse-strewn battlefields. The pattern is repeated in the funeral scene. The chorus of Indian

H.M. Brock illustration for The Last of the Mohicans.

maidens says little about Cora but offers a detailed catalogue of Alice's virtues: "Her ringlets were compared to the exuberant tendrils of the vine, her eye to the blue vault of the heavens, and the most spotless cloud, with its glowing flush of the sun, was admitted to be less attractive than her bloom." Alice is therefore revealed as correspondent of a landscape which throughout the novel serves as a constant reminder of something more ordered, more permanent, more significant than the bloody chaos of the French-Indian war. No matter how admirable to modern readers—or to other characters—Cora is, in contrast, merely another of the book's grotesques. Hopelessly flawed by mixed blood, she is simply too strong, too self-sufficient, too sexual to live. Alice, on the other hand, is Nature; her weakness, her greater ethereality, her "infantile dependency" are apparently the qualities of an ideal woman. Her union with Duncan therefore provides the logical conclusion to Cooper's argument. Together they form a complementary pair, balancing masculine force and feminine spirituality and thus reflecting the interdependent hierarchical order embodied in the distinct but analogous units of class, race, and historical epoch found in the novel.

So at end, it would seem that in *The Last of the Mohicans* Cooper traced a historical process in which a physical, masculine, red culture embodied in the futureless bachelorhood of Uncas, Magua, and Chingachgook gives way to a more spiritual, more feminine, white culture represented by the promising union of Alice and Duncan. In addition, the novel portrays the breakdown of European power in America, and, through the progress of Uncas and Duncan, depicts the supplanting of one native culture by another. The novel therefore concerns not only the last of the Mohicans but the first of the Americans. It is not, then, a historical tragedy but a narrative of natural process, one dealing with the inevitability and desirability of change. Like woodland plants, the Indian rose, flourished, and died; now, the book suggests, the time of the white American has come. Implicit in that historical vision, however, lies the disquieting message that his rule too is no more than a temporary phase. Within the circular movement of the spiral, a beginning predicts its end. In *The Last of the Mohicans,* therefore, inheres a promise of The Last of the Americans. (pp. 117-39)

> *Michael D. Butler, "Narrative Structure and Historical Process in 'The Last of the Mohicans',"* in American Literature, *Vol. XLVIII, No. 2, May, 1976, pp. 117-39.*

PETER VALENTI   (essay date 1979)

[*Valenti is an American educator and critic. In the following excerpt, he considers the conflict in* The Pioneers *between the independent woodsman Natty Bumppo and the need of the pioneer settlements to impose social and physical order on the American wilderness.*]

While concern with natural landscape characterizes much American literature written before 1830, little attention has been devoted to the examination of landscape as a structural concept or as contributory to aesthetic order. American writers adopted many of the aesthetic categories first popularized by the eighteenth-century British taste for natural scenery, although critical consideration has not shown very clearly how the landscape, and the imaginative response to beholding that landscape, can determine linguistic structure, novelistic theme, and narrative progression. That landscape can furnish a structural or thematic principle is apparent in such documents as Crevecoeur's *Letters from an American Farmer* and Bartram's *Travels in North and South Carolina;* perhaps less obvious upon first consideration, though not less crucial, is the importance of landscape as structural device in James Fenimore Cooper's Leatherstocking saga, and particularly in *The Pioneers.*

As Cooper introduced Nathaniel Bumppo to the public in 1823, he also introduced the tragic despoiling of the beautifully promising American landscape as a necessary concomitant to the progress of national civilization. The deep problems which arise from the encroachment of civilization upon the wilderness are embodied in the conflicts between the unwritten codes of woodsmanship and hunting ritual on the one hand and the man-made laws drafted for a frontier society on the other. With the beautiful Hudson River Valley as a backdrop, Cooper presents the violent clash of Leatherstocking's tenets of natural order with Judge Temple's belief in strictly enforced rules. In so doing the novelist shows how the actual physical movement across the North American interior away from the eastern seaboard affects tremendous physical change upon the landscape sacred to Leatherstocking and his blood brother Chingachgook. In Britain and on the continent, the term "picturesque" had been firmly established by 1780 as a method for viewing and evaluating natural scenery against aesthetic norms derived from Burke's categories of sublime and beautiful as well as from actual experience with affecting examples of natural scenery. *The Pioneers* develops response to affective natural scenes as a frame upon which the key situations in the novel are constructed, as an indicator of moral character, and as demarcation of conflicting lifestyles. Picturesque elements characterize this response and demonstrate graphically the tension between the two orders of law.

The term "picturesque" has surely been used with as wide lexical variation as any word. Beyond its most rudimentary definition as "that which pleases in a picture," picturesque suggests a definite category of aesthetic description. While American enthusiasm for this aesthetic category lasted at least until William Cullen Bryant's *Picturesque America* in 1874, the picturesque had been codified in England almost a hundred years earlier. Both William Gilpin and Uvedale Price defined the picturesque in aesthetic essays, though one must seriously question to what extent these conscious critical dicta defined a term already in wide use. Gilpin distinguishes picturesque from beautiful by stressing variety and roughness as characteristic of the former; this art seeks atmospheric qualities which would meld rough multiplicity into a pleasing verbal or visual artifact. Price builds upon Gilpin's theories to characterize roughness as the quality which "conveys . . . irritation, but at the same time . . . animation, spirit, and variety." Roughness offers an alternative to the smooth and pleasing symmetry of the beautiful, but these aesthetic treatises of Gilpin and Price do not tell the entire picturesque story: for the real popularity of the picturesque school lay not in codified dicta but rather in the tours made to spots of great natural beauty.

Versified and more routine prose accounts of travelers' experiences in the British Lake District, Scotland, Canada, or upstate New York obviously satisfied a deep craving which transcended mere curiosity about distant places. Perhaps the most prominent feature of such tours is the sense of excitement at beholding an aesthetically pleasing scene in nature; the traveler hopes that the next bend in the road or the next view through a screen of trees will be a striking one. The activity of the viewer's imagination corresponds to the movement of the trip, of being exposed to new scenes and walking about to arrange a scene for best effect. Moving from one scene or prospect to another stimulates sources of intellectual energy; as Gilpin says of the Highlands of Scotland [in his *Observations on Several Parts of Great Britain, Particularly the Highlands of Scotland*]: "There is something very amusing even in a hasty succession of beautiful scenes. The imagination is kept in a pleasing perturbation while these floating, unconnected ideas become a kind of waking dream and are often wrought up by fancy into more pleasing pictures; than they in fact appear to be, when they are viewed with deliberate attention." External motion demands a correspondent interior action as the imagination works to create striking pictures or images. Landscape experience thus becomes a sort of reverie, a poetic process of dissolution into ideal forms as the consciousness of the beholder plays over the images in the field of vision.

Many readers might agree that such a transforming power characterizes Leatherstocking in his reflective moments, even though one cannot prove that Cooper was familiar with picturesque travel literature by 1823. However, both contemporary British models and the considerable body of literature celebrating New York state further indicate that a certain rubric of response to landscape had become commonplace by 1823. One can see in *The Pioneers* how the language and rhetoric of the picturesque tours underlie the novelistic structure and provide the basic tension in the novel: two prospects frame the novel's most haunting passages in which the senseless destruction of wildlife is vividly depicted.

Movement in various forms constitutes the main activity in the novel: Leatherstocking and the pioneers move westward, though not together. Progress across the landscape, as the pioneers move from one settled area to another, is a form of motion very different from the graceful movements of Leatherstocking and Chingachgook through the forests; yet through these forms of "progress" Cooper juxtaposes the lifestyles that confronted one another in late eighteenth-century America. Forest paths are visible only to Natty; roads cut by settlers are highly visible to all. Gentle gradations of change in the natural scene suggest reverence for a state of nature undefiled by man's civilizing. Experiencing the natural scene can be done as unobtrusively as Leatherstocking's movements through the wilderness, or as eventfully as the inhabitants of Templeton's main street who burn great piles of lumber for fuel. The picturesque traveler or artist would approximate Bumppo's response, for both find aesthetic enjoyment in scenes that have not been physically arranged by man. Where roads would suggest movement across the landscape in a civilized scene, the only movement in a pre-civilized scene would be that of rivers, since the paths of animals in the woods are virtually invisible. Rivers or waterfalls suggest naturally sustained animation in the landscape; where some picturesque art might employ both roads and moving water, Cooper points out how man's attitude toward one necessarily affects the other.

As a cosmic backdrop for man's movement through the natural scene, Cooper suggests a mythopoetic seasonal round in which the novel's action begins in the dead of winter and progresses toward a resolution with the approach of autumn. Leatherstocking stands impotent against the pioneers' relentless movement across New York state. The novel's diction is permeated with the words "motion," "movement," "speed," "rapidity," and "progress." By hewing down trees and erecting houses, the pioneers demonstrate the "wasty ways" which Natty Bumppo opposes as fiercely as he opposes their unremitting motion across the landscape to new settlements. Pioneers move through forests and devastate the wilderness as they go; Natty Bumppo shares with picturesque travelers an enthusiasm for beholding the natural scene as it exists. The former group causes physical change, while the latter makes only mental modification. The settler cuts and clears trees to erect a house and establish a livelihood, while the picturesque traveler imaginatively rearranges verbal or visual scenes which will not affect the elements present in nature. That Cooper keenly felt such a distinction can be inferred from the contrasting views of nature possessed by Judge Temple and Nathaniel Bumppo; the novel's conflict arises from the tragic incompatibility of these two world views.

The opposition is shown most clearly in contrasting picturesque scenes and in architectural modes, both of which categories demonstrate Temple's sympathy for the reshapings wrought by change and progress as opposed to Leatherstocking's reverence for the random natural scene. As the Judge details for his daughter Elizabeth the prospect available from Mount Vision, he emphasizes the changes that he has imposed on the landscape:

> "Unimproved and wild as this district now seems to your eyes, what was it when I first entered the hills! I left my party, the morning of my arrival . . . and following a deer-path, rode to the summit of the mountain, that I have since called Mount Vision; for the sight that there met my eyes seemed to me as the deceptions of a dream. . . . I had met many deer, gliding through the woods, in my journey; but not the vestige of a man could I trace, during my progress, nor from my elevated observatory. No clearing, no hut, none of the winding roads that are now to be seen, were there, nothing but mountains rising behind mountains, and the valley, with its surface of branches, enlivened here and there with the faded foliage of some tree, that parted from its leaves with more than ordinary reluctance. Even the little Susquehanna was then hid, by the height and density of the forest."

Temple asserts the modifications he has imposed on the landscape by first suggesting to Elizabeth that the scene from Mount Vision was infinitely less civilized the first time that he saw it. His tone suggests a negatively delusive, dreamlike quality encouraged by the scene which he feels he must transform into something more readily controlled. Overlayering as he does the virgin wilderness upon the "improved" or "civilized" scene, Temple suggests to his daughter a certain discomfort with the natural scene. He sees a lake—a passive, reflecting body of water—but not the hidden Susquehanna.

In marked contrast, Leatherstocking describes a natural scene dominated by the natural activity of moving water. The scene which most pleases Natty Bumppo is one where he sees beauty in the Burkean sense: order and symmetry, graceful and flowing lines, near and distant orderliness. The spot he calls "Creation!": "The river was in sight for seventy miles, under my feet, looking like a curled shaving, though it was eight long miles to its banks." This view, typical of many such scenes in America, indicates immensity; however, Natty prefers another spot which in its variousness is less sublime than picturesque—"a short two miles back of that very hill, that in late times I relished better than the mountain; for it was more kivered with the trees, and more nateral." From this wonderful spot one can view a lovely stream such as might turn a mill, "But the hand that made the 'Leap' never made a mill!" Edwards is surprised that he has never read of this scene in a picturesque tour book, but

> "I never read a book in my life," said Leatherstocking; "and how should a man who has lived in towns and schools know anything about the wonders of the woods! No, no, lad; there has that little stream of water been playing among them hills, since He made the world, and not a dozen white men have ever laid eyes on it. The rock sweeps like masonwork, in a half-round, on both sides of the fall and shelves over the bottom for fifty feet; so that when I've been sitting at the foot of the first pitch, and my hounds have run into the caverns behind the sheet of water, they've looked no bigger than so many rabbits. To my judgment, lad, it's the best piece of work that I've met with in the woods; and none know how often the hand of God is seen in a wilderness, but them that rove it for a man's life."

While Temple suggests that a landscape can reflect the inroads of civilization, Leatherstocking shows how to preserve the natural order inherent in the scene by respecting the aesthetic unity provided by the animating river. Natty's critical and aesthetic powers would be considered the common sense of an uneducated man; Edwards, as reconciler of the two modes of life represented in the conflict between Temple's laws and Bumppo's beloved landscape, listens in wonderment to Natty's description at the same time he understands that Natty's fond longings can never again be realized. As Elizabeth tells him, even if the forests could be miraculously restored from the clearings, it would be disastrous to the present modes of life in the settlement.

Bumppo's final comment on the striking scene strengthens the reader's sense of forces other than pioneers moving across the New York countryside:

> "I've sat on the shelving rock many a long hour, boy, and watched the bubbles as they shot by me, and thought how long it would be before that very water, which seemed made for the wilderness, would be under the bottom of a vessel, and tossing in the salt sea. It is a spot to make a man solemnize. You can see right down into the valley that lies to the east of the High-Peak, where, in the fall of the year, thousands of acres of woods are before your eyes, in the deep hollow, and along the side of the mountain, painted like ten thousand rainbows, by no hand of man, though without the ordering of God's providence."

Leatherstocking realizes that the water flowing through the virgin wilderness shall one day be turned to more commercial purposes as it will support boats—perhaps even those bringing more settlers to the new world. Unlike Temple's prospect description, in which the Judge does not suggest the Deity, Leatherstocking emphasizes God in His "Creation!"; "and none know how often the hand of God is seen in a wilderness, but them that rove it for a man's life." The passive scene described by Temple is to be acted upon, to be civilized; Leatherstocking's detailing reveres the active force perceptible in and behind the prospect. Natural splendor and natural aesthetic are the work of God, not man, Leatherstocking asserts. Indeed, the magnificence of the view precludes the "hand of man" or any meddling civilization. The random coloring of

nature exhibits true picturesque beauty; perfectly organized symmetry would suggest a formal beauty, and perhaps a grand divine plan, alien to the American picturesque scene. Leatherstocking sees a prospect at the height of beauty as fall approaches; Temple gazes on the "Vision" after the leaves have fallen and he can see more easily how improvements can be made. For Temple, the picturesque moment in a naturally changing scene has tragically passed into a state where improvements and clearings can be envisioned. Even the names of the prospects suggest this contrast: "Mount Vision" carries modern, Babbitt-like connotations of the "man of vision," the businessman who can predict demand profitably. "Creation!" conversely suggests reverence for the work of God, the supreme creator who has provided unity in the multiplicity of natural beauty. Though Bumppo has no guide books or architectural plans to shape his responses, he avails himself of his most basic God-given talents to envision a landscape far more attractive than that offered by Richard Jones with his "square rule" of "composite order."

Plot development also points up the tensions between the two outlooks. The novel opens with a chance meeting upon a road as Leatherstocking and Temple try their rights to a slain deer; the wounded Oliver Edwards goes from Natty's hut to the Judge's house. Though Edwards reconciles the two worlds of settlement and wilderness as represented in the judge and the frontiersman, he also suggests movement into a house characterized by foolish attempts to imitate nature and progress away from a hut designed for the most basic requisites of shelter. These two dwellings comprise one pair of oppositions crucial to the novel's themes; the two picturesque scenes comprise the second pair. The movements back and forth between houses constitute the narrative events of the novel. Oliver moves from Natty's hut to Temple's house, back to Natty's hut and finally, at the novel's end, back again to Temple's house. Temple and Natty view their favorite prospects years before the initiation of the action covered in the novel proper, but these scenes figure prominently in the narrative. At Temple's Mount Vision, Natty first saves Elizabeth from the panther and later meets her there as fire sweeps through the forest and the novel reaches its climax.

Cooper presents *The Pioneers'* most memorable incidents as adventures linking these two prospects. Sandwiched between the extended views are the incidents of the slaughter of passenger pigeons and fish, which demonstrate convincingly the shocking disregard for natural order and wildlife on the part of the despoilers while also suggesting the impotence of such conservationists as Natty or Chingachgook to end the senseless squandering. Oliver and Judge Temple, though they suggest the laws which will govern Templeton and the Otsego region, partake in the fish kill as the exhilarating spirit of the "sport" overpowers them. Also taking a prominent role is the woodchopper Billy Kirby, who loves the wilds at the same time he helps despoil them. His role later becomes central as he must represent the laws of civilization against fellow outdoorsman Natty Bumppo. Thus the seeds of violent combat are sown as the magistrate Hiram Doolittle frees Natty's hounds for the hunt that will land Leatherstocking in prison and as the powers of the law begin militating against Natty. The effects of pioneering and civilization are carried to Natty's hut, where their threat can be purged only by a ritualistic burning. Once Doolittle has attempted to penetrate the cabin's interior to plumb its mysteries, Bumppo cannot return to the same privacy he had previously enjoyed there. Ironically, he tells young Effingham of his ideal prospect at the very same time the representatives of a warped law are violating another natural law: the right of a frontiersman to his solitude.

The picturesque tours suggest a number of ways for a writer to find solace in solitude and in the pursuit of aesthetic fulfillment through natural scenery. Cooper's focus on rivers, particularly the Susquehanna, in the novel parallels the fondness of picturesque writers for rivers as structural devices. Many picturesque writers, in search of suitable structures around which to organize their tours, often followed the course of a river as logical focus for such an expedition. . . . For Cooper, the Delaware and Susquehanna rivers furnish both natural beauty and a form of exterior motion that counterpoints well the movement of picturesque traveler as well as groundbreaking pioneer. The picturesque pilgrim traverses paths and roads with the delicious anticipation of a striking new scene to be encountered at every turn providing an interior animation to match the physical movement across the landscape. Cooper's use of roads suggests the animation not of sensitive beholders but rather of plodding journeymen determined to wrest a living from a hostile environment. The roads which the pioneers tread through the forest floor gradually kill even the trees left standing by incessantly wearing down through the roots and cutting off vital nourishment. The roads, of course, provide access for the settlers; the paths which Natty and Chingachgook pursue through the woods are virtually invisible to the untutored eye.

Chapter XXI, which presents the prospect of Mount Vision, begins with a dissertation on roads as they cut through the forest to allow the pioneers ingress and egress. Cooper prefaces this chapter with a motto from Scott:

> Speed! Malise, speed! such cause of haste
> Thine active sinews never brac'd.

Temple's proud contemplation of the scenes he has transformed so quickly through his introduction of civilization provides an aesthetic analogue to Scott's accounts of conflicts produced by historical development. Activity is associated with change, improvement, and the inroads made on the natural scene sacred to Leatherstocking and Chingachgook. The motions of deer and bear are being replaced by those of new settlers.

Motion is also connected with Natty Bumppo and John Mohegan, though their movement is entirely natural and leaves as little trace as the frail birchbark canoe. This craft's "motion was amazingly rapid" as it noiselessly moves across the water's surface, so smoothly that it seems to be moving above the lake. When Mohegan gives Miss Temple a ride in his canoe, "it appeared to Elizabeth that they glided over the water by magic. . . ." Such motion differs completely from the progress made by the pioneers as they wear more deeply the rough roads and polish the exposed tree roots by their incessant travel. The movement of the seasons brings even more obvious development as ruts deepen and additional fields are tilled. As with the sporting pursuits, the progress must be rapid if it is to please the on rushing pioneers: "But the slow, though certain adventures with a hook and line were ill-suited to the profusion and impatience of the settlers." Too, the pioneers act as a group—as well they might in a situation founded upon democratic ideals—in opposition to the hunt in which Natty engages and which implies the heroic ideal of single combat, even if with a vastly inferior adversary. The solitary bird, deer, or fish is Natty's target. As

certain details of the landscape compose or suggest a pleasing picturesque scene, so does Leatherstocking isolate a suitable object for his hunt. In both, some aesthetic choice—based upon experience and a sense of propriety—will be necessary to avoid the headlong plunge into chaotic composition or senseless destruction.

The scene which Leatherstocking terms "Creation!" suggests even more precisely the relationship between aesthetic response to nature and a moral sense of what occurs in the natural setting. Perhaps the faculty of taste which Natty displays for Oliver Effingham reaches back most obviously to Shaftesbury, whose Characteristics equated morality with beauty as congruent foci of mature aesthetic response. And this sense may well be the main dividing point between law and landscape: the laws of Templeton and the "composite order" of architecture are based only on abstract principles and not on an intuitive sense of what is correct. Cooper forces his reader to ask if this is the price to be paid for wresting democracy out of the wilderness, Natty Bumppo realizes that one day the water will be out in the world of ships and commerce, but here he sees the water in its pristine state as it is formed from rain and run-off, before it runs its logical course. The natural progress of water to sea presents an image of motion-in-stasis which captures perfectly the ongoing force confined within the riverbank. Like Mohegan's canoe, the flowing water does not upset the essential repose of the landscape. Conversely, improvements are decidedly unnatural and show man's egotistical—perhaps immoral—imposition of individual will upon the sancity of nature. Natty's hut might suggest a sacred way station offering comfort and affording a spot for veneration of the area's tremendous natural beauty, since this dwelling is the only evidence Judge Temple finds to show human habitation on his first visit to the area.

But this vision of a beautiful scene reverently recollected is shattered by the cries of Natty's hounds: "These variations in the tones of the hounds passed with amazing rapidity," as Leatherstocking realizes the weaselish Hiram Doolittle has surreptitiously freed the dogs. The pack drives a deer across the lake toward the men who, unable to refrain from logically completing the hunt, paddle after the buck: "The canoe whirled with each cunning evolution of the chase, like a bubble floating in a whirlpool; and when the direction of the pursuit admitted, for a short distance, of a straight course, the little bark skimmed the lake with a velocity that urged the deer to seek its safety in some new and unexpected turn." The beauty of the bubble floating down the coursing stream and the canoe sliding beautifully across the lake stress natural activity, counterpointed by the unavoidably primitive instinct to slay the deer once the dogs have started it. The deer looks for safety, satisfaction, haven in the "new and unexpected turn" suggestive of the picturesque, a diametrically opposed method of traveling. But both travels suggest close affinity to nature and natural forms as opposed to those of lawmakers whose laws are unnecessary, as Leatherstocking soliloquizes, to anyone but a real greenhorn.

Like picturesque writers, Judge Temple and Natty Bumppo offer verbal interpretations of visual scenes in order to convey their reactions. Arresting natural details predominate in both accounts, though significant differences exist. The Judge and Bumppo describe prospects which suggest a shared respect for natural beauty but also an opposed attitude toward change in that natural scene. Temple happily contemplates the effect of his civilizing of the forest, while Leatherstocking reminisces about an Adamic wilderness yet untroubled by human improvers. Framing the key natural incidents of senseless slaughter, these prospects comprise the novel's structural center: after his reminiscences, Bumppo goes down to indulge in those "unlawful" hunting activities which will force him to burn his hut, land him in jail, and ultimately cause him to begin anew on a wilder frontier. The killing of the deer neatly balances the beginning of the novel as well, for in attempting to shoot a deer Judge Temple wounds Oliver Effingham. The wound is symbolically as well as physically dangerous, for it implies that the effect of Temple's hunting diametrically opposes Leatherstocking's. If Oliver is the promise for the future of the American experiment, one can only hope that the results of Temple's laws have no more deleterious effect on young Effingham.

But the killing of the deer suggests other concerns as well. Bumppo is nicknamed "Deerslayer" because of his particular prowess, seen only positively because he exercises sense when hunting and never kills more than he can actually use. He is also called "Hawkeye" and "Pathfinder," two titles which testify to his highly developed visual abilities. William Gilpin, Thomas Pennant, or Alexander Wilson would welcome such powers; as they might, Bumppo applies his powers to surveying prospects such as the "Creation!" and to ferreting out those yet-uncharted wilderness paths which enable him to move about in the nearly impenetrable forests. Only later will the settlers wear roads down through tree roots and kill trees without even chopping them down. Again, Leatherstocking moves insensibly through natural surroundings; civilization lets everyone know where and how it moves. Cooper thus prepares well for the cruelest section of the novel, when the aging Natty Bumppo has his motion and freedom of activity arrested by confinement to the stocks in the center of Templeton. Here he is at last unable to move away from the community for whose coming he has unwittingly prepared but with which he can share no common values.

The structure of the picturesque tour, then, suggests a rhetorical framework which allows Cooper to present his characters responding to a challenging environment at the same time they demonstrate qualities drawn from the sentimental and adventure fiction of the period. Cooper's third novel, ***The Pioneers,*** progresses beyond the study of manners to be found in ***Precaution*** and the chase, hidden identity, and intrigue motifs of ***The Spy*** to probe the nuances of response to a complex new style of life. The picturesque tour offers the suggestion of an aesthetically grounded sympathy for natural landscape and simultaneously provides an analogous pursuit to "view-hunting," or the search for interesting prospects. Cooper's respect for the men—cast in the mold of his father—who establish new communities against considerable adversities also merits respect and suggests genuine sympathy for the figure of Judge Marmaduke Temple. Though landscape cannot continue unchanged once the developers arrive, the vast potential of the American continent cannot be tapped until the forests are at least partially cleared. So the Marxist critic Georg Lukács quotes Maxim Gorky's description of Leatherstocking:

> "As an explorer of the forests and prairies of the 'New World' he blazes new trails in them for people who later condemn him as a criminal because he has infringed their mercenary and, to his sense of freedom, unintelligible laws. All his life he has unconsciously served the great cause of the geographical expansion of material culture in a country of un-

civilized people and—found himself incapable of living in the conditions of this culture for which he had struck the first paths." Gorky shows here very finely how a great historical, indeed world-historical tragedy could be portrayed through the destiny of a mediocre man of the people. Cooper shows that such a tragedy is rendered much more artistically moving if portrayed in a *milieu* where the immediate economic contrasts and the moral ones arising from them grow organically out of everyday problems. The tragedy of the pioneers is linked superbly here with the tragic decline of gentile society, and one of the great contradictions of mankind's journey of progress therewith acquires a wonderful and tragic embodiment.

The social emphasis of Gorky and Lukács dovetails neatly with the picturesque aesthetic to demonstrate Cooper's novelistic artistry. Structurally, the contrast between Temple and Bumppo is expressed through picturesque landscape, social position, and educational level, all of which suggest different veneration of the past.

Artistic contraries dominate the conclusion of the novel. Law and landscape, violently juxtaposed in the clash of Judge Temple and Leatherstocking, are further contrasted in paired incidents involving the killing of the deer and the detailing of arresting prospects. But this conflict is not resolved in Bumppo's final injunction to Mrs. Effingham: "Trust in God, Madam, and your honourable husband, and the thoughts for an old man like me can never be long nor bitter. I pray that the Lord will keep you in mind—the Lord that lives in clearings as well as in the wilderness—and bless you, and all that belong to you, from this time, till the great day when the whites shall meet the red-skins in judgment, and justice shall be the law, and not power." After the finely detailed picturesque scenes previously associated with Bumppo, this generalized homily fails to establish a solution logically derived from the novel's contrasted orders; it would more fittingly have come from Reverend Grant, religious complement to Temple as social pioneer. Such a statement might at first seem to unify the two levels of law, but Cooper's most finely wrought natural scenes belie so oversimplified a resolution. Leatherstocking's benediction thus evokes genuine pathos.

The character of Natty Bumppo strikes a responsive chord in readers throughout the world because he fulfills human desire for a mythic past in which man understands his natural environment and operates in it perfectly. Leatherstocking's inability to function in a prescribed society governed by man-made laws only confirms the tragic conflict between natural and man-made laws. Cooper has created and peopled a mythic Otsego region which fulfills social desire even though that past, that mythic country, never existed in historical fact. The resolution to oppose the movements of the pioneers causes Leatherstocking to leave Templeton for a wilder frontier as the only possible solution. Bumppo's desire to arrest an irresistable force is doomed to failure, as suggested by his passive receding before its onslaught. But he continues to embody that nagging doubt behind the admission that his mode of life, as perversely as it opposes American democratic growth across the continent, is doomed: Edenic natural states *do* promise another beginning with unknown results and offer the opportunity to start anew. To see that the improvements lead to human failure and shortcomings—as they always have—may be a necessary disappointment; the appeal of Leatherstocking and Mohegan is the resistance to this usual moral progress as, remaining just beyond it, they treasure an active life retained in memory. The "ordering of God's providence" does not apply natural rules to human conduct but to random effects. Rules and boundaries confine that richness and complexity, abundantly detailed by such writers as Crevecoeur and Bartram, which characterize the experience of man moving about in the new American landscape. The bursts of light across the landscape and the thrill of individual pursuit are isolated, independent activities which cannot long exist in the clearings of a true democracy. Cooper's obvious sympathy with Bumppo suggests that the building of frontier settlements which the novelist found so exciting must have been tinged with the sense of loss of irreplaceable elements. The enduring mythic appeal of Cooper's literary creations transcends its author's novelistic abilities as it somehow fulfills a desire for a past that never existed. (pp. 191-203)

Peter Valenti, "The Ordering of God's Providence: Law and Landscape in 'The Pioneers'," in Studies in American Fiction, Vol. 7, No. 2, Autumn, 1979, pp. 191-207.

RICHARD SLOTKIN (essay date 1985)

[*Slotkin is an American educator and critic. In the following excerpt, he examines the role of the first three Leatherstocking novels in contributing to the mythologization of American history.*]

The antecedents of the Leatherstocking myth as developed during the colonial period and the early republic had centered on a perennial heroic triad—the captive, the hunter, and the savage. Cooper continued and elaborated this scheme by "doubling" and dividing these basic roles, multiplying the varieties of social type they could be made to represent, thus expanding the stories' ideological references. Likewise, he invented elaborate variations on the "plots" of his source narratives, multiplying and varying the scenarios of captivity and rescue. But these variations were not merely arbitrary manipulations of formal entities. Cooper recognized in these source narratives of the captive, hunter, and savage a paradigm of American history and a fable of moral regeneration. Within this general pattern he integrated three distinct, pre-existing plot formulae or scenarios of interaction, defining and valuing the roles of each of the three heroic figures.

The earliest of these to develop was the "conversion" formula, derived from the religious preoccupation of the Puritans, which centered on the female captive's role in the adventure and saw the outcome of the adventure as a spiritual redemption through suffering and humiliation. A chastened but potentially tragic self-knowledge follows, for the victim's suffering breaks her connections to family and home, and her spiritual redemption orients her away from this world and toward death. The other plot forms are secular variants of the conversion. In the "initiation" story, typified by the narrative of Church and the legends of Boone and Washington, the central figure is the hunter, not the captive; but the experience is still one of self-knowledge achieved and of a new relation to the created universe through the wilderness adventure. The initiation differs from the conversion in seeing divinity as resident in nature itself, rather than in pure transcendence of the world; and the acts that allow the hero to achieve self-transformation involve a willed intimacy with the savage and the wilderness, and then a violent attack on and triumph against those elements.

The third variant, the "success" story, is the most secular of all the formulae, and the only one that works as easily for an adventure behind the cutting edge of the frontier as for one in the wilderness proper. Its prototypes exist in pre-1800 literature—in Cotton Mather's biography of William Phipps, in Benjamin Franklin's *Autobiography* (a classic statement of the type), and in the agrarian imagery of Crèvecoeur—but it would be wrong to say that the success story form was as clearly conventionalized as the conversion and initiation fables, and it was certainly not as closely associated with the Frontier before 1820. The hero of this narrative type is out to change his fortunes through his adventure, and in pursuing his private interest he certainly needs to acquire "know-how"—hence his story often involves an initiation into the secular wisdom of nature. It may also happen that in achieving worldly success, this hero grows in grace—this is certainly the way the story is told by Mather, Franklin, and Crèvecoeur. But the success hero's motives have nothing of the self-abnegation of the captive or the hunter's willingness to risk self for the captive's sake. The success hero is a radical individualist, whose know-how is used not only against the savage but to exploit the gullibility of his fellow man. In the popular literature that developed after Cooper's success, this type of hero was exemplified by the "living legend" Davy Crockett and the fictional Simon Suggs. For these heroes, self-transformation takes the primitive form of learning to be "shifty in a new country," and is consummated by the achievement of upward mobility.

Cooper's genius lay in his ability not only to draw on these patterns, but to integrate them into a single narrative line that runs through the entire series of novels. The romantic "plots" of Cooper's fiction are concessions to the sentimental taste of his audience, and their shapes from novel to novel are (with some exceptions) redundant and predictable. But the narrative subtext, in which Cooper carries forward his integrated retelling of the Frontier Myth, develops and grows from book to book, adding meanings rather than merely repeating them.

In the first three Leatherstocking novels—*The Pioneers* (1823), *The Last of the Mohicans* (1826), and *The Prairie* (1827)—Cooper makes his most sustained and intensive effort to comprehend historical movements through the conventions of literary fiction. To do this, he draws heavily on the symbolic language inherited from the writers of popular narratives (especially captivities), on myth-historical accounts like Filson's *Kentucke,* and on the more sophisticated and "analytical" attempts of writers like Crèvecoeur and ideologists like Jefferson to account for America's peculiar history and destiny. In Cooper's hands the fictive "geography" of Crèvecoeur and Jefferson, with its characteristic association of frontier regions with particular social types or classes, is organized and developed as a literary plot and as a historiographical doctrine. But Cooper's concern is to show not only the existence of different phases or stages in American social development, but to exemplify the processes through which one stage impinges upon and finally replaces another. Crèvecoeur's geopolitical map is an allegorical tableau, stable and relatively free of catastrophic change; Cooper's map is active, with lines that break and shift as human actors cross the boundaries in both directions, pursuing a struggle that will end only when one people and one geographical realm has been eliminated from the map.

Such a vision was not readily compatible with the liberal optimism of the intellectual heirs of Jefferson, nor with the philanthropic and evangelical Christianity of the period. It is a vision at odds with the Jeffersonian belief that all human beings share a common moral sense that is the basis and justification of their right to liberty; and at odds with the missionary impulse of romantic and Victorian America, which sought to extend the blessings of Christianity and liberty to all nations and races. Moreover, Cooper's vision of a historical conflict resolvable only by a war of extermination departs radically from the reconciliationist conventions of the historical romance genre established by Sir Walter Scott and his English imitators. If the myth of the "English nation" was proposed in terms of consensus, that of the American nation was proposed in terms of division and exclusion. Yet Cooper's vision is consistent with the tradition of discourse established by Jefferson and Crèvecoeur and Filson. The difference is that where these writers settled for optimistic readings of the signs on the Dark and Bloody Ground, compartmentalized their treatments of Indian wars and republican politics, or offered histories that were inconclusive about final outcomes, Cooper told a complete tale and did not attempt to palliate the presence of darkness or the likelihood of tragedy.

Cooper makes two contributions to the mythologization of American history: he puts the Indian and the matter of racial character at the center of his consideration of moral questions, and he represents the historical process as essentially a violent one. The two conceptions are logically related in Cooper. The racial character of the Indian shows what man is like in his natural, precivilized state; and while some of his propensities are shared with whites (especially primitive or unsocialized whites), his "gifts" are also peculiarly and permanently his own. It is because racial gifts are unique that different peoples respond differently to the same natural environments, the same ethical questions. And given this difference, if two races come together in the same environment, competition between them is inevitable, accommodation unlikely, and the elimination of one or the other logically necessary for there to be social peace. But the case of the Indian is only the most extreme and dramatic expression of this "truth." It is equally applicable to oppositions within society between contending groups whose divisions appear basic and profound: white masters and black slaves, all masters and all servants, the wealthy and the poor, the propertied establishment and the demagogic under-men greedy for wealth.

Indeed, even sexual relations are potentially explicable by the metaphor. For Cooper and his contemporaries race and sex were twinned metaphors of distinctions rooted indubitably in human nature. The impossibility of a black or an Indian becoming fully "white" in character was likened to that of a woman becoming completely and perfectly virile; and the distinction was extended to underscore the differences in mind that divided the savage and dependent classes from their racial and social superiors. In *Last of the Mohicans* this metaphor is literalized in the creation of a series of racially and/or sexually "mixed" characters, whose blended traits test and prove the validity of racialist doctrine. The key figure is Cora, who is of mixed black and Scottish ancestry, and whose personality is a mixture of feminine sensibility and masculine realism and courage. But an analogous set of issues is represented in the characters of Natty Bumppo (Hawkeye, the Leatherstocking) and Magua—the white man raised among Indians, and the Indian who has attempted to affiliate with the whites. The outcome for each of these mixed characters is fatal or tragic.

What is at stake in this symbolism is an essential feature of democratic theory: the belief that all humans are equally capable of exercising moral freedom and are therefore justified in asserting their right of self-government as citizens of the republic. The breadth or narrowness of the scope of republican citizenship depends upon how one interprets and applies Cooper's Indian-war myth—where one draws the line between redskins and palefaces. As an artist, Cooper devoted himself to the intensive exploration of that myth, and *Last of the Mohicans* sets out its tragic logic more completely than anything else he wrote.

The opening pages of the novel elaborately frame the setting in which the drama will unfold. It is 1757, the era of the French and Indian War, we are in the American wilderness near the shores of the Horican or "Holy Lake," called prosaically Lake George by the English. The French are reported advancing with an army "as numerous as the leaves"—a figure that links them to the brooding, threatening, and yet also "Holy" wilderness. The British under General Webb are represented as fearing this advance, evidence of the "imbecility" of British leadership, which has already produced a series of defeats—which will, as any American reader knows, lead in the end to the Revolution. The two daughters of Colonel Munro, Alice and Cora, together with Major Duncan Heyward of the Royal Americans (like Washington, a "Virginian boy"), alone among Webb's garrison have the courage or foolhardiness to go forward in the face of Montcalm's advance, moved by the daughters' desire to reach their father, who commands Fort William Henry on the Holy Lake. They are joined by the psalm singer David Gamut, whose naive faith in his religion and physical incompetence make him a parodic exaggeration of the Christian and sentimental values which the women embody. His presence suggests Cooper's ambivalence about the very values his heroes will be obliged to defend.

Thus, as we cross the border between civilization and wilderness the "normal" order of sexual and social values begins to be inverted—the fainthearted British soldiers hang back, the women and the minister whom they ought to protect go forward, led by one of the despised Americans. They take with them as guide an Indian named Magua, a savage whose beautiful form and athletic carriage hide a villain's heart. As they prepare to depart, Cora Munro, helplessly fascinated by the movement of Magua's naked limbs, lets fall her veil and we have a glimpse of her:

> . . . in the surprise her veil also was allowed to
> open its folds, and betrayed an indescribable look
> of pity, admiration, and horror, as her dark eye fol
> lowed the easy motions of the savage. The tresses
> of this lady were shining and black, like the plum
> age of the raven. Her complexion was not brown,
> but it rather appeared charged with the color of the
> rich blood, that seemed ready to burst its bounds.
> And yet there was neither coarseness nor want of
> shadowing in a countenance that was exquisitely
> regular and dignified, and surpassingly beautiful.

The curiously negative suggestions about Cora's coloring ("not brown") prepare us for the revelation that she inherits through her West Indian Creole mother a fraction of Negro "blood." This racial "taint" is imagistically linked to her superabundant vitality and sexuality, her voluptuousness and her susceptibility to sensuous appeals. She is spontaneously fascinated by Magua and later by Uncas, the son of Chingachgook, and the novel is enlivened by the persistent erotic tension generated between these three: the darkened beauty, a potential rapist, and a potential lover. Her affections are checked by her reason and conscience, and we racialize these two elements of her character, linking her sensuality with her blackness and her reserve with her whiteness. This suggestive association is reinforced by the presence of Alice, whose mother was white and "without a cross" of any other blood—Alice, who is more child than woman, who gazes at Heyward with "infantile dependency," who is lacking in both the passion and the vitality of Cora. Further, it is Cora—never Alice—who excites lust or loving desire in the hearts of Magua and Uncas, as if darkness in the blood called to its fellow.

That the sentiment of love is a litmus test of racial character is "proven" when Heyward approaches Colonel Munro to seek his daughter's hand. Munro assumes Heyward is asking for Cora, and when Heyward denies this, Munro accuses him of a slaveholder's prejudice against Cora for the faint strain of Negro blood. Heyward denies any knowledge of this fact, and denies as well any prejudice against Cora now that he knows; but the fact is that once he had seen Alice, the question of Cora simply never arose for him. Spontaneously, naturally, the whiteness of Alice speaks to the whiteness of Heyward; no call comes to him from Cora. Cooper is here invoking, in rather a subtle way (for Cooper), the nineteenth-century concept of "natural repugnance" between the races, especially marked (it was asserted) on the part of whites toward nonwhites. The doctrine also held that (as Jefferson said) it was "natural" among nonwhites to depart from "natural repugnance," and to prefer the supposedly superior charms of whites—a "natural" tendency of the lower folk to behave "unnaturally." Thus Cora apparently is more strongly drawn to Heyward than he to her; and thus Magua and Uncas are drawn to Cora.

The romantic complications of the plot serve to establish as a central premise the association of sexual and racial identity, and the linkage of sexual and racial qualities to moral character and psychological structure. The linkage uses sexual analogy to establish the immutability of racial character—nonwhite can become white only to the degree that women can become men. So defined, sexual and racial forces appear in the novel as keys to understanding the larger tendencies that work below and shape the surface of the historical events—specifically the siege and massacre of Fort William Henry, and generally the historical triumph of civilization over savagery.

The true characters of the different races and sexes are not clear at the outset. We do not perceive what the difference between Indian and white cultures and characters is unless we see what happens to those who try to cross the border between them. Magua is such a character—a warrior and chief who is drawn to the whites because of his admiration for their apparent superiority in weaponry and wealth. But Magua, as an Indian, cannot abide British discipline; and when Munro has him whipped for drunkenness, his Indian pride is fatally wounded and he becomes the most cruel and implacable of enemies. There are elements of cultural relativism in Cooper's depiction of this conflict—Magua and Munro simply do not understand each other's ways, and the result is tragedy. However, for Cooper the sources of cultural difference are at bottom a matter of blood. Indians are not only unused to discipline and European ideas of manners and restraint, they are inherently incapable of achieving them. Indeed, the best Indians do not even wish to achieve them: just as the white Hey-

ward is not attracted to the gorgeous but un-white Cora, so Chingachgook and his son Uncas do not share Magua's weak predilection for all things white. However, even these Indians—of the pure and unmixed race of the Mohicans, as Cooper tells us—are tempted by friendship and love to gaze (at least) across the border. From these impulses the tension of the novel arises, and is tragically resolved.

The figure who tests these boundaries most significantly is Leatherstocking. He is a white man raised among Indians, but he continually identifies himself as "a man without a cross." The sobriquet is double in meaning, suggesting his non-Christian nurture (and perhaps his Adamic innocence) but referring directly to the purity of his blood line, the fact that he is a white man with no "cross" of Indian blood. In all matters of skill and outward culture, he has adapted to Indian ways, and this allows him to be the most effective of the white warriors; but inside, in all matters of conscience and affection, he is pure white and highly conscious of that fact. Indeed, he represents the irreducible minimum of white racial character—the white man without the extra support of a civilization. Thus it is he who not only scouts the trails, but also scouts the hidden borders between the races and so defines them. He asserts at every opportunity the doctrine that the "pure" and "unmixed" race is best—whether white *or* Indian; and he has scant sympathy with excessively charitable views of Indian character as voiced by Heyward, Munro, or the two girls. Even to Chingachgook he says, "You are a just man, for an Indian."

Character is revealed by its testing in action, and Cooper's way of doing this can be suggested by a brief look at the episode of the combat at Glens Falls (chapters 6-10). Heyward, Alice, Cora, and the psalmist David Gamut now joined by Leatherstocking, Chingachgook, and Uncas, are besieged on a cave-riddled island in the cataract by Magua's Hurons. Cooper uses the natural setting to establish a thematic grounding for the moral drama that follows. The refuge is set amid waters that are at once natural and unnatural. As Natty tells Cora, the river fabricates images and illusions, it leaps about and changes direction "as if, having broke loose from order, it would try its hand at everything." This quality in rivers, as in men, does not appeal to the purist in Leatherstocking.

With their position hopeless, the besieged confront a moral choice: shall they all perish defending the helpless women and the psalmist, or shall some of them try to escape—either to save themselves or to bring rescue when advantage offers? There occurs a moral test which defines clearly the parameters of racial and sexual character. The women and the clergyman do not have to make a choice: their physical weakness is their fate, they must stay and abide the verdict of the action. Chingachgook is willing and eager to go, since it is perfectly sound within the Indian value system (as Cooper defines it) for a valuable warrior to save himself by abandoning the undervalued females. Cooper's Indians are primitive pragmatists, living according to the "natural law" of a wilderness in which fang and claw rule. But natural law is variable, as we have seen. What is natural for an Indian is not "according to the gifts" of a white man. Heyward cannot leave the women to their unmentionable fate, even though that is the practical course. It is, rather, simply inconsistent with his honor as an officer and a white man to go.

Uncas and Leatherstocking experience the moral conflict. As a white man by birth and gifts, Leatherstocking is reluctant to leave the women; but his wilderness pragmatism, learned among Indians, tells on him, outweighing his white conscience. There is a suggestion that caste as well as race is operative: Natty is no officer and gentleman, and hence is not bound by any code of honor other than Indian pragmatism, which is the antithesis of Christian honor. Still, it is only the prospect that his escape will make possible a later rescue of the women that makes his choice palatable. Uncas ought to feel as his father does; but his attraction to Cora makes him hesitate, and by this we see that his integrity as an Indian has been in some measure breached by love. His behavior, unlike his blood, is no longer unmixed, but like Hawkeye's partakes of both white and Indian elements. While Cooper regards his sympathetic awakening as making him more "advanced" than the rest of his nation, it is also the cause of his downfall.

Among those who are left a further, somewhat more subtle division appears. Although he is a man, Gamut does not "play a man's part" in what follows; and although she is a woman, Cora here shows a capacity for action and courage that is in sharp contrast to Alice's feminine passivity, and suggests her possession of qualities that might almost be called masculine. She urges the Mohicans to leave her, adopting the unsentimental "realism" of Hawkeye. She is indeed a doubly mixed character—a white woman with Negro blood, a female with masculine traits of courage and coolness under stress.

The consequences of these moral choices are evaded in the first part of the novel: the captives are rescued, and make their way to Fort William Henry. There they are besieged, and the incapacity of Webb dooms them to surrender. Montcalm, overawed by Magua, supinely allows the Indians to massacre the refugees from the Fort, and in the melee Magua seizes Alice, Cora, and Gamut and flees into the wilderness.

With this catastrophe, the first volume of the novel ends, and the long pursuit and rescue of the captives begins with a new departure, a new evocation of the deeper and darker wilderness into which the heroes now plunge. This bifurcation of the novel is crucial, for with the massacre we leave the terrain of "history" and enter a world organized by myth. It ceases to matter that the year is 1757, that a certain battle has just been fought. The rescue of the captives, as Cooper well knew, was a motif common to all writing about the frontier from the seventeenth century onward; and the rescue of the daughters of Munro in 1757 is not importantly different in detail or meaning from its probable source—the rescue of Daniel Boone's daughter in 1776, as related by John Filson and others. The narrative finds its cognate structures not in historical accounts, but in the mythic archetype of the captivity narrative, and in a mythological rendering of Indian history based on early anthropological researches. Stepping entirely beyond the border of civilization, we step outside the framework of white history, and into a new framework: the mythologized history of the Indians themselves, played against the white myth of the Indian captivity.

The "historical" framework of Part II is that of "Indian history," as refracted through a pseudo-myth fabricated by Cooper, with borrowings from the writings of Joseph Heckewelder on the Delawares. The pseudo-myth's structure is suggested from the beginning of the novel, when Chingachgook reminds Natty that his people are the "grandfathers" of the Indians, and that he is of the "unmixed" race of chiefs. But the idea is a minor note in the background so long as we are within the frame of white history, worrying about the

French and Indian War. Now it comes into the foreground, and is fully revealed when Uncas declares himself to Tamenund, the ancient chief of the Delawares who have captured our heroes. The old chief's role parallels that of Montcalm, and, like him, Tamenund is based upon a historical figure. An Indian of that name was both prophet and chief, and a role as lawgiver was ascribed to him by whites, who took his name (or a variant) for the Tammany Democratic Club of New York politics. Tamenund reveals that Chingachgook and Uncas are the last heirs of the Mohicans, an ancient race of Indians who once dwelt by the "Salt Lake" or ocean. Through the name of Uncas—borne by all members of the family till they gain another by special deeds—Cooper links his Mohicans with the ancient Uncas who befriended the English, and fought with them in the Pequot and King Philip's wars. Their warlike prowess is, by this evidence, linked with a moral superiority that enabled them to appreciate and stay faithful to the English. But war, white men's diseases, and treachery have diminished the Mohicans, until only Uncas and Chingachgook remain—living, like Natty Bumppo, as adopted Delawares.

According to Cooper, the Delawares themselves acknowledge the royalty of the Mohicans; and the tribe had been a worthy vessel for the blood of the Mohicans until the Delawares fell into a kind of degeneracy, and submitted to the "Mingoes" (Iroquois), earning the shameful epithet of "women." It was this episode of subjection in Heckewelder's *History, Manners and Customs of the Indian Nations* that seems to have been the germ of Cooper's conception of the Delaware, and of the myth-history he borrows and invents for his tribe.

Cooper made serious and detailed use of Heckewelder's observations of Indian customs, manners, and linguistic formulae. But a comparison of *The Last of the Mohicans* with its nominal source reveals that Cooper substantially altered and reinvented Heckewelder's account of Indian history. In Heckewelder it is the Delawares, not the Mohicans, who are the original and "unmixed" race; the Mohicans are described as a late addition to the tribe resulting specifically from intermarriages, and they are represented as possessing (if anything) less courage and grandeur than the Delawares proper. Although sadly diminished, neither Delawares nor Mohicans are on the verge of extinction in Heckewelder's account (written in 1818)—and in fact both tribes survive today. Heckewelder does mention an older, technologically more advanced and physiologically superior tribe, who were the first occupants of the land—the Allegewi (as he calls them), whom we would identify as Mound Builders. But the Delawares were the enemies of these people, not their "grandchildren," and in alliance with the Iroquois they destroyed the Allegewi.

It is clear, then, that Cooper's Indian history is a deliberate and rather elaborate fabrication of "myth" for fictional purposes. Its effect is to unite the fragmentary history of the Indians into a single myth of origin, rise to grandeur, intermarriage, decline and fall—echoing (or, as Cooper would like to suggest prefiguring) the cycle of civilizational rise and fall which was a major concept of contemporary historiography. Cooper's Indian myth is a metaphorical rendering of the pattern of our own civilization, reinforcing the suggestion that in the Indian we see the primitive germ of our own character and fate. In their character as racial "grandfathers" Cooper's Mohicans resemble the various master races cited by historians as the linguistic, cultural, and genetic forebears of the ruling classes or dominant nations of Europe. Like Cooper's Mohicans, these grandfather races—the Aryans, Teutons, the Celts, and so on—were often seen as morally and genetically purer than their technologically more advanced descendants; and like the Mohicans, they were sometimes seen as having been diminished in number or quality by intermarriage or the vicissitudes of war and disease. The idea that their racial career might, like the Mohicans', end in extinction was part of the cyclical theory many racialist historians accepted; and as the nineteenth century went forward, this prophecy of racial mongrelization and extinction became the dominant theme of racialist historiography.

Cooper's projective fantasy of race history requires the representation of the full tragic cycle, and hence the doctrine of extinction is emphasized by him to a degree perhaps greater than that of most prior and contemporary historians. But when Tamenund greets Uncas as a kind of Indian Messiah, we are unmistakably asked to see his role as specifically restorative of the virtues of the Indian "blood" or race; he is not merely to be a new leader and lawgiver, but a genetic renewer, founder and perpetuator of a dynasty that will reverse the course of race-history, drive away the white men and restore the ancient dominion of the red man. The situation is comparable to that in a modern fantasy novel, Tolkien's *Lord of the Rings,* when an heir of the ancient line of the Kings of the Race of Numenor returns to cleanse and restore a darkened world.

This Aryanization of the Mohicans serves to heighten our sense of conflict in the novel. We have left the French and Indian War behind, and at an unfavorable juncture. Now we learn that beneath the surface of that historical combat is a more elemental struggle between savagery and civilization. What is the weak Montcalm against the powerful and subtle Magua? And what would he be as enemy compared to the kingly Uncas? The threat is only implicit, and of course purely novelistic: we know that the English will defeat the French, and that no Indian Messiah will arise to unite the tribes—although our knowledge that Pontiac (1764) and Tecumseh (1809-14) will try lends a degree of credibility to the idea.

If the threat works at all, it is because Cooper has linked the appeal of Uncas-as-Messiah to the erotic appeal of the Uncas-Cora romance. They are the most beautiful and exotic characters in the novel. Uncas is not merely a noble savage, he may be an embryonic god-king, if the prophet Tamenund is to be believed. Cora is regal, brave, clever, evidently possesses all of the queenly virtues to make her a fit mate for a Messianic Uncas. She also combines in her blood the two other racial strains of the New World, black and white. Magua would debase or exterminate these; but in the marriage of Cora and Uncas there would be a fusion, an amalgamation of the warring American races. Thus the union would not be of the lowest types, but of individuals bearing the best of their respective blood lines.

The dynasty of Cora and Uncas becomes part of the Delaware fantasy of what may come from the return of the Last of the Mohicans. Together they may avert the vanishing of the "vanishing American," and make the time of racial history go backward. Both Cora and Uncas are also linked to the fascinating, ubiquitous, and dangerous presence of the "dark" elements in individual psychology. What appeals to Cora from Magua and Uncas, what appeals to Cooper's white reader from Cora—the forbidden, the beautiful-horrible

"other"—also appeals to the reader from the pseudo-myth of the Mohican Messiah. It is the appeal of an alternative world and culture, erotically and socially freer than our own, antithetical to and an escape from the civilization that both sustains and discomforts us. Cooper is playing upon *our* "natural attraction to the unnatural," and does this so successfully that he was misread as an advocate of restoring the primitive rights and powers of the subject tribes.

There is a political dimension to the romance as well. The myth wilderness is the antithesis of the disciplined world of white society—a "natural" environment which stimulates and licenses the most "unnatural" human fantasies and actions. In the wilderness of the second half of *Last of the Mohicans* there is no guarantee that boundaries of race, caste, and chastity will be observed; yet this world is one in which things appear "in their harshest and truest colors." The normal order of white society—the order of the historical, French and Indian War world of the first part—is inverted. In Part I, characters are subordinated according to rank and caste, irrespective of "talent and virtue." Munro commands Heyward; Heyward commands Hawkeye; Hawkeye in some sense commands the Mohicans. In Part II the structure is completely reversed. Even before their true character as Indian royalty is revealed, pragmatic considerations make the Mohicans leaders of the hunt, subject only to their deference to the skill of Hawkeye. Heyward follows Hawkeye, and is followed by Munro—whose inexperience and physical and emotional weakness make him the least effective member of the party. As far as the captives are concerned, in the world of civilization Gamut (as man and clergyman) would presumably act as protector or preceptor to the girls, and Alice might enjoy a marginally higher status than Cora. But in the Indian village Cora is treated as a queen, Alice as a nullity, and the foolish Gamut as a holy madman. Inside this looking glass, only Hawkeye—the white man who knows Indians—remains in a comparable position, neither Indian nor white, neither high nor low.

Much can be made of this inversion. Ideologically it appears to confirm the suggestion of Turner's Frontier Thesis that the wilderness was (or was seen as) a place in which virtue and talents could emerge to prominence over inherited wealth or position. Certainly Cooper saw in the wilderness a fantasy refuge from the class ordering and potential strife that marred civilization—a place in which talent could rise above birth *without* the necessity of revolution or even litigation. But one major effect of the inversion in the novel is to place Cora and Uncas at the heads of their respective worlds, especially after his true character is revealed. This reinforces the possibility of a climactic marriage between them, makes it seem appropriate to the reader, and creates a kind of expectation or wish for it.

We know, of course, that there is no Indian Messiah, that the "Last of the Mohicans" is an elegiac phrase. We may even say that Cooper never loves his Indians so much as when he is watching them disappear, and that for him as for General Sheridan—although with different emphasis—the only good Indians were dead. But it is part of the appeal of the romance to make us wish for something that we know is impossible. However, it is also important to Cooper, for ideological reasons, that he suppress whatever in him wishes for the consummation of Cora and Uncas.

Leatherstocking—with occasional assists from Heyward—has tried to teach us the fundamentals of a "realist's" view of the moral universe. They insist on the superiority of "un-mixed" races, and they see that the conflict between races of unlike "gifts" is inevitable and inherently unlimited. Men must choose between triumph or extermination in such a war; and their choice is paralleled by the moral problem of the females: an either/or choice between surrendering or defending their virginity, or between losing or preserving the purity of the race. But in his response to Tamenund, as in his love for Cora, Uncas is trapped into tragic ambivalence by a fatal mixture of elements that ought to be kept pure. The friend of Hawkeye and the lover of Cora cannot lead Tamenund's Messianic revolution. Therefore it is not Uncas, but Magua who speaks for the irreconcilability of races, and proposes to lead Tamenund's war of extermination against the whites and their black slaves. But Magua is himself a mixed character, and though he echoes Hawkeye's theme of racial purity his own "mixed" character appears to make him excessively, unappealingly racist. He protests Indian superiority too much, compensating for his own sense of shame and inferiority. Hawkeye also is "mixed" in his nurture, but it is part of his "white gifts" to define racial separation in ways we are meant to find more moderate—and paradoxically more effective—in violently eliminating the Indian. Although we hate Magua for killing Cora and Uncas, hate his way of expressing the doctrine of racial purity, and rejoice when Hawkeye picks him off with his Longue Carabine and sends him plunging like Lucifer headfirst into a chasm, there is yet something in us, in Cooper at least, that consents to the effects if not to the deed of Magua.

Although tempted by the alternative history offered by the pseudo-myth of Uncas, we are not only left with the facts of our past, we *ought* (says Cooper) in good conscience and for the sake of the public peace accept those consequences as good. Even if violence must resolve what marriage cannot be permitted to reconcile—the confrontation of racial/sexual opposites—we must return to the doctrine of purity that Hawkeye continually reiterates. By the novel's end all of the mixed characters are either dead—like Cora, Uncas, and Magua—or settled in a path of sterility (like Gamut, Chingachgook, Hawkeye, and Colonel Munro). Only the pure whites, who have never even yearned for a dark lover, will marry and produce heirs. The future belongs to Heyward and Alice. All the color is dead. And although Cooper mourns that loss, he grapples with the need—equally strong as yearning—to disapprove of it.

In the concluding funeral scene, the Indians mourn Cora and Uncas together:

> They pronounced him noble, manly and generous; all that became a warrior, and all that a maid might love . . . He was of a race that had once been lords on the shores of the salt lake, and his wishes had led him back to a people who dwelt about the graves of his fathers [i.e., the whites]. Why should not such a predilection be encouraged? That she was of a blood purer and richer than the rest of her nation, any eye might have seen; that she was equal to dangers and daring of a life in the woods, her conduct had proved; and now, they added, the "wise one of the earth" had transplanted her to a place where she would find congenial spirits and might be forever happy.

They fantasize a union in an Indian heaven beyond the grave—a union too perfect for earth, perhaps, but obviously appropriate in the eyes of the god who had created two such beings.

Munro and Heyward listen uncomprehendingly; but Munro catches the spirit of the prayer, and responds in language that almost seems prophetic of the Fourteenth Amendment: he declares that "the Being we all worship, under different names, will be mindful of their charity; and that the time shall not be distant when we may assemble around his throne without distinction of sex, or rank, or color."

But it is Natty Bumppo—the white man educated as an Indian—who rebukes this extreme statement of religious and social leveling by invoking his version of "natural law." " 'To tell them this,' he said, 'would be to tell them that the snows come not in winter. . . . ' " The Indians have in fact been saying something quite similar, with Natty listening and shaking his head disapprovingly. He simply refuses to translate their song correctly for Munro. Here, as elsewhere in this novel and others, Bumppo is the strictest and most absolute spokesman for racial and social conservatism: "I am a man without a cross."

This consciousness of his race is the trait that keeps Leatherstocking true to his own gifts throughout the vicissitudes of his adventures. He is therefore our guide, not only in woodcraft, but in the interpretation of the two "histories." He, who knows both sides of the race war, declares that war to be in its nature irreconcilable. He, who loves Indians, consents to their demise, although he mourns the passing of Uncas and shares the Indians' fate of disappearing without a trace of progeny in the American future. He will mourn throughout his life, sharing the grief of his beloved Chingachgook; yet in the end, they may well end up in segregated heavens, to be rewarded according to their "gifts."

Although Cooper confirms paternalistic and male-dominant values and confirms racial prejudices in his killing off of Cora and Uncas, he also reveals in them possibilities that transcend the conventional limitations assigned to their sex and race, and gives them a greater emotional appeal than his nominal hero and heroine. If he has preached all sorts of moral precepts to us via Leatherstocking, he has also shown us what his limitations are; and in the funeral scene so juxtaposes the elements as to throw Bumppo's prejudices into stark relief by showing them in a less appealing light than the courtesy of Munro. Like most of us, Cooper would like to have had his dilemmas resolved both ways: the races both reconciled and left separate, the wilderness both civilized and preserved in purity, the Indian forever vanishing yet never lost.

The mythology of race, and the linkage of this myth to a larger myth of progressive history, provided Cooper with a resolution to the contradiction between democratic or egalitarian ideals and the perceived need for subordinating one social class (or race) to another. *Last of the Mohicans* extends this mythology by reaching out to link sexuality to race and class, and through a deliberate act of mythogenesis it becomes his first comprehensive rendering of the whole pattern of his myth of American history.

In his next Leatherstocking novel, *The Prairie* (1827), Cooper elaborates the symbolic language of class, sex, and race, and extends it to a new historical phase and a new social problem. The novel was set on the Great Plains or "Great American Desert," in the years just following the Louisiana Purchase. It was to have been the last Leatherstocking novel, and the hero's death in the final chapter was to have signaled

Reginald Marsh's depiction of an elderly Natty Bumppo, from The Prairie.

the end of the phase of expansion that had begun in the French and Indian War and reached its climax with the removal of the last Indians in the East—an event symbolized in *The Pioneers* by the death of Chingachgook. As in Crèvecoeur, it is nature that determines the social fate of the region. The Great Plains are represented as so arid and intractable to agricultural development that they constitute a permanent barrier to continuation of the frontier.

In this refuge outside the arena of continued historical action, Natty Bumppo has survived his exile from Templeton, and he shares the region with nomadic tribes of horse Indians. Onto this blank screen of desert trundles the caravan of a "squatter" clan, led by Ishmael Bush—a unique combination of the patriarch and the criminal, whose character curiously anticipates the negative stereotypes of John Brown in the late 1850s. Their very presence in this world suggests that they are people whose "gift" it is always to go too far. We learn that they have been driven from the settlements because of their refusal to adapt to the regime of law that must pertain in a postfrontier society—which is what America has become east of the prairie. Thus although they are physically removed beyond the pale of society, the Bush clan brings onto the testing ground of the mythic wilderness the elements within American society that were, in Cooper's view, as

threatful to the Metropolis as Indians and Frenchmen had been to the Frontier.

Here Cooper has succeeded in reducing a variety of social and literary types to a compact symbol system. The two types of savage personality complexly developed in Chingachgook/ Uncas and Magua are formulaically rendered in Hard Heart and Mahtoree. Captain Middleton embodies the military-aristocratic principle promulgated in Duncan Heyward and Oliver Effingham—in fact, he is the direct descendant of Heyward and Alice Munro. Leatherstocking himself is realized here as a mythic figure: his first appearance is out of the rays of the noonday sun, which makes him appear to have colossal stature; and at his death he gives up his ghost to the setting sun, surrounded by worshiping Indians. The principle of "female" civilization is represented by Inez, who is so much the incarnation of the qualities of weakness, refinement, and Christianity symbolized by the type that she verges on parody. The social hierarchy developed in *The Pioneers* but missing from *Last of the Mohicans* is represented here by two groups of plebeian frontiersmen. Paul Hover and his beloved Ellen represent the virtues of the yeoman farmer. Although coarser than Middleton, they recognize their proper social relations, and are deferential to Middleton, Inez, and Leatherstocking.

The Bush clan represents the capacity of the common man for evil, and this quality is symbolically expressed by their display of Indian-like qualities. This is shown first of all by their having captured and carried into captivity the aristocratic Inez—the action that is quintessentially "savage" in Cooper's framework. Their disrespect for the woman is related to the contempt they have for the rights of property established in law. Like Indians, they recognize only the rights, the needs, and the code of their clan. Their idea of justice involves the "savage" principle of revenge, and also recalls a kind of Old Testament eye-for-an-eye code. As squatters they would characteristically plant themselves on land legally owned by someone else; develop or simply occupy it, and file a preemption claim hoping to usurp title. Like the pushing and unscrupulous class they represent, the Bushes have a kind of power and grandeur which is primitive and admirable: they achieve things (whether or not by violent means), they are pioneers, they try to make their lives a fable of "success." But like the Indians they are unsuited to civilization, and having broken trail for the progress represented by the yeomen they now find themselves in exile from society.

In their clannishness, their belief in the revenge code, their primitive style of life, and above all in their role as captors, the Bushes are very much like the Indians. In the past, one might have viewed them as precursors of civilization, as Crèvecoeur did. However, in *The Prairie,* the nation seems to have touched the outer limits of arable land. On the rim of the prairie, America confronts the end of the Frontier as it has been known. Neither the Bushes nor anyone else will be able to plant on the "ocean" of undulating dry prairie that everywhere confronts the eye. Here Leatherstocking finds a last refuge, and the Indians—in diminished numbers and degenerate form—eke out a marginal existence. This is intractable wilderness, pure and simple, from which the actors will recoil once the adventure is done.

Cooper resolves the social/racial tensions of *The Prairie* by the usual means: captivities and rescues, leading ultimately to the union of Middleton and Inez, Paul Hover and Ellen. Leatherstocking dies, honored as a holy man among the remnant of the Indians and mythologized among his own people. The Bushes discover that Abiram, one of their own number, has betrayed the clan for his own self-interest; and the clan slays him, in accordance with its primitive code of justice. But clan justice merely reproduces among whites the vengeance law of savagery. Therefore Cooper must go further to resolve the ideological difficulty posed by the Bush clan. The race tension in *Last of the Mohicans* is resolved by the death of the mediating figures and the "vanishing" of the Indian. *The Prairie*'s class/race tensions are resolved by the vanishing of the Bush clan. The clan returns to the settlements, the older generation broken in spirit and the younger apparently edified by an adventure that has demonstrated the criminal folly of the squatter's code. The triumph of civilization is once again effected by the vanishing of the primitive enemy; although in the case of the squatters, they are only *partly* exterminated, and partly amalgamated. The great promise of the Frontier is that of absolute escape from one's competitors and rivals. (pp. 86-100)

Richard Slotkin, "Ideology and Fiction: The Role of Cooper," in his The Fatal Environment: The Myth of the Frontier in the Age of Industrialization, 1800-1890, *Atheneum, 1985, pp. 81-106.*

FRANK BERGMANN   (essay date 1985)

[*Bergmann is an American educator and critic. In the following excerpt, he examines racial issues in* The Last of the Mohicans.]

I believe that in *The Last of the Mohicans* Cooper says more about the race problem than most critics have conceded, and that he does so with greater art than has generally been acknowledged. Central to my view is the consideration of how Cooper ties together the three concerns given separately in condensed form on the novel's title page: "The Last of the Mohicans; A Narrative of 1757. 'Mislike me not, for my complexion, The shadowed livery of the burnished sun.'" The book's major message is the historical lesson inherent in the disastrous race conflict, a lesson for both Cooper's time and ours; the "narrative" is a more effective and carefully constructed vehicle for Cooper's message than the scoffers would have us believe; and the motto from Shakespeare's *The Merchant of Venice* is more than a pious sentiment engraved upon a stately burial monument. (p. 118)

Cooper designs his story to make the reader give him a hearing; above the story, the plot transmits the values. Outside is the sugar coating, inside the medicine. The apparent problems of the story of *The Last of the Mohicans* have often been ridiculed, and indeed, where is the logic in the girls' desire to join their father at such an inopportune time? They would be much safer in Albany or New York. But we are already asking "why?", which means that we are picking up the plot even as we follow the story. After all, the girls' father might die, and so we have no right to call them imprudent or stupid. If go then they must, at such a time, they would appear to be safest amidst the contingent that marches the high road from Edward to William Henry between sunup and sundown. Duncan Heyward, however, wants to make time and further errs in feeling that Magua is a trustworthy guide. The girls are not properly outfitted: they wear riding veils instead of Allagash hats, slippers instead of Herman Survivors. We worry. Twice during the first half of the book does the story reach a climax, both times linking fear for life with fear for virtue. After Cora has persuaded Leatherstocking, Chingachgook, and Uncas not to await everyone's death at Glens Falls but to run for help, she wants Duncan to join the three. He refuses, because of his military honor—how could he possibly show himself to Munro without the girls?—and because of the likelihood of having to save the girls from "evils worse than death" by killing them before the Mingoes can defile them. Magua's proposal to Cora somewhat later makes death for the party imminent because of Cora's refusal to become his squaw. The daring rescue by Leatherstocking and the two Mohicans, Magua's escape, the tight moment at the old blockhouse, the scene with the French sentinel, and finally the dangerous confusion outside William Henry are further spine-tingling episodes along the simple story line of getting the two girls to their father. The experienced reader knows, of course, that nothing will go really wrong with the girls this early in the book; a glance at the many pages yet to come assures him. At William Henry, the story's expected resolution is briefly unveiled; the girls have joined their father not just to be with him but so that he may promise one of them to Duncan. We may be disappointed that Alice is the one rather than Cora, but precisely because Cooper gives the story this turn do we stay with it. We sense that the deeper implications of Cora's racial background will be addressed beyond Duncan's sidestepping, but the story takes yet another turn: what will become of Cora and whether we will see the wedding of

Duncan and Alice must yield for the time being to the negotiations for the fort's surrender and to the massacre, that is, to the largely historical "narrative of 1757."

It has often been noted that Cooper doubles his story, that the book's center marks the shift from two daughters in search of their father to "the father in quest of his children." There are, nevertheless, major differences between the book's two halves. The initial journey from Edward to William Henry is clearly delimited: twelve miles or so along the road, somewhat more by the forest paths. The journey into the wilderness beyond the Horican, however, is open-ended; whereas the father's whereabouts are known at the outset of the first half, the daughters are we know not where at the beginning of the second half. Not only do we face an away match, so to speak, we do not even know where the opponent's ballpark is. Leatherstocking remarks grimly that by now the girls may be in the wilds of Canada. It is this open-endedness which changes the entire character of the book: in the first half, the story leads us to a white men's fort and the plot makes us think about a white men's war; in the second half, the story leads us into the land of the Indians and the plot makes us think about their lives.

In the first half of the book, cultural comparisons are rare and oblique. The most shocking incident before the massacre is not anything Magua does but instead Chingachgook's murder of the French sentinel. Duncan's presence of mind and Cora's sympathy, as well as their French, get the party past the danger of detection and detention. Then the presumably good (because he helps the girls) Chingachgook kills the sentinel and takes his scalp. Even Leatherstocking is shocked; then he explains rather lamely that it is a worthy deed for an Indian, no matter how reprehensible it would have been for a white man. Yet just before, Leatherstocking relates with almost ghoulish relish an earlier massacre for which he was responsible and in which totally unsuspecting French troops were not made prisoners but instead butchered and dumped into the same Bloody Pond that received Chingachgook's victim, with the only difference being that their scalps were still on their heads. Chingachgook's deed and the terrible slaughter of William Henry's British garrison by Montcalm's Indian allies eclipse the earlier massacre in the reader's mind. The conclusion that the whites are capable of being as savage as the Indians reaches the reader almost subconsciously; since it requires precisely that memory which the story in its onward rush seeks to disable, it is a—high—function of plot achieved virtually in opposition against the very story that generates it.

The novel's second half presents this sort of comparison directly in the story and reserves to the plot even more complex matters. The travel pattern in the second half makes the story into a mechanism of discovery: an object or circumstance encountered along the way becomes itself an insight, frequently explained by Leatherstocking as an answer to a question barely broached in the first half. For example, the fear that Cora and Alice might be raped at Glens Falls is lifted when they are not: whatever might have happened does not happen because Magua happens to have other plans. In the second half we are told that it was not Magua's plans that made the difference but Indian custom of never violating captive women. Munro has been worrying himself sick; he wants his "babes" returned to him "spotless." He and Duncan worry because they know that white warfare—"shame be it to our colour," says Leatherstocking—has at all times given plenty

of evidence that whites consider captive women fair game, evidence that World War II and Vietnam have done nothing to weaken.

Leatherstocking becomes in the second half an interpreter not only of Indian languages but more importantly of Indian customs. Nor does Cooper make his case for Indian civilization by Uncas alone, whom the romantic requirements of the story cast as the epitome of the noble savage; Chingachgook and even the bad (because they do not help the girls) Indians are enlisted. Cooper has the reader observe the warm relationship between Chingachgook and Uncas, the son's instant obedience when the father wishes to end their conversation and go to sleep, the musicality of the Indian language (no bloodcurdling yells or cavemen's grunts here), and the high standards of Indian debate (which Cooper recommends as a model for whites—and who, considering the deplorable lack of decorum in many of today's parliaments in western Europe, including the British, would disagree?). The rape matter, the Indians' not hurting a "non-composser," Leatherstocking's stern lecture to David Gamut on the Indians'—even the Mingoes'—worshiping not idols but "the true and living God" are further lessons for Leatherstocking's white companions and Cooper's readers. The bad Indians, we observe, have rules as strict as those of baseball; Reed-That-Bends looks, so to speak, at three pitches and therefore strikes out: he has dishonored his tribe by cowardice thrice and is therefore summarily executed. Tamenund's Delawares prize justice and go to some length to establish it; they also obey the Indian law of hospitality so scrupulously that the reader thinks immediately of the Christian notion of turning the other cheek.

Most significantly, Cooper makes the anxiety of the white travelers before the uncharted wilderness across the Horican express the anxiety of the white reader before the unfamiliar culture. Duncan and Munro must enter this wilderness to reclaim daughters and bride; the reader must learn about Indian culture to reclaim a vital part of his past. Neither party is qualified; Duncan and Munro must be guided by Leatherstocking and the two Mohicans, the reader by Cooper. The guilt of having lost the girls motivates the two officers; the guilt of having dispossessed and decimated the Indians should motivate the white American reader. Cooper's job is the more difficult of the two: his reader does not wish to go. Hence, the wilderness beyond the Horican becomes the book's second major metaphor, a symbol for the white man's attitude toward Indian life and history in general:

> The party had landed on the border of a region that is, even to this day, less known to the inhabitants of the states, than the deserts of Arabia, or the steppes of Tartary. It was the sterile and rugged district, which separates the tributaries of Champlain from those of the Hudson, the Mohawk, and of the St. Lawrence. Since the period of our tale, the active spirit of the country has surrounded it with a belt of rich and thriving settlements, though none but the hunter or the savage is ever known, even now, to penetrate its wild recesses.

Here and in several of his footnotes of 1831, Cooper makes clear that the locales of the novel's first half—Lake George, Glens Falls, Ballston Spa, all in the southeastern foothills of the Adirondacks—have by 1826 been appropriated by the white man, but the Adirondacks proper have not been. "Sterile" and "rugged," they cannot be made over into a garden, but even travelers do not visit them. It is most revealing that

Cooper does not set Rome or Paris against the Adirondacks but foreign wildernesses instead. The Adirondacks thus are the metaphor for the past one wishes to deny by ignoring it, even while one professes to have an open, exploring mind. They are the blot on the landscapes of the map as well as of the soul. Out of sight, out of mind; in our time, he who visits Auschwitz or Hiroshima is more likely to think about the holocaust than he who spends his vacation exploring Nullarbor Plain or Queen Maud Land, not to mention lounging on the Riviera.

"If it was not for death and marriage I do not know how the average novelist would conclude," says Forster. Uncas and Magua must die, for in 1826 the Eastern Indians are, for all practical purposes, dead. Duncan and Alice must marry, or else most readers hostile to Cooper's teaching will not finish the book. But there is more than death and marriage at the end; they are the winding up of the story, which for this purpose briefly reverts to its erstwhile level. It is the plot which, in taking up the title motto, inquires after the sense of the ending.

Cora bears the full weight of that motto: "Mislike me not, for my complexion, The shadowed livery of the burnished sun." From the beginning, she is the dark lady, no matter how white she may appear, though she seems much better off than Mark Twain's Roxy of *Pudd'nhead Wilson,* for her speech matches her beauty, and she is no slave. She likes Duncan but is too noble to cut in on her half-sister Alice. Uncas and Magua find her attractive, although they see her as white, since Cora's background is revealed only to Duncan, at William Henry, in the privacy of Munro's quarters. From the first, she judges persons by anything but their complexions. She defends Magua against Alice: " 'Should we distrust the man, because his manners are not our manners, and that his skin is dark!' coldly asked Cora"; she says "dark," not "red"! Magua should of course have been distrusted for the likelihood of wanting revenge for the whipping Munro subjected him to. Later, she commends Duncan for his assessment of noble-looking Uncas: " 'Now Major Heyward speaks, as Major Heyward should,' said Cora; 'who, that looks at this creature of nature, remembers the shades of his skin!' " When she rejects Magua's deal—to free the others by becoming his squaw—she conceals "her powerful disgust," which arises primarily from his calculating vengeance. That she has little to hope for becomes clear to the reader in Duncan's interview with Munro when Duncan conceals his prejudice against her blackness by a lie and an encomium of Alice.

Cooper does not solve the complexities of Cora's mixed blood. When she speaks to Tamenund of how " 'the curse of my ancestors has fallen heavily on their child!' " and Tamenund replies with a spirited condemnation of white racial prejudice, the matter is not pursued any further (" 'but why—it is not permitted us to inquire!' " says Cora), and nobody is the wiser. To Magua, her blackness would scarcely have made a difference; what counts for him is that she is Munro's daughter, and her duties as a squaw would have been no different than those of the blacks Magua describes in his speech to the Delawares, " 'to work for ever'." Uncas, Cora's match in nobility of spirit, could not have cared either, though their "future prospects" are denied by Leatherstocking anyway and would have greatly unsettled "the selfcommand of both Heyward and Munro" who, unlike Uncas and Leatherstocking, know that Cora is not pure white.

In not explicitly exploring the ramifications of the racial

problem posed by Cora's background, Cooper clearly considers the attitude of his reader. His immediate goal is a revision of his contemporaries' view—kept alive by the memory of Jane McCrea—of the Indians as unmitigated savages; that goal can be achieved without the detailing of Cora's mixed background (or, better yet, entirely without Cora, since her beauty and death call to mind Jane McCrea's). But Cora and her problem are in the book, which therefore has a goal beyond the immediate one. Cooper's activating the Shakespeare motto is not a matter of story but a subtle enriching of plot; it requires the reader's memory and intelligence of which Forster speaks, although it may also well be comprehended intuitively by the busman's unpretending good nature and decency of character. Except—and because of—Bassanio, Shakespeare's Portia dislikes all suitors *a priori.* She then finds acceptable reasons for disliking them in their shortcomings: who would really wish her a drunkard for a husband? We do not know much about the Prince of Morocco. He is a bit blustering, but apparently he has the record to back it up. We do not know why he courts Portia, nor does it greatly matter, since he chooses the wrong casket anyway. What matters is Portia's reaction. She mislikes him because of his complexion, not because of any character deficiencies. When he honors the stipulations and leaves quickly, like a gentleman, Portia comments: "A gentle riddance. Draw the curtains, go. / Let all of his complexion choose me so."

One is tempted to equate Morocco with Uncas, Portia with Cora—but Morocco is black, not red. His lines are on Cooper's title page because in Cooper's day as in ours, the blacks—unlike the Indians—are alive and numerous. The motto and Cora's being part black in a world that sees the white man triumph over the redskins can have but one message: let us not do unto the blacks as we have done unto the Indians. Hence, the reaffirmation of Leatherstocking's friendship for Chingachgook at the end of *The Last of the Mohicans* becomes the symbol of mutual racial acceptance, an acceptance which today's "black is beautiful" echoes in calling for not a problematic merging but a rightful coexistence. Stripped of their dogmatic use, the lines from Psalm 133 which David Gamut sings at the book's beginning might, more fitting than Tamenund's cyclic epitaph, dismiss the congregation of Cooper's readers at the book's end: "How good it is, O see, / And how it pleaseth well, / Together, e'en in unity, / For brethren so to dwell." That Tamenund's lines do close the book tells us that Cooper is well aware of the realities of history indeed; nevertheless, that awareness does not fetter his imagination. In his Introduction of 1831, Cooper writes that "the business of a writer of fiction is to approach, as near as his powers will allow, to poetry." E. M. Forster . . . [in *Aspects of the Novel*] locates the "spongy tract" that is the novel between "the opposing ranges of Poetry and of History." In moving away from the historical "narrative of 1757" in the second half of *The Last of the Mohicans,* Cooper aspires to poetry and asks for a world more tolerant and more humane than he knew his was and he suspected ours would be. (pp. 119-25)

Frank Bergmann, "The Meaning of the Indians and Their Land in Cooper's 'The Last of the Mohicans'," in Upstate Literature: Essays in Memory of Thomas F. O'Donnell, *edited by Frank Bergmann, Syracuse University Press, 1985, pp. 117-27.*

DONALD A. RINGE (essay date 1988)

[*Ringe is an American educator and critic who has focused on nineteenth-century American literature. In the following excerpt from his biographical and critical study of Cooper, he discusses aspects of plot, theme, and characterization in the Leatherstocking novels.*]

Called "A Descriptive Tale" on its title page, **The Pioneers** draws its fundamental meaning from the description of the society it portrays and the relation of that society to the natural environment—the American wilderness that must be invaded and destroyed if civilization is to spread across the continent. Setting the scene at Otsego Lake (Cooperstown) in 1793-94, Cooper depicts a landscape in the process of change from the untouched wilderness hunted by Leatherstocking and visited by Judge Temple when he came to survey his possessions, to the placid domestic scene of 1823 presented in the first paragraphs of the novel. In 1793 the settlement is already past the frontier stage; the village is secure from Indian attack and the leading citizen has begun to pay some attention to the refinements of life. The gap between the social classes, however, has not yet become so large as to set him completely apart from the rest of the villagers; for, although there is some pretension among the common people, all men can still come together in the tavern without undue restraint on Christmas Eve for a pleasant celebration.

Much of the book indeed suggests a pastoral idyl. Drawing upon James Thomson's *The Seasons,* Cooper takes the reader through most of a year, from Christmas Eve to October, and describes the rural pastimes, like the shooting match for the turkey in winter, or the night-fishing on the lake in summer. Yet the action of the novel is anything but idyllic. Contention erupts in the opening pages when Judge Temple, Leatherstocking and Oliver Edwards all shoot at the same deer, the judge accidentally wounds the young man, and they argue over who has killed the animal. The hostile relations thus established continue throughout the book, for although this conflict is quickly resolved, Edwards and Leatherstocking persist in opposing the judge. They believe he has wrongfully appropriated the young man's inheritance because, after the Revolution, he had bought at a low price the lands of the young man's grandfather, the loyalist Major Effingham, when they fell under the acts of confiscation. Edwards is unaware that the judge considered himself to be holding the land in trust for his old friends, the Effinghams. But the judge had been unable to locate the old major, and he believed that the major's son and grandson had been lost at sea.

This conflict is resolved on the level of plot. Although the return of the lost heir has long been a stock device in fiction, Cooper uses it, as Thomas Philbrick has shown [see Further Reading], for a sound thematic purpose. The central issue involved is the ownership of the land, and several of the characters represent legitimate claims. Judge Temple is, of course, the American entrepreneur who holds title from the state of New York. Major Effingham represents a prior claim derived from royal grants, and since he had been adopted into the Delaware tribe, a right that had been extended to his son and grandson, he and his heirs also represent an even earlier Indian claim. When Oliver Edwards reveals himself, therefore, as an Effingham and the grandson of the major, he is asserting the legitimacy of rights that have long been extinguished in the legal sense, but which the judge, by dividing his estate with him, admits to be morally just. And when Edwards marries the judge's daughter, Elizabeth, all claims are resolved

in their union, and their children will be the heirs of all who have held the land before them.

For the modern reader, however, a much more important theme is presented through the conflict between Judge Temple and Leatherstocking, for it raises significant questions about the westward march of American civilization. The land on which Templeton, the judge's settlement, is built has been occupied for some forty years by the old hunter, who, with John Mohegan, his Indian friend, wants only to live in harmony with his natural surroundings. But the process of change that the judge initiates in settling the land violates the concept of nature that Leatherstocking holds. When the story opens, much of the natural landscape is still untouched. Virgin forest stretches uncut all around the town, pigeons on their annual migrations darken the sky as they fly past by the millions, and fish can be drawn in untold numbers from the lake. But the first ominous note of change has already been sounded. The larger game—most particularly deer—are becoming scarce; the people are making inroads on the forests of sugar maples, which they cut and waste for firewood. Leatherstocking and his Indian friend observe the change and lament it, for the process entails a moral wrong that Leatherstocking cannot tolerate.

The hunter maintains a moral view of nature, and he regards the bounty around him as provided by a beneficent God for man's use. A man is justified, he believes, in using whatever part of nature he truly needs; but he is not free to destroy at will. When he sees the settlers drawing in their seines with hundreds of fish, most of which will be left to rot on the shore, he can only lament the folly of men who can be so lawless in their relation to their natural surroundings; and he is completely disgusted by the wholesale destruction of wildlife and by the cutting of trees. That Leatherstocking is fundamentally right in his view is abundantly demonstrated by the numerous scenes of irrational destruction that Cooper includes in the novel. Billy Kirby, an expert axman who delights in cutting trees, urges the destruction of thousands of pigeons and shoots wildly into the flock in a frenzy of killing; Richard Jones, the judge's cousin and sheriff, actually brings out a swivel gun and lines up his men to fire volleys into the cloud of birds that is passing overhead. Wherever we read in the novel, there are scenes of senseless destruction or of settlers laughing at the idea that game or wood should ever become scarce.

Judge Temple himself clearly sees that such destruction is morally wrong and he is certainly opposed to it. The problem he faces, however, is how to control the waste without curtailing the advance of civilization. The judge's recourse is to civil law, the law of society, which he hopes to bring into accord with the moral law that Leatherstocking is following in his relations with nature. He is pleased to see the state legislature establishing seasons for the taking of game, and he hopes eventually to make it a crime to cut trees wantonly. He enforces the law for the protection of deer with unswerving rigidity, and he demands that the forms of society be respected even though the law be administered for selfish aims by unworthy officers. Thus, when Leatherstocking kills a deer out of season and resists arrest by Hiram Doolittle, who tries to use the law to satisfy his curiosity about what is in Leatherstocking's cabin, the judge insists that the law be rigidly enforced. Judge Temple's position is made doubly difficult in that Leatherstocking has recently saved his daughter, Elizabeth, by shooting a mountain lion which was on the point of attacking her. But he adheres to his decision. Leatherstocking is sentenced to the stocks and publicly humiliated.

The judge's argument in defending his actions is a good one. As he tells his daughter, "Society cannot exist without wholesome restraints. Those restraints cannot be inflicted, without security and respect to the persons of those who administer them; and it would sound ill indeed, to report that a judge had extended favour to a convicted criminal, because he had saved the life of his child." The judge's logic is unimpeachable if men must have discipline imposed on them by external authority, and Marmaduke Temple has seen enough of the men in his settlement to recognize that most will act from selfish motives or be influenced by their overpowering passions before they will exert the kind of self-control that would make the laws of society unnecessary. That Leatherstocking can resist most of the selfish impulses of men makes him only the exception that proves the rule. From his long life in the wilderness, he has learned his true relation to nature and has acquired the humility he needs to discipline himself in the moral code taught him by the Moravian missionaries. But there is no reason to assume that all men will be able to perceive and follow such a system of belief. Human experience, indeed, seems to suggest just the opposite; most men react like Richard Jones, Billy Kirby, or Hiram Doolittle when no longer restrained by civil law.

Society demands, therefore, that the just man be punished that justice may prevail. To be sure, there is strong irony in the fact that Leatherstocking is persecuted for killing one deer out of season when the people of Templeton have slaughtered and chopped with complete impunity merely because they violated no man-made law. But Cooper wastes no sentimental tears on Leatherstocking's fate; for, although the hunter is caught in a cycle of change over which he has no control, he plays a vital part in the process which is ultimately working for good. In the last lines of the novel, Cooper comments on the role that Leatherstocking plays in the American drama. Of his own free will he leaves the settlement and disappears into the woods. "He had gone far towards the setting sun,—the foremost in that band of Pioneers, who are opening the way for the march of the nation across the continent." The asocial man, free from restraint except for those moral imperatives that bind men in all times and places, flees the sometimes unjust restraints of a civilized society. But his flight does him no good; it merely begins the cycle anew and makes it all the easier for those social injunctions to catch up with him. He becomes, therefore, the inevitable herald of the civilization he most wants to avoid.

The end result of this process is, of course, the good society of Templeton; but it need not be bought, Cooper insists, at a price of the rape of the wilderness, the indiscriminate destruction of nature. Men like Richard Jones could learn from Leatherstocking to take the long view and conserve the bounty that has been lavished upon the American settler. If they do not do so—and these are implications that are not fully developed until later tales in the series—the nation itself must eventually suffer the judgment of an exhausted earth. It is in Judge Temple's view, therefore, that the best compromise is to be found. Clearly he is bringing the values of Christian civilization to the wilderness and laying the foundation for a good society. Although he is willing to sacrifice much of nature to social order, he recognizes the values that are being lost and tries to some extent to curb at least part of the wanton destruction. The judge is certainly superior to his cousin

and the other wasteful settlers, none of whom can be trusted to discipline themselves as Leatherstocking has. And, indeed, he is superior to the hunter too in the social values that he always affirms. Judge Temple is, therefore, the first of Cooper's long series of Christian gentlemen on whom he placed his faith for the establishment and maintenance of the good life. (pp. 16-20)

[In *The Last of the Mohicans* (1826) and *The Prairie* (1827), Cooper] further developed the character of Leatherstocking into the mythic figure who eventually dominates the series. He returned, moreover, in both of these frontier stories to the kind of material that had proved so useful in his previous successes—the natural landscape and its relation to the men and women who move through it. In *The Last of the Mohicans,* we enter the untouched wilderness around Lake George during the campaign of 1757, when Leatherstocking, now called Hawkeye, is in his early prime; in *The Prairie,* we are on the Great Plains about 1805, when Leatherstocking, here called only "the trapper," is well past eighty. Both tales pick up the thematic pattern we have already observed in *The Pioneers;* the moral implications of the westward march of civilization which Leatherstocking initiates and which finally destroys his world.

This theme is less apparent in *The Last of the Mohicans* than in the other Leatherstocking tales, and some critics have been content to dismiss the book as almost pure adventure with slight social import. It is true, of course, that the tale says little explicitly about the problem; but when we come upon it from *The Pioneers*—and this is the way it should be approached—we can easily recognize its relation to the earlier novel if we consider the mode of development Cooper uses in each book. *The Pioneers,* "a descriptive tale," is essentially spatial in its development. The settlers have achieved a degree of secure repose, now that they have pushed back the wilderness, driven off hunter and Indian, and begun to develop a civilized social life. The narrative mode of *The Last of the Mohicans,* on the other hand—the pattern of chase, escape, and battle—suggests the fundamental insecurity of the whites when they penetrate the virgin wilderness for the first time and become dependent upon the Indians—and the Indian-like Hawkeye—for survival. Danger greets them at every turn, and their fears are projected through the Gothic images with which Cooper fills the landscape.

In *The Last of the Mohicans* everything is dominated by the virgin forest. The moment Duncan Heyward leads the girls, Alice and Cora Munro, off the main road between Forts Edward and William Henry, he loses control over his environment and becomes an easy prey to the machinations of the evil Magua. From this point to the end of the novel, all the white characters, with the exception of Hawkeye, are at the mercy of the wilderness and its natural, red inhabitants. Even Montcalm and the victorious French cannot completely govern their Huron allies after the evacuation of the fort, and the French commander himself muses about the dangers of setting in motion a process which he cannot control. In the massacre at Fort William Henry, the Indians clearly dominate the whites who have invaded their lands. Indeed, even the English characters who finally succeed in recovering the stolen Alice from the Hurons must rely upon their Indian friends, the Delawares, to escape from being totally destroyed by the wilderness they have penetrated. Without Chingachgook and Uncas, the capable Hawkeye himself could have done little.

Even the scale of events is determined by the untouched wilderness. Whole armies are swallowed up in the living mass of dense vegetation only to emerge as broken and scattered remnants; and the entire struggle between the British and French troops, with their white loyalties to distant kings, seems trivial when viewed in relation to the immense forest that surrounds them. Cooper deliberately draws his landscape on an immense canvas; the vast panorama he pauses to describe when the little party led by Hawkeye approaches the fort for the first time deliberately suggests the immensity of space that surrounds the little fort they see below. The white men, dwarfed by their hostile environment, are incapable of handling it; for the civilized principles they import are of little value here. Overconfident in himself from the very beginning, Duncan Heyward constantly makes errors in judgment until Hawkeye bluntly warns him: "If you judge of Indian cunning by the rules you find in books, or by white sagacity, they will lead you astray, if not to your death." Indeed, the massacre at William Henry speaks eloquently of the irrelevance of the white man's code of honorable surrender in the depths of the forest.

Only Hawkeye, of all the whites, is competent to survive, mainly because his experience in the woods has instilled in him the humility he needs to understand the Indian and to interpret the white and red man to each other. Superstitious, ignorant, and prejudiced though he may be—qualities critics have tended to ignore in him—he perceives as no other white character does his true relation to the immensity of the nature that surrounds him; and his humility lets him see good even in his enemies. He alone sees virtue and justice among the Indians as well as among those of his own color; and, although he always remains true to his race and consistently maintains the superiority of the Christian view, he doesn't make the mistake of completely scorning the heathen. He is willing to learn from them, and his knowledge wins him survival. Yet if Hawkeye's balanced view enables him to cope with his environment and save the other whites from certain destruction, it also sets in motion the chain of events that eventually leads to his degradation in *The Pioneers.*

For the whites, hunted and insecure as they are in this tale of suspense and violence, have already taken the first steps toward complete mastery of the continent. The great tribe of the Delawares has been scattered by the settlers, and their enlistment in the white man's struggle against the Hurons foreshadows the eventual destruction of both. Magua is certainly right in asking the Delaware chiefs why Huron and Delaware should "brighten their tomahawks, and sharpen their knives against each other! Are not the pale-faces thicker than the swallows in the season of flowers?" This question, repeated by Mahtoree in terms of Sioux and Pawnee in *The Prairie,* should, of course, provide a rallying point for the tribes. That it does not is most fortunate for the whites and makes possible the ultimate conquest of the continent in the name of Christian civilization. That it also involves the death of Uncas, son of Chingachgook and beloved foster-son of Hawkeye, is not foreseen by these companions of the woods any more than is their own ultimate degradation. Only Tamenund, in the last pages of the book, can foresee the inevitable: "The pale-faces are masters of the earth, and the time of the red-men has not yet come again."

The Prairie shows the end toward which events are tending and brings the series to its logical point of repose in the great death scene of the trapper in the final pages of the book. The weakest of the three early Leatherstocking tales on the plot level—the kidnaping of Inez and the transporting of her to the trans-Mississippi west are most implausible—*The Prairie* is probably the richest thematically and the most complex intellectually. The relation of man to nature introduced in the two earlier books is further developed in terms of the immensity of the treeless waste of the Great Plains; the rape of the wilderness is described in less equivocal terms than in *The Pioneers;* and the moral view of nature is reaffirmed in the eloquent speeches of the aged trapper. In addition, Cooper goes out of his way to assemble a group of characters who run the whole gamut of American life from the "semi-barbarous" squatter, Ishmael Bush, to the refined Inez and Middleton, with Paul Hover and Ellen Wade forming the intermediate stages. Indeed, Cooper even includes a scientist, Dr. Obed Bat, who, although actually a caricature, must be taken seriously because he introduces a new attitude toward nature, one as much opposed to the old trapper's view as that of the lawless squatter.

As in the previous books, the relation of man to nature is fundamental to the tale, but the landscape is described as even more vast and sublime so that the characters seem all but completely dwarfed and overpowered by the immensity of grass and sky that stretches in every direction. Cooper had never seen the plains. He relied on books to give him the sense of a scene he did not personally know; but . . . he used his sources creatively. The setting of *The Prairie* serves the perfect aesthetic function in the book. Unlike *The Pioneers, The Prairie* depicts a world that man cannot pretend to master, for it is completely beyond his control; and unlike *The Last of the Mohicans,* it presents a gaunt, bare, hostile nature that leaves man naked to the elements. It is clearly a harsher world than that of the two previous volumes in the series.

But in many ways, the book directly complements *The Last of the Mohicans* and completes the cycle begun in it—and sometimes in precisely the same terms. The process that began on the eastern seaboard with the dislocation of the Delawares and the settling of the forest wilderness now moves into its final phase. As in *The Last of the Mohicans,* there is little law but might; and, although many of the whites are now more capable of coping with their environment, fundamentally they must still play one Indian tribe against another to attain their ends. Cooper has been accused of "laziness" in paralleling Hard Heart and Mahtoree with Uncas and Magua, yet the repetition may well have been intentional. If Pawnee against Sioux recapitulates Mohican against Huron, the lesson is unmistakable: only the whites can win. And when the honest Hard Heart refuses to listen to the treacherous Mahtoree, just as the Delawares had ignored Magua's similar plea, he, like them, will be rewarded for his virtue with the degradation of his people. Even the trapper, who always laments the grievous wrong done the red man, never realizes the part he himself plays in bringing about his friends' destruction when he opens the path for the exploiters who follow.

The exploiters in this book, however, are not the settlers of *The Pioneers* who are building homes in the wilderness but their advance guard: Ishmael Bush and his tribe of lawless squatters who admit no authority over themselves, who are anti-social wanderers whose function in the settling of the country is to skim "the cream from the face of the earth" and get "the very honey of nature." If the trapper represents the natural man who has disciplined himself as a result of his moral view of nature and thereby earned his right to freedom, Ishmael Bush is the more usual type who has confused liberty with license, who takes the law into his own hands—as witness his execution of his brother-in-law, Abiram White—and who asserts his own mighty ego as the sole basis for all he does. Completely selfish, Bush and his tribe attack the physical landscape with their axes in much the same way as did the settlers in Templeton, but without their justification of bringing civilization to the wilderness. In effect, they confirm the opinion of Marmaduke Temple that civil law is necessary to keep men in check, for the implication of *The Prairie* is strong that men without civil law are more likely to resemble Ishmael Bush than the trapper. The wasted earth they leave behind them is testimony to their moral state.

A more sophisticated exploiter, but one equally ominous for the future, is Dr. Obed Bat, the satirized physical scientist who accompanies Bush and who is in his own way as egotistical as the squatter. In his assumption of the scientific view toward nature, Dr. Bat believes that all knowledge and power will one day be within the reach of "reasoning, learned, scientific, triumphant man"; and he anticipates the time when science will enable man to "become the Master of all learning, and consequently equal to the great moving principle." Though certainly superior to Bush in education and refinement of character, Dr. Bat, whose name suggests his intellectual blindness, is curiously like him in the assertion of his own ego and in the assumption that his mind and will represent the standard for judging the universe. He is similar to the squatter also in that the removal of civil and religious restraints has encouraged the development of selfish desires, for Dr. Bat is much more interested in garnering personal fame than in modestly increasing human knowledge.

This is not to say, of course, that Cooper denies the legitimate aims of freedom and knowledge in his portrayal of Bush and Bat, for all the evidence of his life and works clearly indicates his devotion to freedom and his respect for true science. What he *is* attacking is the arrogance—both physical and intellectual—of undisciplined men. Through the character of the trapper, he reveals the basis for its control. In *The Prairie,* the trapper is more specifically religious than he had been in the previous books—in *The Pioneers* he had turned away from the Reverend Mr. Grant's church—but his moral view of the world remains unchanged. His experience in the untamed wilderness has convinced him of his smallness in relation to God's universe, has developed in him a deep spirit of humility, and has endowed him with a true sense of his own limitations. Like Bush, he wants no unnecessary laws—the fewer the better—for he knows how men can distort the injunctions of God to their own willful ends. But unlike Bush, he desires his freedom not to gratify his own passionate wishes but to exert willingly that principle of self-discipline and self-government which lies at the heart of both true religion and true democracy.

By the end of *The Prairie,* the problem that Leatherstocking has had to face is abundantly clear. Distrustful of the social and civil law on the one hand, he detests the aberrations of freedom as revealed in Ishmael Bush and Obed Bat on the other. He has achieved the self-discipline he needs to lead a free and asocial life, but he has also learned that few others can attain by themselves the same desirable end. He has sought the woods to practice the kind of life he loves, but every step he takes westward opens a path for the exploiters who follow him. At last, driven to the Great Plains "by a spe-

cies of desperate resignation," he dies physically defeated; but intellectually and morally he still maintains his deeply felt philosophy. That attitude toward the universe which the trapper affirms ought to animate the lives of those who follow him is clearly the meaning of the three books. That human nature being what it is, men will not follow his moral path is equally certain. If they do not, however, men face a serious question of whether or not a free society can survive on a selfishly despoiled and wasted continent. In his three early tales of the wilderness, therefore, Cooper penetrated to the heart of the American experience and raised questions that were to disturb him for the greater part of his career. (pp. 25-30)

[*The Pathfinder* (1840) concerns] the career of Leatherstocking thirteen years after Cooper had laid him to rest on the prairie. . . . The relation to the three early Leatherstocking tales is clear enough, not only in the reappearance of the characters of Natty Bumppo (here called Pathfinder) and Chingachgook but also in Cooper's return to the natural landscape to dominate the tone of his book. Repeatedly stressing the sublimity of both forest and lake, he clearly makes the point that the power of God revealed in each should teach the lesson of humility to all who see themselves in relation to the natural wilderness. The themes of the American waste of nature, of the unjust displacement of the red men, of the march of civilization across the continent, and of the insecurity of the white man in the virgin wilderness are present in *The Pathfinder* as they were in *The Last of the Mohicans* and *The Prairie.* (pp. 61-2)

The real problem of [*The Pathfinder*] is social, but in the "manners" connotation of that word. This primary interest is somewhat obscured by the familiar wilderness material and by the relatively low social position of the characters: they are much below the level of the Effinghams. Nevertheless, their problem is similar. Cooper insists that social station is important at *all* levels of society since class lines exist everywhere; and, although they are not rigidly fixed, they are not to be crossed with impunity. Class, of course, is never purely hereditary with Cooper; for, although one tends to belong to the class of his father, people can rise above or fall below the station into which they were born. Cooper stresses the fact that each person has his appropriate gifts and special knowledge, and that to overstep the limits thus placed on everyone will usually lead to disaster. Cap, for example, is a salt-water sailor who cannot command successfully on Lake Ontario, for his knowledge and experience are not equal to the task. When he tries to command the *Scud* in place of Jasper Western, a Great Lakes sailor, he almost runs the ship aground. It is saved only when Jasper assumes command. In the practical world, each must act in accordance with his talents, knowledge, and experience.

In the less tangible world of social relations, the same truth is equally manifest. Lieutenant Muir, the uxorious quartermaster, has fallen below his proper station because of his numerous marriages and his less formal liaisons with women; Mabel Dunham, the sergeant's daughter, has been educated beyond the point that would make her a suitable match for a common soldier, but she has not attained sufficient knowledge and sophistication to be an officer's lady. Her problem, therefore, is a difficult one; for in a military garrison there are few eligible suitors for her hand. Hence, the central theme of the book is a peculiarly social one—proper marriage for the heroine; but the problem is set against a highly unusual background. In the wilderness outpost, of course, Mabel becomes the center of attention of a wide variety of men. Arrowhead, a Tuscarora chief, is attracted to her; Lieutenant Muir becomes her suitor; and Pathfinder and Jasper Western become rivals for her hand. The former two are obviously unsuitable; and the sergeant, totally unaware of the position his daughter has achieved, and judging suitability solely by his own masculine standards, encourages the suit of Pathfinder. The simple woodsman, for the first time called Adam-like at the very moment that Cooper tries to humanize him, so far forgets himself as to let the sergeant persuade him to hope for Mabel's love.

Cooper's use of Leatherstocking in such a social context has been much commented upon by the critics; and Zoellner, in particular, has pointed out that *The Pathfinder* really does not fit in the overall pattern of the Leatherstocking series [see Additional Bibliography entry in *NCLC,* Vol. 1, p. 229]. Everything that Cooper had written of his character certainly indicated that his forest life, his deep friendship with his male companions, and his function as the symbolic embodiment of the American consciousness forbade his settling down in a cabin with wife and children. Yet Cooper was certainly aware of what he was doing. He makes it abundantly clear that in this novel Leatherstocking is tempted to deny his gifts, to betray his fundamental nature. He allows Jasper Western to win a shooting match when he could easily have defeated him, and he so far departs from his natural path as to remain in the fort with Mabel while Chingachgook is scouting the woods for their Mingo enemies, a dereliction of duty that allows the French to reconnoiter the works with impunity. The Pathfinder has lost his way. He is as much out of his proper place as Cap, Lieutenant Muir, or Mabel Dunham.

Cooper succeeds, nonetheless, in making Pathfinder's attraction to Mabel thoroughly believable, mainly because, despite his desire, he seems somehow reluctant to win her. Though she is closer to him in station than any of the other girls he has met in the wilderness, he only half believes the sergeant when he tries to persuade him that he is a proper match for the girl, and his grotesque reaction—half laughter, half weeping—when he is refused convincingly presents the conflict between the two elements in his character, the social and the asocial. On purely material grounds, the match is unsuitable, for it is beyond belief that Pathfinder could adopt the ways of the settlements for very long. Although the sergeant almost exacts from the couple a death-bed promise that they will marry, Pathfinder learns that Mabel and Jasper are in love, gives up his suit, and sees them happily settled in a cabin on the lake. He perceives the truth about himself: he is born to celibacy in the wilderness and could never hope to reach the level of civilization that Mabel and Jasper represent. His "gifts" forbid that he could ever be content with it. (pp. 62-4)

Cooper insists upon class lines, but he also maintains that they have nothing to do with political democracy or the inherent value of men. Jasper Western is better education and more refined than Pathfinder and, as such, is a better match for Mabel. But he is not necessarily a better man. Jasper and Pathfinder are equal in virtue, though different in talent and experience; both are morally superior to Lieutenant Muir, who has had many material advantages in life. Men are different, are unequal, Cooper argues; and each should organize his life with a clear understanding of both his talents and his deficiencies. Jasper is superior on fresh water, Cap on salt, Pathfinder in the woods. If each but stoops to what he knows and can do, with humble submission to the God revealed in

the sublimity of forest and sea, all will be well. If men fall into the natural classes determined by the function they can fulfill in life, a just society will result. Indeed, some will rise, just as Jasper and Mabel eventually move into the merchant class in New York. It will not be a leveling democracy, however, or one where Steadfast Dodge can operate; it will be truly democratic so long as each is free to find his proper station because of merit alone. (p. 64)

[*The Deerslayer* (1841)] too is concerned less with the march of American civilization than with the question of popular American values. The last of the Leatherstocking tales to be written, though the first in the chronology of the hero's life, *The Deerslayer* is perhaps the best of the series in the complexity of its meaning and in its affirmation of value in American life. Like *The Pathfinder,* it concentrates on lowly characters and is concerned with considerable social import; but it places much more stress upon moral meaning. The book has a strongly religious tone which provides the series with its final note of affirmation.

The setting of the tale is similar to that of *The Prairie* in its almost perfect wilderness state, but the natural landscape is by no means so harsh and forbidding. In contrast to the absolute desolation of the earlier book, the Glimmerglass (Otsego Lake) shines like a jewel in the wilderness of trees that stretches west from the Hudson River halfway across the continent. The dominant mood is peace and serenity; and Cooper pauses frequently to stress the quiet of forest and lake at night, at dawn, at high noon—indeed whenever its peace is not shattered by the crack of a rifle or the shrieks of passionate men. It is a landscape "altogether soothing, and of a character to lull the passions into a species of holy calm." It ought to fill all who perceive it with the feeling of reverence and awe for its Creator that, Cooper writes in the preface, had been the dominant influence on the character of Deerslayer; but unfortunately it does not. "I have only studied the hand of God, as it is seen in the hills and the valleys, the mountaintops, the streams, the forests and the springs," the woodsman once tells Judith Hutter; but he has learned more from such tuition than have most of the other white characters. Like most Americans, they accept as a matter of course whatever is familiar to them and seldom give it a second thought.

The only man-made objects to be seen on the lake are the ark, a large boat, and the castle of Tom Hutter, a house built on piles out on the water. Cooper makes the castle a kind of microcosm of the moral states possible to men in such a setting. At the bottom of the scale are Tom Hutter and Hurry Harry (Harry March), the former an ex-pirate, the latter a woodsman. Hurry in particular illustrates a number of the most unattractive American traits. He takes great pride in his good looks and physical strength, justifies to himself whatever he wants to do, and throws tantrums when thwarted. He is endlessly restless, as his nickname implies, and he considers members of other races as so many animals. He thus represents an unpleasant side of the American character that is still with us.

Moreover, Hurry and Hutter are as economically motivated as any of Cooper's European villains. Since the only value they respect is money, they will do anything to get it—even to killing women and children to collect the bounty placed on Indian scalps. They are literally in business for all they can get out of it; and in the first attack on the Huron camp they almost scalp Hist, Chingachgook's fiancée, who is a prisoner of the Hurons. Judith, too, Tom's older daughter, is a creature who worships the physical, both in her own beauty and in the glitter of the British officers who sometimes visit the lake. Thus, in a setting that should convince all men of the vanity of their selfish motives, all three characters are determined upon their own willful ends.

Opposed to this view is the affirmation of the Delawares, Deerslayer, and Hetty, Tom's younger daughter. The Indians, of course, live in close communion with nature and follow their own red "gifts" to lead a satisfactory life, but one necessarily far below the Christian ideal that Cooper holds up for his readers. Still, the Indians are morally superior to Tom and Hurry. They scalp for glory; but, since they know no better, they cannot really be blamed. Deerslayer and Hetty, however, affirm a higher good. Both are curiously alike in being unreasoning creatures—Deerslayer is simply an uneducated and generally unthinking man; Hetty, simple-minded from birth. Both are frequently described as child-like, and one cannot escape the impression that they have both achieved the happy state (they have become as little children) that the gospels describe as the passport to Heaven. Both are removed from the sophisticated temptations of civilized life, and both are somewhat deficient (Deerslayer is physically unattractive; Hetty, simple-minded) in qualities most frequently praised among men. Despite these handicaps—or perhaps because of them—both try to live their lives in accordance with Christian morality and ethics. As a number of critics have noted, there is a Dostoyevskian quality in these marred but moral beings.

That the completely Christian life which Hetty in particular affirms is all but impossible in a fallen world would seem to be part of the meaning of the book, but the converse is equally true. The totally unchristian life is complete chaos. To illustrate his point, Cooper sends Hetty into the Huron camp to plead for the lives of her father and Hurry, both captured in their scalping expedition against the Indians. Hetty accepts the injunctions of Christ to forgive one's enemies and to turn the other cheek as literal guides to life, and she preaches them to the Indians. She is utterly confounded, however, when Rivenoak, the Huron chief, asks her why the whites do not follow them themselves—a question that a Christian apologist intellectually stronger than Hetty might have trouble in answering. But if Hetty's course is impractical, her words clearly illustrate how far below the Christian ideal her father has fallen, and how richly he deserves the fate that the Indians, rendering simple justice, finally mete out to him: they scalp him alive and leave him to suffer and die.

Between these extremes stands Deerslayer, whose practical experience keeps him from trying to live by the ideal ethics that Hetty preaches but whose Christian training at the hands of the Moravians prevents him from engaging in the ghastly occupation of Tom and Hurry. Rather, he follows, as he tells the Indians, the law of nature (rather than the law of God) "to do lest you should be done by." Deerslayer is on his first warpath; and, as his name implies, he has heretofore been a hunter, not a warrior. Now, in a beautifully written passage . . . , Deerslayer confronts his first enemy, graciously offers him a chance for his life, and by the quickness of his eye (the dying Indian names him Hawkeye) shoots his first human being. In killing him and a second Indian, however, Deerslayer is not the aggressor. To be sure, his actions are something less than the Christ-like turning of the other cheek that Hetty tries to preach to the Hurons. But his actions are

certainly practical—and they have the universal justification of self-defense.

In this practical world, of course, Hetty cannot survive; for, although she bears a charmed life among the Indians, she is totally incompetent to live in normal society; and the man she loves, Hurry Harry, hardly realizes that she exists, so attracted is he to the beautiful Judith. It is appropriate, therefore, that she be killed accidentally in the final fight, just as it is essentially right that the lovely but tarnished Judith be rejected by Deerslayer when she offers him her love. But if Hetty's standards are impractical, it is equally true that civilized society cannot survive with the standards of Tom and Hurry. The worship of the physical to the detriment of the spiritual (the love of things as opposed to the love of principle which Cooper saw everywhere in American life) and the economic motivation that will condone all acts which bring a profit are both wrong attitudes that can only lead to disaster. (pp. 64-8)

A practical compromise between the best and the worst in men is certainly Deerslayer, who is imperfect and fallible but also, in Brady's words, "an embodied conscience for America" [see Further Reading]. He is a man who sees the moral values of the American landscape and who has absorbed enough from the Moravian missionaries to give that perception a definitely Christian tone. He represents a kind of competent humility, unselfish and unconcerned with the impedimenta of American things; and he affirms American principle by calmly and quietly going his way almost instinctively doing what is right. Uneducated and unreasoning, he clearly shows that virtue does not depend on qualities of mind but may well be corrupted by them. Physically unattractive, he illustrates that a beautiful reality may exist behind an unprepossessing exterior appearance. He lacks, of course, the civilizing qualities of Judge Temple in *The Pioneers,* and one cannot escape the conclusion that the ideal American would somehow combine characteristics of the two. Nevertheless, in this final volume of the Leatherstocking tales, Cooper has developed a character who criticizes in all he says and does the evil realities present in American life.

And yet *The Deerslayer* does not end on a truly optimistic note. To be sure, the Glimmerglass returns to its naturally beautiful state, the selfish characters retire to the fort, and Deerslayer and his Indian friends melt into the wilderness. But the reader of the tale knows what is going to happen: the ideas that Deerslayer affirms here and reaffirms in *The Pathfinder* and *The Last of the Mohicans* will be ignored by his fellow Americans. The struggle between white man and red will be re-enacted for over a century. The settlers will come with axe and gun to chop the trees and slaughter the game in *The Pioneers,* and the earth at last will belong to its despoilers. Ishmael Bush is implicit in the characters of Hurry Harry and Tom Hutter, for they are a constant factor in the American scene and become increasingly important as the wilderness is opened. It is with a kind of nostalgia for what might have been that we see Deerslayer, Chingachgook, and Uncas pass into the wilderness at the end of *The Deerslayer;* for this has been the first stage of the struggle, not only between the whites and Indians, but between the values of Deerslayer and those of Harry March. And we know the result of that conflict: the Harry Marches win.

Read in these terms, *The Deerslayer* is a much more significant book than Mark Twain's criticism would have us believe [see *NCLC,* Vol. 1, pp. 208-10]. Indeed, it may well be considered Cooper's masterpiece, for it unites in one well-executed whole the dual streams that had been developing in his work: the sense of the American past in both its temporal and spatial aspects and the question of values as they were developing in contemporary American life. **The Deerslayer** is the logical culmination of the Leatherstocking series. It affirms a set of values that were always implicit in the earlier tales; and, with **The Pathfinder,** it applies them by implication to the contemporary American scene. (pp. 68-9)

Donald A. Ringe, in his James Fenimore Cooper: Updated Edition, *Twayne Publishers, 1988, 151 p.*

FURTHER READING

Allen, Dennis W. " 'By All the Truth of Signs': James Fenimore Cooper's *The Last of the Mohicans.* " *Studies in American Fiction* 9, No. 2 (Autumn 1981): 159-79.

Examines Cooper's treatment of "the semiotic differences between white and Indian cultures, between the worlds, respectively, of language and non-verbal sign" in *The Last of the Mohicans.*

Axelrad, Allan M. *History and Utopia: A Study of the World View of James Fenimore Cooper.* Norwood, Pa.: Norwood Editions, 1978, 231 p.

Study of "Cooper's world view—his cosmology—as it is expressed everywhere in his voluminous writings."

Baym, Nina. "The Women of Cooper's Leatherstocking Tales." *American Quarterly* XXIII, No. 5 (December 1971): 696-709.

Examines the role of women in the Leatherstocking novels.

Beers, Henry A. "James Fenimore Cooper, 1789-1889." *The Critic* 15, No. 298 (14 September 1889): 125-26.

Tribute pronouncing the Leatherstocking novels Cooper's "surest claim to immortality."

Bier, Jesse. "Lapsarians on *The Prairie:* Cooper's Novel." *Texas Studies in Literature and Language* IV, No. 1 (Spring 1962): 49-57.

Contends that a mythic Christian pattern of a fall from grace underlies the action of *The Prairie.*

Blakemore, Steven. "Language and World in *The Pathfinder.*" *Modern Language Studies* XVI, No. 3 (Summer 1986): 237-46.

Considers ways that facility with language affects perception of reality on the part of characters in *The Pathfinder.*

Brady, Charles A. "James Fenimore Cooper, 1789-1851: Mythmaker and Christian Romancer." In *American Classics Reconsidered: A Christian Appraisal,* edited by Harold C. Gardiner, S.J., pp. 59-97. New York: Charles Scribner's Sons, 1958.

Examines Christian themes in Cooper's fiction.

Bush, Sargent, Jr. "Charles Cap of *The Pathfinder:* A Foil to Cooper's Views on the American Character in the 1840s." *Nineteenth-Century Fiction* 20, No. 3 (December 1965): 267-73.

Suggests that the character of Charles Cap in *The Pathfinder* represents aspects of the American national character of the 1840s with which Cooper was dissatisfied.

Canby, Henry Seidel. "James Fenimore Cooper." *Classic Americans: A Study of Eminent American Writers from Irving to Whitman,* pp. 97-142. New York: Russell & Russell, 1959.

Surveys Cooper's career, commending the Leatherstocking novels and citing Cooper's preeminence as a "maker of national epics."

Clark, Robert. "The Last of the Iroquois: History and Myth in James Fenimore Cooper's *The Last of the Mohicans.*" *Poetics Today* 3, No. 4 (Autumn 1982): 115-34.

Posits biographical reasons why Cooper's accounts of relationships between different native American groups and British, French, and other immigrant groups often inverted actual historical accounts.

———, ed. *James Fenimore Cooper: New Critical Essays.* London: Vision Press Ltd., 1985, 208 p.

Includes essays on the Leatherstocking novels by Eric Cheyfitz, Charles Swann, Richard Godden, John P. McWilliams, and Gordon Brotherston.

Cowie, Alexander. "James Fenimore Cooper and the Historical Romance." In his *The Rise of the American Novel,* pp. 115-64. New York: American Book Co., 1948.

Commends Cooper as the first strongly original delineator of the American scene and praises his creation of the character of Natty Bumppo.

Darnell, Donald. "Uncas as Hero: The *Ubi Sunt* Formula in *The Last of the Mohicans.*" *American Literature* XXXVII, No. 3 (November 1965): 259-66.

Contends that the character of Uncas, as the last of his people, embodies the *ubi sunt* ["where are those who lived before us?"] formula and supplants Natty Bumppo as the ostensible hero and central figure of *The Last of the Mohicans.*

———. "*The Deerslayer:* Cooper's Tragedy of Manners." *Studies in the Novel* XI, No. 4 (Winter 1979): 406-15.

Considers issues of social hierarchy central to the plot of *The Deerslayer* and terms the novel a tragedy of frustrated social ambition patterned after the novel of manners.

Dekker, E. "*The Pathfinder:* Leatherstocking in Love." *British Association for American Studies Bulletin,* No. 10 (June 1965): 40-7.

Suggests that Cooper resurrected the character of Natty Bumppo in *The Pathfinder,* thirteen years after depicting his death in *The Prairie,* primarily to recoup the critical and popular regard that had attended the initial Leatherstocking novels and escaped Cooper since.

Flanagan, John T. "The Authenticity of Cooper's *The Prairie.*" *Modern Language Quarterly* 2, No. 1 (March 1941): 99-104.

Examines possible sources for the setting of *The Prairie.*

Franklin, Wayne. *The New World of James Fenimore Cooper.* Chicago: University of Chicago Press, 1982, 275 p.

Offers commentary on Cooper's frontier novels, suggesting that in choosing to write fiction about the expanding American frontier, Cooper "found an opportunity and left a tradition."

Frederick, John T. "Cooper's Eloquent Indians." *PMLA* LXXI, No. 1 (December 1956): 1004-17.

Considers Cooper's representation of native Americans' highly figurative use of English to be accurate and realistic.

Gladsky, Thomas S. "The Beau Ideal and Cooper's *The Pioneers.*" *Studies in the Novel* XX, No. 1 (Spring 1988): 43-54.

Suggests that Cooper's genteel male protagonists, beginning with the character of Oliver Effingham in *The Pioneers,* were offered as desirable models of behavior to his American readers.

Grossman, James. *James Fenimore Cooper.* New York: William Sloane Associates, 1949, 286 p.

Biographical and critical study that includes discussion of the Leatherstocking novels.

Haberly, David T. "Women and Indians: *The Last of the Mohicans* and the Captivity Tradition." *American Quarterly* XXVIII, No. 4 (Fall 1976): 431-43.

Considers the impact of American captivity narratives on *The Last of the Mohicans.*

House, Kay Seymour. *Cooper's Americans.* Columbus: Ohio State University Press, 1965, 350 p.

Examines Cooper's pioneering portrayal of uniquely American characters and situations in his novels. Individual chapters discuss his fictional treatment of women, native Americans, different ethnic groups, and levels of social class. A concluding chapter is devoted to the character of Natty Bumppo.

———. "James Fenimore Cooper: *The Pioneers.*" In *The American Novel: From James Fenimore Cooper to William Faulkner,* edited by Wallace Stegner, pp. 1-12. New York: Basic Books, 1965.

Contends that in *The Pioneers* Cooper took the first steps toward defining the emerging American national character.

Humphrey, William. *Ah, Wilderness! The Frontier in American Literature.* El Paso: Texas Western Press, 1977, 29 p.

Discussion of American frontier literature citing Cooper's pre-eminence in the genre.

Kaul, A. N. "James Fenimore Cooper: The History and Myth of American Civilization." In his *The American Vision: Actual and Ideal Society in Nineteenth-Century Fiction,* pp. 84-138. New Haven: Yale University Press, 1963.

Includes discussion of the Leatherstocking novels as "the clearest statement in literature of the archetypal American experience."

Keiser, Albert. "James Fenimore Cooper." In his *The Indian in American Literature,* pp. 101-43. New York: Oxford University Press, 1933.

Calls Cooper "the writer who more than anyone else impressed his conception of the Indian upon America and the world at large," citing the Leatherstocking tales and six other novels: *Satanstoe, The Chainbearer, The Redskins, The Wept of Wish-Ton-Wish, Wyandotté,* and *The Oak Openings.*

Leisy, Ernest Erwin. "The Pioneer Spirit: J. Fenimore Cooper and Frontier Romance." In his *American Literature: An Interpretive Survey,* pp. 53-60. New York: Thomas Y. Crowell Co., 1929.

Briefly surveys Cooper's frontier novels.

McAleer, John J. "Biblical Analogy in the Leatherstocking Tales." *Nineteenth-Century Fiction* 17, No. 3 (December 1962): 217-35.

Examines Cooper's use of Biblical analogies in the Leatherstocking novels.

Motley, Warren. *The American Abraham: James Fenimore Cooper and the Frontier Patriarch.* Cambridge: Cambridge University Press, 1987, 188 p.

Considers the recurring theme of a patriarchal authority figure in Cooper's frontier novels. Two Leatherstocking novels—*The Pioneers* and *The Prairie*—are included in the study.

Muszynska-Wallace, E. Soteris. "The Sources of *The Prairie.*" *American Literature* 21, No. 2 (May 1949): 191-200.

Suggests that Cooper achieved the "remarkable verisimilitude" of the background of *The Prairie* through extensive research among nonfictional sources.

Överland, Orm. *The Making and Meaning of an American Classic: James Fenimore Cooper's "The Prairie."* Oslo: Universitetsforlaget, 1973, 205 p.

Provides a detailed record of Cooper's life when he wrote *The Prairie,* an examination of Cooper's literary theories, and discussion of the setting, characters, plot, and historical context of *The Prairie.*

Owen, William. "In War as in Love: The Significance of Analogous Plots in Cooper's *The Pathfinder.*" *English Studies in Canada* X, No. 3 (September 1984): 289-98.

Draws analogies between the romantic plot and the military action that are jointly presented in *The Pathfinder.*

Paine, Gregory Lansing. "The Indians of the Leather-Stocking Novels." *Studies in Philology* XXIII, No. 1 (January 1926): 16-39.

Considers the historical accuracy of Cooper's portrayal of native Americans in the Leatherstocking novels and theorizes about sources from which Cooper might have drawn his information about them.

Parkes, Henry Bamford. "Metamorphoses of Leatherstocking." In *Literature in America,* edited by Philip Rahv, pp. 431-45. Cleveland: World Publishing Co., 1957.

Examines the persistence in American popular fiction of a Leatherstocking-like figure—a fugitive from civilization possessed of an innate moral sense that infallibly guides his behavior—citing the cowboy and the private investigator as permutations of this fictional type.

Pearce, Roy Harvey. "The Metaphysics of Indian-Hating: Leatherstocking Unmasked." In his *Historicism Once More: Problems and Occasions for the American Scholar.* Princeton: Princeton University Press, 1969, 357 p.

Considers ways that the Leatherstocking novels depict the historical process, examining in particular the role of Natty Bumppo in facilitating the encroachment of civilization—a process that would ultimately render both himself and the aboriginal inhabitants of the continent obsolete.

Peck, H. Daniel. *A World by Itself: The Pastoral Moment in Cooper's Fiction.* New Haven: Yale University Press, 1977, 213 p.

Study of Cooper's pictorialism focusing on the symbolic use of landscape in the major novels.

Philbrick, Thomas. "Cooper's *The Pioneers:* Origins and Structure." *PMLA* LXXIX, No. 5 (December 1964): 579-93.

Considers Cooper's authorial intent in writing *The Pioneers* by examining his life at the time of its composition, and offers commentary on the settings, plot, and characters of the novel.

Popov, Igor. "The Immortality of the Last Mohicans." *Soviet Literature* 1, No. 430 (1984): 138-42.

Discusses the popularity of *The Last of the Mohicans* and *The Pathfinder* with Russian commentators, including V. I. Lenin and Vissarion Belinsky.

Quinn, Arthur Hobson. "James Fenimore Cooper." In his *American Fiction: An Historical and Critical Survey,* pp. 53-76. New York: Appleton-Century-Crofts, 1936.

Survey of Cooper's career naming the Leatherstocking novels as his best works.

Ringe, Donald A. *The Pictorial Mode: Space & Time in the Art of Bryant, Irving & Cooper.* Lexington: University Press of Kentucky, 1971, 244 p.

Explores the thematic and artistic role of physical description in the literary works of William Cullen Bryant, Washington Irving, and Cooper. The book also addresses the symbolic use of landscape in Cooper's Leatherstocking novels.

Robinson, E. Arthur. "Conservation in Cooper's *The Pioneers.*" *PMLA* LXXXII, No. 9 (December 1967): 564-78.

Examines attitudes toward "the manner in which man regards his natural environment" and the ways that different characters interact with their environments in *The Pioneers.*

Rose, Marilyn Gaddis. "Time Discrepancy in *Last of the Mohicans.*" *American Notes and Queries* VIII, No. 5 (January 1970): 72-3.

Notes that the plot of *The Last of the Mohicans* deviates from the historical sequence of events on which the action of the novel is based.

Rosenzweig, Paul. "*The Pathfinder:* The Wilderness Initiation of Mabel Dunham." *Modern Language Quarterly* 44, No. 4 (December 1983): 339-58.

Interprets *The Pathfinder* as a psychological drama of a young woman's coming of age.

Scheckter, John. "History, Possibility, and Romance in *The Pioneers.*" *Essays in Literature* VIII, No. 1 (Spring 1981): 33-44.

Contends that *The Pioneers* incorporates moral and philosophical dialogue about developing American traditions in a plot modeled on the traditional historical romance.

Scheick, William J. *The Half-Blood: A Cultural Symbol in 19th-Century American Fiction.* Lexington: University Press of Kentucky, 1979, 113 p.

Includes discussion of several of Cooper's characters in an analysis of the figure of the half-breed native American in nineteenth-century American fiction.

Shulenberger, Arvid. *Cooper's Theory of Fiction: His Prefaces and Their Relation to His Novels.* Lawrence: University of Kansas Press, 1955, 105 p.

Examines Cooper's literary theories as explicated in his prefaces to his novels, including discussion of Cooper's 1850 preface to the collected Leatherstocking novels (see *NCLC,* Vol. 1, pp. 205-06).

Slotkin, Richard. "Man without a Cross: The Leatherstocking Myth (1823-1841)." In his *Regeneration Through Violence: The Mythology of the American Frontier, 1600-1860,* pp. 466-516. Middletown, Conn.: Wesleyan University Press, 1973.

Discusses the mythic nature of the Leatherstocking novels and the character of Natty Bumppo.

Sundahl, Daniel J. "Details and Defects: Historical Peculiarities in *The Last of the Mohicans." Rajah: The Rackham Journal of the Arts and Humanities* (1986): 33-46.

Explores Cooper's attitude toward artistic license with historical fact implicit in the action of *The Last of the Mohicans,* suggesting that Cooper "set a high value on the novelist's skill in invention, but the incidents leading to the invention must be sufficiently historical before the romance writer may exercise his fair right to garnish."

Tompkins, Jane P. "No Apologies for the Iroquois: A New Way to Read the Leatherstocking Novels." *Criticism* XXIII, No. 1 (Winter 1981): 24-41.

Counters criticism that characterization in the Leatherstocking novels is stereotypical, suggesting that Cooper's characters are stylized in the manner of mythological figures.

Van Doren, Carl. "James Fenimore Cooper." In his *The American Novel,* pp. 24-50. New York: Macmillan Co., 1936.

Includes discussion of the Leatherstocking novels in an overview of Cooper's career.

Walker, Warren S. "The Tragic Wilderness." In his *James Fenimore Cooper: An Introduction and an Interpretation,* pp. 30-63. New York: Barnes & Noble, 1962.

Discusses the importance of the Leatherstocking novels in shaping American conceptions of early United States history.

Wallace, James D. *Early Cooper and His Audience.* New York: Columbia University Press, 1986, 230 p.

Examines Cooper's development of uniquely American novels and a readership for them.

Wasserstrom, William. "Cooper, Freud, and the Origins of Culture." *The American Imago* 17, No. 4 (Winter 1960): 423-37.

Compares the plot of *The Prairie* to "the mythic primal crime" of revolt against the father described by Freud in *Totem and Taboo* and in *Moses and Monotheism* as an archetype underlying the collective consciousness of humankind.

Immanuel Kant

1724-1804

German philosopher.

Considered one of the most important and influential figures in western philosophy, Kant developed a comprehensive philosophical system in which he analyzed the foundations of metaphysics, morality, and aesthetic judgment. The most important exposition of his ideas can be found in his *Kritik der reinen Vernunft (Critique of Pure Reason), Kritik der praktischen Vernunft (Critique of Practical Reason),* and *Kritik der Urteilskraft (Critique of Judgment).* In *Critique of Pure Reason,* Kant decisively altered the development of modern philosophy by insisting on a separation of the "sensible" and the "intelligible" worlds; in other words, a division between that which can be perceived by the senses and that which can be ascertained only by the intellect, such as the idea of free will. He applied this distinction to the ethical realm in *Critique of Practical Reason,* wherein he argued that an individual's moral decisions are based on rational precepts that are independent of experience in the world and therefore display the exercise of free will. In his study of the basis of aesthetic discrimination, *Critique of Judgment,* Kant continued this line of thinking, suggesting that nature, like humanity, has an ideal purpose—a moral end that is revealed by the overall "fitness of things." While Kant is best known for these three central works, his writings on history, political science, and religion are also considered vital contributions to the development of western thought.

Kant was born in Königsberg in East Prussia (now Kaliningrad in the Soviet Union). His family belonged to the Pietist branch of the Lutheran church, a sect that placed great emphasis on austerity and virtue. Kant's father, a saddler, was of modest means. Through the influence of a local pastor, however, Kant acquired an excellent formal education. From 1732 to 1740 Kant studied at the local Gymnasium, a Pietist school offering intensive instruction in Latin. Thereafter he entered the University of Königsberg, where he studied philosophy, mathematics, and the natural sciences under a young instructor named Martin Knutzen, who first introduced him to the rationalist philosophy of Gottfried Wilhelm Leibniz and Christian von Wolff. Kant's father died in 1746, leaving him without income. Kant found employment as a private tutor for the children of distinguished families, which enabled him to acquire the social graces expected of men of letters at that time. During this period, he published an impressive series of papers on natural history, beginning with *Gedanken von der wahren Schätzung der lebendigen Kräfte (Thoughts on the True Estimation of Living Forces),* a study of kinetic forces. Kant completed his university degree in 1755. He spent the next fifteen years as a non-salaried lecturer, his income derived entirely from modest student fees, and he continued to write prolifically on scientific subjects. In 1764 he published *Untersuchung über die Deutlichkeit der Grundsätze der natürlichen Theologie und der Moral,* a critique of traditional metaphysics as defined by Leibniz, which is considered his most important work of this formative period.

Kant was appointed to the chair of logic and metaphysics at the University of Königsberg in 1770. His inaugural thesis, *De mundi sensibilis atque intelligibilis forma et principiis dissertatio (Dissertation on the Form and Principles of the Sensible and Intelligible Worlds),* published the same year, is important for its distinction between sense and understanding, a key concept in his philosophical system. Kant published very little thereafter until his *Critique of Pure Reason* appeared in 1781, initiating the series of extraordinary works that ultimately brought him widespread recognition as the most original philosopher of the age. For the next twenty years, Kant's reputation as a leading spokesman of Enlightenment thought increased as he continued to write prolifically on philosophy, religion, and political theory. A treatise on theology, *Die Religion innerhalb der Grenzen der blossen Vernunft (Religion within the Limits of Reason Alone),* which denied the supernatural elements of Christianity, resulted in a government ban on future writings by Kant on religious subjects. In *Zum ewigen Frieden: Ein philosophischer Entwurf (A Philosophical Treatise on Perpetual Peace),* he eloquently addressed Europe's political problems, proposing a peacekeeping "league of nations." Around 1800, Kant's health, which had always been precarious, began to deteriorate. After relinquishing his university position in November 1801, Kant rarely left his house and experienced increasing difficulty in following his customary work habits. He died in 1804.

Kant's major philosophical principles are contained in the three *Critiques*. While the first of these works, *Critique of Pure Reason*, has often been criticized for the density of its style, attributed by scholars to Kant's reliance on the scholastic jargon of Wolff and his followers, the clarity and originality of the philosophical concepts articulated in the treatise are universally acknowledged. In *Critique of Pure Reason*, Kant systematically analyzed the foundations of human knowledge about the world. The majority of the book is devoted to a "Transcendental Doctrine of Elements," wherein Kant elaborated his theory of knowledge; this is followed by a much shorter "Transcendental Doctrine of Method," which outlines the proper application of "pure reason." The *Critique's* first part, by far the more important, is divided into three sections—the "Transcendental Aesthetic," the "Transcendental Analytic," and the "Transcendental Dialectic"—that examine the foundations of mathematics, the physical sciences, and metaphysics respectively. In all three areas Kant sought to determine if it was possible to prove the validity of "a priori synthetic statements," that is, philosophical propositions that are not only true without reference to experience, but which also expand our knowledge of experience. In the process, Kant effected what has been called a "Copernican Revolution" in philosophy: whereas formerly philosophers had considered the mind a passive agent whose judgments conformed to objects in the world, Kant believed that innate cognitive faculties actually determine the content of any possible experience, and therefore constitute our knowledge of objects.

Like the first *Critique*, Kant's second major treatise, *Critique of Practical Reason*, is subdivided into a table of "Elements" and a "Methodology," but is much shorter and more comprehensible. While theoretical reason is concerned with the epistemological basis of cognition, practical reason is concerned with the ethical significance of action. In *Critique of Pure Reason*, Kant distinguished between phenomenal and noumenal reality, or that which appears to us through the senses and that which lies behind appearances, which he called "the thing-in-itself." In the second *Critique*, he drew a similar distinction. On a purely phenomenal level, Kant explains, individuals appear to be conditioned by the law of causality, which states that every effect has a predetermined cause. Practically speaking, this would destroy the possibility of freedom. However, Kant also suggests that the individual is also aware of himself or herself as a purely rational, intelligible being. As such, an individual intuits that his or her actions are freely chosen, as they are either conditioned by sensuous motives or grounded in the moral law, the "categorical imperative," which requires us to "act only on that maxim through which you can at the same time will that it should become a universal law." Kant also asserts, in concluding his arguments about freedom, that the concepts of God and immortality, while entertained as a mere possibility for theoretical reason, are necessary for practical reason. This is true, according to Kant, since only a perfect being could conceive of a moral will, and because we naturally believe in an afterlife in which the virtuous are rewarded.

In *Critique of Judgment*, Kant proceeded to a discussion of the relation between freedom and nature. The work is divided into two parts, a "Critique of Aesthetic Judgment" and a "Critique of Teleological Judgment." The first section is devoted to an analysis of the beautiful. Unlike judgments of taste, which are subjective, aesthetic judgments are held by Kant to be universally valid. In the contemplation of a beautiful object, Kant explains, a concord is established between the imagination and the understanding; Kant contends the universal feeling of pleasure that accompanies aesthetic contemplation is the result of an inevitable synthesis of cognitive faculties, which never varies among individuals. In the second part of *Critique of Judgment*, Kant considered the concept of teleology in nature, trying to determine the significance of the fact that in living organisms the parts of the body may be seen simultaneously as means and ends. Kant rejected the then fashionable mechanistic argument as an explanation for the harmony of parts in organisms, as well as the theological argument that it is the product of an intelligent design. Nonetheless, Kant agreed that nature is inherently teleological. He indicates that the understanding, aided by the imagination, acknowledges an "apparent purposiveness" in nature, the ultimate source of which lies beyond the grasp of human perception.

The complexity—and apparent ambiguity—of Kant's arguments concerning aesthetics and teleology in the third *Critique* are indeed typical of his approach to great philosophical issues. While Kant has been criticized for this tendency, as well as for his abstruse, technical literary style, his philosophical works, in particular the three central *Critiques*, continue to be intensely scrutinized by scholars and critics throughout the world, upholding Kant's status as possibly the most original and influential philosopher of the western tradition.

PRINCIPAL WORKS

Gedanken von der wahren Schätzung der lebendigen Kräfte (essay) 1746
  [*Thoughts on the True Estimation of Living Forces* (partial translation) published in *Kant's Inaugural Dissertation, and Early Writings on Space*, 1929]
Allgemeine Naturgeschichte und Theorie des Himmels (treatise) 1755
  [*Kant's Cosmology*, 1900; also published as *Universal Natural History and Theory of the Heavens*, 1968]
Untersuchung über die Deutlichkeit der Grundsätze der natürlichen Theologie und der Moral (treatise) 1764
Beobachtungen über das Gefühl des Schönen und Erhabenen (essay) 1765
  [*Observations on the Feeling of the Beautiful and Sublime*, 1965]
Träume eines Geistersehers, erläutert durch Träume der Metaphysik (satire) 1766
  [*Dreams of Spirit-Seer*, 1900]
De mundi sensibilis atque intelligibilis forma et principiis dissertatio (dissertation) 1770
  [*Dissertation on the Form and Principles of the Sensible and Intelligible Worlds* published in *Kant's Inaugural Dissertation, and Early Writings on Space*, 1929]
Kritik der reinen Vernunft (treatise) 1781
  [*Critique of Pure Reason*, 1838]
Prolegomena zu einer jeden künftigen Metaphysik die als Wissenschaft auftreten können (essay) 1783
  [*Prolegomena to Every Future Metaphysic, Which Can Appear as a Science*, 1819; also published as *Prolegomena to Future Metaphysics* in *Metaphysical Works of the Celebrated Immanuel Kant*, 1836, and *Prolegomena to Any Future Metaphysics*, 1902]
Beantwortung der Frage: Was ist Aufklärung? (essay) 1784
  [*What Is Enlightenment?* published in *Kant's Critique*

of Practical Reason, and Other Writings in Moral Philosophy, 1949]

Idee zu einer allgemeinen Geschichte in weltbürgerlicher Absicht (essay) 1784

　[*Idea for a Universal History from a Cosmopolitan Point of View* published in *Kant On History,* 1963]

Grundlegung zur Metaphysik der Sitten (treatise) 1785

　[*Fundamental Principles of the Metaphysic of Morals* published in *Kant's Critique of Practical Reason, and Other Works on the Theory of Ethics,* 1873; *The Moral Law, or Kant's Groundwork of the Metaphysic of Morals,* 1948; *Foundations of the Metaphysics of Morals* in *Critique of Practical Reason and Other Writings in Moral Philosophy,* 1949; *The Metaphysical Principles of Virtue,* 1964; and *The Metaphysics of Morals,* 1965]

Metaphysische Anfangsgrunde der Naturwissenschaft (treatise) 1786

　[*Metaphysical Foundations of Natural Science* published in *Kant's Prolegomena and Metaphysical Foundations of Natural Science,* 1883]

Kritik der praktischen Vernunft (treatise) 1788

　[*Critique of Practical Reason* published in *Kant's Critique of Practical Reason and Other Writings on the Theory of Ethics,* 1873]

Kritik der Urteilskraft (treatise) 1790

　[*Critique of Judgment,* 1892; also published as *Critique of Aesthetic Judgement,* 1911]

Die Religion innerhalb der Grenzen der blossen Vernunft (treatise) 1793

　[*Religion within the Sphere of Naked Reason* published in *Essays and Treatises on Moral, Political, and Various Philosophical Subjects,* 1798; also published as *Religion within the Boundary of Pure Reason,* 1838; and *Religion within the Limits of Reason Alone,* 1960]

Zum ewigen Frieden: Ein philosophischer Entwurf (treatise) 1795

　[*A Philosophical Treatise on Perpetual Peace,* 1948; also published as *Inevitable Peace,* 1948, and *Perpetual Peace* in *Critique of Practical Reason, and Other Writings in Moral Philosophy,* 1949]

Die Metaphysik der Sitten (treatise) 1797

　[*The Metaphysic of Morals, Divided into Metaphysical Elements of Law and of Ethics,* 1799]

Anthropologie in pragmatischer Hinsicht (treatise) 1798

　[*Anthropology from a Pragmatic Point of View,* 1974]

*Gesammelte Schriften. 23 vols. (treatises, essays, notes, and correspondence) 1902-55

Eine Vorlesung über Ethik (lectures) 1924

　[*Lectures on Ethics,* 1930]

Kant On History (essays) 1963

Kant: Philosophical Correspondence, 1759-99 (letters) 1967

*This collection publishes for the first time Kant's philosophical notes, the *Opus Postumum.*

VICTOR COUSIN (essay date 1840)

[*Cousin was a French philosopher and prose-writer who actively promoted the philosophy of eclecticism in France during the first half of the nineteenth century. Denying that any single philosophical system contained the truth, Cousin freely appro-*
priated elements from the works of German idealists, English empiricists, and French materialists. His most famous works during his lifetime were Cours d'histoire de la philosophie *(1826;* Course of the History of Philosophy*),* Fragments philosophiques *(1826), and* Du vrai, du beau et du bien *(1836;* Lectures on the True, the Beautiful, and the Good*). In the following excerpt, Cousin considers the historical background to Kant's philosophy as well as the literary style and philosophical method employed in the* Critique of Pure Reason.]

Kant first directed his studies to theology and the learned languages: he had an extraordinary talent for mathematics, and he made some discoveries in astronomy. But philosophy presided over all his labors, and, at length, absorbed every other taste. This became his true vocation, and his principal glory. His distinctive character was a scrupulous integrity, and a conscience, honest and unbending, which recoiled from the shameful consequences of the fashionable philosophy. But, on the other hand, his dread of sensualism was hardly surpassed by his fear of the dangerous conclusions—such he regarded them—of the metaphysics of the schools. We may say that Hume was a perpetual spectre to Kant; as soon as he endeavored to take one step backward on the old track, the former appeared, and turned him from his purpose. The whole effort of Kant was to shelter philosophy from the attacks of Hume's skepticism, by giving it a place between the ancient dogmatism, and the sensualism of Locke and Condillac.

But it is particularly in moral philosophy, that Kant, without resorting to the mysticism of the middle ages, has assailed the skepticism of the eighteenth century. At a time when pleasure, interest and happiness were the only topics of discussion in France, Italy and England, a voice was heard at Königsberg, which called back the soul to a consciousness of its dignity; and proclaimed to individuals and to nations, that there was something above the attractions of pleasure and the calculations of interest—a rule, a law, unchangeable and obligatory everywhere, always, in every condition, social or private—*the law of duty.* The idea of duty is the centre of Kant's morality, and his morality is the centre of his philosophy. The doubts which severe metaphysical inquiries create, morality resolves, and, by its light, illumines, at the same time, politics and religion. If there be in man the idea of a law superior to passion and to interest, and his existence is not a contradiction, or a problem which cannot be solved, he must be able to obey that law: if he *ought* he *can:* duty implies liberty. On the other hand, if duty is superior to happiness, it is necessary, in extreme cases, to sacrifice the latter to the former. Still, between the two there is an eternal harmony, which, though disturbed for a moment, reason upholds and imposes even, so to speak, on existence and its author. Hence there must be a God superior to all secondary causes, who will maintain, somewhere, the harmony of virtue and happiness. Hence a God and a life to come. And the idea of duty implies, again, the idea of right. My duty to you is your right in respect to me; and so your duty to me is my right in respect to you. Here we have a social morality, a national right, a political philosophy, widely different from the uncurbed policy of passion, and the tortuous policy of interest.

Such, in a few words, are the noble features of the new system which Kant has given to Germany, and Germany to Europe. It is undoubtedly true that the Scottish philosophers had made a similar attempt. At Edinburgh, the sagacious Reid had conceived almost the same thoughts with the great philosopher of Königsberg. But what was only a rough sketch in Scotland, became a precise and accurate system under the strong hand of Kant. Here is the last step, the highest development of the spirit of the eighteenth century;—the Scottish school being the first step, and the point of departure. Kant crowns and closes the century. I do not hesitate to say that Kant is to this period in philosophy, what the French revolution is in political and social order. Kant, born in 1724, published his *Critique of Pure Reason,* in 1781; his *Critique of Practical Reason,* in 1788; his *Agreement of Religion with Reason,* in 1793; his *Metaphysical Principles of Right,* in 1799; and, after some other works, he died at Königsberg, in 1804. He belonged to the eighteenth century; and, at the same time, he opened another which is called to a very different destiny, both in politics and philosophy. (pp. 284-85)

· · · · ·

[*Critique of Pure Reason*] was a large volume, composed, after the model of the school of Wolf, with great regularity, but with such a profusion of divisions and subdivisions, that the leading thought is lost in the circuit of its long development. In addition to this, the work, unfortunately, was badly written. It is true that there is frequently much spirit in the details, and there are some admirable morsels; but, as the author candidly admits in his preface to the edition of 1787, though there is everywhere great logical clearness, there is little of that other clearness, which he calls æsthetic, and which is created by the art of conducting the reader from the known to the unknown, from the easy to the difficult;—an art which is rare, especially in Germany, and which was entirely wanting to the philosopher of Königsberg. Take the table of contents prefixed to the *Critique of Pure Reason.* It is obvious, that, in respect to logical order, and the connexion of all the parts of the work, nothing can be more luminous, nothing more precise. But take each chapter by itself, and every thing is changed. That order in details, which the chapters ought to exhibit is not here. Every idea is expressed with the last precision; but it is not always in the right place to facilitate its introduction into the mind of the reader. To this defect you may add that of the German language, at this epoch carried to its height;—I mean the excessive synthetic character of the German, which is so strikingly contrasted with the analytic character of the French. But this is not all. Aside from this language, still rude and badly trained to the decomposition of thought, Kant had another language of his own,—a terminology, which, once understood, is perfectly clear and quite convenient, but which, presented bluntly and without the requisite preliminaries, obscures every thing, and gives to every thing a misty and whimsical appearance. Kant issued a second edition of this work in 1787, in which many points were corrected; this second edition is the last word of the author, and it is from this, that all the subsequent editions have been published. (p. 286)

· · · · ·

Kant boldly avows himself a genuine revolutionist. Like Descartes, he despises all the systems which preceded his *Critique.* In respect to past philosophies, he expresses himself in the cutting and haughty tone of the philosophers of the eighteenth century. In speaking with such contempt of previous systems, and in presenting them as a mass of arbitrary hypotheses, which scarcely contain a few truths by accident, it does not once occur to him, that the authors of these systems—Plato, Aristotle, Descartes, Leibnitz—are his equals or superiors. But why should he be respectful to genius? He is not so even to humanity. He does, indeed, accord to man an innate propensity to metaphysics; but it is an unfortunate

propensity, and has produced, hitherto, nothing but chimeras. But he flatters himself, that with him, at the close of the eighteenth century, after three thousand years of useless effort, the true system of metaphysics, for the first time, has begun. In such a purpose, and under such language, we are tempted to imagine the existence of unbounded pride. But no, Kant was the most modest and the most circumspect of men. The spirit of the age was in him. Men can never effect revolutions with small pretensions, and Kant wished to effect a revolution in metaphysics. Like every revolution, this must proclaim the absurdity of every thing which went before: else it would be necessary merely to improve, and not to destroy the whole, as preliminary to rebuilding the whole.

Kant, like Descartes, to whom we must constantly compare him, full of his method, saw nothing besides. It was not of his genius, but of his method that he entertained a high opinion. It is here that he exalts himself; it is here that he triumphs. Descartes has somewhere said, that, in comparing himself with other men, he found himself superior to very few, and inferior to many, and that he owed every thing to his method. Socrates, likewise, two thousand years before Descartes and Kant, refers every thing to his method;—which was substantially the same as that of the French and the German philosopher. This is the true method: it is the psychological method:—which begins with man, with the subject that knows, with the study of the faculty that knows, its laws, its extent and its limits. It commenced with Socrates; it was more fully developed by Descartes; and it became perfect in Kant: in the hands of each, it produced a mighty revolution.

But it does not belong to the same man to begin and to complete a revolution. Socrates was neither Plato nor Aristotle, but the father of both. Descartes, again, was not Leibnitz: and Kant, who laid the foundation of German philosophy, has neither directed nor finished it. This philosophy is moving onward, and it does not seem to have reached its last development. With a better fortune, the French revolution, born at the same time with the philosophical revolution of Germany, departing from almost the same point, the declaration of the primitive and eternal rights of man, independently of all history and all society,—as did the other, from the pure laws of human reason, independently of all experience,—proclaiming alike contempt for the past, and the proudest hopes of the future, has run through, in a few years, its necessary vicissitudes; and we see it now arrived at its goal, tempered and organized in the charter which governs us. The charter of the philosophy of the nineteenth century is not yet written. Kant was not called to this work. His office was very different. It was necessary to effect a revolution against all the false dogmatisms, against the grand hypotheses of the idealism of the seventeenth century, and against the pitiful, and perfectly arbitrary hypotheses of his time: and this enterprise he has accomplished, thanks to the *method* whose character I have now explained. (pp. 286-87)

Victor Cousin, "Kant and His Philosophy," in The American Eclectic, *Vol. I, No. II, March, 1841, pp. 276-87.*

JAMES HUTCHISON STIRLING (essay date 1867)

[*In the following excerpt, Sterling questions the accuracy of commentary by Thomas de Quincey and Samuel Taylor Coleridge on Kant's philosophical ideas.*]

In the remarks of [De Quincey and Coleridge] on the German philosophers, especially Kant, there lies the possibility of certain lights, not unillustrative as well of the one side as of the other, and not unlikely, perhaps, to be of interest to the general reader. It is this reader's ear we would win, then, on this subject, for a few pages.

From De Quincey we quote at once as follows:—

> Kant is a dubious exception. . . . Within his own circle none durst tread but he. But that circle was limited. He was called by one who weighed him well, the *Alles-zermalmender,* the world-shattering Kant. He could destroy: his intellect was essentially destructive. He had no instincts of creation or restoration within his Apollyon mind. . . . [He] exulted in the prospect of absolute and ultimate annihilation. . . . The King of Prussia [was] obliged to level his state-thunders, and terrify him in his advance, else I am persuaded that Kant would have formally delivered atheism from the professor's chair.

Now, on matters German, De Quincey is usually admitted to be a master, and it is hardly indirectly that he himself claims as much; nevertheless, there is not one of these words that deserves not to be negatived. Really, throughout his whole life, the thoughts that lay nearest to Kant were God, Immortality, and Free-will. These to him (*with* Ontology, but only as fore-court) constituted Metaphysic; and to re-establish metaphysic was his single aim. To talk of Kant exulting in the prospect of annihilation, "absolute and ultimate annihilation," is even less relevant than to talk of Galileo rejoicing in the unmoved centrality of the earth; while there are few names in our mouths the addition to which of Atheist were a greater blasphemy. We must look closer, however, at the circumstances of the charge.

There is only a single characteristic in Kant which, on the religious side, has been made a handle of attack; and that is the undoubted supremacy which he awards to morality. Hence probably the imputation of Pelasgianism, as likewise, later, that of Rationalism. Morality with Kant, however, has a width of meaning that is quite peculiar to himself. To him it means that single principle which realised, as alluded to already, the interests of metaphysic. Nay, it was morality—the world of *practice*—that explained to him the *lacunæ* in these respects in the world of *theory* (knowledge), and exhibited these *lacunæ* themselves as a provision of the most indispensable purpose. It is no wonder, then, that Kant valued or *over-*valued morality.

As for Pelasgianism, Rationalism, &c., they concern Theology, and shall be left aside. We may remark only that we have not yet found anywhere in Kant a single word that tends not to re-establish religion and knit us closer to Christianity. From the very surface of his writings, indeed, Kant is seen to form even a contrast to the Voltaires, and others the like, with whom such information as De Quincey's would rashly class him. Kant is no mocker, no Frenchman of the eighteenth century, with a blind prejudice against the religion which he has seen—and because he has so seen it—outraged around him. Kant was piously brought up both by parents and instructors, and religion, with all that concerned religion, remained to him through life the central interest; nor was it aught but venom and vulgarity that brought the charge of heresy against him. (pp. 377-78)

But, as intimated, there is more to strike us still than these

curiously absurd imputations about annihilation and atheism: for, briefly to say it, there is not one word in the whole quotation but jingles false. But, first of all, here is another little quotation with which we shall begin what we have further to say:—"So far from seeing too dimly, as in the case of perplexed obscurity, their defect is the very reverse; they see too clearly, and fancy that others see as clearly as themselves. Such, without any tincture of confusion, was the obscurity of Kant." Further on, too, De Quincey talks of the same as an "elliptical obscurity," links in a chain of thought being omitted.

Style, as we know, is one of De Quincey's familiars: he is not only an admirable stylist himself, but he is also an admirable judge of style. Knowing Kant, then, he must be correct as to Kant's obscurity. Now Kant *is* obscure—even Hegel says so, and he of all men is the best qualified to judge; but Hegel's theory of Kant's obscurity is very unlike De Quincey's. Hegel, in fact, explains it by the words, "Zum Ueberfluss des Beweisens kommt noch der Ueberfluss der Sprache," or, indeed, by the single word "Geschwätzigkeit." Nay, in regard to expressions of Kant, Hegel may be found using such words as "verworrene Schwerfälligkeit." And this is the truth. Kant's obscurity, so far from being produced by "fancying that others saw as clearly as himself," arose, on the contrary, simply from fearing that he should never get others to see at all. Kant's obscurity, so far from "being free from confusion," is full of it—full to "perplexed clumsiness." Kant's obscurity, finally, so far from being "elliptical," is tautological, is produced, not only by "superfluity of proving," but by "superfluity of speech," by mere "loquacity," endless iteration. The irrelevancy that loomed through De Quincey's absurd and impossible charges of atheism, repeats and confirms itself, then, as regards such a palpable matter as style,—where, too, the critic himself is eminently a master and judge.

But, returning to the first quotation, we perceive the teaching of Kant further characterised by De Quincey as only of a negative or destructive nature. "His intellect was essentially destructive," he says; then he talks of "his Apollyon mind," and, of course, he could not miss that everlasting but much misunderstood "Alles-zermalmender." All this again, however, is just the reverse of the truth. The destructive or negative side of Kant's intellect was very subordinate to the constructive and affirmative. Construction, indeed, was his special industry; and, if he possessed any instincts at all, these were they which De Quincey directly denies him—instincts, namely, of "restoration and creation." What can be at all named the negative or destructive side of Kant's industry confines itself almost exclusively to the *Dialectic* of his *first Kritik.* But even there his object, in the end, is not by any means to destroy, but simply to prepare for building—simply to prepare for "restoration and creation." He desires, indeed, to point out what, on certain subjects, speculative reason is qualified to say, and what, on the same subjects, it is not qualified to say; and he hopes that, while he will be thus able, on the one hand, to put a stop for ever to the scandalous *rixæ* of philosophers, he will be able also, on the other hand, to lead us to the only true and valid arguments which can have place in the sphere in question. This is his simple object; and this he conceives himself to have accomplished; and the word "destructive," as applied to that object, would not only have surprised and vexed him, but it is a word totally beside the point which he regarded.

The source of such mistakes as convey themselves by this

word "destructive" of De Quincey, or the phrase of others, that Kant left reason "a faculty of lies," is to be found probably in this, that it is only the latter part of the dialectic of the first *Kritik* which, as more easily written, has been generally read. Thus it becomes intelligible how students, who understood what they read in isolation only and not in connection, were tempted to fly to the unwarrantable conclusion that, because Kant here opposed some of the usual arguments bearing on the existence of God, he sought to discredit this doctrine itself. The reverse was the truth, and Kant here had no object in the end that was not affirmative.

But leaving this, it is certain that, apart from this single *dialectic,* all else in Kant is creative and restorative. In the *æsthetik* and *analytik* of his first *Kritik* [*Kritik der reinen Vernunft*], for example, he creates afresh *ontology,* while his second *Kritik* [*Kritik der praktischen Vernunft*], together with the latter part of the third *Kritik* [*Kritik der Urteils-kraft*] and this very dialectic of which we have just spoken, restores metaphysic, or, to Kant's belief, establishes the existence of God, the freedom of the will, and the immortality of the soul. In the third *Kritik,* further, if there be a certain negative as regards *design,* this negative is again owing to motives sincerely affirmative, and there is much in the criticism that is both penetrating and satisfactory. Moreover, also, it is in this *Kritik* that we have affirmatively enunciated, and for the first time, perhaps, *principles* of the sublime and beautiful, accompanied by surprisingly original and suggestive characterisations of genius and of what concerns the liberal arts. We are not limited to the three *Kritiken,* either, but may refer to his numerous affirmative contributions, as to psychology in his anthropology, to logic in his treatise of that name and elsewhere, and to the principles of politics in various of his minor works. The whole works of Kant, indeed, are such as readily to enable any one conclusively to demonstrate the injustice of applying the epithet "destructive" to such an opulent and affirmative soul; and De Quincey, in the allegations which he has permitted himself, has only perpetrated a crime—a crime not only against Kant and history, but against himself.

To be told so pointedly, too, that Kant's circle was "limited" *grates;* for the vast comprehensiveness of the man lies in the very titles of his books, and we know that, of all modern philosophers, he was the first to exhibit to us the example both of a character and a system that, to speak like Emerson, "came" (as nearly as possible) "full circle."

Then in this circle "none durst tread but he"—the Apollyon, the *Alles-zermalmender,* the shatterer of the world. This is the central weak point, the special *lunes* of the De Quincey nature. De Quincey here has teased up his imagination into the mighty, the monstrous, the vast, the vague; and so he would similarly infect ours. We must watch the limbs of a giant in the gloom—a giant who was alone in his power, but dangerous, destructive, deadly. We take leave to say, however, that this awful being of the imagination, around whom, at the bidding of De Quincey, we are, as it were, to charge the air with the strange, the mystic, the irresistible—with what we name to ourselves, as in reference to De Quincey and in his own word, the "tumultuosissimento," contrasts but oddly with the plain little Königsberg burgher of truth. Within his own circle none durst tread but he! Why, the fact is, that anybody may enter it and pace about it at his ease, if he will but faithfully apply what ordinary faculties have been refused to no one. Kant has certainly left behind him the great-

est philosophical structure that any man, since Aristotle and before Hegel, had been privileged to raise. Still there is nothing supernatural or superhuman in the mental powers by which this was accomplished. Philosophically, Kant is fertile, rich, original, as well in depth as in comprehensiveness, to a degree that surprises: he was the first, as it were, that entered the very temple of metaphysic, and made its whole space his. Still his secret to all this was patient and tenacious thought. A clue was given him by Hume, and his merit was to follow it unweariedly till the whole treasures to which it led lay at his feet. True, original power of faculty was required for this, and such was present from the first; but in this faculty there was nothing of the amorphous, nothing of the incomprehensible, nothing of the hopelessly transcendent, nothing of that which the words of De Quincey would picture. There is nothing of all this, indeed, whether in the thoughts, or in the words, or in the demeanour of the plain, simple, discreet, eminently well-meaning, but somewhat old-maidenish and loquacious, Herr Professor Kant. Kant, indeed, is a lesson of *plainness* to De Quincey. (pp. 379-81)

We shall now turn to Coleridge in similar reference; and shall begin, as after the preceding is but natural, with the peculiarity of his character, in subjection also, like that of De Quincey, to the influences of the time. Here, as there, our tone shall be that of one who loves: we shall no longer see, we hope, however, the divine *nimbus* alone, but something, too, of the man within. We shall remain still, nevertheless, not fuller of frankness than free from grudge. As we have not reviled De Quincey, so neither shall we revile Coleridge. (p. 383)

In Chapter IX. of [Coleridge's] *Biographia Literaria,* we find these:—

> While I in part translate the following observations from a contemporary writer of the Continent, let me be permitted to premise, that I might have transcribed the substance from *memoranda* of my own, which were written many years before his pamphlet was given to the world; and that I prefer another's words to my own, partly as a tribute due to priority of publication, but still more from the pleasure of sympathy in a case where *coincidence* only was possible. . . . In Schelling's *Natur-Philosophie,* and the *System des Transcendentalen Idealismus,* I first found a genial coincidence with much that I had toiled out for myself, and a powerful assistance in what I had yet to do.

One is apt to suppose that there is a tacit reference to Kant here, and that his was the quarry from which Coleridge must have "toiled out" that—whatever it was—of which he speaks. In the same chapter, indeed, he acknowledges himself to be indebted to the "writings of the illustrious sage of Königsberg, more than to any other work," for the invigoration and discipline of his understanding; he boasts (and 1815 is the date) of "fifteen years' familiarity with them;" and he alleges, in explanation of his coincidences with Schelling, that they had both "studied in the same school, and been disciplined by the same preparatory philosophy, namely, the writings of Kant." But if Coleridge admit, in Kant's regard, a like debt with Schelling, it is not so certain that he was fully awake to the truth in either case. We suspect that he did not understand the exact nature of Schelling's obligation to Kant; and that, like most of his countrymen probably, he supposed Schelling to be a great *original* writer, who, of course, read *in* Kant, as in others, but, on the whole, owed his triumph to his own "magical brain." The strict historical connection of the German philosophers was not then well understood in England, and such suppositions were, at least on the part of non-experts, very excusable. Coleridge, then (whether, as a professed expert, excusable or not), will not, as seems likely, by any means, foolishly allow himself to be any deeper in Kant's debt, than he fancies Schelling will. "Yet there had dawned upon me," he cries, "even before I had met with the **Critique of the Pure Reason,** a certain guiding light;" and he lets us know that there were others besides Kant to whom he and Schelling owed inspiration. "Both had equal obligations," he asserts, "to the polar logic and dynamic philosophy of Giordano Bruno;" and then, as regards Behmen (Böhme), while Schelling knows him only recently, coincides with him only incidentally, and can extend to him "only feelings of sympathy," he (Coleridge) reverences him from "a much earlier period," "owes him a debt of gratitude," and has to thank him for "obligations more direct." Coleridge will not attribute to Kant all the glory, then, whether in his own case or in that of Schelling. They had both Bruno, he says; they had both Behmen. Still we may take it for granted that he would have allowed the *greater part* of the glory to have been the due of Kant.

Now, then, returning to our extract, we find the case to stand thus:—Coleridge claims to have virtually preceded and anticipated Schelling through a like knowledge with this latter of Kant, Böhme, and Bruno. Nay, we are given to understand that this is not wonderful, inasmuch as Coleridge, in some respects, had even the advantage of Schelling. This was particularly the case as regards Böhme, and as regards "a certain guiding light." What concerns Böhme may be passed, there is so much else to occupy us. The reader, we dare say, has a very good guess already as to what knowledge of Böhme the works of Coleridge will show, and what those of Schelling; as well as to how it stands with the age, directness, and amount of it in the case of either. As for the "guiding light," in the possession of that light—if it led Coleridge to the results of Schelling in independence of Kant—we may allow him to have been singularly fortunate. Nevertheless, we are disposed to believe that, had he known how the matter really stood with what we call "the strict historical connection," Bruno and Böhme, indeed (though not as co-factors in the same breath with Kant), might have been *mentioned,* but not the "light." A "guiding light" *to* Kant and *beyond* Kant, *before* Kant—that were truly a wonder of wonders!

Coleridge's anticipation of Schelling, now, is contained, it seems, in certain "Memoranda;" and these were written, we are told, "many years before Schelling's pamphlet (a word which runs lighter than 'book') was given to the world." Again, further, the particular "pamphlets," of which, in the case of Schelling, Coleridge avows knowledge, are the *Natur-philosophie,* and the *System des Transcendentalen Idealismus.* It is the matter of these, then, that Coleridge shall have anticipated. Now, the comparison of a few historical dates will put these things in very curious lights.

Coleridge returned from Germany in 1800, where he had resided during fourteen months; and, as was natural to suppose, it is to this date (of 1800) that, in the *Biographia Literaria,* he refers, as we have seen, the commencement of his knowledge of Kant. Now, the *Natur-philosophie* was published in 1797, and the *Transcendentalen Idealismus* in 1800. It is evident, then, that Coleridge's "Memoranda," having been written many years before Schelling's "pamphlet was given to the world," must have been written many years also before 1797,

many years before Fichte (the *first* sketch of whose system dates only from 1794), many years before he knew Kant, or had even learned German, and, indeed (seeing that he was born in 1772), many years before his twenty-fifth year. If the "light" perplexed, these "Memoranda" confound. Written as alleged, their contents are to be supposed accurately represented by this *verbatim* translation from Schelling. Let us assume a mistake in the date, however; let us assume the "many years" not to have existed; and the "Memoranda" to have been written *after* a knowledge of Kant. In that case it must be granted that, between 1800 and 1815, Coleridge had time enough to "toil out" for himself, from Kant, such doctrines as those of Schelling's, and before any actual acquaintance with Schelling, if it were from Kant, directly from Kant, and before any actual acquaintance with Schelling, that such doctrines were to be at all toiled out. But every one in the least acquainted with German philosophy, and its rigid historical sequence, must smile somewhat curiously at the pretensions of any one, even a German, to the evolution of a system from Kant, identical with that of Schelling, without the intervention of the link of Fichte. From Kant to Schelling, Fichte, in fact, is the indispensable bridge. Coleridge, therefore, if he evolved Schelling, must, at least, have previously *known* Fichte. But Coleridge did not know Fichte. His notice of Fichte, in this celebrated Chapter (IX.) is but a word, and representative of little or nothing; while the burlesque is simply childish, and points to an astounded gaping at the outside of the *Wissenschaftslehre,* as its only possible source. Or if Coleridge *evolved* Fichte, where is that evolution represented in his works? Nay, where in his works is that "much that he had toiled out for himself?" where is that which, by Schelling's "powerful assistance," he afterwards did? where is this accomplishment that is like Schelling, and beyond Schelling, to be found represented? Why, nowhere—unless in that astonishing, claimed and unclaimed, attributed and unattributed, piece of transcendental idealism, in reference to which bewilderment reaches its climax, when we read, " 'To remain unintelligible to such a mind,' exclaims Schelling, on a like occasion," and know that *this* is the occasion, and that Coleridge is simply literally translating, even in his notes (as in that one about Leibnitz and Hemsterhuis), *from* Schelling! When he says, then, that he "might have transcribed 'his Schellingianism' from *memoranda* of his own that were written many years before Schelling's *pamphlet* was given to the world," is he not also saying something so delightfully impossible that it is impossible not to smile? But when, further, we see the bland Coleridge politely bowing, and chivalrously waiving the *pas* to Schelling, as preferring "another's words to his own," as "a tribute due to priority of publication," but "still more from the pleasure of sympathy in a case where *co-incidence* only was possible," is it possible to do aught else—in presence of so comical an example of the pure ludicrous—than convert the smile into a downright laugh?

But if Coleridge evolved Schelling without knowing Schelling, he must have evolved him also, not only without knowing Fichte, but without—or rather, let us say, only *with* such knowledge of Kant as gave rise to very strange results; for, however curious be the "light that dawned on him" *before,* scarcely less curious must we pronounce the light that dawned on him *after,* he knew Kant. To illustrate and make good this allegation, we cannot altogether avoid quotations; but, as we shall compress and reduce them to their least, it would be very desirable that the reader keep the original by him. In Chapter IX. Coleridge refers to Kant thus:—

The originality, the depth, and the compression of the thoughts; the novelty and subtlety, yet solidity and importance of the distinctions; the adamantine chain of the logic; and, I will venture to add (paradox as it will appear to those who have taken their notion of Immanuel Kant from reviewers and Frenchmen), the clearness and evidence of the critique of the Pure Reason, &c. . . . took possession of me as with a giant's hand. After fifteen years' familiarity with them, I still read these, and all his other productions, with undiminished delight and increasing admiration. The few passages that remained obscure to me, after due effort of thought (as the chapter on *original* apperception, and the apparent contradictions which occur, I soon found were hints and insinuations referring to ideas which Kant either did not think it prudent to avow, or, &c. . . . He had been in imminent danger of persecution. . . . The expulsion of [Fichte] . . . from the university of Jena supplied experimental proof that the venerable old man's caution was not groundless. In spite, therefore, of his own declarations, I could never believe, that it was possible for him to have meant no more by his Noumenon, or Thing in itself, than his mere words express: or that, in his own conception, he confined the whole *plastic* power to the forms of the intellect, leaving for the external cause, for the materiale of our sensations, a matter without form, which is, doubtless, inconceivable. I entertained doubts, likewise, whether, in his own mind, he even laid *all* the stress which he appears to do on the moral postulates. . . . φωνῆσε συνετοῖσιν: and for those who could not pierce through the symbolic husk, his writings were not intended. Questions which cannot be fully answered without exposing the respondent to personal danger. . . .

This passage, while it proves Coleridge to have seriously occupied himself with the great work of Kant as far as the deduction of the categories, proves him also, however strenuous and persevering his endeavours, to have, in general result, failed. That ease in "the" pure reason to which he pretends, he did not attain. For, in the first place, the ascription to Kant of designful reticence and intentional obscurity is not only unfounded and gratuitous, but its reverse is the truth. Kant's great works are free from any reticence, and as for intentional obscurity, anything wider of the truth it was impossible to *invent*. Kant *is*—but never intentionally—obscure; only from excess of *intention* to be *not* obscure is it that, in effect, he becomes obscure. This Kant knew and lamented; and so it is that he is never done with cries to the excellent "styles" of such men as Reinhold and Fichte to come to his rescue. "Hints and insinuations," then, are quite beside Kant; and, of all works, precisely his contain the least of "symbolic husk." A literal conveyance of his thought, for this he strains; but he never calls on imagination for one that shall be figurative or symbolical. Of the obscurity, a peculiar terminology is certainly one element; but the others, as said, are only diffuseness, prolixity, and repetition. Then the reason alleged, caution in consequence of persecution, is but an anachronism. That poor affair of Hilmer and Hermes in 1794, and still less Fichte's mishap in 1799, could have no influence on events of 1781, of 1788, or even of 1790. Kant, then, far from being anxious to conceal his thought, was, on the contrary, *over*-anxious to express it, and even sensitive to a fault at failure. Before printing, he does not seem to have practised the usual reticence in conversation even; his friend Hippel could, from that source, and in priority to himself, publish some of his most original ideas. Kant, in brief, is the most ingenuous, candid, and loyal of mankind; and Coleridge's long and somewhat equivocal defence of concealment (see his book further) could not possibly have been more misplaced.

In the second place, in his misinterpretation of the obscurities which he himself assigns, lies the proof of Coleridge's failure to understand that single theory of perception which, we may say, is their sole burden. Of the various materials in this theory—noumenon, sensation, intuition, notion of understanding, act of judgment, idea of reason—and of the various syntheses of these, in imagination, in "original apperception," &c., we readily grant the difficulty; but this difficulty Coleridge has not overcome. On the contrary, all these things, which are as windmills of fact, he has only Quixotically converted into giants of dream. This is seen in the very expedient by which he has resolved the obscurity and reticence in question: in superfœtating, that is, these by a fantastic brood of his own, he has, at best, only complimented his imagination at the expense of his understanding. Thus the *noumenon*—which, as but external antecedent known only in its subjective effects, lays Kant under the most significant restrictions, not only in reference to *knowledge,* but in reference to design and beauty—must, according to Coleridge, be to Kant, let him say what he may, the same cunning and unnameable sphinx, or other monster, that it is to himself. Nevertheless, Kant does continue that "plastic power" in the very manner which Coleridge refuses to believe; while, as for "matter without form," it is not easy sufficiently to indicate the constancy and the clearness with which Kant urges that objects which are perceived only through a medium of sense can and must have form only from within. As regards *sensation* and *intuition* (*perception*), on Maass, who is then signalising the commonest Kantian distinctions here, Coleridge will be found (Chapter V.) commenting in such manner as suggests only the blind groping of an unsteady imagination in the dark. These relate, for example, to *matter* (sensation from without) and *form* (perception of time and space from within); now, when Maass remarks that the characters of an object are either individual or common (*i.e.,* either *material* or *formal*), Coleridge appends the comically inapposite comment—"Deceptive; the *mark* (character) in itself is always individual; by an act of the reflex understanding, it may be rendered a sign or general term." In remarking (Chap. XII.) that Kant's intuition is used only "for that which can be represented in time and space," he would have insured perfect correctness, had he added the words, *internally as well as externally;* and, in that case, he would have seen that, in *his* sense, Kant does *not* deny "the possibility of intellectual intuitions." On the contrary, it is on these, and in that sense, that the introduction to the first **Kritik** is largely specially employed. The intellectual intuition which Kant denies to man is that (without medium of sense) which he ascribes to God; and is not what Coleridge supposes—it is, in fact, the "Anschauender Verstand" of which he never caught a glimpse. When, further, he goes on to prefer to Kant's sense of intuition the ordinary English one, he again speaks, surely, in complete unconsciousness of the corresponding theory. Coleridge's knowledge of the remaining elements of this theory—at least, as represented by his intimations in respect to *apperception, imagination,* and the *postulates*—is not unconfirmative of the preceding. *Apperception* is spoken of in the extract as—that which it pretty well is—the obscurity special; but, however absurd it be to attribute it to reticence, to intention, it is infinitely more absurd to *imagine* it into *dream.* In Chap. XII. Coleridge speaks of it thus:—

Here, then, we have by anticipation the distinction between the conditional finite I (which, as known in distinct consciousness by occasion of experience, is called by Kant's followers the empirical I) and the absolute I Am, and likewise the dependence, or rather the inherence of the former in the latter; in whom we live and move. . . .

Kant's "empirical I" is the ego as manifested under affection, while his absolute "I Am" is the pure formal I, or, as he calls it also, the bare "I think,"—that is, the simple reflection I, which, to make them *ours*, "must accompany all our other ideas, is in every experience of consciousness one and the same, and can be itself accompanied by none beyond." It will, perhaps, be admitted, then, that this Orientalizing or Judaizing of the simple identity of every one—this hypostasising of a thought common to all of us indiscriminately, into the awful I Am, is the most extraordinary apotheosis on record. That Coleridge should have converted the obscurity of some half-dozen paragraphs on a point of ordinary psychology into this! No wonder that he conceived Kant, in such a ticklish position, reticent. Indeed, the due reticence might have been fortunate for himself here. On *imagination* we have this:—

> The imagination, then, I consider either as primary or secondary. The primary imagination I hold to be the living power and prime agent of all human perception, and as a repetition in the finite mind of the eternal act of creation in the infinite I Am.

There are those, doubtless, who, in this passage, and others such, have seen only the original and profound depth of Coleridge's own philosophy. There underlies all these wonders, however, nothing but Kant's simple distinction of imagination into *productive* and *reproductive,* and the association of the former with *original apperception*—affairs all of only human quality. A small matter, then, may give birth to the most marvellous spectra in the brain of Coleridge; of which spectra, however, the true names are but distortion and caricature. As for the *notions of understanding,* they belong to the above syntheses; and as for the *act of judgment,* there is nothing special to remark on it. The *ideas of reason,* again, fall, for one part, into the *moral postulates;* and in these Kant shall be to Coleridge insincere. On these, as on a rock, Kant, however, found himself just rescued from a ravening ocean all around; though, too, he thankfully acknowledged a distant gleam of firm land elsewhere. In these dreamy misapprehensions, then, and strange misinterpretations, we may well admire the relation of Coleridge to Kant.

In the third place, the terms with which the extract opens, in regard to the merits of Kant and his works, are not always such as we would expect from an expert. "Compression," as we have seen, even though applied to the thoughts, is a word inapposite. Then, in spite of compression, it is not difficulty that Coleridge finds, but, on the contrary, "clearness and evidence." Hegel, for his part, found the study of Kant "difficult" and "hard;" and humanity in general have called him "dark." But Coleridge's own subsequent words co-here but ill with the general statement. After fifteen years' familiarity with the works of Kant, he still reads them, and with increasing admiration. This is not much: still it is to be said that he who has once mastered such writers as Newton, and La Place, and Aristotle, and Kant, does not usually return to read *in* them, and with increasing admiration, &c. In such cases a return is conditioned by defect of memory, or for the sake of reference. The emotional, the imaginative, the rhetorical, does not exist in Kant; he has no sallies of wit, no novel-

ties of expression, no charm of manner, to attract in his works; and, having once achieved these, his "Principia," we return as seldom to them as the mathematician to his Euclid. It is very different writers that we read *in,* and with increasing admiration, &c. In such phrases, then, we hold Coleridge to speak, not in intelligence, but in the air; as it were, afloat, too, in a canoe of mere literary balance.

Perhaps we have seen in the preceding, not only error, but even a certain disingenuousness. This latter *macula,* at least, is visible elsewhere. In Chapter X., for example, we find Coleridge saying:—

> The very words *objective* and *subjective,* of such constant recurrence in the schools of yore, I have ventured to re-introduce. . . . . I have cautiously discriminated the terms, the reason, and the understanding, encouraged and confirmed by the authority of our genuine divines and philosophers, before the Revolution. . . . . This (Chap. XII.) distinction between transcendental and transcendent is observed by our elder divines and philosophers, whenever they express themselves scholastically. . . . I shall venture (XII.) to use potence, in order to express a specific degree of a power, in imitation of the algebraists. I have even hazarded the new verb potentiate. . . .

Now, to begin with *transcendent* and *transcendental,* these words involve a distinction so absolutely and exclusively Kant's, that, without appealing to the whole subsequent history of philosophy in Germany, we may at once permit ourselves categorically to contradict the statement of Coleridge. Of *reason* and *understanding,* again, we may speak in precisely the same tone. This distinction, also, is Kant's, and Kant's alone; in whom, in fact, we are allowed to see the very process of its birth. Authority, then, is here superfluous; but, were it at all wanted, there is Hegel's, and more than once. (pp. 386-94)

The truth probably is, that Coleridge was not properly a student of philosophy, but rather a reader *carptim.* It pleased him, all the same, to sun himself, as quite a Brobdingnagian student, in the eyes of the innocent reader, by significant smiling nods to the fact of metaphysic and psychology being his "hobby-horse." In like manner it pleased him, too, to yield to such idle subjective fancies of the moment as, "I believe in the depth of my being that the three great works since the introduction of Christianity are Bacon's *Novum Organum,* Spinosa's *Ethica,* and Kant's *Kritik;*" and to console his conscience, when it gnawed, by such images as, "I have laid too many eggs in the hot sands of this wilderness, the world, with ostrich carelessness, and ostrich oblivion." (pp. 395-96)

With faculty and law, mostly of mere receptivity and imaginative suggestion, what system of philosophy *could* Coleridge have thought out for himself? A procession of pictures he could give—to more he was incompetent. (p. 396)

> *James Hutchison Stirling, "De Quincey and Coleridge upon Kant," in* The Fortnightly Review, *Vol. 8, No. X, October 1, 1867, pp. 377-97.*

ERNST CASSIRER (essay date 1918)

[Cassirer, a German-born philosopher and historian, has been called "the last true scion of the classic tradition of German idealism." Initially drawn to the Neo-Kantian school, Cassirer later developed the theory that certain "symbolic forms"—for

example language, myth, art, science, and religion—provide a key towards understanding the underlying content of human mental activity from pre-civilization to the present. Cassirer's principal works include Idee und Gestalt *(1921;* Language and Myth*),* Die philosophie der symbolischen Formen *(1923-29;* The Philosophy of Symbolic Forms*), and* Die philosophie der Aufklärung *(1932;* The Philosophy of the Enlightenment*). In the following excerpt from his pioneering full-length study of Kant's life and work, Cassirer distinguishes the varying literary styles employed by Kant in his critical philosophy, arguing that the discursive style of the* Critique of Pure Reason *accurately represents the overall structure of his thought.*]

If what is said about great thinkers is true, that the style is the man, this aspect of the **Critique of Pure Reason** poses a difficult problem for the biographer of Kant. For nowhere else in the history of literature and philosophy do we find so profound and involved an alteration of style as took place with Kant in the decade between 1770 and 1780—not even in Plato, the style of whose old age, in the *Philebus*, the *Sophist,* or the *Parmenides,* differs so markedly from the manner in which the early dialogues were written. Only with difficulty can one recognize in the author of the **Critique of Pure Reason** the man who wrote **Observations on the Feeling of the Beautiful and the Sublime** or the **Dreams of a Spirit-Seer.** Strictness in abstract analysis of concepts replaces the free play of humor and imagination; a kind of academic ponderousness supplants the reflective grace and cheerfulness of those other books. To be sure, anyone who knows how to read the **Critique of Pure Reason** rightly also finds in it, along with the acuteness and depth of thought, an extraordinary strength of intuition and an exceptional power of linguistic imagery. Goethe said that when he read a page in Kant, he always felt as though he were entering a lighted room. Alongside his skill at exhaustively analyzing the most difficult and knotty complexes of ideas stands Kant's gift for expressing and focusing the comprehensive result of a long deduction and conceptual analysis at one stroke, as it were, in striking images and epigrammatic, unforgettable turns of phrase. On the whole, however, most readers have the overpowering impression that the expository form Kant chose fetters his thought and does not foster its adequate and limpid expression. In his concern for the stability and definiteness of terminology, for exactness in the definition and division of concepts, and for agreement and parallelism of schemata, Kant's natural, lively personal and intellectual form of expression seems struck dumb. He felt this himself, and said so. "The method of my discourse," he remarks in a diary note, "has a prejudicial countenance; it appears scholastic, hence pettifogging and arid, indeed crabbed and a far cry from the note of genius." But it is conscious intent that holds him back from every approximation, from every concession to the note of "genius." He says elsewhere: "I have adopted the scholastic method and preferred it to the free play of mind and wit, although I indeed found, since I wanted every thoughtful mind to share in this investigation, that the aridity of this method would frighten off readers of the kind who seek a direct connection with the practical. Even if I had the utmost command of wit and literary charm, I would want to exclude them from this, for it is very important to me not to leave the slightest suspicion that I wanted to beguile the reader and gain his assent that way, but rather I had to anticipate no concurrence whatsoever from him except through the sheer force of my insight. The method actually was the result of deliberation on my part." His sole ideal now, in the face of which all other claims retreat, is to advance strict conceptual deduction and systematization.

But Kant did not renounce those claims lightheartedly. In the years immediately preceding the composition of the **Critique of Pure Reason,** he was continually occupied with weighing whether and how far it might be possible to give philosophical ideas a popular form, without loss of profundity. "For some time," he had written to Herz in January, 1779, "I have been thinking in certain idle moments about the principles of popularity in the sciences (such as are capable of it, of course, since mathematics is not), especially in philosophy, and I think that I have been able to define from this aspect not just another alternative but an entirely different arrangement from that demanded by the scholastic method, which is still the foundation." In point of fact, the early drafts of the First **Critique** were dominated by this outlook. Along with "discursive (logical) clarity through concepts," they strove for "intuitive (aesthetic) clarity through intuitions," and concrete examples. On this point we find in the preface to the finished book what it was that finally moved Kant to abandon this plan. "For the aids to clearness, though they may be of assistance in regard to details, often interfere with our grasp of the whole. The reader is not allowed to arrive sufficiently quickly at a conspectus of the whole; the bright coloring of the illustrative material intervenes to cover over and conceal the articulation and organization of the system, which, if we are to be able to judge of its unity and solidity, are what chiefly concern us." In the place of the early attempts at an intuitive, generally comprehensible exposition, a deliberate renunciation has taken place: there is no more a royal road to transcendental philosophy, Kant sees, than there is to mathematics.

The deeper reason for this stylistic change, however, lies in the fact that Kant is presenting a completely novel *type of thinking,* one in opposition to his own past and to the philosophy of the Age of Enlightenment—to Hume and Mendelssohn, whom he envies for their way of writing, which is as elegant as it is profound. In the decades of withdrawn, lonely meditation in which Kant forged for himself his special method and questions, he had gradually moved away from the common presuppositions on which the philosophical and scientific thought of his age rested, as if by a silent consensus. He still often speaks the language of this age; he still uses the concepts it coined and the scholastic classifications it enforced in its textbooks on ontology, rational psychology, cosmology, and theology, but the whole bulk of these materials of expression and thought is now put into the service of a completely different goal. For Kant this goal is immutable, but he does not disdain terminological and expository expedients, even though their precision is no longer strictly fitted to his own thinking. In fact, he often prefers to go back to these expedients, hoping to find in them the quickest route to a direct link with the reader's habitual conceptual realm. This very flexibility, however, becomes the source of a multitude of difficulties; precisely where Kant has descended to the standpoint of his age, he has failed to raise the age to his level.

Another factor has to be taken into consideration, one that made an entry into Kant's basic vision difficult for his contemporaries and which has continued to be a source of numerous errors and misunderstandings since then. If one considers only the external form Kant gave his writings, nothing seems to be clearer than that what unfolds before us is a finished, doctrinal system, complete as a whole and in every detail. The materials for its structure lie ready to hand in their totality; the basic outline is sketched out clearly and precisely in all particulars: all that needs be done is to put the pieces together according to the plan. But only when this endeavor is actually undertaken does the full magnitude of the task emerge. Fresh doubts and questions are encountered on every side; it is shown everywhere that the particular concepts we thought we could use as assumptions themselves need definition. The concepts become more and more altered, according to the place they occupy in the ongoing systematic composition of the whole. They are not a stable foundation for the movement of thought from its beginning to its end, but they evolve and are stabilized in the course of this very movement. Anyone who does not keep this tension in mind, anyone who believes that the meaning of a specific fundamental concept is exhausted with its initial definition and who tries to hold it to this meaning as something unchangeable, unaffected by the progress of thought, will go astray in his understanding of it.

Kant's distinctive style as a writer harmonizes with what was observed to be characteristic of him as a teacher. "His lecture," [Reinhold Bernhard] Jachmann says [in his *Immanuel Kant geschildert in Briefen an einen Freund*], "was always perfectly fitted to its material, yet it was not something memorized, but rather a freshly thought-out outpouring of his mind. . . . Even his course on metaphysics, with allowances for the difficulty of the material for the beginning thinker, was luminous and interesting. Kant displayed special artistry in expounding and defining metaphysical concepts, in that he experimented in front of his audience just as if he were starting to think about the subject, gradually adding on new defining concepts, trying out continually improved explanations, and finally passing on to a full conclusion with the concepts perfectly exhausted and illuminated from all sides; he thus not only acquainted the listener who paid strict attention with the matter under discussion but also introduced him to methodical thinking. Whoever failed to grasp this course of his lecture by observing him closely, and took his first explanation as the correct and completely exhaustive one, not making the effort to follow him further, gathered only half truths, as several reports from his auditors have convinced me."

This fate of Kant's auditors has been the fate of many of his commentators as well. If one approaches the definitions of analytic and synthetic judgments, the concepts of experience and of the a priori, the concepts of the transcendental and of transcendental philosophy, as they appear in the beginning of the *Critique of Pure Reason,* with the idea that one is hitting upon ready-minted coins whose value is settled once and for all, then one must inevitably be perplexed by the further progress of the book. It repeatedly becomes obvious that an inquiry which was apparently concluded is taken up again, that an earlier explanation is supplemented, broadened, even entirely transformed, that problems which had just been treated separately abruptly enter into a totally new relationship in which their original meaning is altered. At bottom, however, the only natural and necessary situation is precisely this mutability, since it is a testimony to the fact that we stand here in the midst of a living process and a steady advance of thinking itself. Much that in isolation appears contradictory is illuminated only when it is reintegrated with this flow and interpreted in its whole context. Whereas Kant, on the strength of the synthetic method he uses in the First *Critique,* gradually proceeds step by step from the particular to the whole, the free reproduction of his system must begin with the idea of the whole and specify the meaning of the particular relative to it, in a way analogous to the one he himself

pointed out in the *Prolegomena.* As more and more threads are spun together in this process, at last the ingenious web of concepts stands before us; a retrospective analysis is the converse, disentangling only the major aspects from the numerous complexes of concepts and laying down the broadest principles that guide the idea in all its ramifications and developments. The totality of the particular questions comprised by the system of critical philosophy is never exhausted by this procedure; it must suffice if the general articulation seen by Kant himself as the essential moment and the decisive criterion for judging the unity and the solidity of his doctrine becomes visible and lucid. (pp. 139-144)

Ernst Cassirer, "The Construction and Central Problems of the 'Critique of Pure Reason'," in his Kant's Life and Thought, *translated by James Haden, Yale University Press, 1981, pp. 139-217.*

GEORGE SANTAYANA   (essay date 1920)

[*Santayana was a Spanish-born philosopher, poet, novelist, and literary critic who was for the most part educated in the United States, taking his undergraduate and graduate degrees at Harvard where he later taught philosophy. His earliest published works were the poems of* Sonnets, and Other Verses *(1894). Although Santayana is regarded as a fair poet, his facility with language is one of the distinguishing features of his later philosophical works. Written in an elegant, non-technical prose, Santayana's major philosophical work of his early career is the five-volume* Life of Reason *(1905-06). These volumes reflect the author's materialist viewpoint, which is applied to society, religion, art, and science, and along with* Scepticism and Animal Faith *(1923) and the four-volume* Realms of Being *(1927-40) put forth the view that while reason undermines belief in general, an irrational animal faith suggests the existence of a "realm of essences" which leads to the human search for knowledge. Here, Santayana discusses the contradictions in Kant's philosophy resulting from differences between his critical method and personal values.*]

Kant is remarkable among sincere philosophers for the pathetic separation which existed between his personal beliefs and his official discoveries. His personal beliefs were mild and half orthodox and hardly differed from those of Leibniz; but officially he was entangled in the subjective criticism of knowledge, and found that the process of knowing was so complicated, and so exquisitely contrived to make knowledge impossible, that while the facts of the universe were there, and we might have, like Leibniz, a shrewd and exact notion of what they were, officially we had no right to call them facts or to allege that we knew them. As there was much in Kant's personal belief which this critical method of his could not sanction, so there were implications and consequences latent in his critical method which he never absorbed, being an old man when he adopted it. One of these latent implications was egotism.

The fact that each spirit was confined to its own perceptions condemned it to an initial subjectivity and agnosticism. What things might exist besides his ideas he could never know. That such things existed was not doubted; Kant never accepted that amazing principle of dogmatic egotism that nothing is able to exist unless I am able to know it. On the contrary he assumed that human perceptions, with the moral postulates which he added to them, were symbols of a real world of forces or spirits existing beyond. This assumption reduced our initial idiotism to a constitutional taint of our animal minds, not unlike original sin, and excluded that romantic pride and self-sufficiency in which a full-fledged transcendentalism always abounds.

To this contrite attitude of Kant's agnosticism his personal character and ethics corresponded. A wizened little old bachelor, a sedentary provincial scribe, scrupulous and punctual, a courteous moralist who would have us treat humanity in the person of another as an end and never merely as a means, a pacifist and humanitarian who so revered the moral sense according to Shaftesbury and Adam Smith that, after having abolished earth and heaven, he was entirely comforted by the sublime truth that nevertheless it remained wrong to tell a lie—such a figure has nothing in it of the officious egotist or the superman. Yet his very love of exactitude and his scruples about knowledge, misled by the psychological fallacy that nothing can be an object of knowledge except some idea in the mind, led him in the end to subjectivism; while his rigid conscience, left standing in that unnatural void, led him to attribute absoluteness to what he called the categorical imperative. But this void outside and this absolute oracle within are germs of egotism, and germs of the most virulent species.

The categorical imperative, or unmistakable voice of conscience, was originally something external enough—too external, indeed, to impose by itself a moral obligation. The thunders of Sinai and the voice from the whirlwind in Job fetched their authority from the suggestion of power; there spoke an overwhelming physical force of which we were the creatures and the playthings, a voice which far from interpreting our sense of justice, or our deepest hopes, threatened to crush and to flout them. If some of its commandments were moral, others were ritual or even barbarous; the only moral sanction common to them all came from our natural prudence and love of life; our wisdom imposed on us the fear of the Lord. The prophets and the gospel did much to identify this external divine authority with the human conscience; an identification which required a very elaborate theory of sin and punishment and of existence in other worlds, since the actual procedure of nature and history can never be squared with any ideal of right.

In Kant, who in this matter followed Calvin, the independence between the movement of nature, both within and without the soul, and the ideal of right was exaggerated into an opposition. The categorical imperative was always authoritative, but perhaps never obeyed. While matter and life moved on in their own unregenerate way, a principle which they *ought* to follow, overarched and condemned them, and constrained them to condemn themselves. Human nature was totally depraved and incapable of the least merit, nor had it any power of itself to become righteous. Its amiable spontaneous virtues, having but a natural motive, were splendid vices. Moral worth began only when the will, transformed at the touch of unmerited grace, surrendered every impulse in overwhelming reverence for the divine law.

This Calvinistic doctrine might seem to rebuke all actual inclinations, and far from making the will morally absolute, as egotism would, to raise over against it an alien authority, what *ought* to be willed. Such was, of course, Kant's ostensible intention; but sublime as such a situation was declared to be, he felt rather dissatisfied in its presence. A categorical imperative crying in the wilderness, a duty which nobody need listen to, or suffer for disregarding, seemed rather a forlorn authority. To save the face of absolute right another world seemed to be required, as in orthodox Christianity, in which it might be duly vindicated and obeyed.

Kant's scepticism, by which all knowledge of reality was denied us, played conveniently into the hand of this pious requirement. If the whole natural world, which we can learn something about by experience, is merely an idea in our minds, nothing prevents any sort of real but unknown world from lying about us unawares. What could be more plausible and opportune than that the categorical imperative which the human mind, the builder of this visible world, had rejected, should in that other real world be the head stone of the corner?

This happy thought, had it stood alone, might have seemed a little fantastic; but it was only a laboured means of re-establishing the theology of Leibniz, in which Kant privately believed, behind the transcendental idealism which he had put forward professorially. The dogmatic system from which he started seemed to him, as it stood, largely indefensible and a little oppressive. To purify it he adopted a fallacious principle of criticism, namely, that our ideas are all we can know, a principle which, if carried out, would undermine that whole system, and every other. He, therefore, hastened to adopt a corrective principle of reconstruction, no less fallacious, namely, that conscience bids us assume certain things to be realities which reason and experience know nothing of. This brought him round to a qualified and ambigious form of his original dogmas, to the effect that although there was no reason to think that God, heaven, and free-will exist, we ought to act as if they existed, and might call that wilful action of ours faith in their existence.

Thus in the philosophy of Kant there was a stimulating ambiguity in the issue. He taught rather less than he secretly believed, and his disciples, seizing the principle of his scepticism, but lacking his conservative instincts, believed rather less than he taught them. Doubtless in his private capacity Kant hoped, if he did not believe, that God, free-will, and another life subsisted in fact, as every believer had hitherto supposed; it was only the method of proving their reality that had been illegitimate. For no matter how strong the usual arguments might seem (and they did not seem very strong) they could convey no transcendent assurance; on the contrary, the more proofs you draw for anything from reason and experience, the better you prove that that thing is a mere idea in your mind. It was almost prudent, so to speak, that God, freedom, and immortality, if they had claims to reality, should remain without witness in the sphere of "knowledge," as inadvertently or ironically it was still called; but to circumvent this compulsory lack of evidence God had at least implanted in us a veridical conscience, which if it took itself seriously (as it ought to do, being a conscience) would constrain us to postulate what, though we could never "know" it, happened to be the truth. Such was the way in which the good Kant thought to play hide-and-seek with reality.

Kant had a private mysticism in reserve to raise upon the ruins of science and common-sense. Knowledge was to be removed to make way for faith. This task is ambiguous, and the equivocation involved in it is perhaps the deepest of those confusions with which German metaphysics has since struggled, and which have made it waver between the deepest introspection and the dreariest mythology. To substitute faith for knowledge might mean to teach the intellect humility, to make it aware of its theoretic and transitive function as a faculty for hypothesis and rational fiction, building a bridge of methodical inferences and ideal unities between fact and fact, between endeavour and satisfaction. It might be to remind us,

A portrait of Kant.

sprinkling over us, as it were, the Lenten ashes of an intellectual contrition, that our thoughts are air even as our bodies are dust, momentary vehicles and products of an immortal vitality in God and in nature, which fosters and illumines us for a moment before it lapses into other forms.

Had Kant proposed to humble and concentrate into a practical faith *the same natural ideas* which had previously been taken for absolute knowledge, his intention would have been innocent, his conclusions wise, and his analysis free from venom and *arrière-pensée*. Man, because of his finite and propulsive nature and because he is a pilgrim and a traveller throughout his life, is obliged to have faith: the absent, the hidden, the eventual, is the necessary object of his concern. But what else shall his faith rest in except in what the necessary forms of his perception present to him and what the indispensable categories of his understanding help him to conceive? What possible objects are there for faith except objects of a possible experience? What else should a practical and moral philosophy concern itself with, except the governance and betterment of the human world? It is surely by using his only possible forms of perception and his inevitable categories of understanding that man may yet learn, as he has partly learned already, to live and prosper in the universe. Had Kant's criticism amounted simply to such a confession of the tentative, practical, and hypothetical nature of human reason, it would have been wholly acceptable to the wise; and its appeal to faith would have been nothing but an expression of natural vitality and courage, just as its criticism of knowledge would have been nothing but a better acquaintance with self. This faith would have called the forces of impulse and passion to reason's support, not to its betrayal. Faith would have meant faith in the intellect, a faith naturally expressing

man's practical and ideal nature, and the only faith yet sanctioned by its fruits.

Side by side with this reinstatement of reason, however, which was not absent from Kant's system in its critical phase and in its application to science, there lurked in his substitution of faith for knowledge another and sinister intention. He wished to blast as insignificant, because "subjective," the whole structure of human intelligence, with all the lessons of experience and all the triumphs of human skill, and to attach absolute validity instead to certain echoes of his rigoristic religious education. These notions were surely just as subjective, and far more local and transitory, than the common machinery of thought; and it was actually proclaimed to be an evidence of their sublimity that they remained entirely without practical sanction in the form of success or of happiness. The "categorical imperative" was a shadow of the ten commandments; the postulates of practical reason were the minimal tenets of the most abstract Protestantism. These fossils, found unaccountably imbedded in the old man's mind, he regarded as the evidences of an inward but supernatural revelation. (pp. 170-76)

George Santayana, "Kant," in his Little Essays, *edited by Logan Pearsall Smith, Charles Scribner's Sons, 1920, pp. 170-76.*

NORMAN KEMP SMITH   (essay date 1923)

[*In the following excerpt, Smith compares the varying philosophical positions assumed by Kant in the* Critique of Pure Reason, *the* Critique of Practical Reason, *and the* Critique of Judgment.]

The positive character of Kant's [philosophical] conclusions cannot be properly appreciated save in the wider perspectives that open to view in the **Critique of Practical Reason** and in the **Critique of Judgment.** Though in the **Critique of Pure Reason** a distinction is drawn between theoretical and moral belief, it is introduced in a somewhat casual manner, and there is no clear indication of the far-reaching consequences that follow in its train. Unfortunately also, even in his later writings, Kant is very unfair to himself in his methods of formulating the distinction. His real intention is to show that scientific knowledge is not coextensive with human insight; but he employs a misleading terminology, contrasting knowledge with faith, scientific demonstration with practical belief. (p. lv)

[The] term knowledge has, in the Critical philosophy, a much narrower connotation than in current speech. It is limited to *sense*-experience, and to such inferences therefrom as can be obtained by the only methods that Kant is willing to recognise, namely, the mathematico-physical. Aesthetic, moral and religious experience, and even organic phenomena, are excluded from the field of possible knowledge.

In holding to this position, Kant is, of course, the child of his time. The absolute sufficiency of the Newtonian physics is a presupposition of all his utterances on this theme. Newton, he believes, has determined in a quite final manner the principles, methods and limits of scientific investigation. For though Kant himself imposes upon science a further limitation, namely, to appearances, he conceives himself, in so doing, not as weakening Newton's natural philosophy, but as securing it against all possible objections. And to balance the narrow connotation thus assigned to the term knowledge, he has to give a correspondingly wide meaning to the terms faith, moral belief, subjective principles of interpretation. If this be not kept constantly in mind, the reader is certain to misconstrue the character and tendencies of Kant's actual teaching.

But though the advances made by the sciences since Kant's time have rendered this mode of delimiting the field of knowledge altogether untenable, his method of defining the sources of *philosophical insight* has proved very fruitful, and has many adherents at the present day. What Kant does—stated in broad outline—is to distinguish between the problems of *existence* and the problems of *value,* assigning the former to science and the latter to philosophy. Theoretical philosophy, represented in his system by the ***Critique of Pure Reason,*** takes as its province the logical values, that is, the distinction of truth and falsity, and defining their criteria determines the nature and limits of our theoretical insight. Kant finds that these criteria enable us to distinguish between truth and falsity only on the empirical plane. Beyond making possible a distinction between appearance and reality, they have no applicability in the metaphysical sphere.

The ***Critique of Practical Reason*** deals with values of a very different character. The faculty of Reason, which . . . renders our consciousness a purposive agency controlled by Ideal standards, is also, Kant maintains, the source of the moral sanctions. But whereas in the theoretical field it subdues our minds to the discipline of experience, and restrains our intellectual ambitions within the limits of the empirical order, it here summons us to sacrifice every natural impulse and every secular advantage to the furtherance of an end that has absolute value. In imposing duties, it raises our life from the "pragmatic" level of a calculating expediency to the higher plane of a categorical imperative.

The categorical imperative at once humbles and exalts; it discloses our limitations, but does so through the greatness of the vocation to which it calls us.

> This principle of morality, just on account of the universality of the legislation which makes it the formal supreme determining principle of our will, without regard to any subjective differences, is declared by the Reason to be a law for all rational beings. . . . It is, therefore, not limited to men only, but applies to all finite beings that possess Reason and Will; nay, it even includes the Infinite Being as the Supreme Intelligence.

Consequently, in employing moral ends in the interpretation of the Universe, we are not picturing the Divine under human limitations, but are discounting these limitations in the light of the one form of value that is known to us as absolute.

> *Duty!* . . . What origin is worthy of thee and where is to be found the root of thy noble descent . . . a root to be derived from which is the indispensable condition of the only worth that men can give themselves.

In his earlier years Kant had accepted the current, Leibnizian view that human excellence consists in intellectual enlightenment, and that it is therefore reserved for an *élite,* privileged with the leisure and endowed with the special abilities required for its enjoyment. From this arid intellectualism he was delivered through the influence of Rousseau.

> I am by disposition an enquirer. I feel the consuming thirst for knowledge, the eager unrest to ad-

vance ever further, and the delights of discovery. There was a time when I believed that this is what confers real dignity upon human life, and I despised the common people who know nothing. Rousseau has set me right. This imagined advantage vanishes. I learn to honour men, and should regard myself as of much less use than the common labourer, if I did not believe that my philosophy will restore to all men the common rights of humanity.

These common rights Kant formulates in a purely individualist manner. For here also, in his lack of historic sense and in his distrust alike of priests and of statesmen, he is the child of his time. In the education and discipline of the soul he looks to nothing so artificial and humanly limited—Kant so regards them—as religious tradition and social institutions. Human rights, he believes, do not vary with time and place; and for their enjoyment man requires no initiation and no equipment beyond what is supplied by Nature herself. It is from this standpoint that Kant adduces, as the twofold and sufficient inspiration to the rigours and sublimities of the spiritual life, the starry heavens above us and the moral law within. They are ever-present influences on the life of man. The naked eye reveals the former; of the latter all men are immediately aware. In their universal appeal they are of the very substance of human existence. Philosophy may avail to counteract certain of the hindrances which prevent them from exercising their native influence; it cannot be a substitute for the inspiration which they alone can yield.

Thus the categorical imperative, in endowing the human soul with an intrinsic value, singles it out from all other natural existences, and strengthens it to face, with equanimity, the cold immensities of the cosmic system. For though the heavens arouse in us a painful feeling of our insignificance as animal existences, they intensify our consciousness of a sublime destiny, as bearers of a rival, and indeed a superior, dignity.

In one fundamental respect Kant broke with the teaching of Rousseau, namely, in questioning his doctrine of the natural goodness and indefinite perfectibility of human nature. Nothing, Kant maintains, is good without qualification except the good will; and even that, perhaps, is never completely attained in any single instance. The exercise of duty demands a perpetual vigilance, under the ever-present consciousness of continuing demerit.

> I am willing to admit out of love of humanity that most of our actions are indeed correct, but if we examine them more closely we everywhere come upon the dear self which is always prominent. . . . Nothing but moral fanaticism and exaggerated self-conceit is infused into the mind by exhortation to actions as noble, sublime and magnanimous. Thereby men are led into the delusion that it is not duty, that is, respect for the law, whose yoke . . . they *must* bear, whether they like it or not, that constitutes the determining principle of their actions, and which always humbles them while they *obey* it. They then fancy that those actions are expected from them, not from duty, but as pure merit. . . . In this way they engender a vain highflying fantastic way of thinking, flattering themselves with a spontaneous goodness of heart that needs neither spur nor bridle, nor any command. . . .

In asserting the goodness and self-sufficiency of our natural impulses Rousseau is the spokesman of a philosophy which has dominated social and political theory since his day, and which is still prevalent. This philosophy, in Kant's view, is disastrous in its consequences. As a reading of human nature and of our moral vocation, it is hardly less false than the Epicurean teaching, which finds in the pursuit of pleasure the motive of all our actions. A naturalistic ethics, in either form, is incapacitated, by the very nature of its controlling assumptions, from appreciating the distinguishing features of the moral consciousness. Neither the successes nor the failures of man's spiritual endeavour can be rightly understood from any such standpoint. The human race, in its endurance and tenacity, in its dauntless courage and in its soaring spirit, reveals the presence of a *prevenient* influence, *non-natural* in character; and only if human nature be taken as including this higher, directive power, can it assume to itself the eulogy which Rousseau so mistakenly passes upon the natural and undisciplined tendencies of the human heart. For as history demonstrates, while *men* are weak, *humanity* is marvellous.

> There is one thing in our soul which, when we take a right view of it, we cannot cease to regard with the highest astonishment, and in regard to which admiration is right and indeed elevating, and that is our original moral capacity in general. . . . Even the incomprehensibility of this capacity, a capacity which proclaims a Divine origin, must rouse man's spirit to enthusiasm and strengthen it for any sacrifices which respect for his duty may impose on him.

We are not here concerned with the detail of Kant's ethical teaching, or with the manner in which he establishes the freedom of the will, and justifies belief in the existence of God and the immortality of the soul. In many respects his argument lies open to criticism. There is an unhappy contrast between the largeness of his fundamental thesis and the formal, doctrinaire manner in which it is developed. Indeed, in the *Critique of Practical Reason* the individualist, deistic, rationalistic modes of thinking of his time are much more in evidence than in any other of his chief writings; and incidentally he also displays a curious insensibility—again characteristic of his period—to all that is specific in the religious attitude. But when due allowances have been made, we can still maintain that in resting his constructive views upon the supreme value of the moral personality Kant has influenced subsequent philosophy in hardly less degree than by his teaching in the *Critique of Pure Reason.*

The two *Critiques,* in method of exposition and argument, in general outcome, and indeed in the total impression they leave upon the mind, are extraordinarily different. In the *Critique of Pure Reason* Kant is meticulously scrupulous in testing the validity of each link in his argument. Constantly he retraces his steps; and in many of his chief problems he halts between competing solutions. Kant's sceptical spirit is awake, and it refuses to cease from its questionings. In the *Critique of Practical Reason,* on the other hand, there is an austere simplicity of argument, which advances, without looking to right or left, from a few simple principles direct to their ultimate consequences. The impressiveness of the first *Critique* consists in its appreciation of the *complexity* of the problems, and in the care with which their various, conflicting aspects are separately dealt with. The second *Critique* derives its force from the fundamental conviction upon which it is based.

Such, then, stated in the most general terms, is the manner in which Kant conceives the *Critique of Pure Reason* as contributing to the establishment of a humanistic philosophy. It clears the ground for the practical Reason, and secures it in the autonomous control of its own domain. While preserving to the intellect and to science certain definitely prescribed rights, Kant places in the forefront of his system the moral values; and he does so under the conviction that in living up to the opportunities, in whatever rank of life, of our common heritage, we obtain a truer and deeper insight into ultimate issues than can be acquired through the abstruse subtleties of metaphysical speculation.

I may again draw attention to the consequences which follow from Kant's habitual method of isolating his problems. Truth is a value of universal jurisdiction, and from its criteria the judgments of moral and other values can claim no exemption. Existences and values do not constitute independent orders. They interpenetrate, and neither can be adequately dealt with apart from the considerations appropriate to the other. In failing to co-ordinate his problems, Kant has overemphasised the negative aspects of his logical enquiries and has formulated his ethical doctrines in a needlessly dogmatic form.

These defects are, however, in some degree remedied in the last of his chief works, the *Critique of Judgment.* In certain respects it is the most interesting of all Kant's writings. The qualities of both the earlier *Critiques* here appear in happy combination, while in addition his concrete interests are more in evidence, to the great enrichment of his abstract argument. Many of the doctrines of the *Critique of Pure Reason,* especially those that bear on the problems of teleology, are restated in a less negative manner, and in their connection with the kindred problems of natural beauty and the fine arts. For though the final decision in all metaphysical questions is still reserved to moral considerations, Kant now takes a more catholic view of the field of philosophy. He allows, though with characteristic reservations, that the *empirical* evidence obtainable through examination of the broader features of our total experience is of genuinely philosophical value, and that it can safely be employed to amplify and confirm the independent convictions of the moral consciousness. The embargo which in the *Critique of Pure Reason,* in matters metaphysical, is placed upon all tentative and probable reasoning is thus tacitly removed; and the term knowledge again acquires the wider meaning very properly ascribed to it in ordinary speech. (pp. lv-lxi)

Norman Kemp Smith, in his A Commentary to Kant's 'Critique of Pure Reason', *revised, 1923. Reprinted by Humanities Press, 1962, 651 p.*

JOHN DEWEY (essay date 1924)

[*Dewey was one of the most celebrated American philosophers of the twentieth century and the leading philosopher of pragmatism after the death of William James. Like James's pragmatism, Dewey's philosophy, which he named "instrumentalism," was an action-oriented form of speculation which judged ideas by their practical results, especially in furthering human adaptation to the changing circumstances of existence. Dewey's influence has been felt primarily in the fields of education and political theory. Here, he reviews the historic antecedents of Kant's thought, emphasizing the unresolved tension between traditional and revolutionary elements in his philosophy.*]

A colleague of mine once suggested that old books, philosophic classics, be sent out by philosophic journals for review, to be criticized as if they had just issued from the press. The device would be notable, if it could be acted upon, for bringing to light whatever in the book has stood the test of time as well as whatever is found congenial to contemporary taste and style. The two hundredth anniversary of the birth of Kant, falling in the month of April, suggests application of this method to the thinker who for the past seventy-five years supplied the bible of German thought. It also, however, suggests the difficulty of the task. Most philosophers since the days of the lucky early Greeks have been burdened by the weight of previous writers and the seeming need of carrying their technical apparatus. But no other philosopher has assumed the burden as conscientiously as did Kant. He is so fraught with reminiscence of every other philosopher he has ever read that one is tempted to adopt the statement of an undergraduate who, when asked for the point of interest in Kant, replied that the only interesting thing was how he ever came to be.

There are thinkers full of ancestral piety, and there are thinkers who to themselves at least seem to care nothing for the past, in their eagerness to make a fresh start. It was the fate of Kant, whether fortunately or tragically, to unite the two dispositions in himself. As far as his conscious attitude toward the bases of past thought were concerned, he could hardly have objected to the epithet, given him by his contemporaries, of the "all-destroying;" although he would certainly have added that he had destroyed only to rebuild on surer foundations. But at the same time almost every sentence he ever wrote is charged with reminders of previous thought. These reminiscences form his vocabulary. This is one reason why a whole library of technical commentaries has been written about Kant. But they also affect his way of looking at the world, and his sense of the problems and issues of philosophy—as vocabularies are likely to do. Sometimes one wonders if Kant ever looked a fact of life or nature directly in the face, or in any other way than through the medium of what previous thinkers had said and thought about it. I do not mean that Kant was peculiar in this respect. Philosophers like other professionals and specialists get caught in the intellectual machinery they are operating. Intellectual preparation is indispensable; then it seizes hold of us, and what was to have been a means of direct vision and interpretation becomes an end in itself.

But while Kant was not unique in this respect, he was preëminent. His period was not one of great historical sense; Kant could hardly be expected to have employed a historical method of interpretation. He used the distinctions with which his acquaintance with historical schemes made him familiar; even when he radically changed their meaning he preserved a terminology sanctioned by traditional usage—as for example in his taking over the Aristotelian and scholastic matter and form. He was extraordinarily sensitive to the ideas of every author he studied. He responded to Hume, Shaftesbury, Burke, and Rousseau as well as to thinkers with whom he was congenially much more sympathetic. To raw experience, to experience in mass, he was remarkably insensitive. Even his marked proclivities for social and political reform in the direction of republican freedom and equality, seem to be conditioned by his intellectual response to Rousseau and other writers, rather than to be a direct response to what was going on about him.

At the same time, he gave a new turn to philosophical thinking; there is no doubt about that. He put an end to the old attempt to reach conclusions about matters of existence, whether soul, external nature or God, by mathematical and conceptual reasoning. The reasons he preferred have been punctured by modern mathematicians, but the result remains—that concrete experience, not logical conceptions by themselves warrant statements about matters of existence. At the same time, he shattered traditional empiricism by showing that the sensations upon which it depended require thought to get anywhere. All this part of his undertaking is, however, somewhat technical and professional. The significant human thing is that he made these changes in the interest of a system of belief which would give mechanical science, conceived after the Newtonian pattern, complete sway in all matters of fact, in all matters whatsoever where thinking has a claim to intervene; while he reserved a higher ideal realm with which man's moral and religious interests are concerned, a realm where science has no business to enter and where it could say nothing. This was his great achievement: demarcation of two realms, one of mechanical science, the other of moral freedom and faith, connected yet independent, one beginning at the boundaries of the other.

Thus Kant to himself and to many in his own day was a revolutionary. There is no valid intellectual access, he taught, to the things of ultimate importance to man, the things with which traditional philosophy had been preoccupied, God, the soul, immortality, even the universe as an objective single whole. From this standpoint, all previous philosophy had been on the wrong track; it had been attempting the impossible. But the criticism which proved this conclusion, also proved, it seemed to Kant, the existence of a realm beyond scientific knowledge, a realm of whose being we are assured beyond peradventure by the necessities of moral experience. Nevertheless in his criticisms and constructions he worked with the distinctions, terms and issues of traditional philosophy. He reassorted them to make a new pattern; but he did not draw inspiration from a new and fresh personal partaking in the ultimate sources of new ideas—the realities of first-hand experience. See, he says in effect, the intellectual pieces with which past philosophers were occupied; see how these pieces never fitted together into a world-picture, except with the aid of deep-seated optical illusions. Now put them together in my way, according to my directions, and see how thoroughly and coherently they dovetail into a single picture.

The outcome of Kant's combination of piety toward the old with revolutionary intent was doubtless fortunate for his reputation, and for the influence of his writings for the last century, to an enormous extent in his own country and to some extent throughout the world. Yet it has a tragic phase. Solving a problem by dividing things, putting them in different places where they cannot conflict because they do not touch, is a dangerous procedure. It was a great comfort to many to know they could be as scientific and as mechanistically scientific as they desired in the realm of phenomena, and yet retain intact a superior world of ideal values in which freedom, instead of mechanical necessity, reigned. But the price paid for the comfort was unduly high. Science in such a régime becomes a technical occupation of an intellectual class; it is barren in morals, where fertilization by science is most needed, fruitful only in material appliances and machines used in the material sphere for mundane ends where the world is already too much with us. Morals become an affair of formulas, often sublime in themselves, but without possibility of effective translation, intellectual or practical, into the affairs of the workaday world.

In general, the intellectual problem of Europe since the sixteenth century has been the conflict between inherited traditions and the results and methods of a new science. Even the man in the street is sometimes aware of this conflict, as in the fundamentalist-modernist controversy of the churches. But every philosopher has been confronted on some level of thought with the question.

The theories of the western world, outside of science and industry, are inherited from a spiritual idealism formulated in ancient Greece and taken over by the Christian church in the teachings of the fathers and the schoolmen. But the conceptions of science have seemed to point to a very different kind of world from that depicted in this philosophy. Yet the emotional, religious and moral life of the European world—of which of course America is culturally a part—and to a large extent its artistic activities and achievements, have been deeply intertwined with the view of nature and life which science appears to have discredited.

In some form or other every philosopher from Descartes to Comte, Spencer and Bergson has published a variant version of the terms upon which the tradition incarnate in the higher forms of western life and the new science can meet and get on together:—schemes of reconciliation, of attack by one side upon the other, of compromises with varying degrees of surrender, imposed on this side or that.

Kant sensitively felt the problem and valiantly wrought to solve it. But to many of us it seems increasingly clear that his methods and conclusions only postponed a vital and sincere facing of the question. A destructive revolutionary to many of his contemporaries, he now seems almost wholly on the side of the conservatives. What was revolutionary was largely a professional and technical matter, a transfer of certain issues and ideas from cosmic nature into human nature; it left the mind with no genuinely new ideas with which to meet and confront the predicaments of experience. It did not help men to use science in morals. The transfer was one of those intellectual tours de force that delight professional intellectualists and call out warm adherence and equally ardent opposition.

But the net human outcome was hardly more than a complete separation of the world of ideals and of facts, of moral practice and scientific knowledge, of aspirations and of necessities. Doubtless they had been almost hopelessly confused previously in their relations to each other. Certainly the place and office of each in experience and its relations to the other needed clearing up. But it may be questioned whether confusion is not a more hopeful condition than clear-cut and wholesale separation. Confusion at least implies intersection, and a connection which might render co-öperation possible.

Separation surrenders the concrete world of affairs to the domain of mechanism fatalistically understood; it encourages mechanical authority and mechanical obedience and discipline; while it sheds over a life built out of mechanical subordinations the aureole of a superworldly ideal, sentimental at best, fanatical and deadly at worst. Kant himself was truly a pious, honest and good soul, substantial to a degree. But the record of his influence and its consequences may cause one to wonder whether these qualities, even when combined with industrious learning and assiduous reflection, can compensate for the absence of that kind of intelligence which emerges only when a thinker is a first-hand partaker in the vital intellectual currents and issues of his own day—I do not say in its practical movements. Without knowledge of what has been said and thought, intellectual participation will not go

far or deep. But Kant and the countless tomes written about him, stand a monument to the evil of that too professional and technical intellectual preoccupation which can see the world only at second-hand through problems which the past has formulated, through distinctions which dead thinkers have elaborated. An intellectual revolution is not of necessity a good thing; but a professed revolution compromised from the outset by subjection to the old and traditional is pretty assuredly a bad thing. A revolution in tradition that after all stays within the bounds of tradition is a boon to men who wish to be modern and conservative at the same time; who want to be both scientific and also idealistic in the ways sanctioned by the past. But it only postpones the day of reckoning. It is possible that the Great War was in some true sense a day of reckoning for Kantian thought, and that from henceforth interest in him will openly become more and more antiquarian in nature. (pp. 254-56)

John Dewey, "Kant after Two Hundred Years," in
The New Republic, *Vol. XXXVIII, No. 491, April 30, 1924, pp. 254-56.*

WILL DURANT (essay date 1926)

[*Durant was an American journalist, educator, and historian. He is best known for his eleven-volume nonscholarly series* The Story of Civilization *(1935-75), a collaborative effort with his wife, Ariel. The series was immensely popular, as was Durant's collection of revised lectures,* The Story of Philosophy *(1926). In the following excerpt from that work, Durant questions the verity of Kant's central philosophical tenets while affirming the impact of his ideas on later German philosophers.*]

[How does the] complex structure of logic, metaphysics, psychology, ethics, and politics [in Kant's philosophy] stand today, after the philosophic storms of a century have beaten down upon it? It is pleasant to answer that much of the great edifice remains; and that the "critical philosophy" represents an event of permanent importance in the history of thought. But many details and outworks of the structure have been shaken.

First, then, is space a mere "form of sensibility," having no objective reality independent of the perceiving mind? Yes and no. Yes: for space is an empty concept when not filled with perceived objects; "space" merely means that certain objects are, for the perceiving mind, at such and such a position, or distance, with reference to other perceived objects; and no external perception is possible except of objects in space; space then is assuredly a "necessary form of the external sense." And no: for without doubt, such spatial facts as the annual elliptical circuit of sun by earth, though statable only by a mind, are independent of any perception whatever; the deep and dark blue ocean rolled on before Byron told it to, and after he had ceased to be. Nor is space a "construct" of the mind through the coördination of spaceless sensations; we perceive space directly through our simultaneous perception of different objects and various points—as when we see an insect moving across a still background. Likewise: time as a sense of before and after, or a measurement of motion, is of course subjective, and highly relative; but a tree will age, wither and decay whether or not the lapse of time is measured or perceived. The truth is that Kant was too anxious to prove the subjectivity of space, as a refuge from materialism; he feared the argument that if space is objective and universal, God must exist in space, and be therefore spatial and material. He might have been content with the critical idealism which shows that all reality is known to us primarily as our sensations and ideas. The old fox bit off more than he could chew.

He might well have contented himself, too, with the relativity of scientific truth, without straining towards that mirage, the absolute. Recent studies like those of Pearson in England, Mach in Germany, and Henri Poincaré in France, agree rather with Hume than with Kant: all science, even the most rigorous mathematics, is relative in its truth. Science itself is not worried about the matter; a high degree of probability contents it. Perhaps, after all, "necessary" knowledge is not necessary?

The great achievement of Kant is to have shown, once for all, that the external world is known to us only as sensation; and that the mind is no mere helpless *tabula rasa,* the inactive victim of sensation, but a positive agent, selecting and reconstructing experience as experience arrives. We can make subtractions from this accomplishment without injuring its essential greatness. We may smile, with Schopenhauer, at the exact baker's dozen of categories, so prettily boxed into triplets, and then stretched and contracted and interpreted deviously and ruthlessly to fit and surround all things. And we may even question whether these categories, or interpretive forms of thought, are innate, existing before sensation and experience; perhaps so in the individual, as Spencer conceded, though acquired by the race; and then, again, probably acquired even by the individual: the categories may be grooves of thought, habits of perception and conception, gradually produced by sensations and perceptions automatically arranging themselves,—first in disorderly ways, then, by a kind of natural selection of forms of arrangement, in orderly and adaptive and illuminating ways. It is memory that classifies and interprets sensations into perceptions, and perceptions into ideas; but memory is an accretion. That unity of the mind which Kant thinks native (the "transcendental unity of apperception") is acquired—and not by all; and can be lost as well as won—in amnesia, or alternating personality, or insanity. Concepts are an achievement, not a gift.

The nineteenth century dealt rather hardly with Kant's ethics, his theory of an innate, *à priori,* absolute moral sense. The philosophy of evolution suggested irresistibly that the sense of duty is a social deposit in the individual, the content of conscience is acquired, though the vague disposition to social behavior is innate. The moral self, the social man, is no "special creation" coming mysteriously from the hand of God, but the late product of a leisurely evolution. Morals are not absolute; they are a code of conduct more or less haphazardly developed for group survival, and varying with the nature and circumstances of the group: a people hemmed in by enemies, for example, will consider as immoral that zestful and restless individualism which a nation youthful and secure in its wealth and isolation will condone as a necessary ingredient in the exploitation of natural resources and the formation of national character. No action is good in itself, as Kant supposes.

His pietistic youth, and his hard life of endless duty and infrequent pleasure, gave him a moralistic bent; he came at last to advocate duty for duty's sake, and so fell unwittingly into the arms of Prussian absolutism. There is something of a severe Scotch Calvinism in this opposition of duty to happiness; Kant continues Luther and the Stoic Reformation, as Voltaire continues Montaigne and the Epicurean Renaissance. He represented a stern reaction against the egoism and hedo-

nism in which Helvetius and Holbach had formulated the life of their reckless era, very much as Luther had reacted against the luxury and laxity of Mediterranean Italy. But after a century of reaction against the absolutism of Kant's ethics, we find ourselves again in a welter of urban sensualism and immorality, of ruthless individualism untempered with democratic conscience or aristocratic honor; and perhaps the day will soon come when a disintegrating civilization will welcome again the Kantian call to duty.

The marvel in Kant's philosophy is his vigorous revival, in the second *Critique,* of those religious ideas of God, freedom, and immortality, which the first *Critique* had apparently destroyed. "In Kant's works," says Nietzsche's critical friend, Paul Ree, "you feel as though you were at a country fair. You can buy from him anything you want—freedom of the will and captivity of the will, idealism and a refutation of idealism, atheism and the good Lord. Like a juggler out of an empty hat, Kant draws out of the concept of duty a God, immortality, and freedom,—to the great surprise of his readers." Schopenhauer too takes a fling at the derivation of immortality from the need of reward: "Kant's virtue, which at first bore itself so bravely towards happiness, loses its independence later, and holds out its hand for a tip." The great pessimist believes that Kant was really a sceptic who, having abandoned belief himself, hesitated to destroy the faith of the people, for fear of the consequences to public morals. "Kant discloses the groundlessness of speculative theology, and leaves popular theology untouched, nay even establishes it in a nobler form as a faith based upon moral feeling." This was afterwards distorted by the philosophasters into rational apprehension and consciousness of God, etc. . . . ; while Kant, as he demolished old and revered errors, and knew the danger of doing so, rather wished through the moral theology merely to substitute a few weak temporary supports, so that the ruin might not fall upon him, but that he might have time to escape. So too Heine, in what is no doubt an intentional caricature, represents Kant, after having destroyed religion, going out for a walk with his servant Lampe, and suddenly perceiving that the old man's eyes are filled with tears. "Then Immanuel Kant has compassion, and shows that he is not only a great philosopher, but also a good man; and half kindly, half ironically, he speaks: 'Old Lampe must have a God or else he cannot be happy, says the practical reason; for my part, the practical reason may, then, guarantee the existence of God.' " If these interpretations were true we should have to call the second *Critique* a Transcendental Anesthetic.

But these adventurous reconstructions of the inner Kant need not be taken too seriously. The fervor of the essay on *Religion Within the Limits of Pure Reason* indicates a sincerity too intense to be questioned, and the attempt to change the base of religion from theology to morals, from creeds to conduct, could have come only from a profoundly religious mind. "It is indeed true," he wrote to Moses Mendelssohn in 1766, "that I think many things with the clearest conviction, . . . which I never have the courage to say; but I will never say anything which I do not think." Naturally, a long and obscure treatise like the great *Critique* lends itself to rival interpretations; one of the first reviews of the book, written by Reinhold a few years after it appeared, said as much as we can say today: "The *Critique of Pure Reason* has been proclaimed by the dogmatists as the attempt of a sceptic who undermines the certainty of all knowledge;—by the sceptics as a piece of arrogant presumption that undertakes to erect a new form of dogmatism upon the ruins of previous systems;—by the supernaturalists as a subtly plotted artifice to displace the historical foundations of religion, and to establish naturalism without polemic;—by the naturalists as a new prop for the dying philosophy of faith;—by the materialists as an idealistic contradiction of the reality of matter;—by the spiritualists as an unjustifiable limitation of all reality to the corporeal world, concealed under the name of the domain of experience." In truth the glory of the book lay in its appreciation of all these points of view; and to an intelligence as keen as Kant's own, it might well appear that he had really reconciled them all, and fused them into such a unity of complex truth as philosophy had not seen in all its history before.

As to his influence, the entire philosophic thought of the nineteenth century revolved about his speculations. After Kant, all Germany began to talk metaphysics: Schiller and Goethe studied him; Beethoven quoted with admiration his famous words about the two wonders of life—"the starry heavens above, the moral law within"; and Fichte, Schelling, Hegel and Schopenhauer produced in rapid succession great systems of thought reared upon the idealism of the old Königsberg sage. It was in these balmy days of German metaphysics that Jean Paul Richter wrote: "God has given to the French the land, to the English the sea, to the Germans the empire of the air." Kant's criticism of reason, and his exaltation of feeling, prepared for the voluntarism of Schopenhauer and Nietzsche, the intuitionism of Bergson, and the pragmatism of William James; his identification of the laws of thought with the laws of reality gave to Hegel a whole system of philosophy; and his unknowable "thing-in-itself" influenced Spencer more than Spencer knew. Much of the obscurity of Carlyle is traceable to his attempt to allegorize the already obscure thought of Goethe and Kant—that diverse religions and philosophies are but the changing garments of one eternal truth. Caird and Green and Wallace and Watson and Bradley and many others in England owe their inspiration to the first *Critique;* and even the wildly innovating Nietzsche takes his epistemology from the "great Chinaman of Königsberg" whose static ethics he so excitedly condemns. After a century of struggle between the idealism of Kant, variously reformed, and the materialism of the Enlightenment, variously redressed, the victory seems to lie with Kant. Even the great materialist Helvetius wrote, paradoxically: "Men, if I may dare say it, are the creators of matter." Philosophy will never again be so naïve as in her earlier and simpler days; she must always be different hereafter, and profounder, because Kant lived. (pp. 311-17)

Will Durant, "Immanuel Kant and German Idealism" in his The Story of Philosophy: The Lives and Opinions of the Greater Philosophers, *1926. Reprint by Garden City Publishing Co., Inc., 1930, pp. 276-325.*

BARON VON OPPELL   (essay date 1942)

[*In the following excerpt, Oppell remarks on the similarity of Shakespeare's literary aesthetic to Kant's aesthetic philosophy as expressed in the* Critique of Judgment.]

I might have taken beauty in poetry and philosophy as my thesis, the object of the present enquiry being to discover in philosophical *thought* the same beauty which poetry can *express.* I have chosen Shakespeare as the greatest poet and Kant as one of the profoundest thinkers I know, in order, by reference to the actual example of their works, better to give what can at best be a few suggestive ideas to further reflection on a subject which would need a volume for adequate treatment.

If we hold creative art, and thus poetry as its most perfect expression, in contrast to methodical philosophical thought, they might appear at first like two different worlds. But the greater the poetry and the profounder the philosophy the more will this essential contrast tend to disappear.

Both Shakespeare and Kant bring before you equally the last mystery of human existence, which is the soul of beauty; you can feel it as the background to all Shakespeare's creations and it breaks through at the end of Kant's thought. It is in their way of approaching the unknowable wonder that the fundamental difference between them appears.

Shakespeare *saw* the mystery, saw it from the beginning, without searching for it, and at once. Thus he can let you feel it beyond everything he brings before you from the most ordinary situations to the deepest tragedies—it shines like light from afar on Falstaff as it does on Hamlet. Shakespeare *saw* the wonder and was content with seeing it and rendering it as he saw it. Existence appeared to him in perfect synthesis with himself, and as this harmony was wide enough to embrace all humanity as he found it, the most commonplace human beings equally with the heroes of tragedy, we must identify it with beauty. For beauty may well be described as the perfect synthesis between the percipient and his object, and the greater the contrast to be reconciled the wider will be the harmony and the greater the beauty.

Kant also saw the wonder of this world, but not intuitively. The mental and the sensuous were not one in him as in Shakespeare. Therefore he tried to bring existence into harmony with himself from the mental side alone. In Kant the harmony was consciously willed and relentlessly pursued till at last he attained it in his conception of beauty; in Shakespeare it was there *ab initio.* Thus one might say that the genius of Shakespeare was heaven-born, while that of Kant was the result of strenuous thought, of infinite effort. His was the genius that has been well described as the capability of taking infinite pains.

If we now turn to Shakespeare, one of the first features to strike us is the universal character of his poetry. Not only is there hardly an aspect of human life that he does not touch on, but I can recall no important truth, arrived at by searching philosophical thought, which he does not appear to have felt intuitively, and to which the various characters he brings before you do not in some form give poetical expression. Indeed I might have been tempted to entitle my reflections Philosophy in Shakespeare and Poetry in Kant. But I would thereby only be narrowing and perhaps obscuring my thesis which is really a wider one, namely, to find at the end of Kant's *thought* the same beauty which Shakespeare's poetry *expresses* (embracing as it does the truths of philosophy).

I propose therefore to lay stress on Shakespeare's attaining what is to me the foremost requisite of all creative poetry, just by his purely æsthetic contemplation of human experience. I have never been able to see in the awakening of pity and fear the essential substance of tragic poetry, as advocated by Aristotle. Each time I read again one of Shakespeare's tragedies the less inclined I am to do so. Pity and fear, in the sense of Aristotle, are ethical emotions, and to claim them as essential to tragic art would amount in the end to seeing the moral effect on ourselves as the supreme purpose of poetry. To the extent that poetry aims at producing such effect to that extent does it leave its proper realm. Shakespeare's poetry pursues no aim but that of rendering his æsthetic vision and thus bringing before you the wonder of human existence. Certainly, the pity and fear which the contemplation of this inspires are inseparable from any true rendering of life. Shakespeare lets you pass through these emotions, and the consummate skill with which he arouses them shows how deeply he felt himself the infinite pathos of some of the situations he describes. But his pathos never leads to tears, for he always lets you feel beyond the tragedy of the individual the pathos of all human life. The grandeur of the æsthetic spectacle which arose before him always triumphs in the end; your pity, then, is submerged in the joy of its beauty, but not lost. It is for this reason that as Wordsworth truly says: "Shakespeare's writings, in the most pathetic scenes, never act upon us beyond the bounds of pleasure." When I recall those words of Othello:—

> . . . Oh thou weed!
> Who art so lovely fair and smell'st so sweet
> That the sense aches at thee, would thou hadst ne'er been
>   born.

and then at the end:—

> I kiss'd thee ere I kill'd thee; no way but this
> Killing myself to die upon a kiss.

nothing could arouse both pity and fear to a higher degree. Pity for this man who had, after all, something of nobility in his nature, and fear at the terrible fate which we human beings can bring on ourselves. And yet the total impression which this tragedy leaves in our mind is above all its poetry and beauty. I must resist the temptation to quote further pathetic scenes; many will occur to every lover of Shakespeare. (pp. 166-67)

In trying to find in the thought of Kant the beauty that Shakespeare's poetry expresses, I must naturally turn to his reflections on æsthetic. In so doing, I by no means wish to assert that Kant's theoretical conclusions about beauty were to him the essential part of his philosophy. For next to knowledge for its own sake, which he saw at its highest in defining its limits, the supreme value for Kant was the ethical idea and the law of duty it prescribes, providing as it did for him the only possible God-proof. "Two things there are," says Kant, in a famous passage, "which the oftener and the more steadfastly we consider them, fill the mind with an ever new, and ever rising admiration and reverence: the starry heaven above, the moral law within."

We can find the beauty I am searching for in Kant's entire philosophy, but to my mind above all in the fact that its very profundity—his rare capability of thinking things *to the end*—creates a demand—a *want* to which his reflections on æsthetic in his last work, **Critique of the Power of Judgement** alone could give complete satisfaction. It is therefore *not* for Kant's often questionable opinions on single facts of beauty that I propose to dwell briefly on this, his last work, but in the light of his general philosophy to which the **Critique of Judgement,** by filling a gap in his system, provides what appears to me a needful consummation. (p. 168)

I will repeat here the main features of Kant's thought in so far as they appear to me to lead up to beauty as the satisfaction of a want.

Starting with a methodical investigation of the average human mind, Kant's philosophy is, broadly speaking, an enquiry into the principles we must presuppose (*a priori*) in such mind, to make possible any experience or knowledge whatsoever, be it of facts, *i.e. truth,* as far as we can know it, *goodness* or *beauty*. In accordance with this division, Kant distinguishes three separate faculties of knowledge which "as being determined by different principles" are considered in abstraction from each other.

It is the *Understanding* alone which, with the help of the senses gives us knowledge of facts, makes us acquainted with this world, which is therefore determined by the nature of this Understanding and senses, and is thus a conditioned or phenomenal world. We can only obtain a coherent view of this world, have any rule to guide our actions and thus maintain life, by seeing, "understanding," it as governed by causes and their effects. The sensuous world we know—in Kant's language, Nature,—is thus under the iron law of causation, that is, ruled by Necessity.

The human mind is not content with such a world; it claims that there should be something that is *in itself* apart from our knowledge of it; and that is not the effect of any cause other than itself. It is the faculty of *Reason* which satisfies this demand, in giving us the "ideas" of *God, Freedom* (from the law of Necessity) and (thus also) Immortality. They are termed "ideas" because they cannot, like the "concepts" of the Understanding, be demonstrated by pointing to anything in Nature which corresponds to them; thus they cannot give us any knowledge of facts, yet they are ineradicable from the mind.

Here we find a perfect parallel in one of the most beautiful passages in Shakespeare when, alluding to the song of the spheres, Lorenzo says:—

> Such harmony is in immortal souls;
> But whilst this muddy vesture of decay
> Doth grossly close it in we cannot hear it.

The harmony persists in ourselves though we cannot hear it. Just as the ideas of reason are indestructible, although they can give us no positive knowledge. It is again only the "muddy vesture" we wear as human beings, which obscures what those ideas would tell us.

Reason can, however, continues Kant, give us knowledge of goodness. For its ideas find an outlet by prescribing to man the law of duty; which is simply "the law that a being possessing the ideas of God and Freedom would dictate to himself." In so far as we act and find that we can act, on this law which we impose on ourself, we are *free;* free, I would say, by bringing a new motive into Nature, a new "cause" unknown to her causal Necessity.

Yet there remains in Kant's language, which seems to rise here once more to the poetry of his thought,

> a gulf we cannot see across between the territory of
> the conception of Nature, that is the sensuous, and
> the territory of the conception of Freedom that is
> the supra-sensuous . . . just as if they were two different
> worlds.

It is the pain of this contrast within ourself which, it would appear to me, calls forth a *want* for yet another mode of knowing which might unite these two worlds and thus restore harmony to the mind. But the arising of a want *in itself* in no way implies the possibility of its realisation. Kant derives this possibility from the fact that we are able to act within Nature according to the law of duty. He consequently infers "that we must conceive this Nature of Necessity as in some way conforming to the laws of Freedom."

This conception is given us, continues Kant, by the *"Power of Judgement"* which, when employed to "reflect" on Nature, shows us that even in order merely to "understand" her, to search as we do for her laws, we must have an *a priori* conviction that there *are* such laws; we must regard her as entirely comprehensible to us as if she were the creation of a Mind proceeding on the same principles that we find in our own mind. Thus, although we can never know any *final* purpose of Nature, nor even if there be such purpose, we can yet find "purposiveness" in her perfect adaptation to our mind; which should then be to Reason as well as to the Understanding.

It is this conviction that there should be in the end perfect conformity between Nature and our mind—considered no longer for the sake of "understanding" Nature but merely in its *"effect on ourself,"* on our very *"life-feeling,"* which gives the impulse to the imagination to discover as it were hidden beneath the sensuous world before us, a supra-sensuous substratum, and so to attain this perfect consonance. Thus it would be *this harmony and unity between the sensuous world of Necessity we know, and an ideal world of Freedom beyond our knowledge,* which for Kant constitutes beauty.

It would be difficult to find a more perfect conception of the wide harmony and beauty which Shakespeare's poetry expresses. It is almost as if something of Shakespeare's own inspiration broke through at the end of Kant's searching thought. "Les grandes pensées viennent du cœur," as the French poet Vauvenargues truly observes.

Yet between poetry and philosophy, between Shakespeare's intuitive perception of beauty and Kant's methodical approach to it, there remains a fundamental difference which cannot be better illustrated than by Kant's own reflections on creative genius. I will give a few of what appear to me as his most essential and striking conclusions:

> Genius is a gift of Nature which can never be acquired but with which its possessor is born. Thus genius, as conferred by Nature, is an in-born faculty or power which operates *as Nature does herself.*

In so doing, the man of genius by seeing Nature transforms her and creates as it were *another* Nature out of the stuff this Nature presents to him.

Bearing in mind that Nature in Kant's language designates the world we know—this entire phenomenal existence, this conclusion could not be more perfectly rendered than in Shakespeare's description of the poet:—

> The poet's eye . . .
> Doth glance from heaven to earth, from earth to heaven,
> And as imagination bodies forth
> The forms of things unknown . . .
> . . . turns them to shapes . . .

But it is the poet's individual eye alone which creates these new "shapes," indifferent to what others may see in Nature. Therefore *originality* is claimed by Kant as the first attribute of genius.

> The creator of any product of the imagination which he owes to his genius does not himself know from where the ideas for it came to him, nor is it in his power to alter these ideas or to lay down any

plan or rules for others showing how he arrived at them. They come to him, as the Latin word 'genius' might well imply, from a particular protective spirit (the German word *Schutzgeist*) which inspires him throughout his life.

Thus one might say that the ideas of genius, although itself a gift of Nature, are in a way heaven-born, as coming from an unknown source from which Nature herself originates.

It follows, continues Kant,

> that the works of genius defy imitation; no one can learn how to produce them. Whereas every thought needful even for the greatest achievements of science can be learnt. Whatever can be taught and learnt is not the work of genius. Thus the difference between even a marvellous intellect, as that of a Newton, and any intelligent student of his immortal works is yet only one of degree. The distinction between a man of genius and others who do not possess it is one of kind.

I think it must be admitted that a thinker who could appreciate and grasp the essential attributes of genius so well must have possessed it in some way himself. Incidentally it may be remarked that Kant does not include those capable of appreciating and understanding the creative power of genius among those that differ in *kind* from genius itself.

On the other hand, we have in Shakespeare not only the flashes of heaven-born imagination, as they appear in some of his single passages and in the general plan, what I might call the total creative vision, for each of his great dramas, but we must equally admit his *talent*—the great entirely human intellect needful to bring each whole drama down to every detail into harmony with its inspired total vision, and so to give to his inspiration adequate expression.

Therefore we have in Shakespeare not only genius (as described by Kant) simply rendering a message that comes to him he knows not wherefrom, but you have, in a way, Kant's intellect and his power of searching thought as well. While in Kant over and above this power of strenuous thought—perhaps owing to its being pursued relentlessly, one might say infinitely—something of the inspiration of a Shakespeare would seem, I repeat, to break through in his final conclusions on the nature of beauty.

If it then be admitted, as I have tried to show, that between the great creative poet and the profound thinker—a Shakespeare and a Kant—there is an inward affinity in that they both face the mystery of human existence and thus see the same beauty in the end, it should not be overlooked that there is a considerable difference in the recognition they obtain, and therefore to some extent in the respective effect of their message to mankind. For it is well remarked by Schopenhauer: "The poet leaves it to his audience to follow him as far as they are capable of doing; he may thus satisfy the most different degrees of intellect—even fools and the wisest—at the same time." "The philosopher demands the capability of following his thought throughout to the *end*" in order to understand and appreciate him at all.

The truth of Schopenhauer's contention applies with double force to a universal poet like Shakespeare whose creations embrace nearly every aspect of human life, contrasted with a thinker like Kant who, although equally facing all human existence in the end, approaches it across the intricacies of abstract thought.

There are many people who can follow tragedies like, say, Macbeth or Othello, for the interest of the story, appreciating even to some extent the dramatic conflicts presented to them; there are yet more, down to the most vulgar minds, who can enjoy Falstaff being carried off in "a buck basket rammed in with dirty linen" with the added ethical (!) satisfaction that the poor knight richly deserved his ignominy; who are all of them more or less insensible to the highest beauties in Shakespeare.

On the other hand Kant must necessarily remain for the general public but a name, and the "many" who can understand him at all are more or less limited from the beginning to "professional philosophers." But I cannot help thinking that the proportion of those among them capable of appreciating the poetry of Kant's leading ideas is no greater than among the infinitely wider public who enjoy Shakespeare's plays for the story is the number of such who can rise to his highest beauties. Still, the far wider recognition which the poet can obtain compared to that which falls to the thinker no doubt correspondingly affects what they each in the end have at heart; the giving of their message to mankind. But even though the philosopher's message can never actually reach the world at large, yet I am inclined to agree with Schopenhauer's further observation to the effect that philosophical thought, although imperceptibly and slowly, yet none the less deeply influences the mind of men without their knowing it, and thus determines the course of history.

For the rest I must confess to the rather pessimistic opinion that the mass of mankind will probably always be more or less insensible equally to the beauty of poetry as to that of thought; both are accessible only to the few. But I would venture to assert that anyone capable of fully appreciating the highest beauties in Shakespeare should equally be able, not necessarily to follow all the intricacies of Kant's abstract thought, but to discover for himself, as it were shining through them, the poetry of Kant's great leading idea. One might say: Shakespeare gives you the poetry and leaves it to you to find in it the truths of philosophy; Kant gives you the philosophy and it is for you to see the poetry in it. Those who can do the one should be capable of rising to the other.

Thus both Shakespeare, to whom the riddle of life from its most ordinary aspects up to its deepest tragedies appeared as one perfect vision of beauty, and Kant, relentlessly continuing to think till at the end of thought the same wonder stood before him seem to me to come near attaining what might well be the ultimate purpose of the human mind: in *themselves* by experiencing the purest joy to be found in this world (that of creative inspiration and of strenuous thought) and at the same time by giving this joy freely to all *others* who can rise to sharing it. So is genius, be it Nature's free gift or the reward of infinite effort, as Shakespeare says of mercy:—

Twice blest:
It blesseth him that gives and him that takes.

(pp. 169-73)

Baron von Oppell, "Beauty in Shakespeare and in Kant," in The Hibbert Journal, *Vol. XL, No. 2, January, 1942, pp. 166-73.*

LUCIEN GOLDMANN (essay date 1945)

[*Goldmann, a Romanian-born French sociologist and critic, has written widely on the relation between philosophy and soci-* *ety. In the following excerpt, Goldmann assesses, from a Marxist viewpoint, Kant's contribution to the development of modern European philosophy, asserting that his work inaugurated a new concept of humanity seen as an historical subject who is compelled to progress through time.*]

For Kant, man is a rational being and, since reason implies universality and community, at least in part a 'social' being. He is not an autonomous monad who is only part of the community through his relations with other monads. On the contrary, man is in his very existence part of a greater whole, of a *community,* and thereby, of a *universe.*

Both this community and this universe, however, are *imperfect,* for the actions of man are still dominated by powerful instincts and selfish interests which set him against his fellows and tend towards the disintegration of the community and the universe. Man is an 'unsocial-sociable' being. The selfish and anti-social actions and relations of the individual indicate his *dependence* upon his biological nature and upon the external world and constitute his *heteronomy;* his tendency to strive towards a higher, perfect community constitutes his spiritual and rational nature, his *freedom,* his *autonomy.*

It is the destiny of man as a rational being to strive in all his actions and with all his power towards the realization of a perfect community, of the kingdom of God on earth, of the highest good, of perpetual peace. This he can only do if the understanding does not forbid him to *believe* in and to *hope* for the realization of this community. What now unites men in their thoughts and their actions and constitutes their still imperfect community is universal and *a priori form,* common to all individuals (the pure intuition of space and time, the categories of the understanding, the categorical imperative), and aesthetic judgement, partly formal and partly material, but purely *subjective.* What separates them is empirical matter, differing from individual to individual (sensations, inclinations, selfish interests).

The knowledge and the actions of present-day man are thus limited, *social in their form and unsocial in their content.* His knowledge is merely an *incomplete* determination of appearances in experience, his actions selfish and contrary to the community, for which the universal is no more than a duty, a categorical imperative which is not actually followed. A higher community would make possible qualitatively superior knowledge and action, knowledge which would be the complete determination of things in themselves and a holy will for which there would no longer be an imperative or duties, but only free activity in conformity with the community. Both form and content would be common to all men, uniting them universally in both thought and action, theory and practice.

For Kant, however, all these concepts—perfect community, the kingdom of God on earth, knowledge of things in themselves, the holy will, the unconditioned—are suprasensible ideas which man can never realize here on earth through his will and his action. Because he *must* strive towards them, towards the only real spiritual values, without ever being able to attain them, man's existence is tragic. And Kant sees only two possible grounds for hope that this tragic situation might be overcome: *rational faith* and the still insufficient hope for the future of the human community, *history.*

With this vision of man, Kant had laid the foundations for an entirely new conception of the world. Before him, almost all the really important philosophical systems (with the sole great exception of Spinozism) reduced to two fundamental types. The ancient Greek philosophers and most of those who had lived since the end of the middle ages saw the individual as an autonomous and independent being who, as such, could attain the absolute, or at least the highest conceivable human values. The community, the whole, was for them only a *secondary reality,* the result of the mutual influence of autonomous individuals. The Christian philosophies of the middle ages saw the individual as an imperfect being belonging to a larger whole, and the empirical human community as an imperfect reflection of the kingdom of God. But the perfect whole, the kingdom of God, was for them something real and existent, although transcendent. Faith for them was *knowledge,* a certainty and a consolation, not as for Kant *hope* and a reason for action.

Kant opened the way to a new philosophy which unites the Christian idea of the limitation of man with the immanence of the ancients and the philosophers of the seventeenth and eighteenth centuries in considering the intelligible world, the totality, as a human task, as the object of the authentic destiny of man and the product of human action. Whilst the classical philosophers, starting out from the individual, had been centrally concerned with *epistemology* (rationalist or empiricist) and *ethics* (Stoic or Epicurean), and Christian thinkers, starting out from God, had made *theology* the basis of their systems, Kant for the first time created the possibility of a philosophy based on the idea of the *community* and the *human person,* that is to say, on the *philosophy of history.* It is in this direction that philosophical thought has continued to develop in the works of the three most important thinkers since Kant, in the works of Hegel, Marx and Georg Lukács.

Kant's philosophy was, however, immediately followed in Germany by two systems which, in spite of their undeniable importance, seem to me nevertheless to represent a step backwards from Kant's position, and which indeed Kant recognized as such. These were the systems of Fichte and Schelling, two philosophers whose thought took quite different directions from that of Kant.

Kant's philosophy was much more a beginning than an end, and thus only thinkers who have understood and perceived it as such have been able to appreciate its true philosophical importance. This has been achieved by starting from the most important question left by Kant's philosophy to its successors: *Is the tragedy of human existence really insurmountable? Is there no way for empirical man to achieve the unconditioned, the highest good?*

The principal philosophers of German idealism, Fichte, Schelling and Hegel, as well as its 'materialist heir', Marxism, have been concerned to give a positive answer to this question.

It is impossible here in this conclusion to analyse the factors which explain why the German bourgeoisie of the early nineteenth century could in the long run accept neither the individualist activism of the young Fichte nor the reactionary philosophy of Schelling (a philosophy which presented itself as a conscious reaction against the French Revolution), or why this bourgeoisie which lived in the hope of a progress which it could not itself bring about found its ideological expression in that mixture of a progressive and revolutionary world-view with a reactionary apology for the Prussian state which constituted the Hegelian system. If, however, we ask what is still living and important for us in the thought of

Hegel, its importance seems to me to lie in having overcome the rigid separation between philosophy and empirical anthropology which still dominated the thought of Kant. Hegel consciously made the philosophy of history the decisive element in his system, and thus also incorporated in it the positive empirical sciences of sociology and history.

An even more important step on this road was taken in the work of Karl Marx. Marx was the first of the great thinkers of post-Kantian Germany to spend a large part of his life abroad, in Paris and London, and he was thus able to free himself from the limitations resulting from the specific historical conditions of the Germany of his time. Only with Marx does the union of philosophy with empirical sociology prepared by Hegel take on a truly scientific character.

After Marx, towards the end of the nineteenth century, a perceptible diminution in understanding and in the need felt for a coherent philosophical vision of man and of the universe took place not only in Germany but throughout the whole of European intellectual life. With the sole exception of Nietzsche, official philosophical thought was dominated by 'neo-Kantian' and 'neo-Hegelian' professors to whom can also be added many of those 'Marxists' concerned with philosophy and the history of ideas. It was then that innumerable commentators studied almost every line written by Kant and Hegel and interpreted them in every possible or imaginable way—a labour whose results are so paltry that it is difficult to decide which is the sadder, the incomprehension with which the works of most of the great German poets and thinkers were received by their contemporaries, or the conscious or unconscious impudence with which the *epigoni* trivialized, falsified and 'interpreted' them after their death.

Later, after the First World War, under the influence of the profound social, economic and cultural crisis of Europe, there developed the various forms of the philosophy of feeling, of intuition, of anguish and of despair, typified by the works of Henri Bergson, Martin Heidegger and Jean-Paul Sartre. This is not the place for an analysis of the causes or the consequences of their rise and of their success. (These causes and consequences are today in any case apparent.) What seems to me important, however, is that even before the war there had arisen in France a reaction against this psychosis of anguish and despair, a movement which found its most powerful expression in personalism, as developed around the journal *Esprit.* This had certainly not become a conscious philosophical world-view or a fully developed system. Its most important analyses were to be encountered in conversation with young people who in most cases had not yet published anything. Everything was in the course of development when war broke out. It is today impossible to evaluate philosophical developments over recent years, since the most important contributions may well not have been published.

After the philosophical silence of Georg Lukács which has already lasted for more than twenty years, personalism seems to me to have been the most important philosophical occurrence during the years immediately before the war. Of course, this French personalism sprang from traditions quite foreign to German humanism, and was scarcely aware of its affinity with it. It is thus all the more significant that it arrived spontaneously at the same questions, and indeed usually at similar answers. (pp. 223-28)

I have not the slightest desire to echo the oft-repeated slogan 'Back to Kant'. On the contrary, any going back seems to me a betrayal of the thought of a philosopher who made the future and not the past the centre of his system and who constantly repeated that he wished to teach his students not *a philosophy* but *how to think philosophically*. Our attention should be directed not towards the past, seeking to go 'back to Kant', but forwards towards a better human community; only then shall we be able to see the figure of Immanuel Kant in his true light, to see his living and real significance for the present and for the future. He will appear to us then as one of those great thinkers who took the first difficult steps through the wood and opened the way on which we still proceed. When we see things in this light and focus our attention on the future of the human community, then beside the immense figure of Immanuel Kant many a philosophical celebrity of recent years will fade into insignificance. For nothing deserves the name of philosophy which is not aimed at the liberation of man and the realization of a true community. (pp. 228-29)

> *Lucien Goldmann, in his* Immanuel Kant, *translated by Robert Black, NLB, 1971, 236 p.*

JULIUS EBBINGHAUS   (essay date 1948)

[*Ebbinghaus defends Kant's concept of the categorical imperative against various attacks by Kant's critics.*]

The concept connected by Kant with the phrase 'categorical imperative' seems easy to explain. It means a law valid for the will of every rational being and therefore valid unconditionally. This is in no need of interpretation: it can hardly be misinterpreted. Kant has stated it in the clearest and most intelligible terms. Understanding becomes much more difficult if we are concerned, not merely with the verbal definition, but with the content of the categorical command and with the inferences to be drawn from it. Even specialists have fallen into confusion about these questions and have, as it were, begun to see ghosts in quarters where reason prevails: but, quite apart from this, the doctrine of a categorical imperative inherent in the will of man himself appears at present to meet with most unexpected and most unwanted repercussions in the common opinion, not merely of Germany, but almost of the whole world. To lovers of humanity it may seem a lofty and worthy aim that doctrines elaborated by science and claiming to determine the conduct of every man should gradually spread wider and wider until at last every cottage is illuminated by the light this labour generates. But it also seems as if precisely this welcome process, which has gained greatly in intensity since the eighteenth century, has merely added one more to those evils of civilisation by which mankind is afflicted. When we argue with experts in our own subject, we can pretty well manage at least to be correctly understood and not to be saddled with conclusions in direct contradiction of our own thought; but we are, so to speak, robbed of all protection when matters of controversy among the learned are thrust, through the efforts of more or less unfriendly publicists, upon the wide masses of the educated or half-educated, are there passed from hand to hand, and are finally hurled into a sea of surging passion. This happens most of all when we are concerned with the propositions of a science which—like philosophy—is still having to *fight* for its existence so that attacks upon any doctrinal structure attempted in its name will never fail to find authorities prepared to back them. No matter how ludicrous men may consider the claim of philosophy as a guide to life, they are always ready, when they

have reduced their affairs to utter disorder, to listen to those who find its cause in some philosophy they dislike.

No one need be surprised if in the present miseries of the world voices are raised expressing all too clearly the view that the susceptibility to National Socialism displayed by wide ranges of the German people springs properly from that readiness for unconditioned obedience, that spirit of unconditioned sacrifice, which is undoubtedly demanded by Kant in his law of duty; or at least—not going quite so far—the view that Kant's law voices precisely that Prussian or German inclination for discipline and subjection, that readiness for harshness and rigour, that insensitiveness to all the gentler movements of the spirit, which celebrated their frightful triumphs in the years of Terror. 'All that is worthy of respect in me is my capacity to obey—and the same must hold for you as it does for me'. In these words Friedrich Nietzsche already gave utterance to an interpretation of Kant's ethics in which the above view is anticipated. The morality of the categorical imperative as the morality of the correct Prussian official, who regards his superiors as gods or demi-gods and disdains the pleasures of life as sour grapes—this is one of the travesties into which the greatest achievement in the field of ethics since Plato has been distorted by a sociological treatment that has lost its bearings.

• • • • •

If we turn its own methods upon this treatment itself, we discover behind it a tendency to interpret statements, not by the real necessities which led to them, but by some sort of assumed subjective motive. The law formulated by Kant in his categorical imperative is not one by which any principle whatever to which a man may find himself drawn under conditions of experience—such as obedience to potentates or abstention from the pleasures of life—can be imposed on him categorically. Kant's law is rather a way of expressing the conditions under which alone a principle can have the character of a categorical demand. The categorical imperative is thus conceived as the fundamental principle determining which possible principles can be objectively valid for the decisions of our will as such. When we say it is our duty to do something or to refrain from doing it, we manifestly have in mind such a categorical demand or such an objectively valid principle. Hence we can also say that on Kant's view the categorical imperative contains nothing but the concept of being under a possible moral obligation as such. If he was wrong in maintaining that such a command is binding upon our will, it is not to be inferred that duty must be determined by some other law; what it would mean is that there are no universally valid demands on human behaviour, so far as this depends on our will, and consequently that nothing whatever can be our duty and that we are entirely free to do whatever we may happen to want. We might indeed by acting in this way get entangled in all sorts of disagreeable consequences, or we might be astute enough to find means of escaping these disagreeable consequences; but what Kant maintains is this: The sum total of these means could never have the character of a system of precepts for the will such that men would be under an objective obligation to obey them; nor could a necessary harmony of these means be discovered (independently of a categorical imperative) such that it would be free from all possible conflict of the will with itself and with the will of others.

We can sum all this up in the proposition that the categorical imperative determines the concept of duty *solely as regards*

sonal interest, which he nowhere else recognises as a moral criterion, be all of a sudden taken here as decisive?' This is a repetition of John Stuart Mill's criticism—except that the forecast is reversed. Kant cannot possibly be free to appeal to personal interest (in happiness), says Simmel. He must inevitably appeal to happiness, says Mill, when he wants to come down to concrete events; and Mill's follower, Fr. Jodl (*Geschichte der Ethik,* II, 1889), repeats: 'In alleging reasons that make the universalisation of immoral maxims impossible, the decisive word in Kant's own exposition is kept for "empirically material" principles—not, however, the principle of general happiness, but rather of the most commonplace egoism'.

Do such principles really have the last word? The opinion that they do rests manifestly on Kant's argument that we cannot will hard-heartedness as a law because we should then rob ourselves of all hope of (possible) help even when we stood in need of it. Naturally, this can be a reason only for an agent to whom personal happiness is an end. But certainly it cannot be said that personal happiness *to the exclusion of the happiness of others* must be his end, and therefore that his interest in happiness must be a *selfish* interest if it is to prevent him from making his own possible need irremediable by a decision of his own will. What can be said is this. Whether he subordinates his whole interest to his own happiness as a supreme principle or considers also the happiness of others, he cannot possibly will, *so far as his happiness is an end for him,* to be abandoned in his need by all who could save him, and consequently he cannot will his own unhappiness. This is a purely analytic proposition: its truth is in no way affected by questions about the principle on which he acts. Hence Jodl's contention—that here 'the most commonplace egoism' has the decisive word—is false.

Nevertheless—it may be insisted—the whole business still leaves a disagreeable aftertaste. The reason why we cannot will hard-heartedness as a law is simply that we must be afraid of damaging ourselves if we do so. 'Here it is stated as plainly as can be', says Schopenhauer in his prize essay *Über die Grundlage der Moral,* 'that moral obligation rests entirely on a presupposed reciprocity. Hence it is completely egoistic and is to be understood as a form of egoism that prudently commits itself to a compromise on the condition of reciprocity'. If we abandon this condition and imagine a man who assumes (rightly or wrongly) that he will never get into a position where he is in need of help, such a man can perfectly well agree that everybody should act on the maxim of hard-heartedness. Admittedly, if a man is prepared to act on the maxim of kindness only so far as he can in this way purchase the kindness of others, and if he would immediately withdraw his assent to this maxim as soon as he believed himself immune from need—such a man would be an egoist. But if he wills kindness only under such reservations, can he be said to will it *as a law?* Obviously he will never once show kindness himself except in so far as readiness on the part of others to help him will be its outcome. This is precisely the 'reciprocity' that Schopenhauer has in mind; but he fails to notice that if a man shows kindness only on condition that others are kind to him, his maxim of kindness is such that, if it were made into a law, it would remove the possibility of kindness altogether. For if every one makes his kindness depend on another's being kind to him, it is obvious that there is no possibility of anyone being kind at all.

Equally astray is the contention that if we feel ourselves im-

mune from need, we can perfectly well will *the maxim of indifference* as a law. This maxim *as a law* would run as follows—Every one who feels himself immune from need may be deaf to the need of others. It is manifest that however immune from need we may imagine ourselves to be, we *cannot* will this law. The reason is that the universalised maxim of the hard-hearted, let him turn and twist as he will—and indeed every case in which no help is given to him—does not hold subject to the condition on which he agreed to do it, namely, that *he* should be immune from need. *Everybody* is authorised by the maxim to refuse help so far as he himself is immune from need—without regard to the position of the man to whom help is refused. Consequently a will which wills the maxim of hard-heartedness as a law necessarily contains in itself a will to be abandoned in the not absolutely impossible case of the agent's own need, and therefore it is a will in conflict with itself.

Naturally this is based on 'reciprocity'—not, however, as Schopenhauer thinks, on the arbitrarily arranged reciprocity of a deal in cattle, but on a situation entirely withdrawn from human choice, namely, that 'help' is a human relation with two terms: there is always one partner who gives help and another who receives it. Consequently nothing can alter the fact that if we lay down conditions for giving help, we also lay down conditions for receiving help. Hence if I wish the condition under which I can agree to the impossibility of receiving help to remain in force when my maxim about giving help is made universal, I must incorporate this condition in the maxim itself. The maxim will then take this form: I will never help any one who is immune from need. That such a maxim can be willed as a law without the slightest difficulty is certainly not a proposition that Kant would have been anxious to deny.

The series of fallacies into which Kant's critics fall again and again could never have been constructed but for a failure to observe that in a decisive passage in the ***Groundwork of the Metaphysic of Morals*** Kant has given the categorical imperative this form—Act only on that maxim *through* which you can at the same time will that it should become a universal law. The word 'through' has not only been disregarded: there has been such a failure to understand it that the patchwork theorists (to use a phrase coined by Professor Paton) have proposed to see in it a textual corruption and to cut it out. This would mean cutting out the very word that first gives the formula its greatest precision. You must be able to will the character of law 'through' the maxim; that is to say, the reason for the possibility of willing the maxim as a law must be found in the maxim itself—not in any external circumstances of the agent which are in no way determined by the maxim. If any one agrees to make the maxim of hard-heartedness universally valid merely because he believes himself to need no help, he makes the possibility of his agreement depend on circumstances which on their side are not determinable by his maxim. For in the principle 'Help yourself' there is no warrant for the ground on which he assents to the universality of the maxim—namely, that he should be free from the need of others' help. Thus he cannot will *through* his maxim that it should become a law; and consequently he cannot conform to the conditions laid down by Kant.

After all this what remains of the charge of egoism? All that remains is this—Kant rests his argument on the supposition that a man cannot in harmony with his own will choose to be abandoned in misfortune by those who could give him help. We have already said that this has nothing to do with egoism. If I have fallen into the water without being able to swim, and champion swimmers are all around me in lifeboats some twenty yards away, is my wish that they should pull me out to be explained only on the ground that I am an egoist— that is, a man who bothers about the need of others only when he can count on getting some advantage out of it for himself? And how is this to be distinguished in principle from any other arbitrary case where a man is in need of help and other people have the power to help him?

But—it will be said—Kant does insist that for the sake of a higher interest we must be prepared to make unlimited sacrifices of our own happiness. He undoubtedly does require this; but what he has certainly never claimed is that we must therefore be prepared to sacrifice our own happiness *as a possible end altogether.* This is precisely the claim he would have had to make if it were to be inferred from his principles that a man must be able to will his own abandonment in need. In that case the categorical imperative would have to forbid a man to make his own happiness an end. How could we possibly find a reason for any such prohibition? One's own happiness as an end is admittedly not the *ground* on which a will can be in law-abiding harmony with itself and with the will of all others; but it does not follow that *by having this end* the will is split in such a way that there could never be any conditions under which the maxim of making one's happiness an end might be willed as a law. If we wanted to take the contrary view, we should have to be able to say that man can make his own happiness an end only by reference to the unhappiness of others or even of himself—only if he is made unhappy by the happiness of others or perhaps by his own happiness at some past or future time. Under special conditions something like this may perhaps actually happen. But no one can say that this is among the universal and necessary conditions of human happiness as such. And consequently we cannot say that the categorical imperative forbids us to make our own happiness an end. We are therefore in error if we take Kant's statement—that a man cannot will his own unhappiness—to be false on the ground that on Kant's own principles a man ought never to make happiness his end and consequently that on these same principles he must be able to will his own unhappiness.

Not only does Kant's statement not contradict the categorical imperative: it is in itself completely justified. Man cannot renounce happiness altogether as a possible end: to have or not to have this end in no way depends on his own choice. Nature forces this end upon him as soon as he begins to have ends at all. We cannot even conceive beyond this end any further motive which might induce him to make this end his own. This is why Aristotle declared happiness to be the final end of man; and he was perfectly right as long as we look for ends only within the bounds of experience. This amounts to saying that the categorical imperative does not prescribe this end to man—at least not directly. But no more does the categorical imperative prevent me—as has just been shown— from treating this end as one which is naturally common to all human beings. The categorical imperative *abstracts from all ends* because, in deriving from it an absolute demand as such, I cannot rest my case on any end that I presuppose; but this does not mean that the categorical imperative demands a will *that has no ends at all* and so wills nothing. It abstracts from all ends—that is, in the present case, it does not say with the utilitarians: 'You must help others in need because by this you will promote your own happiness'. Rather it says: 'You

must help them, whether this promotes your own happiness or not, since to will the maxim of indifference as a law is in contradiction with your inevitable and permissible end, namely, to receive help from them'. When therefore the empiricist E. Becher asserts that if there is no question of consequences, I can will any arbitrary maxim whatever as a law, he must be told that he is a victim of the loose expression 'there is (for Kant) no question of consequences'. If we make this expression precise, it runs as follows: In deciding the unlawfulness of the maxim 'Never help any one in need' there is no question of consequences so far as these concern the *possibility of attaining my own happiness as an end* if this maxim is followed by myself and others. But in coming to this decision there is indeed a question of consequences so far as these concern the possibility *of taking my own happiness,* and consequently my own rescue in distress, *as an end,* if I will the maxim of hard-heartedness as a law. Inability to distinguish these two points of view is the secret—to use the language of John Stuart Mill—of the almost grotesque failure of those who have attempted to criticise Kant's deductions of particular moral duties. The reason why I cannot will the maxim of indifference as a law is not that by so doing I should stand in the way of my own happiness. Whether my chance of happiness will be improved or impaired by freeing every one, and consequently myself, from all obligation to help others depends on circumstances about which there can never be any *a priori* decision. But I can indeed decide *a priori,* as in the case of every analytic truth, that if my will includes a will to be left without help in need, I cannot possibly take happiness as my end and consequently must be able to will my own unhappiness.

With the help of this analysis we must try to penetrate a little more deeply into the seemingly paradoxical mechanism which makes it possible for a will to fall into contradiction with itself by willing that a maxim it can have should be a law. The decisive consideration here is obviously that the will is viewed in a situation where the object of its volition can itself be a volition. I do will my own happiness—there is no further problem in that. I *can,* secondly, will the happiness of others. But, in the third place, in willing my own happiness, I also will on the principle that others should will my happiness. Now if on my side I do *not* will the happiness of others, I cannot (without willing contrary to my own volition) will that my maxim should be acted on by others, and consequently I cannot will that it should be a law. Hence if the categorical imperative is valid, there follows from it *as a definite command* of duty that I must include within my end of happiness the happiness of others.

With this we conclude our discussion of one *example* by which Kant has illustrated the possibility of deriving particular precepts from the categorical imperative. I cannot hope that this discussion will be enough to show in a new light the world-wide practice of talking as if philosophy were not in a position to tell men quite precisely what they ought to do and ought not to do. But perhaps it will be enough to raise doubts about the reliability of those who want to dismiss Kant's moral philosophy and its categorical imperative as a *causa judicata.*

If this is the situation, would it not be better to refrain from dragging questions of philosophy into regions where there may enter even a stray breath of political passion? When Dewey imagined he could find in Kant's moral philosophy a preparation for those outrages against the rights of man by which a crazy political movement has shocked the whole world, he failed to observe that he was talking about Kant exactly as the Janizaries of the tyrant had also talked. So far as I am concerned, I do not think it the function of philosophy to engage directly in man's battle for the rule of law. All that philosophy can do is to bring the struggle of opinions to a theoretical agreement on rational grounds. Even so, the service it renders to mankind is beyond price; for there can be no assurance of a possible peace among men so long as the division of opinion on ultimate matters cannot be settled. Such a settlement is possible only if those who come to these affairs with reasons can have their reasons heard. The task I had set myself was to make it plain that as regards the reasons Kant puts forward in his doctrine of duty he has not been adequately heard and has not been understood at all. (pp. 211-27)

> *Julius Ebbinghaus, "Interpretation and Misinterpretation of the Categorical Imperative," in his* Kant: A Collection of Critical Essays, *edited by Robert Paul Wolff, Anchor Books, 1967, pp. 211-27.*

LEWIS WHITE BECK (essay date 1949)

[*Beck is an American scholar of German philosophy who has edited and translated many of Kant's principal works for English-speaking audiences. Here, Beck affirms Kant's ability to reconcile the prerogatives of science with humanistic interests in the* Critique of Pure Reason.]

There is a saying among philosophers, "You can philosophize with Kant or against Kant, but you cannot philosophize without him." Much truth lies in this adage, even though few thinkers today would call themselves Kantians without much redefinition and qualification. Nor is its truth greatly diminished by the fact that idealism, as it developed from Kant's philosophy, has been on the defensive for nearly a century. But, inasmuch as Kant saw more clearly than anyone else the ultimate problem of modern thought, and devoted to its solution the greatest philosophical genius of modern times, any thinker who ignores Kant proceeds at unnecessary risk.

The ultimate issue which Kant faced consists in the logical incompatability between the objective and subjective conditions of scientific knowledge. It is the disharmony between the object of science and the human ends it is made to serve. In the Renaissance, after Galilei, Descartes, and Newton had banished purpose from nature, nature came to be seen as a vast mechanism. With the replacement of Aristotelian ideas by mechanistic conceptions, science began to achieve unprecedented control over nature. A similar change of viewpoint in Hobbes, Spinoza, and Harvey with regard to man's own body and mind opened the way for analogous advances in the control of man.

But control for what? It is man who develops science and who through it controls nature for his own purposes. There lies the paradox: man is understood as a machine, but the use of his knowledge of himself and of the external world is thoroughly purposive. The problem is more urgent than any other in modern philosophy because the two incompatible convictions—the idea of the world as a vast impersonal order and the idea of knowledge as power—are fundamental to our world view and equally deep-rooted. To the extent that Western civilization is based on science, it rests on a paradox.

Philosophers before Kant who were aware of this problem at-

tempted to solve it in a variety of ways, and many who were not explicitly conscious of its full implications nevertheless developed philosophies which even now sometimes serve as frameworks for attempted solutions. These ventures involved one of four strategies:

> 1. The problem was denied by exempting man from the laws of nature through *ad hoc* hypotheses (Descartes, many orthodox Christian philosophers).
>
> 2. The problem was declared irresolvable and transferred to a higher court of faith (Malebranche, sometimes Descartes, and many orthodox Christian philosophers).
>
> 3. The problem was declared illusory because purpose is not ultimate even in man (Spinoza and Hobbes).
>
> 4. The problem was declared illusory because mechanism is not ultimate even in nature (Leibniz and Berkeley).

All these strategies have one failing in common. Each allays the conflict only by weakening one or both of the contending forces. None of them accepts with "natural piety" the competing claims of man as knower and agent and of nature (including man) as known and mechanical.

Kant's consummate greatness as a thinker is nowhere shown more indubitably than in his acceptance of both knower and known as facts not to be compromised. Though in his philosophy there are elements of each of these four inadequate attempts, they are integrated into a new philosophy which does justice to their antagonistic demands.

In the eighteenth century, the Age of Enlightenment, the main stream of thought was guided by a faith in human reason. It was intellectualistic in its attitude toward revelation and tradition and skeptical of things irrational; it was little interested in the past and exceedingly optimistic about the future.

Kant was in many respects an exemplary philosopher of the Enlightenment. His ***What Is Enlightenment?*** is a document of much diagnostic value to the historian of ideas. Yet he was also the nemesis of Enlightenment as a historical epoch. More than any other philosopher, he placed limits on knowledge without falling into the irrationalism of the forerunners of Romanticism. He exposed the superficiality of the humanistic and intellectualistic optimism of the time without becoming an apologist for the past.

Together with Hume and Rousseau, he subjected current ideas to a searching examination and found them wanting. Hume's demonstration of the nonintellectual foundations of science and Rousseau's nullification of contemporary institutions prepared the way for fundamental changes. These two critics, however, did not constructively replace what they had rejected. Hume was finally left with only a contemplative skepticism, which Kant turned into a justification of science; Rousseau prepared men's minds for the Revolution, but it was Kant's deepening of Rousseau's criticism of law imposed from above that gave philosophical dignity to *liberté, egalité, fraternité.* Indeed, George Herbert Mead, in his *Movements of Thought in the Nineteenth Century,* gave to Kant the title usually reserved for Rousseau, "the philosopher of the Revolution."

This dual relationship of Kant's thinking to Enlightenment

can best be accounted for by his two dominant interests—by his interest in natural science and by his religious allegiance.

More than any other philosopher of the period except perhaps Leibniz, Kant was attentive to the results of the scientific exploration of nature. Even when placing restrictions on science, he seems always to have thought as a scientist. His earliest works were purely scientific in character, and the number of times he compares his procedure to that of the scientist is remarkable. The *Critique of Pure Reason* is a criticism of the metaphysical claims of science, but it is also a defense of it against its internal enemies.

The counterweight to science in Kant's thought is religion. Pietism, an anticlerical movement founded by Spener in the seventeenth century, emphasized the religious and moral responsibility of the individual, the directness of his contact with God, and the importance of good works and quiet faith over ritual and dogma. This religious attitude was instilled into young Kant by his Pietistic parents. But at the same time he learned to dislike the externalized type of Pietism with which he became painfully acquainted in school. Much of his later religious and ethical thought can be understood as a revolt against the externalized and formal Pietism of the Collegium Fridericianum as well as a defense of the sturdy and unpretentious devotion of his family.

For a proper appreciation of Kant's historical position it is necessary to understand his relation not only to these dominant cultural factors but also to four previous philosophies—the rationalism of the Leibniz-Wolff school, German "popular philosophy," British psychological ethics, and the unclassifiable philosophy of Rousseau.

Kant's philosophical training was that of a Wolffian. Christian Wolff, professor of philosophy in the University of Halle, had developed the rationalism of Leibniz into an elaborate and comprehensive system of ideas. Although Kant was almost never an encyclopedic systematizer in Wolff's manner, his formalistic emphasis is undoubtedly in part attributable to his training. Much of his terminology is derived from textbooks of the Wolffian school, regularly used by him for his own lectures. His marginalia to the textbooks of Alexander Baumgarten, a leading Wolffian, are important sources of information on Kant's development.

However, the substance of Kant's philosophy differs widely from that of Wolff. The *Inquiry* of 1764 renounces the Wolffian method of synthesis, and the *Dissertation* of 1770 restricts the scope of metaphysics as conceived by Wolff. It is this kind of metaphysics which is repudiated in the first *Critique.* In ethics Kant rejects the empty formalism, the perfectionistic ideal, and the utilitarian basis of Wolff's system.

The followers of Wolff, the so-called "academic philosophers," were opposed by the "popular philosophers" who rejected the logical rigor of the academic philosophy. Though some of them, influenced by the "encyclopedic" tradition, retained elements of rationalistic metaphysics, they generally preferred appeals to feeling, common sense, and "sound human reason" as criteria of truth. Through their eclecticism and their uncritical enthusiasm for progress and enlightenment, they gained acclaim and popular following. Windelband correctly remarks that the emptier and more superficial their metaphysics became, the greater the role they ascribed to utility; and, as a result, they fell into "the most jejune philistinism and sensible, prosaic commonplace." Kant, especially in the second part of the *Foundations* and in *What Is Orientation in Thinking?* opposed this group even more vigorously than the Wolffians did.

British psychological moralists appealed so greatly to Kant that he has often been regarded as their disciple. But his early acceptance of their theories was not that of a disciple, and the changes he introduced were of central significance. His later rejection of their theory of moral sense and his radically new orientation to moral feeling are apparent throughout the ethical works of the critical period. Kant's relation to Shaftesbury and Hutcheson is somewhat like that of Socrates to the Sophists. Both the British moralists and Kant based their ethics on human nature. But Kant, like Socrates, searched for the essential character of man's nature, a universal law determining its particular manifestations. In the announcement of his lectures for the winter semester of 1765-66, he says this explicitly:

> I shall make distinct the method by which man must be studied, not just man as he is distorted by the variable form which his chance condition impresses upon him and as he has almost always been misjudged even by philosophers, but rather the abiding nature of man and its unique position in creation. . . .

This "abiding nature of man," differently conceived, becomes the central topic in Kant's later ethical works.

The philosopher who had the greatest influence on Kant's ethics was undoubtedly Rousseau. Kant's admiration for Rousseau is most clearly expressed in unpublished fragments in which he speaks of Rousseau's "noble sweep of genius" and of the beauty of the style as so disturbing that he has to read him a long time before he can be reasonable in his approach. According to a well-known anecdote, Kant missed his customary walk on the day *Émile* arrived. Although the published writings on moral philosophy mention Rousseau only a few times, and in the works in the broader field of social philosophy explicit references to him are generally somewhat critical, Rousseau's influence on Kant is obvious.

Hendel finds the dominant motifs of Rousseau's philosophy and life in the "ideas of obligation, contract, equality, freedom." These are likewise central in Kant. For both, the social contract is not a historical fact but a principle of justification, a political postulate. Freedom for both is not just political freedom but a symptom of reason's dominance and, as such, inseparable from moral obligation. Rousseau describes immoral action as a violation of the contract by which the individual is bound to the whole. Immoral action restricts equality by partiality, and it is possible because reason does not free man from the importunities of the senses. The will which engenders moral actions must be independent of personal contingencies. This, for Kant, is the good will, and it is clearly anticipated in Rousseau's general will.

These two analogous concepts reveal at the same time a marked difference in point of view. For Rousseau, the general will is a political ideal which is to serve as a check upon the will of the majority. This ideal underlies the original contract itself, and from it all positive laws derive their justification. In its capacity as the ultimate legal norm, the general will corresponds to "the right" in Kant's philosophy, to which all positive laws must be accommodated. But the good will has a far wider competence than the general will, and this wider competence befits its higher metaphysical status as a fact of pure reason. It is the direct evidence for and the sole condition of morality. Its expression is the categorical imperative and (in politics) the criterion of publicity.

Each of these points of agreement between Rousseau and Kant involves both the universality neglected by British moralists and the concreteness lacking in Wolff's universals. Rousseau sought to discover man's nature by historical analysis. As Kant says, he did not so much wish that man should return to the state of nature as that, from his present position, he should look back upon his natural condition as a means of discovering in himself the universal—the essence of what he is, apart from the various distortions introduced by society. In this way Rousseau succeeded at the precise point where Kant had found Hutcheson and Shaftesbury wanting:

> Among the multitude of forms assumed by man, Rousseau first discovered man's deeply hidden nature and the concealed law by the observation of which providence is justified. . . . God is justified by Newton and Rousseau, and more than ever is Pope's thesis true.

Kant's indebtedness to Rousseau is best stated in a fragment probably dating from the sixties:

> By inclination I am an inquirer. I feel a consuming thirst for knowledge, the unrest which goes with the desire to progress in it, and satisfaction at every advance in it. There was a time when I believed this constituted the honor of humanity, and I despised the people, who know nothing. Rousseau corrected me in this. This blinding prejudice disappeared. I learned to honor man, and I would find myself more useless than the common laborer if I did not believe that this attitude of mine [as an investigator] can give a worth to all others in establishing the rights of mankind.

In this fragment Kant reflects Rousseau's conviction of the superiority of uncorrupted natural feeling over vain pride of intellect, his pessimism concerning progress through enlightenment, and his faith in democracy founded upon moral egalitarianism. It also foreshadows Kant's doctrines of the limits of human reason. The idea of limits of human reason is to be interpreted morally as the primacy of practical reason, a possession of all men and not just of the enlightened few.

From the concept of the limits of human reason—fully developed only twenty years later—flows the philosophical justification for the other views Kant shared with Rousseau. First among these is the moral argument for the existence of God anticipated in *Émile*. In order to voice his protest against contemporary naturalism, Rousseau, lacking speculative power, had to fall back on personal faith. Kant, by formulating and defending a metaphysics that was both a priori and practical, developed Rousseau's insight into an indispensable part of his own more critical philosophy.

In the 1760's, when Kant was studying Hutcheson and Rousseau, he was working on what he intended to be his definitive treatise on ethics, which, with characteristic optimism in matters of authorship, he expected soon to finish. From the fragments that have come down to us we might reasonably suppose that it would apply the method of the *Inquiry,* searching out by analysis the hidden nature of man of which he speaks in the announcement of his lectures for 1765-66. We might expect that the projected work would emphasize the indemonstrability of the ultimate principles of ethics and would support them by arguments not unlike those found in Hutcheson and Rousseau. Or Kant might have developed a speculative metaphysics, also in the manner of the *Inquiry,* which would provide a context for the more empirical ethics.

But something unexpected happened. Kant read Hume, and, before he could go forward with his ethical works, ultimate questions had to be answered. The competence of reason had been radically questioned, and, before the mind could enjoy the luxury of metaphysics, or the security of rational certainty in science or of moral certainty in religion, reason's authority in experience and science's relation to the spirit had to be determined. Only upon a basis so secured would it be possible to found an ethics more than merely edifying. The result of this fundamental investigation was the *Critique of Pure Reason.*

The explicit task of Kant's first *Critique* was to answer the question—restated in more exact terms—which had occupied him in the *Inquiry* of 1764: "How are synthetic judgments a priori possible?" Since all rational knowledge consists of a priori synthetic judgments, failure to answer this question could not but affect every department of thought.

A synthetic judgment is one whose predicate is not contained in the concept of its subject. It *synthesizes* diverse elements into one proposition. For instance, "This table is of oak" is a synthetic judgment, while "This table is a piece of furniture" is analytic, because we find the predicate of the latter by merely analyzing the concept of table.

An a priori judgment is one which applies to all possible experience of a relevant kind without being derived from any particular experience. If a judgment is derived from particular experiences, i.e., if it is a posteriori, we cannot know that it is universally and necessarily true. Now, since mathematics and natural science make statements which we accept as being universally true, their validity cannot be derived from experiences, however often repeated.

All this was well known to Kant's predecessors in the rationalistic school. But Kant discovered that the basic propositions in these fields of knowledge were both synthetic—going beyond the subject—and a priori—requiring no experience to amplify the concept of the subject. Before Kant, "a priori synthetic judgment" would have been considered a *contradictio in adjecto*. If a judgment was synthetic, experience seemed necessary to lead us beyond the concept of its subject. In order to find out what predicate not included actually qualifies it, the object denoted by the subject of the proposition would have to be given in perception. That is to say, a synthetic proposition would have to be an empirical, an a posteriori, proposition.

On the other hand, if a judgment was a priori, it was thought that it had to be analytic, for only by analysis of a given concept could a judgment be made which did not require experience. Thus the rationalistic philosophers who emphasized reason's faculty of reaching true conclusions without sense experience were forced to the conclusion that all final knowledge is analytic.

Kant, originally trained in the rationalistic philosophy of Wolff and himself an able practicing mathematician, only gradually perceived the inadequacies of this view. In the *Inquiry* of 1764 he saw the divergence between mathematical and metaphysical knowledge and made the first hesitant step toward coming to terms with empiricism. In the *Dissertation* of 1770 he discovered that mathematics—the paradigm of rationalistic certainty—was concerned only with appearances.

This was a radical change of view which foreshadowed the further retrenchment of speculation in the *Critique of Pure Reason* eleven years later.

Probably it was only after Kant had begun what might be called his own "palace revolution" within rationalism that he came to know of Hume's work. Hume awoke him from his "dogmatic slumber"—Kant's term for his early faith in the power of reason to give metaphysical knowledge. Yet even if he had not accepted Hume's argument against the possibility of metaphysics, it is probable that Hume's strictures on natural science would have aroused him. For both rationalism and empiricism, if carried to the ultimate, deny the necessity and universality of natural science, and Kant's conviction of the certainty of Newtonian mechanics was too deep to be shaken by any negative conclusions drawn from speculations concerning the human mind. Kant asked *how* synthetic judgments a priori are possible, but *that* they are possible he never seems to have questioned. Instead, he revised the principles of both rationalism and empiricism in the light of a hard fact to which these two schools had not given due regard—the validity and certainty of the synthetic judgments of geometry and physics.

This revision Kant made in his well-known "Copernican Revolution." In a famous passage in the Preface to the second edition of the *Critique of Pure Reason,* Kant compares his new epistemology to the Copernican hypothesis. The predecessors of Copernicus had had difficulty in explaining the apparent motions of the planets on the supposition that they all revolved around the earth. Before Kant, it was similarly impossible in philosophy to explain how there could be a priori knowledge of things on the assumption that knowledge is passive conformity to the object. "Failing of satisfactory progress in explaining the movements of the heavenly bodies on the supposition that they all revolved round the spectator," Kant says, "he [Copernicus] tried whether he might not have better success if he made the spectator to revolve and the stars to remain at rest." Similarly, if the phenomenal characteristics of objects are explained in terms of the behavior of the knowing mind, it is possible to see how knowledge of them can be a priori, for, as objects of knowledge, they must conform to the structure and activity of the knowing mind which make knowledge possible.

One advantage claimed for the rationalistic method lay in the fact that, whereas empiricism had to stop at the limits of sense experience, rationalism was perhaps even more fruitful beyond these boundaries. Under the influence of Hume's criticism of causation, Kant discovered that the rationalistic method accomplished too much: it not only proved theses which transcended possible experience; with equal cogency it proved their antitheses too. The discovery of these antinomies (i.e., conflicts of principles) was the true beginning of Kant's new philosophical development. The antinomies arise from the inadequacy of reason to meet its own demands on thought. Let us see how these antinomies result from the diversity of our cognitive faculties and what they imply concerning the limits of knowledge.

The mind has three cognitive faculties: sensibility, understanding, and reason. Sensibility supplies empirical content or sensation. Understanding links sensations into perceptions and these into objects of knowledge and series of objective events. Sensibility and understanding supply us with a constellation of phenomena under laws; the experience formed by them is empirical nature. Nature comprises series of phenomena in space and time, and these series can and indeed must be infinitely extendable, for every phenomenon has other phenomena as its conditions. There is, in sensibility and understanding and in the world of experience they underlie, no way to arrest this infinite regress of conditions. Reason, however, demands a totality of these conditions, for otherwise all is contingent. This demand cannot be met by a faculty which, like understanding, merely seeks out proximate causes, and proximate causes of proximate causes, and so on. Extending the phenomenal series infinitely (in the antitheses of the four antinomies) is met by the demonstration (in the theses) that the extension under the rules of understanding is inadequate to reason's needs; and, if reason is to reach satisfaction, it must speculate *beyond any possible experience* to find the unconditioned.

In this speculation, reason negates the restriction of the categories to the world of possible experience. A category and its schema are *constitutive* of nature, for nature is simply phenomena under the laws of understanding; but the object of speculation cannot be in time, and therefore the schemata of the categories do not apply to it. It cannot be in time, for then it would be conditioned in an infinite regress; but, as it is not in time, the categories cannot *constitute* it. In spite of this, the categories control our thought about it and are consequently in this function called *regulative ideas.* If the difference between the constitutive categories and the regulative ideas is overlooked, the antinomies cannot be resolved. The rationalistic philosophers had not drawn this distinction, and therefore their speculative metaphysics was ripe for the Kantian critique, which really commences with the demonstration of the antinomies.

While the Copernican Revolution alone might have strengthened Kant's predisposition toward rationalism, discovery of the antinomies showed this philosophy to be inadequate at its crucial point. The Copernican Revolution is a confession that the object is not the determining factor in knowledge; the natural dialectic of reason is proof that speculative theory is not the determining feature in metaphysics. If the object determined knowledge, a priori knowledge would be impossible, and scientific knowledge would be out of the question. If theoretical reason were the only faculty, a true and adequate metaphysics would be impossible, and the supersensuous world would be a mere extension of the world of appearances. And, if this were the true state of affairs, morality would be impossible. For morality, Kant argues, makes demands on men as free agents—demands at variance with the mechanistic world picture of science. It makes demands conflicting a fortiori with a supersensuous world conceived of as a mere extension of nature. The antinomies show that this extension is impossible, and for that reason Kant regarded them as the "most fortunate perplexity" into which pure reason could ever fall.

The antinomies strictly limit theoretical reason to the world of space and time, nullifying all speculative flights from the results of science and all attempts to use scientific method in speculation beyond the limits of sense. But their resolution permits an altogether different use of reason. The occurrence of the antinomies is indicative of reason's broader competence as a faculty not exclusively devoted to cognition.

This is very clear in the third antinomy, the one most directly concerned with ethics. This antinomy arises from the conflict in the idea of causality and is resolved by the distinction between the world of appearances and that of things as they are in themselves. Kant made the discovery that the thesis, which asserts the reality of nonmechanical causes, and its antithesis, which asserts the sufficiency of natural causality, may each be true if their respective scopes are sharply distinguished.

The field of application of each is defined by the nature of the argument supporting it, and neither can be validly employed beyond the area to which the respective proofs extend. The proof of the thesis presents the claim of reason, which requires a sufficient cause of every phenomenon. This sufficient cause cannot be found within phenomena, because a phenomenal cause is the effect of prior events and hence not by itself a sufficient explanation of subsequent phenomena. The proof of the antithesis, on the other hand, represents the interest of the understanding in applying the law of causality to a series of events in time. The argument shows that the assumption of a free cause among phenomena would interrupt the continuity required by natural law. There is no contradiction, however, when the thesis is applied to the relationship between noumena (things-in-themselves) and phenomena (appearances) and the antithesis to relations among phenomena. These separate and distinct but compatible applications are all that is legitimized by these two proofs.

The solution to the third antinomy, therefore, is achieved through a distinction between the world of appearance and the world of supersensuous reality. *This dualism is the necessary presupposition of Kant's ethical theory.* Without it, science would be the only occupation of reason. With it, science is limited in two respects: a boundary is fixed beyond which scientific knowledge cannot aspire and the possibility is established that natural law may not be the only form of causality.

First, by rejecting the presumptions of theoretical reason to a scientific metaphysics, a practical extension of pure reason is made possible. "I have therefore found it necessary," Kant says, "to deny *knowledge,* in order to make room for *faith.* The dogmatism of metaphysics . . . is the source of all that unbelief, always very dogmatic, which wars against morality."

The limitation he places upon theory may be taken negatively or affirmatively, with respect to what it forbids or what it permits. Negatively, it means that reason is incapable of knowledge of God, freedom, and immortality. Regarded in isolation, this stricture has been the occasion of positivistic and fictionalistic interpretations of Kant—the belief that reason's true vocation is found in knowledge and that whatever is assumed in the light of practical demands is fictional and subjective. Yet such interpretations are in complete discord both with the general character of Kant's philosophy and with his personality as a man of deep faith.

In his ethical and religious works, however, the affirmative interpretation—the emphasis on "making room for faith" instead of on "denying knowledge"—is of more central importance. Morality, even in the *Critique of Pure Reason,* is a given fact whose necessity and universality require legitimation just as the apriority of science does. The denial of the possibility of knowledge is not a reluctant admission of reason's impotence but an expression of the moral injunction that we *ought not* to know. Knowledge of the intelligible world would destroy the possibility of free actions and of the faith that moral demands can be met. Thus instead of providing us in a "stepmotherly fashion with a faculty needed for our end," "inscrutable wisdom is not less worthy of veneration in respect to what it denies us than in what it has granted

to us," for only through our theoretical ignorance of our destiny is there proper scope for our practical faith.

The second way in which science is limited is by defending a causality not under natural law. The resolution of the antinomy of causality is necessary for Kant's ethics, for the antithesis, which implies the impossibility of morality, is the inevitable consequence to which theoretical understanding, unrestrained by criticism, leads us. Indeed, Kant says that, if the antinomy could not be resolved, it would be morality and not nature that we should have to surrender. With the demonstration that natural causality is not the only thinkable kind of causality, Kant voided the chief argument against freedom; but this refutation is not by itself enough to establish freedom. The reality of freedom must be shown by indicating it as a necessary a priori condition of a type of experience. In this case the experience to be considered is morality with its universal and necessary injunctions. Morality must be defended against subversive empiricism in the same way mathematics and physics were defended.

This mode of arguing for freedom as the *ratio essendi* of morality is in its turn a Copernican Revolution in ethics. There is a perfect parallelism between the mode of argument and the conclusions in the theoretical and practical phases of Kant's philosophy. In both, reason appears as the lawgiver and as bound by the laws which it gives. Kant clearly compares these two legislative functions: "The legislation of human reason (philosophy) has two objects, nature and freedom, and therefore contains not only the law of nature, but also the moral law, presenting them at first in two distinct systems, but ultimately in one single philosophical system. The philosophy of nature deals with all *that is,* the philosophy of morals with that which *ought to be.*"

Apriority of knowledge can be maintained only by rooting it in understanding; apriority of duty can be preserved only by basing it on an equally pure, but acting, reason. Just as empiricism in epistemology destroys certainty, so empiricism in morality destroys its obligatory character. Any ethics deriving from the idea of the good as happiness dislodges the person from his autonomous position as legislator and destroys both the dignity of the agent and the necessity inherent in moral law.

Hence, in order to justify the phenomenon of moral necessitation, moral will must be identified with pure but practical reason. This pure reason is the same reason that was discovered in the *Critique of Pure Reason,* but it is here acting in a different capacity. It is no longer theoretical, no longer loses itself in transcendent speculation. Only in action can it be adequately manifested. The ideas of reason remain transcendent and problematical to thought, while in action they are concretely effective. Kant says that in the "ought" reason "frames to itself with perfect spontaneity an order of its own according to ideas." Caird has succinctly stated the continuity and difference between the two functions of reason: "Just because reason cannot find its ideal realized in the world, it seeks to realize that ideal for itself."

Not only does the first *Critique* thus erect the framework in which all Kant's subsequent thought naturally fits, but there are several clear indications in it of the specific ethical theses developed later. In 1781 Kant had already passed beyond the moral doctrines of the precritical period, though this transition was a gradual evolution rather than a radical change.

The following specific ethical doctrines are anticipated in the first *Critique:*

1. Moral laws are principles of the possibility of experience, the imperatives being objective laws of freedom.

2. The laws of morality are not empirical and prudential, i.e., they do not show how happiness is obtained, but they contain the a priori conditions of worthiness to be happy. This worthiness, unlike happiness itself, necessarily constitutes a system, a "*corpus mysticum* of the rational beings in it [the world]."

3. The highest good, defined as the proper proportion between happiness and virtue, gives practical confirmation to other ideas that were only problematical to speculative reason, viz., the existence of God and the immortality of the soul. The way in which immortality is postulated in the first *Critique* should be particularly noted: happiness and virtue do not correspond in this life, though reason demands that they should; hence there must be another life. In the second *Critique,* however, the argument is more strictly moral: we are required by moral law to be perfect, and, as this is impossible for a finite sensuous being, a continuation of moral progress *in infinitum* is postulated—a consequence of Kant's view that an obligation is invalid unless it can be fulfilled. (pp. 1-16)

> *Lewis White Beck, in an introduction to* Critique of Practical Reason and Other Writings in Moral Philosophy *by Immanuel Kant, edited and translated by Lewis White Beck, The University of Chicago Press, 1949, pp. 1-49.*

GEORGE SCHRADER (essay date 1949)

[*Schrader argues that Kant's inability to arrive at a single definition for the concept of the "thing-in-itself" results in a number of logical contradictions in his philosophy.*]

The charge has often been made against Kant that it is meaningless to talk about an unknowable thing-in-itself. If the thing-in-itself is totally unknown and intrinsically unknowable, it cannot be known that it exists. One may posit the thing-in-itself as the cause of appearances which are known, but then one is guilty of extending the category of causality beyond the realm of appearances, a procedure which he had explicitly repudiated. The validity of the thing-in-itself for the critical philosophy cannot depend upon its being posited as a separate and distinct entity which stands in the relation of cause to phenomena. Only if the thing-in-itself is also the thing which appears, is Kant's position consistent and defensible.

So far as his critical employment of the concept is concerned, the thing-in-itself is *not* a second object. The thing-in-itself is given in its appearances; it *is* the object which appears. In other words, the object is taken in a twofold sense. There is no contradiction, Kant maintained, in supposing that one and the same will is, as an appearance, determined by the laws of nature and yet, as a thing-in-itself, is free. He never meant to hold that the self of the theoretical reason and the self of the practical reason are two separate and distinct entities. It is one and the same object considered from two perspectives. In this sense the thing-in-itself is purely a limiting concept. So far as the critical method is concerned, objects are always considered from a particular and *limited* perspective, e.g. science, morality, art, et cetera. This is the central

meaning of his theory of appearances. In this employment of the concept it is completely meaningless to speak of the thing-in-itself as a *cause* of appearances. The critical distinction between appearances and things in themselves is not intended to be a distinction between subjective sense data and public objects, but between public objects as given according to two or more modes. This involves no extension of the category of causality beyond appearances. Moreover, it is not open to the charge that an unknown object is given the attribute of existence. The thing-in-itself is *known* as an appearance. By definition that is the only way that it could be known. To say that we know only appearances and not things in themselves is to state an obvious tautology, namely that objects are known only as they are known.

This is, I am convinced, the critical meaning of the concept of the thing-in-itself; yet Kant employs it in quite another way. He sometimes refers to the thing-in-itself as the cause of appearances. On this view appearances are regarded as subjective sense data and things in themselves as independent objects, stripped of all primary and secondary qualities. It is obvious that on this basis the thing-in-itself is a superfluous and meaningless entity. If Kant were to make his critical theory consistent with this exposition, it would be necessary for him to abandon the concept of the thing-in-itself altogether. It is this employment of the concept of the thing-in-itself to establish the existence of unknowable objects which has occasioned so much criticism of Kant's position.

Whatever interpretation of Kant's theory is advanced, it is evident that the concept of the thing-in-itself as the cause of appearances has nothing whatever in common with his critical distinction between appearances and things in themselves. This twofold employment of the thing-in-itself represents one of the fundamental inconsistencies in the *Critique of Pure Reason.* Kant was apparently unaware of the inconsistency even as he effected a revision of the first edition of the *Critique.* If one considers Kant's private views, it is not difficult to understand the reason for this inconsistency. In his private views, he was a confirmed realist throughout the critical period. Apparently he could not resist the temptation to offer a defence of realism, and employed the concept of the thing-in-itself to that end. However, this represents a dogmatic employment of the concept. Such passages must be dismissed as reflecting Kant's private views, but as of little significance for his critical position. In concerning himself with the problem of the perception of objects he was dealing with a secondary problem that is not at all essential to his critical objective. This was the sort of problem which had occupied Locke and Berkeley but which Kant had deliberately avoided. Objectivity does not depend, on Kant's analysis, upon the independent existence of unperceivable entities.

The seriousness of Kant's inconsistency is easily seen when one recognises that, on a critical basis, it is only appearances which are objects. In his references to the thing-in-itself as a cause of appearances, Kant reverses himself, regarding appearances as subjective and the thing-in-itself as the object. Objectivity, in this sense, has none of its critical meaning. Kant's position in maintaining that things in themselves are the cause of appearances, is altogether untenable. However, this clearly does not represent his critical view and should not be regarded as central to his position. Appearances are objects, but not *because* they exist independently. Things in themselves are intrinsically unknowable: hence, they are not *objects,* independent or otherwise.

Kant frequently employs the concept of the transcendental object in such a way as to make it synonymous with the concept of the thing-in-itself. Not only is this obvious from the general context, but Kant himself uses the terms interchangeably. As in the case of the thing-in-itself, the transcendental object has both a critical and dogmatic meaning. In its critical employment it is strictly a limiting concept, while in its dogmatic usage it is regarded as the cause or ground of appearances. In this two-fold meaning, the transcendental object may be regarded as identical with the thing itself. It poses no additional problems of interpretation.

As employed in other contexts the concept of the transcendental object has no relation to the thing-in-itself. As the concept of an object in general which serves to unify the manifold of intuition, it is *a priori* and transcendental. The meaning and function of the *a priori* object is never precisely determined in the *Critique.* In fact, Kant tended to abandon it altogether in the second edition. However, his statements that the transcendental object as an *a priori* concept is *unknowable* have no significance for the knowability of the thing-in-itself. No *a priori* concept or principle is *knowable,* for the determinate empirical content is lacking that is required for knowledge. In discarding the *a priori* concept of the transcendental object Kant was in no way giving up his notion of the thing-in-itself.

Another serious inconsistency in Kant's exposition concerns the possibility of applying the categories to the things in themselves. On the one hand he suggests the possibility of 'thinking' things-in-themselves through the categories, even though no intuition can be given to furnish the necessary empirical content. In other connections he holds that the categories are absolutely without meaning when applied beyond the realm of appearances. Some of his interpreters have concluded that in denying the possibility of applying the categories to things in themselves, Kant was, for all practical purposes, repudiating the notion of the thing-in-itself altogether. There would appear to be a serious dilemma involved in his position at this point. If the categories can be applied to things in themselves, Kant is fundamentally inconsistent with his critical position; if the categories cannot be applied to them, the things in themselves are completely meaningless. The confusion results from Kant's two-fold deduction of space, time, and the categories, and his effort to find a critical basis for his private metaphysical views. His ambivalent position results from his continuing struggle between rationalism and empiricism, between his private metaphysics and his metaphysics of experience.

Although Kant sometimes refers to space and time as the only forms of intuition of which human minds are capable, he never justified or needed to justify any such assertion. On the contrary, his position is intelligible only if that is not actually capable of being proved. The objective deduction of space and time depends upon their being shown to be the necessary *a priori* conditions of mathematics, and, hence, of any mathematical science of nature. If this was not clear in the first edition of the *Critique,* Kant made it explicit enough in the *Prolegomena* and the second edition of the *Critique.* Synthetic *a priori* judgments are held to be possible because of the reality of space and time, the logical conditions of mathematics. If any mathematical knowledge of nature is to be possible, these same logical conditions will be required. In the objective deduction, Kant does not show that space and time are *psychologically* prior to experience, or even that they are *psy-*

chologically necessary in the intuition of objects. It is the existence of mathematical physics which demonstrates the possibility of such synthetic *a priori* judgments of nature. On this basis the forms of intuition are valid only for mathematical knowledge. Beyond that sphere no application whatever can be claimed for them. They cannot be regarded as the exclusive forms of intuition or as the logical conditions for all knowledge, but only for that intuition and knowledge which patterns itself after mathematical physics.

Kant also offered a psychological deduction of space and time, which has little in common with the objective deduction so far as method is concerned. If his method is to be the selective principle, one must choose between these deductions. In view of Kant's explicit statement that the objective deduction alone is essential, this presents no real difficulty. It is unfortunate that the psychological deduction is frequently assumed as the archimedean point for the understanding of Kant's method. The two deductions have quite different implications, particularly for the meaning of the thing-in-itself. Whereas the objective deduction leaves the way open for other modes of intuition and is valid only for mathematical knowledge of nature, the psychological deduction would establish these forms as the only possible modes of human intuition. In the latter instance, either things in themselves must be capable of being intuited under the forms of space and time, or they can never be given in any experience whatever. The only alternative would be that objects which cannot be perceived might still be conceived. At times Kant was not averse to holding this view, unsatisfactory as it proved to be.

The deduction of the categories presents a similar difficulty. On the one hand, Kant presents the categories as the only possible forms of judgment. But he never demonstrates this anywhere in the *Critique* or elsewhere in his writings. This is, in fact, one of the most dogmatic and rationalistic parts of the *Critique of Pure Reason.* The critical or transcendental deduction of the categories consists in their being shown to be the necessary presuppositional concepts of pure science of nature. In the latter instance it cannot be claimed that they are the only forms of judgment, but only that they are required concepts for natural science. Only in so far as knowledge is patterned after mathematical science is the validity of the categories guaranteed. Again these two deductions have different and inconsistent implications. The more dogmatic deduction would postulate the categories as the necessary concepts of any human thought whatever. In this instance either they would have to be applicable to things in themselves, or else things in themselves could not be conceptualised. The critical deduction, on the other hand, would allow for the possibility of other categories for other types of experience. It would even imply the possibility of such concepts. From this standpoint it would be quite dogmatic and altogether uncritical to attempt an extension of the categories beyond appearances—unless some other basis were provided.

Kant had originally held that we can think things in themselves through the categories because of his conviction that the categories are the forms of human thought in general, applicable to any objects whatever. He was not inconsistent in holding that they might be applicable to objects apart from the forms of space and time. Since he admitted that they would be empty apart from some other mode of intuition which remained to be discovered, he was not contradicting himself. However, in maintaining that things in themselves actually could be thought through the categories, indeed must be thought through them, Kant was asserting more than his position would allow. Thus, he was only correcting his position in the direction of greater consistency in amending his statements regarding the application of the categories to things in themselves. So far as the ***Critique of Pure Reason*** is concerned, one has no right to assert that things in themselves are even thinkable through the categories.

His further concern was to avoid any appearance of holding to the rationalist position. If the thing-in-itself is thinkable, that would seem to put Kant in the Leibnizian camp. He was exceedingly anxious to avoid any such semblance. To say that we can have an intelligible concept of something that cannot be empirically given in intuition would seem to be saying that we can know objects by reason alone. The point is that the categories are *derived* from experience and without experience can have no meaning so far as knowledge is concerned. But this is true only in so far as the validity of the categories is dependent upon the objective deduction. They cannot be declared to be meaningless in an absolute sense. It is only that no basis for an extension of their application has been provided in the case of the theoretical reason.

Here Kant was drawn between two poles. His empiricism prompted him to declare the meaninglessness of the categories when extended to things in themselves. Yet, at the same time, he was attempting to provide a basis for just that extension of them in the case of the practical reason. Although no intuition is available for the theoretical reason, the categories might receive empirical meaning through moral experience. Thus the self might be regarded as a substance that is spatial and determined in time for the theoretical reason, and as a simple substance that is free for the practical reason. In holding that things in themselves are thinkable, e.g. God, the free moral self, the world as totality, Kant had the moral part of his philosophy clearly in mind. It is evident that he was not willing to affirm the reality of noumena merely on the basis of their being conceptually intelligible. Nonetheless, it is significant that he speaks of noumena as intelligible cause, as thinkable, if not theoretically knowable. In the pre-critical period he had been convinced that they could be known intelligibly by reason alone. In the critical period he modified this position to hold that they are theoretically intelligible but not theoretically knowable. A further modification is to be found in his rejection of the theoretical significance of the categories beyond the area of experience from which they are derived. Apart from this experience their application is altogether problematic.

The dilemma with respect to the application of the categories to things in themselves is not insuperable. The first part of the dilemma is cleared up by admitting that no claim can be made for the application of the categories to things in themselves so far as theoretical knowledge is concerned. The limitations of the categories is implied in the very method by which they are derived. The inconsistency in Kant's exposition at this point results from a transition in his thought from a dogmatic to a more critical position. The second part of the dilemma is false. The meaning and validity of the concept of the thing-in-itself in no way depends upon an extension of the categories beyond appearances. The thing-in-itself is not actually the *cause* of appearances. Hence, nothing is lost if it is found to be impossible to apply the category of causality to the thing-in-itself. The thing-in-itself is primarily a limiting concept. As such it has no positive or determinate meaning.

Kant's contention that moral experience gives us things in themselves involves an unfortunate use of language. The objects of moral experience are no less phenomenal, on critical grounds, than the objects of theoretical knowledge. If the concepts of the practical reason are transcendentally ideal, which is required if they are *a priori,* their validity is limited to the experience from which they are derived. In this respect they are no different from the *a priori* concepts of the theoretical reason. Actually, it is two sets of phenomenal objects that are involved, rather than appearances and things in themselves. In so far as Kant employed the concept of the noumenon positively to designate objects which belong to an 'intelligible world' he was departing widely from his critical position. There is in evidence here a carry-over of pre-critical language. The question is whether it is merely the language of his rationalistic period that is retained. There can hardly be any doubt that Kant believed that the world postulated by the practical reason is the 'real' world. In holding that it is 'thinkable' he was clinging to an important element of his pre-critical metaphysics. His denial that it can be *known* theoretically only partially suffices to free his position of rationalistic overtones.

Although he insisted that the practical reason is fully autonomous, he apparently believed it necessary to provide a theoretical foundation for the postulates of morality. This dogmatic and rationalistic tendency in Kant's philosophy makes it appear that the practical reason serves only to validate a theoretical metaphysics which was required but not schematised by the theoretical reason. Kant's fondness for architechtonic, his continuing commitment to the fundamental principles of his pre-critical metaphysics accounts for this development. Actually, the practical validity of the postulates of morality in no way depends upon such a theoretical undergirding. Kant's position was ambivalent. He insisted upon the autonomy of the practical reason, declaring that the postulates of morality have no theoretical validity whatever. At the same time, he provided a theoretical foundation for the metaphysics postulated by the practical reason, maintaining that the realm of the practical reason is the 'intelligible' or 'noumenal' world. This is a fundamental inconsistency in his position. The implicit rationalism of his philosophy is only partially concealed by his insistence that the metaphysics of morality is based upon faith rather than knowledge. The term faith is not used in any conventional sense and serves to confuse the function of the critical method as applied to moral experience. Kant was attempting to make a theoretical claim for metaphysical concepts without being willing to accept all of the implications involved.

Only if it is assumed that there are just two modes of knowledge, the theoretical and the practical, is it proper to speak of moral experience as affording access to things in themselves. But even then it is only from the perspective of *science* that the concepts of the practical reason can be said to refer to noumena. Moreover, it would be equally legitimate to refer to the objects of scientific knowledge as noumena when speaking from the standpoint of moral experience. On this assumption, phenomena and noumena, appearances and things in themselves, become complementary terms. Objects as they appear in any other way than in space and time are then regarded as noumenal. Even though Kant appears to have made this assumption, the language is still misleading. Things in themselves can never be known or positively defined either theoretically or practically. In holding that they are given in moral experience, Kant beclouded the whole distinction between appearances and things in themselves.

Kant is, of course, permitted his own use of language. The objection here is not that he employs the term noumena to mean the phenomenal objects of moral experience, but that the means by noumena something other than appearances. It is not at all consistent or justifiable to equate noumena in this sense with things in themselves. The *a priori* concepts of moral experience are valid only for moral experience. That is the central doctrine of the ethics. In insisting that moral experience provides an access, even indirectly, to things in themselves, Kant is over-extending the application of these concepts. To say that the real self, the self *an sich* is a free self, is to make a claim which is altogether unjustified on the basis of Kant's method. The same thing is true of his postulation of God and a purposeful world as noumena. The positivistic metaphysics of the critical philosophy, the metaphysic of experience, embraces morality as well as science. Kant's attempts to give positive meaning to the concept of the thing-in-itself in whatever context represents a compromise with dogmatism and rationalism, a concession to his private metaphysics.

As Kant uses the term faith in referring to the concepts of moral experience, it has little of the traditional meaning and certainly none of the religious meaning which is usually associated with the concept. It is not an irrational faith, a faith that is blind or mystical to which Kant refers. He is at great pains to point out that the faith presupposed by morality is a rational faith (Vernunftglaube). For Kant as a person I suspect that more than rational faith was involved. Thus the term faith has a double meaning for him. It refers to the critical or transcendental meaning and to Kant's private meaning, which was not at all dependent upon his critical analysis. He really tried to say two things which are incompatible: (1) that things in themselves are given in the case of the practical reason; (2) that the concepts of the practical reason have no theoretical validity when extended beyond the moral realm.

There can be little doubt that Kant actually believed that the practical reason gets at the heart of reality, that in a literal sense it presents us with things as they really are. It is the latter aspect of the practical reason, the latter type of faith, which has been most influential in modern theology. One can, if one will, choose to accept Kant's private view as the more significant of the two, but the two views must not be confused. So far as the critical method is concerned, it cannot be maintained that things in themselves are given, positively, unless one means to equate things in themselves with a specific order of phenomena. One may offer the rejoinder that so far as moral experience is concerned it is *as if* things in themselves are given. And I suspect that this is the case. There is an existential element involved in religious faith, perhaps even in religious faith that is based exclusively upon morality. But this proves nothing! Kant should have been the last to conclude from this fact that things *are* actually given as they are in themselves. It is not *psychological* certainty or belief with which Kant is concerned. It is rather the *a priori* principles required by reason in order to account for objective moral experience that are involved. Some post-Kantians have attempted to specify the formal conditions of psychological belief, the *a priori* conditions of religious experience in the subjective sense. But there is little in common between such psychological conditions and the *a priori* principles of the critical philosophy. This is only to restate the point that the Kantian *a priori* is not intended to be psychological in character, whether for science or morality.

There are at least three important ways in which Kant employs the concept of the thing-in-itself dogmatically: (1) in

An eighteenth-century view of Königsberg, the city where Kant was born and lived most of his life.

positing the thing-in-itself as the cause of appearances; (2) in holding that the categories are applicable to things in themselves; (3) in maintaining that the practical reason affords an access to things in themselves. This threefold dogmatic employment of the concept is indicative of the metaphysical undercurrent which runs through the critical writings. Kant was personally convinced of the reality of God as a transcendent being, of the world as teleologically ordered, and of the soul as free. He struggled to avoid any confusion of his private views with his critical position, but was not always successful in keeping them separate. Whereas the concept of the thing-in-itself is always negative and empty, a limiting concept, in its critical meaning, in its dogmatic employment it has positive metaphysical content. The conflict for Kant was not between subjectivism and phenomenalism, but between ontological realism and phenomenalism. If he had ever had the opportunity to reconsider the continuity of his critical writings, there is good reason to believe that he would have found occasion to effect certain changes in order to bring them into greater self-consistency. He would, I am convinced, have found it necessary to eliminate altogether: (1) those passages in which he refers to the thing-in-itself as the cause of appearances; (2) those passages in which he attempts to find a theoretical foundation for the concepts of traditional metaphysics; (3) those passages in which he holds that any one faculty or area of experience affords an access to things in themselves.

Kant might well have written a further treatise on metaphysics in order to consider the positive character of things in themselves. Kantian phenomenalism and metaphysics are not incompatible. Phenomenalism itself becomes dogmatic when it insists that it is *meaningless* to raise questions about the nature of things in themselves. In suggesting the possibility of analogical knowledge as a basis for metaphysical judgments, Kant explicitly recognised this alternative. Moreover, Kant might have attempted to consider experience in its wholeness, taking into account the transcendental principles of the various modes of experience. This would involve the explication of the transcendental concepts which are presupposed by science, morality and art. The critical philosophy always presupposes a rational faculty which is capable of just such an effort. It is not the theoretical reason which criticises the theoretical reason, nor the practical reason which criticises the practical reason, but the philosophical reason which accomplishes both tasks. It is this same faculty which might achieve some synthesis or reconciliation of the theoretical, practical, and aesthetic modes of experience. In the *Critique of Judgment*, Kant attempted something of this sort. By his own admission, he was seeking to find a bridge between the theoretical and the practical reason. However, only a beginning was made; the task remains altogether incomplete. At best one gets some indication of the way in which Kant might have gone about the business of dealing with the various areas of experience synoptically.

The logical development and extension of the critical philosophy in this respect would be an all-inclusive phenomenalism. To the extent that certain of the neo-Kantians have attempted to accomplish this, they have been true to the Kantian methodology. However, if that is one legitimate extension of the critical method it is not the only one permitted. Kant himself was a metaphysician at heart. He was never satisfied to ignore the questions of metaphysics, and it is doubtful if he could ever have been content with an account of experience that was merely phenomenalistic in character. There is

no basis whatever, on Kantian grounds, for the assertion that nonphenomenalistic metaphysics is meaningless. It is only dogmatic and rationalistic metaphysics which is declared to be futile. The implication of the critical philosophy is not to rule out hypothetical metaphysics, to deny the meaning of speculation as to the nature of things in themselves, but only to deny the possibility of certainty in obtaining answers to such questions.

Phenomenalism is impossible as a permanent position for philosophy in that it cuts the nerve of philosophical inquiry. Philosophy, unlike the sciences, is concerned to raise questions about the ultimate. That it may be unable to obtain ultimate answers is no reason in itself to ban such inquiry. On Kantian grounds *certain* knowledge of things in themselves is impossible. Yet even Kant could not avoid raising such questions. How can the notion of a phenomenal self be reconciled with the notion of a free self? How can the concept of a mechanically determined world be reconciled with the concept of an organic and teleological world. These are questions which Kant could not avoid. That he arrived at no conclusive answers is no justification for the conclusion that such inquiry is meaningless. On the contrary, it further establishes the importance and urgency of such inquiry. It may be questioned whether the critical method itself could ever suffice to deal with such questions. It may even be doubted whether Kant was, in attempting to answer these questions, operating as a critical philosopher rather than as a traditional metaphysician. The important point is that while Kant flatly declared that reality in itself is theoretically unknowable, he could not escape trying to formulate meaningful theoretical concepts of it. (pp. 172-88)

George Schrader, "The Thing in Itself in Kantian Philosophy," in Kant: A Collection of Critical Essays, *edited by Robert Paul Wolff, Anchor Books, 1967, pp. 172-88.*

LEWIS WHITE BECK   (essay date 1957)

[*Beck is an American scholar of German philosophy who has edited and translated many of Kant's principal works for English-speaking audiences. Here, Beck elaborates on the four essential arguments of* Perpetual Peace, *asserting that they reveal Kant to be far more pragmatic in his thinking than is commonly assumed.*]

In 1795, Immanuel Kant published his tractate, ***Perpetual Peace: a Philosophical Sketch (Zum ewigen Frieden: Ein philosophischer Entwurf).*** He had enthusiastically adhered to the American cause in the Revolution against England; like many Germans he had welcomed the French Revolution and—unlike them—had remained faithful to its purposes even after the Reign of Terror. For his constancy to revolutionary principles he had come to be called a Jacobin—as unfriendly an epithet as "fellow traveler" is today—and he was under a royal prohibition from writing and teaching on religious subjects. To publish this work in the reign of Frederick William III was an act of courage.

But peace and plans for peace were in the air. Prussia had just made peace with the revolutionary government in France; a people's government had won a victory and the right to exist, not only against the *ancien régime* of France, but against the whole concert of warlike powers of Europe. Kant cannily chose this moment to issue his analysis of the causes of war and the conditions of peace. That it suited the interest of the time is shown by the fact that it was, within a year, translated into both French and English.

The tractate is drawn up in mock-heroic style, with its several sections corresponding to those of the treaties of his day. The witty proem prepares the reader for the hard but just indictment to be brought against the approved statecraft of the warring dynasties of Europe. Yet there is an elevated seriousness in it, befitting its high subject. Kant was a republican and a humanitarian, as deeply committed to a defense of the rights and interests of mankind as any French or American revolutionary. He saw war as the supreme obstacle to be overcome on the hard road toward securing these rights and interests. He was a realistic student of history and politics, and he knew the practical man's deafness to Utopian plans. But he was also the author of a system of moral philosophy which, he believed, provided a philosophical rationale for those practical procedures seen by prophets of peace from Dante to Saint-Pierre, from Rousseau to Wilson and to the authors of the Charter of the United Nations, to be the only ones that can possibly lead to permanent peace.

Perpetual Peace—unlike some of Kant's other works—can be best read just as it is printed: straight from beginning to end. He sets up Preliminary Articles prescribing what states, as they now exist, must do to have peace; then he formulates Definitive Articles of political philosophy, showing what must be the constitution of the states and what must be the structure of a league of nations under international law if peace is to be lasting. He next turns to a study of the conditions which make men and states war-like, and which, he believes, give hope that they will eventually renounce this barbarity. Then there is a demand, in an acute Secret Article, that the philosopher should be heard in times of peacemaking; and the rest of the essay is what he, as a philosopher, has to say about *Realpolitik*, the ethical criteria of political measures, and the moral obligation to seek and preserve peace.

This is the order in which the essay should be first read. But the careful reader will discern a different logic in it. He will see that there are four lines or phases of argument which, in their own arrangement, make Kant's theses clearer than they may be in the treaty-like organization of the text. I shall try to make these four parts clear under the following headings:

PHASE OF THE ARGUMENT	CHIEF PLACES IN TEXT
(1) Anthropological, concerning the place of war and peace in history, and man's natural tendency to peace	First Supplement
(2) Moral-philosophical, concerning the priority of the ethical over mere political considerations, and the ethical ideal of peace	Secret Article, First and Second Appendixes, and the selection from the "Jurisprudence"
(3) Moral-political, concerning the moral foundation of states capable of establishing permanent peace	The Definitive Articles and part of First Appendix
(4) Pragmatical or technical, concerning the ways and means of implementing this ideal in an imperfect world	The Preliminary Articles, and some parts of the Definitive Articles

Of course the rubrics are not quite so sharp and the pattern is not quite so simple; for the arguments, in part interdependent, are not presented in such isolation as this listing might suggest. But the references in the second column are to the chief discussions of the respective topics.

(1) *The anthropological study of war and peace.* Human nature, it is often said, is so depraved that peace is only a futile dream; all idealistic plans shatter on the rocks of unregenerate human nature. Kant, who seems never to have had a sentimental or flattering thought about mankind, nevertheless does not draw this pessimistic inference from his study of the litany of evils which is history. Rather, he argues that it is nature herself (including, of course, human nature as understood by scientists and historians) which is the ultimate guarantor of peace.

Kant is impressed by the natural opposition of man to man, and by what he elsewhere calls their "unsocial sociability," which brings them together and forces them to co-operate in the works of both peace and war. Kant is, of course, opposed to the glorifiers of war who have sometimes claimed him for their own; but he is simply being realistic in recognizing the way in which, in the past, conflict has laid down the conditions on which co-operation, first in small groups and eventually between states, becomes feasible and actual. Even a race of devils, granted only that they are intelligent, would find it possible and necessary to co-operate and establish civil society; and states governed by intelligent devils would themselves in time find it to their interest to form leagues and alliances, to make treaties and fulfill them. How much more is this true of man! Peace is an edifice at whose foundation there are past wars, in which issues decided by force and violence have become the material of laws, subsumed under and refined by compacts, constitutions, treaties, and alliances. Kant believes that this trend, whose dynamics are found in the "mechanism of human passions," can issue in perpetual alliances, the condition of lasting peace.

Not that, as he warns us, human beings are disinterested spectators or passive beneficiaries of an inevitable progress. Peace is a stern moral task, not a shore reached by simply riding on a historical wave. Why, then, this historical, anthropological disquisition with its optimistic conclusion, interrupting, as it seems to do, the political and moral admonitions of the treatise?

Here, as everywhere in Kant, there is a stubborn distrust of fanciful ideals not in contact with the facts of life. In his systematic works on ethics, he always tries to show that it is possible for some law to be obeyed, some ideal to be achieved, before he declares the law to be binding or the ideal valid. That is why, for instance, in the first *Critique* he argues for the possibility of freedom of the will before, in the second *Critique*, he argues for the practicability of the moral law. Similarly here. Here the same realistic compunction makes him try to show that, judged from the standpoint of fact, peace is not a chimerical ideal. If men by nature were so constituted that they must inevitably war among themselves through all time, then the only perpetual peace would be that of the great burial ground of humanity, and the moral law, "There ought not to be war," would be vain. But he attempts, in this historical and anthropological study, to show that, moral considerations aside, man and society are not so constituted; thus his right to discuss the *moral* problem is established.

(2) *The argument from moral philosophy.* Peace cannot be left

entirely to blind nature, and it is too momentous to be entrusted solely to lawyers and politicians acting according to rules of thumb or books of statutes not continuously subjected to moral review. Statements of fact, such as those drawn from the historians' observations, imply no obligatory laws or judgments of value; nor is obligation created by the arbitrary fiat of a sovereign. An obligation is to be justified or "deduced" from principles of pure practical reason, from what Kant calls the "metaphysics of morals." Only the application of moral judgment requires detailed knowledge of men and affairs; the moral principles themselves cannot be extracted from empirical knowledge. Thus ethics, the "science" of the morally necessary, takes precedence over politics, the "art" of the empirically possible. The first question on a political act, therefore, ought not to be "Is it feasible?" but, "Is it right?"

Having shown that peace is not, because of human nature, an impossible ideal, Kant now argues that actions directed toward peace are right and obligatory. There are two premises for this. Neither of them is drawn from attempted answers to the obscure question of what will secure happiness among mankind as a whole; there is nothing utilitarian, in the optimistic manner of the eighteenth century, in Kant's argument. The first premise is the categorical imperative which enjoins us always to act on a maxim of respect for human beings as ends in themselves. Kant says that in warmaking the ruler does not obey this principle, and instead of respecting the citizens as persons, he treats them as things to be used—and used up. The second premise is the juridical principle which underlies the dynamics of government, that men ought to, and as rational beings do, seek to extend the reign of law.

Together these lead to a formula by which the rightness or wrongness of particular political maxims can be judged: this is the *criterion of publicity*. Actions whose maxims cannot be publicly exposed without thwarting the purpose of the action itself are not responsive to the rights of others, and are therefore immoral. Actions are right if they can be fully effective only when their maxim is known to those touched by the action, for in these actions the person is treated as an end in himself. These are actions which the person affected could himself have willed. Their maxim is one which both the agent and patient can regard as a law they would willingly decree for themselves and their fellows. Where such actions are willed, the persons are equal, lawgiving members of a realm of ends.

(3) *The moral-political argument.* The political analogue of the realm of ends is a republic. In a republic, all laws are self-imposed, and government is by the consent of the governed. Only here is there any a priori reason to expect that the rights and interests of men will be honored. Thus Kant sees the moral law and its political corollary, the criterion of publicity, as the key to the constitution and international law which may secure us the blessings of peace.

The three Definitive Articles are moral laws, translated into the language of law and politics. Only the second, the organization of a league of nations, requires special comment here. It should be noted that most of Article II is concerned with the alliance of sovereign states; but at the end Kant says that this will not secure permanent peace. What is needed is actually a "continuously growing state consisting of various nations," in default of which alliances must be established, though they are in constant peril of breaking down. But Kant admits here that there is not the will to establish world gov-

ernment, and elsewhere he says that such a dominion would be administratively unworkable. Therefore the most that men can hope for is a gradual approach to a condition of peace—an ideal to be approached asymptotically.

(4) *The political implementation.* The way to begin is to begin. The first steps must be taken by imperfect, warlike, perhaps despotic, rulers of states whose chief glory is self-aggrandizement. They must be convinced that war is fatal to them, yet inevitable under their usual political practices. Kant believes that slight changes—they undoubtedly appeared slighter in the eighteenth than they do in the twentieth century; they are certainly slight in comparison with the world-shaking, epoch-making revolutions of the Definitive Articles—these slight changes, he says, can reverse this suicidal trend and lead to a climate of opinion in which peace will not be regarded by politicians as a cynical slogan, and as a sweet but empty dream by the citizens. A little of the good faith, intelligence, and common decency which make civil society possible will work a subtle revolution in the ways of diplomacy, and make it a tool of peace and not of war.

One point in these articles is worth special attention: Kant's "realism." Most interpreters of Kant show little awareness of this aspect of his ethics. The argument that, for instance, one ought not tell a lie even to save the life of an innocent person is often taken to be a characteristic and unavoidable feature of Kant's moral philosophy, and it is often thought that nothing can save it from what appears to be this *reductio ad absurdum*. But in some important, though not so well known, ethical writings there is full and clear insistence—which is present at least between the lines of the better-known works—upon the need and rightness of elbowroom for practical, realistic, common sense. A fortiori there is room for it in politics, even moral politics. Kant never forgets that politics is the art of the possible; he asks only that there be a more just estimate of what *is* possible. While not sanguine by nature, Kant is convinced that more is possible than is envisaged in the essentially hopeless political view that war is unending. (pp. vii-xiv)

Lewis White Beck, in an introduction to Perpetual Peace *by Immanuel Kant, edited by Lewis White Beck, Liberal Arts Press, 1957, pp. vii-xiv.*

JOHN KEMP (essay date 1968)

[*In the following excerpt, Kemp assesses Kant's attempt to synthesize in his philosophical system the diverse currents of Enlightenment thought.*]

The mind of a great thinker, contrary to what is sometimes suggested by historians who are interested in sources and origins, is not simply the resultant of a number of forces operating upon it; no matter how carefully and thoroughly one studies the way in which he has been influenced by his early education, by the work of previous or contemporary thinkers, by the social and political conditions of his own times, or by reflection on the history of past events, one will never by this means arrive at more than a superficial understanding and explanation of his thought. On the other hand, no thinker, however great, can escape such influences altogether. A philosopher will ask the questions he does because he believes either that, though important, they have not been asked before or that, although they have been asked by predecessors or contemporaries, they have as yet received no satisfactory answer; and his answers, however original, will preserve some echoes, conscious and unconscious, from his acquaintance with the thought of others.

Kant's general attitude to philosophy follows in many respects the main principles of the movement of thought known as the Enlightenment, especially in its German form. The principle that men should seek as far as possible to find systematically rational solutions to their problems, instead of relying on revelation, tradition, and the like, received its main philosophical support in Germany from Leibniz and his successors, especially Christian Wolff, and more practical support and encouragement from Frederick the Great. The principle was one which Kant earnestly professed and constantly observed, even though his use of reason led him in the end to conclusions which went far beyond those of his contemporaries and immediate predecessors. Some remarks in his essay **What is Enlightenment?** (published in 1784) provide a clear illustration of this attitude. Enlightenment, he explains, consists in a kind of liberation, in man's release from a tutelage or subjection which he has brought on himself.

> Tutelage is man's inability to make use of his understanding without direction from another. This tutelage is self-incurred when its cause lies not in lack of reason but in lack of resolution and courage to use it without direction from another. *Sapere aude!* 'Have courage to use your own reason'—that is the motto of the Enlightenment—

and, one might add, Kant's own.

But this rather cold rationality was supplemented and transformed, especially in Kant's moral and political thinking, by two other factors. First in order of time was his exposure to the influence of the religious movement known as Pietism. This movement, to which his parents belonged and around which his early education was centred, represented an attempt to return to what was thought of as the true Protestant spirit of the Reformation—to a religion in which the individual soul, not the organized church, was all-important, and in which a sense of personal duty and discipline went with a distrust for external religious forms and observances. Kant accepted much of the more negative aspect of this attitude to religion, and never ceased to regard the pietists with great respect, even though they were far too dogmatic and irrationalist in their faith to satisfy him completely. Secondly, there was Rousseau, the reading of whose works in the 1760s, on Kant's own confession, corrected his growing tendency to value intellectual powers more highly than straightforward moral goodness, and encouraged him to search for a moral philosophy which should be based on reason but which should at the same time show how the ordinary unphilosophical man could understand, as well as perform, his duties—a philosophy which should not display any of the condescension so often shown, before and since, by philosophers to their supposed intellectual inferiors. More specifically, Kant derived from Rousseau his picture of human nature as distinguished from the rest of the animal creation, not by man's possession of an intellect but by his possession of freedom, in the sense of the capacity to pursue ends and objectives which he has spontaneously set before himself (animals being limited to the pursuit of ends given them by nature).

In a more narrowly philosophical context, Kant derived from Leibniz and his followers a belief in system as the distinguishing feature of philosophy. The essence of any scientific body of knowledge consists in the fact that it is systematic; common or unscientific knowledge is a mere aggregate of facts.

His own philosophical system or 'architectonic', which has struck many commentators as artificial and valueless, is seen by Kant as providing a basis for philosophical certainty and the resolution of controversy, which he sees as the great scandal of philosophy; the scientific, systematic, and critical investigation of philosophical problems, and especially of the nature and limitations of the human mind, replaces the existing state of war by a state of law and order. And Kant derived from Hume, as he tells us more than once, the impetus for his dissatisfaction with the dogmatic certainties of his philosophical predecessors and contemporaries, and his attempt to resurvey the foundations of the whole philosophical and metaphysical enterprise; from Hume's account of causation came also some hints, at least, towards the Kantian description and deduction of all the categories of the understanding, including that of cause and effect.

These influences, nevertheless, would have come to nothing without the integrating and originating power of Kant's own philosophical intellect. To see the need for a synthesis of all that is best in the outlook of the Enlightenment and all that is best in the thought of Rousseau is one thing; to devise a conceptual system and a philosophical method by means of which the synthesis could be provided is quite another. And while it is easy to say that a body of thought is philosophical only to the extent that it is systematic, the construction of an elaborate and profound system cemented together by acute and lengthy arguments is the most difficult of all philosophical enterprises. Kant, rightly, thought of his philosophy as revolutionary; and the originality of his achievement is emphasized by his often quoted, but sometimes misunderstood, comparison of himself to Copernicus. In the Preface to the second edition of the **Critique of Pure Reason** Kant says that Copernicus, having failed to find a satisfactory explanation of the movements of the heavenly bodies on the traditional supposition that they revolved round a stationary spectator, put forward the suggestion that the spectator revolves and the stars remain at rest. Kant makes an analogous suggestion in respect of metaphysics, viz. that objects, if they are to be known by us, must conform to our intuitions and concepts (i.e. to the conditions prescribed by the nature of human sensibility and understanding), instead of our intuitions and concepts having to conform to objects. On this latter view (universally held up to now) all a priori knowledge of objects would be impossible. The hypothesis of Copernicus was eventually vindicated by Newton: his own 'Copernican' hypothesis, Kant thinks, is vindicated by the arguments of the *Critique of Pure Reason.* It was by the truth or falsehood of this hypothesis and by the success or failure of its demonstration and application in the three **Critiques** and the other major works of the 1780s and 1790s that Kant's philosophical achievement was, in his own judgement, to be assessed. If we accept this judgement, we can hardly regard the critical philosophy as a complete success. Apart from actual mistakes and errors, some of which at least are relatively unimportant and could easily be corrected, it is now clear that Kant was unable in some respects to escape from the assumptions and prejudices of his own day. He takes for granted many positions and attitudes which seemed obviously correct to his contemporaries as well as to himself, but which subsequent thought and practice has shown to be partially, at least, open to question. In the first **Critique** he assumes without hesitation that Aristotelian logic, Euclidean geometry, and Newtonian physics are in essence the last word on their respective subjects; in the second he takes for granted that duty, considered as a sort of command or law, must be the central notion of human ethics, and accepts uncritically the eighteenth-century belief in an unchanging human nature; in the third, he takes for granted that the notions of the beautiful and the sublime comprise the entire field of aesthetics, and seems also to assume without question that art is the imitation of nature. To complain that Kant takes some things for granted is, of course, to complain that he is subject to ordinary human limitations; in reality no philosopher of science, morality, or art can possibly be sure that he has taken account in his philosophy not only of all past and present manifestations of science, morality, or art but of all future ones as well. One may have a right to complain of the over-optimistic tone of some of Kant's claims for the comprehensiveness and completeness of his philosophy; but in spite of this, it is doubtful whether, with the possible exception of Aristotle's, there has ever been a more comprehensive one.

In any case, a philosopher is not in the end to be judged entirely (perhaps not even at all) by the number and importance of his philosophical theses which appear to later generations still to be true. He is to be judged by the originality and range of his thought, by the depth and clarity of his arguments, and by his fecundity as a source of ideas for later thinkers. By these and by any other reasonable standards, Kant is worthy of a place among the very greatest philosophers. (pp. 123-26)

> *John Kemp, in his* The Philosophy of Kant, *Oxford University Press, Oxford, 1968, 131 p.*

HANS REISS (essay date 1970)

[*Reiss examines Kant's philosophy of politics and history.*]

[What] are Kant's principles of politics? They are substantially the principles of right (Recht). The philosophical enquiry into politics must establish which political actions are just or unjust. It must show by what principles we can establish the demands of justice in a given situation. Justice must, however, be universal, but only law can bring it about. A coherent political order must then be a legal order. Just as in Kant's ethics actions ought to be based on maxims capable of being formulated as universal laws, so in politics political arrangements ought to be organised according to universally valid laws. Political action and legislation ought thus to be based on such rules as will allow of no exception. Kant's principles of politics are normative. They are applications of principles of right to experience. Right, in a succinct phrase of Kant's, 'ought never to be adapted to politics, but politics ought always to be adapted to right'.

There is, of course, no reason whatsoever to believe that Kant was not aware that the details of the political situation always vary. His aim, however, was to discover the philosophical foundations on which political actions could, and ought to, be based. Right is to be found only in external relations which are the proper business of politics. External relations are relations which arise because we have possessions, 'an external mine and thine' as Kant calls it. He here uses the terminology of Roman Law for the concept of 'mine and thine' (*meum et tuum*). These relations have to be placed under rules. Politics, as Hobbes had argued, belongs to that sphere of human experience in which man's will can be coerced by another will; for like Hobbes, Kant reduces all action to the will. If coercion is exercised according to a universal principle, it is law. Thus, law is conceived as 'a coercive order'. Legality is therefore the decisive principle in the sphere of politics. The moral decision

of the inner man finds outward expression in legality, i.e. in an action conforming with law. But man's inner life must not be subject to coercion. Because we cannot know for certain anything about another person's inner life, it ought not to be the task of political action or legislation to change or in any way to condition another person's thought. As men we are free. Our freedom implies that we have a hypothetical right to acquire anything in the world of a nature which we are potentially capable of acquiring.

Not only any one particular individual, but all individuals have this right of acquiring possessions. It is the expression of their freedom. Collision between the freedom of one individual and that of others must, however, be avoided. Otherwise there would be chaos and constant strife. The freedom of each individual has consequently to be regulated in a universally binding manner. Thus, external freedom is freedom from any constraint except coercion by law, a freedom which allows each individual to pursue his own ends, whatever they may be, provided that this pursuit leaves the same kind of freedom to all others.

Acquired rights do not, however, belong to us merely by virtue of our humanity. They can be regulated or even curtailed by law. The act of acquisition establishes the right to property. It does not necessarily mean physical possession, but rather an intelligible or noumenal possession independent of time. In order to distinguish my possession from that of others, it is necessary that the choice of others should agree with my own. This condition is only possible under a law regulating possessions. But such a law is not possible in a state of nature, only in a civil society. From the principle that everyone has a right to acquire external possessions, therefore, there arises the command that everyone ought to act in such a way that everyone is able to acquire the external 'His' (or his external possessions). This in turn amounts to a command to enter civil society, to become a member of the state. Or, in other words, when a conflict about external possessions arises, as it inevitably does, a right exists to compel the other person to enter civil society.

In establishing this view of right, Kant is again not concerned with delineating the content of relations between individuals (i.e. the ends which they desire or ought to desire), but only with the form. What matters is the arrangement which establishes that the free actions of one individual 'can be reconciled with the freedom of the other in accordance with a universal law'.

From this conclusion, the universal principle of right can be deduced. It runs: 'Every action which by itself or by its maxim enables the freedom of each individual's will to coexist with the freedom of everyone else in accordance with a universal law is *right*.' This universal principle of right imposes an obligation upon us, but it does not expect, let alone require, us to act in accordance with it. It tells us merely that if freedom is to be restricted in accordance with right and if justice is to prevail it must do so in accordance with this universal principle of right. To restrict freedom in this manner does not entail interfering with the freedom of an individual, but merely establishes the condition of his external freedom.

The universal principle of right is basically only an application of the universal principle of morality, as laid down in the Categorical Imperative, to the sphere of law, and thus also to the sphere of politics. But since it is morally necessary to realise external freedom, we can be compelled by others to carry out our duty of entering civil society. But we do not have to become morally better to enter it; for the political problem must be capable of solution not only by good men, but even by 'a nation of devils (so long as they possess understanding)'.

To restrict freedom except on the basis of the universal principle of right is wrong. It is not only wrong, but will also lead to strife, and thus is self-defeating. He who restricts freedom otherwise, i.e. arbitrarily, violates the freedom of another and abuses his own. To use constraint against anyone who violates the freedom of another is, however, right. The principle of right implies analytically the authorisation to use coercion by means of or on the basis of law against anyone who violates freedom illegitimately.

If this principle is applied to politics it is necessary that there should be established: 'A constitution allowing the *greatest possible human freedom* in accordance with laws which ensure *that the freedom of each can coexist with the freedom of all the others*'. Kant elaborates this principle by saying that it is 'a necessary idea which must be made the basis not only of the first outline of a political constitution but of all laws as well'. This fundamental principle could, by way of analogy, be called the universal principle of political right, although Kant himself does not use this term in the **Critique of Pure Reason** where he discusses it.

From these elementary principles, all other Kantian principles of politics follow—Kant's approach also makes it clear that, for him, the philosophical problem of politics is virtually that of Hobbes, viz. the transition from a state of war to a state of peace and security. But Kant's solution is different.

What further principles did Kant then formulate which ought to govern external relations among men? A state is a union of a group of men under laws. Since laws must then be based on the principle that we ought to be treated as ends and not as means, and since we must be considered as our own law-givers, we should be asked to consider as right only those laws to which we could agree or ought to have agreed if we had been asked to do so. 'For so long as it is not self-contradictory to say that an entire people could agree to such a law, however painful it might seem, then the law is in harmony with right.' An important corollary of this principle is the necessity that all laws be public laws. Any legislation based on a maxim that needs publicity to achieve its end is just.

The sovereign has not only rights, but also duties. He thus has not only the right but also the duty to coerce his subjects by the giving of laws; it is, however, his (moral) duty to treat his subjects as ends and not as means. Kant here is not entirely clear. It is not at all certain whether he refers to the sovereign (legislature) or to the ruler (executive). The sovereign (according to him) can never do wrong; whatever the laws given by him are, they have to be obeyed. But the positive law which is given has still to be judged by the standard found in the principles of right. The ruler cannot be judged by the sovereign since if this were done the legislature would usurp the power of the executive or judiciary which is self-contradictory and thus not right.

The problem of sovereignty, in fact, greatly occupied Kant; for he reverts to it again and again in his unpublished notes. His discussion is not without occasional contradiction, as might be expected from a philosopher wrestling with a problem which he had not solved entirely to his satisfaction. The whole trend of Kant's thinking as revealed in these notes, makes it, however, abundantly plain that, according to him, sovereignty resides or originates in the people which ought to possess legislative power. However, a monarch could possess it as a representative of the people in a derivative form. Yet Kant appears convinced that if the monarch is to exercise this power together with executive powers, his rule is despotic.

It is also the sovereign's (moral) duty to give just laws and to introduce constitutional reforms so that a republican constitution can be established. (The term 'republican' in Kant's writings could be interpreted to represent what nowadays is generally called parliamentary democracy, though it does not necessarily have this connotation.) But the subject cannot coerce the ruler (or sovereign) to exercise these duties. They are therefore not legal, but moral duties for the ruler.

All this also implies that men have inalienable rights. In a state of nature, the war of all against all may prevail, but in a state where men live under law it is different. Men are free, equal and self-dependent. This statement is derived from the idea of freedom. For if all individuals are free, they must necessarily be equally so; for the freedom of all individuals is absolute and can only be universally and equally restricted by law. Each free person must also be self-dependent. The idea of freedom entails the individual's autonomy, for it postulates the individual's power of exercising his will independently, uninhibited by improper constraint.

Kant thus starts his enquiry into politics from the standpoint of the individual. This view reflects his emphasis on the need of the free individual to make decisions, a view which he had propounded in his writings on ethics. The political freedom of the individual can, as we have seen, be understood only in terms of legal arrangements guaranteeing the freedom of all individuals.

But Kant states the political problem in a negative manner. He does not consider it to be the purpose of politics to make people happy. Happiness is subjective. He thus strongly condemns utilitarianism in politics, just as he objects to utilitarianism in pure ethics. This argument, of course, does not mean that he does not wish people to be happy. It only means that political arrangements should not be organised in such a way as to aim at promoting happiness, but that they should permit men to attain happiness in their own way. He thus rules out benevolent despotism as practised, and defended in his writings on politics, by Frederick the Great.

Kant realises, indeed, that it is necessary for the ruler to give such laws and act in such a manner that the subject will not seek to destroy the state and to overthrow the system of laws. For this purpose, men must be treated as ends and not as means. A genuine paradox, the paradox of political freedom, appears to arise. Man's freedom can be safeguarded only by his submitting to coercion; for law presupposes coercion, and thus an infringement of the individual's freedom. Rousseau saw this paradox clearly when he stated at the very beginning of the *Contrat Social* 'Man is born free, and everywhere he is in chains'. He blamed society for this state of affairs. Kant agrees with him in considering this act of coercion to be a result of man's membership of civil society, of his citizenship of the state, but he solves the paradox by seeing it as a necessary condition of civilisation. He resorts to the following explanation. We are free only in so far as, in the case of a conflict of interests, we obey the law to which we would have agreed, i.e. we submit only to coercion which is legally exercised, on the basis of public law given by the sovereign authority. The sovereign ought thus to be obliged to respect the laws which he has given. Kant here differs from Hobbes for whom the sovereign is above the law; law is the sovereign's command to the people. Man, according to Kant, preserves his freedom by remaining his own law-giver. In principle, every subject thus participates in all legislation as a fellow-legislator, and the ruler when legislating ought to respect this right of his subjects. This solution ensures freedom and security for all. Political freedom, then, is independence from coercion by another will.

If freedom is the first principal right of a citizen in a state, equality is the second. Men must be equal before the law; legislation must not make an exception nor must the law be administered so as to allow for exceptions. Kant attacks the entire heritage of feudal privilege, a foremost contemporary issue. He also rules out in principle slavery or any inferior political status for a citizen. But he thinks of political equality only, and does not at all consider the question of economic equality. He does not, however, ignore economic issues entirely. He asserts the right of man to own property. He even goes further; for he makes economic independence a criterion for active participation in political affairs.

The third principal right, independence (or *Selbständigkeit* as Kant calls it), requires that each citizen must have a right to participate in the government. He ought to do this not directly, but indirectly by the exercise of the vote. Each citizen must have one vote, however large his estate may be. No one must, by statute, have more legislative power than has been agreed to by a law concerning the delegation of legislative power. But while every one is free and equal and ought to enjoy the protection of law in these respects, not every one has a right to participate in the making of laws. Kant, if judged by modern criteria, here appears to depart from his own enlightened standpoint. Although in many ways he was ahead of his time, he was not so in all respects. He is still, not surprisingly perhaps, profoundly steeped in eighteenth-century traditions. He may be the philosopher of the American and French revolutions, but it should not be forgotten that the former was essentially a revolution of landowners and the latter a revolution of the bourgeoisie. So Kant, perhaps understandably, differentiates between men of independence and those who have none. He classes those who are independent as *active* citizens and those who are dependent as *passive* citizens. Only active citizens have a right to vote and to legislate. Women are, on principle, disqualified. But any legislation should always be enacted and carried out as if the passive citizens too were participating, for, inherently, they have the same political right as active citizens. The requirements for independence are, for him, partly economic. A man must not be dependent on any one else economically, as a servant or as an employee, for otherwise he cannot freely and independently take part in politics. No self-dependent citizen untainted by crime or insanity can abdicate the duty of participating in legislating. He cannot relinquish this duty even if he were mistakenly to find the spectacle of politics abhorrent and beneath his dignity. For while no one has a right to coerce others except by a public law executed by the sovereign, no one can divest himself of this right either.

These three rights of freedom, equality and self-dependence show that, in a properly organised state, men can find security and justice. Kant differs from Rousseau, since he believes that the state of nature is not a state of perfection. Thus, man is not corrupted by society. On the contrary, society has civilised him. Kant rather agrees with Hobbes that the state of nature is the state of a war of all against all.

What is therefore needed is a will that binds every one equally, i.e. a collectively universal will that alone can give security to each and all. Consequently, everyone has to restrict his freedom so as to make possible the establishment of such a supreme power and to avoid collision with the freedom of others. Kant, following the tradition of his age, uses the analogy of the social contract to explain this existence of the state governing a people by a system of civil law. For Kant, however, the social contract must not be considered a historical fact. On this point, he is quite unambiguous. Any such conception would be fraught with peril; for it is likely to encourage disobedience of, or even active rebellion against, the prevailing law. The social contract must therefore be seen as a practical Idea of reason. (An Idea, for Kant, is not found in experience and can thus be neither proved nor disproved by scientific enquiry, but is a regulative principle of Reason in the light of which experience can be given order and unity, which it would otherwise lack.) It is a practical Idea of reason in so far as it can be applied to the world of practical affairs or to experience, i.e. the phenomenal world; for it allows us to say something about the kind of state which ought to exist, i.e. the state which ought to be established in accordance with the principles of right. The social contract is thus a criterion of political judgement, but it should not lead us to go into historical reasons for the purpose of drawing practical conclusions. The Idea that men have made a contract to establish the state means rather that they have been prepared to submit their own personal will in matters external to them to a universal will. This universal or general will is, of course, the will of reason. It is not the united will of all, even if this were to be found so in fact, nor is it the will of the majority. Kant is again close to Rousseau, but again, where Rousseau is ambiguous, he is decisively clear. He transfers the conception of the general will, which might be embodied in the government, to an Idea of reason which entitles the government to exercise the power of political action, to coerce others according to universal law. He differs cardinally from Hobbes, who ruled out the question as to whether the sovereign could make just or unjust laws as illegitimate; for in Hobbes' view, there can be no such moral yardstick to measure existing laws.

For Kant, the Idea of the social contract also implies the necessity of a civil constitution. While it is necessary and obligatory, as he believes, to establish a civil constitution, it is also the greatest practical problem for mankind to attain this end; for only in a civil society, universally administering right according to law, can freedom exist. Only then does the freedom of one co-exist with the freedom of others. But to find a just government ruling according to a just constitution is not easy. For who is to safeguard the rights of the individual in face of authority? Who will see to it that a just constitution is established and that the government will act in accordance with the principles of right?

There is no perfect solution to the old problem *quis custodiet ipsos custodes?* This means that 'only an approximation to the idea' of a just constitution and a just government is given to us by nature.

According to what principles, then, should a rightful government be organised, even if completely just political arrangements can never be attained? Kant differentiates between the republican form of government, where the executive is separated from the legislature, and the despotic, where it is not. Republican government is impossible in a democracy; for a 'democracy' is necessarily despotic. A power is established where all rule. It means that all take decisions about all and also against any one who decides to differ from the prevailing majority view. It would in fact be a contradiction of the universal will with itself and with freedom.

Republican government, however, is rightful government. A republican constitution is established in accordance with the principles of right if powers independent from one another are set up. First, there is the sovereign, in the person of the legislator who represents the united (or general) will of the people, which, in theory, is the will of reason. The ruler (or regent), i.e. the government or the executive, cannot be the legislator. Finally, neither the legislator nor the ruler can be the judiciary. For interpreting the law and for making individual judgements, an individual justice is required. For this function, a special representative of the people—a court of law or a jury—has to be appointed.

The legislative sovereign power, according to Kant, ought to be vested in the people. He also states that, in practice, the idea can only be approximated to. The most that we can hope for is that this power will be exercised indirectly by representatives of the people. It cannot be expected that all should give laws and agree on legislation. All that can be attained is apparently a representative assembly which will legislate for all. The people as a whole must be expected to agree to this procedure and accept the legislation. They are, of course, bound by it.

Kant does not specify in detail how the representatives of the people ought to exercise their power, nor does he say according to what principle they should be chosen. He does not advocate the rule of the majority, and certainly not its unfettered power to legislate, which would have appeared to him only another form of the arbitrary will in action. He does, however, state explicitly that all should combine to give laws and that legislation is to spring from the united will of all. But he criticises the constitutional practice prevailing in eighteenth-century Britain. For British constitutional monarchy appeared to him merely as a device designed to cloak an autocratic rule. He warns that the danger of a monarch becoming a despot is particularly great, because one man is more easily tempted to become a tyrant. But he also states that where the government is in the hands of the smallest number of people and the representation is at its widest, republican rule will be most easily assured. He even appears to prefer a monarchy to an aristocracy. Yet he appears to be somewhat obscure on this point. The general drift of his argument is clear, however; his use of the term 'republican' shows us that he is basically antimonarchic. And because he knew of the dangers of one man abusing his power, he did not believe, as Rousseau did, that the united will of all could well be represented by one man. There can also be no doubt as to his basic plea for separation of powers and his conviction that the sovereign authority should rest in the people or its representatives. And he is equally clear in his demand that the sovereign must not own any private property so that he may be unable either to exercise private power or to be affected by private interest.

The fundamental element of any republican constitution, however, is respect for law. The subjects as well as the ruler and the sovereign must possess this respect. In the last resort, the subject can be expected to respect those laws in the giving of which he has participated as fellow-legislator. But the subject or citizen must neither rebel against the laws which the sovereign has made nor against the regent who carries them out, whether he likes the laws or approves of the regent or does neither. This attitude is perhaps surprising, especially if we consider Kant's attitude to the French Revolution. It follows, however, from Kant's general conception of the supremacy of law, for to rebel against the supreme power would amount to disregarding, or even overturning the law. This is evil. Kant is most outspoken on this point.

His favourable view of the French Revolution, however, complicated his argument. He tries to give legal status to the revolution by saying that it was not in fact a revolution at all in the legal sense; for the king had surrendered his sovereign power to the Third Estate. This is a dubious contention, though admittedly Louis XVI had abandoned absolute monarchy when he called the States-General. It is, however, doubtful whether he relinquished sovereign power. Kant's argument on this point remains controversial, to say the least, and does not carry much conviction.

According to Kant, the case against rebellion is unambiguous. The people cannot possess a right to rebel. There can be no power to determine what constitutes the right to rebel. Rebellion would upset the whole system of laws. It would create anarchy and violence. It would also destroy the civil constitution which the idea of the social contract demands. For if a constitution contained an article permitting a people to rebel or to depose a sovereign, a second sovereign would thereby be established. This event would be a contradiction. It would, in fact, require a further, third sovereign to decide between the two, which is absurd. There cannot therefore be in a constitution a clause giving any one a right to resist or to rebel against supreme authority. The idea of the civil constitution must be sacred and irresistible. To overthrow the sovereign or the ruler is not only wrong but will also fail to achieve its end; for it does not produce a true reform of thought.

But once a revolution has taken place, attempts to undo it and reestablish the old order are just as wrong, for it is men's duty to obey as citizens. If a government is newly established, as in England in 1688, it has to be accepted and obeyed. On the other hand, there exists no right to punish the ruler for deeds committed as ruler, for the ruler's deeds, in principle, are not subject to punishment. The sovereign cannot be punished for issuing unjust laws or for committing unrightful political actions; for such an endeavour would amount to rebellion while he is in power, and would violate the same principle after he had been deposed.

The sovereign has the right to dismiss the ruler, but he has no right to punish the dismissed ruler for actions committed as ruler. Judicial action against, and punishment of, the ruler are worse than the assassination of a tyrant. In fact, the judicial punishment of a (sovereign) ruler, such as the regicide of Charles I or Louis XVI, is the worst crime imaginable. It is a perversion of the Idea of the law itself.

Kant, however, demands from the sovereign that he should promote a spirit of liberty. Only if it prevails is it likely that the coercive ends of the ruler will not be defeated. The rulers are, in fact, aware of the desire for liberty; for no ruler dares to say that he does not recognize any rights whatsoever in the people, that they owe their happiness exclusively to the government, and that any claims of the subjects to have rights against him are a punishable offence. Rulers dare not say this because a declaration of this kind would make the citizens band together in protest. Yet even if citizens conclude that their happiness could be taken away, they have no right to rebel. Obedience, however, does not mean silence. What must and does remain for the people is the right of public criticism, i.e. not only freedom of the press, but the right of open criticism of the powers that be. Following Voltaire, Kant believed that *'Freedom of the pen* is the only safeguard of the rights of the people'. This is tantamount to demanding an open society, a society which seeks to carry on government and to give laws by a process of free rational discussion.

The right to criticise in public ought, therefore, to be guaranteed by the republican constitution. This right is restricted only by 'respect and devotion towards the existing constitution' of the state in which it is exercised.

To qualify the right of public criticism by the proviso that it should be resorted to only if respect for the republican constitution is not infringed implicitly establishes the principle of the limits of tolerance. This principle amounts to saying that all views must be tolerated provided that they are views which involve the toleration of the views of others. Or, in other words, only those views ought to be tolerated which do not advocate the overthrow of the constitution established according to the principles of right. For anyone publicly to advocate views calculated to overthrow the republican constitution amounts to a demand for violating the principles of right and thus the freedom of others. It is, therefore, legitimate to frame laws which restrict the freedom of the pen in this respect, but in this respect only. Such a law can be made universally applicable. If, on the other hand, violation of a republican constitution and of the principles of right and thus of the freedom of others is advocated, a demand of this kind cannot be given the form of a universal law. For if such a violation were to prevail, chaos, and with it the erosion of all laws, would ensue. A law permitting violation of the constitution and thus of the system of laws itself would amount to a law contradicting itself, which is absurd. It must, however, be made equally clear that this restriction is the only possible one. To restrict public criticism in any other way would amount to violating the principles of right and thus of freedom. And this limitation of public criticism must not be construed to mean that the government has a right to suppress public criticism as such, but only public criticism which has no respect for the constitution (i.e. criticism which amounts to advocating, or involves violation of, a republican constitution). Kant does not lay down the exact limits beyond which it is not legitimate to criticise a constitution publicly. The phrase 'respect' should not be taken to mean that it could be illegitimate to discuss the principles of right and their application in practice in a philosophical manner. But it does suggest that an unreasoned or forcible attack upon a republican constitution and any attempt to establish a rule which does not permit public criticism can, in principle, be legislated against. For such attacks do not carry respect, while a philosophical enquiry into the constitution and the principles underlying it does.

Unfortunately, Kant does not elaborate on this point. He was much more concerned with the problem of his age, with establishing the right of public criticism in face of a paternalistic ruler, and much less with problems of modern liberal democracy, the need to limit this right and to define the limits of tolerance so as to avoid destruction of public freedom by excessive liberality in tolerating views hostile to free public criticism and thus to freedom itself. The limits of public criticism are thus the defences which must needs be erected against those who wish to destroy it, from whatever quarter they may come; but this is the only frontier which requires protection.

Right, however, cannot possibly prevail among men within a state if their freedom is threatened by the action of other states. The law can prevail only if the rule of law prevails in all states and in international relations. Only then are all individuals free; only then does right prevail everywhere. Clearly, the very universality of the demand that right should prevail makes it imperative that it should apply to all men and provide legal protection against all kinds of violence. This is possible only if war is abolished as a means of politics and peace is established and safeguarded on earth according to the principles of right. This is the ultimate problem of politics. Kant had predecessors in this view of international politics, but once again the rigour of his argument and the relentless search for philosophical vindication are unprecedented.

In Kant's view, right can be jeopardised by war or by preparations for war. As he writes in his essay *Conjectural Beginning of the Human Race* (1786): 'It must be admitted that the greatest evils which afflict civilised nations are brought about by war, and not so much by actual wars in the past or the present as by never ending and indeed continually increasing preparations for war.' Neither a republican state (however just its legal arrangements are) nor its citizens are safe unless they avoid conflicts with other states. The only way to do so is by establishing peaceful relations between independent states according to the principles of right. Kant realises, as his ironic preamble to his treatise *Perpetual Peace* indicates, that the ultimate alternative to this view is the graveyard, the death of all, a possibility which has become only too real in this nuclear age of ours.

It is a duty to work towards the establishment of a cosmopolitan society. A world state would be the ideal solution, but states are not likely to agree to a complete surrender of their sovereignty, nor is the territory of the world compact enough to permit control by one supreme authority. (Modern technology has, so to speak, made the world shrink since 1795, but there are still almost insuperable barriers to effective control of the globe by a world government, owing to the diversity of nations.) This positive solution is therefore unrealistic; a negative solution must suffice. As war becomes more and more expensive and as the peoples (not the sovereigns) will have to bear the burden, they will not desire war any more. Necessity will bring about this state of right; for the balance of power is too precarious. Indeed, Kant harshly attacks the concept of the balance of power because it cannot lead to perpetual peace. This state of affairs can be brought about only gradually. It needs a nucleus of republican states. To have a world republic is impossible unless all nations agree to it, which is not very likely. Kant admits that, on the analogy of individuals uniting to form a state, all states might be compelled to unite into a world state governed by law. He points out that states would not wish to abandon their sovereignty. In his view, so it would seem, they are intrinsically incapable of doing so. This is surprising, since for him, as distinct from Fichte or the Romantics, states do not have an unalterable traditional, natural or linguistic basis. Since the states persist, a world state would create only the semblance of public international law; it would, in fact, be likely to result in a particularly oppressive despotism.

What could be brought about is a federation of states which are opposed to war. Again the *a priori* principles of right decide the issue. War is not the right way of settling disputes between nations. Nor is war invigorating or noble. Kant's principles of right demand that the nations agree to laws capable of settling disputes between them and that they be prepared to submit to arbitration according to law. The respect for law which prevails in a republican state makes it incumbent upon its citizens and its government to establish a similar system of law in international affairs.

Kant was thus well aware of the role of power in politics. He was certainly not so naïve as to believe that it would be sufficient to proclaim such rules in order to bring about perpetual peace. But in Kant's view, the sense of right is all-pervasive; for even the mighty tend to appeal to right when they violate law. It is an observation which Machiavelli, though from a completely different standpoint, had also made. Kant therefore thinks it imperative to make men aware of the principles of right and accept the rule of justice.

Kant expressly rejects the rule of expediency in international politics. Men who espouse expediency, however, also have principles, principles which are derived from the view that might is right. Kant shrewdly analyses them. He was indeed aware of customary political practice and he acutely discerned the arguments usually put forward to deceive political opponents.

Kant considers it essential to demonstrate that perpetual peace cannot be established by following the doctrines of expediency which are: *fac et excusa, si fecisti nega* and *divide et impera*. These principles are not objective *a priori* principles of right on which men can agree and act. They involve considering the consequences of one's action and not the maxims of one's action. They are therefore heteronomous, i.e. uncertain and imprecise. It is impossible to agree on them by the use of reason. They do not allow of a philosophical enquiry into politics, nor do they afford points of orientation for rightful political action.

Just as Kant did not write a single masterpiece on political philosophy, he did not write a single comprehensive work on the philosophy of history. We have to turn to the essays **What is Enlightenment?** and **Idea for a Universal History with a Cosmopolitan Purpose** of 1784 and to a section of **The Contest of Faculties** of 1798. What then is his view of history?

First of all, Kant asks whether we can formulate laws in history, just as we can formulate laws in nature, so that we can understand history in the way in which we understand nature. In his view, it is difficult to detect these laws, but perhaps biography—and Kant here takes up a point frequently raised in eighteenth-century German discussions by Mendelssohn, Hamann, and Herder, for instance—may serve as a suitable analogy. Perhaps the general course of history shows a development in mankind similar to that which biography discerns in the individual. If there is progress, this is certainly not due to human wisdom; for even the philosophers, Kant ironically remarks, are not wise enough to plan their lives.

Kant nevertheless sets high standards. He intends to discover the natural laws of history, just as Kepler had discovered the natural laws of the planets. When Kant talks of plans of nature in history, he does not mean that there is an actual legislator or mind called nature which has consciously made a plan to be carried out in history, but merely that if we wish

to understand history as (according to him) we have to, we must resort to an Idea, such as the one that nature has a purpose in history. This Idea cannot be proved or disproved by a scientific enquiry, but without it, we cannot understand history at all. Nor must this Idea be considered to have equal status to a scientific law. Kant adopts a point of view, admittedly a subjective one, from which [as R. G. Collingwood states in his *The Idea of History*] it is not only 'possible, but profitable, and not only profitable, but necessary' to look at the facts of history. Since his main concern is with human freedom, the development of human freedom provides him with the necessary clue. He therefore assumes that a plan of nature must intend the education of mankind to a state of freedom. Or (to put it differently) since nature has endowed man with reason, and since the purpose of nature is to realise man's essence, nature has made man in order that he should become rational. Kant's view that man's essence must be realised follows an argument later developed in the **Critique of Judgment** where Kant had maintained that the teleology of nature is internal, not external. It is also a peculiarity of reason that it cannot be completely realised in the lifetime of an individual, but only in the entire species. This view represents a pivotal point in Kant's philosophy of history. His anthropological studies, to which he devoted much time and energy, had confirmed him in his conception of the unity of mankind. Culture was not the result of individual effort, but was produced by mankind as a whole. Man as a rational being therefore needs to live in a historical process. History is a progress towards rationality, but it must not be thought that this process involves a continuous advance in rationality all the time. In **The Contest of Faculties,** Kant explicitly rejects the suggestion that the question of progress can be solved by appealing to experience. None of the possibilities which he can envisage supplies an answer. The first possibility is that everything is getting worse and worse. He calls it 'terrorism'. This hypothesis does not work, because after a certain stage, things would have become so bad that everything would disintegrate. The second possibility, which is called 'chiliasm', implies that everything is getting better and better, but it is equally mistaken. It is false, because there is evil in any individual which cannot be diminished and because there is good which cannot be increased. To increase the good, man would need to possess more good than he has, which is untenable. The third possibility he calls 'abderitism': this implies that everything gets neither better nor worse, but is simply stagnating. Good and evil seem to neutralise one another. But this is a farcical situation which must be considered unworthy of man.

We must therefore look for a principle outside experience. We can find it in the moral character of man. Outwardly, this moral character is realised in legal arrangements, i.e. by instituting a republican constitution. The French Revolution seems to him to represent this kind of event; for its aims are precisely the establishment of a republican state. To advance the spread of rationality is a moral obligation, for this advance is the only way in which our moral nature can be fully realised. It is our duty to further the establishing of a republican constitution, but it is also our duty to maintain the existing system of laws, whatever its character may be. We may, indeed we ought to improve the existing system of laws by criticism, so that it may approach the system of laws which ought to prevail in accordance with the principles of right. These aims are not chimerical; for the goal towards which history is moving is the establishment of a republican civil constitution. Since it is an ideal, it is not possible to realise

Engraving of Kant by Karl Barth.

it completely, but it can be approached. If it were merely to depend on man's moral decision whether a republican constitution be established, the outlook would indeed be bleak; for we must not expect too much of men. But nature is on our side. History can be interpreted only if we fully understand the conflict among men. Man is not only social, but antisocial too. The unsocial sociability, the mutual antagonism which prevails in society, is thus the means which nature employs to bring about the development of all capacities implanted in men, but only in so far as the antagonism will eventually bring about an order regulated by law: 'Man wishes concord, but nature, knowing better what is good for his species, wishes discord.'

Kant then certainly does not ignore the role which might and strife play in life. Like Hobbes, he sees in the antagonism among men, in the war of all against all, the mainspring for the establishment of a civil society. Logically, this view is in keeping with his assumption that, if history is the process by which man becomes rational, he cannot be rational at the beginning. Consequently, the force which serves as the mainspring of the process cannot be reason. It must be something radically different from it, such as mutual anti-rational antagonism among men.

Kant's philosophy of history is of considerable consequence for his political theory. Rebellion is condemned not only because it runs counter to the principle of law, but also because it is unnecessary in the light of historical development. Progress towards rationality, i.e. the establishment of a republican constitution, cannot be held up for long. To rebel against the powers that be would not hasten this process. It would even be likely to retard it; for rebellion would create a bad exam-

ple. If a ruler sets men free there will usually at first be difficulties, even dangers, but 'men must be free in order to be able to use their power wisely in freedom'. Sooner or later, reason will assert itself and the principles of right will be respected.

Such are the aims and principles of Kant's theory of politics. It is an impressive picture of a world that ought to be governed entirely by the principles of right. It would be easy to be sceptical and to dismiss the attempt as unrealistic. Kant anticipated this objection, and explicitly based his principles not on a high-minded view of man, but on a conviction, doubtless inherited from the Christian dogma of original sin, of the radical evil in human nature. Kant's principles of politics are laid down neither by tradition nor by the sovereign power. They are found neither in experience nor in nature. Like Hobbes, he believes in the power of reason to judge politics. But unlike the principles of Hobbes, they are not the logical consequences of definitions derived from a detached observation of life. They are independent of experience. Kant's principles are not part of an elaborate system of politics, but elementary principles which can help us to guide our actions. They can help us to orientate ourselves in politics if we wish to safeguard our freedom and that of others. They are analogous to the categorical imperative and require universal application. Kant, however, was not concerned with elaborating political programmes. For his conception of political freedom is not positive, but negative. It is concerned with those restraints which the individual must accept in order to avoid conflict with others so that he may enjoy the freedom of moral action.

For Kant, what is true in theory also applies in practice. By practice, he means the activities of practical life in a wide sense. His theory of politics is capable of explaining political life; a theory based on heteronomous elements, i.e. a theory seeking to explain political life by reference to might, is unable to do so; for political life is only superficially concerned with political power. Power cannot be ignored, but the real problem of politics is to ensure right, i.e. law and justice. If we take the dignity of man, his freedom as a rational being, as the starting-point of our enquiry into political practice, only a theory of right based on principles of pure reason is capable of explaining political life. Other theories are false and thus mislead not only in their understanding of political practice, but also in their political repercussions.

The right theory does afford points of orientation for political practice, though it is never by itself enough. Prudence and practical skill are also needed in the conduct of political affairs. Kant was not a blinkered visionary, nor was he even an unpractical utopian dreamer. As a scientist, he had learnt to respect fact. His own philosophical polemics and his attitude to the government of the day reveal a keen awareness of the needs of the actual situation, and he did not resort to lying or to a flagrant compromise with his own principles. He sought to follow the maxim accepted in *Perpetual Peace:* 'Be ye therefore wise as serpents, and harmless as doves.'

Kant should be accorded a prominent place in the history of Western political thought, a place which has far too long been denied to him. He ought to be ranked among the leading political thinkers of all times. Plato, Aristotle, Hobbes are his peers. He is second to none in the acuteness of his thinking. His attempt to formulate rational principles of politics on which all men can, and even ought to, agree of their own accord is as important for the modern world as Hobbes' endeavour to free political thought from the quagmire of tradition and superstition. To read Kant's political writings is to scale the heights of philosophical reflection on politics. His political thought should be of interest to all those who value the use of reason in public life. (pp. 21-40)

Hans Reiss, in an introduction to Kant's Political Writings, *edited by Hans Reiss, translated by H. B. Nisbet, Cambridge at the University Press, 1970, pp. 1-40.*

ALLEN W. WOOD (essay date 1970)

[*In the following excerpt from his full-length study of Kant's philosophy of moral and religious faith, Wood analyzes the logic of Kant's arguments for a transcendental ethical realm that would permit unconditioned human freedom.*]

Kant's moral arguments for God, freedom, and immortality represent an abiding concern throughout his critical works. We find attempts of greater or less clarity and detail to state these arguments in no fewer than eleven of Kant's critical writings, and innumerable allusions to them throughout these writings. Not many of Kant's doctrines were defended more often or at greater length than his doctrine of moral faith. Yet for all of Kant's attention to this subject, and indeed perhaps because of it, we find it extremely difficult to extract from his works any single and coherent account of the line of reasoning with which he attempted to justify moral faith. Very few of Kant's readers seem to have even tried to formulate for themselves in a precise way just what Kant is attempting to show in the moral arguments, and to state clearly just how he tried to show it. And those who do seem to have attempted formulations of this kind appear also to have for the most part concluded that no really valid argument for moral faith can be extracted from Kant's works. But I do not believe that a clear account of the moral arguments is necessarily inaccessible to the patient reader of Kant, and I do think that once a clear account has been arrived at, we shall see that these arguments possess a far greater degree of insight and plausibility than has usually been accorded them.

Before beginning our consideration of the arguments themselves, however, attention must be paid to an important issue in Kant scholarship which relates to our investigation. Erich Adickes, in his pioneering work in editing and interpreting Kant's *Opus Postumum,* concluded that Kant repudiated the moral arguments of his critical period in the *Opus Postumum,* and that he had replaced them with a more "personal" and "subjective" faith in God based on a "subjective awareness" (*subjectives Erleben*) of God in the recognition of the categorical imperative. Adickes' conclusion on this point has been accepted as authoritative by many of Kant's commentators since without their realizing—as I believe Adickes did—how problematic any interpretation of the scattered and enigmatic remarks the *Opus Postumum* must be and how much any such interpretation must be based on a particular reading of Kant's published and relatively clearer works. And Adickes' conclusion—valid or not—has all too frequently been *misused* by Kant's interpreters to suggest that Kant himself might have endorsed their own less than sympathetic readings of the moral arguments, or to explain away their inability to understand these arguments by the claim that they are not a genuine and valid part of the critical philosophy anyway.

More recently, however, Adickes' conclusion itself has been cogently challenged by Schrader and, following him, by Sil-

ber. Schrader argues that Adickes' conclusion is based on insufficient evidence from the *Opus Postumum* itself and is rendered plausible only by Adickes' own highly dubious and highly unsympathetic reading of the moral arguments as they appear throughout Kant's published works. It will not be our task here, happily, to attempt an interpretation of the *Opus Postumum,* or to attempt any direct assessment of Adickes' conclusion or Schrader's response. But I think it can be seen quite simply how the argument of the present essay, if it is correct, does contribute to this discussion.

Even Adickes can find no positive "repudiation" of the moral arguments anywhere in any of Kant's works, including the *Opus Postumum.* Thus he says only that in the *Opus Postumum* the moral arguments "*sind so gut wie vollig verschwunden.*" (Schrader, however, contests even this claim.) It seems to me that the absence of a detailed restatement of the moral arguments in the *Opus Postumum* must be conceded to be a conspicuous one, but by itself it can hardly be conclusive evidence that Kant had repudiated these arguments. And it is plain that Adickes' other grounds for his conclusion rest largely on his own claim that the moral arguments always were incompatible with the critical philosophy, that they undermined the "subjective" character of faith, that they constituted speculative demonstrations of the existence of God and of immortality, and that they represent a "hedonistic intrusion" into Kant's ethics. These, quite clearly, are not claims about the *Opus Postumum* at all, and to assess them requires only a careful examination of Kant's own statements of the moral arguments and of his moral philosophy. Of course, if Kants' moral arguments are as clearly unsound, as obviously incompatible with the critical philosophy, and as inimical to Kant's ethics as Adickes and others have believed, then it would be no wonder if Kant had repudiated them at *some* point in his career. The only puzzling thing in this case is that Kant continued to state and restate these arguments time and time again throughout his critical writings, and to defend them at every turn. The puzzling thing then is only that Kant did not repudiate the moral arguments long before the *Opus Postumum,* and that he did not give a more unequivocal repudiation there.

But if, on the other hand, a closer examination of the moral arguments themselves reveals that they are in fact not incompatible with Kant's philosophy, that they are the natural and proper consequence of his ethics, and that they are as sound and perceptive as anything in his philosophy, then it would be surprising indeed if Kant had ever repudiated them; and we could not in this case take his failure to restate the arguments in the *Opus Postumum* as conclusive evidence that Kant had rejected, for no apparent reason, an important part of his philosophical contribution. We should not expect to find Kant repudiating arguments which are sound and perceptive, and we surely ought not to take such repudiations (even if we were to find them) as Kant's best thinking unless they were supported by even stronger considerations. Now it is clear that, whatever we may say about the *Opus Postumum,* all of the reasoning in favor of *our* rejecting the moral arguments, of *our* regarding them as inimical to Kant's ethics and incompatible with his philosophy, come not from Kant but from the critics of the moral arguments. How sound their reasoning is, we will have some occasion to consider in the present essay.

Kant asserts in many places that his moral arguments are not like the three traditional arguments for God's existence, or any of the speculative arguments for freedom and immortality. He maintains that the arguments he is presenting differ essentially from the traditional ones and, indeed, from any possible speculative or metaphysical arguments. In spite of these assertions, however, the moral arguments are commonly criticized as being "theoretical" in character. Thus Kemp Smith holds the moral arguments to be "illegitimately theoretical" in character and Lewis White Beck claims to have discovered as their "hidden sense" a form of natural theology. It is not uncommon to see Kant as having only deceived himself into thinking that he had formulated an argument which was unlike the traditional ones. Adickes thus bases his claim that Kant "repudiated" the moral arguments in his later life largely on the supposed fact that Kant had finally seen through his own deception:

> Yet it always held for him that he must deny knowledge [*Wissen*] in order to make room for faith [*Glaube*]; only now the earlier practical arguments for God were also counted as knowledge and as such were rejected.

Adickes must have realized, of course, that passages like [the above] were intended by Kant to distinguish the moral arguments (in justification of *faith*) from the traditional speculative ones (which had promised *knowledge* of God). The question, then, is not whether Kant's own views on the relation of faith and knowledge ever underwent any change, but is simply whether the moral arguments *are* in fact (what Kant said they were) justifications of *faith* rather than claims to *knowledge*.

Kant frequently contrasts the moral faith or belief (*Glaube*) which the moral arguments justify with the knowledge or cognition (*Wissen, Erkenntnis*) at which the traditional speculative arguments had aimed. From what Kant says about "faith" and "knowledge" it is evident that they possess both important similarities and crucial differences. Both faith and knowledge are spoken of as ways of "holding" (*Fürwahrhalten*) judgments. Both are also said to be ways of holding judgments which are "valid for everyone" and hence are both justified or "sufficient" (*zureichendes*) ways of holding judgments. Both, that is, are judgments held on account of some good and genuinely "sufficient" reason or ground for holding them. And since they are justified in this way by a "sufficient" ground for holding them to be true, both faith and knowledge are described by Kant as forms of "conviction" (*Überzeugung*) rather than of mere "persuasion" (*Überredung*), and both are opposed to mere "opinion" (*Meinung*), which is the "insufficient" (*unzureichendes*) holding of a judgment. Both faith and knowledge allow us to "assert" (*behaupten*) the judgments which are known or believed true. These judgments presumably are, or may be, *theoretical* judgments in both cases, and this is why Kant says that "theoretical reason," or the *Erkenntnistriebe*, assumes or presupposes the existence of a God and a future life on the basis of the moral arguments. But this does not imply that the arguments themselves are "theoretical" or that they make claims to "knowledge" of any kind.

The crucial difference between "knowledge" and "faith" is the way in which each is regarded as "sufficient":

> If our holding of the judgment be only subjectively sufficient, and is at the same time taken as being objectively insufficient, we have what is termed *believing* [*glauben*]. . . . When the holding of a thing to

be true is sufficient both subjectively and objectively, it is *knowledge* [*Wissen*].

Unfortunately, Kant does not draw the distinction between "subjective" and "objective" sufficiency with the clarity we might wish. In several places, he seems to identify "objective sufficiency" with "being valid for everyone," and suggests that only "objective sufficiency" can give rise to a true "conviction" (*Überzeugung*). But he also asserts that moral faith is "subjectively . . . sufficient absolutely and for everyone" and that it is a form of justified conviction.

A clue to Kant's meaning seems to be provided by his statement that "from a practical point of view the theoretically insufficient holding of a thing to be true can be termed believing." This suggests that Kant does not mean by "objectively sufficient" in this context "valid for everyone," but rather that he means by this term *theoretically* sufficient." Kant is thus entertaining the possibility that there might be a form of justified conviction which is not held on theoretical grounds, but is somehow justified "absolutely and for everyone" on other grounds which are completely "sufficient" but "subjective" in character. If this is so, then it seems to me that what Kant intends to say is something like this: the holding of a judgment is "objectively sufficient" if the grounds for holding that judgment consist in knowledge of, evidence concerning, or reasoning about the *object* (or objects) with which the judgment deals. Such knowledge, evidence, or reasoning dealing with the existence and characteristics of objects is included for Kant in the province of *theoretical* reason. Thus for instance to hold the judgment that God exists on the grounds that one knows, has evidence, or can demonstrate that God exists, would be to hold this judgment in an "objectively sufficient" way, and to have *theoretical* grounds for this judgment. It would also be *knowledge* (*Wissen, Erkenntnis*) that God exists, and not a faith or belief (*Glaube*) in God. Faith, in Kant's view, is essentially different from knowledge, and no theoretical demonstration or even any evidences (*Zeugnisse*) can be presented in support of judgments which are held in this way. Faith, instead, presupposes that the believer be *conscious* of the "objective insufficiency" of the judgment he holds. Kant anticipates at this point the famous remark of Kierkegaard in the *Concluding Unscientific Postscript*:

> If I am capable of grasping God objectively, I do not believe, but precisely because I cannot do this I must believe. If I wish to preserve myself in faith I must constantly be intent upon holding fast to the objective uncertainty, so as to remain out upon the deep, over seventy thousand fathoms of water, still preserving my faith.

Faith for Kant, as for Kierkegaard, is a personal and "subjective" matter. Kant expresses this character of faith when he says that as a result of the moral arguments,

> no one, indeed, will be able to boast that he *knows* that there is a God and a future life. . . . No, my conviction is not logical but *moral* certainty; I must not even say, *It is* certain that there is a God, etc., but only *I am* morally certain etc.

Yet it must not be concluded that faith for Kant is "illogical" or irrational. The moral arguments are intended by him to justify a conviction which is "subjectively . . . sufficient absolutely and for everyone," to show that this conviction is "the most reasonable one for us men" to hold. The moral arguments, then, will not demonstrate *that* there is a God or a future life, nor will they add a single shred of *evidence* in favor of their existence (thus Ewing's comment that Kant's arguments are of "some probability value" could not be more wrong); and yet, on the basis of practical considerations holding for each man personally as a moral agent, Kant proposes to justify and even rationally to require of each man the personal conviction that there exist a God and a future life.

We may well wonder at this point how Kant can possibly hope to justify the holding of a judgment without attempting in any way to offer evidence in favor of its truth. Is such a "subjectively sufficient" holding of a judgment even possible? How can I be required to believe something if no shred of evidence for its truth is set before me? And if I can be so required, why can't I then be "justified" in believing propositions true which I *know* are false? But isn't this absurd? "No indeed," we may be tempted to say, "there can be no such thing as a 'subjectively justified' faith."

Before we content ourselves with this hasty judgment, however, let us at least consider the manner in which Kant himself proposes to justify moral faith. Let us first ask what sorts of "objectively insufficient" beliefs admit of a "subjective" justification. Kant is clearly not trying to justify belief in propositions which are *known* to be false. Nor does moral faith apply, in Kant's view, to judgments which are *known* to be true. If I *know* a proposition to be true, all other considerations relating to my holding it are irrelevant; if I *know* it to be false, no other consideration can possibly justify believing it. Thus belief (*Glaube*) is justifiable as such "only . . . if the insufficiency of [theoretical demonstration] is fully conceded." Kant denies, in fact, that moral faith can apply to *any* judgment which *admits* of theoretical knowledge as to its truth or falsity. In the case of such judgments (e.g., historical judgments) there is no "faith" (*Glaube*) but only "credulity" (*Leichtgläubigkeit*). In the moral arguments, Kant is attempting to justify belief in *transcendent* objects. Objective uncertainty, the inability to demonstrate or give evidence either for or against the existence of these objects, is in this case forced upon us by a conceptual necessity relating to the limitations of our powers of theoretical cognition. A form of justified belief, different from moral faith, can occur, however, also in cases where our objective uncertainty is based only on an insufficiency of empirical evidence. This belief, which Kant calls *pragmatic belief* (*pragmatische Glaube*), is used in the first critique to elucidate the concept of moral belief in an insightful way. Kant describes pragmatic belief as a "contingent belief, which yet forms the ground for the actual employment of means to certain actions." As an example of this kind of belief, Kant gives the following: "The physician must do something for a patient in danger, but does not know the nature of the illness. He observes the symptoms and if he can find no more likely alternative he judges it to be a case of phthisis."

Pragmatic belief, it should be noted, is not itself a means to an end, but a "ground for the . . . employment of means." But it may be strongly objected that this example does not offer us any unique way of justifying beliefs. The only justification for the physician's belief here is the actual evidence in favor of the patient's having phthisis, and his belief is justified only insofar as evidence to this effect is present. Or, indeed, it might be urged (in a vein reminiscent of the intellectual puritanism of W. K. Clifford) that in such a case *belief* is a dangerous luxury on the physician's part, a luxury which he cannot in good faith afford. Such a "belief" may prejudice his

evaluation of new evidence and prevent his impartial weighing of the facts. In good conscience he must simply treat the patient as best he can and suspend judgment about matters of which he has no sufficient objective grounds for belief.

But whatever the merits of this line of reasoning, it quite misses the point of Kant's example. For what concerns Kant in his discussion of pragmatic belief is not the relation between belief (or action) and the evidence which justifies it, but rather a *relation between belief and action themselves,* considered apart from whatever evidence justifies them. Let us consider this point further. Suppose our physician were to announce his intentions to cure a certain patient, and that he were to tell us that he is treating the patient for phthisis. And then suppose that we were to ask him (rather moronically perhaps) whether he *believes* that the patient has phthisis. Now Kant's point is that no matter how much or how little evidence he has for believing the patient to have phthisis, he cannot reasonably give a *completely* negative answer to our question. He might, to be sure, give us some sobering information about how uncertain the situation was, he might say that he didn't *know* or wasn't *sure.* For, as Kant says, "even in his own estimation his belief is contingent only; another observer might perhaps come to a sounder conclusion." But unless he is giving a silly answer to a silly question, he cannot reasonably say simply that he does not believe the patient to have phthisis at all. Not only could he not reasonably tell us that he did believe the patient to have some other disease; but it would also be unreasonable for him to tell us that he had decided to avoid the risk of error by a judicious "suspense of judgment." He incurs the risk of error by his *action,* and he cannot pretend to avoid it by disavowing the belief on which his action is rationally based. Indeed, his "suspense of judgment" would be the most unreasonable attitude of all. For we might imagine a case where the physician had a (perhaps quite strong and objectively well-founded) belief that his patient had a minor ailment, but treated him for a more serious one as a precaution. But of course he could not in such a case disavow *all* claims that the patient might have the more serious disease, and would thus maintain a "contingent" belief in this possibility.

Kant's point here is of course not merely that we may *predict* from the physician's actions and his expressions of intention that he will be found to hold certain beliefs. The point is not that (as a sort of general psychological fact) we find that people who act in certain ways *do* actually hold appropriate beliefs as grounds for the employment of means to the ends they seek. The importance of the relation between belief and action for Kant is that it is a *rational* relation. Kant's point is that a finite rational being acting purposively in a situation always "presupposes," "implies," or "commits himself to" certain beliefs about his situation which form the "ground for the employment of means" to the ends which he has set himself. Much as, according to Moore, a person who asserts that he went to the pictures last Tuesday *implies* that he believes he did; and as, according to Strawson, a person who uses a uniquely referring expression *presupposes* that (in the context of his use of that expression) there is one and only one thing to which the expression applies; so similarly, according to Kant, when a person announces his intentions to pursue a certain end, and undertakes a certain kind of action in pursuit of that end, he *presupposes, implies* or *commits himself* to a belief that the end in question is at least *possible* of attainment through the action he is taking toward it.

It might appear that this relation between belief and action does not apply to every case, or at least that a counterexample to it can be imagined. Suppose, for instance, that I am playing a chess game with the chess champion of the world. I am a novice at chess, and it would not be excessive humility for me to admit that I have absolutely *no* chance of beating the champion, that it is quite *impossible* in fact for me to win (not *logically* impossible, of course, but still quite impossible enough). But even conceding this, I might continue to play as best I can and play to all appearances with the goal of *winning* (I will protect my king, attempt to take my opponent's pieces, and so on). Now here it seems reasonable to describe my behavior by saying, "He is trying to beat the champion, although he knows it is impossible for him to do so." Moreover, it also seems that it is not in the least irrational for me to play against the champion in this way. But here I am, with perfect rationality, pursuing an end (winning the game) while firmly believing that it is quite impossible for me to attain this end, and this would seem to be ruled out by what Kant has said.

It seems to me, however, that this proposed counterexample is mistaken, for the following reasons. In playing chess, I am following a kind of procedure which *might* have any one of a number of purposes. The most obvious one, of course, is to win the game. But if my goal in playing the chess champion were not to *win* but to *draw*, or even just to last more than ten moves, my procedure would be the same—namely, to play as best I can. In many cases of this kind, people perform actions without any clear end in view (which is not to say that they have *no* end). They follow a procedure which leads them in a certain *direction*, but are quite willing to leave how *far* they go in that direction more or less indefinite. It would probably be best to say, then, that in playing the champion, my end is simply to do as well against him as I can. But in cases like this, where no *specific* end has been adopted, of course no *specific* belief can be presupposed as a ground for the employment of means to that end. But this does not show that in those cases where one's end *is* specific, that no such belief is presupposed. Thus if I were to announce that I did actually intend to *beat* the chess champion of the world (and not merely to last ten moves, or to do "as well against him as I can") I *would* have committed myself to the belief that it is possible for me to do so.

There are various accounts which one might give of this relation between belief and action. I do not propose to consider this question in detail, but will try to state what seem to me the two most plausible alternatives, without trying to decide which of them is the more plausible. (Each of them seems to have some support from Kant's texts, but there is no *conclusive* evidence, it seems to me, that he favored either of them.) We might say, on the one hand, that a person who pursued an end *E* but did not believe *E* was possible of attainment was acting "irrationally," involving himself in a "practical contradiction" of some sort. We would be saying, on this account, that by pursuing *E* he had adopted a *commitment* to hold some belief about his situation such that *E* would be possible of attainment according to this belief, but that by not holding that belief he had failed in some way to meet this commitment. We would also say, then, that according to his own beliefs he *should* (in a logical, rather than a moral sense of "should") stop pursuing *E*.

But we might, on the other hand, view the relation between belief and action in a different way. We could say that the be-

havior of a person could not even be called "purposive action" unless he believed the end of his action to be possible of attainment. For this reason, we could say that a person who expressed his intention to pursue an end *E implies* or *presupposes* that he actually does believe *E* to be possible of attainment. And indeed on this account we would regard a remark like "Jones is pursuing *E* but does not believe that it is possible of attainment" as self-defeating, or even as a misuse of language. Hence if a person claims to be pursuing some end *E,* but does not believe *E* to be possible of attainment, we will not say merely that he has failed to meet a commitment; rather, we will say that by failing to believe *E* possible of attainment, he has admitted that he cannot really be pursuing *E at all* and is just confused or even hypocritical if he thinks he is. Thus on this second account an agent's commitment to hold a belief about his situation such as to make his end possible of attainment will proceed from a requirement imposed on any attempt to give a coherent description of his own behavior as purposive action toward the end in question.

In either case, however, it is clear that the commitment of which we speak is not to be regarded as a "moral commitment" or a *duty*. Neither pragmatic belief nor moral faith is a duty in Kant's view, and he regards it as immoral that beliefs of any kind should be imposed on free men as duties. The "belief" of which Kant speaks is rather a *condition* for purposive volition, or for the rationality of that volition, be it moral or immoral.

We are now ready to see how Kant moves from "contingent" pragmatic belief to moral belief, which is said to be "necessary." In contrast to the "contingency" of pragmatic belief, moral belief is "necessary" in two separate and distinct ways:

> [1] The practical point of view is either in reference to *skill* or in reference to *morality,* the former being concerned with optional and contingent ends, the latter with ends which are absolutely necessary. [2] Once an end is accepted, the conditions of its attainment are hypothetically necessary. This necessity is subjectively but still only comparatively sufficient if I know of no other conditions under which an end can be attained. On the other hand, it is sufficient, absolutely and for everyone, if I know with certainty that no one can have knowledge of any other conditions which lead to the proposed end. In the former case, it is merely *contingent* belief; in the latter, it is *necessary* belief.

"Pragmatic belief," as illustrated by Kant's example, is "contingent" in both these ways. The physician is not necessarily acting in obedience to a moral imperative in seeking to cure his patient, so his ends are "optional" and "contingent" in the example. If he finds that it is impossible to cure the patient, he can with perfect rationality abandon his pursuit of this end, and turn his attention to curing another patient, or to relieving the suffering of the doomed man. His belief that the patient has phthisis is also only one possible belief which might be the condition for the employment of means to his end; another physician might judge the patient to have bronchitis, or yet some other ailment, and adopt an altogether different means. The physician's belief is "subjectively but only comparatively sufficient," because it is merely the *best* practical hypothesis *he* can come up with.

Moral faith, according to Kant, is by contrast "necessary" on *both* counts. Our physician might give up his attempt to cure the patient, in which case he would no longer be committing himself to any beliefs about the patient's condition. But, according to Kant, there is one end, called the "highest good," which is "an a priori necessary object of our will and is inseparably related to the moral law." We cannot abandon the pursuit of this end without ceasing to obey the moral law altogether, and this end is therefore *morally* "necessary." The second "necessity" of moral belief involves the conditions under which this end can be thought as attainable. In the case of the physician, many diagnoses were possible, and many different beliefs might have grounded his purposive action. But, Kant claims, in the case of the pursuit of the highest good, only one set of conditions for the practical possibility of this end is thinkable by a finite rational being: and these conditions involve the existence of a God and a future life.

The necessity of moral belief, then, is made to rest on two claims which are taken by Kant from the critical philosophy. Clearly both these claims are open to question. . . . My first task . . . will be to see how Kant employs these claims in his defense of moral faith.

In the Antinomy of Practical Reason, Kant claims that if the highest good is not possible of attainment (as the argument at that point threatens to prove), "then the moral law which commands that it be furthered must be fantastic, directed to empty imaginary ends, and consequently inherently false." Now this statement suggests one possible way in which Kant's two claims may be employed in an argument for "necessary belief" in God and immortality, an argument which would be based on the following principle: If in order to obey a command, I must pursue an end which I cannot conceive possible of attainment, then that command is invalid or "false" and I am under no obligation to obey it. According to this principle we may reason as follows: Suppose I deny either the existence of God or of a future life. Now if I deny either of these, I cannot conceive the highest good as possible of attainment. But if I am to obey the moral law, then I must pursue the highest good. Thus the moral law requires me to pursue an end which I cannot conceive possible of attainment. Therefore, the moral law is "false" and I am under no obligation to obey it. In Kant's view this must lead to an "antinomy," since we have already seen (if we have read the Analytic of the second critique) that the moral law is the condition for all obligation and that this law is unconditionally binding on me.

Beck seems to support this reading of Kant's argument when he says, "In the Dialectic's discussion of the postulates . . . we come to the following situation: Given a practical proposition, Kant argues that it can be valid, even for practice, only if a theoretical proposition is assumed and if this theoretical proposition is known to be neither demonstrable nor refutable as such."

Viewed in this way, the moral arguments can be seen to be *reductiones ad absurdum,* which may be stated thus: If I deny the existence of a God or of a future life, I can be made to deny the validity of the moral law. But I know the moral law to be valid. Therefore, if I am to avoid this contradiction, I must not deny the existence of a God and a future life. But if we view them *precisely* in this way, I think it can also be shown that they are extremely inadequate. For consider: I am told on the one hand that a command is *invalid* if in obeying it one must pursue ends which he cannot conceive possible of attainment; and I am told, on the other hand, that the moral law has been shown in the Analytic of the second critique to be *valid.* Now from this I ought to be able to infer

that in the Analytic of the second critique it was shown that all the ends one must pursue in obeying the moral law are ends which he can conceive possible of attainment. But one such end (the most important one in fact, the highest good) was not even discussed in the Analytic and in fact discussion of it was explicitly postponed until the Dialectic. And no attempt whatever was made in the Analytic to remove this threat to the validity of the moral law. Hence if I really take seriously what Kant says, it follows not that I must believe in a God and a future life, but rather that the argument of the Analytic was *incomplete,* and that the moral law may very well be invalid. As Cohen correctly remarks, the moral law itself would in this case be merely a "postulate."

But it is evident from what Kant says in numerous passages that he does not mean the argument of the antinomy to prove (even as an "illusion") that the moral law is "false" or *invalid.* In the second critique itself, he says: "Duty is based upon an apodictic law, the moral law, which is independent of . . . and needs no support from theoretical opinions . . . in order to bind us completely to actions unconditionally conformable [to it]." And again in the third critique, he asserts that the moral arguments "do *not* say: it is as necessary to assume the existence of God as to recognize the validity of the moral law, and consequently he who cannot convince himself of the first can judge himself to be free of the second."

Kant's misleading way of stating the moral arguments in the second critique seems to me to have been the result of his attempt to state the antinomy of practical reason after the form of the theoretical antinomies in the first critique. The natural dialectic of theoretical reason results from a misemployment of a priori principles, but it never calls these principles into question. And yet it does result in paralogisms, antinomies, unwarranted and contradictory assertions, in *theoretical* errors. Kant seems to have been trying to produce in the antinomy of the second critique also a contradiction between the "truth" of the moral law, proved in the Analytic, and its alleged "falsity." As a contradiction between two assertions, this would constitute also a *theoretical* error. But is the practical dialectic as Kant presents it really a theoretical illusion, a theoretical error? Beck seems unhesitating in his reply to this question:

> The illusions are theoretical illusions about *morality,* not *moral illusions.* . . . Because the illusions to be exposed are theoretical, we cannot expect so much novelty here or advance beyond the first critique as we found in the Analytic. Most of the problems have already been discussed in the Dialectic of the earlier critique, though to some degree with a different outcome.

If what Kant intends to do in the Dialectic of the second critique is to justify belief in God and immortality, then it would seem that a great deal of "novelty" *is* to be expected here. Moreover, Kant's own descriptions of the results of the practical dialectic do not seem to bear out Beck's claim that its errors are only "theoretical" ones. If I were to deny that I can conceive the highest good as possible of attainment, says Kant, then "my moral principles would themselves be overthrown, and I cannot disclaim them without becoming abhorrent in my own eyes." And in the **Foundations,** though Kant speaks in a rather indefinite way about the "dialectic of practical reason," it is evident that such a dialectic does not result in mere theoretical error, but in subjective moral sophistries which "adapt moral laws to our wishes and inclinations" and "pervert their very foundations and destroy their whole dignity."

Kant's clearest statement of the nature of this dialectic, and of the strategy of the moral arguments as a whole is to be found in his *Lectures on Philosophical Theology,* where he says:

> Our moral faith is a practical postulate, through which anyone who denies it can be brought *ad absurdum practicum.* An *absurdum logicum* is an inconsistency in judgments. There is an *absurdum practicum,* however, when it is shown that if I deny this or that I would have to be a scoundrel [*Bösewicht*].

A moral argument is, then, a *reductio ad absurdum.* But it is not a *reductio ad absurdum logicum,* an argument leading to an unwelcome inconsistency in judgments. Rather, it is a *reductio ad absurdum practicum,* an argument leading to an unwelcome conclusion about the person himself as a moral agent.

In order to see how Kant constructs such a *reductio ad absurdum practicum,* we must return to the rational relation between belief and action which we observed in the case of pragmatic belief. We saw that a person who acts in pursuit of an end *E* presupposes, implies, or commits himself to a belief that *E* is at least possible of attainment. Now from this it follows also that anyone who denies that a certain end *E* is possible of attainment thereby presupposes, or implies, that he himself will not pursue *E,* or commits himself not to pursue *E,* so long as he denies that *E* is attainable.

Using this result, we may state Kant's *reductio ad absurdum practicum* as follows: Assume that I deny either the existence of God or of a future life. Now if I deny either of these, then I cannot conceive the highest good to be possible of attainment. If I deny that I can conceive the highest good to be possible of attainment, then I presuppose or imply that I will not pursue the highest good, or commit myself not to pursue the highest good. But if I do not pursue the highest good, then I cannot act in obedience to the moral law. Therefore, by denying the existence of a God and a future life, I have presupposed or implied that I will not obey the moral law, or have committed myself not to obey it. But if I do not obey the moral law, I am a *Bösewicht,* and presumably this is an unwelcome conclusion about myself, and one that I cannot tolerate. I might of course try to say that I will obey the moral law, but just not meet my "commitment" to believe the highest good to be possible of attainment. But in this case I will have to admit that I am acting "irrationally" and that according to my own beliefs I *should* (in a logical, but not a moral sense of "should") give up my pursuit of the highest good and my obedience to the moral law, and *become* a *Bösewicht.* So in either case, my denial of the existence of a God or a future life has led me to an *absurdum practicum.*

In the arguments as we have just stated it, it has been the "denial" of the existence of God and a future life which has led us to an *absurdum practicum.* It might be wondered whether this would satisfy Kant, and whether he might not also want to exclude religious "doubt" as well as "denial." And it might be questioned whether Kant's argument *could* legitimately exclude such doubt, even if Kant would wish it to. There can be no simple answer to these questions, but we will do well to give them some careful consideration. Kant's argument, it might be said, does exclude the *denial* of the existence of

God and a future life; but that this is not the same thing at all as requiring or even justifying a positive *belief* in God and immortality. For if we do not deny the existence of God and a future life, it does not follow that we will affirm their existence. And if we do not deny that the highest good is possible, we need not affirm positively that it is possible either. We might have no opinion as to whether the highest good is possible or not, or indeed we might never have given the matter any thought. And this is at least not so incompatible with pursuing the highest good as would be our positive denial that it is possible. But then we might also have no opinion about whether there exist a God and a future life, or just not think about this question either, and our attitude would not have to lead us to an *absurdum practicum.*

To a certain extent, Kant would agree with this line of reasoning. As a champion of religious toleration, he is more concerned with justifying a proper kind of religious faith than with condemning those who do not believe. There is no doubt, of course, that Kant believes a *dogmatic* atheism to be quite incompatible with obedience to the moral law. But the question of religious *skepticism* is more complex. Kant says in several places that the "minimum" theology it is necessary to have is a belief that God is at least *possible.* This minimum, says Kant, "may . . . serve as *negative* belief, which may not, indeed, give rise to morality and good sentiments, but may still give rise to an analogon of these, namely, a powerful check on the outbreak of evil sentiments."

Religious skepticism, then, is in Kant's view morally tolerable. But it is far from the most tenable of positions. According to Kant, morality requires that we positively pursue the highest good, that we concern ourselves about its attainment and establishment, that we "promote it with all our strength." Now our having "no opinion" or giving "no thought" to the possibility of the highest good may be in a minimal way compatible with pursuing this end; at least such an attitude does not straightforwardly commit us *not* to pursue it. But an attitude of deliberate aloofness, which prefers to have "no opinion" about the possibility of an end, or which never gives the matter any thought, seems to go very badly with "promoting that end with all one's strength." Such aloofness tempts us to accuse the person who adopts it of hypocrisy in saying that his end—of whose very possibility he has no opinion and to which he gives no thought—is an end whose attainment is of vital concern to him. Thus although skepticism may be in a minimal way compatible with pursuit of the highest good, it is far from the most appropriate and rational attitude for the moral man to hold. It is far better—and more honest—for him to recognize the positive commitment he has adopted in choosing to pursue the highest good, and to maintain a genuine belief in God and a future life as conditions for the conceivability of this end as a practical possibility.

The question of religious doubt, however, has another aspect. While Kant does say that the moral arguments justify a *"zweifellosen Glauben,"* he also admits that a truly honest faith may "waver." Kant seems well aware that a faith which is "consciously objectively insufficient," which holds fast to objective uncertainty and preserves itself over seventy thousand fathoms, that such a faith is not, as Tillich has put it, the opposite of doubt, but rather that doubt is an "element" of faith itself. Thus Kant praises a faith which has the courage to cry "Lord, I believe! Help thou mine unbelief." "Doubt" is not a simple concept. The sentence "I doubt it" may be uttered in as many different ways and under as many different circumstances as the sentence "I am afraid." The doubt which is an element of faith is clearly different from the deliberate, habitual, and complacent doubt of the aloof religious skeptic; and the former sort of doubt is clearly compatible with a constant, concernful and devoted pursuit of the highest good in a way that the latter is not.

Now that we have attempted—with some success, I believe—to state the moral arguments in a fairly precise and plausible way, let us return to the question of the personal and "subjective" character of the faith justified by them. Kant of course realizes that a rational *defense* of faith cannot substitute for faith itself, nor can it exhaust the emotional and personal character of faith. The moral arguments aim at justifying not simply the assent to certain speculative propositions, but more fundamentally the adoption of an outlook on the world of moral action itself. The arguments themselves cannot fully describe or present this outlook, but can only show that it is justified and point to its general features. If we do not see this, we will, like C. C. J. Webb, conclude that although Kant's arguments are "consistent," they are "artificial" and "produce no conviction." In Chapter 5, after I have given the arguments themselves a thorough treatment, I will try to describe the outlook of moral faith more concretely. For the present, however, we can see how the moral arguments themselves justify only a faith which is subjective and personal in character.

The moral arguments depend for whatever force they may have on my regarding the conclusion that I am (or am committed to be) a scoundrel as an unwelcome and unacceptable conclusion, an *absurdum practicum*. If I am willing to tolerate this conclusion, if I candidly admit that I am a ruthless villain, concerned wholly with my own private welfare and unconcerned with the furtherance of justice or the improvement of my moral character, then Kant's arguments are powerless to persuade me of anything. Kant recognizes this fact, and notes that moral faith is adopted "freely" and "voluntarily," and that the moral arguments are binding "only for moral beings." For it is only if I freely choose to lead a life in conformity with the moral law, and to pursue the ends it sets for me, that I can be threatened by the practical absurdity of the conclusion that I am a scoundrel. In this way, the moral arguments depend for their impact upon my personal moral decision and can justify and require moral faith only if I allow them to do so by choosing to act in conformity with my duty. Their "sufficiency absolutely and for everyone" depends upon the universal validity of the command of duty itself, but does not in any way alter the fact that it is only the personal decision to *do* one's duty which makes a subjective justification of faith possible. The moral arguments, then, do justify a "subjective" faith, in that they are founded not on objective proof or evidence but on a personal, but rationally commanded, decision to adopt a morally upright course of life.

Thus far in our discussion, we have neglected Kant's moral argument for freedom, and have spoken only of the arguments for God and immortality. Since the postulate of freedom is not properly part of Kant's philosophy of religion as such, we will not be dealing with it in as much detail as we will deal with the other two postulates. But freedom is closely associated with the postulates of God and immortality, and therefore deserves our consideration also. Kant himself, indeed, accords the postulate of freedom fundamental importance, and even bases the other postulates on it:

> The concept of freedom, insofar as its reality is proved by an apodictic law of practical reason, is the keystone of the whole architecture of the system of pure reason and even of speculative reason. All the other concepts (those of God and immortality) which . . . are unsupported by anything in speculative reason now attach themselves to the concept of freedom and gain, with it and through it, stability and objective reality. That is, their possibility is proved by the fact that there really is freedom, for this idea is revealed by the moral law.

This passage might tempt us to think that our belief that we are free is somehow certified in a stronger way than our belief in God and immortality. We might think that freedom is known as the "fact of pure reason" which Kant speaks of in the second critique and elsewhere. And we might even be tempted to think that freedom is known "directly" by a special kind of experience, perhaps by means of a *"subjectives Erleben,"* as Adickes claims we are aware of God according to the **Opus Postumum.** Kant of course never uses such language, either in the **Opus Postumum** or anywhere else. But it would also be fundamentally un-Kantian to think that we could be aware of freedom in this way. For even if there were an *"Immanenz Gottes im Menschengeist"* or an *Erleben* of free will, we could not know these queer feelings to be evidences of God or freedom without an intellectual intuition; but at no time in his critical period did Kant hold that we are capable of knowledge of this kind.

A look at Kant's texts on the "fact of pure reason"—whatever he may mean by that expression—shows that this "fact" is not usually freedom at all but rather the moral law, or our rational awareness of it. Kant does say sometimes that freedom and the moral law are "identical," and this seems to be the reason why he places freedom in the category of *res facti* in the third critique (and Kant is careful to emphasize the uniqueness and the nontheoretical character of this "fact"). But if these remarks are intended to express anything more than that "freedom and the moral law reciprocally imply each other," then Kant never substantiates this further claim.

The moral argument for freedom must rest, then, on the way in which it "reciprocally implies" the moral law. But Kant can no more hold that the *validity* of the moral law depends on the objective reality of freedom than he could hold that it depends on the objective reality of God or immortality:

> The question . . . is whether our *knowledge* of the unconditionally practical takes its inception from freedom or from the practical law. It cannot start from freedom, for we neither know this immediately, . . . nor infer it from experience. . . . Had not the moral law already been distinctly thought in our reason, we would never have been justified in assuming anything like freedom.

The moral law, as has been said, and as we shall see later, commands us to pursue the highest good. But more fundamentally than this, it commands us to *will* in a certain way. It commands us to will *autonomously,* to *determine* our will by the legislative form of its maxim, rather than by the end we adopt. But, says Kant, "the conception of this form as a determining ground of the will is distinct from all determining grounds of events in nature according to the law of causality." Therefore, moral volition in general can be conceived possible only in the case of a being whose will can be determined by grounds which are *not* events in nature. But this kind of will is a *free* will. Freedom is then the condition which must be assumed, presupposed, and believed of our own will if moral volition in general is to be conceived as a possibility for us. The postulate of freedom thus gives "stability and objective reality" to the ideas of God and immortality in the sense that only a will which is free can will autonomously and thus make the highest good its end. Thus the furtherance of this end in obedience to the moral law presupposes a kind of volition which can be conceived possible only if freedom is postulated.

Kant's argument for freedom can thus be stated analogously to the moral arguments for God and immortality: Suppose I deny that my will is free. If I deny this, I must deny that I can conceive the possibility of my willing autonomously. But in order to obey the moral law, I must will autonomously. Therefore, if I deny that my will is free, I am committed to deny that I do (or even can) obey the moral law. But I am rationally aware that I am unconditionally obligated to obey the law. Thus if I deny that I am free, I am committed to deny that I can do what I am unconditionally obligated to do. This conclusion is presumably an *absurdum practicum,* a conclusion about myself as a moral agent which I cannot tolerate. Therefore, I postulate and believe that I am free, even though I can neither demonstrate that I am free nor produce evidence that I am free. The moral argument for freedom is thus also a *reductio ad absurdum practicum,* and is essentially similar to the moral arguments for God and immortality. It differs from them, however, in that it does not require the doctrine of the highest good, which is crucial for the *absurdum practicum* arguments both for God and for a future life. (pp. 10-37)

> *Allen W. Wood, in his* Kant's Moral Religion, *Cornell University Press, 1970, 283 p.*

FREDERICK P. VAN DE PITTE (essay date 1971)

[*In the following excerpt from his full-length study of Kant's anthropological writings, Van de Pitte argues that Kant's ethical philosophy is fully compatible with traditional Christian theology.*]

The extent to which Kant's awareness of the powers and limitations of man moulded his thought is strikingly brought to light in his works on religion. . . . Religion does not provide Kant with the foundation of his moral theory. In typical unorthodox fashion, Kant has reversed the ordinary relation of these disciplines, and has based his entire religious position on his moral doctrine and, in particular, on the moral nature of man.

In several of his works, and especially in the *Critique of Pure Reason,* Kant had occasion to discuss possible proofs for the existence of God. In every case, he found it necessary to reject any proof from the natural order and, in spite of his personal religious convictions, such rejections troubled him not at all. In fact, as he points out in one place, such a proof would be of little value. For even if the concept of an original Being could be established by a purely theoretical path, i.e., the concept of such a Being as mere cause of nature,

> it would afterwards be very difficult—perhaps impossible without arbitrary interpolation—to ascribe to this Being by well-grounded proofs a causality in accordance with moral laws; and yet with-

out this that quasi-theological concept could furnish no foundation for religion.

Kant, therefore, approaches the matter from the aspect of morality.

Our . . . investigation of Kant's ethics leaves no room for doubt that consciousness of moral law is a most vital element in his thought—it is an absolute fact of pure practical reason upon which we can base the entire system of morality. And it is on this same base that Kant builds the framework of his religious thought. The cornerstone of this additional structure is the concept of the highest good: the morally rational ideal of the complete and perfect goal of human life.

In the *Critique of Practical Reason,* Kant points out that man as an individual is unable to attain perfection in this world; for the supreme condition of the highest good is the complete fitness of intentions to the moral law, and this involves a degree of perfection which is impossible for a rational being in the world of sense. But if this condition cannot be satisfied, then the highest good cannot be attained, and that would be absurd; for the moral law commands us to promote the highest good. It must therefore be possible to meet this condition. But we can conceive it as possible "only in an endless progress to that complete fitness; on principles of pure practical reason, it is necessary to assume such a practical progress as the real object of our will." But such a progress is possible only if we presuppose the infinitely enduring existence and personality of the same rational being—what is normally referred to as the immortality of the soul. "Thus the highest good is practically possible only on the supposition of the immortality of the soul, and the latter, as inseparably bound to the moral law, is a postulate of pure practical reason." Kant finds it possible, then, through the concept of immortality, for man to achieve virtue—but that would still not be the full realization of the highest good.

In order to achieve that ultimate state (the sharing in the *summum bonum* in the intelligible world), both virtue and happiness are required: the former is moral worth attained through obedience to the moral law; the latter, "the condition of a rational being in the world in whose whole existence everything goes according to wish and will." Virtue, of course, is the more important of the two. Kant still maintains that man must do his duty out of pure respect for the moral law rather than from any inclination toward satisfying the self or attaining happiness. But, while virtue is the supreme good, it is not the complete and perfect good. For man's conception of the highest human good requires happiness as well as virtue. Such happiness would, in a rational moral world, correspond to the degree of virtue—always being subordinate to virtue—and at the same time would constitute a perfect whole with it.

Man requires this conception of the highest good in order that he be assured of the systematic order of the universe in accordance with moral purposes. As T. M. Greene expresses it:

> Unless man can be assured by faith in the *Summum Bonum* that he is living under a just moral order and can thus be saved from inhibiting fear that virtue itself may in the end be of no avail, he has not the heart to exert himself to the performance of duty.

But how is this combination of virtue and happiness to be attained? Virtue is attained by acts of the will, but happiness depends upon the order of things in the world of nature as well. And the causality of nature is of a different order. "Hence there is not the slightest ground in the moral law for a necessary connection between the morality and proportionate happiness of a being which belongs to the world as one of its parts and as thus dependent on it." But in the practical order of things, in which man is commanded to strive for the highest good, such a condition is a necessary postulate: we *should* seek to further the highest good, therefore it must at least be possible. "Therefore also the existence is postulated of a cause of the whole of nature, itself distinct from nature, which contains the ground of the exact coincidence of happiness with morality."

In Kant's view, then, the highest good is possible only on the supposition that there is a supreme cause of nature in which there is causality corresponding to the moral intention. But that would imply two things: A being which is able to act in accordance with the idea of laws is an intelligence, or a rational being; and secondly, in such a being, the causality according to laws is his will. "Therefore, the supreme cause of nature, in so far as it must be presupposed for the highest good, is a being which is a cause (and consequently the author) of nature through understanding and will, i.e., God." Thus, if we accept the dictates of the moral law, and the possibility of their fulfillment, we must accept the existence of God. Kant completes his argument: "As a consequence, the postulate of the possibility of a highest derived good (the best world) is at the same time the postulate of the reality of a highest original good, namely, the existence of God."

For Kant, then, the concepts of immortality and of God are necessary in order to guarantee, respectively, virtue and happiness, the two ingredients of the highest good. Kant is careful to point out here that, on the basis of this argument, it is *morally* necessary to assume the existence of God, and thus it is a subjective need rather than an objective duty. But moral necessity is quite sufficient for Kant's purpose—establishing the reality of God and of the immortality of the soul for the moral order.

Kant affirms strongly that this moral proof for the existence of God is superior to any other possible form. And he gives good reasons to support his contention. He points out, for instance, that if a theoretical argument were to be used to establish the existence of God, it would then be necessary to adjust morals in accordance with theology. We can readily see that such a state of affairs would be impossible for Kant to accept, since it would violate his entire conception of reason. For such a morality would undermine the internal, necessary legislation of reason, and would do so invalidly, since the theology on which it was based would be in violation of the limits placed upon speculative reason. But the reason which Kant gives for rejecting such a procedure is that it would ultimately undermine religion itself. He points out that, in such a system, "whatever is defective in our insight into the nature of this Being must extend to ethical precepts, and thus make religion immoral and perverted."

Since Kant's efforts in the first *Critique* were explicitly directed toward convincing us that man's knowledge is restricted to the realm of possible sense experience, it is not surprising that he expresses very little opinion concerning the nature of God, or of the future state of man. Regarding the latter, he said at one time: "We know nothing of the future, and we ought not to seek to know more than what is rationally bound up with the incentives of morality and their end." In his lec-

tures on the philosophy of religion, however, Kant indicated that he did not think that man should expect a radical change in the next life. "Rather, experience of his state on earth and the ordering of nature in general gives him clear proofs that his moral deterioration . . . as well as his moral improvement . . . will continue endlessly, i.e. eternally." But Kant makes no attempt to extend this observation.

Because of the manner in which he arrives at the postulate of the existence of God, however, Kant is now able to say slightly more about the nature of God. In order to fulfill the role of guarantor of the highest good, He must be moral, so as to make the coordination of virtue and happiness possible; He must be intelligent, or capable of conceiving laws, both natural and moral; He must be endowed with a will capable of acting according to an ideal, both for the creation of the world, and for the achievement of the highest good. On the basis of these properties, necessary to the concept of God as postulated, other properties can be determined as logically implied correlates. For in considering the concept of God in relation to the object of practical reason, we find that the moral principle admits of an author of the world having the highest perfection.

> This Being must be omniscient, in order to be able to know my conduct even to the most intimate parts of my intention in all possible cases and in the entire future. In order to allot fitting consequences to it, He must be omnipotent, and similarly omnipresent, eternal, etc. Thus the moral law, by the concept of the highest good as the object of a pure practical reason, defines the concept of the First Being as that of a Supreme Being.

And this awareness of a supreme being, Kant emphasizes again, cannot be achieved through a consideration of physical causality, or any of the speculative procedures of reason.

Kant sees great value in the fact that reason cannot attain to ideas of the supersensible except through its practical, moral application. For this limitation prevents man from carrying theology into theosophy—"transcendent concepts which confound reason"—or from falling into demonology—"an anthropologic way of representing the highest being." At the same time, it prevents religion from becoming theurgy—"a fanciful belief that we can have a feeling of other supersensible beings and can reciprocally influence them"—or degenerating into idolatry—"a superstitious belief that we can please the Supreme Being by other means than by a moral sentiment."

But while practical reason guards us against such distortions, man is ever subject to the tendency to give content to his conception of God, and this tendency, if not carefully guarded, can also undermine morality. Therefore, Kant carefully defines the few properties which must be posited of God in His relation to man. Naturally, Kant's choice is of strictly moral properties. God, he tells us,

> . . . is the only holy, the only blessed, and the only wise being, because these concepts of themselves imply unlimitedness. By the arrangement of these He is thus the holy lawgiver (the creator), the beneficent ruler (and sustainer), and the just judge.

These attributes, Kant assures us, contain everything in virtue of which God is the object of religion. Naturally, he feels that man should not concern himself with attributes of God which are not appropriate to God as the object of religion;

for such properties can have no practical significance for man, and speculation concerning them is useless.

The strictness of Kant's position is moderated somewhat in his lectures on religion. We find him saying that while we should "in theory" carefully purify our conception of God of all anthropomorphic encrustations, "one may, from a practical consideration, think to oneself and represent to others such predicates (as God's immortality, i.e., His eternity) in human fashion, if the idea of God thereby attains to a greater power and strength for our morality." Human motivation thus takes on more significance when Kant's statements are directed to an actual audience. We even find him saying to his students that the postulate of God is essential to morality, "for otherwise all the subjectively necessary duties which I am under obligation as a rational being to perform lose their objective reality." Here, morality for its own sake is temporarily forgotten. "Why should I make myself worthy of happiness by means of moral conduct if there exists no Being who can secure me this happiness?" And, at another time, "if morality can offer me no prospect that my need to be happy will be satisfied, neither can it command me." These remarks are very much unlike the more cautious formulation of the written works. Yet, on the basis of these explicit statements in his lectures, Kant has been accused of hedonism for placing virtue in a merely instrumental relation to happiness. Such a conclusion does not seem warranted.

If, however, we are interested in mentioning exceptions to Kant's customary pattern of thought, we certainly must consider the *Opus Postumum.* For in his closing years, Kant went precisely to the opposite extreme. He then decided that his ethical proof for the existence of God was unsatisfactory, and took up the difficult task of redefining his faith in God, and of attempting to establish it on a firmer foundation. Adickes maintains that Kant's primary reason for making this radical change was the desire to eliminate from his ethical system whatever elements of heteronomy and hedonism had come into it through his doctrine of the highest good. To achieve that end, Kant returned to a strict interpretation of man's relation to the moral law, emphasizing that man must act solely out of regard for the categorical command of practical reason, and for no external end whatever. Man may, however, as a religious person, recognize "that the ideals and ends which he has himself imposed, are also God's ideals, ends, and laws, and through this recognition his motives to do good are appreciably strengthened." Any mention of happiness, however, would be out of place in Kant's later work. Thus, we see him reacting in the *Opus Postumum* to errors which may have arisen from the rather lenient formulation of his position in a few exceptional statements in the lectures. But neither of these two extremes represent the more widely recognized moral teaching of Kant.

It is safe to say that Kant's general conception of the relation between God and man is essentially expressed in the passage from the *Critique of Practical Reason* cited above: God is the holy lawgiver, the beneficent ruler, and the just judge. Here the relationship is perfectly expressed in neat, legalistic language which, better than anything else, aptly characterizes Kant's religious thought. For in this relationship man can only be the receiver of laws, the ruled, and the judged. Because God is for Kant solely a postulate of practical reason, there is no basis for adopting toward Him an attitude of worship or love, as between persons. Religion, therefore is almost reduced to morality.

The word "almost" is important here, for many authors blatantly accuse Kant of completely identifying religion and morality. Rosenkranz, for example, says that "Kant fell into the one-sidedness of absorbing religion in morality." And somewhat later: "Now if religion is entirely absorbed by morality, then the relation of man to God as a personal Being ceases. He may believe in God; morality does not forbid this. But it is superfluous. It is not necessary." According to Rosenkranz, then, Kant has deprived man of God in the traditional sense. "Conscience is his God. The most essential thing is the conception of the highest good, of the categorical imperative, of the maxim." But this kind of statement only emphasizes the degree to which Kant's thought can be misinterpreted; for while part of what is said here is true, more is either misleading, or explicitly false.

Kant leaves himself open to such criticism when he speaks of religion as "morals in reference to God as legislator." If the statement is taken literally, it would reduce religion to a subcategory of morality—an appropriate arrangement for a system in which the very existence of God is a postulate based on the fact of morality. At the very least, it is clear in Kant's discussion of ethics that morality depends solely upon man's consciousness of the moral law, never in any sense upon religion. But the emphatic statements of Rosenkranz fail to take into consideration many other aspects of Kant's thought.

The error in Rosenkranz' position is made obvious by an examination of any of Kant's major works. The concluding chapters of each of the three *Critiques* deal explicitly with man's religious aspirations, and it is clear from Kant's discussion in each work that he is vitally concerned to establish religious values on a firm foundation. Nor can it be consistently maintained that these religious values are reducible to pure morality.

In many places it is clearly expressed that religion is something *added* to morality—something which adds greatly to the significance of morality. In the second *Critique,* Kant says that morality is not really the doctrine of how to make ourselves happy, "but of how we are to be worthy of happiness. Only if religion is added to it can the hope arise of someday participating in happiness in proportion as we endeavored not to be unworthy of it." In the *Lectures on Ethics,* he says: "Morality as such is ideal, but religion imbues it with vigour, beauty, and reality." Kant makes it clear, moreover, that the relation between morality and religion is not merely one of convenience to make the former palatable. Wherever he discusses the two disciplines, he emphasizes that morality leads *necessarily* to religion.

Kant's conception of religion, then, is vital to his thought—but it is never permitted to assume importance apart from morality. It seems obvious to Kant that nothing glorifies God more than that which is most treasured in the world: "respect for His command, the observance of sacred duty which His law imposes on us, when there is added to this His glorious plan of crowning such an excellent order with corresponding happiness." The rigor of Kant's personal ethic is clear as he concludes: "If the latter, to speak in human terms, makes Him worthy of love, by the former he is object of adoration." Love, therefore, has its place in Kant's thought, but adoration, based on respect for God's law, must retain its primacy.

The religious position of Kant becomes more understandable when we realize what it was he was attempting to combat. The kind of religion which he repudiated was entirely deserving of his criticism. Two aspects of religion are mentioned in the lectures on ethics: piety and bigotry. Obviously, these two categories contrast Kant's own conception of religion with what he sometimes observed in others. "Piety, which is practical, consists of obeying the divine laws for the reason that God wills it; bigotry is zeal in the worship of God which uses words and expressions of devotion and submission in order to win God's favor." Certainly the latter cannot be construed as worship of God, for it implies that morality is unnecessary and that we can win God over to our side by flattery. "We imagine God to be like an earthly lord and we treat him as such; we seek to please Him with flattery, praise, and obsequious servility."

But by this attack Kant does not mean to undermine the devoutness of a truly religious man. "Devoutness," he says, "is an indirect relation to the heart of God, which seeks to express itself in action to make the knowledge of God work effectively upon the will." Thus, it is not action in itself, but rather a method of securing readiness for action. And the action for which it prepares us, "the putting into practice of the moral law, the doing of what God wills us to do," is what constitutes true religion. Devoutness, therefore, is seen as providing the drill through which we acquire the skill necessary for such action. "By means of it we seek to have the knowledge of God so impressed upon us that it acts as an incentive to us to give effect to and practice the moral law."

To clarify his position, Kant employs the example of a person interrupted in prayer by someone in need of assistance. Since devotional exercises are intended for the acquisition of good habits, i.e., performing proper deeds, this opportunity would provide an occasion for fulfilling the purpose of devotion. It would be foolish, therefore, to refuse to aid the supplicant because one should not be disturbed while at prayer. "Devotion as a separate pursuit, as an occupation in itself, has no point."

The point is well taken, and the serious student of religion finds little to quarrel with in this version of Kant's morality. True, he completes the discussion by stating that, because devotion is geared to action, we no longer need it when we have established the habit of doing good. But this observation is merely the logical implication of the thoughts already expressed, and not at all a suggestion that devotion is unnecessary in achieving virtue. It seems legitimate to conclude, therefore, that those, like Rosenkranz, who claim that religion holds no real significance for Kant are engaged in special pleading or, at the very least, they are grossly oversimplifying Kant's religious position.

There is no need for us to consider in detail Kant's thoughts on revealed religion, or to examine his attitude toward specific churches. It will suffice to mention that, in general, he favored the Christian religion. He was thoroughly familiar with the Bible and employed its basic concepts in both his written works and his lectures. Nonetheless, shortly before his death he said: "Were the Bible not already written, it would probably not be written anymore." With respect to churches, he applied one rule. Insofar as they advance morality, they are good; to the extent that they substitute mechanical observance for morality, they are evil.

Kant's lack of interest in revealed religion is explained by some writers as a result of his ignorance of theology. While he had been familiar with the Bible and the catechism from the time of his early youth, he did not continue his studies in later years. Stuckenberg mentions that "although he sub-

jected theology to severe criticism, he did not make it a subject of careful study." Kant's biographer, Borowski, also remarks on this deficiency in Kant's background, contrasting it with the otherwise universal character of his learning. "Theological investigations only, of whatever kind they might be, especially exegetics and dogmatics, he never touched." The point is well emphasized by his remark that Kant, before writing *Religion Within the Limits of Reason Alone,* "carefully read one of our oldest catechisms, namely, the *Basis of Christian Doctrine,* which appeared in 1732 or 1733."

It is difficult to conceive of Kant as being quite so narrow with respect to a discipline which he considered vital, but the testimony of his friends cannot be ignored. And, of course, it must be admitted that, if Kant were really rather badly informed on theological matters, it would go a long way toward explaining his obstinate stand on some religious issues. But while these considerations are enlightening, they bear no important relation to Kant's anthropology, and we must return to our central theme.

There is no difficulty in establishing a connection between Kant's thought on religion and his anthropological work. In the first part of *Religion Within the Limits of Reason Alone,* for example, we find a discussion of the conflict of good and evil in man, which is a clear reflection of conclusions in *Anthropologie,* Part II, Section E: "The Character of the Species." In *Religion,* also we find constant allusion to the customs and religious practices of peoples around the world, and a discussion of the merits and shortcomings of these practices in relation to morality. On the whole, we are inclined to agree with Erdmann that the entire work has an anthropological form which is only slightly obscured by the external protestations of its rational religious purpose.

But there is a more interesting aspect to Kant's religious thought: it contains the first presentation of man as both a subjective and an objective phenomenon. The "complete conception of man" . . . begins now to take on significant form. In earlier works we have seen an analysis of man's rational capacity, and—in relation to morality—the internal struggle of his sentient and rational powers. But only in Kant's religious doctrine do we find the analysis of man as a rational subject combined with the explicit analysis of man's objective position in the order of reality. In this context we see man as related to nature, to his fellowman, and to God. Kant presents man as superior to nature—indeed, as the purpose of nature—because he shares in a moral realm which transcends nature. Man stands in a social, and thus a moral, relationship with other men, directed toward the realization of the kingdom of ends. And finally, man is seen as related to God in the order of reality, with this Supreme Being serving as both the object of his respect and adoration, and the hope of his ultimate attainment of the highest good.

In a sense, then, we might be inclined to feel that Kant's religious thought is the key to his anthropology, since only in the religious context does man take on full dimension. But Kant would be extremely dissatisfied with such an interpretation. For anthropology in its full philosophical sense deals with the facts of human nature as participating in both the sensible and intelligible worlds. Religion on the other hand, is a postulate of practical reason, based on the moral law which *is* a fact of human experience. Therefore, because the concepts of religion are derived from human experience, they cannot serve as the logical basis for the investigation of man. Rather, it is necessary for Kant to find that religion, through morality, is based upon a conception of human nature as a part of a logically ordered reality. Religion can crown human experience, and add significance to it, but it can never serve as a foundation upon which anthropological conclusions could be based.

It is important to note, finally, that the relation between Kant's anthropology and his religious thought can provide an insight into the perspective which Kant had in regard to his work as a whole. He was very much concerned to show an integrated pattern of reality, man's position within that pattern, and the knowledge which man could attain of his relation to other aspects of the pattern. The last point, man's knowledge of his relation to reality, is especially important, since only after it is attained can man properly establish the criteria in terms of which he must seek fulfillment. (pp. 82-93)

Frederick P. Van de Pitte, in his Kant as Philosophical Anthropologist, *Martinus Nijhoff, 1971, 120 p.*

STEPHAN KÖRNER (essay date 1981)

[*Körner outlines the essential components of Kant's transcendental idealism.*]

Kant's Copernican revolution in philosophy consists in asking and answering two kinds of questions which, borrowing terms from the Roman jurists, he calls "questions of fact" (*quid facti*) and "questions of legality" (*quid iuris*). The former concern factual claims to the effect that all rational beings in their thinking—theoretical, practical, aesthetic, or teleological—accept certain judgments or employ certain concepts. The latter questions concern the justification of the factual claims. The Copernican revolution is based on an entirely new conception of philosophy and philosophical method which Kant describes as critical or transcendental.

Within the theoretical sphere, that is to say, mathematics, natural science, and commonsense thinking about what is the case, Kant's factual claims include three theses about synthetic judgments a priori—a judgment being synthetic if, and only if, its negation is not self-contradictory and a priori if, and only if, it is logically independent of any judgment describing a sense experience. He claims (1) that there are synthetic judgments a priori; (2) that there is one and only one internally consistent set of them; and (3) that it has been completely exhibited in the *Critique of Pure Reason.* (It comprises all axioms and theorems of Euclidean geometry, all true arithmetical propositions, and certain assumptions of Newtonian physics, such as the principles of causality, of the conservation of substance, and of continuity.)

Kant's attempted justification of these three claims—of existence, uniqueness, and completeness—is a characteristic and important instance of a transcendental justification. It presupposes that we have objective experience or experience of objects and that within it we can distinguish what is given to the senses (its sensory or a posteriori content) from what, although not so given, is yet ascribed by us to the objects (its nonsensory or a priori form). And it consists in producing, or trying to produce, a cogent argument to the effect that the a priori features of objective experience are necessary conditions of its objective character. Transcendental arguments are thus based on the twofold conviction that an experience without—or deprived of—these features is not "a possible objective experience"; and that, in another succinct, if rather metaphorical, Kantian phrase "we can have a priori knowledge

only of those features of the things which we ourselves put into them."

The fundamental tasks of the *Critique of Pure Reason,* namely the factual exposition and transcendental justification of the system of (theoretical) a priori judgments in its uniqueness and completeness, involve the subsidiary tasks of expounding and transcendentally justifying the system of the Categories, which Kant also regards as unique and complete. The Categories, for example, causality and substance, are concepts which occur in nonmathematical, synthetic a priori judgments; which are a priori in the sense of being applicable to, but not abstracted from, sense experience; and which in being applied to what is given to the senses confer objectivity upon it. Kant calls the transcendental justification of the Categories their transcendental "deduction." In doing so he again adopts and adapts a technical legal term from those jurists who mean by "deduction" the demonstration that what has been established as being *de facto* the case is also appropriate *de jure.* In this sense of the term a deduction may, but need not, coincide with a logical deduction.

The theses of Kant's First *Critique* which have just been outlined have all been subjected to various—in some cases very different—interpretations, criticisms, and modifications. In considering them it is advisable to observe the Kantian distinction between questions of fact and factual claims on the one hand and questions of legality and transcendental justification on the other. As regards the interpretation of Kant's factual claims to have expounded the unique and complete system of synthetic a priori judgments and Categories, there is hardly any disagreement among the commentators. There is, on the other hand, sharp disagreement about the correctness of these factual claims—even among philosophers who accept Kant's distinctions between synthetic a posteriori and synthetic a priori judgments and between a posteriori and a priori concepts.

The main reason for their disagreement lies in their different reactions to post-Kantian developments in mathematics and physics. These are on the one hand the discovery of non-Euclidean geometries, together with the incorporation of one of them into the general theory of relativity, and on the other hand the discovery of quantum mechanics, which—at least in its dominant interpretation—is incompatible with the Kantian a priori principles of causality and continuity. According to these reactions we may distinguish between Kantian absolutists who accept Kant's factual claims in their original form (e.g., Leonard Nelson and the so-called Göttingen school); neo-Kantian absolutists who accept Kant's uniqueness claim, but replace his system of synthetic a priori judgments and Categories by a different one (e.g., some Anglo-American analytical philosophers); and neo-Kantian pluralists who reject his claims of uniqueness and, hence, of completeness (e.g., Hermann Cohen and the so-called Marburg school, of which Cassirer was a prominent member).

Turning to Kant's transcendental justification of his factual claims, especially his transcendental deduction of the Categories, one is immediately struck by exegetic divergences which are radical and irreconcilable. For the pluralists, who deny Kant's uniqueness claim, a transcendental deduction of a unique system of Categories and, hence, of universally and necessarily true synthetic a priori judgments is impossible—whatever the alleged nature of such a "deduction" may be. To express the matter in accordance with Kant's quasi-legal terminology, the pluralists hold that since the *quaestio facti* has to be answered in the negative, that is to say, since the factual claim has to be rejected, the *quaestio iuris* does not arise (or, in a phrase of the Roman jurists, *cadit quaestio*).

In the most common contemporary interpretation, Kant's transcendental deduction of the Categories is seen as an attempted logical inference from 'x is capable of objective experience' to 'x is capable of objectifying (transforming, unifying, organizing, into an objective phenomenon) a spatiotemporally ordered, subjectively given manifold by applying *the* Categories to it.' Of Kantian and neo-Kantian absolutists, who accept the uniqueness claim for Kant's or some other system of Categories, some consider this logical inference to be valid, others consider it invalid but remediably so, while still others consider it irremediably invalid. Thus many analytical philosophers with Kantian sympathies argue that the logical inference can be validly reconstructed if the Kantian set of Categories is replaced by another. An exception is C. D. Broad, who suggests that the invalid logical inference can at best be replaced by a more modest probabilistic argument. Lastly, Leonard Nelson and his followers, though accepting Kant's factual claims, regard his transcendental deduction as an instance of the irremediably invalid logical fallacy of a vicious infinite regress. According to Nelson, Kant's correct factual claims can be justified only by showing that the Categories are applicable to an originally obscure, nonpropositional cognition, in the same way that the a priori concepts of arithmetic and geometry are applicable to the nonpropositional intuition of time and space.

In order to understand Kant's thought and influence it is important to separate his fundamental conviction that "we can have a priori knowledge only of those features of the things which we ourselves put into them" from his absolutist claim that what we so put into them is determined for all times and for all rational beings. For, although the fundamental conviction, which is common to all versions of transcendental idealism, may well have inspired the absolutist claim, it is compatible with a pluralistic assumption of alternative and even changeable systems of a priori concepts and judgments.

To the distinctions drawn by the *Critique of Pure Reason* within the sphere of theoretical thinking between the a posteriori and merely subjectively given features, which are its matter, and the a priori, objective features, which are its form, there correspond analogous distinctions drawn by the *Critique of Practical Reason* within the sphere of practical thinking and by the *Critique of Judgment* within the spheres of aesthetic and teleological thinking. Within the practical sphere the difference between a posteriori matter and a priori imposed and organizing form manifests itself in the contrast—and conflict—between desires and inclinations on the one hand and the moral will and moral duties on the other. In the sphere of aesthetic experience it manifests itself in the contrast between the pleasant and the beautiful. Like the factual claims and justifications of the First Critique, Kant's factual claims about the a priori features of morals, aesthetics, and teleology have been subjected to very different interpretations and criticisms. And these have again suggested proposals for various reforms, ranging from versions of neo-Kantian absolutism, over versions of a pluralistic neo-Kantian pluralism, to outright rejections of the transcendental approach in these fields.

Kant's transcendental or critical method is his most distinctive contribution to philosophy, a discipline which has always been very conscious of its dependence on "the correct meth-

od." But many of his other original ideas have proved hardly less influential. Examples of Kantian themes in recent philosophy that stem from the First *Critique* are the antilogicist analysis of arithmetic and the identification of physics with Newtonian physics. The former has not only become a central topic in the philosophy of mathematics but has, through its acceptance by Hilbert and Brouwer, influenced the course of mathematics itself. The latter has become important in the philosophy of science, in particular in the discussion of quantum physics, for example, Einstein's rejection of its indeterministic implications. An example of a Kantian theme stemming from the Second *Critique* is the discussion and rejection of utilitarianism in ethics, and hence in political philosophy, where—possibly under the influence of new developments in welfare economics—the conflict between utilitarian and antiutilitarian analyses of justice has again become central.

Kant's Third *Critique* has been comparatively neglected by contemporary philosophers, even by those whose main concern is with aesthetics. A probable reason for this neglect is the widely accepted view that Kant's *Critique of Judgment* owes its existence less to his philosophical insight and originality than to his idiosyncratic devotion to philosophical architectonics. (pp. vii-xii)

Stephan Körner, in an introduction to Kant's Life and Thought *by Ernst Cassirer, translated by James Haden, Yale University Press, 1981, pp. vii-xxi.*

ROGER SCRUTON (essay date 1982)

[*In the following excerpt, Scruton elucidates the conceptual framework of the* Critique of Judgment.]

The *Critique of Judgement* is a disorganised and repetitious work, which gains little from Kant's struggle to impose on its somewhat diffuse subject-matter the structure of the transcendental philosophy. A contemporary who attended Kant's lectures on aesthetics recorded that 'the principal thoughts of his *Critique of Judgement* [were] given as easily, clearly, and entertainingly as can be imagined'. Kant was seventy-one when he came to write the work, however, and there seems little doubt that his mastery of argument and of the written word were beginning to desert him. Nevertheless, the third *Critique* is one of the most important works of aesthetics to have been composed in modern times; indeed, it could fairly be said that, were it not for this work, aesthetics would not exist in its modern form. Kant's most feeble arguments were here used to present some of his most original conclusions.

Kant felt the need to explore in the *Critique of Judgement* certain questions left over from the first two *Critiques.* Moreover he wished to provide for aesthetics its own 'faculty', corresponding to understanding and practical reason. The faculty of judgement 'mediates' between the other two. It enables us to see the empirical world as conforming to the ends of practical reason, and practical reason as adapted to our knowledge of the empirical world. Kant believed that 'judgement' has both a subjective and an objective aspect, and divided his *Critique* accordingly. The first part, concerned with the subjective experience of 'purposiveness' or 'finality', is devoted to aesthetic judgement. The second, concerned with the objective 'finality' of nature, is devoted to the natural manifestation of design. I shall concentrate on the first, which suffices in itself to bring the critical system to its conclusion.

The eighteenth century saw the birth of modern aesthetics. Shaftesbury and his followers made penetrating observations on the experience of beauty; Burke presented his famous distinction between the beautiful and the sublime; Batteux in France and Lessing and Winckelmann in Germany attempted to provide universal principles for the classification and judgement of works of art. The Leibnizians also made their contribution, and the modern use of the term 'aesthetic' is due to Kant's mentor A. G. Baumgarten. Nevertheless, no philosopher since Plato had given to aesthetic experience the central role in philosophy that Kant was to give to it. Nor had Kant's predecessors perceived, as he perceived, that both metaphysics and ethics must remain incomplete without a theory of the aesthetic. Only a rational being can experience beauty; and without the experience of beauty, rationality is unfulfilled. It is only in the aesthetic experience of nature, Kant suggests, that we grasp the relation of our faculties to the world, and so understand both our own limitations, and the possibility of transcending them. Aesthetic experience intimates to us that our point of view is, after all, only *our* point of view, and that we are no more creators of nature than we are creators of the point of view from which we observe and act on it. Momentarily we stand outside that point of view, not so as to have knowledge of a transcendent world, but so as to perceive the harmony that exists between our faculties and the objects in relation to which they are employed. At the same time we sense the divine order that makes this harmony possible.

Kant's aesthetics is based on a fundamental problem, which he expresses in many different forms, eventually giving to it the structure of an 'antinomy'. According to the 'antinomy of taste' aesthetic judgement seems to be in conflict with itself: it cannot be at the same time aesthetic (an expression of subjective experience) and also a judgement (claiming universal assent). And yet all rational beings, simply in virtue of their rationality, seem disposed to make these judgements. On the one hand, they feel pleasure in an object, and this pleasure is immediate, not based in any conceptualisation of the object, or in any inquiry into cause, purpose or constitution. On the other hand they express their pleasure in the form of a judgement, speaking 'as if beauty were a quality of the object', thus representing their pleasure as objectively valid. But how can this be so? The pleasure is immediate, based in no reasoning or analysis; so what permits this demand for universal agreement?

However we approach the idea of beauty we find this paradox emerging. Our attitudes, feelings and judgements are called aesthetic precisely because of their direct relation to experience. Hence no one can judge the beauty of an object that he has never heard or seen. Scientific judgements, like practical principles, can be received 'at second hand'. I can take you as my authority for the truths of physics, or for the utility of trains. But I cannot take you as my authority for the merits of Leonardo, or for the beauties of Mozart, if I have seen no work by the one or heard none by the other. It would seem to follow from this that there can be no rules or principles of aesthetic judgement. 'A principle of taste would mean a fundamental premise under the condition of which one might subsume the concept of an object, and then, by a syllogism, draw the inference that it is beautiful. That, however, is absolutely impossible. For I must feel the pleasure immediately in the perception of the object, and I cannot be talked into it by any grounds of proof'. It seems that it is always experience, and never conceptual thought, that gives the right to

aesthetic judgement, so that anything which alters the experience of an object alters its aesthetic significance (which is why poetry cannot be translated). As Kant puts it, aesthetic judgement is 'free from concepts', and beauty itself is not a concept. Hence we arrive at the first proposition of the antinomy of taste: 'The judgement of taste is not based on concepts; for, if it were, it would be open to dispute (decision by means of proofs)'.

However, such a conclusion seems to be inconsistent with the fact that aesthetic judgement is a form of *judgement*. When I describe something as beautiful I do not mean merely that it pleases *me:* I am speaking about it, not about myself, and if challenged I try to find reasons for my view. I do not *explain* my feeling, but give *grounds* for it, by pointing to features of its object. And any search for reasons has the universal character of rationality. I am in effect saying that others, in so far as they are rational, ought to feel just the same delight as I feel. This points to the second proposition of Kant's antinomy: 'the judgement of taste is based on concepts; for otherwise . . . there could be no room even for contention in the matter, or for the claim to the necessary agreement of others'.

Kant says that the judgement of beauty is grounded not in concepts but in a feeling of pleasure; at the same time this pleasure is postulated as universally valid, and even 'necessary'. The aesthetic judgement contains an 'ought': others ought to feel as I do, and to the extent that they do not, either they or I am wrong. It is this which leads us to seek reasons for our judgements. The terms 'universality' and 'necessity' refer us to the defining properties of the a priori. It is clear that the postulate that others ought to feel as I do is not derived from experience: it is, on the contrary, a presupposition of aesthetic pleasure. Nor is it analytic. Hence its status must be synthetic a priori.

The argument is very slippery. The 'necessity' of the judgement of taste has little to do with the necessity of the a priori laws of the understanding, nor does its universality issue in a definite principle. Kant sometimes recognises this, and speaks of aesthetic *pleasure* rather than aesthetic judgement as universally valid, and so a priori. Nevertheless, he was convinced that aesthetics raises precisely the same problem as all philosophy. 'The problem of the critique of judgement . . . is part of the general problem of transcendental philosophy: How are synthetic a priori judgements possible?'

Kant offers a 'transcendental deduction' in answer. It is only fifteen lines long, and wholly inadequate. He lamely says: 'what makes this deduction so easy is that it is spared the necessity of having to justify the objective [application] of a concept'. In fact, however, he argues independently for an a priori component in the judgement of taste, and for the legitimacy of its 'universal' postulate.

Kant's concern is, as always, with objectivity. Aesthetic judgements claim validity. In what way can this claim be upheld? While the objectivity of theoretical judgements required a proof that the world is as the understanding represents it to be, no such proof was necessary for practical reason. It was enough to show that reason constrained each agent towards a set of basic principles. In aesthetic judgement the requirement is weaker still. We are not asked to establish principles that will compel the agreement of every rational being. It is sufficient to show how the thought of universal validity is possible. In aesthetic judgement we are only 'suitors

A profile drawing of Kant.

for agreement'. It is not that there are valid rules of taste, but rather that we must *think* of our pleasure as made valid by its object.

Kant distinguishes sensory from contemplative pleasures. The pleasure in the beautiful, although it is 'immediate' (arising from no conceptual thought), nevertheless involves a reflective contemplation of its object. The pure judgement of taste 'combines delight or aversion immediately with the bare contemplation of the object . . . '. Aesthetic pleasure must therefore be distinguished from the purely sensuous pleasures of food and drink. It can be obtained only through those senses that also permit contemplation (which is to say, through sight and hearing).

This act of contemplation involves attending to the object not as an instance of a universal (or concept) but as the particular thing that it is. The individual object is isolated in aesthetic judgement and considered 'for its own sake'. But contemplation does not rest with this act of isolation. It embarks on a process of abstraction which exactly parallels the process whereby practical reason arrives at the categorical imperative. Aesthetic judgement abstracts from every 'interest' of the observer. He does not regard the object as a means to his ends, but as an end in itself (although not a moral end). The observer's desires, aims and ambitions are held in abeyance in the act of contemplation, and the object regarded 'apart from any interest'. This act of abstraction is conducted while focusing on the individual object in its 'singularity'. Hence, unlike the abstraction that generates the categorical imperative, it leads to no universal rule. Nevertheless, it underlies the 'universality' of the subsequent judgement. It is this which enables me to 'play the part of judge in matters of

taste'. Having abstracted from all my interests and desires, I have, in effect, removed from my judgement all reference to the 'empirical conditions' which distinguish me, and referred my experience to reason alone, just as I refer the ends of action when acting morally. 'Since the delight is not based on any inclination of the subject (or on any other deliberate interest) . . . he can find as reason for his delight no personal conditions to which his own subjective self might alone be party'. In which case, it seems, the subject of aesthetic judgement must feel compelled, and also entitled, to legislate his pleasure for all rational beings.

What aspect of rationality is involved in aesthetic contemplation? In the 'subjective deduction' of the first ***Critique,*** Kant had argued for the central role of imagination in the 'synthesis' of concept and intuition. Imagination transforms intuition into datum; we exercise imagination whenever we attribute to our experience a 'content' which represents the world. When I see the man outside my window, the concept 'man' is present in my perception. This work of impregnating experience with concepts is the work of imagination.

Kant thought that imagination could also be 'freed from' concepts (that is, from the rules of the understanding). It is this 'free play' of the imagination that characterises aesthetic judgement. In the free play of imagination concepts are either wholly indeterminate, or if determinate not applied. An example of the first is the imaginative 'synthesis' involved in seeing a set of marks as a pattern. Here there is no determinate concept. There is nothing to a pattern except an experienced order, and no concept applied in the experience apart from that indeterminate idea. An example of the second is the 'synthesis' involved in seeing a picture as a face. Here the concept 'face' enters the imaginative synthesis, but it is not applied to the object. I do not judge that this, before me, is a face, but only that I have imaginative permission so to see it. The second kind of 'free play' is at the root of our understanding of artistic representation. Kant was more interested in the first kind, and this led him to a formalistic conception of the beautiful in art.

The free play of the imagination enables me to bring concepts to bear on an experience that is, in itself, 'free from concepts'. Hence, even though there are no rules of taste, I can still give grounds for my aesthetic judgement. I can give reasons for my pleasure, while focusing on the 'singularity' which is its cause.

Kant valued art less than nature, and music least among the arts, 'since it plays merely with sensations'. Nevertheless the example of music provides a good illustration of Kant's theory. When I hear music I hear a certain organisation. Something begins, develops, and maintains a unity among its parts. This unity is not indeed *there* in the notes before me. It is a product of my perception. I hear it only because my imagination, in its 'free play', brings my perception under the indeterminate idea of unity. Only beings with imagination (a faculty of reason) can hear musical unity, since only they can carry out this indeterminate synthesis. So the unity is a perception of mine. But this perception is not arbitrary, since it is compelled by my rational nature. I perceive the organisation in my experience as objective. The experience of unity brings pleasure, and this too belongs to the exercise of reason. I suppose the pleasure, like the melody, to be the property of all who are constituted like me. So I represent my pleasure in the music as due to the workings of a 'common sense', which is to say, a disposition that is at once based in experience, and common to all rational beings.

But how is it that the experience of unity is mixed with pleasure? When I hear the formal unity of music, the ground of my experience consists in a kind of compatibility between what I hear and the faculty of imagination through which it is organised. Although the unity has its origin in me, it is attributed to an independent object. In experiencing the unity I also sense a harmony between my rational faculties and the object (the sounds) to which they are applied. This sense of harmony between myself and the world is both the origin of my pleasure and also the ground of its universality.

> . . . one who feels pleasure in simple reflection on the form of an object, without having any concept in mind, rightly lays claim to the agreement of everyone, although this judgement is empirical and a singular judgement. For the ground of this pleasure is found in the universal, though subjective, condition of reflective judgements, namely the final harmony of an object . . . with the mutual relation of the faculties of cognition (imagination and understanding), which are requisite for every empirical cognition.

It seems, then, that our pleasure in beauty has its origin in a capacity, due to the free play of imagination, first to experience the harmonious working of our own rational faculties, and secondly to project that harmony outwards on to the empirical world. We see in objects the formal unity that we discover in ourselves. This is the origin of our pleasure, and the basis of our 'common sense' of beauty. And it is 'only under the presupposition . . . of such a common sense that we are able to lay down a judgement of taste'.

Kant distinguishes 'free' from 'dependent' beauty, the first being perceived wholly without the aid of conceptual thought, the second requiring prior conceptualisation of the object. When I perceive a representational picture, or a building, I can have no impression of beauty until I have first brought the object under concepts, referring in one case to the content expressed, in the other to the function performed. The judgement of such 'dependent' beauty is less pure than the judgement of 'free' beauty, and would only become pure for the person who had no conception of the meaning or function of what he saw. The purest examples of beauty are therefore 'free'. Only in the contemplation of such examples are our faculties able to relax entirely from the burdens of common scientific and practical thought, and enter into that free play which is the ground of aesthetic pleasure. Examples of this free beauty abound in nature, but not in art.

The unity that we perceive in the free beauties of nature comes to us purified of all interests: it is a unity that makes reference to no definite purpose. But it reflects back to us an order that has its origin in ourselves, as purposive beings. Hence it bears the indeterminate marks of purpose. As Kant put it, aesthetic unity displays 'purposiveness without purpose'. Aesthetic experience, which leads us to see each object as an end in itself, also leads us to a sense of the purposiveness of nature.

The perception of 'purposiveness', like the regulative ideas of reason, is not a perception of what is, but a perception 'as if'. However, it is an inescapable 'as if': we *must* see the world in this way if we are to find our proper place in it, both as knowing and as acting creatures. Aesthetic judgement, which delivers to us the pure experience of design in nature, frees

us both for theoretical insight and for the endeavours of the moral life. It also permits the transition from the theoretical to the practical: finding design in nature, we recognise that our own ends might be enacted there. Moreover, and again like the ideas of reason, the concept of purposiveness is 'super-sensible': it is the idea of a transcendental design, the purpose of which we cannot know.

Aesthetic experience is the vehicle of many such 'aesthetic ideas'. These are ideas of reason which transcend the limits of possible experience, while trying to represent, in 'sensible' form, the inexpressible character of the world beyond. There is no true beauty without aesthetic ideas; they are presented to us both by art and by nature. The aesthetic idea imprints on our senses an intimation of a transcendental realm. The poet, even if he deals with empirical phenomena, 'tries by means of the imagination . . . to go beyond the limits of experience and to present [these things] to sense with a completeness of which there is no example in nature'. This is how Kant explains the effect of aesthetic condensation. For example, when Milton expresses the vengeful feelings of Satan, his smouldering words transport us. We feel that we are listening not to this or that, as one might say, 'contingent' emotion, but to the very essence of revenge. We seem to transcend the limitations contained in every natural example and to be made aware of something indescribable which they palely reflect. When Wagner expresses through the music of *Tristan* the unassuageable longing of erotic love, it is again as though we had risen above our own circumscribed passions and glimpsed a completion to which they aspire. No concept can allow us to rise so far: yet the aesthetic *experience,* which involves a perpetual striving to pass beyond the limits of our point of view, seems to 'embody' what cannot be thought.

Kant attempts, then, to move from his philosophy of beauty to an account of our relation to the world which will be free of that limitation to our own perspective which he had argued, in the first **Critique,** to be a necessary condition of self-consciousness. In aesthetic experience we view ourselves in relation to a transcendental, or supersensible, reality which lies beyond the reach of thought. We become aware of our own limitations, of the grandeur of the world, and of the inexpressible good order that permits us to know and act on it. Kant has recourse to Burke's distinction between the beautiful and the sublime. Sometimes, when we sense the harmony between nature and our faculties, we are impressed by the purposiveness and intelligibility of everything that surrounds us. This is the sentiment of beauty. At other times, overcome by the infinite greatness of the world, we renounce the attempt to understand and control it. This is the sentiment of the sublime. In confronting the sublime, the mind is 'incited to abandon sensibility'.

Kant's remarks about the sublime are obscure, but they reinforce the interpretation of his aesthetics as a kind of 'premonition' of theology. He defines the sublime as 'that, the mere capacity of thinking which, evidences a faculty of mind transcending every standard of taste'. It is the judgement of the sublime that most engages our moral nature. It thereby points to yet another justification of the 'universality' of taste, by showing that, in demanding agreement, we are asking complicity in a moral sentiment. In judging of the sublime, we demand a universal recognition of the immanence of a supersensible realm. A man who can feel neither the solemnity nor the awesomeness of nature, lacks in our eyes the necessary sense of his own limitations. He has not taken that 'transcendental' viewpoint on himself from which all true morality springs.

It is from the presentiment of the sublime that Kant seems to extract his faith in a Supreme Being. The second part of the *Critique of Judgement* is devoted to 'teleology': the understanding of the ends of things. Here Kant expresses, in a manner that has proved unsatisfactory to many commentators, his ultimate sympathy for the standpoint of theology. Our sentiments of the sublime and of the beautiful combine to present an inescapable picture of nature as created. In beauty we discover the purposiveness of nature; in the sublime we have intimations of its transcendent origins. In neither case can we translate our sentiments into a reasoned argument: all we know is that we know nothing of the transcendental. But that is not all we *feel.* The argument from design is not a theoretical proof, but a moral intimation, made vivid to us by our sentiments towards nature, and realised in our rational acts. It is realised in the sense that the true end of creation is intimated through our moral actions: but it is seen that this intimation is of an ideal, not of an actual, world. So we prove the divine teleology in all our moral actions, without being able to show that it is true of the world in which we act. The final end of nature is known to us, not theoretically, but practically. It lies in reverence for the pure practical reason that 'legislates for itself alone'. When we relate this reverence to our experience of the sublime, we have a sense, however fleeting, of the transcendental.

Thus it is that aesthetic judgement directs us towards the apprehension of a transcendent world, while practical reason gives content to that apprehension, and affirms that this intimation of a perspectiveless vision of things is indeed an intimation of God. This is what Kant tries to convey both in the doctrine of the aesthetic ideas and in that of the sublime. In each case we are confronted with an 'employment of the imagination in the interests of mind's supersensible province' and a compulsion to 'think nature itself in its totality as a presentation of something supersensible, without our being able to put this presentation forward as objective'. The supersensible is the transcendental. It cannot be thought through concepts, and the attempt to think it through 'ideas' is fraught with self-contradiction. Yet the ideas of reason—God, freedom, immortality—are resurgent in our consciousness, now under the guise of imperatives of action, now transformed by imagination into sensuous and aesthetic form. We cannot rid ourselves of these ideas. To do so would be to say that our point of view on the world is all that the world consists in, and so to make ourselves into gods. Practical reason and aesthetic experience humble us. They remind us that the world in its totality, conceived from no finite perspective, is not ours to know. This humility of reason is also the true object of esteem. Only this is to be reverenced in the rational being, that he feels and acts as a member of a transcendental realm, while recognising that he can know only the world of nature. Aesthetic experience and practical reason are two aspects of the moral: and it is through morality that we sense both the transcendence and the immanence of God. (pp. 79-91)

> *Roger Scruton, in his* Kant, *Oxford University Press, Oxford, 1982, 99 p.*

LEWIS WHITE BECK (essay date 1984)

[*Beck is an American scholar of German philosophy who has edited and translated many of Kant's principal works for En-glish-speaking audiences. Here, Beck outlines the epistemological, moral, and aesthetic dimensions of Kant's philosophical system, affirming the relevance of his ideas to the modern world.*]

The publication of Immanuel Kant's *Critique of Pure Reason* two centuries ago concerns a wider public than the professional philosophical community. Although the *Critique of Pure Reason* was written almost exclusively for the professional philosopher, it was nonetheless the foundation for most of Kant's other writings, nearly half of which were addressed to the general learned public.

Great philosophers such as Kant speak not just to the professoriate, but to all who agree with Socrates that the unexamined life is not worth living. Accordingly, in his own work Kant explicitly distinguished between the "interests of the school" and the "interests of humanity." The interests of the school are those of professional philosophers. Kant believed that the interests of the school were subordinate to the interests of humanity though, in the long run, important to them. As a young man Kant wrote in a private jotting:

> By inclination I am an enquirer. I feel a consuming thirst for knowledge, the unrest which goes with the desire to progress in it, and the satisfaction which comes with every advance in knowledge. There was a time when I believed that this constituted the honor of humanity, and I despised the people, who know nothing. . . . [But] I have learned to honor man, and would find myself more useless than the common laborer if I did not believe that this attitude of mine [as an enquirer] can give a worth to all others, in establishing the rights of mankind.

Kant openly sympathized with both the French and the American revolutions, at a time when expressions of such sympathy were in Germany personally hazardous. When he wrote of "the rights of mankind," he certainly meant political and legal rights of the kind that those revolutions were meant to secure. But Kant's conception of rights was much more than political. Political rights were, he thought, essential to all others; they were conditions for the exercise of other rights—the rights of people to enlighten themselves, to use their talents freely in the discovery of truth, and to develop their moral character. All of these constitute the calling (*Bestimmung*) of man.

To determine the calling of man, philosophy is needed. Around the time Kant wrote the note just quoted, he also remarked, "If there is any science which man stands in need of, it is one which teaches him to occupy properly the place assigned to him in creation, and one from which he can learn what he must be, in order to be a man. *But what is man?* This is the principal question of philosophy, and it epitomizes three preliminary questions: What can I know? What ought I to do? What may I hope?" To each of these questions a great *Critique* is devoted, but only the entire corpus is adequate to answer the principal question. The three preliminary questions have definite answers in their respective *Critiques;* nowhere is there a simple, explicit answer to the principal question. Yet Kant's answers to the first three queries point unmistakably to an answer to the ultimate question, for there is a single common theme running through all the *Critiques* that leads always to the same reply to the question, What is man?

In the philosophy of science Kant effected what has been

called (though not by him) the Copernican Revolution. Copernicus found that the phenomena of planetary astronomy can best be understood by taking into account the movements of the earth. The real motion of the astronomer who observes the skies introduces an order into the observations that would not be there if the earth itself stood still, or if the astronomer denied its motion. The movement of every perceiving subject must be reckoned in with the movements observed, in order to discover the real motion of the object one is observing.

Kant drew a fruitful analogy between terrestrial motion and other factors which, from the side of the observer, determine in part both the subjective and the objective (that is, the intersubjective) aspects of what is observed. The knowing subject can understand any phenomenon of the world (whether or not it involves motion) only if he takes account of his own contribution (whether the parallax of his own motion, or some other factor). The observer's contribution is not just the relatively unimportant, that is, nonexplanatory secondary qualities, but the most objective of all properties and structures, the formal characteristics of experience and its underlying laws. These are, as it were, read into experience by the intellectual and operational acts of the observing and explaining mind. Therefore, Kant says, "The understanding derives its laws (*a priori*) not from nature, but rather prescribes them to nature." By subsequent experience we are instructed as to what specific generalizations and laws obtain, as specifications of a priori concepts such as cause, substance, magnitude, and position. Nature, says Kant, is "the existence of things so far as it is determined by universal laws"; accordingly, the human mind can be regarded not only as the legislator or the lawgiver of nature, but as the creator of nature—not of the stuff of nature, of course, for the human mind is finite and must work with material supplied by some unknown source—but of nature considered as a system existing under laws the knowledge of which gives nature whatever intelligibility it exhibits. (When the German idealists denied the limitations Kant placed on our cognitive capacity, they thought of the mind as being the creator of nature in a much more extravagant sense. Kant should not be blamed for their excesses, which in fact he tried to prevent.) Kant stands between the doctrine of Nicolas of Cusa and Vico that *verum et factum convertuntur* (truth is what is made, we can know only what we can make), and Nietzsche's profound aphorism, "Bevor 'gedacht' wurde, muss schon *gedichtet* worden sein" (Before something is 'thought' it must first be *composed*).

The only science Kant knew was Newtonian; the only geometry, Euclidean; the only logic, Aristotelian. Because all of these have been superseded or revised, it is sometimes said that the *Critique of Pure Reason,* which supported them, was a defense of lost causes. Nevertheless, the epistemological foundations Kant supplied to Newtonian physics and Euclidean geometry are reminders that non-Newtonian physics and non-Euclidean geometries also stand on epistemological foundations. The latter are not self-explanatory and self-justifying; they must be, in Kant's language, transcendentally deduced. It is a point of dispute in modern philosophy of science whether the foundations needed for these new disciplines are more like or more unlike those of the Kantian model of classical physics. Whether like or unlike, a treatise analogous to the *Critique of Pure Reason* needs to be written after every scientific revolution. The resemblances between the *Critique of Pure Reason* and modern positivistic, operationalistic, and model theories are striking, for all these con-

temporary theories emphasize one Kantian theme: the ways in which the mind's own activities in inquiry are projected into and reflected back by nature. Naturally this Kantian theme has been modified, and most of these modifications move in the same direction; that is, away from what Stephan Körner has called Kant's uniqueness-thesis, in other words, the doctrine that there is only one way of organizing experience so that we can make any knowledge-claims, even false ones. No doubt the rigidity of the Kantian transcendental apparatus must be relaxed, alternative category systems must be conceded, knowledge itself must be relativized according to changing cultural systems. The creative activity of minds—the central thought in the *Critique of Pure Reason*—is made perhaps even more pervasive by those who undertake these revisions than it was by Kant himself: whereas the creativity in Kant's account is somewhat abstract and transcendental, modern studies of conceptual change emphasize the actual historical, social, and personal factors, and give empirical meaning to the notion of cognitive creations. These changes do not evade the issue that led Kant to write the *Critique,* namely, How can free creations of the mind have objective validity? This question remains, even when the concepts Kant thought of as unique creations of the mind have long since been shown to have alternatives or, indeed, have been replaced by others in the progress of science.

Contemporary sociology of knowledge emphasizes cultural factors in the creation and acceptance of alternative portrayals of the world. Kant, on the other hand, was aware of only one system of grammar. He also thought—perhaps in part for that reason—that there was only one type of cognizing mind, only one system of scientific knowledge. He overlooked the variable social dimensions of thought and was little interested in the philosophy of language (in fact, little interested in language itself, which he seems to have regarded as hardly more than a transparent medium). Because he presented his categorical system as a "transcendental grammar," Kant appears to belong to the tradition Noam Chomsky has called "Cartesian linguistics."

But anti-Cartesian linguistics also may have Kantian sources, as seen originally in the work of Kant's disciples Herder and Humboldt and in this century in that of the neo-Kantians Georg Simmel and Ernst Cassirer. Alternative pictures of the universe and of society depend upon the symbol systems in use, which determine the a priori features of experiences accepted into the communication network. Whether or not a single universal grammar exists, the linguistic turn in philosophy a generation ago was an analogue of the Copernican Revolution, with or without the uniqueness-thesis. Whether the epistemological center (like the sun in Copernican astronomy) is a single universal grammar or whether there are at the ultimate depths diverse and irreducible systems of semiotic rules, the a priori forms of experience of the world correspond to the forms in which this experience is articulated and communicated. We see only what we can say.

Each culture, each scientific paradigm, each linguistic system requires something analogous to a *Critique of Pure Reason* in order to understand how its principles and rules are projected into its cosmological and cultural conceptions. It was no surprise to me, therefore, when Ernest Gellner recently counted Kant as chief among the ancestors of structuralism.

Just as Kant's Copernican Revolution taught that the scientific thinker gives the form of lawfulness to the events in nature, reads the law into nature, as it were, and then specifies the variables by empirical research, an analogous revolution occurs in Kant's moral philosophy, which I call the Rousseauistic Revolution. Rousseau, Kant's favorite modern author, wrote: "Freedom is obedience to a law which man gives to himself." Rousseau meant this primarily in a political sense, and the idea was the basis of his theory of self-government. Only by participation in government and not by mere tacit consent is political authority justified. Kant developed this political theory further than Rousseau did, and he also developed it into a philosophy of morals.

The moral law, which philosophers before Kant had found in what they considered to be the will of God, or the law of nature, or the human desire for happiness, he found (using a political metaphor) in autonomy. Perhaps for the first time, a clear conceptual distinction was drawn between morality and prudence raised to an almost transcendental elevation. Prudence is reasonable adherence to policies for reaching desired and desirable ends; morality is adherence to a maxim out of respect for its status as a law for rational beings. Respect is a unique feeling evoked only by a law which, having no prudential sanctions, is an expression of one's rational capacity shown both in making and judging knowledge-claims and in reaching and justifying practical decisions. I can *obey* laws out of concern with reward and punishment, and if I am prudent I usually do so; but I can *respect* them only if their origin in my own rational lawgiving capacity humbles my merely prudential concerns.

There is an analogy between moral principles and the categorial principles in the first **Critique.** The only theoretical law or principle I can acknowledge as a priori necessary is one my understanding prescribes to nature. 'Acknowledge as necessary' is the first **Critique**'s epistemological analogue of moral 'respect' in the second **Critique.** Autonomy is a fundamental condition of both cognitive and practical activity; because the *word* did not come into Kant's vocabulary until after 1781, many readers have missed the *thing* in the first **Critique.** Yet the analogies are vivid. Pure practical reason stands in the same relation to the moral realm (the realm of ends) as pure understanding does to the realm of nature. Both are sources of a priori laws. One exacts our obedience in interpreting nature, which we regard as equivalent to nature's own obedience to law. The other exacts our obedience in the pursuit of happiness, human rights, and virtue, regardless of whether nature responds favorably to our efforts, or thwarts them. Whether virtue is rewarded with happiness is something that does not lie with man; what is within his power, and what he ought to undertake, is to be *worthy* of happiness. Obedience to a law given by one's rational nature is a necessary condition of such worthiness, but it is neither necessary nor sufficient for the attainment of other human goals.

Many have objected that Kant held obedience to be so high a virtue—indeed the only virtue—that he regarded the origin and consequences of a law as morally irrelevant. Therefore, it has been held, he could not distinguish between legitimate and illegitimate laws, could not condemn fanaticism devoted to some immoral goal, and could not morally criticize any actual government or resist any actual tyranny. Paradoxically, the friend of the American and French revolutions has been seen as a defender of political absolutism.

I must grant that there are paradoxes in Kant's political philosophy, especially in his adherence to the Lutheran position on the unrighteousness of rebellion, which led him into some not very edifying casuistry. Nevertheless, Kant always clear-ly distinguished between the moral law, which derives from reason, and the positive law, which arises from empirically determined power-relations. Even in his casuistical accounts of the misadventures of the French Revolution he never failed to give priority to the moral: "Politics," he says, "must always bend its knee to morality." The law we respect is no arbitrary edict with sanctions of reward and punishment; rather, it is a law of a kind we as impartial lawgivers prescribe, or at least could prescribe, for ourselves. It is a maxim made under the veil of empirical ignorance, with the moral innocence of the dove instead of the political wisdom of the serpent. A law of this kind arises, and is valid, only insofar as it is reasonable. 'Reasonable' here means far more than merely self-consistent; it means constrained by the universal rights and serviceable to the universal interests of mankind. The moral law, then, is not an absolutized positive law, but rather a rational criterion of the legitimacy of statute law. Moral law is the rationalized and secularized form of the law of God or the law of nature, and fulfills much the same functions that these venerable concepts had served as constraints on arbitrary political power.

I have just compared Kant's theory to the traditional doctrines of the law of nature or the law of God, but one might better ask, What is *living* in Kant's moral philosophy? Indeed, there has been a revolution in the moral life just as great as the revolution in the scientific world-picture, and one may well believe that Kant's humanistic ethic with its Jewish, Christian, and Stoic components and Protestant Prussian coloration is as antiquated as the Euclidean geometry and Newtonian physics to which Kant adhered. Nowadays we do not have his faith in the rationality and universality of morality. The very word "rationalization" expresses psychoanalytic suspicions, and the Kantian equation of moral actions with actions done out a punctilious sense of duty or out of pure reason is hardly persuasive today. We see many factors as limitations on human freedom that were morally irrelevant for Kant.

Such reservations appear to me to be legitimate and important, and yet are somewhat superficial, because they misread Kant as a casuist and do not touch the principal points of his moral philosophy. After every moral revolution a new **Critique of Practical Reason** ought to be written, or at least Kant's own ought to be reread. Our present-day ethical views, however far from Kant's they may be, need philosophical foundations not found in clinical psychology or modes and fashions; they need what Kant perhaps misleadingly called a "metaphysics of morals." The foundations of every ethics are to be found in conceptions of an ideal human nature. It is possible that Kant conceived this nature too rationalistically in trying to establish an ethics valid for all rational beings and not for human beings alone, but the metaethical structure of ethical systems based upon quite different ideals of human nature may well be Kantian.

People often indignantly contrast *Kantian* ethics with *human* ethics and say of the former, "It may be right in theory, but will not hold in practice." Against this objection, recall Kant's rejoinder to those who presumed to criticize Plato on the sorry pretext of the impracticality or unfeasibility of his political theory: "Nothing indeed can be more injurious or more unworthy of a philosopher than the vulgar appeal to so-called adverse experience. Such experience would never have existed at all, had history followed the prescriptions of Plato." Per corollary, one ought not object to the Kantian moral philosophy on grounds of its impracticality, but rather one ought to use it as an admonition against actual tendencies that do not aim to establish the kingdom of God on earth (or, in Kantian language, the realm of ends), in which rational beings will be treated as ends in themselves, and not as means only.

One of the strangest phenomena in the history of thought is that Kant led a revolution in our conception of art. It is strange because it was so unlikely: in his entire life, Kant probably never had an opportunity to see a fine painting or hear a good performance of great music. His Copernican and Rousseauistic revolutions were historically conservative; they did not revolutionize science or morals but provided new and revolutionary foundations for the science and the moral ideals already current. His aesthetic revolution, on the other hand, was a renunciation of the critical standards of his time. It prepared the way for artistic developments that occurred after he wrote, and, in the case of German romanticism, in part *because* of what he wrote.

Here again we meet with an analogue of the Copernican Revolution. M. H. Abrams, writing of Wordsworth, says that "the Copernican revolution in epistemology— . . . the general concept that the perceiving mind discovers what it has itself partly made—was effected in England by poets and critics before it manifested itself in academic philosophy." But in Germany the revolution in aesthetics came first, in Kant's academic philosophy.

Kant turned against two dominant aesthetic principles that had governed European thought on art, if not art itself: that art is the imitation of nature (*ut pictura poesis*) and that the purpose of art is moral edification. Kant rejected both principles because they confined art and made it parasitic upon either knowledge or morals. Kant is clear and convincing in his rejection of theories that the aesthetic response is a response to the information-content of a work of art. He saw that aesthetic value is attached to the syntactic, not the semantic, dimension of meaning. Only in that way is the artist free to create something "purposive, [but] without purpose."

One cannot maintain that Kant was completely successful in separating moral from aesthetic interests. Perhaps he was not sufficiently independent of the critical thought of his time to have made a clean break between them. It is not clear whether, given the rest of his theory, he should have, or could have, done so. Historically, however, the principal thrust of Kant's arguments has been in the direction of the emancipation of art from extra-artistic criteria, whether of factual truth or moral value.

Kant replaced the two standard critical principles of his time—the imitation of nature, and the moral edification of the audience—with his theory of genius. Genius is a law unto itself, and it creates a second nature, not just a copy of a first nature. The German romantic movement developed its program from Kant's philosophical emancipation of art through genius. Because the excesses of romantic genius were distasteful to Kant, some may believe that the romantic and other later anticlassical movements in art have made his aesthetic theory as obsolete as they view his defense of Newtonian physics, Christian ethics, and Roman law. After all, Kant's taste was for tulips and arabesques; what could he have seen in Duchamp's *Nude Descending a Staircase*?

Nineteenth- and twentieth-century revolutions of thought about art (perhaps with the exception of the Marxist) appear to be pushing to an extreme what was implicit in Kant's own theory; that is, the doctrine of the autonomy of art, its freedom from nonartistic concerns, or art for art's sake. The creativity of the artist, not the contingent occurrence of beautiful objects and the talent to reproduce them faithfully on canvas, is the decisive condition of aesthetic excellence. If we imagine Kant's coming back to life and visiting our museums and laboratories, I suspect that, after an initial shock and a little time to get his bearings, he might be as much at home in the one as in the other. And I even suspect that in the art gallery he would be more comfortable with *Nude Descending a Staircase* than with Titian's nudes, because his theory of human beauty is not, at least in any obvious way, consistent with his formalistic analyses, which apparently fit arabesques better than they do human portraits. Designs, without representational content or moral message, which present or stimulate the free play of imagination were the paradigms of Kant's aesthetic theory, and are especially characteristic of much post-Kantian art.

From the foregoing, a common theme may be seen in Kant's work in science, morals, and art. The same theme underlies his theories of mathematics, history, religion, and politics. All his works lead to the same answer to the question, What is man? That answer is, man is creator. To Kant's Copernican and Rousseauistic revolutions, therefore, I would add a third: his work also represents a Promethean Revolution in philosophy. It was Prometheus who seized the prerogative of the gods and gave it to humankind. Through possession of fire, everything else could be created. Certainly the Prometheus role is not without its mortal danger; the ancient hero suffered martyrdom, and Prometheanism leads to the vice of hubris. Kant avoided both the fate and the vice by never forgetting that man is a finite-all-too-finite being, and that the world created by man is a human-all-too-human world—indeed, a world of appearance, the basic conditions and materials of which lie beyond the limits of human knowledge and power. Man is no god, but in his creativity he may be godlike, and many of the tasks previously assigned to god in the creation and governance of the world are reassigned by Kant to man.

The world man orders, or seeks to order, is only the known part of the unknown all. Kant was the anthropologist of a race that dwelt in "the land of truth"—the "land of truth" is man's realm, man is the lawgiver in it. But the "land of truth" is only an island, surrounded by "a wide and stormy ocean, the native home of illusion, where many a fog-bank and many a swiftly melting iceberg give the deceptive appearance of farther shores, deluding the adventurous seafarer ever anew with empty hopes, and engaging him in enterprises which he can never abandon and yet is unable to carry to completion." The cultivation of this island and the exploration of this ocean is the calling of man. In these dual efforts of *Aufklärung*, the human race stands alone and independent: "Nature has willed that man, by himself, should produce everything that goes beyond the mechanical ordering of his animal existence, and that he should partake of no other happiness or perfection than that which he himself, independently of instinct, has created by his own reason."

Were it not for the words "happiness" and "reason" in this quotation, you might have thought that I was quoting a rather prosaic Sartre. The autonomy of the individual in creating out of chaos the world in which one is to live is as characteristic of Kant's teaching as it is of that of the modern existentialist thinker. But "happiness" and "reason" cannot be left out of the quotation. For Kant, only reasonable human beings, in spite of all their errors, can create a world in which there is some chance for well-being and happiness, and only the criticism and discipline of reason can lead toward the requisite wisdom.

Like the present, the Age of Reason had its irrationalists. The German Enlightenment had its Counter-Enlightenment just as we have a counterculture. Kant lived in an age that was changing just as rapidly and violently as ours, in which tradition was under as serious a challenge as now, in which it was just as questionable as it is now what should be saved in established institutions and practices and what should be changed or rejected. There were those in his day, as in our own, who were brought to skepticism by the knowledge explosion and by conflicts in values. There were people, even in Königsberg, who had no faith in the life of reason and took refuge in irrationalistic enthusiasms and superstitions. The Germans had a name for this rebellion: *Sturm und Drang.* (The very name sounds frightening.) Kant saw Storm and Stress as a threat to the progress of knowledge and to civilized life, which depends upon that progress. What Kant said in 1786 is as portentous now, because something like *Sturm und Drang* is still with us. These words were addressed to the people of Storm and Stress, but they may be meant also for us:

> Friends of the human race, and of that which is holiest to it! . . . Do not wrench from reason what makes it the highest good on earth, the prerogative of being the final touchstone of truth. If you do this, you will become unworthy of freedom, and lose it, and bring misfortune to those who want to use freedom in a lawful manner to secure the good of mankind.

(pp. 17-30)

Lewis White Beck, "What Have We Learned from Kant?" in Self and Nature in Kant's Philosophy, edited by Allen W. Wood, Cornell University Press, 1984, pp. 17-30.

ROBIN M. SCHOTT   (essay date 1987)

[*Schott analyzes Kant's theory of human sensibility, arguing against his radical separation of sensibility from knowledge.*]

Kant's treatment of sensibility reflects an ascetic tradition inherited from both Greek and Christian sources, which views the body, sexuality, and in particular women's sexuality as a source of pollution. According to this tradition, thought must be divested of the pollution of sensuous existence, in order to achieve the purity associated with truth. Kant's ascetic heritage leads him to distance large portions of sensibility from contributing to knowledge. His hostility to sensuous existence is expressed not only in his desensualization of sense experience, but in his assumption that affective responses have no bearing on cognition.

Although Kant identifies sensibility with intuition in the *Critique of Pure Reason,* elsewhere he recognizes a broader notion of sensibility. In the first *Critique,* Kant defines sensibility as the faculty through which objects are given to us. He writes, there are "two stems of human knowledge, namely *sensibility* and *understanding. . . .* Through the former, objects are given to us; through the latter, they are thought." Sensibility, in this context, refers to intuition as the model of empirical apprehension. However, in the Introduction to the *Metaphysics of Morals,* Kant characterizes sensibility in a more inclusive manner. He depicts sensibility in the following way:

> On the one hand, it can be referred to an object as a means toward cognizing it . . . here sensibility, as the receptivity for a representation that is thought, is sense. On the other hand, the subjective element in our representations may be such that it cannot become a factor in cognition . . . in this case the receptivity for the representation is called feeling.

Despite Kant's recognition that empirical receptivity includes both sense experience and feeling, he adamantly rejects the latter as a component of knowledge. Whenever he mentions feelings in the *Critique,* Kant emphasizes their irrelevance to knowledge. For example, in the Transcendental Aesthetic, he specifically excludes feeling and volition from intuition. He refers to "everything in our knowledge which belongs to intuition—feelings of pleasure and pain, and the will, not being knowledge, are excluded." Later in the *Critique* he repeats that "feeling is not a faculty whereby we represent things, but lies outside our whole faculty of knowledge." Thus, sensibility, as a faculty of knowledge, is only a restricted portion of our total sensible apparatus. These restrictions are evident not only in the distancing of feeling from cognition, but in Kant's analysis of intuition as the mode of immediate apprehension.

In the *Critique of Pure Reason,* Kant identifies the cognitive portion of sensibility with intuition. In the opening passage of the Transcendental Aesthetic, Kant defines intuition in the following way: "In whatever manner and by whatever means a mode of knowledge may relate to objects, *intuition* is that through which it is in immediate relation to them . . . But intuition takes place only in so far as the object is given to us." Kant's claim that intuition stands in immediate relation to the given object suggests that sensibility provides the raw material for empirical knowledge, independent of any theoretical constraints. But Kant is not merely imposing categories of the understanding onto natural sensibility. Intuition is not immediate in an experiential, but only in an analytical sense. Elsewhere, in referring to his method of analysis, Kant comments that his goal is to "isolate sensibility" by taking away all other components of knowledge. This method of isolation is modelled on the method of chemical reduction Kant mentions in the Preface. But if intuition is an *isolated* form of sensibility, it cannot refer to the immediate apprehension of an object. Instead, intuition is itself structured by Kant's theory of sensation.

By reducing sensibility to intuition, Kant implies that observation is primary for knowledge. Kant uses intuition, "Anschauung," to refer to the entire content of experience. But the commonly used word for sense perception is "Empfindung." "Anschauung" means to look at or view; "Schau" is a view or exhibit. By choosing "Anschauung" as the name for sensation, Kant suggests that looking at or viewing is paradigmatic for sense-perception in general. Therefore, the perceiver's relation to the object is that of a spectator.

Kant takes observation as fundamental for knowledge in general, in order to achieve the exactness of knowledge promised by the scientific method. But this procedure attests to a hostility towards the body. In the act of looking, we are less aware of our body than, for example, in the act of touching. In discussing the sense of sight in the *Anthropology,* Kant writes:

The sense of sight, while not more indispensable than the sense of hearing, is, nevertheless, the noblest, since, among all the senses, it is farthest removed from the sense of touch, which is the most limited condition of perception. Not only does sight have the greatest radius of perception in space, but it also receives its sense organ as being least involved (because otherwise it would not be mere sight). Consequently, it comes nearer to being a pure intuition (the immediate idea of a given object without admixture of evident sensation).

The virtue of sight is not only its range. Amongst all the senses, it is the one in which the body is least involved in perceptual awareness. For Kant, awareness of our physical involvement actually distorts knowledge of an object. He stresses the importance of excluding awareness of our senses in the following comment: "When the sensation, however, becomes so strong that the awareness of the activity of the organ becomes stronger than the awareness of the relation to an external object, then outer perceptions are changed into inner perceptions." Since inner perceptions contribute nothing to knowledge, one must distance bodily awareness from sensible apprehension in order to have knowledge of the external world.

Kant contrasts the sense of sight with the sense of touch, which is the "most limited condition of perception." The restricted nature of touch is due not only to its narrow spatial scope, but to the involvement of the sense organ in this experience. Unlike sight, touch cannot be thoroughly purified of any "admixture of evident sensation." Touch contributes to knowledge only insofar as it is completely devoid of any pleasureable sensation. Kant describes it as follows: "The sense of touch lies in the fingertips and their nerve endings, and enables us to discover the form of a solid body by means of contact with its surface." In his view, touch only contributes to knowledge of the formal properties of an object. Since perceiving the texture of an object depends on our sensual awareness, it is excluded from the noetic dimension of sense experience.

Since the senses of taste and smell in no way provide knowledge of the spatio-temporal form of an object, they are considered completely non-noetic. Kant describes them as "subjective senses," in which, "the idea obtained from them is more an idea of enjoyment, rather than the cognition of the external object." Kant thereby establishes an opposition between the idea of enjoyment and the cognition of the external object. He considers the subjective senses to be the "senses of pleasure," indicating that pleasure derives solely from the subject's relation to his sense organs, not to outer objects. Since pleasure is cut off from the perception of an external object, it becomes a completely solipsistic experience. In the first *Critique,* in speaking of taste, and colors, Kant remarks,

> They are connected with the appearances only as effects accidentally added by the particular constitution of the sense organs. Accordingly, they are not a priori representations, but are grounded in sensation, and, indeed, in the case of taste, even upon feeling (pleasure and pain) as an effect of sensation.

The feelings of pleasure and pain (Lust und Unlust) are a secondary, subjective response to the primary perception of the object, which is devoid of pleasure. When Kant speaks of intuition as the "immediate" relation to the object, therefore, he is referring to perception in this primary sense. In other words, the cognitive portion of sensibility, to which Kant ascribes the immediate apprehension of an object, excludes the feeling of pleasure as a subjective interference with external sensation.

Kant's distinction between intuition and feeling implies that the primary experience of an object resides in an objective perception which is contrasted with subjective feeling. But why does Kant assert this priority of objective, desensualized perception? This distancing of feeling from cognition entails a suppression of large portions of one's sensible apparatus from one's immediate apprehension of the world. Kant's analysis of sensibility posits a disengagement from the world, which cannot unquestioningly be accepted as the paradigm of knowledge.

Kant's exclusion of feeling from intuition has consequences not only for his analysis of perception, but for his treatment of both feeling and desire. His discussion of human nature in the *Anthropology from a Pragmatic Point of View,* is not merely an addendum to his picture of human knowledge. It provides the substantive correlate to his model of cognition. In the Introduction to the *Anthropology,* Kant describes his projection in the following way:

> A systematic doctrine containing our knowledge of man (anthropology) can either be given from a physiological or a pragmatic point of view . . . pragmatic knowledge of man aims at what man makes, can, or should make of himself as a freely acting being.

Kant's empirical characterization of human nature is based on his ideal of man as a free, rational being. Thus, his approach to human sensibility, in its broad sense, is systematically related to his conception of rationality. In order to gain knowledge, the subject must comport himself in a particular way. Kant's treatment of feelings shows the practical consequences of this posture. His notion that affective responses have no bearing on cognition has become virtually a presupposition in subsequent philosophical thought. Since his paradigm of knowledge appears to us as natural, the more vividly one conveys the implications of Kant's view, the better one is able to critically evaluate it.

Emotion (Affekt) and passion (Leidenschaft) share, in Kant's view, certain disagreeable features. In the third book of the *Anthropology,* Kant writes, "To be subject to emotions and passions is probably always an illness of mind because both emotion and passion, exclude the sovereignty of reason." He repeatedly uses the metaphor of illness to describe these feelings. He writes,

> Emotion works upon the health like a stroke of apoplexy; passion works like consumption or atrophy. Emotion is like an intoxicant which one has to sleep off, although it is still followed by a headache; but passion is looked upon as an illness having resulted from swallowing poison.

Again, "passion is regarded as an insanity which broods over an idea that is imbedding itself deeper and deeper." Finally, "Passion, on the other hand, no man wishes for himself. Who wants to have himself put in chains when he can be free?" In contrast to this unpleasant disturbance, Kant describes the Stoic ideal of apathy:

> The principle of apathy, that is, that the prudent man must at no time be in a state of emotion, not even in that of sympathy with the woes of his best

friend, is an entirely correct and sublime moral precept of the Stoic school because emotion makes one
(more or less) blind.

Thus, Kant's hostility towards emotion derives from an ascetic tradition with which he explicitly identifies himself.

Kant defines emotion in the following way: "Emotion is surprise through sensation, whereby the composure of the mind
(animus sui compos) is suspended." The conception of emotion as "surprise" suggests that feeling is foreign to our normal condition. One must recover from emotion, the way one
sleeps off a drunken bout. Emotion, therefore, is a temporary
state, which has no continuity with our past or future awareness. Kant's definition of emotion as "surprise through sensation" implies that emotion is a response to something in the
external world. It follows the sensation of an object, in contrast with desire, which precedes the representation. Yet
Kant elsewhere insists that emotion has no intrinsic relation
to an external object. In his view, feeling "contains only the
relation of a representation to the subject." In other words,
affective responses, though stimulated by sensation, are not
determined by the character of the perceived object. Furthermore, since emotion is a disruption of our normal state, affect
cannot be determined by our subjective state. Kant's conception of emotion deprives him of any means of providing either
an objective or subjective explanation of affect. Emotion appears as a strictly arbitrary occurrence. He cannot give an account of why one responds with either joy or melancholy in
a given situation. Thus, emotion, in Kant's view, can never
be considered an appropriate response to a person or an
event.

In emotion, according to Kant, the composure of the mind
is suspended. Kant refers to the "Fassung" of the mind,
which literally means the grasping or seizing. In other words,
our normal state is one in which reason has seized control.
Since emotion and passion threaten the sovereignty of reason,
they must be excluded from ordinary consciousness. Kant's
demand for rational control echoes the Calvinist imperative
to rationalize every moment of existence. For the Calvinist,
the natural man becomes transformed, eliminating any trace
of spontaneity. Similarly, Kant's principle of apathy and self-
control implies that emotion must be completely repudiated
by the rational man.

Despite Kant's ideal of apathy, he recognizes that the feelings
of pleasure and pain are necessary for life. He writes, "Gratification is the feeling of advancement; pain is that of a hindrance of life. But the life (of the animal) is, as physicians
have also noticed, a continuing play of the antagonism between these two feelings." Kant, furthermore, notes that pain
is the more valuable feeling. He states that "Pain is the incentive to activity, and above all, in activity we feel that we are
alive; without such a good, inertia would set in." Kant actually perceives positive feelings of joy to be life-threatening. He
comments, "one can see from the death lists that more persons have lost their lives suddenly on account of exuberant
joy than on account of sorrow." In other words, Kant's valu-
ation of apathy corresponds to the pained and melancholy
disposition with which he identifies himself.

Kant's splitting off of feeling from the perception of an object
relegates feeling to a strictly subjective domain. In Kant's
view, feeling is an inner state of consciousness which illumines nothing about the external world. His description of
feeling as subjective and blind implies that it cannot express

one's response to another person or thing. Nor can feeling reveal anything about the subject's own intentions. In the
Metaphysics of Morals, Kant comments that feeling in no
way contributes to knowledge, "not even the cognition of our
own state." Feeling is not only distanced from objective perception, but even from one's own state of self-awareness.

This treatment of emotion presents feelings in greatly modified form. For example, the definition of emotion as "surprise
through sensation" cannot elucidate the meaning of anxiety.
For Kant, the feeling of anxiety is circumscribed by the metaphor of an intoxicant. It appears as a harmful indulgence,
which reveals nothing about one's relationship to self or
other.

Kant defines joy as that emotion "which motivates the subject to remain in the state in which he currently finds himself." According to this definition, joy appears as a wholly
self-related experience. But this definition is thoroughly inadequate. For example, a mother may feel a great joy when her
child brings home his/her first drawing from school; whereas
a visiting neighbor would not feel so moved. The mother's
feeling is motivated by her involvement with the child, who
has drawn the picture. Her feeling of joy is not strictly self-
related, but derives from the particular relation and situation
in which she finds herself. The neighbor, who observes the
same child and the same picture but who does not share this
mother-child bond, can remain indifferent. Furthermore, the
mother's joy does not imply that she wants to remain in the
state in which she currently finds herself. On the contrary,
this situation is special because it is a precursor of the growing independence of the child, who will eventually outgrow
this need to bring home drawings. Indeed, implicit in the
mother's joy is the knowledge that this condition will be superseded. Kant's general definition of emotion as "surprise
through sensation" is likewise misleading. The mother's ordinary consciousness is not suspended in this joyful encounter.
Rather, her normal state of mind, her recognition of herself
as a mother, is the precondition for this emotion.

Kant's definition of emotion, furthermore, omits any role for
sensuality. Surely, even the mother's joy has a sensual component. This child who hugs and kisses and cries and dirties
is a physical presence for the mother. Sensual pleasure is even
excluded from Kant's discussion of the feelings of pleasure
and pain (Gefühl der Lust und Unlust). The pleasure provided by the senses is limited to playing games, watching a
drama, reading a novel, and the greatest pleasure in life of
all—relaxation after work. For example, Kant speaks of
work as a "troublesome occupation (unpleasant in itself and
delightful only in its success), so that relaxation, through the
mere disappearance of a long hardship, turns into sensible
pleasure, that is, cheerfulness, because otherwise there would
not be anything enjoyable". No doubt many a reader of the
Critique of Pure Reason wished that Kant had taken a more
positive pleasure from his work, for then the task of unraveling the *Critique* might have been less arduous. The pleasure
in all of these activities, according to Kant, derives from the
play of opposing emotions. Although Kant defines gratification (Vergnügen) as a pleasure of sensation, the pleasure consists not in the sensation, but in its effect on the mind. Even
sensuous pleasure, therefore, is distanced from the immediate
experience of an object.

Kant's examination of emotion portrays the ideal man as a
highly disciplined, apathetic creature, who values pain above
pleasure, whose greatest enjoyment consists in the relaxation

following work, and who finds no place for love in his life. The *Anthropology* is a graphic picture, not only of Kant's own disposition, but of the consequences of his analysis of cognition. It reflects the turning away from pleasure and love which has characterized the ascetic tradition.

Kant's analysis of emotion presupposes an opposition between feeling and truth. He treats emotion as a subjective effect, which interferes with knowledge. But emotion is also a means of apprehending persons and things. If, for example, you give me something, my feelings of warmth and appreciation are an appropriate response to your act. This feeling of warmth is not an irrational disturbance of a pure intuition, but is itself a mode of recognition. Kant's exclusion of emotion and pleasure from intuition reflects the ascetic commitment to purify reason from sensuous existence. But this exclusion of sensuality and affect suggests that Kant's conception of rationality is not defined by purely rational interests. It is motivated, in part, by a hostility to the body. In other words, one must reject Kant's claim that his model of knowledge seeks pure truth, which emotion distorts. His restriction of the cognitive portion of sensibility to intuition itself expresses an interest in selecting from and modifying the real.

Kant treats emotion as irrational because it distorts "objective" perception. But one must question whether rationality is best defined by the parameters of a purified, desiccated intuition. One might consider rationality, instead, as that which articulates one's experience. Emotions which express one's intentions, or one's recognition of another, are rational for us, in a way in which Kant's notion of intuition is not. The restricted form of sensibility which Kant includes in intuition may itself be experienced as an irrational violation of our sensible apprehension.

Like feeling, desire in Kant's analysis is excluded from immediate apprehension. Kant defines desire in the following way: "Desire is the power of the subject to determine itself through the representation of something future as an effect of its idea." Desire, in Kant's view, is a mode of self-determination. He comments that the possibility of having a desire "precedes the representation of its object." In other words, desire is not a response to an object, but an impulse to gain possession of one. What the subject seeks in the object of desire is the realization of his own power. Since desire is not a response to the presence of an existing object, the object of desire appears to the subject as a mere idea. When this object is finally achieved, the subject seeks a new object, in order to prove to himself his capacity for self-determination. Because the desiring subject is exclusively concerned with his own power of representation, desire cannot serve as a mode of recognition of another person, as it does in Hegel's analysis of desire. For Hegel, the human struggle for recognition takes place through a desiring relation to another. And since desire is oriented solely towards a future object, which appears as a mere idea, the object of desire is presented in a desensualized form.

Since desire in Kant's view cannot contribute to the recognition of persons, sexual desire is viewed as reducing persons to objects. In sexual passion, according to Kant, one uses another person in order to satisfy one's natural instincts. Desire is not directed towards the loved one as a person, but only as an object of gratification. Kant writes, "when love has been satisfied (by indulgence), the desire, at least with regard to the very person involved, ceases altogether." Kant views erotic desire to be fundamentally opposed to human dignity, to debase another person as an object for one's own uses. In the

Lectures on Ethics, Kant comments, "there is no way in which a human being can be made an Object of indulgence for another except through sexual impulse." He continues,

> Sexual love makes of the loved person an Object of appetite; as soon as that appetite has been stilled, the person is cast aside as one casts away a lemon which has been sucked dry. Sexual love can, of course, be combined with human love and so carry with it the characteristics of the latter, but taken by itself and for itself, it is nothing more than appetite. Taken by iself it is a degradation of human nature; for as soon as a person becomes an Object of appetite for another, all motives of moral relationship cease to function, because as an Object of appetite for another a person becomes a thing and can be treated and used as such by every one. This is the only case in which a human being is designed by nature as the Object of another's enjoyment. Sexual desire is at the root of it; and that is why we are ashamed of it, and why all strict moralists, and those who had pretensions to be regarded as saints, sought to suppress and extripate it.

Since sexual desire is objectifying, the only vehicle for "true human love" is "practical love," dictated by the moral law. Love which arises from feeling or inclination is "pathological," because it cannot be commanded by law. Human love, therefore, is not only de-sexualized, but "admits of no distinction between types of persons, or between young and old." This conception of love means that we will the same love towards our intimate friends as towards a stranger or enemy. Since I can only love the person as a moral agent, according to Kant, I do not love their generosity or stubbornness or loyalty. And since sexual love is objectifying, there is no place in Kant's system for love of persons with empirical qualities. No wonder Charlotte von Schiller said of Kant that since he was not able to feel love, there was something defective in his nature. Kant considers sexual desire to be an instinct which serves "nature's end" and not "what we have devised ourselves as its end". By defining sexuality as strictly natural, the historical circumstances determining sexual relations are asserted to be natural phenomena. For example, Kant asserts woman's character to be wholly defined by natural needs, in contrast to man's character. Woman's lack of self-determination, in his view, is intrinsic to her nature. He writes, "Nature was concerned about the preservation of the embryo and implanted fear into the woman's character, a fear of physical injury and a timidity towards similar danger. On the basis of this weakness, the woman legitimately asks for masculine protection." Because of their natural fear and timidity, women are viewed as unsuited for scholarly work. Kant mockingly describes the scholarly women who "use their books somewhat like a watch, that is, they wear the watch so it can be noticed that they have one, although it is usually broken or does not show the correct time." Kant's remarks in the *Anthropology* on women echo his sentiments in the *Observations on the Feeling of the Beautiful and the Sublime.* In that early work, Kant notes,

> A Woman who has a head full of Greek, like Mme. Dacier, or carries on fundamental controversies about mechanics, like the Marquise de Chatelet, might as well even have a beard, for perhaps that would express more obviously the mien of profundity for which she strives.

In Kant's view, women's philosophy is "not to reason, but to sense." And he adds, "I hardly believe that the fair sex is capable of principles." No wonder that, under these conditions, the woman "makes no secret in wishing that she might rather be a man, so that she could give larger and freer latitude to her inclinations; no man, however, would want to be a woman."

In Kant's view, matrimony is the only solution to the inevitable objectification and degradation involved in sexual desire. Kant writes:

> If I have the right over the whole person, I have also the right over the part and so I have the right to use that person's organa sexualia for the satisfaction of sexual desire. But how am I to obtain these rights over the whole person? Only by giving that person the same rights over the whole of myself. This happens only in marriage . . . each of them undertaking to surrender the whole of their person to the other with a complete right of disposal over it.

Sexual gratification can be legitimately gained only if two individuals each have the "right of disposal" over the other's person. Kant treats sexuality as residing solely in the sexual organs, to which one must gain access. It is a "part" of a person the way shoes are a part of one's wardrobe. In Kant's view, sexual desire does not pervade the sensibility and relationships of an individual, but can be neatly compartmentalized in the organs of the lower body. Although Kant recognizes sexuality as part of the totality of the person, he does not consider it intrinsic to one's humanity. (pp. 213-24)

Kant argues that the suppression of sexuality is a legitimate response to the objectification implicit in sexual desire. But his treatment of sensibility itself establishes the conditions for this objectification. By distancing desire from sensible apprehension, Kant precludes it from serving as a vehicle for human relationships. Kant's hostility towards sexuality echoes that of the Christian ascetics, who rejected sexuality as a means of expressing human love. Rather than accepting this ascetic suppression of sexuality as necessary for human dignity, one should question the operation performed by Kant on sensibility. By distancing feeling and desire from sensible apprehension, he creates the conditions for the conception of emotion as irrational, and of erotic desire as objectifying.

Kant's commitment to the suppression of sexuality echoes the ascetic concern to escape embodiment and sensuality. Ascetic self-denial offers a means to control those factors of existence which appear threatening: the uncertainty of life, the promise of mortality implicit in sexual activity. Kant's analysis of the transcendental conditions of knowledge, which exist prior to and independently of any particular human experience, provide an unchanging certainty, and immortality in the system of truth which is not possible in human life itself.

But if Kant's theory of knowledge is built on this distancing of life, and on a suppression of erotic factors of existence, it cannot support its claim to arise from a pure interest in knowledge, free of empirical motive. On the contrary, Kant's emphasis on purity in his analysis of cognition expresses a will to exclude certain things from the purview of cognition. This mode of knowledge does not express pure truth, in contrast to the distortions threatened by feeling and desire. Rather, Kant's exclusion of large portions of sensibility from contributing to knowledge reflects a disengagement from the world, which is itself a form of defense and control. (p. 225)

Robin M. Schott, "Kant's Treatment of Sensibility,"

in New Essays on Kant, *edited by Bernard den Ouden, Peter Lang, 1987, pp. 213-26.*

STEPHEN F. BARKER   (essay date 1987)

[*Barker discusses the integral relationship between Kant's thought structures and his literary style, focusing on the meaning and significance of the metaphorical literary devices employed in the* Critique of Pure Reason.]

Immanuel Kant stands as a giant figure in eighteenth-century thought. His long period of intellectual creativity extends through the middle and later part of the century. He led an isolated and personally uneventful life at a remote provincial university far from the centers of European culture—yet through the power and originality of his ideas he changed philosophy decisively and assured himself a central place in its history. He has come to be widely regarded as the greatest of the eighteenth-century philosophers, and many view him as the greatest philosopher of the whole modern era. His *Critique of Pure Reason* is his largest, most formidable, and most influential work. Whether or not we agree with its metaphysical and epistemological doctrines, we must respect it as a crucial text in the history of modern philosophy. The thought of earlier modern philosophers can be seen as leading toward the *Critique,* while nineteenth-century philosophy must be seen as deriving from Kant's work.

Yet, despite its greatness, the *Critique of Pure Reason* is not a well-written book, and Kant himself was aware of this. He tells us in the Preface to the second edition that he cannot regard himself as possessing the talent for lucid exposition. As regards the *Critique,* he leaves to others "the task of perfecting what, here and there, in its exposition, is still somewhat defective." But others never satisfactorily performed this task of polishing the expository style of Kant's first *Critique* while leaving its doctrines intact; we still have to acquire our knowledge of Kant's ideas directly from his text.

Its literary deficiencies are considerable. Occasional eloquent passages and vivid figures of speech are insufficient to overcome the turgidity and heaviness of Kant's style. His sentence structure is one negative factor: his sentences often run on at intolerable length, with clauses so intertwined and involuted that the reader cannot keep track of their grammar (once in a while even the author loses the thread). Kant's heavy use of abstract nouns is another factor: his discussion proceeds always in abstract terms, and the reader must struggle to grasp the diffuse ballet of abstractions which Kant stages. Concrete examples are rarely offered to illustrate the abstract points. Kant's reliance upon an extensive technical vocabulary of philosophical jargon is a related factor: he borrows many technical terms from more scholastic predecessors and coins many others. He takes little care to illustrate to his readers (or to himself) what these technical terms are supposed to mean: he is content to define some of his technical terms by means of others, as though this would make everything clear. Yet another factor is Kant's notorious "architectonic," the elaborately structured logical arrangement according to which he groups his sections and subsections in a pattern of twos, threes, and fours, each part supposedly paralleling and counterbalancing others in a rigidly prescribed way. He maintains that this structure must necessarily be exactly as it is; yet there are strong signs of arbitrariness in the structure—the contents of some subsections are perfunctory or atrophied, while the contents of others struggle to burst out of the Procrustean limits within which Kant tries to confine them.

Readers of today, looking back at Kant's *Critique of Pure Reason,* may well feel a strange mismatch between the impressive quality of many of Kant's ideas and the unimpressive or even repellent quality of much of his literary expression. How can a philosopher of the first rank be so inept and unsatisfactory an expositor of his own ideas? How can ideas of such depth and originality be trapped in so clumsy and wooden a text? The contrast is extreme and perplexing.

In discussing this apparent mismatch between the thought of Kant's *Critique of Pure Reason* and its textual expression, I shall argue that the contrast is less surprising and incongruous than at first appears. Several kinds of interconnections exist between Kant's thought and his literary style; attention to these interconnections will help us see that the character of his style largely derives from the state of his thought. I hope that Kant the thinker and Kant the writer will then be seen in clearer relation to one another, making more understandable how these two aspects of his activity belong to one and the same author. (pp. 75-6)

In the medieval world, the older and more long-established a scheme of practices or ideas was, the more it was regarded as worthy of acceptance and respect. This deferential attitude toward tradition began to be undermined in the early modern period by leading thinkers who challenged received opinions in theology and natural science, in political thought and philosophy. In the eighteenth century, with the Enlightenment, the critical examination of received opinions came to be regarded as a central task necessary for human intellectual progress.

Speaking of the eighteenth century, Kant says, "Our age is, in an especial degree, the age of criticism." No longer are traditional ideas to be endorsed merely because they are traditional. Henceforth, all doctrines which present themselves for our acceptance must be subjected to independent rational scrutiny. Only if they meet the tests which reason imposes can they be entitled to receive the intellectual assent of human beings who are now autonomous in their thinking.

In his *Critique of Pure Reason* Kant is concerned with only one of what he regards as the two great aspects of human thinking. He is one of the first philosophers to make a sharp logical distinction between thought about what *is* the case and thought about what *ought* to be the case (the twentieth-century distinction between "facts" and "values" grows out of Kant's distinction). The ancients had distinguished between the active life and the contemplative life, but they did not suppose that there is any deep logical difference between knowledge about what is the case and knowledge about what ought to be the case. Kant regards this as a fundamental distinction. For him, when we think about what is the case we are seeking "theoretical" knowledge, and the task of the sciences is to amass knowledge of this type. Knowledge of what ought to be the case Kant regards as an utterly different type of knowledge. He calls it "practical" knowledge, and the task of ethical, legal, and political thinking is to formulate knowledge of this type. The *Critique of Pure Reason* is concerned with theoretical knowledge, its aim being to examine the functioning of the faculty of reason in its theoretical employment. The practical employment of reason—that is, the pursuit of practical knowledge—Kant deals with in other books, especially in his *Critique of Practical Reason.*

Now, what sort of difficulty forces upon us the need for a critique of reason in its theoretical employment? There is no serious doubt concerning the ability of the human mind to achieve some theoretical knowledge. Two fields in which Kant considers that much rationally impeccable knowledge is to be found are mathematics, as begun by the Greeks, and natural science, as developed by Galileo and Newton. Kant holds that in both these areas knowledge is attained by objective methods upon which all human beings must agree; this knowledge fully measures up to rational standards. However, Kant thinks that philosophers have not yet adequately explained how and why this success is achieved in mathematics and natural science. So a philosophical account is needed of how theoretical knowledge can be achieved there. Such an account will do away with the groundless doubts which some skeptical thinkers have raised concerning this knowledge. But a more serious problem concerns the field of metaphysics, the central part of traditional philosophy. Down through the centuries, metaphysicians have claimed to be able to attain universal and necessary truths, truths that are nontrivial and embody important information about the nature of reality. But in metaphysics, Kant declares, the situation is much worse than in mathematics and natural science, for metaphysics is the scene of endless unresolved controversies. In metaphysics, every claim is met by a counterclaim, and no sound rational method has been developed for settling these disagreements in an objective manner.

Kant sees two great schools of thought among his predecessors in philosophy. On the one hand, the rationalists, such as Descartes and Leibniz, glibly put forward propositions about the nature of reality; they say that their propositions are self-evident truths that reason has the inherent power to grasp. But they can offer no proof or other justification for their specific claims, and their appeal to self-evidence is ultimately sheer dogmatism. Metaphysics as they pursue it can never become a sound branch of knowledge, because their procedure is arbitrary and lacks rational support. They offer no reason why the nature of reality need conform to their ideas about it.

On the other hand are the empiricists, such as Locke, and especially Hume. They object to the dogmatism of the rationalists, and they try to substitute for it a reliance upon sense-experience. All nontrivial knowledge must be derived from sensory observations, they hold. Yet sense experience will at best yield merely probable generalizations; knowledge drawn from sense experience will lack the certainty required by metaphysics. So Kant thinks that the viewpoint of empiricism leads inevitably toward skepticism concerning the possibility that metaphysics can become a rationally acceptable field of knowledge.

Philosophy of the past has thus reached an impasse, Kant believes. The rationalists rightly see that metaphysics must make universal and necessary claims about reality, but they make their claims dogmatically. The empiricists rightly see that dogmatism is insufficient, but they move toward skepticism.

Kant's aim is to find a position in philosophy that will synthesize what is best in rationalism with what is best in empiricism, while establishing from a higher standpoint the way in which metaphysics can genuinely become rational knowledge, within limits. In order to do this, Kant conducts a critique of the human capability to have knowledge. This begins with a critical scrutiny knowable are formulated and the status of metaphysics established.

Kant's critical inquiry leads him to a scheme of philosophical ideas intended to provide an account of human theoretical knowledge, making clear the limits within which knowledge is possible and beyond which it is not possible. Kant thinks that characterizing these limits will explain how mathematics and natural science succeed as forms of knowledge, and it will also explain to what extent metaphysics can succeed as a legitimate field.

Crucial to Kant's results is his distinction between what he regards as the two basic faculties in the human mind. These are "sensibility" and "thought." Sensibility is our passive ability to receive sensations which are forced upon us by some outer reality. Thought is the active ability to organize sensations under concepts, producing thoughts (judgments) about what is the case. Neither thought nor sensation alone will suffice, for "sensations without concepts are blind," while "concepts without sensations are empty." Only when these two faculties both function within our minds can there arise within us that special kind of self-conscious awareness which is knowledge.

But this leads to a further distinction basic for Kant between "phenomena" and "things in themselves." Things in themselves are independently real beings in their own right, which do not need to be perceived or thought of by us in order to be what they are. Phenomena are things as they appear to us; they consist of patterns of passively received sensations which we in thought actively group together under concepts.

Phenomena are always necessarily spatial and temporal in form, Kant holds. Nothing can appear to us except as occupying some volume of space at some point of time. Moreover, we are able to know for certain about the character of space and time. Kant's view is that we do so in geometry (which describes space) and in arithmetic (which describes counting, the basic procedure in time). Kant insists that we possess a priori knowledge of space and time: the knowledge we have of geometry and arithmetic involves universal and necessary truths which could not be attained merely by generalizing from particular sense experiences. We possess this knowledge of space and time, Kant argues, and the only possible explanation of how we can have it is that space and time are essential forms of our human sensibility. Thus, in understanding mathematics we are understanding the fixed and fundamental character of our own minds, as regards their sensibility.

This leads to Kant's doctrine of the ideality of space and time. They are forms of our human sensibility—and nothing more than this. They are not forms to which things in themselves conform. Reality outside our human minds is neither spatial nor temporal in character. So mathematics achieves its certainty through confining itself to the study of the human forms of sensibility rather than of things in themselves. The truths it achieves hold absolutely for all possible human experiences, but they do not hold at all of things as they are in themselves.

Natural science is in a similar situation. It achieves certainty in its grasp of the laws of nature, especially the laws of mechanics, Kant says, because these laws of nature reflect the laws of thought according to which our thought-processes work in organizing our spatiotemporal sense experiences. Any spatiotemporal phenomenon that we can be aware of must conform to these laws, which our minds impose upon

phenomena. But the absolute certainty here is achieved by limiting these laws to phenomena; the laws of nature, as we can know them, have no application to things in themselves.

There thus develops a deep chasm in Kant's philosophy. On the one side is the realm of phenomena, which includes all that we could possibly have scientific knowledge of. On the other side is the realm of things in themselves, which are completely unimaginable by us, as they lack all the spatiotemporal characteristics in terms of which we experience. Things in themselves cannot be studied by science, and human beings can have no theoretical knowledge of them.

Metaphysics, therefore, cannot be a field in which we gain knowledge of things in themselves. The rationalists were wrong to suppose so. However, it is possible for metaphysics to attain universal and necessary truths, if it confines itself entirely to phenomena. The "metaphysics of nature," according to Kant, can deal with some of the most general aspects of the way in which human minds arrange and structure their experience of spatiotemporal phenomena. It can establish laws about the deterministic interconnection of all events in nature, and about how all spatiotemporal events in nature must pertain to phenomenal substance, whose quantity stays always constant. Here the mind can know such principles about nature, because nature is not independently real, but is the systematic order which the human mind imposes upon its sensations.

Turning now to Kant's writing style, let us first consider his use of metaphors. At various places in Kant's writing vivid figures of speech are developed at considerable length. Kant apparently regarded these as important to good exposition— as providing memorable decoration for the philosophical points being made. These figures of speech occur most often in introductory and concluding passages, where Kant is not making new philosophical points but is setting the stage for a new discussion or summarizing what he has completed.

One vivid metaphor is that of the voyage of discovery. Kant had a lively interest in travel, even though he never did any; some of his most popular lectures at the University of Königsberg dealt with the geography and peoples of exotic regions. Since he lived in a port city and entertained sea captains at lunch, the metaphor of the voyage must have had a special meaning to him. He speaks of his philosophical undertaking as a long and dangerous sea expedition through unknown and dangerous waters, in the course of which unknown lands are to be located and their contours charted. Kant thinks of his work as having successfully completed this voyage of discovery, charting the territories of human knowledge and returning safely to make known to the rest of us these new discoveries in philosophical geography. In a further development of the metaphor, he speaks of David Hume, the empiricist, as having "run his ship ashore, for safety's sake, landing on scepticism, there to let it rot." Here Kant is not denigrating Hume's work; indeed, elsewhere Kant says that Hume "first awakened me from my dogmatic slumbers." It was to Hume's credit that he understood the need for such a philosophical voyage and embarked on it even though he lacked the staying power to complete it successfully.

Another of Kant's metaphors is that of territorial sovereignty. This is akin to the metaphor of the voyage of discovery for both are geographical. But the metaphor of territorial sovereignty emphasizes the concept of a legal right to rule over a territory, rather than merely the geographical delineation of contours. A legal right to exercise sovereignty over a territory is a right to plenitude of power there. It is a *de jure* right, and must be contrasted with *de facto* possession, which can derive from usurpation. One has the right to sovereignty over a territory only if one derives this right from a legitimate source. The genuineness of one's title is therefore crucial. This metaphor enters Kant's discussion because he wants to speak of the human faculties as sovereign in their own territories: each faculty has its proper sphere or realm in which to rule. The faculty of thought exercises legitimate sovereignty over the realm of possible experience; this is the territory where it is entitled to rule. Here it may lay down universal laws which govern the structure of all that we can experience. Because it can do so, it can know ahead of time that all within its realm will be subject to these laws, and thus our a priori metaphysical knowledge concerning such matters as causality and substance is accounted for.

The metaphor of sovereignty is also supposed to suggest the source of the error and illusion which continually creep into philosophy: when one faculty has usurped some of the territory of another, or when one faculty tries to extend its rule beyond the legitimate boundaries of all human faculties, then confusion, misunderstanding, and error arise in philosophical thinking. So the metaphor of territorial sovereignty shows that harmony among the faculties will require that each stay within its legitimate territory and not intrude upon any other.

The metaphor of sovereignty leads into the Kantian metaphor of a legal case being judged in court. Both of these types of metaphor involve the idea of legal right. However, the courtroom metaphor more vividly reflects the ongoing stages of a philosophical inquiry. The latter is compared to a legal process in which a question is brought before a judge, who hears witnesses and surveys evidence before reaching the verdict. The judge must distinguish between questions of fact (*"quid facti?"*) and questions of law (*"quid juris?"*), and the record of the case and the judge's verdict will preserved for future reference. In speaking of his critical inquiry Kant especially uses the metaphor of the courtroom: the claims of metaphysics to be able to attain knowledge are to be brought before the bar of reason, and a verdict rendered as to their legitimacy. Kant pictures reason in the role of judge, presiding over this legal process. When the case is over and the claim concerning metaphysics has been adjudicated, once and for all, then the transcript of the process (the **Critique of Pure Reason** itself) is to be "deposited in the archives of Pure Reason."

In a central section of the **Critique of Pure Reason,** entitled "Deduction of the Categories," Kant tries to prove that the faculty of thought has its logical patterns ("categories") which it must impose upon any sensory material of which it can have conscious knowledge. He holds that the presence of these patterns is what enables us to know a priori that in the realm of phenomena all events must be causally interconnected (the principle of determinism) and must involve enduring substance which cannot be created or destroyed (the conservation of matter). That such metaphysical principles are knowable concerning the realm of possible experience is of great importance to Kant. He calls this part of his argument a "deduction," borrowing this term from the traditional German legal usage. There, a "deduction" was a legal document purporting to establish a claim to a title of nobility, with its associated rights of ownership and rule. In the still feudal political society of Germany were many princelings and

many titles of nobility, great and small. Claims must often have come into conflict, and courts would have been accustomed to dealing with them. A "deduction" would trace the lineage of the claimant, showing him or her to be of legitimate descent and the true heir to the title and rights at stake. In terms of this metaphor, Kant is seeking to adjudicate the claim of human thought to achieve metaphysical knowledge through its categories. Kant's "deduction" is the attempt to exhibit the legitimacy of this claim.

While these metaphors which Kant employs decorate his exposition, their role is more than decorative, for were Kant's project not explained through metaphors like these it would be so abstract that we should scarcely be able to understand it. But do these metaphors provide us with an appropriate understanding of Kant's project? How apt are the metaphors? There are difficulties with them.

The metaphor of geographical discovery is vivid in its comparison of Hume and Kant with da Gama, Columbus, and Magellan. But we must remember that the "territory" which the philosophical traveler explores is not a real territory spread out in space which one traverses rapidly or slowly. It is an abstract logical "territory" consisting of distinctions among faculties and types of knowledge.

The metaphor of the courtroom is also vivid. But it too is potentially misleading, for it fails to bring out the full peculiarity of Kant's inquiry. According to Kant, the human mind itself, through rational thinking, is to undertake this critique or "trial" of its rational capacity to know. Thus, the same faculty which is the subject of the inquiry is to conduct the inquiry. The critical philosophy which Kant aims to develop will be a theory produced by the thinking part of the mind concerning how the thinking part of the mind operates and what its limits are. Thus, Kant's metaphor of the courtroom conjures up a most unusual "courtroom" indeed. In it, the human power of thought must play *all* the chief roles: it must be at once the judge (who presides and will render the verdict), the plaintiff (who complains against the pretensions of metaphysical knowledge), and the defendant (who stands accused of fraudulently purveying metaphysics as knowledge). In the "trial" which Kant envisages, reason sits in judgment over its accusations against itself. This is a peculiarly self-reflexive situation. In legal terms, it raises serious problems of conflict of interest: Can reason give itself a fair and impartial hearing? This self-reflexive situation vitiates the courtroom metaphor. We must not take the courtroom idea too seriously if we are to make sense of Kant's philosophy.

In many ways the **Critique of Pure Reason** is an abstract and dry book. It was Kant's intention to write an austere work of technical philosophy in which fundamental problems about knowledge and reality would be attacked and solved. Nevertheless, as the book is written, there peers forth between the lines something of a narrative story. The story has a cast of characters and the rudiments of a plot. The hinted presence in this dry work of these narrative elements is surprising, but it can be explained as a consequence of the very austerity which Kant tries to practice. This austerity defeats itself, for author and reader both find themselves reading into the abstract account a more personal story.

The various faculties of the mind are the dramatis personae of the **Critique of Pure Reason.** Kant's way of writing about these faculties inevitably suggests personification of them. He did not exactly intend to personify them: he would have denied that they are persons, and he would have wanted to regard the language of personification as a merely figurative and decorative aspect of his exposition. Yet this language is deeply rooted in his text, and if he could have rewritten the book eliminating it, a very different work would have resulted. We are entitled to regard the personification of the faculties as a significant component of Kant's exposition.

The cast of characters in Kant's drama includes in starring roles three aspects of the faculty of thought: understanding, reason, and judgment. Each is an active power of the mind to arrange the material of consciousness in logical order. Because they are active in this way, the implicit suggestion is that they are to be regarded as masculine.

Of these three, understanding (*Verstand*) has to be viewed as the sober, responsible paterfamilias. It has a legitimate and useful occupation, imposing its categories upon the sensory material with which it is confronted, so as to produce is law within the realm of possible experience, where its concepts belong. Like a good citizen, it knows its station and its duties, and does not try to range beyond its proper limits.

Reason (*Vernunft*) is the faculty of thinking in a different and much more adventurous aspect. Reason, Kant says, has an innate drive to seek completion in its explanations. But within the realm of possible experience where understanding rules, whenever we start asking for the causes of present phenomena we are led back to earlier phenomena on which they depend, and these in turn lead us back to other still earlier phenomena: we never find any first cause, or ultimate explanation, in this series. Reason is dissatisfied with this and so postulates a first cause outside the series, beyond the realm of possible experience. Thus arises the idea of God, an idea which reason frames in its quest for complete knowledge and final explanation. But to have theoretical knowledge that a God exists we would have to be able to have sense experience of Him, since concepts without sensations are empty. The idea of God is postulated in the first place as an idea of something wholly beyond the realm of possible experience; the consequence is that humans cannot have theoretical knowledge that God exists. Thus, reason has gone off on a quixotic search for the unfindable, a search which inevitably fails, but which reason by its very nature cannot abandon. This is what Kant calls the "Transcendental Dialectic"—the fierce but fruitless struggle of reason to gain theoretical knowledge beyond the realm of possible experience.

If understanding is to be regarded as the sober, respectable, stay-at-home aspect of the faculty of thought, then reason is to be regarded as the errant, disturbed uncle in the family, whose ambitions are utterly beyond what he can ever achieve. He is admirable for his Faustian striving, but pitiable for his inevitable failure to achieve the goals he sets for himself. He cannot hold a solid job making a steady contribution, but always must be disrupting the equilibrium of the family with his yearning after unreachable ideal goals.

The faculty of judgment (*Urteilskraft*) is the third of Kant's aspects of the faculty of thought. Judgment is the power of the mind to subsume particular experiences under a general concept or rule. For example, if the mind has the concept of circularity, then it must rely upon its faculty of judgment to enable it to detect that a particular experience is indeed an experience of a circle. Kant does not have much to say in the *Critique of Pure Reason* about this faculty, or about how it works. He describes it as an innate gift; those in whom this

power of judgment is weak have a lack which can never be made good, he says. So he is thinking of judgment as a sort of male younger cousin to understanding, a cadet faculty whose power is a mysterious and inexplicable gift.

However, in his later work, the *Critique of Judgment,* Kant develops his account of judgment more fully and assigns it additional responsibilities. There it emerges that judgment has a creative, important job to perform in dealing with material that is intractable to the operations of understanding. It turns out that the appreciation of beauty is the work of the faculty of judgment, as is the awareness of purposiveness in nature (teleology). So in the third *Critique* judgment comes into its own with tasks to perform in areas of human experience outside natural science, the special domain of understanding. Judgment does not compete with understanding or come into any conflict with it, but works in a quite different way in different areas. It is freer and more original in what it does, a sort of bohemian faculty, while understanding is rigid and mechanical in application of its own strict laws.

On the distaff side in Kant's drama, we encounter sensibility (or "receptivity"). This is the mind's ability to receive sensations through being affected by things in themselves. As we saw, for human beings sensibility is necessarily spatiotemporal in its form. Sensibility is the wife and helpmeet of understanding. Each is incomplete without the other. Understanding needs sensibility to provide it with material to organize; sensibility profusely produces formless material which requires the disciplinary activity of understanding to put it in order. Sensibility is richly productive, like a primal Earth-Mother; but what it produces is utterly chaotic until the firm hand of understanding is laid upon it.

So far as theoretical knowledge is concerned, sensibility and understanding are a fairly happily united couple, each doing what it does best and welcoming the other as complementary to itself. However, a coldness and distance marks their relationship. Judgment is constantly called upon to mediate between them; apparently they find direct communication with one another very difficult.

A final character, imagination, needs to be mentioned. Kant says that it is passive and partakes of the character of sensibility, but works closely under the direction of understanding. It helps judgment with the obviously difficult task of mediating between sensibility and understanding. The most important function of imagination is to create the full-blooded awareness that we have of phenomena as possessing aspects that we are not at the moment sensing. For example, in seeing what one takes to be a building, one is sensing at most the front side of its outer surface; to be aware of it as a building one must imagine it as having back surfaces and insides. The faculty of imagination must provide this awareness, but it is required to work strictly to the requirements of understanding as regards scientific laws—merely fanciful imagining is not what is called for. Kant is apparently thinking of imagination as the dutiful daughter of understanding and sensibility, a daughter who mostly forgoes fanciful reveries and devotes herself primarily to the blind labor her father orders in furtherance of his project of developing theoretical knowledge.

We may think of the *Critique of Pure Reason* as the story of this family. They have their family troubles—conflict occurs between idealistic reason and prosaic understanding, and coldness and estrangement occur between understanding and sensibility. But they have also their domestic harmony when they work cooperatively. Insofar as there is a plot in the *Critique of Pure Reason,* it has to do with how this family evolves its cooperative harmony despite the estrangement and conflict, overcoming both understanding's coldness toward sensibility and the disruption brought about by reason's ill-starred but inexpugnable drive toward ultimate reality. The resolution of these problems comes through the attainment by the family as a whole of a deeper knowledge of themselves. By learning to recognize and to accept their own capabilities and limitations, they can achieve an adequate harmony with one another. This is possible, although they all know that reason by its nature is doomed never to be able altogether to give up its yearning for theoretical knowledge of the ultimate, even after it has been forced to recognize that this can never be satisfied.

In thus describing the *Critique of Pure Reason* as though it were a soap opera, I am going beyond Kant's actual words. The drama is there only between the lines, as hinted at by the language of personification which Kant employs. While this sort of philosophical drama is only implicit in Kant's text, it will become more explicit a little later in Hegel's *Phenomenology of Mind,* where the whole book is frankly written as if it were a story of the mind's progress through many stages toward ultimate self-awareness. Hegel's story differs from Kant's, though, because Hegel sees no possible barriers to a final perfect harmony within the mind, with full gratification of all its desires for knowledge. Also, for Hegel, the various faculties of the mind do not remain fundamentally separate individuals but appear only as passing phases of the basic ongoing activity of consciousness. Hegel's story is more romantic and optimistic than Kant's, but Kant's is more like real life.

The quality of writing in Kant's *Critique of Pure Reason* varies considerably. Even at his best, Kant is hardly outstanding as a stylist, and he is seldom able to keep writing at his best for long. But brief passages occur of great eloquence, good-sized paragraphs where the writing is vivid and polished, and long sections where literary difficulties at least are not oppressive. Yet there are other sections where the writing is most burdensome to a reader. The quality of the expository style is inversely correlated with the difficulty for Kant of the philosophical problems he is treating.

The Preface to the *Critique* (in both editions) is readable and lively and shows Kant at his expository best. Here his writing is fluent and graceful, with striking figures of speech which students of Kant remember gratefully. Later on, the long section entitled "The Dialectic of Pure Reason" is adequately written, on the whole. It deals with the logical errors into which reason falls when it leaves the realm of possible experience and tries to establish conclusions about the nature of things as they are in themselves. The ideas in this part were worked out by Kant comparatively early, and this portion of the *Critique* presumably was written some years before the publication of the book. It probably went through various drafts, and Kant may have worked a long time on revising and polishing it to make his presentation clear and readable.

Kant's sections entitled "Transcendental Aesthetic" and "Transcendental Analytic" are much less ingratiating as literary productions. These sections are more central to Kant's basic doctrine, and working them out seems to have given him much trouble. The Transcendental Aesthetic deals with space and time as forms of human sensibility. Its presentation

is crabbed, awkward, and obscure. Kant's crucial points are tersely expressed, are not well related to the rest of the book, and make difficult going for readers. The Transcendental Analytic deals with the understanding and its categories. Here Kant is trying to work out his central thoughts about the operations of understanding and how these can yield metaphysical knowledge. His exposition is very difficult.

Within the Transcendental Analytic, one long part is especially notorious: the "Transcendental Deduction of the Categories." Here Kant tries to prove the a priori necessity of the pure concepts of the understanding. He tells us that this section cost him the greatest pain and difficulty to compose, and his ideas in it must have been late in reaching their final form. Here his sentence structure is at its heaviest and most awkward, his paragraphs are not well organized, and his abstract jargon is difficult to penetrate.

We can better appreciate Kant's situation if we realize that in this portion of the *Critique* he was locked in a titanic struggle with the difficulty of his philosophical thoughts. He was trying to formulate and establish an original, profound theory about the functioning of consciousness. Putting it into words was a task requiring heroic exertions.

We should also bear in mind the conditions under which Kant wrote. He worked alone; none of those who knew him and wrote accounts of his life mentions any secretary or even copyist. His habits were of legendary regularity, and he worked on his philosophical writing for only a few hours each morning, the rest of his day being reserved for lecturing, social activity, his walk, and reading. So we must suppose that with quill pen he wrote out all preliminary drafts of material and the final draft of the completed work. This was a monumental task, and we must not be surprised that he did not find time to polish his prose as much as we could wish.

Kant's philosophical ideas began to crystallize for him only in middle age, and as they did so his plans for philosophical writing became more grandiose. His plan for the *Critique of Pure Reason* grew and expanded, and he became convinced of the need to write other works to develop and complete the system of philosophy of which his first *Critique* was to be the foundation. The fear that he might not live to complete his work troubled him, this must have made him write more rapidly and with less attention to style. We must suppose that this fear moved him at last to forge ahead with publishing a final draft of the first *Critique,* even though its exposition was still imperfect. To have taken additional years in refining the literary quality of this very long book would have prevented Kant from getting to the further writing on which his heart was now set. These considerations can help us to understand some of what we cannot enjoy in Kant's writing.

The table of contents of the *Critique of Pure Reason* exhibits Kant's idea that an elaborate logical structure must be present in his philosophical material. This is the "architectonic": Kant's logical pattern of sections and subsections paralleling one another in complex array. To a twentieth-century reader the pattern looks forbidding, alien, and pointless. It seems an arbitrary and willful imposition upon the subject matter. And this bad impression is made still worse when we notice how Kant's architectonic often is out of step with the philosophical ideas which it tries to dragoon into position.

One aspect of this strain between the architectonic form and its philosophical content is that some of the headings which Kant feels bound to list end up with little material falling under them. This is especially noticeable in the final section of the book, the "Transcendental Doctrine of Method," which appears tacked on artificially. It altogether lacks the weight and interest of the earlier parallel part of the book, the "Transcendental Doctrine of Elements." Its final sections, especially the "History of Pure Reason," are strangely short and have slight content. Was Kant rushing to finish the book? If so, why did he include these sections at all?

Another way in which the strain between architectonic form and philosophical content shows itself is in those places where the ideas being treated in one section refuse to remain confined and boil over into other sections. For example, the section entitled "Antinomies of Pure Reason" is supposed to be about the idea of the world as a whole; but its fourth part (the fourth antinomy) raises the question of the existence of God, a question which is supposed to be reserved for discussion in the "Critique of Speculative Theology." In subtler ways, the ideas of the Transcendental Aesthetic refuse to remain separated from those of the Transcendental Analytic, and to make headway toward understanding Kant's philosophy one must deny the sharp distinction which Kant's exposition would erect between the ideas of these sections.

What are we to make of the architectonic? We can better understand this aspect of Kant's style if we see it in relation to one of his fundamental philosophical assumptions: the transparency to itself of the mind's cognitive functioning. This doctrine is not very plausible to twentieth-century readers, who are more inclined to think of the mind as having hidden unconscious depths in which it conceals its operations from itself. But for Kant the transparency of the mind in its knowing activities is an obvious assumption. The assumption is associated with the tradition of German rationalistic philosophy, and it is necessary for the type of inquiry into the mind which Kant aims to conduct.

"Transparency" is not Kant's word, but it is a suitable term for expressing this doctrine. The doctrine is that the mind can understand its own cognitive operations in a thoroughgoing fashion and can know that it has succeeded in doing so. Nothing in the cognitive functioning of one's mind can be ultimately hidden from one's self-conscious rational scrutiny. Outer things in themselves may be unknowable, and even the real nature of one's own mind, as a thing in itself, may remain unknowable. But the workings of the mind, as regards all cognitive activity, cannot be unknowable.

This doctrine of transparency underlies Kant's dedication to architectonic. If the truth about the mind's cognitive operations is all to be knowable, it must be systematic: it cannot consist of a job-lot of unrelated independent facts, for then there could never be any guarantee that one's knowledge of them was complete—one might always have over-looked some. Only if these truths about the mind all hang together in a tight logical network can we be assured that knowledge of some of these truths must in principle lead to knowledge of them all. Only then can the critique of pure reason be a task which we can be confident of being able to complete successfully.

Seen in this perspective, Kant's architectonic is a necessary aspect of the special and remarkable task of criticizing reason. Even if his architectonic classifications creak and wobble in many places, Kant will not abandon them, for he is absolutely confident that an architectonic must exist that is objectively the same for all human minds as they study their men-

tal activity. "Pure reason," he says, "is by its nature architectonic."

In his philosophical writing Kant only rarely gives examples to illustrate his philosophical points. Where examples do occur, they usually are perfunctory and are presented with little detail. This makes much trouble for the reader who is trying to grasp Kant's meaning, for Kant's abstract way of stating his points frequently leaves them floating in air. The reader must endeavor to supply illustrations and examples but often finds this difficult to do, as one cannot always divine Kant's intentions.

Kant's use of technical jargon compounds the difficulty. A barrage of technical germs occurs: *representation, intuition, phenomena, noumena, inner sense, outer sense,* and many others. Some of these terms are defined, but always only cryptically and darkly, and usually via other technical terms. Such arid definitions are of only limited help to the reader. How one would like to have had varied examples and illustrations to make clearer the meanings of the technical terms.

It is on principle that Kant refrains from supplying more than perfunctory examples. Unfortunately, his view of philosophical communication is that it ought to be abstract. He scornfully says that examples are the "go-cart of judgment," implying that only children need to receive explanations in terms of examples. Mature thinkers are supposed to be able to think abstractly, and for them illustrations are to have an inessential, merely decorative function, making the prose more elegant and enjoyable perhaps, but adding nothing to its cognitive content.

The philosophical point here is deep and important, relating to communication. Is it enough, in discussing abstract matters, to rely upon abstract terms and abstract definitions? Kant probably has in mind the success of pure mathematics, where the greatest mathematicians often do the least to illustrate and explain their theorems in language accessible to the nonspecialist. These mathematicians achieve their scientific results without making concessions to the frailties of readers. Their readership is small, but their scientific eminence is high. Now, Kant himself emphasizes that mathematical thinking differs in basic ways from philosophical thinking (he supposes that mathematics has to deal with our "pure intuitions" of space and time, whereas philosophy does not); but for Kant philosophy even less than mathematics need concern itself with giving examples and illustrations.

In twentieth-century philosophy it is Wittgenstein, above all, who has illuminatingly emphasized the crucial role of examples in philosophical discussion. If one chooses too meager or one-sided a diet of examples, he says, one's philosophical ideas will become hopelessly distorted. Wittgenstein's view of what is involved in philosophical understanding is far more wholesome than Kant's on this matter. However, Kant's procedure in his use of examples springs from his deep-rooted conception of understanding and communication in philosophy. It is not heedlessness, carelessness, or haste which drives him to proceed as he does. (pp. 77-91)

I have been discussing a number of the unsatisfactory aspects of Kant's expository writing. I have not argued that Kant's writing is good; no one will want to hold him up, overall, as a literary paragon to be emulated. But the weaknesses, defects, and peculiarities of his writing style can to a considerable extent be explained in terms of aspects of his thought. Some of them spring from the strain and difficulty he was experiencing in formulating his thoughts, while others are consequences of philosophical principles which he maintains. Seeing traits of Kant's style as thus associated with aspects of his thought can help us better appreciate the ***Critique of Pure Reason*** as the monumental intellectual achievement that it is. Also, it can help us to understand how Kant the author and Kant the thinker are very much one and the same person. (p. 92)

> *Stephen F. Barker, "The Style of Kant's Critique of Reason," in* The Philosopher as Writer: The Eighteenth Century, *edited by Robert Ginsberg, Susquehanna University Press, 1987, pp. 75-93.*

FURTHER READING

Acton, H. B. *New Studies in Ethics: Kant's Moral Philosophy.* London: Macmillan and Co., 1970, 71 p.
  Critical and historical assessment of Kant's ethical philosophy.

Beck, Lewis White. Introduction to *Prolegomena to Any Future Metaphysics,* by Immanuel Kant, pp. vii-xx. New York: Liberal Arts Press, 1951.
  Explains the historical context and philosophical intentions of the *Prolegomena.*

————. *A Commentary on Kant's "Critique of Practical Reason."* Chicago: University of Chicago Press, 1960, 308 p.
  Study of Kant's second *Critique,* placing the treatise in its historical context and assessing "the contents of this work on their philosophical merits."

————. *Studies in the Philosophy of Kant.* Indianapolis: Bobbs-Merrill Co., 1965, 242 p.
  Collection of previously published papers that survey all aspects of Kant's philosophy.

————. "Kant." In his *Early German Philosophy: Kant and His Predecessors,* pp. 426-501. Cambridge, Ma.: Harvard University Press, 1969.
  Study of Kant's critical system of philosophy, emphasizing the historical origins of his principal ideas.

————, ed. *Kant Studies Today.* La Salle, Ill.: Open Court, 1969, 507 p.
  Collection of essays by leading Kant scholars.

————, ed. *Proceedings of the Third International Kant Congress.* Dordrecht, Holland: D. Reidel, 1972, 718 p.
  Selected papers delivered at the 1970 Kant congress.

Bird, Graham. *Kant's Theory of Knowledge: An Outline of One Central Argument in the "Critique of Pure Reason."* London: Routledge & Paul, 1962, 210 p.
  A detailed exposition of Kant's epistemology.

Broad, C. D. *Kant: An Introduction.* Edited by C. Lewy. Cambridge: Cambridge University Press, 1978, 319 p.
  Contains transcripts of a series of lectures delivered at Cambridge in the early fifties by Broad, as well as reprints of his earlier articles that address central issues raised in Kant's three main *Critiques.*

Burch, Robert. "Kant's Theory of Beauty as Ideal Art." In *Aesthetics: A Critical Anthology,* edited by George Dickie and R. J. Sclafani, pp. 688-703. New York: St. Martin's Press, 1977.
  Refutes Donald Crawford's contention that "Kant's own work

provides an almost perfect example of the gap between traditional philosophical aesthetics and art criticism" (see Crawford entry below).

Caird, Edward. *A Critical Account of the Philosophy of Kant, with an Historical Introduction.* Glasgow: James Maclehose, 1877, 673 p.
  Considered one of the finest nineteenth-century commentaries on Kant.

Cassirer, Ernst. *Rousseau, Kant, and Goethe.* Princeton: Princeton University Press, 1947, 98 p.
  Relates Kant's philosophy to the work of Jean-Jacques Rousseau and Johann Wolfgang von Goethe.

Cassirer, H. W. *A Commentary on Kant's "Critique of Judgment."* 1938. Reprint. New York: Barnes & Noble, 1970, 412 p.
  Explication of the third *Critique,* offering "plain exposition unmixed with praise or blame."

Cohen, Ted and Guyer, Paul, eds. *Essays in Kant's Aesthetics.* Chicago: University of Chicago Press, 1982, 323 p.
  Collection of articles that examine issues related to Kant's aesthetic theories.

Coleman, Francis X. J. *The Harmony of Reason: A Study in Kant's Aesthetics.* Pittsburgh: University of Pittsburgh Press, 1974, 221 p.
  Evaluates the logic of Kant's argumentation in the *Critique of Judgment.*

Crawford, Donald W. *Kant's Aesthetic Theory.* Madison: University of Wisconsin Press, 1974, 189 p.
  Analysis of the *Critique of Judgment,* focusing on the development of Kant's notion of "the nature and importance of aesthetic experience."

Ewing, A. C. *A Short Commentary on Kant's "Critique of Pure Reason."* Chicago: University of Chicago Press, 1938, 278 p.
  Introduction to the *Critique of Pure Reason.*

Fackenheim, Emil L. von. "Kant's Concept of History." *Kant-Studien* 48, No. 3 (1956-1957): 381-98.
  Exposition of Kant's theory of history, affirming that "Kant views history as a necessary development toward rationality and freedom."

Galston, William A. *Kant and the Problem of History.* Chicago: University of Chicago Press, 1975, 290 p.
  Examines the "complex problems associated with the concept of history . . . ; problems that seemed . . . to have found their first recognizably modern expression in the historical essays of Kant."

Gram, Moltke S., ed. *Kant: Disputed Questions.* Chicago: Quadrangle Books, 1967, 313 p.
  Collection of articles, many by prominent critics of Kant, that discuss various issues related to the *Critique of Pure Reason.*

Greene, Theodore M., and Silber, John R. Introduction to *Religion Within the Limits of Reason Alone,* by Immanuel Kant. pp. vii-cxxiv. 1934. Reprint. New York: Harper and Brothers, 1960.
  Two essays. The first, by Greene, focuses on the historic context and biographical elements of the *Religion;* the second, by Silber, on the ethical component of Kant's religious thought.

Guyer, Paul. *Kant and the Claims of Taste.* Cambridge, Ma.: Harvard University Press, 1979, 447 p.
  Considers the role of Kant's theory of taste in the formation of his aesthetic philosophy.

Heidegger, Martin. *Kant and the Problem of Metaphysics.* Translated by James S. Churchill. Bloomington, Ind.: Indiana University Press, 1962, 255 p.
  Assesses Kant's contribution to the development of modern metaphysical thought.

Jones, Hardy E. *Kant's Principle of Personality.* Madison: University of Wisconsin Press, 1971, 163 p.

Inquiry into Kant's ethical doctrines, emphasizing the importance of the categorical imperative.

Knox, Israel. "Kant's Aesthetic Theory." In his *The Aesthetic Theories of Kant, Hegel, and Schopenhauer,* pp. 9-68. New York: Columbia University Press, 1936.

Examines the metaphysical foundations of Kant's aesthetic theories.

Körner, S. *Kant.* Harmondsworth, Middlesex: Penguin Books, 1955, 230 p.

General introduction to Kant's philosophy.

Kroner, Richard. *Kant's Weltanschauung.* Translated by John E. Smith. Chicago: University of Chicago Press, 1956, 118 p.

Probes the relation between Kant's philosophical ideas and his complex world view.

Laberge, Pierre; Duchesneau, Francois; and Morrisey, Bryan E., eds. *Actes du congrès d'Ottawa sur Kant dans les traditions anglo-américaine et continentale tenu du 10 au 14 Octobre 1974/Proceedings of the Ottawa Congress on Kant in the Anglo-American and Continental Traditions Held October 10-14, 1974.* Ottawa: University Of Ottawa Press, 1976, 541 pp.

Transcripts of readings held at the Congress by a distinguished group of Kant scholars addressing a wide range of issues.

Meredith, James Creed. Introduction to *Kant's Critique of Aesthetic Judgement,* by Immanuel Kant, pp. xvii-cixx. Oxford: Clarendon Press, 1911.

Explication of Kant's third *Critique.*

Paton, H. J. "Kant on Friendship." *Proceedings of the British Academy* 42 (1956): 45-66.

Considers Kant's views on friendship and personal relations, arguing that for Kant "moral action has a common form however much its matter varies."

———. *Kant's Metaphysic of Experience.* 2 vols. London: George Allen & Unwin, 1936.

Analysis of the first half of the *Critique of Pure Reason* that is intended "not to advocate a particular theory, but rather to place the student in such a position that he can set aside the theories of others and read Kant intelligently for himself."

———. *The Categorical Imperative.* Chicago: University of Chicago Press, 1948, 283 p.

Elucidates the complex structure of Kant's moral philosophy, focusing on the *The Metaphysics of Morals.*

Paulsen, Friedrich. *Immanuel Kant: His Life and Doctrine.* New York: Charles Scribner's Sons, 1902, 419 p.

Considered one of the most reliable sources of biographical information on Kant.

Penelhum, Terence, and MacIntosh, J. J., eds. *The First Critique: Reflections on Kant's "Critique of Pure Reason."* Belmont, Ca.: Wadsworth Publishing Company, 1969, 146 p.

Collection of articles on the *Critique of Pure Reason* intended as a guide for the undergraduate student of Kant.

Ross, Sir David. *Kant's Ethical Theory: A Commentary on the "Grundlegung zur Metaphysik der Sitten."* Oxford: Oxford University Press, 1954, 96 p.

Clarifies the main points of Kant's moral philosophy.

Saner, Hans. *Kant's Political Thought: Its Origins and Development.* Translated by E. B. Ashton. Chicago: University of Chicago Press, 1973, 374 p.

Introduction to Kant's political philosophy that seeks to "lay the foundation for an exegesis of Kant's political thought that can dispense with preconceived guidelines from elsewhere."

Shell, Susan Meld. *The Rights of Reason: A Study of Kant's Philosophy and Politics* Toronto: University of Toronto Press, 1980, 205 p.

Study of Kant's political philosophy, focusing on his "understanding of the relation between man and nature, as it bears on his philosophy of right."

Walsh, W. H. *Kant's Criticism of Metaphysics.* Edinburgh: University Press, 1975, 265 p.

Evaluates the central arguments of the *Critique of Pure Reason.*

———. "Kant's *Critique of Pure Reason:* Commentators in English, 1875-1945." *Journal of the History of Ideas* XLII, No. 4 (October-December 1981): 723-37.

Critical résumé of significant commentary on the *Critique of Pure Reason* published in English from 1875 to 1945.

Ward, Keith. *The Development of Kant's View of Ethics.* Oxford: Basil Blackwell, 1972, 184 p.

Study of Kant's moral philosophy that aims to "put the well-known doctrines in the overall context of Kant's developing philosophy."

Warnock, G. J. "Kant." In *A Critical History of Western Philosophy,* edited by Paul Edwards, pp. 296-318. London: Collier-Macmillan 1964.

Critical exegesis of Kant's three main philosophical treatises.

Wolff, Robert P. "Kant's Debt to Hume via Beattie." *Journal of the History of Ideas* XXI, No. 1 (January-March 1960): 117-23.

Argues that Kant's knowledge of David Hume's *Treatise of Human Nature* (*1739-40*) was derived from his reading of the Scottish philosopher James Beattie's *Essay on the Nature and Immutability of Truth* (*1770*).

———. *The Autonomy of Reason: A Commentary on Kant's "Groundwork of the Metaphysic of Morals."* New York: Harper & Row, 1973, 228 p.

Detailed technical analysis of this treatise.

———. *Kant's Theory of Mental Activity: A Commentary on the Transcendental Analytic of the "Critique of Pure Reason."* Gloucester, Mass.: Peter Smith, 1973, 336 p.

Textual commentary on the Transcendental Analytic, focusing on Kant's definition of pivotal terms.

James Clarence Mangan

1803-1849

Irish poet, translator, short story writer, and essayist.

Mangan is best remembered for his adaptations of Gaelic, German, and Middle Eastern ballads and poems, the best of which are regarded as original works superior to their sources. Praised for their lyricism, Mangan's adaptations and original poems are typically melancholic in tone, often treating themes of lost youth, lost love, and Irish patriotism. His work is now considered an important force in the shaping of modern Irish literature, and was especially influential during the Irish Literary Renaissance of the late nineteenth and early twentieth centuries.

The son of a grocer, Mangan was born on Fishamble Street in a Dublin slum. Through his early schooling, he formed an interest in languages, learning Latin, Spanish, French, and Italian, and later studied German under the tutelage of a priest. Due to his father's repeated business failures, Mangan left school in order to support his family, working as a copyist in a scrivener's office for seven years, and then for three years as a clerk in a law office. Loathing the tedium of his work and frustrated by his continuing poverty, he began using alcohol and, according to several scholars, opium to escape his unhappiness. During this period, Mangan wrote his earliest poems, many of which were published under various pseudonyms. Although details are scarce, in his twenties Mangan evidently courted a socially prominent young woman who eventually rejected him, and critics cite the experience as greatly influencing the themes of despair and irreclaimable love in his subsequent poetry.

In the early 1830s Mangan was hired as a cataloging assistant by the Trinity College library, and began publishing his interpretations of German and Irish poems in Dublin journals. These works brought him to the attention of the director of the Irish Ordnance Survey who offered him an assignment in the historical department. There he became acquainted with eminent Gaelic scholars, through whom he acquired knowledge of the old Irish bardic tradition and stories of ancient Irish life. Eventually the survey lost funding for Mangan's position, and he thereafter subsisted primarily on fees paid for his contributions of poetry and prose works to Dublin publications. His poems appeared in the *Nation* and other Irish nationalist periodicals, and his name became associated with the Young Ireland cultural and political movement of the 1840s, although scholars debate the extent of his political commitment. *Anthologia Germanica—German Anthology,* which contains Mangan's translations of German poetry, appeared in 1845 and was the only collection of Mangan's work published during his lifetime. He died during one of Dublin's worst cholera epidemics, yet some biographers have suggested that he actually died of starvation resulting largely from his chronic alcohol and drug use.

Mangan's poems are typically divided into three categories: Irish, Middle Eastern (often denoted as Oriental), and German, depending on the sources of their inspiration. His poetry based on Irish lyrics includes some of Mangan's most highly regarded work, even though most commentators contend

that he knew little Gaelic. Based loosely on literal prose translations of old Irish ballads, poems such as "O'Hussey's Ode to the Maguire" and "Dark Rosaleen" are esteemed for their powerful rhythms, which closely resemble those of the original works, and for passionate imagery that evokes traditional national heroes and the Irish landscape. "Dark Rosaleen," in its depiction of romantic love, is often interpreted as an allegorical lament for the demise of Ireland's past glory and national spirit. It is generally considered Mangan's masterpiece, earning the praise of English poet Lionel Johnson as being "among the great lyrics of the world, one of the fairest and fiercest in its perfection of imagery and rhythm; it is the chivalry of a nation's faith struck on a sudden into the immortality of music." Mangan's Oriental poems present themes and settings from Persia, Turkey, and other Middle Eastern lands. Like his Irish lyrics, poems such as "The Time of the Barmecides" and "The Karamanian Exile" convey a sense of regret and a nostalgia for a past era. Although Mangan first submitted these works to journals as translations, he attributed virtually all of them to apocryphal sources, and critics now view these poems as original. The majority of his German translations are regarded as more closely following their primary sources, and although his renderings of minor German romantic poets are particularly respected, they have received little critical attention.

Mangan employed a variety of rhyming and metrical techniques in his original poems, and he has been compared with his contemporary Edgar Allan Poe for the use of reiterated refrains and internal rhymes in his poetry. Praised for their lyrical intensity, his original poems are characterized by a sense of regret and misery that is viewed as highly autobiographical. "The Nameless One," in particular, is regarded as representative of Mangan's own voice and is lauded for the personal agony and alienation it expresses. Mangan's unfinished autobiography similarly conveys his sense of isolation, and, in its depiction of tormented genius, encourages the critical perception of Mangan as a *poète maudit* ("accursed poet"). His prose fiction, in contrast to much of his other work, is light in tone and includes whimsical tales that depict fantastic, mysterious happenings. Both Mangan's stories and essays are noted for a sharp attention to language and the use of playful puns.

The subjective aspect of Mangan's work, his unfortunate personal history, and his efforts to revive the Irish bardic tradition in English earned him recognition from William Butler Yeats and James Joyce, bringing him much critical attention at the turn of the century. Although commentators criticize his oeuvre as uneven in quality, Mangan is esteemed for his inventive treatment of translation sources and for his skillful adaptation of the conventions of romantic poetry to express his personal suffering.

PRINCIPAL WORKS

Literæ Orientales (poetry) 1837-46; published in journal *The Dublin University Magazine*
Anthologia Germanica—German Anthology. [translator] 2 vols. (poetry) 1845
Anthologia Hibernica (poetry) 1847; published in journal *The Dublin University Magazine*
The Poets and Poetry of Munster (poetry) 1849
Poems (poetry) 1850
The Tribes of Ireland [adaptor; from a satire by Aenghus O'Daly] (satire) 1852
Poems by James Clarence Mangan (poetry) 1859
James Clarence Mangan: His Selected Poems (poetry) 1897
Poems of James Clarence Mangan (poetry) 1903
The Prose Writings of James Clarence Mangan (short stories and essays) 1904
The Autobiography of James Clarence Mangan (autobiography) 1969
Selected Poems of James Clarence Mangan (poetry) 1973

FOREIGN QUARTERLY REVIEW (essay date 1845)

[*The following unsigned review unfavorably assesses the works collected in* Anthologia Germanica—German Anthology.]

[Mangan's **German Anthology**] is a reprint of poems that have appeared from time to time within the last ten years in the *Dublin University Magazine,* and contains specimens of the lyric poetry of Schiller, Uhland, Tieck, Kerner, Bürger, Goethe, Rückert, Freiligrath, &c. &c. The following lines from Uhland are a fair sample of the merits and defects of the collection:—

'Auf der Ueberfahrt'

Ueber diesen Strom, vor Jahren,
Bin ich einmal schon gefahren.
Hier die Burg im Abendschimmer,
Drüben rauscht das Wehr, wie immer.

Und von diesem Kahn umschlossen
Waren mit mir zween Genossen:
Ach! ein Freund, ein vatergleicher,
Und ein junger, Hoffnungs reicher.

Jener wirkte still hienieden,
Und so ist er auch geschieden,
Dieser brausend vor uns allen,
Ist im Kampf und Sturm gefallen.

So, wenn ich vergangene Tage
Glücklicher, zu denken wage,
Muss ich stets Genossen missen,
Theure die der Tod entrissen.

Doch was alle Freundshaft bindet
Ist, wenn Geist zu Geist sich findet.
Geistig waren jene Stunden,
Geistern bin ich noch verbunden.

Nimm nur, Fährmann, nimm die Miethe,
Die ich gerne dreifach biete,
Zween die mit mir überfuhren,
Waren geistige Naturen.

'Spirits Everywhere'

A many a summer is dead and buried
Since over this flood I last was ferried;
And then, as now, the noon lay bright
On strand, and water, and castled height.

Beside me then in this bark sat nearest
Two companions, the best and dearest.
One was a gentle and thoughtful sire,
The other a youth with a soul of fire.

One, outworn with care and illness,
Sought the grave of the just in stillness;
The other's shroud was the bloody rain,
And thunder-smoke of the battle-plain.

Yet still when memory's necromancy
Robes the past in the hues of fancy,
Me dreameth I hear and see the twain
With talk and smiles at my side again.

Even the grave is a bond of union,
Spirit and spirit best hold communion.
Seen through faith, by the inward eye,
It is *after* life they are truly nigh.

Then, ferryman, take this coin, I pray thee,
Thrice thy fare I cheerfully pay thee,
For though thou seest them not, there stand
Anear me two from the Phantomland.

There is much to commend in these lines, but they are disfigured also by no slight faults. Not to dwell on the pleonasm, not authorised by analogy or custom, that occurs in the first line, we have here examples of a radically vicious system of translation, which runs through the whole work. Mr. Mangan in his preface speaks of his translations as 'faithful to the spirit, if not always to the letter, of their originals.' They are very often neither the one nor the other. He takes many unwarrantable liberties with his authors, mutilates and interpolates, and falsifies them by an exaggeration that not seldom produces a burlesque effect where a grave one was intended. In the poem before us Mr. Mangan (not Uhland) lays down the strange doctrine that the death of our friends not only does not prevent all companionship between their souls and ours, but that it even brings us into closer communion with them! The following is a literal version of the fourth and fifth German stanzas:

> Thus ever, when I venture to think on bygone happier days, must I miss companions, dear ones snatched from me by death. But what binds all friendship fast is when spirit meets spirit. Spiritual were those vanished hours: with spirits I am still connected.

The sentiment here expressed is natural and touching; that which the translator has substituted for it is extravagant and false. Uhland says he has lost friends, but not wholly lost them, for memory still makes them present to his spirit: Mr. Mangan asserts that the death of friends is no loss at all, but an absolute gain to the affectionate survivor.

Seeing how grossly the translator has misrepresented the leading idea of the original poem, it is perhaps superfluous to remark on the bad effect of the phrase 'outworn with care and illness,' introduced for the rhyme's sake into the third stanza. There is nothing like it in the German, which merely states that the elder friend's way of life had been quiet, and his departure consonant with the calm tenor of his days. Why cloud this image of serenity with thoughts of bodily and mental suffering, and thereby weaken the contrast between the respective lives and fates of the elder and the younger man? A true artist would have seen the value of this contrast, and how it helps the imagination to realise more distinctly each of the two portraits presented to it.

One more specimen of what Mr. Mangan understands by fidelity to the spirit of his original. In our number for January last, and in *Tait's Magazine* for the following February or March, will be found versions of Freiligrath's celebrated poem, entitled 'The Lion's Ride,' both of them tolerably close. A perusal of either will enable the English reader to guess whether or not Freiligrath's canvass errs on the side of tameness, and needs to have its effect heightened by the addition of more glaring colours. Here is a literal translation of the first verse:

> Desert-king is the lion. Is it his pleasure to speed through his domain? He betakes him to the lagoon, and lies down in the tall sedges. Where gazelles and giraffes drink he crouches among the reeds. Trembling above the mighty one rustles the leaf of the sycamore.

Mr. Mangan's improvement upon the verse is as follows:

> What! wilt thou bind him fast with a chain?
> Wilt bind the King of the Cloudy Sands?
> Idiot fool!—he has burst from thy hands and bands,
> And speeds like Storm through his far domain.
> See! he crouches down in the sedge,
> By the water's edge,
> Making the startled sycamore boughs to quiver.
> Gazelle and giraffe, I think, will shun that river.

This is not gilding refined gold, but plating it with copper; not painting the lily white, but plastering it with red ochre. (pp. 238-40)

A review of "German Anthology," in The Foreign

Quarterly Review, *Vol. XXXVI, No. LXXI, October, 1845, pp. 238-40.*

THE DUBLIN REVIEW   (essay date 1845)

[*The following excerpt from an unsigned review praises* Anthologia Germanica—German Anthology.]

Poetical translations from the foreign languages, especially the German, have multiplied so rapidly of late years, that the English reader is often bewildered in attempting to make a selection. There are at least a dozen English versions of Goethe's *Faust;* nearly twice the number of Schiller's "Song of the Bell"; and even the less remarkable poems of both authors have been, in most instances, repeatedly translated. Still the rage for translation seems to have been confined to these and a few other poets; while the public has been left in comparative ignorance of a host of other writers equally original, little less gifted, and, if less prolific, certainly not less necessary for a proper estimate of the national literature of Germany.

[*Anthologia Germanica*] will introduce the reader to many poets who are comparatively unknown, but whose acquaintance notwithstanding, will, we make no doubt, prove little less agreeable than that of the old and traditionary representatives of German literature. The translations, with one single exception, are reprinted from a series of papers in the *Dublin University Magazine.* But the intervals of publication were distant and irregular; the papers were scattered through nearly twenty volumes of this periodical, and the author has done good service to the public in reprinting them in this neat and convenient form, in which they assume, for all practical purposes, the character of a new and independent work. Indeed, we have no hesitation in saying, that the ***German Anthology*** is destined to take its place in the very highest rank of poetical translations. Mr. Mangan's mind is precisely of that plastic character which is indispensable for spirited and truthful translations. He possesses, in a high degree, the art of thoroughly divesting himself, in his capacity of translator, of every individuality of thought and of manner, and becoming, so to speak, the mere instrument of the author whom he translates. The moment he takes up the pen, he forgets himself altogether; or rather he, as it were, converts himself into his original thinking and writing in a new language; so that not alone the thought, but the words, the form, the style, the manner, the very metre, are faithfully rendered back. With him translation is a mere process of fusion; but the metal is recast in precisely the same mould, and preserves not alone the substance, but the most minute and delicate peculiarities of form which characterised its original structure.

And this faculty is still more extraordinary when exercised, as here, upon an almost endless variety of subjects. That a translator, by long study and fervent admiration of a single author, or even of several authors belonging to the same school and resembling each other in the general character of their compositions, should become thoroughly familiar with that character, and as it were, come to form his thoughts habitually in the same mould, is natural enough, and can be easily understood by any one who has at all studied the art of composition. But Mr. Mangan has tried his hand on more than forty different models, and appears equally at home with all. With that strange faculty of which naturalists tell, his pen seems to take its colour from the food it feeds upon—it is pious and didactic with Hölty or Klopstock—humorous and burlesque with Dunkel—it plunges into the depths of mysticism with De la Motte Fouqué—and laughs at the world with Kotzebue or Bürger. The writer is a complete literary Proteus. He appears to be equally in his element among the fairy tales of Schnezler, and the philosophic reveries of Schiller or Goethe; and after throwing his whole soul into one of the fiery philippics of Freiligrath or Kerner, can return to dream over the melancholy sentimentalism of Tieck, or Simrock, or Rückert, as though he had lived his life long in those dreamy halls,

> Where melancholy music ceaseless swells.

Indeed, we have seldom, perhaps never, met any writer who possesses in a higher degree that mastery over the varieties of metre and the proprieties of poetical phraseology, which supplies, as it were, the mechanical tools of the poet. The reader of Anster's *Faust,* for example, cannot fail to be struck with the evidence of this power which is displayed in that wonderful poem. But if he turn to the original, he will find that this luxuriance and versatility is for the most part Dr. Anster's own—the sparkling and bubbling up of the well-spring of genuine poetry, which refuses to be confined within artificial boundaries. Though his own versification is extremely varied, he seldom follows the variety of the original. But it is not so with the author of the **Anthology.** To him it appears a matter of complete indifference into what form of metre he may throw his thoughts; and the great charm of his versification is, that throughout all its varieties it preserves its freedom, its liveliness, and above all, its perfect propriety.

We have often, therefore, been tempted to regret, that a writer possessing a faculty so rare among the poets of this country—one too which lends such a charm to the lighter pieces of our German neighbours—should not have done something in the line of original English poetry, if it were only to prove that the language is not unsusceptible of similar varieties of poetical structure. But we are inclined, on reflection, to doubt whether this extraordinary power of imitation is compatible with great originality of poetical genius. The vine-branch can climb the rock, or creep along the plain—its tendrils will follow the upright course of the poplar, or twine among the twisted branches of the mulberry; but by itself it is helpless and intractable—and perhaps the mind which habituates itself to borrow inspiration from another, and moulds itself into the fashion of another's thought, is only following therein a hidden instinct, which warns it that it was not destined to labour alone, and is not possessed of resources for great original conceptions. (pp. 312-15)

A review of "German Anthology," in The Dublin Review, *Vol. XIX, No. XXXVIII, December, 1845, pp. 312-31.*

THE CHRISTIAN EXAMINER (essay date 1865)

[*In the following excerpt, the critic evaluates* Poems by James Clarence Mangan.]

In respect to the preservation of her ancient ballads and poetry, as in many another, Ireland has been singularly unfortunate: with airs of the most wild and plaintive beauty, equal, and in many respects superior, to those of Scotland,—every one of which undoubtedly had words attached,—there is very little remaining save the music, which can now never be lost. The poetry, which was handed down from mouth to mouth, has almost entirely perished, with the extinction of Erse as a dialect, almost in our own day. The few scattered fragments that have been preserved, even in the clumsy translation that most of them have received, show what a treasure has been irrecoverably lost.

Mangan translated a number of pieces from the Erse . . . , but without any of heartiness or feeling necessary: singular to say, he did not even understand the language that he ventured to transcribe, being furnished with a literal prose translation of the words, by a friendly co-laborer in the library. Mangan's translations, although they reflect almost literally the intensely realistic expressions and allegorical repetitions of the originals, are almost entirely destitute of their sweetness and tender pathos, which [Irish poet Samuel] Ferguson so clearly reproduces: they are too much like the literal versifying of a schoolboy's task, as thus in the old tale of **"The Forgotten Wedding Day,"** or **"Rory and Darborgilla:"**—

> Know ye the tale of the Prince of Oriel,
>   Of Rory last of his line of Kings?
> I pen it here as a sad memorial
>   Of how much woe reckless folly brings.
>   • • • • •
> But hear ye further! When Cairtre's daughter
>   Saw what a fate had o'ertaen her Brave,
> Her eyes became as twin founts of water,
>   Her heart again as a darker grave.

This is scarcely an improvement on the literal prose translation. How differently Ferguson would have mellowed the sad sweetness of the original into his numbers may be seen in the "Lament of Deirdre for the Sons of Usnach." Or perhaps the best example of the difference in their styles might be **"The Fair Hills of Ireland,"** which was translated by both.

But, passing by these as unworthy of the skill and taste of the translator, and the spirit of his subjects, we come to the translations of the German, which form the bulk of the volume. These again are very unequal, as was to have been expected from so much task-work; but among them are some of the finest gems of poetry, that seem to have almost received additional lustre from their setting in a new language. The very measure and melody of Ludwig Tieck's "Herbstlied" are thus marvellously transferred:—

> A little bird flew through the dell;
> And, where the failing sunbeams fell,
> He warbled thus his wondrous lay:
> 'Adieu! adieu! I go away:
>   Far, far
> Must I voyage ere the twilight star.'
>
> It pierced me through, the song he sang,
> With many a sweet and bitter pang:
> For wounding joy, delicious pain,
> My bosom swelled and sank again.
>   Heart! heart!
> Is it drunk with bliss or woe thou art?
>
> Then, when I saw the drifted leaves,
> I said, 'Already Autumn grieves.'
> To sunnier skies the swallow hies:
> So Love departs and Longing flies,
>   Far, far
> Where the Radiant and the Beauteous are.
>
> But soon the sun shone out anew,
> And back the little flutterer flew:
> He saw my grief, he saw my tears,
> And sang, 'Love knows no Winter years.'
>   No! no!
> While it lives, its breath is Summer's glow!

The translations include specimens from the whole range of modern German poetry, with one exception and a singular one,—that of Heine, none of whose poems appear: yet it would seem, that the melancholy madness, and despairing, bitter mirth of his lyrical drops of gall, would have been in perfect unison with the spirit of Mangan. Perhaps their highly concentrated essence and perfect finish deterred, or their edges, too sharp for his own heart, forbade them to be meddled with in the way of task-work. Not only do we find here the higher names in German poetry, but some that do not rank above the common herd in their own country; as, for instance, many of "raw-head-and-bloody-bones" sentimentalities of the once popular Swabian school of minor poetry,— Dr. Justinus Kerner and the like, representing the "Mysteries of Udolpho" and "Castle Spectre" school of English literature. These, in many instances, are so transfigured and beautified, that the original authors would find it difficult to recognize their offspring. In fact, Mangan by no means considered himself bound to give a literal version in cases like these, often changing the whole structure, melody, and purport of his subject; so that little remained save the title, or interpolating his own fancies, when and where he pleased: this, which would be sacrilege in the case of Goethe and Schiller, is easily pardoned as regards the works of authors that have been justly consigned to almost total oblivion. The following little gem, from Kerner, deserves the credit of an original poem:—

"The Poet's Consolation"

What though no maiden's tears ever be shed
  O'er my clay bed,
Yet will the generous Night never refuse
  To weep its dews.

And though no friendly hand garland the cross
  Above my moss,
Still will the dear, dear moon tenderly shine
  Down on that sign.

And if the saunterer by songlessly pass
  Through the long grass,
There will the noontide bee pleasantly hum,
  And the warm winds come.

Yes—you at least, ye dells, meadows, and streams,
  Stars and moonbeams,
Will think on him whose weak, meritless lays
  Teemed with your praise.

That he understood the true value of such maudlin sentimentalists may be seen by an extract from one of his own poems, to which it is time we now turned:—

Did I paint a fifth of what I feel,
  Oh, how plaintive you would ween I was!
But I won't, albeit I have a deal
  More to wail about than Kerner has!
Kerner's tears are wept for withered flowers,
  Mine for withered hopes: my scroll of woe
Dates, alas! from youth's deserted bowers
  Twenty golden years ago!

Yet may Deutschland's bardlings flourish long!
  Me, I tweak no beak among them; hawks
Must not pounce on hawks: besides in song
  I could once beat all of them by chalks.
Though you find me, as I near my goal,
  Sentimentalizing like Rousseau,
Oh, I had a grand Byronian soul
  Twenty golden years ago!

Tick-tick, tick-tick!—not a sound save Time's,
  And the wind-gust as it drives the rain:
Tortured torturer of reluctant rhymes,
  Go to bed, and rest thy aching brain!
Sleep no more the dupe of hope and schemes;
  Soon thou sleepest where the thistles blow:
Curious anticlimax to thy dreams
  Twenty golden years ago.

The translations included in [*Poems,* 1859] under the head of Persian, Ottoman, Coptic, are undoubtedly his own. On one occasion, being asked how he could credit such gems to [Persian poet Shams ud-din Mohammed] Hafiz, replied that Hafiz paid better than Mangan, and that any one could see that they were only *half his*. His professedly original poems are very few in number, comprising less than thirty pages of this volume; but in them he poured out his soul as man has seldom done, and on them must his claim to be considered a poet rest. It must not be forgotten in the contemplation of these, that the man was a wreck, body and mind, a once stout-built argosy, but utterly and hopelessly wrecked; that he pursued poetry,—translating we mean,—which gave him command of rhyme, only as a means of bread. These are not the theatrical *morbidezza* of a Byron or a Poe, but, like the lamentations of the lonely Job, only the irrepressible moans of his own soul. He reports the horrors and visions that lie in the world of his experience of sorrow, with a realistic intenseness of expression that Browning could alone rival, with a wonderful skill of melody, and capricious variety of rhyme, peculiar to himself, and occasionally flashing into an expression of living fire, as of the hypocrites, who—

  Would look in God's face
  With a lie in their eyes.

A specimen, by no means the best, but characteristic in every point, will give a better idea of the qualities of his poetry than the most labored analysis, and also serve as an autobiography of the life, which we have endeavored to sketch. It is entitled **"The Nameless One;"** and with it we shall close our brief record.

Roll forth, my song, like the rolling river
  That sweeps along to the mighty sea:
God will inspire me while I deliver
  My soul of thee!

Tell thou the world, when my bones lie whitening
  Amid the last homes of youth and eld,
That there was one once, whose veins ran lightning
  No eye beheld.

Tell how his boyhood was one drear night-hour;
  How shone for him, through his griefs and gloom,
No star of all, Heaven sends to light our
  Path to the tomb.

Roll on, my song; and to after-ages
  Tell how, disdaining all earth can give,
He would have taught men, from Wisdom's pages,
  The way to live.

And tell how, trampled, derided, hated,
  And worn by weakness, disease, and wrong,
He fled for shelter to GOD, who mated
  His soul with song:

With song which alway, sublime or vapid,
  Flowed like a rill in the morning beam;
Perchance not deep, but intense and rapid,
  A mountain stream.

Tell how this Nameless, condemned for years long
    To herd with demons from hell beneath,
Saw things that made him, with groans and tears, long
    For even death.

Go on to tell how, with genius wasted,
    Betrayed in friendship, befooled in love,
With spirit shipwrecked, and young hopes blasted,
    He still, still strove;

Till, spent with toil, dreeing death for others,
    And some whose hands should have wrought for him
(If children live not for sires and mothers),
    His mind grew dim.

And he fell far through that pit abysmal,
    The gulf and grave of Maguire and Burns,
And pawned his soul for the devil's dismal
    Stock of returns:

And yet redeemed it in days of darkness,
    And shapes and signs of the final wrath;
When Death, in hideous and ghastly starkness,
    Stood on his path.

And tell how now, amid reck and sorrow
    And want and sickness and houseless nights,
He bides in calmness the silent morrow,
    That no ray lights.

And lives he still then? Yes! Old and hoary
    At thirty-nine, from despair and woe,
He lives, enduring what future story
    Will never know.

Him grant a grave to, ye pitying noble,
    Deep in your bosoms! There let him dwell!
He, too, had tears for all souls in trouble,
    Here and in hell.

                                            (pp. 205-11)

"James Clarence Mangan," in The Christian Examiner, *Vol. LXXIX, No. CCLI, September, 1865,
pp. 200-11.*

DANIEL CONNOLLY (essay date 1880)

[*In this excerpt, Connolly discusses Mangan as an unjustly neglected poet and presents an overview of his major works.*]

The name of Clarence Mangan is a familiar one, we suspect,
to but few American readers, and fewer still, in all probability, are they who possess any knowledge of his dark and desolate life. He died some thirty years ago, and mankind has
since been too busy with other things to give much heed to
the memory of an obscure poet. For Mangan, genius though
he was, and notable as were the results of his literary labor,
passed his days, nevertheless, in the by-ways of poverty and
seclusion, and left the world with hardly a hope or wish that
his name would ever be honored for the work he had done.
A more dismal, dreary life than his no poet ever lived. Even
the dim career of Poe was bright and pleasant by comparison.
There were at least some rays of sunshine there, but Mangan's days were all a succession of cloud and darkness. Constantly pressed by necessity, with the shadow of want ever
haunting his footsteps, his home a cheerless place where
brightness never came, he drifted gloomily on, now advised
and now pitied by his friends, till at last it was announced in
some of the Dublin newspapers that Clarence Mangan was
no more. The notice of his death did not attract much attention, for, even in the city in which his whole life had been

passed, Mangan was but little known. He was only a sorrowful poet, regarded by many as merely a melancholy dreamer,
and such men occupy but a small place in the thoughts of
those among whom they live.

It is an open question among many of his countrymen whether Mangan was not as good a poet as Ireland has produced.
This point is one which it is not now worth while to discuss,
but it may at least be said that Mangan's mind had a broader
scope than that of any other Irish poet. The genius of Moore
undoubtedly rose to loftier flights of sentiment; Goldsmith
was more placid, gentle, and philosophical; Griffin may have
written with a more tender pathos; Davis with greater ardor
and a more headlong patriotic passion; Prout and Lover with
more quaintness and certainly with more humor. Mangan
was unlike any of these. His muse was in the main dreary and
dismal, breathing a spirit of utter desolation. It was but rarely
that a gleam of humor broke through the somber shadows of
his verse. O'Connell once likened the smile upon an adversary's face to a silver plate on a coffin. The same ghastly simile might be applied to Mangan's occasional attempts at lightness. They were much like glints of phosphorus in a graveyard. He was essentially sad, weird, and gloomy, yet warmly
passionate at times, withal, and capable of uttering with tremendous force the aspirations of a lofty soul borne down by
trial and sorrowing on the brink of despair. In the field wherein he labored he was unquestionably great, and entitled to a
distinction entirely his own. (p. 558)

If all the original and translated poems of Mangan were collected, they would fill a six-hundred-page volume of ordinary
dimensions. His translations of German poems make altogether about three hundred pages. These were published a
few years before his death, under the title of **German Anthology,** and attracted some attention from European critics.
They are chiefly from Schiller, Goethe, Uhland, Kerner,
Freiligrath, and Rückert, though ballads and legends of
many minor poets are also given. It is somewhat singular
that, although Mangan had thoroughly familiarized himself
with the French language, French poetry does not appear to
have had any especial charm for him. No doubt the peculiar
mysticism of German verse was more in harmony with his
singular mind than the buoyant, happy spirit of French writers; but, nevertheless, it is strange that he neglected the latter,
except to read them. He also translated, or is supposed to
have done so, from the Ottoman and Arabic. It may be, however, that in the case of poems from these languages—
accepting, for the nonce, the hypothesis that they actually are
translations—Mangan obtained thought and subject through
prose adaptations made by others, and then constructed the
forms in which they have since been known. This, it seems,
was his mode of translating the ancient Celtic bards, of whose
language, strange to say, he did not understand a word. Competent judges pronounce Mangan's versions of old Irish
poems remarkable for fidelity to the originals, yet there is
good authority for saying that he could no more have read
one of the originals than he could have converted Greek into
Chinese. Among his literary friends in Dublin were some accomplished Irish scholars who made free translations of certain old Irish songs and ballads, which Mangan then turned
back into verse, giving it such form as seemed best suited to
the subject. If he translated from the Ottoman and Arabic at
all, it was probably in the same way.

But there is some reason to doubt that his poems purporting
to be translations from these languages had any ulterior ori-

gin whatever. They are thought by many of his admirers to be exclusively his own creations. They certainly have much of the spirit of productions avowedly his own. Their burden is plaintive regret for pleasure long passed away, interwoven with philosophic comment on the cares and disappointments of life. Almost all of Mangan's confessedly original poems have this peculiarity, and herein lies the chief reason for suspecting that the poems credited to Oriental languages, which he can hardly be supposed to have understood, are, in fact, outgrowths of his own mind. **"The Karamanian Exile"** (Ottoman), **"The Wail and Warning of the Three Khalendeers"** (Ottoman), and **"The Time of the Barmecides"** (Arabic), bear a strong family likeness to the poems which Mangan is known to have evolved from his own inner consciousness. One stanza of each may be given here to show the fine sweep and free rhythm of his easy verse:

There's care to-night in Ukhbar's halls,
    Karaman!
There's hope too for his trodden thralls,
    Karaman! O Karaman!
What lights flash red along yon walls?
Hark! hark!—the muster-trumpet calls!
I see the sheen of spears and shawls,
    Karaman!
The foe! the foe!—they scale the walls,
    Karaman!
To-night Murad or Ukhbar falls,
    Karaman! O Karaman!

•　•　•　•　•

La' laha, il Allah!
Ah! for youth's delirious hours,
    Man pays well in after-days,
When quenched hopes and palsied powers
    Mock his love and laughter days!
Thorns and thistles on our path
    Took the place of moss for us
Till false Fortune's tempest wrath
    Drove us from the Bosphorus.
    La' laha, il Allah!
The Bosphorus, the Bosphorus!
When thorns took place of moss for us,
    Gone was all! our hearts were graves
    Deeper than the Bosphorus!

•　•　•　•　•

Then youth was mine, and a fierce wild will,
    And an iron arm in war,
And a fleet foot high upon Ishkar's hill,
    When the watch-lights glimmered afar;
And a barb as fiery as any I know
    That Koord or Beddaween rides,
Ere my friends lay low, long, long ago
    In the time of the Barmecides—
Ere my friends lay low, long, long ago
    In the time of the Barmecides!

Mangan's translations of German poems probably possess more literary merit than any other part of his work. Not only is the general meaning of the originals accurately given, but also the special distinguishing quality. In some instances, it is true, he departed somewhat from the form before him, but rarely for any other purpose than to amplify and embellish. Occasionally a quaint thought or fancy of his own is introduced, and in all such instances the addition is seen to be an improvement. This is especially the case in his rendering of Rückert's "Ride round the Parapet," a romantic legend of fair lady and gallant knights, which Mangan so elaborated

and ornamented that the original seems but a mere framework by comparison. This poem is one of rare beauty, and should be more widely known than it is. Schiller's "Lay of the Bell," a poem which makes over four hundred lines in the translation, is the most ambitious of his efforts, and generally ranks as his best. It certainly is as good an English version as any that has been made—not strictly literal, perhaps (Mangan, like all men of erratic genius, had strong antipathy to the system of square and rule), but retaining all the beauty and faithfully following the thought of the original. In rendering the poems of Schiller and Goethe, he adhered more closely to his text than in the case of other German poets, doubtless because he knew their work was already perfect. Yet, even in their case, his exuberant imagination sometimes soared above the rich lines before him. This tendency to more profuse expression is well illustrated in his translation of Schiller's fine poem of "The Unreal," which was also translated by the late Lord Lytton. The mere verbal form of the English translator is more literal than Mangan's, but it is doubtful if Schiller himself would have been better pleased with it. A comparison of Bulwer's opening with Mangan's can hardly be unfavorable to the latter. Of this, however, the reader may judge:

BULWER.
The suns serene are lost and vanished
    That wont the paths of youth to gild.
And all the fair ideals banished
    From that wild heart they whilom filled.
Gone the divine and sweet believing
    In dreams which heaven itself unfurled!
What godlike shapes have years bereaving
    Swept from this real workday world!

•　•　•　•　•

MANGAN.
Extinguished in dead darkness lies the sun
    That lighted up my shriveled world of wonder;
Those fairy bands imagination span
    Around my heart have long been reft asunder.
Gone, gone, for ever, is the fine belief,
    The all-too-generous trust in the Ideal;
All my Divinities have died of grief,
    And left me wedded to the Rude and Real.

Goethe's poems do not seem to have had as much attraction for Mangan as those of other German authors. The number translated is comparatively small, and these may be called unimportant. The principal one is the "Lay of the Captive Count," which Mangan renders with a very sweet and natural tenderness. This is not at all his usual manner, yet among his German translations there are several short poems in which delicate sentiment finds expression in language fully worthy of the subject. But it is in rendering legends whereof the special quality is weird romanticism, or poems illustrating the vague, restless yearning of spiritualized natures for the ideal, that Mangan is at his best. "The Specter Caravan," by Freiligrath, a poem that has frequently appeared in "poets' corners" of American newspapers, is a good specimen of his aptness in producing ghastly verbal effects. "The White Lady," by the same author, again shows him to advantage, though not in exactly the same manner. The burden of this poem is profound sadness. The spirit of a sinful woman, doomed to wander "in darkness to and fro," appears nightly to young and old, making constant moan of her woes, beseeching prayer, and warning her kindred of the wrath to come. A single verse will suffice to indicate its character:

O God! O God! the coming hour arouses even the dead!
Yet the living still can slumber on like things of stone or
    lead;
The dry bones rattle in their shrouds, but you, you make
    no sign—
I dare not hope to pierce your souls with these weak words
    of mine;
Else would I warn from night to morn; else cry:
    'O Kings, be just!'
Be just, if bold! loose where you may! bind only
    where you must!'
      O pray for Lady Agnes!
      Pray for the soul of Lady Agnes!

This refrain, which is continued throughout, gives the whole poem a most impressive effect. Mangan was evidently more at home with the German poets than with any others—the ancient bards of his own country, perhaps, excepted. Richter's "New Year's Night of a Miserable Man"; Uhland's "Jeweler's Daughter" and "Durand of Blonden"; Bürger's "Demon Yager"; "The Four Idiot Brothers" and "The Ghost-Seeress of Prevorst," by Kerner; Simrock's "O Maria Regina Misericordiæ"; "And Then No More" and "Gone in the Wind," by Rückert; Immermann's "Student of Prague"; "The Midnight Review" by Baron von Tedlitz, and Giebler's "Charlemagne and the Bridge of Moonbeams," are all finely rendered, especially those in which somber melancholy predominates. "And Then No More" seems to have served the translator as a medium for the expression of his own sense of utter desolation . . . [after an unhappy love episode in which Mangan was rejected by a woman from a socially prominent family]. It is evident that these lines take color from the experience through which he had passed:

I saw her once, one little while, and then no more;
'Twas paradise on earth awhile, and then no more:
Ah! what avail my vigils pale, my magic lore?
She shone before mine eyes awhile, and then no more.
The shallop of my peace is wrecked on beauty's shore,
Near Hope's fair isle it rode awhile, and then no more!

Although Mangan took no active part in Irish political affairs, he was not content to be merely a silent witness of the events of his time. It was during the closing years of his life that the Young Ireland party, which made the abortive revolutionary attempt of 1848, came into existence, and among the leaders of that party, especially those connected with the nationalist press of Dublin, were some of the few intimate personal friends he ever had. Most of his Irish poems, original and translated, were first published in the press in question, and served in no small degree to arouse the spirit that culminated in the attempted rebellion. His *Irish Anthology* is probably the best metrical key to the old poetical literature of Ireland that is known at the present time. It has already been said, as on good authority, that Mangan did not understand the Irish language, yet his translations of the old Irish poets are notable for fidelity, not so much in mere verbal form as in purpose and spirit, to the original text. Most of the "Laments" and ballads changed by him into English meter date back to feudal times, and many are characterized by a simplicity that often borders on the ludicrous. This peculiarity is also found in old English poetry as well as in the Irish, and merely illustrates the steps of progress in the art of poetical construction. A great deal of the very old poetry that people sometimes praise is appreciated more for its age than for intrinsic merit.

Mangan's mode of adapting from the Irish was at once novel and illustrative of his singular genius. Taking the prose trans-lations given him by Irish scholars, he set to work to turn the material into English verse, which should be strictly faithful in general character to that of the Celtic bards; and the singular faculty which he possessed of putting himself in the place of the writers, and vividly imagining the customs and circumstances whereby they were influenced, enabled him to reproduce the exact spirit of the originals. Here, for instance, is a verse from a **"Lament for Sarsfield,"** which shows the poet's fidelity even in preserving crudity of manner:

I'll journey to the north, over mountain, moor, and wave;
'Twas there I first beheld, drawn up in file and line,
The brilliant Irish hosts—they were bravest of the brave,
But alas! they scorned to combine!
    Ohone! ullagone!

The expression in the line italicized is peculiarly Irish, as is also the very odd mixture in the italicized part of the following, to which Mangan himself invited attention:

To the heroes of Limerick, the city of the fight,
Be my best blessings borne on the wings of the air!
We had card-playing there o'er our camp fire at night,
And the Word of Life, too, and prayer!
    Ohone! ullagone!

Mangan was well fitted by nature to interpret the melancholy tone that pervades most of the old poetry of Ireland. That tone was in harmony with his own life, and he doubtless found a certain pleasure in making it reëcho in the lines which brought him a mere subsistence. Wailing and lamentation form the burden of ancient Irish song, and these never found more sympathetic expression than in the verse of Mangan. At times he could at least affect lightness and merriment, but the pretense is so plain that even the most careless reader must observe it. All the circumstances of his life were gloomy and depressing, and it is not strange that the sense of isolation and dreariness which was always with him found voice in almost every effort of his pen. Not that he made a practice of obtruding his own sorrows on the public, and inviting sympathy. Weak poets frequently do this, but Mangan was not of their class. The plaintive spirit of his muse comes rather from an organic melancholy of nature than from a desire to parade his individual griefs. His disposition was always retiring, even shrinking, and so unwilling was he to have others know his regrets and their causes, that even the nearest of the few close friends he had knew but little of his inner life. It was his custom, even before he became a slave to opium and alcohol, to avoid companionship, and pass his hours in dreary seclusion. Men who mingle freely with their fellows are always more cheerful than those who do not. Mangan was almost a hermit; hence, partly at least, the somber color of his mind. Yet he could, and frequently did, escape from this condition, and rise to heights wherefrom could be seen shapes and scenes of wondrous beauty. Although, as has been said, the prevailing tone of his poems is one of deep melancholy, yet the expression is often startlingly passionate, and in many instances beautifully ardent and tender. Thus, in the poem of **"Dark Rosaleen,"** one of the many allegorical names for Ireland, he breathes the very spirit of devoted affection:

Over dews, over sands,
    Will I fly for your weal:
Your holy delicate white hands
    Shall girdle me with steel;
At home in your emerald bowers,
    From morning's dawn till e'en,
You'll pray for me, my flower of flowers,

My Dark Rosaleen!
My fond Rosaleen!
You'll think of me through daylight's hours,
My virgin flower, my flower of flowers,
My Dark Rosaleen!

I could scale the blue air,
I could plow the high hills,
Oh! I could kneel all night in prayer
To heal your many ills!
And one beamy smile from you
Would float like light between
My toils and me, my own, my true,
My Dark Rosaleen!
My fond Rosaleen,
Would give me life and soul anew,
A second life, a soul anew,
My Dark Rosaleen!

The warmth and melody of these lines fully equal the same qualities in the best of Moore's national songs.

Like all poets who write and publish in haste, Mangan had the fault of carelessness. His lines are frequently uneven, and in some instances the thought is confused. Doubtless he often wrote, under stress of necessity, when his mind was not in proper condition for the task. But considering the lamentable habits he had formed, and the wretched, desolate emptiness of his life, it is remarkable that his work is even so regular and well sustained as it is. Between his labors, habits, and character, and the labors, habits, and character of Poe, there were many points of resemblance. Both wooed a melancholy muse, both were hopelessly addicted to dissipation, and both were gloomily introspective. Mangan, however, was much superior to Poe in moral attributes, although at times he allowed himself to fall to the lowest depth of debasement. Poe had a more lurid imagination, but Mangan possessed a power of expression not in any way inferior to that of the author of "The Raven." His thoughts did not equal those of Poe in weirdness, but often their intensity was startling. For terrible, ghastly earnestness, **"The Nameless One,"** which recounts his own miseries and presents an almost appalling picture of abandonment and desolation, would be difficult to equal in any language. (pp. 559-63)

The dust of Clarence Mangan lies near that of Daniel O'Connell, in Glasnevin cemetery. He died as he had lived, in wretchedness and obscurity, but with an abiding religious faith which at least partially lighted the last dark days of his life. It would be too much to claim for him a place among great poets, but it is not too much to say that he possessed poetical talents of a higher order than many writers whose names have been rendered familiar to mankind by their works. Except among his own countrymen, his name is little known. (p. 563)

Daniel Connolly, "An Unappreciated Poet," in Appleton's Journal, n.s. Vol. IX, No. 54, December, 1880, pp. 558-63.

W. B. YEATS (essay date 1887)

[*The leading figure of the Irish Literary Renaissance and a major poet in twentieth-century literature, Yeats was also an active critic of his contemporaries' works. As a critic he judged the writings of others according to his own poetic values of sincerity, passion, and vital imagination. In the following excerpt, Yeats evaluates Mangan's life and literary career.*]

One thing is to be remembered concerning Mangan. Unlike most poets, his childhood was not spent among woods and fields, with Nature's primitive peace, and ancient happiness. He had no early dream—no treasure-house of innocent recollection: his birthplace sooty Fishamble-street [in Dublin]—his father a grocer, who boasted that his children would run into a mouse-hole to escape him. His school, round the corner in Saul's-court, in those days given over to clothes-lines and children and sparrows, and now abolished to make room for Lord Edward-street. From here he was transferred to a scrivener's office, his family having come down in life and now depending in the main on him. Concerning his office companions, he himself has left something on record in that strange fragment of autobiography prefixed to the *Poets of Munster:*—

My nervous and hypochondriacal feelings almost verged on insanity. I seemed to myself to be shut up in a cavern with serpents and scorpions, and all hideous and monstrous things, which writhed and hissed around me, and discharged their slime and venom upon my person.

Yet, likely enough, these office companions were by no means bad fellows. From time immemorial the children of genius have got on ill with the children of men. King Alfred let the cakes burn, and the housewife did her best to lead him a life of it; for her the smoke and smother of her burnt cakes, for him the fiery dream and the tremendous vision. Seven years Mangan spent in this office, three more as an attorney's clerk; yet acquired, after his day's work, much polyglot knowledge of foreign tongues, loving especially to read about the strange and mysterious—contributed largely to the *Dublin Penny Journal* and other papers poems, acrostics, &c. Meanwhile the cloud had drawn closer and closer about him; already he had written **"The Dying Enthusiast"** and **"The One Mystery,"** all but the saddest of his songs. His style was fully developed, with its energy and old-fashioned directness. Of late the muse has left her ancient ways, and is now a lady of fashion, learned in refined insincerities and graceful affections, smiling behind her fan—*ça ira.*

Whatever fragment of inbred happiness remained to his spirit, that had asked all things and was given routine and ill health, was lost now; he loved and was jilted; concerning the object of his love, rumour has contradictory voices, beautiful and *spirituelle,* says [Irish patriot John] Mitchel, by no means so, says my informant. One thing alone seems pretty certain, she was a Miss Stackpoole (now for the first time named) of Mount Pleasant-square, one of three sisters.

A short dream this love affair of Mangan's. Before long between him and his Eden was the flaming cherub and the closed gate. I have heard a curious story, which I give for what it is worth, of his rushing with drawn knife at one who had spoken ill of his faithless "Frances;" now, if not before, he sought the comfort of rum, and some say also, opium—

And when the inanity of all things human,
And when the dark ingratitude of man,
And when the hollower perfidy of woman
Comes down like night upon the feelings—

What cure for this? Why, rum and water. So writes he in one of his strange latter poems [**"Broken-Hearted Lays"**]. (pp. 115-16)

Towards the last Mangan commenced his autobiography, or "confession," as he called it. But, haunted by apparitions, as he believed, and overpowered by his ever-growing misery, he could no longer at all do that which was so difficult to calm Goethe—distinguish between fact and illusion. When this was pointed out to him he bid them destroy what he had written. Fortunately this was not done, and it remains not so much a record of his early life as a wonderful piece of the sorrow of his latter, that had stained even memory its own colour.

For days he would disappear, living in a barn or some such place, drinking and brooding. His haunts were ever the lowest taverns. I read in Mrs. Atkinson's *Biography of Mary Aikenhead,* that once he was brought to St. Vincent's Hospital. "Oh! the luxury of clean sheets!" he exclaimed. The man with the "face handsome in outline, bloodless, and wrinkled, though not with age," and the "blue eyes, distraught with the opium eater's dreams," and the "heavy lids," appears to have proved a somewhat troublesome patient. Said one of the sisters—"These poets have nerves in every pore." Yet, withal, he does not seem to have been so much a weak character as a man fated. He had powerful convictions, political and other; and convictions bear the same relation to the character as thoughts do to the intellect. In all he wrote there was a sort of intensity, not merely of the intellectual or of the aesthetic nature, but of the whole man; and supreme misery, like supreme happiness, or supreme anything, seems only given to the world's supreme spirits.

At last death released him from his misery. He died of cholera in the Meath Hospital. I have it from one who had it from the doctor in attendance, that when he was dead his face became beautiful and calm. When the contorted soul had gone, the muscles relaxed, and the clay returned to its primal innocence.

Other poets have found refuge from their unhappiness in philosophic subtleties and aeriel turnings and pirouettings of the spirit. But this man, Mangan, born in torpid days in a torpid city, could only write in diverse fashions, "I am Miserable." No hopes! No philosophy! No illusions! A brute cry from the gutters of the earth! and for solace or rather for a drug—this [from **"The One Mystery"**]—

No more, no more, with aching brow,
    And restless heart, and burning brain,
We ask the When, the Where, the How,
    And ask in vain.
And all philosophy, all faith,
    All earthly—all celestial lore,
Have but one voice, which only saith—
    Endure—adore.

His work is divided into translations from the German, the Irish, and poems from apocryphal Persian or other sources, and original poems in the main personal. Pages there are abundantly wearying and hollow, but whenever there are thoughts on the littleness of life or the short time its good things stay with us, or the vanity of all subtile and sad longings, or if there be any fragment of ghostly pageantry, then from beneath the pen of this haunted (for so he believed) and prematurely aged man, the words flowed like electric flashes. I do not find as much beauty in his oriental poems as others do, though they, like his Irish poems, have a certain radiant energy. Of these last, **"My Dark Rosaleen,"** is quite wonderful with the passionate self-abandonment of its latter stanzas. But powerful and moving more than anything else that he has done are his few personal poems **"Twenty Golden Years Ago,"** with its beautiful ending—

Soon thou sleepest where the thistles blow,
    Curious anti-climax to thy dreams,
Twenty golden years ago . . .

"Nameless," and, many say "Siberia," for that Siberia where the White Tzar sends so many of his wisest and best, seems a sort of type of that Siberia within, where his thoughts wandered and murmured, like outlaws cast from the world's soft places for some unknown offence—

Pain as in a dream,
    When years go by,
Funeral paced yet fugitive,
When man lives and doth not live,
    Doth not live nor die.

But far the strongest of all his poems is **"Nameless."** He who has once learnt this poem will never forget it; it will stay with him with something of the eternity of painful things. Many poems as delicate and fragrant as rose-leaves we soon forget—they vanish with the coquetry of joy. All the great poems of the world have their foundations fixed in agony—not that this is, in the highest sense, a great poem; it is a great lyric, an altogether different thing.

I know not whether I may not seem to have over-valued Clarence Mangan. No, I am not impartial—who is? Under even the most philosophic utterance is a good dose of personal bias. There is no impartial critic save Time, and he only seems so, maybe, because there is no one to accuse him.

Plainly, this scrivener's clerk brought one thing into the world that was not there before, one new thing into letters—his misery—a misery peculiar in quality. He never lost belief in happiness because he was miserable, or faith in goodness because his life was spent among the taverns. He had not that solace.

He can never be popular like Davis, for he did not embody in clear verse the thoughts of normal mankind. He never startles us by saying beautifully things we have long felt. He does not say look at yourself in this mirror; but, rather, "Look at me—I am so strange, so exotic, so different." (pp. 116-19)

W. B. Yeats, "Clarence Mangan," in his Uncollected Prose: First Reviews and Articles, 1886-1896, Vol. 1, *edited by John P. Frayne, Columbia University Press, 1970, pp. 114-19.*

LOUISE IMOGEN GUINEY   (essay date 1897)

[*Guiney was an American poet, essayist, and critic who won recognition for her delicate, Old English–style ballads and poems written in the manner of the seventeenth-century Cavalier poets. Guiney's poetry reflects both her reverence for the Catholic tradition and her deep religious faith. Her critical efforts were often directed toward restoring the reputations of neglected literary figures. Guiney edited a selection of Mangan's poems and wrote a lengthy biographical and critical study introducing the volume. In the following excerpt from that study, she assesses Mangan's Irish and Oriental poems and compares his works to those of Edgar Allan Poe.*]

On the principle that "it has become almost an honor not to be crowned," the name of James Clarence Mangan may be announced at once as very worthy, very distinguished. He is unknown outside his own non-academic fatherland, though he bids fair to be a proverb and a fireside commonplace, much as the Polish poets are at home, within it. Belonging to an age which is nothing if not specific and departmental, he has somehow escaped the classifiers; he has never been run through with a pin, nor have his wings been spread under glass in the museums. It was only yesterday that Mangan took rank in *The Dictionary of National Biography,* in Miles' *Poets of the Century,* and in a new edition of *Lyra Elegantiarum.* In Allibone's *Dictionary of Authors* he has but hasty mention, and a representation as unjust as possible in H. F. Randolph's *Fifty Years of English Song.* He is absent from the *Encyclopedia Britannica.* Even Mr. J. O'Kane Murray's obese volume, *The Prose and Poetry of Ireland,* has contrived to live without him. Palgrave, Dana, Duyckinck, and the score of lesser books which are kind to forgotten or infrequent lyres, know him not; Ward's *English Poets* has no inch of classic text to devote to him. Nor is Mangan's absence altogether or even chiefly due to editorial shortcomings. The search after him has always been difficult. During his lifetime he published only a collection of translations, and his original numbers were left tangled up with other translations, by his own exasperating hand. . . . So it is, and so, perhaps, it must be. Our time adjusts merit with supreme propriety, in setting up Herrick in the market-place, and in still reserving Daniel for a domestic adoration. Apollo has a class of might-have-beens whom he loves; poets bred in melancholy places, under disabilities, with thwarted growth and thinned voices; poets compounded of everything magical and fair, like an elixir which is the outcome of knowledge and patience, and which wants in the end, even as common water would, the essence of immortality. The making of a name is too often like the making of a fortune: the more scrupulous contestants are

> Delicate spirits, pushed away
> In the hot press of the noonday.

Mangan's is such a memory, captive and overborne. It may be unjust to lend him the epitaph of defeat, for he never strove at all. One can think of no other, in the long disastrous annals of English literature, cursed with so monotonous a misery, so much hopelessness and stagnant grief. He had no public; he was poor, infirm, homeless, loveless; travel and adventure were cut off from him, and he had no minor risks to run; the cruel necessities of labor sapped his dreams from a boy; morbid fancies mastered him as the rider masters his horse; the demon of opium, then the demon of alcohol, pulled him under, body and soul, despite a persistent and heart-breaking struggle, and he perished ignobly in his prime. (pp. 3-6)

His work, at its worst, has the faults inseparable from the conditions under which it was wrought: it is stumbling, pert, diffuse, distraught. What Mr. Gosse has named the "overflow," the flux of a line-ending into the next line's beginning, so that it becomes difficult to read both aloud, and preserve the stress and rhyme,—this bad habit of good poets, completely ruins several of Mangan's longer pieces. He had in full that racial luxuriance and fluency which, wonderful to see in their happier action, tend always to carry a writer off his feet, and wash him into the deep sea of slovenliness. Mangan's scholarship, painfully, intermittently acquired, never distilled itself into him, to react imperiously on all he wrote, smoothing the rough and welding the disjointed. Again, his mental strength, crowded back from the highways of literature, wreaked itself in feats not the worthiest: in the taming of unheard-of metres, in illegal decoration of other men's fabrics, in orthoepic and homonymic freaks of all kinds, not to be matched since the Middle Ages.

He delights in creating oceans of this sort of thing (1835):—

> Besides, of course, heroically bearing
> The speech, half-sneer, half-compliment, of Baring,
> And standing the infliction of a peel
> Of plaudits from Lord Eldon and Bob Peel.

Or this (1839):—

> The wretch, who rescued from the halter, still
>   Will kill,
> Or he, who after trampling tillages,
>   Pillages villages,
> Has less of guiltiness than one who when
>   Men pen
> Such rubbish as the dullest must despise,
>   Cries "Wise!"

What he alleges, with truth, in a posthumous fragment, of Maginn, may be reverted to himself: "He wrote alike without labor and without limit. He had, properly speaking, no style; or rather, he was master of all styles, though he cared for none." The legerdemain he shows in handling our flexible language, is hardly so admirable as it has been said, on excellent authority, to be. His compound rhymes, his unearthly opulent metres, are indeed extraordinary; but their effect is often gained by illegitimate means. Mangan has no philological scruples, no "literary conscience," whatever. Does he need a rhyme, he invents a word, chooses one which is archaic, or gives to a known one some grotesque turn; he has prefixtures and elisions ever on duty; his musicianly ear cannot be relied upon to keep him always clear of English sibilations; he frequently loses his sense of the place and time to stop; and when he attempts recognized forms, as in the sapphics (with breath-catching rhymes!) of his own **"Lurelay,"** or the alexandrines of Freiligrath's spirited

> Bound, bound, my desert barb from Alexandria!

the result is somewhat fearsome, to say the least. While a poet subdues technical difficulties by overriding their laws, success so obtained must be ruled out of court. However, a born metrist he was, though a perverse one. From his very first appearances in print, as a young boy, he displays as his essential characteristics, imagination, and the greatest verbal dexterity. A good proportion of his poems are informal exhibitions by a virtuoso, a game of all miracles known to writing man. His best burlesque rivals Butler's and Thomas Hood's, which is the same as saying that it attains the front rank. But we cannot endure mediocre burlesque in the author of **"Dark Rosaleen."** His prose, nearly always, is forced, and defaced with tedious puns. The painful mummery of some pages (of which, it is but fair to recall, their author had never the revision, and which should not have been, nor should be reprinted) is not representative of anything but the awkwardness that comes at intervals over Mangan, and stands between him and his angel,

> When the angel says, "Write."

As an essayist, despite some fine flashes, he is hardly worth preserving. Nor can it be denied that the same element of restlessness and strain, a sort of alloy from the frightful poverty and degradation nigh it, gets at times even into much of Mangan's golden poetic work. "Hippocrene may be inexhaustible," he says quaintly, "but it flows up to Us through a pump." Did ever the Virgilian distinction spring from a houseless Muse, half-fed? The marvel, rather, is that the spirit in Mangan so often surmounts the most appalling obstacles known to the human mind.

Mitchel, who had unerring literary acumen, detected in him the conflict of "deepest pathos and a sort of fictitious jollity." At times, he says, the poet breaks into would-be humor, "not merry and hearty fun, but rather grotesque, bitter, Fescennine buffoonery, which leaves an unpleasant impression, as if he were grimly sneering at himself and all the world, purposely spoiling and marring the effect of fine poetry by turning it into burlesque, and showing how meanly he regarded everything, even his art wherein he lived and had his being, when he compared his own exalted ideas of art and life with the littleness of all his experiences and performances." Mitchel was thinking, in all probability, of the ruinous but very clever postlude to **"The Broken-Hearted Song,"** and the interpolation of Yankee dialect in a lyric raucously beginning,

> O hush such sounds!

To such spoliations his words apply. But there is a vast deal of facetious excellence in Mangan. Amid less felicitous drollery, the reader can take pleasure in a snatch of triumphant parody on Moore, and a recurring chorus which is a real gold nugget of comic opera:—

> So spake the stout Haroun-al-Raschid,
> With his jolly ugly hookah in his hand!

Will it be believed that Mangan was a choice librettist, without his opportunity? Were he earning his living in the same walk to-day, Mr. W. S. Gilbert might look to his laurels. Some of his nonsense runs for all the world like a Gilbert and Sullivan "topical song," in long rattling declamatory lines, of wit and animation all compact. Behold the exhumed precursor of *The Mikado!* The Gilbertian accent is unmistakably prefigured, in Mangan's humorous hours. Sundry lines need but to put in an appearance at the Savoy Theatre, and be welcomed at once as long-lost fathers, by all the six-time A-major *presto e staccato* tribe modern playgoers know so well:—

> As backward he staggered
> With countenance haggard,
> And feelings as acid as beer after thunder,
> 'Twas plain that the dart which had entered his heart
> Was rending his physical system asunder!

and so on; for there is no dearth of it. (pp. 57-63)

Running into twilight fields of his own, as was his wont, he dedicated exquisite work, albeit a trifle schismatical, to the ancient literature of his country, in the day of its last splendid but brief revival. Several scholars, among them the great Eugene Curry of Mr. Matthew Arnold's admiration, furnished Mangan, toward the end of his life, with literal drafts in English of the many ballads taken down from the lips of the peasants, which he was to render for publisher O'Daly of Anglesea Street and for the Gaelic and Archæological societies; and within these outlines he built up structures not untrue to their first design. Mr. J. H. Ingram, editing Mangan's twelve poems for the third volume of Mr. Alfred H. Miles's collection, *Poets of the Century,* and basing all his facts, if not his judgments, on Mitchel, calls these renditions from the Irish "spiritless." Some persons may think that there is a breathless grandeur in Mangan's chanting of the hymn of Saint Patrick, **"At Tarah To-Day,"** and that a less "spiritless" thing never came into being. It was with such deep-mouthed apostrophes that he was best fitted to cope. He was able to try them again in a translation sacred to war, as the other is sacred to Christian peace: **"O'Hussey's Ode to The Maguire"**: rude heroic strophes bursting from the heart of the last hereditary bard of the great sept of Fermanagh, as late as the reign of Charles the First, while the courtly lyres of England were tinkling a cannon-shot away. Quite as good as these, in its province, is the sarcastic rattle of **"The Woman of Three Cows." "My Dark Rosaleen"** is worth them all, "on a pinnacle apart." It was written by a worthy contemporary of Shakespeare, an unknown minstrel of the Tyrconnell chief, Aodh Na Domhnaill (Hugh Roe, or the Red, O'Donnell), who put upon the lips of his lord, as addressed to Ireland, the love-name of "Roisin Dubh," the Black-Haired Little Rose. More exact versions of this symbolic masterpiece have since been made, but the stormy beauty of Mangan's lines does away with considerations of law and order. (pp. 69-70)

Of [**"My Dark Rosaleen"**], and of two or three others from a kindred source, Mr. Maurice Leyne wrote in a supplement to *The Nation,* long ago:

> Their beauty can scarcely be exaggerated. To compare with them any actual remains which we have of the Jacobite poetry would be extravagant. They are what an Irish bard might have written if to the deep vague love of country, the longing, the dreaminess, the allegoric expressions of his art, were added all that modern culture can give of distinctness of feeling and sequence of idea. We have other poets who have caught with wonderful fidelity and felicity the Gaelic turns of thought and the structure of the language; but in Mangan the very Gaelic heart seems poured out.

Mangan, however, was not always a successful conductor of sounds reaching him obliquely, through the stout persons of Irish scholars. Certain numbers, such as **"O'Hussey's Ode,"** and **"Prince Aldfrid's Itinerary,"** are modelled, with the most astonishing closeness, on faithful unrhymed renditions in *The Penny Journal* (1832) and *The University Magazine* (1834). But no critic can set Mangan's flat and passionless **"Eileen Aroon"** beside the wonderful strain of Carroll O'Daly, or prefer **"The Fair Hills of Ireland,"** charming as that is, to Sir Samuel Ferguson's

> A plenteous place is Ireland for hospitable cheer,

which has the advantage, in this instance, of greater literalness. And comparison is least possible between the two native translators, when it comes to the "Boatman's Hymn," yet sung, in vernacular snatches, off the wild western coast. Not only is the Fergusson version a hundred-fold more pleasing, but it is, in equal measure, more Gaelic. It rushes along like the wind scooping the dusky Kerry sails.

> Bark that bears me thro' foam and squall!
> 'Tis you in the storm are my castle wall.
> Tho' the sea should redden from bottom to top,
> From tiller to mast she takes no drop.
> On the tide-top, the tide-top,
> Wherry *aroon*, my land and store!
> On the tide-top, the tide-top,
> She is the boat can sail *go leor*.

How does Mangan start off with this finest of open-air themes?

> O my gallant, gallant bark!
> Oft, a many a day, and oft
> When the stormy skies above are dark,
> And the surges foam aloft,
> Dost thou ride

In thy pride
O'er the swelling bosom of the sea;
Tho' lightning flash
And thunder crash,
Still, my royal bark, they daunt not thee.
Yeo-ho, yeo-ho!
The bar is full, the tide runs high.
So! ready hand, and steady eye,
And merrily we go.

And at the close, in the apostrophe to the Atlantic crag
(which one poet salutes as

Whillan ahoy! old heart of stone,

and the other, *more suo,* as

Dark Dalán, colossal cliff,)

as well as in the whimsical outcry of the fishermen terrified
at the speed of "Wherry *aroon,*" it is easy to decide which
translator attains to the sailor-like and singable, and which
remains merely literary. I cannot think that Sir Samuel Fergusson ever yielded, in power of interpretation, to Mangan,
in any single case where they chose to handle the same originals. Despite it, we have not from him, nor could we have
had, a **"Dark Rosaleen."** Mr. Maurice Leyne, in the illuminating article quoted a moment ago, speaks of Mangan's as
a typically Irish temperament: "a temperament," according
to another sociologist, "which makes both men and nations
feeble in adversity, and great, gay, and generous in prosperity." Is he so generic? It is impossible to think of any class or
race of Mangans. Like Swaran in "Ossian," he "brings his
own dark wing," whereas some readers have asked for references, antecedents, certificates. Or perhaps, to say that such
a one is Celtic, is to put him back among the indescribables.
One Wilson, a phrenologist, made in the February of 1835 a
professional examination of Mangan's beautifully-shaped
head, with this recorded result.

> Constructiveness is hardly developed at all; on
> which account he would not have a genius for
> mechanism or invention generally, but he would
> possess the power of magnifying, embellishing, and
> beautifying in the highest degree. A tendency to ex-
> aggerate and amplify would pervade whatever he
> undertook.

Here we have, disguised as a communication from the physical sciences, a remarkable bit of literary criticism. The verdict
is perfectly true, though opium had helped to make it so.
Mangan was not least Irish ("Oriental" Irish) in this, that he
loved expansions and dilutions, and could not forbear yoking
quantity with quality. (pp. 77-81)

The question of Mangan's Oriental "translations" is one of
keen interest. He is not known to lovers of poetry, because
he played tricks masterly as any of Chatterton's, and because,
unfortunately for the vindication of his genius, his tricks have
never been discovered and explained, when they were suspected; and some who have written of him have left it to be
inferred that he was more of a wiseacre, and less of an organic
force, than he was. His obliging labor of transposing the
Welsh, Danish, Frisian, Swedish, Russian, and Bohemian
(for he solemnly pretends to deal in all of these) is pure
blague. (p. 90)

Whenever he puts on a turban, natural to him as was the hi-
mation to Keats, mischief is afoot. He did not wear it "for
the grandeur of the thing," like a greater poet, poor Collins,

who, in his last days, confessed to the Wartons his suspicion
that his *Oriental Eclogues* were, rather, his Irish Eclogues.
"Translation's so feasible!" Mangan exclaims in a jolly passage wherein he blames other bards who do not dedicate
themselves, for the hungry public's sake, to that excellent diversion. Lamb himself had no more fun out of Ritson and
John Scott the Quaker, than Mangan has out of his poems
by Selber, with notes by Dr. Berri Abel Hummer. The nomenclature of some of his puppets is quite too daring. Berri
Abel, Ben Daood, and Bham-Booz-eel are bad enough, but
Baugtrauter is notorious. He declared continually that his
"translations" were not rigidly exact, or he refused altogether
to gratify the curiosity of his audience. "It is the course that
liberal feeling dictates," he says, with a strict humor worthy
of Newman, "to let them suppose what they like." And all
the time he is enriching them and cheating himself, adorning
the annals of reversed forgery, and cutting off from the circulation of his mother-tongue some of its most original accents.
He produced several Ottoman "proverbs," in the September
of 1837, which are the everyday saws of our western civilization served with spice. Reduced to their lowest terms, these
mystical mouthings grin at one like a bottled imp. "Speech
is Silver, but Silence is Golden," they say; "Enough is as good
as a Feast"; "The Pot calls the Kettle Black"; "A Bird in the
Hand is Worth Two in the Bush"! Mangan took tremendous
delight in throwing dust in devoted eyes. It is within reason
that in his roaring stanzas dedicated **"To the Ingleeze Khafir,
Djaun Bool Djenkinzun,"** the dear and dunderheaded gentleman addressed might miss the point altogether. It would not
be so conceivable that he hood-winked also the Trinity Fellows at his elbow, were it not for two considerations. In the
first place, nobody was especially well acquainted with him;
he was intangible. As none could affirm with authority
whether he had but one coat in his wardrobe, or where and
how he kept his distressing relatives; so none could track his
elusive mental habits, and say, "This knowledge, and not
that, has he acquired." Again, specialists do not grow on
every bush, even in Trinity. The names of authors whom he
cited, Mehisi, Kemal-Oomi, Baba Khodjee, Selim-il-Anagh,
Mustafa Reezah, Burhan-ed-Deen, Mohammed Ben Osman,
Ben Ali Nakkash (may their tribe decrease!) were not illuminating; neither were the mottoes in good Arabic, but somewhat irrelevant to their purpose, with which he prefaced his
apocrypha. He attributes one strain to a sixteenth-century
Zirbayeh, another to Lameejah, a third to a phonetic nightingale called Waheedi. He abstracts from a manuscript in possession of "the queen of Transoxiana" one of the loveliest of
his songs, and fathers it upon Al Makeenah, a fighting bard
of his fancy. Once he was brought to task for concealing himself under the cloak of Hafiz, whereupon he replied that any
critic could discern that the verses were only Hafiz! His custom was to leave Hafiz alone, with Saadi and Omar, these
being persons somewhat familiar to the general. The poets he
courts are more preciously private to himself than ever Cyril
Tourneur was, years ago, to the elect. Some of their names
stand out memorably bright, and only just beneath those of
the splendid phantom Mirza Schaffy, and the Haji-Abdu el-
Yezdi, who had some reality so long as Sir Richard Burton
lived. The attention of a competent Orientalist may never
have been drawn to specifications which would at once throw
the unwary off the trail; but it is likely that they passed with
modest minor scholars who would have suspected anybody
of this roguery sooner than innocent bespectacled Mangan.

It is as a son of the Prophet that he claims his full applause.
"Al Hassan" is more than equalled by **"The Wail and Warn-**

ing of the Three Khalendeers" (which Thackeray would have relished had he known it), by **"The Time of the Barmecides,"** the vehement **"Howling Song of Al Mohara,"** and others, drawn, like these, from the impossible Persian, and many of which are only to be found scattered up and down the capital-lettered yellow pages of extinct provincial journals.

It is more than likely that his taste for Eastern poetry, gratified under such ironic conditions, was in Mangan a reaction from the little he knew of the bardic antiquities of his own Ireland; for he appears to have been much attracted to Vallencey's most tenable theory that the Milesians were the lost tribe of Israel. The all-but-identity of the typical Turkish wail:—

> Wulla-hu, wulwulla-hu!

with the more melodious Gaelic

> Ullu, ullalu!

fascinated him; and he used both rather too freely. Working on Shane O'Golain's "Lament" in 1848 he took fire, at three o'clock of a Friday morning, and resolved to give as good as he got. "I will shortly send you," he writes to his patron, "a funeral wail from the Turkish, on the decease of one of the Sultans. The spirit of the composition closely resembles what we meet with in similar Irish poems." (Marry come up! so it must, slyest of Mangans.) This was probably the **"Elegy for Sulieman the Magnificent,"** a fairly unimpressive production. With his genius for analogies, the "translator" found ancient Irish, at second-hand, as Oriental as need be. Adjurations, apostrophes, superlatives, monotones, reiterations, vague but bold colors, belonged, as outstanding features, to both languages; and to all these characteristics his own habits of speech and thought were congenial.

What Matthew Arnold said of the Celtic literature in general, may apply to Mangan's share in it. "It is not great poetical work; but it is poetry, with the air of greatness investing it." His Eastern fictions, like most of his Western ones, deal usually with a mood of reminiscence and regret, and they have the arch and poignant pathos in which English song is not rich. The mournful echo of days gone by, the light tingeing a present cloud from the absent sun, are everywhere in Mangan's world. He looks back forever, not with moping, but with a certain shrewd sense of triumph and heartiness. . . . He delivers a lament as if it were a cheer; in his strange temperament they blend in one. It is clear to posterity that this looking back on rosy hours is a sham, a poet's fantasy. What idyllic yesterday cradled and reared so ill-adventured a soul? Out of his imagination his "rich Bagdad" never existed; though it be cherished there as only the solitary and disregarded intelligence can cherish its ideal, he is lord of it yet, and can bid it vanish, at one imperious gesture of relinquishment. Down tumbles Bagdad! The crash thereof is in the public ears; and who will refuse to believe that there was a Clarence Mangan who knew something of the blessed Orient, something, too, of felicity, even though it passed?

With his provoking banter, in April of 1840, he calls attention, in a magazine, to **"The Time of the Barmecides,"** a composition of his own, which he had given to the same pages just a year before, and which he had bettered infinitely, meanwhile, by a few discreet touches. Starting off with a motto (obviously of his own manufacture), that

> There runs thro' all the dells of Time

> No stream like Youth again,

he proceeds to explain the second appearance of his favored lyric. "It was published some months back, but in such suspicious company that it probably remained unread, except by the very few persons who have always believed us too honorable to attempt imposing on or mystifying the public. We now, therefore, take the liberty of reintroducing the poem to general notice, embellished with improvements, merely premising that if any lady or gentleman wishes to have a copy of the original (or, indeed, of any originals of our oversettings), we are quite ready to come forward and treat: terms cash, except to young ladies." With talk of such vain and transparent nonsense, Mangan attempts to parry his rightful praise. He would have us think that to his laborious searching and transcribing, "with the help," as he says, of "punch and patience," we are indebted for the existence of his finest work. But the punch is direct from Castaly's well, and the patience covers the rapturous drudgery known to all true art. What held him back from acknowledging his own homespun glories was a trait both of shyness and of perversity. He must have been conscious that his rhythms were nothing short of innovations. Nearly everything which bears his name has a voluptuous dance-measure which no one had written before: a beauty so novel and compelling, that it is remarkable it has lacked recognition. With characteristic shrinking, Mangan sealed his charter of merit to supposititious ancients and aliens. Perspicacious readers are besought to consider it less likely that in one poet was a voice of such individuality that it breaks forth through a hundred disguises, than that bards resident through the ages in the four zones, Jew and Gentile,

> Bold Plutarch, Neptune, and Nicodemus,

are the co-heirs of the self-same astonishing style. (pp. 92-100)

Mangan's shibboleth is the refrain. The refrain is characteristic, in some shape or other, of all old poetry. It belongs to Judea and Greece, no less than to northern France, to the England of the Percy Reliques, and the Persianized Germany of Mangan's study. After a long lapse, it had its first full modern use in "The Ancient Mariner," and in the peculiar cadence of all Coleridge's stops and keys. The fact that at divers periods, fashions of thoughts and speech infect the air, is a vindication of many laurelled heads; for it is a theory which pinches nobody. Almost on the same morning, within twenty years of Coleridge's retirement to Highgate, Mrs. Browning, Mangan, and Edgar Allan Poe were involuntarily conspiring to fix and perpetuate a poetic accident, destined to its subtlest and not wholly unforeseen collateral development in Rossetti. Among these, Mrs. Browning invented and foreshadowed much, but with a light hand. Poe's ringing of the word-changes is, on the other hand, so bold, that any successor who approximates his manner is sure now of smiling detection and discouragement. Whatever recalls

> Come, let the burial rite be read,
> The funeral song be sung!
> An anthem for the queenliest dead
> That ever died so young;
> A dirge for her, the doubly dead,
> In that she died so young,

is all very fine, we say, but it will not do; the thing was done to perfection once: we must let Poe reign in his own kingdom. Let us have a care lest we are letting Poe reign in Mangan's kingdom. The unmistakable mark of Poe's maturer poetry, the employment of sonorous successive lines which cunningly fall short of exact duplication, belongs also to Mangan, in the same degree. There is this passage of his, for instance, in the reverie of the wayfarer beside the river Mourne, who longs for everlasting rest delayed, and who hears, in answer, a prophetic voice from the martyred tree in the saw-mill:—

> "For this grieve not; thou knowest what thanks
> The weary-souled and the meek owe
> To Death!" I awoke, and heard four planks
> Fall down with a saddening echo,
> I heard four planks
> Fall down with a hollow echo!

And one verse out of the powerful many which bear the burden of "Karaman!" will serve to illustrate the point yet more clearly:—

> I was mild as milk till then,
> I was soft as silk till then;
> Now my breast is like a den,
> Karaman!
> Foul with blood and bones of men,
> Karaman!
> With blood and bones of slaughtered men,
> Karaman, O Karaman!

Were it not for the imperfect rhyme in the "Saw-Mill" stanza, any critic would attribute all the lines cited to Poe, both for manner, and for perfect mastery of ghastly detail.

It happens that the Muse over in Dublin has the advantage of priority. Poe's maiden work has not the lovely tautology which has since been associated with his name. Judging by the pains which he took to dissect the rainbow of his genius in his "Philosophy of Composition," he would have us assured that "The Raven" was his earliest experiment in the values of that saying-over or singing-over which, like a looped ribbon, flutters about the close of so many of his posthumous verses. Moreover, "The Raven" was "only that and nothing more." Poe's own thrilling tale of "Ligeia," dating from 1838, provided every one of the "properties" essential to the effect of "The Raven," and even the same psychological situation. It is not inconceivable that the prose was converted into poetry, exclusively for the purpose of trying a rash harmonic experiment on an approved instrument. At any rate, the element in the great lyric which was not already in "Ligeia," is precisely this haunting iteration of sweet sounds. (pp. 100-03)

Having once mastered his invention, Mangan, in the end, came near being mastered by it. He imported a sort of stammering into many of his renderings from foreign languages, to the conceivable amazement of dead authors; and the catchword of a stanza was often multiplied until it attained the numerical importance of Mozart's triumphant *Amens*. No one will deny that the *Schwertlied* itself gains by this vandalism. Poe, in this respect, is merely Manganesque. In *The Dublin University Magazine,* during the years when Poe was attaining his zenith of success, figure successive specimens of the unchanged art of the man who had the start of him by at least five years; for **"The Barmecides"** was in print in 1839, and **"The Karamanian Exile,"** a finished model of its kind, was contemporary with the as yet cisatlantic "Raven," and the predecessor of "Ulalume," "Lenore," "Eulalie," "For Annie," and the rest. (pp. 106-07)

Clarence Mangan, shrinking like the Thane before the super-

natural "All hail hereafter!" is the true founder . . . of the most picturesque feature in modern verse.

While Poe links himself for good with his immediate predecessors in "The Haunted Palace," "The City by the Sea," and the opening of "Al Aaraaf," and so falls gracefully into his dynastic place, Mangan has wayward secondary leanings, sometimes to the whimsical, affectionate temper of Béranger, sometimes to the bare strength of the Elizabethans themselves, as in his lines where Fate

> Tolls the disastrous bell of all our years,

a line as unlike as possible to

> Helen, thy beauty is to me
> Like those Nicean barks of yore.

He is addicted to compound words; and in such mongrel usages as "youthhood," "gloomsomely," and "aptliest," he makes straight for the pitfalls dug for the radiant intelligence of Mrs. Browning. Poe is too "dainty, airy, amber-bright," for sophomoric blunders, for wretched puns, for breathless haste, for dactyls maimed and scarred in the wars. He never makes Mangan's lunges; his every cæsural pause is fixed by conclave of the Muses. And there is over all his entrancing work an air of incomparable self-attentiveness, a touch of satisfied completion, as of a *coquette bien chaussée, bien gantée.* The other's charm is less urban:

> A winning wave, deserving note,
> In the tempestuous petticoat.

The two Celts had much, very much, in common; Poe's Attic taste, sprung from his fortunate training, is responsible for most of the difference. To affirm of him, as has often been done, that he worshipped beauty with his whole soul; that he loved the occult sciences, the phrenologists, and the old mystics; that his existence was but an affecting struggle with the adversaries of darkness; even that he was of a frail physique, his forehead high and pale, the lower part of his face sensitive and dejected;—this is to describe Mangan equally well. They had kindred dreams; they were haunted by the same loathing of the "dishonor of the grave"; they died, under almost identical circumstances of pain and mystery, in the same year. Their respective sense of humor was unevenly apportioned. In point of achievement, too, or of the forces which make achievement possible, they are hardly to be compared. Poe was ever the artist; his imagination was not only sumptuous, but steadfast; his utterances were fewer, and had finality. In the moral contrast, it is the Irish poet who gains. Poe, with his manifold gifts (if we may pervert the terms of Lamb's theological thesis *not* "defended or oppugned, or both, at Leipsic or Göttingen") was "of the highest order of the seraphim illuminati who sneer." He nursed grudges and hungered for homage; he was seldom so happy as in a thriving quarrel. Mangan was a pattern of sweet gratitude and deference, and left his art to prosper or perish, as Heaven should please. (pp. 108-11)

He died, not companionless, with Emily Brontë, Hartley Coleridge, and Thomas Lovell Beddoes, in 1849: three spirits of lavish promise, defrauded and unfulfilled like his own, yet happier than he, inasmuch as they have had since many liegemen and rememberers. Let him come forward at last in a quieter hour, with his own whimsical misgiving manner, or with questions pathetically irrelevant, as one whom the fairies had led astray:—

O sayest thou the soul shall climb
The magic mount she trod of old,
Ere childhood's time?

He has been, for a half-century, wandering on the dark marge of Lethe. It will not do, as yet, to startle him with gross applause. Otherwise, his gratified editor would like to repeat, introducing Clarence Mangan, the gallant words with which Schumann once began a review of the young Chopin: "Hats off, gentlemen: a Genius!" (pp. 111-12)

> *Louise Imogen Guiney, "James Clarence Mangan: A Study," in* James Clarence Mangan: His Selected Poems, *edited by Louise Imogen Guiney, Lamson, Wolffe & Co., 1897, pp. 3-114.*

FRANCIS THOMPSON (essay date 1897)

[*Thompson was one of the most important poets of the Catholic Revival in nineteenth-century English literature. Often compared to the seventeenth-century metaphysical poets, especially Richard Crashaw, he presented the characteristic themes of spiritual struggle, redemption, and transcendent love in poetry and prose noted for rich verbal effects and a devotion to the values of aestheticism. The following excerpt is from Thompson's favorable review of* James Clarence Mangan: His Selected Poems, *edited by Louise Imogen Guiney. For Guiney's discussion, see excerpt above.*]

When the editor of a "popularised" edition of Chaucer requested by letter from a well-known author his support for the project in question, the author sublimely answered, that "he did not want Chaucer popularised, he wanted to keep Chaucer for himself and a few friends." . . . What has this to do with Mangan? What is he to Chaucer, or Chaucer to him? Simply this, that I and a few friends have for a number of years felt a kind of private proprietorship in Clarence Mangan. We cannot all appropriate Chaucers; so we were humbly content with our Mangan. Even we did not know much about him. We only knew him as the author of three or four poems, not all of which we greatly admired. One was an imperfect, but deeply felt and moving poem on his own misfortunes [**"The Nameless One"**], ending with a noble stanza:

Him grant a grave to, ye pitying noble,
    Deep in your bosoms; there let him dwell.
He, too, had tears for all souls in trouble
    Here—and in hell.

There could be no suspicion of pose, for the poet had lived and died in the deepest misery. The other, **"Dark Rosaleen,"** was a splendid and impassioned love-song, a fantasia on an old Irish poem addressed to Ireland under the allegory of a woman. A fantasia, I call it, for it was expanded with a freedom and originality which left translation panting behind. It is too long to quote, and single stanzas would only scandal the torrent vehemence of the whole. This was all we knew of him; but outside his own countrymen we met none who knew as much. Therefore we possessed him, and imparted him to those poorer than ourselves. Of late years I dreaded that our monopoly was coming to an end. I surmised that he would presently go forth to the English public in a volume, and the critics would find he had the Gaelic glamour, or some other infectious complaint. And I did not think Mangan would at all like it. Now here is [*James Clarence Mangan: His Selected Poems,* a volume] issued by Mr. John Lane, with a preface by Miss Louise Imogen Guiney, an American essayist and poetess. When I had timidly glanced through her pages, and

satisfied myself that there was no Gaelic glamour, even in a suppressed form, I was able to read the preface with a heart at ease. And now I am reconciled to the failure of my monopoly. (p. 241)

In some respects I confess to a disappointment [in the poems]. There is no other outburst of swiftness and passion like the **"Dark Rosaleen."** The best of them are dreamy, deficient in substance, passion, or imagery, depending for their effect almost solely on metrical melody. Yet some of them are undoubtedly noticeable. They would be remarkable for one thing alone—the discovery (pointed out by Miss Guiney) that Mangan had elaborated the artifice of the reiterated refrain, exactly in the manner of Edgar Poe, *before the date* when Edgar Poe first began to use it. In fact, the whole manner of the best poems is so startlingly like that of Edgar Poe that it is difficult to resist the suspicion that Poe somehow came across specimens of them, and turned the discovery to account with his usual unscrupulousness and power. Take an example cited by Miss Guiney:

The pall of the sunset fell
Vermilioning earth and water;
The bulbul's melody broke from the dell,
A song to the rose, the summer's daughter!
The lulling music of Tigris' flow
Was blended with echoes from many a mosque
As the muezzin chanted the *Allah-el-illah:*
Yet my heart in that hour was low,
For I stood in a ruined Kiosk:
O my heart in that hour was low,
For I stood in the ruined Kiosk
Of the Caliph Moostanzar Billah;
I mused alone in the ruined Kiosk
Of the mighty Moostanzar Billah.

Again, take this from the song of a dying Arab, **"The Last Words of Al-Hassan":**

The wasted moon has a marvellous look
Amiddle of the starry hordes;
The heavens, too, shine like a mystic book
All bright with burning words.
The mists of the dawn begin to dislimn
Lahara's castles of sand.
Farewell! farewell! mine eyes feel dim:
They turn to the lampless land.
'Llah Hu!
My heart is weary, mine eyes are dim,
I would rest in the dark, dark land!

The **"Karamanian Exile"** has the same note, in yet another arrangement, as a stanza will show:

O none of all my sisters ten,
Karaman!
Loved like me my fellow-men,
Karaman, O Karaman!
I was mild as milk till then,
I was soft as silk till then;
Now my breast is as a den,
Karaman!
Foul with blood and bones of men,
Karaman!
With blood and bones of slaughtered men,
Karaman, O Karaman!

Let me quote one more stanza from another poem, for the sake of its pictorial expression, and I have done:

The silks that swathe my hall divan
Are damascened with moons of gold;

(Allah, Allah hu!)
Musk-roses from my gulistan
Fill vases of Egyptian mould.
(Allah, Allah hu!)
The Koran's treasures lie unrolled
Near where my radiant night-lamp burns;
(Allah, Allah hu!)
Around me rows of silver urns
Perfume the air with odours old.
(Allah, Allah hu!)
But what avail these luxuries?
The blood of him I slew
Burns red on all; I cry therefore,
All night long, on my knees,
Evermore:
Allah, Allah hu!

It will be clear from these extracts that the man who could thus anticipate Poe's metrical feats, though chiefly self-educated, in a country where literary culture could hardly be said to exist, and where there was nothing which we should call literary society; and who yet showed in conception and expression so trained and literary a sense, was of no common gifts. He has, too, something of Poe's atmosphere, if his imagination is weaker. As to that, it is clear his imagination must have been literally starved. (pp. 241-42)

Francis Thompson, "Excursions in Criticism: II—Clarence Mangan," in The Academy, *Vol. 52, n.s. No. 1325, September 25, 1897, pp. 241-42.*

THE ATHENAEUM   (essay date 1897)

[*The following unsigned review challenges the favorable evaluation of Mangan's work by Louise Imogen Guiney in her appreciative study introducing* James Clarence Mangan: His Selected Poems (*see excerpt dated 1897*).]

A charmingly bound volume, with a graceful drawing by Mrs. Clement Shorter, this book comes on the avowed mission of rescuing from oblivion the works of an Irish poet, opium-eater, and drunkard. While it is true that one's knowledge of a man's sins should not prejudice one against his art, yet, on the other hand, the fact that a man was deficient in the rudiments of decency and self-command is no good reason for extolling his verses. . . . Of course sympathy attaches itself to the unfortunate and the fallen, but sympathy for the man has no place beside criticism of the artist. James Mangan must be judged on his merits, just as though he had been a respectable person, a churchwarden, and president of a temperance league.

Miss Guiney proudly tells us that "he has somehow escaped the classifiers; he has never been run through with a pin, nor have his wings been spread under glass in a museum." With all respect to author and biographer, we would suggest that many a meadow-brown or garden-white enjoys a like immunity, and finds no food for pride in an escape shared by so many of his kind.

The few to whom James Mangan is known know him chiefly by his poem **"My Dark Rosaleen,"** a song full of fire, and commanding a certain respectful admiration, which is considerably modified when the reader learns that all which has worth in **"My Dark Rosaleen"** is stolen from the Gaelic, and that in the theft the jewels have been dimmed. Miss Guiney obligingly supplies a literal translation of the Gaelic, which is in its rough unrhythmic form a far finer poem than Mangan's English transcript.

Far be it from us to deny to this obscure author certain gifts—fire, force, and a peculiar and startling earnestness. But these qualities are blurred by a constant wash of weakness—the result of his fatal and unresisted fluency. Many of his poems are extremely interesting as expressions of thought and emotion. Among works of art they have no place. Miss Guiney's enthusiasm has led her to quote "the gallant words with which Schumann once began a review of the young Chopin: 'Hats off, gentlemen: a genius!' " Applied by the risen sun to the rising star, these words are generous and becoming; spoken by Miss Guiney of James Mangan, they are merely absurd. This unfortunate Irishman had talent, and talent which in brighter circumstances might have found expression in work far more valuable than any fate ever allowed him to produce. Genius he had not. One mark (the greatest) of genius is the production of memorable lines—lines which at once catch the ear, and irrevocably fix themselves in the recollection—lines which, once read, are never to be forgotten. Read Mangan's poems from beginning to end, and when you have closed the book you shall find abiding with you no single line. An impression of confused and misspent effort will remain—nothing more.

In her zeal for the glorification of her author, Miss Guiney does not even hesitate to suggest that to him Edgar Allan Poe owes his trick of reiteration, and asserts that "any critic would attribute" the following lines "to Poe, both for manner and for perfect mastery of ghastly detail":—

I was mild as milk till then,
I was soft as silk till then,
Now my breast is like a den,
Karaman!
Foul with blood and bones of men,
Karaman!
With blood and bones of slaughtered men,
Karaman, O Karaman!

"The . . . mark of Poe's maturer poetry, the employment of sonorous successive lines which cunningly fall short of exact duplication, belongs also to Mangan *in the same degree.*" Does it? Let genius speak for itself in the few lines which Miss Guiney herself quotes:—

Come, let the burial rite be read, the funeral song be sung,
An anthem for the queenliest dead that ever died so young,
A dirge for her, the doubly dead in that she died so young!

Perhaps the most interesting thing in the book before us is the purely biographical poem called **"The Nameless One,"** and here the interest is not in the poetry, but in the biography. The comic verses which please Miss Guiney will seem to English readers almost intolerable. (pp. 667-68)

A review of "James Clarence Mangan: Poems and a Study," in The Athenaeum *No. 3655, November 13, 1897, pp. 667-68.*

LIONEL JOHNSON   (essay date 1898)

[*An English poet and critic, Johnson is considered one of the most important figures associated with the Decadent and Aesthetic movements of the 1890s. Like many of his contemporaries in those movements, he lived an eccentric life and died young, producing a small but distinguished body of works that reflects his deep interest in medieval literature and thought and demonstrates two major influences: Walter Pater's aestheti-*

cism and the poetry of the Celtic Revival. In the following excerpt, Johnson lauds Mangan's major works.]

No one can thoroughly realize Mangan's life without some knowledge of Dublin: not knowledge of Ireland at large, for Mangan had practically none, save by reading; but knowledge of that Dublin "dear and dirty," splendid and squalid, fascinating and repulsive, which was Mangan's from the cradle to the grave. There is there an unique piteousness of poverty and decay, a stricken and helpless look, which seem appropriate to the scene of the doomed poet's life. It was a life of dreams and misery and madness, yet of a self-pity which does not disgust us, and of a weakness which is innocent; it seems the haunted, enchanted life of one drifting through his days in a dream of other days and other worlds, golden and immortal. . . . His miseries, which dictated to him that agonized poem, **"The Nameless One,"** were primarily of his own creation, realities of his own imagination, and, therefore, the more terrible: they were the agonies of a child in the dark, quivering for fear of that nothing which is to him so infinitely real and dread a "something." For Mangan's childhood, boyhood, first youth, though hard and harsh, were not unbearably so; many a poet has borne far worse, and survived it unscathed. A rough and stern, rather than cruel, father; office drudgery with coarse companions; stinted, but not insufficient means; a general absence of congenial sympathy and friendship,—these are rude facts to face; but even a poet, all nerves and feeling, need not find life a hell because of them, the world a prison, all things an utter darkness of despair. And even Mangan's failure in love, whatever be the truth of that obscure event, would hardly account, by its own intrinsic sadness, for his abysmal melancholy and sense of doom. . . . Beyond a doubt, his temperament, immeasurably delicate and sensitive, received from its early experiences a shock, a shaking, which left him tremulous, impotent, a leaf in the wind, upon the water. His first sufferings in life were but the child's imagined ghosts; but the "shock to the system," to his imaginative sensitive temperament, was lasting, and he lived in a *penumbra* of haunting memories and apprehensions. In Browning's words, it was:

> The glimmer of twilight,
> Never glad confident morning again!

Life had struck him in his affections and emotions: he could never recover from the blow, could but magnify it in memory and imagination, conceive himself marked by it, go apart from the world to hide it, go astray in the world to forget it. That was Mangan's tragedy.

But he did not suffer it to cloud his poetry with darkness of expression at any time, nor, at its finest times, with darkness of theme or thought. It forced him into writing a deal of unworthy clever stuff, and a deal of excellent work far below his highest ability and achievement. But not a faint shadow of unhappiness dims the radiance of his **"Dark Rosaleen,"** its adoring, flashing, flying, laughing rapture of patriotic passion. It is among the great lyrics of the world, one of the fairest and fiercest in its perfection of imagery and rhythm; it is the chivalry of a nation's faith struck on a sudden into the immortality of music. And Mangan's next glory, his version of **"O'Hussey's Ode to the Maguire,"** is no less perfect upon its lower, yet lofty, plane. A certain Elizabethan poet has this pleasing stanza upon the Irish of his day, as he viewed them:

> The Irish are as civil, as
> The Russies in their kind;
> Hard choice, which is the best of both,

Each bloodie, rude, and blind!

The **"Ode to the Maguire"** gives the noble side to the question, a ferocity that is heroic, in lines of the largest Homeric simplicity and greatness; and as the **"Dark Rosaleen"** sings the devotion of a nation to their country in oppression, so this chants that of a follower to his chief in defeat; but in neither is there the note of despair, in both is the note of glory. Other of Mangan's poems upon Ireland, original or based upon Gaelic originals, have a like lustrous quality: he loved to lose himself in Ireland's past and future, and thereby made poems which will have helped to make the future Ireland. Upon such work as this he left no mark of his mental miseries and physical dishonours; indeed, his poems, though often tragic with sorrow, or trivial with levity, or both at once, are always pure and clear in every sense: in poetry, at least, he lived an innocent life. Besides his own Ireland, there were two chief worlds in which he loved to wander: the moonlit forests of German poetry, often painfully full of "moonshine," and the glowing gardens or glittering deserts of the Eastern, the "Saracenic" world. He wished, half-whimsically and half-seriously, to make his readers believe that he knew some dozen languages; certain it is that he had a strong philological instinct, and much of that aptitude for acquiring a vast half-knowledge of many things not commonly known, which he shares with the very similar, and dissimilar, Poe. But his "translations" from many tongues, even when, as in the case of German, he knew his originals well, were wont to be either frank paraphrases or imitations, often to his originals' advantage. Some of his work in this kind is admirable, and of a cunning art: the work of a poet to whom rhythm and metre, with all technical difficulties and allurements, are passionately interesting; yet we regret the time spent upon most of them, and lost to his own virgin Muse. He seems to have felt that he was content to earn the wages upon which he lived from hand to mouth, by such secondary work, as though he despaired of attempting, or preferred to keep in sacred silence, his higher song. He has given us little of that. A selection from his poems can be bought for sixpence, and one could spare, it may be, a hundred out of its one hundred and forty-four pages. But what remains is, in its marvellous moments of entire success, greater than anything that Ireland has yet produced in English verse, from Goldsmith to Mr. Yeats. (pp. 218-22)

> *Lionel Johnson, "Clarence Mangan," in his* Post Liminium: Essays and Critical Papers, *edited by Thomas Whittemore, Elkin Mathews, 1911, pp. 218-22.*

JAMES JOYCE (essay date 1902)

[*Joyce is one of the most prominent and influential literary figures of the first half of the twentieth century. Many critics maintain that his experiments in prose, particularly in the advancement of the interior monologue, both redefined the limits of language and re-created the form of the modern novel. In his critical writings, Joyce displayed a subjective view of the works he examined, favoring those associated with the school of psychological realism. In the following excerpt, Joyce defines Mangan's strengths and limitations as a poet and discusses his place in Irish literature.*]

[Mangan's] writings, which have never been collected and which are unknown, except for two American editions of selected poems and some pages of prose, published by Duffy, show no order and sometimes very little thought. Many of his essays are pretty fooling when read once, but one cannot but discern some fierce energy beneath the banter, which follows up the phrases with no good intent, and there is a likeness between the desperate writer, himself the victim of too dexterous torture, and the contorted writing. Mangan, it must be remembered, wrote with no native literary tradition to guide him, and for a public which cared for matters of the day, and for poetry only so far as it might illustrate these. He could not often revise what he wrote, and he has often striven with Moore and [Edward Walsh, the Irish poet] on their own ground. But the best of what he has written makes its appeal surely, because it was conceived by the imagination which he called, I think, the mother of things, whose dream are we, who imageth us to herself, and to ourselves, and imageth herself in us—the power before whose breath the mind in creation is (to use Shelley's image) as a fading coal. Though even in the best of Mangan the presence of alien emotions is sometimes felt, the presence of an imaginative personality reflecting the light of imagination beauty is more vividly felt. East and West meet in that personality (we know how); images interweave there like soft, luminous scarves and words ring like brilliant mail, and whether the song is of Ireland or of Istanbul it has the same refrain, a prayer that peace may come again to her who has lost her peace, the moonwhite pearl of his soul, Ameen [in **"The Last Words of Al-Hassan"**]. Music and odours and lights are spread about her, and he would search the dews and the sands that he might set another glory near her face. A scenery and a world have grown up about her face, as they will about any face which the eyes have regarded with love. Vittoria Colonna [Michelangelo's inspiration] and Laura and Beatrice—even she upon whose face many lives have cast that shadowy delicacy, as of one who broods upon distant terrors and riotous dreams, and that strange stillness before which love is silent, Mona Lisa—embody one chivalrous idea, which is no mortal thing, bearing it bravely above the accidents of lust and faithlessness and weariness; and she whose white and holy hands have the virtue of enchanted hands, his virgin flower, and flower of flowers, is no less than these an embodiment of that idea. How the East is laid under tribute for her and must bring all its treasures to her feet! The sea that foams over saffron sands, the lonely cedar on the Balkans, the hall damascened with moons of gold and a breath of roses from the gulistan—all these shall be where she is in willing service: reverence and peace shall be the service of the heart, as in the verses **"To Mihril"**:

> My starlight, my moonlight, my midnight, my noonlight,
> Unveil not, unveil not!

And where the music shakes off its languor and is full of the ecstasy of combat, as in the **"Lament for Sir Maurice Fitz-Gerald,"** and in **"Dark Rosaleen,"** it does not attain to the quality of Whitman indeed, but is tremulous with all the changing harmonies of Shelley's verse. Now and then this note is hoarsened and a troop of unmannerly passions echoes it derisively, but two poems at least sustain the music unbroken, the **"Swabian Popular Song,"** and a translation of two quatrains by Wetzel. To create a little flower, Blake said, is the labour of ages, and even one lyric has made Dowland immortal; and the matchless passages which are found in other poems are so good that they could not have been written by anyone but Mangan. He might have written a treatise on the poetical art for he is more cunning in his use of the musical echo than is Poe, the high priest of most modern schools, and there is a mastery, which no school can teach, but which

obeys an interior command, which we may trace in **"Kathaleen-Ny-Houlahan,"** where the refrain changes the trochaic scheme abruptly for a line of firm, marching iambs. [The line is: "May he show forth His might in saving Kathaleen Ny-Houlahan!"]

All his poetry remembers wrong and suffering and the aspiration of one who has suffered and who is moved to great cries and gestures when that sorrowful hour rushes upon the heart. This is the theme of a hundred songs but of none so intense as these songs which are made in noble misery, as his favourite Swedenborg would say, out of the vastation of soul. Naomi would change her name to Mara, because it has gone bitterly with her, and is it not the deep sense of sorrow and bitterness which explains these names and titles and this fury of translation in which he has sought to lose himself? For he has not found in himself the faith of the solitary, or the faith, which in the middle age, sent the spires singing up to heaven, and he waits for the final scene to end the penance. Weaker than Leopardi, for he has not the courage of his own despair but forgets all ills and forgoes his scorn at the showing of some favour, he has, perhaps for this reason, the memorial he would have had—a constant presence with those that love him—and bears witness, as the more heroic pessimist bears witness against his will to the calm fortitude of humanity, to a subtle sympathy with health and joyousness which is seldom found in one whose health is safe. And so he does not shrink from the grave and the busy workings of the earth so much as from the unfriendly eyes of women and the hard eyes of men. To tell the truth, he has been in love with death all his life, like another [Keats, as identified by the critic] and with no woman, and he has the same gentle manner as of old to welcome him whose face is hidden with a cloud, who is named Azrael [the angel of death in Mohammedan mythology]. Those whom the flames of too fierce love have wasted on earth become after death pale phantoms among the winds of desire, and, as he strove here towards peace with the ardour of the wretched, it may be that now the winds of peace visit him and he rests, and remembers no more this bitter vestment of the body.

Poetry, even when apparently most fantastic, is always a revolt against artifice, a revolt, in a sense, against actuality. It speaks of what seems fantastic and unreal to those who have lost the simple intuitions which are the tests of reality; and, as it is often found at war with its age, so it makes no account of history, which is fabled by the daughters of memory, but sets store by every time less than the pulsation of an artery, the time in which its intuitions start forth, holding it equal in its period and value to six thousand years. No doubt they are only men of letters who insist on the succession of the ages, and history or the denial of reality, for they are two names for one thing, may be said to be that which deceives the whole world. In this, as in much else, Mangan is the type of his race. History encloses him so straitly that even his fiery moments do not set him free from it. He, too, cries out, in his life and in his mournful verses, against the injustice of despoilers, but never laments a deeper loss than the loss of plaids and ornaments. He inherits the latest and worst part of a legend upon which the line has never been drawn out and which divides against itself as it moves down the cycles. And because this tradition is so much with him he has accepted it with all its griefs and failures, and has not known how to change it, as the strong spirit knows, and so would bequeath it: the poet who hurls his anger against tyrants would establish upon the future an intimate and far more cruel tyranny.

In the final view the figure which he worships is seen to be an abject queen upon whom, because of the bloody crimes that she has done and of those as bloody that were done to her, madness is come and death is coming, but who will not believe that she is near to die and remembers only the rumour of voices challenging her sacred gardens and her fair, tall flowers that have become the food of boars. Novalis said of love that it is the Amen of the universe, and Mangan can tell of the beauty of hate; and pure hate is as excellent as pure love. An eager spirit would cast down with violence the high traditions of Mangan's race—love of sorrow for the sake of sorrow and despair and fearful menaces—but where their voice is a supreme entreaty to be borne with forbearance seems only a little grace; and what is so courteous and so patient as a great faith?

Every age must look for its sanction to its poetry and philosophy, for in these the human mind, as it looks backward or forward, attains to an eternal state. The philosophic mind inclines always to an elaborate life—the life of Goethe or of Leonardo da Vinci; but the life of the poet is intense—the life of Blake or of Dante—taking into its centre the life that surrounds it and flinging it abroad again amid planetary music. With Mangan a narrow and hysterical nationality receives a last justification, for when this feeble-bodied figure departs dusk begins to veil the train of the gods, and he who listens may hear their footsteps leaving the world. But the ancient gods, who are visions of the divine names, die and come to life many times, and, though there is dusk about their feet and darkness in their indifferent eyes, the miracle of light is renewed eternally in the imaginative soul. (pp. 78-83)

> *James Joyce, "James Clarence Mangan," in his* The Critical Writings of James Joyce, *edited by Ellsworth Mason and Richard Ellmann, The Viking Press, 1959, pp. 73-83.*

D. J. O'DONOGHUE (essay date 1904)

[O'Donoghue was an Irish critic who wrote extensively on Mangan's life and works and edited volumes of his poetry and prose. In the following excerpt, he presents an overview of Mangan's prose writings.]

To expect a serious work in prose from Mangan would be useless; all he wrote in that medium was intended merely to amuse the reader of the moment. Hence much of [*The Prose Writings*] is purely topical, ephemeral in treatment, evanescent in interest; but it is all stamped with his peculiar qualities, such as they are. It is often defaced by mannerisms, and made trivial by an irresistible tendency to punning; but all know who knew Mangan that to look for uniformly lofty thoughts and lofty expression would be counting without their author. Nevertheless, how eminently characteristic much of this prose is! Perhaps he is at his best in his serious manner in the brilliant **"Chapters on Ghostcraft,"** whose incompleteness is to be deplored; but even here the quaintness breaks through the effort at restraint. In **"A German Poet,"** on the other hand, he is seen in his gayest vein. This is the real Mangan, quizzical and yet critical, half-humorous, half-serious. One feels the influence here of a writer with whom he had much in common—Charles Lamb. This piece reminds me very much of that charming essayist and critic, and, if it is not heresy to say so, one detects the influence of De Quincey in **"An Extraordinary Adventure in the Shades,"** and of Coleridge and Maginn in **"A Sixty-Drop Dose of Laudanum,"** which might be described as an amalgam of [Coleridge's] "Table Talk" and [Maginn's] *Maxims of Sir Morgan O'Doherty*. It is certainly no exaggeration to say that some of the "drops" would not be unworthy of Coleridge, while others read amazingly like Maginn.

The writers, however, who (unfortunately, as I think) had the most marked effect upon Mangan were William Godwin and Charles Robert Maturin. For them and their gloomy school Mangan always had a notable fancy. Godwin's *St. Leon* he knew almost by heart, and there are many evidences of his knowledge and appreciation of, or at any rate interest in, Maturin's works. In stories like **"The Thirty Flasks"** there is a decided flavour of what may be called this pseudo-Byronic school. For Byron's poems Mangan expressed an unstinted admiration. His high regard for that poet is explicable, but one wonders at the astonishing influence on so keen a critic as Mangan of such faint adumbrations of Byron. But in a whimsical passage in one of his articles he defends his many queer views, literary and otherwise:

> My mode of forming an opinion suiteth myself and scandaliseth nobody. I take a few facts, not caring to be overwhelmed by too many proofs that they are facts. With them I mix up a dish of the marvellous—perhaps an old wife's tale, perhaps a half-remembered dream or mesmeric experience of my own, and the business is done. My conclusion is reached and shelved, and must not thenceforward be disturbed. I would as soon think at any time afterwards of questioning its truth as of doubting the veritable existence of the barber's five brothers in the "Arabian Nights," or the power of Keyn Alasnam, King of the Genii. There it is, and an opponent may battle with me anent it if he pleases. I manage to hold my ground by the help of digressions and analogies.

What I have said elsewhere of one phase of this poetical output of Mangan applies equally to much of his prose. Just as he loved doggerel for its own sake, and always wrote it consciously—he may even be said to have raised the art of writing it to a fine art, for even his doggerel is generally distinguished—he seems to have deliberately cultivated the art of writing trivially on trivial matters. When so much pompous and portentous absurdity is written so seriously, this is no small achievement. Mangan's **"Treatise on a Pair of Tongs"** is particularly Manganesque in this respect. Like Swift's "Meditation on a Broomstick," it is a parody on the solemnity of certain metaphysicians, who waste an infinite deal of thought and time in proving what nobody desires to have demonstrated. Mangan's amazing fertility and facility as a writer not unnaturally tend to occasional diffuseness. One sometimes feels that he could go on for ever in his discursive and allusive way. In one of his articles he says:

> A sea of argument stretches out before us, and the waves thereof curl about our feet. But we forbear to plunge in. Reflection recurs, and we receive a *check* on the *bank*.

Thus he explains to his readers how he spares them many other pages of disquisition. One can imagine after reading Mangan's prose what wonderful monologues they were which he used to deliver to his intimates, monologues which the latter remembered with much vivid pleasure in after years. Some of his early sketches are undoubtedly spun out beyond reasonable limits. Accepting one of these pieces in June, 1832, the editor of the *Comet* reminded him that it was "one hundred per cent better to give a good thing in one column than in two." As to that, however, Mangan probably held his own opinion. His perversity—a prevailing characteristic—had to be reckoned with. This characteristic has undoubtedly done much to prevent Mangan from finding universal recognition. He falls short of one's conception of a true or great artist. But so far as his poetical work is concerned, Mangan must be either accepted with all his mannerisms or absolutely ignored. For his prose—well, it is simply the prose of a remarkable poet, a delightful spirit, and, in any event, one of the quaintest and most interesting figures in Irish literary history. (pp. vii-x)

> D. J. O'Donoghue, in a preface to The Prose Writings of James Clarence Mangan, 1904. Reprint by AMS Press, 1978, pp. vii-x.

HENRY W. NEVINSON (essay date 1904)

[*An English journalist, Nevinson earned a wide reputation as a war correspondent covering the Greco-Turkish war of 1897, the Boer War, and World War I, among other conflicts. He is best remembered for his autobiographical writings, but also wrote volumes of biography, criticism, social commentary, and poetry. In the following excerpt, Nevinson examines "Dark Rosaleen" in the context of Irish culture.*]

There is in Ireland an intention of putting up a memorial to Clarence Mangan, if only money enough can be collected. Whether, in the present state of art, a monument is of any advantage to the world, and whether poets who boast of work more durable than bronze had not better be satisfied with that kind of durability—these are questions for artists. But there can be no doubt that, if any country ought to put up memorials to its poets, Ireland owes one to Clarence Mangan.

He was one of those peculiar plants of genius that produce only one perfect flower. He gave every promise of a poet, it is true. The sketch of him taken by Sir Frederick Burton as he lay dead in a Dublin hospital (whether he died of cholera or starvation is a nice point for discussion) shows a clear-cut face of great refinement and sensitiveness—a face like Schiller's, and having something in common with the faces of all lyric poets. We read of the brilliant and dreamy blue eyes, of the hair so abundant and so bright with gold before misery whitened it. His very dress was lyrical. The accounts left by his few friends, Gavan Duffy among them, all agree upon the steeple-crowned hat with its immense brim, the tightly-buttoned coat that had once been a kind of drab, the little blue cloak, hardly reaching to the waist, the baggy trousers made for someone better fed, and the enormous umbrella which he kept tucked under the cloak so that it looked like a bagpipe.

The apparition is poetic enough, and it seems never to have varied, except that under opium and drink it grew rather more spectral and dingy, till suddenly it vanished underground. In external circumstance also, Mangan enjoyed every poetic advantage. He was born poor and remained so; he was well-read; he was unmarried; and he lived to forty-six. Nor was his genius hindered by lethargy, or indifference, or any over-scrupulous criticism of himself. He was, on the contrary, rather peculiarly fertile, and Mr. D. J. O'Donoghue, to whom we owe the new edition of his writings [*The Prose Writings of James Clarence Mangan*], as well as the biography published a few years ago, has discovered over 800 of his poems that appeared in print. So far from being barren, all

his work shows the facility and exuberance of a man who writes with ease, and enjoys writing. There was nothing exiguous or stinted about him, and yet, though he was quite unaware of it himself, he reached high excellence only once.

His devoted admirers, of whom I am one, may bring up strong instances to the contrary. They may call to mind poems still familiar to the literary circle in Dublin, such as **"O'Hussey's Ode to the Maguire,"** with its fine ending, so prophetic of De Wet:

> Hugh marched forth to the fight—I grieved to see him so
>   depart;
> And lo! to-night he wanders frozen, rain-drenched, sad,
>   betrayed—
> But the memory of the lime-white mansions his right hand
>   hath laid
>   In ashes warms the hero's heart!

Or they may call to mind the lament that, like the wood-pigeon, keeps asking, "Where, Oh, Kincora?" or the Turkish song of **"Karaman,"** or the Arabic **"Howling Song of Al-Mohara,"** or the personal sorrow of **"The Nameless One"**:

> Him grant a grave to, ye pitying noble,
>   Deep in your bosoms! There let him dwell!
> He, too, had tears for all souls in trouble,
>   Here and in hell.

Or they may call to mind the regret for the days of the **"Barmecides,"** so productive of Irish parody; or the more genuine part of **"Twenty Golden Years Ago,"** not unlike one of Béranger's smiling lamentations over lost youth:

> Wifeless, friendless, flagonless, alone,
>   Not quite bookless, though, unless I choose,
> Left with nought to do, except to groan,
>   Not a soul to woo, except the Muse—
> O! this, this is hard for *me* to bear,
>   Me, who whilom lived so much *en haut*.
> Me, who broke hearts like chinaware
>   Twenty golden years ago.

I will go further than other admirers, and add the **"Lullaby,"** in which the rod of Moses, the diamond sceptre of Pan, and the Golden Fleece are mingled, in true Irish prodigality, with the glaive of O'Dunn, Diarmid's sword, and Queen Eofa's jewels, as the best possible gifts to keep the baby quiet:

> And Conal's unpierceable shirt of mail,
> And the shield of Nish, the prince of the Gael,
> These twain for thee, my babe, shall I win,
> With the flashing spears of Achilles and Finn,
>   Each high as a pine;
> O, hushaby, hushaby, child of mine!

For such poems as these, Mangan would be remembered, as he is remembered, in any circle that made a special study of Ireland's literary spirit. Owing to that "Celtic Revival" which has been the one spiritual event of the last ten years, it is quite likely that some of them may appear in our recognized anthologies, and the name of Mangan will become familiar to the English child as one of poor, slovenly, drunken and incapable old Ireland's awful warnings.

By most people, even by admirers, the rest of Mangan's work will never be heard of again. Like all the Irish poets of his time, Mangan was much hampered, even in the use of words. They were writing a foreign language, and working on false models. For they had forgotten their own tongue, and the true power of English was hidden from them by the poetic artifice of their day. Take Mangan on his ordinary level, as in **"The Geraldine's Daughter"**:

> A beauty all stainless, a pearl of a maiden,
>   Has plunged me in trouble, and wounded my heart;
> With sorrow and gloom is my soul overladen,
>   An anguish is there that will never depart.

Any Irishman of sixty years ago could have gone on like that to the other side of Godspeed. And to me—perhaps to me alone—there is a certain attraction about that kind of verse, the attraction of a genuine, though slightly faded, gentility. It reminds me of the modest little houses which are still seen in the sweetly mouldering suburbs of Dublin, bearing on their gate-posts of corroded stucco the titles of "Talavera," "Khyber Pass," or "Maharajpore," to recall the poor, battered, old hero who so trustfully served the foreign and dominant race, and inscribed those proud titles as his sufficient reward. Over such gate-posts, such verses, the sensibility of forty years ago would have shed a tear; and still the angels give them a smile of passing recognition.

But in **"The Dark Rosaleen"** we have no time to think about forms and words. Critics may tell us there are echoes of a foreigner's English in it still. That does not matter now. The dawdlers in the suburbs of literature may drowse over such things if they please. They may debate with tepid industry whether it was Mangan or Poe who first invented the obvious characteristics of the metre. In **"The Dark Rosaleen"** we have passed beyond such things. We are borne away to a circle of passion from which tasteful criticism is seen fluttering with all its trumpery in the Paradise of Fools. The winds and stars are round us, and "red lightning lightens through the blood." We have passed into a world of nobler vision, where we behold Ireland incarnate again under the symbol of the Black Little Rose—the *Roisin Dubh*—just as she once appeared to Costello of Ballyhaunis, Red Hugh O'Donnell's wandering singer, who first made that song of such finely woven duplicity that the dull invaders never could be quite sure whether it sang of treason or of love. That early singer, in peril of his life, had said:

> Oh, little rose,
> Let there not be sorrow upon you for what has happened;
> The priests are coming over the waves, they are moving
>   upon the sea
> Your pardon will come from the Pope of Rome in the
>   East,
> And Spanish wine will not be spared for my Dark Little
>   Rose.

It was from that verse that Mangan began:

> O my Dark Rosaleen,
>   Do not sigh, do not weep!
> The priests are on the ocean green,
>   They march along the deep.
> There's wine from the royal Pope
>   Upon the ocean green;
> And Spanish ale shall give you hope,
>   My Dark Rosaleen!
>   My own Rosaleen!
> Shall glad your heart, shall give you hope,
> Shall give you health, and help, and hope,
>   My Dark Rosaleen.

The Gaelic poet, whose name is a shadow, went on:

> It was a long course over which I brought you from yester-
>   day to this day.

Over mountains I went with you, and by sails across the
>   sea,
> The Erne I passed at a bound, though it was great with
>   flood,
> And there was music of strings on each side of me and my
>   *Roisin Dubh.*

Then Mangan sings:

> Over hills and through dales
>   Have I roamed for your sake;
> All yesterday I sailed with sails
>   On river and on lake.
> The Erne at its highest flood
>   I dashed across unseen,
> For there was lightning in my blood,
>   My Dark Rosaleen!
>   My own Rosaleen!
> Oh! there was lightning in my blood,
> Red lightning lightened through my blood,
>   My Dark Rosaleen!

Intermingling the note of human love as though to lead the insensate enemy astray, Costello sings:

> I would walk the dew with you and the desert of the
>   plains,
> In the hope to win love from you, or part of my desire.
> Sweet little mouth! you promised you have love for me.
> Oh, she is the flower of Munster,
>   My Dark Little Rose!

But from a further depth of passion comes Mangan's cry, and the ruler must be dull indeed to miss the rebel's devotion here:

> Over dews, over sands,
>   Will I fly for your weal:
> Your holy delicate white hands
>   Shall girdle me with steel.

The figure of a country rises like a religious vision before some soldier-saint in a ruined chapel of the forest or among Irish hills. She is the Black Rose, the Secret Rose, holy as the Rose of Bethlehem. The poet is enamored of her, as ancient citizens were enamored of a city, but it is with a passion how much more tender and profound! She is no imperial state, standing in white-columned security over the seas which her fleets command; but a sly and fugitive spirit, her beauty remains unseen by all except her worshippers. To strange eyes she looks a mournful and profitless thing. Full of sad memories, reviled and held up to derision, bound, tortured, and spat upon, called out to make sport with her wit, starved and driven through the earth, in turn half-strangled and cajoled as a pleasing strain for the nurseries of her tormentors, even to her lovers she takes the disguise of the Little Old Woman, the Kathleen na Houlihan, who sits uncomforted beside the world's highway, or crouches muttering over the peat-fires of her hearth, while under those worn rags, and under the disguise of that wrinkled skin, is hidden the pure form of that Dark Rose whose heart is the consecrated shrine of joy and sorrow:

> All day long, in unrest,
>   To and fro do I move.
> The very soul within my breast
>   Is wasted for you, love!
> The heart in my bosom faints
>   To think of you, my queen,
> My life of life, my saint of saints,
>   My Dark Rosaleen!
>   My own Rosaleen!

To hear your sweet and sad complaints,
My life, my love, my saint of saints,
   My Dark Rosaleen!

The poem first appeared in *The Nation,* the rebel newspaper
of "Young Ireland." It was in 1846, perhaps the blackest year
in the unbroken storm of Ireland's history since the Invasion.
It may have been for that very reason that the **"Dark Rosaleen"** so far surpassed anything else that Mangan ever wrote.
In the Introduction which John Mitchel, himself one of the
greatest writers in *The Nation,* prefixed to the selection from
Mangan's poems which was published ten years after his
death [see Further Reading], we find a sentence which, perhaps, explains why it is that this poem stands alone and apart,
as something in an utterly different rank of excellence, from
the rest of Mangan's work. Mitchel speaks first of the poet's
poverty-stricken and miserable life, of his shy and sensitive
nature; "modestly craving nothing in the world but celestial,
glorified life, seraphic love, and a throne among the immortal
gods"; and then, as an explanation of his entire neglect by English critics, he adds:

> Mangan was not only an Irishman,—not only an
> Irish papist,—not only an Irish papist rebel;—but
> throughout his whole literary life of twenty years
> he never deigned to attorn to English criticism,
> never published a line in any English periodical, or
> through any English bookseller, never seemed to be
> aware that there was a British public to please. He
> was a rebel politically, and a rebel intellectually and
> spiritually,—a rebel with his whole heart and soul
> against the whole British spirit of the age.

It was because Mangan found in **"The Dark Rosaleen"** the
fullest expression of that lifelong rebellion that the poem is
on quite a different level to the rest of his work. In this alone
he passed beyond the ordinary themes and exercises of poetic
talent—the amorous addresses, the regrets for the past, the
translations from foreign tongues, over which he wasted so
much of his life. In nearly all his other verses, he is untrue
to himself and only plays the common literary part. They are
sometimes pretty, sometimes "literature," and they are never
anything greater. But here he gathers up all the deepest forces
of his nature, to give us, just for this once, the assurance of
something more than a literary man. In this cry of rebellion,
prompted by a devotion like a lover's, but more generous and
of nobler mood, we find at last the essential spirit of the poet.
He was a rebel with his whole heart and soul, says John
Mitchel. And his rebellion was inspired by the vision of that
sorrowful but endearing shape which was his country—that
beggar queen, starving and glorified—that saint of saints,
whose spirit shone in gleams of opal. Like himself, she was
abused, ruined, and despised, but the light that burned in her
heart, burned in his as well. So to her feet he brought his one
great gift, and there he uttered the words which expressed the
whole purpose of his scorned and distracted life:

> But yet will I rear your throne
>   Again in golden sheen;
> 'Tis you shall reign, shall reign alone,
>   My Dark Rosaleen!
>   My own Rosaleen!
> 'Tis you shall have the golden throne,
> 'Tis you shall reign, and reign alone,
>   My Dark Rosaleen!

• • • • •

The Judgment Hour must first be nigh

Ere you can fade, ere you can die,
   My Dark Rosaleen!

(pp. 252-59)

Henry W. Nevinson, "The Dark Rosaleen," in The
North American Review, *Vol. 179, No. 2, August,
1904, pp. 252-62.*

ERNEST BOYD (essay date 1922)

> [*An Irish-American writer and translator, Boyd was a promi-
> nent literary critic known for his erudite, honest, and often sa-
> tirical critiques. His important survey,* Ireland's Literary Re-
> naissance, *presents Mangan and Samuel Ferguson as the
> major precursors of the literary revival in Ireland, and in the
> following excerpt from that work, Boyd discusses the patriotism
> expressed in Mangan's poetry based on Gaelic sources.*]

The poets of *The Nation* [an Irish nationalist periodical], for
all their intensity of patriotic feeling, followed the English
rather than the Celtic tradition, their work has a political
rather than a literary value, and bears little upon the development of modern Irish verse. The literature of the Revival is
no longer concerned with the political revolt against England. It has lost the passionate cry of aggressive patriotism,
the wail of despair, and has entered into possession of the vast
field of Irish legend. Here, in the interpretation of the Celtic
spirit, it has found a truer and more steadfast expression of
Irish nationality. The circumstances propitious to such outbursts as characterised the patriot poets of the mid-
nineteenth century have altered. Patriotic revolt is not a sufficient guarantee of good poetry, and the Irish Muse has found
a quieter and more lasting inspiration. With the exception of
Mangan, none of *The Nation* poets has left work whose appeal is likely to endure. Mangan was something more than
a patriot, he was a poet of genius, and his work has a value
transcending that of the writers with whom he was accidentally associated. In him one can detect the presence of influences which were absent from the work of his contemporaries, and which make him the true father of the modern
poets. Contact with the pure stream of Irish culture, Gaelic
literature, so moulded the mind of the poet as to constitute
his work the first utterance of Celtic Ireland in the English
tongue. Patriot though he was, like Davis, McGee and the
others, he required the stimulus of some ancient Gaelic song
or legend to bring out the great power that was in him. Even
the essentially patriotic and familiar **"Dark Rosaleen"** owes
its existence to Mangan's reading of "Roisin Dubh," the
work of an obscure Elizabethan bard. It was not, moreover,
until he had produced two less felicitous versions that he attained the perfection of form in which it is now best known.

The existence of these three versions, written at considerable
intervals, indicates to what extent Mangan's imagination was
haunted by this song. As he brooded over its passionate
theme, becoming more deeply stirred by its beauty, his soul
vibrated to the music of the Gaelic minstrel, until, carried
away by his awakened inspiration, he gave his noble and almost perfect rendering. A comparison of these versions, verse
by verse, reveals everywhere the same differences; the contrast between translation and inspiration is in every line. As
the poem departs more and more from the text, it comes
nearer and nearer to the conception of the Gaelic poet, and
becomes at the same time an original creation. In exchange
for verbal fidelity Mangan offers such personal contribution
as "your holy delicate white hands," nowhere to be discovered in the text. In short he treats his subject as the moderns

have treated theirs. The latter, absorbing the legends and stories of their country, have identified themselves with the spirit of Ireland's past, and renewed the tradition of Irish literature. Mangan, however, was not always so happily inspired by Gaelic themes, and in many instances his successor, Samuel Ferguson, has surpassed him, without possessing more than a tithe of his poetic genius. Ferguson's profound knowledge of Irish often enables him to succeed, in a measure, where Mangan has failed. Owing to the absence of inspiration to compensate for the lack of scholarship, Mangan's **"The Fair Hills of Ireland"** is inferior to Ferguson's "The Fair Hills of Eire, O." Mangan has notes which Ferguson could never hope to reach, but his fire is spasmodic, and flickers in a manner utterly incompatible with the steady, if somewhat dead, level of Ferguson's work. His finest achievement is **"Dark Rosaleen."** Noisy and sincere patriotism were then, and have since been, the frequent inspiration of Irish poetry, but that wonderful paraphrase has a beauty and a poignant intensity which have never been equalled.

The squalid shiftlessness of Mangan's own life made him the responsive interpreter of Ireland's sorrowful history of former splendour contrasted with an ever-present misery. Here he could lose himself in the hopes, laments and memories of the Gael, and satisfy the vague longings of his idealism. Weak and purposeless himself, he had not that joy of living which alone can create eternal beauty. It was only when he caught the fervour of some old Irish poet that he became truly inspired. Even then, he could not say yea to life. As in his original work, so in his poems of Gaelic origin, his themes are of sorrow, despair and death. His verse is filled with tears, and seems, as it were, the *caoine* of an entire race. Apart from Gaelic sources Mangan is as commonplace as Moore. His work is often shallow and arid, filled with rhetoric which not even his unusual command of rhyme and rhythm, his skilful versification, can conceal. He was devoid of the self-control which enables the great artist to select and fashion his material at will. His genuine culture and love of literature constituted him a somewhat unique figure in his time. In him the authentic voice of Celtic Ireland was heard for the first time in Anglo-Irish poetry, and he indicated the way of escape from the dominance of England, which his successors have followed. (pp. 17-20)

Ernest Boyd, "Precursors," in his Ireland's Literary Renaissance, *revised edition, Alfred A. Knopf, 1922, pp. 15-25.*

PADRAIC COLUM (essay date 1933)

[*An Irish poet, dramatist, editor, and critic, Colum was one of the major writers of the Irish Literary Renaissance. He was most noted for his efforts to make better-known the varied heritage of Irish literature through his writings and public lectures, but he is perhaps most important as a historical dramatist who established many precedents for the Irish national theater. Colum's poems incorporate his knowledge of dramatic technique, and have been praised for avoiding the nationalistic didacticism prevalent in the poetry of many of his contemporaries. In the following excerpt, he examines the themes and poetic techniques of Mangan's major poems.*]

"I would far and away prefer," Mangan said of himself, "being a great necromancer to being a great writer or even a great fighter. My natural propensities lead me rather to seek out modes of astonishing mankind than of edifying them." And John Mitchel when he discovered him on the top of a ladder in the library of Trinity College was induced to picture him in a way that makes us think that he looked the part he wanted to play. The blanched hair was totally unkempt; the corpse-like features still as marble; a large book was in his arms, and all his soul was in the book. "I had never heard of Clarence Mangan before, and knew not for what he was celebrated; whether as a magician, a poet, or a murderer; yet took a volume and spread it on the table, not to read, but with a pretence of reading to gaze on the spectral creature upon the ladder." Like a magician dispossessed for a while of his arcane powers Mangan chants:

> Solomon! Where is thy throne? It is gone in the wind.
> Babylon! Where is thy might? It has gone in the wind.
> Like the swift shadows of Noon, like the dreams of the
>   Blind,
> Vanish the glories and pomps of the earth in the wind.

It goes on, this threnody, for nine stanzas, all the rhymes being on the insistent "wind." And **"The Howling Song of Al-Mohara"** might have been made by a magician who had come out of his cell to seize upon words and poetic forms and make of them things to astonish us:—

> My heart is as a House of Groans
> From dusky eve to dawning grey;
>   Allah, Allah hu!
> The glazed flesh on my staring bones
> Grows black and blacker with decay;
>   Allah, Allah hu!
> Yet am I none whom Death may slay;
> I am spared to suffer and to warn;
>   Allah, Allah hu!
> My lashless eyes are parched to horn
> With weeping for my sin alway;
> Allah, Allah hu!
> For blood, hot blood, that no one sees,
> The blood of one I slew
> Burns on my hands I cry therefore
> All night long, on my knees,
>   Evermore,
>   Allah, Allah hu!

For eight long stanzas this goes on. In **"The Karamanian Exile"** there is again the sense of a magician desperately transforming himself into a poet in order to lament an exile from a country he knew when he had feelings rather than powers:

> I see thee ever in my dreams,
>   Karaman!
> Thy hundred hills, thy thousand streams,
>   Karaman! O Karaman!
> As when thy gold-bright morning gleams,
> As when thy deepening sunset seams
> With lines of light thy hills and streams,
>   Karaman!
> So thou loomest on my dreams,
>   Karaman! O Karaman!

But he is looking back to a country in which there is not one lovable presence:

> Of late my thoughts rove more among
> Thy fields: o'ershadowing fancies throng
> My mind, and texts of bodeful song,
>   Karaman!
> Azreel is terrible and strong,
>   Karaman!
> His lightning sword smites all ere long,
>   Karaman! O Karaman!

As we think of him after reading these poems we note a curious thing: Mangan looks out on lands that are all waste, in which there is no green nor familiar thing. Constantly he does this. He tries to give an impression of an Irish landscape in a poem. And the only object that is familiar in that landscape is an ancient pillar-tower—nothing else, no spring nor field, gives him the sense of homeland:

> This is some rare clime so olden,
> Peopled, not by men, but fays;
> Some lone land of genii days,
> Storyful and golden!

"A Vision of Connaught in the Thirteenth Century" renders a Connaught that is as empty of familiar sights as Karaman. Indeed it is through his power of visualizing a waste—sometimes a bright waste, sometimes a dark waste—that gives his **"Siberia"** actuality as of a country travelled in and discovered to be a place where there can be no hope, no movement:

> And the exile there
>   Is one with those;
> They are part, and he is part,
> For the sands are in his heart,
>   And the killing snows.
>
> Therefore, in those wastes
>   None curse the Czar.
> Each man's tongue is cloven by
> The North Blast, that heweth nigh
>   With sharp scymitar.
>
> And such doom each drees,
>   Till, hunger-gnawn,
> And cold-slain, he at length sinks there,
> Yet scarce more a corpse than ere
>   His last breath was drawn.

We have to note in this poem, a poem that has extraordinary volume in its shortness, a carelessness that often mars Mangan's achievement, as if he had no art after a veritable inspiration had flagged on him—"And cold-slain he at length sinks there"—that "at length" is prosaic to the last degree.

He has a mood in which the sense of loss is softened and humanized. Such a mood is in **"The Time of the Barmecides"** and **"Twenty Golden Years Ago,"** the one with its soldierly Arabian, and the other with its romantic German atmosphere. **"The Time of the Barmecides"** is splendid for its flashing images, for its manly fervour, for its stanzas that move as with a warrior's stride:

> One golden goblet illumined my board,
> One silver dish was there;
> At hand my tried Karamanian sword
> Lay always bright and bare;
> For those were the days when the angry blow
> Supplanted the word that chides—
> When hearts could glow—long, long ago,
> In the time of the Barmecides;
> When hearts could glow—long, long ago,
> In the time of the Barmecides.

"Twenty Golden Years Ago" is again a looking backwards; it has humorous mournfulness, and humour is a scarce quality in Mangan's poetry. There is humour in another of his notable poems, in **"The Ride Round the Parapet,"** humour and gusto displayed in high-stepping, romantic stanzas.

An estimate of Mangan as a poet generally begins with an appreciation of his Irish poems. I have approached him through his non-Irish meaning to come to his other work with some freshness. His poems were published in magazines between 1832 and 1849, the year of his death. One of his first, I find, is an address to his native land. If published now amongst anonymous work this particular poem would not be attributed to James Clarence Mangan; it contradicts what his biographer and editor, D. J. O'Donoghue, says (although he admits it into the definite edition he does not seem to have given this poem any attention). "Yet, while always maintaining his own fatalistic outlook for himself, he was ever optimistic as regards Ireland—a feeling evinced over and over again in this volume, and as potent in his earlier as in his latest poems. He saw no hope for himself—he felt that there was but one inevitable result for him—but his hope for Ireland never faltered throughout his long career." But what does Mangan actually say in this early poem?

> The harp remaineth where it fell,
> With mouldering frame and broken chord;
> Around the song there hangs no spell—
> No laurel wreath entwines the sword;
> And startlingly the footstep falls
> Along thy dim and dreary halls.
> Thou art forsaken by the earth,
> Which makes a by-word of thy name;
> Nations, and thrones, and powers whose birth
> As yet is not, shall rise to fame,
> Shall flourish and may fail—but thou
> Shalt linger as thou lingerest now.

It would be hard for a poet to be less optimistic about his country. The establishment of the journal to which he contributed much of his poetry—*The Nation,* may have made him more hopeful about Ireland, more eager in the national cause. But it is worth noting that **"To My Native Land"** has more spirit, sincerity and finer metrical structure than the poems which have a more encouraging note—**"Soul and Country," "The Warning Voice," "A New Year's Lay," "A Highway for Freedom," "Irish National Hymn," "The Peal of Another Trumpet," "Hymn for Pentecost"**—the last is a prayer for a miracle to save the land. At the bottom of his heart, it would seem, Mangan had no more hope for Ireland than he had for himself.

A sense of something left for ever desolate and yet with power to inspire undying devotion—out of that sense come the two greatest of his Irish poems, the **"Ode to the Maguire,"** and **"The Lament for the Princes of Tyrone and Tyrconnell."** I place the **"Ode to the Maguire"** first. The verse is like the storm that spends its fury upon the chieftain addressed; it rises and falls, pauses and lashes out. Ostensibly in regular verse it has the flowingness of an improvisation; indeed, it is free verse contained in a formal framework, for there is a wide range of different stress between—

> The tempest-driven torrent deluges the mead

and—

> Through some dark wood, 'mid bones of monsters,
>   Hugh now strays.

Mangan could have made himself an innovator in metrics if he had had associates who could recognize and appreciate his departures from verse-norms. This ode is as remarkable for its fine structure as for its metrical arrangements. In the opening line the poet declares the homelessness of his master—

> Where is my Chief, my Master, this bleak night, *mavrone!*

Then it is as if there was nothing in the world but the elements—the deluging rain, the lightning, the cold that makes the night deathly. Before he appears in that desolation the Chieftain is hailed in images that are close to the elements—

> Were he even a wolf ranging the round green woods,
> Were he even a pleasant salmon in the unchainable sea,
> Were he even a wild mountain eagle, he could scarce bear, he,
> This sharp, sore sleet, these howling floods.

In the next stanza he is speaking of the defeated warrior simply. But as he speaks of him the man's stature grows and he becomes equal to the elements that once more break in upon the poet's senses.—

> That his great hand, so oft the avenger of the oppressed,
> Should this chill, churlish night, perchance, be paralysed by frost—
> While through some icicle-hung thicket as one lorn and lost,
> He walks and wanders without rest.

The fury of the elements abates and the flood is only domestically destructive—

> The lawns and pasture-grounds lie locked in icy bonds
> So that the cattle cannot feed.

> • • • • •

> It penetrates and fills the cottagers' dwellings far and wide—
> Water and land are blent in one.

Then, suddenly, we are reminded of the world in which Hugh Maguire strays "lorn and lost"—a line suffices to show how remote and alien that world is—

> Through some dark wood, 'mid bones of monsters, Hugh now strays.

From that on the man is the equal of the elements—

> And though frost glaze to-night the clear dew of his eyes,
> And white ice-gauntlets glove his noble fine fair fingers o'er,
> A warm dress to him is the lightning garb he ever wore,
> The lightning of the soul, not skies.

The **"Ode to the Maguire"** is superb for the elemental rush of the lines, for the sense of boundlessness that it gives; through it, too, comes something of the masculine, extravagant world of the Gaelic bards.

Beginning as an address to a lone figure in an alien land, **"The Lament for the Princes of Tyrone and Tyrconnell"** tells of memoried places, of battles won and lost, and names with loyalty and devotion "the princes of the line of Conn" whose decease marks the passing of the old aristocratic Ireland. It is a poem that can hardly appeal to one who is not devoted to the Irish tradition. But to one who has such devotion it stands as the most memorable of Irish poems. Conventional arrangements of conventional words occur over and over again in it—"Such blow the blood of Conn, I trow, Could ill have borne." "Red would have been our warriors' eyes Had Roderick found on Sligo's field A gory grave." We accept these without disapprobation because the whole lament is so impassioned and sustained—the conventionalities are swept along in the flow of the verse. Mangan, whose interest in actual buildings can be discovered in several of his poems, is nobly architectural in this poem. He rears what is really a memori-

al. The stanzas are like columns bearing up and distributing a weight of grief. Each long stanza is designed to give the rise and pause of lamentation and each is so well built into the whole that the lamentation lifts itself again and again after one has thought that the climax has been reached. **"The Lament for the Princes of Tyrone and Tyrconnell"** has splendid structure.

But Mangan's architectural power is not in evidence in **"Dark Rosaleen."** The stanzas are finely built, but each is complete in itself and does not go to make an organisation. No stanza adds to the one that is before it, each is static till the final one when the prophecy of wrath and deliverance breaks through the protestations of tenderness. For this reason **"Dark Rosaleen"** for all its exaltation and prophetic fervour is not a masterly poem. But what exaltation is in this poem where patriotic feeling is transmuted to devotional ecstasy! "Roisin Dubh" which was only a "secret" name becomes transmuted into an esoteric, into a sacred name in the wonderful litany that is **"Dark Rosaleen."**

With **"Kathaleen-Ny-Houlahan"** and the **"Farewell to Patrick Sarsfield"** Mangan goes from the elaborately contrived bardic poetry to the poetry of the folk—one is the folk reflection of **"Dark Rosaleen"** and the other of **"The Lament for the Princes of Tyrone and Tyrconnell."** Here prophecy is more simple and lament more spontaneous. The music of **"Kathaleen-Ny-Houlahan"** is lilting like country music, and Mangan has never shown himself more of an artist than in the way he makes the light-footed syllables prophesy "the coming-to of Kathleen Ny Houlahan," when "woollen plaids would grace herself and robes of silk her child." It is the most spontaneous and the happiest of Mangan's poems. **"Farewell to Patrick Sarsfield"** has behind it more humanity than is behind the rest of Mangan's verse: one can visualize some old wayfarer who has been through that disastrous war making up those fervent and extravagant lines for some wayside crowd who are stirred into enthusiasm for the departed hero,—

> May the white sun and moon rain glory on your head,
> All hero as you are and holy man of God—

And ending with the outburst that makes no account of actual conditions in the fervency of its hero-worship—

> And I never can believe that my fatherland can fall
> With the Burkes and the Decies and the son of Royal James,
> And Talbot, the captain, and Sarsfield above all,
> The beloved of damsels and dames!

Here is a Mangan who is able to express the loyalties, the fervencies, the extravagancies of the Irish folk.

In the definite edition produced by D. J. O'Donoghue about 180 pieces are given. I would not have Mangan represented by more than fifteen poems. And I would not include certain poems that are regarded as noteworthy by Mangan's admirers. I would not include **"The Nameless One"** for I cannot help regard it as anything more than a piece of rhetoric. I would not include **"Kincora"**: reading it after the **"Lament for the Princes of Tyrone and Tyrconnell"** I feel that its movement is monotonous and its characterizations and descriptions purely conventional; if this is a translation of an official poet's lament—MacLiag's—for King Brian, it was originally a purely official piece of work. I would include **"The Testament of Cathaeir Mor"** for this piece is vigorous and picturesque, but not **"A Vision of Connaught in the Thirteenth Century"** for, to my mind, this piece fails after the chiming stanza that opens it. The Irish group in the selection would be **"The Lament for the Princes of Tyrone and Tyrconnell," "Ode to the Maguire," "Dark Rosaleen," "Kathaleen-Ny-Houlahan," "Farewell to Patrick Sarsfield," "The Testament of Cathaeir Mor"**; the German group would include **"Twenty Golden Years Ago," "The Ride Round the Parapet," "I Saw Her Once," "Gone in the Wind"**; there would be **"Siberia,"** and in the Oriental group **"The Howling Song of Al-Mohara," "The Karamanian Exile," "The Time of the Barmecides,"** and the epigram **"To Amine."** It would be a small but a very important collection.

So far I have made no note of the fact that James Clarence Mangan and Edgar Allan Poe were writing at the same time and that both strove for novel effects through repetition and refrain. Mangan had no chance of reading Poe, but Poe had a chance of reading some of Mangan's pieces in *The Dublin University Magazine.* I do not believe that any influence went from one to the other, it can be taken for granted that they arrived at like musical effects in their verse as they arrived at like humourless grotesqueness in their essays, by being likeminded: they were men who were curiously alike in their temperaments and their fortunes. And I have made no reference to the fact that with one exception the fifteen poems I have listed are supposed to be based on originals in other languages. It is undoubtedly true that Mangan's genius was such that it needed a pattern given to it to begin to operate. But it was a genius that could transcend the pattern given; it could make something out of what it operated on that was original in the highest sense, in the sense of bearing the stamp of unique personality. These poems of Mangan's are not translations even though "from the Irish," "from the German," "from the Arabic," "from the Turkish" are written above them. In the case of the Oriental languages, the ascription of a poem to one or the other of them was probably one of Mangan's modes of astonishing mankind. (pp. 32-40)

Padraic Colum, "James Clarence Mangan," in The Dublin Magazine, *Vol. VIII, n.s. No. 2, April-June, 1933, pp. 32-40.*

JAMES KILROY   (essay date 1971)

[In the following excerpt from his study of Mangan's life and literary career, Kilroy focuses on Mangan's original poems and prose writings.]

Mangan's original poems have received less critical attention than his translations, but a number of them deserve careful reevaluation. Like the translations, they are often experimental in technique, and employ a wide range of metrical and stanzaic schemes. In subject matter, they range from humorous extravaganzas to religious and patriotic verse.

Mangan's earliest published poem is **"Genius,"** which he included in the portion of his *Autobiography* that has survived. It is most fascinating as it reveals the talents and attitudes of the poet at age sixteen. Already he saw himself as burdened by his exceptional gifts. He recognized that not all his suffering was imposed by others who misunderstood his sensitive nature; his sorrows, he saw, resulted primarily from his inner "unshared shroudedness of lot." The verse form of the poem is rhymed iambic pentameter and the rhyme scheme is simple and functional, marking off the major divisions of the poem. The first eight lines form one unit, sustained by a clear rhyme

scheme. The next ten lines begin with the same end rhyme and form a second distinct unit. There follows a four-line transitional section with alternating lines of rhyme. And the poem closes with a seven-line section composed of facing rhymed triplets, followed by a strong, final alexandrine. In its total effect, it is a highly polished, clear and forceful poem, particularly when considered as an instance of Mangan's juvenilia.

"The Nameless One," composed in 1842 or thereabouts, is also autobiographical and treats the sufferings of his childhood and his present state. But despite the enormous popularity of this poem, second in that respect only to **"Dark Rosaleen,"** it now seems self-pitying and morbid. His assessment of his own poetry is accurate, at least in describing the bulk of his composition; he calls it "perchance not deep, but intense and rapid." And as a biographical source the poem does convey the horror with which Mangan viewed life and the longing he felt for death.

The taste for the morbid seen in that poem seems to have begun early. In **"Lines, Written at Seventeen,"** which is not included in O'Donoghue's edition of the poetry, Mangan dwells on death in a grim way:

> The sun's rich rays have often thrown
>   A gleam upon the lonely tomb,
> And all without hath brightly shone
>   While all within was ghastly gloom.
>
>   • • • • •
>
> Thus may a transient smile impart
>   Its radiance to the care-worn cheek
> While all within the tomb-like heart
>   Is dark and drear and coldly bleak.

Some of the gloom may be attributed to the cynicism of the very young. But the subject occurs often; **"Rest Only in the Grave"** concludes that neither wealth nor love nor any activity can provide the peace for which he is seeking. Only death can grant it.

This morbid strain is seen in a number of his other original poems. **"The Dying Enthusiast"** expresses the poet's longing for "Prison-bursting death." But the tone of this poem is assertive and the strong rhythm set by opening each line on a stressed syllable does not seem inappropriate. Again, the rhyme of lines of uneven length serves to divide the poem into units, with each stanza leading up to the cry, "Oh! no! no!" for its final line. **"The One Mystery"** also bewails man's state:

> No more, no more—with aching brow
>   And restless heart, and burning brain,
> We ask the When, the Where, the How,
>   And ask in vain.

But the language is unoriginal and the sentiment seems shallow.

In **"A Broken-Hearted Lay"** Mangan expresses his rejection of "the inanity of all things human," and specifies the two things which most plague him in his life: "the dark ingratitude of man" and "the hollower perfidy of woman." He concludes that all that awaits him in his future life are pain, bitterness, "torturing thoughts that will not be forbidden, / And agonies that cannot all be hidden!" In the poem written on the death of Catherine Hayes, a young girl he had once taught, he sees death as a deliverance and "this blank world a prison and a grave." Therefore, he cannot regret that she

A death portrait of Mangan by Sir Frederick W. Burton.

escaped while life still seemed a joy. The concluding stanza of **"Life is the Desert and the Solitude"** serves as a summary of this common theme in Mangan's verse:

> Alas! for those who stand alone—
>   The shrouded few who feel and know
> What none beside have felt and known
>   To all of such a mould below
> Is born an undeparting woe,
>   Beheld by none and shared with none—
> A cankering worm whose work is slow,
>   But gnaws the heart-strings one by one,
> And drains the bosom's blood till the last
>   drop be gone.

Despite the impressive effect achieved by using a much longer line to close each stanza, the diction and sentiments of this poem are unconvincing. Mangan is seen here in his weakest position, and the grief, which was no doubt sincere, and the impression of futility, which is undeniably felt, become shrill and whining when repeated in so many poems.

However, all of the poems quoted on this subject are the products of the 1830s or earlier. In the last ten years of his life, Mangan became more positive, although not optimistic, in his poetry. If he never changed his view of life as an extended torture, he saw his role as a more active one: that of seer or prophet, particularly of Ireland's destiny.

Ireland had been the subject of some of his early poetry also. **"To My Native Land"** appeared in 1832, but it carries no strong conviction, relying as it does on stock images of harps and empty halls. From the 1840s, when he became involved with the Young Ireland group, even though his association was never a close one, his verse becomes more convincingly patriotic and more assertive in other ways as well. (pp. 47-51)

The continued appeal of Mangan's patriotic poems cannot be denied. **"Dark Rosaleen"** and **"The Warning Voice,"** when recited with unashamed gusto, can still send shivers up the spine of even the most apolitical man of the 1970s. Rudi Holzapfel, one of the most talented of the young poets writing in Ireland today, and himself a highly respected Mangan scholar, calls Mangan Ireland's greatest poet, barring none. Clearly it is his patriotic appeal which Holzapfel has in mind when he writes [in "Dangerous Hero," *Hibernia* XXXII]:

> Mangan is a dangerous hero. If you like Synge you can always go to the Aran Islands and curse Manhattan to the roar of the Western Sea; if you like Joyce you get drunk in his Martello Tower and spew it all out at Forty Foot. If you like Yeats you can sit in the shadow of Ben Bulben and read A. Norman Jeffares. But if you like Mangan you start to weep the wrongs and woes of Erin, and you

reach for your pike. That is the difference. It is one hell of a difference.

It is not surprising that Mangan took up the subject of Ireland's sorrows. It would be more remarkable if an Irishman, no matter how alienated from human society, could ignore the horrors of the late 1840s, when famine and several waves of cholera epidemics racked the country. Between 1845 and 1851 approximately a million died and about another million emigrated, so that the population of Ireland was reduced by one-fourth in that short span of time. Those who survived did so only after severe suffering. In the single year 1849 almost one million Irishmen were kept in a workhouse for some period.

"The Warning Voice," one of Mangan's best patriotic poems, was written in 1846, at the start of this bleak period. The pervading rhythm of the poem is anapestic; rhyme is frequent and up to the last stanza the lines are usually only two stresses in length. But the emphasis on fewer words in each line allows the poem to grow in intensity. Textbook descriptions of various metrical effects claim that anapestic verse has the effect of being light and lilting. But the final six lines of this poem show how strong and majestic it can be:

> So, howe'er, as frail men, you have erred
>   Your way along Life's thronged road,
> Shall your consciences prove a sure guerdon
>   And tower of defence,
>   Until Destiny summon you hence
> To the Better Abode!

Leading up to this conclusion, the poem speaks to the people of Ireland, recognizing their causes for sorrow and foreseeing even further hazards ahead, until in the next generation some peace may reign.

The moving effect on modern readers is due to a number of rhetorical techniques and devices, such as the use of direct address, repeated parallel structures and personification. The poem opens with an appeal to the reader:

> Ye Faithful—ye noble!
>   A day is at hand
> Of trial and trouble,
>   And woe in the land!

The parallelism of the first line is echoed in the alliteration of the third. The rhyme is strong: the last accented syllable always has a rhyme within the stanza. But the stanzas progress in length, so that the last of the five stanzas is almost four times as long as the first. By this, as well as by the parallel structures of so many statements, a climax is built up to in the last stanza, which sets forth the message of following the course of virtue. The message is neither explicit nor detailed; a clear course of action is not prescribed; but the cadence of the verse is so strong and the diction is so elevated that its effect is strong nevertheless.

"A Voice of Encouragement—A New Year's Lay" appeared in *The Nation* on January 1, 1848, in the middle of the Famine. The verse form is unusual: primarily dactylic measure with six stresses in each line, an unusually long line. Mangan's awareness of the horror of the Famine is painful to the reader:

> Friends! the gloom in our land, in our once bright land grows deeper.
> Suffering, even to death, in its horriblest forms, aboundeth;

> Thro' our black harvestless fields, the peasants' faint wail resoundeth.
> Hark to it, even now! . . . The nightmare oppressed sleeper
> Gasping and struggling for life, beneath his hideous bestrider,
> Seeth not, dreeth not, sight or terror more fearful or ghastly
> Than that poor paralysed slave! Want, Houselessness, Famine, and lastly
> Death in a thousand-corpsed grave, that momently waxeth wider.

But worse than that, in terms of the future, is the irresponsibility of Ireland's leaders, who have despaired and surrendered their ideals. Nevertheless, Mangan counsels hope and activity. The Carlylean advice of working and fulfilling one's duty reminds us of Mangan's very Victorian attitudes. Like Carlyle and his English contemporaries, Mangan sees himself as a poet-prophet. Once again, the conclusion is not any clearly stated solution. Images of the coming millennium are given, to be heralded by **"The Envoy"**:

> Cloaked in the Hall, the Envoy stands, his mission unspoken,
> While the pale, banquetless guests await in trembling to hear it.

The atmosphere of confusion and suffering which precedes the coming reign of peace and justice prefigures Yeats's poems of his middle period. The scenes described in such poems as "Easter 1916" and "The Second Coming" are not far in tone from those described by Mangan:

> Slavery debased the soul; yea! reverses its primal nature;
> Long were our fathers bowed to the earth with fetters of iron—
> And, alas! we inherit the failings and ills that environ
> Slaves like a dungeon wall and dwarf their original stature.
> Look on your countrymen's failings with less of anger than pity;
> Even with the faults of the evil deal in a manner half tender;
> And like an army encamped before a beleaguered city,
> Earlier or later you must compel your foes to surrender!

Although his political message is not made specific in these poems, Mangan had allied himself with the Young Ireland movement by this time. But by 1849, the group was disbanded and its efforts toward a revolution had failed. Mangan seems disheartened but not yet hopeless in **"Soul and Country,"** which was published during the last year of his life. The previous year of revolutions on the continent gave signs that "a struggling world would yet be free / And live anew." But so far it had not been accomplished, and, in Ireland, prospects were more dim than ever before. The second stanza reads:

> Look round, my soul, and see and say
>   If those about thee understand
>   Their mission here;
> The will to smite—the power to slay—
>   Abound in every heart and hand,
>   Afar, anear.
> But, God! must yet the conqueror's sword
>   Pierce *mind*, as heart, in this proud year?
>   O, dream it not!
> It sounds a false, blaspheming word,
>   Begot and born of mortal fear—
>   And ill-begot.

Much of the power of this stanza, and the entire poem, results from the air of desperation and confusion. Bitter rhetorical questions are asked and answers are attempted. Even the last statement, in which "begot" is repeated, with an ironic twist, well fits the mood of resentment. By now, no political formulae can be found that can solve the immense problems; in the last stanza of the poem, Mangan turns to religious faith as the only possible source of help. But the conclusion is staggering in its force:

> Beseech your God, and bide your hour—
> 　He cannot, will not, long be dumb;
> 　　Even now His tread
> Is heard o'er earth with coming power;
> 　And coming, trust me, it will come,
> 　　Else were He dead!

The force of the last line, with all its desperation, is accumulated partly by its irregular meter. This is probably the strongest, most moving of Mangan's poetic statements.

"A Vision of Connaught in the Thirteenth Century" was written several years earlier, and illustrates a more fanciful side of even his political verse. It describes a dream vision which reminds us of Coleridge's "Kubla Khan" in its odd imagery:

> Then saw I thrones,
> 　And circling fires,
> And a Dome rose near me, as by a spell,
> 　Whence flowed the tones
> 　　Of silver lyres,
> And many voices in wreathed swell;
> 　And their thrilling chime
> 　　Fell on mine ears
> As the heavenly hymn of an angel-band—
> 　"It is now the time,
> 　　These be the years,
> Of Cáhal Mór of the Wine-red Hand!"

The lines are written in accentual verse with two and four stresses in each line, and the rhyme scheme is simple and functional. But the poem is too short; hardly is the scene described, and some premonitions of impending defeat given, when the speaker ends his dream and the poem concludes.

A completely different kind of poem is **"Gasparo Bandollo,"** which is a narrative poem set in Italy. In the *Autobiography* Mangan indicated that his own father had much in common with the title character of this poem. In it, a fugitive Italian patriot, Sevrini, is betrayed by Giambattista, the son of the title character. When the father learns of his son's act, he disowns him and shoots him, while the son kneels before him begging for mercy. At the end, the focus is on Gasparo, who is left suffering and hopeless, not because he did the wrong thing, but because there seems to be nothing left for which to live. The situation reminds us of Matthew Arnold's "Sohrab and Rustum" and, as in that poem, images of water symbolize man's destiny. The poem ends:

> Onwards in power the wide flood rolls
> Whose thunder-waves wake evermore
> The caverned soul of each far shore,
> But when the midnight storm-wind sweeps
> In wrath about its broken deeps,
> What heart but ponders darkly over
> The myriad wrecks those waters cover!
> It is the lonely brook alone
> That winds its way with Music's tone
> 　By orange bower and lily-blossom,
> And sinks into the Parent Wave,

> Not as worn Age into its grave,
> 　But as pure Childhood on God's bosom.

This is a late poem, written in the last few years of his life; it is more restrained in its use of rhyme and rhythm. The relevance of the Italian uprising to Ireland's politics in the late 1840s is evident enough, but it is not belabored in any way. Rather the theme shifts from political concerns to personal loss, and finally to the consolation of religious faith.

Mangan's life was short, and at his death his poetry was at a point of great promise. He wrote a good deal—too much perhaps—and shows remarkable versatility both in subject matter and technique. Experiments in practically every metrical and stanzaic form abound in his work, and the devices of rhetoric as well as of versification are employed in a startling variety of manners. Although his poems of patriotism and his translations have been stressed in this survey, his religious poetry and humorous verse also deserve rereading. Of the latter category, **"A Fast Keeper"** is representative. It plays on a single pun of "Lent," and complains of his loss of some money loaned to his friend Bentley. One other, **"The Metempsychosis,"** based on a poem by Ignaz Castelli, holds a natural fascination for any reader of Joyce's *Ulysses*. But it is also a pure tour de force, playing with rhyme in a manner matched only by Ogden Nash:

> To go on with my catalogue: what will you bet I've seen a
> Goose, that was reckoned in her day a pretty-faced young
> 　woman?
> But more than that, I knew at once a bloody-lipped hyena
> To've been a Russian Marshal, or an ancient Emperor
> 　(Roman)
> All snakes and vipers, toads and reptiles, crocodiles and
> 　crawlers
> I set down as court sycophants or hypocritic bawlers,
> And there I may've been right or wrong—but nothing can
> 　be truer
> Than this, that in a scorpion I beheld a vile reviewer.

"To Joseph Brenan" is one of Mangan's final compositions. It was written within a month of his death, in reply to that poet's tribute to Mangan, published in *The Irishman*. In Brenan's poem Mangan is praised for his delicate use of sound, and for its embodiment of meaning. He is likened to Prospero and to Swedenborg, and is praised in particular as a scholar of German literature. In Mangan's reply, Brenan is compared briefly with Shelley, but then the poem turns to Mangan's defense of his own life. He agrees that he has worked hard at his poetry, despite his own weaknesses. Often he has been close to despair, but he was rescued by his faith. In imagery similar to that of Francis Thompson's "The Hound of Heaven," God is portrayed as tracking him down and saving him from total defeat. For himself, he sees a clear duty: "to live a bard, in thought and feeling . . . to act my rhyme, by self-restraint." (pp. 52-60)

• • • • •

In 1904, D. J. O'Donoghue, Mangan's biographer and the editor of the most comprehensive edition of his poems, published a collection of a dozen of his prose pieces. In his introduction to the volume, O'Donoghue is modest in his claims for the prose: "The reader will hardly expect to find anything so distinguished as in the *Poems*—the magical power which enabled Mangan to rise from height to height of poetical achievement is almost altogether absent." Admittedly, the strong political themes that inspire his best original poetry do not appear in his prose. And it is true that the author's verbal facility is less exercised in the prose than in his best poems. But the prose writings do exhibit their author's broad interests and love of word play, as well as his bizarre sense of humor. So entertaining, in fact, are some of the prose pieces that they do not deserve to be filed away only in an edition so long out of print.

Two of the prose works in O'Donoghue's edition are short stories reminiscent of stories by Gothic novelists, like Charles Maturin or Edgar Allan Poe. They treat the same central subjects that appear in so much of Mangans' work: the alienated man, damned to wander alone because of some demonic curse; the unhappy love affair; and the desperation of a man under heavy debts.

"The Thirty Flasks" centers on a young man, Basil Von Rosenwald, who has lost all his valuables and accumulated huge debts at gambling. To pay off what he owes, Basil is directed by a friend to a mysterious rich man of untold wealth and unknown background. An air of mystery is set as the friend admits that he has sent two others to the man before: one is dead and another has entered a monastery. But Basil does go to the Nabob, despite some misgivings. When he arrives at the house, Basil is shocked by the man's grotesque appearance: he is dwarfish, deformed, hardly human. The Nabob claims to be Basil's own brother who he had understood was dead; but the Nabob tells a story of being kidnapped and sold as a slave. Eventually, he claims, he got to India and spent ten years there studying magic.

Without hesitation, the Nabob offers to give Basil one thousand ducats, providing that for such amount, he will drink a flask of some mysterious and magical potion, the Black Elixir. The result is predicted: each flask he drinks will transfer one inch of his height to the Nabob, who, at three and a half feet, wants to grow to Basil's six foot height. In order to keep off his creditors and to gain the hand of Aurelia Von Elsberg, his beloved, Basil does drink one flask, and suffers what seem to be only momentary effects. After drinking a second flask the next day, he goes into a trance, described as much like an opium dream. But soon the threatened effects become evident: Basil realizes that he is losing inches steadily.

Before he completely loses his identity, that is, after he has taken twenty-nine flasks, Basil discovers that the Nabob is really the Oriental magician Maugraby. At almost the last moment, Basil is saved: he learns from a stranger that he has inherited a huge fortune. The stranger goes with him to see Maugraby, and once there confronts the magician with what he knows. On being discovered, the Nabob uses magic to escape: he blows up house and all, but when the dust settles, Basil is again six feet tall. All ends happily, with Basil and Aurelia married, and the magician still plying his tricks in Alexandria.

However silly the story line is, the plot moves quickly and suspense is well maintained right to the end. But Mangan cannot resist verbal play, even when it detracts from the tone of the story. The money lender dunning Basil is named Herr Grabb and the stranger who confronts Maugraby is called Rubbadub Snooksnacker Slickwitz. The narrative moves along with regular asides and humorous turns:

> He got up and dressed himself and shaved—or shaved and dressed himself, we forget which—and then he actually breakfasted; and if the curious in dietetics are agog to know of what his breakfast consisted we will gratify them:—it consisted of one

colossal roll and butter, two hen eggs, three slices of Westphalia ham, and four cups of Arabian coffee—a breakfast we undertake to recommend to themselves, the curious aforesaid. After he had finished his last cup, it is a fact that he drew his chair to the fire and deposited his toes on the fender; and, settled in that position, began to pick his teeth and think of Aurelia.

More serious and more remarkable for its biographical relevance is the story entitled **"The Man in the Cloak."** Mangan himself used that appellation as the author of **"My Bugle and How I Blow It,"** and in that essay analyzed the implications of each important word in the phrase. Autobiographical associations occur in this story also, although they are oblique.

The story opens with a scene of Johann Klaus Braunbrock, a bank cashier, forging a draft as part of his embezzlement plan. He is interrupted by a stranger who demands that a check in his name be cashed; he signs the check merely "M.— The Man in the Cloak." As the plot proceeds, the title character reappears several times; each time he reveals that he knows more about the crime Braunbrock is committing. His identity is never revealed, except for his initial, "M," and the fact that he is an Irishman. He indicates that he knows all and can do anything, but, he says, "I cannot conquer my own destiny." Frequent allusions to the devil and demons are made, and his damned state becomes evident.

Once he has stolen the money, Braunbrock has planned to elope with the woman he loves, Livonia. But when he visits her it is revealed that she loves someone else and feels only contempt for the bank clerk. He takes her to the theatre, where the Man in the Cloak again confronts him, and accuses him of forgery. To show what lies ahead, the stranger magically portrays Braunbrock's crime on the stage; there, after stealing the money, Braunbrock is shown apprehended and imprisoned. It is all a vision created by the mysterious stranger, but it has the intended effect: Braunbrock makes some sort of a secret pact with the Man in the Cloak. Immediately, police arrive, arrest the stranger for Braunbrock's crimes, and take him away. However, when they arrive at the police station, the body they had tied up and taken has become only a scarecrow made of a pile of straw, rags, and a pumpkin.

As a result of the secret agreement, Braunbrock himself becomes the Man in the Cloak. He turns on Livonia, discovers her lover in a closet, and predicts that man's capture for his recent treasonous activities. He is vicious in denouncing the faithless, deceiving woman he had loved. But left alone, Braunbrock is seen to have inherited nearly limitless powers and wealth. Predictably, all pleasure soon palls as he becomes more aware of his damned state.

Like his predecessor, he must find a victim who will release him from the curse and take it on himself. One night he has a dream about the man from whom he inherited his title and his doom; he sees him in the Church of St. Sulpice at Paris. He leaves immediately for that place, but when he arrives he finds that the man he is looking for is now dead; a priest tells him that the man's name was . . . Melmoth. After wandering through his miserable life, that man had died penitent and forgiven.

The priest convinces Braunbrock also to pray, which he does, and feels great relief. But the curse is not lifted until he meets Malaventure, a Persian, who agrees to sell his soul, and take on the curse. After this, the talisman of the curse changes hands several times and, it is reported, its progress may have stopped in one man's suicide in the Seine.

That Mangan associated the cursed wanderer with himself is apparent from his descriptions and the force with which he describes that doomed state:

> The enormous nature of his power only made him acquainted with the essential desolation of heart which flows from being alone in the universe and unsympathized with by others. The relations that had existed between his finer faculties and the external world gradually suffered an awful and indescribable change. Like his predecessor, he could in an instant transport himself into the blooming valleys of the East, or the swarthy deserts of Africa; the treasures of the earth were his, and the ocean bared her deeps, teeming with gold and lustrous jewels, before him. But the transitions and vicissitudes by which mortals are taught to appreciate pain and pleasure, and the current of life is guaranteed from stagnating, were lost to him.

As in the previous story, however, Mangan cannot resist puns, and succumbs to one even at one of the most dramatic moments in the story. Braunbrock is challenged to a duel by Livonia's lover:

> "Draw this instant, I say!"
>
> "You would have better success in calling on me for a song; though we are in a drawing room . . . I have never learned to draw, though singing and dancing are very much in my way,—favorite amusements of mine."

Most remarkable about this story is the real artistry of the narrative technique. The story opens with a scene of activity diminishing and narrowing to the scene of Braunbrock alone in his "temporary prison," nervously perpetrating the forgery. Throughout the tale only the scenes of most striking action are presented, while much is left unsaid. The central issue of the diabolic contract is not fully revealed until the end of the story, and even then there are details which mystify, such as the final passage. After finishing the story, Mangan adds a newspaper account of an astrologer inquiring about the suicide which ended the main plot. This eccentric German attempts to analyse the action in terms of astrology and the mystical theories of Jakob Boehme, the sixteenth-century German philosopher. However, his interpretations are only laughed at, and he leaves. Rather than merely being appended to the story, the astrological reference seems to add a comment on the whole mystery, since the German remarks on Jupiter being an arch-demon, and somehow determining what has occurred. All elements of the story: the fantastic, the mysterious, the autobiographical and the humorous aspects blend to form a single memorable work.

In forms other than short stories, Mangan wrote on a wide variety of subjects. His affinities to German writers of his day are evident in his essay, **"Chapters on Ghostcraft,"** in which he discusses the issues arising from Justinus Kerner's books on the Ghost Seeress of Prevorst and similar books on the Supernatural. However sincerely Mangan was interested in the subject, his treatment of it in this essay is playful and ironic. He comments on the spreading refutation of non-belief in ghosts, "incredulism," and quotes extensively from the amazing or amusing ghost stories recounted by "Madame Hauffer, High Priestess of Mysticism." In his playful manner, as well as in the sincerity of some parts of the essay, Mangan here

reminds us of Carlyle in *Sartor Resartus*. Like Carlyle's editor, the narrator of this essay addresses his audience as "spectacled reader," talks to him as an equal about a variety of the most esoteric subjects, and yet speaks with a moralizing, almost evangelistic fervor about following certain ethical rules. A paragraph from the conclusion illustrates some of these parallels:

> Perpend and ponder this well, ye whose knowledge of "many exterior matters," as the mystery of punch-mixing and the like, is at present your sole boast and glory! Ah! think upon the Purgatorial Realm, wherein is no punch; wherein what spirits there are must perforce form an amalgam, not with sugar and hot water, but with phosphorus and hot sulphur! And consider, while consider you may, whether it may not be worth making some slight sacrifice of the comforts of your Soulish Man here, to escape from the necessity of being hereafter condemned to wander in the shape of your Ghostial Man, to and fro in miserable darkness, helpless, restless, guideless; with that *Accusing Numeral* for ever before your eyes, and legions of black and darkest-grey spectres for ever making mockery of your most forlorn and doloriferous condition!

"The Three Half Crowns" is a review of a sonnet sequence written by Gian Battista Casti on the subject of his debt in that amount. In his review, Mangan quotes with enthusiasm a series of the sonnets covering the author's growing mania as his creditor duns him for this insignificant debt. Although an English translation of "I Tré Giuli" by Montagu Montagu had been published in London in 1826 and reappeared in 1841, Mangan has made up his own versions, and the review becomes simply a tour de force, in which Mangan quotes twenty-two sonnets, each one having a different rhyme scheme, except for three perfect Italian sonnets. Playful as the subject and his treatment of it are, there is no doubt that the sorrows of the debtor would have had some personal significance for Mangan, who was only rarely out of debt.

The most characteristic prose work by Mangan is the pastiche, **"A Sixty-Drop Dose of Laudanum,"** that series of sixty aphorisms, parables and jokes which reveal the lively mind of Mangan. Here, as in his poetry, humor and incisive portrayals of human nature are blended in a loose but always amusing work. Because Mangan's prose works are so long out of print, as well as for the pleasure, the quotation of a few of them is in order:

> If you desire to padlock a punster's lips never tell him that you loathe puns: he would then perpetrate his atrocities for the sake of annoying you. Choose another course: always affect to misunderstand him. When an excruciator has been inflicted on you, open wide your eyes and mouth for a minute, and then, closing them again abruptly, shake your head, and exclaim, "Very mysterious!" This kills him.

> • • • • •

> The most opaque of all the masques that people assume to conceal their real characters is enthusiasm. In the eyes of women enthusiasm appears so amiable that they believe no imposter *could* counterfeit it: to men it seems so ridiculous that they are satisfied nobody *would*.

> • • • • •

No neglect, no slight, no contumely from one of his own sex can mortify a man who has been much flattered and courted by women. No matter from what source it may emanate, he will always and necessarily attribute it to envy.

• • • • •

Writing a poem for the sake of developing a metaphysical theory, is like kindling a fire for the sake of the smoke.

Mangan's prose now seems very much the product of its time; in its stylistic peculiarities, its mixture of wild humor with mysterious happenings, and particularly in its insistent moral tone, the prose reminds us of Carlyle's *Sartor Resartus*. Like his Scottish contemporary, Mangan shows a keen perception of human folly and social injustice. Of course, the Irish writer is more playful and less systematic in his exposition, and he has left no major work of prose comparable to so many of Carlyle's.

One composition in prose does rank with the best of his poetry: his **Autobiography,** which is, unfortunately, incomplete. But in that work, Mangan's skill as a prose writer is undeniable: he evokes vivid pictures and expresses strong convictions in an unusual but haunting style. The account of his early years there presented is as artistic as any of his lyric poems, and the conviction of his own doom, as well as the equally strong belief in God's providence, unifies even the autobiographical fragment so that it becomes more than merely a source of biographical information, but an integral and artistic work.

No more extended summary of the significance of the life and writings of James Clarence Mangan is needed than the tributes printed in *The Nation* shortly after his death:

> He has faults, which he who runs may read, mannerism, grotesque, and an indomitable love of jingling; he often sins against simplicity, but the inexpiable sin of commonplace no man can lay to his charge.

• • • • •

> It is enough . . . to say that Mangan, a man of great gifts and great attainments, lived a pauper and a drudge, and died in a hospital. To most he was but a voice which has now ceased for ever. . . . To death he had long looked forward.

(pp. 61-71)

James Kilroy, in his James Clarence Mangan, *Bucknell University Press, 1971, 74 p.*

ANTHONY CRONIN   (essay date 1973)

[*In the following excerpt from his preface to* Selected Poems, *Cronin identifies Mangan as a modern poet.*]

Some twenty years or so after James Clarence Mangan's death, the young Arthur Rimbaud, who, of course, had never heard of him, invented the notion of the poet as *maudit,* "accursed." Suffering was an essential part of his role, and it was actually necessary for the poet to deliberately become *"le grand malade, le grand criminal, le grand maudit."* Part of the concept, subsequently developed by Verlaine, and adopted, consciously or otherwise, by many poets, (the otherwise often leading to strange results) was that of the poet as scape-

goat, who, by sin and circumstance, getting himself into trouble and generally bashed around, atoned in some way for the sins and hypocrisies of society. It was primarily related to the obvious hypocrisies of bourgeois society, which was felt by both parties to the contract to be deeply in need of such an animal as a scapegoat. One says both parties for, of course, society gleefully, if inchoately, adopted the idea.

Thus, every country has its sacrificial poets. France has Baudelaire, Verlaine, and Rimbaud himself. America got off to a good start with Edgar Allan Poe and kept it up with Hart Crane and others. If the major English poets of the nineteenth century were far too disposed towards comfort to accept the role of scapegoat, in the nineties a whole generation, including Ernest Dowson, Lionel Johnson and Oscar Wilde cheerfully rushed in to supply a long-felt want. (p. 11)

And Ireland? Well, Ireland has James Clarence Mangan; and, though the poet himself frequently waved aside the proffered purple, Patrick Kavanagh. The late Brendan Behan somewhat incongruously tried to get in on this act too. The role as such is not in fact a dishonourable one, and the idea has much to commend it. It was invented by a considerable fellow and poets understand it. Of course, suffering is not enough. As has often been made clear, anybody who has money enough to go out and collect a hangover, or get himself muddled up sexually, can do the suffering. Still, there is some sort of necessity in the thing, a religious necessity felt by the poets, whatever about society's motives. They are, I suppose one could demonstrate, a perfect perversion of certain religious feelings. And the idea of poet as *maudit* is also a modern one, related to the industrial revolution, materialism, progress and, of course, to the loss by the poet of his true, or at least his old, role. To make the claim for Mangan that he partially at least knew what it was all about, is to suggest that he was a modern poet.

He has, of course, been ill served by the anthologists, all of them content to take in each other's washing. The representation of Mangan in Irish anthologies would seem extraordinarily repetitive, except that everything in Irish anthologies seems so. **"My Dark Rosaleen,"** whatever else one thinks of it, is not a modern poem: that is to say it does not relate to any experience realised by anybody walking the streets today. A product of two romanticisms, the literary one and the nationalist one, it is a fair old performance of a kind, but anybody who thinks of Ireland as a maiden, "a saint of saints," making "sweet and sad complaints," whose "holy delicate white hands" will "girdle him with steel," wants to have the general mechanism of his sensibility examined.

Nor is Mangan well served by his own prolixity and general indeterminacy of purpose and style. Yeats pointed out quite properly that the establishment of a style, even though it might vary at periods of the poet's life, was half the battle. He also remarked rather sadly on the fact that it is possible to bring to birth in verse only a very small amount of one's personality. Mangan seems most of the time not to be making any attempt to bring the whole man in. Part of the trouble here is that he was in fact early in the game with a specifically modern notion: that of operating behind masks and personae. All those fake or partial translations, the pretence that poems were from the Ottoman, the Turkish, the Persian, the Arabic, the German, the Irish even (of which he knew very little) may be seen as a rudimentary attempt to use the mask in what is really quite a modern way: the way it is used in "Homage to Sextus Propertius," etc.

At least once he used it superbly. **"Twenty Golden Years Ago,"** attributed to the non-existent Selber, in other words the self, is an astonishingly modern poem and it establishes Mangan at once as a contemporary whose pain and remorse we can understand. The circumstances are not his but they are real. The imagery is urban; there are no stock properties; no grots, vales or bowers, and nothing, from the coffee in the cup onwards, is too mundane to be worthy of inclusion. The tone is kept low deliberately; the self-mockery is unindulgent and bitterly ironic, in fact we might almost be in the country of Laforgue, Corbiere and the Eliot of "Prufrock"; there is no romantic agony, but there is a real agony all the same; and it jumps out of the pages that surround it in poor Mangan's works.

He wrote really a great many more good poems than the anthologists seem to be aware of, but only once did he equal this. **"The Nameless One"** seems to me to be the only occasion on which he drops the masks entirely, including the romantic masks, Byronic and otherwise, that the poor fellow, in his general weakness of poetic will, perhaps did not know he was adopting. It might be thought to begin badly with the rhetorical apostrophe to the song to "roll forth . . . Like a rushing river," etcetera, but the rhythm, even if it is only a slight variation on stock rhythms, is altogether Mangan's own. Here is the personal rhythm that is the sure mark of the genuine article. The tone is rhetorical, but it is extraordinary how mundane circumstance prevails at the same time. He admits to the drink, "gulf and grave of Maginn and Burns"; he tells us his age and condition, "old and hoary at thirty-nine"; and he tells us what his life is like: "want and sickness and houseless nights." There is nothing rarer in poetry than a successful cry from the whole encircumstanced heart. This is one.

These two poems seem to me to be not only the first two modern poems written in Ireland in the English language, but among the first in that language anywhere. For once Mangan gets his real agony on paper and it is a modern agony. It is extraordinary that they should have been written in the eighteen forties. Between the drink and the opium and a hideous romantic love of despair, poor Mangan brought a lot on himself, and he rarely succeeded in bringing that self to poetic birth. The suffering in **"The Nameless One"** has a terrible intensity. He was, if the concept has any truth in it, *maudit* all right. (pp. 11-13)

> Anthony Cronin, in a foreword to Selected Poems of
> James Clarence Mangan, *edited by Michael Smith,
> Gallery Press, 1973, pp. 11-13.*

DIANE E. BESSAI (essay date 1975)

[*Bessai traces the development of imagery and political allegory in successive versions of "Dark Rosaleen."*]

There is persistent belief that the patriotic poems which name Ireland allegorically as Roisin Dubh or any of its English variations such as Little Black Rose or Dark Rosaleen, draw on a centuries-old tradition of mystical association of Éire with rose symbolism. While there is certainly an ancient literary formula for personifying the nation in a variety of feminine forms, this particular version bears close examination because, contrary to the common assumption, it appears to have been grafted on that tradition at a relatively modern stage in the development of this type of nationalistic verse.

Actually the rose as a symbol of Ireland is primarily an Anglo-Irish development, although it corresponds to the truly ancient habit of mind cited by T. F. O'Rahilly, [in his "On the Origin of the Names Érainin and Ériu," 1943] as surviving from "the idea of Ireland as a woman wedded to her rightful king." As O'Rahilly also notes, the figure of Éire varies over the centuries in accordance with the vicissitudes of Irish history, ranging from spouse, to widow, even to harlot in dalliance with foreigners. With the Jacobite sympathies in the 18th century, Éire becomes a mournful, would-be bride awaiting marriage to a Stuart exile, a version of the allegorical convention notably characteristic of the popular *aisling* or visionary poem of that era. Many of these, as well as others of a similar patriotic nature, become generally available to English speakers through the translations provided in Hardiman's *Irish Minstrelsy* (1831), Walsh's *Irish Popular Songs* (1847), and Daly's *Poets and Poetry of Munster* (1849).

James Clarence Mangan is the translator-poet perhaps most responsible for the transmission of this Irish convention into English. In his translations for Daly and others, he covered the whole range, of "secret name" verse—"treasonous" sentiments disguised allegorically—with his renditions of songs and *aislingi* that personify Éire by such names as Kathleen O'Holahan, Moirin O'Cullinan, Celia O'Gara, and Little Black Rose. His **"Dark Rosaleen,"** in particular, became the classic expression in the English of Irish sorrow and hope. He called it a translation of a presumably 17th-century original said to celebrate the heroic loyalties to Ireland of Red Hugh O'Donnell in the Nine Year's war against the forces of Elizabeth I. In keeping with this hint, the modern anthologist Kathleen Hoagland, in fact, attributes the Irish poem specifically to Owen Roe Mac Ward, last bard of the O'Donnells. While the looseness of Mangan's translation has often been noted by editors and commentators, the assumption has been usually made that the convention he uses of representing Éire in the figure of the black rose is of some antiquity. Many have used the image since Mangan—de Vere, Carbery, Pearse, Plunkett and Yeats—on that same assumption. In the process Rosaleen, or Little Black Rose, has indeed become a standard allegorical representation of Éire.

The causes for the development of this synthetic dimension to the tradition seem to be rooted in several factors. The overriding one is the traditional habit of mind, as noted by O'Rahilly, that has conditioned editors, poets, and translators alike into assuming a rose mythology, and thereby contributing to it. Another rests in the freedom and poetic license inherent in translation itself, particularly under the influence of the nationalist climate of 19th-century Ireland, which was both political and literary, and led to the self-conscious assimilation of native subject matter and forms. A third, more specific factor lies in the practice of song-writers borrowing old airs for new words, thereby transmitting the names of older songs to new ones of a patriotic nature. Taking all these considerations into account, this study attempts to unravel the convoluted history of the Little Black Rose. The first phase centers on the role of Mangan and his amazing power to combine traditional and contemporary forms and sentiments in the poem **"Dark Rosaleen."** (pp. 62-3)

The original poem from which Mangan claimed to have translated **"Dark Rosaleen"** was entitled "Roisin Dubh." This seemingly simple fact, however, is much complicated by the number of extant variants of the poem that in turn may be responsible for the variety of confusing editorial and critical comment on the subject. Yet Mangan himself did as much as any one to spread the confusion. In a note accompanying his poem's initial publication in *The Nation* (May 30, 1846) he represents **"Dark Rosaleen"** as "translated from the Irish" from an original which

> purports to be an allegorical address from Hugh to Ireland on the subject of his love and struggles for her, and his resolve to raise her again to the glorious position she held as a nation before the irruption of the Saxon and Norman spoilers.

The source for Mangan's information is most likely James Hardiman's allegorical interpretation in a note to the Irish and English "Roisin Dubh" included in *Irish Minstrelsy* (1831). Although Hardiman placed the poem in a section of the collection entitled "Sentimental Song" he expressed the belief that the text was a forgotten allegory that expressed "strong political feelings" as "a personal address from a lover to his fair one," although now it clearly was or had become a "plaintive love ditty." Hardiman continues:

> It was composed in the reign of Elizabeth of England, to celebrate our Irish hero, *Hugh Ruadh O'Donnell,* of Tyrconnell. The toils and sufferings of the patriot soldier, are throughout described as the cares and feelings of an anxious lover addressing the object of his affection. The song concludes with a bold declaration of the dreadful struggle which would be made before the country should be surrendered to the embraces of our hero's hated and implacable rival.

Hardiman's translator, Thomas Furlong, whose English version appears occasionally in collections of Irish verse to this day, is somewhat ambivalent in his rendition. He seems to be trying to achieve a satisfactory balance between wistful love poem and the buried allegory supposedly inherent in it. While Mangan's Irish source for **"Dark Rosaleen"** is the same text, the two English versions are only generally comparable. Mangan shows none of Furlong's equivocation. His poem is without question a strong expression of the patriot-lover's passionate avowals to the beloved nation in the anticipation of violent upheaval. In other words, there seems a strong possibility that, in their own ways, both Hardiman and Mangan were responsible for creating, rather than recovering, a political allegory out of this particular text, so leaving Furlong somewhere in the middle, not quite sure which direction to take.

An important phase in this allegorizing process occurred, paradoxically, when Samuel Ferguson published his series of critiques of Hardiman in *The Dublin University Magazine* in 1834. Ferguson was convinced that Hardiman and his translators were motivated by a combination of Irish-Catholic bigotry and a specious sense of literary decorum. Deploring the English renditions, Ferguson included in his essays a number of his own carefully literal translations for the benefit of the non-Irish reader. "Roisin Dubh" was one such of these and this was to become the specific source for Mangan's **"Dark Rosaleen."** This is deeply ironic insofar as Ferguson made this particular translation in order to refute Hardiman's editorial claim about the political significance of the poem. He dismisses the Red Hugh associations as charming fantasy. According to his interpretation, the poem is not about a patriot's devotion to his country at all, but about a priest who is overcome with desire for a girl described as black-haired Rose. He is now awaiting some sort of dispensation from

Rome so that he might enjoy his love to the full. As Ferguson translates and explains the poem, it is one of several examples he finds in the song tradition expressing the typical Irish lover's consuming passion, "be he priest or parson, layman or divine." Ferguson sees a "bold priest" who "would neither shun his pleasure nor despair of getting pardon for his sin." The precise context of his discussion—and perhaps the hint for a reading of the poem which would seem outrageous at the time—is the examination of "The Maid of Ballyhaunis," attributed to a Father Costello who also has a lady love. Ferguson translates this poem with some relish, since Hardiman's sense of Irish decorum permitted him to give the Irish text only, and includes a note that Costello left the country "to avoid the object of his sinful passion." Protestant Ferguson rather admires Roisin's lover for wanting it both ways.

It is not necessary to accept Ferguson's interpretation absolutely to see that he raised, nevertheless, some grave doubts about the poem's originally being a patriotic allegory. Before examining Mangan's case for following and, indeed, extending Hardiman's interpretation, and at the same time using Ferguson's love-poem translation, it is useful to compare the English texts of Furlong and Ferguson as a telling indication of the first stage in the allegorization process permitted by the license of translation. In some sense Furlong gave Mangan the precedent for his endeavor, if not the English text. To begin with, Furlong's translation compared to Ferguson's is emotionally underplayed, partly perhaps for the sake of literary decorum, but most particularly because Furlong was supposedly working on a chastely impassioned address to the beloved Éire in the guise of a love song. On the other hand, Ferguson's is a frank presentation of an anguished commitment to an unrequited love, as indicated for example, in stanza three:

> You have killed me my fair one: and may you suffer dearly for it!
> And my soul within is in love for you, and that neither of yesterday nor today:
> You left me weak and feeble in aspect and in form:
> Do not discard me, and I pining for you, my Roiseen dubh.

Furlong writes more lyrically, but conventionally. He still maintains the idea of an unfulfilled love, but in languishing rather than passionate tones:

> Though wearied, oh! my fair one! do not slight my song,
> For my heart dearly loves thee, and hath loved thee long;
> In sadness and in sorrow, I still shall be true.
> And cling with wild fondness around my Roisin Dubh.

Ferguson's idea of the dispensation is puzzling perhaps, but a certain plausibility emerges with his version of the first stanza as,

> O rose bud, let there not be sorrow on account of what happened to you:
> The friars are coming over the sea, and they are moving on the ocean:
> Your pardon will come from the pope and from Rome in the East,
> And spare not the Spanish wine on my Roiseen dubh.

Since Hardiman did not attribute any special meaning to "friars," "pope," "Rome" and "Spanish wine," Furlong, if anything, deemphasizes them:

> Oh! my sweet little rose, cease to pine for the past,
> For the friends that came eastward shall see thee at last;

They bring blessings and favours the past never knew,
To pour forth in gladness on my Roisin Dubh.

Indeed, it may well have been Mangan who first divined an allegorical significance to these supposed allusions. He makes his own point about them in a further passage of his note to **"Dark Rosaleen"** in *The Nation:*

> The true character and meaning of the figurative allusions with which it abounds, and to two only of which I need refer here—viz., the "Roman wine" and "Spanish ale" mentioned in the first stanza—the intelligent reader will, of course, find no difficulty understanding.
>
> (pp. 64-7)

Although for a number of years before **"Dark Rosaleen"** Mangan had been publishing poems from the Irish, it is not generally accepted that his knowledge of the Irish language was very great. His most authoritative biographer, D. J. O'Donoghue, believes that it was sometime in 1846 before Mangan began the study seriously. His method of translation was to rely on literal renditions provided through his association with such scholars as O'Donovan and O'Curry. For what became the posthumous *Poets and Poetry of Munster,* O'Donoghue states that Mangan worked from time to time for small sums of money on prose versions provided by John Daly, the book's editor and publisher. O'Donoghue views these as still in "more or less prosaic form" as "mere drafts for future consideration," perhaps accounting for the fact that none of the poems appeared in Mangan's lifetime. Given their method of rendition, it is almost certain that they precede **"Dark Rosaleen"** and the period when Mangan began working more directly from the Irish. Two of the translations of the Munster poems have specific bearing on the present study because they indicate Mangan's familiarity with other variants of the Roisin tradition. Also, combined with Daly's editorial notes, which Mangan may or may not have seen, they cast an interesting light on the evolution of the Roisin complex as it enters Anglo-Irish literature.

The first is entitled **"Ros Gheal Dubh"** ("Black-Haired Fair Rose"), and is accompanied with a brief note on its title, which "is supposed to be one of these names which Ireland is known in the language of allegory." Its third stanza more than echoes stanza one of the Hardiman-Furlong text with its supposedly allegorical references to help coming from abroad. In Mangan's words:

> O, Roisin mine! droop not nor pine, look out so dull!
> The Pope from Rome hath sent thee home a pardon full!
> The priests are near: O! never fear! from Heaven above
> They come to thee—they come to free my *Roisin Dubh!*

Also, the last stanzas of both easily suggest political meaning by their prophecy of universal violence for her protection, if necessary. But the stanza of **"Ros Gheal Dubh"** that least of all sustains an allegorical interpretation, and is unparalleled in "Roisin Dubh," is the second:

> My friends! my prayers for marts and fairs are these
>   alone—
> That buyers haste home ere evening come, and sun be
>   gone;
> For, doors, bolts, all, will yield and fall, where picklocks
>   move—
> And faith the Clerk may seize i' the dark, my *Roisin Dubh!*

Mangan's rendition of these lines indicates the strain of his attempt to generalize into allegory, a problem recalling of

Furlong's problem with "Roisin Dubh." This becomes evident when comparing them to a more precise rendering by Edward Walsh, in *Irish Popular Songs* (1847), who, while believing implicitly in the allegorical significance of this variant, did not gloss over its anomalous details in support of that belief:

> If to the fair you would repair
> To sell your flocks,
> I pray secure your every door
> With bolts and locks;
> Nor linger late from the guarded gate,
> When abroad you rove,
> Or the clerk will play through the live-long day,
> With *Ros geal dubh!*

The second variant printed by Daly, interestingly enough, needs no glossing over to make it allegory. It has all the obvious characteristics of this mode in popular patriotic verse, although is perhaps a little more specific in content than most. Its title is **"Roisin Dubh,"** but it has no other resemblance to Hardiman's text. (pp. 69-71)

Yet the first variant [Daly] prints is more clearly a song that could be "now known by the peasantry merely as a love song," as Hardiman had claimed for his variant. It is possible to speculate that Daly's second variant, which is clearly allegory, was written by a poet who was not reviving a tradition, but unwittingly laying the basis for the development of one. How this happened could be very simply explained by the fact that, according to musicologist Donal O'Sullivan, patriotic songs take their name for Ireland from the name and air of older love songs. At the initial stage of adoption, the name itself is an indication of the air to which the new patriotic song is to be sung. Eventually the name becomes incorporated into new variants and becomes a new version of the personification of Éire. One might speculate that Hardiman knew of such a poem as Daly was later to print because undoubtedly the transmission of the name Roisin through the air to a patriotic version had already taken place by the time of *Irish Minstrelsy.* He may therefore have assumed that his text, perhaps chosen because it is a far better poem, was of the same patriotic convention. Thus, his translator Thomas Furlong can be seen attempting to make a love poem into as much of an allegorical poem as he could with the text and editorial ideas he had at hand.

Donal O'Sullivan's general theory of this process helps to account for the romantic intensity of the patriotic invocation to the beloved nation, as well as the wide variety of names by which she is addressed. However, by no means does it discount the force of O'Rahilly's point about the traditional habit of mind in which the ancient convention of allegorizing Éire is rooted. The process outlined above helps to determine the particular form the allegorical figure takes. In this case, deriving from Roisin love-song traditions, she becomes the beautiful sorrowing object of dedicated but unrequited love, a creature beset by enemies from which the lover hopes to rescue her.

In the more formalized *aisling,* current in the 18th century, in which by the same process Éire has also often acquired the various "secret names," the relationship between beloved and admirer is somewhat more restrained. The poet is presented as either wandering sadly about the countryside, or awakening from a deep sleep, when suddenly he beholds the appearance of a goddess-like creature who tells him of her lamentable condition. He is awed by her amazing beauty which he elaborately describes, as for example in the following passage from Timothy O'Sullivan's "Sighile ni Gara," as Mangan translated in *Poets and Poetry of Munster:*

> Her eyes, like twin stars, shone and sparkled with lustre;
> Her tresses hung waving in many a cluster,
> And swept the long grass all around and beneath her;
> She moved like a being who trod upon ether,
> And seemed to disdain the dominions of space—
> Such beauty and majesty, glory and grace,

In **"The Vision of Conor O'Sullivan"** the dreamer is struck into an attitude of adoration at the sight of her:

> Bowing down now, before her so lowly,
> With words that came trembling and slowly,
> I ask'd what her name was, and where I might worship
> At the shrine of a being so holy!

Seldom does he express personal aspiration for her love, but rather expresses a fervent hope for the restoration of her glory with the return of her Jacobite lord. In two notable examples her supernatural qualities are pronounced. In the early "Brightness of the Bright" ("Gil na Gil") by Eoghan O'Rahilly, and "A Vision of Ireland" by John Claragh Mac-Donnell, she has the aspect of a fairy woman who leads the poet to the strange confines of her otherworld home for the recital of her afflictions. That Mangan was thoroughly familiar with the *aisling* form is evident from the variety of such poems he translated, not only for Daly, but for the various periodicals in which he published during his life-time. **"The Dream of John Macdonnell,"** for example, appeared in *The Nation* a fortnight previous to **"Dark Rosaleen."** In a careful examination of **"Dark Rosaleen"** itself, it becomes apparent that elements of the conventions of the *aisling* as well as the patriotic love-poem had their influences on that composition.

First of all, it may be pointed out, however, that Mangan's poem satisfies Hardiman's editorial requirements for a patriotic Roisin love-poem very well. Drawing rather freely on Ferguson's literal translation of Hardiman's text, and deliberately ignoring Ferguson's interpretation, it becomes, in O'Donoghue's words "a transformation of an undoubtedly good love-song into a much finer and grander poem—a national apotheosis. It is to all intents and purposes an original poem." Thus, in a comparison to Ferguson's translation, he says:

> Now, Mangan's **"Dark Rosaleen"** has only a remote resemblance to the literal version just quoted. To be sure, he mentions the Erne, and the plough, and the Pope and the Spanish ale; but what splendid use he makes of them! Mangan's poem is an allegory—Dark Rosaleen being Ireland, the priests and foreign auxiliaries coming to her aid, and the wine and Spanish ale allusions to the weapons and other expected assistance from Spain and Italy.

Imogen Guiney, in her Mangan study of the same year [see excerpt dated 1897], made the questionable judgment, repeated several times by writers since, that the two earlier Roisin translations for Daly are directly related to the making of **"Dark Rosaleen."** After quoting parts only of the translation of **"Ros Gheal Dubh,"** she writes,

> The theme had taken hold of Mangan's imagination. Last of all, in 1845, or after, with the right mood of selection upon him, and with the warm consciousness at heart of the docility of the one style he had made his own, the poet fused together

the best in the Roisin ballads, and broke into the inebriating music of **"My Dark Rosaleen."**

This is somewhat misleading. The only influence of these two texts discernable is of a very general nature. There are certain elements in common between the Hardiman "Roisin Dubh" and **"Ros Gheal Dubh."** These in turn are, of course, found in **"Dark Rosaleen."** The curious second stanza of **"Ros Gheal Dubh,"** however, is conveniently omitted by Guiney in making her point. Clearly the allegorical version of "Roisin Dubh" offers Mangan nothing specific beyond the obvious justification for a tradition of nationalist sentiments. Indeed, it was Ferguson who supplied the essentials for **"Dark Rosaleen."** There is enough similarity between his literal version and the new poem to indicate that Mangan referred in some way to the poetic ideas of the former in a fairly orderly manner, except to reverse the order of stanzas four and five. Like Furlong, but without Furlong's ambivalence between love poem and allegory, he took what he wanted, modified what he pleased, and left what was of no poetic use to him. His motives were unashamedly nationalistic, as his interest in the Young Ireland movement in these years might well indicate. He made his note to accompany the first publication of the poem into a key for an interpretation that, in respect to the Rome and Spanish references, went further than even Hardiman's suggestion for allegory. Thus the poem begins:

> O my Dark Rosaleen
> Do not sigh, do not weep!
> The priests are on the ocean green,
> They march along the Deep.
> There's wine . . . from the royal Pope,
> Upon the ocean green;
> And spanish ale shall give you hope,
> My Dark Rosaleen!

The problematic "pardon" emphasized by Ferguson is transformed into the less ambiguous "wine," and the drinking of "spanish ale" signifies the "hope" of the nation rather than the anticipated celebration of two lovers free to enjoy their love.

However, these allegorized details in themselves do not account for the peculiar power of the poem. For generations readers have responded to the figure of Dark Rosaleen as embodying the sorrow of Éire and the selfless devotion of her loyal adherents in their most moving and traditional form. Nor is this accountable to some nebulous fusing of the best of the Roisin songs, as Guiney and others have thought. The force of **"Dark Rosaleen"** rests in the remarkable assimilation of the love-poem features of the original Irish text and a number of elements from the *aisling* convention that Mangan knew well. The love-poem structure avoids the rhetorical unreality of the *aisling* poet's formulaic expression of adoration, transformed here as it is into intimate feeling. The beloved herself is no longer the merely conventional challenge to the decorative writing that characterizes the typical *aisling,* although Dark Rosaleen is elevated to the same spiritualized conception as that visionary figure. The wistful longings of Penal times with their unreal focus on the Jacobite hope are redirected to emphasize the willing martyrdom of the patriot-poet himself for the salvation of his beloved. Even the deference to Rome and Spain is a token only.

The patriot-lover of **"Dark Rosaleen"** speaks, in stanza two, of a passionate, dream-like journey taken on behalf of the beloved:

Over hills and thro dales,
Have I roamed for your sake;
All yesterday I sailed with sails
On river and on lake.
The Erne, . . . at its highest flood,
I dashed across unseen,
For there was lightening in my blood,
My Dark Rosaleen!

The basis for this is in Ferguson's second stanza:

The course is long over which I brought you from yester-
    day to this day—
Over the mountains I went with her, and under sails
    across the sea:
The Erne I passed at a bound, though great the flood,
And there was music of strings on each side of me and my
    Roiseen dubh.

However, there are two modifications in Mangan: the first the suggestion of travelling for the sake of the beloved instead of with her; and the second the idea of dashing "unseen" across the Erne as a variation from "at a bound." In a general way, Mangan's rendition recalls John MacDonnell's magical dream journey inspired by a tantalizing vision of a beautiful banshee. Before finding her in the otherworld hall at "The royal towers of Ival," he searches all Ireland for her:

And first I turned to the thunderous North,
To Gruagach's mansion kingly;
Untouching the earth I then sped forth
To Inver-lough, and the shingly
And shining strand of the fishful Erne, . . .

In **"Dark Rosaleen,"** unlike Ferguson's version, Mangan extends the idea of restless movement—as if a perpetual journey—into the next stanza as well to link its motive to the love agonies caused by her "sweet and sad complaints," this last a phrase reminiscent of the usual *aisling* lady's lament over her sufferings and indignities. Thus, stanza three reads:

All day long, in unrest,
To and fro, do I move.
The very soul within my breast
Is wasted for you, love!
The heart . . . in my bosom faints
To think of you, my Queen,
My life of life, my saint of saints,
My Dark Rosaleen!
To hear your sweet and sad complaints,
My life, my love, my saint of saints,
My Dark Rosaleen!

The epithets of endearment suggest the same genus as the divinity who inspires the worship of Conor O'Sullivan, as cited above, or the lady of "Patrick Condon's vision" who is "meek as a vestal, yet grand as a Queen." The speaker in Ferguson's rendition is by no means as idealistic or selfless in his explosive cry: "You have killed me my fair one; and may you suffer dearly for it!" His soul loves, but his body is weakened from pining. As throughout his poem, Mangan elevates the worldliness of romantic sexuality to a plane of spirituality without loss of emotional intensity.

Stephen Gwynn has praised the inventiveness of Mangan's imagery in stanza five for its striking expression of commitment with,

Over dews, over sands
Will I fly for your weal;
Your holy delicate white hands
Shall girdle me with steel.

Even this is rooted to a degree in the *aisling* tradition where hands are one of the features sometimes emphasized in the elaborate description. It is instructive to see, however, the way Mangan's imagery creates a kind of holy embrace out of the frank physical desire of the corresponding love-poem stanza that reads:

I would walk the dew with you and the desert of the
    plains,
In hope that I would obtain love from you or part of my
    desire,
Fragrant little mouth! You have promised me that you
    had love for me:
And she is the flower of Munster, she my Roiseen dubh.

Similarly, there is a striking transmutation from amorous to spiritual intensity in stanza six. The devoted priest-lover perhaps "would plough against the hills" for his love, would make her a gospel "in the middle of the mass," would make "delights behind the fort." But for Mangan such sacrilege is neatly turned into the suggestion of a grail-vigil:

I would scale the blue air,
I would plough the high hills,
Oh, I could kneel all night in prayer,
To heal your many ills!

Yet both lover and patriot seem to suffer most from the beloved's lack of response. Ferguson's lover's hopes are charged with conditionals, and Mangan concludes the present stanza with:

An one . . . smile from you
Would float like light between
My toils and me, my own, my true
My Dark Rosaleen!
My fond Rosaleen!
Would give me life, a soul anew
My Dark Rosaleen!

Love unrequited becomes patriotic dedication as yet unrewarded. The unobtainable, perhaps wilful mistress becomes the enigmatic, tantalizing, also totally demanding spirit of Ireland. The rash violence in the climactic hyperbole of the last stanza in both renditions confirms allegiance to a cause whose outcome is agonizingly uncertain. In the love-poem the speaker becomes passionately protective in language suggesting cataclysmic upheaval in nature "before [you] shall perish, my Roiseen dubh," which may be read as the lover's final, irrational cry in the face of the longings and uncertainties that reverberate throughout. In **"Dark Rosaleen,"** the patriot-lover's devotion meets similar uncertainties. Just "a beamy smile" would give him "A second life and soul anew," but Rosaleen gives little indication of response to these fervent blandishments and his longing to serve her. She stands removed and self-absorbed in her sorrow, accepting without question her suppliant's praise of her ennobling allurements. Mangan's conclusion develops from Ferguson's with the even greater violence of unmistakable patriotic intention in lines such as,

The earth shall rock beneath our tread,
And flames wrap hill and wood,
And gun-peal and slogan-cry
Walk many a glen serene.
Ere you shall fade, ere you shall die,
My Dark Rosaleen!

Yet what the love-poem source has done is help express the peculiarity of much Irish patriotic sentiment. It is bound up with what Yeats later called the traditional martyrdom that he himself well illustrated in the play *Cathleen ni Houlihan.* Indeed, it may have been this same awareness that influenced the figure of his own rose of *The Wind among the Reeds* poems which, for all its differences of intention from the patriotic rose tradition, is also remote and unattainable while demanding the utmost dedication from the votary. Mangan's conclusion to **"Dark Rosaleen"** is the same irrational cry as that of Ferguson's lover. It speaks of total adherence to a cause that is never won and a hope that is never questioned. Ireland becomes a supremely suitable subject for a tangled poem about unrequited love.

In 1899, Yeats made some comment in his notes to *The Wind among the Reeds* on the several ways the rose had been used before in Irish verse in both English and Irish, suggesting the possibility of a mythological source for the symbolism:

> If the Rose was really a symbol of Ireland among the Gaelic poets, and if 'Roseen Dubh' is really a political poem, as some think, one may feel pretty certain that the ancient Celts associated the Rose with Eire, or Fotla, or Banba—goddesses who gave their names to Ireland—or with some principal god or goddess, for such symbols are not suddenly adopted or invented, but come out of mythology.

Given Yeats' strong interest in Irish traditionalism, this particular assumption is not surprising, nor is it by any means imperceptive. While rose symbolism does not appear to come out of Celtic mythology explicitly, to this degree Yeats is right: "such symbols are not suddenly adopted or invented." The tradition for personifying Ireland had to be there, particularly as it was in the 18th century through the "secret name" convention drawn from love song material, before Hardiman could interpret "Roisin Dubh" as a patriotic poem. Freedom in translation created the justification for such an interpretation of the Roisin motif, with contemporary national sentiment as the specific motive. The particular form patriotism takes in the renditions of the Roisin material is more emotionally intimate and politically convincing than the Jacobite reliques, and therefore attracted a variety of writers to adopt it for patriotic lyrics of various sorts. While in the Irish street ballad poetry of the 19th century the rose is still the English emblem it had always been, the appeal of Mangan's poem seems to have been responsible for establishing the black rose as indubitably Irish. (pp. 72-80)

> *Diane E. Bessai, " 'Dark Rosaleen' as Image of Ireland," in Eire-Ireland, Vol. X, No. 4, Winter, 1975, pp. 62-84.*

ROBERT WELCH   (essay date 1976)

[*Welch discusses Mangan's transformation of traditional Gaelic works into poems that reflect modern social and political themes in Ireland.*]

Through the familiarity of constant reference [to Irish topographical and antiquarian lore in the work of the Irish Ordinance Survey, one of Mangan's employers], the facts and obscurities of Irish history gained immediacy and imaginative reality. Mangan had his own way of responding to fact and obscurity, but the painstaking inquiry and the deciphering of texts stimulated his interest in the Gaelic past and its poetry.

Already he had published a good deal of verse translation from the German in the *Dublin University Magazine* and else-

where. Under the influence of the scholars on the Ordnance Survey, he began to translate from the Irish, a language he did not know. [Ordnance Survey scholar and antiquary Eugene] O'Curry, and to a lesser extent [archaeologist and historian John] O'Donovan, supplied him with literal versions of Gaelic poems and, presumably, a certain amount of background information about the originals. The scrutiny given to place names in the Ordnance Survey office can be seen influencing the rich chording of the proper nouns in Mangan's version of Pierce Ferriter's **"Lamentation for the Death of Sir Maurice Fitzgerald"**:

> Far on Carah Mona's emerald plains
> Shrieks and sighs were blended many hours
> And Fermoy in fitful strains
> Answered from her towers.
> Youghal, Keenalmeaky, Emokilly,
> Mourned in concert, and their piercing *keen*
> Woke to wondering life the stilly
> Glens of Inchiqueen.

The *Irish Penny Journal,* founded by Gunn and Cameron in 1840, which harked back to Petrie's *Journal* of the early 1830's in that it too had an antiquarian and Gaelic bias, afforded Mangan a market for his developing interest in verse translation from the Irish. This journal published most, if not all, of Mangan's first versions of Gaelic poems made while he worked in the Ordnance Survey. These included **"The Woman of the Three Cows,"** **"An Elegy on the Tironian and Tirconnellian Princes Buried at Rome,"** the **"Lamentation of Mac Liag for Kincora,"** and **"Kathaleen-Ny-Houlahan."**

At this time Mangan knew no Irish, and it seems unlikely that he ever had more than the merest superficial knowledge of the language. Although he says in a letter to the publisher James MacGlasham that he is giving lessons in German and Irish to a number of pupils, Father [C.P.] Meehan, who knew him well, says "he never Learnt Gaelic." This lack is less important than would be imagined. For Mangan, translation rarely involved a close and rigorous attention to the original. He worked happily with literal versions, and ran division on the groundwork they supplied as he pleased. This, according to Dryden in his "Preface to Ovid's *Epistles*" is what an "imitation" does, and many of Mangan's versions can be seen as imitations in this sense of the word. Mangan himself, although he abounded in notions on the matter, had no set theory or procedure for verse translation. His confusion becomes evident in his differing attitudes to John Anster's well-known translation of Goethe's *Faust*. In the *Dublin University Magazine* for 1836 he praises this work as "the most finished and faithful of all the translations," whereas in 1849, in a sketch of Anster contributed to the *Irishman*, he writes:

> Dr. Anster has not merely translated *Faust:* he has done much more—he has translated Goethe—or rather he has translated that part of the mind of Goethe which was unknown to Goethe himself . . . he has actually made of Goethe the man whom his German worshippers claim him to be—he has created a souch under the ribs of that Death which they have revered as a Jupiter—he is, in short, the *real author* of *Faust*.

The two statements contradict each other. The second one, although it does not easily yield a precise meaning, has more to do with what Mangan thought about verse translation than it has to do with Anster's version of *Faust*. Despite the vagueness, two ideas detach themselves and tremulously float clear: translation involves a high degree of imaginative penetration and appropriation, and translation involves the translator's own personality to such an extent that the text frequently becomes original poetry in its own right.

Mangan, with his taste for the exotic and the strange, revelled in the rich ancestral vocabulary of the older Gaelic poems he came in contact with, and in their curious and elaborate systems of imagery. The assonantal and accented lines of 18th-century verse appealed to his taste for the long resonant English line. Also, he found the whimsical capering of Aindrias Mac Craith and Séan Ó Tuama to his taste. Most of all, however, he took to the great Gaelic laments in which the Gaelic poets made their country's state their own despair. Their grief found an echo in Mangan's own despair, and their catalogues of sorrow called forth Mangan's huge rhetorical talents.

O'Curry supplied the literal version of Eoghan Ruadh Mac an Bháird's "A bhean fuair faill ar an bhfeart" out of which Mangan shaped his **"Elegy on the Tironian and Tirconnellian Princes."** Mac an Bháird's lament for Rory O'Donnell, Cathbhar his brother and Hugh O'Neill is addressed to Nuala, surviving sister of Rory. In a letter to Charles Gavan Duffy, then editor of the *Belfast Vindicator,* Mangan whimsically describes his translation of Mac an Bháird's poem as a "transmagnificanbandancial elegy" and as a "perversion from the Irish . . . which is admired by myself and some other impartial judges." Mac an Bháird's Gaelic expresses its grief in compressed allusive statements while the dignified movement of the *deibhidhe* metre and the traditional nature of the images invests the poem with a calm, restrained severity. One quatrain reads:

Dias do'n triúr soin tarla istigh
clann Aodha ard-fhlaith Oiligh,
ua do'n Aodh soin duine dhíobh—
cuire nárbh aosta i n-imshníomh!

O'Curry's literal version of this, which Mangan worked from, would have read substantially like the following:

Two of that three who happened here (were of)
The race of Hugh, the high prince of Aileach, One
of those (two) was nephew to that Hugh—A warrior not experienced in grief.

As *materia poetica* this does not look very promising. However, Mangan, his imagination aflame with the vision of Mac an Bháird's grief being poured out on the Janiculum in Rome, where the Earls lie buried, transformed the meagre facts of the literal version by erecting a stately and magnificent configuration of lament around them. The details now march in the dress of Mangan's fluent and stately rhetoric:

The youths whose relics moulder here
Were sprung from Hugh, high Prince and Lord
       Of Aileach's lands;
Thy noble brothers, justly dear,
Thy nephew, long to be deplored
       By Ulster's bands.
Theirs were not souls wherein dull Time
Could domicile Decay or house
       Decrepitude!
They passed from Earth ere Manhood's prime,
Ere years had power to dim their brows
       Or chill their blood.

Strictly speaking, this can only be satisfactorily thought of as original poetry, in that it completely and successfully transforms O'Curry's unpromising literal material. For example, out of the last phrase of the translated quatrain Mangan fash-

ions the ornate music of the second half of his stanza. It is original poetry firmly rooted in Gaelic tradition. It is a hybrid compounded of what Mangan imagined the Gaelic to be like, on the basis of the literal rendering, and his own talent for eloquent declamatory rhetoric. However, it should not be thought that Mangan's eloquence relies on a rich but thoughtless music. He can marshall his rhythmic fluency to throw into sharp relief the totally resonant and intelligent verb or adjective, as he does in the last line of the stanza quoted, where the word "chill" comes as a shock after the open, generous music of the preceding lines. He achieves something of the same sharp, clear effect with the adjective "embellished" in the following quatrain from his version of Maolmuire mac an Bháird's lament over the ruins of Donegal Castle:

Oh! who could dream that one like him,
One sprung of such a line as his,
Thou of the embellished walls, would be the man to dim
Thy glories by a deed like this!

According to Fr. Meehan, Mangan used a literal version by John O'Donovan for this lament. Eugene O'Curry, who supplied the literal versions for the **"Elegy on the Princes,"** **"Kincora,"** and **"Woman of Three Cows,"** strangely enough endorsed Mangan's free versions, but found it necessary to state that the originals were just as good as the English reworkings. In a letter to Thomas Davis he wrote:

> It so happens that Mr. Mangan has no knowledge of Irish, nor do I think he regrets that either. . . . It was I translated these poems (the 'Elegy,' 'Woman of Three Cows' and 'Kincora') . . . from the originals—that is, I turned the Irish words into English words and Mr. Mangan put these English words, beautifully and faithfully, as well as I can judge, into English rhyme. If I have not made a faithful translation, then the versification is not correct, for it contains nothing but what is found in the translation, nor does it contain a single idea that is not found, and as well expressed, in the original.

Here O'Curry seems to say, though not without some mysterious equivocation in the last sentence, that Mangan's versions remained faithful to the versions supplied. However, John O'Donovan differed in his opinion of them. In a letter, also to Thomas Davis, defending his own translations against Davis's charges of stiffness and formality, he spoke of Macpherson and Mangan in the same breath, though neatly avoiding an explicit comparison between the two writers:

> I know English . . . about six times better than I know Irish, but I have no notion of becoming a forger like Macpherson. The translations from the Irish by Mangan . . . are very good; but how near are they to the literal translations furnished to Mangan by Mr. Curry? Are they the shadow of the shade?

Mangan gave the shades fresh corporeality, but his creations have a markedly different aspect to the original substance. (pp. 37-42)

Mangan's second great burst of translating activity came in 1846, a year that saw the production of a long list of impressive poems. They included among the translations from the Irish, **"Dark Rosaleen," "O'Hussey's Ode to the Maguire," "A Cry for Ireland," "A Lamentation for Sir Maurice Fitzgerald," "A Farewell to Patrick Sarsfield,"** and among the original poems **"Siberia," "To the Ingleeze Khafir,"** and **"A**

Vision of Connaught in the Thirteenth Century." Around this time Mangan wrote to Charles Gavan Duffy, editor of the *Nation,* to which he contributed, saying: "I will begin in earnest to labour for my country henceforward." At this time his work became at once more passionately violent and more oblique. Compared with the great brooding but resigned laments of the early 1840's, **"An Elegy for the Princes"** and **"Kincora"** for example, his work now contains more personal fire and anger, distanced however by the consistent use of mask and metaphor.

Ireland at the time lay in the grip of the Famine, and this context should be borne in mind when reading **"Siberia,"** which appeared in the *Nation* on April 18, 1846. In this light Siberia becomes a powerful metaphor that draws together the stricken state of the country and Mangan's own psychological state, after the manner of such Gaelic poets as Fearflatha Ó Gnímh, Dáibhí Ó Bruadair, Aogán Ó Rathaille:

> In Siberia's wastes
> The Ice-wind's breath,
> Woundeth like the toothèd steel.
> Lost Siberia doth reveal
> Only blight and death.

and:

> Therefore in those wastes
> None curse the Czar.
> Each man's tongue is cloven by
> The North Blast, who heweth nigh
> With sharp scymitar.
>
> And such doom each drees,
> Till, hunger-gnawn
> And cold-slain, he at length sinks there,
> Yet scarce more a corpse than ere
> His last breath was drawn.

"To the Ingleeze Khafir, Calling Himself Djaun Bool Djenkinson" has often been seen as a typical piece of Manganesque extravaganza, but it appeared in the same number of the *Nation* as **"Siberia"** did, among accounts of starving families living in caves, and Limerick counting its dead—hardly a context for whimsy, even for Mangan. In fact the title could read, translated from Mangan's somewhat Joycean pun, "To the English Caffler, [colloquial Anglo-Irish, for a blackguard], Calling Himself John Bull Jenkinson." The poem becomes a savage but masked cry of hate against the English and their way of life beginning

> I hate thee Djaun Bool,
> Worse than Marid or Afrit,
> Or corpse-eating Ghoul!
> I hate thee like sin,
> For thy mop-head of hair,
> Thy snub nose and bald chin,
> And thy turkey-cock air;
> Thou vile Ferindjee!

and continuing:

> I spit on thy clothing,
> That garb for baboons,
> I eye with deep loathing
> Thy tight pantaloons.

This obliqueness, which allows the poet to be hard-hitting and savage because he can pretend to be saying something entirely innocuous, had been a favorite device of Gaelic Jacobite poetry. A similar but far less ironic mask can be found at

work in **"A Vision of Connaught in the Thirteenth Century,"** published in the *Nation* in July of 1846. Ostensibly, the poem concerns Connaught of the 13th century, which Mangan imagines as a kind of Golden Age.

> The sun with wondrous excess of light
> Shone down and glanced
> Over seas of corn. . . .
> And a Dome rose near me, as by a spell,
> Whence flowed the tones
> Of silver lyres,
> And many voices in wreathèd swell.

However, the light darkens, and silence descends, breaking the harmonies of the "wreathèd swell." A change has come

> From light to darkness, from joy to woe!
> King, nobles, all
> Looked aghast and strange:
> The minstrel-group sate in dumbest show!
> Had some great crime
> Wrought this dread amaze,
> This terror? None seemed to understand.

The minstrel group struck dumb calls to mind the cloven tongue of **"Siberia."** [Irish painter and antiquary George] Petrie, when trying, in his collection of Irish music, to describe the effect of the Famine on the life of the country, speaks of the "awful, unwonted silence, which during the Famine . . . almost everywhere prevailed." This, Petrie continues, gave "a deeper feeling of desolation than any other circumstance." **"A Vision of Connaught"** concludes with two images: that of an alien sun glaring down on once rich fields, and that of a skeleton presiding over the waste, silent land:

> . . . the sky
> Showed flecked with blood, and an alien sun
> Glared from the north,
> And there stood on high,
> Amid his shorn beams, a skeleton!

This grisly sentinel, the blight-ridden wastes of **"Siberia,"** the cries of hate in **"To the Ingleeze Khafir,"** and the consistent obliqueness—these form the imaginative background to Mangan's translations from the Irish of 1846.

The 1846 translations achieve an oblique intensity because, while they allow Mangan to be both national and personal at once—"When I translate from the Irish" he wrote, "my heart has no pulses except for the wrongs and sorrows of my native land"—they also provide a comfortable distance from himself by allowing him to pretend he is someone else. Mangan found translation's mask attractive, as it seemed to free him from the agonizing toils of his own brittle personality. In 1850 the *Irishman* posthumously published a self-portrait of Mangan. Again, pretending to be someone else, he initialled this E. W., pointing to Edward Walsh, his contemporary and fellow translator. Mangan writes of himself:

> It is a strange fault, no doubt, and one that I cannot understand, that Mangan should entertain a deep diffidence of his own capacity to amuse or attract others by anything emanating from himself. But it is a fact. I do not comprehend it, but he has mentioned it to me times without number. . . .
> People have called him a singular man but he is rather a plural one—a Proteus, as the *Dublin Review* designates him. I confess that I cannot make him out; and I incline strongly to suspect that there must be something that is dark and troubled in his

mind—perhaps a something very sore and very heavy on his conscience.

Translation gave the "singular" man not only plurality, but a degree of objectivity that freed him from the tremors of his private grief and agony. The mask he gave anger in **"To the Ingleeze Khafir"** and the metaphors he elaborated in **"Siberia"** and **"A Vision of Connaught"** served similar purposes. In 1846 the mask of translation seems to come closest to his personal lineaments: the rhetoric flows, the images burn with clarity, and the words fall with an ardor beyond that supplied by the ordered sonorities of intelligent music.

Not long after Davis's death in September, 1845, John Mitchel's writings in the *Nation,* the staff of which he had recently joined, began to take a revolutionary turn. The Famine exacerbated his anger, but as early as November, 1845, he wrote in the *Nation* of the possibilities for ambush the new railways under construction provided. Mangan, who had contributed to the first number of the *Nation,* seems to have come under Mitchel's influence and certainly shared his rising anger and frustration as the country's miseries deepened. Mangan's version of **"O'Hussey's Ode to the Maguire"** images the Irish warrior pitted against a malign and pitiless nature:

Where is my Chief, my Master, this bleak night, mavrone!
O Cold, cold, miserably cold is this bleak night for Hugh,
Its showery, arrowy, speary sleet pierceth one through
    and through,
Pierceth one to the very bone!

Maguire's consolation in this inhospitable terrain lies partly in the fact that he can remember more pleasant days. Also, the memories of destruction he has made, and of revenge he has taken, serve to calm his heart:

Hugh marched forth to the fight—I grieved to see him so
    depart;
And lo! to-night he wanders frozen, rain-drenched, sad,
    betrayed—
*But the memory of the lime white mansions his right hand
    hath laid
In ashes warms the hero's heart!*

Duffy, the editor of the *Nation,* who remained fairly moderate despite Mitchel's radicalism, rejected **"O'Hussey's Ode to the Maguire,"** as did the more conservative *Dublin University Magazine,* edited by James MacGlashan. However, it did appear later that year in H. R. Montgomery's *Specimens of the Early Native Poetry of Ireland* (1846).

Mangan based his version of the **"Ode"** on a literal prose rendering in Ferguson's articles on Hardiman in the *Dublin University Magazine* for 1834. The last quatrain of the prose rendering provided Mangan with the groundwork for the stanza about the warming memory of mansions laid in ashes:

Hugh, marched, though it grieved me, with his host to bat-
    tle,
And his tresses softly curling are hung with ice—
*Cause of warmth to the hero are the shouts of war,
And the many mansions lime-white which he laid in ashes.*

Mangan's version remains remarkably close to this. However, he neglects the "tresses" hung with ice in favor of the more congenial idea of the chieftain betrayed and desolate: ". . . to-night he wanders frozen, rain-drenched, sad, betrayed. . . ." Despite departures of this kind, mainly to emphasize the theme of betrayal, Mangan retains much of the

spirit of the prose he worked from. This, unfortunately, only very inaccurately translates the Irish. A correct literal translation of the stanza in question reads: "Because of Maguire's circuit, throughout the west of the fair sunsetland many is the court in flames, many the territory without heir or great-grandson." This has little to do with comforting memories of great destruction made, with betrayal, or indeed with softly curling "tresses." As Osborn Bergin pointed out, in Mangan's version ". . . the great captain who is ravaging Desmond is turned into a poor wanderer, lonely, persecuted and betrayed, cheered only by memories and warmed only by 'the lightning of the soul'." Certainly Mangan wrote well of betrayal, loss, and persecution, but the prose version he worked from had already misinterpreted the original. In the Irish, the following quantrain describes Maguire's hand:

Bos tláith na dtachar n-édtláth,
sion oighridh da fhúaighealtáth
re crann rionnfhuar geaol gceise
ionnfhuar dh'Aodh san oidhcheise.

Bergin's literal version of this reads: "Gentle hand versed in ungentle strife, icy weather welding it tight against the slender shaft of a cold-pointed spear—bitter it is for Hugh tonight." The version Mangan worked from read as follows: "His kind-dealing hand which punished cruelty. By frost made numb; Under some spiked and icicle-hung trees—Oh! bleak and dreary is this night for Hugh!" The hand has been invested with a spurious morality: "bleak and dreary" have totally different overtones to "ionnfhuar" ("bitter") and the "cold-pointed spear" has been completely missed. It has become an "icicle-hung tree," which in turn becomes a "thicket" in Mangan, where Maguire, now the possessor of a hand that often avenged the "oppressed," wanders "lorn and lost"—a fascinating, highly successful metamorphosis.

That his great hand, so oft the avenger of the oppressed,
Should this chill, churlish night, perchance, be paralysed
    by frost—
While through some icicle-hung thicket—as one lorn and
    lost—
He walks and wanders without rest.

The *Nation* did publish **"Dark Rosaleen"** on May 30, 1846. Here, in contrast to the desolation of **"O'Hussey's Ode"** Mangan gives expression to a feeling of deperate hope, of violent triumph. The last stanza attains a blood-drenched apocalyptic intensity:

O! the Erne shall run red
With redundance of blood,
The earth shall rock beneath our tread,
And flames wrap hill and wood,
And gun-peel, and slogan cry,
Wake many a glen serene,
Ere you shall fade, ere you shall die,
    My Dark Rosaleen!
    My own Rosaleen!
The Judgment Hour must first be nigh,
Ere you can fade, ere you can die,
    My Dark Rosaleen!

As with **"O'Hussey's Ode,"** Mangan based his version on a prose rendering, in Ferguson's 1834 Hardiman articles in the *Dublin University Magazine,* which translates the Irish with considerable accuracy. Hardiman, when he published "Róisín Dubh" in his collection, thought it "an allegorical ballad, in which strong political feelings are conveyed. . . . The allegorical meaning had been long since forgotten, and the verses are now remembered . . . as a plaintive love ditty." However, Ferguson took issue with this. To him the song was what it seemed, a love song, but the love song of a Catholic priest, waiting for a dispensation from the Pope so that he might marry. Ferguson gives his priest the following sturdy advice: he should "pitch his vows to the Pope, the Pope to Purgatory, marry his black rose-bud, and take a curacy from the 'next Protestant rector'." While he bases his poem on Ferguson's prose rendering, Mangan not surprisingly ignores this interpretation and resurrects the political allegory. He stresses the images of blood, carnage, natural disturbance and violence, which both the Irish and Ferguson's prose contain, but they hold a less central place there. In the stanza quoted, for example, the English rendering suggests the images of the Erne running red with blood, and of the earth shaking, but in Mangan the earth "rocks" because of a martial "tread," and the "gun-peal and slogan cry" which follows comes entirely from Mangan. His imagination effects a similar transformation in the second stanza. The source reads:

> The course is long over which I brought you from yester-
> day to this day—
> Over mountains I went with her, and under sails across
> the sea:
> The Erne I passed at a bound, though great the flood,
> And there was music of strings on each side of me and my
> Roisin dubh.

Out of this Mangan fashions the fury of:

> Over hills and through dales
> Have I roamed for your sake;
> All yesterday I sailed with sails
> On river and on lake.
> The Erne at its highest flood
> I dashed across unseen,
> For there was lightning in my blood
> My Dark Rosaleen!
> My own Rosaleen!
> Oh! there was lightning in my blood,
> Red lightning lightened through my blood,
> My Dark Rosaleen!

The word "unseen," unprecedented in Ferguson's version, makes the traveller conspiratorial, but the major departure from the source comes in the next line: "For there was lightning in my blood. . . ." This note of angry rebellion, which looks forward to the apocalyptic images at the end of the poem when the Erne is mentioned again, once struck, fires Mangan's imagination and climbs into heady, incantatory refrain.

1846 also saw the publication of **"A Farewell to Patrick Sarsfield,"** which later appeared in O'Daly's *Poets and Poetry of Munster.* The translation shares the same note of anger and violence found in **"O'Hussey's Ode"** and **"Dark Rosaleen,"** save that here, at times, it attains an almost shrieking intensity.

> But O'Kelly still remains, to defy and to foil;
> He has memories that hell won't permit him to forget,
> And a sword that will make the blue blood flow like oil
> Upon many an Aughrim yet.

Memories seem important to Maguire and O'Kelly; they console the one and feed the anger of the other. Mangan's sympathies and his personality drew him closer to Mitchel than to Duffy and, when Mitchel and Devin Reilly broke with the *Nation* in 1846 to found the *United Irishman,* Mangan allied himself with them.

What can be considered as Mangan's third series of translations appeared in what he called *Anthologia Hibernica,* echoing his *German Anthology* (1845), in the *Dublin University Magazine* for 1847. In his introductory note, Mangan dedicates his talents "exclusively to the service of our country." Furthermore, he thinks he sees a new era approaching for its literature. Generally speaking, the translations themselves suffer from florid metrical ingenuity. In the following, for instance, Mangan tries to do the impossible with repetition and refrain.

> Oh!—thou Ocean of blue billows
> Billows, billows,
> Oh! thou Ocean of blue billows
> From Cork Harbour to Bearhaven
> A curse this blessed night lies on thy flood,
> For with its wave is blent the pure heart's blood
> Of that Chief whose hand and raven
> Locks the storm-wind pillows!
> Storm-wind pillows.

Here the incantatory effects, so successful in **"Dark Rosaleen,"** have gone completely astray. Rhythm attempts too great a degree of complexity and confusion follows. When Mangan writes well, his verse has a musical inevitability and cumulative power, when badly the music cracks, and frequently the ludicrous and the embarrassing seep through. However, the *Anthologia Hibernica* contains a number of interesting pieces, among them **"The Lament of King Cormac,"** which contains the following lines:

> Three causes there be,
> That have wrecked my Ship's Anchor
> Of Wedlock for me—
> Lies, Coldness, and Rancour.

His version of **"The Lass of Carrick"** and **"Ellen Bawn,"** both taken from Walsh's *Irish Popular Songs* (1847), have some merit, although the former translates the simple freshness of the Gaelic into a metre that is, to say the least, startling in its eccentricity.

> O, have you been in Carrick and have you met her?
> You know my love all beauty and all grace!
> Forth from her eyes come flowing Bright threads that fet-
> ter
> The hearts of all who gaze upon her face!
> The fairest, rarest flower is she
> In Banba's bloomful gardens glowing;
> The wondrous living Apple-tree,
> Whose golden fruit keeps ever glowing.
> O tell me, tell me, have you met her,
> And does my long, long tarrying fret her?

The translations Mangan made for O'Daly, his publisher, can be considered as his fourth and last group of translations. These eventually formed part of two separate publications: *Poets and Poetry of Munster,* edited by O'Daly himself in 1849, and *The Tribes of Ireland,* edited by John O'Donovan and published in 1852, three years after Mangan's death.

Mangan had begun his versions for O'Daly's collection of the Munster poets as early as 1846 and worked on them on and off until his death in 1849. Working in collaboration with O'Daly drew Mangan into closer contact with the literal details, but more especially with the rhythms of the Gaelic originals. For this reason some of the versions appear shackled and cumbersome. Also, many suffer from a malformed diction due perhaps to haste in composition, as Mangan, occasionally at least, made a translation for ready cash. However, it appears that O'Daly took some trouble to ensure that Mangan got as accurate an idea as possible of the Gaelic rhythms. One of O'Daly's correspondents, Patrick Forhan from Dingle, Co. Kerry, in a letter containing a number of other translations, included an English version of a poem called "Síos Cois na Trágha" made to the air of the original "merely to give Mr. Mangan an idea of the metre." Due to the close attention Mangan, under O'Daly's guidance, paid to the Gaelic rhythms, a number of the versions in the collection rise above competence to achieve a vivid musicality. His translation of **"A Lament for Kilcash"** reads:

> Oh! sorrow the saddest and sorest!
> Kilcash's attractions are fled—
> Felled lie the high trees of its forest,
> And its bells hang silent and dead.
> There dwelt the fair lady, the Vaunted,
> Who spread through the island her fame.
> There the Mass and the Vespers were chanted,
> And thither the proud earls came.

This captures quite successfully the rush of the Irish rhythm and its capacity for effortless statement. . . . O'Daly's literal version, which Mangan worked from, would have read something like the following:

> What shall we henceforth do for timber, The last of the woods is down? There is no mention of Kilcash or its household, And its bells will not be rung forever; That place where the heavenly lady used live, Who had reputation and merriment over women, Earls used come from over the sea to it, And the sweet Mass used be said.

Also, Mangan's frequently underrated version of Aogán Ó Rathaille's "Gile na Gile," though it does not attempt any extensive mirroring of the complex system of parallel assonance, does have considerable firmness, grace, and emphasis.

> There a wild and wizard band with mocking fiendish laughter
> Pointed out me her I sought, who sat low beside a clown;
> And I felt as though I never could dream of Pleasure after
> When I saw the maid so fallen whose charms deserve a crown.
>
> Then with burning speech and soul, I looked at her and told her
> That to wed a churl like that was for her the shame of shames,
> When a bridegroom such as I was longing to unfold her
> To a bosom that her breath had enkindled into flames.

During 1849, the last year of his life, Mangan versified O'Donovan's literal translation of Aenghus na nAor Ó Dálaigh's bitter satire called *The Tribes of Ireland.* When O'Daly published it in 1852 he faced the Irish text with O'Donovan's prose version and printed Mangan's none too faithful rendering towards the close of the volume. Ó Dálaigh's poem—specially commissioned, O'Donovan says, by Lord Mountjoy and Sir George Carew to foment national disorder—attacks all four of the Irish provinces for their inhospitality. Mangan crams his verse with the concrete emblems of meanness taken from O'Donovan's prose: lean goats, watery whey, bread thinner than the fins of a fish, and so on. However, he allows the bitter acerbic wit of Ó Dálaigh's poem, captured to a certain extent in O'Donovan's rendering, to run to a not unsuccessful whimsy. O'Donovan's translation of Ó Dálaigh's attack on the district of Blarney and Beare reads:

> Three reasons why I shunned
> The district of Bantry and Beare,
> (They use) brown, soft, lumps, without taste,
> Long division, and milk-and-water.

Out of this Mangan makes:

> Three reasons there were why I lately withdrew
> In a hurry from Bantry: its want of a pantry
> Was one; and the dirt of its people was two;
> Good heavens! how they daub and bespatter
> Their duds! I forget the third reason. No matter.

Aside from this fantastic strain, the poem also indicates how deeply the living images of the Famine had penetrated his consciousness in the last years of his life. In the following, for example, whimsy cracks into nightmare:

> O'Reilly the feeble, the palsied, the old,
> The most wretched of wretches the earth can behold;
> Dines along with his dumb sons, whose glazed eyes and lank wet
> Chin and cheeks, makes his dinner a sort of death's banquet.

Mangan's translations from the Irish accomplished two things. Firstly, with him, translation from the Irish became an intensely personal affair: it gave release to one of the deeply rooted aspects of his personality, his "plurality" as he called it himself. Through it he could don the mask and avail himself of the structure of someone more creatively "forthright" than himself. Secondly, he brought a freedom of approach to verse translation from the Irish, so that frequently the question arises as to whether what he did at his best can fruitfully be seen as translation at all. This, while strictly speaking playing havoc with the original Irish, freed the old verse to new uses and experiences through the transforming power of Mangan's restless imagination. (pp. 43-55)

> *Robert Welch, " 'In Wreathed Swell': James Clarence Mangan, Translator from the Irish," in* Eire-Ireland, *Vol. XI, No. 2, 1976, pp. 36-55.*

DAVID LLOYD (essay date 1987)

[*In the following excerpt from his study* Nationalism and Minor Literature: James Clarence Mangan and the Emergence of Irish Cultural Nationalism, *Lloyd examines Mangan's treatment of Irish nationalist ideals in his poetry and his method of translating Gaelic poems into English.*]

Mitchel's introduction to his edition of the **Poems** [1859] inaugurated the still conventional view that Mangan's earlier poetic career was a preparation for the fullest expression of his poetic gifts under the influence of the Young Ireland movement in the 1840s. His association with this movement began in 1842 with his ditty **"The *Nation's* First Number"** and lay dormant until his most productive years from 1845 to his death in 1849, during which he wrote regularly for that and other nationalist journals. During these years he encountered much newly researched Gaelic material and experienced the full horror of Ireland's economic and political condition during the Famine. But, given the aptness of this configuration of factors to the formation of a committed nationalist poetry, what is most striking when Young Irelanders write about Mangan is the extent to which they register the poet's refractoriness, his reluctance to commit himself fully to the nationalist cause. Mitchel's account, written ten years after his transportation, gives the nationalist myth of the writer as martyr integrated and explained in the moment of his engagement in the cause, and representative of the general fate of his nation. [Irish nationalist journalist] Charles Gavan Duffy's account of Mangan's relation to the Young Ireland movement is more sober and fits more closely with the pattern of the poet's life insofar as we can establish it:

> I thought the gifted and gallant young men associated in the enterprise, who were afterwards known as "Young Irelanders", would bring him companions for his mind and heart for the first time and that his slumbering nationality would be awakened by their design to raise up their country anew and place a sceptre in her hands. But his habit of isolation had hardened, he shuddered at the idea of social intercourse.

Duffy anticipates in the individual poet a latent "spirit of the nation," which might be revived in association with the collective labor of the nationalist movements. What he encounters instead is not merely indifference to nationalism as such but a "habit of isolation" that refuses any association whatsoever.

An earlier account, the obituary for Mangan published in the new series of the *Nation* in September 1849, makes some attempt, in a more overtly religious rhetoric, to reconcile the conflicting images of Mangan as writer and as man:

> Melancholy in anyone, most tragic in a man of genius is it to see the separation between the speculative and active powers, the curse of the fall, become an utter divorce, and the will lie prostrate and impotent beneath the feet of tyrannic habit—to see fancy, imagination, poetic susceptibility still subsisting, and at a breath giving forth music to delight and benefit mankind, while the Man, the lord of these, is drifting hopeless and powerless to ruin and death.

Reconciliation falls short in separation, his fall remaining unredeemed by the ethical act of reintegration with the nation. In an essay that has maintained that "in Mangan the very Gaelic heart seems poured out," it becomes essential to separate the spirit of the writing from the figure of the writer, the latter isolated, drifting, unethical, mortal, the former immortal and ethical in its effects. As with Ireland itself, the actual outer form belies the transcendent spirit it conceals.

Many attempts were made to persuade Mangan to produce nationalist literature more than sporadically, and to conform to the nationalist ideal of writing. But even the ballads and poems that are most frequently read as the evidence of Mangan's nationalist tendencies are marked internally by the disintegration that nationalist-oriented accounts of his writings seek in one way or another to overcome. The fissure that the *Nation* article imposes between man and writing or Mitchel depicts as being resolved by political commitment is in fact intrinsic to the structure of those writings. Comparing passages from such poems with examples selected almost at random from *The Spirit of the Nation,* or even from the prose of Mitchel's own exhortatory editorials, one is struck at first by the rhetorical similarities:

> Know, then, your true lot,
>   Ye faithful, though few!
>   Understand your position,
>   Remember your mission,
> And vacillate not,
>   Whatsoever ensue!

> Alter not! Falter not!
>   Palter not with your own living souls!
>
>   (Mangan)

> Stand together, brothers all!
>   Close together, close together!
> Be Ireland's might a brazen wall—
>   Close together, tight together!
> Peace! no noise!—but, hand in hand,
> Let calm resolve pervade your band. . . .
>
>   ("Theta")

> Yes! with our fellow-citizens rests now the fate of Ireland. If they quail, or shrink, vacillate, pause, postpone, or exhibit the slightest weakness—if they balk the hopes of a single Irishman, or give one enemy another chance to scoff, 'twere better they had remained slaves, contented in their slavery, or, being discontented, had hanged themselves.
>
>   (Mitchel)

Viewed in the context of Mangan's poem as a whole, however, a tension can be seen to subsist between an imperative voice that mimes the nationalist projection of unification into the future, and a present tense in which an accumulation of substantives mimes the situation that evokes that projection, the perpetual *imminence,* that is, of the realization of the *immanent* idea of the nation. The nationalist's present is depicted as a perpetual labor in perpetual suspension. For each generation of readers of **"The Warning Voice,"** the suspension is to be repeated:

> To *this* generation
> The sore tribulation,
> The stormy commotion,
> And foam of the Popular Ocean,
>   The struggle of class against class;
> The Dearth and the Sadness,
>   The Sword and the War-vest;
> To the *next,* the Repose and the Gladness,
>   "The Sea of clear Glass,"
>   And the rich Golden Harvest!

If, as at the end of the **"Irish National Hymn,"** Mangan continually assumes the privilege of "one whom some have called a Seer," he is most typically a prophet who intimates but does not see, stressing the gap that persists between expectation and event:

> And I heard, as I guessed,
>   The far-echoing sound
> Of a trumpet, with tones,
>   And lightnings and thunders,
> As ye read of in John's
>   Revelation of Wonders.
> What meant they? I trow not.
>   What next might befal?
>   And how ended All?
> This, too, friends, I know not—
> For here were my cords
>   Of Sleep suddenly broken
>   The bell booming Three;
> But there seemed in mine ears,
>   As I started up, woken,
> A noise like fierce cheers,
>   Blent with the clashing of swords,
>   And the roar of the sea!

Exactly at the point where the significance of the vision—final defeat or final victory, hell or apocalyptic prelude to a new earth—seems about to be grasped and controlled, the vision is interrupted. With that refusal to endow his "vision" with its expected meaning, Mangan introduces a disarming, distancing irony, one compacted by the ambivalence of "as I guessed," "seemed in mine ears," "a noise like." The poem's dream is described as "a Stream / That in vain seeks the light," and that "mocks our control" (stanza 1).

Constantly opposed to nationalist projections, which come gradually to appear as misrecognized alienation from the plenitude they pursue, is the figure of the poet who stresses his irredeemable alienation. **"A Voice of Encouragement"** begins expressly with the assertion that the speaker is "a man unworthy to rank in your number," "his music and diction / Rather . . . fitted, alas! to lull to, than startle from, slumber." The uneven faltering "numbers" of Mangan's nationalist poems reflect that act of self-subtraction from the nationalist vision—which depends, after all, on the "cords / Of Sleep." In the fuller context of the nationalist ballads, this self-subtraction, which operates precisely through emphasis on the singularity of the writer, functions simultaneously as a critique of nationalist politics and aesthetics.

"Self-subtraction" in this context becomes a parodic version of the ethical self-effacement called for by the nationalist literary program. Rather than project perfect integration, Mangan insists on the ineradicable residue of a self-conscious and alienated selfhood which cannot be assimilated to "the spirit of the nation." And his failure to integrate aesthetic representation with ethical action, "To live [his] poetry—to act [his] rhyme," is what most troubles his nationalist contemporaries. Nor is their unease unwarranted: Mangan's writing, in its recalcitrant insistence on the inassimilable remainder, intimates that their utopia of identity will only be achieved over the poet's dead body and suspends the issue of nationalist politics in protracted speculation.

The nationalist recourse to the ballad form as one in which the individual is effaced in order to permit the reproduction of a national spirit is largely determined by the need to overcome the break in continuity that the loss of Gaelic as a national language entails. From the outset there exists an intimate connection between the composition of "original" ballads and the translation of those Gaelic poems on which the former are supposedly modeled. That connection goes beyond the relation of model to imitation, however, insofar as the demand made of the translator repeats that made of the balladeer—that he should become the transparent medium for the spirit of the nation. An article in the *Nation* [10 October 1846] praises both Mangan and [Samuel] Ferguson for exactly that quality, noting only how one arrives there through study, the other simply through identifying with his nation:

> Whether in translation or original, they seem almost alone in the art of reproducing for us the inner heart and outward vesture of the bygone ages of Ireland, that lie so obscure for us. Yet between them there is a large difference—Ferguson seems to have rendered himself, by zealous study, as familiar with old Irish ways as Walter Scott with those of the middle ages. Mangan, on the other hand, seems rather to penetrate without study, and by the instinct of the poet and his own Irish sympathies, into the feelings and sorrows of those too sorrowing times.

This contemporary judgment is almost entirely reversed by a recent critic writing on Mangan and Ferguson:

> So that when Ferguson turns to versifying a selec-

tion of poems from Hardiman's collection, his intention is in no way that of Mangan, who always wished to make his originals as expressive of himself as possible. . . . Ferguson had that kind of personality which expresses itself in impersonality, in a kind of self-effacement, so that he makes an excellent translator, remaining absolutely true in as many particulars as possible, to the spirit, tone and rhythm of his originals, and to their curious, if at times chaotic image sequences.
> We get, in the appendix affixed to the four Hardiman articles, twenty translations which are as faithful to their Irish originals as it is possible to get in English versions. Here, the act of the imagination is one of transparency, of self-denial, curiously analogous in its self-surrender to that "negative capability" of which Mangan was incapable. [Robert Welch, *Irish Poetry from Moore to Yeats*]

The difference between the two assessments pivots at least in part on a difference of opinion as to the nature of Mangan's self: to the nationalists, Mangan's true self is that in him which can be identified with Ireland, while to Welch it is that which intrudes uncomfortably to obscure the "transparency" of the ideal translation. But in that notion of "transparency," the opposed evaluations meet around a common expectation.

Welch is of course right to locate an ideal of transparency at the center of Ferguson's theory of translation. What is not so clear in his account of Ferguson is the close bond between the ideal of the translations and the political theory of the articles to which they form a practical appendix. The "Hardiman articles" which Welch mentions were a series of articles published in the *Dublin University Magazine* as a review of the Irish antiquarian James Hardiman's collection of Gaelic poetry, *Irish Minstrelsy*. Hardiman's aim was, quite explicitly, to vindicate the Irish poets "against the ignorance and prejudice by which they have been assailed, particularly during the last century." Accordingly, he published the originals in parallel text, facing English versions by a team of translators who versified the Gaelic in a mode that uneasily combines the conventions of late Augustan descriptive verse with those of Romantic meditative and ballad poetry. The Gaelic is thus thoroughly "anglicized," but Hardiman's political sentiments are revealed time and again in the extended notes he appends to the text.

Ferguson's articles on the *Irish Minstrelsy* seek accordingly to depose Hardiman as authority, displacing his "spirit of petty anti-Anglicism" and his poetry's "scheme of dissension" with "the reconciling strength of an honest literature." Ferguson's aim was to present a theory of the gradual development of the native Irish loyalties from the immediate clan to the idea of a constitutional monarchy, obliging a transition from investment in the sensuous to investment in the supersensuous. Knowledge thus becomes unifying rather than—as with Hardiman—divisive and sectarian. The ideal of transparent translation repeats this theory at two levels. In the first place it ensures a continuous transition into which no arbitrariness enters, rather than furnishing a perpetual reminder of the nation's separation from its past. In the second place, the ideal of transparency allows for the undistorted reproduction in English of the essential quality of the Gael, which, for Ferguson, as for Arnold some thirty years later, is "sentimentality." That being the case, the ascertaining of that quality, in which translation plays a fundamental role, is a crucial stage in the process of cultivating its growth in the right direction. If Ferguson finds that "their sentiment is pathetic" and that "desire is the essence of that pathos," his mission will be to direct that "desire" away from a lost past and toward the idea of unity.

Providing, in the first Hardiman article, prose translations of Irish poems that represent "the words, and unmutilated thoughts, and turn, and expression of the original," Ferguson is obliged to observe that "the idiomatic differences of the two languages give to the translation an uncouth and difficult hesitation, which in the original did not affect the Irishman." But by the time Ferguson comes to write his verse translation, the "uncouthness" of the prose translation has become an essential part of the verse in rhythm and idiom, reflecting exactly Ferguson's idea of the primitive but powerful sentiments of the Irish race. Hardiman's edition is criticized for failing to communicate this: "All the versifiers seem to have been actuated by a morbid desire, neither healthy nor honest, to elevate the tone of the original to a pitch of refined poetic art altogether foreign from the whole genius and *rationale* of its composition." In opposition to that "foreign," "morbid desire," Ferguson's style is a clear medium through which the *living* genius of the Irish race can express itself, "unrefined" and, ultimately, as raw material to be worked on in the service of a political end.

Is it then the case that Mangan, contrariwise, allows his personality to intrude upon his translations. . . . Any reading of Mangan's Gaelic translation is immediately vexed by the question as to whether he actually knew Gaelic. There is some small evidence that Mangan began to study Irish seriously in the late 1840s, having already toyed with it earlier in the 1830s, but it seems that his understanding of the language even then must have been rudimentary and faulty at best. Certain it is, however, that on a number of occasions Mangan availed himself of the versions he found in Ferguson's Hardiman articles, in order to produce his own poems. These versions, taken from Ferguson and written in reaction to his manner, are among the most frequently cited of Mangan's Irish translations, and generally regarded as his most "successful." Given the representative nature of Ferguson's practice as a translator, a detailed comparison of the versions is instructive with regard to the distinctiveness of Mangan's practice.

Perhaps the most celebrated of Mangan's translations from the Gaelic is **"Dark Rosaleen."** In addition to the best-known version, which was published with that title in the *Nation* of 30 May 1846, Mangan wrote two other versions entitled **"Roisin Dubh"** (Dark-Haired Rose), published in the **Poets and Poetry of Munster,** but according to O'Donoghue representing earlier versions of the poem. Mitchel in his introduction to the **Poems** collates these two versions "to illustrate his method of translating" but does not elaborate on what he intends to illustrate. No single original of the poem can be established, but the various versions form part of a tradition of similar personifications of Ireland, cognate with the better-known "Kathleen ni Houlihan." Ferguson provides only a prose version of this poem, but the ordering of its seven stanzas and their thematic concerns suggest that this—perhaps with the Irish text given in Hardiman—may have been Mangan's primary source. Ferguson's translation involves him in an attempt to refute Hardiman's assertion that the poem is an allegorical political ballad concluding "with a bold declaration of the dreadful struggle which would be made before the country should be surrendered to the embraces of our hero's hated and implacable rival":

This, says Mr. Hardiman, is an allegorical political ballad—it seems to us to be the song of a priest in love, of a priest in love, too, who had broken his vow, of a priest in love who was expecting a dispensation for his paramour, of a priest in love who was willing to turn ploughman for his love's sake—nay to practice the very calling of a priest to support her.

Ferguson's insistence begins eventually to trip over itself, and remains a little unconvincing, if only because, whatever the original intention, Hardiman's "allegory" will inevitably be read into "Roisin Dubh." Ironically, Ferguson may even have helped that reading, given that, for obvious reasons, he translated fairly literally as "Your pardon will come from the pope [sic] and from Rome in the East" (stanza 1), the Gaelic "Tiocfaidh do phádún ó'n b-Pápa, a's ó'n Ró'imh an-oir," which Hardiman's translator Furlong had blurred into the lines: "For the friends that come eastward shall see thee at last; / They bring blessings—they bring favours which the past never knew."

Mangan's celebrated version takes up Hardiman's reading of the poem, a point which Mangan makes quite explicit in a prose introduction, where he even stresses obliquely what is, in fact, supplementary allegorical allusion: "The true character of and meaning of the figurative allusions with which it abounds, and to two only of which I need refer here—the 'Roman wine' and 'Spanish ale' mentioned in the first stanza—the intelligent reader will, of course, find no difficulty in understanding." The singular density of this version is perhaps attributable to his synthesizing of the two views of the poem, as love song or allegory, which Ferguson and Hardiman opposed to each other. It is in these opposite directions that his other versions respectively tend. One stresses the element of the love relationship that Ferguson perceived:

> I dashed through Erne:—the world may learn the cause from
>   *Love;*
> For light or sun shone on me none, but *Roisin Dubh!*

The other stresses the personification of the land as Roisin, and the apotheosis this involves:

> O never mourn as one forlorn, but bide your hour;
> Your friends ere long, combined and strong, will prove their
>   power.
> From distant Spain will sail a train to change the scene
> That makes you sad, for one more glad, my Dark *Roisin!*

From the synthesis of the two interpretations emerges a poem in which the heavily stressed internal rhyme scheme of the other versions, which tends to break each line into segments, modulates into a series of tonal variations on the vowels of the first lines, which contain its thematic statement:

> O my Dark Rosaleen,
> Do not sigh, do not weep
>   (stanza 1)

> 'Tis you shall reign, shall reign alone,
>   My Dark Rosaleen!
>   My own Rosaleen!
>   (stanza 4)

> And gun-peal, and slogan cry,
>   Wake many a glen serene,
> Ere you shall fade, ere you shall die,
>   My Dark Rosaleen!

My own Rosaleen!
(stanza 7)

The tonal pattern of **"Dark Rosaleen"** repeats formally the suspension of the speaker's desire around the apotheosized woman in whom "life, love and saint of saints" (stanza 3) are condensed, a suspension which is echoed in the verbal dominance of futures which are almost conditionals. In this respect, Mangan's poem becomes the great nationalist ballad it has been taken to be: not as an exhortation, but as a representation of the asymptomatic progress of the nationalist project toward an idealized land whose domain is always in the future. The perception of the stasis or suspension at the core of this process is peculiarly Mangan's.

That quality of suspension is, and has often been noted to be, the dominant quality of the most highly regarded of Mangan's Gaelic translations. Padraic Colum has noted the "architectural" qualities of **"Dark Rosaleen"** and of the **"Lament for the Princes of Tyrone and Tyrconnell."** Welch also, in the course of a very fine analysis of the rhythmic scheme of the latter poem, remarks that its success derives from the fact that it is "static." And, as [Jacques] Chuto has remarked, in this poem, as in **"Dark Rosaleen,"** it is to the conditional mood that Mangan turns. The dominant trait of Mangan's writing in the Irish translations, which incline constantly toward elegiac models, is indeed this quality of suspension, the speaking voice caught between a lost ideal past and an apotheosized future, neither of which is approachable except in the conditional mood. But to understand the recurrence of this pattern in Mangan's work as the manifestation of a peculiar disposition, which precedes as a source the utterance that is the poem, is to draw on a theory of writing that is particularly questionable in the area of translations. Not only must the vexed question as to the relation of a source poem to its translation or to the translator be thrown open, but the probable *function* of specific deviations, inevitable as these are in any translation, has to be foregrounded before they can legitimately be identified with the expressive drives of the writer.

This problem of the identification of the writer with his object is one of the primary concerns of another poem based on Ferguson and Hardiman, Mangan's **"Lament over the Ruins of the Abbey of Teach Molaga."** The possibility of subjecting this poem to widely differing readings is already apparent in the gulf between Hardiman's and Ferguson's commentaries. For Hardiman, it is predominantly a lament for one of the "appalling monuments of the ravages committed by the first protestant reformers." Ferguson grants Hardiman's account of the poem, but once again appropriates his original to exemplify the loyal attachment of the Irish to their inherited beliefs. The poem becomes, for all its anti-Protestant sentiments, a kind of "neutral ground," as Protestant meets Catholic on the basis of shared feeling: "we would be men without hearts if we could not appreciate such a melancholy and touching complaint as this sweet elegy." The parallel, established by Hardiman in his note, between the destruction of the abbey and the dispossession of the Irish poet Collins's family by a "ruthless band of privileged marauders," the "Act of Settlement Men," is not mentioned in Ferguson's commentary. Rather, Collins's decline is generalized in both versions of his translation.

The parallel between abbey and poet, however, is much more insistently established *formally* in both of Ferguson's versions than in that of Hardiman's translator, Thomas Furlong. The latter, indeed, provides a fine illustration of the tension that subsists between the tenor of Hardiman's commentaries and the "refined," Englished style of the versifications. A considerable instability of diction is apparent throughout Furlong's version. On the one hand, a Romantic convention of the solitary mourner finds its appropriate descriptive diction and rhythms:

> The wind with silent wing went slowly by,
>   As though some secret on its path it bore:
> All, all was calm—tree, flower, and shrub stood still,
> And the soft moonlight slept on valley and on hill—
> (stanza 2)

On the other, the soliloquy is reminiscent of eighteenth-century moral verse in its vestigial antithetical forms and circumlocutory diction:

> Where far from crowds, from courts and courtly crimes,
> The sons of virtue dwelt, the boast of better times.
> (stanza 3)

> The hissing weasel lurks apart unseen,
> And slimy reptiles crawl where holy heads have been.
> (stanza 9)

Where the uneasy relationship between two modes leaves the parallel between Furlong's poet and the ruined abbey to be rather insecurely tacked on at the end of the poem, Ferguson's version repeats and reorganizes a parallelism that has been available throughout the poem, between the present and former states of the abbey. The speaker's dead friends and children, "powerless and corrupting" in the abbey, leave him as soulless and cut off from continuity as the ruin itself, its "abbot, rule, and order" reduced to "a heap of clayey bones" (stanzas 19 and 16). His heart, his capacity for feeling, shrunk to the dimensions of a nut, only "Death's deliverance were welcome," allowing him to merge finally with the abbey which is his image (stanza 20). Effectively, Ferguson depoliticizes the poem by universalizing the condition of decay and converting abbey and poet into each other's reflection: victims alike of an ineluctable natural process, the specific cause of the decay of each—British imperialism—is elided.

Turning to Mangan's version, we may observe that the differences to be traced there from Furlong's and Ferguson's versions go far beyond his much stronger stress on Catholic rite and the responsibility of "brutal England's power" for the ruination of the abbey (stanzas 8, 9, 17). Already in the first stanza, Ferguson's "Meditating and reflecting" is replaced by a speaker whose "soul and strength lay prone." The "proneness" of the subjected soul to color its objects with its own emotions is hinted in the fifth stanza:

> The memory of the men who slept
> Under those desolate walls—the solitude—the hour—
> Mine own lorn mood of mind—all joined to o'erpower
>   My spirit—and I wept!

The overpowered spirit subsequently envisions a quasi-paradisal former state of the abbey, "yonder Goshen," where "unity of Work and Will / Blent hundreds into one" (stanzas 6-10). The vision is, however, already suspect, "yonder Goshen" having been the place of refuge that turned to slavery for the children of Israel. Not only is this merely the *thought* of the speaker; it is, furthermore, anxiously "burdened" with the swift passage of time: "With Charity and the blessed spirit of Prayer / Was each fleet moment *fraught*." An ambiguity of mood—indicative or subjunctive—attaches to this Paradise's triumph over misfortune, which is, after all, dependent on the "fortunate stars": "their fortunate stars / *Had* triumphed o'er all ill!" These ambiguities issue in the change that is the concern of the subsequent stanzas (11-15).

The deviation from Ferguson's version is equally striking: in place of the parallel established in the latter between the two *states,* and maintained within and between the stanzas of the poem, Mangan's change appears as a *process.* The ruined abbey, already perceived in the fourth stanza as "crumbling to slow decay, the remnant of that pile," becomes involved in a continuing process of degradation which is mimed in the sequence of the speaker's perceptions of it. Hardiman, deriving his information from a pair of guidebooks, had stressed in his note that "the building, though unroofed, is entire" and offered a lengthy description of its continuing magnificence. Ferguson's version of the poem mentions successively all the elements of the building as still standing, though ruined. Mangan's speaker's attention, however, shifts progressively from "its mouldering walls" and "pillars low," overgrown by grass and gowan, to the "unsightly stones" choking its wells and the completion of the building's razing by the elements:

> Tempest and Time—the drifting sands—
> The lightning and the rains—the seas that sweep around
> These hills in winter nights, have awfully crowned
>   The work of impious hands!
>
> (stanza 13)

The source poems, including Collins's, had all posed the abbey's survival of natural forces against its destruction by the impious. Here, finally, the "monumental shapes" have "vanished all," and the poet is left contemplating the "whitening bones" of its former inhabitants.

If the poet's feelings find vent briefly in a furious cry against the English tyranny (stanzas 16-17), that outcry is immediately perceived to be misplaced, the change being within the poet even more than without:

> Alas! I rave! . . . if Change is here,
> Is it not o'er the land? Is it not too in me?
> Yes! I am changed even more than what I see.
>   Now is my last goal near!

The dimness that had been attributed to the ruin (stanza 4) is now on the speaker's eyes (stanza 19), and Mangan gives an ironic turn to an inconsistency that had passed unobserved by the other translators: the abbey is the vision of a *blind* man ("Gone is the use of eye and ear," Ferguson, stanza 19, rhymed version). In the final stanza of Mangan's version, which has no equivalent in the Irish or in any other version, a suspension is introduced that arrests the speaker's suicidal wish:

> I turned away, as toward my grave,
> And all my dark way homeward by the Atlantic's verge,
> Resounded in mine ears like to a dirge
>   The roaring of the wave.
>
> (stanza 20)

Death is suspended as a mere simile, "as toward my grave," the poet's return being only "homeward." And if the blind poet, on his "dark way," still insists on a natural correlative for his feelings, it mocks his hopes as another semblance, "like to a dirge," its *re*sounding" only an echo of the heavily appropriated "dreary, shingly, billow-beaten shore" of the opening stanza.

In its first publication in the *Nation,* the absence that underlies the poet's appropriation of the ruin is nicely confirmed and repeated in a footnote that provides an ironic contrast to Hardiman's recourse to guidebooks: "Literally 'The House of (St.) Molaga,' and now called Timoleague. Our readers will find its position on the Map of Munster." At this point Mangan's ironic play becomes particularly intricate. Where the other translators of the poem had simply adopted the anglicized form of the name, Mangan here reverts to the Gaelic name, only to find himself obliged to retranslate it. Since the place-name is metonymically derived from that of the abbey itself, the full title of Mangan's poem becomes implicitly absurd, given that it only makes sense so long as the anglicized transliteration disguises the meaning that full translation foregrounds. Similar gestures are found throughout the ballads of the *Nation,* with the difference that nationalist balladeers tend to be content merely to revert to a superficial rewriting of the anglicized name in Gaelic orthography. Retained or restored in this form, the Gaelic name becomes a picturesque index of Irishness, appearing to localize and reroot an English writing while actually seeking to master the otherness of Gaelic speech and culture and assimilate it to an English literary culture. The peculiar vacillation that results, between an ineradicable alienation and a process of familiarization, produces a significant index of the contradictions that trouble the nationalist project for a representative Irish literature. (pp. 78-93)

Translation itself, then, embodies a duplicity which can stand as the approximate index of a contradiction that, in varying degrees, afflicts all nationalisms. Devoted to the unification of a people by the revitalization of a hypothetical past unity, cultural or political, nationalism depends nonetheless on exactly those forces that tend to deracinate a people and that, by instigating an uneven process of modernization, fragment those social structures which come to appear in retrospect as the expression of a coherent and unified national consciousness. Translation, envisaged in both nationalist and unionist cultural thought as an unrefractive medium that restores continuity with the past and transmits the national spirit untransformed, involves for all that an assimilation of alien material in a process of cultural homogenization that is utterly foreign to the older culture. Invoked as a mode of return and reintegration, translation, even by virtue of those very terms, enacts and accentuates the dislocation out of which the dream of unification arises. In the specific context of Ireland, the common assumptions that underlie the cultural theories of both unionist and nationalist politics serve to illuminate their mutual ideological dependence on an expansive administration, without whose instrumental drive to integrate Ireland into the Empire neither the means nor the recipients for the dissemination of alternative ideologies of integration would have existed. (pp. 94-5)

> *David Lloyd, in his* Nationalism and Minor Literature: James Clarence Mangan and the Emergence of Irish Cultural Nationalism, *University of California Press, 1987, 257 p.*

FURTHER READING

Andrews, Jean. "James Clarence Mangan and Romantic Stereotypes: 'Old and Hoary at Thirty-Nine.' " *Irish University Review* 19, No. 2 (Autumn 1989): 240-63.

Asserts that Mangan maintained a religious orthodoxy and celibacy that hindered him from understanding "the darker depths of Romanticism though he assumed its outward trappings" in his life and works.

Cain, Henry Edward. *James Clarence Mangan and the Poe-Mangan Question.* Washington, D.C.: Catholic University of America, 1929, 93 p.

Compares Mangan and Edgar Allan Poe, concluding that while their lives and works show similarities, "there is no direct or indirect evidence to support the contention that one influenced the other." The dissertation also includes a discussion of Mangan's German translations.

Chuto, Jacques. "Mangan, Petrie, O'Donovan, and a Few Others: The Poet and the Scholars." *Irish University Review* 6, No. 2 (Autumn 1976): 169-87.

Focuses on Mangan's Irish works and the role played in their production by prominent Gaelic scholars of the era. Chuto asserts that Mangan did not always rely on literal translations supplied by scholars, but, rather, translated for himself late in his career. For an opposing viewpoint, see MacMahon, cited below.

———. "The Sources of James Clarence Mangan's Oriental Writings." *Notes and Queries* 227, No. 3 (June 1982): 224-28.

Traces many of the sources of Mangan's *Literæ Orientales* to Joseph von Hammer-Purgstall's four-volume *Geschichte der Osmanischen Dichtkunst* (1836-38), a work containing German translations of the poetry of Middle Eastern writers.

Donaghy, Henry J. *James Clarence Mangan.* New York: Twayne Publishers, Inc., 1974, 141 p.

Quotes from Mangan's major works, notes his influence on other writers, and offers a selected bibliography in a study of his life and writings.

Duffy, Charles Gavan. "Personal Memories of James C. Mangan." *The Dublin Review* 142, No. 285 (April 1908): 278-94.

Reminiscence of Mangan by his friend and colleague, Irish nationalist journalist Charles Gavan Duffy (1816-1903).

Feeley, John. "James Clarence Mangan in Joyce's 'The Dead.' " *English Language Notes* XX, Nos. 3-4 (March-June 1983): 27-30.

Suggests that Joyce's writings on Mangan indicate that he used elements of Mangan's life and personality to create the character Michael Furey in his short story "The Dead." For Joyce's discussion of Mangan's work, see excerpt dated 1902.

Graves, Alfred Perceval. "James Clarence Mangan: Poet, Eccentric, and Humorist." *The Cornhill Magazine* n.s. 77, No. 21 (March 1898): 328-39.

Summarizes Mangan's life and literary career in a review of *James Clarence Mangan: His Selected Poems* and *The Life and Writings of James Clarence Mangan.*

Hess, M. Whitcomb. "James Clarence Mangan: A Story of Triumph." *The Catholic World* CLXIX, No. 1,011 (June 1949): 185-90.

Praises Mangan's life and literary career in a tribute occasioned by the centenary of his death.

Lloyd, David. "James Clarence Mangan's Oriental Translations and the Question of Origins." *Comparative Literature* 38, No. 1 (Winter 1986): 20-35.

Examines the translation process used by Mangan in *Literæ Orientales,* quoting from his commentary published with the poems in the *Dublin University Magazine.*

McCall, John. *The Life of James Clarence Mangan.* Dublin: Carraig Books, 1882, 31 p.

Appreciative examination of Mangan's life and literary career.

MacDonagh, Thomas. *Literature in Ireland: Studies Irish and Anglo-Irish.* Dublin: The Talbot Press, 1916, 248 p.

Presents brief commentary on several of Mangan's works in a survey outlining the distinctive qualities of Irish literature written in English.

McKiernan, Eoin. "James Clarence Mangan: Ireland's 'German Poet.' " In *Anglo-German and American-German Crosscurrents,* vol. 1, edited by Philip Alison Shelley, Arthur O. Lewis, Jr., and William W. Betts, Jr., pp. 39-70. Chapel Hill: University of North Carolina Press, 1957.

Maintains that through his German translations Mangan served as an intermediary of German literature in Ireland.

MacMahon, Peter. "James Clarence Mangan: The Irish Language, and the Strange Case of *The Tribes of Ireland.*" *Irish University Review* 8, No. 2 (Autumn 1978): 209-22.

Scrutinizes the sources of *The Tribes of Ireland* and disputes the assertion made by Jacques Chuto (cited above, 1976) that Mangan knew Gaelic. According to MacMahon, "Mangan's knowledge of Irish was negligible, and remained so until his death."

Magalener, Marvin. "James Mangan and Joyce's Dedalus Family." *Philological Quarterly* XXXI, No. 4 (October 1952): 363-71.

Argues that Joyce used aspects of Mangan's life to form the characters Stephen and Simon Dedalus in *A Portrait of the Artist as a Young Man* and *Ulysses.*

Mitchel, John. Introduction to *Poems of James Clarence Mangan,* by James Clarence Mangan, edited by D. J. O'Donoghue, pp. xxvii-xlvii. Dublin: M. H. Gill & Son, 1910.

Biographical introduction which originally appeared in Mitchel's collection of Mangan's poems published in 1859.

Monahan, Michael. "A Group of Irish Poets." *The Forum* XLVIII (November 1912): 565-83.

Includes a section devoted to Mangan, focusing on patriotic elements in his adaptations of Irish works.

O'Brien, John J. "Mangan and Poe." *The Catholic University Bulletin* XV, No. 2 (February 1909): 139-55.

Elaborates on the "curious parallelism" between Mangan and Edgar Allan Poe.

O'Connor, R. F. "James Clarence Mangan." *The American Catholic Quarterly* XXVIII, No. III (July 1903): 435-55.

Commentary on Mangan's life and literary career, focusing on his alleged alcoholism and opium addiction and on his relation to members of the Young Ireland cultural and political movement.

O'Donoghue, D. J. *The Life and Writings of James Clarence Mangan.* Edinburgh: Patrick Geddes & Colleagues, 1897, 250 p.

Quotes extensively from Mangan's autobiographical writings, letters, translations, and verse in a seminal study of his life and literary career.

———. Preface to *Poems of James Clarence Mangan,* by James Clarence Mangan, edited by D. J. O'Donoghue, pp. xi-xxvi. Dublin: M. H. Gill & Son, 1910.

Evaluates Mangan's works and provides biographical information.

Rafroidi, Patrick. *Irish Literature in English: The Romantic Period (1789-1850).* 3 vols. Atlantic Highlands, N.J.: Humanities Press, 1980.

Comments on Mangan's autobiographical writings and major Irish poems, with a biographical summary and list of his published works.

Rogers, Cameron. "Mangan and His Rosaleen." *The Saturday Review of Literature* II, No. 33 (13 March 1926): 625-26.

Sympathetic biography presenting an overview of Mangan's literary career.

Shannon-Mangan, Ellen. "A Letter and a Poem: New Sources for the Life of Mangan." *Eire-Ireland* 21, No. 1 (Spring 1986): 6-15.

Calls for revision of biographical and critical assessments of Mangan based on evidence provided in previously overlooked documents.

Sillard, P. A. "Clarence Mangan and His Poetry." *The Westminster Review* 149, No. 5 (May 1898): 648-54.

Appreciative sketch praising Mangan's poetry and translations.

Thompson, Francis. "James Clarence Mangan" and "A Bewildered Poet." In his *Literary Criticisms*, edited by Terence L. Connolly, S. J., pp. 362-67, 367-70. New York: E. P. Dutton & Co., 1948.

Contains two essays on Mangan: the first discussing his literary career (see excerpt dated 1897); the second presenting general biographical information.

Thompson, Francis J. "Poe and Mangan, 1949." *The Dublin Magazine* n.s. XXV, No. 5 (January-March 1950): 33-40.

Examines possible literary cross-influences between Mangan and Edgar Allan Poe.

———. "Mangan in America, 1850-1860: Mitchel, Maryland and Melville." *The Dublin Magazine* n.s. XXVII, No. 3 (July-September 1952): 30-41.

Charts the critical reception of Mangan's poetry in the United States during the decade after his death.

Review of *The Autobiography of James Clarence Mangan,* by James Clarence Mangan, edited by James Kilroy. *The Times Literary Supplement,* No. 3,507 (15 May 1969): 528.

Summarizes Mangan's life, stressing his unhappiness.

Welch, Robert. "James Clarence Mangan: 'Apples from the Dead Sea Shore.' " In his *Irish Poetry from Moore to Yeats,* pp. 76-115. Totowa, N. J.: Barnes & Noble Books, 1980.

Studies the themes and political implications of Mangan's versions of German, Oriental, and Gaelic poems, emphasizing their presentation of self-identity.

Williams, Alfred M. "James Clarence Mangan." In his *The Poets and Poetry of Ireland,* pp. 325-35. Boston: James R. Osgood & Co., 1881.

Offers biographical information and a small selection of Mangan's works in an anthology of Irish verse that includes historical and critical essays.

Yeats, William Butler. "Clarence Mangan's Love Affair." In his *Uncollected Prose, Vol. 1: First Reviews and Articles, 1886-1896,* edited by John P. Frayne, pp. 194-98. New York: Columbia University Press, 1970.

Focuses on Mangan's alleged love affair and suggests biographical causes behind the melancholic tone of his poetry in an essay that originally appeared in *United Ireland* (22 August 1891). For Yeats's discussion of Mangan's work and its significance, see excerpt dated 1887.

Hannah More

1745-1833

English dramatist, poet, essayist, tract writer, and novelist.

One of the most popular authors of her time, More initially gained renown as a dramatist and poet, and later as a writer of political and religious tracts and essays on religion, morality, and education. Early in her career she found support for her work among the Bluestockings, a group of writers and intellectuals of the second half of the eighteenth century who held meetings intended to provide a forum for women to discuss literature and art with men. Although she was especially praised for her dramas, she eventually rejected the theater as a morally corrupting influence and devoted herself to encouraging ethical reform through her essays and the stories she published as *Cheap Repository Tracts.*

More was the daughter of a Bristol schoolmaster who tutored her in reading, mathematics, and Latin, giving her an education far more extensive than what was usually offered to girls in the mid-eighteenth century. However, she was so adept at her studies that her father feared overeducating her in subjects he considered the province of men and discontinued her lessons in mathematics before she was ten years old. At the age of twelve, she was sent to a boarding school for girls that had been recently established by her eldest sister. She wrote her first drama, *The Search after Happiness,* at the age of seventeen, intending it as a suitable replacement for the "improper" dramas often used to instruct young ladies in recitation. After completing her studies, she served as an instructor in her sister's school for several years, resigning her position in 1767 when she became engaged to a wealthy landowner. After six years of postponements by her fiancé, More broke off the engagement, and later accepted an annuity from him as compensation for her lost time. Now free from financial concerns, More dedicated herself to literary pursuits. *The Search after Happiness* was successfully performed in Bath in 1773, and More was well received by literary society in London when she made her first visit there later that year. She made the acquaintance of prominent writers associated with the Bluestockings, including Samuel Johnson and Elizabeth Montagu, who welcomed her into their circle. More became close friends with the actor David Garrick, and consulted with him during her composition of *Percy,* a tragedy concerned with the destructive nature of jealousy. He not only supported its production with his influence in the theater, but also wrote the prologue and epilogue. A popular success for its engaging plot and emotional power, *Percy* established More's reputation as a writer.

After Garrick's death in 1779, More became less socially active. While her religious beliefs had always kept her from dances, card-playing, and other activities she considered frivolous or dissolute, she now also refused to attend the theater because she believed that its stimulation of the imagination was corrupting. As a result, she ceased writing plays for performance in favor of those, such as her *Sacred Dramas,* which were intended to be read rather than performed. Nevertheless, she continued to frequent Bluestocking gatherings, praising the members and their recognition of the place of women in intellectual discourse in her poem *The Bas Bleu.*

In 1785 More moved to a cottage near Bristol and thereafter she visited London infrequently. Focusing on religious and moral issues, she wrote such essays as *Thoughts on the Importance of the Manners of the Great to General Society* and *An Estimate of the Religion of the Fashionable World.* More published these volumes anonymously because she feared the reaction of her friends to these works, which criticized their way of life, and because she felt that a woman might not be taken seriously on these subjects. However, the books were very well received, and she went on to publish several more volumes on moral and educational reform. In her essays, More frequently combined progressive ideas with conservative goals. For example, she advocated a more extensive and rigorous education for females, although maintaining that women should use this education only in their traditional domestic roles. Similarly, she advocated teaching the poor to read, and established Sunday schools throughout the Bristol area toward this end; however, her ultimate goal was to instill in the lower classes values of frugality, piety, and acceptance of their position in life. Although resistance to educating the poor existed, More's schools were generally successful, with high enrollment and the approval of many in the upper classes.

In 1794 More began publishing a series of *Cheap Repository*

Tracts to counteract the influence of French revolutionary politics on the working classes, as well as to offer a pious alternative to what she considered the morally harmful fiction available to the poor. She designed the tracts to compete with the inexpensive, entertaining chapbooks that had been popular with working-class readers for years, couching conservative politics in short, entertaining stories. Immensely popular, over two million copies were published in the first two years. More stopped writing the tracts when the threat of French revolutionary ideas subsided, although others imitated her style and format for years.

In 1808 More published her only novel, *Cœlebs in Search of a Wife,* in which she adapted what she considered a decadent genre to moral purposes. The novel combines the story of Cœlebs's search with instructions for young men and women on how to lead pious and productive lives, and for parents on how to raise their children. Although some critics condemned the novel as religious fanaticism and others felt that nothing could counteract the degenerate influence of novels, most approved of More's mixture of religious instruction and narrative. The novel was phenomenally popular, selling out twelve editions in its first year. More continued to write essays on religion and morality until illness prevented her in 1825. She died in 1833.

Most critics divide More's career into two phases: her Bluestocking writings and her religious writings. Although her poems and dramas were extremely popular and highly acclaimed during her lifetime, after her death these works fell into critical disfavor and were often ridiculed for sentimentality, superficiality, and lack of wit. Recent evaluations have found her poems and dramas interesting in their reflection of late eighteenth-century values and concerns, but mediocre in their style and content. Critical reaction to More's religious writings followed a similar cycle of great praise followed by criticism and ridicule, and are studied today for their value as historical documents and their role in literary history. In particular, her tracts are considered to have been important in popularizing the short story form with English and American readers, and her novel *Cœlebs in Search of a Wife* has been credited with helping to reconcile religious readers to what had been regarded as a spiritually injurious genre of literature.

Critics today agree that More's greatest achievement lies in her wide-ranging influence on her contemporaries, noting that she was unusual for an author of her time in having written successfully for readers of both the upper and lower classes. Feminists consider her writings and life to have been important in the advancement of women's education and in challenging attitudes about women's intellectual competence. Her efforts to educate the poor and to engender moral reform reached many through her Sunday schools, her stories, and her essays. Although many of More's works do not address modern concerns, Edmund Gosse explains that they "responded with adroitness to the immediate instincts of her own generation."

PRINCIPAL WORKS

The Search after Happiness: A Pastoral Drama (drama) 1773

The Inflexible Captive: A Tragedy (drama) 1774

Sir Eldred of the Bower and the Bleeding Rock: Two Legendary Tales (poetry) 1776

Essays on Various Subjects, Principally Designed for Young Ladies (essays) 1777

Ode to Dragon, Mr. Garrick's House-Dog, at Hampton (poetry) 1777

Percy: A Tragedy (drama) 1777

The Fatal Falsehood: A Tragedy (drama) 1779

Sacred Dramas: Chiefly Intended for Young Persons, the Subjects Taken from the Bible (dramas) 1782

Florio: A Tale for Fine Gentlemen and Fine Ladies. The Bas Bleu; or, Conversation (poetry) 1786

Slavery (poetry) 1788

Thoughts on the Importance of the Manners of the Great to General Society (essay) 1788

Bishop Bonner's Ghost (poetry) 1789

An Estimate of the Religion of the Fashionable World (essay) 1791

Village Politics, by Will Chip (tract) 1792

The Shepherd of Salisbury Plain (tract) 1794

Cheap Repository Tracts (tracts) 1795-97; also published as *Stories for the Middle Ranks of Society, and Tales for the Common People* [revised edition], 1818

Strictures on the Modern System of Female Education with a View of the Principles and Conduct Prevalent among Women of Rank and Fortune. 2 vols. (essay) 1799

Hints towards Forming the Character of a Young Princess. 2 vols. (essay) 1805

Cœlebs in Search of a Wife: Comprehending Observations on Domestic Habits and Manners, Religion and Morals (novel) 1808

Practical Piety; or, The Influence of the Religion of the Heart on the Conduct of the Life. 2 vols. (essay) 1811

Christian Morals. 2 vols. (essay) 1813

An Essay on the Character and Practical Writings of St. Paul. 2 vols. (essay) 1815

Moral Sketches of Prevailing Opinions and Manners, Foreign and Domestic: With Reflections on Prayer (essay) 1819

Bible Rhymes on the Names of All the Books of the Old and New Testament, with Allusions to Some of the Principal Incidents and Characters (verse) 1821

The Spirit of Prayer (essay) 1825

The Feast of Freedom; or, The Abolition of Domestic Slavery in Ceylon (essay) 1827

The Works of Hannah More. 11 vols. (poetry, dramas, essays, and novel) 1830

Memoirs of the Life and Correspondence of Mrs. Hannah More. 2 vols. (letters) 1837

THE MONTHLY REVIEW, LONDON (essay date 1778)

[*In the following excerpt from a review of More's* Percy, *the critic compares the drama to its source,* Gabrielle de Vergy, *and praises its sentiments and language.*]

Although this publication [*Percy: A Tragedy*] carries no name in the title-page, it cannot properly be called anonymous, since the last leaf announces several other productions *lately published by the same* AUTHOR; some of which, if not all, we remember to have come forth as the avowed works of Miss Hannah More, an ingenious female, of Bristol.

A *very laconic* advertisement, immediately preceding the piece, acquaints the Reader, that 'the French drama, founded on the famous old story of *Raoul de Coucy,* suggested to the Author some circumstances in the *former part* of this tragedy.' The French drama here *obscurely* alluded to, is the *Gabrielle de Vergy* of M. de Belloy, the popular author of *the Siege of Calais,* and other tragedies; to one of which our stage is indebted for the well-received drama of *the Grecian Daughter.*

Gabrielle de Vergy is the undoubted parent of **Percy,** not having given birth only to 'some circumstances in the *former part* of the tragedy,' but having manifestly engendered the whole. Such, however, is the operation of time, that French tragedy is now become too *horrible* for the English stage, and Miss More thought herself obliged to soften some of the leading incidents in the drama of M. de Belloy: a singular change of taste in two rival nations!—unless we solve the miracle by reflecting that *Gabrielle* is the work of a man, and **Percy** the production of a lady: the result is, that Miss More's tragedy is the most delicate, M. de Belloy's the most nervous.

Percy, however, holds no contemptible station in the ranks of modern tragedy. The fable is, with much address, accommodated to the 'old story' of Chevy Chace; the characters, with the happy addition of Lord Raby, are copies from Belloy; the sentiments are, many of them, natural and delicate; and the language, in general, is flowing and easy, though not totally free from female prettinesses. . . . (p. 23)

> *A review of "Percy: A Tragedy," in* The Monthly Review, *London, Vol. LVIII, January, 1778, pp. 23-6.*

HORACE WALPOLE   (letter date 1785)

[*An English author, politician, and publisher, Walpole is best known for his memoirs and voluminous correspondence, which provide revealing glimpses of life in England during the last half of the eighteenth century. He was a close friend and correspondent of More's for twenty years. In the following letter to More, Walpole praises the variety of More's talents and particularly, the humor of an anonymous, satirical letter she had sent to him. She had ridiculed the fashion of adopting French idioms into the English language by creating an example of the corrupted language of the future.*]

Had I not heard part of your conversation with Mrs Carter the other night, Madam, I should certainly not have discovered the authoress of the very ingenious anticipation of our future jargon. How should I? I am not fortunate enough to know all your talents—nay, I question whether you yourself suspect all you possess. Your **Bas Bleu** is in a style very different from any of your other productions that I have seen—and your intuition into the degeneracy of our language has a vein of humour and satire that could not be calculated from your **Bas Bleu,** in which good nature and good humour had made a great deal of learning wear all the ease of familiarity. I did wish you to write another **Percy**—but I beg now that you will first produce a specimen of *all* the various manners in which you can shine; for since you are as modest as if your issue were illegitimate, I don't know but, like some females really in fault, you would stifle some of your pretty infants, rather than be detected and blush.

In the mean time, I beseech you not only to print your "Specimen" of the language that is to be in fashion, but have it entered at Stationers' Hall, or depend upon it, if ever a copy falls into the hands of a fine gentleman yet unborn, who shall be able both to read and write, he will adopt your letter for his

own, and the galimatias will give the *ton* to the Court, as *Euphues* did near two hundred years ago; and then you will have corrupted our language instead of defending it—and surely it is not *your* interest, Madam, to have pure English grow obsolete!

If you do not promise to grant my request, I will show your letter everywhere to those that are worthy of seeing it—that is indeed, in very few places—for you *shall* have the honour of it. It is one of those compositions that prove themselves standards, by begetting imitations; and if the genuine parent is unknown, it will be ascribed to everybody that is supposed (in his own set) to have more wit than the rest of the world. I should be diverted, I own, to hear it faintly disavowed by some who would wish to pass for its authors—but still there is more pleasure in doing justice to merit, than in drawing vain pretensions into a scrape; and therefore I think you and I had better be honest and acknowledge it, though to you (for I am out of the question but as evidence) it will be painful; for though the proverb says, tell truth and shame the devil, I believe he is never half so much confounded, as an amiable young gentlewoman who is discovered to have more taste and abilities than she ever ventured to ascribe to herself even in the most private dialogues with her own heart; especially when that native friend is so pure as to have no occasion to make allowances even for self-love. For my part, I am most seriously obliged to you, Madam, for so agreeable and kind a communication, and am with sincere regard

> Your most grateful and obedient humble servant,
> HOR. WALPOLE
> (pp. 226-27)

> *Horace Walpole, in a letter to Hannah More on April 5, 1785, in his* Horace Walpole's Correspondence with Hannah More, *W. S. Lewis, Robert A. Smith, and Charles W. Bennett, eds., Yale University Press, 1961, pp. 226-27.*

ZACHARY MACAULAY   (essay date 1809)

[*A close friend of More's and a fellow Evangelical, Macaulay was unaware that More was the author of* Cœlebs in Search of a Wife *when he wrote a review of it for the* Christian Observer. *In the following excerpt from that review, Macaulay analyzes narrative form, characterization, and style in order to evaluate the work's success in combining religious instruction with fictional narrative.*]

It may be very true that novels are mischievous; but we cannot allow this work [**Cœlebs in Search of a Wife; comprehending Observations on Domestic Habits and Manners, Religion and Morals**] to be called a novel. "Definitions indeed are dangerous," and therefore we shall not hazard them;—it is plain, however, a composition should not be denominated by reference to a single feature or quality, but according to its really prevailing character. Who, for instance, would speak of Boëthius's *Consolation of Philosophy,* as a poem, though it contains a good quantity of verses? Who calls the *Jerusalem Delivered* a romance? Yet it is full of tales of wonder. At the least, works should not be miscalled; for the learned tell us, that names are things. If they belong to no species, let them remain unclassified. In novels, as in dramas, the author *teaches by examples.* Whether he wishes to instruct or amuse, it is by a fable, artfully inlaid with incidents and characters, that he principally works. This is his machinery; and though many a grave and pithy sentence may be dropped in the course of the story, the distinctive character of the book remains, and nobody mistakes it for a treatise in philosophy. The work now under review is of a different kind. The object of the writer evidently was, not to construct an interesting fable, but to communicate a variety of religious, moral, and economical truths, in an easy and agreeable manner. Essays are formal; sermons are dull; and the question-and-answer way is babyish. A narrative affords facilities which cannot otherwise be secured; and for this reason, and for this reason only, it seems to have been adopted. It is merely a frame-work for better things. Some characters are of necessity introduced; but for the most part they are mere visitors, and neither hasten nor retard the action of the piece. They are principally employed to exemplify or illustrate the precepts which are inculcated; as a father, in an evening walk with his son, diversifies the conversation by remarks on the objects around him.

We think, then, that if this work is censured merely as a novel, it will be blamed for being what it is not. That it partakes slightly of the character and peculiarities of that species of composition, is true; and it may probably, therefore, in the same proportion, share its disadvantages. Still it should in fairness be considered, whether more is not gained than sacrificed by this arrangement. At the least, the author is entitled to have the merits of his execution weighed against the faults of his design; and if such a process be instituted, he can have little reason to fear the result.

The story, which the author under review has selected for his purpose, is a very simple one. Cœlebs, himself one of the principal actors, is the narrator. He is a young man not quite four-and-twenty, and remarkably steady for his years; of a plain understanding, excellent principles, and four thousand pounds a-year. The work is a journal of his adventures.— Having the misfortune to lose his parents, home became dull; and he thought, as youths of his age are apt to think, that a wife would be very agreeable. Like other youths too, he sketched an image of excellence suited to his taste; "She must be elegant, or I should not love her; sensible, or I should not respect her; prudent, or I could not confide in her; well-informed, or she could not educate my children; well-bred, or she could not entertain my friends; pious, or I could not be happy with her." Strange to relate, Westmoreland did not contain such a paragon; so the post-chaise was ordered, and drove straight to London. The young adventurer was landed at Sir John Belfield's in Cavendish Square, an old friend of his father's, where he met with an hospitable reception; and at this house he passed the principal part of the time spent in the metropolis. . . . The weeks in town produced nothing of importance, but were diversified by visits, in which the reader is introduced to various ladies in high life, and to a Mrs. Ranby at Hampstead; for, by some odd accident, Cœlebs generally finds himself in female society. The men, we suppose, were at White's, or the House of Commons.

Cœlebs had wished to visit London, but he had no thoughts of resting there. He had promised his father not to suffer his affections to be engaged, till he had seen Mr. Stanley in Hampshire. To the Grove therefore he goes, and finds a paradise; a father, a mother, and six lovely daughters practising every virtue, and enjoying the most genuine happiness. This family is drawn for a model of domestic perfection and felicity. The purest Scriptural piety, unwearied beneficence, sense, taste, spirit, mutual affection, humility, every grace and every virtue, are here found united in admirable symmetry, and embellished by all the gifts of nature and of fortune. The imagi-

nation is delighted, and longs to detain for ever the seraphic vision. What could Cœlebs do? Lucilla Stanley was just nineteen; pious, gentle, elegant, intelligent; and the very air of the Grove breathed love. Within a few weeks a declaration was made to Mr. Stanley; but as the feelings of forty-six and twenty-four are not perfectly sympathetic, a month's novitiate was enjoined, greatly to the discomposure of the young lover, but greatly to the relief and benefit of the reader; who is the gainer, by this arrangement, of at least four hundred pages of excellent composition, besides being rescued awhile from the perils of an *eclaircissement*. The interval is filled with visits and conversation; in which many of the neighbouring families bear a part; some interesting histories are told, and much admirable truth inculcated. The arrival of the Belfields at the Grove adds to the general happiness; and every thing goes on so smoothly, that we almost hoped the love affair had been forgotten: but, alas! before the month expires, the fatal moment is accelerated by the *gaucherie* of a baby sister. Thanks to the mercy of our author, all is over in an instant. Lucilla seems to have thought very little about the matter; but as Cœlebs had behaved with propriety, and the match was unexceptionable, she referred it to her parents, and the rest was soon settled. Mr. Stanley judged it right that the union of the young people should be postponed for three months; so, as the affair happened last autumn, we suppose they were married a little before Christmas.

So simple a tale as this affords very little room for praise or censure. There is enough of it to furnish an outline, and a point of convergence, which is all that the author's plan required; and the preceptive parts are not choaked with incidents. It is difficult to say who is the hero of the tale. The rival claimants are Cœlebs and Mr. Stanley; though, to say the truth, there is very little of the heroic in either of them. The critics would hold this uncertainty to be a fault; but, as the same defect is attributed to the *Pharsalia* and the *Paradise Lost,* a writer of the nineteenth century may submit to share their disgrace. The story, however, has one prime excellence. It is perfectly in nature; and not only that (for nature may be any thing), but it is drawn from the very best model. Certainly it is not romantic, yet we cannot but think a true taste will contemplate with great delight the picture of quiet goodness here presented to us. Surely to a Christian's eye, Lucilla praying by the side of her poor cottager ought to appear a more sublime and interesting object, than even Clementina in her madness, or Corinne in the Capitol.

The characters introduced in this work are numerous, and of very different degrees of excellence. Some of them are certainly drawn with great force and spirit; but a severe critic would perhaps say, that those intended as warnings are over-coloured, and the models not coloured at all. Yet this is a defect which it is more easy to observe than avoid; for all strong painting borders on caricature; and real goodness is like perfect beauty, which commonly seems inanimate upon canvas.

Cœlebs, the narrator, the lover, and perhaps the hero of the work, would have appeared to more advantage, if the story had been told by another. However, we think him very good and very sensible, admirably suited for domestic life in the county of Westmoreland, though not quite equal to the bustle and activity of London. We should have liked a little more fire at four-and-twenty; but there is no having contradictory excellencies, and his piety is worth a thousand dazzling qualities. Yet Cœlebs has faults which must not be wholly overlooked. He is given to prosing, is not very delicate, and has a low suspiciousness about him that is exceedingly unamiable. He is perfectly possessed too with the idea, that, wherever he goes, mothers and daughters are throwing out lures. The Ranbys, the Fenthams, the Flams, not to mention the *belles* of Westmoreland, are all angling for Mr. Cœlebs. Really he should not have believed his friends, when they talked such nonsense to him.

Mr. Stanley, one of the leading figures of the piece, is a portrait which it required something more than genius, enriched by observation, to execute; for as Milton declares that no one can be a poet who is not himself the epitome of a good poem, so we may venture to say, that he who could sketch this exalted character must have felt in his own bosom the power of holiness;—that he is himself, in some measure, the great sublime he teaches. This eulogy is not bestowed rashly; and we do not believe it will be thought extravagant by any one who considers, not only the varied excellencies combined in Mr. Stanley, but the admirable skill with which they are proportioned. Any body can take a heap of Christian graces, throw them carelessly together, and, calling his image a god, command the people to fall down and worship; but so to distribute the elements of moral and intellectual greatness, that every part of the figure shall be in perfect symmetry, yet the whole swelling with divinity, is a task of a far higher kind, and demands not only a knowledge of the doctrines and precepts of Christianity, but an experimental acquaintance with their separate and their combined influence on the heart. We need hardly add, that piety—pure, vital, practical piety—is the governing principle of Mr. Stanley's character. He lives only to the glory of God and the good of man; and these great ends he prosecutes with combined ardour and intelligence; with unwearied diligence, steady temper, discretion, and humility. The march of his virtues is like the course of nature, silent and effective. Though his character is full of force, its powers are rather felt than seen: without prominence, without bustle, they remind us of those matchless pieces of ancient sculpture, whose expression is calm greatness, the union of energy and repose.

Lucilla is Mr. Stanley grown young, and softened into a woman. Pious and humble, active and intelligent, adding grace to virtue, and the more lovely, because unconscious of her loveliness, she appears a seraph "just lighted on this orb, which she hardly seems to touch." There is a charm in youthful piety, thus associated with elegance and gentleness, and decently attired in the soft veil which modesty throws around it, which no words can adequately paint. Every eye turns to it with rapture, and every heart does willing homage. Lucilla has only one defect—she wants a little of her father's self-possession. Not that a girl of nineteen should have too much; but Lucilla puts the sugar into the cream-pot, and the tea into the sugar-dish, and runs out of the room, because her baby sister tells that she reads Latin. She blushes and cries too on every occasion, and sometimes when we really think the matter was not very moving; though if she had blushed deeply at one of the questions proposed to her by Cœlebs, we could have forgiven it. These overt acts of sensibility, we suspect, are commonly less a proof of fine feeling than of want of self-government; and though it is both proper and pleasing for a man of sense to give an arm to his companion through the rough walk of life, yet if she knock her foot against every pebble in the path, the journey will prove wearisome to both.

Angelic as Lucilla's character really is, we are not without fears that the men will think it insipid. There is no helping

this; very good people are apt to seem insipid. Religion is such a neutralizer of the character, that, unless pious women are loved for their piety, they must often be content to be passed by altogether. Consider St. Paul's account of female graces—shame-facedness and sobriety; the ornament of a meek and quiet spirit—how exceedingly uninteresting! There is hardly a Madona on canvas that does not want intelligence; and we suspect if this writer were arraigned for the insipidity of Lucilla's character before Guido and Raphael, his sentence would be a very mild one. We have sometimes thought that persons of eminent holiness are like pellucid bodies, which philosophers tell us contain more matter than opaque ones; but every part being justly distributed, the light passes freely through, nothing detains the eye, and they are as if they were not. (pp. 109-13)

[We think that the author's powers] are rather historical than dramatic. He conceives well, and describes forcibly; but he wants ductility for the stage. He has not, in much perfection, that Proteus-power, which enables a writer to transform himself into every shape and form he wishes to exhibit: the dialogues, therefore, with all their merits, are not very characteristic. In this respect our author is the very opposite of Miss Burney, who is perfectly at home in company, but writes indifferently in her own person.

We are sorry to see this writer adopting, even partially, the practice of nic-naming his personages. We have Mrs. Comfit and the Miss Rattles, and Signor Squallini, &c. This is one of the bad fashions that Ben Johnson contributed to make popular, but it really is only fit for children on Twelfth-night.

We can afford no more space to the plot and characters of this work. They are merely auxiliary to the main design; and therefore we repeat our humble remonstrance against the work being objected to as a novel. If, however, a novel it must be called, as we are not contentious about names, then we venture to hint that it ought not to be condemned as uninteresting. The author could easily have given it more poignancy; but, we are bold to say, he has made it as interesting as he intended. His *first, great* object was to instruct; and having ventured, with a just confidence in his own powers, to seek assistance in this undertaking from the most dangerous of all allies, his saga-city enabled him to discover how delicate a management was necessary to prevent his object being defeated by the very means he had adopted for securing it. We feel great admiration at the skill he has shown in extricating himself from this difficulty. A little more complication of incident, a little more intensity of passion and feeling, would have completely ruined his project. The work would have been a novel; a mere novel;—interesting, and useless. Surely much reasoning is not needed to convince us how idle it is for a writer of romance to attempt to be sententious. Who ever reads the didactic parts of an attractive novel? Who *can* read them? Who even knows that they exist? When the feelings are roused and the fancy fired, they will brook no delay; the mind, pressing impetuously forward, hurries to the conclusion; and truth, wit, learning, elegance, are alike thrown aside as trifling and obtrusive. Even the rich landscape-painting of Mrs. Radcliffe is felt as an incumbrance. The Pyrenean heights, the Alpine forests, and laughing plains of Lombardy, are alike cast into the shade by the lurid flames her imagination kindles around them. Yet what a pencil was her's! with powers to adorn all that is elegant, and darken all that is awful; to exhibit, with rival genius,

Whate'er Lorrain light sketch'd, with softening hue,

Or savage Rosa dash'd, or learned Poussin drew.

We feel bound, therefore, to render to this author high praise for his discriminating judgement in the conduct of a very delicate and difficult enterprize. He has succeeded. His work is both interesting and instructive. Yet we would caution others not to enter rashly on the same project—to be quite sure they possess his genius before they imitate his example. The Pelian javelin was only to be wielded by the arm of Achilles. (pp. 114-15)

Divinity is an odd ingredient in a work of imagination; yet the author of these volumes has ventured on this novelty; and those who think the practice strange, may perhaps be reconciled to it by the justness of the sentiments thus introduced. The theology of Cœlebs is drawn immediately from the Scriptures; not loose and general, like the creed of the world, in which all truths have equal weight, like bodies in an exhausted receiver, because indeed none have any; not warped from its just symmetry by the disproportioned size of a favourite doctrine: but pure, just, elevated, and comprehensive; without bigotry, without enthusiasm. Neither is it unnaturally torn away from that code of Christian morals, which is the very body in which it lives, and every part and member of which it inspires with life and action. Unless, indeed, Christian doctrines and Christian practice are thus united, neither can be fully understood or justly exhibited. Like the great chemical agents in nature, they are incapable of existing in separation; and in these volumes we see them, with delight, always allied in the closest amity. (pp. 115-16)

The style of this work is, in general, animated and correct; not remarkable for grace, but in the earlier parts full of life, and in the latter easy and copious. It is principally defective in variety; a fault much felt in the dialogues, where the whole company, old and young, belles and beaux, gentle and simple, talk as if sentences, cut into lengths, had been delivered out to them from a magazine. Yet there is a spirit in the composition which keeps the attention ever wakeful. The language is often choice, always appropriate.

Of the defects of this work, we have already taken some notice; and certainly, for those who wish to make sport, a religious novel is so open to ridicule, that Momus himself could not desire a better laughing-stock. But the office of censure has, for us, no charm, except the ease with which it is executed; and it is pitiful to jest, where we should listen and be wise. Yet there are a few particulars to which we wish to advert; and we have sufficient confidence in the candour and good sense of this writer, to be persuaded that he will be rather gratified than offended with ingenuous criticism.

We object then, first and vehemently, to the title of these volumes. A squire of Westmoreland may go *in search* of grouse or woodcocks; but, to beat about thus for *a wife,* is not altogether so well imagined. Girls may be thought fair game; yet they are not quite on a level with red-legged partridges.

The author's dread of romance, though just and salutary, has made him, we think, incline a little to an opposite fault. The young lover is not merely steady, but has a drawling gravity about him that is tiresome. He is in danger of being a sad proser at fifty. Even the angel Lucilla might have had more play of fancy and features, without losing any thing of her dignity.

In the second volume, the conversations are both too long and too monotonous. We suspect that the writer grew a little tired before his task was finished.

We think accomplishments are rather undervalued in this work. Artist ladies, indeed, are like their own performances, fit only to be shewn to connoisseurs; yet surely music and drawing, at least, are innocent and elegant attainments. To consider them as of prime importance is silly; to let them engross our time or feed our vanity is sinful;—but it really seems hard on Lucilla, who has a fine ear and correct eye, not to allow her to cultivate graces for which she is naturally qualified, merely because she had five younger sisters to attend to. We say of accomplishments, what the writer himself says of poetry,—"To raise and purify the amusements of mankind, is surely not only to give pleasure, but to render service. It is allowable to seize every avenue to the heart of a being prone to evil; to rescue him, by every fair means, not only from the degradation of vice, but from the dominion of idleness."

We have to complain, occasionally, of some want of taste and delicacy, probably the effect of inadvertence. Cœlebs, in particular, is apt to be vulgar. He talks of the amusements of a religious family *smacking* of their religion; of the *live-stock* of Eden, &c.; and once, when Lucilla smiles on him, we find him exclaiming in his heart, "Lord Staunton, I defy thee!" To speak honestly, after many efforts, and some self-reproach, we still find it difficult to be quite reconciled to this youth. Lucilla, perhaps, will improve him.

Amidst a great deal of excellent wit, there are a few failures; and though the allusions shew the mind of the writer to be enriched with very varied information, there is perhaps rather too much display of knowledge.

We have spoken of the defects of this work; but how shall we find proper terms in which to speak of its merits? The sentiments expressed in **Cœlebs** are so congenial to those which we have ever approved and laboured to inculcate, that an eulogy passed on this writer would be an eulogy on ourselves. To say all we feel, would appear both adulation and vanity; to say less, would be unjust. We must be content, therefore, to deny to ourselves the most pleasing of all offices, and leave the reader to collect our opinion from the general tenor of this article. Yet, if it were permitted us to express the feelings of delight, admiration, and gratitude, with which we have perused these volumes—delight in anticipating their usefulness, admiration at the genius and virtues of the author, and gratitude for the consecration of such talents to the cause of truth—the writer would not think us either jealous or insensible of excellence.—May the Father of all Goodness bless this work to his glory, in the advancement of piety and happiness. To Him, doubtless, it is an acceptable sacrifice; and what are the applauses, even of the wise and good, compared with his favour, "in whose presence is life, and at whose right hand are pleasures for evermore?" (pp. 120-21)

> *Zachary Macaulay, in an originally unsigned review of "Cœlebs in Search of a Wife," in* The Christian Observer, *Vol. VIII, No. 1, January, 1809, pp. 109-21.*

SYDNEY SMITH   (essay date 1809)

[*An English cleric, essayist, and lecturer, Smith founded the* Edinburgh Review *in 1802 to provide a forum for liberal and Whig opinions. While his active campaigns for such causes as*

Catholic emancipation and Church reform and against slavery and prisons earned him a reputation as a humane man, he was also known for his keen wit. In the following review of Cœlebs in Search of a Wife, *Smith severely criticizes both the literary aspects of the novel and the moral principles on which it was based.*]

This book [*Cœlebs in Search of a Wife; comprehending Observations on Domestic Habits and Manners, Religion and Morals*] is written, or supposed to be written (for we would speak timidly of the mysteries of superior beings), by the celebrated Mrs. Hannah More! We shall probably give great offence by such indiscretion; but still we must be excused for treating it as a book merely human,—an uninspired production,—the result of mortality left to itself, and depending on its own limited resources. In taking up the subject in this point of view, we solemnly disclaim the slightest intention of indulging in any indecorous levity, or of wounding the religious feelings of a large class of very respectable persons. It is the only method in which we can possibly make this work a proper object of criticism. We have the strongest possible doubts of the attributes usually ascribed to this authoress; and we think it more simple and manly to say so at once, than to admit nominally superlunary claims, which, in the progress of our remarks, we should virtually deny.

Cœlebs wants a wife; and, after the death of his father, quits his estate in Northumberland to see the world, and to seek for one of its best productions, a woman, who may add materially to the happiness of his future life. His first journey is to London, where, in the midst of the gay society of the metropolis, of course, he does not find a wife; and his next journey is to the family of Mr. Stanley, the head of the Methodists, a serious people, where, of course, he does find a wife. The exaltation, therefore, of what the authoress deems to be the religious, and the depreciation of what she considers to be the worldly character, and the influence of both upon matrimonial happiness, form the subject of this novel—rather of this *dramatic sermon.*

The machinery upon which the discourse is suspended, is of the slightest and most inartificial texture, bearing every mark of haste, and possessing not the slightest claim to merit. Events there are none; and scarcely a character of any interest. The book is intended to convey religious advice; and no more labour appears to have been bestowed upon the story, than was merely sufficient to throw it out of the dry, didactic form. Lucilla is totally uninteresting; so is Mr. Stanley; Dr. Barlow still worse; and Cœlebs a mere clod or dolt. Sir John and Lady Belfield are rather more interesting—and for a very obvious reason, they have some faults;—they put us in mind of men and women;—they seem to belong to one common nature with ourselves. As we read, we seem to think we might act as such people act, and therefore we attend; whereas imitation is hopeless in the more perfect characters which Mrs. More has set before us; and therefore, they inspire us with very little interest.

There are books however of all kinds; and those may not be unwisely planned which set before us very pure models. They are less probable, and therefore less amusing than ordinary stories; but they are more amusing than plain, unfabled precept. Sir Charles Grandison is less agreeable than Tom Jones; but it is more agreeable than Sherlock and Tillotson; and teaches religion and morality to many who would not seek it in the productions of these professional writers.

But, making every allowance for the difficulty of the task which Mrs. More has prescribed to herself, the book abounds with marks of negligence and want of skill; with representations of life and manners which are either false or trite.

Temples to friendship and virtue must be totally laid aside, for many years to come, in novels. Mr. Lane, of the Minerva Press, has given them up long since; and we were quite surprised to find such a writer as Mrs. More busied in moral brick and mortar. Such an idea, at first, was merely juvenile; the second time a little nauseous; but the ten thousandth time, it is quite intolerable. Cœlebs, upon his first arrival in London, dines out,—meets with a bad dinner,—supposes the cause of that bad dinner to be the erudition of the ladies of the house,—talks to them upon learned subjects, and finds them as dull and ignorant as if they had piqued themselves upon all the mysteries of housewifery. We humbly submit to Mrs. More, that this is not humorous, but strained and unnatural. Philippics against frugivorous children after dinner, are too common. Lady Melbury has been introduced into every novel for these four years last past. Peace to her ashes! . . .

The great object kept in view throughout the whole of this introduction, is the enforcement of religious principle, and the condemnation of a life lavished in dissipation and fashionable amusement. In the pursuit of this object, it appears to us, that Mrs. More is much too severe upon the ordinary amusements of mankind, many of which she does not object to in this, or that degree; but altogether. Cœlebs and Lucilla, her *optimus* and *optima,* never dance, and never go to the play. They not only stay away from the comedies of Congreve and Farquhar, for which they may easily enough be forgiven; but they never go to see Mrs. Siddons in the Gamester, or in Jane Shore. The finest exhibition of talent, and the most beautiful moral lessons, are interdicted, at the theatre. There is something in the word *Playhouse,* which seems so closely connected, in the minds of these people, with sin, and Satan,—that it stands in their vocabulary for every species of abomination. And yet why? Where is every feeling more roused in favour of virtue, than at a good play? Where is goodness so feelingly, so enthusiastically learnt? What so solemn as to see the excellent passions of the human heart called forth by a great actor, animated by a great poet? To hear Siddons repeat what Shakespeare wrote! To behold the child, and his mother—the noble, and the poor artisan,—the monarch, and his subjects—all ages and all ranks convulsed with one common passion—wrung with one common anguish, and, with loud sobs and cries, doing involuntary homage to the God that made their hearts! What wretched infatuation to interdict such amusements as these! What a blessing that mankind can be allured from sensual gratification, and find relaxation and pleasure in such pursuits! But the excellent Mr. Stanley is uniformly paltry and narrow,—always trembling at the idea of being entertained, and thinking no Christian safe who is not dull. As to the spectacles of impropriety which are sometimes witnessed in parts of the theatre; such reasons apply, in much stronger degree, to not driving along the Strand, or any of the great public streets of London, after dark; and if the virtue of well educated young persons is made of such very frail materials, their best resource is a nunnery at once. It is a very bad rule, however, never to quit the house for fear of catching cold.

Mrs. More practically extends the same doctrine to cards and assemblies. No cards—because cards are employed in gaming; no assemblies—because many dissipated persons pass their lives in assemblies. Carry this but a little further, and we must say,—no wine, because of drunkenness; no meat, because of gluttony; no use, that there may be no abuse! The fact is, that Mr. Stanley wants not only to be religious, but to be at the head of the religious. These little abstinences are the cockades by which the party are known,—the rallying points for the evangelical faction. So natural is the love of power, that it sometimes becomes the influencing motive with the sincere advocates of that blessed religion, whose very characteristic excellence is the humility which it inculcates.

We observe that Mrs. More, in one part of her work, falls into the common error about dress. She first blames ladies for exposing their persons in the present style of dress; and then says, if they knew their own interest,—if they were aware how much more alluring they were to men when their charms are less displayed, they would make the desired alteration from motives merely selfish.

"Oh! if women in general knew what was their real interest! if they could guess with what a charm even the *appearance* of modesty invests its possessor, they would dress decorously from mere self-love, if not from principle. The designing would assume modesty as an artifice; the coquet would adopt it as an allurement; the pure as her appropriate attraction; and the voluptuous as the most infallible art of seduction."

If there is any truth in this passage, nudity becomes a virtue; and no decent woman, for the future, can be seen in garments.

We have a few more of Mrs. More's opinions to notice.—It is not fair to attack the religion of the times, because, in large and indiscriminate parties, religion does not become the subject of conversation. Conversation must and ought to grow out of materials on which men can agree, not upon subjects which try the passions. But this good lady wants to see men chatting together upon the Pelagian heresy—to hear, in the afternoon, the theological rumours of the day—and to glean polemical tittle-tattle at a tea-table rout. All the disciples of this school uniformly fall into the same mistake. They are perpetually calling upon their votaries for religious thoughts and religious conversation in every thing; inviting them to ride, walk, row, wrestle, and dine out religiously;—forgetting that the being to whom this impossible purity is recommended, is a being compelled to scramble for his existence and support for ten hours out of the sixteen he is awake;—forgetting that he must dig, beg, read, think, move, pay, receive, praise, scold, command and obey;—forgetting, also, that if men conversed as often upon religious subjects as they do upon the ordinary occurrences of the world, that they would converse upon them with the same familiarity, and want of respect,—that religion would then produce feelings not more solemn or exalted than any other topics which constitute at present the common furniture of human understandings.

We are glad to find in this work, some strong compliments to the efficacy of works,—some distinct admissions that it is necessary to be honest and just, before we can be considered as religious. Such sort of concessions are very gratifying to us; but how will they be received by the children of the Tabernacle? It is quite clear, indeed, throughout the whole of the work, that an apologetical explanation of certain religious opinions is intended; and there is a considerable abatement of that tone of insolence with which the improved Christians are apt to treat the bungling specimens of piety to be met with in the more antient churches.

So much for the extravagances of this lady.—With equal sincerity, and with greater pleasure, we bear testimony to her talents, her good sense, and her real piety. There occurs every now and then in her productions, very original, and very profound observations. Her advice is very often characterised by the most amiable good sense, and conveyed in the most brilliant and inviting style. If, instead of belonging to a trumpery gospel faction, she had only watched over those great points of religion in which the hearts of every sect of Christians are interested, she would have been one of the most useful and valuable writers of her day. As it is, every man would wish his wife and his children to read *Cœlebs;*—watching himself its effects;—separating the piety from the puerility;—and showing that it is very possible to be a good Christian, without degrading the human understanding to the trash and folly of Methodism. (pp. 60-5)

Sydney Smith, "Hannah More," in Famous Reviews, *edited by R. Brimley Johnson, Sir Isaac Pitman & Sons, Ltd., 1914, pp. 60-5.*

THE MONTHLY REVIEW, LONDON (essay date 1820)

[*In the following excerpt from a review of More's* Moral Sketches, *the critic finds fault with some aspects of More's religious beliefs.*]

Among the literary ladies of the present day, Mrs. Hannah More merits a place of high distinction, for the ability which she has displayed and the effect which she has produced. Indeed, few persons of either sex have exerted themselves with more assiduity and perseverance, in a cause which to her appears that of pure religion and unsophisticated truth. Her writings on religious and moral topics, though often elevated neither in the matter nor in the style above the level of any ordinary capacity, have experienced a wide and extensive circulation: they have been read both by the high and by the low, by the rich and by the poor; and it is to be hoped that the sentiments and the conduct of many persons, in both classes, can bear testimony to the good which they have produced. We give Mrs. More credit for the best intentions: we commend both her honesty and her zeal; and we believe that she has been habitually actuated by the truly noble desire of making her writings subservient to the promotion of piety, and the increase of righteousness. While, however, we bestow this praise on the purity of her motives and the integrity of her character, we trust that we shall not be deemed uncandid if we contest the truth of some of her opinions, and the justness of some of her inferences. (pp. 164-65)

It is well known that, in her religious tenets, Mrs. More is a strenuous advocate for the controverted doctrines which are more exclusively inculcated by those who are termed "Evangelical Preachers." These doctrines she deems the essentials of Christianity; and, in course, the faith which she recommends does not rest on that broad basis which is made up of a few simple principles, but is of a more complicated and less comprehensive kind. The great article of religious belief which is taught in the Gospel, as Mr. Locke has demonstrated in his "Reasonableness of Christianity," is that "Jesus is the Messiah," or that he was commissioned by God to reveal his will to mankind; and, as far as faith is concerned, what other article of belief is requisite to make a man *a Christian?* With this great fundamental principle of belief, however, Mrs. More would connect many others, of a more doubtful nature and a more polemical kind. The religion, which she so zealously teaches, is founded on the innate depravity of man; and of this innate corruption of human nature, she says,

> That it is a doctrine which meets us in one unbroken series throughout the whole sacred volume; we find it from the third of Genesis, which records the event of man's apostacy, carried on through the history of its fatal consequences in all the subsequent instances of sin, individual and national, and running in one continued stream from the first sad tale of woe, to the close of the sacred canon in the Apocalyptic vision.

> And to remove the groundless hope, that this quality of inherent corruption belonged only to the profligate and abandoned, the Divine Inspirer of the sacred writers took especial care, that they should not confine themselves to relate the sins of these alone.

> Why are the errors, the weaknesses, and even the crimes of the best men recorded with equal fidelity? Why are we told of the twice-repeated deceit of the father of the faithful? Why of the single instance of vanity in Hezekiah? Why of the too impetuous zeal of Elijah? Why of the error of the almost perfect Moses? Why of the insincerity of Jacob? Why of the far darker crimes of the otherwise holy David? Why of the departure of the wisest of men from that piety, displayed with sublimity unparalleled in the dedication of the Temple? Why seems it to have been invariably studied, to record with more minute detail the vices and errors of these eminent men, than even those of the successive impious kings of Israel, and of Judah; while these last are generally dismissed with the brief, but melancholy sentence, that they did that which was evil in the sight of the Lord; followed only by too frequent an intimation, that they made way for a successor worse than themselves? The answer is, that the truth of our universal lapse could only be proved by transmitting the record of those vices, from which even the holiest men were not exempt.

With respect to this doctrine of *'innate depravity,'* streaming through the whole sacred volume in the way which is asserted by the present writer, we shall only say that, in the work which was published on this subject by Dr. John Taylor of Norwich, that learned divine was not able, in the whole compass of the Old and New Testament, to discover more than five or six texts that give any direct countenance to such a doctrine; and even these, when carefully examined and critically explained, will be found to afford it no support. Yet, if we were to omit the doctrine of innate depravity, of the Atonement, and other matters of uncertain speculation, in our account of the essentials of Christianity, Mrs. More would call this *generalizing* religion, against which she warns her readers . . . ; for she says that *'a general religion is no religion at all.'* We would ask Mrs. More, if 'a general religion is no religion at all,' what will become of the religion of Jesus? That religion is certainly a general religion. It is universal in its principles, and suited to the universal wants of mankind; it contemplates God as the universal Father; and it regards all mankind as his common progeny. It says that God made of one blood all the nations that dwell on the earth; and that, in every country under heaven, "he who worketh righteousness is accepted of him." When Christ was asked which was the great commandment in the law, he said, "Hear, O Israel! the Lord thy God is one Lord, and to love him with all the heart and with all the mind is the first and great commandment: and the second is like unto it, Thou shalt love thy

neighbour as theyself: on these two commandments hang all the law and the prophets." Is not this to say, these two commandments are the substance of all true religion, and comprehend all that is essential for man as the rule of his conduct towards his Father in heaven and his fellow-creatures on earth? Yet what are these two commandments but *'a general religion?'* What are they but a religion which is not exclusively confined to any particular people, country, or government; which is not compatible only with particular habits and institutions, but which, like the air that we breathe or the water that we drink, is suited to the moral wants of all mankind, in all ages, countries, and climes, whatever institutions they may cherish, or under whatever governments they may live? If this be not 'a *general* religion,' we know not what a general religion is; and yet will Mrs. Hannah More now tell us that this is no religion at all?

The Christian doctrine is more particularly distinguished by one great generalizing principle, which causes all diversities of faith, as far as they are grounds of dissension, to disappear; and which unites in the sympathies of peace men of the most discordant sentiments. What principle is this? It is CHARITY. This is the bond of perfectness; and we ask the pious author of these **Moral Sketches** whether this *Charity,* as it was taught by Christ, and afterward extolled by St. Paul, be not a *generalizing principle?* Does it not tend to compress every creed into its minimum of articles? Does it not make the love of God and of man so operative in the heart, and so comprehensive in the mind, as to render us in a great measure indifferent to modes of faith? For is not Charity, when invested with all its divine attributes, as they have been described by St. Paul, more transcendant in its nature than even the most orthodox sublimities of faith? If the abstractions of Faith, Hope, and Charity could be embodied in a visible form, would not Charity cause the other two to fade in their beauty and wane in their lustre by its side?

Nearly half of this volume is occupied with *'Reflections on Prayer,'* which exhibit abundant proof of the devotional zeal of the author, and of her earnest, and we trust hallowed desire to diffuse this zeal among her fellow-creatures. Mrs. M. would willingly make us more of a praying people, in order, no doubt, to give additional encouragement to the cultivation of those virtues, without the continual growth of which in our hearts and lives we pray in vain. We have not, however, met with anything new in this part of Mrs. More's work; for, indeed, what could she state on such a subject which had not been repeatedly observed before? If we grant that much of it is *well said,* and that Mrs. More has here made some of her remarks glitter with ornament or sparkle with vivacity, still, in general, we must think that the pious author indulges too much in the declamatory style. The progress of her mind over a subject which has so often occupied her thoughts, and with which she has long been so intimately familiarized, is like that of the charioteer whose horses whirl his car along without regarding the rein.

"Fertur equis auriga, neque audit currus habenas."

Among the author's 'Reflections,' we meet with some on the Lord's prayer, which is very properly considered 'as a model both for our devotion and our practice.' If she had taken that view of this prayer to which we have been accustomed, she would have found in it the principles of *'general religion,'* which, as we have previously remarked, she has described as *'no religion at all:'*—but the Lord's prayer contains none of those *doctrinal peculiarities,* in which, according to Mrs.

More, and others of her school, the essence of Christianity consists. God is represented as the universal Father,—the great object of man's devotional reverence,—of his filial love, and his entire dependence;—while that spirit is impressed towards our fellow-creatures which inclines us to overlook their faults, and to live in charity with all men. This is *'general religion;'* and is it not the religion of Christ? We quote a passage from this part of the work, in which some of the remarks are in unison with our own, though we do not bestow much praise on the diction:

> In the Lord's prayer may be found the seminal principle of all, the petitions of a Christian, both for spiritual and temporal things; and however in the fullness of his heart he will necessarily depart from his model in his choice of expressions; into whatever laminæ he may expand the pure gold of which it is composed, yet he will still find the general principle of his own more enlarged application to God, substantially contained in this brief but finished compendium.
>
> Is it not a striking proof of the Divine condescension, that, knowing our propensity to err, our blessed Lord should Himself have dictated our petitions, partly perhaps as a corrective of existing superstitions, but certainly to leave behind him a regulator by which all future ages should set their devotions? and we might perhaps establish it as a safe rule for prayer in general, that any petition which cannot in some shape be accommodated to the spirit of some part of the Lord's prayer may not be right to be adopted. Here temporal things are kept in their due subordination; they are asked for in great moderation, as an acknowledgement of our dependence on the Giver. The request for the Divine intercession we must of course offer for ourselves, as the Intercessor had not yet assumed his mediatorial office.
>
> There is in this prayer a concatenation of the several clauses, what in human composition the critics call concealed method. The petitions rise out of each other. Every part also is, as it were, fenced round, the whole meeting in a circle; for the desire that God's name may be hallowed, His will be done, and His kingdom come, is referred to, and confirmed by the ascription at the close. If the kingdom, the power, and the glory are His, then His ability to do and to give, are declared to be infinite.

We shall now conclude our notice of a publication which, though written at an advanced period of life, exhibits no decline in the intellectual powers of its author. She is not less mistress of her subject, or of herself, than in her former productions. She possesses the same stock of sentiment, and the same fluency of style: her mind is not a fountain in a state of exhaustion, but the spring still flows without any deficiency of water, of sound, or of foam. (pp. 170-74)

> *"Mrs. More's 'Moral Sketches'," in* The Monthly Review, *London, Vol. XCI, February, 1820, pp. 164-74.*

AMERICAN QUARTERLY REVIEW   (essay date 1834)

[*In the following excerpt from a review of the* Memoirs of the Life and Correspondence of Mrs. Hannah More, *the critic surveys More's writings.*]

In her seventeenth year, [More] published a small dramatic poem, entitled *Search after Happiness.* We find little concerning her for ten years after this publication. She was probably engaged, together with her sisters, in the "useful and honourable occupation of school teaching." She was also, during this period, occupied with an *affaire du coeur,* which terminated unpropitiously; but from that time she gave herself up to the requirements of fashionable and literary society, until, after a lapse of years, a change came over the spirit of her thought.

She visited London in 1774, and immediately became acquainted with a number of living authors, the choice writers of the day. Of all those with whom she then associated, Dr. Johnson seems to have exerted the greatest influence over her mind. (p. 522)

The high favour with which she was received induced her to try her strength in another poem, entitled **"Sir Eldred of the Bower,"** which was attended with flattering success. Her work afforded a bountiful theme for literary and social talk. Read, criticised, and amended in these small circles, it not only brought additional consequence to the writer, but received itself substantial benefit from the corrections. No one was more lavish in its praise at these parties, than Johnson, who, in fact, wrote a stanza for it. (p. 524)

She was led to a design of furnishing something for the stage, and in pursuance of it produced *Percy.* [David Garrick] wrote the prologue and epilogue, prepared it for representation, and gave out to the world the high sanction of his approval. Its success was greater than that of any tragedy for many years. Home's tragedy of Alfred had just been brought out, but had lived only three nights. The profits of the copyright of *Percy* and of the authoress's nights of representations amounted to near six hundred pounds,—a large sum, even in those days of theatrical glory and patronage. It was extremely grateful to her feelings. She declares to one of her sisters, that "one tear is worth a thousand hands, and I had the satisfaction to see even the men shed them in abundance." Again she writes, "I was much diverted at the play the other night; when Douglas tears the letter which he had intercepted, an honest man in the shilling gallery, vexed it had fallen into the husband's hands instead of the lover's, called out, 'Do pray send the letter to Mr. Percy.' I think some of you might contrive a little jaunt, if it were only for one night, and see the *bantling.*" We find her, in a few years, firmly resisting all importunities to attend the theatre, even for the purpose of witnessing the inimitable Siddons in her own *Percy.*

Another tragedy which she had written, was delayed in its representation, by the death of [Garrick], her kind friend, in 1779. . . . [*Fatal Falsehood*] was shortly after produced and met with a reception hardly inferior to her first. (pp. 525-27)

Sacred Dramas and *Sensibility* were published together, in 1782. Her first decidedly ethical work was not printed till six years after, when she gave to the world her *Thoughts on the Importance of the Manners of the Great to General Society.* In this work she confines herself to what she considered prevailing, practical evils. The great beauty and merit of this and her other productions of the same description, consist in that pure and consistent regard and reverence which she manifests for the practical precepts of Christian morals. "Fine people," she writes, "are ready enough to join you in reprobating vice; for they are not all vicious; but their standard of right is low, it is not the standard of the Gospel." Points of doctrine she rarely touches upon. To enforce a due consideration of the Sabbath, or an observance of the propriety of conduct towards inferiors in the smallest things, are themes more congenial to her pen than subjects of lofty speculation. The *Manners of the Great* was published anonymously, and without her communicating her design to a single person, except the bookseller; not, however, through fear of consequences to herself, as the censor of the class in which she mingled, but lest, as she modestly expresses it, they might "bring her proverbs to confute her life,"—an unjust supposition of her own. But, *ex pede leonem;* her friends immediately detected her, and congratulations poured in upon her from every quarter.

At this time and with this work, commenced that influence which, throughout the remainder of her long life, she exerted so beneficially upon the moral character of her countrymen. It was her fortune at all periods to command their attention; and, what does not always happen to the children of genius, to deserve it. She addressed herself to every class of society, and adapted her works to the comprehension of all. How far national character may be affected by such writers, cannot of course be precisely determined; but among those who have exercised such a power, Mrs. More certainly occupies the first place. The influence of her writings was not confined to her own country; it has operated as beneficially upon ours. To the present generation, both there and here, her tracts are among the earliest of their recollections. (p. 531)

The blow that Miss More had struck against the laxity of morals and Christian practice among the higher classes of English society, by her *Manners of the Great,* was followed up in 1790 by another, in a work, entitled *An Estimate of the Religion of the Fashionable World.* Within two years this publication reached a fifth edition; which, considering the boldness with which she attacked the corruptions of the day, and the uncompromising religious attitude which she assumed, was certainly remarkable. Consistency is the beauty of character; and will gain respect even among those whose prejudices are strongly opposed to him or her who exhibits it, or to the doctrine inculcated.

A critical juncture, which was to give employment to the best minds of England, to preserve the established order of things, and which elicited the talents of Hannah More in a line still different from any in which she had exerted them, had now arrived. The revolutionary principles of France were gaining ground in England; and gloomy apprehensions were entertained of the safety of the government, by its friends. The republicans of the country were moving; and the doctrines of their brethren across the channel gaining daily proselytes. The popularity of Mrs. More among all classes, her knowledge of human nature, the practical style of her writings, pointed her out as a suitable person to publish something to counteract this tide of opinion. Although she declined complying with the many importunities which were made to her on this subject, she secretly composed the dialogue of *Village Politics, by Will Chip,* and in order to avoid suspicion, sent it to one who was not her regular publisher. It enjoyed a great run; and is considered to have operated very effectually for the purpose for which it was intended.

Mrs. More was no friend to the principles under which our country came into political existence. With her, republicanism was synonymous with disorder. She admired nothing that tended to destroy distinctions of rank and title. It was the breaking up of the foundations of religion as well as civil society, to produce equality in the privileges of government and political rights. It was, indeed, a part of her education

not only to distrust but to oppose innovation. These sentiments were confirmed in her by her associations and companionships. Her friends were among those interested in the institutions of the land. We readily, therefore, find an excuse, if one were expected, for her political opinions.

Yet the madness of the French revolutionists was calculated to excite the fears of the friends of popular rights, as well as to furnish their enemies with opportunity and means to oppose them. They were not content to overturn thrones and to break sceptres, but they sought to overthrow the altars of God. The speech of M. Dupont before the National Convention, on the 14th December, 1792, was the declaration of national atheism. The object of this motion, in the language of Mrs. More, was not to dethrone kings, but HIM by whom kings reign. It did not excite the cry of indignation in the orator, that Louis the Sixteenth reigned, but that the "Lord God omnipotent reigneth!" Nature and Reason were the gods of their vain idolatry; transferring the worship which could not derogate from the dignity of man or endanger his natural and social rights, to empty names, possessing no power in themselves, and as agents or instruments feeble and limited. The cause of liberty was hurried into an extreme. They flew from despotism, but so rapidly as to pass by the resting place of freedom,—that point where the requirements of our social state, and the possession of individual power, harmonize.—Liberty, in religion, is toleration coupled with equal privileges;—the power of obeying the dictates of conscience and reason without restraint and without partiality. Atheism has no more to do with it, than anarchy has with political freedom. It may be as enslaving and intolerant in its practice as any sect of religion ever has been, in the worst days of priesthood or New England witchcraft. Its principles are more so; for not being founded on the love of virtue, or on an accountability for our acts, but on faulty nature and circumscribed reason, it acknowledges passion and sanctions prejudice. It was the great rock upon which the republicans of France fatally struck.

Innumerable small publications, pamphlets, tracts, &c. not only propagating doctrines hostile to the government, but the principles of infidelity, appeared and were distributed to the poor, at prices which enabled all who felt disposed, to possess them. In order to counteract their irreligious tendency, Mrs. More proposed to herself an arduous and extensive task—the production of three tracts, consisting of stories and religious characters, every month, and adapted to the comprehension of the poorer classes, by a lively and popular style. *The Shepherd of Salisbury Plain,*—a tract more read than any thing of the kind in the English language, and a multitude of others not inferior in merit, emanated from her pen. Two millions of these publications were sold in the first year. (pp. 532-34)

With all these tasks upon her hands,—the charge of her schools, which now embraced between fifteen hundred and two thousand children, and of her tract repository system,—she still found leisure to furnish the world with another of those valuable works in the series which commenced with her *Manners of the Great.* This was her *Strictures on Female Education.* (p. 535)

In 1805 she published *Hints towards Forming the Character of a Young Princess,* with a view to the education of the late Princess Charlotte of Wales. In 1809 appeared her *Cœlebs in Search of a Wife;* a work which ran through twelve editions in less than a year. It was translated into French; and in this country, during her life, not less than thirty editions of it appeared. Of this production of her pen, it may be justly said that it deserved all the popularity it received. It was an attempt at prose fiction,—a walk in which she had not as yet tried her powers. Lucilla, the heroine, is a pattern of female excellence,—a character congenial to our thoughts and feelings, and formed upon those active principles of Christianity which render their subject practically wise and efficiently useful.

Madame de Stael, who has been so much idolized by her admirers, and who has been placed in the very highest rank of female intellect, has afforded the biographer of Mrs. More an occasion to compare her Corinne with the Lucilla in *Cœlebs.* In any attempt of this kind, the distinguishing features of the minds of these two authoresses, will furnish us with valuable means to execute it. Madame de Stael possessed a lively imagination. She was ever disposed to reach after something novel and striking; she did not look upon human nature as it really exhibited itself. As a critic she despised all rule; rejected all canons; and built up a system—or, more rightly, perhaps, an irregular superstructure of her own. As a moralist she was inconsistent, generally faulty, and frequently dangerous. Hannah More possessed a mind less soaring,—one that found employment in objects immediately around her. She dealt but little in speculation. Her aim was to be useful; to correct evils that presented themselves to her daily observation. She invariably referred herself—her thoughts and actions, to one standard—that of scriptural truth. Her morality was religious, springing from the heart. Madame de Stael was the more daring, ambitious, and philosophical genius; Mrs. More was more retired, discreet, and practical. Both are great in their respective spheres; and both, by their writings, exerted a permanent influence upon the opinions of mankind. Taking these characteristics and keeping them in view, we may readily suppose the nature of Corinne and that of Cœlebs. Madame de Stael uses invention for the purpose of exhibiting the character; Mrs. More employs it for the purpose of conveying instruction. The one has embellished the heroine, made her an unearthly personage; the other presents her as she may be, and looks to the result. Corinne is a sentimentalist, a philosophical pretender; Lucilla a picture of domestic virtue and religious excellence. It is the brilliancy and vanity of the female sex which we find exemplified in the former; its beauty and tenderness in the latter. Each character is a partial counterpart of its author. Mr. Roberts has judiciously remarked, in reference to Lucilla, that "no writer could have moulded such a character with thoughts so tender, and principles so firm; and with all the qualities appropriate to the sex, so tempered and so balanced, but one who found the model, at least in many of its features, reposited on her own bosom." (pp. 537-38)

[More's] religious views were simple. She did not involve herself in the perplexities of doctrines; but deeply studied the practical precepts of the Gospel. Calvinism or Arminianism troubled her little; though she undoubtedly had her peculiar tenets on these points. With her, the great duty was to lay herself and her talents at the foot of the cross, with the same abasement and self-renunciation, as her more illiterate neighbour. It was to teach charity, practise love, and to correct the folly and wickedness of man's heart. Her respect for the Sabbath was most sacred. It excites more remark in her correspondence than any one other injunction of the Scriptures. Upon her first entrance into the gay and fashionable world, when Sunday seemed a favourite day for parties, she recorded her sense of its sinfulness. Speaking of the first and only en-

gagement of the kind at Mrs. Montagu's, she said, (1775) "I *did* think of the alarming call, 'what doest thou here, Elijah?'" From this time forward to her death, her efforts were unceasing to prevent the breaking of God's holy day. She was, however, no friend to austerity. She thought it to be the duty of men to be pleasant, cheerful, and even gay. Those who were the contrary she considered as abusing their powers and injuring the cause of religion. But, those who would know her peculiar sentiments on religious subjects, cannot be satisfied with any epitome which we may present: they must seek that knowledge in the work itself; and in her own productions, especially her latest, *Practical Piety, Christian Morals,* and *Moral Sketches.*

The works just referred to have placed the name of Hannah More in the very highest class of ethical and religious writers. Although she had outlived the generation in which she first appeared as a candidate for public favour, as a writer, still she remained in the succeeding one the most popular author in the description of writing in which she exerted herself, of all of her countrywomen or countrymen. In these works it was her object to elevate the standard of religion; to bring it home to the person and individual. She endeavours to give the peculiar doctrines of Christianity; and to show their superiority to all other religious systems. She strives to correct prevailing errors of opinion: manifesting here, as throughout her whole life, a solicitude to remedy those evils which were of immediate bearing on society. (pp. 542-43)

> *A review of "Memoirs of the Life and Correspondence of Mrs. Hannah More," in* American Quarterly Review, *Vol. XXXII, No. 32, December, 1834, pp. 519-44.*

LEIGH HUNT   (essay date 1847)

[*An English poet and essayist, Hunt is remembered as a literary critic who encouraged and influenced several Romantic poets, especially John Keats and Percy Bysshe Shelly. Hunt produced volumes of poetry and critical essays and, with his brother John, established the* Examiner, *a weekly liberal newspaper. In his criticism, Hunt articulated the principles of Romanticism, emphasizing imaginative freedom and the expression of a personal emotional or spiritual state. Although his critical works were overshadowed by those of more prominent Romantic critics, such as his friends Samuel Taylor Coleridge, William Hazlitt, and Charles Lamb, his essays are considered both insightful and generous to the fledgling writers he supported. In the following excerpt from a discussion of British poets, Hunt evaluates More's poem* Florio.]

It is the first time we ever read any [verses by Hannah More]; and she has fairly surprised us, not only with some capital good sense, but with liberal and feeling sentiments! How could a heart, capable of uttering such things, get encrusted with Calvinism! and that, too, not out of fear and bad health, but in full possession, as it should seem, both of cheerfulness and sensibility! Oh, strange effects of example and bringing up! when humanity itself can be made to believe in the divineness of what is inhuman! "Sweet Sensibility!" cries our fair advocate of eternal punishment—

> Sweet Sensibility! thou keen delight!
> Unprompted moral! sudden sense of right!
> Perception exquisite! fair virtue's seed!
> Thou quick precursor of the liberal deed!
> Thou hasty conscience! reason's blushing morn!
> Instinctive kindness ere reflection's born!

Prompt sense of equity! to thee belongs
The swift redress of unexamin'd wrongs!
Eager to serve, the cause perhaps untried,
But always apt to choose the suffering side!
To those who know thee not, no words can paint,
And those who know thee, know all words are
    faint.

And again:—

Since life's best joys consist in peace and ease,
And tho' but few can serve, yet all may please,
O let th' ungentle spirit learn from hence,
A small unkindness is a great offence.

The whole poem, with the exception of some objections to
preachers of benevolence like Sterne (who must be taken, like
the fall of the dew, in their general effect upon the mass of
the world) is full of good sense and feeling; though what the
fair theologian guards us against in our estimation of com-
plexional good nature, is to be carried a good deal farther
than she supposes. "As Feeling," she says,—

————tends to good, or leans to ill,
It gives fresh force to vice or principle;
'Tis not a gift peculiar to the good,
'Tis often but a virtue of the blood;
And what would seem Compassion's moral flow,
Is but a circulation swift or slow.

True; and what would seem religion's happy flow is often
nothing better. But this argues nothing against religion or
compassion. Whatever tends to secure the happiest flow of
the blood provides best for the ends of virtue, if happiness be
virtue's object. A man, it is true, may *begin* with being happy,
on the mere strength of the purity and vivacity of his pulse:
children do so; but he must have derived his constitution
from very virtuous, temperate, and happy parents indeed,
and be a great fool to boot, and wanting in the commonest
sympathies of his nature, if he can continue happy, and yet
be a bad man: and then he could not be bad, in the worst sense
of the word, for his defects would excuse him. It is time for
philosophy and true religion to know one another, and not
hesitate to follow the most impartial truths into their consequences. If "a small unkindness is a great offence," what
could Miss Hannah More have said to the infliction of eternal
punishment? Or are God and his ways eternally to be represented as something so different from the best attributes of
humanity, that the wonder must be, how humanity can survive in spite of the mistake? The truth is, that the circulation
of Miss More's own blood was a better thing than all her doctrines put together; and luckily it is a much more universal
inheritance. The heart of man is constantly sweeping away
the errors he gets into his brain.

There is a good deal of sense and wit in the extract from *Florio, a Tale for Fine Gentlemen and Fine Ladies;* but Miss
More is for attributing the vices of disingenuousness, sneering, and sensuality, to freethinkers exclusively; which is disin-
genuous on her own part; as if these vices were not shared by
the inconsistent of all classes. She herself sneers in the very
act of denouncing sneerers; nor did we ever know that a joke
was spared by the orthodox when they could get one. (pp.
156-58)

Leigh Hunt, *"Specimens of British Poetesses,"* in his
Men, Women, and Books: A Selection of Sketches,
Essays, and Critical Memoirs, Vol. II, *Smith, Elder
and Co., 1847, pp. 110-59.*

AUGUSTINE BIRRELL (essay date 1894)

[*Birrell was an English statesman and essayist. Although politics was always his primary concern, he gained modest repute
as a literary critic with his 1884 volume of essays,* Obiter Dicta,
*and he wrote several biographies of prominent English authors.
Contemporary critics, however, tend to devalue his nonaca-
demic, subjective, and sometimes precious approach to literature. In the following excerpt, Birrell ridicules More's works.*]

An ingenious friend of mine, who has collected a library in
which every book is either a masterpiece of wit or a miracle
of rarity, found great fault with me the other day for adding
to my motley heap the writings of Mrs. Hannah More. In
vain I pleaded I had given but eight shillings and sixpence for
the nineteen volumes, neatly bound and lettered on the back.
He was not thinking, so he protested, of my purse, but of my
taste, and he went away, spurning the gravel under his feet,
irritated that there should be such men as I.

I, however, am prepared to brazen it out. I freely admit that
the celebrated Mrs. Hannah More is one of the most detestable writers that ever held a pen. She flounders like a huge
conger-eel in an ocean of dingy morality. She may have been
a wit in her youth, though I am not aware of any evidence
of it—certainly her poem, ***Bas Bleu,*** is none—but for all the
rest of her days, and they were many, she was an
encyclopædia of all literary vices. You may search her nineteen volumes through without lighting upon one original
thought, one happy phrase. Her religion lacks reality. Not a
single expression of genuine piety, of heart-felt emotion, ever
escapes her lips. She is never pathetic, never terrible. Her
creed is powerless either to attract the well-disposed or make
the guilty tremble. No naughty child ever read *The Fairchild
Family* or *Stories from the Church Catechism* without quak-
ing and quivering like a short-haired puppy after a ducking;
but then Mrs. Sherwood was a woman of genius, whilst Mrs.
Hannah More was a pompous failure.

Still, she has a merit of her own, just enough to enable a mid-
dle-aged man to chew the cud of reflection as he hastily turns
her endless pages. She is an explanatory author, helping you
to understand how sundry people who were old when you
were young came to be the folk they were, and to have the
books upon their shelves they had.

Hannah More was the first, and I trust the worst, of a large
class—"the ugliest of her daughters Hannah," if I may parody a poet she affected to admire. This class may be imperfectly described as "the well-to-do Christian." It inhabited snug
places in the country, and kept an excellent, if not dainty,
table. The money it saved in a ballroom it spent upon a green-
house. Its horses were fat, and its coachman invariably present at family prayers. Its pet virtue was Church twice on Sunday, and its peculiar horrors theatrical entertainments, dancing, and threepenny points. Outside its garden wall lived the
poor who, if virtuous, were for ever curtsying to the ground
or wearing neat uniforms, except when expiring upon truck-
le-beds beseeching God to bless the young ladies of The
Grange or the Manor House, as the case might be.

As a book ***Cœlebs in Search of a Wife*** is as odious as it is absurd—yet for the reason already assigned it may be read with
a certain curiosity—but as it would be cruelty to attempt to
make good my point by quotation, I must leave it as it is.

It is characteristic of the unreality of Hannah More that she
prefers Akenside to Cowper, despite the latter's superior

piety. Cowper's sincerity and pungent satire frightened her; the verbosity of Akenside was much to her mind:

> Sir John is a passionate lover of poetry, in which he has a fine taste. He read it [a passage from Akenside's *Pleasures of Imagination*] with much spirit and feeling, especially these truly classical lines:
>
> > *Mind, mind* alone—bear witness, earth and heaven—
> > The living fountains in itself contains
> > Of Beauteous and Sublime; here hand in hand
> > Sit paramount the graces; here enthroned
> > Celestial Venus, with divinest airs,
> > Invites the soul to never-fading joy.
>
> "The reputation of this exquisite passage," said he, laying down the book, "is established by the consenting suffrage of all men of taste, though, by the critical countenance you are beginning to put on you look as if you had a mind to attack it."
>
> "So far from it," said I [Cœlebs], *"that I know nothing more splendid in the whole mass of our poetry."*

Miss More had an odd life before she underwent what she calls a "revolution in her sentiments," a revolution, however, which I fear left her heart of hearts unchanged. She consorted with wits, though always, be it fairly admitted, on terms of decorum. She wrote three tragedies, which were not rejected as they deserved to be, but duly appeared on the boards of London and Bath with prologues and epilogues by Garrick and by Sheridan. She dined and supped and made merry. She had a prodigious flirtation with Dr. Johnson, who called her a saucy girl, albeit she was thirty-seven; and once, for there was no end to his waggery, lamented she had not married Chatterton, "that posterity might have seen a propagation of poets." (pp. 278-81)

I still maintain that Hannah More's works in nineteen volumes are worth eight shillings and sixpence. (p. 283)

> *Augustine Birrell, "Hannah More," in his* The Collected Essays & Addresses of the Rt. Hon. Augustine Birrell: 1880-1920, Vol. 1, *Charles Scribner's Sons, 1923, pp. 278-83.*

CHAUNCEY BREWSTER TINKER   (essay date 1915)

[*A distinguished American educator, Tinker was instrumental in acquiring for Yale University the world's largest collection of writings on his two greatest subjects: James Boswell and Samuel Johnson. As an editor and writer, Tinker is particularly remembered for his collected* Letters of James Boswell *(1924) and his popular biography* Young Boswell *(1922). In the following excerpt, Tinker discusses the works More wrote during her association with the Bluestockings and records the Bluestocking reaction to them.*]

Miss Hannah More had larger ambitions and more varied talents than the other bluestocking authors. She wrote poems lyrical, occasional, and narrative; she wrote dramas tragic, classical, and sacred; and she wrote essays and critiques of conduct. In all her earlier work she was assisted and inspired by the bluestockings. She was their chosen poet. She represented them in print as Mrs. Montagu represented them in the salon. She celebrated them all in verse, and dedicated in turn to Mrs. Boscawen, Mrs. Montagu, and Mrs. Vesey. It is with this earlier period of her career that we are exclusively concerned; the voluminous works which the lady produced

after her separation from the bluestockings form no proper part of our inquiry.

Miss More's relations with the bluestockings began in 1774, soon after her arrival in London. The exact date of her first visit to the metropolis is uncertain. Her biographer, Roberts, who seldom gives himself any concern with dates, says that this took place in '1773 or 4'; but inasmuch as Miss More dedicated her **Inflexible Captive** to Mrs. Boscawen as early as March 1, 1774, the former date would appear the more probable. Her introduction to the *literati* was due to Garrick, whose interest in Miss More had been roused by her description of his acting in *Lear*. By 1775 Hannah More was a recognized member of the circle that surrounded Mrs. Montagu. Her poems, **Bas Bleu** and **Sensibility,** . . . were composed directly in their honour; but works of a more public appeal created no less enthusiasm among these ladies. Thus her ballad, **Sir Eldred of the Bower,** which appeared in 1775, was greeted by Mrs. Montagu in her most extravagant manner. She admired 'the spirit and fire of the gothic character' in the tale; the simplicity of the plot, the depiction of ancient manners (save the mark!), the primitive sentiments, and the characterization—all these challenged the critical approval of Mrs. Montagu. The tale of **The Bleeding Rock,** in the same volume, she esteemed no less highly. 'Your Rock,' she wrote, 'will stand unimpaired by ages as eminent as any in the Grecian Parnassus.' Such was the measure of bluestocking praise. But the poems had a sanction more important than this. They were read by a larger circle, Reynolds, Garrick, and Johnson; they became the 'theme of conversation in all polite circles.' Johnson could repeat all the best stanzas by heart. He read both poems with the author, made some alterations in **Sir Eldred,** and even—as was his custom with poems submitted to his judgment—added certain lines to it.

The poems belong to the Gothic school, and may well have been suggested by Percy's *Reliques;* Johnson's interest in them would be hard to understand were they not the production of a woman whom he playfully termed 'the most powerful versificatrix' in the language. But the bluestockings loved romance and the primitive world to which they thought it introduced them. The fact that this world, as conceived by Hannah More, has no remote similarity to our own made it only the more conformable to bluestocking standards of the antique. In reading this lady's poems and plays one is constantly reminded of those still-popular engravings of the eighteenth century, in which distressed virgins, in carefully studied poses, cast their melting eyes up to heaven. They live in bowers; refer to themselves in the third person, as the 'sad Elwina' and 'the distressed Julia'; and when disappointed in love, or (to speak in their own idiom) when their flame is not reciprocated, immediately go mad, and after a painful scene before the footlights complete their career by sudden death. Their lovers are of sterner stuff. They seek wars in distant climes, disappear for long periods of time, and are reckoned dead, only to reappear just as some domestic tragedy is reaching its climax; they are for ever drawing their swords—frequently to plunge them into their own bosoms. Miss More made full use of the poetic license which governs this pasteboard world. Her characters are burdened with no human motives, and it is idle to seek for related cause and effect in their conduct. But morality flourishes. Thus in **Sir Eldred** we learn the dangers of jealousy:

> The deadliest wounds with which we bleed
> Our crimes alone inflict;
> Man's *mercies* from God's hand proceed,

His *miseries* from his *own.*

But as the hero never once in the course of the poem acted like a human being, the force of the moral is somewhat impaired.

In 1777 Miss More essayed a higher flight. She had written dramas in her school-teaching days, and now, with the assistance of Garrick, produced a romantic tragedy, entitled **Percy.** Its title, if not its contents, indicates the influence of Home's *Douglas.* The situation in this play, venerable in romance, deals with two rival houses, those of Percy and Douglas, a heroine forced into an unwilling marriage with the rival of her lover, who has been killed in the Crusades. The distressed heroine and the returned lover (who had not really been killed) meet in a garden-bower:

PERCY.	Am I awake? Is that Elwina's voice?
ELWINA.	Percy, thou most adored—and most deceived!
	If ever fortitude sustained thy soul,
	When vulgar minds have sunk beneath the stroke,
	Let thy imperial spirit now support thee.—
	If thou canst be so wondrous merciful,
	Do not, O do not curse me!—but thou wilt,
	Thou must—for I have done a dreadful deed,
	A deed of wild despair, a deed of horror.
	I am, I am—
PERCY	Speak, say, what art thou?
ELWINA.	Married.
PERCY.	Oh!

It is unnecessary to follow the course of the tragedy; for the reader's own imagination will suggest it.

The play was a success in every way. It ran for twenty-one nights. No tragedy for years had been so successful. Mrs. Barry was at her finest in the mad-scene at the end. The author made nearly six hundred pounds. The play was translated into German, and acted with success in Vienna. The bluestockings were triumphant. Mrs. Montagu appeared repeatedly in her box at Covent Garden. Mrs. Boscawen, who could carry Duchesses to the theatre with her, sent the author a wreath of bay. Mrs. Delany invited her to dinner. Garrick, who had written the prologue, introduced her to Home, thus presenting 'Percy to the Douglas.'

In **Percy** Miss More reached the summit of her early achievement, and the book is still sought by collectors. Readers, if in an indulgent mood, will perhaps agree with Walpole, who found the play better than he expected, and, though devoid of nature, not lacking in good situations. Severer folk will side with Mrs. Thrale, who considered it foolish, and thought Fanny Burney ought to be whipped if she did not write a better. The truth probably lies between the two opinions. To the eighteenth century the piece certainly seemed to have merit. At any rate, it was popular enough to be revived in order that Mrs. Siddons might appear as Elwina. Had it survived to the mid-nineteenth century it might have proved useful as a libretto for Bellini or Donizetti. In the coloratura woes of the modern *diva,* the distressed Elwina would have found her perfect interpretation.

Garrick was so pleased with the success of **Percy** that he urged Miss More to write another tragedy. The result was **The Fatal Falsehood,** a romantic tragedy of the same sort. It was acted late in the spring of 1779, some months after the death of Garrick, and, though it did not duplicate the success of the earlier play, was enthusiastically received. With its production Miss More's connection with the London stage came to an end.

The Fatal Falsehood sinks far below the level of **Percy.** It probably suffered from the lack of Garrick's revising hand; though it is doubtful if even his genius could have introduced any semblance of reality into a series of situations so preposterous. Miss More is usually content to depend upon accident as the source of her dramatic effects; but in **The Fatal Falsehood** she attempted to depict in Bertrand a villain as subtle as Iago. Although he analyzes himself and his motives in a series of soliloquies, he remains a tangle of absurdities, and all the action of the piece, which flows from him, must be similarly described.

Miss More's dramas, as well as her poems and essays, were intended to serve the cause of virtue, about which all bluestockings were seriously concerned. Even the plays are filled with a sort of portable morality in the shape of maxims:

> The treacherous path that leads to guilty deeds
> Is, to make vice familiar to the mind.

Miss More never escaped from the office of preceptress; the forming spirit of all her work is that of the Young Ladies' Academy.

In the same year which saw the production of **Percy,** she put forth a volume entitled **Essays on Various Subjects, principally designed for Young Ladies.** The book is of the same sort as Mrs. Chapone's *Letters:* it warns young women to be modest, to avoid envy, and guard against the 'obliquities of fraud' in lovers. Allowing for its hopelessly narrow view of life, it may be granted that the advice is sound enough. But the bluestockings never realize that good advice is the cheapest commodity in the world.

Florio, a tale somewhat inappropriately dedicated to Walpole, is a sort of parable in verse, designed to enforce such lessons as are conveyed in the **Essays.** The hero, once a slave to frivolous society, is converted by reading Johnson's *Idler* and inspecting the beauties of Nature under the direction of his mistress.

With **Florio** we reach a period in Miss More's literary career and the end of what may be called the bluestocking influence on her work. Her pietism, which had amused Garrick, was now becoming chronic. She declined to go and see Mrs. Siddons as Elwina, because it is wrong to attend the theatre. She deplored the singing, dancing, and feasting in which London indulged after King George's recovery of his sanity. She even objected to the phrase *merry Christmas,* as being bacchanalian rather than Christian. Walpole, who was naturally distressed by all this, made a charming attack on Miss More's Low Church faith in the Ten Commandments, and pointed out to her that she was guilty of the Puritanical heresy. The truth is that Miss More's sense of responsibility to society at large was weighing on her mind. In 1788 she published a serious call to a more solemn view of life in her **Thoughts on the Importance of the Manners of the Great to General Society,** and definitely embarked upon her career as preceptress in public morality. Meanwhile she was drawing steadily away from her fashionable friends. At last she came to think any association with them almost wicked. On March 12, 1794, she wrote in her diary:

> Dined with friends at Mrs. ____. What dost thou here, Elijah? Felt too much pleased at the pleasure expressed by so many accomplished friends on seeing me again. Keep me from contagion!

Whatever may have been the influence of the bluestockings upon others, there can be no doubt that for Hannah More it had been an excellent corrective. It had at least prevented her from comparing herself to Elijah. (pp. 180-88)

> Chauncey Brewster Tinker, "Bluestockings as Authors," in his The Salon and English Letters: Chapters on the Interrelations of Literature and Society in the Age of Johnson, *The Macmillan Company, 1915, pp. 166-88.*

EDMUND GOSSE   (essay date 1927)

[*Gosse's importance as a critic is due primarily to his introduction of Henrik Ibsen's "new drama" to English audiences. He was among the chief English translators and critics of Scandinavian literature, although his other works include such diverse subjects as John Donne, Thomas Gray, and Sir Thomas Browne. In the following excerpt, Gosse compares twentieth-century reactions to More's works with the reception they received in her own time.*]

On the first page of Mr. Brimley Johnson's pleasant selection from the *Letters of Hannah More* [see Further Reading], the Editor abruptly states that "her one novel is deservedly unread." Just that! I do not raise my feeble voice against so stringent a verdict, although I think that "deservedly" is rather harsh, but when Mr. Johnson does not proceed to give even the title of this "one novel," I feel hurt, because *Cœlebs in Search of a Wife* took a considerable place in my own youthful economy. Novels were excluded from my Plymouth Brother home, as being essentially "worldly" in their tendency, and that *Cœlebs* lurked in my father's swept and garnished library I can only account for by presuming that it was looked upon as a work of pure edification. It was a story, it is true, but devoted to reflections on religion and morals, while its author was a tried Evangelical. But the moralising part of the book made no impression on my infant mind, which was fascinated by the pictures of frivolous society and even perilous intrigue which were introduced (I feel sure) to indicate what should be avoided. These I revelled in, at that tender age, as being essentially "worldly," but I will not disturb the ancient illusion that *Cœlebs in Search of a Wife* was rather naughty. I shall never read it again. If I were alone with *Cœlebs* on a desert island I would not read it. I deliver it over to the scorn of Mr. Brimley Johnson, but again I ask, Why "deservedly"?

Hannah More is a curious instance of an author whose works were immensely read in her own time, and were sold to a degree then almost unparalleled, yet have now become unreadable. Her *Letters* are the best of them, and that is because these are really conversation and illustrate her character. That is all that we can say survives of Hannah More; character and conversation, herself and her friends. The mass of her writings, of which no bibliographer has yet dared to give a complete list, is quite alarming, and she poured it out in an unbroken stream of strictures on Female Education and Practical Piety, and Reflections on Prayer, and Moral Sketches for more than fifty years.

She fought with "Jacobins and Levellers," and with every sort of profligate and idler, as with beasts at Ephesus. She was the perfect Evangelical warrior, "clad in shining biblical armour," dauntless in resisting every inroad of Satan into society. She was particularly fierce after 1795 in resisting the French variety of Satan. She did it because she zealously believed her message and thought it was her duty to distribute it, but she was amply and uniformly rewarded. It is said that of her *Shepherd of Salisbury Plain* more than a million copies were sold. Hannah More, in an age when women had little chance of success, rose from nothing at all to wealth. In spite of her hospitality and her lavish benevolence, she was worth £30,000 when she died, and she had made it all by her pen. Mr. Brimley Johnson rather severely calls her "scribbling Hannah," but she scribbled to some tune.

She did not, however, scribble for the twentieth century. It is difficult to suppose that one human being breathes who has read *The Influence of Religion on the Conduct of Life,* which made a sensation, in two volumes, in 1811. Even to think of it now induces a faintness at the heart. Nor is there any hope of popular revival for an *Estimate of the Religion of the Fashionable World,* issued anonymously in 1791. Yet when these and a multitude of similar works were published they were snapped up like hot cakes. Of *Cœlebs* itself, the "deservedly unreadable," ten editions were sold in the year of publication. (This was 1809. In his introduction Mr. Brimley Johnson gives no dates, not even the date of Miss More's death, 1833. I like an introduction to be informative.)

With this complete disappearance of her published writings, it might seem that the writer, too, would disappear, but this is not the case. Miss Hannah More lives, and will always live, in the gossiping annals of her age, as a bluestocking, as the friend of great wits, and as an educational reformer. We no longer regard her as a great author, but we shall always think of her as a personage. (pp. 145-47)

The literary value of Miss Hannah More's writings has ceased to exist. At the best, they were what is called "occasional," and responded with unconscious adroitness to the immediate instincts of her own generation. Her disquisitions on morals and piety were edifying in the highest degree, and not oily or priggish, yet of a kind no longer capable of stirring the pulse or the conscience. Even in her own day there were those who resented her cascade of lukewarm eloquence. Fanny Burney, always inclined to the sub-acid, remarked that in her hortatory pamphlets Miss More "points out imperfections almost unavoidable, with amendments almost impracticable." The ungrateful Mrs. Anne Yearsley, the milk-seller poetess, was extremely rude, and there was a clerical enemy, calling himself the Rev. Archibald Macsarcasm [see Further Reading], who pursued her with the venom of a gad-fly. But, on the whole, the long life of Hannah More was as happy and successful as it was innocent and useful. (p. 151)

> Edmund Gosse, "Hannah More," in his Leaves and Fruit, *William Heinemann Ltd., 1927, pp. 143-52.*

M. C. MALIM   (essay date 1933)

[*In the following excerpt, Malim discusses More's influence on the education of women.*]

In the childhood of the writer there was a very pleasant Old Georgian dining-room in a house in an English county-town. It looked out into a walled, green garden, and was furnished with old mahogany; the mantelpiece was decorated with Nankeen vases, and in the centre was a little statuette of an ancient lady clad in a flowing gown and close-fitting frilled cap, ensconced in an upright armchair. This effigy, one was told, represented Mrs. Hannah More, and a difficulty was presented to the mind by the dignified prefix before the name of this excellent lady, who, it appeared, had done nothing to deserve it!

Mature views of life have revealed the fact that there was much else existent in the society of the little town which stood for Mrs. Hannah More's posthumous presence in it. It was another *Cranford,* where traditions of past generations lingered, overlaying, rather than annihilating, one another. You had only to scratch the surface a little, and you were back in the world of Queen Anne! But *on* the surface the monumental institutions, among which the life of two younger generations eddied, were those of the period just after the Napoleonic Wars. Our *Cranford,* like Mrs. Gaskell's, was the home of many old maiden ladies of the middle class, the lives of some of whom were ruled by a strict etiquette of manners and by equally austere canons of moral and religious obligation. These, it seems to me, were the outcome of the system of adolescent training formulated by Hannah More, who presided on more than one mantelpiece, and whose influence on the education of Englishwomen was greater than is generally recollected.

She herself belonged to a much earlier age, and her long life was a bridge that spanned a whole flood of rapid development in English life and thought. She was born in the year of the last Jacobite rising; the nurse of her childhood had cared for Dryden in his last illness; two of her great-great-uncles had been captains in Cromwell's army: and she died in the year after the passing of the Reform Bill, having enjoyed the friendship of the abolitionists of West Indian slavery and having been herself a pioneer in the education of the poor, and a reformer of the education of well-to-do middle-class girls, as well as the real protagonist, though quite unconsciously, in the movement towards the liberation of women from the tradition that restricted their activities to the household. (pp. 329-30)

It was in connection with . . . [her] Sunday School work that Hannah began to write her Village Tracts and Tales. The latter, which are terribly moral little narratives of cottagers, strike one as altogether artificial; but they may, perhaps, have suggested to labouring folk that they were capable of a hitherto undreamt-of range of life. The Tracts were written in a purely didactic strain and in Johnsonian periods. Anyhow, the voluminous sale of these writings proves to us that they met some need of the time. And no one could grudge to Hannah More the pecuniary success that made it possible for her to move to a larger house, called Barley Wood (near Wrington), where all her sisters lived with her in repose and comfort. There they entertained the various members of the "Clapham Sect," including young Tom Macaulay, who was Mrs. Hannah More's pet, much as she had been Dr. Johnson's. That fact illustrates the fashion in which her life bridged the transitional period between two ages; for Macaulay was representative of the age ushered in by the French Revolution, an age of war between political ideals and of clamorous controversy about the fundamental things of life; while his old friend had been born too early to be accessible to the changes in the atmosphere of thought, and looked with abhorrence on the new spirit of revolt and doubt.

Notwithstanding, she was anxious for reform in one direction, that of girls' education, a subject on which she was qualified to speak. She expressed her views in a serious volume entitled *Strictures on the Modern System of Female Education,* and, again, in her curious novel, half didactic and half satirical, which was written in 1809 and has the merit of reflecting very clearly some phases of the English society of the era of the Napoleonic Wars, when her mind was still extremely alert. Probably her true sphere in literature was satire; and *Coelebs in Search of a Wife* has a considerable degree of living interest. The book purports to be the autobiography of a young, a very young and very ingenuous, gentleman of the name of Charles; who, after the death of his parents, sets out on a tour among the houses of their acquaintance, the unavowed object of which is to find a wife. Charles has been bred up by his father's injunctions concerning matrimony, aided by his mother's pithy comments on her own sex, to require a paragon; and in the end he finds her, and her name is Lucilla.

The war meets us on the threshold of the adventure, and anticipates us when we pass from London to the country. During our own Great War it became habitual to us to conclude that, because we meet with few allusions to them in contemporary fiction, the Napoleonic Wars engrossed the public mind very little. But Hannah More's writings give a different impression. Not only were her plans for her Sunday School enterprise, described in a letter of 1792, crossed by the reflection: "If I live and have health and money, and the French do not come," but her novel leaves us with the feeling that, seventeen years later, the European situation had become only more engrossing to her and her neighbours. We could fancy that it was a "morning paper" of 1918 that Charles' host "explored," if it were not for the clear proof that our young gentleman had never heard of a *ration-card:*

> To a speculative stranger a London day presents every variety of circumstance in every conceivable shape of which human life is susceptible. When you trace the solicitude of the morning countenance, the anxious exploring of the morning paper, the eager interrogation of the morning guest; when you hear the dismal enumeration of losses by land, and perils by sea, taxes trebling, dangers multiplying, commerce annihilating, war protracted; invasion threatening, destruction impending; your mind catches and communicates the terror, and you feel yourself "falling with a falling state."

> But when, in the course of the very same day, you meet these gloomy prognosticators at the sumptuous, not "dinner," but hecatomb, at the gorgeous fête, the splendid spectacle; when you hear the frivolous discourse, witness the luxurious dissipation, contemplate the boundless indulgence, and observe the ruinous gaming; you would be ready to exclaim, "Am I not supping in the Antipodes of that land in which I breakfasted?"

> If you observed the overflowing subscriptions raised, the innumerable societies formed . . . the palace-like structures erected; and all this to alleviate, to cure and even to prevent every calamity which the indigent can suffer, or the affluent conceive . . . would you not exclaim with Hamlet, "What a piece of work is man!"

In the country, among the acquaintance of Lucilla's family, we encounter a Squire of the John Bull breed, boisterous, unpolished, and lacking in high sentiment, but actuated by a plain, practical motive of patriotism, in virtue of which he declines to indulge his daughter with the Season in Town, insisting that while taxes are so high the welfare of his farms and his tenantry demands that he shall keep his private expenses down.

There is one touch in which we can still perceive the underlying poignancy: Lucilla's father relates of certain ladies whose conduct he holds up as a warning against the instability of the ill-trained feminine mind, that he had actually heard them interrupt (with muttered requests to each other for scissors and thread) the reading of the first news of the battle of Trafalgar, and Nelson's death.

It is Lucilla's father and mother who are the principal characters of the book. They are the pattern Gentleman and Lady because they have educated their daughters aright. Hannah More had a very lucid idea of what should be the exact object and scope of every young lady's education, and brought a surprising—if uneven—amount of psychological insight to bear on them, in elaborating her system. The sole object of education was the development of Christian character. But there was some recognition of utilitarian values in the assumption that its secondary purpose was the production of such a type of Christian character as would fit a young person to fill adequately an appropriate sphere of life. Miss More thus shows the influence of John Locke's principles, which held the field in English education till the theories of Kant and Pestalozzi began to make themselves felt. A young lady was to be educated to become an excellent wife, mother, mistress of the household, and lady bountiful. For this vocation certain attainments were necessary: a knowledge of Christian doctrine in the special form advocated by our authoress, which was more philosophical than evangelical doctrine as we know it; a sound understanding of other people's dispositions; a knowledge of household management; the acquirement of elegant manners and deportment (including the art of dressing); and the cultivation of the habit of employing time to advantage.

But beyond all this, and of far more importance, was the development and discipline of the native powers of the child, especially from what we should call the psychological point of view. Of course the exemplary parent spoke far too many words of exhortation, out of season, and the child was taught to practise a too perpetual and minute self-analysis; but there was something to be said for a method that inhibited self-satisfaction. Moreover, Hannah More had a firm grasp of two important principles of education; she realised the part played by indirect influence in the formation of character, not the influence only of daily habits and example, but of moral assumptions implied in the stimulus of certain rewards and punishments; and again she insisted that mental development was as essential to the development of character as moral training.

The general prejudice of the time against the thorough intellectual development of women is illustrated by the apology offered by Lucilla's father for having taught Latin to this one daughter, in recognition of her unusual ability. But for all, reading was to be constant and varied though not voluminous. *Non multa sed multum legere*. She did not altogether underrate the need for amusement; but that also was to be subject to discipline and was much restricted in quality. All theatres, private theatricals, dancing and cards were to be eschewed, as definitely wrong; and music and painting, which were regarded more as pastimes than study, were not to ab-

sorb much time. Children and young ladies were to have plenty of outdoor occupations; they are pictured as having access to spacious gardens and meadows and country lanes. They were to ride in the lanes, to study the form of the flowers in the fields, and tend those growing in the garden. Their walks and rides were, also, to be guided by an altruistic aim; they were to make friends with the cottagers who were their fathers' dependants, and especially with the children in the village school, whom, as they grew older, they were to help to instruct. In the garden they were to entertain their grown-up relations and friends at occasional *al fresco* "feasts," which were to be entirely their own affair, affording a pleasant surprise to their guests. Thus to some extent they were allowed initiative; but on the whole Hannah More's system lacked an outlet for spontaneous mental energy, particularly of the imaginative kind.

Notwithstanding, she had generated a force which was to revolutionise the lives of Englishwomen, and their opportunities. For when she died at Clifton in September 1833 her influence on the education of girls of the leisured classes had become immense, and she had not only exalted the function of household administration and the care of children to the level of a vocation, if not of a fine art, but had popularised philanthropy as a distinct calling; she had instilled into the mind of a weighty section of English society the idea that no character can be formed, nor work achieved, without systematic thinking. She was thus the forerunner of Ruskin, of Miss Octavia Hill, of Miss A. J. Clough and Miss Emily Davies. (pp. 332-36)

M. C. Malim, "Hannah More: 1745-1833," in Contemporary Review, *Vol. CXLIV, September, 1933, pp. 329-36.*

M. G. JONES (essay date 1952)

[In the following excerpt, Jones evaluates More's religious writings in terms of typical criticisms of Evangelicalism.]

When the nineteenth century got into its stride, Hannah More's close association with Evangelicism brought her under criticism of the same nature as that to which it was exposed. That Evangelicism was, in Mr Gladstone's words, 'a strong, systematic, outspoken and determined reaction against the prevailing standards both of life and preaching' which exercised a profound influence on spiritual understanding and moral conduct, conferred on it no immunity from harsh and prolonged criticism. The doctrines which Miss More expounded were regarded as rigid and narrow. She had followed Wilberforce in the emphasis which he laid upon the need for precise and definite doctrine. The 'peculiar doctrines of Christianity', defined by him in the *Practical View* as the corruption of man, the efficiency of the Atonement, the sanctifying influence of the Holy Spirit, and the unqualified prediction of eternal punishment for those who refused Christ's offer of Redemption, were her peculiar doctrines. She said nothing on the doctrine of the Trinity or of the Incarnation, and barely mentioned the life of Christ leading up to the Atonement. *Christus Redemptor*, not *Christus Consummator*, defined her doctrinal position. The doctrine of eternal punishment cannot have failed to trouble her profoundly, as it could not fail to trouble all religious minds, but she accepted it without submitting it to the grave inquiry of nineteenth-century thought. In the eyes of later generations of religious men she represented a restricted and above all a disproportionate view of Christian doctrine.

Moreover the Evangelical Plan was open to adverse criticism on counts other than that of doctrine. Neo-Anglicanism asserted that Evangelicalism had neglected the Catholic aspects of the Christian system. It is true that Evangelicals laid little emphasis on the Church as a divine institution; the organization of episcopacy was apparently a matter of secondary importance to them, and, with notable exceptions, sacramental observances were not stressed in their teaching. They conceived of religion primarily as a subjective relationship between the individual soul and God. Hannah More's teaching, no less than that of her fellow Evangelicals, was open to criticism on these lines. She was not, it is clear, indifferent to the Church principle of episcopacy; she had a genuine attachment to apostolic order; she had expounded a view of the visible Church in her *Hints;* but the Catholic aspects were not stressed in her teaching. 'Christianity', she said, 'is not a religion of forms and modes and decencies: it is being transformed into the image of God.' She referred her readers to Chapter XX of the *Strictures* as the expression of her faith, and drew from Miss Charlotte Yonge a sharp and pertinent Anglo-Catholic criticism of her book.

> Considering that the authoress believed herself a thorough church-woman her views in the latter chapters of her book are curiously lacking in any references to church ordinances, or the means of grace. She had said nothing which was not borne out by the Articles and the Liturgy. The point was what she had *not* said.

Equally open to the animadversions of the new age was the philosophical weakness of her homiletical writings. Always apparent, it became conspicuous in an age alive with new intellectual life and possessing in the historic method a new apparatus for finding and assessing truth. It would be unfair to condemn Hannah More for her ignorance of evolutionary theories which were to revolutionize nineteenth-century thought, or for her unwillingness to apply the remarkable work in Bible criticism, which marked the new age, to the explanation and interpretation of the traditional biblical narrative. These things were in the future. But, except in the *Hints,* there is no evidence that the new trends of thought, new widening of horizons in the last twenty-five years of her life, of which she cannot have been unaware, received a welcome. Yet Coleridge, whom she knew personally, pleading for a more profound religious philosophy, was not a dumb oracle in these years, and Dr Marsh had translated Part I of Michaelis's *Introduction to the New Testament, with Notes of his own* in 1793. It might have been expected that any contribution which could explain and interpret the Scriptures to an earnest biblical student would have met with a measure of interest and acceptance. There is no sign of this in her writings. On the contrary she expressed in no measured terms her abhorrence of the 'new philosophical and theological speculations'.

> Novelties in the sciences and in the arts may be . . . beneficial. Every invention may be an improvement; but in religion they are delusions. Genuine Christianity is not, as one class of men seem to suppose, a modern invention; serious piety is no fresh innovation. 'That which was from the beginning declare we unto you' are the words of inspiration . . . Though Holy Scripture was given to be searched [it] was not given to be criticized . . .

> Christianity is no appropriate field for the perplexities of metaphysics . . . It is not to be endured . . . to hear questions on which hang all our hopes and fears speculated upon as if they were a question of physics or history.

Such an attitude of mind helps to explain her failure to make any permanent contribution to theological thought, and goes some way to justify Mark Pattison's harsh criticism of Evangelicalism in the 'thirties:

> In 1833 Evangelicalism was already effete. The helpless imbecility of Evangelical writing and preaching, their obvious want of power to solve or even to apprehend the questions on which they were nevertheless perpetually talking; their incapacity to explain the Scripture while assuming the exclusive right to it; their conceit of being able to arrive at conclusions without premises, in a word their intellectual weakness contributed very greatly to the fall of the Evangelical school before a better informed generation of men.

To Hannah More could be applied the criticism to which Evangelicals were exposed. She too had divorced piety from intellect.

The divorce, which it is impossible to deny, has been attributed by some of the critics of the Evangelicals to their lack of intellectual capacity. Hannah More's life as a leading Evangelical of her day throws some doubt on this estimate. She did not lack intellectual capacity. Her long and sustained friendships with men and women of outstanding qualities of mind, 'worldly' as well as 'sober', their eager desire for her opinion and support on matters secular as well as religious, the breadth of her reading, the spirited comments on men and books in her letters, and the recognition by her most adverse critic of the 'very profound remarks scattered throughout her writings' absolve her from this condemnation. Nor can a lack of power in discussing 'theological speculations' be charged against a woman who talked and corresponded with Alexander Knox and Bishop Jebb. There is in her writings none of the contempt for things of the intellect attributed to the Evangelicals of her day. 'I put religion on my right hand and learning on my left. Learning should not be despised even as an auxiliary.' Yet the works of her pen, by which posterity has judged her, involved no 'intellectual exercise' and reveal no sustained intellectual power which would be of permanent value to religion. She allowed no criticism of the Bible narrative, no truck with history or the historic method. She did not 'unite the pair so long disjoined, knowledge and vital piety'.

Nor did her writings admit critical appraisement of the Church she revered. She appeared insensitive to the Church's forgetfulness of its traditional social mission and was untroubled by its 'acquiescence in the conventional ethics, class-consciousness and economic inequalities of the age'. Her occasional strictures, tempered by deference, were reserved for the individual servants of the Church who neglected their duties to their flocks. Her writings offered no help wherewith the Church could meet the new liberalism and all-powerful agnosticism of the coming age.

Hannah More's distrust of intellect *applied to religion* is the explanation of the poverty of her homiletics. The strength of her teaching, as that of her fellow Evangelicals, lay in its appeal to the hearts and consciences of men to live the Christian life. In her devoted efforts to save men's souls she had concentrated all the powers of her mind on piety, mistrusting intellect as its indispensable companion in Christian apologetics. During the troubled years of the 'nineties when she could not make her peace with God, she had found it so difficult to live the Christian life that she had renounced all secular interests, and although in later years the discipline of life and religion taught her to modify her extravagance and she began again to read secular literature, the same unwillingness to allow intellect to impinge on piety is apparent in her later works. 'That I have added to the mass of general knowledge by one original idea, or to the stock of virtue by one original sentiment I do not presume to hope. But that I have laboured assiduously to make that kind of knowledge which is most indispensable to common life familiar to the unlearned and acceptable to the young . . . I will not deny to have attempted.' To this end theological and historical speculations were unnecessary. 'I know no way of teaching morals but by infusing principles of Christianity, nor of teaching Christianity without a thorough knowledge of Scripture.' This was to her the work of supreme importance. All else was relatively valueless. 'Search the Scriptures, seek the help of the Holy Spirit, follow Christ's example in well-doing and stretch every faculty in the service of the Lord.'

This simple and sincere teaching came also under criticism of a new kind. John Foster's memorable essay *On the Aversion of Men of Taste to the Evangelical Religion* had already revealed and deplored the rapid development of a conventional phraseology among Evangelicals, closely connected, Foster insisted, with their lack of 'intellectual exercise'. Hannah More's essay on **High Profession and Negligent Practice** treated the same subject in a similar manner. She protested against the 'Phraseologists' who, desiring a reputation for holiness, 'picked up the idiom of a Party' and 'indulged in spiritual gossiping with a lack of taste and breeding'. To them she ascribed the unjust association which persons of refinement made between religion and bad taste. But Miss More herself was not free from the same failing. Honest and sincere, she did not always manage to avoid party slang and sanctimonious phrase. Her didactic writings and her letters are remarkably free from cant, but they are not free from religious pedantry, nor from the mannerisms which the 'unco guid' of her day introduced into common parlance. Lady Chatterton, the warm admirer of a woman who, in her opinion, was entitled to the reverence of succeeding generations, referred regretfully to the kind of 'fat complacency' which Hannah More used in speaking of the Evangelical faith. This it was, perhaps even more than her narrow doctrine and neglect of Catholic aspects, which offended subsequent generations. To her contemporaries the idiom was common form. Posterity denounced it as cant. (pp. 230-35)

M. G. Jones, in her Hannah More, *Cambridge at the University Press, 1952, 284 p.*

FORD K. BROWN (essay date 1961)

[*In the following excerpt, Brown surveys More's tract writing.*]

Before [William Wilberforce's] *Practical Christianity* came out in 1797 Hannah More had published a series of incomparable statements of political Christianity in defending her country against the destructions of the French Revolution. This was a signal service to the great cause, and to the nation if her friends were right in considering her the chief agency in checking the flood of philosophy, infidelity and disrespect for inherited privilege that poured fearfully across the Channel from 1790 on.

The honour of raising Mrs More's pen to this task was Bishop Porteus's. In casting about for means of combating that tide of evil he struck on the idea of some cheap literature that would urge piety and subordination in an attractive form suitable to the people. It occurred to him that Hannah More was peculiarly qualified to write such works because of her knowledge of the inferior orders gained in the Somerset schools. Having herself noted the necessity of such literature—the poor could get radical works cheap but had to pay several shillings for the moral tales of Mrs Sarah Trimmer, who furthermore was a High Churchman—Mrs More, after declining the task at first, 'scribbled a little pamphlet called **Village Politics, by Will Chip**'. 'It is as vulgar as heart can wish; but it is only intended for the most vulgar class of readers. . . . Rivington [the publisher] sends me word that "they go off very greatly, and the purchasers are people of rank".' 'It flew with a rapidity which may appear incredible', her biographer Roberts says, '. . . into every part of the kingdom. Many thousands were sent by government to Scotland and Ireland. Numerous patriotic persons printed large editions of it at their own expense; and in London only, many hundred thousands were soon circulated.' Roberts was probably right about the circulation. **Village Politics** was caught up avidly and reprinted by the government, by loyal associations and loyal individuals to be sold or given away (neither Mrs More nor her bookseller made anything by it, a bad aspect of reform that turned out later to be unnecessary). Her authorship was soon known. '**Village Politics** is universally extolled', Porteus wrote, 'it has been read and greatly admired at Windsor, and its fame is spreading rapidly over all parts of the kingdom.' 'Mr Cambridge says that Swift could not have done it better. I am perfectly of that opinion. It is a master-piece of its kind.'

This little tract deserves some examination, as the first of a long series that gave Hannah More an audience much greater than she reached in her less vulgar works, fantastically successful as they were, and established her beyond question, and very likely for all time, as the world's leading practitioner in this kind of art. Fortunately they are a matchless statement of the least dissimulating kind, wholly authentic in every part and respect, of Evangelical views on all pertinent moral, social, political and religious topics. It was obvious that to fight off the contamination of the French Revolution two points had to be stressed. The inferior ranks had to be led to see that French philosophy was bad and that English conditions were good. The first was not hard, the poor having little knowledge of such speculation and less interest in it, and it was made easier by a well-established principle. This is the principle that as pitch defiles and evil corrupts, any sensible moral person will avoid all contact with spiritual as well as physical contamination. It is well stated in Mrs More's **History of Mr Fantom the New-Fashioned Philosopher,** in which rash William Wilson the footman is debauched by radical philosophy and dies on the scaffold while prudent Mr Trueman wisely does not read works attacking religion or government. 'I have made it a rule never to cast my eyes on any thing which I know to be of a corrupt tendency; sinful curiosity was the sin of the first woman, and it is still one of the unhappy effects of that original offence.' Thus Mrs More, having read nothing at all of most of her antagonists' writings, had a telling advantage: she could with perfect sincerity state their doctrines just as she supposed them to be.

On the other hand her arguments that the English working class were well off were pretty much circumscribed by facts that the inferior ranks were closely familiar with. Unfortunately too, severe as times were in the early 1790's, they grew worse. Prices rose, unemployment increased, taxes rose to unheard-of-levels and the price of proper food, clothing and fuel to prohibitive levels. An unparalleled series of terrible winters made matters still worse (the point of Wordsworth's *Goody Blake and Harry Gill* of 1798). In the blindness of the great to the causes (humanly speaking) of such things, or their indifference, or equanimity of some sort, we see most clearly the strange callousness to human suffering that is an outstanding characteristic of the age. It is perhaps illustrated in the 'long and placid' life of Lord Sidmouth. As Home Secretary through a good part of the period, he was responsible for the imprisonment for political reasons of scores of his fellow Englishmen and the execution of several, and told his physician Sir Henry Holland 'that no events of the day had ever ruffled his night's sleep'. To many besides the Evangelicals there seemed nothing to be done—the existing order being divinely instituted—but to urge the use of food substitutes (there is a large literature on the subject), stress the compensatory advantages of the British constitution, preach resignation and point out that the rich too were enduring hardships.

Two unhappy circumstances made the situation graver. Thanks to the Evangelicals and dissenters and against the strong opposition of the Regular clergy and laity, many of the poor had been taught to read. In her own schools Mrs More had taken every precaution, but no one had ever struck on a way of teaching the poor to read the Bible without enabling them to read Tom Paine too. A more dangerous difficulty was that possibly because of the inherent fascination of evil to sinful man the atheists seemed more zealous in presenting their case than good people, the inferior ranks more attentive to radical propaganda than to loyal. Worthy Mr Trueman noticed that if he and his friend Mr Fantom 'set out with talking of trade or politics, of private news or public affairs, still Mr Fantom was . . . sure to end with a pert squib at the Bible, a vapid jest on the clergy, the miseries of superstition, and the blessings of liberty and equality. "Oh!" said Trueman to himself, "when shall I see Christians half so much in earnest? Why is it that almost all zeal is on the wrong side?"'

Village Politics, by Will Chip takes the form of a dialogue between honest Jack Anvil the blacksmith and Tom Hod the mason, not a bad fellow but misled by Tom Paine. A few excerpts will show reason for Bishop Porteus's admiration, though perhaps the cool judgment of times not so immediately vexed by the French Revolution will not insist on Richard Owen Cambridge's comparison with Dean Swift.

Tom Hod wants Liberty and Equality, a new Constitution (*Jack Anvil:* 'Indeed! Why I had thought thou hadst been a desperate healthy fellow. Send for the doctor directly.') and the Rights of Man. But if he wants a reform, he should mend himself, and if he wants a general reform, then every one should mend one. To imitate the French is folly, as they 'began all this mischief at first in order to be just what we are already'. The French are now free . . . to rob and kill whom they will. They had a poor sort of religion, but bad is better than none. When Tom Hod defends Paine's doctrine that as all men should be free the gaols should be torn down, Jack Anvil counters with the equality before the law of rich and poor in England: 'I may go to law with Sir John at the great

castle yonder.' That appears to be satisfactory to Mrs More, and we must believe she had not heard Horne Tooke's remark that the courts were indeed open to rich and poor, like the London Tavern. She makes good use too (together with all other conservative writers of the period) of the hanging of Earl Ferrers for the murder of his steward (of course not the Evangelical Earl Ferrers of Wilberforce's day).

Like Mrs More, Jack Anvil has not read *The Rights of Man;* but also like Mrs More, he knows a good deal about Paine's doctrine. It is so foolish that 'if this nonsensical equality was to take place', he could take away all Tom Hod's property because he is stronger. We come to some Christian lessons about these matters that quite finish off Tom Paine with his insistence that there should be no gaols, no taxes, and no government at all.

> TOM. But I say all men are equal. Why should one be above another?
>
> JACK. If that's thy talk, Tom, thou dost quarrel with Providence, and not with government. For the woman is below her husband, and the children are below their mother, and the servant is below his master.
>
> TOM. But the subject is not below the king: all kings are 'crowned ruffians'; [Mrs More's note: a popular phrase at that time] and all governments are wicked. For my part, I am resolved I'll pay no more taxes to any of them.
>
> JACK. Tom, Tom, if thou didst go oftener to church, thou wouldst know where it is said, 'Render unto Caesar the things that are Caesar's'; and also, 'Fear God, honour the king'. *Your* book tells you that we need obey no government but that of the people; and that we may fashion and alter the government according to our whimsies; but *mine* tells me, 'Let every one be subject to the higher powers, for all power is of God; the powers that be are ordained of God; whosoever therefore resisteth the power, resisteth the ordinance of God'. Thou sayest, thou wilt pay no taxes to any of them. Dost thou know who it was that worked a miracle, that he might have money to pay tribute with, rather than to set you and me an example of disobedience to government? an example, let me tell thee, worth an hundred precepts, and of which all the wit of man can never lessen the value. Then there's another thing worth minding; when Saint Paul was giving all those directions, in the Epistle to the Romans, for obedience and submission; what sort of king now dost think they had? Dost think 'twas a *saint* which he ordered them to obey?
>
> TOM. Why, it was a kind, merciful, charitable king, to be sure: one who put nobody to death or to prison.
>
> JACK. You was never more out in your life. Our parson says he was a monster—that he robbed the rich, and murdered the poor—set fire to his own town, as fine a place as London—fiddled to the flames, and then hanged and burnt the Christians, who were all poor, as if they had burnt the city. Yet there's not a word about rising.—Duties are fixed, Tom—laws are settled; a Christian can't pick and choose, whether he will obey or let it alone.

Jack Anvil does not pretend that 'our great folks' are a bit better than they should be, but 'they'll answer for that in another place'. They could set us a better example about going to church, but still 'hoarding's not the sin of the age: they don't lock up their *money*—away it goes, and every body's the better for it'. 'It all comes among the people. Their very extravagance, for which, as I said before, their parsons should be at them, is a fault by which, as poor men, we are benefited; so you cry out just in the wrong place.' The 'private vices, public benefits' argument is one of Mrs More's favourites, under various names and taken in various ways. In *Mr Fantom,* after William the footman has been corrupted by Paine and Godwin, he serves dinner in a very drunken condition. He has often heard Mr Fantom say private vices are public benefits, 'and so I thought that getting drunk was as pleasant a way of doing good to the public as any'. Taken as true or as false this argument was effective in Mrs More's hands.

Without the great and their wealth of course the poor would have nothing.

> Their coaches and their furniture, and their buildings and their planting, employ a power of tradesmen and labourers. Now in this village, what should we do without the castle? Though my lady is too ranti-polish, and flies about all summer to hot water and cold water, and fresh water and salt water, when she ought to stay at home with Sir John; yet when she does come down, she brings such a deal of gentry, that I have more horses than I can shoe, and my wife more linen than she can wash. Then all our grown children are servants in the family, and rare wages they have got. Our little boys get something every day by weeding their gardens; and the girls learn to sew and knit at Sir John's expense, who sends them all to school of a Sunday besides.

Furthermore,

> when this levelling comes about, there will be no infirmaries, no hospitals, no charity-schools, no Sunday-schools, where so many hundred thousand poor souls learn to read the word of God for nothing. For who is to pay for them? *Equality* can't afford it; and those that may be willing won't be able.

Jack's strongest or at least most typical argument is that although this nonsensical equality 'would not last while one could say Jack Robinson',

> suppose it could—suppose, in the general division, our new rulers were to give us half an acre of ground apiece; we could, to be sure, raise potatoes on it for the use of our families; but as every other man would be equally busy in raising potatoes for *his* family, why then, you see, if thou wast to break thy spade, I, whose trade it is, should no longer be able to mend it. Neighbour Snip would have no time to make us a suit of clothes, nor the clothier to weave the cloth; for all the world would be gone a digging. And as to boots and shoes, the want of some one to make them for us would be a still greater grievance than the tax on leather. If we should be sick, there would be no doctor's stuff for us; for doctors would be digging too. And if necessity did not compel, and if equality subsisted, we could not get a chimney swept, a lamp lighted, or a load of coal from pit, for love or money.

'I have got the use of my limbs, of my liberty, of the laws, and of my Bible', says Jack Anvil.

> The first two I take to be my *natural* rights; the two last my *civil* and *religious* rights: these, I take it, are the *true Rights of Man,* and all the rest is nothing but nonsense, and madness, and wickedness. . . . Instead of indulging discontent, because another is richer than I in this world (for envy is at the bottom of your equality works), I read my Bible, go to church, and look forward to a treasure in heaven.

Mrs More's authorship of *Village Politics* caused great happiness among her friends, and King George too is said to have been delighted with it. It should be pointed out, however, in justice, that the 'all the world would be gone a digging' argument was not actually hers. She was given it by Sir William Weller Pepys, one of the leading Evangelical philanthropists and a very active supporter of Wilberforce's moral and religious societies. Mrs More was not alone in understanding that pitch defiles.

Of course no one knew better than Hannah More that the church 'needed amending as well as attending' or was doing more to amend it, or that the sinecurists, placemen and pensioners were indefensible parasites, the rotten boroughs rotten, the Parliament corruptly constituted and corrupt. Who had blocked every serious effort against fashionable adultery and the slave trade, for taxation on fashionable luxuries and the enforcement of Sabbath observance? It was probably the necessity of disguising such beliefs in exhorting the lower orders that led her always to speak deprecatingly of these works and her friends to refer to them facetiously. They were only intended for the most vulgar classes. But if she did not for an instant believe all she patriotically advanced for the improvement of the discontented inferior ranks she believed a large part of it implicitly, and her belief was shared by Newton and Wilberforce. If none of the Evangelicals of this period who recorded their political views expressed them with such crass candour or in terms so suitable to the vulgar, the number of those who did not agree with Mrs More was tiny. (pp. 123-30)

Mrs Hannah More's political doctrine for the lower orders was naturally not full and thorough, necessarily being in a striking dramatic form and enforcing only the simplest elementary concepts; but in proceeding to examine it further we may have the fullest confidence, even apart from the testimony of great and wholly unqualified Evangelical applause, that it will contain nothing that is not sound Evangelicalism.

In 1794 at the continued entreaties of Porteus and many others she undertook to write or get friends to write for her three tracts a month, similar to *Village Politics,* for the duration of the crisis. In four years, with the help of Miss Patty and an occasional outside contributor, she turned out a lengthy series of moral, loyal and religious pieces, enough to make three thick little volumes when collected. Old Archbishop Moore headed a committee that bribed hawkers to sell them, for a penny or halfpenny, and worked to get them into display windows in place of radical and atheistic propaganda. Helped by the crisis and the Spirit of the Age, the committee did its work well. In these tracts Mrs More had her greatest audience. Few other people had had one like it.

The high point was reached in 1795. In April, Dr Stonhouse, himself author of *Materials For Talking Familiarly With Children of All Ranks,* wrote with something like awe of the astounding demand. 'After the sale of two hundred and eleven thousand, sixty thousand are now bespoke.' Three months later, 'Seven hundred thousand of Mrs Hannah More's

Tracts have been sold, and the demand still so great, that they cannot be printed fast enough. Hazard [one of Mrs More's three publishers] says, a million will have been sold before the end of next month. No such sale has ever been heard of in the annals of England.' They had sold over two millions by the end of the year, 'besides very large numbers in Ireland'.

Mrs More called them the Cheap Repository Tracts, a name soon contracted into Cheap Repository.

These little stories fall into two groups, one designed for the middle ranks, the other for the inferior, both constructed on the fundamental principle that virtue comes only from the Christian religion. In the tales of the second group particularly, which continue to be as vulgar as heart could wish, there is usually a good parish priest or member of the upper classes, worthy and charitable, with a virtuous (and rewarded) member of the inferior ranks, and an impious, dissolute or radical (and punished) member of the inferior ranks. Mrs More's language is simple, vigorous and even racy, with a kind of humour and pungency and what may be called a moral dramatic quality. It would have been beyond flesh and blood for her to keep from preaching, especially as she was accustomed to preach a good deal to her schools, and once in a while it is badly overdone. In *The Two Wealthy Farmers* poor Mr Bragwell receives from good Mr Worthy the most ponderous burden of reproof ever given to any character in fiction. But on the whole the stories deserved their immense reputation. Considered merely as art they were beyond the range of Mrs Trimmer, a respectable but not gifted woman, and in fact beyond the range of anyone else who has appeared in the field. It seems probable that we will not look upon their like again.

Of course subtlety would have been worse than useless. The circumstances were pressing, the artist's method strong and direct. Her good and bad characters are immediately identified in the simplest way by their introduction as good Mr White and bad Mr Black or in some equally understandable fashion. Mrs More as a rule gets quickly to the point and the reader is left in no perplexity as to what is right and what wrong. Mr Bragwell's 'natural disposition was not particularly bad, but prosperity had hardened his heart'. 'Poaching Giles lives on the border of one of those great moors in Somersetshire.' 'Hester Wilmot was born in the parish of Weston, of parents who maintained themselves by their labour; they were both of them ungodly, it is no wonder therefore they were unhappy.' 'John Wilmot was not an ill-natured man, but he had no fixed principle.' 'Mr Johnson on the Saturday evening reached a very small inn, a mile or two distant from the Shepherd's village; for he never travelled on a Sunday without such a reason as he might be able to produce at the day of judgment.' 'William was a lively young servant, who lived in a great but very irregular family.' 'A barrow-woman, blessed be God and our good laws, is as much her own mistress on Sundays as a duchess.' 'But if religious persons will, for the sake of money, choose partners who have no religion, do not let them complain that they are unhappy; they might have known that beforehand.' 'Jolly George, as we used to call him, the ring-leader of all our mirth, who was at the bottom of all the fun and tricks, and wickedness, that are carried on within these walls, Jolly George is just dead of the jail distemper!'

Mrs More writes with vigour and pertinency, and even her longer and more deliberate sentences are nearly always crowded with substantial matter. 'It was the custom in that school, and an excellent custom it is, for the master, who was

a good and wise man, to mark down in his pocket-book all the events of the week, that he might turn them to some account in his Sunday evening instructions; such as any useful story in the newspaper, any account of boys being drowned as they were out in a pleasure-boat on Sundays, any sudden death in the parish, or any other remarkable visitation of Providence; insomuch, that many young people in the place, who did not belong to the school, and many parents also, used to drop in for an hour on a Sunday evening, when they were sure to hear something profitable.'

Mrs More's sardonic criticisms of such things as contemporary novels and education in young ladies' seminaries are the work of an intelligent, observant, informed woman. As her friends believed, she knew far more than most the manners of the great and the rural inferior. Her characters are accurately reported and her ideas sensible within the Evangelical framework. With the possible exception of some basic religious, moral and political concepts, which cannot, however, unfortunately, be abstracted from these tales and leave much behind, everything in them is above criticism. Her novice piece *Village Politics* was not only foolish but artless. In the later tales there is less arguing, more conflict, more objective virtue or radicalism. The moral is pointed out in most not by reasoning but by visible results. Black Giles falls while thieving and is killed; honest William Wilson the footman, ruined by Godwinian doctrine, is hanged. Patient Joe the Newcastle coal-miner, who believes all is for the best, steadfastly endures the profligate wit of idle Tim Jenkins, who mocks at the Bible. Joe's lunch is stolen by a dog. Leaving Tim in the pit, laughing and swearing and asking if that too is for the best, Joe hurries off after his lunch, and returns to find the pit fallen in and Tim crushed. In *The Two Shoemakers,* James Stock, honest and pious, rises to affluence, while his fellow apprentice idle Jack Brown sinks lower and lower, haunts evil resorts, plays fives, patronizes jugglers and mountebanks, goes to fairs, and at last is ruined, though helped as much as is prudent by James Stock. It is in *The Two Shoemakers* that Mrs More quotes a stanza of 'that beautiful hymn so deservedly the favourite of all children':

> Not more than others I deserve,
> Yet God hath given me more;
> For I have food while others starve,
> Or beg from door to door.

Hester Wilmot, in *The Sunday School* and *The History of Hester Wilmot,* refuses to eat cakes and drink ale at the fair, becomes an underteacher in the Sunday school and has prospect of further promotion. Mrs More did not necessarily think that because Hester was virtuous there would be no more cakes and ale, having indeed no objection to either; but she did object to fairs opening on Sunday evenings.

Mrs More is at her best in such a piece as *Black Giles the Poacher: containing some Account of a Family who had rather live by their Wits than their Work,* one of her most spirited tales. It exhibited a knowledge of the life of the poor, in villages and cottages, together with the shifts, wiles, tricks and devices of the lawless poor, that came close to going beyond the knowledge of such things that a respectable member of society could with propriety have. It was this sort of knowledge too that led her friends among the great to refer to Cheap Repository facetiously. Black Giles and Tawney Rachel his wife bring their offspring up to be beggars and pilferers. Their son Dick is 'the best of Giles's bad boys', and when Black Giles and his lads profit by poor widow Brown's absence, at church, to steal all her finest apples it is eventually too much for Dick. Giles plants some of the apples in the home of Samuel Price, a very honest carpenter in the parish, and his son Tom is accused of the theft. Tom Price is the best boy in the school, has once given Dick a piece of his own bread and cheese, and has also saved him from drowning; and when Mr Wilson the worthy clergyman has got Dick into the Sunday evening school, and the master there has shown that the theft of the redstreaks, on a Sunday, has probably broken no fewer than five of the commandments, Dick cannot hold fast to his evil ways.

> 'If the thief,' the master continues, 'to all his other sins, has added that of accusing the innocent to save himself, if he should break the ninth commandment, *by bearing false witness against a harmless neighbour,* then six commandments are broken for an *apple*! But if it be otherwise, if Tom Price should be found guilty, it is not his good character shall save him. I shall shed tears over him, but punish him I must, and that severely.'—'No, that you sha'n't,' roared out Dick Giles, who sprung from his hiding-place, fell on his knees, and burst out a-crying, 'Tom Price is as good a boy as ever lived; it was father and I who stole the apples!'

It would have done your heart good to have seen the joy of the master, the modest blushes of Tom Price, and the satisfaction of every honest boy in the school.

With *A Cure for Melancholy (Shewing the Way to Do Much Good with Little Money)* we rise to a more serious doctrinal level. It was written during the 'scarcity' of 1794, one of three extremely severe winters in the first half of the decade. Mrs Jones, a worthy widow, is anxious to do good in the parish, but has no money. It was fortunate for her that the vicar of Weston was a pious man. (Though careful to introduce exemplary clergymen in these tales, Mrs More as we know was not of the opinion that all clergymen in English parishes were exemplary. Though she tried hard to keep views peculiar to Evangelicalism out of these tracts, once in a while something like the pious vicar shows up.) Through him Mrs Jones learns how she can help the poor greatly without money, by benevolent exertions.

Mrs More's statement of good Mrs Jones's activities and aims is the clearest autobiography and the whole story one of the fine pictures of Evangelicalism at work among the humble. 'Her chief aim was the happiness of her poor neighbours in the next world; but she was also very desirous to promote their present comfort: and indeed the kindness she shewed to their bodily wants gave her such an access to their houses and hearts, as made them better disposed to receive religious counsel and instruction.' Apart from the gift of her own moral and religious example and exhortation, Mrs Jones though without funds succeeds in bestowing four considerable benefactions on the parishioners: she gets the blacksmith to inform on Mr Crib the baker whose loaves are light, and succeeds in having sounder views adopted on the necessity and morality of the informer's office; she gets the Squire to fine shopkeepers who keep open on Sundays; she helps in the suppression of superfluous public houses; and she urges and demonstrates the avoidance of expensive foods such as butter, tea, milk and meat, and the use of cheap recipes.

Mrs Jones does other good things too. She 'took care never to walk out without a few little good books in her pocket to give away. This, though a cheap, is a most important act of charity; it has various uses; it furnishes the poor with religious knowledge, which they have so few ways of obtaining; it counteracts the wicked designs of those who have taught us at least one lesson, by their zeal in the dispersion of *wicked* books,—I mean the lesson of vigilance and activity; and it is the best introduction for any useful conversation which the giver of the book may wish to introduce.' 'Thus Mrs Jones, by a little exertion and perseverance, added to the temporal comforts of a whole parish, and diminished its immorality and extravagance in the same proportion.'

One could wish, though it is futile at this point, that sometimes Mrs More could have thought of charities without 'uses'. But that would have been opposed to a very basic principle.

Such tracts were devoted chiefly to pointing out the rewards of piety, virtue and orderliness and the punishments of irreligion and profligacy. An important section of Cheap Repository dealt primarily with economic instruction in a way begun by Mrs Jones, that is, told the poor how to get along on their few shillings a week. The destitution of unskilled labourers in particular, at the end of the century and from then on through the Evangelical campaign, was very severe, as we are told again and again in Mrs More's pages, not only in the children's favourite hymn. In Mrs Jones's parish and elsewhere in Mrs More, fuel was almost unobtainable for the inferior orders and no poor woman could buy milk, 'as the farmers' wives did not care to rob their dairies. This was a great distress, especially when the children were sick.' Mrs Trimmer observed during these years that many of the families of her husband's labourers (at Brentford) were clothed in rags picked up on the roads and sewn together. There were few country labourers' families, according to the testimony of these worthy ladies, that could afford fuel, shoes for the children, or anything but desperate substitutes for good food. It is in 1795, the worst of these years, that rioting advances in Mrs More's stories to the position of the worst sin. Her charitable worthy people, always anxious to share their last penny with the deserving unfortunate, deny their charity to rioters first, passive malcontents second, and profane swearers, drunkards and Sabbath-breakers third. It is also at this time that Mrs More enunciates her doctrine about honest and prudent informers without malice or bitterness.

Her solution of the evils of extreme indigence, while laying no hand on the political and economic institutions of the land, which are a dispensation of Deity, was twofold and correct in each part. The poor were guilty of too great regard for appearances and of worldly-mindedness, and they had not learned a truth stated long before, in a general way, by an earlier philosopher, that happiness can be attained as easily by decreasing desire as by increasing gratification. It might have occurred to Mrs More that waste and economic folly could reasonably have been expected from 'ignorant' and untaught people, neglected by church and state, but it does not seem to have done so. Hardly anything shocked her so much as the observation that even families living in squalor, clad in filthy rags and without fuel for heat, often had white bread, tea, butter, joints and ale. The less terribly indigent they were, the more waste. When Mrs More and Miss Patty extended their school system to the glass factory at Nailsea they found high wages (ten or eleven shillings a week instead of seven or eight) and 'luxurious' eating and drinking—'the body scarcely covered, but fed with dainties of a shameful description.' 'The high buildings of the glass houses ranged before the door of these cottages', Miss Patty's journal continues, 'the great furnaces roaring—the swearing, eating and drinking of these half-dressed, black-looking human beings, gave it a most infernal and horrible appearance. One, if not two, joints of the finest meat were roasting in each of these little hot kitchens, pots of ale were standing about, and plenty of early delicate-looking vegetables. . . . We were in our usual luck as regards personal civility, which we received even from the worst of these creatures, some welcoming us to "Botany Bay", others to "Little Hell", as they themselves shockingly called it.'

Mrs More had three arguments against such indulgence. First, it shows poor judgment: it would be better to have plainer food and more fuel and clothing. Second, such luxury is worldly-minded, forbidden by the Bible and disrespectful to one's betters (hence the shamefulness of the dainties at the glass factory). Third, there are other dishes equally appetizing and more becoming to one's inferior rank. Her specific reply to the winter of 1795, when sheep froze in the fields and farmers could not hire labourers unless they made an effort to make work indoors, was *The Second Part of Tom White the Postboy; or, The Way to Plenty.* This tract, which may be described without a bitterness that would be pointless at this time as one of Mrs More's most terrible works, appeared in Cheap Repository in the middle of the winter. As with so many of these tales, indeed nearly all, the difficulty in describing *The Way to Plenty* (which is done, it is hoped there is no real need of saying, in Mrs More's words) is to determine which sentences must be left unquoted. Through virtue and piety, Tom White has become a respectable farmer. Sober and temperate, he is active and healthy as a natural consequence; industrious and frugal, he has become prosperous. That is not a certain rule, although the ordinary course of Providence, for God is sometimes pleased for wise ends to disappoint the worldly hopes of the most upright men. Tom refuses to sell his corn at a seaport at a high price, knowing it is intended for illicit export; he threshes a small part of it at a time and sells it to the neighbouring poor at less than the market price. He lets his labourers plant potatoes for their own use in his waste bits of ground, and gives up his dogs, which eat food that can be given to the poor (a point stressed by the Evangelical and other philanthropists). He joins in subscriptions for the deserving unfortunate, in the form of selling them rice and coarse bread at reduced prices, naturally wishes his labourers not to go to the public house and is particularly set against the hearty celebration of rural holidays. In pressing a variety of practical counsels on the poor, Tom is abetted by his wife, a very worthy woman, and by the vicar, Dr Shepherd, Mrs More's usual exemplary clergyman. Dr Shepherd is very charitable and condescending; in fact with the exception of Mr Johnson in *The Shepherd of Salisbury Plain* he is Mrs More's most condescending character. He lectures all good poor people tirelessly on their duty to themselves and their betters, and is noteworthy for uttering one of Mrs More's finest things when he tells the honest wives of the shilling-a-day labourers that their unusual hardships of this winter are particularly valuable as 'prosperity had made most of us careless'.

> My good women, I truly feel for you at this time of scarcity; and I am going to show my good will, as much by my advice as my subscription. It is my duty, as your friend and minister, to tell you, that one half of your present hardships is due to bad management. I often meet your children without shoes and stockings, with great luncheons of the

very whitest bread, and that three times a day. Half that quantity, and still less if it were coarse, put into a dish of good onion or leek porridge, would make them an excellent breakfast. Many too, of the very poorest of you, eat your bread hot from the oven; this makes a difference of one loaf in five; I assure you 'tis what I cannot afford to do.

Mrs White warmly supports Dr Shepherd in demanding that white bread be given up. Furthermore tea is not only expensive but is slop. It requires a deal of costly sugar and is bad for the stomach. Two pounds of fresh meat cost less than one pound of butter and give five times the nourishment. If the gentry would buy only prime cuts, and not take the cheap, coarse and inferior joints for soups and gravies, the poor could get them instead of good pieces.

> Dry peas, to be sure, have been very dear lately; but now they are plenty enough. I am certain then, that if a shilling or two of the seven or eight was laid out for a bit of coarse beef, a sheep's head, or any such thing, it would be well bestowed. I would throw a couple of pounds of this into the pot, with two or three handsful of gray peas, an onion, and a little pepper. Then I would throw in cabbage, or turnip, and carrot, or any garden stuff that was most plenty; let it stew two or three hours, and it will make a dish fit for his majesty. The working men should have the meat; the children won't want it; the soup will be thick and substantial, and requires no bread.

Rice pudding is even cheaper, for anyone who can get skim-milk. Half a pound of rice, Mrs White says, two quarts of skim-milk, and two ounces of brown sugar; cost not above sevenpence. But more than half a day's wage at that, and Mrs More knew well, having frequently pointed it out herself, that no one could get milk except through the kindness of a charitable farmer. There is still another objection. At this point in *The Way to Plenty* one of the less worthy poor summons the hardihood to complain that all this leaves the fuel problem unsolved.

> Bless your heart, muttered Amy Grumble, who looked as dirty as a cinder-wench, with her face and fingers all daubed with snuff; rice milk indeed! It is very nice to be sure for those who can dress it, but we have not a bit of coal; rice is no use to us without firing. And yet, said the doctor, I see your teakettle boiling twice every day, and fresh butter at thirteen pence a pound on your shelf. O dear sir, cried Amy, a few sticks serve to boil the teakettle. And a few more, said the doctor, will boil the rice milk, and give twice the nourishment at a quarter of the expence.

The poor are not allowed to depart with their subscription until Dr Shepherd has warned them that only those who come to church should come for alms. He concludes his exhortation with the one rule from which their benefactors will never depart: 'Those who have been seen aiding or abetting any riot, any attack on butchers, bakers, wheatmows, mills or millers, we will not relieve; but with the quiet, contented, hard-working man I will share my last morsel of bread.' It is clear that that should be taken as the natural exaggeration of a warm-hearted man.

No account of these moral writings, and as far as that goes no account of English letters during this period that pretends to any thoroughness, could leave out the work of sustained and unequalled greatness of its kind with which Hannah

More crowned Cheap Repository. With *The Shepherd of Salisbury Plain* she rose to a lonely level, for it has no competitor. The greatest of Mrs More's tracts and of all tracts, it towers over similar works like another *Agamemnon*, a flawless masterpiece perfect in conception and in execution, likely to remain forever peerless on a height the moral tale will not reach again.

The Shepherd of Salisbury Plain came from Mrs More's pen in 1794. It should be mentioned that the circumstances and character of the Shepherd were taken from a living model. He was discovered by Sir James Stonhouse's curate Stedman when entering on his curacy at Cheverel. His name was David Saunders. He was of the neighbouring parish of West Lavington, and he used to keep his Bible, Stedman recorded, in the thatch of his hut on the Plain.

As usual Mrs More gets quickly to the point. Her second sentence introduces her exemplary character of the upper classes, Mr Johnson, riding across the Plain slowly that he might have leisure to admire God in the works of his creation. A 'very worthy charitable gentleman', Mr Johnson is said to have been a portrait of Stonhouse. He meets the Shepherd, a clean, well-looking, poor man about fifty years old. His coat has been patched so often that the original colour cannot be made out, his stockings are entirely covered with darns of different coloured worsted, but have not a hole in them. His shirt, though nearly as coarse as the sails of a ship, is as white as the drifted snow. This is a plain proof of his poverty, but equally of the exceeding neatness, industry and good management of his wife. 'A poor woman who will be lying a-bed, or gossiping with her neighbours when she ought to be fitting out her husband in a cleanly manner, will seldom be found to be very good in other respects.'

Mr Johnson accosts the Shepherd with asking what sort of weather it will be on the morrow. 'It will be such weather as pleases me', answers the Shepherd. Although his tone is mild and civil, Mr Johnson naturally thinks he has mistaken his man. He is soon set right. 'Because', the Shepherd continues, 'it will be such weather as shall please God, and whatever pleases him always pleases me.'

That being quite another thing, Mr Johnson benevolently engages the Shepherd in conversation. 'Your's is a troublesome life, honest friend.' The Shepherd defends his calling in a humble but spirited fashion. His tasks are not nearly so toilsome as those assumed by the Great Master for his sake; he is exposed to cold and heat but not to great temptations. 'Besides, Sir, my employment has been particularly honoured— Moses was a shepherd in the plains of Midian.' Furthermore, it was to shepherds that the angels appeared in Bethlehem. 'Here the shepherd stopped, for he began to feel he had made too free, and had talked too long.' Mr Johnson, however, 'desired him to go on freely, for that it was a pleasure to him to meet with a plain man, who, without any kind of learning but what he had got from the bible, was able to talk so well on a subject in which all men, high and low, rich and poor, are equally concerned'. The Shepherd, reassured, enlarges on the generosity of the rich in modern times, the privileges of poverty, and the importance of its place in the Scriptures. 'Sir, I wonder all working men do not derive as great joy and delight as I do from thinking how God has honoured poverty!'

Turning to his own circumstances, he shows the greatest contentment and happiness in the face of many difficulties, which are appropriate enough to his station in life but nevertheless seem to be severe, even in Mrs More's description.

> 'I have but little cause to complain, and much to be thankful; but I have had some little struggles, as I will leave you to judge. I have a wife and eight children, whom I bred up in that little cottage which you see under the hill about half a mile off.'—'What, that with the smoke coming out of the chimney?' said the gentleman. 'O no, Sir,' replied the Shepherd, smiling, 'we have seldom smoke in the evening, for we have little to cook, and firing is very dear in these parts. 'Tis that cottage which you see on the left hand of the church, near that little tuft of hawthorns.'

The Shepherd of Salisbury Plain is full of wonderful things perfectly said, but even so benevolent Mr Johnson's reply has special distinction:

> 'What, that hovel with only one room above and below, with scarcely any chimney? how is it possible you can live there with such a family!'

> 'O! is it very possible and very certain too,' cried the Shepherd. 'How many better men have been worse lodged! how many good christians have perished in prisons and dungeons, in comparison of which my cottage is a palace!'

Mrs More proceeds to a relentless and fearful picture of humble economy punctuated with condescending admiration. The Shepherd's wife is sickly, there are no gentry in the parish, and they have no help except a shilling now and then from the curate. The Shepherd's hovel—as he calls it later, realizing how he has presumed in calling it a cottage—costs him fifty shillings a year, his wage is one shilling a day. The three children under five are no help to him, but before they are six his little girls are making first a halfpenny and then a penny a day knitting. The boys keep the birds off the corn, for which the farmers may give them a penny or even twopence a day, and sometimes a bit of bread and cheese into the bargain.

> While they were in this part of the discourse, a fine plump cherry-cheek little girl ran up out of breath, with a smile on her young happy face, and without taking any notice of the gentleman, cried out with great joy,—'Look here, father, only see how much I have got!' Mr Johnson was much struck with her simplicity, but puzzled to know what was the occasion of this great joy. On looking at her he perceived a small quantity of coarse wool, some of which had found its way through the holes of her clean, but scanty and ragged woolen apron. The father said, 'This has been a successful day indeed, Molly; but don't you see the gentleman?' Molly now made a curtsey down to the very ground; while Mr Johnson inquired into the cause of the mutual satisfaction which both father and daughter had expressed, at the unusual good fortune of the day.

> 'Sir,' said the Shepherd, 'poverty is a great sharpener of the wits.—My wife and I cannot endure to see our children (poor as they are) without shoes and stockings, not only on account of the pinching cold which cramps their poor little limbs, but because it degrades and debases them; and poor people who have but little regard to appearances, will seldom be found to have any great regard for honesty and goodness; I don't say this is always the case, but I am sure it is so too often. Now shoes and stockings

being very dear, we could never afford them without a contrivance. I must shew you how I manage about the shoes when you condescend to call at our cottage, Sir; as to stockings, this is one way we take to help to get them. My young ones, who are too little to do much work, sometimes wander at odd hours over the hills for the chance of finding what little wool the sheep may drop when they rub themselves, as they are apt to do, against the bushes. [Mrs More's note: This piece of frugal industry is not imaginary, but a real fact, as is the character of the Shepherd, and his uncommon knowledge of the Scriptures.] These scattered bits of wool the children pick out of the brambles, which I see have torn sad holes in Molly's apron to-day; they carry this wool home, and when they have got a pretty parcel together, their mother cards it; for she can sit and card in the chimney corner, when she is not able to wash, or work about house. The biggest girl spins it, the little boys knit stockings for themselves while keeping cows or at night, and what the girls and their mother knit is for sale, to help pay the rent.'

Mr Johnson lifted up his eyes in silent astonishment at the shifts which honest poverty can make rather than beg or steal; and was surprised to think how many ways of subsisting there are, which those who live at their ease little suspect. He secretly resolved to be more attentive to his own petty expences than he had hitherto been; and to be more watchful that nothing was wasted in his own family.

Perhaps it is just another of those painful blemishes in the nature of things as they are rather than as they should be that in so far as Mr Johnson and others of his superior station did that, they were rendering null and void Jack Anvil's only remotely admissible argument in favour of the upper classes, in *Village Politics,* that their extravagance benefits all the poor. (pp. 134-48)

Cheap Repository was discontinued in 1798 when the flood of French principles was believed to have fallen off. Before then and long afterward many a conservative and respectable voice was raised in grateful praise. 'The sublime and immortal publication of the "Cheap Repository", I hear of from every quarter of the globe', Bishop Porteus wrote in 1797. 'I am . . . determined to eat nothing but Mrs Jones's cheap dishes all this winter.' His playful manner should not be misunderstood; he believed Mrs More's tracts were the chief influence in preventing the spread of revolutionary ideas among the poor. Many were far from facetious about these tracts. There is a story of William Jay, the noted nonconformist divine of Bath, weeping as he read Mrs More's tale of the honest shepherd, and years later William Wilberforce declared that he would rather go up to render his account at the last day carrying with him *The Shepherd of Salisbury Plain* than with all the volumes of Sir Walter Scott's works, 'full as they are of genius'. (pp. 150-51)

> *Ford K. Brown, "Citizenship in Heaven," in his* Fathers of the Victorians: The Age of Wilberforce, *Cambridge at the University Press, 1961, pp. 123-55.*

SAM PICKERING (essay date 1977)

[*In the following excerpt, Pickering asserts the importance of More's* Cœlebs in Search of a Wife *in establishing the novel as a respectable genre.*]

In *Novels of the Eighteen-Forties,* Kathleen Tillotson wrote

that Walter Scott, more than any other writer, was responsible for the novel's becoming respectable reading in the nineteenth century. Breaching the moral opposition to the genre, Scott opened the way for Dickens, and by mid-century the novel was the dominant literary form. Following the footsteps of writers such as Anthony Trollope, Mrs. Tillotson's history of the novel has become a critical commonplace. And certainly the sale of Scott's novels support her theory. *Waverley* (1814), for example, sold 6000 copies in six months; *Rob Roy* (1818), 10,000 in a fortnight. However, despite these phenomenal figures, I think that the way for the novel's respectability and resulting general acceptance by reading public, was paved, not by Scott, but by Hannah More. Combining religious lessons with a novelistic narrative, Mrs. More's *Coelebs in Search of a Wife* was the first nineteenth century novel to be accepted enthusiastically by the large religious reading public. Introducing the novel to many readers, *Coelebs* prepared the public for Scott, whose concerns if not particularly theological were at least moral.

Discussing Scott in 1847, *Fraser's Magazine* declared that just thirty years before "every novel came into the world with a brand upon it." Although forty years would have been more accurate, *Fraser's* was essentially correct. In its first issue (1805), the *Eclectic Review,* a journal for conservative dissenters, maintained that only a novelist's mental limitations controlled "the mischief" he could create. In the same year, the *Christian Observer* condemned novels out of hand, declaring they vitiated the taste and blunted the benevolent affections through "unnatural excitement" and raising "extravagant ideas in the mind."

The novel had not always stood in such poor stead with religious readers. Prior to the French Revolution, most members of the Established Church thought that literature, and especially the novel, would become a guide to Christian living in the nineteenth century. In the late seventeenth and early eighteenth centuries, Anglican latitudinarians had become a powerful force in the Established Church. These broad church divines turned English Christianity into a moral system emphasizing charity instead of Christ and goodness instead of grace. Spontaneous affection and personal benevolism became the hallmarks of the Christian. "The frame of our nature so disposeth us," wrote Isaac Barrow, "that our bowels are touched with sensible pain upon the view of any calamitous object: our fancy is disturbed at the report of any disaster befalling any person; we can hardly see or read a tragedy without motions of compassion."

This latitudinarian theology spread beyond the Church. The cult of sensibility and the man of feeling were direct shoots off Barrow's "motions of compassion." Mirroring latitudinarian concerns, criticism demanded that the novel be a parable, teaching Christian charity. For the most part, novelists either believed or quietly accepted the broad church morality. As a result readers had little difficulty in fitting, for example, two of the century's most popular novels, Richardson's *Pamela* and Mackenzie's *The Man of Feeling,* into theological perspective. Despite the many *Shamela*-like parodies, the vast majority of readers thought *Pamela* a morally beneficial work. Although he was Richardson's friend, Aaron Hill's enthusiastic reaction to the novel was typical. "It will live on thro' posterity, with such unbounded extent of good consequences that twenty ages to come may be the better and wiser for its influence," Hill wrote, exclaiming that "who could have dreamt he should find under the modest disguise of a *novel* all the soul of religion, good-breeding, discretion, good-nature, wit, fancy, fine thought and morality?"

The Richardson-Mackenzie latitudinarian sensibility dominated the novel throughout the eighteenth century. And although reactions to the novel occurred, criticism remained comparatively mute until the French Revolution. However with the Revolution, critical good will toward the novel was dispersed, and the novel became known as "one of the most universal as well as most pernicious sources of corruption among us." At the beginning of the revolution, a strong parliamentary party believed a Jacobinical conspiracy was trying to overthrow Britain by spreading seditious writings among the lower classes. Fear of seditious writings soon led to irrational fear of all writing. Moreover, the novel's broad church morality was no longer respectable. Reacting against the Revolution, Britain swung sharply to the theological right, with the result that latitudinarianism became identified with Socinianism. Holding that the Constitution rested on both Church and State, Edmund Burke said that Socinians were Jacobins trying to undermine the Constitution. If they were not stopped, Burke argued, they would destroy every British establishment and then rebuild the state on a French model encompassing Tom Paine's doctrines.

Instead of looking back to English divines or to Richardson and Mackenzie, critics of the novel now found the source of the genre's excessive sentiment in Rousseau. From Rousseau and his followers came characters who practised "superfluous acts of generosity" while "trampling on obvious and commanded duties," who combined "inflated sentiments of honor with actions the most flagitious," and who taught that no duty existed which was "not prompted by feeling" and impulse was "the main spring of virtuous actions while laws and religion" were "only unjust restraints."

This statement by Hannah More in her popular *Strictures on the Modern System of Female Education* (1799) was representative of religious readers' disapproval of the novel at the turn of the century. This disapproval, however, rested on shaky theoretical grounds. During the 1790's Hannah More and her friends at Clapham had written the *Cheap Repository Tracts.* Aimed at the lower classes whom the Claphams feared were susceptible to French doctrines, many of the *Tracts* were short novels teaching sound politics and religion. Moreover the *Tracts* were an amalgam of latitudinarian heterodoxy and Church of England orthodoxy. The doctrines of the atonement, original sin, and justification by faith alone were alongside Barrow's "motions of compassion" and Richardson's "Virtue Rewarded."

In 1798 after more than two million *Tracts* had been sold and when an English revolution appeared unlikely, the Claphams stopped publishing the *Tracts.* However the Claphams' success served as an example for other groups with political, but primarily religious, axes to grind. In the first decade of the century, millions of tracts repeating the successful Clapham formula were published by groups who condemned novels based on a similar formula.

The effect of the *Cheap Repository Tracts* and their "progeny" is incalculable. But since the *Tracts* were most often distributed in the Sunday Schools, Britain's most effective educational system in the 1790's, I think that tracts taught a generation of Britons how to read and how to judge literature. These "new" readers read *Coelebs* as an extended tract and enthusiastically withdrew it from the circulating library.

After *Coelebs,* they turned to Scott; and together with their children, later they formed the base of Dickens's early popularity.

If tracts had indirectly prepared the way for *Coelebs* with "new" readers, the spirit of the age had prepared the way with the 220,000 people in the higher and middle classes whom Francis Jeffrey thought read for instruction or amusement. The Napoleonic wars and religious controversy were the two most discussed topics of the day. In an era in which methodist preachers were accused of being "instruments of Jacobinism," when the Archbishop of Canterbury said that Catholic emancipation would provoke the animosity which existed before the Reformation, and when the Prime Minister debated if the Pope were the beast with seven heads or just one of the heads in the Book of Revelation, the stage was set for general interest in a religious novel.

Nevertheless if nineteenth century readers were psychologically prepared for a religious novel, Hannah More was not sure she should write such a book. Religious readers still accepted her *Strictures,* and as late as June 1808, the *Christian Observer* wrote that novels produced "a disinclination to regular industry" and quickened "the appetite for low and vicious pursuits." However, Mrs. More's chagrin at the growth of circulating libraries outweighed her disapproval of the novel. As early as 1775, Sheridan's Sir Anthony Absolute had denounced the circulating library as "an evergreen tree of diabolical knowledge," blossoming throughout the year. Although comic, Sir Anthony's denunciation pointed to a serious concern with the effects of circulating libraries. In the first decades of the nineteenth century, this concern grew. As taxes for the Napoleonic wars and higher book prices coincided with greater literacy, middle and lower class Britons could not afford to buy many books. To fulfill the demand for inexpensive reading, circulating libraries multiplied. Evangelicals believed the libraries' indiscriminant circulation lists now threatened British morality, much as seditious writings had threatened the Constitution in the 1790's. As she had done with the *Cheap Repository Tracts,* so Hannah More now rose to the occasion, writing *Coelebs* as a paradigm of what the novel could and should be. Hopefully *Coelebs* would establish the religious novel as a staple of the circulating library and like the *Tracts* "counteract the delusive and irreligious spirit" of the age.

Describing both the good Christian life and an evangelical courtship, *Coelebs* was built around a series of situations which illustrated the material and spiritual benefits which accrued to those who accepted "true" religion. Each situation was followed by a sermon which served as a coda, and sermon by sermon, the novel advanced through all possible sins. Today *Coelebs* is dated, and it is almost impossible to understand the excitement when it appeared. Published anonymously, speculation over *Coelebs*'s author stirred up public controversy. A run-away best seller, "all the world" was "mad to read it." Eleven editions appeared in nine months, and rumor said that the book was printed simultaneously at three different locations.

In the first quarter of the nineteenth century, no novel was so widely reviewed as *Coelebs.* Most reviews were enthusiastic and favorable. The stodgy *British Critic* had "never read a work which" combined "the *utile cum dulci* more completely than *Coelebs.*" Writing that every part of *Coelebs* tended "to good," other journals recommended "its perusal to every virtuous family in the British Empire." After pointing out a minor flaw, the *Scots Magazine* waxed wildly meta-phorical, saying: "But in Coelebs, as in Achilles, there is but a heel that is vulnerable; and after our severest operation, he looks better than before. Winnow this book as we please, there remains a full and nutritious grain behind. Its feathers may be plucked, but it only tends the better to lay bare a plump and full fed body which when scientifically served up will, we surmise, afford as savoury and satisfying a repast as ever touched the table, or pleased the plate of an intellectual epicure." Rhapsodically the *Christian Observer* ended its review [see excerpt by Macaulay dated 1809] with a prayer: "May the Father of all goodness bless this work to his glory, in the advancement of piety and happiness. To Him doubtless, it is an acceptable sacrifice; and what are the applauses even of the wise and good, compared with his favour, in whose presence is life and at whose right hand are pleasures for ever more?" Even more remarkable was the forty-three line poetic tribute in the *Poetical Magazine* to "The Unknown Author of Coelebs." The "floating novels of the day" had corrupted the young virgin, the servant wench, the prentic'd lad, and student for the bench. Previous novelists had forgotten the soul. "None dar'd to take Religion for a theme, but dipped their pens in Error's wandering stream." According to the *Poetical Magazine, Coelebs* was the first novel to speak of divine truths and explain the Christian covenant between God and man.

The few journals that condemned *Coelebs* did so primarily on the grounds of its religiosity. For the most part these journals were politically conservative. Unfairly they identified Mrs. More's brand of evangelical Anglicanism with methodism. Broadly labelling all dissenters methodists, hidebound Tories argued that dissenters undermined the Constitution by separating themselves from the Established Church. One periodical asserted that the sentiments taught by *Coelebs* were "those of methodism with all its vile cant and its holy perversion." Mixing personal with religious attacks, another periodical wrote that although Coelebs tried to reverse the strategem of Achilles, by disguising himself in the dress of a young man of twenty-five, his "eagerness to grasp the quill of religious controversy" betrayed the illusion and sent "him forth to the holy wars in the shape of an old lady of seventy." The *London Review* said that *Coelebs* was a novel for "conventiclers and suckling none but the babes of grace with the pure milk of divine love." In the midst of a quarrel with the Clapham sect, Sydney Smith flayed *Coelebs* in the *Edinburgh Review* [see excerpt dated 1809]. After calling the novel a "dramatic sermon," Smith lefthandedly apologized, writing that if Mrs. More had not belonged to a trumpery gospel faction and had not degraded the human understanding to the trash and folly of methodism, she would have been one of the most valuable writers of the day.

Although overstated, these unfavorable reviews underlined the reason for *Coelebs* sensational sales. Most readers and journals thought the meshing of religion and the novel constituted a new literary genre. The *Monthly Magazine* and the *Scots Magazine* were uneasy with "the plan of mixing up religion" with the novel. The *London Review* said that *Coelebs* should have been called "Serious Dialogues on Faith and Good Works" while the *Critical Review* said that *Coelebs* was "not so much a regular story as a series of conversations." Unsure of what it was, the *Monthly Review* weakly called *Coelebs* "something" which assumed "the form of a novel." In contrast the *European Magazine*, publishing its review late in 1809 after most reviews of *Coelebs* has already appeared,

printed a long apologia in which they proved that "conveying instruction through the medium of a tale" had a long and respectable past, in which Bunyan, Defoe, and Richardson loomed. Despite this justification of *Coelebs,* however, the journal was ambivalent toward the novel as a respectable literary form. Finally, though, the *European Magazine* concluded that there were some subjects not grave enough for the pulpit but which became "excellent materials in the hands of a novelist."

The breaking down of nineteenth century moral barriers between the novel and the sermon lay behind *Coelebs's* success and the periodicals' uneasiness. In a harsh but perceptive review, the *Universal Magazine* said that *Coelebs's* "extraordinary sale" could be "accounted for upon the same principles as that of the Evangelical Magazine or any antinomian tract." The novel found "purchasers among those, the majority of whom would discard with pious indignation a Shakespeare or a Milton from the shelves."

The *Universal Magazine* erred in discounting the "fashionable world" which also read *Coelebs* eagerly, but the journal was right in believing that *Coelebs* was the first novel thought morally respectable by nineteenth century religious readers. The *Christian Observer* typified the religious world's changed attitude toward the novel. Founded in 1802 by the evangelical Anglicans at Clapham, the *Observer* was the best religious magazine in Britain during the first quarter of the nineteenth century. Since its founders had written the ***Cheap Repository Tracts,*** its unfavorable attitude toward the novel involved critical hairsplitting. Recognizing that many tracts were actually short novels, in the name of critical consistency, Zachary Macaulay, the editor, reviewed few tracts during the *Observer*'s first years. Like other religious periodicals, the *Observer*'s objections to the novel were based on two critical commonplaces. First by appealing to readers' feelings, the novel stimulated the imagination. Once the imagination was aroused, right reason and the Hebraic code of morality were neglected. Second, and this is related to the first, orthodox Christianity demanded that one know one's self. Self-knowledge convinced man of his innate depravity, the first step toward salvation. By turning man's eye outward to an imaginary world, the novel undermined self-knowledge and concomitantly Christianity.

Despite this philosophic disapproval, it was only a matter of time until religious journals reviewed novels. Like the *Observer* periodicals such as the *Methodist Magazine* and the *Evangelical Magazine* filled their pages with religious biographies and accounts of foreign travel, which often read like sentimental tales or picaresque novels. When these journals reviewed books which were novels, they expediently declared that the work being reviewed was not a novel but instead was "original." Such intellectual elephant-swallowing caused strains, and the hope that the "right sort" of novel would be published lay between the lines of many articles. As a result when *Coelebs* appeared, reviews such as that in the *Observer* were embarrassingly effusive.

For Macaulay, *Coelebs* was a new genre, an "interesting fable" communicating "a variety of religious, moral, and economical truths in an easy and agreeable manner." In contrast to the ordinary novel, Mrs. More's characters, Macaulay wrote, were introduced not for themselves but "to exemplify or illustrate the precepts which are inculcated, as a father in an evening walk with his son diversifies the conversation by remarks on the objects around him." If *Coelebs* partook "slightly of the character and peculiarities" of the novel, this advantageously broadened the book's appeal. Writing that the "first, great object" of the author was to instruct, Macaulay lectured other novelists, saying things as: "We have often wondered that novel-writers, careless as they are of every thing but how they may surprise or please, should never have suspected that the infusion of religious principles and feelings into the character of a heroine would add greatly to the interest of the piece."

Macaulay wrote that the story itself had the "one, prime excellence" of being "perfectly in nature." Romance did not undermine the book's lessons as it did in Mrs. Radcliffe's novels, for example, where "the lurid flames" of her imagination kindled all about them. Instead of stimulating the imagination, Mrs. More's characters were signposts pointing the way to heaven. Mr. Stanley the father of Lucilla, the girl Coelebs married, was Macaulay wrote, "a portrait which it required something more than genius enriched by observation to execute; for as Milton declares that no one can be a poet who is not himself the epitome of a good poem, so we may venture to say that he who could sketch this exalted character must have felt in his own bosom the power of holiness;—that he is himself, in some measure, the great sublime he teaches."

The whole review was cut from this panegyrical cloth, and for a journal, formerly hostile to the novel, was remarkable. A critical Rubicon had been crossed; and the *Observer,* like thousands of readers who had opposed the novel on moral grounds, now found itself reading and praising *Coelebs.* Urging Hannah More to write another novel, James Stephen said that he hoped *Coelebs* "would not be left like a pilgrim in the African forest, to be followed and surrounded by monkey imitators without a companion from the same rational stock to support him in his pious enterprise." Stephen was disappointed. Mrs. More never wrote another novel, and monkey imitators abounded. But more importantly, *Coelebs* had paved the way for Scott and a wider acceptance of the novel in Britain. After praising the benefits *Coelebs* "conferred upon the world," the *Observer,* fifteen years later, significantly regretted that the reading of religious novels had broken "the barrier which has hitherto been maintained between the habits of *bona fide* Christians and the habits of worldly society."

Only after *Coelebs* broke the barrier was Scott's "correct morality" accepted. "Go where you will," a reviewer wrote in 1822, "a Waverley novel peeps forth; you will find it on the breakfast table and under the pillow, concealed in the desk of the clerk and the till of the shopman, in the sleeve of the gownsman and the pocket of the squire, on the barouche-box and in the sword-case, by daylight, by lamp-light, by moonlight, by rush-light, ay, even among the Creek Indians has been seen a volume of these far-famed tales, beguiling the tedious hours of the daughter of an Alabama planter as she sat down with her coffeepot by the evening fireside in the recesses of an American forest." Certainly Scott was a better novelist than Hannah More, but his phenomenal success and the popularity of the novel in the nineteenth century resulted in part from *Coelebs's* making the novel respectable reading for a large part of the British public. (pp. 78-85)

> *Sam Pickering, "Hannah More's 'Coelebs in Search of a Wife' and the Respectability of the Novel in the Nineteenth Century," in* Neuphilologische Mitteilungen: Bulletin de la Société Néophilologique, *Vol. LXXVIII, No. 1, 1977, pp. 78-85.*

MITZI MYERS (essay date 1982)

[In the following excerpt, Myers compares Mary Wollstonecraft's and More's respective suggestions for change in female education and status.]

"Changes of Times, and Fashions, still demand / New Lessons to instruct the Female Band," remarked one mid-century conduct book writer. No period more aptly illustrates his observation than the revolutionary decades, which witnessed an energetic proliferation of both radical and conservative directives to women. The conventional interpretation of the new lessons for females in that time of convulsive change has recently been reiterated by Lawrence Stone, whose formulation follows closely that of Maurice Quinlan forty years since. Quinlan's pioneering inquiry into how Victorianism antedated Victoria locates the nineties as a "turning point in English social history," the era when a conservative corpus of manners was fathered by reaction to the revolution and mothered by educators like Hannah More who lauded a newly created standard of womanly excellence, the "model female." Quinlan reads the *Rights of Woman* as sui generis, a radical call for female self-assertion which leagued all other preceptors against the rebel Wollstonecraft. Stressing the importance of extreme femininity and urging women to be a species apart, they called upon their audience "to accept [woman's] subordinate position and to stake all upon the bargaining power of . . . sexual attraction. It was to be," says Quinlan, seriously misrepresenting their stance, females' "one forte, guarded by rules of decorum and made mysterious by the disguise of frailty."

The Family, Sex and Marriage, Stone's massive study of English domestic history, similarly confers a symbolic value on More's popularity. Stone draws a sharp dichotomy between woman's status in the eighteenth-century ambience of "affective individualism" ("relative" equality, companionate marriage, sexual permissiveness) and her devaluation and subordinance in the Evangelically fueled resurgence of patriarchalism which he finds characteristic of the nineteenth. The remarkable success of More's fictionalized conduct book *Coelebs in Search of a Wife* (1808)—it sold eleven editions in nine months, thirty before More's death—Stone believes, "marks the end of an era in husband-wife relations: the Amelia Rattles were out, the Lucilla Stanleys were in." (Since More's anti-heroine Amelia is "boisterous," a "hoyden," "a mass of accomplishments . . . without one particle of mind, one ray of common sense, or one shade of delicacy," any student of eighteenth-century feminine exemplars must wonder when she was ever in.) *Coelebs,* says Stone, "celebrates the ideal woman . . . devoted to domestic duties, religious, modest in dress, silent unless spoken to, deferential to men, and devoted to good works." The brand "new ideal of womanhood" iconized in More's Lucilla "involved total abnegation, making the wife a slave to convention, propriety, and her husband." For Stone, late-eighteenth-century feminism thus "died a swift and natural death, not to be revived again until the twentieth century." More recently and more demeaningly yet, Lynne Agress's *The Feminine Irony* indicts en masse late eighteenth- and early nineteenth-century women writers as "devil's disciples" for perpetuating a "passive, inferior, feminine stereotype" rather than protesting the second-class standing they inherited from an imperfectly illumined Enlightenment. Again, More is the premier villain; Wollstonecraft, the lonely exception.

Modern scholarship, then, myopically reproduces the anti-

Jacobin opposition of More and Wollstonecraft, the contrast between the bishop and the hyena in petticoats epitomized in Walpole's letters or Richard Polwhele's *The Unsex'd Females*. Rightly emphasizing the ferment over womanhood seething in the nineties, Quinlan and Stone reincarnate as new what were old standards, familiar favorites in the conduct book repertoire of femininity, while failing to consider the positive redirections factored into the ostensible traditionalism of reformers like More. Conversely, overaccenting Wollstonecraft's iconoclasm obscures the degree to which her demands are typical of a wide spectrum of women writers. In the nineties, in fact, female educators of every stripe—from radicals like Catherine Macaulay Graham, Wollstonecraft, Mary Hays, and Anne Frances Randall (who was probably Mary Robinson), to moderates like Clara Reeve, Maria Edgeworth, Anna Laetitia Barbauld, Priscilla Wakefield, and Mary Ann Radcliffe, to religionists like Sarah Trimmer, More, and Jane West—vigorously attacked the deficiencies of fashionable training and values. In their different ways, they seek to endow woman's role with more competence, dignity, and consequence. Downgrading the ornamental and pleasing to magnify the useful and moral, they dwell on the disjunction between functional education for ethical living and the current "phrenzy of accomplishments" geared merely to seduce success in a disadvantageous marriage market. Female instructors in general were increasingly prodding their auditors to take responsibility for realizing their own potential, to become self-improved, albeit modest, mistresses of their own—and the nation's—destiny. Such women, gently or stringently reformist in orientation, had female co-workers, discreet rebels among the horde of novelists overtly preoccupied with propriety, and notable male contemporaries like the Evangelical Thomas Gisborne as well as numerous nineteenth-century successors.

Situating these variant models of female reform within a theoretical context based on current work in social anthropology offers a more sensitive and nuanced approach than clichés of bifurcation reducing most women to passive victims, to mindless mouthpieces of patriarchal attitudes. Edwin and Shirley Ardener's analysis of dominant and muted groups draws attention to the subtleties and ambiguities of belief systems generated by the culturally inarticulate. Subordinate groups like women must shape their world views *through* the dominant models, transforming their own perceptions and needs as best they can in terms of received frameworks. If women's alternative or counterpart models are not acceptably encoded in the prevailing male idiom, female concerns will not receive a proper hearing. Women's ways of ordering, of making significant their situation, must thus be carefully disinterred from the dominant structures which muffle them. Even though female models of reality and desire mostly follow the ground rules, their unique deviations from the norms make a woman's world of difference. Women's interpretations of their roles are not fully coincident with men's. If writers enjoin the primacy of familial duties, as do both More and Wollstonecraft, they may yet invest women's roles with powerful, even subversive meanings quite different from conventional ascriptions of weakness and public insignificance. Since female models characteristically operate in terms of strategically redefining and rescripting traditional markers, the linguistic surface of such sexual pronouncements must be carefully scrutinized for imperfect integrations, submerged conflicts, covert messages—for all the meanings which hover interstitially.

Not only do the texts of prescriptive works demand solicitous sifting, but their contexts, their membership in wider ideological movements, also require investigation. In an important essay focusing modern reexamination of Evangelicalism, for instance, Gerald Newman persuasively questions the orthodoxy of such polemicists as More, concluding that they did "much more indeed to subvert the established order than to uphold it" and that the neopuritans "should be regarded as moral and social revolutionaries." Masters and mistresses of propaganda specializing in fifth column tactics, they obeyed the injunction to be "wise as serpents, and harmless as doves," infiltrating and undermining the traditional order from within through their genius for organization and for manipulation of public opinion. The revised view of Evangelicalism as a militant vanguard of emergent middle-class consciousness convincingly demonstrates how diverse anti-French political strategies (whether anti-old or anti-new regimes) mutated into a much broader social and moral critique of aristocratic mores and modes, paving the way for progressive nineteenth-century liberalism. To downplay political hostilities and connect middle-class groups seldom considered together is to illuminate the pervasiveness and the ideological significance of reformist ethics as an agent of the class redistribution of moral authority necessary for fundamental social change.

Although Newman cites "the puritanical strictures on upper-class habits laid down equally by Mary Wollstonecraft and Hannah More," he does not pursue his insight to probe the intersection of moral reform, class tension, and gender consciousness. Yet, despite the fulminations Wollstonecraft occasioned (and these derived even more from her checkered life than from her work), what most strikingly emerges from close interrogation of competing radical and Evangelical domestic ideologies is the similar psychological and emotional dynamic, the unexpected congruence of the ideals and programs expressed in such politically polar works as Wollstonecraft's *Rights of Woman* (1792) and More's ***Strictures on the Modern System of Female Education*** (1799), *Coelebs* thematic precursor. (The same might be said for the works of the radical Mary Hays and the orthodox Jane West.) "It is amazing," observed their contemporary Mary Berry, studying More and Wollstonecraft in tandem, how much the two "agree on all the great points of female education. H. More will, I dare say, be very angry when she hears this." No doubt, for More emphatically refused to read Wollstonecraft and thought her a dangerous malcontent. Nevertheless, the parallels between the two texts extend far beyond their mutual insistence on the radical renovation of female education and manners as prerequisites to a moral restructuring of society.

Wollstonecraft's enlightened womanhood and More's doctrines of Evangelical femininity, her authoritative codification of woman's sphere, responsibilities, and powers, demonstrate alike the extent to which reformist educators had assimilated and were purveying the ascendant bourgeois ethic sanctifying useful industry and family, an ideology which was at that historical juncture for the most part progressive, criticizing, not celebrating the status quo. But at the same time—and this is a crucial point—female moral reformers were recasting that ethic in women's terms for women's benefit, suiting to their own needs the general middle-class protest against aristocratic license and inutility and inflecting bourgeois modes to fit the feminine sphere of endeavor. Moral reform, radically or Evangelically permuted, offered such activist ideologues a body of legitimating imperatives and a vocabulary for venting female dissatisfaction and rendering telling critiques of a society governed by worldly libertine males, as well as for formulating counterpart models based on middle-class female values and priorities. For them, to reform is to reform. Applying the corrective insights stimulated by woman's unsettled status in a transitional era, they ask what constitutes the good society and how women can further it. Significantly, their social strictures both partake of and subtly subvert certain constituents of the bourgeois nexus. Proponents of the humanizing values associated with home, they do not endorse domesticity as decorative gloss or quiescent retreat. Rather, they interpret domestic culture as proffering active roles, constructive channels through which women can aid in revitalizing the world to conform to the values of home, not the materialistic marketplace. Defining domesticity in terms of social responsibility, they negotiate available ideologies into habitability.

Combatants for the allegiance of their increasingly leisured, marginally educated countrywomen, Wollstonecraft and More both strive to replace the regnant ideal of pliant, unproductive urbanity with socially functional middle-class models. Had More looked into Wollstonecraft, she would have discovered an analysis of contemporary female frivolity, incompetence, and maldirected energies, of "weak and wretched" women, commensurate with her own, as well as a similar idealistic myth of what properly fortified female minds might accomplish: a more respectable and powerful status underscoring women's need for purposeful, nationally significant work (whether charitable or paid) and endowing them with weighty authority as mothers and educators, a reordering of the state through the wise nurture of children, a reining in of male behavior and attitudes to a chaste and modest single standard. The "ideal of passive womanhood" frequently attributed to the Evangelicals is very much a misnomer. For at the heart of both More's and Wollstonecraft's works lies a pattern of female domestic heroism, an image of activity, strength, fortitude, and ethical maturity, of self-denial, purity, and truth. It is God, however differently envisioned, who empowers what are essentially revivified spiritual ideals. If life is probationary, an education for immortality, then woman is not mere flesh for male consumption, not a being delimited by sexual attraction (as Quinlan would have it), but a creature of rationally educable mind and aspiring soul, a potent spiritual agent whose most exigent duties are personal improvement and social regeneration.

Both women thus challenge popular conduct book recommendations for feminine training and behavior—hide your wit, your learning, your health—and define themselves in opposition to the usual arts of flattery, dissimulation, and manipulative pleasing, signaling women's restiveness in their elegant niche and implicitly querying Stone's optimistic conclusions about eighteenth-century female status. Indicting what they call the Mohammedan view of woman as docile matter catering to masculine appetite (perhaps best exemplified in Rousseau's Sophia), they claim homage not to charm and modish graces, but to mind and moral excellence. They deplore a female education fixated on the body and senses, for moral reform entails mental enlargement, a puritan work ethic of the mind. Finding women's brains and morality in a state of ill repair, both prescribe a regimen of rigorous ethical and intellectual cultivation to exercise the faculties of readers starved on elegant abstracts, vitiated by "stupid novelists" and artificial male gallantry. They go in for "dry tough

reading" and bracing character formation. If they appropriate bourgeois stress on motherhood, they infuse the evolving ideal with spiritual and mental backbone and public import, each writer transforming the parable of the talents into an exemplum of maternal heroism and power. If they push the middle-class virtues of accountability, diligence, discipline, and order, they also deride social emulation and self-indulgence to preach a genuine upward mobility—that of the soul. More does not hew to the orthodoxly genteel line on woman's role any more than does Wollstonecraft, nor is her "new ideal" wholly retrograde. She inculcates not passive submission, but reasoned acquiescence to established custom, and that only up to a point. As with Wollstonecraft, and with comparable important consequences, her ultimate frame of reference is non-secular. Evangelical spiritual egalitarianism, like feminism, offers a path to autonomy and transcendence of sex. It is no accident that both like to cite that fruitfully ambiguous verse "be not conformed to this world."

Each preceptor in her own way is a reformer who works to extend female agency through the moral revision of conventions. Wollstonecraft's radicalism, for example, is firmly embedded within the bourgeois paradigm. Modifying middle-class domesticity to fit her own purposes, she creates an alternative, potentially revolutionary female ideology within a scaffolding of cultural givens. Like such other mentors as Jane West, she makes an initial point of addressing not ladies, but "those in the middle class, because they appear to be in the most natural state." For men at least, the necessity of exertion ensured the "notorious" consequence that "the middle class contains most virtue and abilities." But its women "ape the fashions of the nobility," fall prey to "factitious manners" imported from aristocratic France, and, exasperatingly, all yearn to be "ladies. Which is simply to have nothing to do." In fact, she concludes, her own "observation with respect to the middle rank, the one in which talents thrive best, extends not to women." Since static women will halt all progress, the *Rights of Woman* is designed to remedy this unhealthy enervation by guiding them back to nature, reason, and virtue, to the "severe duties" and "domestic pleasures" of Wollstonecraft's desideratum: "more observant daughters, more affectionate sisters, more faithful wives, more reasonable mothers—in a word, better citizens." She tirelessly contrasts duty and diversion, the life styles of enlightened domesticity and elite gallantry. Women are to shun the stigmata of the frivolous great world—dress, pleasure, and sway—relishing instead the "minutiae of domestic taste," the "simple grandeur" of "dignified domestic happiness." Pointedly reversing aristocratic attributes—sensuality, indolence, luxury, privilege—the new woman's world projected by middle-class radicalism exalts modesty for both sexes, serviceable work, education, and, above all, mothering.

Wollstonecraft asserts (if sometimes without elaboration) many claims integral to modern feminism, suing for coeducation, economic independence, legal equality, and freer access to jobs and professions, yet, despite her often inflammatory rhetoric, the core of her manifesto remains middle-class motherhood, a feminist, republicanized adaptation of the female role normative in late eighteenth-century bourgeois notions of the family. Nature enlists women to fulfill "peculiar duties": "the rearing of children, that is, laying a foundation of sound health both of body and mind in the rising generation, has justly been insisted on as the peculiar destination of woman." In accordance with this female destiny, women are naturally "susceptible of the attached affections." Indeed, though Wollstonecraft derides sexual virtues and sentimental propaganda casting all women in one languid mold, she also affirms, taking for granted the female's primary responsibility for child care, that "whatever tends to incapacitate the maternal character, takes woman out of her sphere." No more than More (or, for that matter, Mill) does she aspire to pluck most women out of their families or dissever them from their relative duties.

On the contrary, Wollstonecraft aggrandizes, heroizes the maternal mission, elevating woman's status by making her familial roles the linchpin of a new society. Although she does not suggest that woman's only possible place is the home, motherhood provides a pervasive rationale for better education, as well as for civil existence and work. The more enlightened understanding women acquire, the more they will take to those offices nature annexes to their gender. As "active citizen," the average woman will advance the common welfare by managing her family, educating her children, and assisting her neighbors, also standing ready for work outside the home to facilitate family maintenance if necessary. In thus carrying out her communal obligations, she eludes the spirit of degrading dependence and self-respectingly earns her keep, while also developing her own autonomous moral character. Like Mill, Wollstonecraft has recently been faulted as a feminist theorist for failing to challenge the nuclear family as an institution or to question its constraints on female life. Her acceptance of natural sex roles, of rationalized marriage and motherhood as public service in the national interest, it is argued, limits her application of egalitarian principles to women. But for Wollstonecraft, nature and reason validate the bourgeois family as a key corrective to the sins of an oppressive, class-bound establishment. Only through training generations of reform-oriented citizens can the "pestiferous purple" of rank and riches ultimately be exorcized. Her vision of radical progress, of "public freedom and universal happiness," depends on the private virtue nourished by chaste fathers and "patriot" mothers. Marriage civilizes man, families school humanitarian republicans, and domestic affections cement the general good. Her radical politics operates through the militant moral posture inherent in middle-class ideology.

Intent on reinventing bourgeois domestic conventions in women's favor, Wollstonecraft elides any possible antagonism between their "first duty . . . to themselves as rational creatures" and their next "as citizens, . . . that, which includes so many, of a mother." The text cancels conflict between individual autonomy and corporate duty in declaring, for instance, that "the being who discharges the duties of its station is independent." Such configurations illuminate Wollstonecraft's argumentative and emotional logic, revealing how her expressivism was tempered by and shaped through current models of public belief. Critic of sexual stereotyping though she was, Wollstonecraft's feminism is very much conditioned by and justified in terms of revisionist bourgeois ideology, that idyll of a harmonious and socially productive domesticity which haunted her imagination and punctuates her text. On the one hand, even the eighteenth-century's foremost female radical equates private need and public contribution, demands no rights without concomitant duties. Her translation of feminism into the language of social purification and spiritual endeavor demonstrates the female strategy of self-assertion through virtue, of being good as potential power. "I will be *good,* that I may deserve to be happy," she was to write in the greatest psychic crisis of her life. On the other hand, Wollstonecraft's tailoring of her con-

ceptual framework shows how female marginality clarifies moral insight, evolving dynamic models of resistance within a dominant superstructure.

If Wollstonecraft's new society predicates the ultimate deletion of the great as a class (servants and the poor perdure—their lot is commiserated with but not resolved), More embarks on a reclamation project. A firm believer in the efficacy of example to chasten or corrupt, she shepherded the *ton* toward social helpfulness and the "almost sacred joys of *home.*" "Reformation must begin with the GREAT," she intones, or the reformer merely throws "odours into the stream while the springs are poisoned." Lamenting that the "middle orders have caught the contagion" of fashionable emulation and that "this revolution of [their] manners" has almost rendered obsolete the adage " 'most worth and virtue are to be found in the middle station,' " she scolded women of rank and fortune into trading their lazy Frenchified habits for the strenuous exertion of feminine influence in her *Strictures,* while establishing a voguish pattern of bourgeois domestic culture in *Coelebs.* Like Wollstonecraft, she posits a reform or ruin dichotomy, attesting women's potency to undermine or save their country. They bear, in More's view, special civil and social responsibilities. Yoking gender and regeneration, she proclaims that educated women's moral force, by example and exhortation (she herself was a formidable model), can resurrect society on a Christian basis. *Strictures,* for instance, opens with an invigorating evocation of female power, urging women to its "most appropriate" exercise: "to raise the depressed tone of public morals." Trafficking in mere manners is a "low mark, a prize not worthy of their high and holy calling." Her terminology of moral reform insists on female agency; her works comprise a practical, comprehensive program for converting the standard *topos* of feminine influence from pacifying sham to redemptive fact. Not only must patricians embrace middle-class and Christian values, but men, forsaking aristocratic male honor, must also accede to the feminization of their ethos in the name of Jesus. More's conflation of Christian and feminine virtues to female advantage cuts two ways, enduing women with quiet strength and courage and weaning men from their lax codes to that of the domestic milieu. She adjures females to self-discipline, but the worldly latitude forbidden them is not allowed to men either and what is good for women is also salutary for men.

More's subsumption of the feminine in the Christian is the root of her pious, public-spirited tour de force. Supplely preserving conventional appearances, she gives them a new direction, not only investing woman's traditional province with national relevance but also expanding her sphere. In line with general Evangelical professionalization, she ennobles woman's work into a vocation: "the profession of ladies . . . is that of daughters, wives, mothers, and mistresses of families." But women are not, cloistered, to renounce the outside world. Rather, following More's incessant emphasis on active virtue, they are to broaden their nurturing and reformative functions: the "superintendance of the poor" is "their immediate office"; *charity is the calling of a lady; the care of the poor is her profession.*" More inoculates everyday routine with aggressive virtue: women must not only discountenance vice, for example, but debar the guilty rake from society. One historian of feminism remarks that, "without in the least intending" it, devout women like More and Sarah Trimmer who mapped out new female fields were really fomenting mid-Victorian feminist revolt. She had in mind More's manifold philanthropical contributions, both personal and authorial—what might be labeled social feminism—but in fact the drift of More's explicitly conservative message is toward a liberating reworking of feminine ideology. She avers not only women's capability to define their own sphere—an issue of autonomy however bounded that sphere—but also their fitness for ethical stewardship. A partisan of her sex amply possessing Evangelic tactical shrewdness, More was a female crusader infinitely more successful than Wollstonecraft or any other competitor. She furbishes her goals in palatable form and hones those ideals paid cultural lip service to achieve her own ends, playing within the rules of the game while taking on the substantive reorganization of the dominant male culture's beliefs and values. Underneath its discreet surface, a More text is alive with submerged power, not that derived of dominance but a positive power of ability, competence, energy—a negative power of refusal, the right, indeed duty, to say no to custom, on Christian grounds of course. (A complete analysis of the complex rhetorical counterpoint through which she manages to convey female power while upholding sexual complementarity and deftly sidestepping impropriety would require a separate essay.) Rhythmically alternating the systole of ingratiating genuflection and the diastole of combative assertion, it is also predictably rife with latent contradictions and undrawn conclusions.

Yet More clearly offered much to her readers—a diet of "wholesome occupation, vigorous exertion, and systematic employment" seasoned by "rational and domestic enjoyments." The comment of a young American attuned to nuance is instructive: "what an important sphere a woman fills! how thoroughly she ought to be qualified for it—but I think hers the more honourable employment than a man's for all men feel so grand and boast so much—and make such a pother about their being lords of the world below . . . oh every man of sense must humbly bow before woman. She bears the sway, not man as he presumptuously supposes." Outlining the advantages of separate spheres, of women's role as "lawful possessors of a lesser domestic territory," More persuasively infuses their domestic vocation with social and political resonance. Nor is the Evangelical view of marriage she presents a regression to patriarchy. If she likes to talk of mutual dependence, she is a firm advocate of companionate marriage. Her heroine Lucilla Stanley may be too good for modern tastes, but she is indisputably a woman of character, a wife to be consulted, not dictated to. Participating in "all the dignity of equality," she is "not only the associate, but the inspirer of [Coelebs's] virtues"—his "coadjutress," "directress," and "presiding genius." More's stress on philanthropy also spoke to female needs, as Wilberforce's reflection on the improved status of unmarried women indicates: "formerly there seemed to be nothing useful in which they could naturally be busy, but now they may always find an object in attending the poor." His diagnosis is echoed more ambivalently by that astute observer Lucy Aiken (Mrs. Barbauld's niece), who traced the overexuberances of the charitable "rage" to More, but knew "no one circumstance by which the manners, studies, and occupations of Englishwomen have been so extensively modified, or so strikingly contradistinguished from those of a former generation." They were, she thought in 1842, a hardier, more active lot.

Female activity and usefulness are indeed More's forte. Accepting constraints, she construes them as moral heroism, delivering the expected, but on her own terms: let girls "not be instructed to practise gentleness merely on the low ground of its being decorous and feminine and pleasing, and calculated to attract human favour," as the male conduct book writers she sardonically paraphrases counsel, but "on the high principle of obedience to Christ . . . a perfect pattern of imitation." The "divine Alchymy" of vital religion dilates female prerogative, licenses therapeutic moral imperialism, for in religion women are men's full equals, in truth their superiors and guides. Christianity generously reimburses women for earthly handicaps (a topic on which More can be tart) and opens a lawful avenue to achievement. More's Christian heroism is daily, domestic, full of small private amendments with public reverberations—requisite for men but peculiarly suited to the women whose ascriptive meekness and charity Christianity so strikingly ranks above society's rougher male standards. In her pre-Evangelical days, More had likened women to fine porcelain vases on high shelves, but 1799 pleaded for "a patriotism at once firm and feminine for the general good," for the "young Christian militant" who could "awaken the drowsy spirit of religious principle." When, in an England trembling before "the most tremendous confederacies against religion and order, and governments, which the world ever saw," More pronounced religious rebirth the one thing needful, it is not surprising that she tapped a receptive female constituency eager to believe that on their influence depended "the very existence" of civilization, that the "dignity of the work" to which they were summoned was "no less than that of preserving the ark of the Lord." Doing the good work of moral reform, they enrolled as Providence's agents.

Moral reform, then, was the complex issue of the day, and it was preeminently a female issue, witnessing the dialectic through which women, enmeshed in ideologies, use cultural definitions to try to shape their own lives, partly complying with and partly taking charge of their destinies. However amenable to variant subplots, it both testifies to female agency and ratifies woman's socially functional centrality. Though their remedies differ in many details, Wollstonecraft and More each diagnose England's moral—and almost mortal—illness in analogous terms. Perceiving a society infected with fashionable corruption, both preach a militantly moral middle-class reform grounded in women's potentiality. Delineating a female vision of the world, they put familial experience first. It is certainly true that conservatives identified feminists and male radicals who dared to reassess family structure and the relationship between the sexes as a threat. Terrified of collapse on the home front, they shored up domestic verities to strengthen the nation for its external battles. As the *Annual Register* spelled out, "The grand spring and cement of society is, the divine principle of love, branching forth from conjugal into parental, fraternal, and filial affection, an attachment to kindred, neighbours, countrymen." Because domesticity and patriotism were thus inextricably joined, women, sex, and the family were thematic obsessions of anti-Jacobin polemic. The foundations of national morality were laid in private families: the home was fount of civic virtue, custodian of social stability, bulwark against political subversion. But radicals like Wollstonecraft (and Hays) were equally anxious for a renovated domestic ideal: marriage, says Wollstonecraft, is the "cement of society," the "foundation of almost every social virtue." For each side, then, woman's role as "chaste wife, and serious mother" is pivotal.

Both More and Wollstonecraft also avow the wider warrant of female example to effect national change and spur women to "labour by reforming themselves to reform the world."

Anti-sensuality, pro-chastity, both orchestrate modesty, self-control, and purity as human values rather than primarily feminine ones. Women were no longer to be merely the customary refiners of manners and the victims of those duplicitous manners, not the votaries of love, but the reformers of male and female morals alike and the beneficiaries of those reformed morals. Seeking to remodel traditional sexual codes and ethical systems to satisfy the needs of the time, radicals and Evangelicals alike were assailing the double standard of aristocratic French gallantry and immorality, espousing moral reform for all classes and sexes. Such alternative (but not mutually exclusive) domestic ideologies as More's model of Evangelical femininity and Wollstonecraft's rational womanhood are parallel, even symbiotic, female responses to political upheaval, attempts to take advantage of national unease to repattern domestic life through new schematic images of social order. Both were part of the larger and eventually successful bourgeois campaign to rehabilitate a degenerate culture through propaganda for enlightened domesticity and societal reform. If the demands of such radicals as Wollstonecraft for equal political rights were premature, their demands for forceful female social leverage and for freedom from sexual exploitation were not. From the positive perspective of moral reform, the doctrines of femininity are more profitably viewed not as the unequivocal opposite of feminism in the nineties, but rather as a perhaps necessary precondition to, a stage of preparation for, nineteenth-century feminism. (pp. 200-12)

> *Mitzi Myers, "Reform or Ruin: 'A Revolution in Female Manners'," in* Studies in Eighteenth-Century Culture, *Vol. 11, edited by Harry C. Payne, The University of Wisconsin Press, 1982, pp. 199-216.*

OLIVIA SMITH (essay date 1984)

[*In the following excerpt, Smith assesses More's skill in writing conservative tracts for the poor.*]

Thomas Paine was confident that the distribution of his works would give the radicals an important advantage: 'As we have got the stone to roll it must be kept going by cheap publications. This will embarrass the Court gentry more than anything else, because it is ground they are not used to.' The head start which he envisioned lasted only a short while. In November 1792, the Association for Preserving Liberty and Property against Republicans and Levellers (more simply, the Association) was formed to imitate the techniques of radical political groups. The cheap distribution of pamphlets and the publication of resolutions encouraging other loyalist clubs rapidly established a network which greatly surpassed that of the London Corresponding Society. Although the question of whether or not the government instigated the Association is unresolved, it is clear that the Association's activities were co-ordinated with government action, that its ability to distribute pamphlets depended on the government's assistance, and that its adherents in Parliament—Pitt, Burke, Windham, and Grenville—enhanced its power. Aided by an extensive education and armed with literary traditions and conventions of language, conservatives had the advantage over radicals, who were frequently less formally educated and who were attempting to adapt literacy to a new and unfamiliar purpose.

Each side, however, began from a contradictory position. Radicals needed to prove that they were not vulgar, but as the notion of vulgarity was a linguistic one, they could not write in 'mere native English' without demonstrating their vulgarity. Conservatives, who wished to forestall the growth of democratic ideas among the audience, did not want to extend either political awareness or literacy. Pamphlets produced locally could discourage literacy by employing a dialect form of English such as *A Wurd or 2 of Good Counsel to about Hafe a Duzzen diffrant sortes o Fokes* (Birmingham, 1791). Such material did not grant its audience practice in reading which would contribute to their ability to understand other writings. Tracts intended for national distribution had to rely on other means—the simplest being to recommend that their readers not read. The *Liberty and Property* series, which was energetically distributed through the two thousand branches of the Association and through churches, taverns, coffee houses, factories, and barber shops, portrays employers advising their workers to concentrate on financial self-improvement and not to damage themselves by spending time with books: 'I seldom read anything except my Bible and my Ledger'. The debate between the two parties had its own life, however, and in one aspect the opposing sides acted in unison. They responded quickly to each other's writings, and the audience gained in knowledge and numbers by the urgent need to answer the opposition. (pp. 68-9)

Between 1795 and 1797 Hannah More wrote approximately fifty of the Cheap Repository Tracts, editing and publishing a total of one hundred. She was well suited for such an enterprise. The Bishop of London, ever busy with propaganda, recognized that her founding of the Mendip Valley schools gave her an unusual knowledge of the lives and conversations of working people. From the start she was scornful of fashionable English and preferred the greater simplicity of earlier eighteenth-century writing. Her preference for the 'courtly ease of the style of Addison, the sinewy and clear precision of Swift' brought her own writing closer to the vernacular than that of many of her contemporaries. As a published poet and former friend of Lord Monboddo, Samuel Johnson, and Bishop Lowth, she did not need to prove her ability to succeed in a literary world nor did she particularly want to once she became more religious. Being female, she was by definition not a writer of the hegemonic language. During the Blagdon controversy, when the extremity of conservative rhetoric accused even her of being a radical, More was unwilling to defend herself in print and insisted that she did not initiate any activities without masculine encouragement. Believing in the 'defenseless state of our sex' as she then put it, she did not think of language as a means of asserting her value in a public sphere. She thought of writing for the poor as an act of humility appropriate to both her gender and her faith.

Hannah More's writing exemplifies the limited dignity that conservatives could convey to their audience, while it avoids some of the worst characteristics of conservative prose: she does not make jokes at the expense of her readers; she does not advocate hatred of radicals, distrust of one's peers, or scorn for social inferiors; and she does not imply that the efforts which her readers expend make no difference to their character. Unlike radical writers, she does not need to demonstrate the superiority of her language to that of the audience. Even when discussing the difference between the language of her social class and that of the audience, she abstains from using refined language. Describing a well-educated man's inability to explain religion to his servant, she states, 'though his meaning was very good, his language was not always plain; and though the *things* he said were not hard to be understood, yet the words were, especially to such as were very ignorant'. Compared to both radical and conservative writings, this is exceptional and a self-conscious *tour de force*. Moreover, the statement disagrees with familiar notions of language on several counts. Complexity is described as irrelevant to meaning, the inability to speak plainly is portrayed as a limitation of the refined speaker's, and the ignorance of the listeners does not imply their moral deprivation. Because Hannah More did not believe in widely current notions of vulgarity, she had exceptional freedom as a writer. Her Cheap Repository Tracts contrast sharply with both conservative and radical literature in the simplicity of the language, the portrayal of the poor as individuals, the use of credible dialogue, and the particularized portrayal of various situations, including different trades. Tracts describe apprenticeship, a family which breaks the game laws, being a servant, working in a coal-mine, an impoverished widow, getting drunk and attending an anti-Paine riot, and the process of weaving. The characters, the settings, and many of the events are realistic:

> Jack, who, with all his faults, was a keen, smart boy, took to learn the trade quick enough, but the difficulty was to make him stick two hours together to his work. At every noise he heard in the street, down went the work—the last one way, the upper leather another; the sole dropped on the ground, and the thread he dragged after him, all the way up the street. If a blind fiddler, a ballad singer, a mountebank, a dancing bear, or a drunk were heard at a distance—out ran Jack—nothing could stop him.
> **(The Two Shoemakers)**

This is Hannah More at her best, portraying ordinary work in detail, village life as potentially exciting, and a character who is both specific and familiar. The tracts can bring dignity to labour, unspectacular characters, and ordinary settings by the degree of attention which the author manifestly gives them.

Realism breaks down, however, as More relentlessly demonstrates that the poor exist to be saved by the upper classes. In a *Lancashire Collier Girl,* an allegedly true story, a nine-year-old girl works in the mines. Her father dies, her mother becomes insane, and the girl's strength is ruined by her work. For years, she supports her mother and her siblings until a wealthy man learns about her history and employs her as a servant. The easy gesture of his charity is less impressive than the girl's ability to survive despite overwhelming odds and to continue caring for other people. *The Shepherd of Salisbury Plain* is based on a real shepherd named David Saunders. In the story, the shepherd's poverty is vividly described: his eight children, his rudimentary cottage, and his inability to procure sufficient food and medicine. A wealthy gentleman advises him to start a Sunday school, arranges it for him, and pays him a regular salary: 'I am not going to make you rich but useful'. The real David Saunders had sixteen children, he thought of starting a school on his own initiative, he was probably paid by his students, and he did not achieve the financial security of his fictional counterpart. The capability of himself and of the collier girl before her rescue portrays a strength which More did not want her audience to have; that is, she wanted them to endure, but not to manage for themselves. She sometimes travels this fine line with astounding lack of tact, cheering on the poor for the suffering that enables the rich to be virtuous. The basic plot of a poor person saved by the chance arrival of a generous and wealthy man

occurs over and over again. In the ballad, *The Riot, or Half a Loaf is Better than no Bread* (1795), written during a severe famine, labourers sing their willingness to starve:

> Besides I must share in the wants of the times
> Because I have had my full share in its crimes,
> And I'm apt to believe the distress which is sent
> Is to punish and cure us of all discontent.
> So I'll work the whole day, and on Sunday's I'll seek
> At church how to bear all the wants of the week.
> The Gentlefolks too will afford us supplies;
> They'll subscribe—and they'll give up their
>   puddings and pies.

The unprecedented attention which More pays to her readers, thus comes with great cost—that of permitting her to quiet them by eventually betraying the recognition that she originally granted. The individuality of her characters dissolves as so many of them weep in gratitude. More attempts to take the discontent out of misery by this simple plot and also by the relentlessness of her tone and diction. The purity of her language, where every word means precisely what it says, implies that meaning on all levels is unquestionable. Word falls after word into its appointed place without question, stress, or ambiguity. The flow and certainty of the language is still soothing, in its lullaby way, and in a time of political disruption it would have been more so. Compared to the hysterical style and tone of the Association's tracts, Hannah More's are like oil upon the waters.

Having an unconfused concept of her readers, Hannah More knew how to address them. Whether discussing inexpensive radical writings or her own tracts, More describes them as 'alluring'. She considers the effectiveness of writings addressed to the audience to be of a particular kind—a matter of catching attention through the appetites of her readers. This leaves her in the odd position of describing her relation to her audience as one of righteously seducing people who have no control over their passions: 'Alas! I know with whom I have to deal, and I hope I may thus allure these thoughtless creatures on to higher things'. This potentially dangerous relation between a female author and her readers is secure only when the poor are pathetic and manipulable. Behind Hannah More's evident attention to the lives of her readers lies the quiet and usually unstated fear that they will disrupt the social system by becoming self-sufficient. Her diary entry of 2 November 1794 records her complex attitude towards her students, and will serve to describe her attitude towards her reading audience as well: 'Oh Lord, grant that this people may never rise up in judgement against me, and that, with all the advantages of knowledge and education, I may not fall short of these poor ignorant creatures.'

From the start, however, Hannah More's version of the vulgar life and language was regarded more highly by the upper than the lower classes, who went at them somewhat desperately. Two million tracts had been distributed by March 1796 but in January of that year Hannah More was worried that they were not reaching their intended readers. To remedy this, she decided to publish expensive editions in order to finance cheaper ones which would undersell the chap-books. In addition, she planned to distribute tracts to charity school children in London with the particular intention of reaching their parents: 'and we should thus get them introduced among a greater number of the lower class than we have yet been able to do'. The tracts were distributed through the army and navy, prisons, work-houses, factories, and parishes, as well as by private families. Despite this enthusiastic activity, little evidence exists of the tracts being bought for their own enjoyment or even of being ordered by the booksellers without solicitation. Albert Goodwin's claim that they 'outsold even Paine' disregards too many differences in the distribution of their work. He is comparing the sales figures of a hundred entertaining tracts that were given away through large institutions to that of political essays that were sold inexpensively at great legal risk. One claim to their effectiveness is the story of rioters near Bath who disbanded after 'a gentleman of fortune' distributed her ballad, *The Riot, or Half a Loaf is Better than No Bread*, and induced the riotous colliers to sing it together. The Bishop of London wrote that a Quaker bookseller in York gave the tracts away to poor people who said they loved them, but such comments are noticeably rare. William Cobbett wrote More a letter in praise of them, but he was soon to change his mind: 'This flatterer, on coming to England joined Mr Bere's party and became my mortal enemy'.

Although very little praise from her intended audience was recorded, there were also few angry comments, such as those by William Hone and William Cobbett in 1817. Then, political turmoil again prompted Hannah More to write, but her writings had little effect. Her famous tract, *Village Politics,* which appeared in the *Liberty and Property* series, was rewritten as *Village Disputants;* she wrote some more tracts, and she contributed to the weekly, *Anti-Cobbett,* but these writings were powerless against the convincing radical publications of that time. The end of the eighteenth century appears to have been her moment. Her writings stand out for several reasons: because the radical press could not develop adequate fictional forms, because the alarmist portrayals of the Association required an antidote, and because the passage of the Two Acts dealt a heavy blow to the opposition. In the late 1790s, the several currents of alarmism, the awkward relation of radicalism to literature and conventions of language, and the passage of repressive legislation were all moving in her favour. Hannah More's ability to write simple, calming, and vividly detailed stories describing the lives of the poor might have comforted readers who had been publicly defined as immoral, vicious, and incapable of self-control by the *Liberty and Property* series. Without question, however, they comforted wealthier readers who grasped on to her tracts to allay fears which former conservative tracts had done their best to instill. Coming after the hysteria of the 1790s and before the even greater repression of 1800, her gentle propaganda was a harbinger of the encroaching silence. (pp. 91-6)

Olivia Smith, "The Pamphleteers: The Association, the Swinish Multitude, Eaton, More, and Spence," in her The Politics of Language: 1791-1819, *Oxford at the Clarendon Press, 1984, pp. 68-109.*

FURTHER READING

Addleshaw, S. "Hannah More, Blue-Stocking and Reformer." *Church Quarterly Review* CXVIII, No. CCXXXV (April 1934); 57-79.
    Biographical and critical sketch which explains More's immense popularity in her own day.

Aikin-Sneath, Betsy. "Hannah More (1745-1833)." *London Mercury* XXVIII, No. 168 (October 1933): 528-35.
    Tribute to More on the centennial of her death. The author concludes, "Had Hannah More been more progressive, she would have called forth less censure from later generations, but she would have been less effective in her own time."

Aldridge, Alfred Owen. "Madame de Staël and Hannah More on Society." *Romantic Review* XXXVIII, No. 4 (December 1947): 330-39.
    Compares Mme. de Staël's and More's views on English and French society and politics, focusing on their criticisms of national character.

Armstrong, Martin. "In Darkest Mendip." *London Mercury* IV, No. 24 (October 1921): 602-12.
    Chronicles the institution of More's Sunday schools, describing the values More wished to impart to the students.

Avery, Gillian. *Childhood's Pattern.* London: Hodder and Stoughton, 1975, 256 p.
    Frequent reference to More within a discussion of Sunday schools and the type of literature developed for their students.

Bennett, Charles H. "The Text of Horace Walpole's Correspondence with Hannah More." *Review of English Studies* n. s. III, No. 12 (October 1952): 341-45.
    Discusses More's correspondence with Walpole, criticizing William Roberts, the official biographer of More, for altering the contents, dates, and order of her letters in his work *Memoirs of the Life and Correspondence of Mrs. Hannah More.*

Bodek, Evelyn Gordon. "Salonières and Bluestockings: Educated Obsolescence and Germinating Feminism." *Feminist Studies* 3, Nos. 3-4 (Spring-Summer 1976): 185-99.
    Compares the eighteenth-century French salon to the English Bluestocking clubs, emphasizing the important role these meeting places had in providing advanced education for women and challenging traditional views of women. Bodek also describes More's accomplishments and the support she received from her association with the Bluestockings.

Courtney, Luther Weeks. *Hannah More's Interest in Education and Government.* Waco, Texas: Baylor University Press, 1929, 61 p.
    Discusses More's views on increasing education for women and the poor and her accomplishments in this area, but criticizes her fundamental conventionality.

Dobbs, Jeannine. "The Blue-Stockings: Getting It Together." *Frontier* I, No. 3 (Winter 1976): 81-93.
    Describes the advances the Bluestockings made for women's education and social position.

Forster, E. M. "Mrs. Hannah More." In his *Abinger Harvest,* pp. 241-48. New York: Harcourt, Brace and Co., 1936.
    Biographical sketch which praises More's charm and her affectionate work with the poor.

Hunt, Margaret. "Literary Success a Hundred Years Ago." *Littell's Living Age* XXXII, No. 1, 894 (2 October 1880): 48-53.
    Harsh evaluation of More's career.

Johnson, R. Brimley. Introduction to *The Letters of Hannah More,* edited by R. Brimley Johnson, pp. 1-16. New York: Dial Press, 1926.
    Evaluation of the life and works of More, concentrating on her character and personality.

Knight, Helen C. *A New Memoir of Hannah More; or, Life in Hall and Cottage.* New York: American Tract Society, 1862?, 282 p.
    Sympathetic biography which emphasizes More's religious beliefs.

"A Word for Hannah More." *Littell's Living Age* 200, No. 2,594 (24 March 1894): 707-12.
    Biographical sketch which disputes the prevailing image of More as a "strait-laced, narrow-minded country dame."

MacSarcasm, Archibald [pseudonym of William Shaw]. *The Life of Hannah More with a Critical Review of Her Writings.* London: T. Hurst, 1802, 208 p.

Scornful evaluation of More's character and works.

May, G. Lacey. "Hannah More." In his *Some Eighteenth-Century Church-Men: Glimpses of English Church Life in the Eighteenth Century,* pp. 166-84. London: Society for Promoting Christian Knowledge, 1920.

Biographical sketch which highlights More's Evangelical influence on both the rich and the poor of her time.

Meakin, Annette M. B. *Hannah More: A Biographical Study.* London: Smith, Elder, and Co., 1911, 415 p.

Anecdotal biography of More which includes excerpts from her correspondence.

Pickering, Sam[uel], Jr. "The First Part-Issue of New Fiction." *English Language Notes* XIII, No. 2 (December 1975): 124-27.

Contends that Victorians' familiarity with More's tracts, which often continued a story through several pamphlets, led to their acceptance of books issued in parts.

————. "*The Cheap Repository Tracts* and the Short Story." *Studies in Short Fiction* XII, No. 1 (Winter 1975): 15-21.

Demonstrates that the tracts written by More and others accustomed Victorians to short prose narratives, thus preparing them for the development of the modern British and American short story.

————. "The Sunday School Movement: New Readers and the Novel" and "*Cœlebs in Search of a Wife,* and *Waverly.*" In his *The Moral Tradition in English Fiction, 1785-1850,* pp. 11-64, pp. 89-106. Hanover, N.H.: The University Press of New England, 1976.

Contends that More's tract writing and didactic novel *Cœlebs in Search of a Wife* promoted the respectability of fiction to the religious and morally strict section of the population who believed that stories had a corrupting influence.

Rosman, Doreen M. " 'What Has Christ to Do with Apollo?': Evangelicalism and the Novel, 1800-30." In *Renaissance and Renewal in Christian History: Papers Read at the Fifteenth Summer Meeting and the Sixteenth Winter Meeting of the Ecclesiastical History Society,* edited by Derek Baker, pp. 301-11. Oxford: Basil Blackwell, 1977.

Explains the Evangelical stance against novels and describes the importance of More's religious tracts in overcoming that prejudice.

Yonge, Charlotte M. *Hannah More.* Boston: Roberts Brothers, 1888, 227 p.

Biography of More which includes assessments of her works.

Alexander Pushkin

1799-1837

(Full name Alexander Sergeyevich Pushkin; also transliterated as Pushchkin, Púshkin, Pouchkin, Poushkin, Púskin, Pùshkin, Puškin, Pushkine) Russian poet, dramatist, short story writer, novelist, essayist, and critic.

The following entry presents criticism of Pushkin's novel *Yevgeny Onegin* (1833; *Eugene Onegin*). For additional information on Pushkin's career and *Eugene Onegin,* see *NCLC,* Vol. 3.

Pushkin's renown as the national poet of Russia is largely based on *Eugene Onegin.* Labeled a "novel in verse" by Pushkin, *Eugene Onegin* is a story of twice-rejected love set against a detailed picture of Russian life in the early nineteenth century. Though the plot of *Eugene Onegin* is relatively simple, its style and narrative method are regarded as exceedingly complex, and the work has elicited a variety of interpretations. Its technical precision, consisting of fourteen-line stanzas of rhymed iambic pentameter, combined with its psychological characterization and obvious Byronic influences, have led some critics to view *Eugene Onegin* as a transitional work between the classicism of the eighteenth century and European Romanticism. Other critics, however, have interpreted *Eugene Onegin* as primarily an autobiography, as first and foremost a brilliant lyrical poem, or as a parody of the creative process. While the complexity of *Eugene Onegin* admits of these varied readings, it is generally agreed that the work's historical accuracy and realistic presentation of scene and character provided the model for the modern Russian novel.

Eugene Onegin was written over an eight year period and most scholars see the work as a close reflection of Pushkin's personal and artistic development during this time. Pushkin began writing *Eugene Onegin* in 1823 while stationed with the army corps in Kishinev in southern Russia, where he had been banished by the Foreign Ministry for politically suspect poems he had composed while attending school in Moscow and while working as a civil servant in St. Petersburg. As he had in St. Petersburg, in Kishinev Pushkin immersed himself in a life of gambling, drinking, and consorting with women. The first chapter of *Eugene Onegin* reflects this period of carefree existence with its lighthearted and highly humorous portrayal of Onegin's excessive lifestyle in St. Petersburg. In 1824, Pushkin's reputation as a political liberal caused him to be discharged from his government position, and he was exiled to his mother's estate, Mikhailovskoe, in northern Russia. Though his two years in Mikhailovskoe were spent under constant threat of censorship, they were creatively productive for Pushkin; he composed three additional chapters of *Eugene Onegin,* as well as the important historical drama *Boris Godunov.* In 1826, Pushkin was pardoned by the new czar, Nicholas I, but, still subject to close police surveillance, he wandered aimlessly between Moscow and St. Petersburg, resuming his dissipated lifestyle, though with considerably less enthusiasm. Biographers note that Pushkin's youthful enthusiasm had already begun to flag in Mikhailovskoe, possibly as a result of the failure of the 1825 Decembrist uprising, and his restlessness is reflected in the increasingly somber

tone of the final chapters of *Eugene Onegin,* the last of which he completed in October 1831.

The individual chapters of *Eugene Onegin* were published in Russian journals between 1825 and 1832, with the first complete edition of the novel appearing in 1833. Pushkin originally planned *Eugene Onegin* on a much larger scale, but condensed his story to ten chapters as he wrote, the last two of which were fragmentary and not included in the final text. The last planned chapter, written in a coded language, contained scathing remarks against Czar Alexander I and addressed Onegin's involvement in the Decembrist uprising. Pushkin later supposedly burned this section of the novel because of the potential adverse effects on his writing career.

The story of *Eugene Onegin* opens with an account of Onegin's hedonistic existence in St. Petersburg, where he is living the life of a bon vivant, indulging in gourmet food, society balls, and nightly outings at the opera and theater. After some time, Onegin becomes bored with this way of life and leaves St. Petersburg for the Russian countryside to claim his inheritance from a dying uncle. He soon becomes acquainted with his neighbor Lensky, an idealistic poet and student who has recently returned from a German university. Despite the differences in their personalities—Onegin's blasé egotism is a sharp contrast to Lensky's naive romanticism—the two establish a solid friendship. Through Lensky, Onegin is introduced to Madame Larin and her two daughters, Olga and Tatyana. Shy and provincial, Tatyana immediately falls in love with the cosmopolitan Onegin and writes an impassioned letter to him professing her love. Onegin responds with a condescending lecture, bluntly telling her that there is no hope for a union between them. Aggravated by the confinement of his parochial surroundings, Onegin grows tired of his rural lifestyle. At a local party, more out of boredom than maliciousness, Onegin flirts with Olga, who is betrothed to Lensky. Outraged at this violation of his honor, Lensky challenges his friend to a duel. Although Onegin is certain that he could smooth the affair over with a few words of explanation, he accepts the challenge, declaring, "I absolutely have to do this because, otherwise, fools whom I despise will whisper and snicker." The confrontation takes place and Lensky is killed. Onegin, despondent and disillusioned over the senseless incident, departs for a period of extended travel and soul-searching. Several years pass and Onegin returns once again to St. Petersburg. One evening at a society ball he notices among the guests Tatyana, now married to an elderly aristocrat who is a prominent member of St. Petersburg society. The earlier plot is reversed and Onegin finds himself desperately in love with the sophisticated Tatyana. His numerous letters entreating her to abandon her husband and return to the country with him remain unanswered. Finally, Onegin confronts Tatyana, who admits that although her feelings for him have not changed over the years, she will not betray her commitment to her husband: "I love you . . . but I'm another's pledged; and I to him stay constant till I die." The story ends with the understanding that the two lovers will never meet again.

Initial critical response to *Eugene Onegin* was for the most part negative. Many early Russian reviewers attacked Pushkin for what they felt was his inconsequential plot and dull characterization. One critic claimed that *Eugene Onegin* contained "no thoughts, no feelings, only pictures." The first favorable response from a major critic came from Vissarion Belinsky, whose 1844 essay calling *Eugene Onegin* "an encyclopedia of Russian life" emphasized the historical significance of the novel and extolled it as an affirmation of Russian culture. In 1865, Dmitry Pisarev responded to this praise with an essay in which he attacked Belinsky for glorifying a work that neglected important social issues in order to focus on the eccentricities and excesses of one childish man. Pisarev accused Pushkin of using "the whole arsenal of his talent to put to sleep social consciousness." In 1880, Fedor Dostoevsky helped to restore *Eugene Onegin* to its status as a work of national importance in a speech delivered at the dedication of the Pushkin monument in Moscow. Viewing the novel as central to the spiritual identity of Russia, Dostoevsky called Tatyana "the apotheosis of the Russian woman" and praised her as morally superior to Onegin, who had been corrupted by European values. A number of later critics have shared Dostoevsky's allegorical interpretation of *Eugene Onegin*. According to this reading of the work, the cosmopolitan Onegin, with his individualistic values and wandering nature, represents Western ideals. In contrast, Tatyana symbolizes the Russian values of constancy, loyalty, and faithfulness. Tatyana's rejection of Onegin, then, metaphorically implies Russia's (and Pushkin's) cultural rejection of the West.

Twentieth-century criticism of *Eugene Onegin* has focused on its influence on the development of the modern Russian

novel, as well as on its complex style and narrative method. Critics stress that, despite its verse form, *Eugene Onegin* set the model for later Russian fiction with its psychologically intricate portraits of its hero and heroine, its detailed picture of urban and rural life in nineteenth-century Russia, its realistic dialogue, and its narrative structure, divided into scenes rather than episodes, which was characteristic of the eighteenth-century picaresque tradition. Pushkin's multi-faceted narrative method, too, has been a common subject of discussion. His frequent authorial intrusions and digressions on the actual process of composing *Eugene Onegin* have led some critics to describe *Eugene Onegin* as a parody of the creative process similar to Laurence Sterne's *Tristram Shandy*. *Eugene Onegin* has also been praised for its stylistic brilliance. Commenting on Pushkin's versatile use of language, Louis Kronenberger remarked, "There is, indeed, almost every species of good writing—dark and bright, mocking and tender, gay and serious, brilliant and passionate—in this remarkable novel in verse." The subtle nuances of Pushkin's style have made accurate translation of *Eugene Onegin* nearly impossible, and critics agree that much of the beauty of Pushkin's verse has been lost in foreign-language editions. These problems of translation have prevented Pushkin's writings, including *Eugene Onegin,* from being appreciated internationally on the level of Fedor Dostoevsky, Leo Tolstoy, and Ivan Turgenev. Nevertheless, *Eugene Onegin* remains one of Russian literature's most important works because, as D. S. Mirsky stated, "Pushkin's picture of Russian provincial life laid its impress on all the main line of Russian novelists from Lermontov to Chekhov. The characters of Onegin and Tatiana were the direct ancestors, the authentic Adam and Eve of the Mankind that inhabits Russian fiction. And the muffled, unhappy ending . . . became the standard ending of all Russian novels."

ALEXANDER PUSHKIN   (letter date 1825)

[*In the following excerpt from a letter to Alexander Alexandrovich Bestuzhev, written sixteen months after declaring that he was writing* Eugene Onegin *"in the style of* Don Juan," *Pushkin denies any similarities between the two works.*]

Your letter is very intelligent, but all the same you are mistaken, all the same you are looking at **Onegin** from the wrong point of view, all the same it is my best work. You compare the first chapter with *Don Juan*. Nobody esteems *Don Juan* more than I do (the first five cantos; I have not read the others), but there is nothing in common with **Onegin** in it. You talk of the Englishman Byron's satire and compare it with mine, and demand of me the very same thing! No, my dear fellow, you want too much. Where do I have *satire*? There is not even a hint of it in **Evgeny Onegin.** My embankment would crumble if I were to touch satire. The very word *satirical* ought not to appear in the preface. Wait for the other cantos. . . . Oh! If I could only lure you to Mikhaylovskoe!. . . You would see that if **Onegin** is to be compared at all with *Don Juan,* then perhaps in one respect: which is the nicer and more charming (*gracieuse*), Tatiana or Julia? The first canto is simply a rapid introduction, and I am satisfied with it (which very seldom happens with me). (pp. 209-10)

Alexander Pushkin, in a letter to Alexander Alexan-

drovich Bestuzhev on March 24, 1825, in The Letters of Alexander Pushkin, *3 vols., translated by J. Thomas Shaw, 1963. Reprint by The University of Wisconsin Press, 1967, pp. 209-10.*

DMITRY PISAREV (essay date 1865)

[*Pisarev was the most radical of a group of mid-nineteenth-century Russian writers known as the Civic Critics. In his critical writings, Pisarev followed the precedent set by Nikolay Chernyshevsky and Nikolay Dobrolyubov of subordinating literary interpretation to the analysis of social and political content. Pisarev's aesthetic stance was more extreme than that of his predecessors, however, and his uncompromising rejection of traditional notions of the value of art and literature made him notorious during his lifetime as a leader of the nihilist movement. In the following excerpt, Pisarev contends that Vissarion Belinsky's famous article terming* Eugene Onegin *"an encyclopedia of Russian life" (see NCLC, Vol. 3, pp. 417-21), is misleading. He argues that* Onegin *is not an accurate representation of Russian society, but rather a depiction "of some Arcadia at the dawning of the Golden Age" that focuses too much attention on the frivolous and superfluous lifestyle of one misguided man. Pisarev's essay first appeared in 1865.*]

According to Belinsky, "***Eugene Onegin*** is Pushkin's most sincere work, the most beloved child of his imagination. Here everything mirrors the poet; the work embodies his feelings, his concepts, his ideals." Let us see whether Pushkin's novel really merits the high acclaim accorded it by our great critic. First of all, we must decide just what sort of person Pushkin's hero is. Belinsky insists that Onegin is not of the ordinary run of men: "He is not cut out to be a genius, he does not aspire to be a great man, but the inertia and banality of life oppress him." Pushkin himself treats his hero with respect and love:

His features fascinated me,
His bent for dreamy meditation,
His strangeness, free of affectation,
His frigidly dissecting mind.
He was embittered, I maligned;
We both had drunk from Passion's chalice:
In either, life had numbed all zest;
Extinct the glow in either breast;
For both, too, lay in wait the malice
Of reckless fortune and of man,
When first our lease of life began.

He who has lived and thought can never
Look on mankind without disdain;
He who has felt is haunted ever
By days that will not come again;
No more for him enchantment's semblance,
On him the serpent of remembrance
Feeds, and remorse corrodes his heart.
All this is likely to impart
An added charm to conversation.
At first, indeed, Onegin's tongue
Used to abash me; but ere long
I liked his acid derogation,
His humor, half shot-through with gall,
Grim epigrams' malicious drawl.

How often summer's radiant shimmer
Glowed over the Nevá at night,
Her cheerful mirror but aglimmer
With Dian's image—and the sight
Would hold us there in rapt reflection,
Aware again in recollection
Of love gone by, romance of yore;
Carefree and sentient once more,
We savored then, intoxicated,

The night's sweet balm in mute delight!
As some fair dream from prison night
The sleeping convict may deliver
To verdant forests—fancy-lorn
We reveled there at life's young morn.

(I, 45-47)

In these stanzas, however, Pushkin keeps using elastic words which in and of themselves have no defined meaning and which consequently can be interpreted in a variety of ways. A man possesses a frigidly dissecting mind, he has drunk from passion's chalice, he has lived and thought and felt, the glow within his breast is extinct, in him life has numbed all zest, the malice of men and reckless fortune lies in wait for him. All these words could be applied to a man of importance, to an outstanding intellect, even to a historical figure who tried to bring people to their senses but was misunderstood, mocked, or cursed by his narrow-minded contemporaries. Belinsky was deceived by these fine elastic words—by the very words which he himself as a thinker and a doer was accustomed to using to denote a real, live human being, and he regarded Onegin favorably. He boldly assumed that Onegin was not one of the crowd, that he was not an ordinary person. But Belinsky was wrong. He believed Pushkin's *words* and overlooked the fact that all too often people utter fine words without clearly understanding what they mean, or they attribute to such words some narrow, paltry meaning. Let us ask ourselves: *What* had made Onegin's mind frigid? *What* had made him drink from passion's chalice? *On what* had he spent his ardor? *What* did he mean by the word *life,* when he said to himself and to others that life had numbed all zest? *What* does it really mean, in Pushkin and Onegin's language, to *live,* to *think,* and to *feel*?

The answers to these questions must be sought in the description of those diversions which Onegin indulged in from early youth, diversions which finally gave him a case of the blues. In Chapter I, beginning with stanza 15 and extending all the way to stanza 37, Pushkin describes a day in the life of Onegin, from the moment he wakes up in the morning to the moment he lies down to sleep, which is also in the morning. While still abed, Onegin receives three invitations to parties. He gets dressed and in his morning attire goes out to parade on the boulevard

Till the repeater's watchful peal
Recalls him to the midday meal.

He then goes to dine at the restaurant Talon, and, since it is winter, his beaver collar conveniently glistens with a hoarfrost dusting [I, 16]. This memorable incident prompted Belinsky to note that Pushkin possessed an amazing ability "to make the most prosaic objects seem poetic." If Belinsky had lived longer he would have renounced these aesthetic ideas and realized that the ability to celebrate beaver collars is hardly a great achievement.

Having celebrated Onegin's beaver collar, Pushkin goes on to celebrate all the foods which await Onegin at Talon. The dinner is not bad. There is bloody roast beef, a truffle which Pushkin for some reason calls "youth's delight," deathless pie Strasbourg, bold Limburger cheese, luscious gold pineapple, and cutlets which are sizzling and so greasy that a lot of champagne has to be downed [I, 16-17]. Regrettably, Pushkin does not explain in what order these poetic objects are served, and thus it is the duty of antiquarians and bibliophiles to fill in this important gap through painstaking research.

Dinner is not yet finished, the sizzling grease of the cutlets is not yet doused in waves of champagne (what brand you may well ask; this is also a very interesting problem for assiduous commentators), when the repeater's peal informs Onegin that a new ballet has begun [I, 17]. As the exacting arbiter of the stage, as the fickle worshiper of charming actresses, and as established freeman of the wings [I, 17], Onegin rushes off to the theater. (Here I suddenly realize to my horror that we have absolutely no idea what color Onegin's horse was and that very likely no commentator, no matter how hard he tries, will be able to solve this great mystery for us.) Entering the theater, Onegin begins to display the frigidity of his mind. Having scrutinized all the tiers, he seems bored by the gowns and faces. In Pushkin's words, he had "seen it all" [I, 21]. Absentmindedly he glances at the stage, then turns away with a yawn, and says:

> . . . "In all things change is needed;
> On me ballets have lost their hold;
> Didelot himself now leaves me cold."

(I, 21)

Here Pushkin seemed to sense that he had put his hero in a rather ludicrous position. After all, people who really have frigidly dissecting minds do not waste their irony poohpoohing the balletmaster Didelot and the gowns of society women. So Pushkin appended the following humorous note to stanza 21: "A trait of chilled sentiment worthy of Childe Harold. The ballets of Mr. Didelot are full of liveliness of fancy and extraordinary charm. One of our romantic writers found in them much more poetry than in the whole of French literature." Obviously, through this note Pushkin wanted to show that he himself did not take Onegin's sally seriously and that he did not consider it a sign of real disenchantment. But the note has little effect on the discerning and distrustful reader. He realizes that apart from amusing sallies Onegin's frigidly dissecting mind does not produce anything at all. In I, 21, Onegin negates the ballets of Didelot; in III, 4-5, Onegin negates bilberry elixir, Olga's beauty, the moon, and the sky. And these infrequent, harmless sallies totally exhaust the malice of Onegin's grim epigrams, with which Pushkin tried to frighten us in I, 46. Nothing more malicious or grimmer ever emerges from Onegin's lips. If all of Onegin's epigrams were really this malicious and grim, no wonder Pushkin grew accustomed to them so quickly.

Onegin continues to exude disenchantment as he leaves the theater, while cupids, devils, and monkeys prance and swoop behind the footlights [I, 22]. Since he is not interested in their prancing and swooping, he goes home to dress for a ball and then off to dance until the wee hours of the morning. While Onegin is preening before the mirror, Pushkin transforms the combs, files, scissors, and brushes which adorn the boudoir of the "philosopher at age eighteen" [I, 23] into poetic objects. Very likely Onegin appeared to be a philosopher because he had so many combs, files, scissors, and brushes. But Pushkin does not want to be outdistanced by Onegin in philosophical matters, and so he categorically states that philosophical truth which was so much to Pavel Kirsanov's liking, that one can be moral and capable and still have manicure on one's mind [I, 25]. This great truth Pushkin supports with another, even greater truth. "Why," he asks, "vainly chide one's age?" (Obviously, if one is indifferent to manicured nails it means that one is a reactionary and an obscurantist.) "Custom," continues Pushkin the philosopher, "is lord of all mankind" [I, 25]. It goes without saying that custom will al-

ways be lord to *such* philosophers as Onegin and Pushkin. Regrettably, the number of such philosophical gems begins to diminish. Pushkin would like to go on uttering philosophical truths, but Onegin is already dressed and has driven off to the ball *in a headlong flurry* [I, 27; the italics are Pisarev's]—very likely, a consequence of the frigidity of his mind. Of course, Pushkin hurries after him, and so the stream of philosophical truths dries up for a while.

At the ball we completely lose sight of Onegin and have absolutely no idea how his indisputable superiority over the crowd of vulgar men manifested itself. Escorting his hero into the ballroom, Pushkin falls to reminiscing about feet and passionately recounts how he once enviously watched "the waves repeat / Their onrush of tumultuous motion / To stretch in love about her feet" [I, 33]. The skeptical reader will perhaps doubt that waves could actually stretch *in love* about her feet, but I assure such an uncultured reader that here prosaic waves are transformed into a poetic object and therefore it is very laudable of the poet to ascribe to them—for poetic effect, of course—love for woman in general or her feet in particular. After Pushkin has explained to readers that he adores little feet much more than lips, cheeks, or breasts, he remembers his hero and takes him home from the ball and tucks him into bed while working-class Petersburg is already beginning its day. When Onegin wakes up, the same thing begins all over again. He goes out to walk on the boulevard, then off to dine at Talon, then to the theater, then home to dress for a ball, then off to the ball, and finally home to sleep.

And so Onegin eats, drinks, criticizes ballets, dances whole nights away—in a word, leads the good life. His consuming interest is the "science of tender passion" [I, 8], which he pursues assiduously and with great success. But was Onegin "content with his condition?" asks Pushkin [I, 36]. It turns out that Onegin was not content, and this leads Pushkin to conclude that Eugene is on a higher level than the contemptible, self-complacent crowd of vulgar men. As we have seen, Belinsky agrees with this conclusion, but I, to my great regret, must disagree with both our greatest poet and our greatest critic. Onegin's boredom bears no resemblance to real dissatisfaction with life. Here there is not even the slightest trace of an instinctive protest against those unbearable rituals and attitudes which the silent majority accepts—out of habit, out of sheer inertia. Onegin's boredom is nothing more than the physiological consequence of a very disorderly life. This boredom is simply a variant of what the Germans call *Katzenjammer*, a condition which usually visits every rake the next day after a good bout of drinking. Man is so constituted that he cannot continually gormandize, get drunk, and study the "science of tender passion." Even the strongest organism breaks down or at least grows weary when it enjoys the gifts of nature to excess. (pp. 43-7)

[Let] us see what means Onegin adopted to overcome his *Katzenjammer* and reconcile himself once more to life. When a man has become sick and tired of life's pleasures and senses that he is young and strong, he inevitably begins to look for something challenging. A time of serious reflection sets in. He examines himself; he examines society. He carefully weighs his own abilities. He sizes up the obstacles which he will have to struggle to overcome and the needs of society which beg to be answered. Finally after long reflection he reaches a decision and begins to act. Life shatters his plans. It tries to deprive him of his individuality, to water down his convictions and make them like everyone else's. But he stubbornly fights for his intellectual and moral independence, and in the un-avoidable struggle that ensues the magnitude of his own pow-ers is revealed. When a man has graduated from this school of reflection and hard knocks, we have the right to ask if he stands head and shoulders above the conforming, idle masses or not. But so long as a man has not undergone this reeduca-tion, he is like an infant—in an intellectual and moral sense. If a man who is weary of life's pleasures does not even know how to find this school of reflection and hard knocks, then we can definitely say that this embryo will never become a thinking person and consequently will never have a legitimate reason to look with contempt on the idle masses. Onegin is one of these eternal and hopeless embryos:

> Apostate from the whirl of pleasure,
> He did withdraw into his den
> And, yawning, reached for ink and pen.
> He tried to write—from such tenacious
> Endeavor, though, his mind recoiled;
> And so the paper stayed unsoiled.

(I, 43)

Onegin does not suffer from boredom because he cannot find some kind of intellectual activity to occupy himself or be-cause he is a higher nature, but simply because he has extra money lying in his pocket which allows him to eat a lot, to drink a lot, to pursue the "science of tender passion" and as-sume all sorts of expressions—depending on the effect he wants to create. Nothing has made his mind frigid. It is sim-ply untouched and totally undeveloped. He has drunk from *passion's chalice* to the extent that this is part of the "science of tender passion," but he has absolutely no understanding of other, stronger passions—like the consuming passion for an idea. He has wasted the *glow* within his *breast* on boudoir scenes and masquerade balls. If Onegin thinks that *life has numbed him,* he is thinking utter nonsense. A person who has really been numbed by life does not gallop off in pursuit of an inheritance from a dying uncle. To *live,* in Onegin's lan-guage, means to parade on the boulevard, to dine at Talon's, to frequent the theater and go to balls. To *think* means to crit-icize Didelot's ballets and to call the moon insipid because it is too round. To *feel* means to envy the waves which stretch out at the feet of a good-looking woman.

Onegin goes off to the country, only to discover that he is bored there as well. His young neighbor Lensky becomes his friend and companion. If we analyze the conversations they have, we are forced to conclude that they do not talk about any lofty subjects at all and that Pushkin has absolutely no idea what it means to carry on a serious discussion, one lead-ing to true reflection, that he has no notion what it means to have real and deeply felt convictions. In Onegin's relation-ship with Lensky, Pushkin wanted his hero to reveal grace and gentleness of character. Pushkin, who was well versed in grace and gentleness and completely ignorant of convictions, did not stop to think that in endowing his hero with these re-fined traits he was condemning him to pathetic insipidity so that he could only chatter on about the weather, the merits of champagne, and—oh, yes—Oleg's treaties with the Greeks. If Onegin had really had any convictions, then, out of affection for Lensky, he would have tried to share openly with the youth his own views on life and to dispel those youthful delusions which sooner or later are so ruthlessly de-stroyed by the contemptible prose of everyday life. But be-cause Onegin was undeveloped and totally lacking in convic-tions, he practiced the celebrated policy of concealment and

pedagogical deceit, which all parents and teachers who pos-sess warm feelings and narrow minds practice with their charges.

Lensky challenges Onegin to a duel because he becomes infu-riated by the attentions Onegin showers on Olga, his intend-ed, at Tatyana's name-day party. After Onegin has received Lensky's "urbane, high-minded, and polite" challenge [VI, 9] from the latter's second, Zaretsky, he, like the model dandy he is, does not demand any further explanations but answers in an urbane, high-minded, and polite manner that he is "at Lensky's command" [VI, 9]. Zaretsky departs, and Onegin, "left alone with his soul" [VI, 9], begins to think that he has committed a lot of blunders. Onegin is dissatisfied with him-self. Pushkin observes:

> And rightly so: for self-indicted
> In secret court, he could defend
> But little, and was sternly cited
> For many wrongs: First, that a friend,
> Who loved so tenderly and gently,
> Last night was duped so nonchalantly.
> And second: if that friend had been
> A silly ass, well, at eighteen
> He could be pardoned. Not to mention
> That he, who dearly loved the youth,
> Ought to have proved himself in truth
> No helpless play-ball of convention,
> No gamecock bristling with offense,
> But man of honor and good sense.
>
> He could have curbed his angry feeling,
> Instead of snarling; have appeased
> That hot young spirit by appealing
> To reason, friendship—had he pleased.
> "But it's too late; that chance was squandered . . .
> And now, to make things worse," he pondered,
> "We're saddled with this dueling hawk,
> Sharp, fond of gossip, quick to talk . . .
> The best, of course, is to ignore him;
> But still, one will not be exempt
> From snickers, whispers, fools' contempt . . ."
> Our god, Good Repute, rose before him,
> To which we feel our honor bound:
> This is what makes the world go round!

(VI, 10-1)

You see, Eugene dearly loves the youth. Moreover, the stern indictment handed down by the secret court of his conscience tells him that a man of honor and good sense would not bris-tle with offense and would not permit himself to shoot at an eighteen-year old who had made a fool of himself. On one scale Onegin places the life of the youth he dearly loves and the sensible demands of honor and good sense—those de-mands that were sternly formulated by the secret court. On the other Onegin places the whispers and snickers of fools which the dueling hawk and gossip Zaretsky would be only too happy to provoke—the dueling hawk who in Onegin's own opinion would be best ignored. The second scale is heavi-er and immediately tips the balance. The observant reader quickly sizes up the situation and surmises just how capable Onegin is of love and how highly he values his own self-esteem. "I must kill my friend," Onegin reasons. "I must show the secret court of my conscience that I am a man with-out honor and good sense. I absolutely have to do this be-cause, otherwise, fools whom I despise will whisper and snicker."

From the way Onegin reasons, it is obvious that the words

"friend," "conscience," "honor," "good sense," "fools," "contempt" do not have any real meaning for him. Oppressed by intellectual emptiness and the prejudices of society, Onegin has irreparably lost his ability to feel, to think, and to act without seeking the approbation of that crowd of vulgar men he so utterly despises. Onegin's own ideas, feelings, and desires are so weak and amorphous that they cannot possibly have any appreciable effect on his actions. In any case he acts just the way the crowd demands that he act. In fact, he does not even wait for the crowd to state its demand; he guesses it in advance. With the abject servility of a slave, raised in slavery from the cradle, he anticipates all the desires of this crowd, which, like a pampered master, does not even take notice of the sacrifices its faithful slave Onegin makes in order to buy the right to stay in its good graces.

The question arises: How should Pushkin have regarded Onegin's servility? I think he should have sensed the profound humor implicit in this trait, that he should have used the whole arsenal of his talent to expose the ludicrous aspects of this servility. He should have derided it, trivialized it, vilified it—without showing the slightest bit of sympathy for that vile cowardice which makes a sensible man play the role of a harmful idiot, just so he will not be subjected to the timid ridicule of real idiots who are worthy of utter contempt. If the poet had acted this way, he would have rendered a great service to social consciousness. He would have compelled the masses to make fun of those forms of ignorance and conformity which they are all too accustomed to regard with indifference—and sometimes even favorably.

But did Pushkin act this way? No, he acted just the opposite. In his assessment of Onegin's situation he revealed himself to be one of the crowd. He used the whole arsenal of his talent to turn a petty, cowardly, spineless, idle dandy into a tragic figure, exhausted from battling the inordinate demands of people and the age. Instead of telling the reader that Onegin is spineless, ludicrous, and contemptible because he kills his friend to please fools and scoundrels, Pushkin says: "This is what makes the world go round"—as if to refuse an utterly absurd challenge is to break a universal law.

Thus, Pushkin elevates those types and those traits which in and of themselves are base, banal, and contemptible and uses the whole arsenal of his talent to put to sleep social consciousness. A true poet would awaken and educate social consciousness through his works. Pushkin stifles personal initiative, disarms personal protest, and reinforces the prejudices of society—those very prejudices which every thinking person is called upon to eradicate. *"This is what makes the world go round,"* Pushkin naively confesses. You see, for him the whole world is concentrated in those exclusive circles of fashionable society where people worship "Good Repute" and out of reverence for it go against their own convictions and exchange shots with their friends.

After Lensky's death, Onegin sets out to travel across Russia. Everywhere he goes, he frowns and groans; everywhere he goes, he gazes with ridiculous contempt on the pursuits of the idle public. Finally he reaches such absurd extremes that he begins to envy the sick and wounded he sees taking mineral baths in the Caucasus:

> Engrossed in bitter meditations
> Amidst this melancholy crew,
> Onegin looks with wry impatience
> Upon the waters dim with dew
> And thinks: why could not I be blessed

> With such a bullet in my chest?
> Why am I not a senile coot
> Like that poor sack of landed loot?
> Why, like the alderman from Tula,
> May I not lie there stiff with gout?
> Could not at least my shoulder sprout
> Rheumatic pains? O Lord and Ruler,
> I'm young, and life is strong in me,
> And what's ahead? Ennui, ennui!

(I, 14)

Belinsky's comments apropos of these ridiculous complaints are extremely curious. They clearly reveal the profound sincerity of our great critic, his extraordinary truthfulness, and his remarkable credulity—his willingness to take for gospel truth every word a man says, even those which are the crudest, most obvious lies, the most impudent form of charlatanism. Obviously Belinsky mistook Onegin for someone else—for example, for Beltov, the civil servant who did not serve out his fourteen years and six months. But, see here, Beltov did not waste his youth seducing inveterate coquettes. He was incapable of vile cowardice; he could not have killed a friend. He never lamented the fact that he did not have a bullet in his chest. He never envied an alderman from Tula or a senile coot. In short, Beltov is as far from Onegin as Beltov's creator, Herzen, is from Pushkin.

I simply cannot understand how Belinsky could have confused these two totally different types. Onegin is nothing more than a Mitrofan Prostakov decked out in the fashion of the 1820s. Even their ways are almost the same. Mitrofan says: "I don't want to study, I want to marry." And Onegin studies the "science of tender passion" and draws mourning crepe around all the thinkers of the eighteenth century [a reference to I, 44]. Beltov is quite the opposite. He, together with Chatsky and Rudin, represent the agonizing awakening of the Russian consciousness. These are thinking people, people who are capable of loving passionately. If they are bored, it is not because their minds are idle but because the questions long ago resolved in their own minds cannot even be raised in real life.

The day of the Beltovs, the Chatskys, and the Rudins was over the moment the Bazarovs, the Lopukhovs, and the Rakhmetovs came on the scene. But we, modern realists, sense our kinship with this type, which has had its day. We recognize that the Chatskys, the Beltovs, and the Rudins are our forerunners. We respect and love them as our teachers, and we understand that, without *them, we* would not be here. Absolutely nothing, however, binds us to the Onegin type. We are not obligated to it in any way. It is a completely sterile type, capable of neither development nor rebirth. Onegin's boredom cannot give rise to anything except absurd and vile acts. Onegin is bored like a fat merchant's wife who has drunk three samovars of tea and complains about the fact that she cannot drink thirty-three. If a man's belly did not have its limits, then Onegin would not be bored. Belinsky loves Onegin because he mistakes him for someone else, but the same cannot be said of Pushkin.

We have analyzed the hero of Pushkin's novel. Now we must decide whether Belinsky was right when he extolled **Onegin** as an "encyclopedia of Russian life," as "an act of consciousness for Russian society."

If consciousness means that society is fully aware of its needs, sufferings, prejudices, and flaws, then on no account can *Eu-*

gene Onegin be called an "act of consciousness." Pushkin's attitude toward the phenomena of life he portrays is so biased, his ideas about the needs and moral obligations of men and citizens are so vague and misleading that the "beloved child" of Pushkin's muse acts on the reader like a soporific drink, which is so delightful that a man forgets everything he should constantly be mindful of and is reconciled to everything he should tirelessly oppose. *Eugene Onegin* is nothing more than a vivid and glittering apotheosis of the dreary and senseless *status quo*. All the pictures in this novel are drawn in such bright colors, all the dirt of real life is so carefully pushed to the side, the profound foolishness of our morals and manners is made to look so grand, the tiny mistakes are laughed at so good-naturedly, the poet himself leads such a gay life and breathes so easily, that inevitably the impressionable reader imagines that he is the happy inhabitant of some Arcadia at the dawning of the Golden Age.

Suppose you would like to find out how educated people in the 1820s spent their time, the encyclopedia of Russian life will answer that they ate, drank, danced, frequented theaters, fell in love and suffered—now from boredom, now from the pangs of love. "Is that all?" you will ask. "That's all," the encyclopedia will answer. "That's very jolly," you will think, "but not entirely believable." You will learn almost nothing that would tell you about the physiology or the pathology of society in that period. You will definitely not find out what ideas or illusions informed that society. You will definitely not find out what gave it meaning and direction or what fostered apathy and absurd behavior. You will not get a historical picture. You will only discover a collection of outdated costumes and hairdos, outdated menus and playbills, outdated furniture, and outdated grimaces. Everything may be described in an extremely lively and playful manner—but so what? In order to create a historical picture one must be not only an attentive observer but also a real intellect. One must be able to select from the variety of persons, ideas, words, joys, sorrows, stupidities, and base deeds that which epitomizes the character of a given period, that which leaves its mark on all the secondary phenomena, that which influences and shapes all the remaining spheres of private and public life.

It was Griboedov who accomplished this enormous task for Russia in the 1820s. So far as Pushkin is concerned, I have to say it: he did not come anywhere close to accomplishing this task. He did not even have any real notion what this task was. First of all, his choice of a hero is very unfortunate. In a novel which purports to depict the life of an entire society at a particular stage in its development, the hero must either be the kind of person who typifies the *status quo* or the kind of person who bears within himself the seeds of the future and who clearly understands the real needs of society. In other words the hero must be either a knight of the past or a knight of the future, but in any event a person who is active, who has some goal in life. Only the life of an active person can clearly reveal the merits and shortcomings of society's machinery and morals.

If the critics and the public had understood Pushkin's novel the way he himself understood it, if they had regarded it as an innocent and frivolous piece like *Count Nulin* or *Little House in Kolomna,* if they had not put Pushkin on a pedestal, which he did not in the least deserve, if they had not thrust on him great tasks, which he did not know how to undertake, did not want to undertake, and never even thought of under-

taking, then I would not have taken it upon myself to upset the sensitive souls of the Russian aesthetes with my irreverent articles on the works of our so-called great poet. But unfortunately in Pushkin's day the public was so undeveloped that it mistook polished verses and vivid descriptions for great events in its intellectual life.

Twenty years passed, and a first-rate critic undertook to resolve the question of Pushkin, a critic who was an honest citizen and a real intellect. I am speaking of Vissarion Belinsky. It would seem that he should have been able to resolve this question and assign Pushkin the modest place in the history of our intellectual life which he rightfully deserves. However, just the reverse happened. Belinsky wrote eleven excellent articles on Pushkin, pouring into them lots and lots of good ideas concerning the rights and duties of man, relations between men and women, love and jealousy, private and public life, but the question of Pushkin's place in the history of our intellectual life was completely fogged. To readers and perhaps even to Belinsky himself it seemed that Pushkin had generated all these remarkable ideas. In fact, however, they were entirely Belinsky's, and most likely they would not have pleased the poet at all. Belinsky exaggerated the significance of all of Pushkin's major works and ascribed to each of them some serious and profound meaning which the author himself never intended and was incapable of articulating.

As essays, Belinsky's articles on Pushkin were extremely useful and promoted the intellectual development of our society. But these articles also did their share of harm, because they extolled an old idol and entreated people to enter an old temple which harbored food for the imagination but no food for the intellect. Belinsky loved the Pushkin he himself created, but many of Belinsky's fervent followers have fallen in love with the real Pushkin in his natural and unadorned dress. They have begun to extoll the weak aspects of the poet's works, those very aspects which Belinsky either ignored or interpreted in his own way. As a result, Pushkin's name has become the banner of incorrigible romantics and literary philistines. All of Apollon Grigoriev's criticism and that of his followers is based on the notion of universal love, which allegedly permeates Pushkin's works.

At the same time these romantics take refuge in Belinsky's great name, hoping that it will act as a lightning rod and save them from being suspected of having philistine tastes and tendencies. "We are one with Belinsky," the romantics say, "and you, nihilists or realists, are simply egotistical brats, trying to get the public's attention by flaunting your irreverence for esteemed authorities."

We hope to prove to the public that old literary idols crumble as soon as a serious critic turns his attention on them. As for Belinsky's estimable name, it will ring out against our literary enemies. Although we part company with Belinsky in small matters, although we find that he is excessively trusting and too impressionable, we come much closer than our opponents to sharing his fundamental convictions. (pp. 47-55)

Dmitry Pisarev, "Pushkin and Belinsky: 'Eugene Onegin'," in Russian Views of Pushkin's "Eugene Onegin", *edited and translated by Sona Stephan Hoisington, Indiana University Press, 1988, pp. 43-55.*

VIKTOR SHKLOVSKIJ   (essay date 1923)

[*In the following excerpt, Shklovskij suggests that, in writing* Eugene Onegin, *Pushkin borrowed a variety of parodic devices from Laurence Sterne's* Tristram Shandy. *This essay was first published in 1923 in the volume* Ocherki po poètike Pushkina.]

[In] *Eugene Onegin* . . . we are able to detect a number of devices akin to those of the world's most paradoxical author, [Laurence] Sterne, the creator of *Tristram Shandy* and *A Sentimental Journey.* (pp. 68-9)

Eugene Onegin, like *Tristram Shandy,* is a parodistic novel; moreover, in both works the target of parody is neither the mores nor the social types of an age, but the technique of the novel itself, its very structure.

Let me briefly recapitulate the composition of *Tristram Shandy.*

Instead of the conventional pre-Sternean device of beginning a novel with a description of its hero or his situation, *Tristram Shandy* begins with an exclamation: "*Pray, my dear,* quoth my mother, *have you not forgot to wind up the clock?*"

We know neither the identity of the speaker nor what the clock is all about. It is only on page 9 of the novel that the query is clarified.

Eugene Onegin begins similarly. The scene opens on the chronological midpoint of the novel, with a dialogue in which the identity of the speaker is held in abeyance. "Now that he is in grave condition, / My uncle, decorous old prune" etc.

The speaker is identified in the next stanza: "Thus a young good-for-nothing muses." There follows a description of the hero's upbringing. It is only in the fifty-second stanza of chapter 1 that we find a comprehensive clarification of the opening lines.

> And as he had anticipated,
> His uncle's steward soon sent news
> That the old man was quite prostrated
> And wished to say his last adieus.
> In answer to the grievous tiding,
> By rapid stage Eugene came riding
> Posthaste to honor his behest;
> Prepared, in view of the bequest,
> For boredom, sighs, and simulation,
> And stifling yawns well in advance
> (With this I opened my romance):

Thus our attention is called to a rearrangement of the time sequence. In Sterne's *Tristram Shandy* separate parts of the novel are likewise reshuffled. The dedication, for instance, is found on pages 15-16. Moreover, the author remarks that such an arrangement violates three basic requirements, those of "matter, form, and place." The preface occurs in chapter 64 and runs from pages 170 to 179. In Pushkin the dedication appears in the fifty-fifth stanza of chapter 7. . . . (pp. 69-70)

The unusual structure of *Eugene Onegin* and the Sterne-like quality of Pushkin's devices have already impressed more than one critic. "In addition to all its other qualities, *Eugene Onegin* is characterized by a truly amazing method of composition that contradicts all the basic rules of writing," wrote Pavel V. Annenkov in his *Materials for the Biography of A. S. Pushkin.*

It is a measure of how tradition-bound is our approach to

Pushkin that we should have turned the novel's masterfully contrived muddle into a canon.

Similarly Arab scholars construed as norms all Mohammed's deviations from the standard language of his time. And today we eulogize Pushkin's serenity and classicism, even as he confronts us with turmoil. (p. 70)

The lyrical digressions in *Eugene Onegin* are yet another Sternean element. The novel's plot is remarkably simple. The epic retardation results from the fact that while Tatjana loves Onegin, Onegin does not love her; and when he does fall in love with her, Tatjana rejects him. (p. 71)

Pushkin was aware of the nature of his novel's basic plot and underscored its schematic quality by the use of symmetry. Tatjana writes a letter to Evgenij. He appears and lectures her. A corresponding movement occurs when Onegin sees Tatjana, writes her a letter, visits her—and she lectures him!

Tatjana's letter to Onegin and his to her, as well as their respective harangues, exhibit a number of parallels. Since I cannot list them all here, I shall content myself with citing only the concluding scenes:

Chapter 4, stanza 17:

> Quailing
> Tatjana listened to him preach;
> From streaming tears her sight was failing;
> She scarcely breathed, bereft of speech.

Chapter 8, stanza 48:

> She left. Eugene stood robbed of motion,
> Struck dumb as by a thunderbolt.
> Yet in his heart, what stormy ocean
> Of feelings seething in revolt!

In both instances the stanzas that follow use the device of the poet's taking leave of his hero and usher in a digression.

Such is the less than intricate scheme of the novel.

But taking his cue from Sterne—most likely through the mediation of Byron, who had elaborated the same technique in verse—Pushkin rendered his novel extraordinarily complex by his use of digressions. These digressions cut into the body of the novel and push aside the events.

The true plot of *Eugene Onegin* is not the story of Onegin and Tatjana, but a playing with this story. The real content of the novel lies in its formal patterns, while the plot structure itself is used the way Picasso uses real objects in his paintings.

First we get, as in Sterne, an event from the middle of the plot; then a description of the hero's setting; the setting expands and crowds out the hero; the theme of "little feet" enters; and finally the poet does return to his hero. "But what about Onegin?"

The same kind of return to the hero occurs in chapter 4, stanza 37: "Well, and Onegin? Brothers, patience!"

These exclamations remind us that we have once again forgotten the hero. The reminder occurs after a digression of sixteen stanzas.

Incidentally, the riddle of the omitted stanzas in *Eugene Onegin* might also be solved in light of Sterne's influence. As is well known, a number of stanzas in *Eugene Onegin* are omitted, notably 13, 14, 39, 40, and 41 of chapter 1. Most characteristic of all is the omission of stanzas 1-6 in chapter 4.

In other words, the beginning of the chapter has been omitted!

Yet there is no break in the action. All Pushkin has done is to abandon Tatjana, underlining the conventionality of the device by a thoroughly Sternean gesture:

> But by your leave, I feel unequal
> Just now, dear friends, to adding more
> To all that has been said before,
> And tell this chance encounter's sequel;
> I need to rest and have some fun;
> Some other time I'll get it done!

Likewise, the first movement of chapter 4 has to do not with action, but with Onegin's musings. The connection of these stanzas (7-9) with Evgenij is weak; what we find is authorial ruminations like those in stanza 11 of chapter 1. (pp. 71-3)

We know that several of the "omitted stanzas" were never written. Once again, I feel, Pushkin is playing with the novel's plot. In a like manner Sterne "omitted" whole chapters of a prose work.

The fact that *Eugene Onegin* was never finished may also be accounted for by Sterne's influence. We will recall that *Tristram Shandy* ends as follows: "*L—d!* said my mother, *what is all this story about—A Cock and a Bull*, said Yorick—*And one of the best of its kind, I ever heard.* The End."

A Sentimental Journey ends thus: "So when I stretch'd out my hand, I caught hold of the Fille de Chambre's . . . "

Of course, biographers are convinced that death befell Sterne at the very moment he was stretching out his hand, but, since he could have died only once and has left us two unfinished novels, it may be handier to assume the use of a certain stylistic device.

The device Pushkin employed to conclude his story differs from the corresponding device in Sterne. Sterne will sometimes break off a story, offering as his reason the fact that the final portion of the manuscript has been lost (for example, the interpolated novella in *A Sentimental Journey*). Gogol inherited the same device, justifying it on the same grounds. Pushkin simply breaks off his narrative, emphasizing the deliberateness of the interruption:

> Blest he who left in its full glory
> The feast of life, who could decline
> To drain the brimming cup of wine,
> Refused to read life's waning story,
> And with abrupt resolve withdrew,
> As I from my Onegin do.

(pp. 73-4)

Let me raise an intriguing question: was *Eugene Onegin* meant to be taken seriously at all? To put it crudely, did Pushkin weep over Tatjana, or was he making light of her? Russian literature, with Dostoevsky as its head, insists that Pushkin did indeed weep.

And yet *Eugene Onegin* is replete with parodistic devices. If its plot does not collapse as does that of *Tristram Shandy*, this is most readily explained by the fact that *Eugene Onegin* is not simply a novel but a novel in verse—"a devil of a difference," as Pushkin himself put it.

Already Aristotle had urged the poet to pay special attention to parts of the composition that are short on action. In general it would seem that the amount of effort expended on the work is a definable, or at any rate, a finite quantity. If one part of the work is strengthened, another is apt to be weakened. In *Eugene Onegin* the parodistic treatment of the plot is rendered less obtrusive by an intricate stanzaic pattern with an abrupt break before the last two lines, which are linked by rhyme and contain either a summation of the stanza or, more often, its pointed resolution. For example, "There I myself once used to be: / The North, though, disagrees with me."

The choice of words in *Eugene Onegin* is also highly parodistic. We encounter at this level a plethora of barbarisms, arbitrarily introduced and deliberately underscored:

> *Madame* first watched him competently.
> From her *Monsieur* received the child;
> The boy was likeable, though wild.
> *Monsieur,* a poor abbé from Paris, etc.
>
> . . . . .
>
> But *pantalons, gilet* and *frack*—
> With such words Russian has no truck,
> For as it is, I keep inviting
> Your censure for the way I use
> Outlandish words of many hues
> To deck my humble style of writing,
> Although I used to draw upon
> The Academic Lexicon.

By mentioning the Academy dictionary, Pushkin once again calls attention to the exoticism of foreign words with which his text is studded.

Pushkin's notes to *Eugene Onegin* in general smack of parody. Onegin's phrase "Didelot himself now leaves me cold" is provided with the following gloss. "5. A trait of chilled sentiment worthy of *Childe Harold*. Didelot's dances are marked by sprightly imagination and extraordinary charm. One of our romantic writers found in them much more poetry than in all of French literature." Note especially the parodistic sentence structure. Pushkin speaks of the name "Tatjana" as exotic. While in **"Poltava"** the historical name of Kochubej's daughter Matrëna was changed to the conventionally romantic Marija, the name "Tatjana" in Pushkin's time sounded more like a challenge than a stylization.

> Tatjana was her name . . . I grovel
> That with such humble name I dare
> to consecrate a tender novel.
> What if it's fragrant with a peasant
> Antiqueness, if it does recall
> The servant quarters? . . .

Pushkin provided this passage with the following commentary: "The most euphonious Greek names such as Agathon, Philatus, Theodora, Thekla are used with us only among the common people." Pushkin had a special reason to mention the name "Agathon":

> . . . the girlish treble sounds
> more tearful than the reed-pipe's blowing.
> "What is your name?" He stares, and on
> He strides, replying: "Agathon."

Since the latter passage is less traditional, less quotable, as it were, than the passage about Tatjana's name, its odd, not to say, comic flavor is more readily apparent.

Rhymes in *Eugene Onegin* are frequently parodistic. Proper names are often rhymed: Ovid, Gris, Shakhovskoj, Cleopatra, Byzantium, Juvenal, Theocritus, [Adam] Smith, Kaverin, Knjazhnin, Terpsichore, Venus, Flora, Bentham, Diana, Apollo, Albion, Salgir. (All examples are drawn from chapter 1).

At times the rhyme underscores its own triteness:

> Oh dreams, my dreams, where is your sweetness?
> Oh youth's (the rhyme fair beckons) fleetness.

> . . . . .

> At last a crackling frost enfolded
> Fields silvered o'er with early snows:
> (All right—who am I to withhold it,
> The rhyme you knew was coming—*Rose*).

In *Eugene Onegin* similes, generally rare in Pushkin, also tend toward parody. Sometimes they are motivated by being assigned to a protagonist.

> . . . Olga's blended
> Of peach and cream, as round and soft
> As that insipid moon aloft
> On that insipid dome suspended.

This is a curious example of a "discarded" simile. The comparison is not made, only the slot for it is provided.

> The blissful and benignant juices
> Of Veuve Cliquot or of Moët
> Their effervescent froth and tinkle
> (Symbolical of what you will) . . .

This empty comparison is, it would seem, unique in poetry.

Thus, in a cursory survey in which even the digressions have scarcely been analyzed, it has been possible to indicate that elements of parody deeply inform the whole structure of Pushkin's novel in verse. It is true that Pushkin himself would appear to treat Tatjana in a grave and sympathetic manner:

> Tatjana, Tanja, whom I cherish!
> My tears now flow with yours; the sands
> Are running out, and you must perish
> At our modish tyrant's hands.

> . . . . .

> But stay; I feel an urgent need
> To vary this unwholesome ration
> With taste of lovers' happiness;
> I am constrained, I will confess,
> My gentle readers, by compassion;
> So bear with me and let it be:
> My Tanja is so dear to me!

Yet the tone of these excerpts, just as the reference and the apostrophe to the critic in stanza 32 of the same chapter is pure Sterne; sentimental play and play with sentimentality.

Likewise, the following description of Tatjana with its blatantly archaic diction clearly verges on parody:

> And all the while the moon was shining
> And in its fallow gleam outlining
> Tatjana's cheek with sickly glare,
> The loose profusion of her hair.

(pp. 75-8)

Pushkin's sentimental treatment of Lenskij is also a singular

instance of play. The motif of the city dweller's sorrow at the poet's grave is a recognizable stylistic convention, and the twice-repeated exclamation in stanzas 10 and 11 of chapter 7 seems to hark back directly to Sterne's cry, "Poor Yorick!"

Now, why is it that *Eugene Onegin* was cast in the form of a Sternean novel/parody? The appearance of *Tristram Shandy* was due to the petrification of the devices of the traditional *roman d'aventure*. All its techniques had become totally ineffectual. Parody was the only way to give them a new lease on life. *Eugene Onegin* was written . . . on the eve of the rise of new prose. Poetic molds were cooling off. Pushkin was dreaming of writing a prose novel—rhyme bored him.

Eugene Onegin is like that "eccentric" who appears toward the end of a variety show and exposes all the tricks of the foregoing act. (p. 79)

> *Viktor Shklovskij, "Pushkin and Sterne: 'Eugene Onegin',"* translated by James M. Holquist, in Twentieth-Century Russian Literary Criticism, *edited by Victor Erlich, Yale University Press, 1975, pp. 63-80.*

BORIS BRASOL   (essay date 1937)

[*In the following excerpt, Brasol discusses numerous aspects of* Eugene Onegin, *including its historical background and accuracy, its influence on other prominent Russian writers, and its autobiographical content.*]

Which one of the great works of Poushkin should be considered the greatest?—This is largely a matter of opinion, since in our poet's artistic heritage there are so many perfect creations that it is, indeed, difficult to select among them any particular one in preference to others, equally ingenious and beautiful. Here we have to contend with a typical case of *embarras de choix*.

Still, it is undeniable that in *Eugene Onegin,* Poushkin has expressed himself more freely and more exhaustively than in any other of his major poems.

> "*Onegin*"—says Bielinsky—"is Poushkin's most intimate creation, the most beloved child of his fantasy, and there are but few works in which a poet's personality would be drawn out with such a completeness, so serenely and lucidly, as Poushkin's ego has been reflected in *Onegin.* Here is his whole life, his soul, his love; here—his sentiments, conceptions and ideals." [see *NCLC,* Vol. 3, pp. 417-21].

But *Eugene Onegin* is not a mere autobiographical account or an author's confession about the things he had dreamed in the days when he was young. In this work, Poushkin carved the characters out of the very flesh of Russian life, which he depicted so truthfully that he who wishes to comprehend Russia's past must begin with the study of *Eugene Onegin.* Here, we find unfolded a multi-colored picture of Russia's town and country, with a mass of living detail which, like sweet-scented flowers, are freely strewn all over the vast grounds of a virtuosic narrative outliving the wear and tear of fading time.

Like one of those Bartalozzi mezzotints, the general tone of this famous novel is graceful, humorous and light, here and there, touched in gold of the rising sun's first smiling beams, or tipped with silver of sighing sorrow—illusions and disillusions fused together, just as in everybody's experience, and just as smiles and sorrows were part of Poushkin's own life. For there is, in this work, a great deal of autobiographical material which the poet does not bashfully conceal from his audience even when he happens to reveal some trait of his intrinsic deviltry. Take these lines:

> By Fate Eugene was safely guided:
> To *Mádame* first he was confided,
> And then *Monsieur* took care of him.
> The child was sweet, but full of whim.
> *Monsieur l'Abbé,* a humble Frenchman,
> In order not to tire the child,
> Instructed him in manner mild,
> Becoming his indulgent henchman.
>
> . . . . .
>
> But when, in line with nature's fashion,
> Upon Eugene youth cast her grace—
> The age of hopes and tender passion—
> *Monsieur* was told to quit his place.

This certainly is suggestive of Poushkin's own childhood.

In the history of Russia's intellectual development, *Eugene Onegin* became a landmark of major moment. As Professor Kluchevsky said:

> This was an event of our youth; a biographical trait of ours; a break in our growth similar to that which is occasioned by college graduation or the first love.

Poushkin devoted at least eight years of his life to the moulding and remoulding of *Eugene Onegin,* which is a novel of eight chapters in verse and rhyme. In the days when the work was originally conceived, Poushkin was still living through his Byronic period, and Byron's impress upon the character of Eugene is quite obvious. But here, again, Poushkin succeeded in preserving his independence of an artist, and the complex type of Onegin himself comprises many psychological ingredients and historical antecedents, all of which stand in no relation to the Byronic philosophy.

Nor was Poushkin at all sure as to which anthropological class his hero really belonged. Half-seriously he asked these questions:

> What is he then?—An imitation?
> A worthless phantom?—Or perhaps,
> Just one of Moscow's many chaps
> In Harold's guise?—Or a translation
> Of other people's whims and moods?

No doubt, Childe Harold's mantle was an important feature in Onegin's attire. But there is a long genealogical history behind Onegin—a past evolution which dates back to the early part of the Eighteenth Century: the fathers of the Russian Onegins began their studies under Elizabeth; they completed their education under Catherine, and leisurely slumbered through their senescence under Alexander. This genetic background constitutes a peculiar mixture of Peter's stern traditions, Voltaire's skepticism, the grand covenants of Racine, and the petty vices of a wealthy aristocracy which bred on *dolce far niente* and was nourished by gaunt serfdom.

Nor is there any question that in his descending lineage Onegin was the forefather of a whole company of wanton heroes, such as Lermontov's Pechórin, Goncharóv's Raisky, Turgenev's Roudin and Lavretzky, Dostoievsky's Raskolnikov, and so many others. In this or that sense, in one mea-

sure or another, they are all afflicted with a marked inferiority complex, which has been fitly stated in the well-known sentence:

> We are born for daring impulses,
> But achievement—is not our realm.

Polished and smart, but superficial and carefree, Onegin is a legitimate son of Russian nobility as it used to be in those remote days. A child "of luxury and play", the "eighteen year old philosopher" began to burn the candle of his life at an age when he should have been diligently attending school, and he grew fatigued even before he had done anything to be tired of.

The scope of Onegin's education was neither too extensive nor too profound. But he did, from his early youth, master "the science of tender passion", and all the subtle little tricks of deceiving and intriguing the fair sex, now by passionate declarations, and now, by pensively eloquent silence. A habitué of the ballet, Eugene grew fond of that half-veiled life "behind the scenes", those theatrical *dessous,* which are artfully concealed from the eyes of the uninitiated.

The radical commentators of the Sixties accused Poushkin of having almost glorified in Onegin the model of a socially useless creature. But they seem to have overlooked the fact that Poushkin himself, when portraying his hero, entertained no illusions concerning the actual meaning of his moral character. Obviously, it was for this reason that he selected as an epigraph to the opening chapter of the novel this citation from a private letter:

> Absorbed by vanity, he also possessed that kind of arrogance which made him view with equal indifference the bad things as well as the good—an attitude which was due to a feeling of superiority, imaginary perhaps.

Poushkin clearly understood that, by introducing Onegin to his readers, he was giving a vivid picture of those idle strata of Russian, or if you please, European society, whose existence was an incarnation of nothingness, and whose would-be disappointments—or to use the then fashionable term—whose "spleen", was the natural outgrowth of incurable indolence and lack of mental culture. Onegin's main trouble is that he has no aim in life, and he drifts along from day to day, according to Ruskin, "without fear, without pleasure, without horror, and without pity."

This vacuity of the spirit prompts him to give vent to hopeless lamentations:

> Oh why, like Tula's poor taxator,
> Am I not lying paralyzed?
> Why am I not, at least, chastised
> By rheumatism?! . . . Oh Creator!
>
> . . . . .
>
> The ill are happy: They can figure
> That o'er them hangs Fate's heavy glaive,
> But I am young and full of vigor!
> I'm bored, and craving for the grave!

Fate interrupts the monotonous diversity of Onegin's social adventures on the Neva banks, and chance transplants him to his estate where he begins to dwell in dull seclusion. But soon he meets Lensky, a young poet, an admirer of Schiller and an adept of Goettingen's devious ideals. Between the two a friendship develops and, for a while, both seem pleased with each other.

Through Lensky, and on his insistence, Onegin makes the acquaintance of the Larins, an old-fashioned, simple, but hospitable family, in whose bosom there grow two lovely field flowers, two fair sisters—Olga and Tatiana.

Of Olga Poushkin gives this picture:

> She, ever modest, bashful seeming,
> And always bright as sun at morn;
> As naïve as a poet's dreaming,
> And sweet, as when love's kiss is born;
> Her eyes as deep as heaven's blue;
> Her smiles, her locks of golden hue;
> Her maiden stature, voice and glance,—
> All that is Olga:—Choose by chance
> Some novel cheap, her portrait's there;
> 'Tis very pleasing; I admit
> I once was quite in love with it.
> But now its sight I cannot bear.

But Lensky *is* in love with Olga. They are even engaged, and soon the link of two loving hearts will be made stronger— who knows?—by the nuptial tie. Though charming, Olga is a *terre à terre* creature. Her feelings are shallow, light her moods, and, inconsequentially, she flits about like an iridescent butterfly.

How different Tatiana!—Timid as a doe in dreamy woods, she has never taken any fancy to the vivacious games of her youthful companions. She prefers pensive solitude, and even within the fold of her own family she seems a stranger.

> But pensiveness, her true attendant,
> From tender days of cradle age,
> In hours of leisure, bright and splendent,
> Dream feasts for her did often stage.

Always meditating over something, always sorrowful and wistful, Poushkin tells us about Tatiana that

> . . . her tender little fingers
> Despise the needle, as she lingers
> O'er silken patterns all aflame,
> And drowsy linen on the frame.

Since childhood, Tatiana has had an almost mystical adoration of Nature. Fond of her silent park and the golden fields around,

> She loved to watch the morn's slow wading,
> Awaiting dawn's first smiling glance,
> When from the sky line, pale and fading,
> Stars disappear in choral dance.

As she grew older, Tatiana, just as Poushkin himself, contracted the delightful but somewhat dangerous habit of reading—a tendency which, in her case, could be hardly conceived as congenital, since

> She always had a strong addiction
> To reading novels, soft and stern,
> She was in love with dreams, with fiction,
> Rousseau and Richardson, in turn;
> Her father, not a social climber,
> Was just a simple good old-timer,
> And while in books he saw no wrong,—
> For reading his distaste was strong.

Then comes the romance, an immortal *page d'amour* of a maiden's heart.

"Elle était fille, elle était amoureuse."—Desperately Tatiana falls in love with Onegin, and after much fear and hesitation, she writes him a letter full of sentimental emotion. She knows that she is breaking all conventions, and she even starts her confession with a pathetic self-indictment:

> I write to you! Is more required?
> Can lower depths beyond remain?—
> 'Tis in your power, if desired,
> To crush me with a just disdain.

Alas! Her love evokes no echo in Onegin's sophisticated heart, and in a chilly sermon, he tells her:

> I love you with a love of brother,
> Still stronger is my love, maybe.

He confesses that "he is not created for beatitude", nor adapted to the delights of domesticity. He wants to be free, and freedom—he argues—is incompatible with nuptial shackles.

Heartbroken, Tatiana listens to Onegin's lesson. She firmly knows that, having once given her heart to Onegin, she will never love again:

> *Das giebt's nur einmal!*
> *Das kommt nicht wieder. . . .*

Deep is her wound, and it will never quite heal. For Tatiana's heart is not governed by fleeting caprice or transient whims. Tatiana is a Russian woman whose heart, though soft and yielding, is firm and faithful; to her, self-sacrifice is not a pose or mood, but rather an irresistible response to love and duty. Tatiana is that captivating symbol of Russian womanhood which found its further interpretation in other dear images— in Turgenev's Lisa, Tolstoy's Natásha, Goncharóv's Vera, and Dostoievsky's Sonya. They all are victims of love, and of what they conceive to be their duty. Theirs is proud and concentric suffering; theirs is pain caused by eccentric circumstances, desecrating the "holy of holies" of their loyal hearts.

Onegin's and Tatiana's paths seem to be parting forever: *He* leaves her—still "absorbed by vanity", still wearing Childe Harold's moody mantle, with a mind perhaps more arid than ever, after his duel with Lensky, whom he so cruelly insulted and so wantonly killed; *She* is left by him—with a bleeding, but loving heart, determined to forget, ready to forgive, with a firm resolve to fulfill her duty, trying though it be.

In the ever-flowing tides of Time, as Heraclitus used to call it—"in the ceaseless flux of changes"—events appear and disappear, but life rolls its waves just the same.

A few years after Onegin's departure, Tatiana, acceding to the entreaties of her family, marries a brilliant General of high standing. Now, admitted to the Imperial Court, Tatiana shines as the brightest star in the aristocratic constellation of the Northern capital. And it so happens that Onegin, who, for years, has heard nothing about her who chose him for the hero of her dreams, returns to St. Petersburg after having wandered long and uselessly throughout Russia. Again, he is attracted by the luster and shine of social life; again, he divides his time between one ball and the next, while, *entre poire et fromage*, again, he feels ready to resume his amorous career.

Yet, Fate rules differently: At one of the social affairs, he sees a woman: She is "all harmony, all wonder." Surrounded by an admiring crowd and flattered by those who themselves are used to nothing but flattery, she displays her grace with divine indifference and calm. Onegin is thrilled, and he learns that this is Tatiana. Now he begins to worship her, whom in days past, he had treated as a *quantité négligeable*. Now he is in love, but

> Not with that girl so shy and bashful,
> So poor, and simple, and in love,
> But with a princess unaffected,
> A goddess, perfect and selected,
> Of the majestic Neva shores.

Onegin's passion for Tatiana leaps and bounds. But she remains indifferent, cold and deaf. He writes her letter after letter, tender, flaming, apologetic. He confesses:

> Once having met you, by mere fortune,
> Your love I marked. To my misfortune,
> Take heed of it I did not dare.
> That feeling then I have arrested;
> My freedom, worthless and detested,
> To lose, alas! I did not care.

His letters are ignored. The tortures of unreturned love grow so acute that he retires from society, and lives in solitude through the slow-creeping Winter. He fears he is going mad, but Poushkin, with his usual sense of humor, remarks that

> . . . how it happ'd he did not know it:
> Long winter months began to wane,
> Yet he did not become a poet,
> Nor did he die nor grow insane.

Now Onegin makes his last effort to win Tatiana's affection: Once more he sees her, and kneeling before her, he eloquently tells her of his love and sufferings and dreadful regrets about the fatal error which, years ago, when he first met her, he had so carelessly committed.

Sadly and silently, Tatiana listens to this impassioned confession. Then she renders her final verdict. But how different is her rebuttal from that of Onegin's first lecture on a maiden's ethics! Hers are words permeated with sighs of a wounded heart:

> Enough! Arise. I feel I must
> Reveal my thoughts for this may lessen
> Your pain. You will recall the day,
> When in the park, by fate's strange way,
> Together we were brought. Your lesson
> I then, alas! was doomed to learn.
> And yet, today, it is my turn.
> Onegin, then I was so youthful,
> And better then I was, maybe.
> I lovèd you, and I was truthful,
> But in your heart—what did I see?
> What was its answer?—Condemnation:
> A maiden's humble fascination,
> Her love, to you, were far from new.

And then Tatiana asks Onegin what petty whim had brought him to her feet: She suspects that he is more fascinated by the brilliant setting, in which he found her, than by anything that is truly part of her own self. To Tatiana the tinsel of her weary life, the frippery of the fatiguing masquerade are of no value or attraction. If it were only possible, she would gladly abandon all the splendor of her gleaming life

> For silent bookshelves, dreamy parks,
> And our humble rural dwelling.

She tells Onegin that she still loves him, but having once

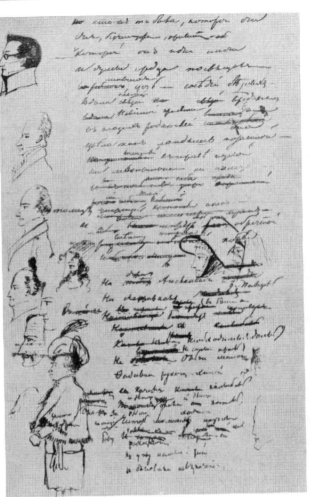

Manuscript page of Eugene Onegin.

pledged her loyalty to another, she must and will forever remain true to him.

Abruptly Poushkin draws the curtain, but before leaving his heroes to their fate, he heaves a sigh of regret, sounding a lamenting note on that which to himself was dear and yet had vanished, like a dream, into the all-engulfing Nirvana of the past:

> But they to whom, at gath'rings gay,
> The early strophes I have read. . . .
> These are no more, those—far away,
> As Sádi once so aptly said.
> Without them was Onegin moulded.
> And thou, who hast to me unfolded .
> Tatiana's beautiful ideal. . . .
> Yes, much did fate relentless steal! . . .
> Ah, happy he who early goes
> And leaves the feast of life divine,
> Who does not drain its cup of wine,
> Nor read its novel to the close,
> And swiftly parts with it, as I
> To my Onegin bade goodbye.

(pp. 172-86)

*Boris Brasol, "Chapters from 'The Mighty Three',"
in* Pushkin: The Man and the Artist *by Martha*

Warren Beckwith and others, The Paisley Press, Inc., 1937, pp. 99-186.

F. D. REEVE (essay date 1967)

[In the following excerpt, Reeve assesses different interpretations of Eugene Onegin, *arguing that the work combines romantic and realistic literary traditions, and that it set a unique precedent for the work of Fedor Dostoevski, Leo Tolstoy, and Boris Pasternak.]*

Eugene Onegin has been given many sorts of readings, has been called a study of the tranquil life of early nineteenth-century Russian gentry and an autobiography, a purely lyric poem. Indeed, the novel admits both extremes, and one is encouraged in such a reading by the legendary aspects which the figure of Pushkin has taken on. Never mind the statues of him all over the world or the continual editions of his works; speeches like Dostoevsky's at the 1880 celebration (in which Dostoevsky said that Pushkin was a prophecy and a revelation [see *NCLC*, Vol. 3, pp. 424-26]), or the special 1899 Imperial edition for the army to mark the centennial of his birth, suggest the myth of a man greater than the writer, of a writer who became greater than anything he wrote about. The myth is partly substantiated by Pushkin's dynamism, by his keen and even scholarly interest in Russian history, to which he felt closely tied. Unlike Dostoevsky, a professional man of letters, he was an aristocrat, a liberal, at times the "gay blade" he called Onegin (and as he called himself in some of his short lyrics). He was also a literary man, an editor, who in 1836 founded *The Contemporary,* the most important literary journal in Russia in the nineteenth century. His discovery of the world of literary realism, quite unlike the worlds of *Adolphe* and of *Beppo* from which he partially and very obviously derived (or, as Dostoevsky would have said, came out from under), was built around understanding of the isolated individual as a social force, a cognitive agent determined by and in turn determining his environment. The environment becomes significant only to the degree that it is realized in the individual's performance.

A common view of **Eugene Onegin** is that it remains an encyclopedia of Russian life. Belinsky shared this view, emphasizing, in the spirit of his interpretation of Hegelian philosophy, the exemplification in the book, through opposition between Onegin and society, of the conflict between spirit or consciousness and actuality, of the dichotomy between romantic terms and everyday details. Belinsky, and others, considered Onegin a superior type, typicalness of character being for them the criterion of a book's excellence. Such a criterion is admissible only if the function of literature is to educate; for Belinsky, it was. Though Onegin may successfully represent a type, the type which he represents is not "typically Russian," and—to follow the argument out—the "real hero" of the novel, the typical and genuine Russian, is Tatyana.

On the other hand, for Brodsky and other critics, the novel is a literary monument, its importance guaranteed by its prominent features: its intimacy, its artistic effects, and its contrasting use of the romantic and naturalistic styles of storytelling.

The opening stanza of Chapter III, on Tatyana, set against the first chapter on Onegin, reports the basic pattern and helps establish the rhythm of the novel, even as it rubs against the formality of the pattern. A colloquial conversation is housed in the intricate iambic tetrameter stanzaic scheme rhyming ababccddeffegg. Superficially, and then finally, the hero is characterized by social judgment of his social function:

> "Where, now? I'm tired of these poets."
> "Good-bye, Onegin, I have to go."
> "I'm not keeping you, but tell us
> Where you spend your evenings out."
> "At the Larins." "You really don't!
> For Heaven's sake! It must be hard
> For you to knock off evenings there?"
> "Not at all." "I don't see why.
> I picture how the whole thing is:
> First of all (listen: right?),
> There's a simple Russian family,
> Much cordiality to guests,
> Preserves, and endless conversation
> About the rain, the flax, the barnyard. . . ."

(III, 1)

The novel is framed by the lists of Onegin's reading; the characters are defined by identification with literary tradition. Tatyana's bovarysm brings to life the romantic mode which Pushkin is transforming:

> Fancying the heroine
> Of her beloved books was she—
> Clarissa, Julie, or Delphine—
> Tatyana wandered in the woods
> Alone, the dangerous book in hand. . . .

(III, 10)

The eleventh stanza outlines the moralistic novel of the eighteenth century; the twelfth stanza, the "new novel" of Lord Byron's "despondent romanticism"; the thirteenth, in a tone of light irony and with cultural pride, Pushkin's program. The three novels which are listed as defining Tatyana—*Clarissa Harlowe* (1748), *La Nouvelle Héloïse* (1760), *Delphine* (1802)—encompass both the sentimental and the romantic moralities and, all three, tell of unhappy, unsuccessful loves. The crossed plot of Rousseau's novel, Julie's faithfulness to her unloved husband when her beloved St. Preux has returned, is close to the Tatyana-Onegin plot, but only as idea. Julie's father compels her obedience, prevents her marriage to her beloved; Tatyana fails to attract Onegin. In **Eugene Onegin** the plot is not manipulated by opposition between social conformity and the "free emotions of the heart" but depends on the dramatic decisions of two independent actors, who are not ruled by their time but who embody their time. By the end of the novel, Onegin's position is hopeless; Tatyana's, strong. Psychology has replaced conventional morality. Motivation has replaced machination. And the study of Onegin's and Tatyana's motivation is itself part of the study of cultural tradition, which the novel also is.

That Tatyana with her bovarysm and Onegin with his adaptation of the romantic mode are three-dimensional figures (and not psychological instances, like some characters in Tolstoy novels, for example) is pointed up by the flatness of Olga and of Lensky. Again, the sharpest definition of the frame within which the characters move is made by literary reference. Mocking the misquotes of half-educated literary pretenders, Pushkin has Lensky ineptly say over General Larin's grave:

> Poor Yorick! *he said despondently . . .*

(II, 37)

and adds a footnote to refer the reader not to Shakespeare but to the four chapters in Sterne's *A Sentimental Journey* in which the parson gets the name of Yorick and in which the count says of the parson's talk, "*Voilà un persiflage!*" Olga does not imagine herself a literary heroine come to life; on the contrary, she is described as being the model for any heroine in literature:

> As gentle as a lovers' kiss,
> Her eyes as azure as the sky,
> Her smile, her flaxen locks of hair,
> Her movements, voice, her slender waist—
> All that was Olga . . . but just you take
> Any novel and you'll find
> Her portrait: it is very sweet;
> I used to like it much myself,
> But now it bores me beyond belief.
> Reader, if you please, allow
> Me to describe the older sister now.
>
> (II, 23)

That Olga is a flat character assists the construction of "plot," of course, and helps overcome the romantic-sentimental story. The advantage of a stock character is recognizability. Within limits, the stock character is easily maneuvered. Or the author can, if he pleases, easily move around it. Pushkin uses figures of conventionality and uses Tatyana as a conventional figure, at the name-day party in Chapter V, as excuses for Onegin's "perhaps imaginary" sense of superiority. Onegin's condescending caricaturization of the guests, including Tatyana next to him, his own "composing," unlike Pushkin's sympathetic irony, only exposes his improper superciliousness:

> Now, triumphing ahead of time,
> He started drawing in his mind
> Caricatures of all the guests.
>
> (V, 31)

Lensky is a modish and, therefore, false poet. Olga is a conventional and, therefore, unreal girl. Onegin is an egotistic and, therefore, inconstant friend. Literature and literary sources define them, define Tatyana, shape the novel. The stanza form of the verse is one source of pattern. The literary form, which in turn is held against its sources—

> The frost's already stinging noses
> And blanketing the fields with white . . .
> (The reader wants the rhyme of roses;
> Here, damn it, hurry up and take it!)
>
> (IV, 42)

—is one source of rhythm. All together, we have the pattern and the rhythm of an ordering of the conversation which proceeds from the language of the court, the talk of the town, the examples of intellectual tradition. As a lyric narrative, *Eugene Onegin* is equally a reformation of a literary genre. It is also an effort to create a literary genre, the socially apt realistic novel in the nineteenth century. It is an attempt to give a novel . . . a social function so that it may as much illuminate the possibilities of the future as illustrate the failures in the past.

An outline of the "plot" says little that is relevant to understanding the book. There is here no succession of events such as that by which Macbeth or Don Quixote or Tom Jones measured their progress. In that sense, there is no progress, no motion here at all (as there is none in any of Dostoevsky's novels). What shapes the book, finally, is our awareness of the movement in coincidence of natural and human events—for example, of the occurrence in winter of the nameday party, the meaning of which is revealed only in the dream symbolism of stanzas 43-45 in Chapter V. The "climax" of the novel, in Chapter VI, turns around Lensky's death, the whole story of the duel, the analysis of the poet's role, and the implied delineation of the role of what we might call the lady of the house, Pushkin's Muse. Chapter VII, on the two sisters, begins with an apostrophe to winter. Chapter VIII, the denouement, is the story of the second rejected love, Onegin's. It begins with autobiography (for example, the lines in stanza 2 on Derzhavin), encompasses Pushkin's relation to the Muse (for example, stanza 4), and includes reminiscences of young manhood which frame the story (the "lost youth" of stanzas 10-11), a condensation of Onegin's travels (stanzas 12-13), and a definitive description of the reality of the ideal woman, Tatyana become a lady (stanza 14).

The shift in character and in "plot" leads to a shift in style. Onegin's appeal to Tatyana in Chapter VIII is preceded by a stanza practically in prose identifying the state of mind which produced the letter. The novelist's real friend, it turns out, is no *semblable*, is Eugene Onegin done over by the poet in this book. The question of purpose in the rhythm of the novel suddenly raises anew the issue of motivation. Contrary to the romantic notion, the beautiful, Pushkin says, is not the thing itself, necessarily, but the purity or excellence of the artist's emotion about it, of his understanding of it. In Chapter VIII, stanzas 15-16, Pushkin says he likes the word *vulgar* but cannot translate it, that it is "a new word among us." In a letter to his wife in 1833, he said, "You know how I dislike anything that smacks of the Moscow debutante, anything that's not *comme il faut*, anything that's *vulgar*." What the poet possesses is his language, and Pushkin's controversy with Shishkov (see, for example, VIII, 14) followed from his effort to make the language vital so that it, too, like clothes and manners, would aptly reflect the culture of an age. A man's language is himself and encompasses him. Language goes beyond the poet and stays.

Pushkin believed what Flaubert said later, that the artist ought not to appear in his work any more than God in nature. God is outside the world of Flaubert's novels and rules that world by law; the reader must infer (as for *Salammbô* or *Madame Bovary*) the moral system. Law, for Pushkin, is inadequate and inaccurate (one of the themes of **Dubrovsky**). The god of art, much like the life force of which Pasternak speaks, *is* nature, is continually re-creating it in terms of its whole moral system, by the validity of the artist's talent: his imagination, his kindness, his courage, his skill.

> But I withdrew from their alliance
> And ran far off . . . she followed me.
> How often the caressing Muse
> Enchanted me on my silent way
> By the magic of a mysterious tale!
>
> (VIII, 4)

In the opening stanzas of Chapter VIII, which recapitulate Pushkin's own travels, his own autobiography, homage to the Muse is equated with service to the poet's countrymen. Brodsky points out that in the fifth stanza of this chapter the manuscript contains a line, later deleted, which refers to the influence on Pushkin of the national minorities he met in the south of Russia and to his own allegiance to social reform:

> And she forsook the speeches of gods
> For barren, alien, pagan tongues,
> For the literature of precious freedom. . . .

Brodsky reads this as indication that Pushkin was intellectually and emotionally in sympathy with the uprisings of the early nineteenth century. I should read it as also an acknowledgment in social terms of that freedom of which Tatyana dreamed but which she found was inaccessible.

The novel seems to offer a moralistic finale: Tatyana pledges faithfulness forever to her husband. Perhaps she is not pledging herself but simply stating her condition. The steam roller of conventions has blindly and inexorably reduced Onegin and his values to its own. The deviation has occasioned its own disaster, mild compared to Anna Karenina's but akin to what Flaubert said of Emma Bovary: "Elle retrouvait dans l'adultère toutes les platitudes de mariage." This is the most painful condition: rebellion is finally subject to the same terms as that against which it was undertaken. This is the final irony. Onegin is left by the author in a "disastrous moment," is turned into a move in a literary game. The catastrophe of the classical hero (Achilles, Oedipus) expresses the preservation of the tribe or of the state; in the world of literary realism, the catastrophe of the hero expresses the loss of the self.

The measure of Pushkin's protest against society, the instrumentality for altering social perceptions, the source of tragedy in the novel, is Tatyana's capacity for love, her love affair. The beautiful dreamer, the beautiful innocent is crushed by the distorted ambitions of people who have only a little power and who, to live, must assert it. Man's rebellion cannot succeed, neither Tatyana's nor Onegin's nor Pushkin's; society constrains suffering; the love affair appears in the end to have been impossible from the start. Correspondingly, the author has three roles: he narrates the sequence of events; he is friend to Onegin; he comments, as a social agent, on his own life, on his past, on Russian history and speech, on his sense of Russia's destiny. The narrative proper includes the author's ironic attitude toward the characters' motivation. Its lyric and autobiographical digressions are serious treatment of the same theme.

The novelist, to cite Auden's poem,

> . . . must
> Become the whole of boredom, subject to
> Vulgar complaints like love; among the just
>
> Be Just, among the Filthy, filthy, too,
> And in his own weak person if he can
> Must suffer dully all the wrongs of man.

The novel, which has predominated in those times and places when the individual's privacy has been publicly subverted either by social institutions or by a prevailing "philosophy," requires that the Many be suffering. The development of the modern novel, following *Don Quixote,* and of the contemporary novel, following the nineteenth-century Russians, coincides with the individual's loss of identity and his deepest illusion of freedom. Each novelist must create his own function for himself. The distinguishing characteristic of *Eugene Onegin* and of the other great Russian novels is that, in their study of society, they come to a deep and final judgment.

Onegin is the sophisticated, half-foreign, frustrated, withered, artificially passionate Byronic hero. Lensky, also half-foreign, is the impossibly Germanic romantic idealist. Tatyana is the native Russian, placid, overly simple, naïve, fresh, with Rousseau-like natural charm, who in the end becomes grand. They are held together by the social aptness of the

poet's language. Through them the poet has touched on the possibilities within which human life may occur. Intimately tied to life by the conditions under which he lived (for example, the autobiographic passages in the novel) and by history itself (*The Negro of Peter the Great*), but alienated by the disparity between prevailing norms and the final values which sanction human activity. Pushkin drew a portrait of his time and of its typically dominant figure, in which he emphasized (in eighteenth-century style) the difference between their actions and their claims and (in romantic style) the difference between their actions and their potential, and defined (in realist style) the difference between the figures and the age, on the one hand, and between the figures and himself, on the other, asserting the importance and social usefulness of his artistic labor because of its preservation of the fundamental values for human life and its exposure of all false claims and spurious understandings. Beyond the saccharine, illusioned romanticism of Rousseau's or Richardson's novels and the disillusioned romanticism of Byron's or Constant's, there is the realism of Pushkin's, reporting the intelligence of discrepancy, the final accommodation to fact.

Eugene Onegin is not just a story of a socially realistic hero, nor is it a Byronic imitation. It is the narrative of the struggle by an individual against his socially determined limitations, of the development of character in the movement determined by social life. It is "the new novel," the study of the world of the family, leaning not backward on *Adolphe* or *Don Juan* but leading forward, both by theme and by narrative expansiveness, to *Fathers and Children,* to *The Idiot,* to *Anna Karenina*—and, finally, to *Doctor Zhivago,* our contemporary "novel in prose." (pp. 34-44)

> *F. D. Reeve, " 'Eugene Onegin'," in his* The Russian
> Novel, *Frederick Muller, 1967, pp. 14-44.*

JOSEPH P. MANSON   (essay date 1968)

[In the following excerpt, Manson analyzes the narrative structure of Eugene Onegin, *demonstrating ways in which Pushkin used contrasting themes and opposing character traits to add meaning to his story.]*

Puškin's Novel in Verse, *Evgenij Onegin,* was written over the course of eight years (1823-1831). During this time, the author's concept of the plot and characters underwent many changes which considerably influenced the development of the poem's narrative structure. The changes are attested by extant original drafts and completed but excluded sections of poetry contained in volume six of Puškin's complete works published by the Soviet Academy of Sciences in 1937. Such major plot elements as "The Duel" and "Onegin's Journey" were accepted or rejected by the author only after large sections of the poem had already been completed and published. Puškin had been working on the novel for several years before certain critical points of characterization in regard to both Onegin and Tat'jana achieved final form. The artistic integrity and unity of the completed work is all the more remarkable in view of this gradual development.

The plot of *Evgenij Onegin* is extremely simple. A girl falls in love with a young man who rejects her. After she has married another, the young man falls in love with her but she rejects him. On the basis of this narrative frame, Puškin created a poem which develops with the restrained and measured beauty of a classical symphony. The whole is filled with deep passions, suffering and emotional conflict but is constantly modulated by the objectivity of gentle irony and an essential counter-point of contrasting thematic elements.

Counter-point of contrasting thematic elements is the key to Puškin's narrative technique within his verse novel. It is most apparent in the two major dramatic episodes, Tat'jana and Onegin's confrontations in the Larins' garden and later in a Moscow drawing-room. Although the narrative reversal that Puškin achieved between these scenes is, in its own way, a unique literary *tour-de-force,* both episodes are convincing and impress the reader with their profound psychological truth. One easily accepts the speedy development of passion within the country-girl, Tat'jana, who has had no actual experience of erotic emotions but, on the contrary, has formed her heart and mind on romantic novels. Without having previously found an object worthy of her devotion, she had developed a firm belief in the sacred character of undying love. What more likely object might she choose than the handsome, sophisticated young man from Saint Petersburg who had a proper romantic "pallor" and suitable "disdain" for life's trivialities? Onegin becomes for her a type of deity to whom she can look up. . . . (p. 201)

Onegin, on the other hand, would contradict his character if he could bring himself to accept this young girl's too readily offered love. In contrast to her lack of experience, he has had far too much. He has learned all the tricks of conquering female hearts, both simple and sophisticated. Love has become for him not an exalting, self-sacrificing emotion but a means of proving his own ability to overcome coquettish resistance and to satisfy selfish whims, a lethargic shuffle between two poles. . . . (p. 202)

Onegin in his disillusionment cannot see any difference between the love that Tat'jana offers so quickly and that which had sated him in Saint Petersburg. Fortunately for Tat'jana, he has tired of taking advantage of young girls. With his shallow experience in a certain kind of love, he warns her against other men, thinking that all men would see in her passion that which he might allow himself to see if he had not decided to abandon the pursuit. . . .[In] the first confrontation, Puškin has established the basic kernel of the plot. The reader will not see Onegin and Tat'jana alone together again until the very end of the novel. Without a multiplication of vindictive colloquies and with an almost total absence of standard *scènes-à-faire,* Puškin will draw his narrative to the point where the situation of the first confrontation is apparently completely reversed. The mastery of the achievement lies in the fact that both confrontation scenes are true to characterization and setting. The contradictory outcome of the two scenes is due to motivation arising from exactly the same personality complexes in each case. The irony is further enriched by the fact that Onegin rejects Tat'jana in her native environment, the country, while she will reject him in his, the urbane world of brilliant high society.

Puškin has posed for himself an intricate narrative problem. After portraying the development of an unhappy romance in the country, he undertakes to portray an unhappy romance in the city using the same characters with their narrative positions reversed. The Onegin of chapter one looks upon everything with condescension from the heights of a self-assured superiority. He disdains Lenskij's idealism no more or less than Tat'jana's romanticism. The Onegin of the second confrontation is abased and looks up to the object of his passion. He who formerly posed the riddle is to be baffled by the cold serenity of the country-girl-turned-princess. His ironic attitude has disappeared. Tat'jana, on the other hand, may now look down upon him from a valid position of greater moral integrity. Her love, which had been one of adulation for a superior being, has become a love tempered by suffering and mixed with pity.

A narrative fabric of counter-point justifies the major contrasts of the love plot. To begin with, Puškin introduces a second pair of lovers, Lenskij and Ol'ga. The love counter-point is established on two levels—that of plot-action in the narrative parallels of the two affairs and that of character. Onegin's character stands out more clearly against the background of his friend, Lenskij, just as Tat'jana is seen more clearly by contrast with her sister, Ol'ga. The clarification of personality works in opposite directions for the two main characters. Onegin's poverty of soul is emphasized by Lenskij's enthusiasm while Tat'jana's depth of feeling is opposed to Ol'ga's lightmindedness. The contrast is subtly enhanced by its presentation in the country rather than in the city where the novel began. In Petersburg, Onegin's natural environment, his disenchantment seems almost a positive quality when opposed to the spiritual vacuity of the society around him. In the country, it becomes evident that the disenchantment stems from a deep interior emptiness rather than from any combination of external conditions.

As Puškin portrays the love of Lenskij and Ol'ga, he stresses the fact that Lenskij is the more ardent of the pair. Ol'ga is too superficial and flighty to experience a deep passion while Lenskij's inexperienced, idealistic heart can not know any other kind. Tat'jana and Onegin's love is a perfect balance and counter-point to this. Like Lenskij, Tat'jana is consumed by love and willing to abase herself completely to realize its fulfilment. Onegin, however, like Ol'ga, is incapable of a "Grand Passion." He is so thoroughly imbued with an artificial society's fear of showing the slightest enthusiasm that he pretends not even to have noticed which of the sisters is Tat'jana when he first sees them. . . . Onegin continues his pose of blasé nonchalance by taunting Lenskij that, as a poet, he should prefer Tat'jana who sits "sad and silent as Svetlana" to the prosaically pretty Ol'ga.

The contrast of the couples is built on a very complex counter-point. Lenskij-Onegin and Tat'jana-Ol'ga are character oppositions. Within the love scheme, however, Lenskij-Tat'jana and Onegin-Ol'ga are oppositions. The counterbalance of the two love affairs is the dynamic basis of the first half of the novel.

The unraveling of the essential narrative problem of reversal begins with Tat'jana's dream. In solving the problem, Puškin uses as his primary instrument the character of Onegin but his character as it is gradually discovered by Tat'jana. Until the dream, Tat'jana has seen in Onegin her Ideal and a superior being. The dream is the first hint of a darker, destructive side to the person of her Ideal. As a device, the dream operates on the subconscious level. Psychologically, it indicates that Tat'jana had previously apprehended some flaw in Onegin which she had repressed but which continued to haunt the deepest recesses of her mind. From the external narrative point of view, it prepares the reader for the unexpected presentation of Onegin as the murderer of his friend (the dream-Onegin stabs Lenskij with a knife). After the description of Onegin in the first two chapters, some objective element must forewarn the reader of the duel. If this element were presented on the conscious level of action before the duel, it would destroy the delicately balanced fabric of relations between the four protagonists. The revelation of Onegin's character through the subtle device within Tat'jana's subconscious is balanced and reinforced by an element on the conscious level of recognition. When Tat'jana visits Onegin's house in the country, she undergoes an experience which relates within the novel's structural counter-point directly to the psychic experience of the dream. As Onegin's hidden potential for evil was revealed to Tat'jana by an intuitive perception, now the shallowness of his soul is revealed by the portrait of Byron, the bust of Napoleon and the particular passages in his books which most impressed him. . . . After the duel, it is within the counter-point of these two revelations, the dream and the visit, that Puškin finds the narrative means of justifying Tat'jana's reversal in the final confrontation. She has come to understand her hero at last. Although she understands him, however, she does not stop loving. . . . Her heart has been given and, "condemned by fate," she cannot redeem her feelings. Nevertheless, she will never again look to Onegin with that self-abasement which marked their first meetings. The essential difference in the Tat'jana of chapter eight is not the rank and dignity of a princess. It is rather that change which has taken place in her love and understanding. Some have accused Puškin of neglecting the "objective correlative" for the superficial change in Tat'jana which is effected by her new position in life. The more important change in her, however, is well justified and the justification lies in the counter-point of the two revelation episodes.

The duel in chapter six is a central plot device from a mechanical point of view. It is a climactic motive which effects the transition from the rising development of the novel's first half to the rapid descent toward the denouement. As a mechanism of the plot structure, it eliminates Lenskij from the novel. Ol'ga is thereby free to meet and marry another man and also to be removed from view. The technical use of these two characters has achieved its purpose and they are no longer necessary for the further development of the novel. This technical consideration does not, of course, consider the broader artistic aims involved. Onegin's acceptance of the challenge through fear of society's censure is a means of throwing greater light on his character. His unhesitating readiness to shoot the poet also throws his character into broader relief while counter-balancing Tat'jana's dream image of him. The fact that Ol'ga marries another so quickly after the duel emphasizes the constancy of her sister who is true to her one love in spite of shattering revelations and his culpable involvement in the tragedy.

The primary value of the duel as a narrative device, however, is in its effect on Onegin. Mechanically, it forces him to leave the country. This provides the freedom necessary for Puškin to transport Tat'jana to Moscow where she marries and becomes a member of the *beau monde*. In regard to Onegin, personally, it is the crucial experience which drains him of his irony and superior attitude. He has murdered a friend because of the petty considerations of an artificial milieu which he had haughtily undertaken to despise. . . . When he reappears in Moscow, he bears little external resemblance to the brash young scapegrace of Petersburg. . . . The duel, therefore, although it does not contribute directly to the love plot, is still one of the most important narrative devices within the structure of the novel. Just as the two revelations justify the Tat'jana of chapter eight, the duel justifies the changed Onegin.

By the time Puškin comes to the depiction of the second confrontation, he has already solved his basic narrative problem of reversal by this series of artistic contrasts and oppositions. His technique throughout the last chapter is particularly striking. All secondary characters have been removed. In the center of the action remain only two—Onegin and Tat'jana. The tone of the chapter is melancholy and restrained. The ebullience and humor of the earlier sections are completely missing. Tat'jana is an established luminary of society, a lady of quiet dignity and inner beauty. Onegin, on the contrary, is a stranger. As he becomes wildly enamored of the "new" Tat'jana, the basic counter-point is fulfilled. Onegin was indifferent but now loves; Tat'jana was overwhelmed by passion but now is calm enough to reject the man she still longs for. The question to be considered is whether Onegin and Tat'jana have really changed in their essential elements. Onegin had been indifferent to a retiring young girl in the country. He completely misunderstood her and was unable to appreciate her real beauty of soul. Now he loves—but he loves a princess who dictates to society, who is cold, superior and aloof. True to character, Onegin does not reflect that he has nothing to offer her but infamy and shame. Divorce, of course, was out of the question. With the same lack of concern about consequences with which he shot Lenskij, he now hopes to make Tat'jana party to a conventional "liaison." He still does not know or love her real self. The Onegin of the first chapter might have gone about this conquest of a haughty princess in just the same way. His feeling may now be stronger but his passion is not noble. It does not respect the honor and happiness of its object. Tat'jana, with the still intact simplicity of her romantic soul, fortified by a deep awareness of the true Onegin, refuses his love. To accept it would contradict all the truth of her character. She too is the same but now has more experience, understanding and perception. The surface reversal is achieved but stands in artistic tension with the inner reality which is based on a delicate consistency of characterization throughout. It is difficult to imagine a more artistically satisfying solution of the narrative problem which Puškin had set for himself. (pp. 202-06)

Joseph P. Manson, "Puškin's 'Evgenij Onegin': A Study in Literary Counter-Point," in Studies Presented to Professor Roman Jakobson by His Students, *edited by Charles E. Gribble, Slavica Publishers, Inc., 1968, pp. 201-06.*

LOUIS KRONENBERGER (essay date 1969)

[*A drama critic for* Time *from 1938 to 1961, Kronenberger was a distinguished historian, literary critic, and author highly regarded for his expertise in eighteenth-century English history and literature. Among his best-known writings are the nonfiction accounts* Kings and Desperate Men: Life in Eighteenth-Century England *(1942), which examines British culture of that century, and* Marlborough's Duchess: A Study in Worldliness *(1969), a biography of the wife of the first Duke of Marlborough. Of his critical work, Kronenberger's* The Thread of Laughter: Chapters on English Stage Comedy from Jonson to Maugham *(1952) and* The Republic of Letters *(1955) contain some of his best literary commentaries. In an assessment of Kronenberger's critical ability, Jacob Korg states: "He interprets, compares, and analyzes vigorously in a pleasingly epigrammatic style, often going to the essence of a matter in a phrase." A prolific and versatile writer, Kronenberger also wrote plays and novels and edited anthologies of the works of others. In the following excerpt, he summarizes the plot of* Eugene Onegin, *at the same time analyzing Pushkin's attitude to-*

ward Onegin by contrasting him with Lensky and Tatyana. Kronenberger also praises Pushkin's diverse writing styles and ability to vividly portray nineteenth-century Russian life.]

Next to a few of the greatest works of poetry and drama, what I could most wish to read and fully appreciate in the original is Pushkin's—I abandon at once the Russian spelling—*Eugene Onegin.* And of these things Pushkin's is the most completely frustrating, for though my Greek is much worse than spotty and my Italian covered with rust, at least I know a little how Homer and Aeschylus and Dante tend to sound in the original, I have a faint sense of the greatness of the Greeks in their own language and a fair sense of Dante in his. But with Pushkin, with *Onegin,* one is encountering something so special that to know no Russian is a double loss: one is not just deprived in translation of much of what makes him uniquely great, one is equally deprived of what makes him constantly delightful. In a translation such as Babette Deutsch's, which at its best has real virtues, we are made to feel the *fact* of Pushkin's greatness, but are never quite given what constitute great effects; again, for a number of lines or a stanza or two, we savor what makes him delightful, but then what we get is spruce, or jingly, or a little verbose. The translator of Pushkin is to be sympathized with: that special amalgam of gifts which, to be approximated in English, seems to involve comparing Pushkin successively with Horace, Byron, Keats, Stendhal, André Chénier, Praed, and Tolstoy; an amalgam, moreover, that has made Pushkin both the prime figure of Russian poetry and the forefather of the Russian novel, not to speak of his being the inspiration of Russian opera—*Ruslan and Ludmila, Pique Dame, Onegin, Boris Godunov,* and *Coq d'Or.* This amalgam is of course what baffles the translator and hence robs the English reader of Pushkin's very essence. However much we may lose of Dostoevsky or Tolstoy, we have a full sense of what makes them great and individual; even with Chekhov there is not the equal loss of verbal magic or unparaphrasable effect, and in a first-rate production, something of what is lost can be regained.

Pushkin's very special qualities, and special effects, in *Onegin* seem to have baffled even the Russian imitators who sought to capture them. *Onegin,* says Prince Mirsky [see *NCLC,* Vol. 3, pp. 431-37], demanded "two qualities that are extremely rare in conjunction—a boundless spontaneous vitality and an unerring sense of artistic measure." This is to say that he was as natural a genius as he was instinctive an artist, as creative as self-critical, as free-flowing as channeled. Such a combination of genius and artistry brings, above all others, Mozart to mind. But though this is to indicate the marvelous rareness of Pushkin's gifts, it is not quite to define the special nature of his poem—or, as it might better be called, his novel in verse; and here Edmund Wilson [see *NCLC,* Vol. 3, pp. 438-40] is more immediately helpful, when in the matter of *Onegin* he speaks of Pushkin's "peculiar combination of intensity, compression and perfect ease." Intensity and ease are not often happily married; yet they pretty plainly seem so here: the intensity we must at times infer, the perfect ease we can, I think even in translation, feel. Which suggests another combination, and one no less remarkable—the happy marriage here of poet and novelist, of something more than poet and storyteller; of someone who achieves magical effects with language, atmosphere, the visible world, while simultaneously telling a story, developing a theme, creating and counterpoising characters, projecting in the most vivid fashion social and personal scenes. *Eugene Onegin* is not only a novel of manners in all that it pictures of high life, of domestic life,

of country life, of bachelor life; it is a novel of contrasted attitudes and temperaments, and thus of contrasted values: Eugene and Tatyana and, to a lesser degree, Lensky are as representative figures and as differing natures as we can ask for in good fiction. But we get them with all the vivid force that we ask for in good poetry; and again with all the brilliance that we can ask for in gay and witty writing, and in a polished and worldly writer.

Onegin opens briskly, indeed at a kind of gallop; for Eugene, a gay young dog and dandy, is bounding along to the bedside of a dying uncle, whose heir he is to be, and reflecting as he rides:

> My uncle's shown his good intentions
> By falling desperately ill;
> His worth is proved; of all inventions
> Where will you find one better still?
> He's an example, I'm averring;
> But God, what boredom—there, unstirring
> By day, by night, thus to be bid
> To sit beside an invalid:
> Low cunning must assist devotion
> To one who is but half alive:
> You puff his pillow and contrive
> Amusement while you mix his potion:
> You sigh and think with furrowed brow
> "Why can't the Devil take you now?"

Thus in a single stanza we are given one of the most worldly of situations and easy and sophisticated of tones, together with something of the character of Eugene himself. That a rich uncle one is inheriting from should be dying in the country is a great bore for a dashing young man about town, who, we are told,

> keen as brandy
> Went forth in dress—a London dandy,
> His hair cut in the latest mode;
> He dined, he danced, he fenced, he rode.
> In French he could converse politely,
> As well as write; and how he bowed!
> In the mazurka, 'twas allowed,
> No partner ever was so sprightly.

He was not without accomplishments:

> with the spark of a bon mot
> He set the ladies' eyes aglow;

He could

> Quote Virgil, not a long selection,
> And always needing some correction
>
> . . . . .
>
> Theocritus and Homer bored him
> If true delight you would afford him
> You'd give him Adam Smith to read.
> A deep economist, indeed,
> He talked about the wealth of nations;
> The state relied, his friends were told,
> Upon its staples, not on gold . . .
> His father listened, frowned and groaned
> And mortgaged all the land he owned.

But his principal accomplishment was l'amour—

> He early played the fond deceiver
> And feigned the pang of jealousy,
> Rejoiced the fair one but to grieve her,
> Seemed sunk in gloom, or bold and free.

Which made for an active life:

> After an evening's dissipation
> He will lie late, and on his tray
> Find notes piled high. What—invitations?
> Three ladies mention a soiree,
> Here is a ball, and there a party,
> His appetite for pleasure's hearty—
> Where will my naughty lad repair?
> For he is welcome everywhere.

And we follow him as he promenades, and sets forth in the snow at dusk in a sleigh, to where "Glass after glass is drained"; and goes on to the theater and the ballet,

>   to taste the blisses
> And breathe the free air of the stage,
> To praise the dancer now the rage
> Or greet a luckless Phèdre with hisses:
>
> The theatre's full, the boxes glitter,
> The stalls are seething, the pit roars,
> The gallery claps and stamps, atwitter,
> The curtain rustles as it soars;

and afterward,

> The house rocks with applause; undaunted,
> And treading toes, between the chairs
> Onegin presses; with his vaunted
> Aplomb, he lifts his eye-glass, stares
> Askance at fair, unwonted faces,
> Remarks the jewels and the laces,
> And notes complexions, with a sneer
> Briefly surveying every tier.

All this eventually begins to pall. Seduction, says Pushkin, ceased to be amusing, and

>   he could make no bon mot
> Or wash things down with Veuve Clicquot
> When his poor head began to ache;
> And though he was an ardent rake,
> The time came when he quite abhorred
> Even the pistol and the sword.

It was an age of Byronism and English fashions; and as against that female ailment, the vapors, he had that male malaise, the spleen. True, says Pushkin,

> He spared us one piece of folly:
> Although he grew more melancholy
> He did stop short of suicide.

He scorned women, and locked himself in to read and write. But after a short time,

> He's done with women, and it looks
> As though he's also done with books.

Society and solitude, gaiety and gloom, had about equally, now, left this intelligent, but dilettantish, this appreciative but Byronically posturing young man at loose ends. At just this point, our dissatisfied worldling and equally dissatisfied flee-the-worldling is summoned to his uncle's bedside; but this time the new form of boredom he seems faced with is spared him. When he reaches his uncle's country house, his uncle is already dead.

He takes possession of his uncle's estate and attempts the business of managing it:

> His early years were all a waste,
> And this routine was to his taste.

adding:

> For two days he found it quite diverting . . .
> The third day interest abated
> And he was not the least elated
> By grove and stream and field and steep—
> They only sent him off to sleep.

Fortunately, in his new boredom, he meets a young neighbor, a poet named Lensky, fresh from a German university and filled with German idealism. Lensky, who in his romantically exalted fashion has long loved and been faithful to a "nice" uninteresting girl, seems to Eugene incredibly naïve, but he is likable and a new type and they see a good deal of each other. And when Onegin goes visiting Lensky's girl with Lensky, he meets her sister Tatyana, a strange shy wildly romantic girl—

> She is the novelist's creation:
>   Julie, Clarissa or Delphine;
> She wanders with imagined lovers
> Thru silent woods, and she discovers
> Her dreams in every circumstance
> Of some imported wild romance.

Tanya, at first sight of him, falls passionately in love with Eugene: Werther, Grandison, St. Preux, all the romantic heroes,

> All these our tender dreamer fused
> Into one image . . .
> Onegin's form, Onegin's face.

But though Onegin had noticed her as a hundred times more interesting than Lensky's choice, he had not been personally aroused; and the poor girl goes about for days, in a fever and torment, waiting for him to come visiting again. When he does not come, she pours out her love in a movingly honest and impassioned letter to him. Two or three days later he does come to see her, with a sense of the beauty of her letter, with decent feelings and honest words—*if* he wanted to marry, it is she he would choose:

> If for a moment I found pleasure
> In cosy scenes of fireside life,
> You, you alone would be my wife.

But, he goes on,

> I must confess, though loth to hurt you,
> I was not born for happiness;
> I am unworthy of your virtue;
> I'd bring you nothing but distress.
> My conscience speaks—pray let me finish;
> My love, first warm, would soon diminish:
> Our marriage would mean misery,
> Then you will weep, but who supposes
> Your grief will bring me to remorse?
> I shall lose patience, then, of course:
>
> What is there more to be lamented
> Than this: a household where the wife
> Whose spouse has left her, discontented,
> Grieves for the wretch throughout her life?
> While the dull husband . . . jealous in a frigid way
> Can only curse his wedding day.
> And I am such.

And in taking his leave he preaches self-control to the half-out-of-her-senses, tear-blinded girl.

He sees her again at a big party that her family gives, and she is again all hot and cold in his presence. And, finding the party—which Lensky had dragged him to—boring, he revenges himself by idling flirting with Lensky's girl. He has dance after dance with her, he makes up to her with all his dash and charm: so that Lensky in a heartsick rage leaves the party and straightway challenges Eugene to a duel. Realizing how wrong his behavior has been, Eugene is ready to make things up, but then begins to worry that by not going through with the duel he will make a fool of himself, be subject to whispered jokes and to that worldly scorn that is bred of worldly quarrels. And so he meets Lensky and indeed, by rather dishonorably raising his pistol while the distance is still being paced off, shoots him dead before Lensky can even aim. And it becomes apparent that subconsciously Onegin has resented Lensky even while liking him—has resented his feeling an unselfish love, as he could not do; his being a poet, as he could not be.

Onegin now goes away from his place in the country, and Tatyana in time goes to it in all its desertedness, goes day after day, reading the books in Onegin's fashionable library. She refuses other suitors, and at length her mother takes her to Moscow, where she goes out into society and is eventually married to a general. When in due time Onegin himself appears in Moscow, he discovers that she has become a poised, splendid, much-admired great lady. Eugene would now make up to her but she ignores him; he writes letters to her but she does not answer them; and after a period of self-immolation he goes one day to her house, finds no one at the door, walks in, encounters her reading the letters he has been writing to her, and falls at her feet. She is momentarily touched, but then she makes him get up and recalls to him the reversed scene when she, in spirit, was on her knees before *him* and he read her a sermon. *That* she can forgive him, for he was honest:

> Far from Moscow's noise and glitter
> You did not like me . . . That was bitter
> But worse what now you choose to do!
> Why do you pay me these attentions?
> Because society's conventions,
> Deferring to my wealth and rank,
> Have given me prestige? Be frank!
> Because my husband's decoration,
> A soldier's, wins us friends at Court,
> And all would relish the report
> That I had stained my reputation—
> 'Twould give you in society
> A pleasant notoriety?

Even the old harshness of speech, she adds, is preferable to "this insulting passion." And she goes on to say that all her present splendor means nothing to her, that she would give everything to be back in the country where she first met him. But now it is too late:

> Now my fate is quite decided,
> I was in too much haste, I fear;
> My mother coaxed and wept; the sequel
> You know: besides, all lots are equal
> To hapless Tanya . . . Well, and so
> I married. Now, I beg you, go.
> I know your heart; I need not tremble
> Because your honor and your pride
> Must in this matter be your guide.
> I love you (why should I dissemble?)
> But I became another's wife:
> I shall be true to him through life.

> She went. Onegin stood forsaken,
> Stood thunderstruck. He could not stir.
> By what a storm his heart was shaken:

> What pride, what grief, what thoughts of her!
> But are those stirrups he is hearing?
> Tatyana's husband is appearing.
> At this unlucky moment, we
> Must leave my hero, ruefully,
> For a long time . . . indeed, forever.

This seems to me, in its suddenness and theatricality, and at the same time its artistic completeness, one of the great leavetakings in literature. Pushkin need say no more; he in a sense dismisses his hero at the same moment that Tatyana does. "Onegin's portrait," as Pushkin says, "has been finished." It has been done with quick, light, creative strokes that are at the same time incisive ones. Onegin is the young worldling par excellence of a certain class and period, temperament and taste. He is no mere society playboy or rake, leading a life of wholly frivolous pleasure; himself intelligent and perhaps not ungifted, a man capable of sensitive perceptions who has come under the spell of Byronism, Onegin is perhaps best described as a dandy-dilettante. It is not simply the activities of a dashing young man of the world that engross him, but rather the attitudes. It is not the vulgar fashions that he cares about, but the picturesque and recherché ones. His is the essential dandyism that regards dress as not just decorative or becoming or beautiful, but as expressing a mood or portraying a role; everything, indeed, is to be significantly stylish, symbolically expressive. His in the same way is a dilettantism that turns to art most readily when he is out of sorts or at loose ends; you cannot imagine him normally staying away from a ball to read a book, except as a pose, except that it may make for publicity. Yet he gets pleasure, a right and educated pleasure, from books, indeed from the arts generally; he does not just ogle ballet girls, he appreciates the ballet. He enjoys the advantage of having one foot in the social world and one in the artistic; but more than this in the end is an advantage, it is a misfortune. For he is never quite happy, or entirely at home, in either world: the social world that suffices for the ordinary playboy must all too often bore him, while the world of seclusion, of thought and expression and feeling, must all too often leave him restless. For such a dandy-dilettante, his greatest advantage is really his youth and his personal dash and charm: they shelter his shallowness, they embellish his poses, they even make him cut a figure of sorts. But the truth is that for all his desire to be expressive, there is little to express; he can only adopt attitudes, enact roles, stage-light situations. For achieving his effects, he is dependent upon the very society that he pointedly eschews or showily turns his back on; just as, in his dilettante moods, he models himself on the fashionable writers he has read or met. Tatyana, examining the books in his country house,

> found the margins most appealing:
> The pencil marks he made with care
> Upon the pages everywhere
> Were all unconsciously revealing:
> A cross, a question mark, a word—
> From these the man might be inferred.

For an Onegin, the world is too much with him even when he has taken leave of the world. It is not only that whenever he goes in for the simple life he is deeply aware that he has gone in for it, but also that as soon as it becomes a way of life—as soon as there are no new fields or paths or brooks to discover, no new romantic views or picturesque customs to be found—he turns bored. He does not like solitude, he likes the idea of liking it. He cannot be simple, he can only be *sim-*

pliste. In the same way, he perhaps cannot be truly unhappy, he can only be Byronically melancholy, self-dramatizingly sad. At his best, he has a real air; very often he has only affectations. At his best, he has sensitive feelings about life, sensitive reactions to situations; but he is oftener sensitive about the kind of figure he will cut, the kind of impression he will leave behind. He is thus not only a man of the world, but the world's man, its ultimate slave, its eventual faintly tragic victim. If such a dandy-dilettante is a good deal of an eternal type, in another way he is a pure period type; but Pushkin, with his brilliant vivacity and superb detail, has given Onegin, if no full face, at least a profile of his own.

And Pushkin, best of all, has dramatized—and simultaneously criticized—Onegin's make-up by bringing it into crucial relations with others, by setting it against first Lensky and then Tatyana. At the first, and even the second, glimpse Onegin shines by contrast; he has what the other two lack, all the social graces; he has dash and poise, an air of wit, of cultivation, of connoisseurship; he is the kind of man who, in a pinch, can convey a critical judgment simply by looking bored. Obviously, too, Lensky admires him, and Tatyana loves him at first sight. Yet we have but to note just once his behavior toward Lensky, and just once his behavior toward Tanya, to get to the root of him. He knows how wrong he was with Lensky's fiancée at the ball, he knows too how shamefully absurd it would be to go through with the duel, yet the thought that by not doing so may invite a few sniffs and sneers from society is enough to make him change his mind. In the same way, as Tanya points out, his feverish pursuit of her as a Moscow great lady is predominantly a desire to publish his conquest of her and add to his reputation as a society rake. These two things are the key to his character and the measure of his limitations; they epitomize him, they type him. In that sense they are a more decisive criticism of the essential Onegin than something as shocking as his not giving Lensky quite an even chance in the duel, for in this he unconsciously seeks revenge that is a form of tribute, in this he is actuated, without knowing it, by envy. In the same way, by refusing Tanya's love, by refusing to marry her, though the consequences were to be grave, he was being honest about himself, and was only dishonest when pursuing her as a great lady.

When I say the consequences of Onegin's refusing Tatyana's love were to be grave, I mean chiefly in terms of Tatyana. Hers, as between the two, is both the moral and the personal victory; hers, by Onegin's standards, is indeed a dazzling success story; but it is she who is the truly tragic figure of the story, from being pushed into so unwanted a role and coming to live so wasted a life. In the shy girl we first meet, who is incapable of pretense or concealment, and whose untutored heart bursts with the most passionate love for Onegin, we have also a type, and also a period type. But in her passionateness, and in the poetic accuracy and delicacy of her creator's perceptions, we have suddenly a human being—one of those figures who stay with us not from how thoroughly we know them but from how intensely we feel them; not in detail, but in essence. The Tanya whom Eugene suddenly encounters as a great lady is someone whom *we* suddenly encounter in the same way: we have not watched her working into a new role, and when in the great scene she speaks to Onegin for the first time since he has again become aware of her—and for the last time, it is to be assumed, in their lives—every word is crucial, a false sentence, even a few wrong syllables, can be fatal. For she is grown into the kind of woman she should never have

been, playing a part she seemed in no way ever able to play; and with a calm glacial dignity she refuses for good and all the man she still loves. The scene not only has a great moral force: *that* it might possess from the nature of the situation and the poet's power of words; it has also a convincing trenchancy, an exalting stature, as between man and woman no less than between differing natures and ways of life. The poet triumphs here by his boldness, his succinctness, his speed, by compressing the whole psychological analysis into a few salient facts, a few freighted speeches, a recollection of what was, a recognition of what is: a novelist would not have been so daring, nor trusted to so little; nor, without the heightening power of verse, have been capable of so much.

It has been well said that Pushkin's greatness in creating Tatyana lay in his almost miraculous ability to make of her at the end a virtuous wife and yet neither a prig nor a puritan; nor, we might add, a conscious martyr. Perhaps, best of all, he does not let the spirit of the final scene sound the final note of the story: he resumes the light, informal manner of so much of the book, the briskness and gaiety acquiring now a wistfulness, the modest ending having its own kind of human magnificence. In Pushkin's diminuendos, we sense something of Turgenev and, with a lesser kinship, of Chekhov. And it is a commonplace that the Tanya-Onegin relationship—the weakling and the woman of strength, the worldling and the woman of character—has been a recurrent one in Russian literature. But, as Prince Mirsky has said, "the classical attitude of Pushkin, of sympathy without pity for the man, and of respect without reward for the woman, has never been revived."

I have summarized this story at considerable length, I have quoted from it in considerable detail, because it seems to me that Pushkin managed to enfold his criticism in his chronicle. For all the personal, or seemingly personal, comments that he introduces, for all his quick sallies and short sermons, his asides and digressions, it is in this tale of Onegin and his way of life, as set lightly against Lensky, and graphically against Tanya, that we find our whole sense of comparative values. To be sure, the more than eight years that Pushkin spent in writing his poem also chronicle the moral and artistic growth of the poet himself. The young man who, inspired by Byron's *Don Juan,* set light-heartedly to work on *Onegin*—with his own kind of dazzling youthful gifts—was far removed from the mature artist who wrote the final scenes; and in that sense, we may doubt whether the young man would have had the moral insight, let alone the creative power, to tell the story quite as it came to be told, or to be concluded. We might say that, in a sense, the account of Onegin's deterioration is the mark of Pushkin's development; that the protagonist and his creator started off in a strong autobiographical alliance, as both of them dashing, privileged young men of the world, and increasingly diverged as Pushkin learned from life and from his endowments as a student of life and a writer, while, with no such endowments, Onegin acquired no such knowledge either. In Pushkin's own life there was enormously much, of course, of Onegin's—in his youth Pushkin drank and gambled, danced and fought duels, had a succession of love affairs, attacked autocracy and epigrammatically thumbed his nose at the Czar, and was more or less exiled with an army appointment in southern Russia. As the politically agitated years passed, he became much less of a firebrand; he returned to Moscow, a gayer blade than ever, and more than ever a social success, and finally met and married a beautiful young girl, who with the passing years proved flagrantly unfaithful, which provoked the duel that caused Pushkin's death. This is the Onegin side of Pushkin's story; but the whole other side of Pushkin's life, the political troubles and financial debts, the vagabond streak and clutter of adventures and experiences, and above all his position in the literary world and his considerable productivity, contributed equally if less directly to the writing of *Onegin* and the insight with which it was written; while beyond that there was the ever more deft and accomplished artist.

There is, indeed, almost every species of good writing—dark and bright, mocking and tender, gay and serious, brilliant and passionate—in this remarkable novel in verse; writing that proclaims Pushkin's knowledge of human nature, his acute observation of the physical world, his thorough familiarity with sophisticated life and the social scene; writing that at the same time, in a rather taxing fourteen-line stanza, can be wonderfully lyrical, immensely poetic, or have the crackle of epigram, the ballroom gloss of *vers de société*. No other criticism of worldliness, no other taking the measure of a worldling can so draw blood from the worldling's own weapons, his insouciance, his suavity, his dash. No one, more than Pushkin, has so brilliantly described the social scene or so ably appraised it, but it is the measure of the poem's high excellence that it describes and appraises so much else, and can elsewhere be as intense and poetic as here it is glittering and sharp.

Let me quote a few of the ways in which, even at brief length and in translation, Pushkin excels. Here is pure society verse, pure portrayal of manners:

> They take her to the Club for dances,
> The rooms are thronged and hot and gay.
> The blare, the lights, the shining glances,
> The couples as they whirl away,
> The lovely ladies' filmy dresses,
> The balconies where such a press is,
> The young and hopeful brides-to-be,
> Confound the senses suddenly.
> Here dandies now in the ascendant
> Show off their impudence, their vests,
> Their monocles that rake the guests.
> And here hussars on leave, resplendent
> And thunderous, flock eagerly:
> They come, they conquer and they flee.

And here is Pushkin, not high and Keatslike in poetic description, but homely and domestic, rather after the fashion of the Dutch genre painters:

> Here's winter! . . . The triumphant peasant
> Upon his sledge tries out the road;
> His mare scents snow upon the pleasant
> Keen air, and trots without a goad;
> The bold *kibitka* swiftly traces
> Two fluffy furrows as it races;
> The driver on his box we note
> With his red belt and sheepskin coat.
> A serf-boy takes his dog out sleighing,
> Himself transformed into a horse;
> One finger's frostbitten, of course,
> But nothing hurts when you are playing;
> And at the window, not too grim,
> His mother stands and threatens him.

From these translated quotations alone, one might deduce no more than Pushkin's great adroitness in small ways, and fine eye for detail. But in the original I would suppose that from just such passages there emerged a marvelous expressiveness, a delicate play of mind, a large gift of observation, things that exceed the most accomplished lightweight, that indeed stamp Pushkin as not a lightweight. And how little he was one stands forth when we recall that these quotations are hardly more than garnishing for a poem that exhibits great mastery of narrative, of characterization, of theme; and that, for all it may pause or digress, has beyond its shapeliness an organic form. We can only praise and value Pushkin the more for his gaiety and elegance and his dandyism since they did not prevent his achieving in the same work what would not only father much important fiction but was in itself important fiction. Certainly the great scenes in the story of Eugene and Tanya—the first meeting; Tanya and her nurse; the scene in the garden; Tanya's journey to Moscow; and the final scene in Moscow—certainly these scenes, to re-dignify a much-abused word, are unforgettable. (pp. 161-80)

> *Louis Kronenberger, " 'Eugene Onegin'," in his* The Polished Surface: Essays in the Literature of Worldliness, *Alfred A. Knopf, 1969, pp. 161-80.*

JOHN FENNELL (essay date 1973)

[*In the following excerpt, Fennell addresses the multi-faceted role of the narrator in* Eugene Onegin *and examines Pushkin's two contrasting writing styles, the poetic and the prosaic.*]

The immensely complex work that is *Evgeny Onegin* has engendered a bewildering variety of critical interpretations. It has been called 'an encyclopaedia of Russian life' (Belinsky [see *NCLC,* Vol. 3 pp. 417-21]), 'first of all and above all a phenomenon of style . . . not "a picture of Russian life" ' (Nabokov [see bibliography of Further Reading]), 'the first Russian realistic novel' (Gor'ky) and even 'the first truly great realistic creation of all world literature in the nineteenth century' (Blagoy), 'a broad and just portrayal of the world of lies, hypocrisy and emptiness' (Meylakh), 'the most intimate of all Pushkin's works' (Blagoy again), 'a novel of parody and a parody of the novel' (Shklovsky [see excerpt dated 1923]). The problem of interpretation is not simplified, as it rarely is, by Pushkin's various extraneous utterances. In a letter of 4th November, 1823 written just after the completion of Chapter I, for instance, he describes his work as 'not a novel but a novel in verse—the devil of a difference! Like *Don Juan*', while eighteen months later he writes: 'you compare the first chapter of my novel with *Don Juan*. No one respects *Don Juan* more than I do . . . but it has nothing in common with *Onegin*.' In his 'Preface' to *Evgeny Onegin,* added to the work in 1827, he talks, with enraging vagueness, of 'multicoloured chapters, half funny, half sad, of the common people (*prostonarodnykh*), ideal, the carefree fruit of my enjoyments'.

We may be able to get a clearer idea about the nature of *Evgeny Onegin,* if we consider Pushkin's attitude, as expressed *within* the work, to the narrator, to his characters, to the events described, to the reader, and above all to the novel, if not to poetry itself. This relationship is remarkably intricate and, it would appear at first sight, contradictory: the distance between the narrator and the object of his narrative seems now vast, now tiny; the identification of Pushkin with the narrator—now credible, now suspect; the narrator himself—now ironic and detached, now passionate and involved.

Evgeny Onegin is the most 'intrusive' of all Pushkin's works: the narrator continually thrusts himself to the fore. From time to time he may retreat into the wings in order to describe an action or let his characters speak for themselves. But never for long. Back he comes, often with what looks like unquenchable garrulity, to chat, to comment, to explain, to reminisce, and to treat his readers to huge asides.

Now had Pushkin confined his narrative method to objective, impersonal 'showing' (e.g. 'It is now dark: [Evgeny] gets into a sleigh. "Look out, look out!", the shout rings out' etc., etc., 1/16), to omniscient 'telling' or interpretation (e.g. 'The Russian *khandra* [spleen, ennui] overcame him little by little', 1/38) and to an intimate author-reader relationship used for commenting or for shifting the story forward ('But what of my Onegin?', 1/35), then we might have been able readily to suspend our disbelief and to accept the illusion of the story's reality and the credibility of the author. But Pushkin complicates matters. Towards the end of Chapter I he introduces himself as a *character* in the story.

Up to this point Pushkin has already laid the foundation for the character of Evgeny by closely observing his behaviour and the workings of his mind. At the same time he has given us a great deal of information about himself—about his spleen, boredom, indifference, about his love of pleasure and his rakish life, about his infinite regret for the past and his 'romantic' amours, about his habits, his likes and dislikes, and so on. Then, in Stanza 45, he informs us: 'I made friends with him at that time' (i.e. during Evgeny's period of boredom with life in St. Petersburg—*before* the action of the story begins), and proceeds to compare his own character with Evgeny's, to reminisce on their meetings together and finally, in Stanza 51, to part from him ('But we were separated by fate for a long time'). Except in the 'Fragments from Evgeny's Journey', 'Pushkin', the character in the story, never emerges again.

From the narrative point of view this unmotivated parting of 'Pushkin' and Onegin is essential, and we are obliged to forget 'Pushkin': the subsequent story could not have been told by an 'I' who personally knew one of the characters, unless all pretence of omniscience were dropped. 'Pushkin', the friend of Evgeny, could not have done what only Pushkin the author could do—namely pry into his characters' minds, record their thoughts in monologues and observe their behaviour when out of Evgeny's presence. Why then does Pushkin introduce this perplexing ghost?

Of course it might be explained by 'carelessness' (cf. 'the carefree fruit of my enjoyments' of the 'Preface') or speed of writing, an unwillingness at this early stage of the novel to think ahead to future technical complications; or it might even be attributed to a slapdash, devil-may-care touch of Byronism. But although such carelessness could easily have been removed, Pushkin made no attempt to eliminate Evgeny's awkward friend from the story at a later date; indeed he included in his original eighth chapter (replaced by the present Chapter 8 and printed separately as 'Fragments from Onegin's Journey') the so-called 'Odessa stanzas' in which Pushkin again appears briefly as a character in his own right: 'I lived at that time in dusty Odessa . . .' Perhaps the real reason for the inclusion, or at any rate the ultimate retention, of this additional 'character' was in fact to blur or destroy the illusion of reality? A consideration of Pushkin's authorial intrusions in the novel as a whole may help us further in this direction.

Why does Pushkin intrude at such length and with such frequency throughout the work? Two obvious answers present themselves. First of all, a 'novel in verse' or a 'free novel', as Pushkin called it (8/50)—that is, a novel bound by no limits, no rules of genre, a novel 'like *Don Juan*' in fact—was the ideal vehicle for personal commentary. There were no tiresome conventions to hem the author in. Here was an opportunity to discourse on subjects which intrigued, worried, fascinated or puzzled him, to go off on seemingly arbitrary and capricious tangents in any direction, to expatiate on love, literature, art, society, fate, women, friendship and so on.

Of course such garrulity is deceptive. However capricious Pushkin's disquisitions appear at first glance, they are in fact carefully woven into the fabric of the novel. What looks like a loose clutter of structural units separated by rambling digressions turns out, on closer scrutiny, to be a work of classical tautness and proportions. Time and again the narrator intrudes not just to indulge in compulsive ad-libbing, but to move the narrative, to change the subject and the mood, to increase or decrease the tempo, even to explain away narrative difficulties. One example will suffice. In Chapter 4 a series of seemingly irrepressible discourses on random topics turns out to be a skilfully controlled bridge-passage between one theme and another. After describing with sentimental clichés and devastating irony (4/25, 26) how Lensky and Ol'ga pass their time together, Pushkin slips into a light, bantering digression on albums (4/27-30)—still in the same 'stylistic key' as the Lensky-Ol'ga theme, though with slightly more sophistication and wit. Gradually the subject changes and with it the tone: from albums to madrigals, from madrigals to elegies, from elegies to odes; and by Stanza 32 we are involved in an esoteric literary debate (32, 33). In the following stanza (34), subtly linked with its predecessor by two splendidly conventional lines aping the periphrastic formulae of the eighteenth-century ode . . .

> An admirer of fame and freedom,
> In the excitement of his stormy thoughts.

Pushkin returns to Lensky, but only to deflate him in the next two lines: . . .

> Vladimir might have written odes,
> But Ol'ga would not have read them.

The mock-serious digression which follows, with its four lines of conventional poetic jargon: . . .

> And indeed blessed is the modest lover
> Who reads his daydreams
> To the object of his songs and love,
> A pleasantly-languorous beauty!

capped by two of down-to-earth deflation: . . .

> Blessed . . . though perhaps she
> Is diverted by something quite different.

remind us that we are once more back in Pushkin's own intimate world. This is confirmed by Stanza 35, which is full of homely simplicity (*staroy nyane* [old nanny]; *skuchnogo obeda* [boring dinner]; *zabredshego soseda* [a neighbour who has dropped in]; *pugayu stado dikikh utok* [I scare a flock of wild ducks]) mixed with irony and wit: again the mock serious 'poetic' is punctured by the simplicity of the 'prose'. The periphrastic: . . .

> But I [read] the fruits of my fantasies
> And of my harmonious devices

is followed by . . .

> Only to my old nanny

and nine more equally unaffected 'prosaic' lines, while the concluding couplet consists of the lofty, archaic, Derzhavin-like: . . .

> Hearkening to the chant of sweet-sounding strophes

followed by the artless: . . .

> They fly away from the banks.

This combination of cosiness and irony, simplicity and bathos, attunes us for the Onegin theme which follows immediately (Onegin in the country, leading a life similar to Pushkin's at Mikhaylovskoe). The transition is complete. The digressions have guided us from one major theme to another.

We have seen that authorial intrusions in *Evgeny Onegin* are used both as an outlet for Pushkin's views on a variety of topics and as a structural device. But a third use can also be discerned: the 'lyrical author' is displayed, it seems, in order to create a sense of what one critic has called the 'second reality', or the reality of the creative process. Now *Evgeny Onegin* is a highly 'literary' work. It is full of allusions to authors, books, styles, genres, literary conflicts; it contains parodies, imitations, quotations; there are obscure esoteric references to literary circles. It is a work which needs a commentary to enable the reader to unravel the more abstruse allusions. As such it might be considered an imitation of *Don Juan,* and indeed the literariness of *Don Juan* no doubt attracted and influenced Pushkin. But Pushkin takes his 'literariness' a stage further. He makes the reader constantly aware of the poet in the background, manipulating, creating, comparing, and thus points up the conventional nature of the 'first reality' of the work, the reality of the plot, the love story, the setting; he undermines reality, as it were. A landscape, for example, is not necessarily painted to provide a backcloth against which the *personae* are going to perform. It is painted rather as a model of the artist's style and technique. Take for example the beginning of Chapter 5. Tat'yana wakes up in Stanza 1 to see a wintry landscape from her window. We *believe* in the scene as she is made to witness it: in other words, the illusion is created because we see it through her eyes. But with the first word of the second stanza this is no longer the case. The exclamatory *Zima!* [Winter!] makes us immediately aware that it is now Pushkin the artist intruding with a *generalized* picture of winter, just as 'concrete' and 'realistic' as the catalogue of objects viewed by Tat'yana in Stanza 1, but no longer forming a realistic setting for the characters or the action of the story. As if to drive this point home, Pushkin starts Stanza 3 with a comment on his painting ('But perhaps pictures of this kind will not attract you: all this [you will say] is lowly nature; there is not much that is elegant here'), and even goes on to compare his technique with that of his contemporaries Vyazemsky and Baratynsky. In other words we are made to feel that the nature picture of Stanza 2, for all its 'realism', is not part of the décor at all, but an example of Pushkin's art. Pushkin is showing us what he can do. Our attention is distracted entirely from Tat'yana, who has to be artificially re-introduced in Stanza 4 ('Tat'yana . . . loved the Russian winter') before we can be lulled back into the illusion of the Tat'yana setting.

The same sort of thing occurs in Chapter 4. Having described Onegin's country life and habits with intimate and convincing detail (4/37, 39), Pushkin moves over to the changing seasons and in Stanza 41 produces another 'model', another realistic and 'concrete' picture, this time of autumn. And again we realize that this is not a setting for Evgeny at all, but a set-

piece as it were. The point is emphasized by Pushkin in the following stanza where he interrupts his highly realistic description to make a jocular comment in parenthesis: . . .

> And now the brittle-hard frosts have set in,
> Shining silver amidst the fields . . .
> (The reader is already expecting the rhyme 'roses';
> Here you are then, take it quickly!)

(In Russian 'roses' rhymes with 'frosts'.)

Of course this is not to say that we are never aware of the setting or that the characters always perform against an artificial background. Again and again we are made to feel the atmosphere, the physical presence of the characters against a material setting. But we are never allowed to enjoy the illusion for long, for the illusion is always being undermined by the stylistic devices of the author, just as it was undermined by the early introduction of 'Pushkin' the friend of Evgeny. One may be carried away by the tense atmosphere of the duel—by the cold technical brilliance of the pistol-loading scene (6/29), by the doom-laden movements of the contestants moving heavily towards each other (*Pokhodkoy tverdoy, tikho, rovno* . . . [With firm gait, calmy, evenly . . .] 30), the awful finality of dead Lensky's immobility and the blood 'steaming' from his wound (32); but the final feeling one carries away from the scene is one not of pity, anguish, horror, but of amazement at Pushkin's poetic versatility. In what should be one of the most solemn moments of the whole poem, Pushkin pours forth a 'torrent of unrelated images' and second-hand clichés to describe poor dead Lensky in his own style: . . .

> The young singer
> Has found an untimely end.
> The storm wind blew, the fair blossom
> Faded at the dawn of day,
> The flame on the altar went out! . . .

and then follows it up with the great extended image of the empty house—quiet, utterly simple, majestic and haunting: . . .

> Now, as in a deserted house,
> All within is both quiet and dark;
> It has become silent for ever.
> The shutters are closed. With chalk the windows
> Are whitened. The owner is not there.
> But where she is God knows. All trace is lost.

'Pushkin's own contribution, a sample as it were of what *he* can do', as one critic has remarked. We have been involved not so much in the events as in the manner of their telling. We have been made conscious—and this time without any intrusive hint from the author—of Pushkin's manipulation of style and poetic technique. (pp. 36-44)

In no other work does Pushkin allow his consciousness of *style* to be felt so acutely by the reader as in *Evgeny Onegin.* Our attention is constantly being drawn to the technique of description, to the manipulation of phraseology, to the choice of colours for townscapes and landscapes, to the choice of syntax for action, movement, conversation, to the choice of clichés for objects of parody and ironic treatment. Yet it is difficult to label the various styles, to talk of the 'Romantic', or the 'mock-classical', or the 'realistic', because these terms are often imprecise, and one particular 'style' may consist of a deliberate mixture of diverse elements. It would perhaps simplify the problem if we were to consider two main 'manners' of writing which seem to run through *Evgeny Onegin,*

Pushkin at Mikhailovskoe.

sometimes exclusive of each other, sometimes temporarily coalescing, but for the most part in strict juxtaposition, if not actual conflict. The problem is to supply them with a name: one might be called loosely the 'poetic' manner, the manner typical of Pushkin's own early effusions, of Zhukovsky and the Russian 'pre-Romantics'—the stringing together of periphrases, some from the pseudo-classical treasury of Russian eighteenth-century poetry, some from the Karamzinist school of the beginning of the nineteenth century—of tired stereotypes evocative of sentiment and emotions, of vague polysemantic metaphors depicting the 'inexpressible disturbance of the soul'. The other might be called the 'prosaic' manner—realistic, objective, unemotional, undecorative, concrete, concise, to use a few of the epithets which can be applied to it—the manner with which Pushkin began to experiment in *The Gipsies* for what we called the 'objective narrator's voice' and which is so much in evidence in *Count Nulin, The Little House in Kolomna* and the 'Evgeny passages' of *The Bronze Horseman*.

The most striking element of the 'poetic' manner is the use of clichés formed by joining together mutually evocative adjectives, nouns, verbs and adverbs. The clusters thus formed (particularly if one or all of the elements are 'abstract' or 'subjective') do little or nothing to increase our knowledge of the original concept. Thus, in the field of emotions—the most fertile for such conventional growths—*grust'* [grief] is barely en-

riched by trite epithets like *nezhnaya* [tender], *beznadezhnaya* [hopeless] or *taynaya* [secret], and we know little more about the nature of a person's love when the verb '*lyubit'* [to love], say, is qualified by *tomno* [languorously], *strastno* [passionately] or *plamenno* [ardently]. It is as though the poet has at his fingertips a number of words to express emotions from despair to bliss to which he can add vague, imprecise qualifiers at will. The results are often as meaningless and uninformative as the combination of traditional set themes used by the mediaeval writer to describe a saint's childhood or a battle.

Even more widespread are the conventional periphrases which decorate the 'poetic' style of *Evgeny Onegin.* These range from the heavy classical conceits (*Nemolchnyy shopot Nereidy* [Nereid's unceasing whisper] 8/4; or *Priyut zadumchivykh Driad* [The shelter of pensive dryads] 2/1) to such complex and often subtle combinations as: . . .

> The mysterious shade of the forests
> Was baring itself with mournful sound.

in which the adjectives (particularly *pechal'nym* [mournful] refer rather to the effect produced on the onlooker than to the nouns they qualify; and they include innumerable circumlocutions to describe natural phenomena such as 'the wondrous choir of heavenly luminaries' (5/9) or the bee which 'flies from its waxen cell to fetch the tribute of the fields' (7/1), as well as the ubiquitous images of heat, fire, storm and waves to denote passion.

Pushkin's views on such stylistic artificialities, as far as prose is concerned at any rate, were unequivocal. In an unfinished article written before *Evgeny Onegin* (in 1822) he attacked those Russian writers who, 'considering it base to explain the most ordinary things simply, think to enliven childish prose with additions and flaccid metaphors. They never say "friendship" without adding "this sacred feeling, the noble flame of which etc.". Instead of "early in the morning" they write "barely had the first rays of the rising sun illumined the eastern edges of the azure heaven" . . . I read in a review of some theatre-lover: "this young nursling of Thalia and Melpomene, generously endowed by Apollo"—My God—put "this good young actress".' How can we then explain the profusion of clichés, 'flaccid metaphors' and periphrases which we find in *Evgeny Onegin?* Why is there such an abundance of 'languorous glances', 'tormented hearts' and 'seething passions'? Why 'Diana's face' (1/47) and not the moon? Why the loans from Parny, Millevoye, Zhukovsky, Milonov, Kyukhelbeker and countless other second-rate early Romantics? The answer is to be found in the use which Pushkin makes of his 'poetic' style.

Primarily it is used for parody. In his description of Lensky and Ol'ga, Pushkin mercilessly ridicules them as if to highlight their artificiality, their tawdriness and their insincerity. Lensky pours out his thoughts before the duel in a string of grandiloquent hackneyed metaphors: . . .

> I shall not permit the libertine
> With the fire of sighs and flattery
> To tempt her young heart,
> Nor the despicable poisonous worm
> To nibble at the lily's tender stalk,
> Nor the flower on its second morn
> To fade away still half-unfolded . . .
>
> (pp. 46-8)

The 'poetic' manner, however, is by no means confined to pure parody; we find it used, for example, in passages where no mimicry or outright mockery are intended, but where one may still suspect an ironic attitude of the author to his subject. When Tat'yana's emotions, aroused by her imagination or by her reading of sentimental novels, are uncontrolled, they are given the full 'poetic' treatment. At her nameday party she is so overcome with emotion that she nearly swoons (5/30). Pushkin describes her with two nature similes ('paler than the morning moon, timider than the hunted deer'), talks vaguely of her 'darkling' (*temneyushchikh*) eyes, and finally tosses together the images of fire and tempest to convey her agitation ('passionate heat blazes stormily within her'). Still more banal are the images used to describe her disturbed condition after the rendezvous with Evgeny in the garden (4/23). The 'mad sufferings of love' 'agitate the young soul thirsting for sadness'; Tat'yana 'burns with inconsolable passion'; 'sleep shuns her bed' and her youth 'grows dim'. We have only to compare this stream of romantic exuberance with the phraseology used to depict the Tat'yana of Chapter 8 to realize how effective this 'poetic' style can be for creating an image of immaturity and uncontrolled (and often derivative) emotionalism. When Tat'yana is portrayed as above pettiness, contemptuous of the artificialities of society, mistress of her feelings, *mature*—then the language becomes concrete, prosaic, majestically solemn and icily simple. In Stanza 14 a string of negatives (*ne . . . ne . . . ne . . . , bez . . . bez . . . bez . . . bez . . .*) showing what qualities were absent in her make-up is capped with . . .

Everything about her was quiet, simple

words which not only describe the mature Tat'yana but also the language itself. When Tat'yana meets Evgeny again in Stanza 18, her self-control is brought to light by the absolute calm and simplicity of the vocabulary and syntax: . . .

> But nothing betrayed her:
> She preserved exactly the same tone,
> Her bow was just as serene.
> In very truth, far from shuddering
> Or becoming suddenly pale or crimson,
> She did not even move an eyebrow,
> Nor did she even compress her lips.
>
> (pp. 49-50)

[The principles of the 'prosaic' style are]: elimination of unnecessary epithets; absence of 'abstract' and vague parts of speech, of periphrases, clichés and hyperbole, etc.; economy of words; simplified syntax with a minimum of subordination; frequent enjambement between lines and quatrains; a tendency to catalogue, particularly concrete objects (see especially 7/31, 38). To these can be added a considerable lowering of the tone and the introduction of purely conversational elements—both lexical (vulgarisms) and syntactical (ellipsis, infinitives expressing inceptive past tense, interjections in place of main verbs, frequentative use of perfective verbs, etc.).

The 'prosaic' style is most frequently used for description of action. Interest or excitement is kept at a high pitch by some or all of the devices mentioned above. The classic example is Tat'yana's headlong rush through the garden to meet Evgeny in Chapter 3: . . .

> Suddenly the clatter of horses' hoofs! . . . Her blood froze.
> Nearer and nearer! The horses are galloping . . . And into the courtyard
> [Drives] Evgeny! 'Ah!' [she cries], and lighter than a shadow
> Tat'yana jumps into the other entrance hall,
> From the porch into the courtyard, and straight into the garden
> She flies, she flies; to look back
> She does not dare; in an instant she ran through
> Borders, [across] small bridges, a little field,
> Down the avenue leading to the lake, through a copse,
> Breaking down lilac shrubs,
> Flying over flower-beds towards the brook.
> And gasping for breath, upon the bench . . .
> She fell . . .

Apart from the stereotyped *krov' ee zastyla* [her blood froze], which is still attached by rhyme to the ultra-romantic first two lines of the stanza, the language is very close to common speech. The vocabulary is plain and 'concrete'; the syntax is simplicity itself—verbs are omitted (*i na dvor / Evgeniy!* [into the courtyard—Evgeny!]) or replaced by interjections ("*Akh!*"; *Tat'yana pryg* [Tat'yana jumps]); there is no subordination unless we count the gerunds *letya* [flying] and *zadykhayas'* [gasping for breath]; 'concrete' nouns are piled up (*kurtiny, mostiki, luzhok* . . . [borders, small bridges, a little field] etc.); enjambements—interlinear, interquatrain and even interstanza—completely disrupt the pattern of ordered poetry and break the hypnotic rhythm of the stanza. (pp. 50-2)

'Action' passages are of course not the only vehicles for the 'prosaic' style. Frequently land- and townscapes receive the same treatment—perhaps with less ellipsis, but with an equal simplicity of vocabulary and syntax, a tendency to enjambement and 'cataloguing' and an avoidance of abstract, emotional phraseology—see for example the brittle vivid picture of winter in 5/2, or the 'Flemish' 'farmyard' description (*Lyublyu peschanyy kosogor* [I love a sandy hill-side]) in 'Fragments from Evgeny's Journey,' or again the description of winter in 4/42.

But for the most remarkable examples of simplicity and naturalness of language we must turn to the conversations, particularly to the words of Tat'yana's *nyanya* (3/17-20, 33-5) and Evgeny's housekeeper (7/17-18). Both Filippovna's and Anis'ya's utterances are as far removed from conventional 'poetic' or bookish jargon and as close to popular speech as Pushkin could get without sinking into tedious naturalistic imitation. With customary tact Pushkin avoids pure reproduction of peasant speech. There is no phonetic mimicry, for example. His effects are achieved with the aid of a few 'signal' words (*zashiblo* [I've lost my memory], *byley* [true tales], *nebylits* [fables], *chereda* [sorry pass], *moy svet* [my sweet]—3/17-18; *sizhival* [used to sit], *obedyval* [used to dine], *zhival* [lived], *kostochkam* [dear bones]—7/17-18). Of course it's not just a question of stripping their speech of ornamentation and simplifying the syntax: it is the *rightness,* the *exactness* of so many of the expressions and gestures which in a few words make Filippovna and Anis'ya as memorable as any peasant type painstakingly built up by Nekrasov in hundreds of lines. When for example Tat'yana explains dramatically but imprecisely that she is 'sick at heart': . . .

> O nanny, nanny, I feel miserable,
> I feel sick at heart, my dear;
> I'm about to cry, to sob! . . .

Filippovna's reaction: . . .

> My child, you are unwell;
> The Lord have mercy and save us!

is exactly right. Romantic yearnings are quite beyond her ken: 'sickness of heart', a fevered look and tearfulness are in Filippovna's mind a symptom of physical illness. And when the stuttering confession comes out: . . .

> I . . . you know, nanny . . . I'm in love

the bewildered *nyanya* can only resort to a trembling sign of the cross and a prayer: . . .

> 'My child, the Lord be with you!'
> And the nurse with a prayer
> Made the sign of the cross over the girl with her frail hand.

The 'prosaic' manner is rarely allowed to stand in isolation for long. Time and again it is placed by Pushkin in direct contrast, even in conflict, with the 'poetic'. Tat'yana's flight through the garden (3/38) is sandwiched between lines of striking banality ('her soul ached and her languorous gaze was full of tears'—'her heart, full of torments, keeps a dark dream of hope'); the haunting, liquid, moon-washed picture of Tat'yana and her *nyanya* (3/20) which concludes their first conversation is a strange mixture of well-defined 'Flemish' strokes: . . .

> . . . and on the bench . . .
> With a kerchief on her grey head
> The old woman in her long jacket . . .

and vague blurred pastel shades: . . .

> . . . the moon shone,

> And with dark light illumined
> the pale charms of Tat'yana
> And her loosened hair
> And drops of tears . . .

The 'romantic' concluding couplet: . . .

> And everything slumbered in quiet
> In the light of the inspirative moon—

which sets the seal to the predominantly 'poetic' scene consisted in the original draft of a soft 'moon' line: . . .

> And everything was silent in the moonlight

followed by the stark: . . .

> Only a cat miaowed at the window.

Perhaps Pushkin felt the contrast here to be too strong; at least the revised version left the reader in a certain amount of ambiguity as to the author's attitude to the picture. Unromantic miaowing was too obvious a pointer to authorial irony.

Why this perpetual juxtaposing of stylistically different elements, this conflict between 'poetry' and 'prose'? Is it just to shatter the illusion of reality, to stop the reader from taking this or that character or passage too seriously? Is it to enforce awareness of the artificiality of the 'romantic' or the solemn by placing them cheek by jowl with the 'realistic' or the vulgar? Or is it primarily the result of an overwhelming desire to demonstrate poetic skills, to exhibit art, to revel in words and to show how language, verse, metre and rhyme can be manipulated and moulded to produce certain effects?

We might go one step further and ask: Is not the fundamental theme of *Evgeny Onegin* Pushkin himself? Not necessarily a Pushkin lamenting the irretrievable passing of time and weeping for wasted youth or inability to find a meaning in life, but a Pushkin observing and recording the process of his maturation as a poet and rejoicing in the ripeness of his 'prose' rather than lamenting the greenness of his 'poetry'? The clues are there. The identification of his muse with his heroine in the beginning of Chapter 8 and his comparison in 'Evgeny's Journey' of the exuberance of his 'Crimean period' ('At that time I thought I needed wildernesses, the pearly crests of waves, and the sound of the sea, and rocks piled high, and the "ideal" of a proud maiden, and nameless sufferings'—all the baggage of the Romantic poet) with the sobriety of his mature style ('I have poured much water into my poetic goblet') point unmistakably to his absorption with the question of his development as a poet. Perhaps after all Pushkin meant us to take this 'complex symphony of stylistic layers' first and foremost as a monument of—and to—poetic craftsmanship. (pp. 52-5)

John Fennell, "Pushkin," in Nineteenth-Century Russian Literature: Studies of Ten Russian Writers, *edited by John Fennell, University of California Press, 1973, pp. 13-68.*

RICHARD FREEBORN (essay date 1973)

[*In the following excerpt, Freeborn examines the qualities of* Eugene Onegin *that make it a unique work in Russian fiction. In particular, he discusses Pushkin's playful, witty style, his use of chronology and description to make his novel appear a "replica of history," and his complex characterization emphasizing the role of Fate in the lives of Onegin, Tatyana, and Lensky.*]

No work in Russian literature solicits our attention more charmingly than *Eugene Onegin.* We are invited without preamble, this very instant, to make the acquaintance of Onegin, the author's 'good friend'. His presumably unspoken thoughts about his dying uncle which are given in stanza I contrast ironically with the charming introduction of stanza II. At its very opening the work suggests a playfulness of tone which unites many moods and manners, as the brief dedication says:

> Take this gathering of motley chapters,
> Half-jocular, half-sad,
> Unsophisticated, idealistic,
> The careless fruit of leisure hours,
> Sleeplessness, slight inspirations
> Of callow and long-faded years,
> The mind's chill observations
> And heartache's bitter tears.

The valedictory note to the work (8, XLIX) has a similarly flippant, or not unduly serious, air to it when it refers to the 'careless' lines ('Goodbye. Whatever you have sought of me / Here in these careless lines . . .'). No doubt such playfulness or flippancy hardly need emphasising. They are so natural to the work, so splendidly suited to its graceful precocity, so in keeping with the lilt of the four-foot iambic line (which no translation can ever adequately match), that they provide the natural climate for the proneness to digression and all the personal embroidery of comment and opinion with which Pushkin embellishes his story. Playfulness, flippancy, wit, youthful in their freshness though not always lighthearted in their manner, contribute to the stylistic tone and make it uniquely Pushkinian. It is the poet's charm which welcomes us into the work, his is the Sternian playfulness which holds up the action of his story for fifty stanzas (1, II-LII) while he tells of his hero's upbringing and life in St Petersburg, his are the flippancy, wit and regret which fill the passages of commentary.

Pushkin's relationship to his 'novel in verse' is authoritarian: he is its author and he does not pretend otherwise. It is equally clear that the characters whom he chose to portray and the story in which he involved them, like the form of the work, grew into their final shape by processes which he had not determined at the start. At the end of the first chapter he states that he has already thought about the form or plan for his work (1, LX), but it is likely that this refers only to the general concept of the 'novel in verse' as the story of a hero, Onegin, who leaves St Petersburg for the country and there meets the heroine, Tatyana. The final episode of the 'novel' had probably not been conceived. The penultimate stanza of Ch. 8 (written more than seven years later) virtually admits as much:

> Gone by are many, many days
> Since young Tatyana
> And Onegin with her in a darkling dream
> First came before me—
> And the far horizon of a free-ranging novel
> I could not through the magic crystal
> Clearly yet descry.

In much the same way, and with the utmost playfulness, he does not offer an introduction (*vstuplen'ye*) until the very end of Ch. 7. The form of the work, except in the loose sense of its having been conceived as a 'novel in verse', and the development of the hero and heroine do not, therefore, follow according to a plan but grow of their own volition and almost,

it would seem, in deliberate violation of formal canons. Pushkin played with the form of his work and with the story he was telling much in the way that Sterne played with *Tristram Shandy.* Shklovsky noticed this affinity [see excerpt dated 1923]. He went on to insist that Pushkin's playfulness involved his playing a kind of game with his characters: when Tatyana is in love with Onegin, Onegin is not in love with her, and when he falls in love with her she refuses him. Shklovsky concludes that 'the true subject-matter of *Eugene Onegin* is not the history of Onegin and Tatyana, but a game with this plot'—a conclusion which overemphasises the element of conscious parody in the work, though he is significantly right and evocative in his judgment of the work's experimental originality when he adds that 'the main content of the novel, the elements from which it is constructed, the form of its subject-matter are used much in the same way as are real objects in the paintings of Picasso'.

Two elements seem, despite Pushkin's parade of playfulness, to have a conditioning and disciplining effect on it. The first of these is the simple fact that it was composed in verse. The stanza form obviously establishes a prescribed pattern which Pushkin follows throughout with the exception of Tatyana's letter, the song of the peasant girls (Ch. 3) and Onegin's letter (Ch. 8). The rhythm of the verse gives a homogeneity to the work that is more consistent and pervasive in its effect than any other single identifiable characteristic, infinitely accommodating though it may be. Speaking of the form of Pushkin's stanza, John Bayley [see bibliography of Further Reading] brilliantly reconciles the seeming paradox of regularity and changeability inherent in it by saying: 'Its regularity holds endless permutations of tone, stress, and flow; and yet at the same time the unchanging metrical coordinates of its fourteen lines, rhyming *ababeecciddiff,* lead us with each verse to new contemplation and appraisal of what it achieves.' What it achieves, let it be said at once, is never sombre. It suggests a sprightliness and inherent vivacity even at those moments, particularly at the time of the duel and Lensky's death, when the words and images (e.g. Ch. 6, XXXII) are specifically intended to invoke solemnity. It is a rhythm primarily of the dance, not of the elegy or the ballad or the ode. It can encompass the full range of moods and manners from the pensive or philosophical to the most graceful and active. It achieves its greatest exactitude of effect when it is used for the description of movement, and there is no more startling example of such exactitude than in Ch. 1, XX when Onegin goes to the theatre. Immediately prior to his arrival at the theatre—he arrives late, of course—the ballerina Istomina has come on to the stage:

> The theatre's full; boxes glitter;
> Parterre and stalls—all loudly chatter.
> The Gods impatiently clap,
> And up goes the curtain with a swish.
> Resplendent and light as air,
> Obedient to the magic bow,
> Encircled by a host of nymphs,
> Istomina—alone she waits,
> Poised on one foot upon the stage,
> Then with the other slowly turns
> And quickly jumps, and quickly flies,
> Lightly as down upon Eolus' breath;
> And then she supply bends and weaves,
> And foot on foot she briskly strikes.

So dependent is this stanza for its effect on the rhythm, the verbs of motion in the last half-dozen lines and the onomatopoeia of the rhymes that translation can only offer a poor rendering. Still more difficult to convey is the visual exactitude of Istomina's movements in her dance.

The point is that such a dance rhythm is perceptible in every stanza of *Eugene Onegin.* It is what contributes to the unique stylistic tone which distinguishes the work as Pushkin's. But it has a conditioning effect, as does any kind of style, upon the work as a whole and in particular upon the story of Eugene Onegin's relationship with Tatyana Larina. For the story, in its essentials, resembles one movement in a dance. Onegin and Tatyana, the partners in the story-dance, face each other; Tatyana advances, Onegin withdraws; then, in completion of the movement, Onegin advances, Tatyana withdraws. The movements resemble those of figures on an eighteenth-century musical box. They are prescribed by the dance, predestined by it perhaps, and always governed by the musical-box mechanism which sets them in motion and ends their relationship when the formal cycle of the dance movement has run its course. The combination of dance rhythm and story-dance contributes to the remarkable organic wholeness of *Eugene Onegin.*

The second of the two elements which have a disciplining effect on the work is the attitude which Pushkin deliberately takes towards his characters and the story in which he involves them. Perhaps it is no more than narrative convention for Pushkin to claim, as already quoted:

> Gone by are many, many days
> Since young Tatyana
> And Onegin with her in a darkling dream
> First came before me.

The implication is that, with almost Olympian detachment, he *saw* his hero and heroine as people apart from himself and existing despite himself. The very opening of the work suggests this, with the first stanza of Ch. 1 devoted to the presumably unspoken thoughts of the hero who is first introduced to us in the second stanza. The hero, as it were, comes before the work itself, his thoughts come before he is introduced and his portrait is fully painted (in stanzas II-XLII of Ch. 1) before his story begins; and Pushkin's relationship to him is that of a biographer who was at one time his close friend and who is concerned to describe the most important episode in his life.

Pushkin's attitude to his hero may therefore be called 'objective'. A particular instance of this objectivity is to be found in 1, XLV when Pushkin, in the guise of personified narrator, describes how he made friends with Onegin. In the immediately following stanza he goes on to insist that Onegin is not a self-portrait in the Byronic manner. Throughout the novel Pushkin, as narrator and historical personage, withholds himself from the substance of his fiction, meaning the lives and story of his hero and heroine. Though Pushkin obviously plays a part in his novel, he retains as narrator and commentator a generally impartial attitude to his fiction and by so dissociating himself from it gives it an apparent validity in its own right.

None of which would have much value as comment on Pushkin's achievement were it not for the brilliance with which he has sustained the richness and intricacy of the poetry. Byronic influences fade into pointlessness when the splendour of Pushkin's work is fully acknowledged. Encyclopedic though it may be in its picture of Russian life, the work's claim to literary greatness rests largely on Pushkin's ability to suggest

in words the urban and rural aspects of Russian life. Here is a glimpse of a St Petersburg morning:

> And my Onegin? Half-asleep
> To bed he travels from the ball:
> While Petersburg, the restless place,
> Already wakens to a sound of drums.
> The merchant rises, the roundsman's on his way,
> A cabbie's off to the exchange,
> The milkmaid hurries with her jug,
> The morning snowfall crunching underfoot.
> Shutters are opened; chimney smoke
> Arises in light-blue plumes. (1, XXXV)

Or a picture of Moscow on Tatyana's arrival there from the country:

> Already the columns of the gates
> Shine white ahead; along Tver Street
> A sledge bumps through the ruts.
> Flash by streetmenders, womenfolk,
> Urchins, street stalls, lamps,
> Mansions, gardens, monasteries,
> Bokharans, sleigh-carts, vegetable plots,
> Merchants, hovels, peasantfolk,
> Boulevards and towers and cossack guards,
> Pharmacies and fashion shops
> Balconies and lions on gates
> And flocks of jackdaws on the crosses. (7, XXXVIII)

The details of such glimpses, for all their haphazard juxtaposition of items, evoke clearly enough the pungent sense of early morning in the first instance and the kaleidoscope of Moscow life in the other. Such vigour and concreteness in the words brought a remarkable sense of factuality to Pushkin's descriptions. But richer still are his cameos of rural life, at the coming, for instance, of the fateful snowfall not so long before Tatyana's nameday ball:

> In that year the autumn weather
> Stayed long upon the land.
> Winter was waited for, nature waited—
> Snow fell finally in January
> On the night of the third. Awaking early,
> Tatyana saw through the window
> The outside morning world all white,
> Flowerbeds and roofs and fences,
> Light tracery of frost on glass,
> Trees in a winter silver,
> Magpies enjoying themselves in the yard
> And hills so softly carpeted
> In winter's glistening covering.
> Everything around was bright, was white. (5, I)

Or the coming of spring in that same year, after Lensky's death and Onegin's departure:

> Driven by the rays of springtime,
> The snows from all surrounding hills
> Have run away in muddy streams
> Into low-lying flooded leas.
> With such translucent smiles does nature
> Greet out of sleep the year's new morning;
> Suffused in blue the heavens glitter.
> Still transparent, the woodlands
> Put on a green downiness of leaf.
> The bee in search of fieldfresh gold
> Flies from its waxen cell.
> The valleys dry and put on motley;
> The herds are lowing, and the nightingale
> Has sung already in the night-time quiet. (7, I)

The range of careful, detailed observation in both these pieces mirrors the range of Pushkin's powers, emphasises the lucidity and simple directness of his poet's eye, but notable in each case is the commonsense discipline of a viewpoint: the way in which, in the first instance, we can trace the gradual enlargement of Tatyana's field of vision from the immediate scene of flowerbeds, roofs and fences to the distance of the silvered trees and snow-covered hills; or, in the second, we see how those same snows are now vanished away, but *our* eye (for Tatyana's eye does not now guide us) sees first the distant scene and gradually, abetted by the poet's light underscoring (the 'smiles' of nature, the greeting of the year's morning), traverses the whole open, landscaped scene until the flight of the bee and, more particularly, the lowing of herds and night-time nightingales suggest our immediate vicinity, the sounds immediately around us. The effect of far and near is to give the work at such moments the appearance of a three-dimensional miniature. Verisimilitude is achieved by an act of miniaturisation which, though suggesting a replica, both delights by its faithfulness to detail and yet never quite succeeds in suggesting close-up. A very conscious distance is preserved between the reader and the cleverly scaled-down world of the fiction.

The first chapter opens with a stanza of soliloquy which initiates the action of the novel; but this action is retarded by the *deus ex machina* entrance of the narrator who introduces our mutual acquaintance, the hero, and then proceeds to outline the background scene. The establishment of Onegin in a particular background, and thus the establishment of his validity as a character, is achieved by a technique of documentation. We are given suitably selected facts, or factual details, such as place names, names of people (Istomina, Katenin, Chaadayev), allusions to Europeans famous at the time (Adam Smith, Rousseau, Grimm), lists of foods and wines, descriptions of the theatre, of Onegin's clothes and articles of toiletry, etc. In this way Onegin is provided with a two-fold documentation: his character is given perspective by the biographical details with which Pushkin is careful to introduce him and he is 'placed' in a particular society. A similar objectification of character occurs in Tatyana's case: she is documented not only by the biographical details of her life in the Larin family but also by such 'facts' as the books she reads and a mention of her pastimes. This method naturally sets the characters in their environments and yet by this means individuates them. Validity and authenticity of background provide for validity and authenticity of character: such is the principle behind Pushkin's method. It follows that it is Pushkin's aim to make his fiction appear to be a replica of history.

Moreover, the 'story' in which hero and heroine become involved can be seen to have its special chronology. Onegin probably 'flew in a postchaise through the dust' (1, II) to claim his inheritance from his dying uncle in May 1820. He was probably born in 1796, entered society in 1812, 'killed' eight years in St Petersburg society and left for the country in 1820. Chs. 2, 3 and 4 refer to events occurring during the summer, autumn and (partial) winter of that year. Chs. 5 and 6 are set in January 1821. Tatyana's nameday and ball probably occurred on January 12 and Lensky's death on January 14. Olga was presumably married to a hussar in the summer of 1821 and by the beginning of the next year Tatyana had been carried off to Moscow. She is married to her 'corpulent General' either at the end of 1822 or at the beginning of 1823. Onegin is meanwhile travelling and arrives back in St Petersburg at the beginning of the 1824-5 season. Ch. 8 is devoted to his experiences during that winter and to his last meeting

with Tatyana in the early spring of 1825. The chronological exactness of the novel's story is very striking: it is set in an historical time in an authentic context. The *length* of time occupied by the events—approximately five years, from the late spring of 1820 to the early spring of 1825—implies clearly enough that we are confronted by a chronicle in which events and human relationships may seem to develop without the author's agency and where there is no evidence of a guiding plot or intrigue. The fiction appears to be motivated by the assumption that, as time passes, situations and people change. The situations and personalities of the hero and heroine in 1825 must therefore differ in some significant way from what they were in 1820. The 'interest' of the work—one hesitates to use such an artificial term as plot—consists in detailing and exploring this process of development.

Despite the historicism implicit in this method, Pushkin deliberately embellishes his replica with decorative features which give it a resemblance to historical paintings in the neoclassical manner. Pensive dryads take refuge in the large neglected garden of Onegin's country estate (2, I), or country Priams drive out into the fields in spring (7, IV), just as the classical Muse leads Pushkin to hear the ceaseless whispering of the Nereids on the shores of the Crimea (8, IV). The classical allusions, of which there are so many instances, decorate the text like the classical statues which graced the buildings and walks of Tsarskoye Selo where Pushkin was educated. Although less purely decorative, Pushkin's commentary on his history serves to frame it, to give it topicality and the charm of personal comment. The topical references encompass such matters as the theatre, the use of foreign words or the poor state of Russian roads, while the more intimate forms of commentary touch on the charm of women's feet, the poet's concern with the fate of his own work or his regret at the fading of his youth. The autobiographical character of this strand of commentary is finally justified by the reference which Pushkin makes in the opening stanzas of Ch. 8 to his own upbringing and subsequent exile. All such commentary is digressive, naturally, but it is digressive in Laurence Sterne's sense: 'Though my digressions are all fair, as you observe—and that I fly off from what I am about, as far and as often too as any writer in Great Britain; yet I constantly take care to order affairs so, that my main business does not stand still in my absence.' (*Tristram Shandy*.) Although Pushkin digresses into his own commentary on the theatre (1, XVIII, XIX), Onegin arrives at the theatre in the author's absence. Pushkin digresses into autobiography at the beginning of Ch. 8, but meanwhile Onegin has been on his travels and has returned to St Petersburg.

The 'main business' is of course Eugene Onegin and his relationship with Tatyana. In this sense, the work is roughly divisible into sections comprising the hero's background and character (Ch. 1), the heroine's background and character (Ch. 2), the heroine's confession of love and the hero's rejection of her bold overture (Ch. 4). These are followed by the central climax of the story: Tatyana's nameday ball and the circumstances which provoke the young Lensky into challenging Onegin to a duel, in which Lensky is killed; after which Onegin departs on his travels (Chs. 5 and 6). Ch. 7 is a linkage which both reveals Tatyana's discovery of Onegin and gently shifts the emphasis of the fiction from hero to heroine; and Ch. 8 tells us how Onegin falls in love with Tatyana, only to be rejected by her at their final meeting. (pp. 10-21)

The enigma of Onegin has caused perennial debate. That Pushkin was depicting in him a phenomenon of his time is beyond doubt. In purely literary terms, his genesis may be said to go back to the figure of the Russian officer in his *Kavkazsky plennik* (*The Prisoner of the Caucasus*, 1822). 'I wanted to describe in him,' Pushkin wrote to Gorchakov (letter of October-November 1822), 'that indifference to life and all its pleasures, that premature ageing of the soul, which has become the distinguishing feature of the youth of the nineteenth century.' He failed in his object in *Kavkazsky plennik*, largely because he did not endow his hero with sensibly individual traits. The Prisoner is nameless, a poetic essay in the Byronic manner, having little if any relationship to the Russia of Pushkin's time. From the very moment when he embarked upon his new work, the 'novel in verse', it seems—judging from the many references in his letters—that he regarded it as devoted to a specific named individual: Onegin. It was a work intended to offer a specific portrait—far more specific than the figure of Aleko in *Tsygany* (*The Gypsies*)—of a type of individual who had been conditioned by the social and psychological pressures of an upbringing and life in a particular environment. In other words, Onegin can be taken as a typical example of St Petersburg society in the immediate post-Napoleonic period. His familiar world is the world of St Petersburg; all else—meaning in particular the rest of Russia—is unfamiliar to him. In such lack of familiarity lies his tragedy. But the typicality and the tragedy are separate. In so far as he is typical of the St Petersburg world, Onegin can be assumed to be recognisable as a type to his contemporaries—to Pushkin's readers, that is—and by that token identifiable as a portrait of a public type, a dandy and poseur, who might be said to exhibit in general terms 'that indifference to life and all its pleasures, that premature ageing of the soul' which Pushkin had tried to depict in his earlier portrayal.

If the 'novel in verse' were designed to be no more than a portrait of Onegin as a public type, it could well end at the moment when Onegin leaves for the country. But it is a work which, in the very rhythm of the verse—not to mention the pace of the opening—implies movement, both spatial and temporal, and processes of change and all those inevitable factors which contribute to the movement of peripeteia. Onegin may be typical in the setting of his St Petersburg world, but he is a 'typical exception' in his decision to leave that world. Because he is an exception he is destined for tragedy. He is exceptional in the very simple sense of being, as the second stanza of the novel clearly states introducing him:

> By the almighty will of Zeus
> The inheritor of all his kin.

The circumstance is opportune. His father having recently died with all his estates mortgaged, Onegin hands over what is left of his father's estate to his father's debtors in the expectation that an uncle of his, owner of extensive estates in the country, will shortly die. Since Onegin is the last in the Onegin line, it is not unnatural that his aged uncle, apparently without other descendants, should leave all his property to Onegin, his nephew. Onegin is already racing countrywards when we first meet him and he arrives in the country 50 stanzas later to find (to his relief) that his uncle is already dead. Even though he may actually leave St Petersburg because he cannot afford to stay there, he informs Pushkin, his 'biographer', that he has become bored by society life and seeks freedom. Russian 'spleen', or *khandra*, had taken its toll of him

and in a quasi-Byronic manner he looks to travel as a means of reviving his world-weary spirits.

On the fringes of Onegin's life, impinging no doubt only as playfully upon it as does Pushkin's commentary but framing it no less absolutely, is Fate. It is Fate, we are told, which preserved Onegin as a boy:

> Having served unusually nobly,
> His father lived in debtedness,
> Regularly gave three balls a year,
> And ended up in bankruptcy.
> Fate alone preserved Yevgeny . . .(1, III)

It is also Fate which separated Onegin from Pushkin (1, LI). In both instances Fate is identifiable with death; death separates him from his father and the death of his uncle separates him from Pushkin. Death accompanies Onegin in his life like Fate. The death of his uncle takes him into the country and the death of Lensky causes him to leave on his travels. Another but equally powerful aspect of Fate is the despotism of social custom ('*Obychai despot mezh lyudey*', 1, XXV). The observance of social custom dictates the habitual daily round of Onegin's life in St Petersburg. More than this: the despotism of social orthodoxy is an important as Fate, it would seem, in determining Onegin's character and his subsequent behaviour in the novel.

The effect of Fate in the context of social relations is both to condition man to the hierarchical structure and to emphasise the insignificance of his human individuality. In Ch. 2 these issues are presented as man's relationship either to such a human ideal as Napoleon or to such a superhuman notion as Providence. What Pushkin seems to touch on in this chapter is the whole question of heroism as a literary category. Onegin is represented as playing the role of Fate to the serfs on his newly inherited estates who 'blessed their Fate' (2, IV), when he replaced *barshchina* or *corvée* (compulsory labour) with the much lighter *obrok* or quit-rent payment system. By this unconventional act he no doubt deserved his local reputation as 'a most dangerous eccentric', but he could quote Adam Smith in justification. No matter how unsociable Onegin may seem to his neighbours, to the young poet Lensky he is condescending but friendly. The introduction of Lensky into the fiction is the point at which not only Onegin's image of himself, but also Pushkin's image of himself as poet, comes for the first time under close scrutiny in a contrast between innocence and maturity, youthful idealism and world-weary scepticism.

The ostensible friendship which springs up between Onegin and Lensky, whether or not it may have any basis in autobiographical fact, is qualified at the outset by the categorical Pushkinian stricture that friendship is impossible (see 2, XIV). Looked at without prejudice, human beings regard all other human beings as worthless; we alone are whole numbers; all of us aspire to be Napoleons, for whom the millions of two-legged creatures are simply our tools. Although Onegin was more tolerant than many, in general he despised humanity and to this extent conformed to the sceptically conventional view of mankind defined above. For his serfs, being their master, he played the role of Fate, just as conventions, social or otherwise, had their part to play in determining his own destiny, his view of mankind and his view of himself. He was exceptional only in having a high regard for certain people and in being able to respect another's feelings as he respected the feelings of the young Goettingen-educated Lensky.

It is clear that when he writes about Lensky Pushkin's tone verges on an amiable mockery that must in part be due to the mature poet's sceptical amusement at a likely younger—and much less talented—version of himself. The poet's cloudless innocence and romantic ingenuousness were originally, it seems, to have been given the hallmark of élitism, but Pushkin omitted lines in which he expanded on Lensky's belief in the 'chosen ones of Fate' (1, VIII). Where Lensky's view of humanity is pitifully exalted, Onegin's is callously cynical and Pushkin's view of his own creation unites scorn at its anachronism (for Lensky, whether as a 'romantic' poet or a version of the poet's younger self, is hardly timely) with fondness for this young man's vulnerability. Lensky's role in the novel is to be a victim—victim alike of Olga's spurious charms and Onegin's egoism, but chiefly victim of his own romantic illusions and perhaps also of Pushkin's part-regretful, part-sceptical abandonment of youthful idealism. His portrait, however delightful, is designed primarily to suggest the transience of all things human, just as his primary function in the novel is to be a means of transition from Onegin to the Larins.

Via Lensky, then, and Olga, his fiancée, we are introduced to Tatyana. She is both typical of her sheltered country world and an exception to it, as was Onegin to his. Formidably exceptional in her pensiveness, she renounced all playing with dolls, all embroidery, all playing at tag, but took delight (for want, one can only suppose, of television) in watching the rising sun from her balcony or, in winter, its setting (2, XXVIII). She was presumably typical of many other provincial young ladies of her age in her love of novels. After her fashion she was a book-worm, and it is through her reading, as it were, especially of Richardson, that we move by easy stages to her mother and her father and the domestic routines of their world. The yearly round of the Larin family matches the daily round of Onegin's life in St Petersburg society and helps to point up the fact that this chapter is as introductory as Ch. 1, offering in this case a picture of the country life of hero and heroine as the first chapter offered a picture of the urban life of the hero and his creator.

The final stanzas of the chapter, however, which comment on the death of Tatyana's father, Dmitry Larin, already hint at the tragedy of the human condition, the endless cyclic process by which in life's furrows the generations are harvested moment by moment, for through the mysterious will of Providence they arise and mature and fall, and others come to take their place (2, XXXVIII). The youthfully epicurean philosophy of the opening chapter is taken a stage further here by Pushkin's private view of life's vanity, its meaningless and its ephemeral character, to which he opposes, let it be noted, no Christian belief in the immortality of the soul. No God, certainly no all-merciful Creator, presides over Pushkin's world. The only immortality for which he can hope is that which his verses may obtain for him; the only God he offers to his characters in his fiction is that of Fate.

At the beginning of Ch. 3 Onegin accompanies Lensky on his visit to the Larins, there meets Tatyana, whom he at once prefers to the insipid Olga; and Tatyana instantly falls in love with him. Perhaps Onegin was originally intended to reciprocate the feeling. Conclusions were quickly drawn: everyone believed that Onegin was destined to be Tatyana's fiancé (*'Vsye stali tolkovat'* . . . '3, VI). She is given the role of Onegin's betrothed in everyone's gossip about her, much as Onegin himself was assumed by St Petersburg society to be a dandy and 'pedant'. With whom, though, does Tatyana fall in love? Having even less knowledge of Onegin's world than he has of hers, she can judge what he is or might be only through the heroes of the novels she has read. These fall into two categories. All the heroes of the romantic novels become fused for her into the figure of Onegin, even if he was really no Grandison (3, VIII, IX, X): it may also be assumed that Tatyana had read some of the Gothic horror novels 'which can disturb a young girl's sleep' (3, XII), though Vladimir Nabokov [see bibliography of Further Reading] argues that we should not identify Tatyana with this 'young girl' (*otrokovitsa*).

What happens at this point is that Onegin seems to assume in Tatyana's eyes a two-fold image which combines the heroic image of Romantic fiction with that of a modish tyrant. Pushkin connives at this ambivalence by feigning to shed tears over entrusting her Fate to a fashionable tyrant (3, XV). When she writes her letter to him, naïvely and impetuously confessing her love, she admits that she could never have given her heart to another, that her whole life has been a guarantee of her meeting with him, that all this has been willed for her by some higher power, that she has seen Onegin in her dreams, that, in other words, she is 'fated' to love him. Yet who is he?

> Who are you: my guardian angel,
> Or an insidious seducer?

She begs him to resolve her doubts. Even so, she commits her Fate to this enigmatic hero and begs for his protection. Because she is alone, misunderstood, intellectually unawakened, she appeals to him to respond to her heartfelt hopes and in her shame at having written such a confession she calls upon his sense of honour.

Added depth, even a kind of third dimension, has now been given to the characterisation through the way in which Onegin is presented from Tatyana's point of view. The shift in viewpoint is used sparingly, but it is telling in the specific sense that it accentuates the difference between hero and heroine and their misconceptions about each other. When the confrontation occurs, at the end of Ch. 3, after Tatyana has waited so anxiously for Onegin's reply, we notice that the drama of it is heightened when he is seen through her eyes as he stands in the pathway of the garden like some threatening apparition. The shift in viewpoint is suggested rather than stated. We witness the event like *voyeurs* at a cranny; and with the imagery of trapped butterfly and trembling hare in the penultimate stanza and Pushkin's deliberate curtailment of the scene at the chapter's end, there is no doubt that Onegin has acquired a sombreness of aspect, accompanied by suggestions of the demonic, which had not previously been his and which can only be satisfactorily explained by assuming that Tatyana projects her fearful anxieties into what she sees.

Pushkin carefully suggests this by introducing in the following chapter a brief emotional biography of Onegin (4, IX) which explains that he was clearly no Melmoth or vampire. Though he had fallen victim in his first youth to uncontrolled passions, his amorous affairs had soon begun to possess little more importance for him than any other kind of entertainment, such as an evening's whist. Social orthodoxy dictated as much: Onegin was 'pampered by life's customary usage' (*'privychkoy zhizni izbalovan'*), we are told. We are also told that Onegin was touched by Tatyana's letter, so that when they meet he matches like with like, making a perhaps rather sententious confession of his own, the gist of which is that he is not destined to know marital bliss, that her tears will not touch his heart but simply infuriate him, that he is gloomy, taciturn, irritable and prone to jealousy whereas she has a pure ardent soul, simplicity and intelligence—surely therefore Fate has not destined her for such a one as him. He admits to loving her like a brother, but she will probably exchange her present dreams for other dreams, as a tree changes its leaves each spring. Finally he urges upon her the need for self-control. Almost at once Pushkin makes the point, button-holing the reader as he does so, that this was not the first time Onegin had demonstrated the straightforward nobility of his soul.

There is irony in this remark as there is irony in the whole situation. Had not Tatyana forced the issue by writing her letter to Onegin, there would have been no reply and perhaps no story. Equally, had she not led such a sheltered life and become so affected by the potent images of her novels, she would not have fallen in love and written the letter. And Onegin, for his part, had he not killed eight years in society and thus wasted the finest flowering of his life (4, IX) would perhaps not have responded with such cold-hearted *hauteur* to the ardent Tatyana's confession. The ironic Pushkin now lightly insists that one should love only oneself; indulgent egoism is the only worthwhile emotion. Onegin at once illustrates these precepts by making summer bathing and autumnal wine-tastings with Lensky a substitute for happiness. He rejects Tatyana now, but will pine for her four chapters and four years later, when he sees her in St Petersburg. Now the happiness of love reciprocated is enjoyed only by Olga and Vladimir Lensky. The northern summer, that 'caricature of southern winters' (4, XL), as Pushkin reminds us, soon enough becomes autumn, until the turning of the year and the next chapter brings the snowfall of January; and the relationship between Onegin and Tatyana, brief enough by any standard, becomes frozen forever in a tragedy of misapprehensions.

With the coming of the snow, all the participants in the little drama can be seen to have become frozen into their particular roles and none can act, it would seem, in any but a preordained fashion. The crisis is precipitated by the one occasion in the work—Tatyana's nameday ball—when each of the major characters is obliged to make public demonstration, as it were, of their mutual exclusivity and incompatibility. Tatyana, alarmed by the portentous character of her dream, to which the dream-book of Martyn Zadeka can offer no clues (though Nabokov suggests otherwise), is obviously in a high state of nerves. The causes, then, of the ensuing events lie in Tatyana's failure to understand the true nature of Onegin, in Onegin's failure to come to terms with his environment, in Lensky's failure to make a balanced judgment, in Olga's failure to observe her duty to her betrothed. For all the apparently chance occurrence of these failures on this one occasion, they are obviously more than momentary aberrations.

It has to be assumed that Tatyana's rural upbringing, her limited knowledge of the world and her essential purity of heart are factors that make her incapable at this stage of understanding the real Onegin. So Onegin may be assumed to be mentally, morally and physically incapable of feeling himself part of the society into which he has been transplanted on the death of his uncle. Lensky's youth and romantically poetic nature would not allow him to see in Olga anything but the

most perfect example of womanhood: his judgment was entirely at the mercy of his idealistic illusions. Olga, it seems, was not naturally inclined to feel any profound sense of duty towards her betrothed, for soon after Lensky is killed, though she weeps a little, she is married off to a hussar. In their mutual failure of understanding, all four characters, but especially Onegin and Tatyana, contribute directly to the central moment of the novel's action, its central climax: the duel and the death of Lensky.

So Onegin, irritated by the sight of Tatyana's tears at the nameday feast, vows to have his revenge on the young Lensky who had persuaded him to attend, and he therefore makes a point of dancing with Olga. Lensky, deeply offended, leaves the ball early and the following day challenges Onegin to a duel. The duel occurs early the next morning. Throughout, what seems to matter most is public opinion, what other people think. Onegin blames himself for making light of young love, acknowledging that Lensky at eighteen could be forgiven for making a fool of himself, but public opinion, the social norm, will never forgive (6, X, XI). Lensky must die to prove the point. Instead of the conventional elegiac passages which might be expected on such an occasion. Pushkin, as if perhaps aware that his romantic young poet is anachronistic, muses on the likely futures awaiting the young man: a future of renown and immortality as a great national poet (6, XXXVII) or a future as a man who parted from the Muse, married, had children, contracted gout at forty and died finally in bed surrounded by children, tearful women and apothecaries. The youthful, the romantic ideal is contrasted with the mature, sceptical likelihood; both combine in this 'novel in verse' to form a pattern of 'prose in poetry' as closely woven as the texture of the verse. For what Pushkin suggests is that our lives follow conventions and that the 'they' who create such conventions behind the scenes—the gossip-mongers, the social law-givers—are the source of the tragedy. He makes this clear in lines omitted from the end of Ch. 6 where he explains what he means by the 'quagmire' of society in which he swims, as does everyone else (*V sem omute, gde s vami ya/Kupayus', miliye druz'ya!*). His romantic Lensky would no doubt have fallen victim to the conventional quagmire as did Pushkin himself.

The final two chapters reveal by their greater maturity of both style and content the true novelty and originality of Pushkin's enterprise in *Eugene Onegin.* The events are simple enough: Onegin leaves the district after Lensky's death and six months or so later Olga marries. Tatyana meanwhile, still obsessed by thoughts of Onegin, visits his house one evening. She knows that she must hate him as a murderer and yet she still cannot penetrate his enigma. She is a poor chorusfigure for the puzzled reader, though such puzzlement is largely of her own making. She begins to understand on her second visit to Onegin's house a little of his pose (we assume it is mostly guesswork on her part, because she is not allowed to see Onegin's *Album*) but whether he is a melancholy and dangerous eccentric, a creation of heaven or hell, an angel or a scheming devil, an imitation, a Moscovite in Childe Harold's Cloak or a parody she cannot tell: she does not find the *right word* for him (7, XXIV, XXV). Solitary, apparently uncomprehending, less affected, it seems, by Lensky's death than by Onegin's departure yet fundamentally unmoved by either, as pensively devoted to nature now as she was before Onegin's arrival, she disregards the social norm and accepts only the conformity of personal conscience. She is taken off to Moscow, and in the final stanza of Ch. 7 Pushkin congratulates his heroine on her conquest.

The rise to dominance of Tatyana in the novel is marked by an accompanying increase of nostalgia and regret in the tone of Pushkin's commentary. We have to assume, no matter how remote as readers we may seem to be from access to her thoughts, that Tatyana changes, if only through growing wiser, in her transference from the country to the capital. The commentary at the opening of Ch. 8 suggests clearly enough both how greatly Pushkin himself may seem to have changed in the course of his seven-year travail over his work and how closely he now identifies his much-travelled Muse with his metamorphosed heroine (8, V, VI), even though his Muse is the more adaptable of the two. Tatyana, like his own youth, is now more than ever precious to the poet; Onegin, on the contrary, though equally an aspect of the poet's past, is faintly mocked as out-dated in his modishness (8, VIII) and finally categorised by the commentary as immature:

> Blessed he who in youth was young,
> Blessed he who in due time matured,
> Who gradually the cold of life
> Learned with the years to endure. (8, X)

> But sad it is to think that vainly
> Was youthfulness once given us,
> That we've betrayed it hour by hour,
> That it has quite deceived us;
> That all our fondest wishes,
> That our fresh young dreams,
> Have perished in quick succession
> Like leaves that fall and rot in autumn. (8, XI)

Pushkin's regret at such wasted youth leads almost immediately into the condemnation of Onegin:

> Onegin (again I take him up),
> Killing his friend in a duel,
> Living without aim, without effort
> To the age of twenty-six,
> Languishing in idle ease
> Workless, wifeless, unoccupied,
> Was Onegin: good-for-nothing. (8, XII)

A tone of gentle mockery surrounds the Onegin of the novel's final chapter and contrasts with the fond, stately magniloquence which characterises all that Tatyana does and says. Though so silent until the last chapter she achieves a quite startlingly dominant presence in the fiction. Her pensiveness gives her whole character bell-like resonances of memory and experience that echo back to her own country girlhood. Simultaneously she acquires a universal appeal which removes her beyond the confines of her specific Russian background. She has the strange allure of someone permanently innocent who naturally shows up the idle sophistications and pretensions of maturity. As Belinsky pointed out, she understands and knows herself as little as she knows and understands Onegin, and though she discovers that Onegin is not what she first imagined him to be she never relinquishes that unselfconsciousness which is the key to her purity and completeness as a literary image [see *NCLC,* Vol. 3, pp. 417-21]. This image we find mirrored in the heroines of Turgenev, but, as if in its coming of age a literature must inevitably become self-conscious, the later images are all flawed by conscious straining towards such an ideal. The effect of such straining can be clearly seen in the souring of the Romantic ideal of innocence which occurs in an Oblomov or a Myshkin. In these heroes the innocence becomes inseparable from a state of retarded

development. It has little in common with the spontaneous, assertive virtue of Tatyana which unselfconsciously proclaims its ideal in *Eugene Onegin* and finds its purest reflection in later literature in the corporate principle governing the instinctive Rostov view of the world in *War and Peace.*

Returning to St Petersburg, Onegin discovers Tatyana is the wife of his former friend, the corpulent General. We do not really know why Onegin should have gone on his travels; perhaps he had never intended to do more than spend a winter on his uncle's estates before embarking on his tour of Russia in the spring of the year that Lensky dies; it is unclear why he should spend three-and-a-half years on going such relatively short distances. On the principle that travel broadens the mind, he is presumably a trifle wiser, or perhaps absence from the *beau monde* of St Petersburg has made him emotionally more susceptible. Whatever the reason, he falls passionately in love with Tatyana—not with the Tatyana whom he had rejected earlier but with the imperious, remote beauty in to whom she has been transformed by her marriage and the sumptuous surroundings of the imperial capital. Pushkin carefully underlines the moral that, like Eve, all people wish for what they have not got—unless they have the forbidden fruit, paradise is not paradise for them (8, XXVII).

Although surrounded in St Petersburg by the social throng, Tatyana remains as ever a solitary, temperamentally remote from the *beau monde* as she is morally above it. Her reaction therefore to Onegin's love for her, sympathetic and understanding though it may be, is tinged with anger (8, XXXIII). He demeans himself in her eyes by such a display of passion for her. In their last encounter the most pointed of the things she says—and this is the only time she speaks to Onegin, so far as we know, during the entire work—is contained in the rhetorical assertion that her shame in succumbing to his advances would surely be noticed by all and would lend Onegin a certain alluring esteem in the eyes of society. How can he, a man of such heart and intellect, be slave to such a shallow feeling? (8, XLIV, XLV)

What she appeals to in him, and what she upholds in herself, is a morality that transcends convention. Her final words are a statement of her moral duty, in that Fate has ordained she should be given to another, to whom she will be faithful for the rest of her life. The triteness of these sentiments should not be allowed to obscure the declaration of private morality which the words clearly express. It has to be assumed that Tatyana is the touchstone of true moral good sense by which the moral worth of the hero is to be judged. Both may be caught in the toils of that Fate which is reality itself, or so Belinsky would have us believe, surrounding both hero and heroine like the air they breathe, but what is most real in terms of human experience in the whole of *Eugene Onegin* is this moment when Tatyana, though she loves him deeply, feels in duty bound to reject Onegin's love for her and all possibility of their mutual happiness. The experience is essentially private, between private individuals; it is not comprehensible, we must assume, in terms of *beau monde* morality, nor is it explicable in terms of the differing social backgrounds which initially give rise to the tragedy of misapprehensions. Tatyana at least is capable of understanding Onegin and makes a conscious act of rejection which she may justify by referring to Fate but cannot mitigate. She has said: No. The finality of that negative at this dramatic moment cuts her off from her past, precludes future hope, annihilates happiness and upholds a solitary moral right that defies social casuistry and all temporisings of the conscience.

The final scene of the meeting between Onegin and Tatyana has a psychological and dramatic profundity which is to serve as a model for all future developments in the Russian novel. Relying little in construction on coincidence or plot, the Russian novel, in its greatest examples, is a form designed to enact a situation, a particular scene, a present dramatic immediacy in which the lives and spirits of human beings are suddenly penetrated, illuminated and laid bare. Pechorin's discovery of himself, Chichikov's ultimate discomfiture, the meaning of Oblomov's dream, Raskolnikov's disenchantment, Andrey Bolkonsky's knowledge of love in death, Pierre Bezukhov's discovery of God in life are all offered to us as moments of revelation when the meaning of each life is dramatically illuminated. The history of the evolution of the Russian nineteenth-century novel may be seen as an ever deeper penetration into the privacy of human experience or an ever greater intrusion in to the intimacies of private rooms. There is always a clear opposition between public and private areas of experience, but there is also an equally clear assumption that, though the areas interpenetrate, the public facade requires to be known before the private life can be revealed. In each case the private dilemma mirrors the divisiveness of society; in each case it asserts its independence of social causes. We leave Onegin at the moment when his irrelevance to society is a great deal less real to him than his irrelevance to Tatyana; whether or not he is superfluous in social terms matters less than his private failure to transcend the conventional *comme il faut* of the St Petersburg world where he and Tatyana confront each other as equals. What Tatyana asserts—and what other heroes and heroines of the Russian novel will assert—is the privacy of conscience, the singularity of all moral awareness and certitude, the discovery of the single, unique moral self which opposes and withstands the factitious morality of the mass, of society, humanity or the general good. (pp. 23-37)

> *Richard Freeborn, " 'Eugene Onegin','' in his* The Rise of the Russian Novel: Studies in the Russian Novel from "Eugene Onegin" to "War and Peace", *Cambridge at the University Press, 1973, pp. 10-37.*

J. DOUGLAS CLAYTON (essay date 1975)

[*In the following essay, Clayton studies Pushkin's use of imagery in* Eugene Onegin *and compares the novel to William Shakespeare's* A Midsummer Night's Dream.]

Much of the critical debate in the Soviet Union concerning Pushkin's *Eugene Onegin* has in recent years centred on the propagation of the view that this verse novel represents a shift in the development of the author towards realism. It seems to me that because of the polemical force of this position, certain aspects of the work as a poetic statement, of the poem *qua* poem, have been neglected. It is my purpose in this study to refocus attention back on these aspects, emphasizing certain poetic devices which Pushkin develops into a subtle and suggestive pattern. What follows is based on the premise that Pushkin's use of detail is by no means accidental, and that the detail in *Eugene Onegin* is elaborated into a complex web of correspondences and associations which serve to deepen and enrich the poetic statement.

The first of these aspects which merits our attention is the recurrent use of certain colours and associated floral imagery,

notably the red and white which interplay in the descriptions of Ol'ga and Tat'iana. As they are originally presented, Ol'ga is the red-cheeked sister whose colour is contrasted with Tat'iana's pallor. Of Tat'iana the poet writes: "Neither with her sister's beauty / nor with her sister's rosy freshness / would she attract one's eye." This association of pallor with the young Tat'iana is reinforced by the recurrent emblems of pallor which surround her: stars, candles, snow, mist, a pale horizon, the silvery pre-dawn light, but most of all the moon. In his initial description of the heroine, the poet contrives to combine most of these elements in a single passage:

> She on the balcony
> liked to prevene Aurora's rise,
> when, in the pale sky, disappears
> the choral dance of stars,
> and earth's rim softly lightens,
> and, morning's herald, the wind whiffs,
> and rises by degrees the day.
> In winter, when night's shade
> possesses longer half the world,
> and longer in the idle stillness,
> by the bemisted moon,
> the lazy orient sleeps,
> awakened at her customary hour
> she would get up by candles.
>
> (Two: XXVIII: 1-14)

Such is the initial description of Tat'iana given by the poet, prior to her love for Eugene. The whiteness of her countenance and the emblems which surround her bespeak purity and chastity. Hence we are not surprised when her role in the novel turns out to be that of the chaste heroine, faithful to her husband.

There is, however, one point in the novel where this chastity is placed in jeopardy, namely the point where Tat'iana falls in love with Onegin and sends him her letter. It is significant that this event brings a sharp change from the emblems of pallor to those of fire, suggestive of passion. These fire emblems are introduced in Chapter Three:

> The time had come—she fell in love.
> Thus, dropped into the earth, a seed
> is quickened by the fire of spring.
>
> (Three: VII: 6-8)

By implication the "fire of spring" is preceded by the snows of winter, i.e., the chastity of maidenhood. Similarly, in the previously quoted passage, where Tat'iana rises before the dawn, an alternation takes place: pre-dawn whiteness/redness of dawn. Thus the development of passion in the chaste Tat'iana is paralleled by a like progression in the imagery.

The emblems of fire which surround Tat'iana and signal her passion for Onegin are confined to Chapters Three and Four, reaching a climax in the scene where she seals the letter to Onegin:

> By turns Tat'iana sighs and ohs.
> The letter trembles in her hand;
> the rosy wafer dries
> upon her fevered tongue.
> Her poor head shoulderward has sunk;
> her light chemise
> has slid down from her charming shoulder.
> But now the moonbeam's radiance
> already fades. Anon the valley
> grows through the vapor clear. Anon the stream
> starts silvering. Anon the herdsman's horn

wakes up the villager.
Here's morning; all have risen long ago:
to my Tat'iana it is all the same.

(Three: XXXII: 1-14)

This scene is a conscious modification by the poet of the previously quoted passage on the balcony. The emblems of passion—inflamed tongue and rose-coloured wafer—are supplanted towards the end of the stanza by the wonted symbols of pallor. In this case no mention is made of the dawn, since its redness would disturb the impression sought by the poet of the fading of a passionate impulse in the cold pre-dawn light.

The passion smoulders on after Tat'iana's interview with Onegin in the garden, but the poet suggests, likewise, the return of the pallor:

Nay poor Tat'iana more intensely
with joyless passion burns . . .
Alas Tat'iana fades away,
grows pale, is wasting, and is mute!

(Four XXIII: 6-7, XXIV: 1-2)

It is this customarily pale Tat'iana who persists throughout the rest of the book. The dying echoes of the colour theme are to be found in Chapter Eight, where Tat'iana turns neither pale nor red at the sight of Onegin (Eight: XIX) although in the last scene Onegin finds her "unadorned, pale," (Eight: XL: 11), a suitable guise for the wrenching finale,

Pushkin's sketch for the first chapter of Eugene Onegin.

where chastity prevails and Onegin's proffer of love is rejected.

Thus the colours red and white are both used emblematically in connection with Tat'iana to denote the interplay of passion and virtue in her. The same colours are also used in the portrayal of her sister Ol'ga, where they serve rather different purposes. As we have seen in the passage where the two sisters are introduced to the reader for the first time, their complexions are contrasted: Ol'ga is red-cheeked, whereas Tat'iana is pale. From this initial association of ruddiness with Ol'ga, we may conclude that her nature is more lusty, and that her attitude towards the opposite sex less constant and timid than that of her sister. It therefore comes as no surprise when Ol'ga, a few months after the death of her fiancé, marries a hussar. Indeed, by indulging in the flirtation with Onegin at the name-day party, Ol'ga actually provokes the quarrel which leads to Lenskii's death. On this occasion too her face is flushed with (sexual) excitement:

and bright glows
on her conceited face
the rosy flush.

(Five: XLIV: 8-10)

Ol'ga is constrained to blush again at the end of Tat'iana's dream:

Ol'ga flits in to her
rosier than Northern Aurora
and lighter than a swallow.

(Five: XXI: 10-12)

Like Tat'iana, Ol'ga had tried to dream about her future husband. The reader is left to speculate on the exact cause of the flush on her face when she awakes, but no doubt some kind of sexual excitement is again implied.

In this context it is instructive to note the association of floral imagery with Ol'ga as she is perceived by her parents and by Lenskii:

She under the eyes of her parents
bloomed like a hidden lily-of-the-valley
which is unknown in the dense grass
to butterflies or to the bee.

(Two: XXI: 11-14)

This flower/butterfly image is recalled in a digression on Lenskii's happiness over his impending marriage to Ol'ga:

Blest hundredfold is he who is devoted
to faith; who . . .
in the heart's mollitude reposes . . .
as a butterfly
absorbed in a spring flower.

(Four: LI: 3-8)

Important here is the whiteness of the lily-of-the-valley, connoting a rustic version of that chastity represented by the haughty lily, and also the passivity of the flower, which accepts equally the attentions of moth and bee. While the whiteness of the flower is a conventional expression of that purity which Lenskii and Ol'ga's parents see in her, the different visitors which the flower entertains are a sly hint by Pushkin that Lenskii's view is not entirely correct: she is equally amenable to the attentions of Lenskii, Onegin, or a certain hussar. This floral imagery is resumed in the justification which Lenskii makes for his impending duel with Onegin:

I shall not

. . . let a despicable, venomous
worm gnaw a lily's little stalk,
nor have a blossom two morns old
wither while yet half grown.

(Six: XVII: 6, 9-12)

Lenskii here exalts Ol'ga from lily-of-the-valley to pure lily, but the connotations of chastity are equally clear. As it turns out, he is fatally wrong. It is Ol'ga's lack of chastity and constancy which lead him to his death. The whole point of Lenskii is that the view of life which he expresses in his poetry is totally conventional. His description of his "muse" Ol'ga as a pure lily, as a faithful maid who will visit his urn (Six: XXII: 6-14), is remote from the reality of the flirtatious, easily aroused, inconstant girl which Ol'ga really is.

Thus it can be seen that the alternations of red and white in the complexions of Tat'iana and Ol'ga and the associated floral imagery are not haphazard, but correspond to the design of the novel as a whole, and modify it. Tat'iana's face is only enflamed with passion during the height of her infatuation for Onegin in Chapters Three and Four. Otherwise, the pallor of chastity is her emblem. Ol'ga, on the other hand, is a red-cheeked girl who appears several times before the reader with a flush of sexual excitement on her face, and who proves to be far from constant in her affections despite the wishful comparison of her by her parents and Lenskii to the floral emblems of chastity.

Corresponding to the floral emblems associated with Ol'ga is a set of animal images which Pushkin uses to describe Tat'iana. Whereas Ol'ga is seen as a flower, blooming and willingly yielding its secrets to those that wander its way, Tat'iana is seen as a timid doe. Thus, in giving his initial characterization of his heroine in Chapter Two, the poet calls her "Sauvage, sad, silent, / as timid as the sylvan doe" (Two: XXV: 5-6). The comparison is repeated in the scene where Onegin sits down opposite Tat'iana on her name-day. Here she is "more tremulous than the hunted doe" (Five: XXX: 3). In addition to these overt comparisons, there are two more passages where the image of the hunted animal is recalled in connection with Tat'iana. Firstly there is the scene in Chapter Three where, having heard Onegin's horse entering the yard, Tat'iana rushes through the garden to escape him. The long list of obstacles which she circumnavigates—flowerbeds, alley, copse—suggests the speed of her flight. When she reaches the supposed sanctuary of the bench, she stops and tries to compose herself, half-fearful, but also, one suspects, half-hopeful that Onegin may appear. The doe image is recalled in the nature of her flight past the obstacles, and by the way she bursts through the thicket of lilac: "she breaks the lilac bushes as she flies" (Three: XXXVIII: 12). The image is pleasantly modulated by the comparison of her to a hunted hare:

. . . thus
a small hare trembles in the winter corn
upon suddenly seeing from afar
the shotman in the bushes crouch.

(Three: XL: 12-14)

The second passage is the first part of Tat'iana's dream, in which the image is transposed onto a winter landscape. Here Tat'iana resembles a hunted creature as she struggles through thickets and snowdrifts, pursued by the bear.

If Tat'iana is the timid doe, the prey, then Onegin is the hunter. This is suggested, at least, by the imagery of the first chase

through the garden. Yet despite her fears, Onegin does not pursue Tat'iana at this point, being only interested in her after her marriage to Prince N. The reason for this lies in a further development of the hunt imagery associated with husbands and marriage. In a chapter entitled "Amur i Gimenei" of his book *O Pushkine*, V. Khodasevich examines Pushkin's general attitude towards marriage and marital constancy. He writes: "Educated in the literary traditions of the 'gallant century,' Pushkin almost from childhood developed a sympathetic attitude towards 'lovers,' and a contemptuous one towards 'husbands'." Indications of such an attitude abound in *Eugene Onegin*. Thus, we learn of the relations between Onegin and husbands:

But you, blest husbands,
you remained friends with him:
him petted the sly spouse,
Faublas' disciple of long standing,
and the distrustful oldster
and the majestic cornuto . . .

(One: XII: 7-12)

Significantly, it is after the death of Lenskii that the author chooses to expound on Onegin's pleasure in the art of cuckolding:

With an insolent epigram
'tis pleasant to enrage a bungling foe;
pleasant to see how, bending stubbornly
his buttsome horns, he in the mirror
looks at himself involuntarily
and is ashamed to recognize himself . . .
Still pleasanter—in silence to prepare
an honorable grave for him . . .

(Six: XXXIII: 1-10)

Onegin appears interested less in seducing wives than in cuckolding husbands. It is the "sight" of a husband wearing the horns—time-honoured emblem of cuckoldry—which gives him pleasure. The horns, or antlers, of the betrayed husband appear as the symbol of this pleasure at strategic places throughout the poem.

From this we may deduce an instructive irony in the likening of Tat'iana to a "doe." She is afraid of Onegin, because she loves him and because she realizes her vulnerability, should he choose to "hunt" her, but in fact he is not interested in her because she is not married and therefore has no husband to cuckold. Only when he sees her after her marriage to Prince N is he attracted to her—perhaps by the possibility of cuckolding her husband. (In fact, of course, Pushkin creates a further irony here, for Onegin really does love her, but is forced to act out the role of the unsuccessful seducer—of a woman he could have married. The change in Tat'iana, from the timid doe, the "prey," into a woman able to resist the huntsman and thus save her husband from the "antlers," this change is the crucial element in the ironical dénouement.)

Thus the novel is based on a sexual hunt, with wives as the does, husbands as the stags, and single men such as Onegin as the hunters. It is a hunt which leads to the destruction of the chastity of the wife and the integrity of the marriage, if not to the physical destruction of the husband in a duel. In the first seven chapters of the poem, it is Lenskii, not Tat'iana or her husband, who is the object of the hunt, as far as Onegin is concerned. We recall that, in the elegy addressed, apparently, to Ol'ga, which Lenskii writes on the eve of the duel, he declares: "I'm thy spouse!" (Six: XXII: 14). We have also noted above that the stanza in which Pushkin describes the pleasures of cuckoldry is placed immediately after the depiction of the duel and is inspired by Lenskii's fate. Clearly, to Onegin, as to Pushkin, Lenskii is a husband to be aroused by some piece of arrogance and then destroyed. The impression that Lenskii, arrayed in his mind's eye in a set of antlers, is being hunted by Onegin, is reinforced by the imagery which Lenskii uses in his elegy: "Whether I fall, pierced by the dart, or whether / it flies by—all is right" (Six: XXI: 9-11). The hunting image of the arrow finds a gloomy echo in the simile used to characterize the speed of the horses bearing Lenskii's body home: "and like an arrow off they fly" (Six: XXXV: 14).

Behind the sets of colour, flower, animal and hunt images which we have traced in *Eugene Onegin,* there is another set of "icons" which must be examined for their role as an element of embroidery and enrichment, namely the series of allusions to the classical deities which adorn the work. The most notable of these arises from the association of Tat'iana with the moon. Her very pallor appears to be a reflection of the moon that reigns over her most of the times that she appears before us. For example, it is the moon that watches when she writes to Onegin. As the fateful night begins, the moon appears: "Night comes, the moon / patrols the distant vault of heaven" (Three: XVI: 8). Then, when her old nurse goes away: "all's still. The moon gives light to her" (Three: XXI: 8). Only after she seals the letter to Onegin does the moon, that has seemed to inspire such "lunacy" in the young girl, fade: "But now the moonbeam's radiance / already fades" (Three: XXXII: 8-9). In this scene Tat'iana truly seems possessed by the moon, almost as if in a trance. The lunar associations are echoed in Chapter Five, where the superstitions of the country village lend force to our image of a girl possessed:

> Seeing all at once
> the young two-horned moon's visage
> in the sky on her left,
> she trembled and grew pale.
>
> (Five: V: 12-VI: 1)

> Tatiana . . .
> . . . trains a mirror on the moon,
> but in the dark glass only
> the sad moon trembles. . . .
>
> (Five: IX: 4-8)

The role of the moon in the fate of Tat'iana appears crucial. She is captured in the moon's spell in an enchanted world from which she will only escape through the death of Lenskii and Onegin's departure. The lines "Réveillez-vous, belle endormie" (Five: XXVII: 8) have more than a passing significance in the light of this.

An important hint as to how we are to interpret this power of the moon is found in one description of Tat'iana:

> Alone, sadly by Dian's beam
> illumined at the window, poor Tat'iana
> is not asleep
> and gazes out on the dark field.
>
> (Six: II: 11-14)

The moon, Pushkin reminds us, is the emblem of Diana, goddess of both hunting and chastity. The mention of Diana in this context also calls to mind a line in the poem where the poet, concerning his preferences in females, refers to "Diana's bosom, Flora's cheeks" (One: XXXII: 1). The whiteness of Diana's breast is associated with Tat'iana, while Flora's rosy cheeks remind us of Ol'ga and the floral imagery connected

with her. Thus the line seems to sum up the contrast between the two sisters.

From this discussion it can be seen that the poem is saturated with iconographic references and emblems which fit into a total significative pattern and serve to enrich the poetic statement. The question of the source of these icons and emblems is one which clearly requires exhaustive scrutiny. The classical origin (via Western European literature) of much of them—e.g., the references to the goddesses—is apparent, although there may also be Russian folklore elements involved, perhaps in the attention given to the moon, and the tradition of characters turning into animals (Tat'iana's dream) which we find as early as the *Lay of Igor's Campaign.* The highly original and systematic use of the emblems, especially the hunt/moon/Diana/chastity set must surely be an expression of Pushkin's poetic genius.

Although it is not feasible to enter here into a detailed commentary on the possible sources of Pushkin's emblems in *Eugene Onegin,* it does seem appropriate to evaluate the possible traces of the reading of one literary work which has never been discussed in relation to the poem, and which may be added to the list of literary sources used by the poet in its making. The work in question is Shakespeare's *Midsummer-Night's Dream.*

On the question of the earliest reading by Pushkin of Shakespeare, Alekseev writes: "Unfortunately we do not know and are hardly likely to establish in the future the sequence of Pushkin's acquaintance with the works of Shakespeare in the years 1824-25. We can only guess that by this time Pushkin had already managed to study not only all the basic plays of Shakespeare, but also his poems and perhaps even the sonnets." Thus even if Pushkin had come to *Midsummer-Night's Dream* at a comparatively late time, it could still have had an influence on the evolution of *Eugene Onegin,* written between 1823 and 1831. That Pushkin was very taken up by the Shakespeare play is indicated by the fact that he later advised Vel'tman to adapt it as an opera, advice which Vel'tman carried out. Iu. D. Levin comments: "The great poet Pushkin dreamed of the creation of a brilliant, enchanting, fantastic opera based on the Shakespearean comedy." One is reminded by this remark of the gay theatrical scenes in Chapter One of *Eugene Onegin.*

There are a number of features which *Midsummer-Night's Dream* and *Eugene Onegin* have in common. Firstly, there is the situation of the "crossed lovers." At the beginning of the play, both Lysander and Demetrius love Hermia. The love of Hermia for Lysander and Helena for Demetrius indicate, however, the "ideal" coupling with which the play will end. The effect of Puck's magic is to have both Lysander and Demetrius fall in love with Helena, bringing a confrontation which almost leads to a duel:

> *Lysander:* Hélène, je t'aime; sur ma vie, je t'aime; je jure sur ma vie, que je veux perdre pour toi, de convaincre de mensonge celui qui osera dire que je ne t'aime pas.
>
> *Demetrius,* to Helena: Je te proteste que je t'aime plus qu'il ne peut t'aimer.
>
> *Lysander:* Si tu parles ainsi, retirons-nous, et prouve-le-moi.

A comparable "crossed lovers" situation is found in *Eugene Onegin,* when Onegin courts Ol'ga at the name-day party, breaking the Onegin-Tat'iana, Lenskii-Ol'ga pattern. The difference is that in the poem a duel does indeed result from the mismatch, and the ideal coupling is never achieved. Similarly, whereas the forced marriage of Hermia against her will to Demetrius is averted, the marriage of Tat'iana to the general becomes a reality which prevents her eventual ideal coupling with Onegin. Shakespeare manipulates his plot to avert the threatened tragedy, while Pushkin precipitates the tragedy of the forced marriage. One might say that the pattern in *Eugene Onegin* is contrapuntal to that in *Midsummer-Night's Dream:* when the characters awake in the latter, all is resolved; when Tat'iana awakes from the spell of Diana, she has to face the sobering reality of an arranged marriage.

Another important feature in both works is the dream motif. As has already been noted, Tat'iana acts in her love for Onegin as if in a trance or dream. Thus, she writes in her letter to Onegin: "revive / my heart's hopes with a single look / or interrupt the heavy dream" (Three: Tat'iana's letter: 72-74). The dream is, likewise, the central device in *Midsummer-Night's Dream,* and, like Tat'iana, the lovers—Hermia, Helena, Demetrius, and Lysander, as well as Titania—are forced to do strange things in the "dream" reality. The similarity is reinforced when we realize that Triquet's words "Réveillez-vous, belle endormie . . . belle Tatiana" (Five: XXVII: 8, 14) echo closely those of Puck: "Allons, ma chère Titania; éveillez-vous, ma douce reine." The dream device is focused in *Eugene Onegin* in Tat'iana's dream in Chapter Five, which contains certain elements reminiscent of *Midsummer-Night's Dream.* Thus, the pursuit of Tat'iana by a bear, and the quasi-human monsters in the hut recall the transformation of Bottom, and the threatened mating of the heroine with an animal: Tat'iana with the bear, and Titania with Bottom. Similarly, the panic-stricken flight of Tat'iana from the bear recalls Hermia's plight as she seeks Lysander:

> Jamais je ne fus si lasse, jamais je ne fus si désespérée: déchirée par les ronces, je ne peux ni aller, ni me traîner plus loin: mes jambes ne peuvent suivre le pas de mes désirs.

Tat'iana, too, is overcome by this lassitude (Five: XIV). There is another similar flight in *Midsummer-Night's Dream* when Thisbe flees from a lion:

> Cette terrible bête, qui, de son nom, s'appelle un lion, fit reculer, ou plutôt épouvanta la fidèle Thisbé venant dans l'ombre de la nuit; et en fuyant, elle laissa tomber son manteau.

Beyond the resemblance of these devices, one is struck by the similarity of the iconological references and imagery in the two works. Although, as Pushkin himself points out (Two: XXIV), "Tat'iana" is an old Russian name, one is tempted to believe that he was led to choose the name partly for its similarity to Titania, especially because Titania is one of the names given to Diana. The association of Diana with chastity is specifically referred to in *Midsummer-Night's Dream.* Theseus, for example, offers Hermia the option "ou bien à épouser Démétrius, comme il le désire; ou enfin à prononcer, sur l'autel de Diane, le voeu qui consacre à une vie austère et à la virginité." The reference to Diana is reinforced by numerous mentions of the moon. For example, in Act III, Scene I, Quince and Bottom and Snug discuss the need to have the moon shine in through the window as they enact their playlet. Likewise, the image of the moon shining in the window on Tat'iana fascinated Pushkin. It occurs in Chapter Three (XXXII), and a picture of the scene drawn by Pushkin is

found in the manuscript. In Act III, Scene I, Titania makes explicit the association of the moon with chastity:

> La lune paraît nous regarder d'un oeil humide; et lorsqu'elle pleure, les petites fleurs pleurent aussi et regrettent quelque virginité violée.

In Act V, Scene I, the remark by Moonshine "Cette lanterne vous représente la lune et ses cornes" and Demetrius' reply "il aurait dû porter les cornes sur sa tête" seem to point to the mention of the "two-horned moon's visage" (Five: V: 13) and the numerous references to the antlers as the symbol of cuckoldry in *Eugene Onegin.*

The cumulative effect of the similarities enumerated suggests that *Midsummer-Night's Dream* was a considerable source of poetic inspiration for Pushkin in the creation of *Eugene Onegin.* The principal borrowings appear to be the Diana/moon/chastity complex, the role of the dream in the poem, and the human-to-animal transformation, as well as certain minor poetic details. Structurally, the poem may also owe to Shakespeare the shift of attention from the upper to the lower classes—from the fate of Tat'iana, Ol'ga, Onegin, and Lenskii to the images of the peasant girls picking berries, Tat'iana's old nurse, and other mentions of the peasantry. However, unlike Shakespeare, Pushkin does not weave these images of the lower classes into an independent subplot (Bottom, Snug, Quince). As usual, he took from his literary sources those elements which served his purpose, but, in the case of Shakespeare's play, without the sense of irony or parody which frequently accompanied such borrowings. (pp. 53-64)

> *J. Douglas Clayton, "Emblematic and Iconographic Patterns in Pushkin's 'Eugene Onegin': A Shakespearean Ghost?," in* Germano-Slavica, *No. 6, Fall, 1975, pp. 53-66.*

ROBERTA CLIPPER-SETHI (essay date 1983)

[*In the following excerpt, Clipper-Sethi traces the influence of early nineteenth-century Russian drama on the dialogue, characterization, and plot of* Eugene Onegin.]

Russia did not see a successful, original novel until long after the genre had developed in Western Europe. And yet, when it did appear, the Russian novel was almost immediately equal to the French and English classics of this most popular form of literary expression in the nineteenth century. In so little time, how did the Russians solve the problems of their fiction? Namely, how did they discover a literary idiom capable of suggesting both artifice and mimesis at the same time? What enabled some of their writers to break from an awkward, imitative narrative tradition and to create excellent original novels? (p. 397)

The belated development of a Russian novel has encouraged investigations of the genre in Europe for models by which the Russians renewed their narrative tradition. Yet, one of the main reasons why a Russian novel did not appear until the nineteenth century was slavishness to the plots, characters and even individual scenes of European fiction. Moreover, the very nature of the genre as an illustration of the languages, personalities, milieux and ideals of its writers and readers bound novelists to their own traditions and times, enhancing the value of what native sources they had. Native precedents must have been instrumental in the discovery of novelistic techniques appropriate to Russia. A study of the possible sources of one of the first modern Russian novels might help to explain how the genre evolved there.

The models *Eugene Onegin* provided—a narrative structured as a series of confrontations, the Russian anti-hero and strong heroine—have established it as a prototype of the Russian novel in spite of its verse form. Puškin himself called it a "novel in verse". In fact, the range of its style has affinities with the genre as it developed in Europe: an all-inclusive genre, the novel grew precisely by incorporating the techniques and concerns of all of the forms of expression at its disposal. Puškin is at once serious and comic; beginning with chatter, he ends with a lyrical digression. His point of view is narrative at times, at others dramatic, defined so by his characters' distinctive idioms. Moreover, what distinguishes *Eugene Onegin* from previous Russian fiction parallels that which differentiates the post-Renaissance novel from its narrative ancestors. Puškin abandons the diffuse, episodic formulae that had guided the picaresque authors of an earlier age and even the narrative poets of the eighteenth and early nineteenth centuries for a compact, complex structure organized as a novel is, according to consistent themes and intents—an education, a series of causes and effects. His characters are fuller, more realistic than those of his narrative predecessors. Employing a language virtually unique to Russian fiction, he is among the earliest to imitate speech successfully, both in his characters' discrete monologues and dialogues and in the authorial address itself. His language, like his settings and situations, mimics that of his readers.

Though the mature literatures of France, England and Germany inspired Puškin vitally, they could not begin to account for his innovations in terms of his own culture. In fact, in choosing verse Puškin may have been responding more strongly to the unique state of Russian literature in his day than to Byron's treatment of the narrative tradition. While Europe had already learned to respect the artistic value of prose as much as that of verse, Russians were still arguing that prose was only appropriate for empirical or merely popular writing at the beginning of the nineteenth century. Puškin himself was not convinced that prose could be a suitable vehicle for his novel. On the other hand, *Eugene Onegin's* realism and the novelty of its plot structure, characterizations and even language qualify its debt to Russian verse narration. Puškin refuses to heighten experience in the manner of contemporary Russian narrative poetry. He abandons as well the episodic structure, stereotypical characters and elevated diction of the tradition. While lyricism is hardly foreign to *Eugene Onegin,* the influence of lyric poetry upon it can only be as limited as the genre itself, unable to provide models for characterization or plot construction. However, Russian verse was thriving in another form of expression that Puškin knew—drama.

Puškin wrote *Eugene Onegin* as he thought a novel should be told, with "chatter". Initially his desire to avoid a Byronic association of the author-narrator with the protagonist might have led him to differentiate Onegin's voice from that of the narrative persona, but he also gave Lenskij and Tat'jana distinctive styles of speaking, thus composing the novel of the very effects of dialogue and monologue.

Bachtin regards such "dialogization" a device of all novels, uniquely enabling them to embrace the methods of other genres. However, while he recognizes that the language of *Eugene Onegin* is superior to not only the outmoded literary Russian, but even the spoken usage of its day, he does not consider the influence upon it of the highly developed and unusually mimetic idiom of contemporary Russian comedy. He is surprisingly conventional in this regard. Despite the constraints that the Soviets have imposed upon comparative study, canonic Russian criticism has been less reluctant to admit the influence of foreign traditions upon Puškin than that of his own early nineteenth-century theater. This prejudice stems from the criticism of the mid-nineteenth century, which affected Russian literary history similarly to the way in which neoclassicism had prevented the appreciation of Shakespearean drama before romanticism rehabilitated it. In rejecting the possibility that inferior works can influence a classic, Puškin's critics proved more proud than he was, as his well-documented debt to the lesser poet Byron should demonstrate. Nor was the theater of Puškin's experience as poor as Russian criticism has maintained. Its contemporaries recognized the comparative value of comedy in particular: its characters and plots successfully captured the spirit of the times, and its style was surprisingly graceful for its day. The most popular playwrights had discovered how to adapt spoken Russian to verse even before Puškin had begun to experiment with it.

Puškin's method of rendering dialogue in verse, his deft manipulation of rhythm and rhyme within a mimetic conversation, appears highly developed only in terms of the Russian narrative tradition of his experience. As Šachovskoj's *Her Own Family; or, The Married Fiancée* shows as early as 1818, the dramatists were the real pioneers of this technique, so necessary to the success of verse comedy. (pp. 397-400)

The influence of the Russian theater on the characterization of Onegin enabled Puškin to go beyond the traditional, stock figures of Russian fiction and their European cousins. Using Onegin's very manner of speaking not only to reveal his nature, but to undercut him as a social type recalls a balance of ridicule and sympathy characteristic of Russian comedy. With Lenskij too Puškin is able to elicit both sympathy and scorn in the manner of his dramatic predecessors. Lenskij's personalized poetic speech defines him as a hopelessly naive, but compelling product of a Germanic, sentimental education. While Puškin's schoolmate and fellow poet, Kjuchel'beker, appears the most likely model for his fictional poet, Šachovskoj had provided Puškin with both the type and a means of presenting him in his literary satires. Lenskij only refers to Puškin's contemporary by way of the theater.

Tat'jana's family, as typical, landed provincials, also seems to have come to the novel directly from life, but a chief source of its familiarity in a literary context was the stage. The fact that Puškin called them the "Prostakovs" in his first drafts links them with Fonvizin's provincials of the same name in the play, *The Minor*. Nevertheless, Puškin complicated the satirical Prostakovs. He gave Tat'jana's mother some models from the novels of her experience—the Richardsonian sentimental heroines of the eighteenth century. Likewise he explained Tat'jana's errors of judgment as inspired by her reading of the next generation of novelists, contrasting her with Onegin by providing folkloric motifs for her spontaneous action. Tat'jana's sister, Ol'ga, is initially the heroine of "any novel". But Puškin inherently dramatizes his characters and overturns the European allusions by letting their own speech and behavior expose and ridicule them. Curiously, the dramatic use of speech is less important in Tat'jana's characterization than in Onegin's. Nevertheless, Puškin is able to present her as dramatically as his males through an external perspective akin to a staged scene.

Concentration upon dialogue and monologue is the most direct way to capture the vivacity of the stage in a novel. Nonetheless, drama may also provide precedents for the visual perspectives of some novelistic scenes. Ballet or pantomime, silently representing emotions on stage, might have inspired Puškin's classic control of description, precision and concentration, especially evident in the immediate, visual impression of Tat'jana. Her confrontation with Onegin in the third chapter (66-73) begins with her exclamation, announcing Onegin's arrival, without ostensible narrative explanation. Omitting a direct description of her mental state does not limit the portrayal of her personality, but allows Puškin to approach a visual perspective as closely as a narrative medium will allow. His precise, evocative language prevents a narrative voice from distancing the reader. After Tat'jana's speech directly expresses her escape to the garden, an essentially narrative description begins. At this point a song interrupts the continuity. Like the digression and the chapter break that follow, this seemingly superfluous material certainly inhibits the dramatic effect. Transparent description and the inclusion of Tat'jana's reactions may have drawn the reader's identification with her point of view, allowing a dramatic revelation of the action, but Puškin undercuts his own apparent intention and denies the readers' expectations to tease his readers with his very artistry. On another level, however, his inclusion of the song may reveal the theatrical basis of Puškin's inspiration. Its pastoral innocence, like its folkloric derivation and its sociological message, which Puškin inserts in parentheses, recalls the material of late eighteenth-century comic opera. Puškin may have been led by the staged quality of his scene and the similarity of its setting to that of pastoral drama to remember a component of the same theater. The ensuing interruption—Onegin's soliloquy at the beginning of the next chapter—is itself reminiscent of the stage.

A synthesis of dramatic dialogues, characters and scenes, *Eugene Onegin* explores the effect of stereotypical behavior, born of the misconceptions of Onegin, Lenskij and even Tat'jana, upon their personalities and lives. In comedy, especially Russian salon comedy of Puškin's time, the very illusions of the characters determine the plot. The elaborate mistake, whether enacted through planned ruses or simply the blindness of the characters, must be resolved by the end of the play, through ridicule or enlightenment. Tat'jana becomes a woman because Onegin had humiliated her and because she finally adopts principles appropriate to her situation. Onegin is ridiculed despite Puškin's sympathy for him because he does not.

Puškin's native comedy may have been more influential than the psychological novel of the West as it had developed to the 1820's in inspiring his choice of a courtship plot as a vehicle for illustrating manners and character. The compact comic structures enabled him to concentrate the episodic prescriptions of the Byronic narrative poem; his inclusiveness and his ironic reversal of convention allowed him to go beond the comedic plot itself.

Puškin bases *Eugene Onegin* upon three interrelated developments, each instilling in his reader the hope that a traditionally comedic outcome will resolve opposition and misunderstanding; then he denies the expectations that he creates. The structures he overturns are common to his native theater. No matter how satiric a play was, it always involved the resolu-

tion of a couple's difficulties. Like the stylized romance of comedy, the idyllic, quasi-folkloric nature of Tat'jana's love prepares the reader for a happy ending, her marriage to Onegin, but Puškin internalizes the traditional obstacle as Onegin's psychological impotence and refuses to remove it. At the same time inverting the comedy precludes a strictly tragic outcome.

Like the dramatists, Puškin begins with an exposition of the protagonist. The displaced citified dandy, like the Europeanized Russian of *The New Sterne,* finds himself and his modish misperceptions among unsympathetic provincials. The ensuing conflict points out his ridiculousness in a series of representative scenes. By exposing the artificiality of Onegin's actions, as in his rejection of Tat'jana and the duel, Puškin undercuts his standards of behavior. Puškin's greater talent and the comparative complexity of his medium allow a more convoluted and subtle kind of ridicule than that of the more overtly satiric dramatist.

Eugene Onegin ends with Tat'jana's growth to maturity. Her situation and the representation of Muscovite society recall the urbane sophistication of Russian comedy of intrigue. Puškin defined salon comedy by its portrayal of love and deception. His plot correspondingly represents Onegin's blindness to his true feelings for Tat'jana. Traditionally comedies of adultery ridiculed the husband, but true to his habit of reversing the convention and his initial intention to satirize the protagonist à la the comic dramatists, Puškin embarrasses Onegin. In contrast Tat'jana's fidelity elevates the arranged marriage. Again, Puškin inverts the inevitable expectations for a comic resolution implied by his model, then prevents a tragic denouement by simply abandoning his hero and concluding the novel.

Not to forget the duel between Tat'jana's rejection and her refusal of Onegin, even Lenskij's demise evolved according to a comedic model. Despite the foreshadowing suggested in Tat'jana's dream, the characters' farcical behavior before the duel seems to prepare for the traditional surprise resolution of a jealous misunderstanding, as in plays like *The Feigned Infidelity.* Onegin's personality again prevents the essential action. Puškin realizes not only the ridiculous proportions of his protagonists' behavior, but its potential for harm. At the same time he is quick to avoid a tragic climax by including a cynical denouement, which explains what little posterity may have lost with Lenskij, certainly how little Ol'ga lost.

Puškin's conversational verse, his dramatic characterizations and his romantic, satiric plot reveal his debt to the contemporary Russian stage, the influence of which freed him from narrative conventions that would have limited his originality and significance. In fact, the dramatization of narrative fiction may have initiated the technical renewal of the genre as a whole, as the most important, most novelistic innovations of the earliest novels of France and England have clear precedents in their native theater. Moreover, what was learned has a long tradition in the nineteenth century novel: the use of dialogue and monologue to create character and relate events, the division of narrative not into episodes, but into scenes and the construction of the narrative according to the conventions established by comic and tragic plot. (pp. 405-08)

Roberta Clipper-Sethi, "A Lesson for Novelists; or, The Dramatic Structure of 'Eugene Onegin'," in Russian Literature, *Vol. XIV, No. 4, November 15, 1983, pp. 397-411.*

J. DOUGLAS CLAYTON (essay date 1985)

[*In the following excerpt, Clayton summarizes divergent critical interpretations of* Eugene Onegin, *and then undertakes his own analysis of the ultimate meaning of the work, examining Pushkin's use of opposites, the political and social significance of the novel, and its importance as a lyrical poem.*]

When one surveys the critical literature, some of it brilliant, which has been produced on **Onegin,** one is, ultimately, left dissatisfied. The levels of complexity of the work, its technical feats, its repleteness with literary allusion, and its ironies are so complex that any critic who feels that he has unravelled even some of them is likely to be seduced by a sense of achievement into not pursuing the final question of the meaning of the work. One is inclined to believe that this is not an accident. Because of its 'battle with the critics' mode, because of the careful veiling of detail about the author-narrator, because of the contradictory ironies which are made to resonate, it appears as if the author has deliberately—or perhaps because of the circumstances of the creation of **Onegin**—tried to defend himself against any ultimate judgment about the meaning of it all. (p. 187)

Some attempts have been made to approach the problem of meaning through the categories of 'comedy' and 'tragedy.' There is in **Onegin** a deep melancholy that leads some to speak of tragedy. Others, e.g., Hoisington and Shklovskii [see excerpt dated 1923], would see **Onegin** as a comic work. Chumakov tries to resolve the paradox by speaking of the double note of melancholy at the end of Chapter Eight, balanced by the joy of poetic return to the world of youth in Odessa in the "Journey." His comment would appear to be as close to a definition of the tone as we could reasonably expect to get. Yet—it *is* only a definition of tone, which is to say that to accept it as all one can say on the subject is to beg a number of important questions which Pushkin's work poses directly or indirectly and which therefore deserve to be answered.

Perhaps one should begin by discussing the irony, since it is the directedness of it, and the bracketing-off of any characters and emotions that are proof against it, that may tell us where to seek the central kernel of positive experience. As Shaw points out, there are certain experiences which Pushkin recalls with enjoyment and which distinguish him from Onegin (who is the centre of the irony): the theatre, Italian music, the Russian countryside, the Russian language (albeit with a French accent). A good part of the aesthetic pleasure of reading **Onegin** derives from the description of these, but mostly it comes from the sheer joy of the Russian verse, its musicality and vitality, which tell us of them. The poem is the celebration of certain pleasures—not all, and not necessarily, Russian, we note—which are, for Pushkin, equated with or serve as metaphors for poetry. More than that, however, it is the power of poetry—to transfix, to compel, to recreate life in memory and imagination—that lies at the heart of the work. Pushkin makes it clear from the stanzas in Eight where Onegin is smitten by love for Tat'iana that for him poetry *is* morality, it is remorse, and it is the overcoming of the formal automatization of life. The ball, the duel, the seduction, the empty and malicious rituals by which humans control and destroy each other—these are the outward forms imposed on life which must be broken through if one is to be truly alive. Poetry is the force which can do this.

The dichotomy of imposed form and life is therefore something that is central to **Onegin:** whether it be in the prose/poetry opposition . . . , or in the behaviour of Onegin with his reverses from natural behaviour to the automatic, or in Tat'iana at the end—loving one man, married to another. The dichotomy is made emblem in the contrast of red and white, flush and pallor, passion and chastity, warmth and cold, south and north, which runs through the work to such an extent that we must consider it a leitmotiv. Lenskii's blood in the snow is emblematic of life petrified by death, the rose on a girl's cheek bitten by frost, Italy exiled to Russia, perhaps even the mix of African and Russian blood in Pushkin's veins.

Beyond these minor manifestations of the categories of opposites which inform **Onegin,** there is one figure who is Pushkin's inspiration in the work, namely Tat'iana (whose opposite is, of course, the eponymous hero). Tat'iana is the personification of the poetic for Pushkin: closely related to the muse-figure, she is Russia, she is constancy, she is the nymph of the birch forests and the lakes. The real drama of the poem is, I would suggest, not Onegin's and Tat'iana's love for each other, but Pushkin's love for Tat'iana—a secret, undemanding love, nurtured from afar. It is Tat'iana who is his 'true ideal.' She overcomes the corrosive negativeness of Onegin and triumphs, although that triumph is a pyrrhic one, for her relationship to it at the end is the analogue of the opposition of Pushkin's poetry and the demonic—keeping it at bay but far from vanquished.

In addition, Tat'iana is the antidote for Pushkin to the visions of the faithless female, the Helen, the adultress whose waywardness destroys her husband. Pushkin, we recall, was switching roles precisely at the time when the last chapter was being written—from young philanderer and seducer of other people's wives to the husband of the beautiful young Natal'ia Goncharova and potential cuckold. Tat'iana is an attempt to realize in concrete form the ideal of womanhood—an ideal in whose existence Pushkin had to believe if he were to survive. Yet Pushkin is curiously reticent about Tat'iana. As I have said, she is an ideal whom he admires from afar, and becomes, after all, the wife of N, not of the poet. The career of Prince N, likewise, is very different from that of the poet and is treated half-ironically, half-enviously as the paradigm of success. The final situation of N and Tat'iana suggests the isolation and exclusion of the poet (and, we might add, of his creation Onegin)—an isolation which is made only more profound by the mention of missing friends.

Ultimately, if one leaves aside the ephemeral pleasures of friendship, wine, the opera, and the theatre, the poet appears as a figure for whom existential happiness is unattainable save in his poetry. The message of the poem is a pessimistic one: love, that chimaera of the poet's world, is in reality either impossible or at best brings not fulfilment but unhappiness. The poetry that makes life so meaningful for Pushkin is likewise that which separates him from so much of it. It is Tat'iana who manages the impossible—to survive in society and yet retain her soul, a feat which seems beyond the poet in a world he so clearly detests. Here the figure of Tat'iana seems to be 'wish fulfilment' on the part of the poet; that is to say, the imposition of an ideal on a less than happy reality. Is such a purity as hers really possible—or desirable? Is it truly possible for Tat'iana to remain free of all the corruptions that surround her? In my reading the Tat'iana of Chapter Eight remains the Madonna, the angel of Pushkin's lyrical symbolism, and the enigmatic qualities that permit her to exist at all in the novel are never really motivated.

A remarkable aspect of **Onegin** is the fact that the poet has been able to weave his narrative out of something so insubstantial. If we were to resume the plot of the novel in a sentence, it would be: 'two people meet and nothing happens.' If we were to imagine ourselves into the position of an outside observer, a frequenter of society gatherings, perhaps, then we would know nothing at all of Onegin's encounters with Tat'iana. We would know that the beautiful Princess N had married, perhaps also that Onegin had killed someone in a duel over her sister, and we might even realize, if we were perspicacious, that Onegin was one of her many admirers. We would know nothing of the inner drama that takes place in the hearts of the two individuals. It is this inner drama, a drama in which nothing happens (but everything happens), that forms the stuff of the novelistic plot. The situation is more than a little reminiscent of David Lean's film *Brief Encounter,* which is equally a film about nothing. Where in the film the camera is the observer, registering the expression on the heroine's face as the express races past, so in **Onegin** Pushkin is our ghostly viewing-piece as he secretly admires her from afar. In this way Tat'iana serves as a metaphor for the intimacy of Pushkin's poetry—the simple external appearance belies the complex inner content. Among other things, the inner drama is suggestive of the poet's own rejection of the search for fame (*slava*) (which had been, we recall, the goal of Lenskii), in favour of a quasi-Horatian withdrawal.

On the question of death and life hereafter, Pushkin seems unequivocal—if we are to seek any fulfilment, then it must be in this world. The oblivion which swallows Lenskii (and which, the author tells us in the last stanza of Eight, we must be ready to embrace without fear) is as total as that nothingness which surrounds the few sketchily drawn episodes of **Onegin.** The brevity and incompleteness of **Onegin** thus serve as a kind of metaphor for Pushkin's vision of human existence. Piety, when it exists, is a female quality which Tania finds in her nurse, but Pushkin insists on the importance of morality, which is 'in the nature of things' (to quote the epigraph) and is inherent in Pushkin's notion of the noble life. To ignore it is to court eternal confusion, the state in which Onegin is left at the end of Eight.

There remains the vexed question of the extent to which we may trace in **Onegin** Pushkin's political stance in the years after the Decembrist uprising. The contrast between public appearances and private emotions is clearly important here, but so is the attitude of Tat'iana towards Onegin at the end, for in her refusal of Onegin and her decision to remain faithful to her husband it is possible to read, as Belinskii did, a metaphor of the acceptance or acquiescence by Pushkin in the political realities of Russia under Nicholas I. Such an interpretation has not been current in Soviet criticism since the publication of the number of *Literary Heritage* (*Literaturnoe nasledstvo*) devoted to Pushkin, in 1934. Public acquiescence by Pushkin, private sympathies with the Decembrists, but a view that all that is past, and moreover, that to revolt against authority—symbolized here, as Belinskii thought, by the institution of marriage—is immoral, a quasi-Napoleonic act of self-aggrandizement: all these can be traced in **Onegin** and serve to shape its final outcome in Chapter Eight. Pushkin was the scion of a declining family of nobility, a man poised between his impatience with the régime and the petty humiliations that it inflicted upon him as a writer and a person, and his patriotic feelings towards his country. Pushkin does not find, and does not offer, a solution to these contradictions. They are enshrined in the final scene between Onegin and Tat'iana: the predicament of the demon in love with the angel. No outcome is possible. The demon is petrified into immobility. Similarly, the Pushkin of the 1830s was an individual petrified by the contradictions of his social and existential circumstances, contradictions that proved unresolvable by any other outcome than death. I would argue that we must read **Onegin,** like a lyrical poem, as a sort of map of Pushkin's existential predicament, and, beyond that, as a symbolic representation of the dilemma of his whole class—forced to acquiesce in a system to which they owed their privileges yet which exacted a heavy price for them in terms of the abasement of that individualism and self-assertion which they imbibed from Western European culture. better, documenting the intimate life and cares of the poet Pushkin, hinting, also, at the life of the man himself, and serving as the vehicle for flights of Russian poetry that have remained unsurpassed. It is here, I believe, that we must seek the ultimate importance of the work, and the reason that it has succeeded in captivating and fascinating generations of Russian-speakers. . . . [It] is in reading the work as poetry, as a piece whose structure is the analogue of a lyrical poem, that we can penetrate to the heart of it and grasp the uniqueness of a work which, despite its imperfections and contradictions, proved an extraordinary beginning to an extraordinary literary century. (pp. 188-94)

J. Douglas Clayton, in his Ice and Flame: Aleksandr Pushkin's "Eugene Onegin", *University of Toronto Press, 1985, 224 p.*

FURTHER READING

Bayley, John. *"Evgeny Onegin."* In his *Pushkin: A Comparative Commentary,* pp. 236-305. Cambridge: Cambridge University Press, 1971.

   A two-part discussion of *Eugene Onegin,* examining its place among the great novels of European literature and its elements of parody.

Čiževsky, Dmitry. Introduction to *Evgenij Onegin: A Novel in Verse,* by Alexander Sergeevich Pushkin, edited by Dmitry Čiževsky, pp. ix-xxx. Cambridge: Harvard University Press, 1953.

   A study of *Eugene Onegin* focusing on its rhythmic form and rhyme scheme and its relationship to Russian Romanticism. Čiževsky also provides a brief publication history of the work and a survey of initial critical reaction.

Clayton, J. Douglas. "The Epigraph of *Eugene Onegin:* A Hypothesis." *Canadian Slavic Studies* V, No. 2 (Summer 1971): 226-33.
   Examines the significance of the French epigraph that appears at the beginning of *Eugene Onegin.*

Eidelman, Nathan. *"Evgeni Onegin:* The Puzzle of the Tenth Chapter." *Soviet Literature* 10, No. 331 (1975): 29-33.
   Raises questions concerning the existence and possible whereabouts of the tenth chapter of *Eugene Onegin,* which Pushkin supposedly burned.

Gibian, George. "Love by the Book: Pushkin, Stendhal, Flaubert." *Comparative Literature* VIII, No. 2 (Spring 1956): 97-109.
   Contends that the protagonists of *Eugene Onegin, Le rouge et le noir,* and *Madame Bovary* form their concepts of love through literature.

Gregg, Richard A. "Tat'yana's Two Dreams: The Unwanted Spouse and the Demonic Lover." *The Slavonic and East European Review* XLVIII, No. 113 (October 1970): 492-505.

Analyzes the psychological implications and various interpretations of Tatyana's dream sequence.

Gustafson, Richard F. "The Metaphor of the Seasons in *Evgenij Onegin*." *The Slavic and East European Journal* VI, No. 1 (1962): 6-20.

Suggests that Pushkin used the transition of the seasons and descriptions of nature in *Eugene Onegin* to express the passage of time.

Hoisington, Sona Stephan, ed. *Russian Views of Pushkin's "Eugene Onegin"*. Translated by Sona Stephan Hoisington. Bloomington: Indiana University Press, 1988, 199 p.

Reprints important commentary by Russian critics on *Eugene Onegin,* including essays by Vissarion Belinsky, Dmitry Pisarev, Fedor Dostoevsky, Mikhail Bakhtin, and Yury Lotman.

Katz, Michael R. "Love and Marriage in Pushkin's *Evgeny Onegin*." In *Oxford Slavonic Papers,* n.s. Vol. XVII, edited by J. L. I. Fennell, I. P. Foote, and G. C. Stone, pp. 77-89. Oxford: Clarendon Press, 1984.

Discusses Tatyana's motivation for rejecting Onegin's marriage proposal.

McLean, Hugh. "The Tone(s) of *Evgenij Onegin*." In *California Slavic Studies,* Vol. VI, edited by Robert P. Hughes, Simon Karlinsky, and Vladimir Markov, pp. 3-15. Berkeley and Los Angeles: University of California Press, 1971.

Studies the complex tone of *Eugene Onegin,* particularly Pushkin's mixture of "jocularity and lyricism."

Nabokov, Vladimir, trans. *Eugene Onegin: A Novel in Verse,* by Alexander Pushkin. 4 vols. Bollingen Series LXXII. New York: Pantheon Books, 1964.

Nabokov's translation of *Eugene Onegin.* Volumes 2 and 3 of this four-volume edition are devoted to Nabokov's analysis of the work, which Anthony Burgess termed "a massive act of copulation with scholarship."

Posin, J. A. "Pushkin and Onegin as Viewed by Two Generations." In *Slavic Studies,* edited by Alexander Kaun and Ernest J. Simmons, pp. 132-45. Ithaca, N. Y.: Cornell University Press, 1943.

Examines *Onegin* criticism written by the early Russian critics Vissarion Belinsky and Dmitry Pisarev. While the article focuses on the methods of the two critics, the juxtaposition of their views on Pushkin is valuable to an understanding of the work.

Schmidgall, Gary. "Peter Ilyich Tchaikovsky: *Eugene Onegin*." In his *Literature as Opera,* pp. 217-46. New York: Oxford University Press, 1977.

Contrasts Pushkin's conception of *Eugene Onegin* with Tchaikovsky's interpretation of the story in his opera of the same name. The critic argues that Tchaikovsky's opera is a too serious, literal, and emotional rendering of the story, which Pushkin meant as a romantic satire.

Simmons, Ernest J. *Pushkin.* Cambridge: Harvard University Press, 1937, 485 p.

An authoritative biography by a noted Pushkin scholar.

Todd, William Mills, III. "*Eugene Onegin*: 'Life's Novel'." In his *Fiction and Society in the Age of Pushkin: Ideology, Institutions, and Narrative,* pp. 106-36. Cambridge: Harvard University Press, 1986.

Explores ways in which life and literature merge in *Eugene Onegin.*

Vickery, Walter N. "Byron's *Don Juan* and Puškin's *Evgenij Onegin*: The Question of Parallelism." *Indiana Slavic Studies* IV, (1967): 181-91.

Addresses the much studied relationship between *Eugene Onegin* and *Don Juan,* focusing on similarities of plot and character and problems related to genre.

Woodward, James B. "The 'Principle of Contradictions' in *Yevgeniy Onegin*." *The Slavonic and East European Review* 60, No. 1 (January 1982): 25-43.

Surveys various critical approaches to the explanation of the contradictory statements in *Eugene Onegin.*

José Rizal

1861-1896

(Born José Protacio Mercado y Alonzo Realonda) Filipino novelist, poet, essayist, and dramatist.

Rizal has long been revered as the national hero of the Philippines. His two novels, *Noli me tangere (The Social Cancer)* and its sequel *El filibusterismo (The Reign of Greed),* in which he calls for an end to the abuses suffered by Filipinos under Spanish colonial rule, marked a turning point in the history of the Philippines: many historians claim they served as a catalyst in the 1896 Philippine Revolution, which brought an end to the Spanish regime, and they are widely regarded as the most influential works in Filipino literature. In addition, Rizal was the first writer to vividly depict Filipino life and customs and his novels helped shape the country's nationalism. Today, he remains the subject of fervent patriotism and the most prominent literary figure to ever emerge from the Philippines.

Born in the province of Laguna in the northern Philippines, Rizal was the seventh of eleven children in an affluent family of rice farmers. Rizal's mother was well educated and taught her son to read by the age of three. As a child, Rizal composed poetry and demonstrated considerable talent as a writer, completing a full-length play by the time he was eight years old. In 1872, Rizal went to Manila to attend the Ateneo Municipal, a prestigious Jesuit school, where he studied the classics and was an avid reader of European Romantic authors. At sixteen, he enrolled in the University of Santo Tomas to study medicine. While pursuing his scientific interests, Rizal continued to write, composing numerous poems, dramas, and essays, many of which were labeled subversive by the Spanish Civil Guard for their criticism of the Spanish regime. At an early age Rizal had become acutely aware of the injustices the Spanish authorities were capable of in their dealings with the Filipinos. When he was a child his mother was falsely accused of a crime, imprisoned by the Civil Guard, and subjected to humiliating treatment while detained. At school in Manila, Rizal was exposed to more racial prejudice. In one instance, Rizal had anonymously entered a poetry contest and received a first place award only to have it taken away when the judges learned that he was Filipino. In an essay he wrote: "In the University, I got to understand better in what sort of world I was. In it there were privileges for some and rules for others, and assuredly the discrimination was not based on capacity." Biographers agree that the persecution Rizal suffered in Manila was a deciding factor in his decision to continue his education abroad.

In 1882 Rizal left Manila for Europe, spending the next seven years attending universities in Madrid, Paris, Heidelberg, and Berlin. Rizal continued his study of medicine, specializing in ophthalmology, and maintained his literary interests, reading widely and becoming fluent in twenty-two languages. While in Europe, Rizal worked for reforms in his homeland, regularly contributing articles to *La Solidaridad,* a Filipino propaganda newspaper published in Madrid that petitioned for the civil rights of all people of the Philippines. In the most famous of these essays, "La indolencia de los Filipinos" ("The Indolence of the Filipinos"), Rizal attributed the al-

leged passive nature of the Filipino people to government oppression, not racial inferiority. In 1887, Rizal published his first novel, *Noli me tangere,* a biting satire on the corruption of the Hispanic friars and racial prejudices of the Spanish colonial government. The same year, Rizal began to work on its sequel, *El filibusterismo,* which was completed and published, through the donations of friends, in 1891. Because of the antigovernment feelings expressed in them, Rizal's novels were banned in the Philippines by the Censorship Commission, who labeled his work "libelous, immoral and pernicious." Despite this censorship, hundreds of copies of *Noli me tangere* were illegally circulated throughout the country, inciting a spirit of solidarity never before felt among the people of the Philippines.

In 1892 Rizal moved back to Manila, where he founded *La Liga Filipina,* an organization that stressed the importance of national unity and encouraged gradual political reforms through peaceful agitation. Deeply influenced by the Enlightenment principles of such Western liberal thinkers as Jean Jacques Rousseau and Voltaire, Rizal appealed to reason, not revolution, as a means of alleviating the plight of the Filipino people. Despite his nonviolent tactics, Rizal was considered a threatening presence by the Spanish authorities and later that year was exiled to Dapitan, a remote village in the southern Philippines. Here, Rizal practiced medicine and was actively involved in the opening of new schools and the teaching of improved agricultural methods. After four years in exile, Rizal was granted permission by the Spanish government to serve as an army doctor in the Cuban revolution. Within days of his release, the Spanish authorities became aware of the existence of a secret Filipino revolutionary group, the Katipunan, who, upon being discovered, instigated the 1896 revolt against Spain. Despite having spent the preceding years in relative isolation, Rizal was named as an accomplice in the insurrection. En route to Havana, his ship was intercepted by Spanish authorities and he was returned to the Philippines, where he faced false charges of inciting rebellion and was subsequently sentenced to death. The night before his execution, Rizal wrote his most famous verse, "Mi ultimo adios" ("My Last Farewell"), which has become the national poem of the Philippines. The next morning he was shot by a firing squad at Bagumbayan field in Manila.

In a letter to a friend, Rizal described the purpose of his two novels: "I have endeavored to answer the calumnies which for centuries had been heaped on us and our country; I have described the social condition, the life, our beliefs, our hopes, our desires, our grievances, our griefs; I have unmasked hypocrisy which, under the guise of religion, came to impoverish and to brutalize us." In *Noli me tangere* and *El filibusterismo* Rizal directs his attack at two targets, the Spanish Civil Guard and the friars, who controlled the Philippine church and owned most of the land in the country. *Noli me tangere* takes place during the last years of the Spanish colonial regime in the Philippines and addresses the conflict between the laws of the Spanish government and the native lifestyle of the Filipinos. The plot focuses on the actions of Crisostomo Ibarra, a Filipino student who has just returned from Europe to work for social reforms in his native country. Throughout the novel, Ibarra and his fiancée, Maria Clara, suffer the persecution of the Spanish authorities. Ibarra narrowly escapes death when a plot to kill him as he lays the cornerstone of a new school is thwarted by his companion, Elias. When a Spanish friar, Padre Damaso, publicly ridicules the name of Ibarra's father, Ibarra strikes him, and as a result is excommunicated from the church. Abandoning all hopes of marrying a religious outcast, Maria Clara seeks solace by entering a convent, only to endure more suffering when she is sexually abused by the priests. In the end, Ibarra is driven from his country when he is falsely implicated in a local uprising, and Maria Clara becomes insane as a result of her mistreatment at the convent. *El filibusterismo* tells of the return of the exiled Ibarra in the guise of a merchant named Simoun. Although conceivably the same character, Simoun is more revolutionary than the staunch pacifist Ibarra. Simoun defends the violent overthrow of the Spanish regime, viewing it as an example of the evolutionary theory of survival of the fittest. Critics have linked this dichotomy of philosophies to Rizal's own inner struggle with the notion of violence as a means of reform. Despite his steadfast belief in passive resistance, Rizal acknowledged the likelihood of revolution as the only end to Spanish rule in the Philippines. The autobiographical content of both novels is also evident in Rizal's characterization. Critics have noted the obvious comparison between Rizal and his fictional hero Ibarra and the uncanny foreshadowing of Rizal's own fate. The character of Maria Clara is generally seen as a representation of Rizal's one-time fiancée Leonor Rivera, who ended their relationship because of Rizal's political entanglements. The subplot of the tragic story of Sisa, a helpless victim of the corrupt political system

who suffers false accusations and public degradation at the hands of the Civil Guard, bears striking similarities to the mistreatment of Rizal's own mother.

Because Rizal is primarily recognized as a patriotic figure, critical reaction to his works has often been characterized by nostalgic bias. Regarded as a national hero in the Philippines, Rizal has been the subject of a great number of biographies by Philippine writers and his novels are taught in many schools. The publication of the English translations of Rizal's novels in 1912 sparked widespread interest in his writings in Europe and America. Some critics have complained that Rizal's importance as a political figure has overshadowed the value of *Noli me tangere* and *El filibusterismo* as literature and have demonstrated how he effectively used such devices as characterization, symbolism, and satire in presenting his political message. It is generally acknowledged, however, that Rizal's political contributions far outweigh his literary significance, and he is primarily praised for his vivid depictions of Filipino customs and for his influence on the future of his country. As the Filipino scholar León Ma. Guerrero wrote: "Few novels, except perhaps the now much disparaged *Uncle Tom's Cabin*, have made a more shattering impact on the society in which they were conceived than the *Noli me tangere* and *El filibusterismo*."

PRINCIPAL WORKS

Noli me tangere (novel) 1887
    [*The Social Cancer*, 1912; also published as *The Lost Eden*, 1961]
El filibusterismo (novel) 1891
    [*The Reign of Greed*, 1912]
Epistolario Rizalino. 6 vols. (letters) 1930-38
Las poesías de Rizal (poetry) 1946
Memorias de un estudiante de Manila (unfinished autobiography) 1949
    [*The Young Rizal*, 1950]
The Rizal-Blumentritt Correspondence. 2 vols. (letters) 1961
Rizal's Complete Poetical Works: 1869-1896 (poetry) 1976

HUGH CLIFFORD (essay date 1902)

[*In the following excerpt, Clifford emphasizes that Rizal's importance as an historical figure has made it difficult for critics to accurately estimate his literary achievements.*]

The tragedy and the pathos of Rizal's own story has cast something of a glamour over his literary work, to the confusion and bedazzlement of his critics. He has been proclaimed as a genius: ***Noli Me Tangere*** and its successor, [***El Filibusterismo***], have been made the subject of almost hysterical praise; and quite recently a writer, who is usually a model of sanity and self-restraint, has committed himself to the statement that "the palpitating life in these stories can only be equalled in the best literature of other lands." The fact is that Rizal was a genius, not because he produced works of genius, but because, like Tennyson's "divinely gifted man," he "burst his birth's invidious bars"; and indeed it is barely possible to form a completely sane estimate of the value of his books as literature, so strong is the bias of wonder that their author should have been a scion of the Malayan race.

To me, after reading much that Rizal wrote with interest and sympathy, it seems that his novels are to be regarded, not as works of fiction, but as supremely able political pamphlets. He writes well, fluently, with point, occasionally with finish; he has at his command a certain grim humour; but he lacks all power of construction, he can neither conceive nor depict a character that lives, as live, for instance, the characters of Scott or Thackeray, or even Trollope, and, like the little girl in the nursery rhyme, his people, "when they are good, are very, very good, and when they are bad they are *horrid.*" On the other hand, he knows and loves the Philippines and the Filipinos; he describes the lives of the people with detail, truth, and picturesqueness; and he has sufficient of skill and power to excite the interest of his readers in his impeachment of Spanish rule, and to quicken their sympathies for the brown folk who groaned beneath that tyranny. (pp. 623-24)

[Rizal's] novels represent the alpha and omega of his achievement: they were at once the glory and the price of those who hailed him as their prophet, and the crown of his offending in the sight of the men who regarded him as a dangerous firebrand. One must not only examine the books themselves, but must recognise what their publication meant to the bulk of educated Filipinos, and to the authorities that governed them. And here judgment must be aided by an impartiality at once dispassionate and critical, for the glamour which tragedy has cast over Rizal and all his ways and works has blinded his biographers, and has made of them, not sane historians, but fierce partisans. (p. 624)

> *Hugh Clifford, "The Story of José Rizal the Filipino," in* Blackwood's Edinburgh Magazine, *Vol. CLXXII, No. MXLV, November, 1902, pp. 620-38.*

THE NATION, NEW YORK   (essay date 1913)

[*In the following review of* The Social Cancer *and* The Reign of Greed, *the anonymous critic discusses Rizal's political position and commends the sensitivity of his novels, noting their importance as documents of Filipino life.*]

[*The Social Cancer* and *The Reign of Greed*] are two books that every American should read; not simply because a Malay novelist is a great curiosity, but because these romances contain a serious exposition of the conditions which prevailed in the Philippines just before the American occupation. Those who readily believe in racial superiorities and inferiorities may find in these novels some stimulus to reflection. For here is a Filipino, with no European blood in his veins, who writes with the compelling charm of a Galdòs, who has a considerable store of European culture and a perfect understanding of European ideals; who strikes chords of emotion that no American could find exotic; who believes passionately in all that Western civilization stands for, and whose appeal for the fraternity of races has not a trace of cowardice or pose.

We feel even that if José Rizal seems foreign to us at all, it is because certain literary motives that in the West have become sodden from over-cultivation return in his works with the fresh sincerity of youth. Few of our contemporary novelists could describe with such true exultance the beauty of Oriental moonlight, a tropical spring, all that distinctive local environment that so moves men like Pierre Loti or Lafcadio

Hearn. This exquisite delicacy, so characteristic of Rizal's temperament, is all the more remarkable when we try to estimate the amount of furious passion that must have been behind his novels. For, after all, they are romances of most sombre outline, and their tragic appeal is intensified by the apparent effort for reserve, for sobriety, and kindliness of judgment.

A Spanish imperialist would, of course, maintain that Rizal's novels are a gross slander on Spanish rule, and that his execution in 1896 was justified by his revolutionary associations and by the inflammatory spirit of his works. We are probably still too close to the events involved to reach valuable conclusions on such questions. But we should observe that the major theses of Rizal are distinctly pro-Spanish in every essential. He attempts to prove first that everything good in Filipino civilization is due to Spain; and then that permanent advancement must come not from political convulsions, not from endless and abortive revolutions, but from an assimilation of Spanish civilization which automatically will place the Filipinos on a footing of equal opportunity with their rulers. So his great case against the Spanish is their refusal to disseminate their civilization, their use of the Islands preëminently for commercial and social exploitation, their exclusion of them from a respectable place in the Spanish Empire, and their inhibition of any national spirit, among the natives. He is fighting less for Filipino independence than for a Spanish school system on democratic lines.

We believe that this is the only fair interpretation of Rizal's position in his novels; though it must be confessed that the emotions aroused by them are not those best suited to guiding pacific reforms. If we are to believe his biographers, his own life experiences have entered too directly into the principal episodes of his books not to have left in them some of the wild passions which his own sufferings, ending in martyrdom, must have created. And perhaps the calm reflection that shapes the plot around a constructive plan for social betterment in his countrymen, is obscured by the violent emotional reactions caused by the narrative of oppression, sorrow, and death. We can see how a remote public might find here a strong dose of melodrama. But if these episodes are based on facts, and some of them are documented by Rizal himself, how are we to calculate the effect they must have had on a suffering people knowing them to be true?

This portrayal of Filipino life gives permanent interest to these books. The characters are taken from every branch of society, including the Spaniard of noble ideals and the native of barbarous instincts. We are not sure that psychologically these people are very deeply or acutely drawn; but their exteriors at least are real and vivacious. If we do not carry away from among them any lasting friendships, we do gain a picture of life in the Philippines that is varied and complete. (pp. 35-6)

> *A review of "The Social Cancer" and "The Reign of Greed," in* The Nation, *New York, Vol. XCVI, No. 2480, January 9, 1913, pp. 35-6.*

BOSTON EVENING TRANSCRIPT   (essay date 1913)

[*In the following review of* The Social Cancer *and* The Reign of Greed, *the anonymous critic stresses the importance of the two novels as unique documents of the suffering of the Philippine people under Spanish rule.*]

Whatever [*The Social Cancer* and *The Reign of Greed*] may purport to be as novels, they are the most powerful statement that has come to our ears of government abuses in the Philippines. When we have finished reading the two books we can scarcely wonder that the author was put to death for writing them. No government capable of such abuses would dare to show its face if it did not execute anyone who ventured to make public such appalling revelations of its iniquity. The books are vivid with life and filled with the minds of these people—the desire to revolt, and the hopelessness, the utter helplessness of it all, the curse which his birth laid upon the "Indian." It is gruesome in many places, as in the graveyard scene, where the year-old corpses are being disinterred to make way for new ones, and the scene between Basilio, his little brother, and the sacristan. Horror broods on every page. Not even the beautiful Maria Clara is free from it, but is its chosen victim.

The author of these two novels shows a thorough knowledge of all the intricacies of the Philippine questions at that date, and as though from bitter experience he places upon them the sacred and bloody seal of truth. The books should be known, for no other reason than as a justification of all that our Government is trying to do and has done, to better the lives of the people in the Philippines.

> *"Two Philippine Novels," in* Boston Evening Transcript, *Part 45, February 21, 1913, p. 4.*

THE NEW YORK TIMES (essay date 1913)

[*In the following anonymous review of* The Social Cancer *and* The Reign of Greed, *the critic praises Rizal's writing style but emphasizes the historic significance of the novels over their literary value.*]

In 1887 *Noli me Tangere,* a book written by a young man from the Philippines who was studying medicine in Germany, was printed in Berlin and was introduced surreptitiously into the Philippine Islands. A few years later the author's second book, *El Filibusterismo,* was published in Ghent, and, like its predecessor, secretly sent back home. At the end of the year 1806, less than two years before Spain lost the Philippines, José Rizal, author of the two "unpatriotic" volumes, and more or less frank revolutionist, was executed in Manila. In his preface to the English edition of the young insurrectionist's books, published here as *The Social Cancer* and *The Reign of Greed,* Charles Derbyshire, the translator, calls the killing of Rizal "Spain's political suicide in the Philippines."

His two books are thoughtful, earnest, well-written studies of social conditions in a time that already seems very long ago. For us their interest is historic—all the more impressively so in that the manner of Spain's occupation of the Philippines was in itself an anachronism. The time of which José Rizal wrote is past—it ended fifteen years ago. There are parts of his books that read like a record of mediaeval oppression.

The author's shafts of attack are directed especially against the friars. He is unhesitating in his exposure, however, of whatever he believes to be evil in Philippine society. His style is clear, ironic, sometimes picturesque. *The Social Cancer* is the more interesting story; its narrative of the misfortunes of a pair of lovers separated by political and religious oppression, has a real plot. *The Reign of Greed* is written with more political force and less charm, and is almost without incident. The translator has supplied an excellent introduction, and the

books themselves are interesting reading, not as novels, but as history.

> *"A Modern Martyr's Books," in* The New York Times, *March 2, 1913, p. 111.*

SALVADOR P. LOPEZ (essay date 1940)

[*In the following essay, Lopez suggests that, while many readers have held up the famous heroine of Rizal's novels, Maria Clara, as the ideal Filipino woman, she was more likely intended as a satiric figure parodying the weaknesses of women. Lopez's essay was first published in 1940 in his* Literature and Society.]

There is no more significant inquiry that can be made into the literary work of Jose Rizal than his conception of the character of Maria Clara. No other character in Philippine literature has had a more pervasive influence on the thought-life of the Filipino people than this famous heroine of Rizal.

Filipino womanhood is even now at the crossroads of modernity and conservatism, slightly bewildered, and not knowing exactly which way to turn. Lured on the one hand by the attractions of the new emancipation, she is on the other hand as yet too strongly attached to a lingering ideal of Filipino womanhood to brush aside the traditional conception of her sex which she imbibed with her mother's milk.

For decades since Maria Clara was created by the genius of the great patriot, we have heard the name of this heroine spoken now in reverent whispers, now in a gush of romantic idealism. She has been celebrated in song and oratory as the paragon of Filipino womanhood. Whenever it seemed that the modern Filipino girl was becoming too vital, too progressive or too daring, prophets of execration and doom were not lacking to hold up the figure of Maria Clara anew and to whisper her name as if it were an incantation to drive away an evil spirit.

That was the accepted interpretation of the character of Maria Clara. Everyone thought that Rizal intended to set her up as an ideal for the women of his country, the noblest blossom of Filipino womanhood. Was she not the fiancee of the hero of the novel in which he tried to bare the soul of his people through the sufferings of his own soul? Did not even this hero himself seem to be moulded upon Rizal's own personality, the author weaving into this hero's thoughts, pains and tribulations, the deep notes of his own anguish? Did he not imbue Maria Clara with loyalty and modesty, which are the two cardinal virtues of our women?

There seemed to be no escape from the only conclusion to which the answers logically led. It was evident, according to this view, that Rizal had intended Maria Clara to be a model Filipino woman—loyal to the point of selflessness, modest to the point of weakness.

So did the legend become firmly imbedded in the Filipino mind—of Maria Clara against whose assumed perfections all the weakness of present-day women are to be measured, whose virtues are a mirror whereon other women might look at their own reflection and blush in shame.

Let us try to subject this legend to closer examination. We shall not tear away the canvas from the wall of memory where Rizal hung it for the contemplation of posterity. We shall only take it down with reverent hands so that at the close range we may judge whether the portrait was drawn by a loving or by a satirical hand.

Let us consider the original inspiration of Maria Clara. Rizal makes her the daughter of a Spanish priest, thus placing a double handicap upon her as a would-be model Filipino woman. For that automatically makes her a *mestiza* and an illegitimate child. It is true that he gives her the virtues of modesty and loyalty. But in an age which compelled a woman to remain in the background, these qualities were not virtues born of interior strength. And while Rizal surrounds the figure of Maria Clara with the aura of romanticism (as in her love scenes with Crisostomo Ibarra), he also places her in questionable situations with another priest. All in all, the character of Maria Clara is far too weak to justify her being held up as a model for the women of our country. Her loyalty is the loyalty of the vanquished in spirit, her modesty the modesty of the timid.

To insist that Rizal meant to put up a woman of this type as an ideal for future generations of Filipino women to imitate, is to place a miserable estimate upon the prophetic insight of Rizal. Surely, the man who wrote **"The Philippines a Century Hence"** and **"The Indolence of the Filipino"** could not have made the mistake of putting up as an ideal a type of womanhood that the twentieth century was certain to outmode. Rizal knew that the new century was going to be a century of unprecedented progress in all lines of human endeavor. He knew that the new age would witness the emergence of a new woman enjoying privileges and responsibilities of which before she was not even aware. Having lived for many years in Europe and having visited America shortly before the turn of the century, he could not have missed the clear portents of the new womanhood that was soon to arise.

It is difficult to believe that, with this background, Rizal could ever have fallen into the error of setting up a feeble and invertebrate woman as the model for the women of his country. He wanted his countrymen to be robust and powerful in spirit; he could not have wished his countrymen to become exactly the opposite. His famous letter to the women of Malolos shows clearly that his conception of Filipino womanhood was enlightened, and that while he deplored none of their old virtues, he insisted that new and more vital qualities be added to these.

We are left with the surmise that Rizal most probably intended the character of Maria Clara not as a glorification of the women of his time but rather as a satire upon their foibles and weaknesses. To point out that her figure is touched with the sublimity of the author's conception, is merely to say that Rizal succeeded as an artist in creating a character that is fundamentally unsound without being contemptible, that is weak and yet appealing.

The character of Maria Clara inspires not scorn but sympathy born of understanding. We realize that Rizal probably intended to use the type of womanhood she represented for a definite purpose, even as Cervantes used the character of Don Quixote to laugh the romantic knight out of court forever.

Maria Clara was the forerunner in fiction of that woman who, in 1896, betrayed the secret of the Katipunan to the priest of Tondo. You find in her the same feebleness, the same helplessness, the same fear—none of the qualities that were possessed by Princess Urduja of ancient Pangasinan or by Tandang Sora of the Revolution or by Teodora Alonso, Rizal's own brave and gallant mother.

Other times, other heroes and heroines. In the regime upon which this nation has but recently entered, we shall need a type of Filipino woman as unlike that of Maria Clara as possible—energetic, enterprising, progressive and with a mind of her own. (pp. 81-4)

Salvador P. Lopez, "Maria Clara—Paragon or Caricature?," in Rizal: Contrary Essays, *edited by Petronilo Bn. Daroy and Dolores S. Feria, Guro Books, 1968, pp. 81-4.*

RAFAEL PALMA   (essay date 1949)

[*In the following excerpt, Palma analyzes the delineation of character in* Noli me tangere, *focusing on Rizal's presentation of Elias.*]

Noli Me Tangere is a novel with a weak plot that is developed around the figure of Crisostomo Ibarra, a Spanish *mestizo* educated in Europe. He has recently returned to his native land and, aspiring to elevate his people, strives for their education by means of a school project. Upon so slim a foundation one would believe that the author could not construct a costly and solid platform. But Rizal succeeded in making his plot interesting without distorting Philippine life; and brought it to a climax in a tragic manner which holds the reader in suspense and moves him.

Ibarra, although a friend of the authorities and of the people, does not succeed in carrying into effect his simple project. During the laying of the corner stone of the school building, someone desirous of getting rid of Ibarra causes a mishap from which, luckily, Ibarra is saved by Elias. At the banquet following the "accident" Ibarra is grossly insulted by one *reverend* whom he knocks down in a moment of confusion and nearly stabs with a table knife. Later an uprising is fomented in the town, in which Ibarra is implicated. Once in jail he escapes and dodges the persecution of the agents of public order, thanks to the assistance of Elias, who sacrifices his own life for him.

That is the novel; but what is most admirable and fascinating about it is the exposition of Filipino types taken from life. The foreigner who has neither resided in the Philippines nor put himself in contact with the Filipinos will neither fully understand nor feel any very great interest for the little personages that flit across the pages of the book and reveal the peculiar psychology of the *indio*. The pomposity, the false appearance, the submissiveness and obedience to the friars of those who do not wish to be disturbed in the least in their well-being and comfort, have their prototype in Captain Tiago. The *gobernadorcillo* personifies the nullity, the despotism towards those below, and the blind obedience to the caprices of those above. In contrast to this, and as if to redeem it, we find the *teniente-mayor* Don Filipo, who represents dignity, courtesy, and probity in authority. Father Damaso and Father Salvi are prototypes of the "friarocracy" of those days. They are outwardly very religious and devoted, supinely intolerant, vain, arrogant, and lacking consideration; inwardly, greedy, immoral, corrupt, and hypocritical. The philosopher Tasio is the educated man who dreams of a distant future, so distant that he cannot reach and see it, for which reason he masters a system of hieroglyphics and writes for a more advanced generation.

Among the feminine types there is Maria Clara, the ideal, the poetical, the pure and virgin dream, the fidelity in love, who prefers to seclude herself in a nunnery rather than break her pledge. Sisa is the humble and simple woman of the town, defenseless victim of social injustices. Doña Victorina represents the crazy and ludicrous pro-Hispanism, who detests the *indios,* although herself an *india,* and despises their dress, their language, and their customs. Doña Consolacion is the imprudent woman, foul-mouthed, arbitrary, and depraved.

Elias is perhaps the most "novelesque" personage of the *Noli Me Tangere,* much more so than Ibarra. He personifies all the virtues of the villager: gratitude, abnegation, sacrifice, and devotion to his country. He is created with the love and affection of the author. His past, forged from ignominies, is terrible. A grandfather falsely accused of incendiarism is flogged publicly and escapes to the mountains where, miserable and wounded to the soul, he hangs himself. The wife, compelled to find a living for the family, first prostitutes herself and later is imprisoned for the death of her husband because she did not report it to the authorities. A son of this unfortunate couple becomes a bandit and goes from province to province, sowing hate and terror everywhere, but at last falls into the hands of justice. His head, severed from his mutilated trunk, is hung in a basket from the branch of a tree before the hut of his mother, who dies from the shock. Another son flees from so much outrage and, after wandering for a long time, establishes himself in an unknown town; by dint of work and economy he succeeds in raising a little capital and becomes engaged to marry. When he is about to marry, his frightful past is discovered, and he is prosecuted and sent to jail. As a result of his relations with the girl, twins were born: a boy and a girl, who grew up happy. Their happiness did not last long because, once more, the past, gravitating on them as an accursed inheritance, was discovered anew by the authorities. The girl lost her sweetheart and died, murdered or drowned in an overflow of the lake; the boy wandered from town to town, fleeing justice, hating and hated by all. This is Elias.

Elias vindicates the ignorant, vicious, lazy, and egoistic Filipinos that abound in the novel. Although his education has been slight, the injustices which had befallen his poor family have enlarged and sharpened his intellect and have made him hate the social conditions in which he lives. But, unlike many who distrust but do nothing to improve that condition, he is an optimist like modern reformers. He trusts in Ibarra, in God, in the government of the metropolis, in almost all except the military men and the friars. He hates and punishes the wicked. He pities and joins those persecuted by the authorities. In a word, he is a restless, free spirit who has suffered much from the malice and iniquity of men; who, nevertheless, does not seek reparation nor vengeance but, with a kind of piety and mysticism, seeks to put into play all possible human resources to prevent any increase in the number of criminals and unhappy persons victimized by the gear of social injustices and prejudices.

One cannot be certain whether Elias was a fiction or a reality. The majority of the characters of the *Noli* evidently are sketches or pictures taken from life. But Elias surpasses them by his spiritual traits, his contrasts of light and shade, his dramatic surroundings—for all of which, it may be said, he is not a model hewn from reality, but a pure, allegorical creation. It is possible, however, for Elias to be a personage who has lived, thought, and suffered like many Filipinos of his time. He may be a portrait not of any specific person, as in the cases of Capitan Tiago, Doña Victorina, Father Damaso, and others, but of a personage whose antecedents and traits of character were taken from different people. The misfortunes of

Elias are perhaps not those of one single family or of many families, but the summation of the sufferings, the vague aspirations, and the prejudices of his epoch. He could be any one of the friends and acquaintances who followed Rizal, who approved his ideas as a redeemer, who suffered with him the misfortunes of the country, and who sought with unction and faith a miraculous balm for the wounds afflicting the social organism that was his country.

The Filipino of that epoch was considered an unlikely character for a novel. Those who represented him as a nonentity naturally could not believe in the real existence of Elias. For this reason Rizal undoubtedly created this mysterious and romantic personage who brings to mind some of Victor Hugo's characters, a mixture of bandit and savior, convict and patriot at the same time, who mocks the sacred character of priest and *alférez,* and respects the enemy of his family even to the extent of saving him from death. A paradoxical figure, yet a human being, who lives in tatters like a beggar, but aspires to demolish with his heavy mallet the firm bulwarks of the Pulpit and the Throne.

And for that reason Elias will always be a figure admirable, romantic, and subjugating; he will appeal to all the sympathies and tender feelings of the Filipino heart. What matters his enigmatic origin and his indefinable position, when he is a social worker who suffers, struggles, and endeavors to ameliorate the present and illuminate the utter darkness of the future? He will be a pariah, but he will see to it that the others are not. The curate and the *alférez* will persecute him and curse him; but he, like a shadow, will be present and be invisible at the same time. The machinations of the powerful can do nothing against him; he shall discover all their plans and frustrate them. When they believe they have Ibarra lodged in jail, Elias shall facilitate his flight and shall let himself be killed so that the other may be free and flee. Elias shall die rather than surrender himself to his enemies, arranging for the cremation of his body on a pyre so that his remains and his grave shall not be profaned. And thus ends that obscure yet luminous life, leaving the reader with a bitter taste of irony and of sadness for the memory of a hero of liberty who disappeared mysteriously in the night "without seeing the dawn of day shine upon his native country."

These are the principal personages. The rest of the cast is roughly sketched. The *hermanas terceras,* Tia Isabel, Crispin, Basilio, Cabesang Tinong, Tano, the old lieutenant, the *alférez* Guevara with his inseparable Doña Consolacion, and others who figure in the novel are mere caricatures, rough sketches of a reality, which pass before the view with the velocity of a motion picture.

The theme of the *Noli Me Tangere* is that there are men in the Philippines—like those who exist in other parts of the world—with their longings and passions, their loves and prejudices, their vices and virtues, that have been formed by a defective education that recognizes in them only the imitative and atrophied virtues of the lower animals; that there is no difference between the distinct social strata of the Filipinos and those of other countries; that what makes the Filipino appear of limited intelligence is the effect of the education he receives; that, although the Filipinos have some vices and defects, they are not those which the Spanish writers attribute to them, like Gaspar de San Agustin, Casimiro Herrero, Sinibaldo de Mas, Cañamaque, and others; that there is no stimulus to worth nor to merit, on the contrary, when a Filipino rises above the heap, he is ridiculed and made the object of mockery unless he serve the friars. Many Filipinos are persecuted or implicated in false conspiracies or exiled from their towns for maintaining their rights. The public administration does not rest on the confidence but on the fear of the people; the friars are availed of as counselors in everything that signifies reforms, and no liberal reform is carried out to which they are opposed.

The novel shows that the friar-priests have made of the Catholic religion an instrument of domination and have prostituted it with many exterior practices which only serve to foster the appearances of worship and to enrich the orders. The civil guard does not protect the peaceable citizens and the humble classes; they lend protection only to the friars and the Spaniards. The Filipinos, contaminated by the airs of superiority of the Spaniards, despise their own countrymen and make themselves ridiculous with their pretensions at false imitation. Rizal tried to show that there was no filibusterism in the Philippines, but that there would be, if the abuses and excesses of the friars and of the Government should force the Filipinos to it.

These are the conclusions, more or less general, that are deduced from the pages of the *Noli Me Tangere,* and with reason the author could say in his prologue that he has tried "to reproduce the condition of his country faithfully and fearlessly, and has raised part of the veil that hides the evil, sacrificing all to truth, including his self-love." (pp. 73-8)

> *Rafael Palma, in his* The Pride of the Malay Race: A Biography of José Rizal, *translated by Roman Ozaeta, Prentice-Hall, Inc., 1949, 385 p.*

NICK JOAQUIN   (essay date 1955)

[*In the following excerpt, Joaquin argues that the patriotic fervor inspired by Rizal has overshadowed the literary merit of his novels, emphasizing that, as satiric comedies,* Noli me tangere *and* El filibusterismo *are comparable to the works of Charles Dickens and Evelyn Waugh. Joaquin's remarks first appeared in* Katha I *in 1955.*]

Rizal re-read today is Rizal "discovered"—as a novelist, a modern novelist. His two novels, *Noli Me Tangere,* and *El Filibusterismo,* have suffered sadly from his reputation as a patriot. You don't go to a great national hero for a funny story; you go to admire, contemplate, worship, and gather pearls of wisdom. Rizal's books have been so beatified, so canonized, so enshrined, that they have almost ceased to belong to literature. What's worse, they've been called such names as "The Bible of the Race"—the sort of epithet a book finds hard to live down. It took the Bible many, many centuries to get itself read simply for pleasure—as all good books should be. Rizal will probably find the going even tougher. Nationalism—in our part of the world, anyway—is on the rise; and the Rizal novels are bound to get holier and holier instead of less so. The time may come, in fact, when a prospective reader will have to wash his hands, incense his person, and genuflect, before reading a passage from the sacred text. Rizal's title for his first novel may be prophetic.

As it is now, who reads Rizal? Everybody. And everybody's always urging everybody else—especially the helpless young—to read him. It's becoming a sort of sacred duty among us Filipinos. And that's exactly how we read him: as a duty, a tribal duty; and to have our minds elevated, our patriotism intensified. And because we have to write a theme

in school about him; or because we're tracking down a quotation; or because we're ghost-writing for some politician who'd like to mouth a few lofty utterances by the Pride of the Malay Race.

In short, nobody reads Rizal.

Nobody thinks of those two books as novels—like *Gone with the Wind,* and *St. Elmo* and *For Whom the Bell Tolls*—novels that are funny and sad and exciting and enjoyable. All novels are written to be enjoyed. But when we want to curl up with a good book, do we think of Rizal? Alas no. We sit down to study Rizal. But we don't take his books to bed with us like we do Margaret Mitchell's.

The result is very sad. You should never deliberately sit down to read a book for some high and noble purpose. (That's what I call reading a book in cold blood.) If you do, you are bound to get bored—though you may refuse to admit it even to yourself. When you finally do admit it, you may blame the book for having bored you. You may accuse it of being dull, over-rated. But it may not be the book's fault at all. To approach a book with awe is fatal.

I'm not sure that something of the sort has not already begun to happen with Rizal. Already some critics have attacked his novels on literary grounds. They say that the plot is preposterous, and borrowed from Dumas; that the characters are caricatures; that the writing is pedestrian. Many young people, who were made to read Rizal in a state of stupefied awe practically indistinguishable from boredom, will suddenly realize that it was boredom, and will join, with eager cries for relief, in the icon-smashing. All this may be for the best. When these books have been knocked down from the altar they may find their way back to the shelf and some curious ignorant boy may pick them up and start reading them with no thought for their message or purpose—simply for the pleasure of reading. And that boy is going to have one hell of a good time. For both these books—but the *Noli* especially—are first-rate comic novels—fast, funny and outrageous—novels, in fact, of the same kind as and almost in the same class with Dickens and the early Evelyn Waugh.

If Rizal did borrow from Dumas, it's amazing what he did with it. He took a creaky, lugubrious melodrama and turned it into a crisp, ironic social-problem novel. He picked up Edmond Dantes and transformed him into a Candido. His novels—or his novel, rather—the two books are really one story—is Dumas as Aldous Huxley or Evelyn Waugh might have written it: tongue in cheek. It has bite, it has fun, and—most important of all—has audacity. Who among our modern literary social reformers would dare couch his message in the form of an outrageous cloak-and-dagger romance? Rizal did—and got away with it. He had little to learn about narrative. He was a born novelist—and might have been a great one if he had been less of a patriot.

See how he starts his books with a bang. It usually took Dickens a dozen chapters to unroll the plot and march out the characters. Rizal had just as varied a group of dramatis personae; but, in both his books, the scene is set, the characters are assembled, the antecedents emerge, and the plot's aboiling, in the very first chapter. And with the very first chapter, he astounds, tickles, fascinates and dazzles with the brilliance and audacity of his invention.

In the *Noli,* for instance, there's the delicious hair-splitting little sermon by Fray Sybilla: "*Debemos distinguir en las pala-*

bras de Fray Damaso las del hombre de las del sacerdote . . . En las del hombre hay que hacer una sub-distincion: las que dice ab irato, las que dice ex ore pero no in corde, y las que dice in corde." Could mockery be sweeter? And Rizal closes the chapter with a gem of huge inspired silliness that, to my ear, sounds like pure Waugh. Fray Sybilla has remarked that it was in the fourteenth century that a Franciscan invented gunpowder; whereupon Doña Victorina inquires with great interest: *"En el siglo catorce? Antes o despues de Cristo?"* How Rizal must have roared when he wrote that!

The ninth chapter of the *Noli* (Cosas del Pueblo) must be cited as proof of Rizal's mastery of the novel—of his economy, his quick eyes, and the richness of his novelistic imagination. The brief chapter begins with Fray Damaso arriving at Captain Tiago's house; we are then taken into the Dominican convent to witness the enigmatic scene in the dying friar's cell; suddenly we are in Malacañan, listening to the jests of the captain-general; and finally we come back to Captain Tiago's house to find him angrily blowing out the candles lighted for Ibarra's safety on the road. The crucial event in this chapter—the conversation between Fray Damaso and Capitan Tiago—we have not been allowed to witness at all; but the quick transitions, the counter-pointing, the snatches of casual dialogue, the expert, rapid piling-up of details—we hear even the clinking of coins in the convent—bespeak a novelist who knows exactly what he's doing.

This brief perfect chapter might be used as a model in classes for writing. I once re-read it a dozen times at one sitting, fascinated by its mechanics, always with the same astonished delight. But there are other chapters just as wonderful: the Junta, for example, as the tribunal (Chap. XX); and the entire section dealing with the picnic, where Rizal did his most limpid writing; and the uproarious chapter on the battle between the alferez and his woman; as well as every single scene in which the incomparable Doña Victorina appears.

As far as I'm concerned, Doña Victorina is one of the great comic creations of all literature—on a par with Mrs. Malaprop, Mrs. Micawber, and the nurse in Proust. She's now usually cited as the symbol of the Filipino's slavish, cringing attitude towards the Westerner—and I really don't know why. For Doña Victorina may ape the Westerner and wear preposterous costumes and false curls: but she's not slavish, she does not cringe—not before the genuine Europeans, nor before the friars, nor even before the captain-general. It's her poor devil of a Spanish husband who does the cringing—at her feet. She rules him with a terrible fist. And if she's typical of the "slavish" Filipino of those times maybe we need more of her kind in these times. I wish Rizal had written an entire book about her. I'd willingly give up both the books he did write for that one book he didn't write. It would have been a comic masterpiece.

Over the figure of Maria Clara—whom, after Doña Victorina, I consider Rizal's most successful creation—there has been a worse misunderstanding, a double one. The nineteen-twenties turned her into a sentimental stock-figure; in reaction, some critics of the succeeding generation have knocked her down from her pedestal, branding her a caricature, not a paragon, and an obsolete ideal. They allege that not being a "pure blood" Filipina, she should not be urged as a model for Filipino women—a line of reasoning that automatically excludes from our emulation not only Rizal's fictitious heroine; but Rizal himself, as well as Burgos, Quezon, Arellano, and a host of our other national heroes. They are

dismayed that Rizal should have made a mestiza his heroine; but seem quite undisturbed that his hero should also be a mestizo. They assert that, being a friar's lovechild, Maria Clara is far from being an ideal, merely an object of disgust; and that Rizal (apparently without the slightest sense of chivalry or mere justice; since he is willing to visit the sins of the father upon an innocent girl) was really holding her up to our scorn, not our sympathy—an assertion that makes me wonder if these critics have ever read the book. For anybody that read the book cannot but feel that the author seems to have fallen in love with his heroine. The pen that's usually so sharp and acid suddenly turns tender and mellifluous whenever it deals with Maria Clara. Whenever Maria Clara appears on the scene, the prose, so hard and controlled elsewhere, trembles into poetry. (pp. 19-23)

And yet, these critics are not really attacking Maria Clara, not the Maria of Rizal anyway. Rizal nowhere announced that he was going to depict an "ideal woman" or an "ideal Filipino woman"—whatever that may be. Being a true novelist, he set out to create just one particular person, a single definite individual—and he succeeded so well that his heroine has become a folk-figure, the only one of all his characters who has attained this highest form of literary immortality. Between the first and second part of *Don Quixote,* the folk took over and recreated its hero; when Cervantes wrote the second part he was already dealing with another, larger hero, a folk-figure, only partly his creation. Similarly, the folk took over the recreated Maria Clara; unfortunately, there had been, in the meantime, a sudden shifting of cultures: Maria Clara was recreated as a Victorian—which she never was, nor any of her contemporaries for that matter.

The Philippines never actually experienced the Victorian Age. When Rizal said that the Philippines of his era was a hundred years behind in time, he was absolutely right. For Rizal, that was cause for lamentation; for us, from our happier vantage-point in time, it may be cause for relief—for the Philippines, by being "backward" escaped some of the ponderous horrors of Victorianism. We may be said to have leapt straight from the 18th to the 20th century, from the age of romanticism and the Revolution to the age of politics and anxiety. However, we did not—and it would have been impossible to—completely escape Victoria. Sometime during the last of the nineteen-hundreds and the first of the nineteen-twenties a generation [that] was being nourished on Mr. Longfellow, Mr. Bryant and Mr. Tennyson, that was being taught to appreciate such books as *Pollyanna, Silas Marner, Rebecca of Sunnybrook Farm,* and the Elsie Dinsmore series, suddenly developed Victorian taste and attitudes. The Señoritas became very genteel indeed; and the señoritas became addicted to blushing and fainting at the least provocation. The era of America's "Manifest Destiny" in the Philippines was a sort of Victorian twilight of the Middle Ages.

It was during this mock-Victorian twilight that Maria Clara was turned into a mock-Victorian ideal—by a people that had gone all the way back to the ABC's of a new culture, that had forgotten or were ignorant of the days of Revolution, and that were naturally and consequently rather unsure of their standards and of their taste. Each refined señorita of the nineteen-twenties simpering in a Maria Clara costume helped to distort the image of the vital vigorous girl that Rizal created. There was nothing of the girly-girly, of the limp and languid in Rizal's Maria Clara. Compare her to her contemporaries in English or American literature: to the Little Nells and

Doras and Agneses of Dickens, or to the now incredible heroines of American novelists like Dean Howells, who blushed and averted their eyes at the most innocent mention of bedrooms. No wonder Howells raved over Rizal's novels! What a relief for that haunted Puritan to read a book in which there was no Puritanism, no Victorian coyness, and where the women were women, not stuffed skirts.

The Maria Clara of Rizal, a mere girl, is subjected to the most awful and brutal and staggering revelation imaginable—a revelation that could crush even a mature man. She staggers, but she isn't crushed; she stands up under the blow. Is that the "spineless" woman she is now declared to be? Imagine her Victorian counterparts having to undergo such an ordeal! To save her lover, and to save her mother's name, she agrees to marry, in cold blood, a man she does not love, even at the risk of inviting the contempt of the lover she's trying to save. This, remember, is the decision of a mere chit of a girl. Is that an example of the vacuity and immaturity of the women of those days? When she learns that her lover is dead, she defies even her real father: she will marry no one, she will enter a nunnery. You may question her decision, but you cannot question that she has a mind of her own and that she seems capable of bending the will of others to her own. Where, then, is the slave and chattel of men in this proud, passionate girl?

There is, in fact, nothing at all of the Maria-Clairsh in Maria Clara—no, nor in any of the other women in Rizal. Where's the frailness and limpness in Doña Victorina or in the alferez' woman or in Sinang, Victoria, Iday and Nenang? But we have lumped all the women of that time—who must surely have been as various and complex as the women of any other time—into our saccharine idealization of the Rizal heroine; and it is this stock-figure that the critics have been attacking with such relish. Rizal saw a woman who was firm, clean, honest, graceful, devout, dignified, modest, tender and true; and if, as some say, our generation must now consider such a woman "obsolete," then God help our generation!

The dismay expressed by some people over the fact that such a patriotic man as Rizal should have made a mestiza his heroine strikes at the creative freedom of a writer; for it implies that a writer—or a Filipino writer anyway—should write to flatter the national ego and not to satisfy his own particular creative impulses, that he's not free to create the people he wants, and for reasons he need not explain, define, or apologize for.

I have dealt at length on Maria Clara because there has been, I think, the most misunderstanding about her and because the namby-pamby figure she has become may be frightening some people away from Rizal, who might enjoy reading him if they could only discard their old misconceptions of his novels. To prospective re-readers, I say: Forget all the solemn nonsense your school teachers and professional patriots have said about these books. Discover them for yourself. Don't read them because you think you ought to. Read them as you would read a new book by Waugh or Thurber, knowing just what to expect but also knowing you'll be surprised and delighted anew. Read them for laughs, and, I assure you, you'll find them great fun. (pp. 25-7)

Nick Joaquin, "The Novels of Rizal: An Appreciation," in José Rizal: A Collection of What People Have Said and Written about the Filipino National Hero, *edited by Sixto Y. Orosa, Manor Press, Inc., Publishers, 1956, pp. 19-27.*

JAMES A. MICHENER (essay date 1961)

[*Michener, among the most popular American novelists, is known primarily for his historic epics chronicling the events of a place and a people from prehistoric times to the present. He first gained attention with his 1947 Pulitzer Prize-winning collection of short stories,* Tales of the South Pacific, *and has continued to enjoy success with such panoramic works as* Hawaii *(1959),* The Source *(1965),* Centennial *(1974), and* Chesapeake *(1978). In the following forward to* The Lost Eden, *a translation of* Noli me tangere, *he commends Rizal for his adept portrayal of Filipino life and calls the novel a "national monument" to the Philippines.*]

In 1896, two years before United States intervention freed the Philippine Islands from the Spanish domination under which they had existed for nearly five hundred years, an armed revolution broke out. Led by Filipino patriots, it was both premature and unsuccessful. Its repression was bloody, and for the two-year interregnum between this abortive revolution and the American invasion it seemed as if the gracious islands had subsided once more under the somnolent dictatorship of Spain.

This curious revolution, so lacking in physical or political success, had an astonishing collateral effect upon Filipino literature, for nine years earlier, in 1887, José Rizal, a brilliant young eye doctor from the Philippines who was undergoing voluntary exile in Europe, had composed a powerful and compelling novel which predicted in minute detail the foundations and the course of the 1896 revolution. Thus the world saw proved once again the fact that real life labors diligently in its determination to mirror art. Today this novel, originally titled *Noli Me Tangere,* is the acknowledged masterpiece of Filipino literature. If any nation can be said to have a single source for its nationalism, the Philippine Republic is such a land, and this novel is the source. In this respect *Noli Me Tangere* is unique.

In form *Noli Me Tangere* is a nineteenth-century Gothic melodrama, filled with eery churches, flashes of lightning, ominous strangers, premonitory whisperings, and almost unacceptable coincidences:

> When everyone knelt and the priests lowered their heads at the *Incarnatus est,* a man whispered in Ibarra's ear: "At the blessing ceremony, stay close to the parish priest, don't go down the excavation, and don't go near the corner-stone. Your life depends on it." Ibarra saw Elias who, having said this, was losing himself in the crowd.

The style of the novel is pleasantly archaic; the reflections of the characters are predictable, and the dialogue has an ancient theatricality in keeping with the Gothic form, as when impassioned lovers greet after the hero has experienced unusual dangers:

> "Crisostomo!" she whispered, full of terror.
>
> "Yes, it is I, Crisostomo," the young man replied gravely. "An enemy, a man who had reason to hate me, Elias, has rescued me from the prison where I was flung by my friends." A rueful silence followed these words.

In structure the novel is well contrived, leading from the general social scenes in Manila to the particular involvements in the provincial capital of San Diego. A numerous cast of characters is kept in control, and their lives are intermingled naturally. Of special value to the pace of the novel are the brilliantly written short scenes like Chapter 15, "The Bell-ringers," or the comic scene in which a pretentious lady is endeavoring to pronounce the name of her country and can come no closer than "Feeleefeens."

In its characterizations *Noli Me Tangere* is worthy of being a national monument; the men and women who populate these pages seem to have come from nowhere but the Philippine Islands. The hero is indeed a young man who reveres his Spanish heritage but who also loves his Filipino homeland. The revolutionary Elias foretells the real-life Aguinaldos who were to follow him. Doña Victorina is a real horror of a provincial beldame trying to live down her Tagalog ancestry.

But it seems to me that what marks this novel is its constant gratuitous flashes of benign insight into various aspects of Filipino life. Often these comments are brief, witty pinpricks for pomposity, as applicable now as when they were written: "The Sabbath day is generally kept holy in the Philippines by going to the cockpit in the afternoon, just as in Spain it is kept by going to the bullring."

Or when another periodic massacre of Chinese is supposed to have taken place: "What a pity!" exclaimed Sister Rufa. "All the Chinese dead before Christmas, when they send us such nice gifts. They should have waited for New Year's Day."

Or when a loving father explains to his daughter the Spanish ideal of a perfect husband: "That is why I sought for you a husband who could make you the happy mother of children who would command, not obey, who would have the power to inflict punishment, not endure it."

Rizal is also exceptionally good in evoking with a few words complete scenes of Filipino life, as in his casual but unforgettable glimpse of a roadside chain gang: "The prisoners were unusually tall men with stern faces, whom Ibarra had never seen smile but whose eyes flashed when the whip fell whistling across their shoulders, or when a passer-by tossed them a cigar butt, damp and shredded, to be picked up by the nearest and hidden in his straw helmet while his fellows watched the other passers-by with unfathomable looks." And at times he interpolates countryside scenes which are almost finished short stories.

Noli Me Tangere is memorable in the history of literature for a special reason. It is the only novel I know that was directly responsible for its author's death, and this gives the work an added tragic dimension. Frequently, when reading this book the reader is tempted to cry, "These things are impossible. They must have been invented!" Yet observe what happened.

At dawn on the morning of December 30, 1896, José Rizal, a handsome young man with a small moustache, a Hapsburg chin and intense, dark eyes was marched onto a parade ground and executed by a firing squad. The very forces that he had railed against in his novel had conspired to destroy him. Reluctantly, he had become the moral hero of the revolution and today he rests as the most exalted figure in the pantheon of the Philippines. In choosing this complex, hesitant, gifted man as their national hero the Philippines have not only done him honor but have created an attractive portrait of their own aspirations. (pp. vi-viii)

> *James A. Michener, in a foreword to* The Lost Eden
> (Noli me tangere) *by José Rizal, translated by Leon
> Ma. Guerrero, Indiana University Press, 1961, pp.
> vi-viii.*

Manuscript cover of Noli me tangere.

CHARLES KAUT (essay date 1962)

[*In this excerpt from a review of the 1961 translation of* Noli me tangere, The Lost Eden, *Kaut emphasizes the anthropological importance of Rizal's work and its impact on the developing culture of the Philippines.*]

Though Rizal is often compared to writers like Dickens, Stowe, or Dumas, he cannot be accurately compared to anyone other than himself because of his unique position as a non-Western writer in 19th century Western literature. For the anthropologist, Rizal is a colleague as well as a source of valuable materials. His novels and other writings are full of ethnographic detail and social observations. His efforts to reconstruct pre-Spanish Philippine culture have made available to us certain important documents relating to the early and pre-Spanish periods. (p. 1090)

The title, *Noli Me Tangere,* has been rendered in English in various ways. Rizal originally took the phrase from John XX:17 where Christ, newly arisen, admonishes Mary Magdalen not to touch him. *Lost Eden* is taken from a poem written in Spanish by Rizal while he was in prison awaiting execution. As the translator tells us in his introductory essay, "Two Novels That Made a Revolution," *Noli Me Tangere* "will always be known to all the Filipinos as the *Noli,*" but *Lost Eden* is quite apt in view of Rizal's message that the Spanish had lost a chance to participate in the building of an exceptional Asian nation.

The plot of the *Noli,* set in the 1880's, concerns the return of a native son from his education in Europe to the city of Manila and a provincial town in Laguna. He is frustrated and defeated in his attempts to work within the framework of Spanish administration for the advancement of his country through education of the common people. The basic theme is social injustice which finally brings the young hero, Ibarra, to his death. As it describes the difficulties of the Filipino at the hands of his Spanish masters, especially the clergy, the story is designed to show that the *Indio* is not a "savage just down from the trees," but a capable human being whose feelings and intelligence should be respected.

In the process of telling his story, Rizal describes in great detail various aspects of 19th century Tagalog life. My feeling is that he is probably at his best in describing the behavior of the upper class (of which Rizal was a member) and bustling social events, such as the town fiesta that provides the setting for a major portion of the novel. Unfortunately, we get only glimpses of the *taong bukid* or peasant, and these of such a highly romantic sort that they do not seem real.

However, almost all segments of the Philippine nation (except Pagan and Moro) have been so deeply influenced by Rizal and his writings that the anthropologist needs an awareness of them. The characters and ideas in the *Noli* and the *El Filibusterismo* have been drilled into several generations of college students, many of whom have returned to teach in rural schools. The books themselves have been widely read, discussed, and reworked for stage productions, movies, short stories, and comic strips. Rizal's novels have, then, been widely used and effective vehicles for presenting ideas that are now firmly established as part of the national ethos. . . . Rizal may not have been an omniscient reporter of his time, but some of his misunderstandings have been translated into social realities as succeeding generations of Filipinos have looked to his descriptions and evaluations of character as models for judgment of their own behavior and that of others. (p. 1091)

> *Charles Kaut, in a review of "The Lost Eden," in* American Anthropologist, *Vol. 64, No. 5, October, 1962, pp. 1090-91.*

CARMEN GUERRERO-NAKPIL (essay date 1968)

[*In the following essay, Guerrero-Nakpil regards Rizal's female protagonist Maria Clara as a harmful role model for Filipino women, citing her submissive character and idealized physical features as undesirable and unattainable standards to which many Filipino women aspire.*]

The greatest misfortune that has befallen Filipino women in the last one hundred years is Maria Clara. I mean this in a very real sense for, in trying to live up to the pattern set by Rizal's beautiful heroine, millions of Filipinas became something other than their real selves.

They forced their persons into the narrow mold of Maria Clara's maidenly charms and became effete and exceedingly genteel caricatures. They affected modesty to an absurd degree and became martyrs to duty and familial love. They tried to disguise their native industry and energy with put-on airs of languidity. And because Maria Clara was ill so often, and

so elaborately sad and tragic, it became vulgar to be healthy and almost un-Filipina to be happy.

It is this melancholy transformation of Maria Clara from paragon to parody that I want to trace briefly here.

To begin with, let me say that I believe there are two popular interpretations of Maria Clara. One, which found favor during the first three decades after the *Noli,* conceived of her as a compendium of all possible feminine virtues, beautiful, demure, tender, docile, pure, everything a woman should be.

The other, of more recent origin, was a reaction to the first. As a result of a "revolution of taste" it views Maria Clara with a jaundiced eye indeed. It calls her obsolete, melodramatic, meaching, and fatuous and finds her fragility mousy, her nobility irritating, her virtue priggish.

I must confess that I am by temperament inclined to the second view. But an objective analysis of Maria Clara as Rizal wrote her and not as clubwomen and their guest speakers on one hand, nor as the aggressive iconoclasts of the thirties, on the other, would have her, seems to indicate that a middle way would be more correct.

Maria Clara, as all successful literary creations should be, was not all of a piece. She was, certainly, a good and beautiful woman, innocent, unselfish, and admirable in many respects. But she was also—and quite indubitably—a silly girl, coy, sentimental, and often rather foolish. She was, as most people are, neither all good nor all bad.

She was so sweet that everyone adored her, so utterly feminine that everyone wished to protect her. She was also strong in adversity. When the shameful story of her parentage was revealed to her, she took it upon herself to shield her real father, her foster father, and her mother's honor. "She staggers, but she isn't crushed," writes Nick Joaquin, "she stands up under the blow. She agrees to marry in cold blood a man she does not love, even at the risk of inviting the contempt of the lover she's trying to save. When she learns that her lover is dead, she defies even her real father; she will marry no one, she will enter a nunnery" [see excerpt dated 1955]. We may disagree with her decisions, as indeed many of us do, but we cannot rightly say that she made them out of weakness. After all, it does take courage to give up a lover, to decide a loveless marriage, and afterwards to take the veil.

Nevertheless, and at the same time, Maria Clara is insufferably soggy and affected. When her sweetheart, just home from Europe, comes to call on her, she rushes to the family oratory and has to be dragged out, head hanging, to greet him. Whenever she hears any piece of bad news, she develops faintness and totters off to her bedroom. She archly pretends to be unworthy of Ibarra's attentions. She appears to be inarticulate and humorless: a priceless comic character like Doña Victorina does not draw the faintest smile or the palest remark from her. One has only to compare her with Sinang, her closest friend, who is direct, outspoken, and alive to the significance and the humor of every situation, to realize how dull and colorless Maria Clara's company must have been. But, worst of all, she fails to respond to the patriotic needs of the hour; at the crucial moment, she does not choose the side of the filibustero, the reformer, the patriot, but the side of the friar and the *peninsular.* She gives her all to have two completely unworthy men: Fray Damaso, the seducer, and Capitan Tiago, the cringing, servile colonial.

How did this commonplace heroine, whose virtues are singularly stereotyped and whose tragedies are ascribable only to fate, ever become apotheosized into the ideal of Filipino womanhood? We owe it to the historical circumstances of Rizal's martyrdom and to the subsequent devotion, more passionate than discerning, to his literary creations. Had Rizal not become the national hero, his heroine would have remained merely one more character in our little-read Spanish literature, to be encountered by chance in the romantic labyrinths of an old-fashioned novel, to be dissected perhaps by a few esoteric critics, but surely dismissed by a new generation of readers.

We cannot really blame Rizal. There is little evidence that he tried to enshrine Maria Clara as the ideal or, even, the typical Filipina. It is more probable that he merely created a single individual character out of a woman in his own life. Perhaps Rizal tried to write out his own frustration and to purge his own heart-break from the unfortunate affair with Leonor Rivera, the woman whom he called "my only illusion." We have reason to suppose that Leonor was the prototype for Maria Clara; she, too, sacrificed her sweetheart, although her motives were less pure and pressing than those the novelist attributes to his creation. Rizal never did attempt to make Maria Clara into the Filipino woman. She was simply a woman he had loved. She was not even his own ideal—many men, after all, give their hearts to women whom their minds find inadequate. We must go to the **"Letter to the Young Women of Malolos"** to know the measure of the women Rizal really admired. In that letter he urged his young countrywomen to be bold, aggressive, industrious, to get rid of the inhibiting ties with religion and convention. The *Epistolario Rizalino,* too, contains evidence of the type of woman he believed his country needed. While in Germany, for example, he wrote his sister Maria to tell her of the ingenuity and the industry of the *frauleins;* he urged his sisters towards self-improvement, and he was surely their inspiration when they joined the Katipunan and the Masonic Order. Rizal's own mother was as dissimilar as possible from Maria Clara, and we know that he adored her. Doña Teodora was a down-to-earth, enterprising, incredibly brave woman with a respect for the intellect and intellectual accomplishment. She recognized, although it brought her pain, the value of hatred and rebellion. We can only imagine how different Rizal and our country would have been if Rizal had had a Maria Clara for a mother.

Then, too, Rizal was perhaps merely following the literary conventions of the period: the literature of his time was full of haunted, gentle, ill-starred heroines. Dickens, Dumas, Tolstoy, whom Rizal admired, respected the fashion that ordained that heroines must be true, good, and beautiful—and also a little limp and vapid. Rizal's Maria Clara, perhaps, merely succumbed to the dictates of literary vogue.

But we can blame the generation of Filipinos who came after Rizal. Had they been less sentimental and more clear-headed about Maria Clara, things would have been different. Instead of seeing Maria Clara whole, instead of admiring the woman entire, they made the mistake of idealizing her external traits. Instead of giving their attention to her strength, her nobility, her inherent stubbornness, they made a cult out of her capacity for blind obedience, for fainting and blushing. Thus, their women moved quickly from a studied to a habitual demureness, and the nation soon had many millions of mincing, smirking, doltish parodies of Maria Clara.

Maria Clara also influenced, and for the worse, our feminine standard of beauty. She was a *mestiza* and therefore, white, "perhaps too white" is Rizal's own phrase, light of hair, "almost blonde," with huge eyes which were "almost always cast down" and a perfect nose. Rizal himself called her features "semi-European," and while this circumstance was clearly called for by the novel's plot, yet it was unfortunate for Filipino beauty. For, in portraying his heroine in this guise, Rizal set up, unwittingly, one likes to think, a standard of feminine beauty that was untypical and unreal.

By trying to look like Maria Clara, Filipino women have lost the warm naturalness of their Asian personality. Because Maria Clara was fair, they have hidden their golden skin under rice-powder, and, lately, make-up; because Maria Clara's hair was curly, they twisted their hair with curling irons, ribbons, and chemicals and succeeded only in frizzing it; because Maria Clara's eyes were round and long-lashed, their own Oriental almond eyes fell into disrepute, and because Rizal called Maria Clara's European nose "the correct profile," everything else became incorrect and therefore deplorable. Because Maria Clara's mouth was small and dimpled, thousands of Filipinas have gone through life compressing their generous Asian lips into prim and ridiculous rosebuds. We have all seen this kind of mimicry in old family albums—our mothers and grand-mothers, powdered, frizzed, and over-dressed, gazing foolishly at a paper moon and, when we come to think of it, looking painfully out of character.

The cult of Maria Clara has contributed to the development of many disagreeable traits and attitudes in the Filipino woman. One may cite a diehard refinement and of the *comme il faut,* such as ostentatious costumes and jewelry, the *duenna,* the avoidance of industry or anything that might possibly be called work, the cultivation of idleness and leisure.

Another is the exaggerated emphasis on the maidenly proprieties, the coy look, the half-smile, the dislike to appear too eager or too forward, the excessive regard for appearance. Also, its corollary: the prescribed rituals of Victorian Courtship, with its elaborate hypocrisy and formality. What tribulations have been heaped on generations of Filipino suitors because Maria Clara never met Ibarra's eyes directly!

Another and even more deplorable result is the Filipino women's fondness for sentimentality, for the mawkish and the banal. Conventional Filipinas, more's the pity, have a propensity for being sticky-sweet, for tears and signs, as well as saccharine situations and expressions. Maria Clara once more!

But the most unfortunate of all of Maria Clara's legacies was the masochistic attitude. Because of Maria Clara millions of Filipinas learned to enjoy suffering and humiliation. They took up their crosses and followed her to the apotheosis of romantic sanctification. They embraced, with as many pretty tears as Rizal's heroine, hardships and tragedies which they could have, and should have, avoided; they gave up sweethearts and love marriages; they suffered in silence and renounced all unladylike pleasures. They denied themselves every kind of joy, wallowed in self-pity, gorged themselves on their delicious miseries. And in so doing made everyone around them miserable: we all know how hard it is to live with a woman who is bent on immolating herself. Self-sacrifice can be the cruelest form of tyranny.

It is this element of guilt and disaster in the attitude of Filipino women that we must lament most. It is so well rooted in our *mores* that the average Filipina—though she may not have read through Rizal's novels—has a compulsive sense of sin and doom, of sadness and shame. She feels obliged to see terror in the delights of love and sex, and to offset this, as Maria Clara did, by a kind of frantic piety.

I risk the dangers of simplification willingly when I say that all this came about because Maria Clara—a literary creation who has become a "folk-figure"—had a priest for a father, an adulteress for a mother, and a radical for a sweetheart, and because, caught in the meshes of a patriot-novelist's plot, she made a talent for unhappiness her greatest virtue. (pp. 85-91)

Carmen Guerrero-Nakpil, "Maria Clara," in Rizal: Contrary Essays, *edited by Petronilo Bn. Daroy and Dolores S. Feria, Guro Books, 1968, pp. 85-91.*

PETRONILO BN. DAROY (essay date 1968)

[*In the following essay, Daroy examines the relationship between politics and literature in Rizal's life.*]

As a writer, Rizal is a victim of the patriotism of our scholarship, just as he was of the colonial and illiberal policies of Spain. In the Philippines, he has been regarded exclusively as a political figure. The fact is that what he said in his defense was true: that he was never directly engaged in political activities. Unlike Bonifacio or Mabini, Rizal never became directly involved in a political movement. His relationship to the Revolution was indirect. He did nothing more than write. Even his involvement in the *Liga,* an organization which was dissolved four days after its formal founding, consisted in nothing more than the writing of its constitution and bylaws. Rizal was a writer and he was persecuted as such by the Spanish colonial government.

It is therefore surprising that this fact is usually ignored by our scholars. It is true that Rizal himself was partly responsible for this confusion. In his letters, his conversation, and in his shorter and occasional articles, he was full of concern for the native society and these nationalistic interests are projected into the thoughts and motives of the important characters in his novels. But a writer need not be talking always about writing and literature; very few writers do; and to regard Rizal exclusively as a patriot on the basis of his interest in nationalism, is like accepting Aesop as a zoologist because he wrote about animals.

Rizal was an engaged writer and this is one reason for his continuing relevance. His literary taste was rather narrow, and, in certain cases, a bit mediocre. He thought *Uncle Tom's Cabin* was a great work of art and, yielding to a romantic sense of himself, identified himself with Eugene Sue's *Wandering Jew.* His poetry is remarkable for its confusion of metaphors, for its excessive rhetoric, and for its mere commemorative value. But he had definite convictions about art. In sculpture, he had a preference for the allegorical in favor of plastic values, and indeed, it was the allegorical implications in Juan Luna's painting, "The Spoliarium," that appealed most to him. He saw in it the blending of two cultures, the Occidental and the Oriental; he also made the inference that the painting suggested a theory of history, perceiving in it the mythical quarrel of generations—of father and son—and extending the meaning to imply the passing away of Spain's authoritarian rule in the country. Culture, Rizal said, still speaking of Luna's painting during the banquet held in honor of Luna and Hidalgo in Madrid—advances dialectically and

the contact between our Oriental and the Hispanic cultures gave us "life, liberty, and civilization," and woke us up from our Asiatic "slumber."

These ideas are obviously extraneous to the painting. I cannot see how the representation of dying gladiators, being dragged by Roman soldiers, could suggest this complex theory. But the speech also implied Rizal's theory of art: he said that art must not simply aim to please; it must be an instrument for political action.

To Rizal, therefore, the artist must take issues with politics and social institutions. His aim is not merely to delight—an aesthetic popularly held by Walter Pater and Oscar Wilde in about the same era. The writer, on the contrary, must be a critic of society. This formulation virtually recalls Matthew Arnold, but there is a point in which Rizal goes beyond Arnold's belief that literature should be a "criticism of life." Rizal thought that criticism must inevitably lead the mind to certain conclusions and must seek to realize reforms within the practical terms of politics. He dismissed Pedro Paterno's *Ninay* as a mediocre work; it did not grapple with the problem of politics and evil; it did not express any partisanship in the issues that confronted the society it tried to present. For Rizal, the writer must be a partisan, and it is in terms of the partisanship that he must be judged. The writer acts through literature; this is his way of expressing his interest in freedom; being able to address himself to the freedom of others.

This is not to say that Rizal was indifferent to formal considerations. Although he wrote his brother Paciano that to be a writer one does not have to bother so much about style, human liberty being a more important issue, he was also quick to perceive the stylistic excellence of Marcelo H. del Pilar's *La Soberania Monacal.* For that matter, Rizal valued del Pilar's critical opinions. After the publication of *El Filibusterismo* he sent del Pilar a copy, expecting him to review the book in *La Solidaridad.* Rizal anxiously waited for the review, and when del Pilar failed to write it, giving the book merely a notice in *La Solidaridad,* Rizal resented it and considered it an affront.

The quality and content of Rizal's novels, therefore, derived from literary criteria, not just the expression of an individual patriotism. His interest in the colonial question reflected the sort of responsibility he attached to his role as writer. He was serious about this responsibility; he believed it should be exercised in defense of the rights of man, which is to say, that it should be expressed in antagonism against coercive institutions and against the policies of an authoritarian politics. I think this is the reason why Rizal is consistently misinterpreted. He expressed himself in the concrete. From his letters to Father Pastells we know that he was not a Platonist and that he did not believe in ideals as abstraction. He knew that freedom must be defended in concrete terms. Consequently, its enemies must be isolated and defined in the particularity with which they manifest themselves in politics and in society. The colonial situation in the Philippines at the time dramatized the issue of freedom and political authoritarianism, and it was in terms of this concrete situation that Rizal expressed his commitment as a writer.

In the history of literature, it is not unusual to find politics claiming the attention of the novelist and to see him creating a formal narrative structure, through a series of correlatives, out of the specific details, implications, and aspects of the subject. Sometimes the novelist engages the subject explicitly, as in *Darkness at Noon,* giving us to understand that the situation he depicts derives from an immediate fact in contemporary history. Then, it is also the case that presentation of the subject is metaphorical in which the fictional situation is an analogy of what is happening in life or in a particular generation. *The Magic Mountain* is an example of this.

Rizal's novels belong to the former category. They happen also to have practical aims; they intend to realize social and political reforms. The Board of Censors was correct in its evaluation of the *Noli.* It is a subversive book; its sequel, the *Fili,* is even more radical.

But these novels are radical in more than the political and practical sense. They are radical in a very literary sense. Next to Burgos' *La Loba Negra,* they brought Philippine literature to the status of modernity by breaking away from the stale literary conventions popular at the time. Rizal was not the first Filipino writer to have used politics as the subject of literature. Balagtas' *Florante at Laura* is a political poem, but Balagtas was content to adopt the conventions of the *corrido* and *awit.* Balagtas confined himself to questioning the morality of the ruling authority in the country; he did not attempt to break away from the traditional literary techniques.

The novels of Rizal are important in the sense that they created a new literary canon: a way of observing details, of organizing the continuity of narrative actions, of constituting characters and analyzing their motives different from the established terms of the literature of the time. *Noli Me Tangere* and *El Filibusterismo* belong to the category of realism and naturalism and to the tradition of literature that began with Balzac and Zola.

Like Balzac, Rizal is interested in depicting houses, personal ambitions, and such details of life as the way of making friends and treating one's enemies; the concern with one's public image; the importance that people attach to what they consider are the extensions of their personalities such as the furniture in the sala, their clothes and dresses, their manner of speech, their husbands or their wives. The documentary tendency extends even to the measurement of houses; the statistics of indulgencies and the reproduction of misspellings and grammatical mistakes in personal letters. The concern with facts is of course an aspect of realist literature, but, as with Balzac, Rizal uses them not merely to achieve specificity in the drama of situations, but to realize the abstract nature of the social process.

The *Noli* is not about Ibarra, it is about society, and in the first paragraph of the novel the state of things in society is at once established: its "parasites," and social-climbers responding to Capitan Tiago's invitation to the banquet he is giving in honor of Ibarra. Then the central metaphor is established. The house of Capitan Tiago, like his country, is open to everything except commerce and bold and new ideas. This analogy is expanded later on: something is wrong with the structure of the houses; it significantly leans to one side, and the novel raises the question of blame but suspends final judgment on the source of responsibility for this faulty structure—whether it was the fault of a cross-eyed architect or due to the natural conditions of the country, the earthquakes and the typhoons. It is the intention of the novel to search for a resolution of this question, so, for the moment, it tries to expand further the house-country analogy by noting the decor in Capitan Tiago's sala: the furniture is imitative and it is

Capitan Tiago's pride to tell his guests that the chairs are "European." The decor is a motley of Christian, pagan, and Oriental art: paintings of miraculous saints, Chinese porcelain and, in the window, a stuffed *botete.* We are also told that Capitan Tiago takes a pragmatic view with regards to the importance of his saints.

This confusion of the religious sentiment is recapitulated in the latter part of the novel, in the description of the religious procession. Here again we notice the confusion of symbols; the peculiar adaptation by the natives of the Christian cult.

As against this confusion and chaos in culture, Rizal counterpoints the stability of Nature. The description of the town of San Diego in Chapter X focuses on the surrounding landscape and trees; the house and the churchtower stand out in the lush greenery. From this angle of vision the perspective descends to reveal the forest and, for the first time we have the menacing hints of violence and death introduced into the domain of nature. We come to know later that these dark hints actually foreshadow Elias' story in Chapter L where the violence of society and politics is enacted in the stillness and solitude of the forest.

The dialectics of the novel is developed through the juxtaposition of Nature and society. Nature is associated with survival and revivification: Ibarra saves Elias from drowning during the picnic; the caves and the forests are the refuge of "criminals"; Tasio instructs Ibarra on politics by pointing to the plants in his garden, etc. Then, as counterpoint to the picnic incident, Elias saves Ibarra during the chase on the lake by jumping from the boat and swimming ashore in order to divert the attention of the pursuer.

A different implication of "nature" is presented in terms of the characters: Maria Clara is an "unnatural" daughter; Doña Victorina tries to disguise her natural self and becomes grotesque. Among the characters, disguise is a common propensity: Don Tiburcio passes himself off as a doctor; Doña Victorina threatens to reveal the "humbug" of her cousin, Linares; Padre Damaso dissimulates his paternity of Maria Clara. Here it is the conventions of society, the demands of morality, that compel the concealment of the natural, rendering the characters either grotesque, effete, or detestable.

On yet a different level, the whole authority of society in the novel is unnatural in the sense that it is artificial, an imposition. In **"The Indolence of the Filipinos,"** Rizal implies his acceptance of Montesquieu's climatic theory of government. Laws must evolve from the necessary conditions of a community. Thus he implies, in the Philippines, the conditions of labor are different and, therefore, the productive capacity of the natives must not be judged in the quantitative terms of more temperate zones. Also, labor laws should be adjusted to the natural realities of the country. The conflict between the colonial laws and the indigenous realities of life in the Philippines constitutes the central theme of the *Noli.*

The colonial order implicitly assumes that the natural condition of the natives was evil, or at any rate, not promotive of civilization. Hence it had to be rectified, curbed by the ethos and morality of a different religion, by the colonial laws, and by a colonial educational system. After the publication of the *Noli,* Rizal worked on the annotation of Morga's *Sucesos.* He meant to provide the Filipinos, he said, a sense of the past; to give them an awareness of what they were before the colonial conquest, the culture they had, the gods they worshipped, and the morality that governed the system of relationships in their society. The colonial regime thwarted the natural development of the indigenous culture and, consequently, created a crisis in life and society. Nationalism was a way of restoring the natural condition of the Filipinos; consequently, the revolution that is hinted at in the *Noli* and developed fully in the *Fili* was a means of regaining the Filipino identity in the natural state of his sovereign community. The Filipinos were born free, but in the colonial *status quo* everywhere he was in chains.

In Rizal's terms, freedom is associated with the condition of life enjoyed by the Filipinos before the colonial conquest. Spain tried to destroy everything associated with this life and in *Tagalog Nobility,* Rizal showed how the Spanish conquest was not merely political. It also destroyed the native traditions: our songs, our literature, our myths and our beliefs. Now and then the native aspects would manifest itself, turning into a travesty the European culture which we were forced to adopt. But the suppression of the native culture, as Rizal tried to show in **"The Philippines Within A Century,"** was also bound to create violence. The native aspects would break through the colonial crust and this even would be a positive thing.

In the *Fili* revolution is presented as an assertion of the natural rights of the natives. Its logic and inevitability is affirmed after all the liberal reformatist issues have been shown as invalid to the situation of society in the novel. "Hispanization of rights" (Simoun's phrase) and assimilation, for instance, are criticized by Simoun in his first conversation with Basilio. These will be unnatural because it will simply result in the substitution of native values, including "the structure of our thoughts," with foreign aspects. Simoun insists on the retrieving of the native identity: Aspire to be yourselves, he told the students through Basilio.

In spite of the intimate associations between revolution and the reassertion of natural rights in the novels, however, Rizal did not argue for a return to nature in the terms we usually encounter it in Western literature. In Western literature, the assertion of "nature" or "naturalness" or of freedom usually takes the form of a rejection of social conventions and the affirmation of the more anarchic impulses of man. We find the arguments in favor of the darker, usually repressed, instincts in André Gide, in Nietzsche, and in D.H. Lawrence. There is something of the prudish in Rizal: in Dapitan, he wanted the women to cover their legs with stockings. And throughout his system of thought, he accepted the validity of government and laws. In the novels, he is concerned with the passage of the individual from the natural to the civil state and in his examination of the colonial situation, he did not go beyond the terms of the social contract. In the *Fili,* revolution is a political, not a metaphysical concept. It deeply implicates economic issues.

El Filibusterismo investigates social injustice in relation to the concept of property. It is sharp in its delineation of classes and the first chapter immediately gives us the state of stratification in the society. The boat *Tabo* is the ship of state, symbolically divided into upper and lower decks, the passengers in these divisions corresponding to the social classes in conflict in the novel. On the upper deck are the bourgeois, indolent, full of stupid notions, arrogant, and bored. On the lower deck are of course the lower classes, the laboring mass, and free to go up and down are the students and Simoun—the liberals and the revolutionary.

The novel shows up the liberal argument as empty, utopian, and abstractly idealist. In fact Simoun used these terms in his conversation with Basilio in the grave yard of Sisa. The liberals are alienated from the masses; they are full of generalizations and they remain unaware of the revolutionary ferment in their society. Up to a certain point—until the interview of Isagani with Señor Pasta—Rizal allows the liberal argument to have a certain force. But the role of liberalism in the social question is never allowed to dominate the argument of the novel, for the main argument of the novel rests on the question of property. The revolution in the novel does not suggest it would settle this question, although its recruits come from the dispossessed, like Basilio. It ultimately becomes an anarchic plan, bereft of ideology.

Against the background of Simoun's revolutionary plans, two main ideas are made to counterpoint each other: one is connected with the plight of Cabesang Tales; the other one has something to do with Simoun's jewels.

Cabesang Tales cultivates a piece of land which turns out to belong to a religious corporation. Unable to pay the rent which the friars increase every year, he finally goes to court. He is defeated in the case and is evicted from the land. The novel raises the question: What criteria should determine the right to property and rejects the legal consideration (possession of title) in favor of a more practical consideration? Property should belong to one who can make it socially useful. The friars had allowed the land to remain idle; Cabesang Tales, on the other hand, had made it productive and used the benefits that derived from it to improve the condition of his family, to send his granddaughter to school and, by paying the rent, partly contributed to the welfare of the state.

Contrasted with Cabesang Tales' relationship to the land are the jewels of Simoun. Simoun uses his jewels to corrupt the officials of the colony and to excite the greed of the masses. In the Chapter "Wealth and Want," he uses the conspicuous value of his jewels to make the masses feel more acutely their misery. In the novel, the jewels have a negative value: they serve no purpose except to promote corruption and greed. In the end, the jewels are thrown into the sea by Padre Florentino with the invocation that they should remain in the depths until someone with a better purpose should find it fit to fish them out.

What this purpose is, Padre Florentino does not say and the novel fails to be explicit. We know only that it should not be the sort of purpose that Simoun had put them to. It should not be for the purpose of confusing the ends of revolution, nor for the sake of arbitrarily promoting the instinct for violence and rapacity even if these be directed against a corrupt regime and a decadent society. It is at this point that we begin to perceive how limited, indeed, was Rizal's radical viewpoint. But this limitation refers only to his politics and does not condemn his achievement in literature. Rizal's politics transcends the mere nationalist cant of his contemporaries like Lopez-Jaena of whom he said that one does not know whether he (Lopez-Jaena) wanted to get drunk in order to be eloquent or cultivated his eloquence in order to get drunk, and the mediocre patriotism of most of the scholars who have studied him. As a writer, Rizal showed how inevitable it is that the writer should be drawn to consider politics and statecraft; he also demonstrated how literature could rise above a certain aesthetic level when it examines the concepts, the intellectual formulations that oppose or guide man's particular existence in culture. (pp. 128-38)

Petronilo Bn. Daroy, "Politics as Literature," in
Rizal: Contrary Essays, *edited by Petronilo Bn.
Daroy and Dolores S. Feria, Guro Books, 1968, pp.
128-38.*

ELLIOTT C. ARENSMEYER (essay date 1970)

[*In the following excerpt, Arensmeyer evaluates Rizal's talent
as a novelist, examining such aspects of* Noli me tangere *and*
El filibusterismo *as plot, characterization, humor, theme, and
style. He concludes that, while Rizal demonstrates a mastery
of these elements, he lacks the "universal vision" found in the
works of Leo Tolstoy, Charles Dickens, Honoré de Balzac, and
Émile Zola.*]

The novel is said to be a narrative arranged in time sequence.
To tell a story is the fundamental purpose of the writer. In
the end, a novel will stand or fall on the universal criteria of
plot, people and purpose achieved. There are, of course, secondary considerations such as power of prophecy, pattern,
fantasy, rhythm and style. All novels have a purpose, most
present a point of view, and all should reveal a certain
amount of life at their source. This is the basic difference between straight, historic narration and creative fiction. In the
end a writer is judged by whether he has created or recorded.
Comparisons between one author and another are often odious and always controversial. Thus, it is not valid to judge
José Rizal against the achievements of his fellow writers, but
it is wise to judge his novels according to the criteria above.
In this fashion it is possible to decide if he has recorded or
created.

Rizal wrote his two novels with a simple and direct purpose
in mind: to bring his people out of their long medieval twilight dominated by the last medieval power in Europe, Spain,
and into the dynamism and intellectual excitement of the
nineteenth century European world. It is not an exaggeration
to say that Rizal, in the end, died for Europe and was, from
birth to death, a man of Europe. Although he spoke for an
oriental people he was neither caught up in the passivity of
the Indian Tagore, his contemporary in national feeling, nor
in a torturous duality between an old, static culture and a new
scientific pragmatism as were the Japanese intellectuals of the
Meiji period. Rather, he was a Mazzini and a Zola . . . entirely measurable by Western standards. Rizal was the classic
Good Man who was dedicated to the noblest ends and possessed the art of forceful expression which had been developed by his Jesuit education. His years in Europe allowed
him to develop all his faculties. His keen intelligence gave
him amazing facility in languages and commendable ability
in painting, sculpture and medicine. Rizal, then, is measurable in European terms and the purpose of his novels was to
lay bare a sick and decayed society with all the humor and
mordant facility of a fine novelist.

Neither *Noli Me Tangere* nor *El Filibusterismo* is content
merely to tell a story, although both have taut and, by in
large, satisfactory plots. The *Noli* seeks to expose the
frailocracy of the Philippines and the foibles of governors and
governed alike. It is a novel of both social and political criticism with satiric commentaries on a vast range of colonials
and natives. The *Fili* is perhaps less neat in its purpose. It
shifts from exposé to debate and while its plot is a real "cliff
hanger" its purpose vacillates between Rizal's desire to reject
anarchism as a solution and his desire to promote political
upheaval as the only way for the Filipino to gain freedom. In
the end the purposeful theme which runs through both books

remains the vibrant anti-clericalism which Rizal chose, in
much the same way which his great hero Voltaire chose, to
expose all the evils of his world. Amidst the intricacies in *El
Filibusterismo* of the student plots and twisted designs of the
anarchist Simoun, the friar theme rides high.

> Remove the friar, gentlemen, and you shall see the
> edifice of state tottering for lack of sturdy shoulders
> and hairy legs to support it; life in the Philippines
> will grow monotonous without the merry laughter
> of the playful and carousing friar . . . without the
> daily lively re-enactment of the tales of Boccacio
> and La Fontaine.

One of the basic criteria on which to judge the literary value
of a book is whether the characters are round or flat. That
is, are they constructed on a single quality or can they be easily identified by the reader in their varied qualities of characterization? In *Noli Me Tangere* it is Rizal's avowed purpose
to expose the Friar. Thus we might expect his friar characters
to be flat constructions, bordering on caricature. To a certain
extent the friars in the *Noli* are "types". They are exaggerations of evil and weakness, being lecherous, cruel, false, mur-
derous and proud. The murder of the little boy, Crispin, by
the parish priest is the most savage introduction possible to
the *Noli.* Yet the Fathers Dámaso, Camorra and Sibyla are
entirely human creations and possess an astonishing individuality. Rizal achieves this, in part, by his use of the homely
details of their lives: their appearance, their eating habits and
even their gait. Father Dámaso's chagrin at receiving only a
chicken wing in his soup at the dinner at Captain Tiago's may
make him appear querulous but it also raises him to an entirely human level. It is fair to say that the friars in *Noli Me
Tangere* vibrate with enough vitality to save them from being
flat creations. Their humanity, combined with their utter villainy, is diffused throughout the book. There are friars at
every level of society and only the Filipino secular priest, Father Florentino in the *Fili,* is good. Nevertheless, without the
friars *Noli Me Tangere* would not succeed as a novel and they
must be counted as rounded creations.

The characters of Maria Clara and Crisostomo Ibarra/
Simoun are but faintly realized. It is hard to say whether
Rizal fell into the Victorian trap of having the "good girl" be
vapid and uni-dimensional or whether she was an ironic commentary by the author on the colonial hybrid. This latter possibility is credible but it does not serve to make her character
a satisfactory one to the reader. Ibarra undergoes a metamorphosis from one novel to the next and, in his dual role, serves
the author's purpose well. As Ibarra he is the liberal reformer, perhaps Rizal himself at one stage of his development; as
Simoun he is the destructive anarchist whom Rizal had encountered in Europe. There are qualities of the romantic hero
in both Ibarra and Simoun but in neither characterization
does the figure come to life nor does he rise to a two dimen-
sional creation. Both Maria Clara and Ibarra remain flat.

In writing his two novels in tandem, so to speak, Rizal set
himself a difficult task. He had to create at least one character
who successfully spanned both novels and carried the author's theme by a self-development which was both realistic
and satisfactory. In Basilio, Rizal found his best realized and
most satisfactory hero. From Basilio's introduction in the bell
tower of the church of San Diego to his last appearance in
the streets of Manila, standing indecisive and terror-stricken
with the knowledge of Simoun's deadly lamp, Basilio represents the Filipino in his best and worst aspects and so fulfills

Rizal's final bitter analysis of the effects of colonialization summed up in Father Florentino's pronouncement at the end of *El Filibusterismo,* ". . . whoever submits to tyranny, loves it!" Basilio is a device but a well realized one. In his intelligence and diligence and determination to serve his people as a doctor he falls into the all too human trap of ambition and pride. Although he is willing to risk his medical degree by helping Simoun he is more motivated by revenge for Juli's death than for the cause of freedom. As he fades indecisively out of the book he is more real to us than Simoun whose end is only satisfactory from a moral point of view. Basilio best serves Rizal as a well developed link between the two novels and emerges as the most subtle and best realized of his characters.

One of the finer qualities in Rizal's two novels is the quality of humor. It is sometimes surprising to the twentieth-century reader to discover such a wealth of this quality in the nineteenth century writers. Who among us has not delighted in such comic creations as Joseph Sedley in *Vanity Fair,* Mr. Micawber in *David Copperfield* and Signora Neroni in *Barchester Towers?* What is doubly surprising to us is that José Rizal, reared in the sober and limited atmosphere of the colonial Philippines, possessed the touch of comic genius of his Victorian contemporaries in Europe. Surely the character of Doña Victorina must be elevated to the ranks of her European counterparts. She is a magnificent creation, combining satiric and original characteristics which are consistently raised above the level of caricature. On the surface Doña Victorina is the humorous embodiment of the Filipina who denies her birthright. Her fractured Spanish, heavy makeup to conceal her dark complexion, her obsessive desire to marry a Spaniard and her total insensivity to her own absurdities could have made her a flat and limited creation. Rizal succeeds, however, in elevating her to a minor work of art. This is primarily achieved by her relationship with her poor, unfortunate husband, Don Tiburcio, himself a satisfactory comic character. The physical description of Doña Victorina recalls Dickens' Mrs. Skewton in *Dombey and Son* and is every bit as successful.

> She was more than blowzy; she was overblown. Her abundant hair had dwindled down to a bun the size . . . of a head of garlic; her face was furrowed with wrinkles, and her teeth were growing loose. Her eyes had also suffered considerably; she had to screw them up frequently to be able to see a certain distance away. Only her character remained.

By the single addition, "Only her character remained", Rizal redeems her from caricature. In his superbly balanced description of her intended husband, Don Tiburcio, Rizal further redeems himself from the charge of one level characterization. "He smiled with resignation and called to his aid the spectre of hunger . . . she was a pretentious, domineering, masculine old woman . . . but hunger was even more overbearing, nagging and demanding."

Perhaps the quality which best links Rizal with his European contemporaries is the dark, sexual undercurrent which runs through the two novels. Today it is fashionable to point out that the Victorians (the term is here used to embrace all those novelists who wrote in Europe in the second half of the nineteenth century) were far from being the prudish and repressed human beings that their stereotype has made them. Throughout the novels of Dickens, Zola, Flaubert and Tolstoy runs the theme of women's natural passions stifled and twisted in "good" society. Rizal was keenly aware of the nature of women; his own experience was varied and wide. In creating Salomé and Juli he portrayed children of nature who were freer to give themselves to the men they loved but, in Juli's case, were ultimately destroyed by sick sensuality. Maria Clara, aside from her dark paternity, is the conventional heroine whose body is sacred but whose mind is weak. In a lighter vein Rizal describes the aftermath of the wedding of Doña Victorina and Don Tiburcio and achieves a sardonic commentary on the natural side of life.

> She had a terrible stomach ache on the wedding night, and he, giving thanks to God, showed himself to be solicitous and considerate. The second night, however, he did his duty as an honorable man, and the following morning after gave himself a melancholy smile in the mirror, displaying his toothless gums; he had aged at least ten years.

Throughout the two novels runs the almost obsessive theme of the carnality and lust of the friars. Rizal judges the evils wrought upon the Philippines by pointing out the tortured and hypocritical acts of the spiritual mentors of the Filipinos. Rizal is humorous, yet profoundly bitter, on the subject. In one of the opening chapters of *Noli Me Tangere* Father Salví, tormented by dark thoughts, stalks Maria Clara and her friends as they paddle in a brook; "[their] small, rosy feet playing in the water aroused strange sensations in his starved body and unfamiliar thought and fancies in his feverish mind." Rizal may have felt the unnatural state of the celibate Catholic clergy, especially as he sought to balance the natural aspects of the Filipino countryside with the artifice of Filipino-Hispanic society, but beyond that aspect he felt that the friars' lustful acts were a part of the hypocrisy and evil of Spanish colonial rule. From the act of Father Dámaso's fathering of Maria Clara to the rape and suicide of Juli, sexuality runs as a dark and recurrent theme in Rizal's two novels and serves to bring him closer to the Europe of his day.

So far we have seen that Rizal fulfilled the novelist's task of creating living, rounded characters. In so doing he completed his purpose of exposing the good and the bad, the weaknesses and the strengths and the real and the ephemeral in the colonial Philippines. Often the minor characters such as Doña Consolación, the Three Sisters, old Tasio and Isagani play a minor fugue on the main theme and thus enhance the completeness of the author's exposure. If we have not discussed the success or failure of the plots of the novels it is because, in the end, the melodrama of Maria Clara's fate, the dramatic end of Simoun and the deaths and disappointments of almost all the main characters are all part of Rizal's purpose. The plot fails to stand alone but that does not detract from the excellence of the books. What of the secondary criteria: the strength of prophecy, the pattern and rhythm, the style and, finally, the source of life at the core of the books?

A most satisfactory pattern and rhythm run through the two novels. From the beginning of the *Noli* to the end of the *Fili* this pattern is based on alternative scenes of town and country. For Rizal, Manila held the darkness of colonial rule and the worst of the sycophantic Filipinos lived in a kind of pseudo-European style in the heart of the city. In a description of Captain Tiago's house it is possible to see the absurdity of aping the conqueror's ways in a damp and humid tropical climate. By contrast, in the country scenes in and around Laguna de Bai all is fresh and natural. People live, as far as they are able, as they did before the Spanish came and the rhythm of their country lives is spoiled only by the constabulary and the parish priest. Although not all of the country Filipinos are good, witness the father of Basilio and Crispin, it is the eternal earth mother figures like Sisa and the pure and natural Salomé who carry out Rizal's intention of showing the innate worth of the Filipino. The scenes in *El Filibusterismo* are increasingly set in the city as the story of Simoun becomes more tortured and despairing. The scenes in Kiapo, at the University, in the sinister Chinese Quiroga's house, and finally, as the tale comes full circle back to Captain Tiago's house, it is always the city where the darkest and most evil deeds are plotted and executed. Through both books the river Pasig runs, symbolically polluted at the Manila end, "combining the functions of public bath, sewer, laundry, fishery, waterway and should the Chinese water-pedlar find it convenient, even as a source of drinking water". At the end of the *Fili* Rizal abruptly shifts the scene to the little known East coast of the Philippines and there the rhythm of city and placid countryside is sharply broken by the roar and thunder of the sea.

If the power of prophecy is a canon by which to judge the excellence of a novel it is easily established that Rizal succeeds. By seizing on and rejecting an assortment of heroes and antiheroes Rizal sounds the warning which he himself understood in the end; the warning that everything fails which is founded on hate. The novels are both an incitement to revolution and an indictment against it. Perhaps it is fair to say that the prophecy is not an appeal but a description of the mental climate of revolt. Rizal found, at the end, that life itself has a universal relevance and he died with the last words of Christ on his lips, "Consummatum est". As Rizal forecast in the *Noli,* the Eliases of the Philippines were as doomed to defeat as the Simouns. Rizal was above all a writer and if his prophecy is larded with propaganda, an artist must take issue with political and social institutions. His aim is not merely to delight but to inspire. As he expresses an interest in freedom and reform he becomes a critic of society. Thus, all novels of social realism possess a high degree of prophecy.

The most difficult criteria by which to judge Rizal's success as a novelist is that of style. Rizal's books were written in Spanish, the florid and romantic Spanish of his day. The best English translation available freely admits of paraphrasing, reworking and incorporating. It is evident that all the translations are faithful to story and characters. How much of the highly humorous dialogue and clever juxtaposition is translatable is difficult to say. Nevertheless, the beauty of description defies bowdlerization and Doña Victorina remains Doña Victorina in *Andalusian* Spanish or Filipino English. Humor and truth shine above style and, where writers like Theodore Dreiser and Henry James seldom have humor to save them from their critics, Rizal's wit and eloquence rise above any peculiarities of style.

Rizal had always hoped to touch the heart of Europe with his novels, although the *Noli* was written essentially to "rouse the feelings of my countrymen". In addition, the book was written for Filipinos and Rizal hoped that, above all, it would be read by the Filipinos. It was Rizal's misfortune that the book attracted the most attention among the enraged rulers of the Philippines. The Europeans, aside from genuinely interested and sympathetic friends such as Blumentritt, had little opportunity to read either the *Noli* or the *Fili* as they were published in a limited quantity and in Spanish, never the common language of European intellectuals. Indeed, "The

Noli and the *Fili,* proscribed in the Philippines, unread in the great world of Europe, had failed to arouse the international storm of indignation and sympathy for which he had hoped." In spite of his avowed purpose Rizal remained essentially a European intellectual and however much the two novels form part of the Philippine Independence movement, as novels they belong to Europe.

At the core of both *Noli Me Tangere* and *El Filibusterismo* lies a concern with the historic. Rizal the Scholar hoped to stir European memories with the historian's perspective, stir European hearts with polemics and win European reforms with his timely liberalism. At bottom, Rizal was a Protestant in his timely liberalism. He was also a Protestant in his shining belief in the supremacy of private judgment. At the core of both novels is a reverence for European culture which is matched by a hatred for European colonialism. Possessing at once a deeply Victorian and Teutonic pedantry and scholarly scrupulousness he was saved from self-importance and his books from pomposity by an almost Renaissance humanity, If prophecy is a tone of voice, humility and humor must temper the writer if his tone is to be acceptable. The tone of the *Noli* is racy, pungent and relentless but at the core of both novels lies man himself, and through man, life.

Thus far we have failed to fault Rizal on any of the criteria for the successful novel. What, then, keeps him from having

Manuscript copy of "My Last Farewell."

constructed two "mighty edifices"? In the end it is the smallness of the stage. The London of Dickens, the Paris of Balzac and Zola and the vast Russia of Tolstoy play significant roles in the novels in which they appear. Without comparing Rizal as a novelist to these giants of European fiction we are bound to consider his place and the place of his characters on the world stage. As Charles Reade created a minor masterpiece out of medieval Europe in *The Cloister and the Hearth* so Rizal created two mini-masterpieces out of remote and distant islands. As medieval Europe is remote to us today so the Spanish Philippines was remote to the Europe of the nineteenth century. Rizal was handicapped by a European mentality when he wrote of his homeland and he failed to bring the two together in the same way Reade failed to make medieval Europe contemporary. Both *Noli Me Tangere* and *El Filibusterismo* lack timelessness. They remain remote for the average reader. There is wit, humanity and beauty but the range is narrow. No one who has not lived in the Philippines, and indeed, made a study of her history, can ever fully appreciate the venality of the secular and religious Spaniards, the poignancy of the abused natives and the absurdities of a falsely joined Filipino-Hispanic society. It is not necessary to have lived in Dickens' London or Tolstoy's Tsarist Russia to feel the breadth and sweep of life in their novels. José Rizal, a brilliant, cosmopolitan and heroic figure dedicated his short life to the cause of emancipating his people and in so doing he sacrificed vision for phantasmagoria. His satire is Swiftian but Swift was universal. Rizal belongs to the traditions of naturalism and realism and he even succeeded in harmonizing in himself the influences of Spain and Germany, the two extremes of European thought. But the canvas was small where the man was not. In the end he created the "little mansions" which made the man greater than his literary works, neither of which quite achieved the perfection found in a writer of universal vision. (pp. 742-52)

> Elliott C. Arensmeyer, "Little Mansions: Some Aspects of José Rizal as a Novelist," in Philippine Studies, Vol. 18, No. 4, October, 1970, pp. 740-52.

TEOFILO DEL CASTILLO Y TUAZON AND BUENAVENTURA S. MEDINA, JR.   (essay date 1972)

[*In the following excerpt, Tuazon and Medina survey Rizal's prose and poetry, commenting on his two novels, his autobiography, his most influential essays, and several of his best-known poems.*]

Noli Me Tangere, Rizal's first novel, was written in spirited Spanish prose to unveil the hypocrisy of the authorities and to open the eyes of the Filipinos to the abuses to which they were subjected. It tells the story of a romance set against the background of oppression by petty tyrants. Its principal characters are Crisostomo Ibarra and Maria Clara.

In this novel, several subplots like the stories of Sisa, Filosofo Tasio, de Espadañas, Elias, and others were used by Rizal to paint vividly the oppressive conditions in his country.

Noli Me Tangere is doubtless the best novel ever written by a Filipino. As a powerful and devastating denunciation of the unjust social and political conditions of our country, it ranks with Leo Tolstoi's *Resurrection,* Harriet Beecher Stowe's *Uncle Tom's Cabin,* and Hervey Allen's *Anthony Adverse.* So graphic and vigorous, indeed, is the language and the delineation of character that this novel soon undermined the power of the priests in the Islands and the *caciques,* and contributed

mightily to the immediate downfall of Castilian prestige in the Philippines.

El Filibusterismo is the sequel to *Noli Me Tangere.* It deals with the story of Simoun, the jeweler, and his revolutionary misadventures in the Islands. In *Noli Me Tangere,* Ibarra made good his escape to Cuba and became prosperous and influential with the passing of the years. Eventually, he returned to the Philippines as Simoun, the Jeweler. Simoun's plan was to extricate Maria Clara from the convent and to take vengeance on his enemies through revolution. Thus he sought to contact influential Spanish officials and the oppressed Filipinos as well.

Unfortunately, the well-conceived scheme of Simoun failed. The object of his affection, Maria Clara, died in the convent. Again, his well-drawn plan of murdering high officials of the Spanish Government and of the Church in the wedding of Paulita Gomez was frustrated by Basilio's inopportune revelation of the plot and of Isagani's mad scramble to snatch the dynamite-charged lamp. In like manner, his attempt to escape was rendered ineffectual, for in his pursuit for Tandang Selo in the hills, he had unwittingly placed himself within the firing range of civil guards trying to quell rebellious convicts. Though wounded, Simoun succeeded in dragging himself as well as his wealth into the miserable house of a poor native priest, Padre Florentino, hidden in the forest by the seashore. There, Simoun revealed his true self. Thus ends Rizal's second novel.

To expose effectively the deplorable conditions of his country and to create characters to voice his innermost thoughts, Rizal wrote the stories of Juli and Basilio, Isagani and Paulita Gomez, Cabesang Tales, Señor Pasta, and other victims of maladministration. He created ideal types like those of Padre Florentino and Isagani. With these characters living in his pages, Rizal sought to arouse a national awakening and to evoke a genuine love for our country.

"I would like to give my country," he wrote Dr. Ferdinand Blumentritt, "an example that I do not write for glory and fame, but for my native land and for this reason, I wish that my compatriots would sacrifice their passions for the sake of love of country. I wish that they would not look after their welfare for the sake of honors, employments, gains, adulations but for virtue which distinguish and adorn countries that are free and independent."

El Filibusterismo, although the creation of a more mature artist, lacks some of the qualities that gave *Noli Me Tangere* its unique power and beauty. The main plot is so subordinated to what might be called its nationalistic mission that at times it seems to disappear. Another quality that it lacks is action. In *Noli Me Tangere* what the characters do is important and interesting. But in *El Filibusterismo,* the emphasis is more on what they say and think. Consequently, the lifelike interest of the former is not to be found in the latter.

Character delineation in *El Filibusterismo,* however, is remarkably forceful and clear; and as an arraignment of the social and political evils in the country, the book is almost brutal in its stark reality. This is why Rizal was accused of treason and rebellion by the Spanish Government. It was really because of the devastating effects of his writings. (pp. 145-47)

Memorias de un Estudiante de Manila is an intimate glimpse of Rizal's life as a youngster and as a student. "It pictures," wrote Dr. Vidal Tan, "his loving sensitive nature, the sweet melancholy that seemed to have pervaded his young life, his prophetic awareness of the tragic end to come, his tender affection for his home town, his deeply religious nature, the patriotic ardor that permeated his adolescence, his sweet, delicate first love, his truly Filipino adoration for his mother, and his sense of gratitude towards his parents."

"Filipinas dentro de Cien Años" ("The Philippines a Century Hence") may be read with pleasure in both Spanish and English. As an analysis of Philippine conditions at that time, little is left to be desired in factual account, in clarity of reasoning, and above all, in its prophetic conclusions.

"The Philippines," he wrote, "will remain Spanish if the country be given the life and law of civilization, if the other rights due it are granted (freedom of the press and representation in the Cortes), and if a liberal policy of the government is carried out without trickery or meanness, and without subterfuge or false interpretations."

"Political transformation in the Islands," he added, "will be violent and fatal if it proceeds from the ranks of the people, but peaceful and fruitful if it emanates from the upper class."

To destroy the allegation that the Filipinos were indolent, Rizal wrote the **"Sobre la Indolencia de los Filipinos" ("The Indolence of the Filipinos.")** Without mincing words, he dissected the issue, saying: "The indolence in the Philippines is a chronic malady, but not a hereditary one. The Filipinos have not always been what they are; and witnesses to this fact are all the historians of the first years after the discovery of the Islands."

"Even granted that the Filipinos were indolent," Rizal went on, "who is the indolent person in Manila? Is it the poor clerk who comes at eight o'clock in the morning and leaves at one in the afternoon with only his parasol, who copies, and writes, and who works for himself and for his chief, or is it the chief who comes in a carriage and sits smoking, with his feet stretched out on a chair or a table, and gossips with his friends?"

Rizal is perhaps the most quoted Filipino today. His prose always contains a stirring message that beats upon the pained heart of his people. It is persuasive and highly patriotic. (pp. 147-48)

* * * * *

The poetry of Jose Rizal was mostly written in Spanish. A sprinkling was in Tagalog. Rizal wrote some twenty-two poems while attending the Ateneo de Manila and the University of Sto. Tomas. These poems were written in varying stanzaic arrangements. They were full of apostrophes and classical allusions, exhibiting beautiful conception and perfection in verse form. These are evident in **"A Message of Remembrance to My Home Town," "Along the Pasig,"** and **"Congratulations."** (p. 152)

Considered the crowning glory of his early poetic achievement is **"A la Juventud Filipina."** This poem was Rizal's winning entry in the poetry contest sponsored by the Lyceum of Arts and Letters of the University of Sto. Tomas.

After leaving Manila for Europe to pursue further studies, Rizal wrote **"Me Piden Versos," "A la Srta. C.O.Y.R.," "A las Flores de Heidelberg," "Canto de Maria Clara," "A Mi," "Kundiman," "Flor entre Flores," "Himno al Trabajo,"** and **"El Agua y el Fuego."**

It is observed that Rizal composed but few poems abroad at the height of his creative powers. Sorrow and hard work and unending love for country dominated Rizal's poetry during this period. There was, however, a different Rizal; it was the Rizal who could poetically react to his immediate environment. **"To the Flowers of Heidelberg"** belongs to his classification. This poem was written in 1886. Our sensitive patriot was deeply impressed by the picturesque castle on top the Koenigstuhl, two hundred meters above the German town, and the magnificent sunrise there. The result was a celebration of this historic scene in noble and flowing language.

Rizal wrote his best poetry in Dapitan, Mindanao, and in Fort Santiago, Manila, as a political prisoner. In Dapitan, he wrote five poems: one addressed to his political custodian, Don Ricardo Carnicero; one to his wife, Josephine Bracken; one to his mother, **"Mi Retiro;"** a hymn in connection with the fiesta in Talisay, Dapitan, **"Himno a Talisay;"** and **"Canto del Viajero."**

"Mi Retiro" is a poem composed of twenty-four stanzas describing to his mother the actual world he lived in. **"Canto del Viajero"** was written by Rizal a few days before leaving to become a volunteer physician in war-torn Cuba. It reveals the depth of tragedy which Rizal endured while wandering in a foreign land. Vibrant in appeal and lofty in sentiment, **"Mi Ultimo Adios"** may be regarded as one of the great poems of our time.

"Mi Ultimo Adios," "Mi Retiro," and the novels, *Noli Me Tangere* and *El Filibusterismo* are sufficient to gain for Rizal the glory of a literary giant. No man of letters in our country has lived more beautifully, thought more nobly, and suffered more deeply than Jose Rizal. (pp. 152-53)

> *Teofilo del Castillo y Tuazon and Buenaventura S. Medina, Jr., "Rizal's Prose" and "Rizal's Poetry," in their* Philippine Literature: From Ancient Times to the Present, *Teofilo del Castillo, 1972, pp. 142-51, 152-59.*

JOSÉ BARÓN FERNÁNDEZ (essay date 1980)

[*In the following excerpt, Fernández outlines Rizal's objectives in writing* Noli me tangere, *discussing the success of his efforts to use characterization and setting to depict the struggle of the Filipino people.*]

As Rizal himself explains, he wrote the *Noli* "to awaken the feelings of his countrymen." The book is a denunciation of a political system founded on the privilege of the rulers, discrimination against the ruled, and the perpetuation of the state of ignorance that had indefinitely extended the road to the emancipation and liberty of the Filipino people. For the presentation of his arguments, Rizal chose to depict a series of typical Filipino scenes in which he vividly and realistically describes the classical types in the country during that era, including the Spanish peninsulars, with their virtues and vices. These descriptions reveal his excellent gift of observation. In his criticisms of the religious orders, he directs his attack especially against the Dominicans and the Franciscans, principally in the figure of Father Dámaso whom he presents as an intolerable fanatic and the adulterous father of Maria Clara. The Jesuits, on the other hand, are treated with considerable respect and consideration. The abuses of the police authorities are revealed in the dialogue. The remarks about the *guardia civil* may reflect the wounds left in Rizal's and his mother's hearts by painful experiences with the force.

The description of typical local scenes, done with great vividness and realism, recreates the town fiesta, the pompous and magnificent scenes in the houses of opulent Filipinos, the cockpit, the school teacher and his surroundings, the great church feast, the incidents in the headquarters and lodgings of the *guardia civil,* the stage presentations, etc. In these descriptions of Filipino manners and customs as well as folklore, Rizal speaks through his characters, severely censuring superstition, advocating the fight against ignorance and illiteracy, criticizing political opportunism, the enrichment of some peninsulars—the most ignorant—who, on top of it all, speak ill of the country and its defects. He offers his rationalistic opinion regarding indulgences, the papal bulls, candles that are supposed to drive away the *tulisanes,* the preference for the ringing of bells to the use of lightning rods when there are storms, etc. But, contrary to what many have affirmed, in no instance does Rizal show himself an enemy of Spain nor an advocate of separatism. When asked, during a dinner which country he liked best, Ibarra replies: "Any free country in Europe."

On another occasion, in his idyll with Maria Clara, he speaks of her as the poetic incarnation of the Philippines, "that beautiful country which unites the great virtues of Mother Spain and the beautiful qualities of a young nation, in the same manner as all the beautiful components of the patrimony of both races are united in yourself."

Rizal, in the words of Ibarra, recognizes that the Philippines is religious and loves Spain, but in a discussion with Philosopher Tasio, rich in ideas, the latter replies that although some Spanish ministers did introduce reforms, these were nullified in the lower spheres, due to the over-riding desire for self-enrichment and to the ignorance of the people, who allowed all of these without limit. "The royal decrees will not correct the abuses, as long as the authorities do not see to the implementation, as long as there is no freedom of expression against the tyrants."

Not all the Spaniards that figure in the novel are censured. The Governor-General, Lieutenant Guevarra and Don Tiburcio, among others are presented as worthy, noble and honest persons. The way he describes and delineates the persons of the Governor-General brings to mind the personality of Emilio Terrero, but in the manner of a prophecy, for he had written the *Noli* before he came to know Terrero.

The character of greatest worth is Elias. His humane qualities, his courage, his willingness to give up his life in order to save others, his strong conviction and decisiveness, his honesty and patriotism, make his figure the most outstanding among all the other characters. Since he is a peasant, he represents the Filipino native into whom Rizal has poured all the virtues of the Tagalog race. The dialogues between him and Ibarra are most interesting, showing the ideological differences that separate them as well as the points on which they agree.

Both believe in God; both are rationalists: Elias intuitively, Ibarra due to his cultural and scientific background. The peasant is denied human justice and the right of man to be judged by his equals. He protests the domination of some classes over others. Elias is wanted because of his political ideas; these he presents to Ibarra everytime they meet. Ibarra disputes, although without much force, the most progressive

ideas of Elias, whose arguments are, surprisingly, much more solid than those of Crisóstomo. At no time does he ask for independence, nor does he insult Spain, but attacks the political power of the religious orders, the conversion of honest persons into *tulisanes* because of the conduct of some officials of the administration, the keeping of the people in ignorance and the discrimination between peninsular and Filipino priests. Elías is a native, an *indio,* who speaks the voice of the people. Ibarra is a man very much like Rizal in some aspects: "I have not been brought up among the people, and perhaps I do not know their needs. I have spent my childhood in the Jesuit college; I grew up in Europe, have been educated from books. What the writers have not written I know nothing about."

Some people believe that Ibarra personifies Rizal, and Maria Clara, Leonor Rivera, and Elías, Bonifacio. There are many similarities, but it cannot be accepted that this was in accordance with a preconceived plan of Rizal. Among other reasons, Rizal did not know Bonifacio. Admitting that Ibarra personifies Rizal, the latter has much of Elias, too, in the arguments that arose between the two, Ibarra, in some cases, ends up accepting the thesis of his opponent, either explicitly or tacitly. (pp. 108-10)

Whatever success [Rizal attains in the novel] is the fruit of his innate art, not of his experience. In literary terms, the novel does not reach great heights. Neither the vocabulary nor the style, which lacks conciseness, would have merited for the author a place in the Academy of Languages. The construction is frequently defective, and he is sometimes inclined to the use of *Tagalismos* (corruption of the Spanish by the use of a Tagalog word or part of a word). These lapses are found even in his later works.

All this can be explained: in his 7 years at the Ateneo, he hardly spoke anything but Tagalog, his maternal language, which has no analogy or similarity whatsoever to Spanish, and with a very different spelling and syntax. We may recall that his less than excellent performance during his first year at the Ateneo was due exclusively to his deficient Spanish. Furthermore, when he wrote the *Noli,* he was alternating his study of Spanish with French, and later on, with English and German, each with its own different construction. Besides, when Rizal wrote, he was not moved by literary motives but by the desire to transmit a message to his people that would lead them to liberty by means of education and culture.

In a letter to Ponce from London he says, "One does not write for anything or for anybody but for the cause of our country." In his letters to others, he advised them to write, even if the style be deficient. He himself, with his love of perfection, put his best efforts into polishing his writings, for which purpose he ordered the complete works of Larra (Figaro), whose style he admired tremendously.

The *Noli* expresses the personality of Rizal—a romantic, not in the sense of belonging to the Romantic movement in literature, whose exponents were Mme. de Stael, Victor Hugo and Lamartine, but in the sense that he was a sentimentalist, an idealist, and a dreamer.

Rizal, like Larra, utilized irony, for the latter too had to fight against censorship and resorted to caustic metaphor. From the literary point of view, the best parts of the work are the vivid descriptions of the people's customs and manners, in which he successfully pictures Philippine society, with the minute descriptive details of a keen observer. Into these descriptions he injects his socio-political message, to awaken his people from the lethargy in which they were submerged. (pp. 110-11)

> *José Barón Fernández, in his* José Rizal: Filipino Doctor and Patriot, *edited by Teodoro M. Locsin, translated by Lilia Hidalgo-Laurel, Manuel L. Morató, 1980, 377 p.*

JOSE S. ARCILLA, S.J. (essay date 1988)

[*In the following excerpt, Arcilla outlines various literary devices Rizal used in* Noli me tangere, *emphasizing the importance of the work as propaganda literature.*]

With few exceptions, Rizal wrote explicitly propaganda. His style, therefore, was that of the debater or the polemicist, with all its vices and virtues. His essay, **"Filipinas dentro de cien años,"** for example, has all the prolixity and exaggeration, the ornateness and overstatement of the fanatical pamphleteer or professional agitator. In contrast, his **"Sobre la indolencia de los filipinos"** is more moderate and does not have as much literary embellishment as the first. It is because in the second essay he does not have to prove anything, but merely assert the facts. But his style changes whenever he writes about the friars in the Philippines—his "obsession"— and then his sharp pen is devastating. When it comes to them, Rizal tends to overgeneralize, missing no opportunity to caricature them with gusto.

Undoubtedly abuses were rife in the Philippines in the time of Rizal. But his sweeping condemnations seem unnatural. They seem to prove too much, a tactic we call today "overkill." But to say that in his works the national hero was a nationalist who used innuendo and extreme statements is not to take from them their essential truth. Style is one thing, content is another, and the two must not be confused. Propaganda, like commercial advertising, must be demythologized to be properly understood. So also Rizal's novels must be properly read; otherwise, one misinterprets his mind.

One must also bear in mind that Rizal wrote in nineteenth-century Spanish. Unless one is at home in that florid and romantic language, he is liable to miss the author's intent. Being polemical, Rizal's writings were not scientific historical studies which demand a more disciplined and sparse style, free from literary flairs and florid phrases that betray emotion rather than thought. Still what he wrote are documents of vital historical significance. Properly interpreted, they contain information not at all valueless.

Rizal's *chef-d'oeuvre* are two novels, literary works that entertain while delivering a serious message. Perhaps he could not have done otherwise. He lived in the second half of the nineteenth century, also known as the "age of novels." From the Greek *Daphne and Chloe,* a story of unrequited love, to the eighteenth-century *Emile,* Rousseau's didactic novel, we have a full range of writing that had gradually realized its potential to voice out the conscience of the people. And in the Ateneo, Rizal came to know the language of the muses which he confessed he had learned to love.

He was only twenty-five years old when he finished his *Noli me tangere.* A twenty-five year old writing in a foreign tongue in such a way as to electrify an entire nation could not have been a mere *"mesticillo vulgar,"* as the novel's critics snorted. The style itself does not compare with the best, its grammar leaves much to be desired. As a piece of literature, it will never be included in any Spanish anthology. And if the *Noli* can be rated as Rizal's *magnum opus,* its sequel, *El Filibusterismo* can be called its counterpiece as far as literary merit goes.

The *Fili* is a rather undisciplined outpouring of smouldering hatred, even of seething white-hot anger. In the *Noli,* Doctor Rizal uses the scalpel, deftly handling the sores and weak spots of his patients. But in the *Fili,* the doctor has laid aside his art, and picks up blunt instruments, applies the crudest surgical methods. The scalpel is laid aside, and he has picked up the bludgeon or the sledge hammer. There is haste, impetuosity. Restraint is cast to the winds, caution is gone, like Basilio's prudence which has turned into petulant impulsiveness. For in this novel, Rizal seems to say time is fast running out. At times, the tone is like the "riposte—a sudden thrust after parrying a lunge." But this thrust is like that of a novice fencer who is unfamiliar with the art and can counter only with a "violent blow." Still, as propaganda, the two novels rank among the best.

What did Rizal write? The plot of the *Noli* is rather loose. Juan Crisostomo Eibarramendia (Ibarra, for short) returns home after several years of study in Europe, ignorant of how his father died. In trying to find out what happened, he uncovers corruption and abuse in high and low places of Philippine society. He is most shocked when he finds out his father had died alone in jail, that his corpse had been disinterred and thrown into the lake at the behest of a family friend, Fray Damaso Verdolagas. Instead of exacting vengeance, however, Ibarra decides to do good for the people, certain such would be his father's wish if he were still alive. But he is thwarted at every turn. At the laying of the cornerstone of the school building he is erecting, a contrived accident almost kills him. During the fiesta dinner, Fray Damaso's uncalled for slurs against his family provoke him to attack the priest violently, bringing down upon his head automatic excommunication from the Church, and his marriage to Maria Clara is called off as a result. Later he is implicated in a revolutionary plot, is taken prisoner to Manila, but he escapes through the help of Elias, an outlaw whose grandfather had once been wronged by Ibarra's Spanish grandfather, Don Pedro Eiberramendia. The novel ends with two cryptic episodes. Basilio, the young sacristan, finally catches up with his crazed mother who dies in his arms on recognizing her son. He has no means of burying her, but a wounded, dying stranger appears and directs him to cremate his own and the corpse of Basilio's mother. And in Manila, Maria Clara, a poor Clare after refusing to marry the Spaniard Fray Damaso had chosen for her, escapes one stormy night to the roof of the monastery, seeking refuge in the angry elements from the presumed sexual advances of Fray Bernardo Salvi, promoted to the chaplaincy of the monastery after single-handedly aborting the revolution in San Diego.

The second novel is even less compact. One gets the impression that the dialogue and the action are a pretext to make explicit Rizal's personal debate on violent revolution. Simoun, the main character, is a ruthless plotter, best portrayed in the opening discussion on how to improve communications between Manila and Laguna province. Instead of the slow, winding channel of the Pasig River, he advocates a solution that "would not cost a penny," namely, "dig a canal straight through from the lake to Manila . . . make a new river channel and close up the old Pasig." People would be killed or dislocated, forced labor would have to be used, but that was "the only way to accomplish great works with little means." Anyway, he adds, "the dead are dead; posterity gives its verdict only to the strong." Challenged that the end never justifies the means, he scoffs he has no time for moral platitudes, scandalizing everyone within hearing. His revolution fails in the end, but, instead of regret, he is overcome with despair and commits suicide.

Noli me tangere is rich in imagery and symbolism. One, for example, immediately recognizes in Rizal's grave-digging scene a similar episode in Shakespeare's *Hamlet*. And one cannot help but notice the classical motif of a son going to the depths of Hades in search of his dead father which Rizal imitated to start his story. But unlike the tragic Hamlet, Ibarra is neither beset with doubts, nor does he ever question his role in Philippine society. So much so that he strides through the novel as a noble, all-conquering figure, almost too good to be true. Indeed, he falls short of the classic hero, for Ibarra has no tragic fault that will doom him to a fatal dénouement. His sanitized story weakens whatever cathartic value is left in the plot. But he appears as a breath of fresh air amid the hot stench that inflated the tinsel and bubble of the pretentious and showy life of Manila, where so much store was set on outward appearance and too little on true inner qualities, where men are "turtles . . . classified and valued according to their shells."

An obvious defect of both novels is their extreme wordiness. Action is slow, conversation is long drawn-out, as if the plot unfolds only in order to advance one idea after another. This is especially true with the *Fili*. It is actually an ill-concealed philosophical debate on whether violent revolution is justified or not.

Second, characterization is shallow. Ibarra, as mentioned, is wooden and stiff. His assault on the Franciscan friar who insulted his dead father's memory and its sequel—better, its lack—do not convince and are just a bit too melodramatic to be plausible. Rizal seems never to have realized that a public affront to a priest would not have been settled as easily through the Governor General's immediate personal intervention, no matter how powerful he was, without a formal investigation. If, as the novel seems to imply, the friars enjoyed tremendous power in the Philippines, why did they turn out to be so impotent as to fail to marshall their legal resources against Ibarra the attacker of a friar?

One can always single out the literary defects of the novel, but they are only one side of the picture. Its positive aspects are more abundant, and they explain to a degree the novel's immediate success. Rizal's years at the Ateneo moulded him into a careful writer, and this is shown in the literary devices he employed.

First, the names of his characters are highly symbolic. For one reason or another, Rizal's generation was fond of pseudonyms and meaningful titles. Rizal himself used "Laong Laan" a number of times. Marcelo H. del Pilar was "Plaridel." And in answer to critics of his novel, Rizal made a play on words, choosing meaningful names for his characters. For example, when the Governor General shelved the censors' statement condemning the novel, the Augustinian Fray Salvador Font clandestinely circulated copies of his censure, and Rizal wrote a pamphlet satirizing the Augustinian. In an imagined telephone conversation, *Salvadorcito Tont* is brought to task by his religious superior for accepting a dona-

tion to the Augustinian order, thus compromising their vows of wealth, lust, pride, etc. Note Rizal's meaningful choice of names: "Salvadorcito" or Tiny Salvador (savior), and "Tont," from the Spanish *tonto* (fool) combined with the friar's name "Font."

The main character of the *Noli* is Juan Crisostomo Eibarramendia (Ibarra), obviously named after Saint John Chrysostom martyred in A.D. 389. John is a common name in Christian history, obviously used in honor of the harbinger of the Good News of Christ's coming. Chrysostom means "goldenmouth" from the Greek CHRYSOS = gold, STOMA = mouth, the appellation of the eloquent preacher of the fourth century. What name more apt for the novel's hero, whose words and deeds were a source of hope for the downtrodden Filipino? True to his namesake, Ibarra's words reveal a noble mind and, even in anger, he never descends to vulgarities.

He comes from San Diego, a town whose name reminds one of Spain's Santiago de Compostela, the city that had grown around the famous shrine of the Apostle James (in Spanish, "Santiago") and center of pilgrimage that had united all of western medieval Christendom. As everyone knows, the Latin *Jocobus* is translated into Spanish as *Jacobo, Santiago, Diego* (English, Iago). So, too, in the novel, people flock to San Diego on the town's patronal saint's day.

Don Santiago de los Santos, Capitan Tiago, or in English, James of the Saints, is a perfect foil to the saint. In the Apostle's case, one man was the source of help for practically all of western medieval Europe, but in the novel, help is sought from many for only one man, Capitan Tiago. In keeping with the latter's character, heaven is called upon—more exactly, he bribes those whom he calls his friends in heaven to keep himself safe and sound. At the start of the uprising, he vows more candles, more masses, and bigger fireworks. Religion to him is a question of how much to pay for the favors from heaven.

Fray Damaso Verdolagas recalls the first of two Popes Damasus who reigned in 366-384, the perceptive Vicar of Christ who commissioned his secretary, St. Jerome (*ca.* 345-419/420), to revise the Latin translation of the New Testament basing it on the original Greek text. He reorganized the papal chancery, and was the first to call Rome the "Apostolic See." Because of his liturgical reforms, Latin became the language of the Roman Catholic Church. The second Pope Damasus was pope from 17 July to 9 August 1047, and practically nothing can be said about him. Unlike his namesake, however, Fray Damaso of the *Noli* is an anti-intellectual. His *modus operandi* is to crack the whip, lash out against ambitious young men who pursue higher studies abroad, calling them "daft," "subversive," insolent imps for whom eternal fire and brimstone are ready. Interestingly, while Pope Damasus I was persecuted by his enemies, in the novel, it is the friar who persecutes his enemies. And, of course, "Verdolagas" is the Spanish for the Tagalog *kulasim* or "sour," "acrid," or *kulasiman, gulasiman, ulasiman,* a creeping red-stemmed plant formerly used in salads because of its succulent juice, but now serving only as animal fodder. Ibarra's creator certainly knew his man.

Maria Clara is the third important character in the *Noli*. Together with her Aunt Isabel, the two remind one of the New Testament pair of kinswomen, Mary and Elizabeth, whose sons, Jesus and John, ushered in the new Christian age. Did Rizal have this parallelism when he chose these two names?

And ironically, the background of Ibarra's dream girl, despite her name, is anything but clear!

There are other names. Doña, not Victoria, but its diminutive, "Victorina," petty victory. Alas, she has to be satisfied with her small victory in her desperate catch of that puny derelict of a Spaniard, the lame and toothless Don Tiburcio de Espadaña. *Espadaña* is a plant which they dried before stuffing it into pillows or cushions. Doña Victorina has a perfect cushion for her needs! She also plasters her face with make-up to hide her brown skin, and pitifully gesticulates with her barbarous Spanish, a deeply meaningful symbol of the tragedy of colonial subservience. (pp. 183-88)

And finally, of course, we have Simoun, the main protagonist in the second novel. In choosing this name, did Rizal have in mind that more famous Simon of the New Testament, the one who, impressed by the miracles performed by the prince of the Apostles, offered money in exchange for the power not even the devils enjoy? Their names are spelt a little differently, but both seem to believe that money can provide everything. Would it be reading into the mind of Rizal if we say that he was aware of this parallelism and wanted to condemn the luxury and affluence of the friars so contrary to their professed way of life? to disabuse people of the real value of money, although it is useful in a certain sense? The words he puts in Father Florentino's mouth as he throws away the chest of money brought by Simoun lead us to the conclusion:

> When men should need you [Simoun's money chest] for a purpose holy and sublime, God will raise you from the bottom of the seas. Until then you will do no evil there, you will not thwart justice or incite greed!

A second literary device masterfully employed in the novels is the apothegm, or meaningful sentence. We have already cited one from the opening paragraphs of the *Noli:* "Men are like turtles: they are classified and valued according to their shells." Pretense! Sham! External show and empty facades! As soon as word spreads that Capitan Tiago is hosting a party, everyone sets out to "hunt polish for their boots, collar-buttons and cravats" and rehearse how to "greet their host with the assumed intimacy of longstanding friendship. . . ."

During the party to welcome Ibarra at Capitan Tiago's house, Fray Damaso's indignant challenge to the military officer reveals more than he intends: "Do you think that under my cassock I am less of a man?" The novel will show he *is* a man who can sire a child. But his behavior makes him *less* than one. And unfortunately for him, his priestly consecration should have made him more than a man. Later his fiesta panegyric asphyxiates everyone in the overcrowded church. Only one succeeds in extricating himself, the irreverent Manileño who gets up and walks out, not through the main door which has been locked, but through the sacristy doors, in the full sight of everybody and shocking them with such effrontery. Ibarra, too, is miserable. He listens to every word of the friar, and

> . . . understood the allusions. Under an outward composure, his eyes sought help from God and the authorities, but he found nothing except images of saints and the nodding Governor.

In other words, there was no redemption, no escaping the abusive friar! God is not to be found, only painted wooden images of the saints. Neither is there help from the Governor,

for instead of being inspired, he falls asleep lulled by the constant droning of the friar's unintelligible mouthings. Ibarra feels all alone. And this, precisely, is the tragedy of Philippine society. In the face of friar omnipotence, there is no support or hope of salvation.

Overlooked by many is the final line of the fourth chapter of *Noli me tangere,* in which Lieutenant Guevarra recounts to Ibarra how his father died and was dishonored after his death. It was a shocking revelation to Ibarra who had no words to thank the officer, "but with emotion." Slowly he turns and hails a carriage, inaudibly telling the driver where to take him. And the driver thinks Ibarra "must be just out of gaol." Indeed. During the party in Capitan Tiago's house, no one dared tell him as everyone tried to put up a front and make believe everything was fine. It was when he had gone out, away from the crowd, away from both the adulation and the suspicion awaiting him on his return from Europe that he found the truth, and the realization that Fray Damaso was *not* his family's friend, that the country which from afar had seemed an eden is not so in reality. For the first time he touches the sordidness that has so far spared him. But it was his night of liberation from the prison of his ignorance. And he is now on a voyage of discovery—not of things that will lift him up, but of the social cancer gnawing at the entrails of his own country, "a cancer so malignant that the least touch inflames it and causes agonizing pain. . . . " Because Ibarra will try to cure it, it will cost him dearly.

Though not fully studied, the theme of pretense suffuses every page of Rizal's two novels, but we can just mention one or two examples to illustrate it. In the *Fili* we have "Ben Zayb, the writer who looked like a friar . . . arguing with a religious who in turn looked like a gunner. And in the *Noli* we have Doña Victorina de Espadaña, perhaps Rizal's best aper of Spanish ways.

Events, too, are not what they seem, but are full of pretense and empty show. The several fiestas and parties in the *Noli* are loud and meaningless, and have all the air of "putting on appearances." Capitan Tiago's shell-like house, with its untouched piano, the unappreciated paintings on the wall, the careful attention to what to wear to the party—they all stress what Fray Damaso repeats in another context "what is already patent to the eye." And what of Fray Irene who disguises himself to attend an operetta on the pretext of being its censor? If so, why cover up? If men and events can be one thing, and yet seem to be another, something is definitely wrong. In psychology, they call this an identity crisis. Was this part of the social cancer?

The Spaniards in the Philippines, too, have their identity crisis. This is seen in the anonymous—note how much in keeping with the theme of identity crisis—High Official trying to intercede for Basilio, and admits surprisingly that the native is always on the losing end when foreign officials fall out. The High Official has just been discussing and interceding for Basilio with the Governor General, but he failed because the latter needed a martyr for the "good of the majority . . . the good of all [and] maintain the threatened principle of authority, and preserve and enhance the prestige of the regime." Out of a myopic sense of justice, someone had to die: "that way the punishment turns out to be more salutary and exemplary for it will strike more terror." And so, because he openly sides with the natives, the High Official receives a one-way ticket back to Spain, no doubt, arranged by the Governor. But, before leaving, the Official talks to the native lackey who opens the door as he steps out of the Governor's office: "When you declare yourselves independent some day, remember that there were not lacking hearts in Spain that beat for you and fought for your rights." But the lackey asks uncomprehending, "Where to did you say, sir?" Is Rizal saying communication has broken down between the rulers and the ruled? Worse, that the people have no longer ears or the time to listen in order to know which direction to take?

More than symbolic names or apothegms, Rizal employs to great advantage symbolic episodes, or individual incidents that illumine a wider situation. Multiform vignettes of daily life, they are the details that add up to a perfect picture *ad unguem*.

Maria Clara and the girls are happily chattering along the street when they are stopped by a strange sight. A leper is begging, as is his wont, and Iday explains his plight. She says people suspect he contracted the disease from overstaying in the prison, while others report he was infected by his diseased mother for whom he was caring. Everyone now avoids him, and he is forbidden all human contact. To obtain his daily bread, he leaves out at a distance a basket, and people drop what they set aside for him. One day he happens to be passing by when a small boy falls into a ditch. He instinctively pulls the lad up, but instead of being grateful, the father denounces the leper to the town authorities. The *gobernadorcillo* has him flogged, burning the lash afterwards. Iday dramatizes the end of her story:

> It was horrible! The leper running away, the flogger running after him, and the Mayor screaming: "Let that be a lesson to you! Better to drown than to catch your disease!"

> And Maria Clara whispered, "True!"

In other words, things were so bad in the Philippines that for trying to do good, one is penalized. And Maria Clara, Ibarra's beloved, *agrees*.

In lines that stop short of being maudlin, Rizal illustrates the irony of pretense that wrings the hearts of his readers, one night in Sisa's home. Basilio has just come back from the town, where with his brother he was serving as an altar boy in the parish church. He is late this evening, and his forehead is bleeding from a gunshot wound. He is not hungry, although he has had nothing to eat. Even if he wants to, there is no food, for his worthless father had arrived unexpectedly and, having had his fill, departs as unexpectedly, fondling his game cock. On his way out, Sisa painfully wrings out from him some kind word for his sons. Later, she lies to Basilio to save the boy from the painful realization of how inhuman his father can be. Basilio himself was forced to come home earlier than usual, leaving his brother detained in the priest's house on the charge of having stolen from the priest. Later that night, Basilio has nightmares about Crispin's probable fate. Awakened by his mother, he in turn concocts a lie, painting an idyllic picture to comfort her with the empty unreality of a dream world. Young as he is, he does not want to share his anxieties with her.

> The voice of Sisa called him back to reality.

> "What's the matter? Why are you crying?"

> "I was dreaming," Basilio answered, raising himself, covered with sweat. "Oh, God! Say it was a dream, mother, only a dream."

> "What did you dream?"

> The boy did not answer. He sat up to dry his tears and sweat. The hut was in darkness.

> "A dream, a dream," Basilio repeated in a low voice.

> "Tell me what you dreamed," his mother said when he had gone back to bed. "I can't sleep."

> "Well," he whispered, "I dreamed that we went harvesting, in a field full of flowers. The women had baskets full of grains, and the children, too . . . I don't remember anything more, mother, really I don't."

> Sisa did not insist. She did not believe in dreams.

Alas, the good, the weak, the poor and downtrodden have to dissimulate, to pretend, because life is harsh, and men do not help. One has to cover up, to tell a lie to protect the innocent, one's beloved, although not always successfully when people have lost hope. And Sisa? She has ceased to dream and no longer believes in any. All she can do is "cover up with the ashes of outward indifference the burning emotions of [her] soul lest they be extinguished by careless exposure. . . ."

In the dialogue between Isagani and his favorite friar, the student asks some pointed questions. The sickly—why sickly?—Fray Fernandez is a teacher, having spent his life hoping to educate the Filipinos in justice and self-respect. Now he is hurt that no one is brave enough to say what the students honestly think about the friars. Isagani counters by saying that when the natives are schooled in hypocrisy, in seeking only to flatter the powerful in order to be on their good side no matter what the cost, they will act that way. When free speech and every independent thought is labeled subversive, what is the point of standing up and speaking one's mind? Old, outmoded ideas, false principles, and an embargo on the free employment of the mind is what passes for education, Isagani retorts. Freedom is to man what education is to the mind, and the "opposition of the friars to our education is the source of our discontent." Both men are now fully communicating and words are used to convey thought and attitudes, not to camouflage them. There is now a communion of minds and hearts here, there is no pretense, but honesty, courage to express and face the truth. In general, the student says that his fellows leave the shreds of respectability as long as they are in the classroom where they are endlessly brutalized and the innate desire for knowledge is effectively squelched. Making a mockery of the unlettered native will never help or motivate him to study or improve himself: "You strip him and then mock his nakedness!" The friar replies there are overbearing professors because there are compliant students. There are no tyrants where there are no slaves. Both men finally take leave of each other with a bitter-sweet feeling that their respective friends, alas, will never believe the other exists.

> " . . . it may look as if nothing practical has been gained from our conversation, but something has been achieved. I shall speak to my brethren about what you have told me and I hope that something can be done. I only fear they may not believe that you exist."

> "I fear the same thing," answered Isagani. . . . "I am afraid that my friends will not believe that you exist as you have shown yourself to be."

Was this Rizal's message, that the cancer eating up the victuals of Philippine society has already reached that stage where neither the Filipinos nor the Spaniards believed it was still possible to be good? When hope is gone, the worst will follow.

In the second novel of Rizal, the Governor General goes hunting in Bosoboso, but lady luck is unpropitious to him. He retires to a rest house to play cards with some friars and his other friends, Simoun the jeweller among them. The Governor's secretary is part of the party, for, as Rizal notes with evident sarcasm, his "Excellency was very hard-working and did not waste time so that he attended to official business when he was dummy or while the cards were being shuffled." But even the card game is not going well for the highest official of the land, nor for one of the more loquacious friars. They ask Simoun to join them, and the man says he will be "satisfied with mere words. . . ." Instead of paying in chips, Fray Sibyla will say "I renounce poverty, humility, and obedience for five days." Fray Irene, "I renounce chastity, generosity, etc." In turn, Simoun will offer his diamonds. A high official asks what is to be gained from mere "promises of virtue, prison sentences, deportation and summary executions." Quite a lot, the jeweller answers. After all, he declares,

> . . . in my view the outlaws are the most honest men in the whole country! They are the only ones who really earn their daily rice. Do you think that if I had fallen into the hands of, well, for example, you, Father Irene . . . would [you] have let me go without taking at least half of my jewels?

The trouble is, Simoun goes on, not in the mountains and in uninhabited places, but with the bandits in the towns and the cities, with people like Simoun himself who are "not openly professional bandits; when we become like that and go to live in the forests, that day the country will have been saved, that very day a new society will have been born capable of running its own affairs," and the Governor General can play cards at will. And at this moment, the secretary yawns loudly, raising his arms and stretching his crossed legs, causing laughter in the room. But the Governor did not like the turn of the conversation and, "dropping the cards which he had been shuffling, said half serious and half jolly":

> Come, come, enough with jokes and games. To work, let's go down to some serious work, there is still half an hour before luncheon. Is there a lot of business?

Put bluntly, while the Governor had the entire morning to hunt and play cards, he had only half an hour before the noon meal for some serious work! That, Rizal implied, was part of the social cancer.

Chapters 23 and 24 of the *Noli* describe the fishing expedition a day or so before the town fiesta of San Diego. Everybody was there, even Fray Salvi who followed afterwards. The heart of the episode is the free banter during the meal after the excitement of killing the crocodile that has been eating the fish in the traps. The conversation ranged from the failure of the peace officers to apprehend those who had earlier mauled Fray Damaso to the care shown by Fray Sibyla not to lose a single peso of the Church while losing his two sacristans. In the officer's words.

> "Your Reverence loses a few pesos and my sergeant is routed out of bed to look for them; then Your Reverence loses two sacristans and not a word said.

And you, Mr. Mayor. . . . You must admit that you. . . ."

Without bothering to continue he broke into a laugh, sinking his spoon into the red meat of a wild papaya.

The priest lost his head and blurted out in confusion: "But I'm accountable for the money!"

"That's a fine answer, Father, for a shepherd of souls," interrupted the lieutenant, his mouth full. "A fine answer, indeed, for a man of religion!"

And the give and take continues, each interlocutor freely accusing the other of neglect of duties.

All this took place in the carefree atmosphere of a picnic, outside and away from the town. And, this is the point. At the end of the day, they all return home, "by the light of the torches, huge and crimson in the night. . . . The company scatters, the lights go out, the song dies, the guitars grow silent, as they approach the habitations of men. *Put on your masks: you are again among your brothers,*" Rizal wrote. Why? Was life in the Philippines such that only by pretense one could live in the towns? Or, as Simoun says, was the town the home of the real bandits who are supposed to be brothers of one another? Was it the town, and not the forests or mountains that spawned the real dangers to men?

There are many other similar significant sentences in the novel, but let what we have pointed out suffice. The next literary device used by Rizal is perhaps best exemplified by the sub-plot of Don Tiburcio de Espadaña and his wife.

In chapter 48 of the *Noli,* Don Tiburcio and Doña Victorina pass in front of the commanding officer's house. Doña Consolacion, the officer's wife, happens to be at her window, and Doña Victorina, not liking the way she looks at her, picks up a fight. The officer arrives in time and sides with his wife. Routed and in desperation, Doña Victorina hysterically screams at her husband for not standing up for her honor. Don Tiburcio answers meekly he is afraid they might cudgel him. The dialogue continues:

> "That is why you are a man!"

> "But-b-but I'm lame!"

Overlooked by commentators, the episode shows Rizal using a man's physical disability to satirize the rest of Philippine society. The first thing one notices in this passage is Don Tiburcio's physical defects. Rizal skillfully uses Doña Victorina "who would have preferred a Spaniard who was not so lame, who did not stutter so, who had more hair and teeth, and who sprayed less saliva when he talked . . . a Spaniard who had, as she used to say, more brio and more class. . . ." In approved repetitive propaganda style, the word "lame" is used about ten times. Not only that, the national hero gives Don Tiburcio a lisp, causing him to stammer, a detail to emphasize his lameness.

Like all novelists, Rizal has also to explain de Espadaña's pitiful condition. His story has to be plausible. Thus, the poor man is not a Spanish grandee, not a bemedalled war hero or brave veteran. He is a drifter, one who abhors work, with no personal ambition, i. e., a psychologically lame individual wandering from country to country, and as often frustrated in his efforts. He is the born loser. He settles in the Philippines, because he thinks one has a fighting chance here if he knows some tricks and wiles. Don Tiburcio is seeking, no longer a fortune, but a modicum of comfort, three meals a day and a bed under a roof every night for the few years still remaining to him. He once dreamed of a "girl with a caressing smile." Alas, the smiling girl turns out to be a masculine, pretentious, and domineering hag, for "in this world one cannot live on dreams alone." Ridiculed, he has a quick and ready answer: "Fill my stomach and you can call me a fool." Worse, he is willing to suffer her, even if when "annoyed with him, she snatched the denture out of his mouth and left him looking ghastly for one or two days, in proportion to his crimes." Never mind, for he is hungry. He married her, or more accurately, *she* married him, and to satisfy her, he agrees to pose as a medical doctor. He became an expensive quack, with no one the wiser, an impostor whose total ignorance is craftily camouflaged by his excessive rates willingly shouldered by the pretentious but ignorant rich of Philippine society.

These literary devices—repetition, detailed description, satire, humor, irony—are intended to appeal to the emotions. One is repelled by a "toothless" and "balding" Tiburcio, at the same time that one pities and scorns him. His material and bodily misfortunes are compounded by his moral and psychological shortcomings. Evidently, Rizal wanted this negative reaction from the reader. Is there a symbolic message in Doña Victorina's pathological obsession to shed her brown Filipino skin and her native accent, only to emphasize her being a native *india?* What is the message in her marrying a broken Spaniard who earns a livelihood on the strength of a lie?

Perhaps one of the more dramatic episodes of *Noli me tangere* is the revelation of Maria Clara's origins. We must admit the incident is a bit melodramatic for contemporary tastes, and could stand more improvement from the literary viewpoint. Maria Clara is blackmailed into surrendering Ibarra's written pledge of undying love and loyalty in exchange for her mother's two secret letters revealing her real father. They had been written before she died. Now, given a choice of either marrying Ibarra and have the identity of her real parents exposed, or giving up her love by saving the honor of both her mother and her real father, Fray Damaso, she chose the latter. In admiration, Ibarra manages to blurt out Maria Clara is a "saint."

The incident is a bit too pat, and perhaps too artificial. It can stand literary improvement, for as the critics say, like Homer, Rizal *aliquando dormitat.* But it prepares for the sequel, when Fray Damaso explains himself to his daughter. All he wants, he assures her, is her happiness:

> Could I allow you to marry a Filipino, and see you unhappy as a wife and wretched as a mother? But I could not put your love out of your head. I opposed it with all my strength, I abused all my powers, for your sake, only for yours. If you had been his wife, you would have wept afterwards to see your husband's condition exposed to all manner of persecution without means of defence. . . . I know that your childhood friend was a good man: I loved him as much as I loved his father; but I hated them from the day I saw they were going to make you unhappy. . . .

The temptation to focus only on the friar's sexual misconduct in this episode is strong, and many have succumbed to it. But that is the best way to misconstrue Rizal's mind. I suggest

rather this is perhaps one more of those pithy, but pregnant descriptions of the colonial malaise that was victimizing the Philippines. We can understand how a father can love his child, even if that father happens to be a friar. But can we excuse a racism condoned by the society in which he lived? The native-born *indio* was legally equal to the peninsular Spaniard, equally a citizen of Spain. In cases, as was true of Rizal himself, some of the despised *indios* and Chinese mestizos were more talented than the peninsular Spaniards. But in the second half of the nineteenth century law and theory did not always correspond to reality. Worse, as exemplified by Fray Damaso, certain sectors in the colony had no qualms abusing their position in order to maintain their superiority. Unsure of their inner worth, they made use of external helps, not always moral or licit, to keep up their prestige and "dignity." This indeed was a social cancer!

Rizal's novels, but especially the *Noli me tangere,* are rightly considered an attack against the abusive friars in the Philippines in the last quarter of the nineteenth century. But they are more than that. They are books to "lift a corner of the veil which shrouds the disease" of Philippine society. As is true in every case of cancer, corruption has already spread to the whole organism before it is detected. And when it is, the malady is already beyond cure.

So also, the novels portray evil lurking in all corners and on all levels of Philippine colonial society. And it is to make his readers aware of their extreme situation and of the need to do something about it that prompted the national hero to create these fictional works. It was not always easy for him. As he says in his dedication of his first novel, he is "sacrificing to the truth everything, even self-love. . . ."

To think that the *Noli* is a criticism only of the Spaniards would not be according to the mind of Rizal. It will not do to concentrate on his anti-Spanish barbs, or to miss the symbolism that makes the work such a powerful piece of propaganda. Trying to check the historical reality of the novel as it is written is perhaps self-defeating—for example, identifying Maria Clara, or Crisostomo Ibarra. And like every piece of writing against legally constituted authority, the novels speak covertly, it preaches in secret terms, much like the classic apocalyptic warnings of early Christian history intelligible only to those "who have ears to hear."

And so, one must not only know the main plot of the novel, but also all the minor sub-plots and episodes that support it. One must consider the minutest details and descriptions, and the role they play to convey the single unified message intended by the author. For in good writing, unity is an essential quality. In good writing no word is useless. Everything has a purpose, everything has its place. (pp. 189-99)

Jose S. Arcilla, S.J., "Once More the 'Noli'—with Understanding," in Understanding the "Noli": Its Historical Context and Literary Influences, *edited by Jose S. Arcilla, S.J., Phoenix Press, Inc., 1988, pp. 183-99.*

FURTHER READING

Alzona, Encarnación. *Rizal's Legacy to the Filipino Woman.* Pasay City, Philippines: Encarnación Alzona, 1953, 22 p.
    Outlines Rizal's ideas concerning women and discusses the female characters in *Noli me tangere* and *El filibusterismo.*

Bernad, Miguel A. *Rizal and Spain: An Essay in Biographical Context.* Manila: National Book Store, 1986, 188 p.
    Examines Rizal's relationship with his friend and former teacher, the Spanish priest Father Francisco de Paula Sanchez, and evaluates Rizal's attitude toward the government and people of Spain.

Bonoan, Raul J. "Religion and Nationalism in Rizal." *The Manila Review* 4, No. 2 (June 1978): 15-23.
    Addresses Rizal's religious interpretation of Filipino nationalism.

Coates, Austin. *Rizal: Philippine Nationalist and Martyr.* Hong Kong: Oxford University Press, 1968, 378 p.
    A reliable Rizal biography.

Craig, Austin. *Lineage, Life, and Labors of José Rizal, Philippine Patriot: A Study of the Growth of Free Ideas in the Trans-Pacific American Territory.* Manila: Philippine Education Co., 1913, 287 p.
    The first Rizal biography published in English.

Domingo, Benjamin B. *Rizal in Germany.* 2d ed. Manila: Foreign Service Institute, 1983, 97 p.
    Chronicles Rizal's lengthy stay in Germany, highlighting the considerable impression he made on the people he met there.

Guerrero, León Ma. *The First Filipino: A Biography of José Rizal.* Manila: National Heroes Commission, 1963, 549 p.
    A modern biography written by a prominent Filipino statesman on the centennial of Rizal's death.

Majul, Cesar Adib. *A Critique of Rizal's Concept of a Filipino Nation.* Diliman, Philippines: 1959, 47 p.
    Presents a theory of Rizal's social and political ideology based on his writings and political activity.

———. "Maria Clara's Locket: A Significance." *General Education Journal* 11 (1967): 19-27.
    Analyzes the symbolism of Maria Clara's locket in *Noli me tangere* and *El filibusterismo.*

Pascual, Ricardo R. *The Philosophy of Rizal.* Manila: Pedro B. Ayuda and Co., 1962, 335 p.

Outlines Rizal's social, political, educational, religious, and ethical philosophy.

Quirino, Carlos. *The Great Malayan: The Biography of Rizal.* Manila: Philippine Education Co., 1940, 340 p.
    The first Rizal biography written by a Filipino.

Runes, Ildefonso T., and Buenafe, Mamerto. *The Forgery of the Rizal "Retraction" and Josephine's "Autobiography".* Manila: Pro-Patria Publishers, 1962, 198 p.
    An impassioned argument refuting the claim that Rizal disavowed his loyalty to the Masonic Order before his execution.

Russell, Charles Edward, and Rodriguez, E. B. *The Hero of the Filipinos: The Story of José Rizal, Poet, Patriot and Martyr.* New York: Century Co., 1923, 392 p.
    An account of Rizal's life based on the research of Rizal biographers W. E. Retana and Austin Craig.

Sánchez, Cayetano. "The Franciscans in the Life and Works of Jose Rizal." *Philippine Quarterly of Culture and Society* 11, No. 1 (March 1983): 1-56.
    Examines the significance of Rizal's negative portrayal of Franciscans in *Noli me tangere* and *El filibusterismo.*

Schumacher, John N. "Due Process and the Rule of Law: Three Unpublished Letters of Rizal." *Philippine Studies* 25 (1977): 237-53.
    The first publication of letters Rizal wrote to the Spanish government calling for the release of his exiled brother-in-law, Manuel Timoteo de Hidalgo.

———. "Rizal the Revolutionary and the Ateneo." *Philippine Studies* 26 (1978): 231-40.
    Discusses the correlation between Rizal's revolutionary philosophy and his spiritual beliefs.

Yabes, Leopoldo Y., ed. *José Rizal on His Centenary: Being an Attempt at a Revaluation of His Significance, by Professors of the University of the Philippines.* Quezon City: University of the Philippines, 1963, 269 p.
    A collection of essays on topics ranging from Rizal's philosophy of history to his views on education.

Zaide, Gregorio F. *José Rizal: Life, Works, and Writings.* Manila: Villanueva Book Store, 1957, 295 p.
    A comprehensive biography including commentary on Rizal's travels.